BoatU.S. Coopera
Marinas Near Yo

p to 15% OFF Repairs

Look for the sign and save. Over 900 marinas offer valuable discounts to BoatU.S. Members on fuel, repairs, overnight slips and more.

NORTH CAROLINA

Bath Harbor Marina
Bath (252) 923-5711

Hurricane Harbor
Marina and Boatyard
Bayboro
(252) 745-5483

Jarrett Bay Boatworks
Beaufort
(252) 728-7100

The Boat House at
Front Street Village
Beaufort
(252) 838-1524

Town Creek Marina
Beaufort
(252) 728-6111

River Forest Marina
Belhaven
(252) 943-2151

Joyner Marina, LLC
Carolina Beach
(910) 458-5053

Alligator River Marina
Columbia
(252) 796-0333

International Yachting Ctr.
Columbia
(252) 796-0435

Edenton Marina
Edenton
(252) 482-7421

The Pelican Marina
Elizabeth City
(252) 335-5108

The Boatyard at
Hampstead
Hampstead
(910) 270-2794

Anchors Away Boatyard
Hampstead
(910) 270-4741

Hatteras Landing Marina
Hatteras
(800) 551-8478

Albermarle Plantation
Hertford
(252) 426-4037

Capt. Bob Beck's
Marina Cafe
Jacksonville
(910) 938-2002

Morehead City Yacht
Basin
Morehead City
(252) 726-6862

Portside Marina
Morehead City
(252) 726-7678

Bridge Pointe Marina
New Bern
(252) 637-7372

New Bern Grand Marina
New Bern
(252) 638-0318

Sea Gate Marina
Newport
(252) 728-4126

Ocean Isle Marina &
Yacht Club
Ocean Isle Beach
(910) 579-6440

Whittaker Creek Yacht
Harbor
Oriental
(252) 249-0666

Grace Harbor at
River Dunes
Oriental
(252) 249-4908

Deep Point Marina
Southport
(910) 269-2380

St. James
Plantation Marina
Southport
(910) 253-0463

Holden Beach Marina
Supply (910) 842-5447

Dockside Restaurant &
Marina
Wilmington
(910) 256-3579

Wilmington Marine
Center
Wilmington
(910) 395-5055

Gregory Poole Marine
Service Center
Wilmington
(910) 791-8002

SOUTH CAROLINA

Charleston
Maritime Center
Charleston
(843) 853-3625

Charleston City Marina
Charleston
(843) 723-5098

St. Johns Yacht Harbor
Charleston
(843) 557-1027

The Bristol Marina
Charleston
(843) 723-6600

Toler's Cove Marina
Charleston
(843) 881-0325

UK Sailmakers,
Charleston
(843) 722-0823

Bucksport Plantation Marina
Conway
(843) 397-6300

Dataw Island Marina
Dataw Island
(843) 838-8410

Georgetown Landing
Marina
Georgetown
(843) 546-1776

Hilton Head Harbor
Marina
Hilton Head
(843) 681-3256

Quantum Hilton Head
Hilton Head
(843) 342-6612

Harbour Town
Yacht Basin
Hilton Head Island
(843) 671-2704

Skull Creek Marina
Hilton Head Island
(800) 237-4096

Isle of Palms Marina
Isle of Palms
(843) 886-0209

Bohicket Yacht Club, LLC
Johns Island
(843) 768-1280

Coquina Yacht Club
Little River
(843) 249-9333

Crickett Cove Marina
Little River
(843) 249-7169

Lightkeepers Marina
Little River
(843) 249-8660

Myrtle Beach
Yacht Club
Little River
(843) 249-5376

Fisher's Silver
Coast Marina
Little River
(843) 249-1000

Charleston
Harbor Marina
Mount Pleasant
(843) 284-7061

Marina at
Grande Dunes
Myrtle Beach
(843) 315-7777

Osprey Marina
Myrtle Beach
(843) 215-5353

The Barefoot Resort
Yacht Club
N. Myrtle Beach
(843) 390-2011

Heritage
Plantation Marina
Pawley's Island
(843) 237-3650

Port Royal
Landing Marina
Port Royal
(800) 326-7678

Lemmond's Marine
Tega Cay
(800) 671-4440

GEORGIA

Riverwalk Marina
Augusta
(706) 722-1388

The Old Boat Shop
Buford
(404) 401-1970

Ft. McAllister Marina &
Inn, Inc.
Richmond Hill
(912) 727-2632

Delegal Creek Marina
Savannah
(912) 598-0023

Hogan's Marina
Savannah
(912) 897-3474

Sail Harbor Marina &
Boatyard
Savannah
(912) 897-2896

The Landings Harbor Marina
Savannah
(912) 598-1901

Morningstar Marinas at
Golden Isles
St. Simons
(912) 634-1128

Tybee Island Marina
Tybee Island
(312) 786-5554

Visit www.BoatUS.com/MSL to find more Cooperating Marinas near you.
Only Members get the discounts. Call 800-395-2628 and join TODAY!

BoatUS COOPERATING MARINA

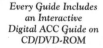

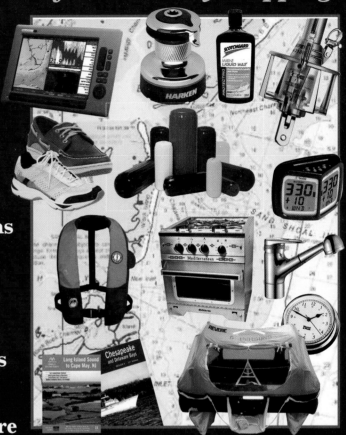

DOZIER'S
WATERWAY® GUIDE
THE CRUISING AUTHORITY

FOUNDED IN 1947

Publisher **JACK DOZIER**
jdozier@waterwayguide.com

Associate Publisher **CRAIG DOZIER**
cdozier@waterwayguide.com

Editor **JANI PARKER**
jparker@waterwayguide.com

Production Artists **REESA KUGLER**
reesa@waterwayguide.com
CAROLYN AUGUST
carolyn@waterwayguide.com

Director of Marketing **MIKE KUCERA**
mkucera@waterwayguide.com

Marketing & Sales Associate **SANDY HICKEY**
sandy@waterwayguide.com

Product Sales Manager **HEATHER SADEG**
heather@waterwayguide.com

Web & News Editor **TED STEHLE**
tstehle@waterwayguide.com

News & Social Media Manager **JANE ANDERSON**
jane@waterwayguide.com

Web Master **MIKE SCHWEFLER**

Accounts Manager **ARTHUR CROWTHER**
accounts@waterwayguide.com

Administrative Assistant **MARGIE MOORE**

Properties Manager **ROBERT MATALIK**

IT/Editoral Assistant **PARKER BOGGS**

BOOK SALES:
www.WaterwayGuide.com
800-233-3359

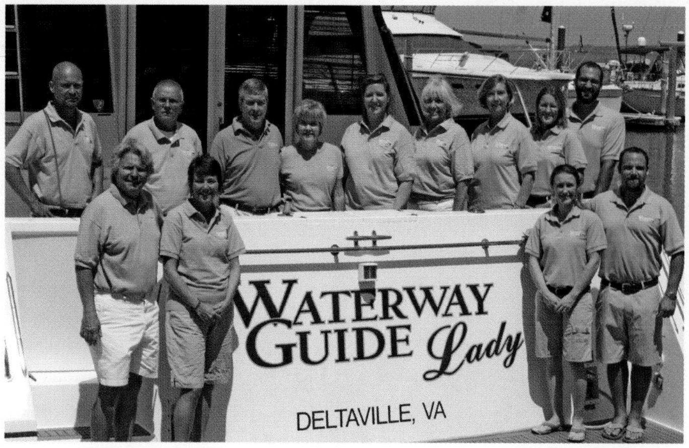

Waterway Guide staff and Dozier Marine Group in Deltaville, Virginia.
Photo by Kylie Everton.

EDITORIAL, CORPORATE & ACCOUNTING OFFICES
Waterway Guide/Skipper Bob Publications
Dozier Media Group, LLC
Send Correspondence to:
P.O. Box 1125
Deltaville, VA 23043
804-776-8999

CONTRIBUTORS

• Chris Caldwell • Kay Gibson
• Mark Gonsalves • Bill Hezlep
• Pepper Holmes • Gil Johnson
• Carl Jordan • Rick Kennedy
• Robert Linder
• Diane & Michael Marotta
• Peter Mitchell • Alan Pereya
• Kip & Larry Putt • Jim Quince

ADVERTISING SALES
GENERAL ADVERTISING INQUIRIES
MIKE KUCERA
mkucera@waterwayguide.com

CRUISING EDITORS

CHESAPEAKE BAY EDITION
JACK & CRAIG DOZIER
BUD & ELAINE LLOYD

ATLANTIC ICW EDITION
BUD & ELAINE LLOYD
JACK & CRAIG DOZIER

NORTHERN EDITION
LARRY & RUTH SMITHERS

BAHAMAS EDITION
JANICE BAUER CALLUM
ROBERT WILSON
JEN & MAXWELL WILLIAMSON

SOUTHERN EDITION
JAY CORZINE
BUD & ELAINE LLOYD

GREAT LAKE EDITION
BOB AND CAROL KUNATH
WALLY MORAN
TED & AUDREY STEHLE

On the cover: An aerial view of Broad Creek, Hilton Head, SC. (Photo courtesy of Mike Kucera.) Ferry Dock at Dawfuskie Island, SC. (Photo courtesy of Mike Kucera.) Swing bridge in North Carolina. (Photo courtesy of Caldwell.)

Price per copy: $39.95. When ordering by mail or telephone, add shipping and handling charges. Direct all orders to: Waterway Guide, P.O. Box 1125, Deltaville, VA 23043; or call 800-233-3359, fax 804-776-6111.

To provide the most complete and accurate information, all facilities have been contacted within the past year. Although facility operators supplied this data, we cannot guarantee accuracy or assume responsibility for errors. Entrance and dockside soundings tend to fluctuate. Always approach marinas carefully. Reference numbers on spotting charts indicate marina locations. Aerial photos are for general overview only and are not to be used for navigation.

Member of National Marine Manufacturers Association – Printed In U.S.A.

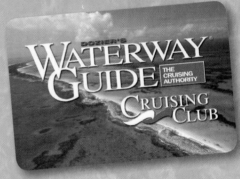

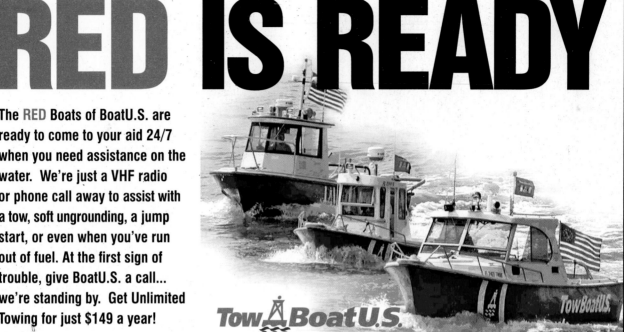

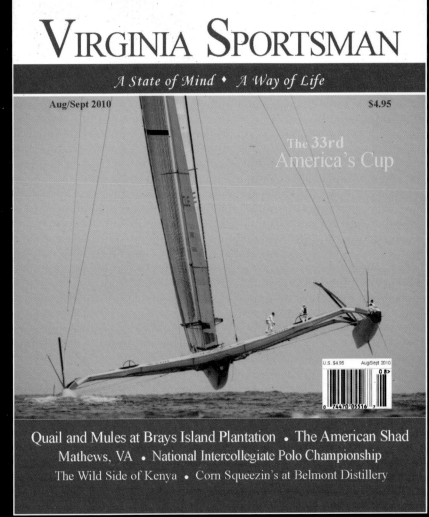

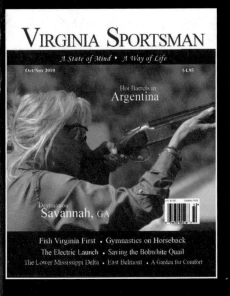

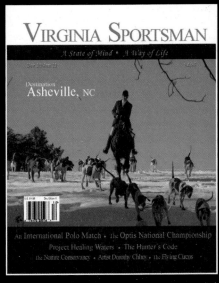

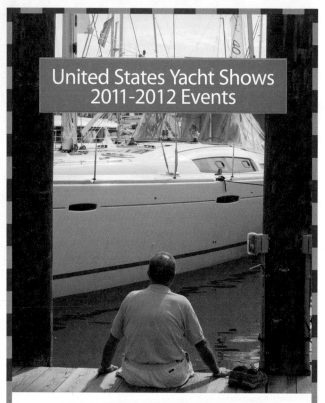

Navigating Your Guide

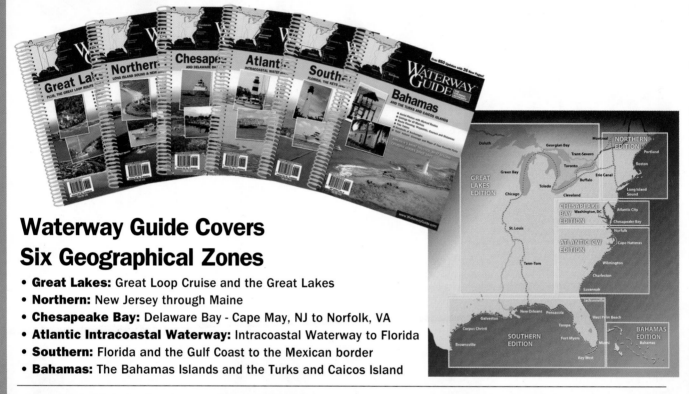

Waterway Guide Covers Six Geographical Zones

- **Great Lakes:** Great Loop Cruise and the Great Lakes
- **Northern:** New Jersey through Maine
- **Chesapeake Bay:** Delaware Bay - Cape May, NJ to Norfolk, VA
- **Atlantic Intracoastal Waterway:** Intracoastal Waterway to Florida
- **Southern:** Florida and the Gulf Coast to the Mexican border
- **Bahamas:** The Bahamas Islands and the Turks and Caicos Island

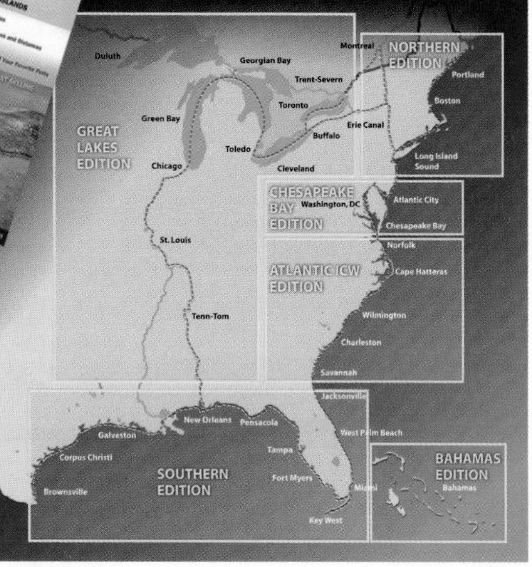

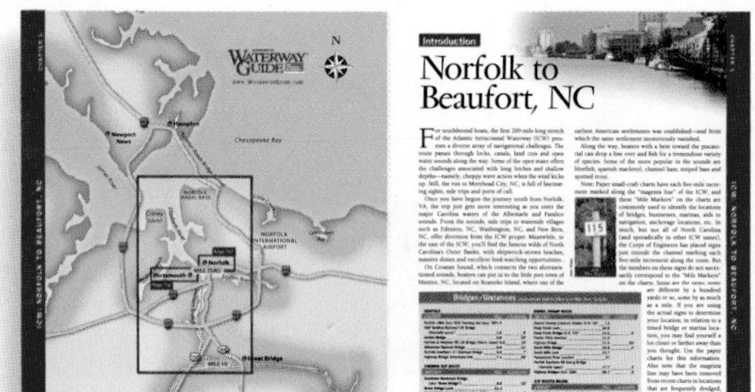

1. Regional Overview

The organization of the guide begins with large geographical regions. Information includes:

- ***Mileage Tables***
- ***Regional Maps***
- ***Bridge Information***
- ***Regional History***

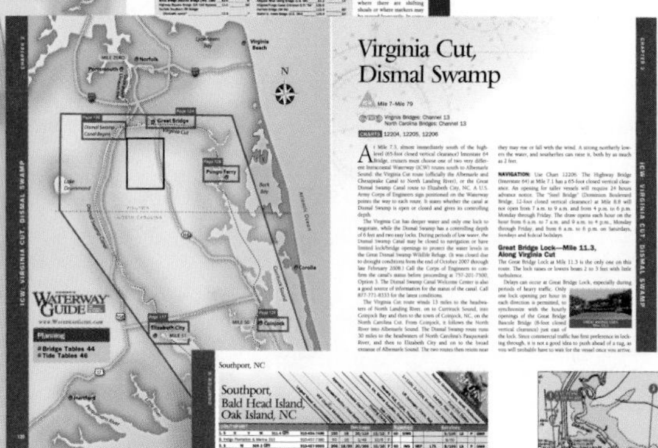

2. Section Contents

Sections focus on smaller areas of geographical coverage within the regions. Sections feature:

- ***Color-coding for Easy Reference***
- ***Detailed, Smaller-scale Maps***
- ***A List of Chapters Within Each Section***

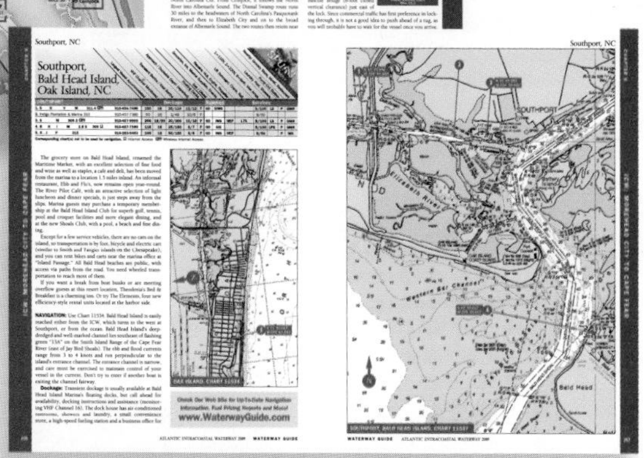

3. Chapters

Chapters focus on even smaller coverage areas within the sections. Chapter information includes:

- ***Aerial Photos With Marked Routes***
- ***Navigational Reports***
- ***Dockage and Anchorage Information***
- ***Goin' Ashore Features for Towns Along the Way***

Marina Listings and Locator Charts

The Atlantic Intracoastal Waterway Guide covers hundreds of marinas with the following information:

- ***Clearly Labeled Charts***
- ***Marina Locator Arrows***
- ***Marina Amenities***
- ***Phone Numbers***
- ***Internet and Wireless Internet Capabilities***
- ***Fuel, Services and Supplies***
- ***GPS Coordinates and Bold Type for Advertising Sponsors***

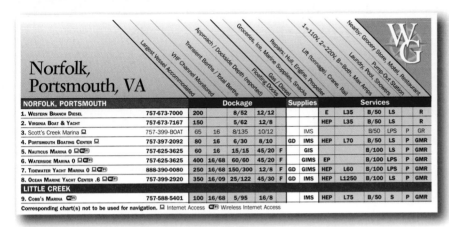

Norfolk, Portsmouth, VA

NORFOLK, PORTSMOUTH		Largest Vessel Accommodated	VHF Channel Monitored	Transient Berths / Total Berths	Approach / Dockside Depth (reported)	Floating Docks	Gas / Diesel	Groceries, Ice, Marine Supplies, Snacks	Repairs: Hull, Engine, Propeller	Lift (tonnage), Crane, Rail	1=110V, 2=220V, B=Both, Max Amps	Laundry, Pool, Showers	Pump-Out Station	Nearby: Grocery Store, Motel, Restaurant
		Dockage					Supplies		Services					
1. **Western Branch Diesel**	**757-673-7000**	**200**		**8/52**	**12/12**				**E**	**L35**	**B/50**	**LS**		**R**
2. **Virginia Boat & Yacht**	**757-673-7167**	**150**		**5/62**	**12/8**				**HEP**	**L35**	**B/50**	**LS**		**R**
3. Scott's Creek Marina 🖳	757-399-BOAT	65	16	8/135	10/12			IMS			B/50	LPS	P	GR
4. **Portsmouth Boating Center** 🖳	**757-397-2092**	**80**	**16**	**6/30**	**8/10**		**GD**	**IMS**	**HEP**	**L70**	**B/50**	**LS**	**P**	**GMR**
5. **Nauticus Marina 0** 🖳 WiFi	**757-625-3625**	**60**	**16**	**15/15**	**45/20**	**F**		**GIS**			**B/100**	**LS**	**P**	**GMR**
6. **Waterside Marina 0** 🖳 WiFi	**757-625-3625**	**400**	**16/68**	**60/60**	**45/20**	**F**		**GIMS**	**EP**		**B/100**	**LPS**	**P**	**GMR**
7. **Tidewater Yacht Marina 0** 🖳 WiFi	**888-390-0080**	**250**	**16/68**	**150/300**	**12/8**	**F**	**GD**	**GIMS**	**HEP**	**L60**	**B/100**	**LPS**	**P**	**GMR**
8. **Ocean Marine Yacht Center .6** 🖳 WiFi	**757-399-2920**	**350**	**16/09**	**25/122**	**45/30**	**F**	**GD**	**IMS**	**HEP**	**L1250**	**B/100**	**LS**	**P**	**GMR**
LITTLE CREEK														
9. **Cobb's Marina** WiFi	**757-588-5401**	**100**	**16/68**	**5/95**	**16/8**			**IMS**	**HEP**	**L75**	**B/50**	**S**	**P**	**GMR**

Corresponding chart(s) not to be used for navigation. 🖳 Internet Access WiFi Wireless Internet Access

Marina and Contact Information (advertising sponsors are bolded) ***Dockage*** ***Supplies*** ***Services***

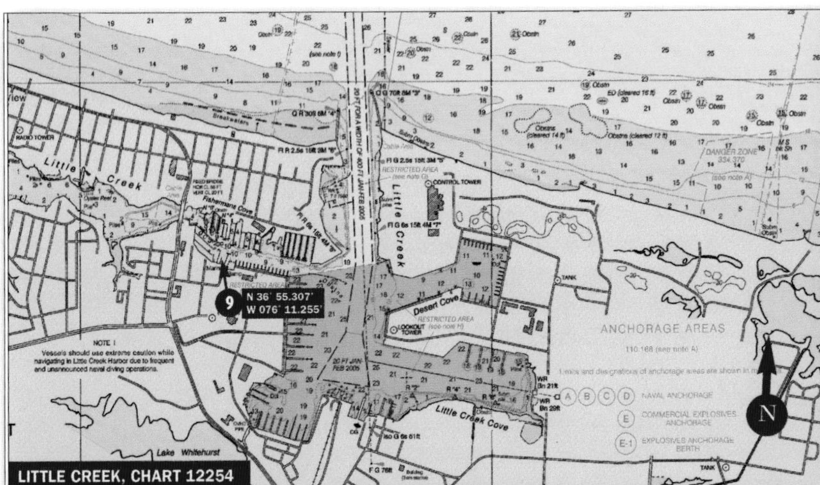

Clearly labeled marina locator charts help tie it all together.

Skipper's Handbook

A whole section with useful boating references.

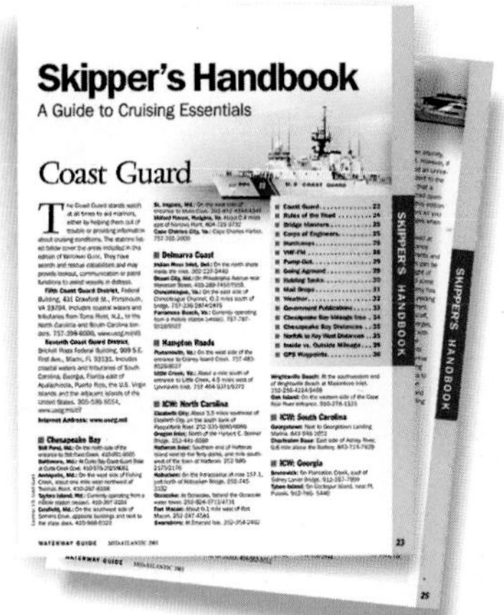

Bridges and Distances

Tables give you opening times and mileage between points.

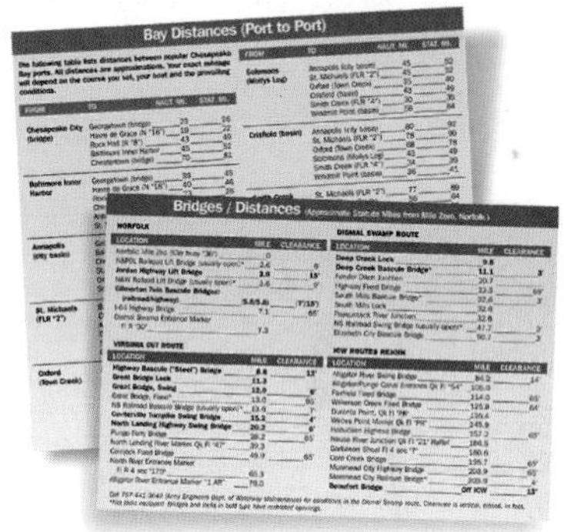

Goin' Ashore

Quick-read features on ports and towns you'll visit along the way.

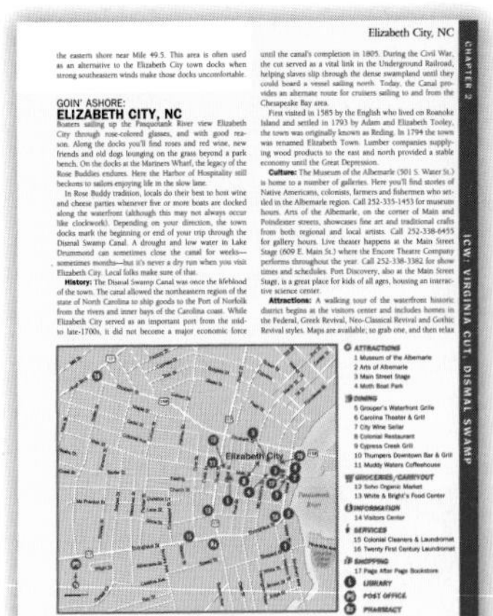

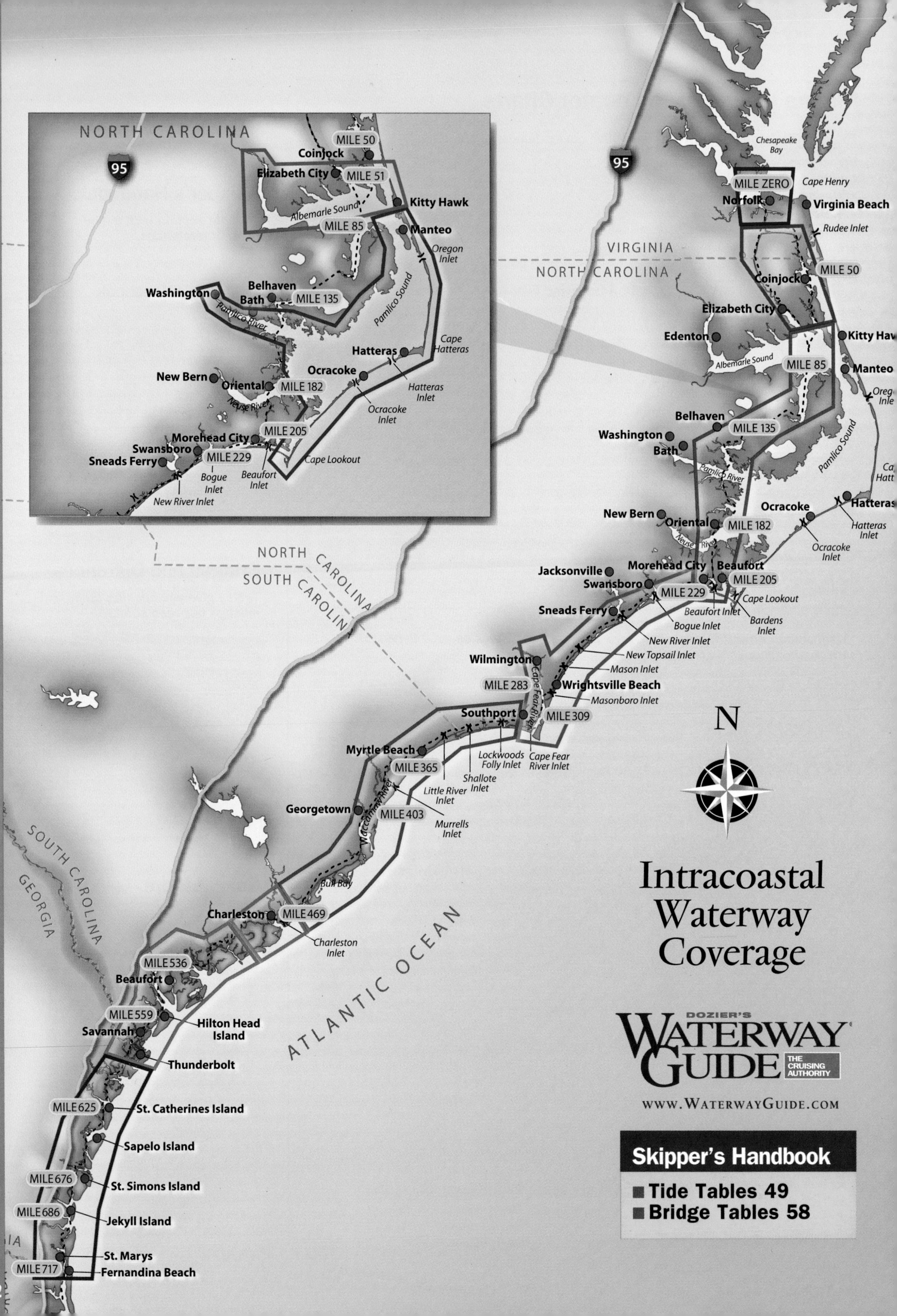

Intracoastal Waterway Coverage

DOZIER'S WATERWAY GUIDE THE CRUISING AUTHORITY

WWW.WATERWAYGUIDE.COM

Skipper's Handbook

Contents

VOLUME 65, NO. 1

DOZIER'S WATERWAY GUIDE® THE CRUISING AUTHORITY
A DOZIER MEDIA GROUP PUBLICATION

Strategically situated at Mile Zero, the "official" beginning of the Atlantic Intracoastal Waterway, Norfolk, VA offers nearly every kind of marine service and equipment, and is an especially good fitting-out place in preparation for the cruise south or north. Norfolk is also an exciting place to visit, with its rejuvenated waterfront filled with shops, restaurants, hotels, museums and historic sites.

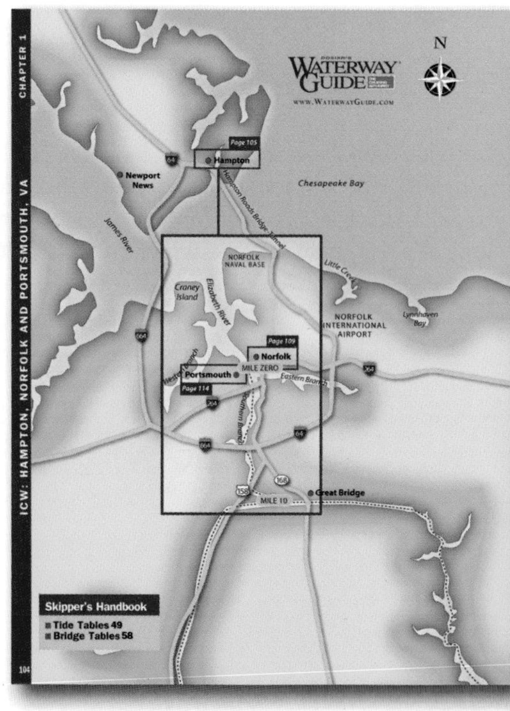

Virginia Cut, Dismal Swamp

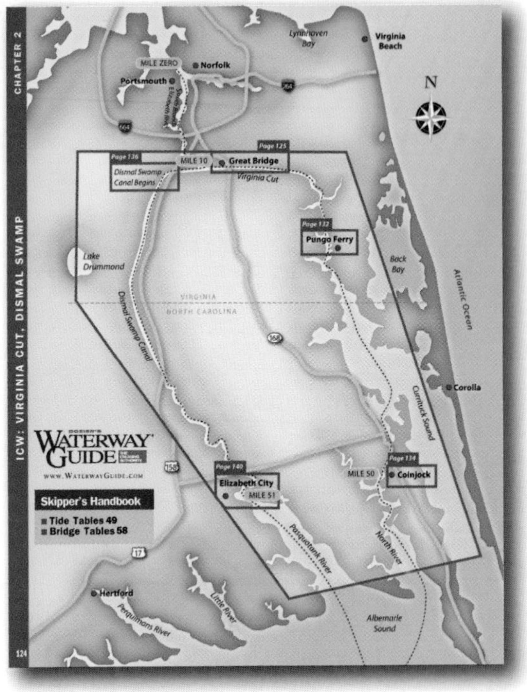

At Mile 7.3, almost immediately south of the high-level (65-foot closed vertical clearance) Interstate 64 Bridge, cruisers must choose one of two very different Intracoastal Waterway (ICW) routes south to Albemarle Sound: the Virginia Cut route (officially the Albemarle and Chesapeake Canal to North Landing River), or the Great Dismal Swamp Canal route to Elizabeth City, NC. A U.S. Army Corps of Engineers sign positioned on the Waterway points the way to each route. It states whether the canal at Dismal Swamp is open or closed and gives its controlling depth.

Sidetrips on the Albemarle Sound

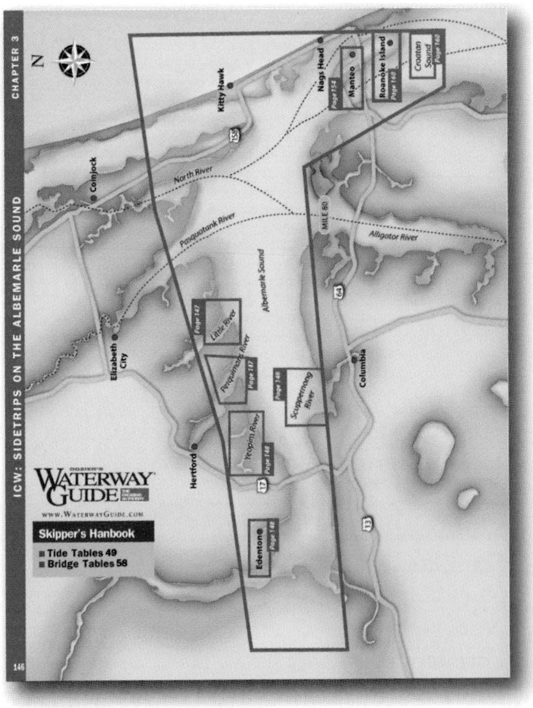

North Carolina's sounds (Inner Banks) and the Outer Banks make a rewarding side trip for those who are willing to depart from the Intracoastal Waterway (ICW) proper. The Albemarle and Pamlico sounds, along with their big rivers, which at times almost become sounds in themselves, are convenient to the ICW and offer isolated side waters and out-of-the-way waterside communities.

Sidetrips on the Outer Banks, Pamlico Sound

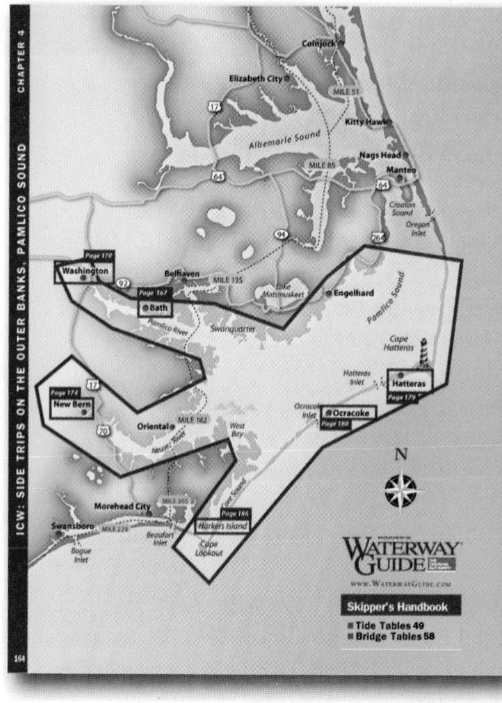

North Carolina's Outer Banks, a long strip of barrier islands, are unlike any other islands along the Mid-Atlantic coast. Vulnerable to wind and wave, they extend in a crescent from the Virginia state line, bending farther and farther out to sea until the strip swings back suddenly at Cape Hatteras, leaving an exposed and dangerous cape.

Albemarle Sound to Beaufort

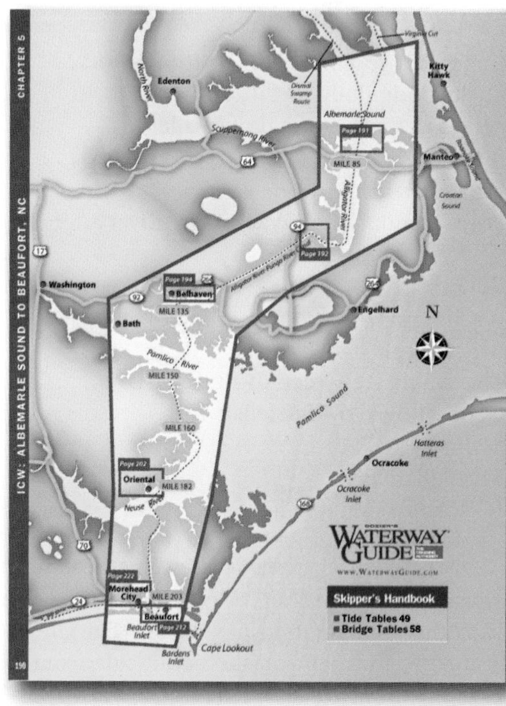

Two boats that opted for either the 79-mile-long Virginia Cut route or the 82-mile-long Dismal Swamp route, respectively, are likely to meet again just north of flashing green "1AR" at the mouth of the Alligator River near Intracoastal Waterway (ICW) Mile Marker 80. Here, on the southern side of Albemarle Sound, the two ICW routes converge.

TABLE OF CONTENTS

Morehead City to Cape Fear

Below Morehead City (Mile 205), the Intracoastal Waterway (ICW) follows Bogue Sound almost 25 miles to Swansboro (Mile 229), the port for Bogue Inlet. The ICW channel to Swansboro is marked with daybeacons and lights; green and red are staggered, with few exceptions.

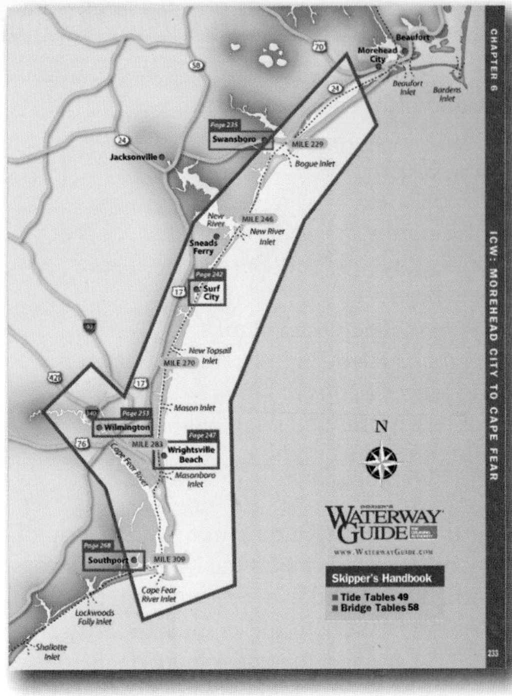

Cape Fear to Charleston

After the swift currents of the Cape Fear River, beyond the Southport area, Intracoastal Waterway (ICW) cruisers will enter an area of the ICW that lives up to its nickname, "The Ditch." A series of beach developments is evident on the ocean side from Oak Island through Long Beach.

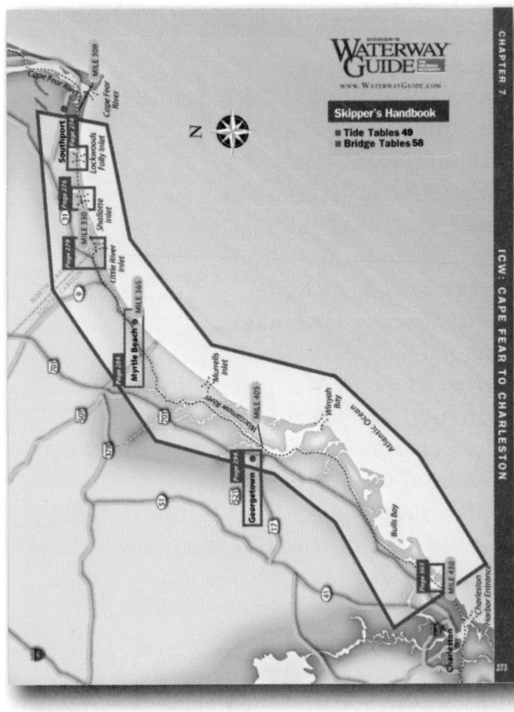

Charleston and Environs

The miles north of Charleston are some of the most scenic on the Intracoastal Waterway (ICW). Here, the dredged ICW channel cuts through low marshy islets, across several small rivers and finally through a long land cut before reaching Charleston Harbor.

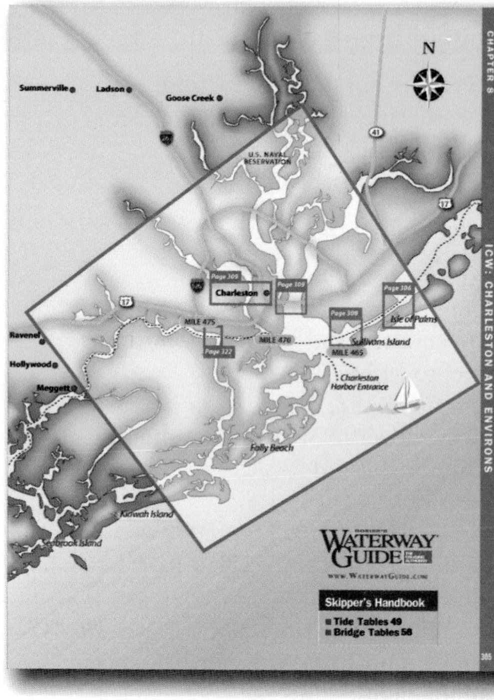

Charleston to Thunderbolt

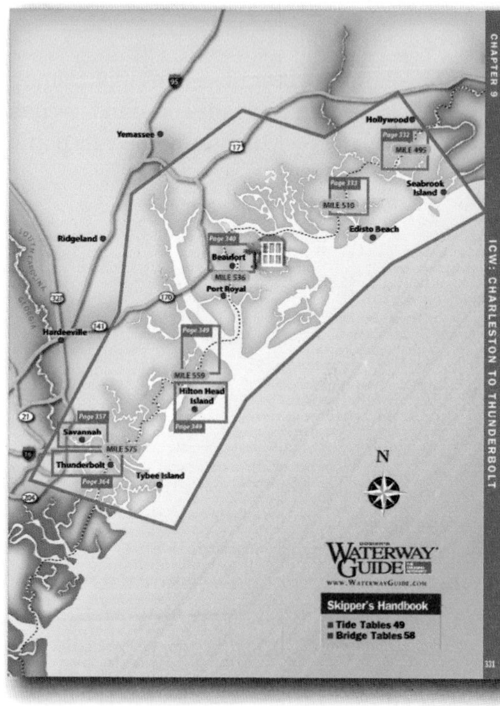

From Elliott Cut, which leads from Charleston, SC south to the Stono River, the Intracoastal Waterway (ICW) route continues along the Stono River for about 12 miles.

Thunderbolt to the Florida Border

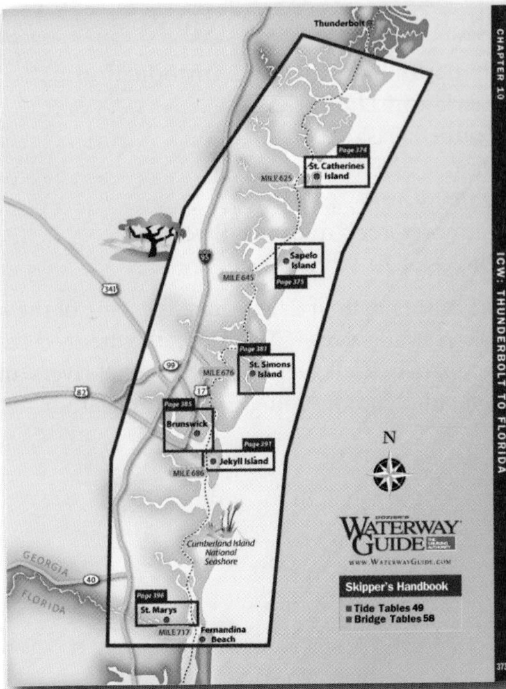

The ICW follows the Bear River as it empties into St. Catherines Sound (Mile 618). This is the first in a series of sounds—connected by rivers—that you will pass through as you transit the Georgia portion of the ICW.

Florida Border to Jacksonville

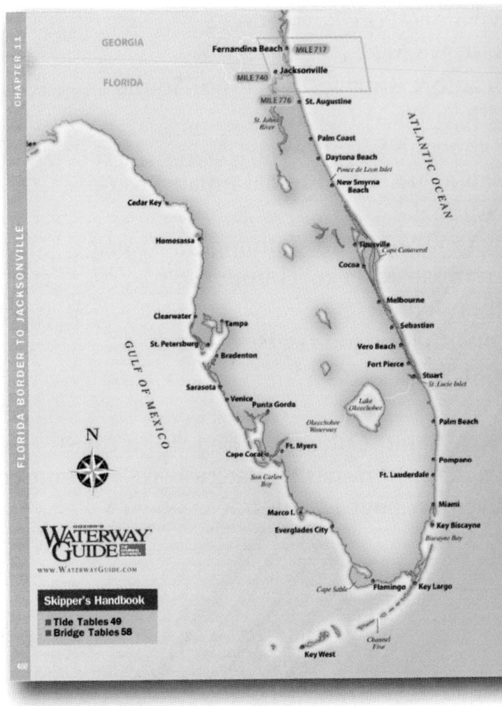

As you cross the St. Marys River and enter the state of Florida, you will notice a change in the characteristics of the Intracoastal Waterway (ICW). Georgia's long, open sounds and wide rivers gradually transform into a series of creeks and rivers connected by narrow land cuts. The ICW crosses several navigable inlets that no doubt attracted the early explorers. The first settlers built strategic, profitable ports along these protected inside waters. Today's cruisers use improved and connected passages that link many of these original settlements.

Navigating Change On the Waterway

We all form personal impressions from our cruising adventures. Comparing other's impressions with our own can be a real eye opener. It's uniquely entertaining and interesting to listen to a first timer's account of their trip up or down the waterway or after they have visited new cruising grounds. It's entertaining because of the level of excitement they come back with—an enthusiasm for the new-found boating lifestyle, new friends and new discoveries. It's interesting because they are eager to relate their impressions and experiences and, from that, they often point out things that we veteran (read: old) cruisers take for granted or don't notice. That's similar to seeing friends every day and not noticing the gradual change in their appearances, as opposed to going to a school reunion where the people we haven't seen for 40 years are barely recognizable.

The changes that have occurred in my lifetime of cruising, starting with my family in the early 50s, are overwhelming when taken all together, but they happened slowly and sometimes were almost unnoticed at the time. Reminiscing over pictures from cruises between the Chesapeake and Florida in the late 60s and early 70s and then comparing that to the same cruise in 2011 really points up a number of major contrasts.

The most obvious change is development along the shore. Areas that were once considered unattractive by homeowners are now prime residential areas. The dredged gut behind Myrtle Beach - Pine Island Cut, the vast salt marshes of South Carolina and Georgia, and low-lying wilderness areas everywhere were once among the vacant stretches of shoreline that seemed destined to remain that way. Other areas, such as the shores of the Indian River in Florida and Manatee Pocket at Stuart, were largely undeveloped, but we knew it was just a matter of time. The effect residential development has had on cruisers is a loss of the sense of adventure in exploring undiscovered lands, which has been replaced with a feel of traveling down main street. Along with development came the loss of many secluded anchorages and restrictions on others. Cruising is still fun and interesting but somewhat different.

There are, of course, many positive changes, such as improved marina facilities, better access to supplies and services and fewer low-rise bridges that require openings. Another positive change, although some may argue this, is that now we can stay in almost constant communication with home, office and friends. In days past, it was not unusual to go for days without making a call from a payphone to report in, something else that has taken away from the sense of adventure and freedom.

One of the most important positive changes, and one that newcomers to boating seem to take for granted, is the revolution in navigation technology. Although a relatively recent change, today it is incomprehensible to think that our pinpoint position will not constantly follow us. Electronic charting has taken the guesswork, preplanning and much of the risk out of cruising. Of course, it has also eliminated a certain amount of skill that was previously required. Previously, along with compass, parallel rules and paper charts, serious cruisers needed the skill of dead reckoning, especially in fog, while night cruising or when out of sight of land. Those situations truly created a sense of adventure and accomplishment at the end of the journey.

Pictured (from left): John Dozier, Ned Dozier, Associate Publisher Craig Dozier and Publisher Jack Dozier, with Scooter and Molly.

I've only scratched the surface, but whether you are new to cruising or a veteran cruiser, you get the idea. Even with all the changes over the years, today's boaters share the same desire for the adventure, discovery, accomplishment, fun and freedom that have always lured people to the water. These are an important part of every boaters dream, and the one thing that fortunately has not changed over the years. For all of us, cruising is still fun and interesting, just somewhat different than before.

At Waterway Guide our interest and excitement is constantly peaked, not only in producing the content we present to you but also in our methods of presentation. In just the past 10 years our print content has grown from 1300 pages to 3000 pages (and growing), plus another 1500 pages in our *Skipper Bob* publications. Just as significant, our methods of delivery have expanded through the addition of WaterwayGuide.com, the Waterway Guide Online Planner, Waterway Guide Face Book, and other developments, in the works including Waterway Guide Ebooks. To handle this continuing growth, we have moved into a new and larger facility in Deltaville, Virginia, and assembled the skilled and dedicated staff needed to accomplish our goals. Now that's exciting!

See you on the water,

Jack Dozier,
Publisher

Cruising Editors

Janice Bauer Callum

Janice Bauer Callum

Janice Bauer Callum and her husband, George, have been sailing together for 45 years. George has a much longer sailing history. In his youth, he sailed the eastern seaboard with his family onboard their 8-meter *Gracious,* and crewed for numerous Chicago to Mackinac races, as well as taught sailing for the Michigan City Yacht Club. Over the years, Janice and George have cruised and raced the Great Lakes, the East Coast, the Caribbean and the Bahamas. When they weren't cruising or racing their sloop, *Morning Glory,* with their three children, Treavor, Heather and Dayne, they were racing windsurfers. Janice was a District Chairperson for the International Windsurfing Class Association for whom she organized races for thousands of sailors and qualified them for the first Olympic sail boarding competition in Los Angeles.

Since their retirement in 2000, Janice and George have been docked on the beaches of Mexico and sailed their Hallberg-Rassy Rasmus, *Calamus,* from the Tennessee-Tombigbee Waterway up and down the eastern seaboard and the ICW to the Bahamas, where they sail several months every year. For the short time that they are not onboard Calamus, they are at their small ranch on Lake Calamus in Burwell, Nebraska—home of the oldest (and only) Windsurfing Rodeo.

Kenneth and Amy Braswell

Kenneth and Amy Braswell

Kenneth and Amy Braswell are WATERWAY GUIDE'S cruising editors for the Albemarle and Pamlico Sounds for the ICW 2012 Guide. Ken and Amy spent weekends growing up on the Pamlico River at their parents respective cottages in view of Indian Island. Marriage led to a succession of sailboats they still own today: a Minisail 14, ComPac 16 (Emanuel Wynn), SunCat 19 (Miss Claire), ComPac 23 (John Newbern) and ComPac 27 (Tryumph II). They enjoy sailing with their Airedale, Kirby, on the Pamlico to Ocracoke, Oriental, Washington and Bath.

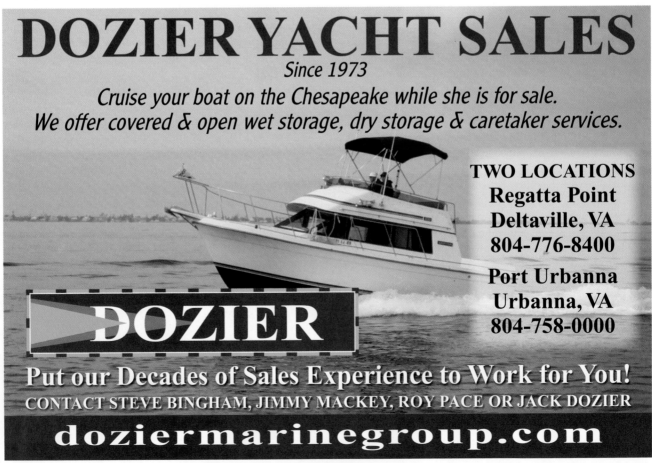

This Fall the Tryumph II will return to the Albemarle Sound in the wake of her namesake, a blockage runner captained by Amy's great-grandfather. When not cruising, Ken is a Plant Manager for a food company while Amy manages a family farm. Ken serves as the Treasurer of the River Rat Yacht Club and Amy serves on the Cruising Committee. Both are involved in Pirates on the Pungo, an annual fundraiser for the Pungo District Hospital in Belhaven.

Jay Corzine

Jay Corzine

Jay began boating on the Great Lakes with his parents aboard a trailerable wood lapstrake cruiser, visiting a number of ports and anchorages. Moving to Fort Lauderdale in the early 60s only led to more fun on the water and larger explorations including the Keys and Lake Okeechobee. Finally, by moving to Texas during the late 1970s, he realized a dream by purchasing his first sailing vessel and sailing Galveston Bay and the Texas coast. Now, with Buffy, his wife of 20 years, also an avid cruiser, they concentrate solely on the Texas coast, making their home in Rockport on Aransas Bay. "We did the cruising thing by spending three years on the east coast and the Bahamas, ranging as far north as Bar Harbor, Maine and as far south as Georgetown, Exuma Islands. It provided a giant step for us in both experience and confidence."

Upon getting his Captain's license in 1997, he became a delivery skipper and tangled with a number of contrary vessels. "Sailboat deliveries usually entail fix and repair in foreign ports before they are able to go to sea. Otherwise, the owners would take them home." The year 2000 found him employed by the currents owners of Bluewater Books and Charts in Fort Lauderdale, Florida, where he became manager of the chart department and specialized in both paper and electronic charts for cruising yachtsmen and Megayacht owners.

In 2009, he self-published the "Guide to Cruising Texas Southern and Central Coast: Brazos Santiago to Galveston Bay" and wrote several articles for Telltales Magazine in Kemah, Texas. His fledgling writing career now includes contributions to WATERWAY GUIDE for the Texas portion of the Southern edition.

Bob and Carol Kunath

Bob and Carol Kunath

Bob and Carol Kunath have owned about a dozen sail and powerboats over the past 40 years. They've ranged from small-lake open boats to those equipped for offshore shark and tuna fishing, to sail and powerboats on Lake Michigan, where they have been cruising for the past 15 years. During those years they have cruised extensively throughout Lake Michigan and the North Channel of Lake Huron. Both are past commodores of the Bay Shore Yacht Club in Illinois and members of the Waukegan, IL, Sail and Power Squadron, where Bob has served as an officer and instructor. He has also contributed to the U.S. Power Squadron national magazine, *Ensign*, and holds a U.S. Coast Guard Master's license.

During 2005, Bob and Carol completed a two-year cruise of the Great Loop in their Pacific Seacraft 38T trawler, *Sans Souci,* logging 9,000 miles on the Loop and many of its side trips. Recently they have resumed cruising all of Lake Michigan, but have plans to expand that area, perhaps back into the rivers of the Midwest or canals of Canada. Bob has also been a seminar presenter at Passagemaker Trawler Fests over the past four years, sharing his knowledge of Lake Michigan. For 2012, Bob and Carol cover Lake Michigan for WATERWAY GUIDE, including Green Bay and Door County.

Bud and Elaine Lloyd

Elaine and Bud Lloyd

Bud and Elaine Lloyd, are the cruising editors for South Florida, the Keys and Okeechobee Waterway. After being long-time sailors (they had several sailboats over the years), the Lloyds decided that in order to do the type of cruising they dreamed of they needed a trawler. *Diamond Girl* is a 36-foot 1990 Nova/Heritage East Sundeck. From their home port of Long Beach, California, they cruised all over southern California and parts of Mexico extensively for over 30 years. After retiring from the printing business in 2005, they decided that it was time to get serious about fulfilling a life-long dream of cruising the Chesapeake Bay and ICW. So in December 2005, they put *Diamond Girl* on a ship and sent her to Ft. Lauderdale, Florida. They have now been cruising on the East Coast for almost 5 years and have found the experience even more rewarding than they ever imagined. They have made several trips up and down the ICW, have spent the summers cruising on the Chesapeake Bay, and have made numerous crossings of the Okeechobee Waterway. Bud and Elaine are full-time liveaboard cruisers and can't wait to see what awaits them over the next horizon. Now the WATERWAY GUIDE has given them the opportunity to write about what they enjoy most…cruising!

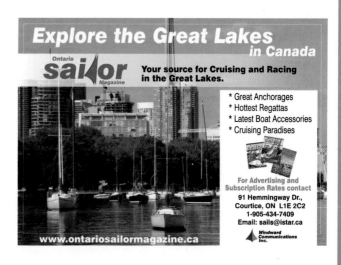

Wally Moran

Wally Moran

Wally Moran has been boating on the North Channel and Georgian Bay since the late 1970s, and has never tired of spending his summers there. "There's always something new to discover up here," he claims. Wally spends his winters cruising south from his northern paradise to the Bahamas, Cuba and the U.S. east coast. When he's not sailing, he writes for SAIL Magazine, and has produced several videos for The Sailing Channel, including "Forbidding, Forbidden Cuba" and "Sailing South, the First Timer's Guide to the ICW."

Larry and Ruth Smithers

Larry and Ruth Smithers

Larry and Ruth Smithers are cruising editors for Waterway Guide's Northern edition from Cape Cod through Maine. They have boated in various capacities since the early 1970s. Serious passionate boating gripped them with the acquisition of *Back Dock,* their 56-foot Vantare pilothouse motoryacht. They quickly discovered that work got in the way of boating. Bidding their land life *adieu* they sold their practice, leased out their home in Wisconsin, packed up and moved aboard to cruise full time in pursuit of high adventure and sunsets worthy of the nightly celebratory conch horn serenade. The Smithers have completed the Great Loop, cruised the Bahamas and, as always, look forward to continue exploring new territories.

Larry spent the first half of his working career in the international corporate world and the last as a chiropractor. He is now retired, a U.S. Coast Guard-licensed captain and can proudly recite the pirate alphabet. Ruth's career was in public accounting. She retired to become a stay-at-home mother, which ultimately evolved into being a professional volunteer and dilettante. She enjoys basket making and her role as "Admiral."

Audrey and Ted Stehle

Audrey and Ted Stehle

Audrey and Ted Stehle are Waterway Guide's cruising editors for the inland rivers and the Tenn-Tom Waterway, from Chicago to Mobile Bay, for the Great Lakes 2012 Guide.

They began boating as sailors in the early 1970s on the Chesapeake Bay and then switched to power after retirement. In addition to extensive cruising of Chesapeake Bay and its tributaries, they have traveled the ICW to Florida many times, completed the Great Loop, cruised the Ohio, Tennessee and Cumberland rivers and made six trips on the Tenn-Tom Waterway. Their Californian 45 is presently on Chesapeake Bay, but plans call for returning it to Kentucky Lake to resume cruising the Cumberland and Tennessee rivers. When not cruising, the Stehles reside in Cincinnati, OH, to be near their children and grandchildren and engage in volunteer work.

Maxwell and Jen Williamson

Jen and Maxwell Williamson

Maxwell and Jen sailed their home waters of the lower Chesapeake Bay for years before deciding to make a drastic lifestyle change in 2009 by moving aboard their Baba 35' Anastasia. While their contemporaries were buying houses and cars, they were selling it all for the dream of cruising. Since then, they have been full-time cruisers traveling up and down the U.S. East Coast, Bahamas and Caribbean. Of all the beautiful places they have visited they still say that their true favorite are the Bahamian Islands. Unlike anywhere else the clear blue water and white sand beaches draw them back year after year. They think cruising is a wonderful way to travel and meet others who share similar interests.

Robert Wilson

Robert Wilson

Robert Wilson has been cruising in the Bahamas from his homeport in Brunswick, GA, for the past nine years. He and his wife, Carolyn, began sailing on Lake Lanier, just north of Atlanta, GA, shortly after they met 25 years ago. Robert is a former employee benefits consultant and is a Past Commodore of the Royal Marsh Harbour Yacht Club in Abaco. Together they have written extensively about their sailing adventures throughout the Bahamas on their 38-foot Island Packet, *Gypsy Common.* Their current boat, *Sea Island Girl*, is a North Pacific 42 pilothouse trawler, which they cruised in the Pacific Northwest along the coast of British Columbia, before shipping the boat to Florida to continue cruising throughout the Bahamas aboard their new trawler.

When not cruising, the Wilsons reside in Atlanta, GA, where Carolyn teaches pre-school, and Robert continues consulting and writing. Robert is Waterway Guide's cruising editor for the northern Bahamas. ■

Things to Know Before You Go

There are many reasons we go cruising, but they can all be summed up in one word—adventure. The thought of casting off the dock lines with a fully provisioned boat and a reasonably blank calendar is intoxicating indeed. Exploring the waters of the Intracoastal Waterway (ICW) can take a lifetime. Let's get started!

For ICW boaters, the ultimate experience is the long-range cruise—the one that continues through several seasons, allowing you to follow the fair weather, from north to south and back again. (Boaters lucky enough to enjoy this lifestyle are often referred to as "snowbirds.") About two weeks into "sweater weather" on the Chesapeake Bay, these cruisers are preparing to head for the warmer climes of North Carolina and ports farther south—much like migratory waterfowl.

Wise skippers schedule their 1,090-mile voyage between Norfolk, VA and Miami, FL so that they neither catch up with the mosquitoes nor get caught by snow. A workable schedule involves dropping Maine astern by the first of September and reaching the Chesapeake Bay by the end of the month, just in time to enjoy the fall foliage. By the time October arrives, the Annapolis Boat Shows get into full swing. After that, it is a good idea to leave Norfolk, and what can be wet, nasty weather, behind you.

Once you have arrived in the Carolinas, the boat will be safe from ice for a time, should you need to leave it moored or docked while you regroup or return home for a visit. Serious snowbirds, however, will be well into Georgia or Florida long before it is time to prepare their Thanksgiving dinners.

The Time Factor

A trip down the ICW can last a few weeks, a month or as long as you choose. It all depends on how fast you go, which route you choose and how long you decide to linger along the way.

If you plan to keep moving under power almost every day—stopping each evening to enjoy the amenities of a

Dinghies at dock ready for departure.
WATERWAY GUIDE PHOTOGRAPHY

marina or anchorage—the following running times are fairly typical. In about two weeks (barring weather or mechanical delays), you can run from the Chesapeake Bay to the Georgia/Florida border. Many ICW cruisers take longer, however, stopping along the way to explore coastal towns and take in the sights. Once in Florida, you can run to southern Miami in an additional week.

It is smart to allow time along the way for sightseeing, resting, waiting out bad weather or making repairs to the boat. Of course, the boat's features and the skipper's temperament will determine whether the pace is fast or slow. Sailboats averaging 5 to 8 knots can cover the same number of miles on a given day as a powerboat that cruises at 20 to 25 knots. The only difference is that the sailboat's crew will have a much longer day underway.

Those who are eager to reach southern waters can cruise the length of Chesapeake Bay in two days or less, while others who want to poke around in the Bay's scores of harbors and gunkholes can spend a month without seeing everything.

First-Aid Basics

A deep cut from a filet knife is normally not a big deal at home where medical help is close at hand, but on the ICW (where you may be a long way from help), you will need to be able to patch yourself up until you can get to an emergency clinic or hospital emergency room. Adequate first-aid kits are essential, along with a medical manual that you can understand quickly; the standard reference is "Advanced First-Aid Afloat" by Dr. Peter F. Eastman. Good first-aid kits can be found at most marine supply stores and better pharmacies or drug stores.

Cruisers who take medication should make sure their current prescription has plenty of refills available so supplies can be topped off along the way. Additionally, make sure crew members are aware of any medication you are on in case you become injured and unable to answer questions regarding your health.

All safety equipment—harnesses, life preservers, jack lines, medical kit—should be in good working condition, within easy reach and ready at a moment's notice. All aboard, both crew and guests, should know where to find the emergency equipment. In addition to having the proper first-aid gear aboard, all aboard should be versed in basic "first responder" procedures, including CPR and making a "May-Day" call on the VHF radio.

Check out our Goin' Ashore sections of this Guide; they provide contact information for local hospitals and emergency clinics. Most importantly, if someone's life is in imminent danger, make a "May-Day" call on VHF Channel 16. This is the best way to get quick help. Making a 911 call on your cell phone is also an option, but not one you should count on because of variable coverage along the ICW by cellular providers.

Boating Education

The most important thing to know before you go is how to operate your boat safely. Operating a boat safely is like operating an automobile safely. Both activities require knowledge, skill and safety awareness. Mastery of these factors leads to a more enjoyable boating experience for everyone on board, and it begins with education.

An effective boating education program begins with an orientation in the equipment involved—the boat, its means of propulsion (sails or engines), instrumentation, and those items that will keep you and any passengers on board safe while underway. The program should include a study of the "rules of the road" which you, as operator, should follow at all times. (Unfortunately, many boaters do not follow the rules because they have never taken a course in boating.) The best programs include hands-on training aboard a vessel while underway.

A good beginners' course is one approved by the State or National Association of State Boating Law Administrators (NASBLA). Such a test is mandatory in some states. A good reference book is *Chapman's Piloting & Seamanship* published by Hearst Marine Books and is available in most bookstores and libraries.

"An educated boater is a safe boater," stated Tom Danti, Dean of Instruction at the *Chapman School of Seamanship*. "Such a boater will be alert and prepared to act effectively should an emergency arise and, in all other respects, make the boating experience an enjoyable one for all on board."

Please note: Each state has its own boater safety regulations. Those with more stringent regulations generally allow exemptions for non-residents who are visiting for a limited (e.g., 45 or 90 days) amount of time. To see state-by-state requirements, visit www.boatus.org/onlinecourse/default.asp.

A Note on Clean Marinas

The next time you pull into your favorite ICW facility, you might want to look around for some indication of it being a designated "Clean Marina." Many states around the country—including those covered in this edition of Waterway Guide—have launched programs in recent years aimed at making marina owners and boaters more aware of how their activities affect the environment. In order for one's marina to be designated a "Clean Marina," the facility's owner has to take a series of steps prescribed by that state's respective program, anything from making sure tarps are laid down when boat bottoms are worked on, to providing pump-out facilities. (The steps were derived

from an Environmental Protection Agency document presented to states across America.)

The underlying principle behind these voluntary, incentive-based programs is this: If the waters we cruise are not clean, then we will cruise elsewhere and the marine businesses in the polluted areas will suffer. The programs represent a nice coupling of economics and environmental management that is catching on with marina owners and boaters alike. So if you see the Clean Marina designation at your favorite facility, rest assured they are doing the right thing for the environment.

Considerations for Sailors

Sailors sometimes worry about travel on the ICW, but unless your mast is higher than 65 feet or your keel draws more than seven feet, the trip is entirely possible and likely easy. Boats that have less than a 6-foot draft usually have few problems, while 5 feet or less is optimum. The truth of the matter is that more sailboats than powerboats can sometimes be seen transiting the ICW.

The Julia Tuttle Bridge in Miami has a 56-foot fixed vertical clearance. Many Gulf Coast bridges have 50-foot vertical clearances, and one bridge across Florida's Okeechobee Waterway is just 49 feet (although a local marina will heel over taller boats using 55-gallon drums of water as ballast to slip underneath it). While overhead power lines are generally quite high, be sure to allow several feet of extra clearance to prevent arcing to the mast. See our bridge tables in the Skipper's Handbook for overhead clearances, opening schedules and mile marker locations. Sailors obviously cannot pace motorboats on plane, but they do have the option of using occasional fair winds to enjoy the quieter ride and save some fuel, often simply by unrolling the jib. Rules forbid sailing through a drawbridge unless a sailboat is without power; notify the bridge tender if this is the case. There may be some good-natured ribbing when a sailboat pulls up to the fuel dock and tops off with 5 gallons instead of 500.

THINGS YOU WILL NEED

To minimize time spent waiting for spare parts—which can be considerable in some areas—WATERWAY GUIDE recommends that cruising boaters take along certain equipment.

Spare Parts

For the engine, bring spare seals for the raw-water pump and an extra water-pump impeller, along with V-belts, points and plugs for gas engines (injectors for diesel engines), a fuel pump and strainer, a distributor cap, fuses, lube oil and filter cartridges. Also, carry a list of service centers for your type of equipment and bring the engine manual and the parts list.

Other things to bring: spare deck cap keys, a head-repair kit, fresh water-pump repair kit, spare hose clamps, lengths of hose and an extra container of fuel. (Keep in mind that, if you want to anchor out, fueling up during the day when there are no crowds at the fuel docks is a good idea.)

Carry a good tool kit with varying sizes of flat- and Phillips-head screwdrivers, socket wrenches (metric and standard), pliers, etc. Remember that all the spare parts in the world are fairly useless without a proper bag of tools aboard to install them with.

For Docking and Anchoring

Your docking equipment should include a minimum of four bow and stern lines made of good, stretchy nylon (each at least two-thirds the length of your boat), and two spring lines (at least 1.5 times the length of your boat) with oversized eyes to fit over pilings. If you have extra dock lines, consider bringing them along with your shore power cord and a shore power adapter or two.

For anchoring, the average 30-foot boat needs 150 to 200 feet of 7/16- to 1/2-inch nylon line with no less than 15 feet of 5/16-inch chain shackled to a 20- to 30-pound plow-type or Bruce anchor—or a 15-pound Danforth-type anchor. Storm anchors and a lunch hook are also recommended. Larger yachts should use 7/8-inch nylon and heavier chain. While one anchor will get you along, most veteran cruisers carry both a plow and fluke-type anchor to use in varying bottom conditions.

Consult a good reference like *Chapman's Piloting* or West Marine's "West Advisor" articles (available online) if you are unsure about proper anchoring techniques and make sure that you master them before setting off down the ICW.

Tenders and Dinghies

A dinghy is needed if you plan to anchor out, gunkhole or carry an anchor to deeper water to kedge off a shoal. Inflatable dinghies are popular, but they require an outboard motor to get them around easily. On the other hand, rowing a hard dinghy is excellent exercise. Check registration laws where you plan to spend any length of time, as certain states (including Florida) have become very strict in enforcing dinghy registration.

Always chain and lock your dinghy when you leave it unattended, even if it is tied off to your boat, as more than one cruiser has woken to a missing dinghy while at anchor on the ICW. Outboard engines should always be padlocked to the transom of your dinghy or on a stern rail, as they are often targets of thieves.

Keeping Comfortable

Another consideration when equipping your boat for a cruise is temperature control inside the cabin. Many powerboats—particularly trawlers—are equipped with an air-conditioner for those hot, steamy nights. Others can get away with fans and wind scoops. When considering heating options for your boat, select something that is not going to suck your batteries dead and, even more important, something that is safe. Many reliable and safe marine propane and diesel heaters are available nowadays for those cruising late into the fall season.

Since the weather can turn chilly or even downright cold in the Carolinas during autumn and in Georgia or northern Florida any time in winter, most seasoned ICW cruisers have full-cockpit enclosures to guard the crew from the elements.

Battling the Sun and Bugs

Cruisers in an open cockpit need the protection of a dodger, awning, or bimini top, not to mention sunscreen and a hat. In fact, many hard-core cruisers have an enclosure that surrounds the entire cockpit. Whatever method, take measures to make sure you are not out in the elements all day without protection if you can avoid it.

You will want a good quality sunscreen on board with you if you have any intention of enjoying the topside portion of your boat. Bug screens for hatches, ports and companionways are a must, as you will want to have the boat open for adequate cross ventilation in warm weather.

Glare off the water can be a major contributor to fatigue. Consider purchasing a quality pair of sunglasses and make sure they are polarized, as this feature removes annoying reflected light from your view and helps prevent long-term damage to your eyes and vision.

Navigating Essentials

Charts for coastal piloting belong at the helm station, not in the cabin, so a clipboard or spray-proof plastic case comes in handy. Many ICW veterans like to use the spiral-bound chart "kits" that feature charts laid out in order according to the ICW route. Since the local conditions change constantly, use only the latest charts, and keep them updated with the U.S. Coast Guard's *Local Notice to Mariners,* which is available online at www.navcen.uscg.gov/lnm. For planning, many charts and nautical publications (Coast Pilots, light lists, tide tables) can be downloaded free of charge via the Internet. See our Skipper's Handbook section for more detail on how to access this valuable information with your computer.

Many cruisers are now equipping themselves with the latest GPS chartplotters and computer-driven electronic gizmos, and while convenient, they are not a requirement for cruising the ICW. Radar is a wonderful aid, not only to "see" markers and other vessels but also to track local storms; probably half of all ICW boats have it. Single-Sideband (SSB) and amateur (ham) radio are excellent for long-range communications, but you can get by without either one on the ICW. You will not want to cruise the ICW without a depth sounder; this item is essential.

You should learn how to operate all of your navigation electronics inside and out before you rely on them for navigation. A dense fogbank is no place to figure out how your navigation equipment works. As always, you should have paper charts available as backup in case your electronic unit malfunctions.

A VHF marine radio is the cruiser's lifeline to the Coast Guard, marinas and other boats and is also necessary for contacting ICW bridges. Mount yours at the helm or keep a handheld unit nearby. Many manufacturers now offer a RAM (remote access microphone) option, which allows the skipper to use the hand unit and control the radio from the helm.

Most cruisers carry cell phones, but you cannot count on coverage everywhere, as these systems are optimized for land users. See the "VHF Radio" section of the Skipper's Handbook located at the front of the book for more detail on VHF radio operation and regulations.

Have a compass adjuster swing (calibrate) your steering compass before departure so you can run courses with confidence. Also, carry a good hand-bearing compass or binoculars with a built-in compass for getting bearings to fixed marks or points ashore.

The Money Issue

Everyone is concerned about money, but when you are a long-range cruiser, the issue becomes a bit more complicated. Luckily, cruisers today can get by with much less cash than in the past. Almost all banks have ATMs. Many grocery stores and drugstores accept ATM and Visa or MasterCard check cards. Remember that most banks will honor the cash-advance feature of Visa and MasterCard. In addition, American Express offices will accept a cardholder's personal check in payment for Travelers checks and will also dispense cash to cardholders.

Most marinas, especially the large ones, accept major credit cards and oil company credit cards for dockage, fuel and marine supplies. Most restaurants, motels and grocery stores will also accept major credit cards. Credit-card statements also serve as excellent records of expenses while traveling.

A majority of banks now offer online banking services that allow you to pay your bills remotely via the Internet. With online banking, you can pay bills, set up new payees, transfer funds, check your balances, and much more. You can also set up recurring payments on an "auto-pay" system that pays your bills automatically every month or when your payee sends your bank an "e-bill."

Do be careful where you conduct your online banking sessions. Many public marina computers "remember" passwords and forms (handy for a thief looking to steal your identity or your money), and many marina Internet WiFi (wireless) connections are not totally secure. It is best to use your own computer that is hooked up to a terrestrial network with your own secure firewall running.

Getting Your Mail

Your incoming mail can be sent to General Delivery in towns where you plan to put in and stay awhile. Many ICW veterans have friends or family at home check their mail and occasionally forward it to them in the next town they plan to pull into. Tell the sender to write "Hold for Arrival" on the envelope, along with your name and your boat's name. Notify the post office that you want your mail held. They will hold first-class mail or forward it to another post office on receipt of a change-of-address card.

The United States Postal Service is now offering a service called Premium Forwarding that is designed to work in tandem with their Priority Mail program. There are also many companies that specialize in forwarding mail and paying bills for ICW cruisers. Simply enter "mail forwarding, bill services" into your favorite Internet search engine for options.

Check the Skipper's Handbook section following this one for mail-drop locations along the ICW, as well a complement of specific details on getting your mail and paying bills.

Waterway Guide Web Updates

Waterway Guide has made so many recent updates to our website (www.waterwayguide.com) that it is hard to know where to begin. We have added Marina Close-ups so you can look ahead to plan your next marina stop with one of our sponsors. Our Waterway Planner can help you plan your trip and locate marinas, bridges/locks and anchorages. The Discussion Board lets you post information about areas through which you are traveling or get information from those traveling ahead of you. These website upgrades strongly focus on reader interaction.

Waterway Guide continues to provide other helpful services on our website: "Navigation Updates" offers the most up-to-date information available on such items as Waterway conditions, changing bridge schedules and hazards to navigation; and "Cruising News" reports events, marina updates, fuel prices and general ICW information. Best of all, these portals are broken into easy-to-follow regions so navigating Waterway Guide's website is even easier than navigating the Waterway. ■

Skipper's Handbook

A Guide to Cruising Essentials

Coast Guard

Photo courtesy: U.S. Coast Guard.

The U.S. Coast Guard is on duty 24 hours a day, 7 days a week to aid recreational boaters and commercial vessels alike. They have search and rescue capabilities, and may provide lookout, communication or patrol functions to assist vessels in distress.

■ Fifth Coast Guard District
(Includes coastal waters and tributaries from Toms River, NJ to the North Carolina/South Carolina border.) **District Office**: Federal Building, 431 Crawford St., Portsmouth, VA 23704, 757-398-6000 or 757-398-6390, www.uscg.mil/d5.

■ ICW: North Carolina (Sector North Carolina)

Sector Field Office Cape Hatteras, NC: 114 Wood Hill Drive, Nags Head, NC 27959, 252-441-0300.

Air Station Elizabeth City, NC: About 3.5 miles southeast of Elizabeth City, on the south bank of the Pasquotank River. 252-335-6333.

Station Elizabeth City, NC: About 3.5 miles southeast of Elizabeth City, on the south bank of the Pasquotank River. 919-335-6086.

Station Oregon Inlet, NC: North of Oregon Inlet and the Herbert C. Bonner Bridge. 252-441-6260.

Station Hatteras Inlet, NC: Southern end of Hatteras Island next to the ferry docks, one mile southwest of the town of Hatteras. 919-986-2175.

Station Hobucken, NC: On the Intracoastal Waterway at Mile Marker 157.1, just north of the Hobucken Bridge. 252-745-3131.

Station Ocracoke, NC: At Ocracoke, behind the Ocracoke water tower. 252-928-3711.

Station Emerald Isle, NC: Near Bogue Inlet. 252-354-2719.

Station Fort Macon, NC: About 0.1 miles west of Fort Macon. 252-247-4583.

Station Swansboro, NC: At Emerald Isle. 252-354-2462.

Station Wrightsville Beach, NC: At the southwestern end of Wrightsville Beach at Masonboro Inlet. 910-256-2615.

Station Oak Island, NC: On the western side of the Cape Fear River entrance. 910-278-1133.

■ Seventh Coast Guard District
(Includes coastal waters and tributaries of South Carolina, Georgia, Florida [east of Apalachicola], Puerto Rico, the U.S. Virgin Islands and the adjacent islands of the United States.)

District Office: Brickell Plaza Federal Building, 909 S.E. First Ave. Miami, FL 33131, 305-415-6730, www.uscg.mil/d7.

■ ICW: South Carolina (Sector Charleston)

Station Georgetown, SC: Just south of the U.S. Highway 17 bridge at Mile Marker 402.1. 843-546-2742.

Station Charleston Base, SC: East side of Ashley River, 0.8 miles above the Battery. 843-724-7600.

■ ICW: Georgia (Sector Charleston)

Air Station Savannah, GA: 1297 N. Lightning Rd. Savannah, GA 31409. 912-652-4646.

Station Brunswick, GA: On Plantation Creek, east of the Sidney Lanier Bridge. 912-267-7999.

Station Tybee Island, GA: On Cockspur Island, near Ft. Pulaski. 912-786-5440.

Additional Resources

U.S. Coast Guard: www.uscg.mil

SKIPPER'S HANDBOOK

Port Security Procedures

Since September 11, 2001, the U.S. Coast Guard and other military organizations have increased their security presence at ports, near military vessels and throughout the length of the Intracoastal Waterway (ICW). The Coast Guard—now a division of the U.S. Department of Homeland Security—requires that all recreational boaters make themselves aware of the existence of security zones, permanent and temporary, before leaving the dock. A claim of ignorance for an infraction will no longer exempt boaters from penalty.

There are several areas along the ICW that require a little forethought and due vigilance on your part. Following the steps in the action plan below will help not only help to ensure a trouble-free journey but should also keep you and your crew out of the headlines.

Prepare:

- Before you leave, check the current charts for the area in which you will be traveling to identify any security areas. Security zones are highlighted and outlined in magenta with special notes regarding the specific regulations pertaining to that area.
- Check the latest *Local Notice to Mariners* (available online at *http://www.navcen.uscg.gov/?pageName=lnmMain* and posted at some marinas) and identify any potential security areas that may not be shown on the chart.
- Listen to VHF Channel 16 for any Sécurité alerts from the Coast Guard (departing cruise ships, naval vessels, fuel tankers, etc.) for the area you will be cruising prior to departure.
- Talk to boaters in your anchorage or marina that just came from where you will be traveling. They will most likely have tips and suggestions on any potential security zones or special areas they encountered on their way.

Stay Alert While Underway:

- Mind the outlined magenta security areas noted on your charts.
- Look for vessels with blue or red warning lights in port areas and, if approached, listen carefully and strictly obey all instructions given to you.
- Keep your VHF radio switched to Channel 16 and keep your ears tuned for bulletins, updates and possible requests for communication with you.
- Avoid commercial port operation areas, especially those that involve military, cruise-line or petroleum facilities. Observe and avoid other restricted areas near power plants, national monuments, etc.
- If you need to pass within 100 yards of a U.S. naval vessel for safe passage, you must contact the U.S. naval vessel or the Coast Guard escort vessel on VHF Channel 16.
- If government security or the U.S. Coast Guard hails you, do exactly what they say, regardless of whether or not you feel they have any merit in their actions.

Sensitive ICW Port Areas:

- **Norfolk, VA –** Large naval installation (Naval Station Norfolk) and support facilities are located north and south of ICW Mile 0 on the Elizabeth River. Keep an eye out for submarines, aircraft carriers and all manner of naval vessels under tow or escort. Keep out of charted security zones where ships are berthed. Vessels also use the entrance to the Chesapeake Bay frequently when returning from the ocean. Containerships and commercial vessels are often under escort in the harbor and in the Chesapeake Bay entrance; stay clear of them at all times.
- **Newport News, VA –** Newport News Shipbuilding (aircraft carriers) is upstream on the James River from Hampton. Keep at least 100 yards away from naval vessels (both underway and berthed).
- **Camp Lejuene, NC –** Marine base is located on ICW near Mile Marker 235. Firing range and Marine base occasionally close the ICW for periods of time during military exercises. Tune radio to AM 530 and keep a lookout for manned boats while transiting this area.
- **Charleston Harbor, SC –** Naval and shipping activity is commonplace in the Cooper and Wando Rivers north of Mile Marker 465 and in the harbor itself toward the Charleston Harbor Entrance.
- **Savannah, GA –** Commercial shipping interests use the Savannah River from the ocean entrance upriver to the Port of Savannah. The ICW intersects this shipping area south of Mile Marker 575 at Fields Cut.
- **Kings Bay, GA –** Trident submarines enter and depart the ICW from north of Mile Marker 710 south to the St. Marys River entrance at the Georgia/Florida state line.

Additional Resources

Department of Homeland Security: *www.dhs.gov*
U.S. Coast Guard *www.uscg.mil*
Local Notice to Mariners: *http://www.navcen.uscg.gov/?pageName=lnmMain*
Atlantic Intracostal Waterway Association: *www.atlanticintracoastal.org*
America's Waterway Watch: *http://aww.aww-sp.com/*

Rules Of The Road

It is all about courtesy. Much like a busy highway, our waterways can become a melee of confusion when people don't follow the rules of the road. But unlike Interstate 95 and its byways, the Atlantic waterways aren't fitted with eight-sided stop signs or the familiar yellow, green and red traffic lights. You will need to rely on your own knowledge to safely co-exist with fellow boaters and avoid collisions.

Most heated waterway encounters can be avoided by simply slowing down, letting the other boat go first and biting your tongue, regardless of whether you think they are right or wrong. Pressing your agenda or taking out your frustrations with the last bridge tender you encountered normally leads to unpleasantness. When in doubt, stand down, and get out of the other guy's way. The effect on your timetable will be minimal.

Anyone planning to cruise our waterways should make themselves familiar with the rules of the road. "Chapman Piloting: Seamanship and Small Boat Handling" and "The Annapolis Book of Seamanship" are both excellent on-the-water references with plentiful information on navigation rules. For those with a penchant for the exact regulatory language, the Coast Guard publication "Navigation Rules: International-Inland" covers both international and U.S. inland rules. (Boats over 39.4 feet are required to carry a copy of the U.S. Inland Rules at all times.) These rules are also available online here: www.navcen.uscg.gov/?pageName=intinland.

The following is a list of common situations you will likely encounter on the waterways. Make yourself familiar with them, and if you ever have a question as to which of you has the right-of-way, let the other vessel go first.

Passing or being passed:

■ If you intend to pass a slower vessel, try to hail them on your VHF radio to let them know you are coming.

■ In close quarters, BOTH vessels should slow down. Slowing down normally allows the faster vessel to pass quickly without throwing a large wake onto the slower boat.

■ Slower boats being passed have the right-of-way and passing vessels must take all actions necessary to keep clear of these slower vessels.

At opening bridges:

■ During an opening, boats traveling with the current go first and generally have the right-of-way.

■ Boats constrained by their draft, size or maneuverability (e.g., dredges, tugs, barges) also take priority.

■ Standard rules of the road apply while circling or waiting for a bridge opening.

Tugs, freighters, dredges, naval vessels:

■ These beasts are usually constrained by draft or their inability to maneuver nimbly. For this reason, you will almost always need to give them the right-of-way, and keep out of their path.

■ You must keep at least 100 yards away from any Navy vessel. If you cannot safely navigate without coming closer than this, you must alert notify the ship of your intentions over VHF radio (normally Channel 16).

■ Keep a close watch for freighters, tugs with tows, and other large vessels while offshore or in crowded ports. They often come up very quickly, despite their large size.

■ It is always a good practice to radio larger vessels (VHF Channel 13 or 16) to notify them of your location and your intentions. The skippers of these boats are generally appreciative of efforts to communicate with them. This is especially true with dredge boats on the Intracoastal Waterway (ICW).

In a crossing situation:

■ When two vessels under power are crossing and a risk of collision exists, the vessel that has the other on her starboard side must keep clear and avoid crossing ahead of the other vessel.

■ When a vessel under sail and a vessel under power are crossing, the boat under power is usually burdened and must keep clear. The same exceptions apply as per head-on meetings.

■ On the Great Lakes and western rivers (Mississippi River system), a power-driven vessel crossing a river shall keep clear of a power-driven vessel ascending or descending the river.

Power vessels meeting one another or meeting vessels under sail:

■ When two vessels under power (sailboats or powerboats) meet "head-to-head," both are obliged to alter course to starboard.

■ Generally, when a vessel under power meets a vessel under sail (i.e., not using any mechanical power), the powered vessel must alter course accordingly.

■ Exceptions are: Vessels not under command, vessels restricted in ability to maneuver, vessels engaged in commercial fishing or those under International Rules, such as a vessel constrained by draft.

Two sailboats meeting under sail:

■ When each has the wind on a different side, the boat with the wind on the port side must keep clear of the boat with the wind on the starboard side.

■ When both have the wind on the same side, the vessel closest to the wind (windward) will keep clear of the leeward boat.

■ A vessel with wind to port that sees a vessel to windward but cannot determine whether the windward vessel has wind to port or starboard, will assume that windward vessel is on starboard tack, and keep clear.

Resources

The Coast Guard publication "Navigation Rules – International-Inland" is available at most well-stocked marine stores, including West Marine (*www.westmarine.com*) and Bluewater Books and Charts (*www.bluewaterweb.com*). These establishments normally stock the aforementioned Chapman's and Annapolis Seamanship books also.

Bridge Basics

Life on the Intracoastal Waterway (ICW) often revolves around bridge openings, and with scores of bridges between Norfolk, VA and Jacksonville, FL, you will likely encounter one or more a day. A particular bridge's schedule can often decide where you tie up for the evening or when you wake up and get underway the next day.

The handy bridge tables farther back in this section are an essential resource for planning your day's travel. Because many bridges restrict their openings during morning and evening rush hours to minimize inconvenience to vehicular traffic, you may need to plan an early start or late stop to avoid getting stuck waiting for a bridge opening. Take a few minutes before setting out to learn whether bridge schedules have changed; changes are posted in the Coast Guard's Local Notice to Mariners reports, which can be found online at www.navcen.uscg.gov.

The easiest way to hail a bridge is via VHF radio. Bridges in most states use VHF Channel 13, while bridges in Florida, Georgia and South Carolina monitor VHF Channel 09. Keep in mind that bridge tenders are just like the rest of us—everyone has their good and bad days. The best way to thwart any potential grumpiness is to follow the opening procedures to the letter and act with professionalism. This will almost always ensure a timely opening.

Bridge Procedures:

■ First, decide if it is necessary to have the drawbridge opened. You will need to know your boat's clearance height above the waterline before you start down the ICW. Drawbridges have "Clearance Gauges" to show the closed vertical clearance with changing water levels, but a bascule bridge typically has 3 to 5 feet more clearance than what is indicated on the gauge at the center of its arch at mean low tide. Bridge clearances are also shown on NOAA charts.

■ Contact the bridge tender well in advance (even if you can't see the bridge around the bend) by VHF radio or phone. Alternatively, you can sound one long and one short horn blast to request an opening. Tugs with tows and U.S. government vessels may go through bridges at any time, usually signaling with five short blasts. A restricted bridge may open in an emergency with the same signal. Keep in mind bridge tenders will not know your intentions unless you tell them.

■ If two or more vessels are in sight of one another, the bridge tender may elect to delay opening the bridge until all boats can go through together.

■ Approach at slow speed and be prepared to wait, as the bridge cannot open until the traffic gates are closed. Many ICW bridges are more than 40 years old and the aged machinery functions slowly.

■ Once the bridge is open, proceed at no-wake speed. Keep a safe distance between you and other craft, as currents and turbulence around bridge supports can be tricky.

■ There is technically no legal right-of-way (except on the Mississippi and some other inland rivers), but boats running with the current should always be given the right-of-way out of courtesy. As always, if you are not sure, let the other guy go first.

■ When making the same opening as a commercial craft, it is a good idea to contact the vessel's captain (usually on VHF Channel 13), ascertain his intentions and state yours to avoid any misunderstanding in tight quarters.

■ After passing through the bridge, maintain a no-wake speed until you are well clear and then resume normal speed.

Bridge Types

Swing Bridges:
Swing bridges have an opening section that pivots horizontally on a central hub, allowing boats to pass on one side or the other when it is open.

Lift Bridges:
Lift bridges normally have two towers on each end of the opening section that are equipped with cables that lift the road or railway vertically into the air.

Pontoon Bridges:
A pontoon bridge consists of an opening section that must be floated out of the the way with a cable to allow boats to pass.

Bascule Bridges:
This is the most common type of opening bridge you will encounter. The opening section of a bascule bridge has one or two leaves that tilt vertically on a hinge like doors being opened skyward.

VHF Communications

Skippers traveling the Intracoastal Watersay (ICW) use their VHF radios almost every day to contact other vessels and bridge tenders, make reservations at marinas, arrange to pass other vessels safely and conduct other business. WATERWAY GUIDE has put together the following information to help remove any confusion as to what frequency should be dialed in to call bridges, marinas, commercial ships or your friend anchored down the creek.

Channel Usage Tips

■ VHF Channel 16 (156.8 MHz) is by far the most important frequency on the VHF-FM band. It is also the most abused. Channel 16 is the international distress, safety and calling frequency.

■ FCC regulations require boaters to maintain a watch on either Channel 09 or 16 whenever the radio is turned on and not being used to communicate on another channel.

■ Since the Coast Guard does not have the capability of announcing an urgent marine information broadcast or weather warning on Channel 09, it recommends that boaters normally keep tuned to and use Channel 16, but no conversations of any length should take place there—its primary function is for emergencies only.

■ The Coast Guard's main working channel is 22A, and both emergency and non-emergency calls generally are switched to it in order to keep 16 clear. Calling the Coast Guard for a radio check on Channel 16 is prohibited.

■ The radio-equipped bridges covered in this edition use Channel 13, except for South Carolina, Georgia, and Florida, which use VHF Channel 09.

■ Recreational craft typically communicate on Channels 68, 69, 71, 72 or 78A. Whenever possible, avoid calling on Channel 16 altogether by prearranging initial contact directly on one of these channels. No transmissions should last longer than three minutes.

■ The Bridge-to-Bridge Radio Telephone Act requires many commercial vessels, including dredges and tugboats, to monitor Channel 13. Channel 13 is also the frequency most used by bridges in Maryland, Virginia, and North Carolina.

Note: The Coast Guard has asked the FCC to eliminate provisions for using Channel 09 as an alternative calling frequency to Channel 16 when it eliminates watch-keeping on Channel 16 by compulsory-equipped vessels.

VHF Channels

09 – Used for radio checks and hailing other stations (boats, shore side operations). Use to communicate with bridges in South Carolina, Georgia and Florida.

13 – Used to contact and communicate with commercial vessels, military ships and drawbridges. Bridges in Maryland, Virginia and North Carolina monitor this channel.

16 – Emergency use only. May be used to hail other vessels but once contact is made, conversation should be immediately switched to a working channel (68, 69, 71, 72, 78A).

22A – Used for U.S. Coast Guard safety, navigation and Sécurité communications.

68, 69, 71, 72, 78A – Used primarily for recreational ship-to-ship and ship-to-shore communications.

VHF Channel 16 – In Case of Emergency

MAYDAY – The distress signal MAYDAY is used to indicate that a station is threatened by grave and imminent danger and requests immediate assistance.

PAN PAN – The urgency signal PAN PAN is used when the safety of the ship or person is in jeopardy.

SÉCURITÉ – The safety signal SÉCURITÉ is used for messages about the safety of navigation or important weather warnings.

Resources

U.S. Coast Guard VHF Channel Listing:
www.navcen.uscg.gov/?pageName=mtvhf

Photo courtesy: Fawcett Boat Supplies Inc.

Hurricanes

With visions of hurricanes Isabel, Katrina, Rita, and Wilma still fresh in the country's collective minds, more folks are tuned into turbulent tropical weather than ever. Hurricanes can create vast swaths of devastation but ample preparation can help increase your boat's chances of surviving the storm.

While all coastal areas of the country are vulnerable to the effects of a hurricane (especially from June through November), the Gulf Coast, Southern and Mid-Atlantic states typically have been the hardest hit. And even cities far from the ocean, such as Annapolis, MD, aren't immune to the damages these storms cause either—Waterway Guide's offices were inundated with more than 4 feet of water from Hurricane Isabel in September 2003.

Hurricane Conditions

■ According to the National Weather Service, a mature hurricane may be 10 miles high with a great spiral several hundred miles in diameter. Winds are often well above the 74 mph required to classify as hurricane strength—especially in gusts.

■ Hurricane damage is produced by four elements: tidal surge, wind, wave action and rain. Tidal surge is an increase in ocean depth prior to the storm. This effect, amplified in coastal areas, may cause tidal heights in excess of 15 to 20 feet above normal. Additionally, hurricanes can produce a significant negative tidal effect as water rushes out of the waterways after a storm.

■ The most damaging element of a hurricane for boaters is usually wave action. The wind speed, water depth and the amount of open water determine the amount of wave action created. Storm surge can transform narrow bodies of water into larger, deeper waters capable of generating extreme wave action.

Storm Intensity

Saffir-Simpson Categories

■ **Category 1** . . . . . . 74–95 mph
■ **Category 2** . . . . . 96–110 mph
■ **Category 3** . . . . 111–130 mph
■ **Category 4** . . . . 131–155 mph
■ **Category 5** . . . . 155+ mph

■ Rainfall varies; hurricanes can generate anywhere from 5 to 20 inches or more of rain. If your boat is in a slip, you have three options: Leave it where it is (if it is in a safe place); move it to a refuge area; or haul it and put it on a trailer or cradle.

■ The National Weather Service reports that wind gusts can exceed reported sustained winds by 25 to 50 percent. So, for example, a storm with winds of 150 mph might have gusts of more than 200 mph.

■ Some marinas require mandatory evacuations during hurricane alerts. Check your lease agreement and talk to your dockmaster if you are uncertain. After Hurricane Andrew, Florida's legislature passed a law prohibiting marinas from evicting boats during hurricane watches and warnings. Boaters may also be held liable for any damage that their boat inflicts to marina piers or property; check locally for details.

■ Rivers, canals, coves and other areas away from large stretches of open water are best selected as refuges. Your dockmaster or fellow mariners can make suggestions. Consult your insurance agent if you have questions about coverage.

■ Many insurance agencies have restricted or cancelled policies for boats that travel or are berthed in certain hurricane-prone areas. Review your policy and check your coverage, as many insurance companies will not cover boats in hurricane-prone areas during the June through November hurricane season. Riders for this type of coverage are notoriously expensive.

Preparing Your Boat

■ Have a hurricane plan made up ahead of time to maximize what you can get done in amount of time you will have to prepare (no more than 12 hours in some cases). You will not want to be deciding how to tie up the boat or where to anchor when a hurricane is barreling down on you. Make these decisions in advance.

■ Buy hurricane gear in advance (even if there is no imminent storm). When word of a hurricane spreads, local ship stores run out of storm supplies (anchors and line, especially) very quickly.

■ Strip every last thing that isn't bolted down off the deck of the boat (canvas, sails, antennas, bimini tops, dodgers, dinghies, dinghy motors, cushions, unneeded control lines on sailboats—everything), as this will help reduce windage and damage to your boat. Remove electronics and valuables and move them ashore.

■ Any potentially leaky ports or hatches should be taped up. Dorades (cowls) should be removed and sealed with their deck cap.

■ Make sure all systems on board are in tip-top shape. Fuel and water tanks should be filled, bilge pumps should be in top operating condition and batteries should be fully charged.

■ You will need many lengths of line to secure the boat—make certain it is good stretchy nylon (not Dacron). It is not unusual to string 800 to 1,000 feet of dock line on a 40-foot boat in preparation for a hurricane.

Hurricanes, cont'd.

■ If you can, double up your lines (two for each cleat), as lines can and will break during the storm. Have fenders and fender boards out and make sure all of your lines are protected from chafe.

■ If you are anchored out, use multiple large anchors; there is no such thing as an anchor that is too big. If you can, tie to trees with a good root system, such as mangroves or live oaks. Mangroves are particularly good because their canopy can have a cushioning effect. Be sure mooring lines include ample scope to compensate for tides 10 to 20 feet above normal. Keep in mind that many municipalities close public mooring fields in advance of the storm.

■ Lastly, do not stay aboard to weather the storm. Many people have been seriously injured (or worse) trying to save their boats during a hurricane. Take photos of the condition in which you left your boat and take your insurance binder with you.

Returning Safely After the Storm

■ Before hitting the road, make sure the roads back to your boat are open and safe for travel. Beware of dangling wires, weakened docks, bulkheads, bridges and other structures.

■ Check your boat thoroughly before attempting to move it. If returning to your home slip, watch the waters for debris and obstructions. Navigate carefully because markers may be misplaced or missing. If your boat is sunk, arrange for engine repairs before floating it, but only if it is not impeding traffic. Otherwise, you will need to remove it immediately.

■ Contact your insurance company right away if you need to make a claim.

Resources

National Hurricane Center:
www.nhc.noaa.gov

BoatU.S. Hurricane Resource Center:
www.boatus.com/hurricanes

WATERWAY GUIDE Navigation Updates:
www.waterwayguide.com

SKIPPER'S HANDBOOK

Four consecutive images of Hurricane Andrew (1992) at 24-hour intervals. Photo courtesy of NOAA.

Hurricane Tracker

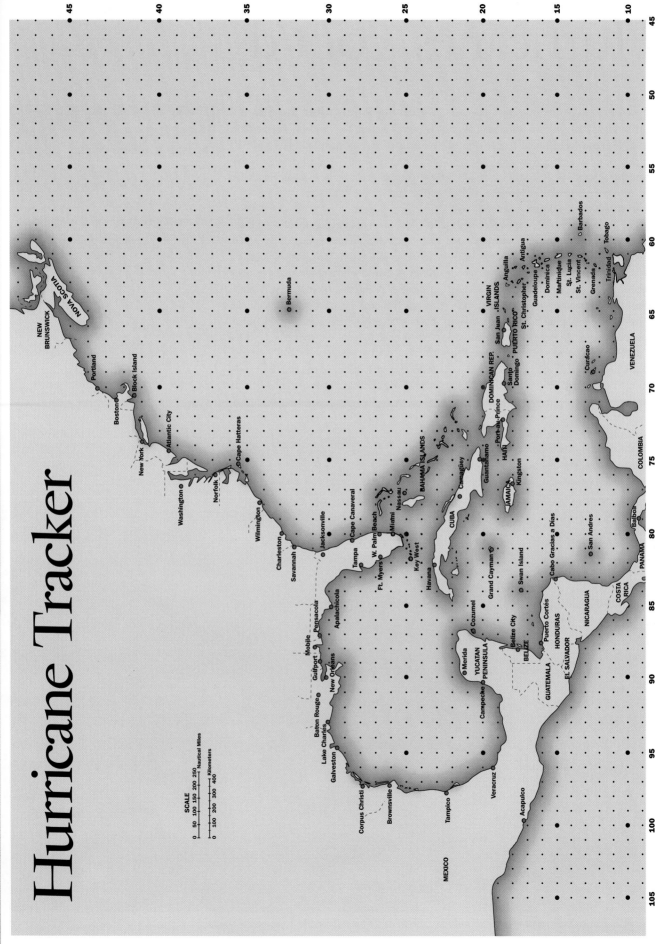

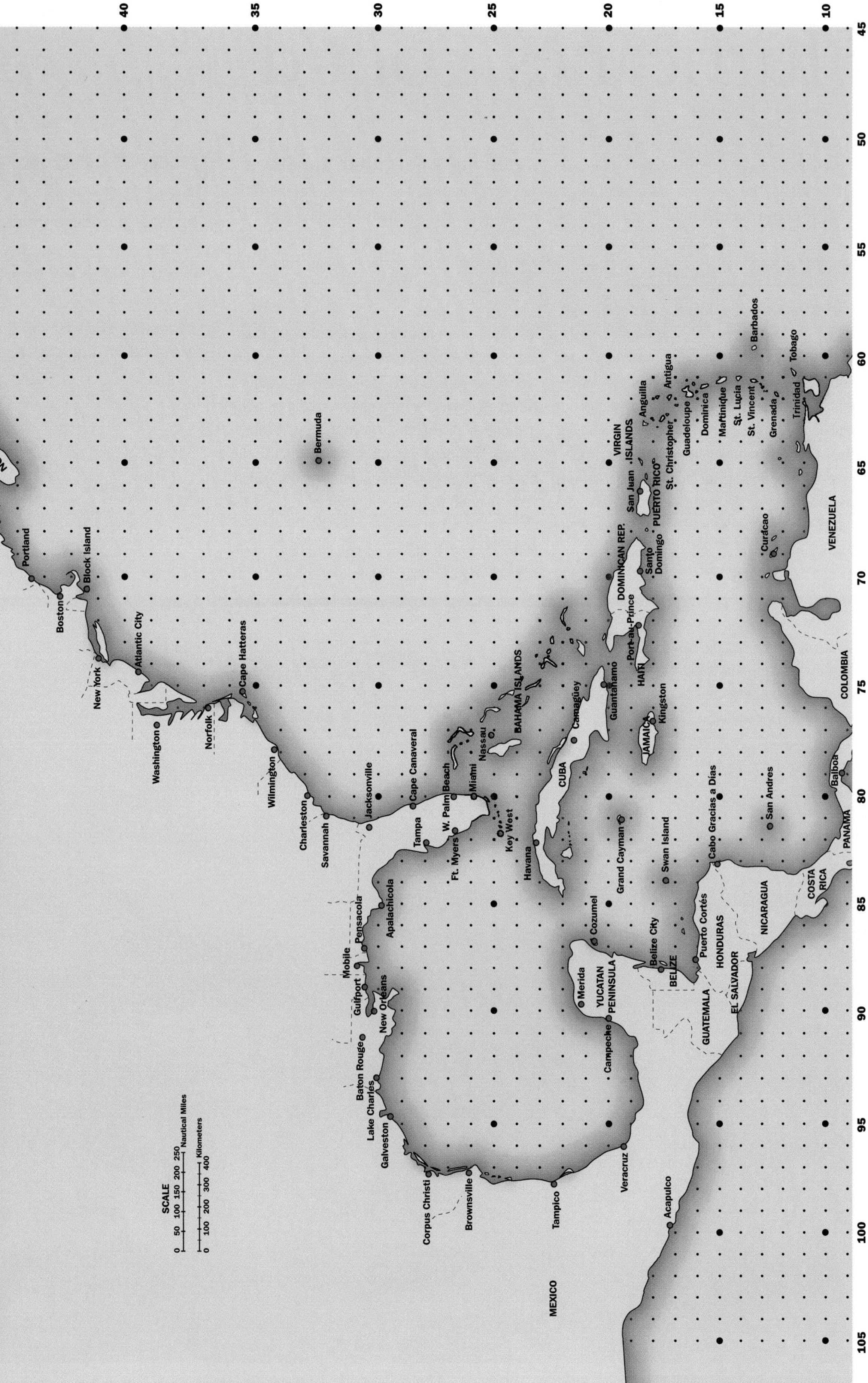
SCALE
0 50 100 150 200 250 Nautical Miles
0 100 200 300 400 Kilometers
45
40
35
30
25
20
15
10
50
55
60
65
70
75
80
85
90
95
100
105
NOVA SCOTIA
NEW BRUNSWICK
Portland
Boston
Block Island
New York
Atlantic City
Washington
Norfolk
Cape Hatteras
Wilmington
Charleston
Savannah
Jacksonville
Cape Canaveral
W. Palm Beach
Miami
Tampa
Ft. Myers
Key West
Apalachicola
Pensacola
Mobile
Gulfport
New Orleans
Baton Rouge
Lake Charles
Galveston
Corpus Christi
Brownsville
Tampico
Veracruz
Campeche
Merida
YUCATAN PENINSULA
Cozumel
MEXICO
Acapulco
Bermuda
Nassau
BAHAMA ISLANDS
Havana
CUBA
Camagüey
Guantanamo
Grand Cayman
JAMAICA
Kingston
HAITI
Port-au-Prince
DOMINICAN REP.
Santo Domingo
PUERTO RICO
San Juan
VIRGIN ISLANDS
Anguilla
Antigua
St. Christopher
Guadeloupe
Dominica
Martinique
St. Lucia
St. Vincent
Barbados
Grenada
Trinidad
Tobago
Curacao
VENEZUELA
COLOMBIA
Swan Island
Cabo Gracias a Días
San Andres
Balboa
PANAMA
COSTA RICA
NICARAGUA
HONDURAS
EL SALVADOR
GUATEMALA
BELIZE
Belize City
Puerto Cortés

Keeping A Weather Eye

While large portions of the Intracoastal Waterway are protected from harsh weather, skippers should always check the latest forecasts before casting off their lines or weighing anchor (especially if hopping offshore). Areas like the Albemarle Sound, Pamlico Sound and Cape Fear River can get nasty in a good blow. You will want to avoid being caught out when you can avoid it.

Staying out of bad weather is relatively easy if you plan ahead. The National Weather Service (NWS) provides mariners with continuous broadcasts of weather warnings, forecasts, radar reports and buoy reports over VHF-FM and Single Side Band (SSB) radio. Reception range for VHF radios is usually up to 40 miles from the antenna site, though Florida stations are frequently picked up in the near Bahamas. There are almost no areas on the U.S. coast where a good quality, fixed-mount VHF cannot pick up one or more coastal VHF broadcasts. Also, there is no substitute for looking at the sky. Afternoon thunderstorms can pop up quickly.

SSB Offshore Weather

SSB reports are broadcast from station NMN Chesapeake, VA and from station NMG, New Orleans, LA. The broadcasts are not continuous, so refer to the latest schedules and frequency lists (see below) to catch them. SSB reports provide the best source of voice offshore weather information. Two major broadcasts alternate throughout the day. The High Seas Forecast provides information for mariners well offshore, including those crossing the North Atlantic Ocean. Coastal cruisers will be more interested in the Offshore Forecast, which includes information on waters more than 50 miles from shore.

The forecast is divided into various regions. Mid-Atlantic cruisers will be most interested in Hudson Canyon to Baltimore Canyon, Baltimore Canyon to Hatteras Canyon, Hatteras Canyon to 31N latitude and the southwest North Atlantic south of 31N latitude and west of 65W longitude.

On the Web:

■ **NOAA National Weather Service:** www.nws.noaa.gov
This site provides coastal and offshore forecasts for the continental U.S. and nearby waters, including Puerto Rico and the United States Virgin Islands, weather maps, station reports and marine warnings.

■ **NOAA Marine Weather Radio:** www.weather.gov/om/marine/home.htm
Provides coverage areas and frequencies for VHF weather radio products in all 50 states.

■ **National Hurricane Center:** www.nhc.noaa.gov
Tropical warnings, advisories and predictions are available here. There is also access to historical data relating to hurricanes and tropical weather. Weatherfax schedules are available online.

■ **National Data Buoy Center:** http://www.ndbc.noaa.gov
This site provides near-real-time weather data from buoys and light stations.

Weather Frequencies

UTC	NMN FREQUENCIES (kHz)	NMG FREQUENCIES (kHz)
0330 (Offshore)	4426.0, 6501.0, 8764.0	4316.0, 8502.0, 12788.0
0515 (High Seas)	4426.0, 6501.0, 8764.0	4316.0, 8502.0, 12788.0
0930 (Offshore)	4426.0, 6501.0, 8764.0	4316.0, 8502.0, 12788.0
1115 (High Seas)	6501.0, 8764.0, 13089.0	4316.0, 8502.0, 12788.0
1530 (Offshore)	6501.0, 8764.0, 13089.0	4316.0, 8502.0, 12788.0
1715 (High Seas)	8764.0, 13089.0, 17314.0	4316.0, 8502.0, 12788.0
2130 (Offshore)	6501.0, 8764.0, 13089.0	4316.0, 8502.0, 12788.0
2315 (High Seas)	6501.0, 8764.0, 13089.0	4316.0, 8502.0, 12788.0

(UTC, or Coordinated Universal Time, is equivalent to Greenwich Mean Time)

VHF-FM Broadcasts/NOAA Weather Radio VHF Frequencies

WX1	162.550 MHz
WX2	162.400 MHz
WX3	162.475 MHz
WX4	162.425 MHz
WX5	162.450 MHz
WX6	162.500 MHz
WX7	162.525 MHz

Going Aground

"Either you've gone aground or you lie," say the old salts, meaning that sooner or later, every boat touches bottom. Of late, cruisers transiting the Intracoastal Waterway (ICW) have found this to be particularly true because of chronically insufficient government funds for dredging.

That said, most of the ICW is lined with soft, forgiving mud (save for some coastal inlet and river areas that are typically sand), so going aground may be an inconvenience, but it is rarely dangerous, let alone life-threatening. Still, it is wise to have a plan of action and basic familiarity with the tried-and-true techniques for getting unstuck from the muck.

To avoid trouble, a prudent mariner will invest a few minutes in research before leaving the dock. For the latest updates on ICW dredging and shoaling, visit www.waterwayguide.com and click on the "Navigation Updates" and "Cruising News" sections. These pages are updated daily with the latest shoaling and dredging updates, which are fed to our main office by Waterway Guide's intrepid cruising editors and cruisers like yourself.

What to do First

■ Throttle back immediately and put the engine into neutral. If under sail, douse and properly stow all sails to avoid being blown farther onto the shoal.

■ Assess the situation. Look back from where you came (it had to be deep enough or you wouldn't be here) and in all other directions for landmarks that might tell you exactly where you are.

■ Determine next the direction to deeper water so you can plan your escape. A quick glance at the GPS and a chart often reveals where you have gone wrong and where the deepest water is relative to your location.

■ When all else fails, it is not a bad idea to sound around the boat with your boat hook (or a fishing rod in a pinch) to determine on which side of the boat is the deeper water. Some skippers carry a portable depth sounder that can work from the dinghy during occasions like this.

■ Determine the state of the tide, especially if you are in an area with a wide range. If it is dropping, you must work fast. If it is rising, you will have some help getting the boat off.

How to Break Free

■ In less severe situations, you may be able to simply back off the bar, but begin gently to avoid damaging the propeller(s).

■ If the tide is low and rising, it may be best to simply set an anchor on the deep side and wait to be floated free. If it is falling and you have a deep-keel boat, be sure that the hull will lie to the shallower side of the shoal so the incoming tide does not fill the cockpit.

■ Sailboats usually come off after turning the bow toward deep water and heeling over to reduce the draft. Placing crewmembers out on the rail works too. Leading a halyard to the dinghy and pulling gently can also provide tremendous leverage for heeling the boat.

■ Keeping wakes to a minimum is common courtesy on the ICW, but a boat aground can actually benefit from the rising motion of a good wake to free itself from the bottom. One commonly used technique is to radio a passing powerboater and actually request a wake. As the waves lift the boat aground, the helmsman should apply throttle and turn toward deeper water. (Passing power boats should never create wake without a request for assistance from the vessel aground.)

■ A powered dinghy can also be used to tow a boat off a shoal. If you know where the deep water is, you can tie a line off to the bow and pivot the boat into deeper water.

■ Kedging, or pulling off with an anchor, is the next logical step. Use the dinghy to carry an anchor (or float it on a life jacket and push it ahead of you while wading and, of course, wearing one yourself) as far into deep water as possible. Then use a winch, windlass or your own muscle to pull the boat into deeper water. You may need to repeat the process a few times, resetting the anchor in progressively deeper water until the boat is free of the bottom.

■ The U.S. Coast Guard long ago ceased towing recreational vessels, but if you are aground and in imminent danger (e.g., aground in a dangerous inlet and taking on water), you may make an emergency request for assistance. Simple ICW groundings in calm weather with no immediate danger do not warrant a call to the Coast Guard.

■ If you need outside help from a commercial towboat or Good Samaritan be sure both of you understand in advance exactly what you plan to do. Fasten the towline to a secure cleat at the bow and stand well clear of the end when it comes taut, as it can snap with deadly force.

Resources

Waterway Guide (Navigation Updates): www.waterwayguide.com
Atlantic Intracoastal Waterway Assn.: www.atlanticintracoastal.org
TowBoatU.S.: www.boatus.com/towing
Sea Tow: www.seatow.com

Getting Your Mail and Paying Bills

One of the most anxiety-inducing issues cruisers face is how to keep their financial life in order while on an extended journey. Luckily, most banks today offer some sort of online banking that allows you to pay your bills with simple Internet access, and post offices will usually hold forwarded mail for transient boaters. With the advent of online banking and new forwarding services from the United States Postal Service (USPS), keeping on top of your bills and important mail need not be a huge hassle.

Options for Mail

General Delivery

■ Use general delivery when you have a person ("mail forwarder") collecting the mail for you at home while you are away.

■ This works best when you are on the move. Your mail forwarder can send bundles of your mail to different post offices ahead of your arrival as you move along the coast. The post office will generally hold these for 10 days.

■ The mail should be addressed as follows:
Your Name
Boat Name
General Delivery
City, State, ZIP Code
"Hold for Arrival" should be printed on both sides.

Premium Forwarding Service

The USPS is now offering a new service called Premium Forwarding that is designed to work in tandem with their Priority Mail program.

■ Once a week, normally on Wednesday, all of your mail is bundled in Priority Mail packaging and sent to you at a single specified temporary address.

■ Premium Forwarding includes most mail that standard forwarding does not normally include like magazines, catalogs and, yes, junk mail.

■ Mail can be sent to a general delivery address (as long as that post office accepts general delivery mail, of course).

■ There is an enrollment fee of $10 and each subsequent weekly Priority Mail shipment costs $10.40. The USPS bills a credit or debit card for each week's delivery fee.

■ Once you pick a temporary forwarding address, it cannot be changed as you and your boat move around. Premium Forwarding is designed for people who will be at a fixed temporary address for at least two weeks.

Standard Forwarding Service

■ Standard mail forwarding will automatically send your mail to a specified address (general delivery addresses included) at no extra charge.

■ Each piece of mail is sent individually, versus the Premium Forwarding service, which sends a single bundle of mail each week on Wednesdays.

■ This does not include magazines, periodicals or junk mail.

Hold Mail

■ You can have your mail held at your home post office from 3 to 30 days and retrieve it when you return.

Paying Bills

■ There are several companies (many online) that will handle paying your bills or forwarding your mail while you are away. Probably the best known is St. Brendan's Isle, which services more than 3,000 of cruisers from its offices in Green Cove Springs, FL. NATO in Sarasota, FL has also been assisting cruisers in getting their mail for decades.

■ If you aren't already doing it and your bank offers it, consider participating in online banking. You can set it up so many of your bills are automatically paid out of your checking account each month.

■ If you have a company that does not work with your bank's online bill pay service, see if they will take a credit card number and have them bill that every month.

■ Many companies will take credit card numbers over the phone for payment.

Resources

United States Postal Service: www.usps.com
St. Brendan's Isle: www.sbimailservice.com
NATO Mail: www.natomail.com

Mail Drops

The following post offices receive and hold mail for transient boaters, are conveniently located (unless otherwise noted) and will hold mail for as long as 10 days. Priority mail generally takes about three or four days to reach you, and the post office may require photo identification, so be prepared. "Hold for arrival" should be printed prominently in several places on the mailing, and a return address always included. If you are expecting more mail, leave a forwarding address with the post office when you move on. Forwarded mail often takes a week or more to arrive at the next destination.

Have your mail forwarder address your mail as follows:

Your Name, Boat Name
General Delivery
City, State, Zip Code

State	Address	ZIP Code
Virginia		
Urbanna	251 Virginia St.	23175
Deltaville	17283 General Puller Highway	23043
Portsmouth	431 Crawford St., Floor 1	23704
*Chesapeake	1425 Battlefield Blvd. N.	23320
North Carolina		
Elizabeth City	1001 W. Ehringhaus St.	27909
Manteo (Chelsey Mall)	212B U.S. Highway 64 & 264	27954
Oriental	809 Broad St.	28571
Beaufort	701 Front St.	28516
Morehead City	3500 Bridges St.	28557
Wrightsville Beach	206 Causeway Drive	28480
Southport	206 E. Nash St.	28461
South Carolina		
*Georgetown (boaters need to send notification letter with signature first)	1101 Charlotte St.	29440
Isle of Palms	1000 Palm Blvd.	29451
*Charleston	83 Broad St.	29402
Beaufort	501 Charles St.	29902
*Hilton Head Island	71 Lighthouse Road, Suite 1	29928
(*Main Branch)	10 Bow Circle	29928
(*Fairfield Station)	213 William Hilton Parkway	29926
Georgia		
*Savannah	2 N. Fahm St., Room 1A	31401

* Post office not within walking distance of the waterfront.

Insurance

Wow! Exciting Insurance News!!!

Are you kidding? What could possibly be exciting about insurance? Well, OK, maybe "interesting" is a better word.

One of the major players in the game has left the field. (See, and you thought insurance folks were making so much money that they didn't know what to do with it all!) They handed a wonderful opportunity to all of the players left in the game, who were nearly beside themselves in trying to scoop up all the folks that were forced back onto the market. If you haven't shopped around for a while, this is the time to get a marine specialist out there testing the waters for you. (We love to get our toes wet so you don't have to.)

Here is a sampling of some of the softening we are seeing from various companies:

1. Now extended navigation available to the Caribbean on this side, or to Costa Rica on the west coast from a couple of additional companies.
2. Some softening of rates.
3. At least two companies now providing actual liveaboard policies to replace Zurich's Quartermaster program.
4. More companies now covering consequential damage. (This is a biggie!)
5. At least one company no longer requires surveys at renewal.

Sometimes, when the new player is part of an 'A'-rated company, that can be a great opportunity for the boat owner. As always, though, you've got to be careful to make sure that the actual insurance company providing the quote is highly rated for its claims-paying ability by at least one of the major rating agencies—AM Best, Standard & Poor, or Fitch Rating.

And, have you been provided with a specimen policy form as part of the quotation? What is absolutely critical for you to remember is that, unlike homeowners or auto policies, marine insurance is not regulated by the States, not regulated by the Feds, not regulated by anyone! So, it is quite likely that the policy form that is being proposed and the premium being quoted have not been reviewed by anyone! So what are your options?

1. If you are able (and can stay awake), you can review the proposed policy yourself to determine if it covers adequately the major items that you wish to have covered.
2. You can hire an attorney to make that determination for you. (This is a contract that has the potential to have a major impact on your life. Just like a life raft, you want to be sure that if you ever have to pull that lanyard that there's really, really something in the container that can save you.)
3. You can secure the quotation through an agent with the long-term reputation to make you comfortable with his or her proposal.

What are the major factors to look for?

1. You want an "All Risk" policy form that states that you are covered for all risk of loss except for perils that are specifically excluded.
2. You want an "Agreed Value" form that agrees to the value of your boat at the time that it is written, not when she is gone.
3. You definitely want a "Replacement Cost" form. This refers to partial losses, which are far, far more common than total losses. There are obviously things with relatively short service lives, like sails, canvas covers, bottom paint, etc., that may be depreciated, but other items should be paid for "new for old" without the words "depreciation" or "betterment" entering into the process. "Actual Cash Value" works quite well for automobiles, for instance, where there are tons of used cars and parts of cars readily available. But, where would you go to find used boat gear specific to your boat?
4. On the liability side of the policy, you want the marine form, titled "Protection & Indemnity." A vessel operating in navigable waters is considered under maritime law to be an entity in the same sense as a corporation would be under common law and can be sued herself.
5. There are lots of other coverages available, but they should never be considered in your selection, nor should you ever make a claim against some of them, even if they are there. Insurance exists to protect you against a financial catastrophe, not a $500 towing claim. If you want coverage for non-emergency towing, join one of the outfits like TowBoatU.S. or Sea Tow.
6. The exception to that applies to liveaboards who need several additional coverages:
    a. Personal Liability – Your liability not related to the boat.
    b. Personal Property – This can be quite extensive and needs to be covered, not just when aboard but also in storage or an automobile, etc.
    c. Loss of Use – Coverage for living ashore while repairs are being made to the yacht.

Please have a great boating season!
Fair winds and following seas,
Al Golden

IMIS (International Marine Insurance Sevices)
110 Channel Marker Way
#200
Grasonville, MD 21638

SKIPPER'S HANDBOOK

Vessel Registration Taxes and Fees by State

Virginia

The first state you will enter on your way south in the ICW is Virginia. There is no requirement in Virginia for documented vessels to be registered, but you may apply for and use a registration sticker when traveling in states that require you do so. "Watercraft currently registered by the owner in another state and not kept in Virginia for more than 90 consecutive days are not required to be registered in Virginia." You will likely not be staying in Virginia for more than 90 days on your passage south, but if you do and yours is not a federally documented vessel, be prepared to pay a fee of $37 for three years for a vessel of 20 to 40 feet and $45 for three years for vessels over 40 feet to register your boat.

Virginia is one of the states that has property taxes. If your vessel is registered in Virginia, is it also assessed property tax based on the locality you select when you register. For example, the tax rate on a pleasure boat for the City of Norfolk was $0.50 per $100 in 2010. Contact the local county office in your jurisdiction for more information.

For more information or to contact the Virginia Department of Game and Inland Fisheries, go to http://www.dgif.virginia.gov/contact/ or call 877-898-BOAT (2628). The mailing address is Richmond Headquarters: 4010 West Broad Street, P.O. Box 11104, Richmond, VA 23230.

North Carolina

Continuing south, you will enter the waters of North Carolina. You need to know that anyone under 26 years of age who is operating a vessel that has a 10 hp engine or greater, must have successfully completed a boating safety course.

If you register a vessel in North Carolina, it can be done for periods of one or three years. One year is $15, while three is $40. Just as in Virginia and many other states, if you keep your vessel in North Carolina for over 90 days, you will be required to register it in that state. This does not apply to a vessel kept on dry land, however, so if you take your boat to North Carolina and haul it for hurricane season, that would not count toward the 90 days. Motorized dinghies fall into the category of vessels that must be registered, as do jet skis. Federally documented vessels do not need to be registered.

North Carolina also has property tax which includes boats; "...all personal property is assessed at 100% of its actual value." As an example, during 2010, residents of Currituck County were charged $0.32 per $100 of valuation. For more information about property taxes, visit the North Carolina Department of Revenue website at http://www.dor.state.nc.us/index.html.

Visit the North Carolina's Wildlife Resource Commission website at http://www.ncwildlife.org/index.htm for more information, or contact them via telephone at 800-NC-VESSEL (800-628-3773). Their mailing address is NCWRC: Transaction Management, 1709 Mail Service Center, Raleigh, NC 27699.

South Carolina

South Carolina's laws are somewhat different from those of Virginia and North Carolina in that "Vessels that are currently registered in another state may operate on South Carolina waters for 60 days before South Carolina registration and numbering is required." Some counties in South Carolina do not require you register your boat until after 120 days. You do not have to title a federally documented vessel in South Carolina.

New registration fees are $40. You can register by mail with the South Carolina Department of Natural Resources, Boat Titling and Registration, P.O. Box 167, Columbia, SC 29202, contact their offices at 803-734-3857 or check out their website at www.dnr.sc.gov. Be aware that South Carolina has a casual excise tax, which caps at $300 and a use tax of 5%. If you have not paid taxes out of state, you must pay this tax at the time of registration.

South Carolina's property tax rate differs somewhat from North Carolina and Virginia in that you will be asked to pay property if your boat remains in the state for longer than 90 days or more than 60 days in a row in one year, whether or not you are a resident of that state. You also cannot get credit for taxes you paid to another state. The rate can be as high as 10.5%, but many counties, such as Georgetown County, passed a 6% county tax instead of enforcing the 10.5%, understanding that many folks live aboard. Individual counties may drop the rate from 10.5 to 6%, and liveaboards may apply for a reduction from 6 to 4%. The South Carolina Department of Revenue's website is http://www.sctax.org/default.htm.

Georgia

Georgia, like South Carolina, also requires that you register your vessel in that state if you remain in their waters for more than 60 days. After that, your registration is good for three years. Vessels 26 to 39 feet will cost you $90 and 40 feet and longer will set you back $150 for the 3-year period.

"Residents and non-residents that own a boat in Georgia...are required to file a return of the fair market value of their boat in the county where the property is located 184 days a year or more (cumulative)." Go to the Georgia Department of Revenue website for more information at https://etax.dor.ga.gov/ptd/adm/forms/pt50m/index.aspx.

More detailed information about Georgia's boating regulations can be found on the Georgia Department of Natural Resources website www.georgiawildlife.com. Their mailing address is Georgia Wildlife Resources Division, 2070 U.S. Hwy. 278 SE, Social Circle, GA 30025. If you want to register by phone, call 800-366-2661.

Florida

We mention Florida here because we briefly cover entry into that state at Fernandina Beach and because you need to be acutely aware of Florida tax and use laws. If your vessel remains in Florida for longer than 90 consecutive days or more than 183 days in the same calendar year, you can be subject to a 6% (fair market value) use tax. If you paid less than 6% tax in the state in which you purchased your vessel, Florida will require you to pay them the difference. There is a cap, however, of $18,000. The Florida laws took effect in July of 2010. There is no property tax charged on boats in Florida, but Florida does require even federally documented vessels to also carry state registration.

Note that all of these states stringently enforce their regulations regarding registering your vessel. In these tough economic times, states are trying to gather all of the financial support they can, and many times, boaters are a ready source of income. Make sure that you display a valid registration sticker from your state and follow your host state's regulations.

Onboard Waste and No-Discharge Zones

Up until the late 1980s, many boaters simply discharged their untreated sewage overboard into the water. After a revision to the Clean Water Act was passed in 1987, the discharge of untreated sewage into U.S. waters within the three-mile limit was prohibited. Shortly thereafter, pump-out stations became a regular feature at marinas and fuel docks throughout the Intracoastal Waterway (ICW).

Simply stated, if you have a marine head installed on your vessel and are operating on coastal waters within the U.S. three-mile limit (basically all of the waters covered in the Guide you are now holding), you need to have a holding tank, and you will obviously need to arrange to have that tank pumped out from time to time.

Government regulation aside, properly disposing of your waste is good karma. While your overboard contribution to the ICW may seem small in the grand scheme of things, similar attitudes among fellow boaters can quickly produce unsavory conditions in anchorages and small creeks. The widespread availability of holding tank gear and shoreside pump-out facilities leaves few excuses for not doing the right thing.

No-Discharge Zones

- No-Discharge means exactly what the name suggests. No waste, even waste treated by an onboard Type I marine sanitation device (MSD), may be discharged overboard. All waste must be collected in a holding tank and pumped out at an appropriate facility.
- There are a number of No-Discharge Zones in the coastal waters that this Guide covers, including the areas in Onslow County and the Cape Fear River, both in North Carolina.
- If you plan to travel outside the coverage area for this Guide, keep in mind that there are some areas (e.g., Lake Champlain, Ontario municipalities) that forbid overboard discharge of any waste, including gray water from showers or sinks. Familiarize yourself with local regulations before entering new areas to ensure you don't get hit with a fine. To see the zones listed by state, go to: http://water.epa.gov/polwaste/vwd/vsdnozone.cfm#nc.

The Law

- If you have a marine head onboard and are operating on coastal waters within the U.S. three-mile limit (basically all of the waters covered in this Guide), you need to have an approved holding tank or Type 1 MSD.
- All valves connected to your holding tank or marine head that lead to the outside (both Y-valves AND seacocks) must be wire tied in the closed position. Simply having them closed without the wire ties will not save you from a fine if you are boarded.
- You may discharge waste overboard from a Type 1 MSD (Lectra-San, Groco Thermopure) in all areas except those designated as No-Discharge Zones. A Type I MSD treats waste by reducing bacteria and visible solids to an acceptable level before discharge overboard.
- While small and inconvenient for most cruisers, "Port-A-Potties" meet all the requirements for a Type III MSD, as the holding tank is incorporated into the toilet itself.

Pump-Out Station and Holding Tank Basics

- Many marinas along the ICW are equipped with pump-out facilities, normally located at the marina's fuel dock. Check the included marina listing tables throughout this Guide for the availability of pump-out services at each facility. Most marinas charge a fee for the service.
- Several municipalities and local governments on the ICW have purchased and staffed pump-out boats that are equipped to visit boats on request, especially those at anchor. Radio the local harbormaster to see if this service is available in the area you are visiting. There is normally a small fee involved.
- You will want to keep an eye out on your holding tank level while you are transiting the ICW, especially if you are getting ready to enter an area where you many not have access to proper pump-out services for a few days. Plan a fuel stop or marina stay to top off the fuel and water tanks and empty the other tank before you set out into the wild.

Marine Sanitation Devices

- **Type I MSD:** Treats sewage before discharging it into the water. The treated discharge must not show any visible floating solids and must meet specified standards for bacteria content. Raritan's Lectra-San and Groco's Thermopure systems are examples of Type I MSDs. Not permitted in No-Discharge Zones.
- **Type II MSD:** Type II MSDs provide a higher level of waste treatment than Type I units and are larger as a result. These units are usually found on larger vessels due to their higher power requirements. Not permitted in No-Discharge Zones.
- **Type III MSD:** Regular holding tanks store sewage until the holding tank can either be pumped out to an onshore facility or at sea beyond the U.S. boundary waters (three miles offshore).

Resources

BoatU.S. Guide to Overboard Discharge:
www.boatus.com/foundation/toolbox/msd.htm

BoatU.S. Listing of No-Discharge Zones:
www.boatus.com/gov/f8.asp

EPA No-Discharge Zones: *http://water.epa.gov/polwaste/vwd*

Federal Clean Vessel Act Information:
http://federalaid.fws.gov/cva/cva.html

Charts and Publications

Charts are must-have for any passage on the Intracoastal Waterway (ICW). Charts are a two-dimensional picture of your boating reality—shorelines, channels, aids to navigation and hazards. Even in an age of electronic chartplotters, most experts agree that paper charts have value and should be carried as a backup. ICW charts incorporate an extremely helpful feature, a magenta line that traces the Waterway's path. Some cruisers call it "The Magenta Highway."

The Internet Age

With widespread availability of the Internet, most all of the publications you will need are available for download from the government in Adobe Portable Document File (PDF) format free of charge. While this is handy, keep in mind that the electronic versions are mainly for reference and planning purposes, as they are not readily accessible while you are at the helm underway.

Once you download them, Coast Pilots and Light Lists can be printed, but since each edition weighs in at about 350-plus pages, they are best viewed online. If you think you will be accessing one of these volumes frequently, buy the bound version from your chart agent.

Most of NOAA's chart catalog is now available for viewing online. Since you can't print these charts, they are best used for planning and reference purposes. Many ICW cruisers hop on their laptops the evening before their next departure and use these online charts to plan out the following day's travel, since they are up-to-date the moment you view them. You can also view the Waterway Planner on our website (www.waterwayguide.com) to plan the next leg of your trip.

NOAA Charts

■ For the ICW, you will primarily use harbor and small-craft charts. Small craft charts are the small, folded strip charts that cover the ICW portion of the coast. Harbor charts, as the name suggests, cover smaller waterways and ports.

■ NOAA Charts are updated and printed by the government on regular schedules—normally every one to two years. (Each new printing is called an edition.)

■ Third-party companies often reproduce NOAA charts into book/chart kit form. Many veteran ICW cruisers use these, as they have all the charts laid out in page order, which means you don't have to wrestle with large folded charts at the helm. Keep in mind that even the latest versions of these charts need to be updated with the *Local Notice to Mariners* to be timely and accurate.

■ Changes to the charts between printings are published in the U.S. Coast Guard *Local Notice to Mariners,* which is available exclusively online at www.navcen.uscg.gov/?pageName=lnmMain.

■ A disadvantage of printed NOAA Charts is that the version on the shelf at your local store may be a year old or more. For the sake of accuracy, it is necessary to check back through the *Local Notice to Mariners* and note any corrections, especially for shoal-prone areas.

■ NOAA's complete chart catalog is also available for viewing as a planning or reference tool online at: http://www.nauticalcharts.noaa.gov/mcdOnLineViewer.html.

■ Even if you have electronic charts on board, you should always have a spare set of paper charts as a back up. Electronics can and do fail. What's more, electronic viewing is limited by the size of the display screen, whereas a paper chart spread over a table is still the best way to realize "the big picture."

Print-on-Demand Charts

■ Print-on-Demand charts are printed directly by the chart agent at the time you purchase the chart. The charts are the ultimate in accuracy, as they are corrected with the *Local Notice to Mariners* on a weekly basis.

■ Print-on-Demand charts are water resistant, and there are two versions with useful information in the margins, including tide tables, emergency numbers, frequencies, rules of the road, etc. One version is for recreational boaters and one for professionals.

■ Print-on-Demand charts are available through various retailers, including Bluewater Books and Charts and West Marine.

Local Notice to Mariners

■ Each week, the U.S. Coast Guard publishes corrections, urgent bulletins and updates in the *Local Notice to Mariners.* One example of this is the removal or addition of a navigational mark. Serious boaters will pencil changes such as these directly on the charts as they are announced.

■ *Local Notice to Mariners* are now available online at www.navcen.uscg.gov/?pageName=lnmMain.

Light Lists

■ Light Lists provide thorough information (location, characteristics, etc.) on aids to navigation such as buoys, lights, fog signals, daybeacons. For the ICW region, use volumes II and III.

■ Light Lists can now be downloaded in PDF format free of charge from the U.S. Coast Guard by visiting: www.navcen.uscg.gov/?pageName=LightLists.

■ Alternatively, you can order or purchase bound copies of Coast Pilots from your chart agent.

Coast Pilots

■ The U.S. Coast Pilot is a series of nine books providing navigational data to supplement National Ocean Service charts. Subjects include navigation regulations, outstanding landmarks, channel and anchorage peculiarities, dangers, weather, ice, routes, pilotage and port facilities.

Charts and Publications, cont'd.

■ For the areas covered in the Atlantic ICW edition of WATERWAY GUIDE, use Volume 4.

■ Coast Pilots can be downloaded free of charge from NOAA by visiting: http://www.nauticalcharts.noaa.gov/nsd/cpdownload.htm.

■ You can order purchase Coast Pilots from your chart agent if a bound copy is more convenient for your use.

Tides and Currents

■ Tide Tables give predicted heights of high and low water for every day in the year for many important harbors. They also provide correction figures for many other locations.

■ Tidal Current Tables include daily predictions for the times of slack water, the times and velocities of maximum flood and ebb currents for a number of waterways, and data enabling the navigator to calculate predictions for other areas.

■ Tide tables and tidal current tables are no longer published by NOS; several private publishers print them now and many chart agents carry them.

■ Additionally, tide and tidal current tables are now available for viewing online at: http://tidesandcurrents.noaa.gov.

Intracoastal Waterway Mileage

Coastwise Distances from Norfolk to Key West

	Chesapeake Bay Entrance 37°56.3' N., 76°176' W.	Norfolk, VA 36°50.9' N., 76°17.9' W.	Diamond Shoals 35°08.0' N., 75°15.0' W.	Morehead City, NC 33°42.8' N., 76°41.8' W.	Southport, NC 33°54.8' N., 78°01.0' W.	Wilmington, NC 34°14.0' N., 77°57.0' W.	Georgetown, SC 33°21.4' N., 79°16.9' W.	Charleston, SC 32°47.2' N., 79°55.2' W.	Port Royal, SC 32°22.3' N., 80°41.6' W.	Savannah, GA 32°05.0' N., 81°05.7' W.	Brunswick, GA 31°08.0' N., 81°29.7' W.	Fernandina Beach, FL 30°40.3' N., 81°28.0' W.	Jacksonville, FL 30°19.2' N., 81°39.0' W.	St. Augustine, FL 29°53.6' N., 81°18.5' W.	Cape Canaveral, FL 28°24.6' N., 80°36.5' W.	Fort Pierce, FL 27°27.5' N., 80°19.3' W.	Stuart, FL 27°12.2' N., 80°15.6' W.	Port of Palm Beach, FL 26°46.1' N., 80°03.0' W.	Port Everglades, FL 26°46.1' N., 80°07.0' W.	Miami, FL 25°47.0' N., 80°11.0' W.	Key West, FL 24°33.7' N., 81°48.5' W.
Norfolk, VA	27																				
Diamond Shoals	117	144																			
Morehead City, NC	222	249	105																		
Southport, NC	315	342	198	133																	
Wilmington, NC	336	363	219	154	21																
Georgetown, SC	365	392	248	184	87	108															
Charleston, SC	402	429	285	220	130	151	79														
Port Royal, SC	465	492	348	284	191	212	141	90													
Savannah, GA	476	503	359	295	206	227	154	102	51												
Brunswick, GA	527	554	410	346	260	281	210	156	110	104											
Fernandina Beach, FL	533	560	416	352	265	286	216	166	120	115	50										
Jacksonville, FL	560	587	443	379	294	315	247	197	152	145	82	53									
St. Augustine, FL	557	584	440	377	296	317	246	199	157	152	90	61	56								
Cape Canaveral, FL	612	639	495	438	367	388	324	283	251	251	195	169	167	120							
Fort Pierce, FL	647	674	530	476	407	428	368	329	298	298	242	216	214	167	69						
Stuart, FL	666	693	549	497	423	444	391	353	324	324	268	242	240	192	91	32					
Port of Palm Beach, FL	678	705	561	509	443	464	407	369	341	340	285	262	259	211	110	52	36				
Port Everglades, FL	720	747	603	550	485	506	449	411	383	382	327	304	301	253	152	94	78	46			
Miami, FL	743	770	626	573	508	529	472	434	406	405	350	327	324	276	175	117	101	68	27		
Key West, FL	881	908	764	711	646	667	610	572	544	543	488	465	462	414	313	255	239	207	165	151	
Straits of Florida 24°25.0' N., 83°00.0' W.	942	969	825	772	707	728	671	633	605	604	549	526	523	475	374	316	300	267	226	211	73

DISTANCES ARE APPROXIMATE; FOR PLANNING PURPOSES ONLY.

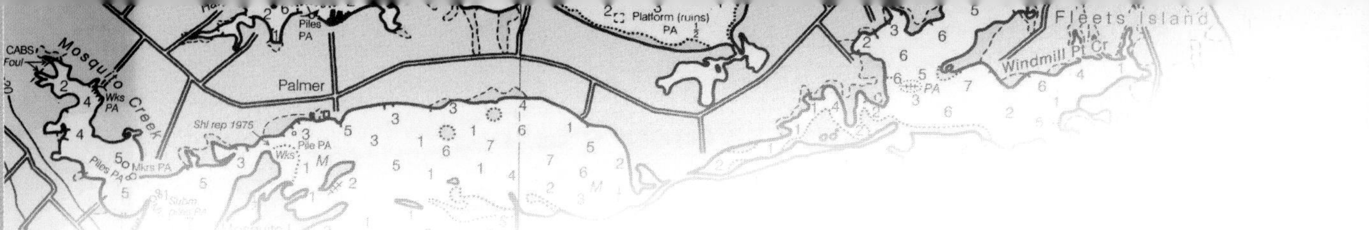

Inside vs. Outside Mileage

Heading north or south, many skippers mistakenly assume that they will shorten their trips by going out to sea and running down the coast. The following chart, which gives the inside-outside distances in nautical and statute miles, inlet to inlet, for the Atlantic Coast from Norfolk to Florida, demonstrates that this is not necessarily true. While outside distances from sea buoy to sea buoy are virtually the same as the Intracoastal Waterway (ICW) distances, the mileage in and out to the buoys adds to the total coastwise figure. Thus, although it is 50 miles from the Georgetown sea buoy to the Charleston sea buoy, the 17 miles out and 14 miles in bring the total mileage to 81, a third more than the ICW distance of 56. And the differences, which may seem insignificant at first, do add up: along the coast, the total Intracoastal mileage is 620; outside the distance measures 758.

Skippers should consider the safety factor as well. Some of the outside stretches are easy while others can be more hazardous; the passage may be safer in the springtime than in the late fall. Watch the weather carefully; it can get uncomfortable outside while the inside passage still seems calm and unaffected. Now that ICW maintenance budgets have been cut, do be prepared to run outside for a day in case the ICW is obstructed locally by a malfunctioning bridge or severe shoaling. Prepare your boat early, plot the course in advance and go only if the forecast is good.

MILEAGES: Inside vs Outside/Nautical Miles (Statute Miles)

NORFOLK, VA TO MOREHEAD CITY, NC
(272.7) Outside ... 237 Inside 178 (204.8)

MOREHEAD CITY, NC TO WRIGHTSVILLE BEACH, NC
City Dock to Sea Buoy...... 6
Sea Buoy to Sea Buoy.... 63
Sea Buoy to Wrightsville Bridge....... 4
(84.0) Outside ...... 73 Inside 70 (80.5)

WRIGHTSVILLE BEACH, NC TO SOUTHPORT, NC
Wrightsville to Sea Buoy... 4
Sea Buoy to Sea Buoy.... 50
Sea Buoy to Southport..... 7
(70.2) Outside ...... 61 Inside 21 (24.1)

SOUTHPORT, NC TO GEORGETOWN, SC
Southport to Sea Buoy..... 7
Sea Buoy to Sea Buoy.... 65
Sea Buoy to Georgetown 17
(102.4) Outside ...... 89 Inside 83 (95.5)

GEORGETOWN, SC TO CHARLESTON, SC
Georgetown to Sea Buoy 17
Sea Buoy to Sea Buoy.... 50
Sea Buoy to Charleston.. 14
(93.2) Outside ...... 81 Inside 56 (64.4)

CHARLESTON, SC TO HILTON HEAD I., SC
Charleston to Sea Buoy.. 14
Sea Buoy to Sea Buoy.... 67
Sea Buoy to Hilton Head 12
(107.0) Outside ...... 93 Inside 82 (94.3)

HILTON HEAD I., SC TO ST. SIMONS I., GA
Hilton Head to Sea Buoy 12
Sea Buoy to Sea Buoy.... 63
Sea Buoy to St. Simons . 10
(97.8) Outside ...... 85 Inside 96 (110.4)

ST. SIMONS I., GA TO FERNANDINA BEACH, FL
St. Simons to Sea Buoy . 10
Sea Buoy to Sea Buoy.... 22
Sea Buoy to Fernandina .. 7
(44.8) Outside ...... 39 Inside 34 (39.1)

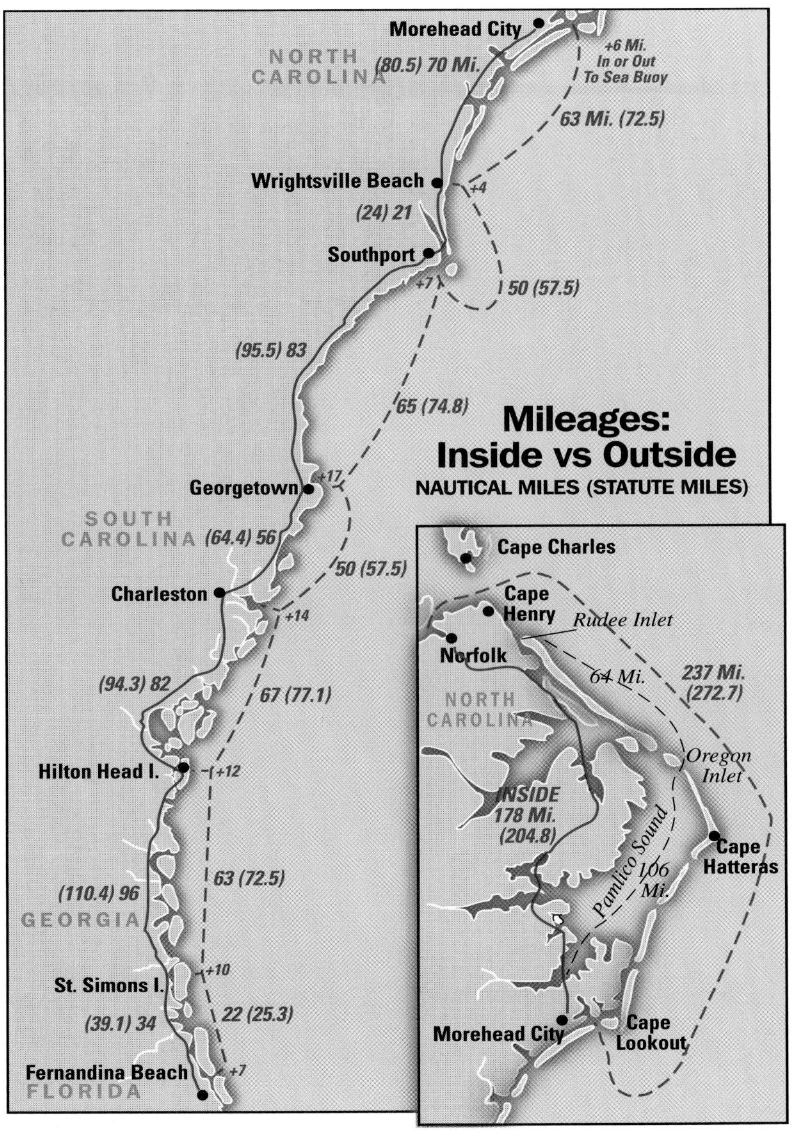

Inside-Route Distances

from Norfolk, VA to Fernandina Beach, FL

STATUTE MILES

	Norfolk, VA	Elizabeth City, NC	Hertford, NC	Columbia, NC	Edenton, NC	Plymouth, NC	Manteo, NC	Belhaven, NC	Washington, NC	Ocracoke, NC	Oriental, NC	New Bern, NC	Beaufort, NC	Morehead City, NC	Swansboro, NC	Jacksonville, NC	Wrightsville, NC	Wilmington, NC	Southport, NC	Little River, SC	Bucksport, SC	Georgetown, SC	McClellanville, SC	Charleston, SC	Beaufort, SC	Savannah, GA	Thunderbolt, GA	Brunswick, GA	Fernandina Beach, FL
Norfolk, VA 36°50.9' N., 76°17.9' W.		89*	102	102	113	121	92	138	180	151	184	207	204	205	230	266	283	314	308	344	377	405	430	467	536	585	583	685	717
Elizabeth City, NC 36°18.1' N., 76°13.0' W.	77*		45	45	55	64	45	91	131	105	136	160	154	157	182	217	235	266	260	296	329	358	382	419	488	536	535	636	669
Hertford, NC 36°11.6' N., 76°28.0' W.	89	39		30	40	48	53	91	132	112	137	160	158	158	184	219	236	267	261	298	330	358	383	421	489	537	536	638	670
Columbia, NC 35°55.0' N., 76°15.4' W.	89	39	26		29	38	52	90	131	110	136	159	157	157	182	217	235	266	260	296	329	357	382	419	488	536	535	636	669
Edenton, NC 36°03.3' N., 76°36.6' W.	98	48	35	25		16	62	100	142	120	145	168	166	167	191	227	245	276	270	306	338	366	391	429	497	547	545	647	678
Plymouth, NC 35°51.8' N., 76°45.6' W.	105	56	42	33	14		70	109	150	130	154	178	175	175	201	237	254	285	280	315	349	376	402	438	508	556	555	656	688
Manteo, NC 35°54.6' N., 75°40.2' W.	80	39	46	45	54	61		81	121	70	105	127	127	127	152	186	205	236	231	267	299	326	352	388	457	506	505	606	639
Belhaven, NC 35°32.1' N., 76°37.4' W.	120	79	79	78	87	95	70		45	49	49	72	70	70	96	131	150	181	175	211	243	270	296	334	402	451	450	551	582
Washington, NC 35°32.6' N., 77°03.7' W.	156	114	115	114	123	130	105	39		69	64	87	85	85	110	146	163	194	189	224	258	285	311	348	417	465	464	565	597
Ocracoke, NC 35°06.8' N., 75°59.1' W.	131	91	97	96	104	113	61	43	60		47	71	68	68	93	129	147	178	173	208	241	268	293	331	399	449	448	549	580
Oriental, NC 35°01.5' N., 76°41.8' W.	160	118	119	118	126	134	91	43	56	41		26	25	25	51	86	105	136	130	166	198	226	251	289	357	406	405	506	537
New Bern, NC 35°06.1' N., 77°02.1' W.	180	139	139	138	146	155	110	63	76	62	23		44	44	69	105	123	154	148	184	216	245	270	307	376	425	423	525	557
Beaufort, NC 34°43.1' N., 76°40.2' W.	177	134	137	136	144	152	110	61	74	59	22	38		3	28	63	81	112	107	143	175	203	229	266	334	383	382	483	514
Morehead City, NC 34°42.8' N., 76°41.8' W.	178	136	137	136	145	152	110	61	74	59	22	38	3		25	61	79	110	105	140	173	200	226	264	331	381	380	481	512
Swansboro, NC 34°41.0' N., 77°07.3' W.	200	158	160	158	166	175	132	83	96	81	44	60	24	22		36	53	84	79	115	147	175	200	238	306	356	353	456	487
Jacksonville, NC 34°44.7' N., 77°26.3' W.	231	189	190	189	197	206	162	114	127	112	75	91	55	53	31		55	86	81	116	148	177	203	239	308	357	356	457	489
Wrightsville, NC 34°13.1' N., 77°48.8' W.	246	204	205	204	213	221	178	130	142	128	91	107	70	69	46	48		31	25	61	94	122	147	184	253	302	300	402	434
Wilmington, NC 34°14.0' N., 77°57.0' W.	273	231	232	231	240	248	205	157	169	155	118	134	97	96	73	75	27		24	60	93	121	146	183	252	300	299	402	433
Southport, NC 33°54.8' N., 78°01.0' W.	268	226	227	226	235	243	201	152	164	150	113	129	93	91	69	70	22	21		36	69	97	122	159	228	276	275	376	409
Little River, SC 33°52.2' N., 78°36.6' W.	299	257	259	257	266	274	232	183	195	181	144	160	124	122	100	101	53	52	31		32	61	86	123	192	241	239	341	373
Bucksport, SC 33°39.0' N., 79°05.6' W.	328	286	287	286	294	303	260	211	224	209	172	188	152	150	128	129	82	81	60	28		28	53	91	159	208	206	308	339
Georgetown, SC 33°21.4' N., 79°16.9' W.	352	311	311	310	318	327	283	235	248	233	196	213	177	174	152	154	106	105	84	53	24		28	64	133	183	181	283	314
McClellanville, SC 33°04.7' N., 79°27.6' W.	374	332	333	332	340	349	306	257	270	255	218	235	199	196	174	176	128	127	106	75	46	24		37	106	155	153	255	287
Charleston, SC 32°47.2' N., 79°55.2' W.	406	364	366	364	373	381	337	290	302	288	251	267	231	229	207	208	160	159	138	107	79	56	32		69	120	119	220	251
Beaufort, SC 32°25.6' N., 80°40.2' W.	466	424	425	424	432	441	397	349	362	347	310	327	290	288	266	268	220	219	198	167	138	116	92	60		49	47	150	181
Savannah, GA 32°05.0' N., 81°05.7' W.	508	466	467	466	475	483	440	392	404	390	353	369	333	331	309	310	262	261	240	209	181	159	135	104	43		16	117	150
Thunderbolt, GA 32°01.5' N., 81°02.8' W.	507	465	466	465	474	482	439	391	403	389	352	368	332	330	307	309	261	260	239	208	179	157	133	103	41	14		101	133
Brunswick, GA 31°08.0' N., 81°29.7' W.	595	553	554	553	562	570	527	479	491	477	440	456	420	418	396	397	349	349	327	296	268	246	222	191	130	102	88		40
Fernandina Beach, FL 30°40.3' N., 81°28.0' W.	623	581	582	581	589	598	555	506	519	504	467	484	447	445	423	425	377	376	355	324	295	273	249	218	157	130	116	35	

NAUTICAL MILES

To use the table, read across to the intersection of the columns opposite the ports between which you are traveling. For example, Morehead City, NC is 445 nautical miles (512 statute miles) from Fernandina Beach, FL. Distances are approximate and for planning purposes only. *Via Dismal Swamp Canal–Call the USACE for status (757-201-7500, ext. 3).

Location	Miles (Statute)
Norfolk	0
Junction VA Cut/ Dismal Swamp Routes	7
Albemarle Sound	65
Alligator River Entrance	79
Pungo River Canal Entrance	105
Pungo River Entrance	127
Belhaven	136
Hobucken	157
Oriental	181
Core Creek	196
Gallant Channel	202
Morehead City	204
Peltier Creek	209
Spooner Creek	211
Swansboro	229
Surf City	261
Wrightsville Beach	283
Carolina Beach Approach	295
Snows Cut	296
Southport	309
Shallotte River	330
Sunset Beach	338
Little River	343
Bucksport	377
Wachesaw Landing	384
Georgetown (entrance)	403
McClellanville	430
Charleston (Municipal Marina)	470
Yonges Island	490
Beaufort, SC	536
Hilton Head Island	557
Harbour Town	565
Daufuskie Landing	571
Thunderbolt	583
Isle of Hope	590
Crescent River	644
Vernon View	596
St. Simons Island	676
Jekyll Island	683
Florida line (St. Marys Inlet)	714

■ WATERWAY GUIDE SOUTHERN EDITION

Location	Miles (Statute)
Fernandina Beach	716
Jacksonville Beach	748
St. Augustine	778
Daytona Beach	830
New Smyrna Beach	846
Titusville	878
Cocoa	897
Melbourne	918
Sebastian Inlet	936
Vero Beach	952
Fort Pierce	966
St. Lucie Inlet	988
Jupiter	1002
Lake Worth Inlet	1018
Palm Beach	1022
Delray Beach	1040
Boca Raton	1048
Pompano Beach	1056
Fort Lauderdale	1065
Hollywood	1072
City of Miami	1090
Dinner Key	1095
Pennekamp Park	1120
Jewfish Creek	1133
Tavernier	1150
Islamorada	1158
Lower Matecumbe Key	1169
Channel Five	1171
Marathon Key	1192
Moser Channel	1197
Harbor Key	1218
Northwest Channel	1236
Key West	1243

GPS Waypoints

The following list provides selected waypoints for the waters covered in this book. The latitude/longitude readings are taken from government light lists and must be checked against the appropriate chart and light list for accuracy. Some waypoints listed here are lighthouses and should not be approached too closely, as they may be on land, in shallow water or on top of a reef. Many buoys must be approached with caution, as they are often located near shallows or obstructions.

The positions of every aid to navigation should be updated using the Coast Guard's *Local Notice to Mariners,* which are now exclusively available via the Internet.

On May 2, 2000, the Selective Availability (SA) degradation of GPS signals was turned off. With SA turned on, users could expect GPS positions to fall within 100 meters of a correct position, 95 percent of the time. Now, with the SA degradation turned off, users should obtain positions accurate to within 20 meters or less.

The U.S. Coast Guard will continue to provide Differential GPS (DGPS) correction signals for those who need positions accurate to within 10 meters or less. Most GPS units require the addition of a separate receiver to obtain DGPS broadcasts.

Hampton Roads to Rudee Inlet

LOCATION	LAT.	LON.
Little Creek Entrance Lighted Buoy 1LC	N 36° 58.083′	W 076° 10.067′
Lynnhaven Roads Fishing Pier Light	N 36° 55.000′	W 076° 04.717′
Cape Henry Light	N 36° 55.583′	W 076° 00.433′
Rudee Inlet Lighted Whistle Buoy RI	N 36° 49.783′	W 075° 56.950′

Albemarle Sound to Neuse River

LOCATION	LAT.	LON.
Albemarle Sound Entrance Light AS	N 36° 03.733′	W 075° 56.133′
Albemarle Sound North Light N	N 36° 06.100′	W 075° 54.750′
Albemarle Sound South Light S	N 36° 01.083′	W 075° 57.617′
Pasquotank River Entrance Light PR	N 36° 09.367′	W 075° 58.650′
Pungo River Junction Light PR	N 35° 22.667′	W 076° 33.583′
Goose Creek Light 1	N 35° 20.400′	W 076° 35.750′
Bay Point Light	N 35° 10.350′	W 076° 30.317′
Bay River Light 1	N 35° 09.800′	W 076° 32.017′
Neuse River Junction Light	N 35° 08.783′	W 076° 30.183′
Whittaker Creek Light 2	N 35° 01.383′	W 076° 41.150′
Smith Creek (Oriental) Channel Light 1	N 35° 00.900′	W 076° 41.467′
Adams Creek Light 1AC	N 34° 58.500′	W 076° 41.767′

Oregon Inlet to Cape Lookout

LOCATION	LAT.	LON.
Oregon Inlet Jetty Light	N 35° 46.433′	W 075° 31.500′
Hatteras Inlet Light	N 35° 11.867′	W 075° 43.933′
Diamond Shoal Lighted Buoy 12	N 35° 09.083′	W 075° 17.550′
Ocracoke Light	N 35° 06.533′	W 075° 59.167′

Beaufort Inlet to Florida Border

LOCATION	LAT.	LON.
Beaufort Inlet	N 34° 38.000′	W 077° 41.000′
(NOTE: This is not the location of a particular buoy.)		
Masonboro Inlet	N 34° 10.000′	W 077° 47.000′
(NOTE: This is not the location of a particular buoy.)		
Frying Pan Shoals Lighted Buoy 16	N 33° 28.783′	W 077° 35.083′
Cape Fear R. Ent. Lighted Whistle Buoy CF	N 33° 46.283′	W 078° 03.033′
Oak Island Light	N 33° 53.567′	W 078° 02.100′
Little River Inlet Lighted Whistle Buoy LR	N 33° 49.817′	W 078° 32.450′
Winyah Bay Lighted Whistle Buoy WB	N 33° 11.617′	W 079° 05.183′
Charleston Ent. Lighted Buoy C	N 32° 37.083′	W 079° 35.500′
North Edisto Rvr. Ent. Lig. Whistle Buoy 2NE	N 32° 31.350′	W 080° 06.850′
South Edisto Rvr. Approach Lig. Buoy A	N 32° 24.717′	W 080° 17.700′
St. Helena Sound Entrance Buoy 1	N 32° 21.667′	W 080° 18.450′
Port Royal Sound Lighted Whistle Buoy P	N 32° 05.133′	W 080° 35.033′
Calibogue Sound Entrance Daybeacon 1	N 32° 02.850′	W 080° 50.533′
Tybee Lighted Buoy T	N 31° 57.883′	W 080° 43.167′
Wassaw Sound Lighted Buoy 2W	N 31° 51.550′	W 080° 53.017′
Ossabaw Sound Ent. Lighted Buoy OS	N 31° 47.800′	W 080° 56.200′
St. Catherines Sound Lighted Buoy STC	N 31° 40.217′	W 081° 00.200′
Sapelo Sound Buoy S	N 31° 31.200′	W 081° 03.900′
Doboy Sound Lighted Buoy D	N 31° 21.233′	W 081° 11.400′
Altamaha Sound Shoal Light	N 31° 18.867′	W 081° 15.333′
St. Simons Sound Lig. Buoy STS	N 31° 02.817′	W 081° 14.417′
St. Andrew Sound Outer Ent. Buoy STA	N 30° 55.550′	W 081° 18.967′
St. Marys Rvr. Approach Lighted Buoy STM	N 30° 42.900′	W 081° 14.650′

Tide Tables

Cape Hatteras Fishing Pier, North Carolina, 2011

Times and Heights of High and Low Waters

Heights are referred to mean lower low water which is the chart datum of soundings. All times are local. Daylight Saving Time has been used when needed.

September

Day	Time (h m)	Height (ft)	Height (cm)	Day	Time (h m)	Height (ft)	Height (cm)
1 Th	0400 1023 0442* 1042*	-0.4 4.1 -0.1 3.5	-12 125 -3 107	16 F	0357 1020 0440* 1032*	0.5 3.4 0.6 2.8	15 104 18 85
2 F	0449 1118 0541* 1135*	-0.3 4.1 0.1 3.2	-9 125 3 98	17 Sa	0431 1100 0522* 1110*	0.6 3.4 0.8 2.7	18 104 24 82
3 Sa	0542 1218* 0645*	-0.1 4.0 0.3	-3 122 9	18 Su	0510 1144 0610* 1154*	0.7 3.3 0.9 2.6	21 101 27 79
4 Su ◐	1234 0640 0122* 0754*	3.0 0.1 3.8 0.5	91 3 116 15	19 M	0554 1234* 0704*	0.7 3.3 1.0	21 101 30
5 M	0141 0745 0231* 0905*	2.8 0.2 3.7 0.6	85 6 113 18	20 Tu ◑	1245 0647 0131* 0805*	2.5 0.8 3.3 1.0	76 24 101 30
6 Tu	0252 0855 0339* 1011*	2.7 0.3 3.6 0.6	82 9 110 18	21 W	0146 0748 0233* 0907*	2.5 0.7 3.3 0.9	76 21 101 27
7 W	0401 1003 0441* 1108*	2.8 0.4 3.6 0.5	85 12 110 15	22 Th	0251 0854 0335* 1003*	2.6 0.6 3.5 0.7	79 18 107 21
8 Th	0502 1104 0535* 1158*	2.9 0.3 3.6 0.5	88 9 110 15	23 F	0355 0959 0432* 1054*	2.9 0.4 3.6 0.5	88 12 110 15
9 F	0554 1157 0622*	3.0 0.3 3.6	91 9 110	24 Sa	0453 1100 0525* 1141*	3.2 0.2 3.8 0.2	98 6 116 6
10 Sa	1240 0640 1244* 0703*	0.4 3.2 0.2 3.6	12 98 6 110	25 Su	0546 1158 0615*	3.6 0.0 3.9	110 0 119
11 Su	0117 0720 0127* 0741*	0.3 3.3 0.2 3.5	9 101 6 107	26 M	1227 0638 1252* 0704*	0.0 3.9 -0.2 3.9	0 119 -6 119
12 M ○	0151 0758 0207* 0816*	0.3 3.4 0.3 3.4	9 104 9 104	27 Tu ●	0112 0728 0146* 0752*	-0.2 4.3 -0.3 3.9	-6 131 -9 119
13 Tu	0223 0834 0245* 0850*	0.3 3.5 0.3 3.3	9 107 9 101	28 W	0158 0818 0239* 0841*	-0.4 4.5 -0.3 3.8	-12 137 -9 116
14 W	0254 0908 0322* 0923*	0.3 3.5 0.4 3.2	9 107 12 98	29 Th	0244 0909 0333* 0931*	-0.4 4.6 -0.2 3.6	-12 140 -6 110
15 Th	0325 0944 0400* 0957*	0.4 3.5 0.5 3.0	12 107 15 91	30 F	0333 1002 0428* 1023*	-0.3 4.5 -0.1 3.4	-9 137 -3 104

October

Day	Time (h m)	Height (ft)	Height (cm)	Day	Time (h m)	Height (ft)	Height (cm)
1 Sa	0424 1058 0527* 1119*	-0.2 4.3 0.2 3.2	-6 131 6 98	16 Su	0357 1028 0457* 1043*	0.6 3.6 0.7 2.7	18 110 21 82
2 Su	0520 1157 0629*	0.1 4.1 0.4	3 125 12	17 M	0436 1111 0543* 1128*	0.7 3.5 0.8 2.6	21 107 24 79
3 M	1221 0622 0102* 0736*	3.0 0.3 3.8 0.6	91 9 116 18	18 Tu	0522 1200* 0634*	0.7 3.4 0.9	21 104 27
4 Tu ◐	0129 0730 0210* 0843*	2.9 0.5 3.6 0.6	88 15 110 18	19 W	1220 0617 1255* 0729*	2.6 0.8 3.4 0.9	79 24 104 27
5 W	0241 0843 0317* 0946*	2.9 0.6 3.5 0.7	88 18 107 21	20 Th ◑	0121 0720 0155* 0827*	2.7 0.7 3.4 0.7	82 21 104 21
6 Th	0347 0951 0417* 1040*	2.9 0.6 3.4 0.6	88 18 104 18	21 F	0226 0829 0257* 0922*	2.8 0.6 3.4 0.6	85 18 104 18
7 F	0445 1051 0509* 1126*	3.1 0.6 3.4 0.5	94 18 104 15	22 Sa	0329 0937 0356* 1014*	3.1 0.5 3.5 0.3	94 15 107 9
8 Sa	0534 1143 0554*	3.2 0.5 3.4	98 15 104	23 Su	0428 1042 0452* 1104*	3.5 0.2 3.6 0.1	107 6 110 3
9 Su	1205 0616 1228* 0634*	0.5 3.4 0.5 3.3	15 104 15 101	24 M	0523 1141 0546* 1153*	3.9 0.0 3.6 -0.2	119 0 110 -6
10 M	1240 0654 0109* 0711*	0.4 3.5 0.4 3.3	12 107 12 101	25 Tu	0616 1238* 0638*	4.3 -0.2 3.6	131 -6 110
11 Tu	0113 0730 0147* 0746*	0.4 3.6 0.4 3.2	12 110 12 98	26 W ●	1241 0707 0132* 0729*	-0.3 4.5 -0.3 3.6	-9 137 -9 110
12 W ○	0144 0804 0224* 0820*	0.4 3.7 0.4 3.1	12 113 12 94	27 Th	0129 0759 0226* 0820*	-0.4 4.7 -0.3 3.5	-12 143 -9 107
13 Th	0215 0838 0301* 0853*	0.4 3.7 0.4 3.0	12 113 12 91	28 F	0219 0850 0319* 0912*	-0.4 4.7 -0.2 3.4	-12 143 -6 104
14 F	0247 0913 0338* 0928*	0.4 3.7 0.5 2.9	12 113 15 88	29 Sa	0310 0943 0414* 1006*	-0.3 4.6 -0.1 3.3	-9 140 -3 101
15 Sa	0321 0949 0416* 1004*	0.5 3.7 0.6 2.8	15 113 18 85	30 Su	0403 1038 0510* 1103*	-0.1 4.3 0.1 3.1	-3 131 3 94
				31 M	0500 1135 0609*	0.1 4.0 0.3	3 122 9

November

Day	Time (h m)	Height (ft)	Height (cm)	Day	Time (h m)	Height (ft)	Height (cm)
1 Tu	1204 0602 1236* 0710*	3.0 0.3 3.7 0.4	91 9 113 12	16 W	0401 1033 0506* 1101*	0.5 3.4 0.5 2.6	15 104 15 79
2 W ◐	0110 0709 0139* 0811*	2.9 0.5 3.5 0.5	88 15 107 15	17 Th	0456 1125 0556* 1159*	0.5 3.3 0.5 2.8	15 101 15 85
3 Th	0218 0820 0242* 0909*	2.9 0.7 3.2 0.6	88 21 98 18	18 F ◑	0559 1221* 0649*	0.6 3.3 0.4	18 101 12
4 F	0322 0928 0341* 1000*	3.0 0.7 3.1 0.6	91 21 94 18	19 Sa	0102 0708 0121* 0743*	3.0 0.5 3.2 0.2	91 15 98 6
5 Sa	0417 1029 0433* 1044*	3.1 0.7 3.0 0.5	94 21 91 15	20 Su	0205 0818 0223* 0837*	3.3 0.4 3.1 0.0	101 12 94 0
6 Su	0405 1021 0419* 1024*	3.3 0.6 2.9 0.5	101 18 88 15	21 M	0305 0925 0323* 0930*	3.6 0.2 3.1 -0.2	110 6 94 -6
7 M	0447 1107 0501* 1100*	3.4 0.5 2.9 0.4	104 15 88 12	22 Tu	0402 1027 0421* 1023*	4.0 0.0 3.2 -0.3	122 0 98 -9
8 Tu	0526 1148 0539* 1134*	3.5 0.5 2.9 0.3	107 15 88 9	23 W	0457 1125 0516* 1115*	4.3 -0.2 3.2 -0.5	131 -6 98 -15
9 W	0602 1227* 0616*	3.7 0.4 2.9	113 12 88	24 Th	0550 1220* 0610*	4.5 -0.3 3.2	137 -9 98
10 Th ○	1208 0637 0104* 0652*	0.3 3.7 0.4 2.8	9 113 12 85	25 F ●	1207 0643 0113* 0703*	-0.5 4.5 -0.4 3.2	-15 137 -12 98
11 F	1242 0712 0141* 0727*	0.3 3.8 0.4 2.8	9 116 12 85	26 Sa	1259 0735 0205* 0756*	-0.5 4.5 -0.3 3.1	-15 137 -9 94
12 Sa	0117 0748 0218* 0804*	0.3 3.7 0.4 2.7	9 113 12 82	27 Su	0152 0826 0257* 0849*	-0.4 4.3 -0.2 3.0	-12 131 -6 91
13 Su	0153 0825 0257* 0842*	0.3 3.7 0.4 2.7	9 113 12 82	28 M	0245 0918 0349* 0944*	-0.3 4.1 -0.1 2.9	-9 125 -3 88
14 M	0231 0904 0337* 0923*	0.4 3.6 0.5 2.6	12 110 15 79	29 Tu	0340 1011 0442* 1041*	0.0 3.8 0.1 2.9	0 116 3 88
15 Tu	0313 0947 0420* 1009*	0.4 3.5 0.5 2.6	12 107 15 79	30 W	0438 1104 0535* 1141*	0.2 3.4 0.2 2.8	6 104 6 85

December

Day	Time (h m)	Height (ft)	Height (cm)	Day	Time (h m)	Height (ft)	Height (cm)
1 Th	0540 1200* 0628*	0.4 3.1 0.3	12 94 9	16 F	0441 1059 0524* 1138*	0.2 3.2 0.0 2.9	6 98 0 88
2 F ◐	1242 0646 1256* 0719*	2.8 0.6 2.9 0.4	85 18 88 12	17 Sa	0542 1153 0614*	0.3 3.0 -0.1	9 91 -3
3 Sa	0142 0752 0152* 0808*	2.8 0.7 2.7 0.4	85 21 82 12	18 Su ◑	1239 0650 1251* 0708*	3.1 0.3 2.8 -0.1	94 9 85 -3
4 Su	0238 0855 0247* 0854*	2.9 0.7 2.5 0.4	88 21 76 12	19 M	0142 0802 0154* 0805*	3.3 0.2 2.7 -0.2	101 6 82 -6
5 M	0328 0951 0337* 0937*	3.1 0.6 2.5 0.3	94 18 76 9	20 Tu	0245 0912 0258* 0903*	3.5 0.1 2.7 -0.4	107 3 82 -12
6 Tu	0413 1040 0423* 1018*	3.2 0.5 2.4 0.3	98 15 73 9	21 W	0345 1016 0401* 1001*	3.8 -0.1 2.7 -0.5	116 -3 82 -15
7 W	0455 1124 0506* 1057*	3.3 0.4 2.4 0.2	101 12 73 6	22 Th	0443 1115 0500* 1058*	4.0 -0.2 2.7 -0.6	122 -6 82 -18
8 Th	0534 1204* 0546* 1136*	3.4 0.3 2.5 0.1	104 9 76 3	23 F	0538 1210* 0556* 1153*	4.1 -0.3 2.8 -0.6	125 -9 85 -18
9 F	0612 1243* 0625*	3.5 0.2 2.5	107 6 76	24 Sa ●	0630 0101* 0650*	4.2 -0.4 2.8	128 -12 85
10 Sa ○	1214 0650 0121* 0704*	0.1 3.6 0.2 2.5	3 110 6 76	25 Su	1246 0721 0150* 0741*	-0.6 4.1 -0.4 2.9	-18 125 -12 88
11 Su	1253 0727 0158* 0743*	0.0 3.6 0.1 2.6	0 110 3 79	26 M	0138 0809 0237* 0831*	-0.6 4.0 -0.4 2.9	-18 122 -12 88
12 M	0133 0805 0236* 0823*	0.0 3.6 0.1 2.6	0 110 3 79	27 Tu	0229 0857 0323* 0921*	-0.4 3.7 -0.3 2.8	-12 113 -9 85
13 Tu	0214 0845 0315* 0905*	0.0 3.6 0.1 2.6	0 110 3 79	28 W	0319 0943 0408* 1012*	-0.2 3.4 -0.2 2.8	-6 104 -6 85
14 W	0258 0926 0355* 0951*	0.1 3.5 0.1 2.7	3 107 3 82	29 Th	0411 1029 0452* 1103*	0.0 3.1 -0.1 2.7	0 94 -3 82
15 Th	0346 1011 0438* 1042*	0.1 3.4 0.0 2.7	3 104 0 82	30 F	0505 1115 0536* 1156*	0.2 2.8 0.1 2.7	6 85 3 82
				31 Sa	0602 1203* 0620*	0.4 2.5 0.2	12 76 6

Cape Hatteras, North Carolina, 2012

Times and Heights of High and Low Waters

January

Day	Time (h m)	Height ft	Height cm	Day	Time (h m)	Height ft	Height cm
1 Su	12:52 AM 07:06 AM 12:57 PM 07:10 PM	2.7 0.5 2.3 0.2	82 15 70 6	16 M	12:17 AM 06:35 AM 12:29 PM 06:42 PM	3.2 0.0 2.6 -0.4	98 0 79 -12
2 M	01:48 AM 08:10 AM 01:52 PM 07:59 PM	2.7 0.6 2.2 0.3	82 18 67 9	17 Tu	01:21 AM 07:47 AM 01:34 PM 07:43 PM	3.2 0.1 2.4 -0.4	98 3 73 -12
3 Tu	02:43 AM 09:10 AM 02:48 PM 08:48 PM	2.8 0.6 2.1 0.2	85 18 64 6	18 W	02:28 AM 08:59 AM 02:43 PM 08:47 PM	3.4 0.0 2.4 -0.4	104 0 73 -12
4 W	03:34 AM 10:05 AM 03:41 PM 09:37 PM	2.9 0.5 2.1 0.1	88 15 64 3	19 Th	03:32 AM 10:05 AM 03:50 PM 09:50 PM	3.5 -0.1 2.4 -0.5	107 -3 73 -15
5 Th	04:21 AM 10:53 AM 04:30 PM 10:23 PM	3.0 0.3 2.1 0.0	91 9 64 0	20 F	04:33 AM 11:04 AM 04:51 PM 10:50 PM	3.6 -0.2 2.5 -0.5	110 -6 76 -15
6 F	05:05 AM 11:36 AM 05:15 PM 11:08 PM	3.2 0.2 2.2 -0.1	98 6 67 -3	21 Sa	05:28 AM 11:57 AM 05:47 PM 11:46 PM	3.7 -0.4 2.6 -0.6	113 -12 79 -18
7 Sa	05:46 AM 12:16 PM 05:58 PM 11:51 PM	3.3 0.0 2.4 -0.2	101 0 73 -6	22 Su	06:19 AM 12:45 PM 06:38 PM	3.7 -0.4 2.8	113 -12 85
8 Su	06:26 AM 12:54 PM 06:39 PM	3.4 -0.1 2.5	104 -3 76	23 M	12:38 AM 07:06 AM 01:30 PM 07:26 PM	-0.6 3.7 -0.5 2.9	-18 113 -15 88
9 M	12:33 AM 07:05 AM 01:32 PM 07:21 PM	-0.3 3.5 -0.2 2.6	-9 107 -6 79	24 Tu	01:27 AM 07:51 AM 02:12 PM 08:12 PM	-0.6 3.6 -0.5 2.9	-18 110 -15 88
10 Tu	01:16 AM 07:44 AM 02:09 PM 08:02 PM	-0.4 3.6 -0.3 2.7	-12 110 -9 82	25 W	02:13 AM 08:33 AM 02:52 PM 08:56 PM	-0.5 3.4 -0.4 2.9	-15 104 -12 88
11 W	02:00 AM 08:24 AM 02:47 PM 08:46 PM	-0.4 3.5 -0.4 2.8	-12 107 -12 85	26 Th	02:59 AM 09:14 AM 03:30 PM 09:39 PM	-0.3 3.1 -0.3 2.8	-9 94 -9 85
12 Th	02:46 AM 09:06 AM 03:27 PM 09:32 PM	-0.4 3.4 -0.4 2.9	-12 104 -12 88	27 F	03:44 AM 09:53 AM 04:08 PM 10:23 PM	-0.1 2.9 -0.2 2.8	-3 88 -6 85
13 F	03:35 AM 09:50 AM 04:09 PM 10:22 PM	-0.3 3.2 -0.4 3.0	-9 98 -12 91	28 Sa	04:31 AM 10:33 AM 04:45 PM 11:08 PM	0.1 2.6 -0.1 2.7	3 79 -3 82
14 Sa	04:29 AM 10:38 AM 04:55 PM 11:17 PM	-0.2 3.0 -0.4 3.1	-6 91 -12 94	29 Su	05:20 AM 11:15 AM 05:25 PM 11:56 PM	0.3 2.3 0.1 2.6	9 70 3 79
15 Su	05:29 AM 11:30 AM 05:46 PM	-0.1 2.8 -0.4	-3 85 -12	30 M	06:14 AM 12:01 PM 06:09 PM	0.4 2.1 0.2	12 64 6
				31 Tu	12:50 AM 07:15 AM 12:54 PM 06:59 PM	2.6 0.5 2.0 0.2	79 15 61 6

February

Day	Time (h m)	Height ft	Height cm	Day	Time (h m)	Height ft	Height cm
1 W	01:48 AM 08:20 AM 01:53 PM 07:55 PM	2.6 0.6 1.9 0.2	79 18 58 6	16 Th	02:13 AM 08:47 AM 02:34 PM 08:36 PM	3.3 0.1 2.3 -0.2	101 3 70 -6
2 Th	02:46 AM 09:21 AM 02:55 PM 08:52 PM	2.7 0.5 1.9 0.2	82 15 58 6	17 F	03:20 AM 09:53 AM 03:43 PM 09:44 PM	3.3 0.0 2.4 -0.3	101 0 73 -9
3 F	03:41 AM 10:14 AM 03:52 PM 09:47 PM	2.8 0.4 2.0 0.0	85 12 61 0	18 Sa	04:22 AM 10:50 AM 04:44 PM 10:45 PM	3.3 -0.1 2.5 -0.3	101 -3 76 -9
4 Sa	04:30 AM 11:01 AM 04:42 PM 10:39 PM	3.0 0.2 2.2 -0.1	91 6 67 -3	19 Su	05:16 AM 11:40 AM 05:37 PM 11:39 PM	3.4 -0.2 2.7 -0.4	104 -6 82 -12
5 Su	05:16 AM 11:42 AM 05:29 PM 11:27 PM	3.2 0.0 2.4 -0.3	98 0 73 -9	20 M	06:04 AM 12:24 PM 06:25 PM	3.4 -0.3 2.9	104 -9 88
6 M	05:58 AM 12:22 PM 06:13 PM	3.3 -0.2 2.6	101 -6 79	21 Tu	12:28 AM 06:48 AM 01:05 PM 07:08 PM	-0.5 3.4 -0.4 3.0	-15 104 -12 91
7 Tu	12:13 AM 06:40 AM 01:00 PM 06:57 PM	-0.5 3.5 -0.4 2.9	-15 107 -12 88	22 W	01:14 AM 07:29 AM 01:42 PM 07:49 PM	-0.4 3.3 -0.4 3.1	-12 101 -12 94
8 W	12:59 AM 07:21 AM 01:39 PM 07:41 PM	-0.6 3.5 -0.5 3.1	-18 107 -15 94	23 Th	01:56 AM 08:07 AM 02:17 PM 08:27 PM	-0.4 3.1 -0.3 3.1	-12 94 -9 94
9 Th	01:46 AM 08:03 AM 02:18 PM 08:26 PM	-0.6 3.5 -0.6 3.2	-18 107 -18 98	24 F	02:37 AM 08:44 AM 02:51 PM 09:05 PM	-0.3 2.9 -0.2 3.1	-9 88 -6 94
10 F	02:34 AM 08:46 AM 02:59 PM 09:13 PM	-0.6 3.4 -0.7 3.4	-18 104 -21 104	25 Sa	03:18 AM 09:20 AM 03:24 PM 09:43 PM	-0.1 2.7 -0.1 3.0	-3 82 -3 91
11 Sa	03:25 AM 09:31 AM 03:42 PM 10:03 PM	-0.5 3.2 -0.6 3.4	-15 98 -18 104	26 Su	03:59 AM 09:56 AM 03:58 PM 10:23 PM	0.1 2.5 0.0 2.9	3 76 0 88
12 Su	04:19 AM 10:20 AM 04:30 PM 10:58 PM	-0.4 2.9 -0.6 3.4	-12 88 -18 104	27 M	04:42 AM 10:34 AM 04:35 PM 11:06 PM	0.2 2.3 0.1 2.8	6 70 3 85
13 M	05:18 AM 11:13 AM 05:22 PM 11:57 PM	-0.2 2.7 -0.5 3.3	-6 82 -15 101	28 Tu	05:30 AM 11:16 AM 05:17 PM 11:55 PM	0.4 2.1 0.2 2.7	12 64 6 82
14 Tu	06:23 AM 12:13 PM 06:20 PM	0.0 2.5 -0.3	0 76 -9	29 W	06:24 AM 12:06 PM 06:07 PM	0.5 2.0 0.3	15 61 9
15 W	01:03 AM 07:35 AM 01:22 PM 07:26 PM	3.3 0.1 2.3 -0.3	101 3 70 -9				

March

Day	Time (h m)	Height ft	Height cm	Day	Time (h m)	Height ft	Height cm
1 Th	12:52 AM 07:26 AM 01:05 PM 07:05 PM	2.7 0.6 1.9 0.3	82 18 58 9	16 F	02:56 AM 09:30 AM 03:27 PM 09:29 PM	3.2 0.1 2.4 0.0	98 3 73 0
2 F	01:53 AM 08:30 AM 02:09 PM 08:08 PM	2.7 0.5 2.0 0.3	82 15 61 9	17 Sa	04:04 AM 10:34 AM 04:34 PM 10:38 PM	3.2 0.1 2.6 0.0	98 3 79 0
3 Sa	02:54 AM 09:27 AM 03:12 PM 09:11 PM	2.8 0.4 2.1 0.2	85 12 64 6	18 Su	05:05 AM 11:28 AM 05:32 PM 11:38 PM	3.2 0.0 2.7 -0.1	98 0 82 -3
4 Su	03:49 AM 10:17 AM 04:07 PM 10:09 PM	3.0 0.2 2.4 0.0	91 6 73 0	19 M	05:58 AM 12:15 PM 06:22 PM	3.2 -0.1 2.9	98 -3 88
5 M	04:39 AM 11:01 AM 04:58 PM 11:02 PM	3.1 0.0 2.7 -0.3	94 0 82 -9	20 Tu	12:30 AM 06:44 AM 12:56 PM 07:06 PM	-0.1 3.1 -0.1 3.1	-3 94 -3 94
6 Tu	05:26 AM 11:43 AM 05:45 PM 11:53 PM	3.3 -0.2 3.0 -0.5	101 -6 91 -15	21 W	01:16 AM 07:26 AM 01:34 PM 07:46 PM	-0.2 3.1 -0.2 3.2	-6 94 -6 98
7 W	06:11 AM 12:24 PM 06:31 PM	3.4 -0.5 3.3	104 -15 101	22 Th	01:59 AM 08:04 AM 02:08 PM 08:23 PM	-0.2 3.0 -0.2 3.3	-6 91 -6 101
8 Th	12:42 AM 06:55 AM 01:05 PM 07:18 PM	-0.6 3.5 -0.6 3.6	-18 107 -18 110	23 F	02:38 AM 08:40 AM 02:41 PM 08:58 PM	-0.2 2.9 -0.1 3.3	-6 88 -3 101
9 F	01:32 AM 07:40 AM 01:47 PM 08:05 PM	-0.7 3.4 -0.7 3.8	-21 104 -21 116	24 Sa	03:17 AM 09:15 AM 03:13 PM 09:33 PM	-0.1 2.8 -0.1 3.3	-3 85 -3 101
10 Sa	02:22 AM 08:26 AM 02:31 PM 08:53 PM	-0.7 3.3 -0.8 3.9	-21 101 -24 119	25 Su	03:54 AM 09:49 AM 03:45 PM 10:09 PM	0.0 2.7 0.0 3.3	0 82 0 101
11 Su	04:14 AM 10:14 AM 04:18 PM 10:45 PM	-0.6 3.1 -0.7 3.8	-18 94 -21 116	26 M	04:33 AM 10:24 AM 04:19 PM 10:46 PM	0.1 2.5 0.1 3.2	3 76 3 98
12 M	05:08 AM 11:05 AM 05:08 PM 11:40 PM	-0.4 2.9 -0.6 3.7	-12 88 -18 113	27 Tu	05:13 AM 11:02 AM 04:56 PM 11:27 PM	0.3 2.4 0.2 3.1	9 73 6 94
13 Tu	06:07 AM 12:00 PM 06:03 PM	-0.2 2.7 -0.4	-6 82 -12	28 W	05:56 AM 11:43 AM 05:37 PM	0.4 2.2 0.4	12 67 12
14 W	12:40 AM 07:12 AM 01:03 PM 07:05 PM	3.5 0.0 2.5 -0.2	107 0 76 -6	29 Th	12:13 AM 06:45 AM 12:31 PM 06:26 PM	2.9 0.5 2.1 0.4	88 15 64 12
15 Th	01:46 AM 08:21 AM 02:14 PM 08:16 PM	3.4 0.1 2.4 0.0	104 3 73 0	30 F	01:05 AM 07:40 AM 01:27 PM 07:24 PM	2.9 0.6 2.1 0.5	88 18 64 15
				31 Sa	02:03 AM 08:38 AM 02:30 PM 08:29 PM	2.9 0.5 2.2 0.4	88 15 67 12

April

Day	Time (h m)	Height ft	Height cm	Day	Time (h m)	Height ft	Height cm
1 Su	03:04 AM 09:35 AM 03:34 PM 09:36 PM	2.9 0.4 2.4 0.3	88 12 73 9	16 M	04:38 AM 10:57 AM 05:13 PM 11:24 PM	3.0 0.1 3.0 0.2	91 3 91 6
2 M	04:03 AM 10:27 AM 04:32 PM 10:39 PM	3.0 0.2 2.7 0.1	91 6 82 3	17 Tu	05:30 AM 11:42 AM 06:00 PM	2.9 0.1 3.1	88 3 94
3 Tu	04:58 AM 11:16 AM 05:26 PM 11:38 PM	3.1 0.0 3.1 -0.1	94 0 94 -3	18 W	12:15 AM 06:16 AM 12:21 PM 06:42 PM	0.2 2.9 0.0 3.3	6 88 0 101
4 W	05:50 AM 12:02 PM 06:17 PM	3.2 -0.3 3.5	98 -9 107	19 Th	01:00 AM 06:57 AM 12:58 PM 07:20 PM	0.1 2.8 0.0 3.4	3 85 0 104
5 Th	12:32 AM 06:40 AM 12:47 PM 07:06 PM	-0.4 3.3 -0.5 3.8	-12 101 -15 116	20 F	01:41 AM 07:36 AM 01:32 PM 07:56 PM	0.1 2.8 0.0 3.5	3 85 0 107
6 F	01:25 AM 07:28 AM 01:32 PM 07:55 PM	-0.6 3.4 -0.6 4.1	-18 104 -18 125	21 Sa	02:20 AM 08:12 AM 02:05 PM 08:31 PM	0.0 2.7 0.0 3.5	0 82 0 107
7 Sa	02:17 AM 08:17 AM 02:18 PM 08:44 PM	-0.7 3.3 -0.7 4.3	-21 101 -21 131	22 Su	02:57 AM 08:47 AM 02:38 PM 09:06 PM	0.1 2.6 0.1 3.5	3 79 3 107
8 Su	03:09 AM 09:06 AM 03:06 PM 09:35 PM	-0.7 3.3 -0.7 4.3	-21 101 -21 131	23 M	03:34 AM 09:23 AM 03:12 PM 09:41 PM	0.1 2.6 0.1 3.5	3 79 3 107
9 M	04:02 AM 09:57 AM 03:56 PM 10:28 PM	-0.6 3.1 -0.6 4.2	-18 94 -18 128	24 Tu	04:11 AM 09:59 AM 03:47 PM 10:18 PM	0.2 2.5 0.2 3.4	6 76 6 104
10 Tu	04:57 AM 10:51 AM 04:50 PM 11:24 PM	-0.4 3.0 -0.4 4.0	-12 91 -12 122	25 W	04:50 AM 10:37 AM 04:25 PM 10:57 PM	0.3 2.4 0.3 3.3	9 73 9 101
11 W	05:56 AM 11:50 AM 05:48 PM	-0.2 2.8 -0.2	-6 85 -6	26 Th	05:31 AM 11:18 AM 05:07 PM 11:40 PM	0.4 2.3 0.4 3.2	12 70 12 98
12 Th	12:23 AM 06:57 AM 12:54 PM 06:53 PM	3.7 0.0 2.7 0.0	113 0 82 0	27 F	06:15 AM 12:05 PM 05:56 PM	0.4 2.3 0.5	12 70 15
13 F	01:27 AM 08:02 AM 02:04 PM 08:04 PM	3.4 0.1 2.6 0.2	104 3 79 6	28 Sa	12:28 AM 07:03 AM 12:59 PM 06:52 PM	3.1 0.4 2.3 0.5	94 12 70 15
14 Sa	02:34 AM 09:06 AM 03:14 PM 09:17 PM	3.2 0.2 2.7 0.3	98 6 82 9	29 Su	01:21 AM 07:55 AM 01:59 PM 07:57 PM	3.0 0.4 2.5 0.5	91 12 76 15
15 Su	03:39 AM 10:05 AM 04:18 PM 10:25 PM	3.1 0.2 2.8 0.3	94 6 85 9	30 M	02:19 AM 08:48 AM 03:00 PM 09:05 PM	3.0 0.3 2.7 0.4	91 9 82 12

May

Day	Time (h m)	Height ft	Height cm	Day	Time (h m)	Height ft	Height cm
1 Tu	03:19 AM 09:40 AM 04:00 PM 10:12 PM	3.0 0.1 3.1 0.2	91 3 94 6	16 W	04:55 AM 11:01 AM 05:32 PM 11:53 PM	2.6 0.2 3.2 0.4	79 6 98 12
2 W	04:18 AM 10:32 AM 04:56 PM 11:14 PM	3.0 -0.1 3.4 0.0	91 -3 104 0	17 Th	05:42 AM 11:41 AM 06:14 PM	2.6 0.1 3.3	79 3 101
3 Th	05:15 AM 11:22 AM 05:50 PM	3.1 -0.3 3.8	94 -9 116	18 F	12:38 AM 06:25 AM 12:19 PM 06:53 PM	0.3 2.5 0.1 3.4	9 76 3 104
4 F	12:13 AM 06:09 AM 12:12 PM 06:43 PM	-0.2 3.1 -0.5 4.2	-6 94 -15 128	19 Sa	01:20 AM 07:05 AM 12:56 PM 07:29 PM	0.2 2.5 0.1 3.5	6 76 3 107
5 Sa	01:09 AM 07:03 AM 01:02 PM 07:34 PM	-0.4 3.2 -0.7 4.4	-12 98 -21 134	20 Su	01:59 AM 07:43 AM 01:32 PM 08:06 PM	0.2 2.5 0.1 3.6	6 76 3 110
6 Su	02:03 AM 07:55 AM 01:53 PM 08:26 PM	-0.5 3.2 -0.7 4.5	-15 98 -21 137	21 M	02:37 AM 08:21 AM 02:08 PM 08:42 PM	0.2 2.5 0.1 3.6	6 76 3 110
7 M	02:56 AM 08:48 AM 02:45 PM 09:19 PM	-0.6 3.1 -0.7 4.4	-18 94 -21 134	22 Tu	03:14 AM 08:58 AM 02:44 PM 09:18 PM	0.2 2.5 0.1 3.5	6 76 3 107
8 Tu	03:50 AM 09:42 AM 03:38 PM 10:12 PM	-0.5 3.1 -0.6 4.3	-15 94 -18 131	23 W	03:51 AM 09:36 AM 03:22 PM 09:54 PM	0.2 2.4 0.2 3.5	6 73 6 107
9 W	04:44 AM 10:38 AM 04:34 PM 11:07 PM	-0.4 3.0 -0.4 4.0	-12 91 -12 122	24 Th	04:29 AM 10:15 AM 04:01 PM 10:33 PM	0.2 2.4 0.3 3.4	6 73 9 104
10 Th	05:40 AM 11:37 AM 05:33 PM	-0.3 2.9 -0.1	-9 88 -3	25 F	05:07 AM 10:57 AM 04:45 PM 11:14 PM	0.2 2.4 0.3 3.3	6 73 9 101
11 F	12:04 AM 06:37 AM 12:40 PM 06:37 PM	3.7 -0.1 2.8 0.1	113 -3 85 3	26 Sa	05:47 AM 11:44 AM 05:33 PM 11:59 PM	0.2 2.5 0.4 3.2	6 76 12 98
12 Sa	01:03 AM 07:35 AM 01:46 PM 07:46 PM	3.4 0.0 2.8 0.3	104 0 85 9	27 Su	06:31 AM 12:35 PM 06:29 PM	0.2 2.6 0.4	6 79 12
13 Su	02:04 AM 08:33 AM 02:51 PM 08:56 PM	3.1 0.1 2.8 0.4	94 3 85 12	28 M	12:48 AM 07:17 AM 01:31 PM 07:32 PM	3.1 0.2 2.8 0.4	94 6 85 12
14 M	03:05 AM 09:27 AM 03:51 PM 10:02 PM	2.9 0.2 2.9 0.5	88 6 88 15	29 Tu	01:43 AM 08:07 AM 02:31 PM 08:40 PM	3.0 0.1 3.0 0.4	91 3 91 12
15 Tu	04:02 AM 10:16 AM 04:45 PM 11:01 PM	2.7 0.2 3.1 0.4	82 6 94 12	30 W	02:42 AM 09:00 AM 03:31 PM 09:48 PM	2.9 -0.1 3.3 0.2	88 -3 101 6
				31 Th	03:43 AM 09:54 AM 04:30 PM 10:54 PM	2.9 -0.2 3.7 0.1	88 -6 113 3

June

Day	Time (h m)	Height ft	Height cm	Day	Time (h m)	Height ft	Height cm
1 F	04:44 AM 10:49 AM 05:27 PM 11:56 PM	2.9 -0.4 4.0 -0.1	88 -12 122 -3	16 Sa	12:12 AM 05:49 AM 11:42 AM 06:23 PM	0.5 2.3 0.2 3.4	15 70 6 104
2 Sa	05:43 AM 11:44 AM 06:23 PM	2.9 -0.6 4.2	88 -18 128	17 Su	12:55 AM 06:33 AM 12:23 PM 07:03 PM	0.4 2.3 0.1 3.5	12 70 3 107
3 Su	12:53 AM 06:40 AM 12:39 PM 07:17 PM	-0.3 3.0 -0.7 4.4	-9 91 -21 134	18 M	01:35 AM 07:14 AM 01:03 PM 07:41 PM	0.3 2.4 0.1 3.5	9 73 3 107
4 M	01:49 AM 07:36 AM 01:33 PM 08:10 PM	-0.4 3.0 -0.7 4.4	-12 91 -21 134	19 Tu	02:14 AM 07:54 AM 01:42 PM 08:18 PM	0.2 2.4 0.1 3.6	6 73 3 110
5 Tu	02:42 AM 08:32 AM 02:28 PM 09:03 PM	-0.5 3.0 -0.7 4.4	-15 91 -21 134	20 W	02:51 AM 08:34 AM 02:21 PM 08:55 PM	0.1 2.5 0.1 3.6	3 76 3 110
6 W	03:35 AM 09:27 AM 03:23 PM 09:55 PM	-0.5 3.0 -0.5 4.2	-15 91 -15 128	21 Th	03:27 AM 09:13 AM 03:01 PM 09:32 PM	0.1 2.5 0.1 3.6	3 76 3 110
7 Th	04:26 AM 10:22 AM 04:18 PM 10:47 PM	-0.4 3.0 -0.3 3.9	-12 91 -9 119	22 F	04:03 AM 09:53 AM 03:43 PM 10:10 PM	0.1 2.6 0.1 3.5	3 79 3 107
8 F	05:18 AM 11:19 AM 05:16 PM 11:40 PM	-0.3 3.0 -0.1 3.6	-9 91 -3 110	23 Sa	04:40 AM 10:36 AM 04:27 PM 10:50 PM	0.0 2.6 0.2 3.4	0 79 6 104
9 Sa	06:10 AM 12:18 PM 06:16 PM	-0.2 2.9 0.2	-6 88 6	24 Su	05:19 AM 11:22 AM 05:17 PM 11:34 PM	0.0 2.7 0.2 3.3	0 82 6 101
10 Su	12:33 AM 07:01 AM 01:17 PM 07:19 PM	3.3 0.0 2.9 0.4	101 0 88 12	25 M	06:00 AM 12:12 PM 06:12 PM	0.0 2.9 0.3	0 88 9
11 M	01:27 AM 07:52 AM 02:17 PM 08:25 PM	3.0 0.1 2.9 0.5	91 3 88 15	26 Tu	12:21 AM 06:45 AM 01:07 PM 07:13 PM	3.1 -0.1 3.0 0.3	94 -3 91 9
12 Tu	02:23 AM 08:42 AM 03:15 PM 09:30 PM	2.7 0.2 3.0 0.6	82 6 91 18	27 W	01:14 AM 07:34 AM 02:06 PM 08:20 PM	2.9 -0.1 3.2 0.3	88 -3 98 9
13 W	03:18 AM 09:30 AM 04:08 PM 10:30 PM	2.5 0.2 3.0 0.6	76 6 91 18	28 Th	02:13 AM 08:28 AM 03:08 PM 09:30 PM	2.8 -0.2 3.5 0.3	85 -6 107 9
14 Th	04:12 AM 10:16 AM 04:57 PM 11:24 PM	2.4 0.2 3.2 0.5	73 6 98 15	29 F	03:16 AM 09:26 AM 04:10 PM 10:38 PM	2.7 -0.3 3.7 0.1	82 -9 113 3
15 F	05:02 AM 11:00 AM 05:42 PM	2.3 0.2 3.3	70 6 101	30 Sa	04:20 AM 10:25 AM 05:10 PM 11:41 PM	2.7 -0.4 4.0 0.0	82 -12 122 0

Heights are referred to mean lower water which is the chart datum of sounding. All times are local. Daylight Saving Time has been used when needed.

Cape Hatteras, North Carolina, 2012

Times and Heights of High and Low Waters

July

Day	Time (h m)	Height (ft)	Height (cm)
1 Su	05:23 AM	2.7	82
	11:25 AM	-0.5	-15
	06:08 PM	4.1	125
2 M	12:40 AM	-0.2	-6
	06:24 AM	2.8	85
	12:23 PM	-0.6	-18
	07:03 PM	4.3	131
3 Tu	01:34 AM	-0.3	-9
	07:21 AM	2.9	88
	01:19 PM	-0.6	-18
	07:56 PM	4.3	131
4 W	02:26 AM	-0.4	-12
	08:16 AM	3.0	91
	02:14 PM	-0.6	-18
	08:47 PM	4.2	128
5 Th	03:15 AM	-0.4	-12
	09:10 AM	3.1	94
	03:08 PM	-0.5	-15
	09:36 PM	4.0	122
6 F	04:03 AM	-0.4	-12
	10:02 AM	3.1	94
	04:01 PM	-0.3	-9
	10:24 PM	3.8	116
7 Sa	04:49 AM	-0.3	-9
	10:54 AM	3.1	94
	04:54 PM	-0.1	-3
	11:11 PM	3.5	107
8 Su	05:35 AM	-0.2	-6
	11:47 AM	3.0	91
	05:49 PM	0.2	6
	11:58 PM	3.1	94
9 M	06:20 AM	0.0	0
	12:40 PM	3.0	91
	06:46 PM	0.4	12
10 Tu	12:46 AM	2.8	85
	07:05 AM	0.1	3
	01:35 PM	3.0	91
	07:46 PM	0.6	18
11 W	01:36 AM	2.6	79
	07:51 AM	0.2	6
	02:30 PM	3.0	91
	08:49 PM	0.7	21
12 Th	02:29 AM	2.4	73
	08:39 AM	0.3	9
	03:25 PM	3.0	91
	09:51 PM	0.7	21
13 F	03:25 AM	2.2	67
	09:29 AM	0.3	9
	04:18 PM	3.1	94
	10:48 PM	0.7	21
14 Sa	04:20 AM	2.2	67
	10:18 AM	0.3	9
	05:07 PM	3.2	98
	11:39 PM	0.6	18
15 Su	05:12 AM	2.2	67
	11:06 AM	0.3	9
	05:52 PM	3.3	101
16 M	12:24 AM	0.5	15
	05:59 AM	2.3	70
	11:52 AM	0.2	6
	06:35 PM	3.4	104
17 Tu	01:05 AM	0.4	12
	06:44 AM	2.4	73
	12:36 PM	0.1	3
	07:14 PM	3.5	107
18 W	01:44 AM	0.2	6
	07:26 AM	2.6	79
	01:18 PM	0.0	0
	07:53 PM	3.6	110
19 Th	02:20 AM	0.1	3
	08:07 AM	2.7	82
	02:00 PM	0.0	0
	08:30 PM	3.7	113
20 F	02:56 AM	0.0	0
	08:48 AM	2.8	85
	02:42 PM	-0.1	-3
	09:08 PM	3.6	110
21 Sa	03:32 AM	0.0	0
	09:29 AM	2.9	88
	03:26 PM	0.0	0
	09:47 PM	3.6	110
22 Su	04:09 AM	-0.1	-3
	10:13 AM	3.1	94
	04:13 PM	0.0	0
	10:28 PM	3.5	107
23 M	04:48 AM	-0.1	-3
	10:59 AM	3.2	98
	05:03 PM	0.1	3
	11:11 PM	3.3	101
24 Tu	05:30 AM	-0.2	-6
	11:49 AM	3.3	101
	05:58 PM	0.2	6
	11:59 PM	3.1	94
25 W	06:16 AM	-0.2	-6
	12:45 PM	3.4	104
	06:59 PM	0.3	9
26 Th	12:53 AM	2.9	88
	07:07 AM	-0.1	-3
	01:45 PM	3.5	107
	08:06 PM	0.4	12
27 F	01:53 AM	2.7	82
	08:05 AM	-0.1	-3
	02:50 PM	3.6	110
	09:17 PM	0.4	12
28 Sa	02:59 AM	2.7	82
	09:07 AM	-0.2	-6
	03:55 PM	3.7	113
	10:26 PM	0.3	9
29 Su	04:07 AM	2.7	82
	10:12 AM	-0.2	-6
	04:58 PM	3.9	119
	11:29 PM	0.2	6
30 M	05:12 AM	2.8	85
	11:14 AM	-0.3	-9
	05:56 PM	4.0	122
31 Tu	12:25 AM	0.0	0
	06:13 AM	2.9	88
	12:14 PM	-0.4	-12
	06:50 PM	4.1	125

August

Day	Time (h m)	Height (ft)	Height (cm)
1 W	01:17 AM	-0.1	-3
	07:08 AM	3.1	94
	01:09 PM	-0.4	-12
	07:41 PM	4.1	125
2 Th	02:05 AM	-0.2	-6
	08:00 AM	3.2	98
	02:02 PM	-0.4	-12
	08:28 PM	4.0	122
3 F	02:50 AM	-0.2	-6
	08:49 AM	3.3	101
	02:52 PM	-0.3	-9
	09:13 PM	3.8	116
4 Sa	03:32 AM	-0.2	-6
	09:37 AM	3.3	101
	03:41 PM	-0.1	-3
	09:56 PM	3.6	110
5 Su	04:14 AM	-0.1	-3
	10:23 AM	3.3	101
	04:29 PM	0.1	3
	10:39 PM	3.3	101
6 M	04:54 AM	0.0	0
	11:10 AM	3.2	98
	05:18 PM	0.3	9
	11:21 PM	3.0	91
7 Tu	05:34 AM	0.2	6
	11:57 AM	3.2	98
	06:08 PM	0.5	15
8 W	12:04 AM	2.8	85
	06:15 AM	0.3	9
	12:46 PM	3.1	94
	07:03 PM	0.7	21
9 Th	12:50 AM	2.5	76
	06:59 AM	0.4	12
	01:40 PM	3.0	91
	08:03 PM	0.9	27
10 F	01:41 AM	2.4	73
	07:49 AM	0.5	15
	02:37 PM	3.0	91
	09:06 PM	0.9	27
11 Sa	02:39 AM	2.3	70
	08:43 AM	0.5	15
	03:34 PM	3.1	94
	10:07 PM	0.9	27
12 Su	03:38 AM	2.3	70
	09:39 AM	0.5	15
	04:28 PM	3.2	98
	11:00 PM	0.8	24
13 M	04:35 AM	2.4	73
	10:33 AM	0.4	12
	05:17 PM	3.3	101
	11:46 PM	0.6	18
14 Tu	05:26 AM	2.5	76
	11:23 AM	0.3	9
	06:02 PM	3.4	104
15 W	12:28 AM	0.5	15
	06:12 AM	2.7	82
	12:10 PM	0.2	6
	06:43 PM	3.6	110
16 Th	01:06 AM	0.3	9
	06:55 AM	2.9	88
	12:55 PM	0.0	0
	07:22 PM	3.7	113
17 F	01:43 AM	0.1	3
	07:38 AM	3.1	94
	01:39 PM	-0.1	-3
	08:02 PM	3.7	113
18 Sa	02:19 AM	0.0	0
	08:20 AM	3.3	101
	02:24 PM	-0.1	-3
	08:41 PM	3.7	113
19 Su	02:57 AM	-0.1	-3
	09:03 AM	3.5	107
	03:10 PM	-0.1	-3
	09:22 PM	3.7	113
20 M	03:36 AM	-0.2	-6
	09:48 AM	3.6	110
	03:59 PM	0.0	0
	10:05 PM	3.5	107
21 Tu	04:17 AM	-0.2	-6
	10:36 AM	3.7	113
	04:50 PM	0.1	3
	10:52 PM	3.3	101
22 W	05:02 AM	-0.1	-3
	11:28 AM	3.7	113
	05:46 PM	0.2	6
	11:42 PM	3.1	94
23 Th	05:52 AM	-0.1	-3
	12:26 PM	3.7	113
	06:48 PM	0.4	12
24 F	12:39 AM	2.9	88
	06:47 AM	0.0	0
	01:29 PM	3.7	113
	07:56 PM	0.5	15
25 Sa	01:43 AM	2.8	85
	07:50 AM	0.1	3
	02:36 PM	3.7	113
	09:07 PM	0.5	15
26 Su	02:53 AM	2.8	85
	08:58 AM	0.1	3
	03:44 PM	3.7	113
	10:15 PM	0.4	12
27 M	04:02 AM	2.8	85
	10:07 AM	0.1	3
	04:47 PM	3.8	116
	11:15 PM	0.3	9
28 Tu	05:07 AM	3.0	91
	11:10 AM	0.0	0
	05:44 PM	3.9	119
29 W	12:08 AM	0.2	6
	06:04 AM	3.2	98
	12:08 PM	-0.1	-3
	06:36 PM	3.9	119
30 Th	12:56 AM	0.1	3
	06:55 AM	3.3	101
	01:01 PM	-0.1	-3
	07:23 PM	3.9	119
31 F	01:39 AM	0.0	0
	07:42 AM	3.5	107
	01:49 PM	-0.1	-3
	08:06 PM	3.8	116

September

Day	Time (h m)	Height (ft)	Height (cm)
1 Sa	02:19 AM	0.0	0
	08:26 AM	3.6	110
	02:35 PM	0.0	0
	08:47 PM	3.6	110
2 Su	02:58 AM	0.0	0
	09:09 AM	3.6	110
	03:20 PM	0.1	3
	09:27 PM	3.4	104
3 M	03:34 AM	0.1	3
	09:50 AM	3.6	110
	04:03 PM	0.3	9
	10:05 PM	3.2	98
4 Tu	04:11 AM	0.3	9
	10:31 AM	3.5	107
	04:47 PM	0.5	15
	10:44 PM	3.0	91
5 W	04:48 AM	0.4	12
	11:13 AM	3.4	104
	05:32 PM	0.7	21
	11:24 PM	2.8	85
6 Th	05:27 AM	0.5	15
	11:58 AM	3.3	101
	06:22 PM	0.8	24
7 F	12:08 AM	2.6	79
	06:10 AM	0.7	21
	12:49 PM	3.2	98
	07:17 PM	1.0	30
8 Sa	12:58 AM	2.5	76
	07:00 AM	0.8	24
	01:45 PM	3.1	94
	08:18 PM	1.0	30
9 Su	01:56 AM	2.4	73
	07:58 AM	0.8	24
	02:45 PM	3.1	94
	09:19 PM	1.0	30
10 M	02:58 AM	2.4	73
	08:59 AM	0.8	24
	03:43 PM	3.2	98
	10:14 PM	0.9	27
11 Tu	03:58 AM	2.6	79
	09:58 AM	0.6	18
	04:36 PM	3.3	101
	11:01 PM	0.8	24
12 W	04:51 AM	2.8	85
	10:53 AM	0.5	15
	05:23 PM	3.5	107
	11:43 PM	0.6	18
13 Th	05:39 AM	3.0	91
	11:43 AM	0.3	9
	06:07 PM	3.6	110
14 F	12:23 AM	0.3	9
	06:24 AM	3.3	101
	12:31 PM	0.1	3
	06:49 PM	3.7	113
15 Sa	01:01 AM	0.1	3
	07:08 AM	3.6	110
	01:19 PM	0.0	0
	07:31 PM	3.8	116
16 Su	01:41 AM	0.0	0
	07:52 AM	3.9	119
	02:06 PM	-0.1	-3
	08:14 PM	3.8	116
17 M	02:21 AM	-0.2	-6
	08:38 AM	4.1	125
	02:55 PM	-0.1	-3
	08:58 PM	3.7	113
18 Tu	03:04 AM	-0.2	-6
	09:25 AM	4.2	128
	03:45 PM	-0.1	-3
	09:45 PM	3.5	107
19 W	03:49 AM	-0.2	-6
	10:16 AM	4.2	128
	04:38 PM	0.1	3
	10:34 PM	3.4	104
20 Th	04:38 AM	-0.1	-3
	11:10 AM	4.1	125
	05:35 PM	0.2	6
	11:29 PM	3.2	98
21 F	05:32 AM	0.0	0
	12:09 PM	4.0	122
	06:38 PM	0.4	12
22 Sa	12:29 AM	3.0	91
	06:33 AM	0.2	6
	01:14 PM	3.9	119
	07:46 PM	0.5	15
23 Su	01:37 AM	2.9	88
	07:42 AM	0.3	9
	02:22 PM	3.8	116
	08:55 PM	0.5	15
24 M	02:50 AM	2.9	88
	08:54 AM	0.4	12
	03:30 PM	3.7	113
	09:59 PM	0.5	15
25 Tu	03:58 AM	3.1	94
	10:04 AM	0.3	9
	04:33 PM	3.7	113
	10:56 PM	0.4	12
26 W	04:59 AM	3.2	98
	11:06 AM	0.3	9
	05:28 PM	3.7	113
	11:45 PM	0.3	9
27 Th	05:52 AM	3.4	104
	12:01 PM	0.2	6
	06:17 PM	3.6	110
28 F	12:29 AM	0.2	6
	06:39 AM	3.6	110
	12:51 PM	0.2	6
	07:01 PM	3.6	110
29 Sa	01:09 AM	0.2	6
	07:22 AM	3.7	113
	01:36 PM	0.2	6
	07:42 PM	3.5	107
30 Su	01:46 AM	0.2	6
	08:02 AM	3.8	116
	02:18 PM	0.2	6
	08:20 PM	3.4	104

October

Day	Time (h m)	Height (ft)	Height (cm)
1 M	02:21 AM	0.2	6
	08:40 AM	3.8	116
	02:59 PM	0.3	9
	08:57 PM	3.2	98
2 Tu	02:56 AM	0.3	9
	09:17 AM	3.8	116
	03:38 PM	0.4	12
	09:34 PM	3.1	94
3 W	03:30 AM	0.4	12
	09:55 AM	3.7	113
	04:19 PM	0.5	15
	10:11 PM	2.9	88
4 Th	04:06 AM	0.5	15
	10:34 AM	3.6	110
	05:01 PM	0.7	21
	10:50 PM	2.8	85
5 F	04:45 AM	0.7	21
	11:17 AM	3.4	104
	05:46 PM	0.8	24
	11:33 PM	2.6	79
6 Sa	05:28 AM	0.8	24
	12:04 PM	3.3	101
	06:36 PM	1.0	30
7 Su	12:22 AM	2.5	76
	06:18 AM	0.9	27
	12:56 PM	3.2	98
	07:31 PM	1.0	30
8 M	01:18 AM	2.5	76
	07:15 AM	0.9	27
	01:54 PM	3.2	98
	08:28 PM	1.0	30
9 Tu	02:20 AM	2.6	79
	08:18 AM	0.9	27
	02:52 PM	3.2	98
	09:22 PM	0.9	27
10 W	03:20 AM	2.8	85
	09:22 AM	0.8	24
	03:48 PM	3.3	101
	10:10 PM	0.7	21
11 Th	04:14 AM	3.0	91
	10:21 AM	0.6	18
	04:39 PM	3.4	104
	10:55 PM	0.5	15
12 F	05:05 AM	3.4	104
	11:16 AM	0.4	12
	05:28 PM	3.5	107
	11:38 PM	0.3	9
13 Sa	05:53 AM	3.7	113
	12:08 PM	0.1	3
	06:15 PM	3.6	110
14 Su	12:21 AM	0.0	0
	06:40 AM	4.1	125
	12:59 PM	0.0	0
	07:01 PM	3.6	110
15 M	01:05 AM	-0.2	-6
	07:27 AM	4.3	131
	01:49 PM	-0.2	-6
	07:48 PM	3.6	110
16 Tu	01:50 AM	-0.3	-9
	08:16 AM	4.5	137
	02:40 PM	-0.2	-6
	08:36 PM	3.6	110
17 W	02:37 AM	-0.3	-9
	09:05 AM	4.6	140
	03:32 PM	-0.2	-6
	09:26 PM	3.5	107
18 Th	03:26 AM	-0.3	-9
	09:58 AM	4.5	137
	04:26 PM	0.0	0
	10:19 PM	3.3	101
19 F	04:19 AM	-0.1	-3
	10:53 AM	4.3	131
	05:23 PM	0.1	3
	11:17 PM	3.2	98
20 Sa	05:17 AM	0.0	0
	11:53 AM	4.1	125
	06:25 PM	0.3	9
21 Su	12:20 AM	3.1	94
	06:21 AM	0.2	6
	12:57 PM	3.9	119
	07:29 PM	0.4	12
22 M	01:30 AM	3.0	91
	07:32 AM	0.4	12
	02:04 PM	3.7	113
	08:34 PM	0.4	12
23 Tu	02:41 AM	3.1	94
	08:46 AM	0.5	15
	03:10 PM	3.5	107
	09:35 PM	0.4	12
24 W	03:46 AM	3.2	98
	09:55 AM	0.5	15
	04:11 PM	3.4	104
	10:29 PM	0.4	12
25 Th	04:44 AM	3.4	104
	10:57 AM	0.5	15
	05:05 PM	3.3	101
	11:16 PM	0.3	9
26 F	05:35 AM	3.5	107
	11:50 AM	0.4	12
	05:53 PM	3.3	101
	11:59 PM	0.3	9
27 Sa	06:19 AM	3.7	113
	12:38 PM	0.3	9
	06:36 PM	3.2	98
28 Su	12:37 AM	0.3	9
	07:00 AM	3.8	116
	01:20 PM	0.3	9
	07:16 PM	3.1	94
29 M	01:13 AM	0.3	9
	07:37 AM	3.8	116
	02:01 PM	0.3	9
	07:54 PM	3.1	94
30 Tu	01:48 AM	0.3	9
	08:13 AM	3.8	116
	02:39 PM	0.3	9
	08:30 PM	3.0	91
31 W	02:22 AM	0.3	9
	08:49 AM	3.8	116
	03:17 PM	0.4	12
	09:06 PM	2.9	88

November

Day	Time (h m)	Height (ft)	Height (cm)
1 Th	02:57 AM	0.4	12
	09:26 AM	3.7	113
	03:55 PM	0.5	15
	09:43 PM	2.8	85
2 F	03:33 AM	0.5	15
	10:04 AM	3.6	110
	04:34 PM	0.6	18
	10:22 PM	2.7	82
3 Sa	04:12 AM	0.6	18
	10:44 AM	3.5	107
	05:16 PM	0.7	21
	11:04 PM	2.6	79
4 Su	03:54 AM	0.7	21
	10:27 AM	3.3	101
	05:00 PM	0.8	24
	10:51 PM	2.5	76
5 M	04:42 AM	0.8	24
	11:14 AM	3.2	98
	05:48 PM	0.8	24
	11:43 PM	2.6	79
6 Tu	05:38 AM	0.8	24
	12:06 PM	3.1	94
	06:38 PM	0.7	21
7 W	12:41 AM	2.7	82
	06:40 AM	0.8	24
	01:02 PM	3.1	94
	07:29 PM	0.6	18
8 Th	01:41 AM	2.9	88
	07:46 AM	0.7	21
	01:59 PM	3.1	94
	08:19 PM	0.5	15
9 F	02:38 AM	3.2	98
	08:50 AM	0.5	15
	02:55 PM	3.1	94
	09:08 PM	0.3	9
10 Sa	03:32 AM	3.5	107
	09:50 AM	0.3	9
	03:50 PM	3.2	98
	09:57 PM	0.0	0
11 Su	04:24 AM	3.9	119
	10:46 AM	0.1	3
	04:42 PM	3.3	101
	10:45 PM	-0.2	-6
12 M	05:15 AM	4.2	128
	11:40 AM	-0.1	-3
	05:34 PM	3.3	101
	11:34 PM	-0.4	-12
13 Tu	06:06 AM	4.5	137
	12:33 PM	-0.3	-9
	06:25 PM	3.4	104
14 W	12:24 AM	-0.5	-15
	06:57 AM	4.6	140
	01:25 PM	-0.3	-9
	07:17 PM	3.4	104
15 Th	01:15 AM	-0.5	-15
	07:49 AM	4.6	140
	02:18 PM	-0.3	-9
	08:10 PM	3.3	101
16 F	02:08 AM	-0.5	-15
	08:42 AM	4.5	137
	03:12 PM	-0.2	-6
	09:05 PM	3.2	98
17 Sa	03:04 AM	-0.3	-9
	09:37 AM	4.3	131
	04:08 PM	-0.1	-3
	10:04 PM	3.1	94
18 Su	04:03 AM	-0.1	-3
	10:34 AM	4.0	122
	05:05 PM	0.0	0
	11:07 PM	3.1	94
19 M	05:07 AM	0.1	3
	11:34 AM	3.7	113
	06:04 PM	0.1	3
20 Tu	12:13 AM	3.0	91
	06:17 AM	0.3	9
	12:37 PM	3.4	104
	07:04 PM	0.2	6
21 W	01:20 AM	3.1	94
	07:28 AM	0.5	15
	01:40 PM	3.1	94
	08:01 PM	0.2	6
22 Th	02:24 AM	3.2	98
	08:37 AM	0.5	15
	02:40 PM	3.0	91
	08:54 PM	0.3	9
23 F	03:21 AM	3.3	101
	09:39 AM	0.5	15
	03:35 PM	2.8	85
	09:42 PM	0.2	6
24 Sa	04:11 AM	3.4	104
	10:33 AM	0.4	12
	04:25 PM	2.8	85
	10:25 PM	0.2	6
25 Su	04:56 AM	3.5	107
	11:20 AM	0.4	12
	05:09 PM	2.7	82
	11:05 PM	0.2	6
26 M	05:36 AM	3.6	110
	12:03 PM	0.3	9
	05:50 PM	2.7	82
	11:42 PM	0.2	6
27 Tu	06:14 AM	3.6	110
	12:42 PM	0.3	9
	06:29 PM	2.7	82
28 W	12:19 AM	0.2	6
	06:51 AM	3.6	110
	01:20 PM	0.2	6
	07:06 PM	2.6	79
29 Th	12:55 AM	0.2	6
	07:27 AM	3.6	110
	01:57 PM	0.2	6
	07:43 PM	2.6	79
30 F	01:31 AM	0.2	6
	08:03 AM	3.6	110
	02:34 PM	0.3	9
	08:20 PM	2.6	79

December

Day	Time (h m)	Height (ft)	Height (cm)
1 Sa	02:09 AM	0.3	9
	08:39 AM	3.5	107
	03:10 PM	0.3	9
	08:58 PM	2.5	76
2 Su	02:47 AM	0.3	9
	09:17 AM	3.4	104
	03:48 PM	0.3	9
	09:39 PM	2.5	76
3 M	03:29 AM	0.4	12
	09:56 AM	3.3	101
	04:27 PM	0.4	12
	10:23 PM	2.5	76
4 Tu	04:15 AM	0.5	15
	10:39 AM	3.1	94
	05:08 PM	0.4	12
	11:11 PM	2.6	79
5 W	05:08 AM	0.5	15
	11:26 AM	3.0	91
	05:53 PM	0.3	9
6 Th	12:05 AM	2.7	82
	06:07 AM	0.5	15
	12:18 PM	2.9	88
	06:41 PM	0.2	6
7 F	01:03 AM	2.9	88
	07:13 AM	0.5	15
	01:15 PM	2.8	85
	07:33 PM	0.1	3
8 Sa	02:03 AM	3.2	98
	08:20 AM	0.4	12
	02:15 PM	2.8	85
	08:26 PM	-0.1	-3
9 Su	03:02 AM	3.5	107
	09:26 AM	0.2	6
	03:16 PM	2.8	85
	09:21 PM	-0.3	-9
10 M	03:59 AM	3.8	116
	10:27 AM	0.0	0
	04:15 PM	2.9	88
	10:16 PM	-0.5	-15
11 Tu	04:54 AM	4.1	125
	11:24 AM	-0.2	-6
	05:11 PM	2.9	88
	11:11 PM	-0.6	-18
12 W	05:48 AM	4.3	131
	12:18 PM	-0.4	-12
	06:07 PM	3.0	91
13 Th	12:06 AM	-0.7	-21
	06:42 AM	4.4	134
	01:11 PM	-0.5	-15
	07:01 PM	3.1	94
14 F	01:00 AM	-0.8	-24
	07:34 AM	4.4	134
	02:03 PM	-0.5	-15
	07:56 PM	3.1	94
15 Sa	01:55 AM	-0.7	-21
	08:27 AM	4.3	131
	02:55 PM	-0.5	-15
	08:51 PM	3.1	94
16 Su	02:51 AM	-0.6	-18
	09:19 AM	4.0	122
	03:46 PM	-0.4	-12
	09:47 PM	3.1	94
17 M	03:48 AM	-0.3	-9
	10:12 AM	3.7	113
	04:38 PM	-0.3	-9
	10:45 PM	3.0	91
18 Tu	04:48 AM	-0.1	-3
	11:07 AM	3.3	101
	05:31 PM	-0.2	-6
	11:46 PM	3.0	91
19 W	05:53 AM	0.2	6
	12:03 PM	3.0	91
	06:24 PM	0.0	0
20 Th	12:48 AM	3.0	91
	07:00 AM	0.3	9
	01:01 PM	2.7	82
	07:18 PM	0.1	3
21 F	01:50 AM	3.0	91
	08:08 AM	0.4	12
	02:01 PM	2.5	76
	08:11 PM	0.1	3
22 Sa	02:48 AM	3.0	91
	09:12 AM	0.4	12
	02:59 PM	2.3	70
	09:01 PM	0.2	6
23 Su	03:41 AM	3.1	94
	10:09 AM	0.4	12
	03:52 PM	2.3	70
	09:49 PM	0.2	6
24 M	04:28 AM	3.2	98
	10:58 AM	0.3	9
	04:41 PM	2.3	70
	10:33 PM	0.1	3
25 Tu	05:11 AM	3.3	101
	11:42 AM	0.2	6
	05:24 PM	2.3	70
	11:15 PM	0.1	3
26 W	05:51 AM	3.3	101
	12:22 PM	0.2	6
	06:05 PM	2.4	73
	11:55 PM	0.0	0
27 Th	06:29 AM	3.4	104
	12:59 PM	0.1	3
	06:43 PM	2.4	73
28 F	12:34 AM	0.0	0
	07:06 AM	3.4	104
	01:35 PM	0.0	0
	07:21 PM	2.4	73
29 Sa	01:12 AM	-0.1	-3
	07:42 AM	3.4	104
	02:10 PM	0.0	0
	07:58 PM	2.5	76
30 Su	01:50 AM	-0.1	-3
	08:17 AM	3.4	104
	02:44 PM	0.0	0
	08:36 PM	2.5	76
31 M	02:28 AM	0.0	0
	08:53 AM	3.3	101
	03:18 PM	0.0	0
	09:15 PM	2.6	79

Heights are referred to mean lower water which is the chart datum of sounding. All times are local. Daylight Saving Time has been used when needed.

SKIPPER'S HANDBOOK

Charleston, South Carolina, 2011

Times and Heights of High and Low Waters

Heights are referred to mean lower low water which is the chart datum of soundings. All times are local. Daylight Saving Time has been used when needed.

September

Day	Time (h m)	Height (ft)	Height (cm)
1 Th	0449 1112 0527* 1123*	-0.5 6.6 -0.2 6.0	-15 201 -6 183
2 F	0540 1209* 0624*	-0.4 6.5 0.1	-12 198 3
3 Sa	1217 0633 0109* 0723*	5.7 -0.1 6.3 0.5	174 -3 192 15
4 Su ◐	0115 0731 0212* 0826*	5.4 0.1 6.2 0.7	165 3 189 21
5 M	0217 0833 0316* 0929*	5.2 0.3 6.1 0.8	158 9 186 24
6 Tu	0321 0938 0418* 1030*	5.1 0.4 6.0 0.8	155 12 183 24
7 W	0423 1040 0516* 1126*	5.1 0.5 6.0 0.7	155 15 183 21
8 Th	0521 1138 0608*	5.2 0.5 6.0	158 15 183
9 F	1217 0615 1230* 0654*	0.6 5.4 0.4 6.1	18 165 12 186
10 Sa	0103 0703 0118* 0737*	0.5 5.5 0.4 6.0	15 168 12 183
11 Su	0145 0747 0203* 0816*	0.4 5.7 0.4 6.0	12 174 12 183
12 M ○	0224 0828 0244* 0854*	0.3 5.8 0.5 5.9	9 177 15 180
13 Tu	0301 0906 0323* 0930*	0.4 5.8 0.6 5.7	12 177 18 174
14 W	0336 0943 0401* 1005*	0.4 5.8 0.8 5.5	12 177 24 168
15 Th	0409 1018 0438* 1040*	0.6 5.8 1.0 5.3	18 177 30 162
16 F	0443 1054 0515* 1115*	0.7 5.7 1.2 5.1	21 174 37 155
17 Sa	0519 1131 0555* 1152*	0.8 5.6 1.3 4.9	24 171 40 149
18 Su	0559 1213* 0640*	0.9 5.6 1.5	27 171 46
19 M	1235 0644 0102* 0732*	4.8 1.0 5.5 1.6	146 30 168 49
20 Tu ◑	0125 0737 0158* 0830*	4.7 1.0 5.6 1.5	143 30 171 46
21 W	0224 0836 0300* 0932*	4.7 0.9 5.7 1.4	143 27 174 43
22 Th	0328 0940 0401* 1031*	4.9 0.8 5.9 1.1	149 24 180 34
23 F	0430 1043 0500* 1127*	5.2 0.5 6.1 0.7	158 15 186 21
24 Sa	0529 1144 0555*	5.6 0.2 6.4	171 6 195
25 Su	1220 0625 1241* 0648*	0.3 6.1 -0.1 6.5	9 186 -3 198
26 M	0110 0719 0136* 0739*	-0.1 6.5 -0.4 6.6	-3 198 -12 201
27 Tu ●	0158 0812 0230* 0830*	-0.4 6.8 -0.5 6.6	-12 207 -15 201
28 W	0247 0905 0323* 0920*	-0.5 7.1 -0.5 6.5	-15 216 -15 198
29 Th	0335 0958 0416* 1011*	-0.6 7.1 -0.3 6.2	-18 216 -9 189
30 F	0425 1052 0510* 1104*	-0.4 7.0 -0.1 6.0	-12 213 -3 183

October

Day	Time (h m)	Height (ft)	Height (cm)
1 Sa	0518 1150 0606*	-0.2 6.8 0.3	-6 207 9
2 Su	1200 0613 1250* 0705*	5.7 0.1 6.5 0.6	174 3 198 18
3 M	1259 0712 0152* 0805*	5.4 0.4 6.2 0.8	165 12 189 24
4 Tu ◐	0202 0815 0255* 0906*	5.3 0.7 6.0 0.9	162 21 183 27
5 W	0305 0920 0354* 1004*	5.2 0.8 5.9 0.9	158 24 180 27
6 Th	0406 1022 0449* 1058*	5.3 0.9 5.9 0.9	162 27 180 27
7 F	0502 1119 0539* 1147*	5.4 0.8 5.8 0.7	165 24 177 21
8 Sa	0553 1210* 0624*	5.6 0.8 5.8	171 24 177
9 Su	1231 0638 1257* 0705*	0.6 5.8 0.7 5.8	18 177 21 177
10 M	0112 0720 0140* 0745*	0.5 6.0 0.7 5.8	15 183 21 177
11 Tu	0150 0800 0220* 0823*	0.4 6.1 0.7 5.7	12 186 21 174
12 W ○	0226 0837 0259* 0900*	0.4 6.1 0.7 5.5	12 186 21 168
13 Th	0300 0912 0336* 0935*	0.5 6.1 0.8 5.4	15 186 24 165
14 F	0335 0947 0412* 1010*	0.6 6.0 1.0 5.2	18 183 30 158
15 Sa	0410 1021 0449* 1044*	0.7 5.9 1.1 5.0	21 180 34 152
16 Su	0447 1058 0528* 1120*	0.8 5.9 1.2 4.9	24 180 37 149
17 M	0527 1139 0612*	0.9 5.8 1.3	27 177 40
18 Tu	1202 0614 1227* 0702*	4.8 1.0 5.7 1.4	146 30 174 43
19 W	1254 0708 0122* 0757*	4.8 1.0 5.7 1.3	146 30 174 40
20 Th ◑	0154 0809 0223* 0857*	4.9 0.9 5.8 1.1	149 27 177 34
21 F	0300 0914 0326* 0957*	5.1 0.8 5.9 0.8	155 24 180 24
22 Sa	0404 1020 0427* 1054*	5.5 0.6 6.0 0.5	168 18 183 15
23 Su	0505 1123 0525* 1148*	5.9 0.2 6.2 0.1	180 6 189 3
24 M	0603 1223* 0620*	6.4 -0.1 6.3	195 -3 192
25 Tu	1241 0658 0119* 0714*	-0.3 6.8 -0.3 6.3	-9 207 -9 192
26 W ●	0132 0752 0213* 0807*	-0.5 7.1 -0.5 6.3	-15 216 -15 192
27 Th	0222 0846 0307* 0859*	-0.7 7.3 -0.5 6.2	-21 223 -15 189
28 F	0313 0939 0359* 0952*	-0.6 7.2 -0.3 6.0	-18 219 -9 183
29 Sa	0404 1034 0453* 1045*	-0.5 7.0 -0.1 5.8	-15 213 -3 177
30 Su	0457 1130 0547* 1141*	-0.2 6.7 0.2 5.5	-6 204 6 168
31 M	0552 1227* 0642*	0.2 6.4 0.5	6 195 15

November

Day	Time (h m)	Height (ft)	Height (cm)
1 Tu	1239 0650 0126* 0739*	5.3 0.5 6.1 0.7	162 15 186 21
2 W ◐	0140 0751 0224* 0835*	5.2 0.8 5.8 0.8	158 24 177 24
3 Th	0240 0854 0320* 0931*	5.2 1.0 5.6 0.9	158 30 171 27
4 F	0339 0955 0412* 1023*	5.2 1.1 5.5 0.8	158 34 168 24
5 Sa	0433 1052 0501* 1110*	5.4 1.1 5.4 0.7	165 34 165 21
6 Su	0423 1044 0447* 1054*	5.6 1.0 5.4 0.6	171 30 165 18
7 M	0509 1131 0531* 1135*	5.8 0.8 5.4 0.5	177 24 165 15
8 Tu	0551 1215* 0613*	5.9 0.7 5.3	180 21 162
9 W	1215 0632 1256* 0653*	0.4 6.1 0.7 5.3	12 186 21 162
10 Th ○	1252 0710 0134* 0732*	0.3 6.1 0.7 5.2	9 186 21 158
11 F	0129 0747 0212* 0809*	0.3 6.1 0.7 5.1	9 186 21 155
12 Sa	0206 0823 0249* 0845*	0.4 6.1 0.7 5.0	12 186 21 152
13 Su	0243 0858 0327* 0920*	0.4 6.0 0.8 4.9	12 183 24 149
14 M	0323 0935 0406* 0957*	0.5 5.9 0.9 4.8	15 180 27 146
15 Tu	0405 1015 0449* 1040*	0.6 5.8 0.9 4.8	18 177 27 146
16 W	0452 1101 0537* 1131*	0.6 5.8 0.9 4.8	18 177 27 146
17 Th	0546 1153 0629*	0.7 5.7 0.8	21 174 24
18 F ◑	1231 0647 1252* 0725*	5.0 0.7 5.6 0.6	152 21 171 18
19 Sa	0135 0753 0153* 0824*	5.2 0.6 5.6 0.4	158 18 171 12
20 Su	0241 0900 0256* 0923*	5.6 0.4 5.6 0.1	171 12 171 3
21 M	0343 1005 0357* 1020*	6.0 0.2 5.7 -0.2	183 6 174 -6
22 Tu	0443 1106 0456* 1115*	6.4 -0.1 5.7 -0.5	195 -3 174 -15
23 W	0541 1203* 0552*	6.8 -0.3 5.8	207 -9 177
24 Th	1209 0637 1258* 0647*	-0.7 7.0 -0.5 5.8	-21 213 -15 177
25 F ●	0102 0731 0151* 0741*	-0.8 7.0 -0.5 5.7	-24 213 -15 174
26 Sa	0154 0824 0242* 0834*	-0.8 7.0 -0.5 5.6	-24 213 -15 171
27 Su	0246 0916 0333* 0926*	-0.6 6.8 -0.3 5.5	-18 207 -9 168
28 M	0337 1008 0424* 1020*	-0.3 6.4 -0.1 5.3	-9 195 -3 162
29 Tu	0429 1100 0514* 1114*	0.0 6.1 0.2 5.1	0 186 6 155
30 W	0523 1152 0605*	0.4 5.7 0.4	12 174 12

December

Day	Time (h m)	Height (ft)	Height (cm)
1 Th	1209 0620 1243* 0656*	5.0 0.7 5.4 0.6	152 21 165 18
2 F ◐	0105 0718 0135* 0747*	4.9 1.0 5.1 0.6	149 30 155 18
3 Sa	0200 0819 0227* 0838*	5.0 1.1 4.9 0.6	152 34 149 18
4 Su	0254 0917 0317* 0926*	5.1 1.1 4.8 0.6	155 34 146 18
5 M	0345 1011 0407* 1013*	5.2 1.0 4.7 0.5	158 30 143 15
6 Tu	0434 1101 0455* 1057*	5.4 0.9 4.8 0.4	165 27 146 12
7 W	0520 1146 0541* 1140*	5.6 0.7 4.8 0.2	171 21 146 6
8 Th	0604 1229* 0625*	5.8 0.6 4.8	177 18 146
9 F	1222 0645 0110* 0706*	0.1 5.9 0.4 4.8	3 180 12 146
10 Sa ○	0102 0725 0149* 0746*	0.0 5.9 0.4 4.8	0 180 12 146
11 Su	0142 0803 0227* 0824*	0.0 5.9 0.3 4.8	0 180 9 146
12 M	0223 0840 0306* 0902*	-0.1 5.9 0.3 4.8	-3 180 9 146
13 Tu	0304 0918 0346* 0941*	0.0 5.9 0.3 4.8	0 180 9 146
14 W	0348 0957 0428* 1025*	0.0 5.8 0.2 4.9	0 177 6 149
15 Th	0436 1041 0513* 1115*	0.1 5.7 0.2 4.9	3 174 6 149
16 F	0530 1131 0602*	0.2 5.5 0.1	6 168 3
17 Sa	1211 0629 1225* 0656*	5.1 0.3 5.4 0.0	155 9 165 0
18 Su ◑	0114 0734 0125* 0754*	5.3 0.3 5.2 -0.1	162 9 158 -3
19 M	0219 0841 0229* 0855*	5.5 0.3 5.1 -0.2	168 9 155 -6
20 Tu	0325 0947 0333* 0956*	5.8 0.1 5.1 -0.4	177 3 155 -12
21 W	0428 1050 0436* 1055*	6.1 -0.1 5.1 -0.6	186 -3 155 -18
22 Th	0528 1148 0535* 1152*	6.3 -0.3 5.2 -0.8	192 -9 158 -24
23 F	0625 1243* 0632*	6.5 -0.5 5.3	198 -15 162
24 Sa ●	1247 0718 0134* 0726*	-0.9 6.6 -0.6 5.3	-27 201 -18 162
25 Su	0139 0809 0224* 0817*	-0.9 6.5 -0.6 5.3	-27 198 -18 162
26 M	0229 0858 0311* 0907*	-0.8 6.3 -0.5 5.2	-24 192 -15 158
27 Tu	0318 0944 0357* 0955*	-0.5 6.0 -0.3 5.1	-15 183 -9 155
28 W	0406 1029 0442* 1043*	-0.2 5.7 -0.1 5.0	-6 174 -3 152
29 Th	0454 1114 0526* 1131*	0.2 5.3 0.1 4.9	6 162 3 149
30 F	0544 1159 0611*	0.5 5.0 0.3	15 152 9
31 Sa	1220 0636 1246* 0656*	4.8 0.8 4.7 0.4	146 24 143 12

Charleston, South Carolina, 2012

Times and Heights of High and Low Waters

January

Date	Day	Time	ft	cm	Time	ft	cm	Time	ft	cm	Time	ft	cm
1	Su	01:13 AM	4.8	146	07:33 AM	0.9	27	01:37 PM	4.5	137	07:46 PM	0.4	12
2	M	02:06 AM	4.8	146	08:31 AM	1.0	30	02:29 PM	4.3	131	08:36 PM	0.4	12
3	Tu	03:00 AM	4.9	149	09:28 AM	1.0	30	03:22 PM	4.3	131	09:27 PM	0.4	12
4	W	03:53 AM	5.0	152	10:22 AM	0.8	24	04:15 PM	4.3	131	10:18 PM	0.2	6
5	Th	04:44 AM	5.2	158	11:11 AM	0.6	18	05:06 PM	4.4	134	11:06 PM	0.1	3
6	F	05:33 AM	5.4	165	11:57 AM	0.4	12	05:53 PM	4.5	137	11:52 PM	-0.1	-3
7	Sa	06:18 AM	5.6	171	12:40 PM	0.2	6	06:38 PM	4.7	143			
8	Su	12:37 AM	-0.3	-9	07:00 AM	5.7	174	01:21 PM	0.0	0	07:21 PM	4.8	146
9	M	01:20 AM	-0.5	-15	07:40 AM	5.8	177	02:01 PM	-0.1	-3	08:01 PM	4.9	149
10	Tu	02:04 AM	-0.6	-18	08:19 AM	5.9	180	02:41 PM	-0.3	-9	08:42 PM	5.0	152
11	W	02:48 AM	-0.6	-18	08:59 AM	5.9	180	03:22 PM	-0.4	-12	09:23 PM	5.1	155
12	Th	03:34 AM	-0.6	-18	09:39 AM	5.8	177	04:04 PM	-0.4	-12	10:08 PM	5.2	158
13	F	04:23 AM	-0.5	-15	10:23 AM	5.6	171	04:49 PM	-0.4	-12	10:57 PM	5.2	158
14	Sa	05:16 AM	-0.3	-9	11:11 AM	5.4	165	05:38 PM	-0.4	-12	11:53 PM	5.3	162
15	Su	06:14 AM	-0.1	-3	12:05 PM	5.1	155	06:32 PM	-0.4	-12			
16	M	12:55 AM	5.3	162	07:17 AM	0.1	3	01:05 PM	4.9	149	07:31 PM	-0.3	-9
17	Tu	02:02 AM	5.4	165	08:25 AM	0.1	3	02:10 PM	4.7	143	08:35 PM	-0.3	-9
18	W	03:11 AM	5.5	168	09:32 AM	0.1	3	03:18 PM	4.7	143	09:40 PM	-0.4	-12
19	Th	04:17 AM	5.7	174	10:35 AM	-0.1	-3	04:24 PM	4.8	146	10:43 PM	-0.6	-18
20	F	05:19 AM	5.9	180	11:33 AM	-0.3	-9	05:26 PM	4.9	149	11:41 PM	-0.7	-21
21	Sa	06:15 AM	6.1	186	12:27 PM	-0.5	-15	06:22 PM	5.1	155			
22	Su	12:35 AM	-0.9	-27	07:06 AM	6.1	186	01:16 PM	-0.7	-21	07:14 PM	5.2	158
23	M	01:26 AM	-0.9	-27	07:53 AM	6.1	186	02:03 PM	-0.7	-21	08:02 PM	5.3	162
24	Tu	02:14 AM	-0.8	-24	08:37 AM	6.0	183	02:47 PM	-0.7	-21	08:47 PM	5.3	162
25	W	02:59 AM	-0.6	-18	09:18 AM	5.7	174	03:28 PM	-0.5	-15	09:29 PM	5.2	158
26	Th	03:43 AM	-0.3	-9	09:58 AM	5.4	165	04:08 PM	-0.4	-12	10:11 PM	5.1	155
27	F	04:25 AM	0.0	0	10:37 AM	5.1	155	04:47 PM	-0.1	-3	10:52 PM	5.0	152
28	Sa	05:08 AM	0.3	9	11:17 AM	4.8	146	05:25 PM	0.1	3	11:35 PM	4.9	149
29	Su	05:53 AM	0.6	18	11:59 AM	4.5	137	06:06 PM	0.3	9			
30	M	12:21 AM	4.7	143	06:42 AM	0.8	24	12:46 PM	4.2	128	06:51 PM	0.4	12
31	Tu	01:12 AM	4.7	143	07:37 AM	1.0	30	01:38 PM	4.1	125	07:42 PM	0.5	15

February

Date	Day	Time	ft	cm	Time	ft	cm	Time	ft	cm	Time	ft	cm
1	W	02:08 AM	4.7	143	08:37 AM	1.0	30	02:35 PM	4.0	122	08:38 PM	0.5	15
2	Th	03:06 AM	4.8	146	09:36 AM	0.9	27	03:33 PM	4.1	125	09:35 PM	0.3	9
3	F	04:03 AM	4.9	149	10:31 AM	0.7	21	04:28 PM	4.2	128	10:30 PM	0.1	3
4	Sa	04:57 AM	5.2	158	11:21 AM	0.4	12	05:21 PM	4.4	134	11:22 PM	-0.2	-6
5	Su	05:47 AM	5.4	165	12:08 PM	0.1	3	06:09 PM	4.7	143			
6	M	12:12 AM	-0.5	-15	06:32 AM	5.7	174	12:52 PM	-0.2	-6	06:55 PM	5.0	152
7	Tu	12:59 AM	-0.7	-21	07:16 AM	5.8	177	01:34 PM	-0.4	-12	07:38 PM	5.2	158
8	W	01:46 AM	-0.9	-27	07:58 AM	5.9	180	02:16 PM	-0.7	-21	08:22 PM	5.4	165
9	Th	02:32 AM	-1.0	-30	08:40 AM	5.9	180	02:58 PM	-0.8	-24	09:06 PM	5.6	171
10	F	03:20 AM	-0.9	-27	09:22 AM	5.8	177	03:42 PM	-0.8	-24	09:53 PM	5.7	174
11	Sa	04:10 AM	-0.8	-24	10:08 AM	5.6	171	04:28 PM	-0.8	-24	10:43 PM	5.7	174
12	Su	05:04 AM	-0.5	-15	10:57 AM	5.3	162	05:17 PM	-0.6	-18	11:39 PM	5.6	171
13	M	06:01 AM	-0.3	-9	11:51 AM	5.0	152	06:12 PM	-0.5	-15			
14	Tu	12:41 AM	5.5	168	07:03 AM	0.0	0	12:51 PM	4.8	146	07:13 PM	-0.3	-9
15	W	01:48 AM	5.4	165	08:09 AM	0.1	3	01:58 PM	4.6	140	08:19 PM	-0.2	-6
16	Th	02:58 AM	5.4	165	09:15 AM	0.1	3	03:07 PM	4.6	140	09:27 PM	-0.2	-6
17	F	04:05 AM	5.5	168	10:18 AM	0.0	0	04:14 PM	4.7	143	10:31 PM	-0.3	-9
18	Sa	05:05 AM	5.6	171	11:15 AM	-0.2	-6	05:14 PM	4.9	149	11:29 PM	-0.5	-15
19	Su	05:59 AM	5.7	174	12:07 PM	-0.4	-12	06:08 PM	5.1	155			
20	M	12:22 AM	-0.6	-18	06:48 AM	5.8	177	12:54 PM	-0.5	-15	06:57 PM	5.3	162
21	Tu	01:10 AM	-0.6	-18	07:31 AM	5.8	177	01:37 PM	-0.6	-18	07:41 PM	5.4	165
22	W	01:55 AM	-0.6	-18	08:12 AM	5.7	174	02:18 PM	-0.6	-18	08:22 PM	5.5	168
23	Th	02:38 AM	-0.4	-12	08:50 AM	5.5	168	02:55 PM	-0.4	-12	09:00 PM	5.4	165
24	F	03:18 AM	-0.2	-6	09:26 AM	5.3	162	03:31 PM	-0.3	-9	09:37 PM	5.4	165
25	Sa	03:56 AM	0.0	0	10:02 AM	5.0	152	04:06 PM	-0.1	-3	10:13 PM	5.2	158
26	Su	04:35 AM	0.3	9	10:38 AM	4.7	143	04:42 PM	0.1	3	10:51 PM	5.1	155
27	M	05:14 AM	0.6	18	11:17 AM	4.5	137	05:19 PM	0.3	9	11:32 PM	4.9	149
28	Tu	05:57 AM	0.8	24	12:00 PM	4.3	131	06:02 PM	0.5	15			
29	W	12:19 AM	4.8	146	06:47 AM	1.0	30	12:49 PM	4.1	125	06:52 PM	0.6	18

March

Date	Day	Time	ft	cm	Time	ft	cm	Time	ft	cm	Time	ft	cm
1	Th	01:14 AM	4.8	146	07:44 AM	1.1	34	01:46 PM	4.1	125	07:50 PM	0.6	18
2	F	02:14 AM	4.8	146	08:46 AM	1.0	30	02:48 PM	4.1	125	08:52 PM	0.5	15
3	Sa	03:16 AM	4.9	149	09:46 AM	0.8	24	03:48 PM	4.3	131	09:54 PM	0.3	9
4	Su	04:15 AM	5.1	155	10:41 AM	0.5	15	04:45 PM	4.6	140	10:52 PM	0.0	0
5	M	05:09 AM	5.4	165	11:31 AM	0.1	3	05:37 PM	5.0	152	11:46 PM	-0.4	-12
6	Tu	05:59 AM	5.7	174	12:18 PM	-0.2	-6	06:26 PM	5.4	165			
7	W	12:37 AM	-0.7	-21	06:47 AM	5.9	180	01:03 PM	-0.6	-18	07:14 PM	5.8	177
8	Th	01:27 AM	-0.9	-27	07:33 AM	6.0	183	01:48 PM	-0.8	-24	08:01 PM	6.1	186
9	F	02:17 AM	-1.1	-34	08:18 AM	5.9	180	02:33 PM	-1.0	-30	08:48 PM	6.3	192
10	Sa	03:07 AM	-1.0	-30	09:05 AM	5.8	177	03:19 PM	-1.0	-30	09:37 PM	6.3	192
11	Su	04:58 AM	-0.9	-27	10:53 AM	5.6	171	05:07 PM	-0.8	-24	11:30 PM	6.2	189
12	M	05:51 AM	-0.6	-18	11:44 AM	5.3	162	05:59 PM	-0.6	-18			
13	Tu	12:26 AM	6.0	183	06:48 AM	-0.3	-9	12:41 PM	5.1	155	06:55 PM	-0.3	-9
14	W	01:28 AM	5.8	177	07:49 AM	0.0	0	01:42 PM	4.8	146	07:57 PM	-0.1	-3
15	Th	02:34 AM	5.6	171	08:52 AM	0.2	6	02:49 PM	4.7	143	09:05 PM	0.1	3
16	F	03:42 AM	5.4	165	09:56 AM	0.2	6	03:57 PM	4.7	143	10:13 PM	0.2	6
17	Sa	04:46 AM	5.4	165	10:57 AM	0.2	6	05:01 PM	4.9	149	11:17 PM	0.1	3
18	Su	05:44 AM	5.5	168	11:52 AM	0.0	0	05:59 PM	5.1	155			
19	M	12:14 AM	0.0	0	06:36 AM	5.5	168	12:41 PM	-0.1	-3	06:50 PM	5.3	162
20	Tu	01:05 AM	-0.1	-3	07:22 AM	5.5	168	01:26 PM	-0.3	-9	07:35 PM	5.5	168
21	W	01:52 AM	-0.2	-6	08:04 AM	5.5	168	02:07 PM	-0.3	-9	08:16 PM	5.7	174
22	Th	02:35 AM	-0.2	-6	08:43 AM	5.4	165	02:46 PM	-0.3	-9	08:55 PM	5.7	174
23	F	03:15 AM	-0.1	-3	09:20 AM	5.3	162	03:22 PM	-0.2	-6	09:31 PM	5.7	174
24	Sa	03:53 AM	0.0	0	09:56 AM	5.1	155	03:56 PM	-0.1	-3	10:05 PM	5.7	174
25	Su	04:30 AM	0.2	6	10:31 AM	4.9	149	04:30 PM	0.1	3	10:40 PM	5.5	168
26	M	05:06 AM	0.4	12	11:06 AM	4.7	143	05:04 PM	0.3	9	11:15 PM	5.4	165
27	Tu	05:43 AM	0.6	18	11:43 AM	4.5	137	05:42 PM	0.4	12	11:53 PM	5.2	158
28	W	06:23 AM	0.8	24	12:23 PM	4.4	134	06:24 PM	0.6	18			
29	Th	12:36 AM	5.1	155	07:08 AM	0.9	27	01:09 PM	4.3	131	07:13 PM	0.7	21
30	F	01:27 AM	5.0	152	08:01 AM	1.0	30	02:04 PM	4.3	131	08:10 PM	0.7	21
31	Sa	02:25 AM	5.0	152	09:00 AM	0.9	27	03:06 PM	4.4	134	09:14 PM	0.7	21

April

Date	Day	Time	ft	cm	Time	ft	cm	Time	ft	cm	Time	ft	cm
1	Su	03:28 AM	5.1	155	10:00 AM	0.7	21	04:09 PM	4.6	140	10:19 PM	0.5	15
2	M	04:30 AM	5.2	158	10:58 AM	0.4	12	05:08 PM	5.0	152	11:22 PM	0.1	3
3	Tu	05:28 AM	5.4	165	11:52 AM	0.1	3	06:04 PM	5.5	168			
4	W	12:20 AM	-0.2	-6	06:23 AM	5.6	171	12:43 PM	-0.3	-9	06:57 PM	5.9	180
5	Th	01:15 AM	-0.6	-18	07:15 AM	5.8	177	01:32 PM	-0.7	-21	07:49 PM	6.4	195
6	F	02:08 AM	-0.8	-24	08:06 AM	5.9	180	02:20 PM	-0.9	-27	08:39 PM	6.7	204
7	Sa	03:00 AM	-1.0	-30	08:56 AM	5.9	180	03:08 PM	-1.0	-30	09:30 PM	6.8	207
8	Su	03:52 AM	-1.0	-30	09:47 AM	5.8	177	03:58 PM	-1.0	-30	10:22 PM	6.8	207
9	M	04:44 AM	-0.8	-24	10:39 AM	5.6	171	04:49 PM	-0.8	-24	11:17 PM	6.6	201
10	Tu	05:38 AM	-0.6	-18	11:33 AM	5.4	165	05:43 PM	-0.5	-15			
11	W	12:14 AM	6.3	192	06:34 AM	-0.3	-9	12:31 PM	5.2	158	06:40 PM	-0.2	-6
12	Th	01:14 AM	6.0	183	07:32 AM	0.0	0	01:33 PM	5.0	152	07:43 PM	0.1	3
13	F	02:17 AM	5.7	174	08:32 AM	0.2	6	02:37 PM	4.9	149	08:49 PM	0.4	12
14	Sa	03:19 AM	5.5	168	09:32 AM	0.2	6	03:41 PM	5.0	152	09:55 PM	0.5	15
15	Su	04:19 AM	5.3	162	10:29 AM	0.2	6	04:41 PM	5.1	155	10:57 PM	0.4	12
16	M	05:13 AM	5.3	162	11:21 AM	0.1	3	05:35 PM	5.3	162	11:53 PM	0.4	12
17	Tu	06:03 AM	5.2	158	12:09 PM	0.0	0	06:24 PM	5.5	168			
18	W	12:43 AM	0.3	9	06:49 AM	5.2	158	12:53 PM	-0.1	-3	07:08 PM	5.7	174
19	Th	01:29 AM	0.2	6	07:31 AM	5.2	158	01:33 PM	-0.1	-3	07:48 PM	5.8	177
20	F	02:12 AM	0.1	3	08:12 AM	5.1	155	02:12 PM	-0.1	-3	08:26 PM	5.9	180
21	Sa	02:51 AM	0.2	6	08:50 AM	5.0	152	02:48 PM	0.0	0	09:03 PM	5.9	180
22	Su	03:29 AM	0.2	6	09:28 AM	4.9	149	03:23 PM	0.1	3	09:37 PM	5.8	177
23	M	04:05 AM	0.3	9	10:04 AM	4.8	146	03:58 PM	0.2	6	10:12 PM	5.7	174
24	Tu	04:41 AM	0.5	15	10:40 AM	4.6	140	04:34 PM	0.4	12	10:46 PM	5.6	171
25	W	05:17 AM	0.6	18	11:16 AM	4.5	137	05:12 PM	0.5	15	11:23 PM	5.5	168
26	Th	05:56 AM	0.7	21	11:55 AM	4.4	134	05:55 PM	0.6	18			
27	F	12:04 AM	5.4	165	06:39 AM	0.7	21	12:39 PM	4.4	134	06:43 PM	0.7	21
28	Sa	12:51 AM	5.3	162	07:28 AM	0.7	21	01:32 PM	4.5	137	07:39 PM	0.7	21
29	Su	01:46 AM	5.3	162	08:22 AM	0.6	18	02:31 PM	4.7	143	08:42 PM	0.7	21
30	M	02:45 AM	5.2	158	09:20 AM	0.5	15	03:34 PM	5.0	152	09:49 PM	0.5	15

May

Date	Day	Time	ft	cm	Time	ft	cm	Time	ft	cm	Time	ft	cm
1	Tu	03:47 AM	5.3	162	10:18 AM	0.2	6	04:35 PM	5.4	165	10:54 PM	0.2	6
2	W	04:48 AM	5.4	165	11:14 AM	-0.1	-3	05:34 PM	5.8	177	11:55 PM	-0.1	-3
3	Th	05:47 AM	5.5	168	12:09 PM	-0.5	-15	06:30 PM	6.3	192			
4	F	12:54 AM	-0.4	-12	06:44 AM	5.6	171	01:02 PM	-0.7	-21	07:25 PM	6.7	204
5	Sa	01:49 AM	-0.7	-21	07:40 AM	5.6	171	01:54 PM	-0.9	-27	08:20 PM	6.9	210
6	Su	02:43 AM	-0.9	-27	08:34 AM	5.7	174	02:46 PM	-1.0	-30	09:14 PM	7.0	213
7	M	03:36 AM	-0.9	-27	09:29 AM	5.6	171	03:39 PM	-0.9	-27	10:08 PM	6.9	210
8	Tu	04:29 AM	-0.8	-24	10:24 AM	5.5	168	04:32 PM	-0.7	-21	11:03 PM	6.7	204
9	W	05:22 AM	-0.6	-18	11:21 AM	5.4	165	05:27 PM	-0.4	-12	11:59 PM	6.4	195
10	Th	06:17 AM	-0.4	-12	12:19 PM	5.2	158	06:24 PM	-0.1	-3			
11	F	12:56 AM	6.0	183	07:11 AM	-0.1	-3	01:18 PM	5.1	155	07:24 PM	0.3	9
12	Sa	01:52 AM	5.7	174	08:07 AM	0.0	0	02:18 PM	5.1	155	08:27 PM	0.5	15
13	Su	02:49 AM	5.4	165	09:02 AM	0.1	3	03:17 PM	5.1	155	09:30 PM	0.7	21
14	M	03:43 AM	5.2	158	09:55 AM	0.2	6	04:12 PM	5.2	158	10:30 PM	0.7	21
15	Tu	04:35 AM	5.0	152	10:45 AM	0.2	6	05:04 PM	5.4	165	11:25 PM	0.7	21
16	W	05:24 AM	4.9	149	11:32 AM	0.1	3	05:52 PM	5.6	171			
17	Th	12:16 AM	0.6	18	06:11 AM	4.9	149	12:16 PM	0.1	3	06:36 PM	5.7	174
18	F	01:02 AM	0.5	15	06:56 AM	4.8	146	12:57 PM	0.0	0	07:18 PM	5.8	177
19	Sa	01:45 AM	0.4	12	07:39 AM	4.8	146	01:37 PM	0.0	0	07:58 PM	5.9	180
20	Su	02:26 AM	0.3	9	08:20 AM	4.8	146	02:16 PM	0.1	3	08:36 PM	5.9	180
21	M	03:04 AM	0.3	9	09:01 AM	4.7	143	02:54 PM	0.1	3	09:13 PM	5.9	180
22	Tu	03:42 AM	0.4	12	09:39 AM	4.6	140	03:31 PM	0.2	6	09:49 PM	5.8	177
23	W	04:18 AM	0.4	12	10:17 AM	4.6	140	04:09 PM	0.3	9	10:24 PM	5.7	174
24	Th	04:55 AM	0.4	12	10:54 AM	4.5	137	04:49 PM	0.4	12	11:00 PM	5.6	171
25	F	05:34 AM	0.5	15	11:33 AM	4.5	137	05:33 PM	0.5	15	11:40 PM	5.5	168
26	Sa	06:15 AM	0.4	12	12:17 PM	4.6	140	06:22 PM	0.5	15			
27	Su	12:25 AM	5.5	168	07:01 AM	0.4	12	01:08 PM	4.7	143	07:17 PM	0.6	18
28	M	01:16 AM	5.4	165	07:51 AM	0.2	6	02:05 PM	4.9	149	08:18 PM	0.5	15
29	Tu	02:12 AM	5.3	162	08:46 AM	0.1	3	03:05 PM	5.3	162	09:24 PM	0.4	12
30	W	03:12 AM	5.3	162	09:43 AM	-0.1	-3	04:07 PM	5.6	171	10:30 PM	0.2	6
31	Th	04:14 AM	5.2	158	10:42 AM	-0.4	-12	05:08 PM	6.0	183	11:33 PM	0.0	0

June

Date	Day	Time	ft	cm	Time	ft	cm	Time	ft	cm	Time	ft	cm
1	F	05:16 AM	5.3	162	11:40 AM	-0.6	-18	06:08 PM	6.4	195			
2	Sa	12:34 AM	-0.3	-9	06:17 AM	5.3	162	12:37 PM	-0.8	-24	07:06 PM	6.7	204
3	Su	01:31 AM	-0.6	-18	07:17 AM	5.4	165	01:32 PM	-0.9	-27	08:03 PM	6.9	210
4	M	02:26 AM	-0.7	-21	08:15 AM	5.4	165	02:27 PM	-1.0	-30	08:59 PM	6.9	210
5	Tu	03:19 AM	-0.8	-24	09:12 AM	5.4	165	03:21 PM	-0.9	-27	09:53 PM	6.8	207
6	W	04:12 AM	-0.7	-21	10:08 AM	5.4	165	04:15 PM	-0.7	-21	10:47 PM	6.6	201
7	Th	05:03 AM	-0.6	-18	11:04 AM	5.3	162	05:09 PM	-0.4	-12	11:39 PM	6.3	192
8	F	05:54 AM	-0.5	-15	12:00 PM	5.2	158	06:05 PM	0.0	0			
9	Sa	12:31 AM	5.9	180	06:45 AM	-0.3	-9	12:56 PM	5.2	158	07:01 PM	0.3	9
10	Su	01:22 AM	5.5	168	07:35 AM	-0.1	-3	01:50 PM	5.1	155	07:59 PM	0.6	18
11	M	02:12 AM	5.2	158	08:25 AM	0.0	0	02:44 PM	5.1	155	08:58 PM	0.8	24
12	Tu	03:02 AM	4.9	149	09:15 AM	0.1	3	03:36 PM	5.2	158	09:56 PM	0.9	27
13	W	03:52 AM	4.7	143	10:03 AM	0.2	6	04:26 PM	5.3	162	10:51 PM	0.9	27
14	Th	04:42 AM	4.6	140	10:50 AM	0.2	6	05:15 PM	5.4	165	11:43 PM	0.8	24
15	F	05:31 AM	4.6	140	11:36 AM	0.2	6	06:01 PM	5.6	171			
16	Sa	12:31 AM	0.7	21	06:19 AM	4.6	140	12:21 PM	0.1	3	06:46 PM	5.7	174
17	Su	01:15 AM	0.6	18	07:05 AM	4.6	140	01:04 PM	0.1	3	07:29 PM	5.8	177
18	M	01:57 AM	0.5	15	07:50 AM	4.6	140	01:46 PM	0.0	0	08:10 PM	5.8	177
19	Tu	02:37 AM	0.4	12	08:33 AM	4.6	140	02:26 PM	0.0	0	08:49 PM	5.8	177
20	W	03:16 AM	0.3	9	09:14 AM	4.6	140	03:07 PM	0.1	3	09:27 PM	5.8	177
21	Th	03:54 AM	0.3	9	09:54 AM	4.6	140	03:48 PM	0.1	3	10:03 PM	5.8	177
22	F	04:32 AM	0.2	6	10:33 AM	4.6	140	04:30 PM	0.2	6	10:40 PM	5.7	174
23	Sa	05:10 AM	0.2	6	11:13 AM	4.7	143	05:16 PM	0.2	6	11:19 PM	5.7	174
24	Su	05:52 AM	0.1	3	11:58 AM	4.8	146	06:05 PM	0.3	9			
25	M	12:03 AM	5.5	168	06:36 AM	0.0	0	12:48 PM	5.0	152	07:00 PM	0.4	12
26	Tu	12:52 AM	5.4	165	07:25 AM	-0.1	-3	01:43 PM	5.3	162	08:00 PM	0.4	12
27	W	01:47 AM	5.3	162	08:18 AM	-0.2	-6	02:43 PM	5.5	168	09:04 PM	0.4	12
28	Th	02:47 AM	5.2	158	09:16 AM	-0.3	-9	03:46 PM	5.8	177	10:10 PM	0.3	9
29	F	03:49 AM	5.1	155	10:16 AM	-0.4	-12	04:49 PM	6.1	186	11:15 PM	0.1	3
30	Sa	04:53 AM	5.1	155	11:17 AM	-0.6	-18	05:51 PM	6.4	195			

Heights are referred to mean lower water which is the chart datum of sounding. All times are local. Daylight Saving Time has been used when needed.

Charleston, South Carolina, 2012

Times and Heights of High and Low Waters

July

Day	Time (h m)	Height (ft)	Height (cm)
1 Su	12:16 AM 05:57 AM 12:17 PM 06:51 PM	-0.1 5.1 -0.7 6.6	-3 155 -21 201
2 M	01:14 AM 06:58 AM 01:15 PM 07:49 PM	-0.4 5.2 -0.8 6.7	-12 158 -24 204
3 Tu	02:08 AM 07:58 AM 02:11 PM 08:43 PM	-0.5 5.3 -0.8 6.7	-15 162 -24 204
4 W	03:01 AM 08:55 AM 03:05 PM 09:36 PM	-0.6 5.4 -0.7 6.6	-18 165 -21 201
5 Th	03:51 AM 09:50 AM 03:58 PM 10:26 PM	-0.6 5.4 -0.6 6.4	-18 165 -18 195
6 F	04:39 AM 10:43 AM 04:49 PM 11:13 PM	-0.6 5.4 -0.3 6.1	-18 165 -9 186
7 Sa	05:27 AM 11:34 AM 05:41 PM	-0.4 5.3 0.1	-12 162 3
8 Su	12:00 AM 06:13 AM 12:25 PM 06:32 PM	5.7 -0.2 5.2 0.4	174 -6 158 12
9 M	12:46 AM 06:58 AM 01:14 PM 07:25 PM	5.4 0.0 5.2 0.7	165 0 158 21
10 Tu	01:32 AM 07:44 AM 02:04 PM 08:20 PM	5.1 0.1 5.2 1.0	155 3 158 30
11 W	02:19 AM 08:30 AM 02:54 PM 09:16 PM	4.8 0.3 5.2 1.1	146 9 158 34
12 Th	03:08 AM 09:18 AM 03:45 PM 10:11 PM	4.6 0.4 5.2 1.1	140 12 158 34
13 F	03:59 AM 10:07 AM 04:35 PM 11:04 PM	4.5 0.4 5.3 1.1	137 12 162 34
14 Sa	04:51 AM 10:56 AM 05:25 PM 11:55 PM	4.5 0.3 5.5 0.9	137 9 168 27
15 Su	05:42 AM 11:44 AM 06:13 PM	4.5 0.3 5.6	137 9 171
16 M	12:41 AM 06:32 AM 12:31 PM 06:59 PM	0.8 4.6 0.2 5.7	24 140 6 174
17 Tu	01:25 AM 07:19 AM 01:17 PM 07:42 PM	0.6 4.7 0.1 5.9	18 143 3 180
18 W	02:07 AM 08:04 AM 02:01 PM 08:23 PM	0.4 4.7 0.0 5.9	12 143 0 180
19 Th	02:47 AM 08:47 AM 02:44 PM 09:02 PM	0.3 4.8 -0.1 6.0	9 146 -3 183
20 F	03:26 AM 09:29 AM 03:28 PM 09:40 PM	0.1 5.0 -0.1 6.0	3 152 -3 183
21 Sa	04:05 AM 10:10 AM 04:13 PM 10:19 PM	0.0 5.1 0.0 5.9	0 155 0 180
22 Su	04:45 AM 10:52 AM 05:00 PM 11:00 PM	-0.1 5.2 0.0 5.8	-3 158 0 177
23 M	05:27 AM 11:38 AM 05:50 PM 11:44 PM	-0.2 5.4 0.2 5.6	-6 165 6 171
24 Tu	06:12 AM 12:29 PM 06:45 PM	-0.2 5.5 0.3	-6 168 9
25 W	12:34 AM 07:02 AM 01:26 PM 07:45 PM	5.4 -0.2 5.6 0.4	165 -6 171 12
26 Th	01:29 AM 07:56 AM 02:27 PM 08:49 PM	5.3 -0.2 5.8 0.5	162 -6 177 15
27 F	02:29 AM 08:56 AM 03:32 PM 09:54 PM	5.1 -0.2 5.9 0.4	155 -6 180 12
28 Sa	03:34 AM 09:59 AM 04:37 PM 10:59 PM	5.0 -0.3 6.1 0.3	152 -9 186 9
29 Su	04:39 AM 11:03 AM 05:40 PM 11:59 PM	5.1 -0.3 6.3 0.1	155 -9 192 3
30 M	05:44 AM 12:04 PM 06:39 PM	5.1 -0.5 6.4	155 -15 195
31 Tu	12:56 AM 06:45 AM 01:02 PM 07:34 PM	-0.1 5.3 -0.5 6.5	-3 162 -15 198

August

Day	Time (h m)	Height (ft)	Height (cm)
1 W	01:49 AM 07:43 AM 01:57 PM 08:26 PM	-0.3 5.4 -0.6 6.5	-9 165 -18 198
2 Th	02:39 AM 08:37 AM 02:49 PM 09:14 PM	-0.4 5.6 -0.5 6.4	-12 171 -15 195
3 F	03:26 AM 09:27 AM 03:38 PM 09:59 PM	-0.4 5.6 -0.3 6.2	-12 171 -9 189
4 Sa	04:11 AM 10:15 AM 04:26 PM 10:43 PM	-0.3 5.6 0.0 5.9	-9 171 0 180
5 Su	04:54 AM 11:02 AM 05:13 PM 11:25 PM	-0.2 5.5 0.3 5.6	-6 168 9 171
6 M	05:36 AM 11:47 AM 06:00 PM	0.0 5.5 0.6	0 168 18
7 Tu	12:07 AM 06:17 AM 12:32 PM 06:48 PM	5.3 0.2 5.4 0.9	162 6 165 27
8 W	12:50 AM 06:59 AM 01:19 PM 07:38 PM	5.0 0.4 5.3 1.2	152 12 162 37
9 Th	01:36 AM 07:43 AM 02:08 PM 08:31 PM	4.8 0.6 5.2 1.3	146 18 158 40
10 F	02:26 AM 08:31 AM 03:00 PM 09:26 PM	4.6 0.7 5.2 1.4	140 21 158 43
11 Sa	03:18 AM 09:23 AM 03:53 PM 10:21 PM	4.5 0.7 5.3 1.4	137 21 162 43
12 Su	04:12 AM 10:16 AM 04:46 PM 11:14 PM	4.5 0.7 5.4 1.2	137 21 165 37
13 M	05:06 AM 11:09 AM 05:37 PM	4.6 0.5 5.6	140 15 171
14 Tu	12:03 AM 05:58 AM 12:00 PM 06:25 PM	1.0 4.8 0.4 5.8	30 146 12 177
15 W	12:49 AM 06:47 AM 12:49 PM 07:11 PM	0.8 5.0 0.2 6.0	24 152 6 183
16 Th	01:32 AM 07:33 AM 01:36 PM 07:53 PM	0.5 5.2 0.0 6.1	15 158 0 186
17 F	02:14 AM 08:18 AM 02:22 PM 08:34 PM	0.2 5.4 -0.1 6.2	6 165 -3 189
18 Sa	02:54 AM 09:01 AM 03:09 PM 09:15 PM	0.0 5.6 -0.1 6.2	0 171 -3 189
19 Su	03:36 AM 09:45 AM 03:56 PM 09:57 PM	-0.1 5.8 -0.1 6.1	-3 177 -3 186
20 M	04:18 AM 10:31 AM 04:45 PM 10:40 PM	-0.2 5.9 0.0 6.0	-6 180 0 183
21 Tu	05:02 AM 11:19 AM 05:37 PM 11:27 PM	-0.2 6.0 0.1 5.8	-6 183 3 177
22 W	05:50 AM 12:13 PM 06:32 PM	-0.2 6.1 0.3	-6 186 9
23 Th	12:19 AM 06:42 AM 01:12 PM 07:32 PM	5.5 -0.1 6.0 0.5	168 -3 183 15
24 F	01:17 AM 07:40 AM 02:16 PM 08:35 PM	5.3 0.0 6.0 0.6	162 0 183 18
25 Sa	02:20 AM 08:42 AM 03:22 PM 09:40 PM	5.2 0.1 6.1 0.6	158 3 186 18
26 Su	03:26 AM 09:48 AM 04:27 PM 10:44 PM	5.2 0.1 6.2 0.5	158 3 189 15
27 M	04:33 AM 10:53 AM 05:29 PM 11:42 PM	5.2 0.1 6.3 0.3	158 3 192 9
28 Tu	05:36 AM 11:54 AM 06:25 PM	5.4 0.0 6.4	165 0 195
29 W	12:37 AM 06:34 AM 12:50 PM 07:17 PM	0.1 5.6 -0.1 6.4	3 171 -3 195
30 Th	01:27 AM 07:27 AM 01:42 PM 08:04 PM	0.0 5.8 -0.1 6.4	0 177 -3 195
31 F	02:13 AM 08:16 AM 02:31 PM 08:48 PM	-0.1 5.9 -0.1 6.3	-3 180 -3 192

September

Day	Time (h m)	Height (ft)	Height (cm)
1 Sa	02:57 AM 09:02 AM 03:17 PM 09:30 PM	-0.1 6.0 0.1 6.1	-3 183 3 186
2 Su	03:38 AM 09:45 AM 04:02 PM 10:10 PM	0.0 6.0 0.3 5.8	0 183 9 177
3 M	04:18 AM 10:26 AM 04:44 PM 10:49 PM	0.1 5.9 0.6 5.6	3 180 18 171
4 Tu	04:56 AM 11:07 AM 05:27 PM 11:29 PM	0.3 5.8 0.9 5.3	9 177 27 162
5 W	05:34 AM 11:48 AM 06:10 PM	0.6 5.6 1.1	18 171 34
6 Th	12:10 AM 06:14 AM 12:32 PM 06:55 PM	5.0 0.8 5.5 1.4	152 24 168 43
7 F	12:54 AM 06:57 AM 01:20 PM 07:44 PM	4.8 0.9 5.4 1.6	146 27 165 49
8 Sa	01:43 AM 07:45 AM 02:12 PM 08:38 PM	4.7 1.0 5.4 1.6	143 30 165 49
9 Su	02:37 AM 08:39 AM 03:08 PM 09:34 PM	4.6 1.1 5.4 1.6	140 34 165 49
10 M	03:34 AM 09:36 AM 04:04 PM 10:30 PM	4.7 1.0 5.5 1.4	143 30 168 43
11 Tu	04:30 AM 10:33 AM 04:57 PM 11:21 PM	4.9 0.8 5.7 1.2	149 24 174 37
12 W	05:23 AM 11:28 AM 05:47 PM	5.1 0.6 5.9	155 18 180
13 Th	12:09 AM 06:14 AM 12:21 PM 06:35 PM	0.8 5.4 0.4 6.1	24 165 12 186
14 F	12:55 AM 07:02 AM 01:11 PM 07:20 PM	0.5 5.7 0.1 6.3	15 174 3 192
15 Sa	01:39 AM 07:48 AM 02:00 PM 08:04 PM	0.2 6.1 -0.1 6.3	6 186 -3 192
16 Su	02:22 AM 08:34 AM 02:49 PM 08:49 PM	-0.1 6.3 -0.2 6.3	-3 192 -6 192
17 M	03:07 AM 09:21 AM 03:39 PM 09:34 PM	-0.2 6.5 -0.2 6.2	-6 198 -6 189
18 Tu	03:52 AM 10:10 AM 04:30 PM 10:22 PM	-0.3 6.6 -0.1 6.1	-9 201 -3 186
19 W	04:40 AM 11:02 AM 05:23 PM 11:13 PM	-0.3 6.6 0.1 5.9	-9 201 3 180
20 Th	05:30 AM 11:58 AM 06:19 PM	-0.1 6.5 0.3	-3 198 9
21 F	12:08 AM 06:25 AM 01:00 PM 07:19 PM	5.6 0.1 6.4 0.6	171 3 195 18
22 Sa	01:09 AM 07:26 AM 02:05 PM 08:21 PM	5.5 0.3 6.2 0.7	168 9 189 21
23 Su	02:14 AM 08:31 AM 03:11 PM 09:25 PM	5.3 0.4 6.2 0.7	162 12 189 21
24 M	03:21 AM 09:38 AM 04:14 PM 10:26 PM	5.4 0.5 6.2 0.6	165 15 189 18
25 Tu	04:26 AM 10:43 AM 05:13 PM 11:22 PM	5.5 0.4 6.2 0.5	168 12 189 15
26 W	05:26 AM 11:42 AM 06:06 PM	5.7 0.4 6.2	174 12 189
27 Th	12:14 AM 06:20 AM 12:36 PM 06:54 PM	0.3 5.9 0.3 6.2	9 180 9 189
28 F	01:01 AM 07:09 AM 01:26 PM 07:38 PM	0.2 6.1 0.3 6.2	6 186 9 189
29 Sa	01:45 AM 07:54 AM 02:12 PM 08:20 PM	0.1 6.2 0.3 6.1	3 189 9 186
30 Su	02:26 AM 08:35 AM 02:55 PM 08:59 PM	0.1 6.3 0.4 5.9	3 192 12 180

October

Day	Time (h m)	Height (ft)	Height (cm)
1 M	03:05 AM 09:14 AM 03:37 PM 09:38 PM	0.2 6.2 0.6 5.7	6 189 18 174
2 Tu	03:42 AM 09:52 AM 04:16 PM 10:15 PM	0.4 6.1 0.8 5.5	12 186 24 168
3 W	04:18 AM 10:30 AM 04:55 PM 10:53 PM	0.6 6.0 1.0 5.2	18 183 30 158
4 Th	04:55 AM 11:08 AM 05:34 PM 11:33 PM	0.8 5.8 1.2 5.0	24 177 37 152
5 F	05:33 AM 11:49 AM 06:15 PM	0.9 5.7 1.4	27 174 43
6 Sa	12:15 AM 06:15 AM 12:34 PM 07:01 PM	4.9 1.1 5.5 1.6	149 34 168 49
7 Su	01:02 AM 07:03 AM 01:24 PM 07:51 PM	4.8 1.2 5.5 1.6	146 37 168 49
8 M	01:56 AM 07:57 AM 02:20 PM 08:47 PM	4.7 1.2 5.5 1.6	143 37 168 49
9 Tu	02:53 AM 08:56 AM 03:17 PM 09:43 PM	4.8 1.2 5.5 1.4	146 37 168 43
10 W	03:52 AM 09:57 AM 04:13 PM 10:37 PM	5.0 1.0 5.7 1.1	152 30 174 34
11 Th	04:47 AM 10:57 AM 05:06 PM 11:28 PM	5.4 0.8 5.9 0.7	165 24 180 21
12 F	05:40 AM 11:53 AM 05:57 PM	5.8 0.4 6.1	177 12 186
13 Sa	12:17 AM 06:31 AM 12:47 PM 06:47 PM	0.3 6.2 0.1 6.2	9 189 3 189
14 Su	01:05 AM 07:21 AM 01:40 PM 07:35 PM	0.0 6.6 -0.1 6.3	0 201 -3 192
15 M	01:52 AM 08:10 AM 02:31 PM 08:24 PM	-0.3 6.9 -0.3 6.3	-9 210 -9 192
16 Tu	02:40 AM 09:00 AM 03:22 PM 09:14 PM	-0.4 7.0 -0.3 6.2	-12 213 -9 189
17 W	03:29 AM 09:52 AM 04:15 PM 10:05 PM	-0.5 7.1 -0.2 6.1	-15 216 -6 186
18 Th	04:20 AM 10:47 AM 05:08 PM 10:59 PM	-0.4 7.0 0.0 5.9	-12 213 0 180
19 F	05:13 AM 11:45 AM 06:04 PM 11:57 PM	-0.2 6.8 0.2 5.7	-6 207 6 174
20 Sa	06:10 AM 12:46 PM 07:03 PM	0.1 6.5 0.4	3 198 12
21 Su	01:00 AM 07:12 AM 01:50 PM 08:03 PM	5.5 0.4 6.3 0.6	168 12 192 18
22 M	02:05 AM 08:17 AM 02:53 PM 09:04 PM	5.4 0.6 6.1 0.6	165 18 186 18
23 Tu	03:11 AM 09:24 AM 03:53 PM 10:02 PM	5.5 0.7 6.0 0.6	168 21 183 18
24 W	04:13 AM 10:28 AM 04:49 PM 10:57 PM	5.6 0.7 5.9 0.5	171 21 180 15
25 Th	05:09 AM 11:26 AM 05:40 PM 11:46 PM	5.8 0.6 5.8 0.3	177 18 177 9
26 F	06:01 AM 12:19 PM 06:26 PM	6.0 0.6 5.8	183 18 177
27 Sa	12:32 AM 06:47 AM 01:07 PM 07:10 PM	0.2 6.1 0.5 5.7	6 186 15 174
28 Su	01:15 AM 07:29 AM 01:51 PM 07:51 PM	0.2 6.2 0.5 5.7	6 189 15 174
29 M	01:55 AM 08:09 AM 02:33 PM 08:31 PM	0.2 6.3 0.5 5.5	6 192 15 168
30 Tu	02:33 AM 08:47 AM 03:12 PM 09:09 PM	0.3 6.3 0.6 5.4	9 192 18 165
31 W	03:10 AM 09:24 AM 03:50 PM 09:47 PM	0.4 6.2 0.7 5.2	12 189 21 158

November

Day	Time (h m)	Height (ft)	Height (cm)
1 Th	03:46 AM 10:00 AM 04:27 PM 10:24 PM	0.5 6.0 0.9 5.1	15 183 27 155
2 F	04:22 AM 10:36 AM 05:04 PM 11:01 PM	0.7 5.9 1.0 4.9	21 180 30 149
3 Sa	05:00 AM 11:14 AM 05:42 PM 11:40 PM	0.8 5.7 1.2 4.8	24 174 37 146
4 Su	04:41 AM 10:55 AM 05:24 PM 11:24 PM	0.9 5.6 1.3 4.7	27 171 40 143
5 M	05:27 AM 11:40 AM 06:10 PM	1.0 5.5 1.3	30 168 40
6 Tu	12:15 AM 06:20 AM 12:32 PM 07:02 PM	4.7 1.1 5.4 1.2	143 34 165 37
7 W	01:11 AM 07:20 AM 01:28 PM 07:57 PM	4.8 1.1 5.4 1.0	146 34 165 30
8 Th	02:11 AM 08:23 AM 02:26 PM 08:53 PM	5.1 0.9 5.5 0.7	155 27 168 21
9 F	03:10 AM 09:27 AM 03:24 PM 09:48 PM	5.5 0.7 5.6 0.4	168 21 171 12
10 Sa	04:08 AM 10:27 AM 04:21 PM 10:42 PM	5.9 0.4 5.7 0.0	180 12 174 0
11 Su	05:03 AM 11:25 AM 05:15 PM 11:35 PM	6.3 0.0 5.8 -0.3	192 0 177 -9
12 M	05:57 AM 12:20 PM 06:09 PM	6.7 -0.3 5.9	204 -9 180
13 Tu	12:26 AM 06:50 AM 01:13 PM 07:02 PM	-0.6 7.0 -0.4 6.0	-18 213 -12 183
14 W	01:18 AM 07:44 AM 02:06 PM 07:56 PM	-0.7 7.1 -0.5 6.0	-21 216 -15 183
15 Th	02:10 AM 08:38 AM 02:59 PM 08:50 PM	-0.8 7.1 -0.5 5.9	-24 216 -15 180
16 F	03:03 AM 09:33 AM 03:52 PM 09:46 PM	-0.7 7.0 -0.3 5.7	-21 213 -9 174
17 Sa	03:58 AM 10:30 AM 04:46 PM 10:44 PM	-0.4 6.7 -0.1 5.6	-12 204 -3 171
18 Su	04:55 AM 11:28 AM 05:42 PM 11:45 PM	-0.1 6.4 0.1 5.4	-3 195 3 165
19 M	05:55 AM 12:26 PM 06:39 PM	0.2 6.0 0.2	6 183 6
20 Tu	12:47 AM 06:58 AM 01:25 PM 07:36 PM	5.4 0.5 5.7 0.3	165 15 174 9
21 W	01:49 AM 08:03 AM 02:22 PM 08:31 PM	5.4 0.7 5.5 0.4	165 21 168 12
22 Th	02:49 AM 09:05 AM 03:16 PM 09:25 PM	5.4 0.8 5.3 0.3	165 24 162 9
23 F	03:44 AM 10:04 AM 04:07 PM 10:14 PM	5.6 0.7 5.2 0.3	171 21 158 9
24 Sa	04:34 AM 10:56 AM 04:55 PM 11:01 PM	5.7 0.7 5.2 0.2	174 21 158 6
25 Su	05:21 AM 11:44 AM 05:40 PM 11:44 PM	5.8 0.6 5.2 0.1	177 18 158 3
26 M	06:03 AM 12:29 PM 06:23 PM	6.0 0.5 5.1	183 15 155
27 Tu	12:25 AM 06:44 AM 01:10 PM 07:04 PM	0.1 6.0 0.4 5.1	3 183 12 155
28 W	01:04 AM 07:23 AM 01:49 PM 07:44 PM	0.1 6.0 0.4 5.0	3 183 12 152
29 Th	01:42 AM 08:01 AM 02:26 PM 08:23 PM	0.2 6.0 0.5 5.0	6 183 15 152
30 F	02:19 AM 08:37 AM 03:02 PM 08:59 PM	0.2 5.9 0.6 4.8	6 180 18 146

December

Day	Time (h m)	Height (ft)	Height (cm)
1 Sa	02:56 AM 09:12 AM 03:38 PM 09:35 PM	0.3 5.8 0.6 4.7	9 177 18 143
2 Su	03:34 AM 09:47 AM 04:14 PM 10:12 PM	0.4 5.6 0.7 4.7	12 171 21 143
3 M	04:15 AM 10:23 AM 04:53 PM 10:52 PM	0.5 5.5 0.7 4.6	15 168 21 140
4 Tu	05:00 AM 11:05 AM 05:35 PM 11:38 PM	0.6 5.4 0.7 4.7	18 165 21 143
5 W	05:50 AM 11:52 AM 06:23 PM	0.7 5.3 0.6	21 162 18
6 Th	12:32 AM 06:48 AM 12:45 PM 07:16 PM	4.8 0.7 5.2 0.4	146 21 158 12
7 F	01:32 AM 07:52 AM 01:44 PM 08:13 PM	5.1 0.7 5.2 0.3	155 21 158 9
8 Sa	02:35 AM 08:59 AM 02:46 PM 09:12 PM	5.4 0.5 5.2 0.0	165 15 158 0
9 Su	03:38 AM 10:03 AM 03:48 PM 10:12 PM	5.8 0.2 5.2 -0.3	177 6 158 -9
10 M	04:39 AM 11:04 AM 04:49 PM 11:10 PM	6.2 -0.1 5.4 -0.6	189 -3 165 -18
11 Tu	05:38 AM 12:02 PM 05:48 PM	6.5 -0.4 5.5	198 -12 168
12 W	12:06 AM 06:35 AM 12:57 PM 06:45 PM	-0.9 6.8 -0.6 5.6	-27 207 -18 171
13 Th	01:01 AM 07:30 AM 01:50 PM 07:41 PM	-1.1 6.9 -0.8 5.6	-34 210 -24 171
14 F	01:55 AM 08:25 AM 02:42 PM 08:36 PM	-1.1 6.9 -0.8 5.6	-34 210 -24 171
15 Sa	02:48 AM 09:18 AM 03:33 PM 09:31 PM	-1.0 6.7 -0.7 5.6	-30 204 -21 171
16 Su	03:42 AM 10:11 AM 04:25 PM 10:26 PM	-0.8 6.4 -0.6 5.5	-24 195 -18 168
17 M	04:37 AM 11:04 AM 05:16 PM 11:22 PM	-0.4 6.1 -0.4 5.3	-12 186 -12 162
18 Tu	05:33 AM 11:56 AM 06:08 PM	0.0 5.7 -0.2	0 174 -6
19 W	12:20 AM 06:32 AM 12:50 PM 07:00 PM	5.2 0.3 5.3 0.0	158 9 162 0
20 Th	01:17 AM 07:33 AM 01:43 PM 07:53 PM	5.1 0.6 5.0 0.2	155 18 152 6
21 F	02:14 AM 08:34 AM 02:37 PM 08:46 PM	5.1 0.7 4.7 0.2	155 21 143 6
22 Sa	03:09 AM 09:33 AM 03:30 PM 09:37 PM	5.2 0.8 4.6 0.2	158 24 140 6
23 Su	04:01 AM 10:28 AM 04:21 PM 10:26 PM	5.3 0.7 4.6 0.2	162 21 140 6
24 M	04:50 AM 11:17 AM 05:09 PM 11:13 PM	5.4 0.6 4.6 0.1	165 18 140 3
25 Tu	05:36 AM 12:03 PM 05:56 PM 11:57 PM	5.5 0.4 4.7 0.0	168 12 143 0
26 W	06:20 AM 12:45 PM 06:39 PM	5.6 0.3 4.7	171 9 143
27 Th	12:38 AM 07:01 AM 01:24 PM 07:21 PM	-0.1 5.7 0.2 4.8	-3 174 6 146
28 F	01:18 AM 07:39 AM 02:01 PM 08:00 PM	-0.1 5.7 0.2 4.8	-3 174 6 146
29 Sa	01:57 AM 08:16 AM 02:37 PM 08:38 PM	-0.1 5.7 0.2 4.7	-3 174 6 143
30 Su	02:35 AM 08:50 AM 03:12 PM 09:13 PM	-0.1 5.6 0.1 4.7	-3 171 3 143
31 M	03:14 AM 09:23 AM 03:47 PM 09:48 PM	-0.1 5.5 0.1 4.7	-3 168 3 143

Heights are referred to mean lower water which is the chart datum of sounding. All times are local. Daylight Saving Time has been used when needed.

Savannah River Entrance, Georgia, 2011

Times and Heights of High and Low Waters

Heights are referred to mean lower low water which is the chart datum of soundings. All times are local. Daylight Saving Time has been used when needed.

September

Day	Time (h m)	Height (ft)	Height (cm)	Day	Time (h m)	Height (ft)	Height (cm)
1 Th	0508 1117 0544* 1134*	-0.8 8.4 -0.3 7.9	-24 256 -9 241	16 F	0505 1105 0529* 1128*	0.8 7.4 1.3 6.6	24 226 40 201
2 F	0557 1215* 0638*	-0.5 8.3 0.1	-15 253 3	17 Sa	0541 1146 0608*	1.0 7.2 1.5	30 219 46
3 Sa	1231 0649 0116* 0736*	7.5 -0.2 8.1 0.5	229 -6 247 15	18 Su	1209 0620 1232* 0651*	6.3 1.2 7.1 1.7	192 37 216 52
4 Su ◐	0130 0746 0218* 0839*	7.2 0.2 7.9 0.9	219 6 241 27	19 M	1256 0705 0123* 0742*	6.2 1.3 7.1 1.9	189 40 216 58
5 M	0230 0849 0319* 0945*	6.9 0.5 7.7 1.0	210 15 235 30	20 Tu ◑	0148 0758 0217* 0841*	6.1 1.4 7.2 1.9	186 43 219 58
6 Tu	0329 0955 0419* 1048*	6.8 0.7 7.6 1.0	207 21 232 30	21 W	0244 0859 0314* 0945*	6.2 1.3 7.3 1.7	189 40 223 52
7 W	0428 1058 0517* 1144*	6.8 0.7 7.6 0.9	207 21 232 27	22 Th	0341 1003 0411* 1046*	6.5 1.1 7.6 1.3	198 34 232 40
8 Th	0526 1156 0611*	6.9 0.7 7.7	210 21 235	23 F	0440 1106 0509* 1143*	6.8 0.7 7.9 0.8	207 21 241 24
9 F	1234 0620 1248* 0700*	0.7 7.1 0.6 7.7	21 216 18 235	24 Sa	0538 1205* 0604*	7.3 0.3 8.2	223 9 250
10 Sa	0120 0709 0135* 0744*	0.5 7.3 0.6 7.7	15 223 18 235	25 Su	1236 0634 0101* 0658*	0.3 7.8 -0.1 8.4	9 238 -3 256
11 Su	0203 0754 0219* 0824*	0.4 7.5 0.6 7.7	12 229 18 235	26 M	0127 0728 0156* 0749*	-0.2 8.4 -0.4 8.6	-6 256 -12 262
12 M ○	0242 0835 0301* 0902*	0.4 7.6 0.6 7.5	12 232 18 229	27 Tu ●	0217 0819 0250* 0839*	-0.5 8.8 -0.6 8.6	-15 268 -18 262
13 Tu	0320 0913 0340* 0938*	0.4 7.6 0.8 7.4	12 232 24 226	28 W	0307 0910 0343* 0929*	-0.7 9.0 -0.7 8.5	-21 274 -21 259
14 W	0355 0950 0417* 1014*	0.5 7.6 0.9 7.1	15 232 27 216	29 Th	0356 1002 0435* 1020*	-0.8 9.0 -0.5 8.2	-24 274 -15 250
15 Th	0430 1027 0453* 1050*	0.6 7.5 1.1 6.8	18 229 34 207	30 F	0445 1056 0527* 1114*	-0.6 8.9 -0.2 7.9	-18 271 -6 241

October

Day	Time (h m)	Height (ft)	Height (cm)	Day	Time (h m)	Height (ft)	Height (cm)
1 Sa	0535 1155 0620*	-0.3 8.5 0.2	-9 259 6	16 Su	0512 1111 0543* 1134*	1.0 7.5 1.4 6.4	30 229 43 195
2 Su	1212 0628 1256* 0717*	7.5 0.1 8.2 0.6	229 3 250 18	17 M	0552 1155 0625*	1.1 7.4 1.5	34 226 46
3 M	0112 0725 0159* 0818*	7.2 0.6 7.9 1.0	219 18 241 30	18 Tu	1221 0637 1247* 0713*	6.3 1.2 7.3 1.6	192 37 223 49
4 Tu ◐	0213 0828 0259* 0921*	7.0 0.9 7.7 1.2	213 27 235 37	19 W	0115 0729 0143* 0809*	6.3 1.3 7.3 1.6	192 40 223 49
5 W	0313 0935 0357* 1022*	6.9 1.2 7.5 1.2	210 37 229 37	20 Th ◑	0214 0830 0241* 0911*	6.4 1.3 7.4 1.4	195 40 226 43
6 Th	0410 1039 0451* 1117*	6.9 1.2 7.4 1.0	210 37 226 30	21 F	0313 0936 0339* 1013*	6.7 1.1 7.6 1.0	204 34 232 30
7 F	0505 1136 0543*	7.1 1.1 7.4	216 34 226	22 Sa	0413 1041 0437* 1111*	7.2 0.8 7.8 0.6	219 24 238 18
8 Sa	1205 0556 1226* 0630*	0.9 7.3 1.0 7.4	27 223 30 226	23 Su	0512 1143 0535*	7.7 0.4 8.0	235 12 244
9 Su	1248 0644 0112* 0714*	0.7 7.5 0.9 7.5	21 229 27 229	24 M	1206 0610 1241* 0631*	0.1 8.2 0.0 8.2	3 250 0 250
10 M	0129 0727 0155* 0754*	0.6 7.7 0.9 7.4	18 235 27 226	25 Tu	1259 0705 0138* 0725*	-0.3 8.7 -0.4 8.3	-9 265 -12 253
11 Tu	0208 0807 0235* 0833*	0.5 7.9 0.8 7.4	15 241 24 226	26 W ●	0151 0759 0232* 0817*	-0.7 9.1 -0.6 8.3	-21 277 -18 253
12 W ○	0245 0845 0314* 0909*	0.5 8.0 0.9 7.2	15 244 27 219	27 Th	0243 0851 0325* 0909*	-0.8 9.3 -0.6 8.2	-24 283 -18 250
13 Th	0322 0921 0351* 0945*	0.6 7.9 1.0 7.0	18 241 30 213	28 F	0334 0943 0418* 1000*	-0.8 9.2 -0.5 8.0	-24 280 -15 244
14 F	0358 0956 0427* 1020*	0.7 7.8 1.1 6.8	21 238 34 207	29 Sa	0425 1037 0509* 1054*	-0.6 8.9 -0.2 7.7	-18 271 -6 235
15 Sa	0435 1032 0504* 1055*	0.8 7.7 1.2 6.6	24 235 37 201	30 Su	0515 1134 0601* 1151*	-0.3 8.5 0.1 7.3	-9 259 3 223
				31 M	0607 1234* 0654*	0.2 8.1 0.5	6 247 15

November

Day	Time (h m)	Height (ft)	Height (cm)	Day	Time (h m)	Height (ft)	Height (cm)
1 Tu	1251 0702 0133* 0750*	7.0 0.7 7.7 0.9	213 21 235 27	16 W	0515 1119 0550* 1150*	0.8 7.4 1.0 6.4	24 226 30 195
2 W ◐	0151 0802 0230* 0849*	6.9 1.1 7.4 1.1	210 34 226 34	17 Th	0607 1214* 0642*	0.9 7.4 0.9	27 226 27
3 Th	0248 0906 0325* 0947*	6.8 1.4 7.2 1.1	207 43 219 34	18 F ◑	1248 0706 0111* 0740*	6.6 1.0 7.3 0.8	201 30 223 24
4 F	0343 1010 0416* 1040*	6.9 1.5 7.0 1.1	210 46 213 34	19 Sa	0148 0812 0210* 0841*	6.9 0.9 7.4 0.5	210 27 226 15
5 Sa	0435 1108 0506* 1128*	7.0 1.4 6.9 0.9	213 43 210 27	20 Su	0248 0919 0308* 0941*	7.3 0.6 7.4 0.2	223 18 226 6
6 Su	0425 1059 0454* 1112*	7.2 1.3 6.9 0.8	219 40 210 24	21 M	0348 1023 0408* 1039*	7.7 0.3 7.5 -0.2	235 9 229 -6
7 M	0513 1145 0540* 1153*	7.5 1.1 6.9 0.6	229 34 210 18	22 Tu	0448 1123 0507* 1134*	8.2 -0.1 7.6 -0.5	250 -3 232 -15
8 Tu	0557 1228* 0623*	7.7 1.0 7.0	235 30 213	23 W	0546 1221* 0603*	8.6 -0.4 7.7	262 -12 235
9 W	1233 0639 0109* 0704*	0.5 7.8 0.9 6.9	15 238 27 210	24 Th	1229 0642 0116* 0658*	-0.8 8.9 -0.6 7.7	-24 271 -18 235
10 Th ○	0113 0718 0149* 0743*	0.5 7.9 0.8 6.9	15 241 24 210	25 F ●	0123 0735 0209* 0750*	-0.9 9.0 -0.7 7.7	-27 274 -21 235
11 F	0152 0755 0227* 0819*	0.5 7.9 0.8 6.8	15 241 24 207	26 Sa	0215 0828 0301* 0842*	-0.9 8.8 -0.6 7.5	-27 268 -18 229
12 Sa	0231 0832 0305* 0855*	0.5 7.8 0.8 6.6	15 238 24 201	27 Su	0306 0920 0350* 0934*	-0.7 8.6 -0.4 7.3	-21 262 -12 223
13 Su	0310 0908 0343* 0930*	0.6 7.7 0.9 6.5	18 235 27 198	28 M	0356 1013 0439* 1028*	-0.4 8.2 -0.1 7.1	-12 250 -3 216
14 M	0349 0946 0422* 1009*	0.6 7.6 0.9 6.4	18 232 27 195	29 Tu	0445 1107 0527* 1124*	0.0 7.7 0.2 6.8	0 235 6 207
15 Tu	0430 1030 0504* 1055*	0.7 7.5 1.0 6.3	21 229 30 192	30 W	0535 1201* 0616*	0.5 7.3 0.5	15 223 15

December

Day	Time (h m)	Height (ft)	Height (cm)	Day	Time (h m)	Height (ft)	Height (cm)
1 Th	1220 0629 1253* 0708*	6.6 1.0 6.9 0.8	201 30 210 24	16 F	0549 1150 0617*	0.3 7.2 0.1	9 219 3
2 F ◐	0114 0727 0144* 0800*	6.6 1.3 6.6 0.9	201 40 201 27	17 Sa	1226 0646 1246* 0712*	6.7 0.4 7.1 0.1	204 12 216 3
3 Sa	0206 0829 0234* 0853*	6.6 1.5 6.4 0.9	201 46 195 27	18 Su ◑	0125 0751 0144* 0811*	6.9 0.5 7.0 0.0	210 15 213 0
4 Su	0257 0929 0324* 0943*	6.7 1.5 6.3 0.9	204 46 192 27	19 M	0226 0859 0243* 0914*	7.2 0.4 6.9 -0.2	219 12 210 -6
5 M	0347 1023 0414* 1030*	6.9 1.4 6.2 0.7	210 43 189 21	20 Tu	0328 1005 0344* 1015*	7.5 0.2 6.8 -0.4	229 6 207 -12
6 Tu	0437 1112 0503* 1116*	7.0 1.2 6.3 0.6	213 37 192 18	21 W	0430 1107 0446* 1115*	7.8 -0.1 6.9 -0.6	238 -3 210 -18
7 W	0525 1157 0551*	7.2 1.0 6.3	219 30 192	22 Th	0531 1205* 0545*	8.1 -0.4 7.0	247 -12 213
8 Th	1200 0610 1241* 0636*	0.4 7.4 0.8 6.4	12 226 24 195	23 F	1212 0629 0101* 0642*	-0.9 8.3 -0.6 7.1	-27 253 -18 216
9 F	1243 0653 0123* 0717*	0.2 7.6 0.6 6.4	6 232 18 195	24 Sa ●	0107 0723 0153* 0735*	-1.0 8.4 -0.7 7.2	-30 256 -21 219
10 Sa ○	0125 0733 0204* 0756*	0.1 7.7 0.4 6.5	3 235 12 198	25 Su	0159 0814 0242* 0825*	-1.0 8.3 -0.8 7.1	-30 253 -24 216
11 Su	0207 0811 0244* 0833*	0.0 7.7 0.3 6.4	0 235 9 195	26 M	0249 0902 0329* 0914*	-0.9 8.1 -0.7 7.0	-27 247 -21 213
12 M	0249 0849 0323* 0910*	0.0 7.7 0.3 6.4	0 235 9 195	27 Tu	0336 0950 0414* 1003*	-0.6 7.8 -0.5 6.9	-18 238 -15 210
13 Tu	0330 0928 0403* 0951*	0.0 7.6 0.2 6.4	0 232 6 195	28 W	0422 1037 0456* 1052*	-0.2 7.3 -0.2 6.7	-6 223 -6 204
14 W	0413 1010 0444* 1036*	0.0 7.5 0.2 6.4	0 229 6 195	29 Th	0507 1124 0538* 1142*	0.2 6.9 0.1 6.5	6 210 3 198
15 Th	0459 1058 0529* 1129*	0.2 7.4 0.1 6.5	6 226 3 198	30 F	0552 1211* 0622*	0.7 6.5 0.4	21 198 12
				31 Sa	1232 0641 1259* 0708*	6.4 1.1 6.2 0.6	195 34 189 18

SKIPPER'S HANDBOOK

Savannah River Entrance, Georgia, 2012

Times and Heights of High and Low Waters

January

Day	Time (h m)	Height (ft)	Height (cm)
1 Su	01:23 AM 07:37 AM 01:49 PM 07:59 PM	6.4 1.3 6.0 0.7	195 40 183 21
2 M	02:13 AM 08:37 AM 02:39 PM 08:52 PM	6.4 1.4 5.8 0.7	195 43 177 21
3 Tu	03:04 AM 09:36 AM 03:31 PM 09:46 PM	6.5 1.3 5.7 0.6	198 40 174 18
4 W	03:56 AM 10:31 AM 04:24 PM 10:37 PM	6.6 1.2 5.8 0.4	201 37 177 12
5 Th	04:48 AM 11:21 AM 05:15 PM 11:26 PM	6.8 0.9 5.9 0.2	207 27 180 6
6 F	05:39 AM 12:08 PM 06:04 PM	7.0 0.6 6.1	213 18 186
7 Sa	12:13 AM 06:25 AM 12:53 PM 06:49 PM	0.0 7.2 0.3 6.2	0 219 9 189
8 Su	12:59 AM 07:08 AM 01:37 PM 07:30 PM	-0.3 7.5 0.0 6.4	-9 229 0 195
9 M	01:44 AM 07:49 AM 02:19 PM 08:10 PM	-0.5 7.6 -0.2 6.6	-15 232 -6 201
10 Tu	02:28 AM 08:28 AM 03:00 PM 08:49 PM	-0.6 7.7 -0.4 6.7	-18 235 -12 204
11 W	03:12 AM 09:08 AM 03:41 PM 09:31 PM	-0.7 7.7 -0.6 6.8	-21 235 -18 207
12 Th	03:57 AM 09:51 AM 04:23 PM 10:17 PM	-0.7 7.6 -0.6 6.9	-21 232 -18 210
13 F	04:43 AM 10:37 AM 05:07 PM 11:08 PM	-0.5 7.4 -0.6 6.9	-15 226 -18 210
14 Sa	05:34 AM 11:29 AM 05:54 PM	-0.3 7.1 -0.5	-9 216 -15
15 Su	12:05 AM 06:29 AM 12:25 PM 06:48 PM	6.9 0.0 6.9 -0.4	210 0 210 -12
16 M	01:05 AM 07:32 AM 01:23 PM 07:48 PM	7.0 0.2 6.6 -0.2	213 6 201 -6
17 Tu	02:07 AM 08:41 AM 02:25 PM 08:54 PM	7.1 0.3 6.5 -0.2	216 9 198 -6
18 W	03:12 AM 09:49 AM 03:28 PM 10:00 PM	7.2 0.2 6.4 -0.3	219 6 195 -9
19 Th	04:17 AM 10:53 AM 04:31 PM 11:02 PM	7.3 -0.1 6.5 -0.5	223 -3 198 -15
20 F	05:21 AM 11:51 AM 05:33 PM	7.5 -0.3 6.6	229 -9 201
21 Sa	12:00 AM 06:19 AM 12:45 PM 06:30 PM	-0.8 7.7 -0.6 6.8	-24 235 -18 207
22 Su	12:55 AM 07:12 AM 01:35 PM 07:21 PM	-0.9 7.8 -0.8 7.0	-27 238 -24 213
23 M	01:46 AM 07:59 AM 02:22 PM 08:09 PM	-1.0 7.8 -0.9 7.1	-30 238 -27 216
24 Tu	02:33 AM 08:43 AM 03:05 PM 08:53 PM	-0.9 7.7 -0.8 7.1	-27 235 -24 216
25 W	03:17 AM 09:25 AM 03:46 PM 09:37 PM	-0.7 7.4 -0.7 7.0	-21 226 -21 213
26 Th	03:58 AM 10:06 AM 04:24 PM 10:19 PM	-0.4 7.1 -0.5 6.8	-12 216 -15 207
27 F	04:38 AM 10:47 AM 05:01 PM 11:03 PM	0.0 6.7 -0.2 6.6	0 204 -6 201
28 Sa	05:18 AM 11:30 AM 05:39 PM 11:49 PM	0.4 6.3 0.1 6.4	12 192 3 195
29 Su	05:59 AM 12:15 PM 06:19 PM	0.8 6.0 0.4	24 183 12
30 M	12:36 AM 06:46 AM 01:03 PM 07:05 PM	6.3 1.1 5.7 0.6	192 34 174 18
31 Tu	01:26 AM 07:40 AM 01:53 PM 07:59 PM	6.2 1.3 5.5 0.8	189 40 168 24

February

Day	Time (h m)	Height (ft)	Height (cm)
1 W	02:18 AM 08:42 AM 02:46 PM 08:57 PM	6.2 1.4 5.4 0.8	189 43 165 24
2 Th	03:12 AM 09:44 AM 03:41 PM 09:56 PM	6.3 1.3 5.5 0.6	192 40 168 18
3 F	04:08 AM 10:41 AM 04:37 PM 10:52 PM	6.4 1.0 5.7 0.3	195 30 174 9
4 Sa	05:03 AM 11:33 AM 05:30 PM 11:44 PM	6.7 0.6 5.9 0.0	204 18 180 0
5 Su	05:54 AM 12:21 PM 06:19 PM	7.0 0.2 6.3	213 6 192
6 M	12:33 AM 06:41 AM 01:07 PM 07:04 PM	-0.4 7.4 -0.2 6.6	-12 226 -6 201
7 Tu	01:22 AM 07:25 AM 01:52 PM 07:47 PM	-0.7 7.6 -0.6 7.0	-21 232 -18 213
8 W	02:09 AM 08:07 AM 02:35 PM 08:29 PM	-1.0 7.8 -0.9 7.2	-30 238 -27 219
9 Th	02:55 AM 08:49 AM 03:18 PM 09:13 PM	-1.1 7.8 -1.0 7.4	-34 238 -30 226
10 F	03:42 AM 09:33 AM 04:01 PM 10:00 PM	-1.1 7.7 -1.1 7.5	-34 235 -34 229
11 Sa	04:29 AM 10:20 AM 04:46 PM 10:51 PM	-1.0 7.4 -1.0 7.4	-30 226 -30 226
12 Su	05:20 AM 11:12 AM 05:34 PM 11:48 PM	-0.7 7.1 -0.8 7.3	-21 216 -24 223
13 M	06:15 AM 12:08 PM 06:27 PM	-0.3 6.8 -0.5	-9 207 -15
14 Tu	12:49 AM 07:16 AM 01:08 PM 07:28 PM	7.2 0.1 6.5 -0.2	219 3 198 -6
15 W	01:52 AM 08:24 AM 02:10 PM 08:36 PM	7.1 0.3 6.3 0.0	216 9 192 0
16 Th	02:58 AM 09:33 AM 03:14 PM 09:45 PM	7.0 0.3 6.3 -0.1	213 9 192 -3
17 F	04:04 AM 10:37 AM 04:18 PM 10:50 PM	7.0 0.1 6.3 -0.2	213 3 192 -6
18 Sa	05:08 AM 11:34 AM 05:20 PM 11:48 PM	7.2 -0.1 6.5 -0.4	219 -3 198 -12
19 Su	06:05 AM 12:26 PM 06:15 PM	7.3 -0.4 6.8	223 -12 207
20 M	12:40 AM 06:55 AM 01:13 PM 07:04 PM	-0.6 7.5 -0.6 7.0	-18 229 -18 213
21 Tu	01:29 AM 07:38 AM 01:57 PM 07:48 PM	-0.6 7.5 -0.7 7.2	-18 229 -21 219
22 W	02:14 AM 08:19 AM 02:37 PM 08:28 PM	-0.6 7.4 -0.7 7.3	-18 226 -21 223
23 Th	02:55 AM 08:57 AM 03:14 PM 09:07 PM	-0.5 7.2 -0.6 7.2	-15 219 -18 219
24 F	03:33 AM 09:34 AM 03:50 PM 09:45 PM	-0.3 6.9 -0.4 7.1	-9 210 -12 216
25 Sa	04:10 AM 10:12 AM 04:24 PM 10:24 PM	0.0 6.6 -0.1 6.9	0 201 -3 210
26 Su	04:45 AM 10:51 AM 04:59 PM 11:05 PM	0.3 6.3 0.2 6.7	9 192 6 204
27 M	05:22 AM 11:33 AM 05:37 PM 11:50 PM	0.7 5.9 0.5 6.5	21 180 15 198
28 Tu	06:04 AM 12:19 PM 06:20 PM	1.0 5.7 0.7	30 174 21
29 W	12:38 AM 06:52 AM 01:09 PM 07:10 PM	6.3 1.2 5.5 0.9	192 37 168 27

March

Day	Time (h m)	Height (ft)	Height (cm)
1 Th	01:31 AM 07:50 AM 02:02 PM 08:10 PM	6.3 1.4 5.5 1.0	192 43 168 30
2 F	02:27 AM 08:55 AM 02:59 PM 09:15 PM	6.3 1.3 5.6 0.8	192 40 171 24
3 Sa	03:25 AM 09:58 AM 03:56 PM 10:16 PM	6.4 1.1 5.8 0.5	195 34 177 15
4 Su	04:23 AM 10:54 AM 04:53 PM 11:13 PM	6.7 0.7 6.2 0.1	204 21 189 3
5 M	05:18 AM 11:46 AM 05:46 PM	7.0 0.2 6.6	213 6 201
6 Tu	12:07 AM 06:09 AM 12:35 PM 06:35 PM	-0.3 7.4 -0.3 7.1	-9 226 -9 216
7 W	12:58 AM 06:57 AM 01:22 PM 07:22 PM	-0.8 7.7 -0.7 7.6	-24 235 -21 232
8 Th	01:48 AM 07:42 AM 02:08 PM 08:07 PM	-1.1 7.9 -1.0 8.0	-34 241 -30 244
9 F	02:37 AM 08:28 AM 02:54 PM 08:53 PM	-1.3 7.9 -1.2 8.2	-40 241 -37 250
10 Sa	03:26 AM 09:14 AM 03:39 PM 09:42 PM	-1.3 7.8 -1.3 8.2	-40 238 -40 250
11 Su	05:15 AM 11:04 AM 05:26 PM 11:35 PM	-1.1 7.5 -1.1 8.0	-34 229 -34 244
12 M	06:06 AM 11:57 AM 06:16 PM	-0.8 7.2 -0.8	-24 219 -24
13 Tu	12:33 AM 07:01 AM 12:55 PM 07:10 PM	7.7 -0.4 6.8 -0.3	235 -12 207 -9
14 W	01:35 AM 08:01 AM 01:56 PM 08:12 PM	7.4 0.1 6.6 0.1	226 3 201 3
15 Th	02:39 AM 09:07 AM 02:58 PM 09:21 PM	7.2 0.3 6.4 0.3	219 9 195 9
16 F	03:44 AM 10:14 AM 04:01 PM 10:31 PM	7.0 0.4 6.4 0.4	213 12 195 12
17 Sa	04:47 AM 11:16 AM 05:03 PM 11:35 PM	7.0 0.3 6.5 0.2	213 9 198 6
18 Su	05:48 AM 12:11 PM 06:02 PM	7.0 0.1 6.8	213 3 207
19 M	12:32 AM 06:42 AM 01:00 PM 06:55 PM	0.1 7.1 -0.1 7.0	3 216 -3 213
20 Tu	01:23 AM 07:30 AM 01:45 PM 07:41 PM	-0.1 7.2 -0.3 7.3	-3 219 -9 223
21 W	02:09 AM 08:12 AM 02:27 PM 08:23 PM	-0.2 7.2 -0.3 7.5	-6 219 -9 229
22 Th	02:52 AM 08:51 AM 03:05 PM 09:01 PM	-0.2 7.1 -0.3 7.6	-6 216 -9 232
23 F	03:31 AM 09:28 AM 03:42 PM 09:38 PM	-0.1 7.0 -0.2 7.5	-3 213 -6 229
24 Sa	04:08 AM 10:04 AM 04:17 PM 10:13 PM	0.0 6.8 -0.1 7.4	0 207 -3 226
25 Su	04:43 AM 10:40 AM 04:51 PM 10:50 PM	0.2 6.5 0.1 7.2	6 198 3 219
26 M	05:18 AM 11:17 AM 05:26 PM 11:28 PM	0.4 6.3 0.4 7.0	12 192 12 213
27 Tu	05:53 AM 11:57 AM 06:03 PM	0.7 6.0 0.6	21 183 18
28 W	12:09 AM 06:32 AM 12:40 PM 06:44 PM	6.8 0.9 5.8 0.8	207 27 177 24
29 Th	12:56 AM 07:16 AM 01:29 PM 07:33 PM	6.6 1.1 5.7 1.0	201 34 174 30
30 F	01:49 AM 08:10 AM 02:23 PM 08:31 PM	6.5 1.3 5.7 1.1	198 40 174 34
31 Sa	02:45 AM 09:11 AM 03:20 PM 09:36 PM	6.5 1.2 5.9 1.0	198 37 180 30

April

Day	Time (h m)	Height (ft)	Height (cm)
1 Su	03:43 AM 10:15 AM 04:18 PM 10:42 PM	6.6 1.0 6.2 0.7	201 30 189 21
2 M	04:41 AM 11:14 AM 05:16 PM 11:43 PM	6.8 0.6 6.6 0.3	207 18 201 9
3 Tu	05:39 AM 12:09 PM 06:12 PM	7.1 0.1 7.2	216 3 219
4 W	12:40 AM 06:34 AM 01:01 PM 07:05 PM	-0.2 7.4 -0.4 7.7	-6 226 -12 235
5 Th	01:35 AM 07:26 AM 01:51 PM 07:56 PM	-0.6 7.7 -0.8 8.2	-18 235 -24 250
6 F	02:28 AM 08:17 AM 02:40 PM 08:45 PM	-1.0 7.9 -1.1 8.6	-30 241 -34 262
7 Sa	03:19 AM 09:06 AM 03:30 PM 09:34 PM	-1.2 7.9 -1.2 8.7	-37 241 -37 265
8 Su	04:10 AM 09:55 AM 04:19 PM 10:26 PM	-1.3 7.8 -1.2 8.7	-40 238 -37 265
9 M	05:01 AM 10:47 AM 05:08 PM 11:20 PM	-1.1 7.5 -1.0 8.4	-34 229 -30 256
10 Tu	05:52 AM 11:43 AM 06:00 PM	-0.8 7.2 -0.6	-24 219 -18
11 W	12:19 AM 06:46 AM 12:43 PM 06:55 PM	8.0 -0.4 6.9 -0.1	244 -12 210 -3
12 Th	01:21 AM 07:44 AM 01:44 PM 07:56 PM	7.6 0.0 6.7 0.3	232 0 204 9
13 F	02:23 AM 08:46 AM 02:45 PM 09:03 PM	7.3 0.3 6.6 0.6	223 9 201 18
14 Sa	03:24 AM 09:49 AM 03:45 PM 10:12 PM	7.1 0.4 6.7 0.7	216 12 204 21
15 Su	04:22 AM 10:48 AM 04:43 PM 11:15 PM	6.9 0.4 6.8 0.7	210 12 207 21
16 M	05:18 AM 11:41 AM 05:37 PM	6.8 0.2 7.0	207 6 213
17 Tu	12:10 AM 06:10 AM 12:28 PM 06:28 PM	0.5 6.8 0.1 7.2	15 207 3 219
18 W	12:59 AM 06:57 AM 01:12 PM 07:13 PM	0.4 6.8 0.0 7.5	12 207 0 229
19 Th	01:44 AM 07:41 AM 01:53 PM 07:54 PM	0.3 6.8 0.0 7.6	9 207 0 232
20 F	02:26 AM 08:21 AM 02:32 PM 08:33 PM	0.2 6.8 0.0 7.7	6 207 0 235
21 Sa	03:06 AM 08:59 AM 03:09 PM 09:09 PM	0.2 6.7 0.0 7.7	6 204 0 235
22 Su	03:43 AM 09:36 AM 03:46 PM 09:45 PM	0.3 6.6 0.1 7.6	9 201 3 232
23 M	04:18 AM 10:12 AM 04:22 PM 10:21 PM	0.4 6.4 0.3 7.4	12 195 9 226
24 Tu	04:54 AM 10:49 AM 04:58 PM 10:57 PM	0.5 6.2 0.5 7.2	15 189 15 219
25 W	05:30 AM 11:27 AM 05:36 PM 11:37 PM	0.7 6.0 0.7 7.1	21 183 21 216
26 Th	06:08 AM 12:09 PM 06:18 PM	0.8 5.9 0.8	24 180 24
27 F	12:23 AM 06:51 AM 12:57 PM 07:05 PM	6.9 0.9 5.9 1.0	210 27 180 30
28 Sa	01:14 AM 07:40 AM 01:51 PM 08:00 PM	6.8 1.0 6.0 1.1	207 30 183 34
29 Su	02:09 AM 08:36 AM 02:47 PM 09:04 PM	6.8 0.9 6.2 1.0	207 27 189 30
30 M	03:05 AM 09:36 AM 03:44 PM 10:11 PM	6.9 0.7 6.6 0.8	210 21 201 24

May

Day	Time (h m)	Height (ft)	Height (cm)
1 Tu	04:03 AM 10:36 AM 04:42 PM 11:14 PM	7.0 0.3 7.1 0.4	213 9 216 12
2 W	05:02 AM 11:33 AM 05:40 PM	7.1 -0.1 7.6	216 -3 232
3 Th	12:15 AM 06:00 AM 12:28 PM 06:37 PM	-0.1 7.3 -0.5 8.1	-3 223 -15 247
4 F	01:12 AM 06:57 AM 01:22 PM 07:32 PM	-0.5 7.5 -0.8 8.6	-15 229 -24 262
5 Sa	02:07 AM 07:51 AM 02:15 PM 08:24 PM	-0.9 7.6 -1.1 8.9	-27 232 -34 271
6 Su	03:01 AM 08:44 AM 03:07 PM 09:17 PM	-1.1 7.7 -1.2 8.9	-34 235 -37 271
7 M	03:54 AM 09:37 AM 04:00 PM 10:10 PM	-1.1 7.6 -1.1 8.8	-34 232 -34 268
8 Tu	04:46 AM 10:31 AM 04:51 PM 11:06 PM	-1.0 7.4 -0.9 8.5	-30 226 -27 259
9 W	05:37 AM 11:28 AM 05:44 PM	-0.8 7.2 -0.5	-24 219 -15
10 Th	12:04 AM 06:29 AM 12:28 PM 06:38 PM	8.1 -0.5 7.0 0.0	247 -15 213 0
11 F	01:04 AM 07:23 AM 01:28 PM 07:36 PM	7.7 -0.1 6.8 0.4	235 -3 207 12
12 Sa	02:01 AM 08:20 AM 02:26 PM 08:40 PM	7.3 0.2 6.8 0.8	223 6 207 24
13 Su	02:57 AM 09:18 AM 03:22 PM 09:45 PM	7.0 0.3 6.8 1.0	213 9 207 30
14 M	03:49 AM 10:13 AM 04:15 PM 10:47 PM	6.7 0.4 6.9 1.0	204 12 210 30
15 Tu	04:41 AM 11:04 AM 05:05 PM 11:41 PM	6.6 0.3 7.1 0.9	201 9 216 27
16 W	05:31 AM 11:51 AM 05:54 PM	6.5 0.3 7.2	198 9 219
17 Th	12:30 AM 06:20 AM 12:34 PM 06:40 PM	0.8 6.4 0.2 7.4	24 195 6 226
18 F	01:15 AM 07:06 AM 01:16 PM 07:23 PM	0.6 6.4 0.2 7.6	18 195 6 232
19 Sa	01:58 AM 07:49 AM 01:57 PM 08:04 PM	0.5 6.5 0.1 7.7	15 198 3 235
20 Su	02:38 AM 08:30 AM 02:38 PM 08:43 PM	0.4 6.4 0.2 7.7	12 195 6 235
21 M	03:17 AM 09:09 AM 03:17 PM 09:20 PM	0.4 6.4 0.2 7.6	12 195 6 232
22 Tu	03:55 AM 09:47 AM 03:56 PM 09:56 PM	0.4 6.2 0.3 7.5	12 189 9 229
23 W	04:32 AM 10:24 AM 04:35 PM 10:33 PM	0.4 6.1 0.4 7.4	12 186 12 226
24 Th	05:09 AM 11:02 AM 05:14 PM 11:13 PM	0.5 6.0 0.5 7.2	15 183 15 219
25 F	05:47 AM 11:44 AM 05:57 PM 11:56 PM	0.5 6.0 0.6 7.1	15 183 18 216
26 Sa	06:29 AM 12:32 PM 06:43 PM	0.5 6.1 0.8	15 186 24
27 Su	12:46 AM 07:15 AM 01:24 PM 07:37 PM	7.0 0.5 6.3 0.8	213 15 192 24
28 M	01:39 AM 08:06 AM 02:20 PM 08:38 PM	7.0 0.4 6.6 0.8	213 12 201 24
29 Tu	02:35 AM 09:03 AM 03:16 PM 09:44 PM	7.0 0.2 6.9 0.7	213 6 210 21
30 W	03:32 AM 10:03 AM 04:14 PM 10:49 PM	7.0 0.0 7.4 0.4	213 0 226 12
31 Th	04:31 AM 11:02 AM 05:13 PM 11:52 PM	7.0 -0.3 7.8 0.0	213 -9 238 0

June

Day	Time (h m)	Height (ft)	Height (cm)
1 F	05:31 AM 12:00 PM 06:13 PM	7.1 -0.6 8.2	216 -18 250
2 Sa	12:51 AM 06:30 AM 12:57 PM 07:11 PM	-0.4 7.2 -0.9 8.6	-12 219 -27 262
3 Su	01:48 AM 07:28 AM 01:53 PM 08:07 PM	-0.7 7.3 -1.0 8.8	-21 223 -30 268
4 M	02:44 AM 08:24 AM 02:48 PM 09:01 PM	-0.9 7.4 -1.1 8.8	-27 226 -34 268
5 Tu	03:37 AM 09:19 AM 03:42 PM 09:55 PM	-1.0 7.3 -1.0 8.6	-30 223 -30 262
6 W	04:29 AM 10:14 AM 04:35 PM 10:50 PM	-1.0 7.2 -0.8 8.3	-30 219 -24 253
7 Th	05:19 AM 11:10 AM 05:26 PM 11:45 PM	-0.8 7.1 -0.4 7.9	-24 216 -12 241
8 F	06:08 AM 12:08 PM 06:18 PM	-0.6 7.0 0.0	-18 213 0
9 Sa	12:39 AM 06:57 AM 01:05 PM 07:12 PM	7.5 -0.3 6.8 0.5	229 -9 207 15
10 Su	01:33 AM 07:48 AM 01:59 PM 08:09 PM	7.1 0.0 6.8 0.9	216 0 207 27
11 M	02:23 AM 08:39 AM 02:50 PM 09:10 PM	6.8 0.2 6.8 1.1	207 6 207 34
12 Tu	03:13 AM 09:31 AM 03:40 PM 10:10 PM	6.5 0.4 6.9 1.2	198 12 210 37
13 W	04:01 AM 10:21 AM 04:29 PM 11:05 PM	6.3 0.4 7.0 1.2	192 12 213 37
14 Th	04:50 AM 11:09 AM 05:17 PM 11:55 PM	6.2 0.4 7.1 1.1	189 12 216 34
15 F	05:40 AM 11:55 AM 06:05 PM	6.1 0.3 7.3	186 9 223
16 Sa	12:42 AM 06:29 AM 12:40 PM 06:51 PM	0.9 6.1 0.3 7.4	27 186 9 226
17 Su	01:26 AM 07:16 AM 01:24 PM 07:35 PM	0.7 6.2 0.2 7.5	21 189 6 229
18 M	02:08 AM 08:01 AM 02:07 PM 08:17 PM	0.6 6.2 0.2 7.6	18 189 6 232
19 Tu	02:50 AM 08:42 AM 02:50 PM 08:56 PM	0.5 6.2 0.2 7.6	15 189 6 232
20 W	03:30 AM 09:22 AM 03:32 PM 09:34 PM	0.3 6.2 0.2 7.6	9 189 6 232
21 Th	04:09 AM 10:00 AM 04:13 PM 10:11 PM	0.3 6.2 0.2 7.5	9 189 6 229
22 F	04:47 AM 10:39 AM 04:55 PM 10:51 PM	0.2 6.2 0.3 7.4	6 189 9 226
23 Sa	05:26 AM 11:21 AM 05:39 PM 11:34 PM	0.1 6.3 0.3 7.3	3 192 9 223
24 Su	06:07 AM 12:09 PM 06:26 PM	0.1 6.4 0.4	3 195 12
25 M	12:22 AM 06:52 AM 01:01 PM 07:18 PM	7.2 0.0 6.6 0.5	219 0 201 15
26 Tu	01:15 AM 07:41 AM 01:57 PM 08:18 PM	7.1 0.0 6.9 0.6	216 0 210 18
27 W	02:10 AM 08:36 AM 02:54 PM 09:23 PM	7.0 -0.1 7.2 0.6	213 -3 219 18
28 Th	03:07 AM 09:36 AM 03:52 PM 10:29 PM	6.9 -0.2 7.6 0.4	210 -6 232 12
29 F	04:07 AM 10:37 AM 04:53 PM 11:32 PM	6.9 -0.4 7.9 0.1	210 -12 241 3
30 Sa	05:07 AM 11:38 AM 05:54 PM	6.9 -0.6 8.1	210 -18 247

Heights are referred to mean lower water which is the chart datum of sounding. All times are local. Daylight Saving Time has been used when needed.

Savannah River Entrance, Georgia, 2012

Times and Heights of High and Low Waters

July

Day	Time (h m)	Height (ft)	Height (cm)	Day	Time (h m)	Height (ft)	Height (cm)
1 Su	12:33 AM	-0.2	-6	16 M	12:51 AM	1.0	30
	06:09 AM	6.9	210		06:42 AM	6.1	186
	12:37 PM	-0.8	-24		12:52 PM	0.3	9
	06:54 PM	8.4	256		07:05 PM	7.4	226
2 M	01:31 AM	-0.5	-15	17 Tu	01:36 AM	0.7	21
	07:09 AM	7.1	216		07:30 AM	6.2	189
	01:35 PM	-0.9	-27		01:38 PM	0.2	6
	07:52 PM	8.5	259		07:49 PM	7.6	232
3 Tu	02:26 AM	-0.7	-21	18 W	02:19 AM	0.5	15
	08:07 AM	7.2	219		08:14 AM	6.4	195
	02:31 PM	-0.9	-27		02:24 PM	0.1	3
	08:46 PM	8.5	259		08:31 PM	7.7	235
4 W	03:18 AM	-0.8	-24	19 Th	03:01 AM	0.3	9
	09:01 AM	7.2	219		08:55 AM	6.5	198
	03:25 PM	-0.8	-24		03:08 PM	0.0	0
	09:38 PM	8.4	256		09:10 PM	7.7	235
5 Th	04:08 AM	-0.8	-24	20 F	03:42 AM	0.1	3
	09:55 AM	7.2	219		09:34 AM	6.6	201
	04:17 PM	-0.6	-18		03:53 PM	0.0	0
	10:29 PM	8.1	247		09:49 PM	7.7	235
6 F	04:56 AM	-0.7	-21	21 Sa	04:22 AM	-0.1	-3
	10:48 AM	7.1	216		10:15 AM	6.7	204
	05:06 PM	-0.3	-9		04:37 PM	0.0	0
	11:19 PM	7.8	238		10:29 PM	7.6	232
7 Sa	05:41 AM	-0.5	-15	22 Su	05:03 AM	-0.2	-6
	11:41 AM	7.0	213		10:58 AM	6.9	210
	05:54 PM	0.1	3		05:22 PM	0.1	3
					11:13 PM	7.5	229
8 Su	12:09 AM	7.3	223	23 M	05:45 AM	-0.3	-9
	06:26 AM	-0.3	-9		11:47 AM	7.0	213
	12:33 PM	6.9	210		06:10 PM	0.2	6
	06:43 PM	0.6	18				
9 M	12:58 AM	6.9	210	24 Tu	12:02 AM	7.3	223
	07:10 AM	0.0	0		06:29 AM	-0.3	-9
	01:24 PM	6.8	207		12:40 PM	7.2	219
	07:33 PM	1.0	30		07:02 PM	0.4	12
10 Tu	01:46 AM	6.6	201	25 W	12:55 AM	7.1	216
	07:56 AM	0.3	9		07:19 AM	-0.2	-6
	02:13 PM	6.8	207		01:37 PM	7.3	223
	08:27 PM	1.3	40		08:01 PM	0.5	15
11 W	02:34 AM	6.3	192	26 Th	01:51 AM	7.0	213
	08:44 AM	0.5	15		08:14 AM	-0.1	-3
	03:01 PM	6.8	207		02:36 PM	7.5	229
	09:24 PM	1.5	46		09:05 PM	0.6	18
12 Th	03:21 AM	6.1	186	27 F	02:50 AM	6.9	210
	09:35 AM	0.6	18		09:15 AM	-0.1	-3
	03:49 PM	6.9	210		03:36 PM	7.7	235
	10:21 PM	1.5	46		10:12 PM	0.5	15
13 F	04:11 AM	6.0	183	28 Sa	03:50 AM	6.8	207
	10:26 AM	0.6	18		10:19 AM	-0.2	-6
	04:38 PM	7.0	213		04:38 PM	7.8	238
	11:15 PM	1.4	43		11:16 PM	0.3	9
14 Sa	05:01 AM	6.0	183	29 Su	04:51 AM	6.8	207
	11:16 AM	0.6	18		11:23 AM	-0.3	-9
	05:28 PM	7.1	216		05:41 PM	8.0	244
15 Su	12:04 AM	1.2	37	30 M	12:17 AM	0.1	3
	05:52 AM	6.0	183		05:54 AM	6.9	210
	12:04 PM	0.5	15		12:23 PM	-0.4	-12
	06:18 PM	7.2	219		06:42 PM	8.2	250
				31 Tu	01:13 AM	-0.2	-6
					06:54 AM	7.1	216
					01:21 PM	-0.5	-15
					07:38 PM	8.3	253

August

Day	Time (h m)	Height (ft)	Height (cm)	Day	Time (h m)	Height (ft)	Height (cm)
1 W	02:07 AM	-0.4	-12	16 Th	01:46 AM	0.6	18
	07:50 AM	7.3	223		07:43 AM	6.8	207
	02:16 PM	-0.6	-18		01:58 PM	0.1	3
	08:30 PM	8.3	253		08:02 PM	7.9	241
2 Th	02:57 AM	-0.5	-15	17 F	02:30 AM	0.2	6
	08:43 AM	7.4	226		08:26 AM	7.1	216
	03:08 PM	-0.5	-15		02:45 PM	-0.1	-3
	09:18 PM	8.2	250		08:43 PM	8.0	244
3 F	03:44 AM	-0.6	-18	18 Sa	03:13 AM	0.0	0
	09:32 AM	7.4	226		09:08 AM	7.4	226
	03:57 PM	-0.3	-9		03:32 PM	-0.2	-6
	10:04 PM	8.0	244		09:24 PM	8.0	244
4 Sa	04:28 AM	-0.5	-15	19 Su	03:55 AM	-0.2	-6
	10:20 AM	7.4	226		09:50 AM	7.6	232
	04:43 PM	0.0	0		04:18 PM	-0.2	-6
	10:49 PM	7.6	232		10:07 PM	8.0	244
5 Su	05:10 AM	-0.3	-9	20 M	04:38 AM	-0.4	-12
	11:07 AM	7.3	223		10:36 AM	7.7	235
	05:27 PM	0.4	12		05:06 PM	-0.1	-3
	11:34 PM	7.2	219		10:52 PM	7.8	238
6 M	05:50 AM	0.0	0	21 Tu	05:22 AM	-0.4	-12
	11:55 AM	7.1	216		11:26 AM	7.8	238
	06:10 PM	0.8	24		05:55 PM	0.1	3
					11:43 PM	7.5	229
7 Tu	12:19 AM	6.8	207	22 W	06:08 AM	-0.3	-9
	06:30 AM	0.3	9		12:21 PM	7.8	238
	12:42 PM	7.0	213		06:48 PM	0.3	9
	06:55 PM	1.2	37				
8 W	01:06 AM	6.5	198	23 Th	12:38 AM	7.3	223
	07:12 AM	0.6	18		06:59 AM	-0.1	-3
	01:30 PM	6.9	210		01:21 PM	7.8	238
	07:42 PM	1.5	46		07:46 PM	0.6	18
9 Th	01:53 AM	6.3	192	24 F	01:37 AM	7.1	216
	07:57 AM	0.8	24		07:56 AM	0.1	3
	02:19 PM	6.9	210		02:23 PM	7.8	238
	08:34 PM	1.7	52		08:51 PM	0.8	24
10 F	02:42 AM	6.1	186	25 Sa	02:37 AM	7.0	213
	08:47 AM	1.0	30		09:00 AM	0.2	6
	03:09 PM	6.9	210		03:25 PM	7.8	238
	09:32 PM	1.8	55		09:57 PM	0.8	24
11 Sa	03:32 AM	6.0	183	26 Su	03:39 AM	6.9	210
	09:41 AM	1.0	30		10:07 AM	0.3	9
	03:59 PM	6.9	210		04:28 PM	7.9	241
	10:30 PM	1.7	52		11:02 PM	0.6	18
12 Su	04:23 AM	6.0	183	27 M	04:41 AM	7.0	213
	10:36 AM	1.0	30		11:12 AM	0.2	6
	04:51 PM	7.0	213		05:30 PM	8.0	244
	11:23 PM	1.5	46				
13 M	05:16 AM	6.1	186	28 Tu	12:00 AM	0.4	12
	11:30 AM	0.8	24		05:42 AM	7.2	219
	05:42 PM	7.2	219		12:12 PM	0.0	0
					06:28 PM	8.1	247
14 Tu	12:13 AM	1.2	37	29 W	12:54 AM	0.1	3
	06:08 AM	6.3	192		06:40 AM	7.4	226
	12:21 PM	0.6	18		01:08 PM	-0.1	-3
	06:32 PM	7.5	229		07:21 PM	8.2	250
15 W	01:00 AM	0.9	27	30 Th	01:45 AM	-0.1	-3
	06:57 AM	6.6	201		07:34 AM	7.6	232
	01:10 PM	0.3	9		02:00 PM	-0.1	-3
	07:18 PM	7.7	235		08:10 PM	8.2	250
				31 F	02:32 AM	-0.2	-6
					08:22 AM	7.8	238
					02:49 PM	0.0	0
					08:54 PM	8.1	247

September

Day	Time (h m)	Height (ft)	Height (cm)	Day	Time (h m)	Height (ft)	Height (cm)
1 Sa	03:16 AM	-0.2	-6	16 Su	02:42 AM	-0.2	-6
	09:07 AM	7.8	238		08:41 AM	8.2	250
	03:35 PM	0.1	3		03:11 PM	-0.2	-6
	09:36 PM	7.8	238		08:59 PM	8.3	253
2 Su	03:57 AM	-0.1	-3	17 M	03:27 AM	-0.4	-12
	09:50 AM	7.8	238		09:27 AM	8.4	256
	04:18 PM	0.4	12		04:00 PM	-0.3	-9
	10:17 PM	7.5	229		09:45 PM	8.2	250
3 M	04:36 AM	0.1	3	18 Tu	04:13 AM	-0.5	-15
	10:32 AM	7.7	235		10:14 AM	8.5	259
	04:59 PM	0.7	21		04:49 PM	-0.2	-6
	10:57 PM	7.2	219		10:33 PM	8.0	244
4 Tu	05:14 AM	0.4	12	19 W	05:00 AM	-0.4	-12
	11:14 AM	7.5	229		11:07 AM	8.5	259
	05:38 PM	1.0	30		05:40 PM	0.0	0
	11:40 PM	6.8	207		11:26 PM	7.7	235
5 W	05:51 AM	0.7	21	20 Th	05:49 AM	-0.2	-6
	11:59 AM	7.3	223		12:04 PM	8.3	253
	06:17 PM	1.4	43		06:34 PM	0.3	9
6 Th	12:25 AM	6.5	198	21 F	12:23 AM	7.4	226
	06:30 AM	1.0	30		06:42 AM	0.1	3
	12:46 PM	7.1	216		01:07 PM	8.1	247
	06:59 PM	1.7	52		07:32 PM	0.6	18
7 F	01:13 AM	6.3	192	22 Sa	01:25 AM	7.2	219
	07:12 AM	1.2	37		07:41 AM	0.4	12
	01:35 PM	7.0	213		02:11 PM	8.0	244
	07:47 PM	1.9	58		08:35 PM	0.9	27
8 Sa	02:03 AM	6.2	189	23 Su	02:28 AM	7.1	216
	08:01 AM	1.4	43		08:47 AM	0.6	18
	02:27 PM	6.9	210		03:14 PM	7.9	241
	08:42 PM	2.0	61		09:41 PM	0.9	27
9 Su	02:54 AM	6.1	186	24 M	03:30 AM	7.1	216
	08:57 AM	1.5	46		09:55 AM	0.7	21
	03:19 PM	7.0	213		04:15 PM	7.9	241
	09:42 PM	2.0	61		10:44 PM	0.8	24
10 M	03:46 AM	6.2	189	25 Tu	04:31 AM	7.2	219
	09:57 AM	1.4	43		11:01 AM	0.6	18
	04:11 PM	7.1	216		05:14 PM	7.9	241
	10:40 PM	1.7	52		11:41 PM	0.5	15
11 Tu	04:39 AM	6.4	195	26 W	05:29 AM	7.4	226
	10:55 AM	1.2	37		12:00 PM	0.5	15
	05:04 PM	7.3	223		06:10 PM	7.9	241
	11:33 PM	1.4	43				
12 W	05:32 AM	6.7	204	27 Th	12:32 AM	0.3	9
	11:49 AM	0.9	27		06:24 AM	7.7	235
	05:55 PM	7.6	232		12:53 PM	0.4	12
					07:00 PM	7.9	241
13 Th	12:23 AM	1.0	30	28 F	01:19 AM	0.2	6
	06:23 AM	7.0	213		07:14 AM	7.9	241
	12:41 PM	0.5	15		01:43 PM	0.4	12
	06:44 PM	7.9	241		07:46 PM	7.9	241
14 F	01:10 AM	0.6	18	29 Sa	02:04 AM	0.1	3
	07:11 AM	7.5	229		08:00 AM	8.1	247
	01:32 PM	0.2	6		02:29 PM	0.4	12
	07:30 PM	8.1	247		08:28 PM	7.8	238
15 Sa	01:56 AM	0.2	6	30 Su	02:45 AM	0.1	3
	07:57 AM	7.9	241		08:41 AM	8.1	247
	02:21 PM	-0.1	-3		03:12 PM	0.5	15
	08:15 PM	8.3	253		09:07 PM	7.6	232

October

Day	Time (h m)	Height (ft)	Height (cm)	Day	Time (h m)	Height (ft)	Height (cm)
1 M	03:25 AM	0.2	6	16 Tu	03:02 AM	-0.6	-18
	09:20 AM	8.1	247		09:06 AM	9.0	274
	03:52 PM	0.7	21		03:42 PM	-0.5	-15
	09:46 PM	7.4	226		09:24 PM	8.2	250
2 Tu	04:03 AM	0.4	12	17 W	03:51 AM	-0.6	-18
	09:59 AM	8.0	244		09:56 AM	9.0	274
	04:30 PM	0.9	27		04:33 PM	-0.4	-12
	10:24 PM	7.1	216		10:15 PM	8.0	244
3 W	04:39 AM	0.6	18	18 Th	04:41 AM	-0.5	-15
	10:38 AM	7.8	238		10:50 AM	8.8	268
	05:07 PM	1.1	34		05:25 PM	-0.2	-6
	11:04 PM	6.8	207		11:10 PM	7.8	238
4 Th	05:16 AM	0.9	27	19 F	05:32 AM	-0.3	-9
	11:19 AM	7.5	229		11:50 AM	8.6	262
	05:44 PM	1.4	43		06:19 PM	0.1	3
	11:46 PM	6.5	198				
5 F	05:53 AM	1.1	34	20 Sa	12:09 AM	7.5	229
	12:03 PM	7.3	223		06:27 AM	0.1	3
	06:24 PM	1.7	52		12:53 PM	8.2	250
					07:15 PM	0.4	12
6 Sa	12:32 AM	6.3	192	21 Su	01:12 AM	7.3	223
	06:35 AM	1.4	43		07:26 AM	0.5	15
	12:52 PM	7.1	216		01:56 PM	8.0	244
	07:07 PM	1.8	55		08:16 PM	0.7	21
7 Su	01:22 AM	6.2	189	22 M	02:15 AM	7.2	219
	07:21 AM	1.6	49		08:31 AM	0.8	24
	01:44 PM	7.0	213		02:57 PM	7.8	238
	07:58 PM	1.9	58		09:20 PM	0.8	24
8 M	02:15 AM	6.2	189	23 Tu	03:17 AM	7.2	219
	08:16 AM	1.6	49		09:40 AM	0.9	27
	02:36 PM	7.1	216		03:56 PM	7.6	232
	08:56 PM	1.9	58		10:20 PM	0.7	21
9 Tu	03:08 AM	6.3	192	24 W	04:15 AM	7.3	223
	09:17 AM	1.6	49		10:45 AM	0.9	27
	03:30 PM	7.2	219		04:52 PM	7.5	229
	09:55 PM	1.7	52		11:15 PM	0.6	18
10 W	04:01 AM	6.6	201	25 Th	05:11 AM	7.5	229
	10:19 AM	1.4	43		11:43 AM	0.8	24
	04:23 PM	7.4	226		05:44 PM	7.5	229
	10:52 PM	1.3	40				
11 Th	04:55 AM	7.0	213	26 F	12:05 AM	0.4	12
	11:18 AM	1.0	30		06:03 AM	7.7	235
	05:16 PM	7.6	232		12:35 PM	0.7	21
	11:44 PM	0.9	27		06:33 PM	7.5	229
12 F	05:48 AM	7.5	229	27 Sa	12:51 AM	0.3	9
	12:13 PM	0.6	18		06:51 AM	7.9	241
	06:08 PM	7.8	238		01:22 PM	0.7	21
					07:18 PM	7.4	226
13 Sa	12:34 AM	0.4	12	28 Su	01:34 AM	0.3	9
	06:39 AM	8.0	244		07:35 AM	8.0	244
	01:06 PM	0.2	6		02:07 PM	0.6	18
	06:58 PM	8.1	247		08:00 PM	7.4	226
14 Su	01:23 AM	0.0	0	29 M	02:15 AM	0.3	9
	07:29 AM	8.4	256		08:15 AM	8.1	247
	01:59 PM	-0.1	-3		02:48 PM	0.6	18
	07:47 PM	8.2	250		08:40 PM	7.3	223
15 M	02:12 AM	-0.4	-12	30 Tu	02:54 AM	0.3	9
	08:17 AM	8.8	268		08:54 AM	8.1	247
	02:51 PM	-0.4	-12		03:27 PM	0.7	21
	08:36 PM	8.3	253		09:18 PM	7.1	216
				31 W	03:32 AM	0.5	15
					09:31 AM	8.0	244
					04:05 PM	0.8	24
					09:56 PM	6.9	210

November

Day	Time (h m)	Height (ft)	Height (cm)	Day	Time (h m)	Height (ft)	Height (cm)
1 Th	04:09 AM	0.6	18	16 F	03:24 AM	-0.8	-24
	10:08 AM	7.8	238		09:36 AM	8.8	268
	04:41 PM	1.0	30		04:09 PM	-0.6	-18
	10:34 PM	6.7	204		09:55 PM	7.6	232
2 F	04:46 AM	0.8	24	17 Sa	04:17 AM	-0.6	-18
	10:47 AM	7.6	232		10:34 AM	8.5	259
	05:17 PM	1.2	37		05:01 PM	-0.3	-9
	11:13 PM	6.4	195		10:54 PM	7.4	226
3 Sa	05:23 AM	1.0	30	18 Su	05:11 AM	-0.2	-6
	11:28 AM	7.4	226		11:35 AM	8.1	247
	05:54 PM	1.3	40		05:55 PM	0.0	0
	11:55 PM	6.3	192		11:55 PM	7.2	219
4 Su	05:04 AM	1.2	37	19 M	06:08 AM	0.3	9
	11:12 AM	7.2	219		12:35 PM	7.7	235
	05:35 PM	1.4	43		06:51 PM	0.3	9
	11:43 PM	6.2	189				
5 M	05:48 AM	1.3	40	20 Tu	12:56 AM	7.1	216
	12:02 PM	7.1	216		07:10 AM	0.7	21
	06:21 PM	1.5	46		01:32 PM	7.4	226
					07:50 PM	0.5	15
6 Tu	12:34 AM	6.2	189	21 W	01:55 AM	7.1	216
	06:40 AM	1.5	46		08:16 AM	1.0	30
	12:54 PM	7.0	213		02:27 PM	7.2	219
	07:14 PM	1.4	43		08:49 PM	0.5	15
7 W	01:28 AM	6.4	195	22 Th	02:51 AM	7.1	216
	07:39 AM	1.4	43		09:21 AM	1.0	30
	01:47 PM	7.1	216		03:20 PM	7.0	213
	08:11 PM	1.3	40		09:43 PM	0.5	15
8 Th	02:22 AM	6.7	204	23 F	03:44 AM	7.2	219
	08:43 AM	1.3	40		10:19 AM	1.0	30
	02:42 PM	7.2	219		04:12 PM	6.8	207
	09:10 PM	0.9	27		10:33 PM	0.4	12
9 F	03:18 AM	7.1	216	24 Sa	04:35 AM	7.4	226
	09:46 AM	0.9	27		11:11 AM	0.9	27
	03:37 PM	7.3	223		05:02 PM	6.8	207
	10:06 PM	0.5	15		11:19 PM	0.3	9
10 Sa	04:14 AM	7.6	232	25 Su	05:23 AM	7.5	229
	10:46 AM	0.5	15		11:58 AM	0.8	24
	04:33 PM	7.5	229		05:49 PM	6.8	207
	11:01 PM	0.1	3				
11 Su	05:09 AM	8.1	247	26 M	12:03 AM	0.3	9
	11:43 AM	0.1	3		06:08 AM	7.7	235
	05:28 PM	7.7	235		12:42 PM	0.7	21
	11:54 PM	-0.3	-9		06:33 PM	6.8	207
12 M	06:03 AM	8.6	262	27 Tu	12:45 AM	0.2	6
	12:38 PM	-0.3	-9		06:50 AM	7.8	238
	06:22 PM	7.9	241		01:24 PM	0.6	18
					07:15 PM	6.7	204
13 Tu	12:47 AM	-0.7	-21	28 W	01:25 AM	0.2	6
	06:56 AM	8.9	271		07:30 AM	7.8	238
	01:32 PM	-0.6	-18		02:03 PM	0.6	18
	07:14 PM	8.0	244		07:54 PM	6.7	204
14 W	01:39 AM	-0.9	-27	29 Th	02:05 AM	0.2	6
	07:49 AM	9.1	277		08:08 AM	7.7	235
	02:25 PM	-0.7	-21		02:40 PM	0.6	18
	08:06 PM	8.0	244		08:32 PM	6.6	201
15 Th	02:32 AM	-0.9	-27	30 F	02:43 AM	0.3	9
	08:41 AM	9.1	277		08:45 AM	7.6	232
	03:17 PM	-0.7	-21		03:17 PM	0.6	18
	08:59 PM	7.8	238		09:09 PM	6.4	195

December

Day	Time (h m)	Height (ft)	Height (cm)	Day	Time (h m)	Height (ft)	Height (cm)
1 Sa	03:21 AM	0.4	12	16 Su	04:01 AM	-0.9	-27
	09:22 AM	7.5	229		10:16 AM	8.2	250
	03:53 PM	0.7	21		04:40 PM	-0.8	-24
	09:45 PM	6.3	192		10:34 PM	7.3	223
2 Su	03:59 AM	0.5	15	17 M	04:52 AM	-0.5	-15
	09:59 AM	7.3	223		11:11 AM	7.8	238
	04:29 PM	0.7	21		05:30 PM	-0.5	-15
	10:24 PM	6.2	189		11:32 PM	7.1	216
3 M	04:39 AM	0.7	21	18 Tu	05:45 AM	0.0	0
	10:40 AM	7.1	216		12:06 PM	7.3	223
	05:08 PM	0.8	24		06:20 PM	-0.2	-6
	11:07 PM	6.1	186				
4 Tu	05:22 AM	0.8	24	19 W	12:29 AM	6.9	210
	11:25 AM	7.0	213		06:42 AM	0.5	15
	05:50 PM	0.8	24		12:59 PM	6.9	210
	11:56 PM	6.2	189		07:13 PM	0.1	3
5 W	06:10 AM	0.9	27	20 Th	01:24 AM	6.8	207
	12:15 PM	6.9	210		07:43 AM	0.9	27
	06:38 PM	0.7	21		01:52 PM	6.6	201
					08:08 PM	0.3	9
6 Th	12:50 AM	6.4	195	21 F	02:17 AM	6.8	207
	07:07 AM	1.0	30		08:46 AM	1.1	34
	01:08 PM	6.9	210		02:43 PM	6.3	192
	07:32 PM	0.6	18		09:03 PM	0.4	12
7 F	01:46 AM	6.7	204	22 Sa	03:09 AM	6.8	207
	08:11 AM	0.9	27		09:47 AM	1.1	34
	02:04 PM	6.9	210		03:35 PM	6.1	186
	08:31 PM	0.4	12		09:56 PM	0.4	12
8 Sa	02:43 AM	7.1	216	23 Su	04:01 AM	6.9	210
	09:17 AM	0.7	21		10:41 AM	1.0	30
	03:02 PM	6.9	210		04:27 PM	6.1	186
	09:32 PM	0.1	3		10:45 PM	0.4	12
9 Su	03:43 AM	7.5	229	24 M	04:51 AM	7.0	213
	10:21 AM	0.4	12		11:30 AM	0.8	24
	04:02 PM	7.0	213		05:18 PM	6.1	186
	10:31 PM	-0.3	-9		11:31 PM	0.2	6
10 M	04:43 AM	7.9	241	25 Tu	05:40 AM	7.1	216
	11:22 AM	-0.1	-3		12:15 PM	0.7	21
	05:02 PM	7.2	219		06:06 PM	6.2	189
	11:29 PM	-0.6	-18				
11 Tu	05:43 AM	8.3	253	26 W	12:16 AM	0.1	3
	12:19 PM	-0.4	-12		06:26 AM	7.3	223
	06:00 PM	7.3	223		12:57 PM	0.5	15
					06:50 PM	6.3	192
12 W	12:26 AM	-1.0	-30	27 Th	12:59 AM	0.0	0
	06:40 AM	8.6	262		07:08 AM	7.4	226
	01:15 PM	-0.8	-24		01:37 PM	0.3	9
	06:56 PM	7.5	229		07:32 PM	6.4	195
13 Th	01:22 AM	-1.2	-37	28 F	01:40 AM	-0.1	-3
	07:35 AM	8.8	268		07:47 AM	7.4	226
	02:09 PM	-1.0	-30		02:16 PM	0.2	6
	07:50 PM	7.6	232		08:10 PM	6.4	195
14 F	02:16 AM	-1.3	-40	29 Sa	02:21 AM	-0.1	-3
	08:29 AM	8.8	268		08:24 AM	7.4	226
	03:01 PM	-1.1	-34		02:53 PM	0.1	3
	08:44 PM	7.6	232		08:46 PM	6.3	192
15 Sa	03:09 AM	-1.2	-37	30 Su	03:00 AM	-0.1	-3
	09:22 AM	8.6	262		09:00 AM	7.3	223
	03:51 PM	-1.0	-30		03:29 PM	0.1	3
	09:38 PM	7.5	229		09:21 PM	6.3	192
				31 M	03:38 AM	0.0	0
					09:35 AM	7.2	219
					04:05 PM	0.0	0
					09:57 PM	6.3	192

Heights are referred to mean lower water which is the chart datum of sounding. All times are local. Daylight Saving Time has been used when needed.

ICW Bridges: Norfolk to Florida

KEY

Statute miles from Norfolk

Closed Vertical Clearance (at center of span)

Bridge: Schedule / Openings

SR=State Route

\# Opening may be delayed up to 10 minutes for approaching vessels that will not reach the bridge for the scheduled time.

* Subject to closure of Dismal Swamp Canal for low water level. Call 757-201-7500, ext.3 (U.S. Army Corps of Engineers) for status.

(VHF) Channels Monitored (by state)

Virginia Channel 13	North Carolina Channel 13
South Carolina Channel 09	Georgia Channel 09

VIRGINIA BRIDGES MONITOR (VHF) CHANNEL 13

2.6 **6'** **Belt Line Railroad Lift Bridge:** Year-round, daily; normally open; announcements on VHF Channel 13, 30 and 15 min. in advance of, and immediately preceding, lowering the span and also after reopening. 757-543-1996 or 757-545-2941.

~~**2.8**~~ 85' **Jordan Highway Lift Bridge (SR 337):** Dismantled.

3.6 **10'** **Norfolk and Western Railroad Lift Bridge:** Year-round, daily; normally open. 757-494-7371.

5.8 **11'** **Gilmerton Bascule Bridge (U.S. 13/460):** Year-round, Mon.-Fri. Closed 6:30 a.m. to 9:30 a.m. and 3:30 p.m. to 6:30 p.m. Opens hourly on the half hour from 9:30 a.m. to 3:30 p.m. Mon.-Fri. and from 6:30 a.m. to 6:30 p.m. Saturdays, Sundays, and federal holidays. Opens on signal at all other times. 757-545-1512.

5.8 **7'** **Norfolk Southern #7 RR Bascule Bridge:** Year-round, daily; normally open; remote operation. 757-924-5320

7.1 **65'** **Highway Bascule Bridge (Interstate 64):** Year-round, Mon.-Fri., except federal holidays. Closed 6:00 to 9:00 a.m. and 3:00 to 6:00 p.m. 757-424-9920.

65' ~~**8.8**~~ **12'** **Dominion Boulevard Bridge (U.S. 17) (aka "Steel Bridge"):** Year-round, Mon.-Fri. Closed 7:00 a.m. to 9:00 a.m. and 4:00 p.m. to 6:00 p.m. Opens on the hour from 6:00 a.m. to 7:00 a.m. and 9:00 a.m. to 4:00 p.m. Weekends and federal holidays, opens on the hour from 6:00 a.m. to 6:00 p.m. Opens on demand after 6:00 p.m. 757-547-0521. Building Double SPAN 6/16

11.3 **Great Bridge Lock:** Opens on the half hour southbound. Timed to open with Great Bridge bascule bridge. 757-547-3311.

12.0 **6'** **Great Bridge Bascule Bridge (SR 168):** Year-round, daily. 6:00 a.m. to 7:00 p.m.: Opens on the hour. 757-482-8250.

13.0 **65'** **Highway Bypass Bridge (SR 168 Bypass):** Fixed.

13.9 **7'** **Chesapeake and Albemarle Railroad Bridge:** Normally open.

15.2 **4'** **Centerville Turnpike Swing Bridge (SR 170):** Year-round, Mon.-Fri., except federal holidays and weekends. Closed 6:30 a.m. to 8:30 a.m. and 4:00 p.m. to 6:00 p.m. Opens on the hour and half hour from 8:30 a.m. to 4:00 p.m. Opens on signal at all other times. 757-547-3631.

20.2 **6'** **North Landing Swing Bridge (SR 165):** Year-round, daily, 6:00 a.m. to 7:00 p.m. Opens on the hour and half hour. 757-482-3081.

28.6 PUNGO FERRY (route 726) FIXED

NORTH CAROLINA BRIDGES MONITOR (VHF) CHANNEL 13

49.9 **65'** **Coinjock Bridge (U.S. 158):** Fixed.

84.2 **14'** **Alligator River Swing Bridge (U.S. 64):** Year-round, daily. Opens on signal. (May not open if wind speed exceeds 34 knots.) 252-796-7261.

DISMAL SWAMP CANAL BRIDGES*

10.5 **Deep Creek Lock:** Lock opens at 8:30 a.m., 11:00 a.m., 1:30 p.m. and 3:30 p.m.

11.1 **4'** **Deep Creek Bascule Bridge (U.S. 17):** Openings coordinated with lock operation. 757-487-0831.

28.1 **0'** **Dismal Swamp Canal Visitors Center Foot Bridge (Pontoon):** Usually open. Call 252-771-6593 to request an opening if closed.

31.5 **65'** **Highway Bridge, Dismal Swamp Canal:** Fixed.

32.6 **4'** **South Mills Bascule Bridge:** Openings coordinated with lock operation. 252-771-5906.

32.7 **South Mills Lock:** Lock opens at 8:30 a.m., 11:00 a.m., 1:30 p.m. and 3:30 p.m. with bridge.

47.7 **3'** **Norfolk Southern Railroad Swing Bridge:** Normally open; hand-operated. 866-527-3499.

50.7 **2'** **Elizabeth City Highway Bridges (U.S. 158):** Year-round, Mon.-Fri. Closed 7:00 a.m. to 9:00 a.m. and 4:00 p.m. to 6:00 p.m., but will open at 7:30 a.m., 8:30 a.m., 4:30 p.m., and 5:30 p.m. if vessels are waiting to pass. 252-331-4772.

NORTH CAROLINA BRIDGES MONITOR VHF CHANNEL 13

113.9 **65'** **Fairfield Bridge (SR 94):** Fixed.

125.9 **64'** **Walter B. Jones Bridge (Wilkerson, U.S. 264):** Fixed.

157.2 **65'** **Hobucken Bridge (SR 33/304):** Fixed.

195.8 **65'** **Core Creek Bridge (SR 101):** Fixed.

203.8 **65'** **Beaufort Channel Hwy. Bridge:** Fixed.

203.8 **4'** **Beaufort Channel RR Bascule Bridge (U.S. 70):** Normally open.

206.7 **65'** **Atlantic Beach - Morehead City Bridge (SR 1182):** Fixed.

226.0 **65'** **Cedar Point Highway Bridge:** Fixed.

240.7 **12'** **Onslow Beach Swing Bridge:** (Use northwest draw.) Year-round, daily, 7:00 a.m. to 7:00 p.m.: Opens on the hour and half hour. 910-450-7376.

252.3 **65'** **Highway Bridge:** Fixed.

260.7 **12'** **Surf City Swing Bridge (SR 50/210):** Year-round, daily, 7:00 a.m. to 7:00 p.m.: Opens on the hour. 910-328-4291. *New High Rise Being Built 6/16

278.1 **65'** **Figure Eight Island Swing Bridge:** Year-round, 24 hours daily: Opens every hour on the half hour. Opens on request weekends and federal holidays. 910-686-2018. (Clearance may be higher than charted.)

283.1 **20'** **Wrightsville Beach Bascule Bridge (SR 74):** Year-round, daily, 7:00 a.m. to 7:00 p.m.: Opens on the hour. 910-256-2886. (Clearance may be lower than charted.)

295.7 **65'** **Snows Cut Highway Bridge (U.S. 421):** Fixed.

311.8 **65'** **Highway Bridge (SR 133):** Fixed.

316.8 **65'** **Swains Cut Highway Bridge (SR 1105):** Fixed.

323.6 **65'** **Highway Bridge (SR 130):** Fixed.

333.7 **65'** **Ocean Isle Bridge (SR 904):** Fixed.

337.9 **65'** **Sunset Beach Bridge (SR 1172):** Fixed.

SOUTH CAROLINA BRIDGES MONITOR VHF CHANNEL 09

347.2 **65'** **Highway Bridge:** Fixed.

347.3 **7'** **Little River Swing Bridge (SR 20):** Year-round, daily: Opens on signal. 843-280-5919.

349.1 **65'** **Myrtle Beach Connector Bridge:** Fixed.

353.3 **31'** **Barefoot Landing Swing Bridge:** Year-round, daily: Opens on signal. 843-361-3291.

355.5 **65'** **Conway Bypass Bridge (U.S. 17):** Fixed.

357.5 **65'** **Grande Dunes Bridge:** Fixed.

360.5 **65'** **Grissom Parkway Bridge:** Fixed.

365.4 **16'** **SCL Railroad Bridge:** Normally open.

365.4 **65'** **Highway Bridge (U.S. 501):** Fixed.

366.4 **65'** **Fantasy Harbor Bridge:** Fixed.

371.0 **11'** **Socastee Swing Bridge (SR 544):** Opens on the hour and 15 minutes thereafter. Use southeast draw. 843-347-3525.

371.3 **65'** **Highway Bridge:** Fixed.

402.1 **65'** **Highway Bridge (U.S. 17):** Fixed.

411.5 **0'** **Ferry Crossing:** Do not try to pass a moving ferry.

458.9 **65'** **Isle of Palms Connector Bridge:** Fixed.

462.2 **65'** **Ben Sawyer Memorial Swing Bridge (SR 703):** Year-round, Mon.-Fri., except federal holidays. Closed 7:00 a.m. to 9:00 a.m. and from 4:00 p.m. to 6:00 p.m. Opens on the hour from 9:00 a.m. to 7:00 p.m. on weekends and holidays. All other times, open on demand. 843-883-3581.

469.9 **67'** **James Island Expressway Bridge:** Fixed.

470.8 **33'** **Wappoo Creek Bridge (SR 107/700):** April 1 to Nov. 30, Mon.-Fri., except federal holidays. Opens on the hour and half hour from 9:00 a.m. to 3:30 p.m. Weekends and holidays: Opens on the hour and half hour from 9:00 a.m. to 7:00 p.m. June 1 to Sept. 30 and Dec. 1 to March 30, Mon.-Fri., except federal holidays: Closed 6:30 a.m. to 9:00 a.m. and 3:30 p.m. to 6:30 p.m. April 1 to May 31 and Oct. 1 to Nov. 30, Mon.-Fri., except federal holidays: Closed 6:00 a.m. to 9:00 a.m. and 3:30 p.m. to 6:30 p.m. 843-852-4157.

479.3 **65'** **John F. Limehouse Hwy. Bridge:** Fixed.

501.3 **65'** **McKinley Washington Jr. Bridge (SR 174):** Fixed

536.0 **30'** **Ladies Island Swing Bridge (U.S. 21):** Year-round, Mon.-Fri., except federal holidays and weekends. Closed 7:00 a.m. to 9:00 a.m., again at 11:00 a.m. to 1:00 p.m., and 4:00 p.m. to 6:00 p.m. Otherwise opens only on the hour. From 6:00 p.m. to 7:00 a.m. opens on signal. 843-521-2111.

539.7 **65'** **McTeer Memorial Highway Bridge (SR 802):** Fixed.

557.6 **65'** **Twin Highway Bridges (U.S. 278):** Fixed.

GEORGIA BRIDGES MONITOR VHF CHANNEL 09

579.9 **65'** **Sam Varnedoe (Causton Bluff) Bascule Bridge (SR 26):** Year-round, Mon.-Fri., except federal holidays. Closed 6:30 a.m. to 9:00 a.m., 4:30 p.m. to 6:30 p.m. Opens only at 7:00 a.m., 8:00 a.m. and 5:30 p.m. during those times. 912-897-2511.

582.8 **65'** **State of Georgia Memorial Bridge (U.S. 80):** Fixed.

592.9 **22'** **Skidaway Bridge (SR 204):** Year-round, Mon.-Fri., except federal holidays. Opens on the hour from 7:00 a.m. to 9:00 a.m. and on the half hour from 4:30 p.m. to 6:30 p.m. Otherwise opens on signal. A high-rise replacement bridge is under construction at this time with a proposed completion date of 2013.

674.5 **65'** **F.J. Torras Causeway Bridge:** Fixed.

684.4 **65'** **Jekyll Island Bridge (SR 50):** Fixed.

Skipper's Notes

Inlets: Norfolk, VA to Florida

For many boaters, the thought of leaving the safe confines of the Intracoastal Waterway (ICW) for the open seas is terrifying. And for most of us, that is as it should be. While the open waters of the Atlantic can be serene, they can also turn deadly, it is no place for the unskilled or poorly prepared.

Yet for those mariners who have the skills, a capable well-found vessel and the mettle to venture out into the deep blue off the coast, the beauty and challenge to be found offshore is reward enough. Nevertheless, Mother Nature is capricious and the National Weather Service is not omniscient. Sometimes a day that begins with clear skies promised by the weatherman ends in tumult, with the captain swearing he will buy a motor home—in Idaho no less—if only he can get safely into port.

And as noted in the previous chapter, it isn't always shorter to run offshore. When you add the distances involved in leaving and returning to the ICW, you are often better off time-wise staying inside. To save any real time, particularly in a slower vessel such as a trawler or sailboat, you will need to run overnight. That means you need someone to spell you at the helm and, very often, only one partner of a cruising couple feels confident with that. Knowing that you have a convenient inlet to duck into should conditions offshore deteriorate certainly adds confidence, as well as an additional margin of safety, to your plans.

Inlets marked: The U.S. Coast Guard marks nearly all the inlets noted here; that was the criteria for inclusion. In many cases, however, NOAA does not chart those marks as they are often moved around to reflect current conditions. These inlets will be obvious on a large-scale chart of the area. If conditions are bad (or worse) when you reach the sea buoy for an inlet, you may find yourself in an untenable position, being driven ashore by wind or waves and unable to find the inlet buoys. It might be far better to remain well offshore in rough conditions, possibly continuing to a better inlet, unless the inlet you are considering is a Class A inlet for big ships, or one of the more easily run inlets, such as Masonboro. Regarding currents, we have listed the average maximums for each inlet when available.

Should you find yourself at an inlet and needing direction, a call on VHF Channel 16 for local knowledge is likely to bring you a response. Sea Tow and TowBoatU.S. are two other knowledgeable sources. The Coast Guard may also be able to assist you. By the way, distances to nearest recommended inlets are generally measured from sea buoy to sea buoy. These are approximate distances for rough planning purposes only and do not relieve the navigators from having to do their own calculations.

Prior to your voyage, there are a number of online sources that can familiarize you with the inlets; the WATERWAY GUIDE website (www.WaterwayGuide.com) has both chart and satellite views of the inlets via the Waterway Planner, plus details from local boaters, both of which are quite useful. Google Earth™ is another possibility, although the images you see may not be up to date. Obviously, this guide can give you helpful advice, particularly on what you will find inside the inlet. And you will need Coast Pilots, which can be downloaded free at www.nauticalcharts.noaa.gov.

With inlets, it is also vital that you keep up with the *Local Notice to Mariners,* which are available online at www.navcen.uscg.gov/ and click on LNMs tab. And the Tide Tables for the areas you are traveling through, of course. For running inlets, these are mandatory.

Some inlets have recent U.S. Army Corps of Engineers surveys in Adobe PDF format, which can be found at www.saw.usace.army.mil. These particular charts, when available, provide waypoint information, although it takes some patience to familiarize oneself with the format. Of particular use are the centerline waypoints and controlling depths they provide within the inlet. The exact locations of all aids to navigation in the inlet are also noted.

Check carefully the date of the survey to determine its applicability for your passage. Inlets, such as Lockwoods Folly, change rapidly, and even recent surveys may be inaccurate.

Offshore runs: There are certain passages that lend themselves to a short offshore run, and this discussion is covered in your Waterway Guide in the Skipper's Handbook section, along with inlet distances, which are very useful for planning purposes. Beaufort, NC to Wrightsville Beach, NC would be one such combination. Both inlets are wide and well-marked and the distance is such that even a sailboat can do the trip without overnighting. (Nevertheless, the sailor will be up long before dawn to make the run, while the powerboater will have had a leisurely breakfast ashore and sundowners at the dock before the sailor reaches the harbor.)

On the other hand, there are passages that don't work well. For example, if you are headed south, you don't want to come in at Beaufort, SC, as it entails a lengthy trip north from the sea buoy at Port Royal Sound. In that case, you would look at Tybee Roads to re-enter the ICW. This series on ICW inlets will assist you in evaluating those choices.

For those willing to do multi-day passages, offshore cruising can slash many days from the slog down the ICW, putting even sailors deep into Florida from Beaufort, NC in less than a week's time. As well, you avoid the challenges of ICW shoaling as well.

Skills, equipment: First, before you begin an offshore passage, take an honest accounting of your vessel, your crew and yourself. Is each of you up to the task? Is the vessel properly outfitted? Do you have the necessary safety equipment, charts, long distance communications gear such as single sideband radio (SSB), an Emergency Position Indicating Radio Beacon (EPIRB) and life raft? Do you and your crew have adequate experience in boating and navigation to attempt an offshore coastal passage? Don't kid yourself here. If you or your vessel aren't up to it, Mother Ocean will find you out, and you will come to regret the choices you have made.

Second, check the weather using as many sources as possible. If you have access to weather routing services, they are a good option, particularly for longer offshore passages. You are seeking a weather window with enough space on each side to get you safely out and back in, with room for unexpected contingencies.

Third, file a float plan with a reliable person. If all your good planning goes awry, this could well be your "ace in the hole" and someone will be able to locate you if you need assistance.

Arrive in daylight: Plan your trip so that you enter in daylight, with the tide, particularly if your boat is slow or underpowered. Remember that wind against tide can create short, steep waves in an inlet that can quickly make even a ship channel impassable for slower boats.

And plan for every contingency while underway. If things start to go wrong, head for that next inlet and deal with the problems from dockside. There are no awards for being foolish when you are offshore.

A safe offshore passage is an accomplishment. You will always remember your first one; the serenity of a calm dark night passage, the thrill of the sun rising after an endless night and the quiet confidence you feel deep inside as you bring your boat to anchor or dockside after many miles outside.

ICW Inlets

Corresponding charts not to be used for navigation.

Lynnhaven Inlet, Virginia

USE CHARTS 12205, 12221, 12222, 12254

(NOT TO BE USED FOR NAVIGATION.) Photo Courtesy of Cloud 9 Photography: Deagle/Kucera.

Sea buoy: There is no sea buoy here, use waypoint 36° 55.35N 76° 05.37W.

Overview: This is a good inlet to use if you are just coming in from an ocean passage or are planning to make a run offshore. It is located just southeast of the Chesapeake Bay Bridge Tunnel, inside Cape Henry.

Cautions and hazards: The straight, dredged entrance channel runs through a series of fixed and floating markers, then passes under a 35-foot fixed bridge. Other than the height restriction, there are no other hazards, except a fairly strong current through the bridge.

Navigation: The inlet was last dredged in late 2009. This is not a jettied inlet like many others. From the waypoint, proceed a quarter mile on a heading of 196° M to G '1L'. Just past red nun "6," you will encounter the fixed bridge with a vertical clearance of 35 feet. Provided you can clear this bridge, you can proceed to starboard for Pleasure House Pt. From there, you can proceed slightly to port then straight up the Lynnhaven River, or turn to port and take the inlet channel back to a number of marinas. Note that there are fixed bridges with 20- to 36-foot clearances to negotiate in this channel, which eventually leads to Broad Bay. There are anchoring possibilities in Broad Bay.

ICW connection: There is none.

Nearest recommended inlets: If you can not clear the bridges in Lynnhaven, you can proceed to Hampton Roads, 13 miles to the west, or proceed out and around Cape Henry to the south for about 14 miles to Rudee Inlet. Note that Rudee Inlet also does not connect with the ICW.

Nearby facilities: Lynnhaven Inlet provides easy and fast access to the Atlantic Ocean, Chesapeake Bay or the ICW via Hampton Roads. Marinas catering to sportfishermen abound. You can find transient berths, fuel, repairs, provisioning and marine supplies. The inlet also provides great access to Virginia Beach, VA.

Historical Note: Lynnhaven Inlet was used by colonials wanting to transit the Bay without being attacked by pirates. The ships would meet here, then travel the Bay together to try to thwart pirate attacks. Unfortunately, the pirates then decided they were easier prey at anchor in the Lynnhaven Bay and would catch them there like fish in a barrel. The English fought back, and a French pirate and his crew were hanged in England.

The inlet was also used during the Revolutionary War as an anchorage for the French fleet. The British hoped to accomplish the same feat as they had with the pirates, but the French helped the Americans defeat the British, which gave them the control of access to the Chesapeake. The British surrendered just five weeks later.

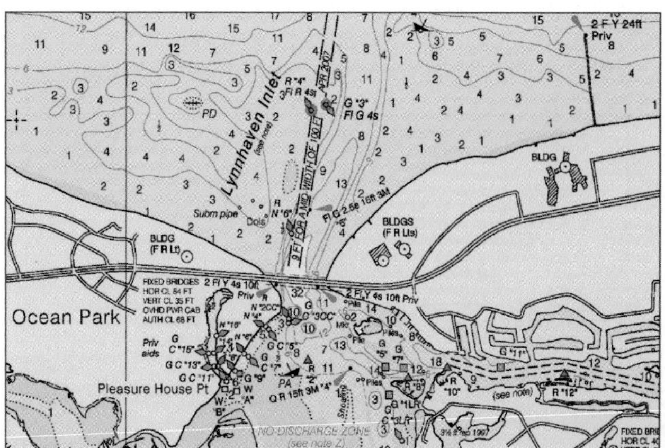

Rudee Inlet, Virginia

USE CHARTS 12200, 12205, 12208

(NOT TO BE USED FOR NAVIGATION.) WATERWAY GUIDE PHOTOGRAPHY.

Sea buoy: Lighted red and white Morse (A) whistle buoy "RI" in position 36° 49.79N 75° 56.95W

Overview: This is a good secondary inlet, particularly if you are staging for a passage to Cape May, NJ or beyond, because of the ease of access to the Atlantic compared to the nearest alternative, the Norfolk-Portsmouth area.

Cautions and hazards: The entrance has twin jetties and is straightforward. At certain times of the day and year, you may encounter a parade of sportfishing boats coming or going. The chart indicates that the inlet is subject to "continual shoaling." We suggest that deeper draft vessels seek local knowledge from the USCG or local towing companies before attempting to enter here due to unconfirmed recent reports of shoaling at the entrance.

Navigation: The inlet was dredged in Spring 2010. Two jetties protect Rudee Inlet. A dredged channel leads between the jetties to a basin just inside, then westward to a safety area about 0.2 miles above the entrance, and then northwestward to Lake Rudee. Lighted buoys and a fixed light mark Rudee Inlet. A lighted whistle buoy is located about one mile east-northeast of the jetties.

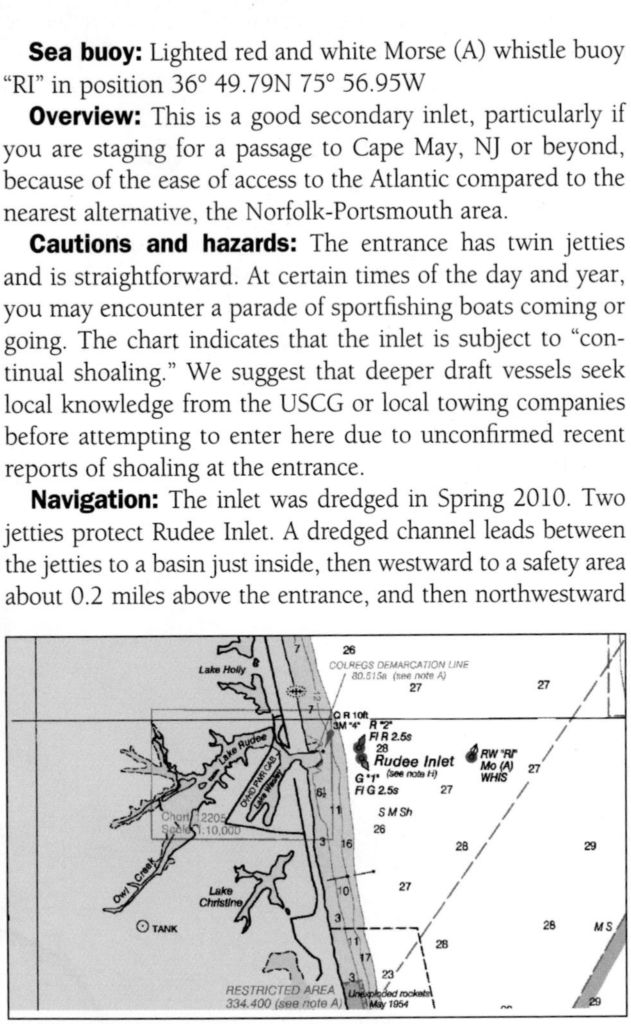

The inlet leads northward to Lake Rudee, and southward to Lake Wesley. Two fixed highway bridges with a vertical clearance of 28 feet cross the arm of the inlet leading to Lake Rudee. Several overhead power and telephone cables with charted vertical clearances of 54 feet cross east of the bridge.

The southward channel to Lake Wesley narrows at one point, shallowing to 7 feet. For tall masted vessels needing out of the Atlantic, this anchorage provides good shelter and avoids the bridge to Lake Rudee.

ICW connection: There is none.

Nearest recommended inlets: About 66 nautical miles to the south is Oregon Inlet, NC, recommended only in good weather and calm seas. Cape Henry, VA is five and a half nautical miles north at the entrance to the Chesapeake Bay.

Nearby facilities: Quick access to the Atlantic Ocean has made Rudee Inlet a haven for serious sportfishing aficionados. A municipal marina and two private marinas are on the north shore of Lake Rudee, west of the bridge. Berths, electricity, gasoline, diesel fuel, water, ice and marine supplies are available; engine and electrical repairs can also be arranged. The amenities of Virginia Beach, VA are nearby. There are no facilities on Lake Wesley.

Historical note: What is now Rudee Inlet began as a manmade drainage culvert. In 1968, the state created the current inlet, part of a $1 million plan to attract boaters. Now, regular dredging is part of a cycle of a system to replenish sand on the beaches of Virginia Beach.

Oregon Inlet, North Carolina

USE CHARTS 12204, 12205

(NOT TO BE USED FOR NAVIGATION.) WATERWAY GUIDE PHOTOGRAPHY.

Sea buoy: Lighted red and white Morse (A) whistle buoy "OI", at 35°47.26 N 75°30.42 W

Overview: Oregon Inlet, about 2.5 miles south of Bodie Island Light, is the most northerly of the Outer Banks inlets and is considered one of the most changeable of all East Coast inlets. Nonetheless, a large number of local sportfishing boats use Oregon Inlet regularly. Coast Guard Station Oregon Inlet is on Bodie Island north of the inlet. This inlet was surveyed in June 2011.

Cautions and hazards: Constant shoaling and strong currents make this inlet difficult at best. Up-to-date knowledge is a must to safely use this inlet. Radio the U.S. Coast Guard station for recent information on the placement of the markers. Do not attempt this inlet in foul weather! You would be far wiser—and safer—to stay well offshore and ride bad weather out. The Coast Guard reports that many smaller fishing boats capsize here each year.

Navigation: From the sea buoy, proceed to 35° 47' 29.530" N 75° 31' 3.238" W and follow the markers in. The channel is roughly SW in 15 feet of water. There are extensive shoals on both sides of the inlet entrance. The inlet shoals from over 30 feet at G "13" to about 10 feet past waypoint 5, then deepens closer to the bridge. Waypoint 7, in over 20 feet of water, is directly in front of the bridge span. The channel under the bridge carries better than 15 feet of water. Get the most recent information and use local knowledge.

On entering Pamlico Sound proper, the route to Oregon Inlet Fishing Center itself is winding, although well marked. Be wary of shoaling in the channel. The previous "route" paralleling the bridge is not viable in anything more than a dinghy.

Average maximum current and direction: 2.1 knots, 202 degrees on the flood; 1.2 knots, 028 degrees on the ebb. Tidal flows of as much as six knots have been reported.

ICW connection: A marked and dredged channel leads south to Pamlico Sound and the ICW.

Nearest recommended inlets: Rudee Inlet at Virginia Beach, VA is 66 nautical miles to the north. Nearby southbound inlets (but not recommended) are Hatteras (59 nautical miles) and Ocracoke (70 nautical miles) inlets. Beaufort, NC is an excellent inlet, but you will need to travel 127 nautical miles, going around Lookout Shoal, to reach it.

Nearby facilities: There are limited transient facilities and fuel at the Oregon Inlet Fishing Center.

Historical note: In 1873, Congress approved and appropriated funds for the building of 29 lifesaving stations, one of which was the Bodie Island Station, located on the south side of Oregon Inlet. In 1883, the station on the north side of Oregon Inlet (also known as Tommy's Hummock) was officially named the Bodie Island Station, and the "old" Bodie Island Station (south of the inlet) was renamed as the Oregon Inlet Station. These are the predecessors to the current Coast Guard Station on Bodie Island.

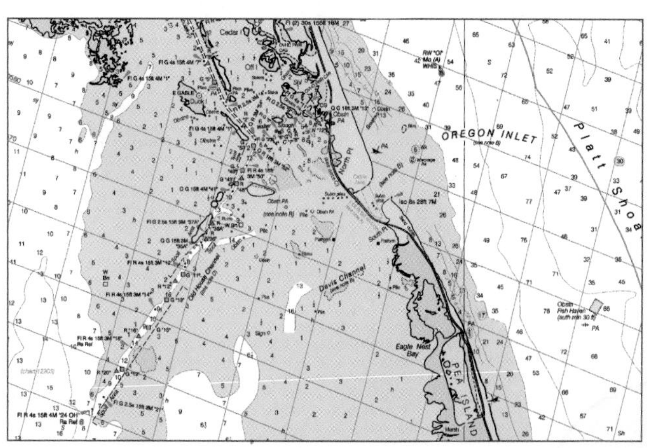

Hatteras Inlet, North Carolina

USE CHART 11555, 12200

(NOT TO BE USED FOR NAVIGATION.) WATERWAY GUIDE PHOTOGRAPHY.

Sea buoy: Lighted red and white Morse (A) whistle buoy "HI", in position at 35°09.97N 75°45.25W just over 1 nm from the inlet.

Overview: From a high point of land in this area, one can see Diamond Shoals, whose constantly breaking waters extend well over 10 miles out into the Atlantic. This is not an inlet for the timid, for the inexperienced and certainly not a choice in any sort of bad weather. Coast Guard Station Hatteras Inlet is located on Austin Creek.

Cautions and hazards: We recommend against using this inlet, as the channel shifts constantly, frequently shoaling to 4 feet. The information in this section is provided with the warning that conditions may render it inaccurate by the time you read it. The Corps of Engineers surveyed this inlet in February 2011 and the inlet chart as a pdf is available at www.saw.usace.army.mil/nav/inlets.htm. It is strongly suggested that you seek local information before using this inlet. Once inside the inlet, depths drop significantly, rendering it of little utility to deep draft cruising boats.

Navigation: This inlet changes frequently, so it is imperative to seek local knowledge before trying to enter. Hatteras Island light at 88 feet (ISO, six seconds) on the east side of the inlet is a conspicuous mark. From the sea buoy, proceed slightly west of north to the entrance markers, which are frequently moved based on recent conditions.

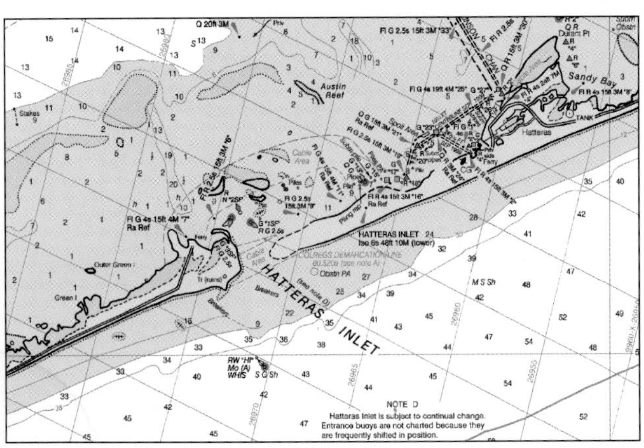

Average maximum current and direction: 2.1 knots, 307 degrees on the flood; 2 knots, 148 degrees on the ebb.

ICW connection: As part of the Outer Banks, this area is quite a distance via the Rollinson Channel from the ICW. Deep draft boats will be unable to reach the channel due to shoal areas on the inside in the vicinity of Hatteras Island light.

Nearest recommended inlets: Oregon Inlet, 59 nautical miles to the north, is a possibility but only with local knowledge. Farther north, Rudee Inlet is 130 nautical miles away, out and around Cape Hatteras but provides no access to the ICW. Southbound, after rounding Cape Lookout Shoals, the deepwater inlet at Beaufort, NC is 67 nautical miles away.

Nearby facilities: Hatteras is a major sportfishing center, and facilities are geared toward these requirements. There is some transient dockage available, along with diesel fuel, gasoline and marine supplies.

Historical note: The first Hatteras Inlet was formed south of the current inlet but closed around 1764. The modern-day Hatteras Inlet was formed on September 7, 1846 by a violent gale. This was the same storm that opened present-day Oregon Inlet to the north. This became a profitable inlet because it gave the Inner Banks a quicker and easier way to travel to and from the productive Gulf Stream fishing waters. Because of the increase in commerce, Hatteras Village Post Office was established in 1858. The initial invasion of the North Carolina coast during the Civil War, called Battle of Hatteras Inlet Batteries, came from Hatteras Inlet. The two Confederate forts guarding the inlet quickly fell. The Graveyard of the Atlantic Museum is also located here.

Ocracoke Inlet, North Carolina

USE CHART 11550, 11555

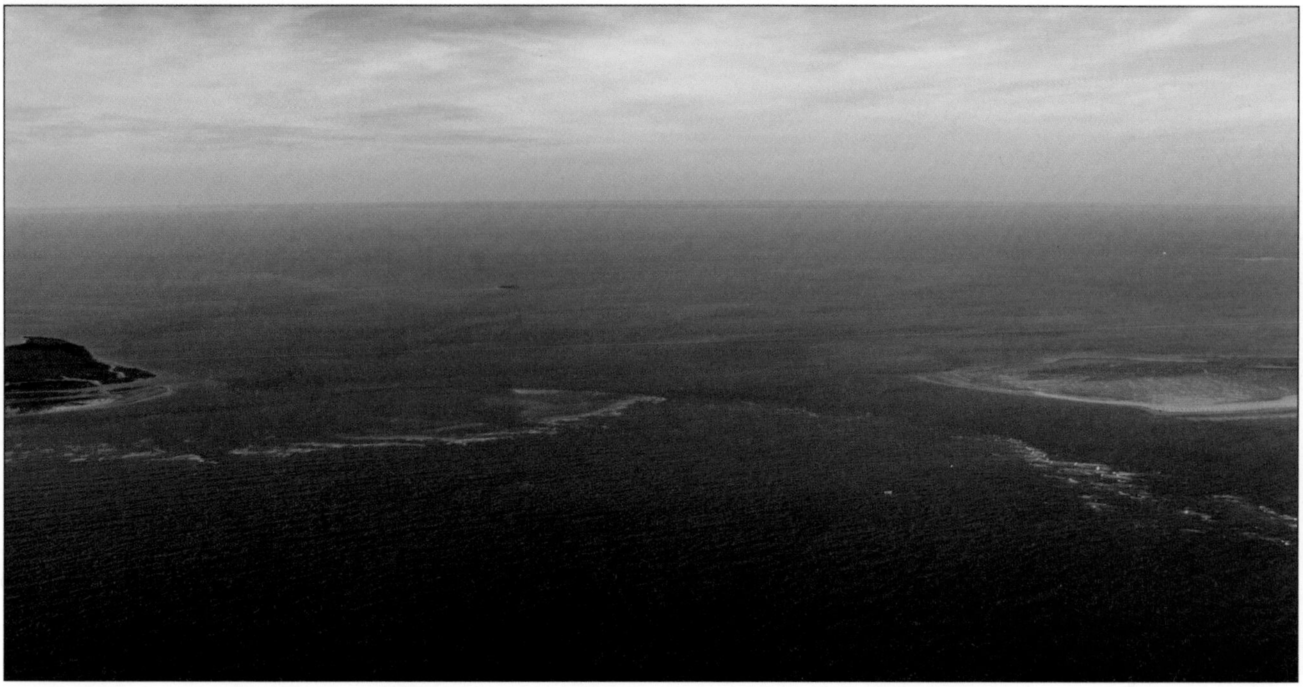

(NOT TO BE USED FOR NAVIGATION.) WATERWAY GUIDE PHOTOGRAPHY.

Sea buoy: Lighted red and white Morse (A) whistle buoy "OC", located at 35°03.11N 75°58.62W.

Overview: This inlet is the most southerly of the Outer Banks inlets. Although protected from the north, shoaling is constant and breakers on both sides are evident in nearly all conditions. This is not an inlet to be attempted under anything but the most benign conditions and, without local knowledge, not even then. Coast Guard Station Ocracoke (a small unit) is located on Ocracoke Island north of the inlet and is subordinate to Station Hatteras.

Cautions and hazards: Due to changing conditions, many aids to navigation are not charted. Contact the local towing operators or Coast Guard Station Ocracoke for local knowledge and up-to-date conditions. Shoaling is constant here and the channel is being redefined regularly.

Navigation: For offshore reference, Ocracoke Light stands 75 feet above the water with a flashing white light on the western part of Ocracoke Island and about three miles northeast of Ocracoke Inlet, south of Silver Lake. Entry is simple, but shoaling on both sides of the channel dictates careful seamanship. Aids to navigation are changed frequently to reflect the changing channel. Average maximum current and direction: 1.7 knots, 0 degrees on the flood; 2.4 knots, 145 degrees on the ebb.

ICW information: This inlet is a good distance off the ICW, but shallow-water navigation through Big Foot Slough Channel and on through Pamlico Sound can get you there.

Nearest recommended inlets: Though poor choices in anything but calm conditions (and using local knowledge), Hatteras and Oregon inlets are nearby to the north at 13 and 71 nautical miles, respectively. Rudee Inlet, VA, is 136 nautical miles out and around Cape Hatteras to the north and has no access to the ICW. Southbound, the distance to Beaufort, NC going outside Cape Lookout Shoals is 64 nautical miles.

Nearby facilities: Ocracoke is part of the Outer Banks islands and mostly home to sportfishermen. Facilities are largely geared to their needs, although there is a full-service marina and an inn. The sunsets are reputed to be magnificent. Those wishing to anchor will find good holding and lots of room in Silver Lake.

Historical note: The residents of this area have stoutly resisted modernization and change and a visit here is very much a trip back to the way it used to be. Ocracoke is part of the area known as the Graveyard of the Atlantic, due to the many shipwrecks over the centuries—thousands according to some sources.

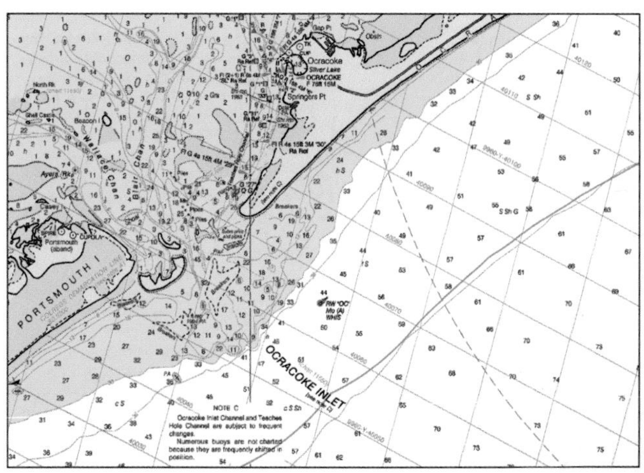

Lookout Bight/Barden Inlet, North Carolina

USE CHART 11544, 11545

Sea buoy: None.

Overview: Barden Inlet is shoal and not advisable for cruising boats. The big ship channel of Beaufort NC is only 6.5 nm miles away and is a much safer choice. Barden Inlet is popular with pleasure boats in good summer weather. The area behind Lookout Bight leading to the inlet offers shelter to all but northerly winds and even then, some shelter can be found within.

Cautions and hazards: There are many shallow, unmarked shoals within Barden Inlet itself. Be wary of strong currents during tide changes.

Navigation: Note: controlling depth of the inlet was 4 feet in 2009. Navigation markers are moved as required to reflect changing conditions.

For Lookout Bight, use the waypoint N 34° 38.260'/ W 76° 32.950'. Proceed to the waypoint from the west or south while staying clear of the shoal building north from Power Squadron Spit, marked by flashing red buoy "4." Once you have cleared flashing red buoy "4," turn to the south into the large basin with 25-foot depths. Barden Inlet is located off to the east, but is shoal.

ICW connection: Neither safe nor practical for cruising boats.

Nearest recommended inlet: Regardless of whether you are north or southbound, continue six and a half nautical miles west to Beaufort, NC to reenter the ICW.

Nearby facilities: None. Anchorage is possible at red daybeacon "6" near Wreck Point in 7 to 14 feet of water.

Historical notes: Home to whalers and Spanish privateers in the 18th century, Lookout Bight is the location of the distinctively diamond-patterned Cape Lookout Lighthouse. The wreck of the schooner Chrissie Wright occurred here on Diamond Shoals, where the entire crew but the cook perished in view of the shore, and rescuers were unable to reach them until the next day due to the large breakers.

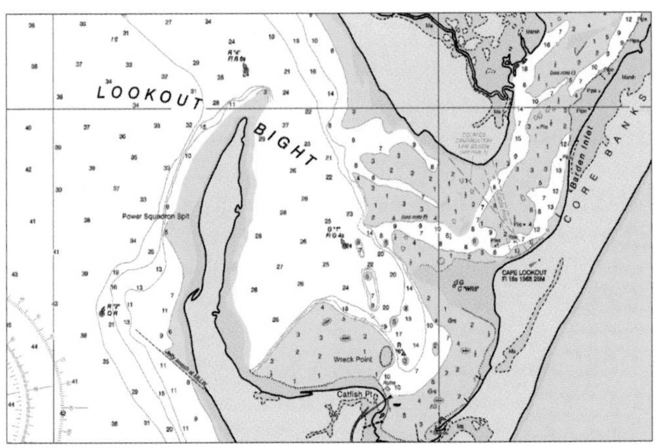

Beaufort Inlet, North Carolina

USE CHART 11544, 11547

(NOT TO BE USED FOR NAVIGATION.) WATERWAY GUIDE PHOTOGRAPHY.

Sea Buoy: Lighted red and white Morse (A) (RACON) whistle buoy "BM" located at 34°34.83N 76°41.55W.

Overview: Beaufort, NC is a big ship inlet—wide, deep and very well marked.

Cautions and hazards: On entering the inlet itself, keep clear of the wide expanse of water to your starboard side, as it is mostly shoal. You will find a great many small-boat fishermen inside and outside of the inlet who will bear watching, particularly past the turning basin heading south to the ICW.

Navigation: As this is a big ship entrance, you can forgo the sea buoy, which is more than five miles out, and start your approach from flashing green buoy "9" and flashing red bell buoy "10", which are just southwest of 34°40 N, 76°40W. From here, follow the markers on a course slightly east of north to quick flashing red "16" on Shackleford Point, then bear west of north. If you are headed for Beaufort itself, take the channel leading to the east side of Radio Island, taking care to round quick flashing red buoy "2." Don't cut flashing red buoy "20" short unless you care to employ local towboat operators. If your destination is Morehead City, bear to port at flashing green buoy "21," and then continue to follow the big ship markers. Shoaling was reported at quick flashing red "16" in March 2009.

Average maximum current and direction: Two knots, 307 degrees on the flood; 1.8 knots, 151 degrees on the ebb.

ICW connection: Proceed to the turning basin (ICW Mile 204) and bear to port if you are heading south on the ICW. If heading north, continue through the high fixed bridge (75-foot vertical clearance) immediately ahead of you. Beaufort is the farthest "northerly" inlet recommended for transient recreational boaters. To the north lie the Outer Banks; rounding them entails a long passage in Atlantic Ocean waters.

Nearest recommended inlets: Barden Inlet is about six nautical miles to the east at Cape Lookout, and though it is no longer considered navigable for cruising vessels, a sheltered anchorage can be found behind Cape Lookout. Bogue Inlet is 20 nautical miles to the southwest. Masonboro Inlet at Wrightsville Beach, NC, a popular passage choice in settled weather, is about 65 nautical miles distant.

Nearby facilities: The marine facilities, especially in Beaufort, are so comprehensive you will want for nothing, including waterfront wireless Internet service. Groceries, hardware and other provisions entail a short trip outside of the downtown area. The nearest West Marine is in Morehead City, a five-minute cab ride from the Beaufort waterfront. Those cruisers anchoring will head for the Beaufort side and anchor in Taylor Creek, a popular and busy anchorage. There is a dinghy dock towards the eastern end of the anchorage.

Historical note: Pirate Edward Teach, popularly known as Blackbeard, lost his ship Queen Ann's Revenge in 1718 after running aground at Beaufort Inlet. There is a fascinating multimedia display at the Beaufort Maritime Museum on his story and the continuing excavation of his vessel. Naval forces off Ocracoke Island later killed Blackbeard, but his head came home through Beaufort Inlet, hanging on the bowsprit of the ship that captured him.

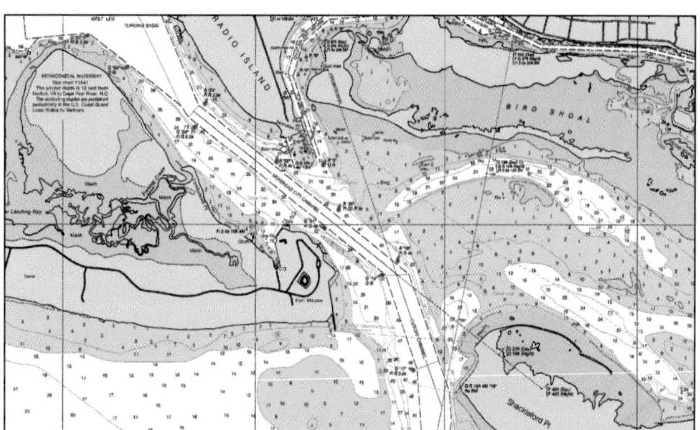

Bogue Inlet, North Carolina

USE CHART 11541

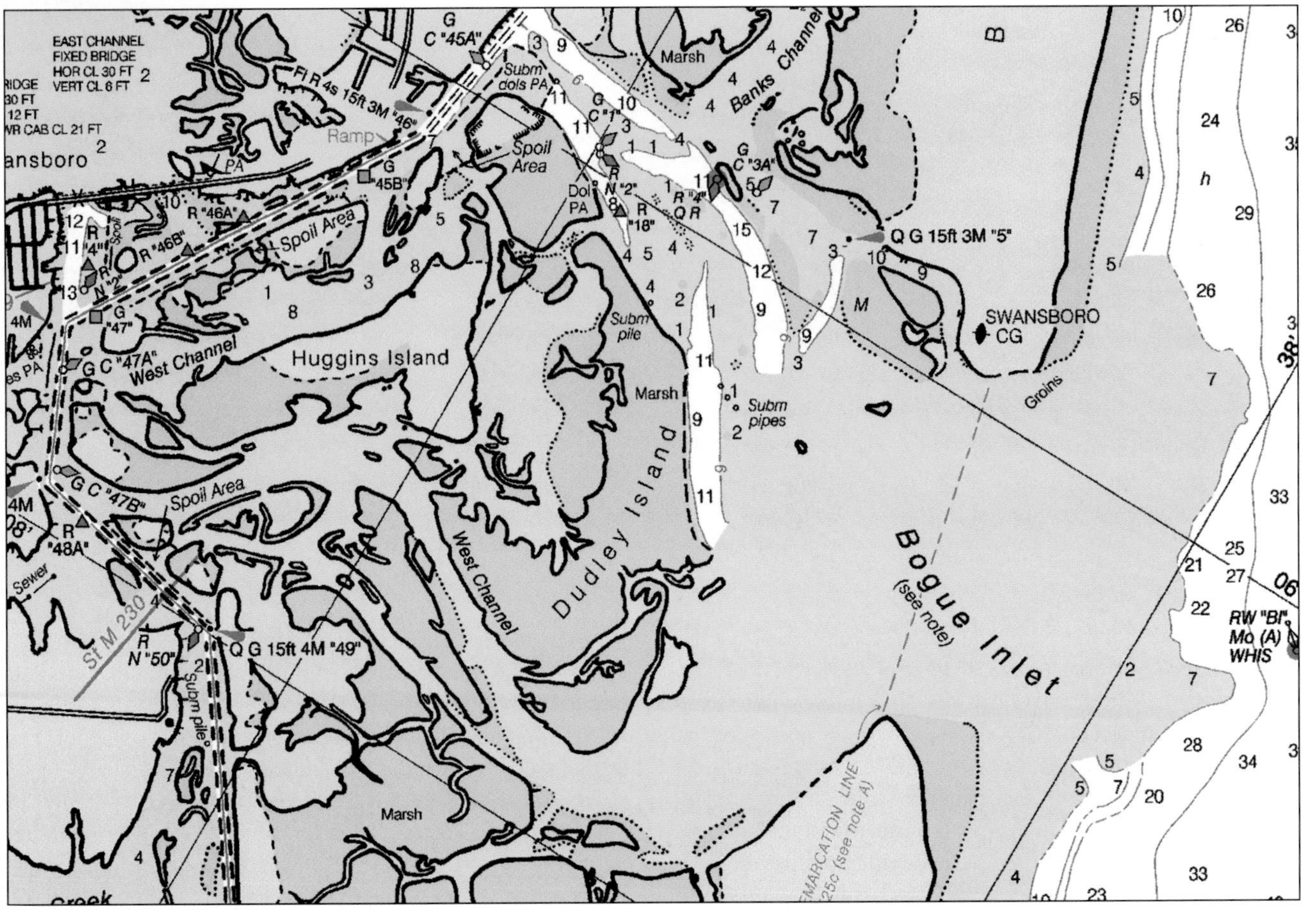

Sea buoy: Lighted red and white Morse (A) whistle buoy "BI" at 34°37.63N 77°06W

Overview: This would be a poor choice of inlets for cruising boats without local knowledge, but Coast Guard Station Swansboro is located on the north side of the inlet, should assistance be required. Shoaling to 2 feet was reported in spring 2011.

Cautions and hazards: We cannot possibly recommend this inlet except in the most dire of circumstances. This is an inlet for which you must have local knowledge, as the entrance is narrow, and the contours are constantly changing, with unlit buoys moved accordingly. It is not suitable for vessels carrying more than 4-foot drafts. Do not attempt this inlet at other than on a rising tide (half-tide or better), and, if at all possible, follow a local boat. If the emergency is medical, wait offshore for the Coast Guard to come to you rather than attempting this entrance. There are breakers on both sides of the narrow channel. If the weather is deteriorating, divert to New River Inlet about 20 nautical miles south.

Navigation: If you are in doubt on your approach to this inlet, use the flashing yellow buoy "A," which is well offshore of the inlet, for your initial approach. The sea buoy itself is about one nautical mile away on a course of 349 degrees magnetic. The inlet runs roughly northeast and the deepest water runs to the northern side of the entrance. Depths inside the inlet are normally 6 feet at mean low water, but be aware that the channel approaching the ICW is quite narrow.

ICW connection: The ICW intersects Bogue Inlet channel at Mile 228.

Nearest recommended inlets: The entrance to Beaufort is 21 nautical miles to the east-northeast. Masonboro, a good secondary inlet, is 44 nautical miles to the southwest.

Nearby facilities: Bogue Inlet leads to the town of Swansboro, NC, and there are several marinas to the south of the inlet. The area offers any marine facilities you may require, although a cab is required for other provisioning. For those anchoring, the anchorage described in the Waterway Guide Mid Atlantic edition, opposite Caspar's Marina, is a popular one.

Historical note: Long an important maritime port, Swansboro was the homeport of the American War of 1812 privateer Snap Dragon, whose captain, Otway Burns, forged a colorful career. Among other incidents of note, he once sunk a boat carrying a group of constables sent to arrest him and, when a lawyer attempted to harass him over his activities, he rowed to shore and pitched the offending gentleman into the river.

New River Inlet, North Carolina

USE CHARTS 11539, 11542

(NOT TO BE USED FOR NAVIGATION.) WATERWAY GUIDE PHOTOGRAPHY.

Sea buoy: Lighted red and white Morse (A) whistle buoy "NR" is located at approximately 34°31N 77°19.5W and is subject to being moved.

Overview: New River Inlet is another inlet that is best left alone by cruising vessels, with serious shoaling on a continuous basis and shoals awash in waves with any sort of sea conditions.

Cautions and hazards: Shoaling, breaking seas, an unmarked fish haven and, according to one source, 4-foot depths at mean high water.

Navigation: Not suitable for cruising boats.

ICW connection: The ICW is about a mile and a half north of the inlet entrance at Mile 227.6.

Nearest recommended inlets: Beaufort, NC is 33 nautical miles to the northeast, while Masonboro Inlet, NC, a good choice in settled conditions, lies 31 nautical miles to the southwest.

Nearby facilities: There are marinas to the north and south of the inlet and a favored anchorage, Mile Hammock, is close by.

Historical note: Camp Lejeune is located nearby and one will often see Marines on exercises. The kids will be thrilled as they roar by in their inflatable vessels, complete with weaponry, or operate tanks or trucks towing artillery on the east side of the ICW. Skippers knowing that this gear constitutes targets for shooting exercises may be a little less sanguine about them, as it could mean the ICW might be closed for a period of time to navigation.

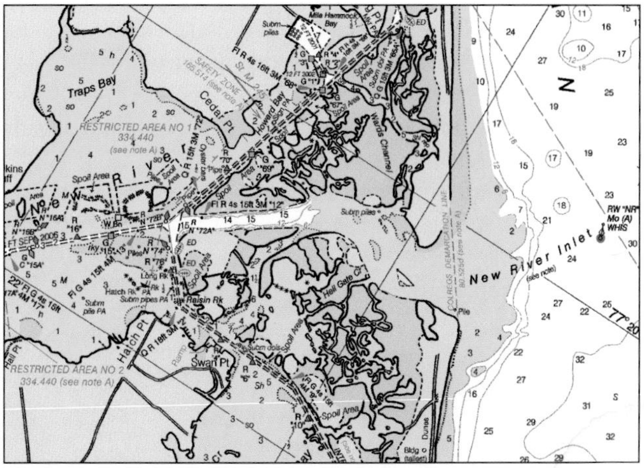

New Topsail Inlet, North Carolina

USE CHART (Uncharted, Use 11541 to Approach.)

(NOT TO BE USED FOR NAVIGATION.) WATERWAY GUIDE PHOTOGRAPHY.

Sea buoy: Lighted red and white Morse (A) whistle buoy "NT" at 34°20.10N 77°38.56W.

Overview: New Topsail Inlet is primarily used by local fishermen and although some reports state entry is possible, this is not a reasonable route for vessels with more than a 4-foot draft to reach the ICW, particularly if there is any sea at all. Given that Masonboro Inlet is close by to the south, we cannot recommend this inlet for cruisers.

Cautions and hazards: New Topsail Inlet is noted for changing drastically after storms and is not recommended for strangers. It has extensive breakers and shoaling.

Navigation: Seek local knowledge. Controlling depth in December 2007 was 6 feet.

ICW connection: A long and narrow shoal channel leads to the ICW at Mile 263.7.

Nearest recommended inlet: Masonboro Inlet is 12.5 nautical miles to the southeast. Beaufort Inlet is 50 nautical miles to the northeast.

Nearby facilities: See Masonboro Inlet.

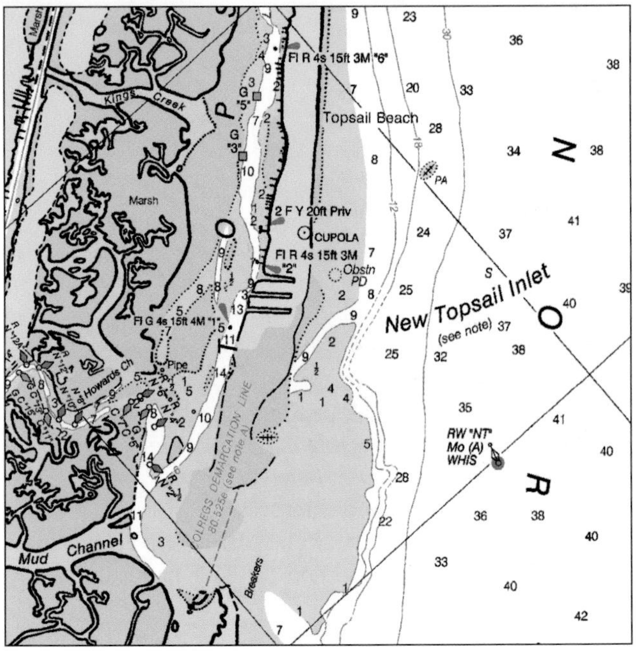

Mason Inlet, North Carolina

USE CHART (Uncharted, Use 11541 to Approach.)

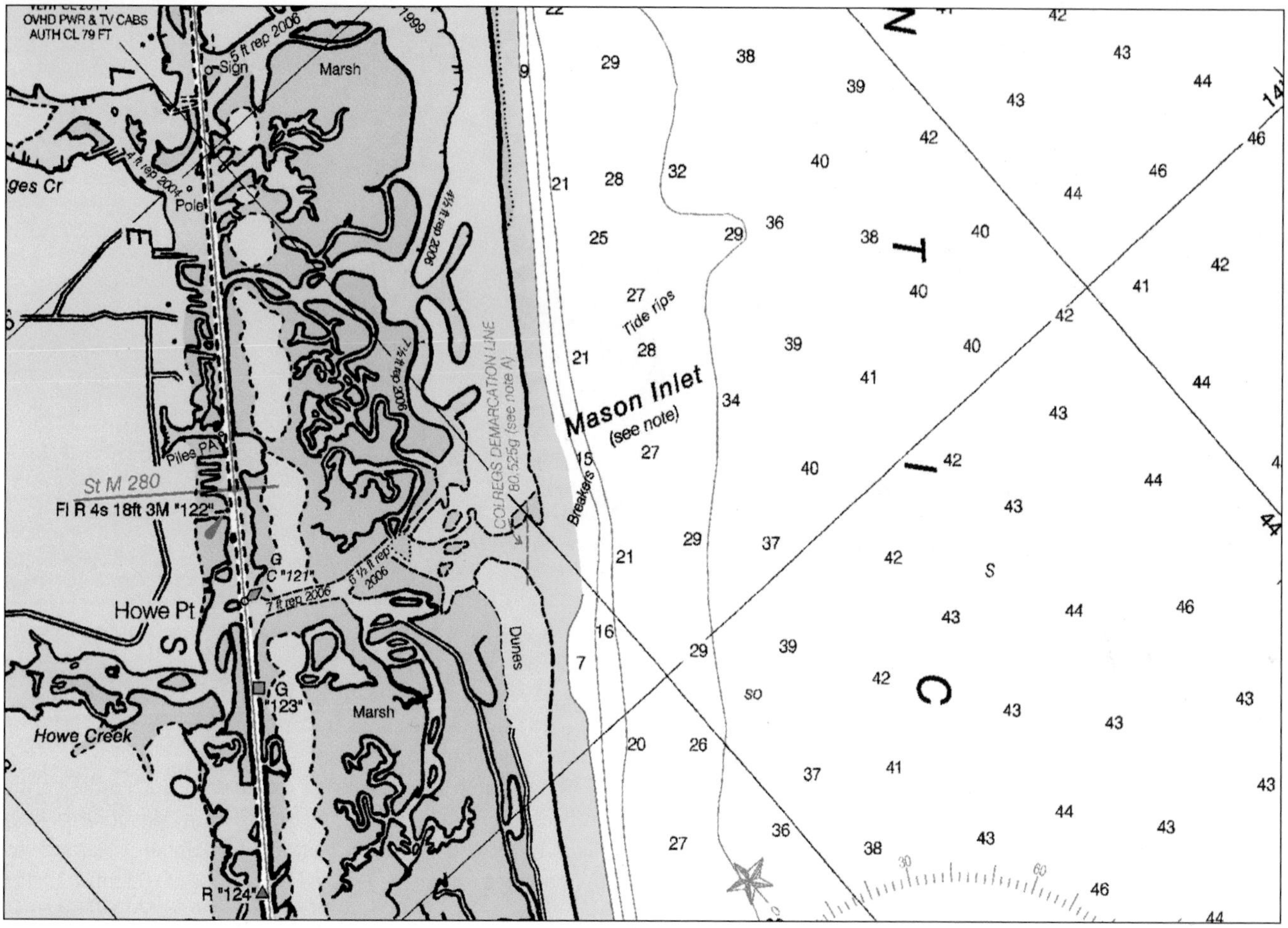

Sea buoy: None.

Overview: Waypoint N 34° 14.500'/W 077° 45.640' is .4 nautical miles from the inlet. A February 2010 survey by the Army Corps of Engineers indicates a 12-foot controlling depth at the ICW/inlet crossing. Local fishermen primarily use Mason Inlet, and although there are reports stating entry is possible, this is not a reasonable route for vessels carrying over 4r feet of draft to reach the ICW, particularly if any seas are running. Given that Masonboro Inlet is close by to the south, we cannot recommend this inlet for cruisers.

Cautions and hazards: There are extensive breakers and shoaling at the inlet. In August 2007, local reports gave depths of 4 to 7 feet at mean low water in the center of the channel.

Navigation: Unknown at present.

ICW connection: Vessels entering via these inlets must cruise a long narrow and shoal channel to reach the ICW just past Mile 280.

Nearest navigable inlets: Masonboro Inlet is four nautical miles to the south.

Nearby facilities: See Masonboro Inlet.

Historical note: In March 2002, Mason Inlet was cut through at a location about 3,500 feet northeast of what was then Mason Inlet. A week after the successful opening of the new inlet, the old Mason Inlet was closed. This engineering work, sponsored by local interests, was in response to the southward migration of Mason Inlet over the years to the point where it was threatening to undermine the Shell Island Resort and community to the south.

Masonboro Inlet, North Carolina

USE CHART 11541

(NOT TO BE USED FOR NAVIGATION.) WATERWAY GUIDE PHOTOGRAPHY.

Sea buoy: Lighted red and white Morse (A) whistle buoy "A" at 34°10.6N 77°47.87W

Overview: Masonboro Inlet is the first major inlet south of Beaufort, NC and is popular with sportfishermen. It is an uncomplicated entrance protected by jetties on both sides and has good depths within.

Cautions and hazards: There are no particular difficulties with this inlet, although a southeasterly wind can cause difficult conditions for smaller boats.

Navigation: From the sea buoy, the jetties lie to the northwest and are unmarked. Once inside, if you are headed to Wrightsville Beach, NC, bear to starboard at green and red daybeacon "WC" and then turn to port at Motts Channel a bit farther up. If Masonboro is your destination, continue straight ahead.

ICW connection: ICW Mile 285 lies straight ahead past Shinn Creek after entering.

Nearest recommended inlets: Masonboro is a good inlet for faster boats or for early-rising sailors or trawler skippers wanting to get off the ICW to or from Beaufort, NC, which is just under 65 nautical miles to the northeast. Some slow-boat skippers make this an overnight passage, arriving at either end shortly after sunrise.

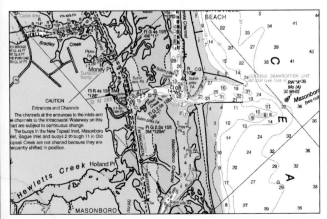

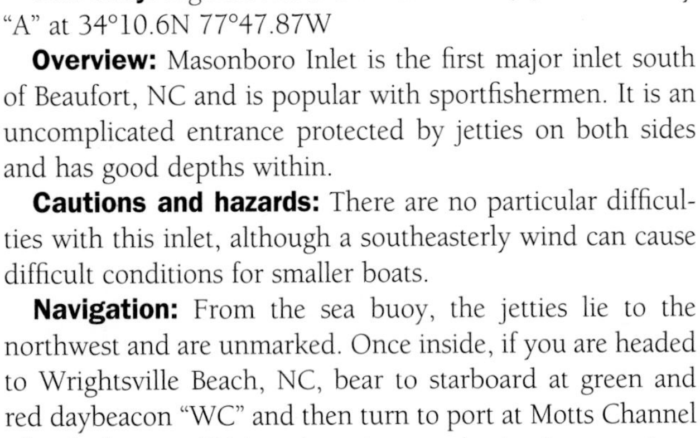

Though the Cape Fear River entrance lies 25 miles to the south as the gull flies, getting there from Masonboro Inlet means having to go around Frying Pan Shoals, making the outside distance to the Cape Fear entrance 85 nm. In flat calm weather, the trip could be shortened to 65 nm by coming inside of R '2FP' but we do not recommend this as it is quite shoal here.

Carolina Beach Inlet is six nautical miles to the south, but a wiser and quicker course is to continue on the ICW from Masonboro, enter the Cape Fear River through Snows Cut, catch the outgoing tide and proceed to Southport (or detour upriver to visit Wilmington).

Nearby facilities: Coast Guard Station Wrightsville Beach is at the southern end of Wrightsville Beach at Masonboro Inlet just past red daybeacon "10." There is a full range of facilities in the area, including several marinas and a West Marine less than a mile from the ICW. You will also find restaurants, banking, hardware stores and a convenient nearby location for propane refills. For those wanting to anchor, follow the channel towards Wrightsville Beach but continue straight ahead towards the low fixed bridge. Anchoring is excellent in 10 feet or more of water. The town has a free dinghy dock near the bridge.

Historical note: In November 1862, Union warships forced blockade running British schooner F.W. Pindar aground at the inlet and sent a boat crew to destroy the vessel. The boat swamped, and the crew was captured after successfully firing on the schooner. In the same month, the Union Navy ran the British bark Sophia aground and destroyed her near the inlet as well.

Carolina Beach Inlet, North Carolina

USE CHARTS 11534, 11539

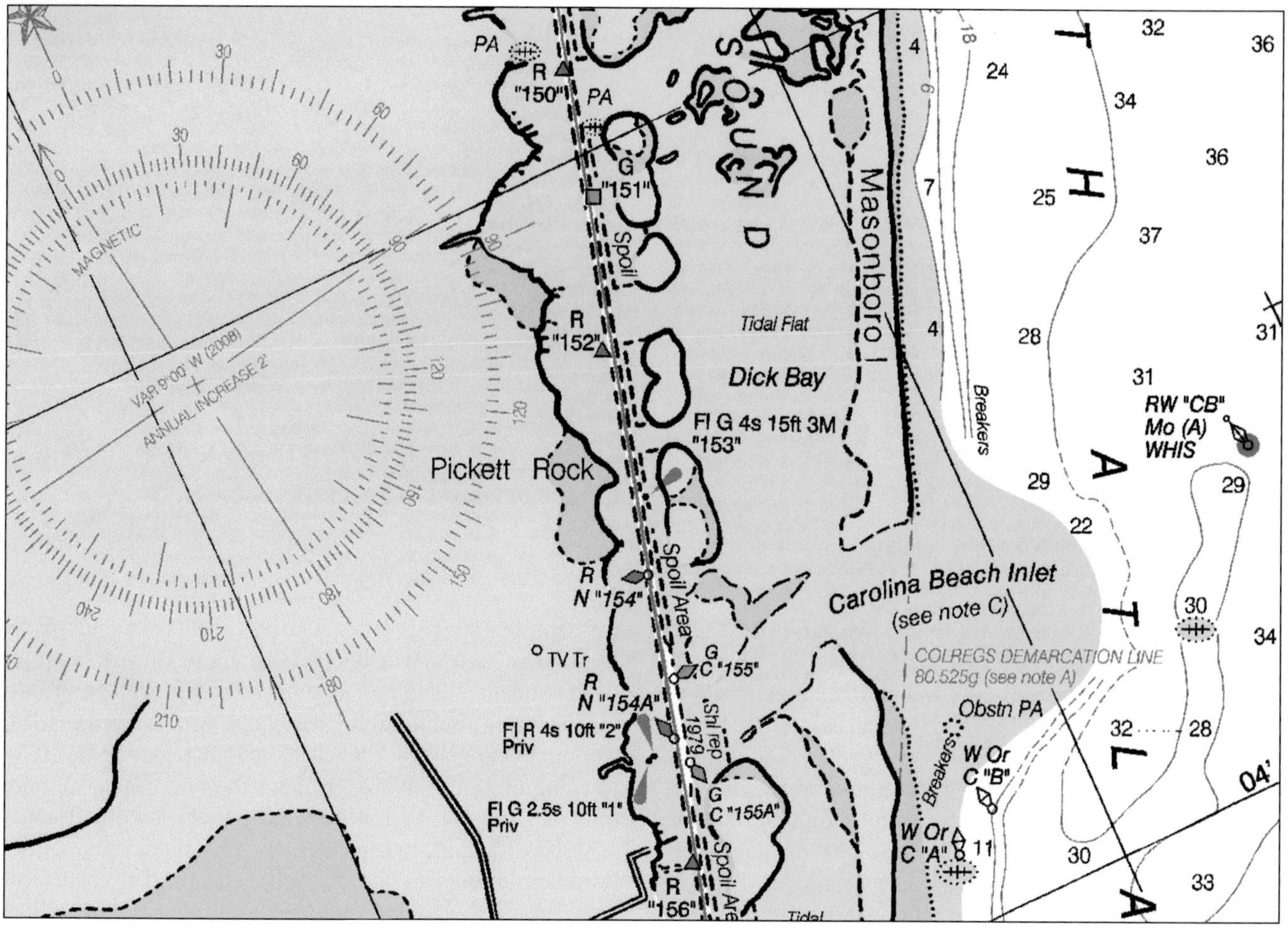

Sea buoy: Lighted red and white Morse (A) whistle buoy "CB" at 34°04.74N 77°51.19W.

Overview: Due to shifting sands, the entrance buoys to this inlet are not charted. With Masonboro Inlet nearby, there is no reason for cruisers to transit through to the ICW via this inlet. The ICW inside the inlet has been subject to shoaling in the recent past. A call to the local towboat operators is advised when passing through here.

Cautions and hazards: The channel connecting to the ICW had a controlling depth of 7 feet as of May 2011. Breaking waves are present throughout the inlet in most conditions.

Navigation: Not recommended for cruising boats. A USACE survey shows waypoints through the inlet and is available at http://www.saw.usace.army.mil/nav/INLETS/Carolina_Beach/cbix_2011-05-09ad.pdf. Note that conditions here change rapidly, the survey may be out of date by the time you arrive. Local knowledge is mandatory here.

ICW connection: The channel intersects the ICW at Mile 293.5.

Nearest navigable inlets: Masonboro Inlet is 7 nautical miles to the north, while the entrance to Beaufort, NC is 61 nautical miles to the northeast. The Cape Fear River is south of here but requires rounding Frying Pan Shoals, making for a very long trip.

Nearby facilities: As a busy resort, Carolina Beach has many restaurants and grocery stores. An excellent, if often crowded, anchorage may be found in the bight behind the barrier beach, which is entered by going straight after flashing green "161" if you are southbound. Taking Snows Cut to starboard heading south, there is a state-run marina at the junction of the cut and the Cape Fear River which has finally reopened after several years being closed. The entrance is reportedly only 4 feet deep and dockage is limited to vessels 40 feet and under.

Historical note: Shoaling closed the original Carolina Beach Inlet in the early 1900s. It was blasted open again with explosives in 1952.

Cape Fear River, North Carolina

USE CHART 11536, 11537

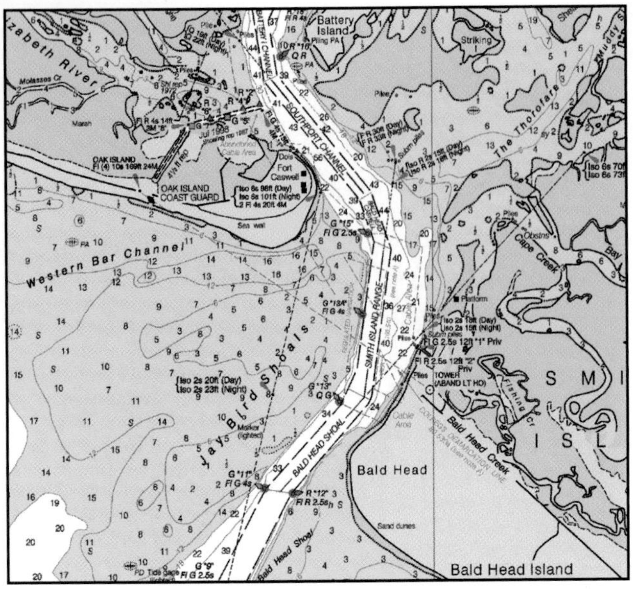

Sea buoy: Lighted red and white Morse (A) (RACON) whistle buoy "CF" at 33°46.28N 78°03.02W.

Overview: Cape Fear Inlet is a well-marked big ship channel that is protected from the north and an easy entrance day or night.

Cautions and hazards: Daytime entrances are straightforward. As this is a busy inlet, keep a constant watch posted for big ships using it. As many as a half dozen freighters may pass by in an hour while transiting Cape Fear River. The current here is very strong; time your entrance to take advantage of the tides.

Navigation: This inlet was dredged in May 2009. The sea buoy is five miles out in deep water. Cruisers can approach using the waypoint 33°50.37N 78°01.78W, which is close aboard red buoy "8" where the surrounding waters begin to shallow. From flashing red buoy "8," proceed slightly east of north to quick flashing red buoy "10" and then to quick flashing red buoy "12," where you can pick up the Bald Head Shoal Range.

ICW connection: The entrance meets up with the ICW at Mile 308.5. Heading north, the ICW follows the big ship channel toward Wilmington. To head south on the ICW, bear to port at Southport itself. For those headed north, wisdom dictates using the ICW here to avoid a significant detour around Frying Pan Shoals, which extend 30 miles out into the Atlantic. Those northbound in slower boats would be well-advised to check the tides before attempting the Cape Fear River's strong currents, which will make a significant dent in your progress if they are against you.

Average maximum current and direction: 2.2 knots, 034 degrees on the flood; 2.9 knots, 190 degrees on the ebb.

Nearest recommended inlets: The Cape Fear River is a good inlet for snowbirds heading south, with several good inlets to duck into should conditions deteriorate. The first is Little River Inlet, SC, which is about 24 nautical miles to the west-southwest. This takes you past the Lockwood's Folly and Shallote inlets, which have been known in years past for severe shoaling. The best option, however, is Winyah Bay, SC (65 nautical miles to the sea buoy), with its well-marked shipping channel. The drawback is that rejoining the ICW to continue south involves coming back north over 8 miles into the inlet, or 15 miles if Georgetown is your destination. Northbound, meanwhile, any coastal passage requires rounding Frying Pan Shoals, so the most prudent tactic is to continue northward on the ICW and use Masonboro Inlet at Wrightsville Beach, NC as your jumping-off point to go offshore to Beaufort NC.

Nearby facilities: There are several marinas in the Southport area with complete facilities for cruisers. The town of Southport itself is a pleasant stopover, with an attractive and charming downtown. For provisioning, you will need to hail a taxi, as grocery stores and other necessities are outside of the downtown. You may be fortunate enough to be offered a ride from one of the locals who are quite friendly.

The small anchorage inside Southport Harbor will hold two or three boats carefully anchored in about 6 to 7 feet of water. Dredging of the harbor has been discussed but not yet accomplished. There are several anchoring possibilities to the south alongside the ICW. There is nothing to the north for cruisers until the entrance to Snows Cut, where a small state marina offers transient dockage.

Historical note: Cape Fear's moniker comes from the fearsome Frying Pan Shoals offshore. This area marks the southern border of the Graveyard of the Atlantic. Bald Head Lighthouse, long known as "Old Baldy," was North Carolina's first lighthouse, dating back to 1796. Legendary 19th-century single-hander Joshua Slocum came ashore in this region while returning from South America in a small vessel he built and wrote about in his book "Voyage of the Liberdade."

Lockwoods Folly Inlet, North Carolina

USE CHARTS 11534, 11536

(NOT TO BE USED FOR NAVIGATION.) WATERWAY GUIDE PHOTOGRAPHY.

Sea buoy: Lighted red and white Morse (A) whistle buoy "LW" at 33°53.85N 78°14.11W

Overview: When ICW boaters discuss shoaling inlets, Lockwoods Folly has been a name that comes up frequently. A U.S. Army Corps of Engineers survey of December 2009 indicated a controlling depth of 6 feet at mean low water. Local small-craft fishermen are the primary users of this inlet.

Cautions and hazards: This is an extremely narrow inlet with rapidly changing shoals and is enclosed by breakers at virtually all stages of tide and wind. There are four historic wrecks just off the channel proper, three of which show at low water.

Navigation: Not recommended for cruising vessels. This inlet is solely for smaller local craft.

ICW information: The inlet connects directly to the ICW near Mile 320. The inlet/ICW junction was dredged in early 2009, and a November 2009 survey indicated depths of 10 feet at mean low water.

Nearest recommended inlets: The entrance to Cape Fear River is 10 miles to the southeast. If pressed, Cape Fear is the best option, regardless of whether your ultimate destination is north or south.

Nearby facilities: There are marinas to the north and south of the inlet, with provisioning nearby.

Historical note: Lockwoods Folly Inlet was the scene of several Civil War confrontations. In an area noted as the Cape Fear Civil War Shipwreck District, which crosses the inlet itself, are the wrecks of Lisa Marie, Elizabeth, Iron Age and Bendigo. The name "Lockwood's Folly" came about when a certain Mr. Lockwood built himself a boat, which happened to have a draft too great to transit the inlet. Some things haven't changed.

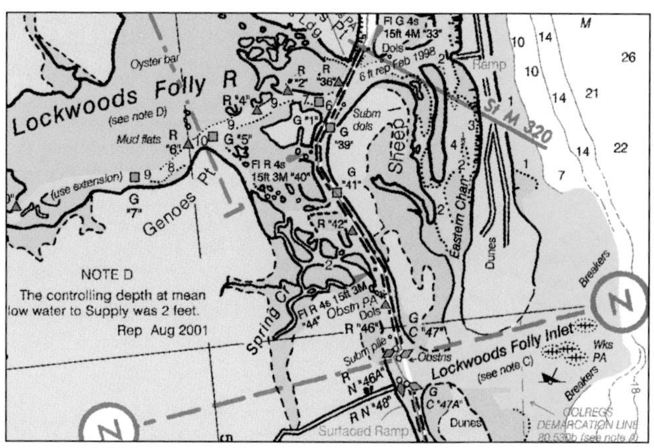

Shallotte Inlet, North Carolina

USE CHARTS 11534, 11536

(NOT TO BE USED FOR NAVIGATION.) WATERWAY GUIDE PHOTOGRAPHY.

Sea buoy: Lighted red and white Morse (A) whistle buoy "SH" in position 33°53.0N 78°22.88W

Overview: Shallotte Inlet is the next inlet south of Lockwoods Folly. This inlet is another that is used by local small-craft fishermen and is not for cruisers, although with a controlling depth of between three and 4 feet and over 4 feet at mean high tide, one could conceivably enter at high tide. But we do not advise it, even if following a local vessel.

Cautions and hazards: This is another extremely narrow inlet with rapidly changing shoals.

Navigation: Not recommended for cruising vessels.

ICW connection: The inlet connects directly to the ICW near Mile 330. The inlet/ICW junction was dredged

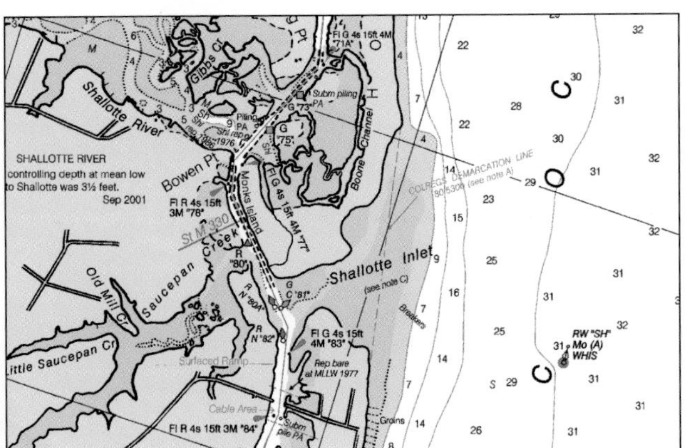

in March 2009 and has depths of 12 feet at mean low water from a Corps of Engineers survey done at that time.

Nearest recommended inlets: The entrance to Cape Fear River is 17 miles to the east. The entrance to Winyah Bay is 56 nautical miles to the southwest. Both are deepwater and marked for big ship traffic.

Nearby facilities: There are marinas to the north and south of the inlet, with provisioning nearby.

Historical notes: The entire coastal area was a hotspot of activity during the Civil War. The Union gunship Penobscot, at 158 feet in length, destroyed her first Confederate vessel, the schooner Sereta, which went aground and was abandoned off Shallotte Inlet in June 1862. In November, the Penobscot forced the British ship Pathfinder aground at Shallotte Inlet and then destroyed her. Penobscot was known as the "90 day gunship" for the length of time it took to build her.

Little River Inlet, South Carolina

USE CHARTS 11534, 11535

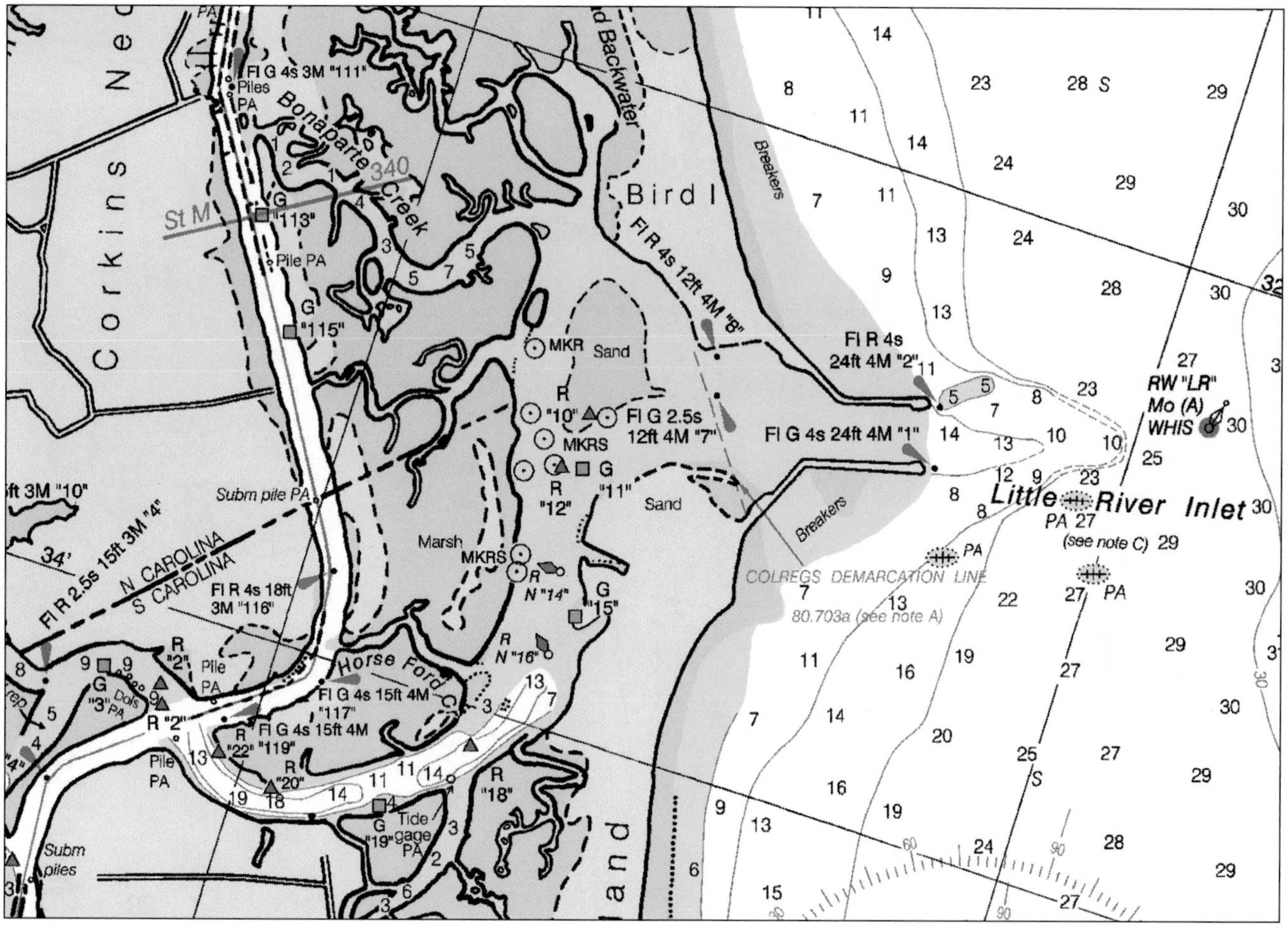

Sea buoy: Lighted red and white Morse (A) whistle buoy "LR" in position 33°49.89N 78°32.43W

Overview: Little River Inlet is deep, wide and busy, with a steady flow of tourist and fishing boats. It presents little difficulty in most conditions.

Cautions and hazards: There is a 5-foot shoal just off the east (starboard on entry) jetty that is awash with breaking waves in the right conditions. Two gambling cruise ships use the inlet several times a day. The chart shows three submerged wrecks near the entrance.

Navigation: From the sea buoy, proceed to the entrance markers on the ends of the twin breakwaters, keeping clear of the shoal to your northeast. The inlet then sweeps west with depths of 10 feet at mean low water. The channel is well marked with a controlling depth of 10 feet and should present no difficulties.

ICW connection: The inlet joins the ICW a little more than one nautical mile to the north at Mile 343. This junction was dredged in early 2009.

Nearest recommended inlets: The sea buoy for Winyah Bay lies 47 nautical miles to the southwest. The Cape Fear River entrance is 24 miles to the east. Both are well marked and deep.

Nearby facilities: The town of Little River is to the south. There are several marinas here—check the marina listings in this Guide for details on available services. An excellent anchorage is located in the Calabash River at the junction of the ICW. Pay attention to the markers here, as the ICW and channel red markers are easily confused.

Historical note: Because of the marshes surrounding Little River, the area received little land traffic until roads were built in the 1920s. Along with the safety afforded by the harbor, it became somewhat of a haven for pirates and smugglers. Following the arrival of some "northerners" after the War of 1812, the town was known as "Yankee Town," certainly not a name fondly accepted by those born there.

Murrells Inlet, South Carolina

USE CHARTS 11534, 11535

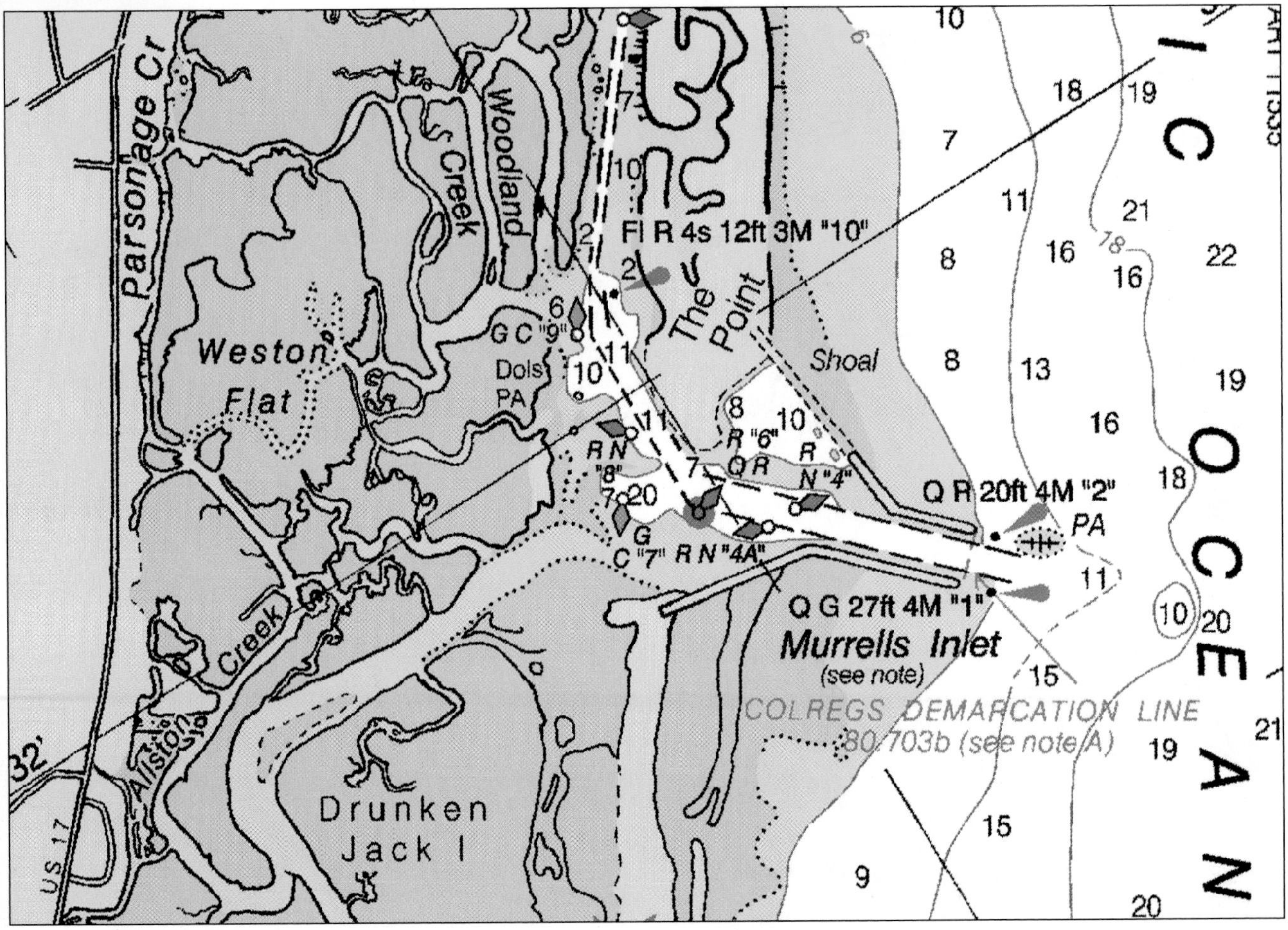

Sea buoy: Lighted red and white Morse (A) whistle buoy "MI" in position 33°30.65N 79°00.74W

Overview: Murrells Inlet, with no connection to the ICW, is used largely by local sportfisherman. In case of need, it is an easy and well-marked entrance with jetties on both sides.

Cautions and hazards: The charts show a shipwreck approximately 500 feet to the southeast of the northernmost jetty. The channel shoals considerably after flashing red light "10."

Navigation: From the sea buoy, run a course of about 325 degrees magnetic for 1 nm toward the jetties (marked with quick flashing green "1" and quick flashing red "2"). The channel turns to starboard at quick flashing red buoy "6" and narrows substantially after green can buoy "9" although the channel continues for some distance further.

ICW connection: Does not connect to the ICW.

Nearest recommended inlets: Winyah Bay is 20 nautical miles to the south. The entrance to Cape Fear River is 51 nautical miles to the northeast over Long Bay. Both have deep, well-marked shipping channels.

Nearby facilities: There are marinas with limited transient facilities within the inlet. The area is known for its seafood restaurants. There is no anchorage within the basin.

Historical note: Close by Murrells Inlet lies Drunken Jack Island—and Drunken Jack.

Legend has it that a pirate was accidentally marooned with nothing but a supply of rum. When the ship finally returned, all they found were empty bottles of rum and the bones of poor Jack. The island is also another of those reputed to contain Blackbeard's treasure.

Winyah Bay Entrance, South Carolina

USE CHART 11532, 11535

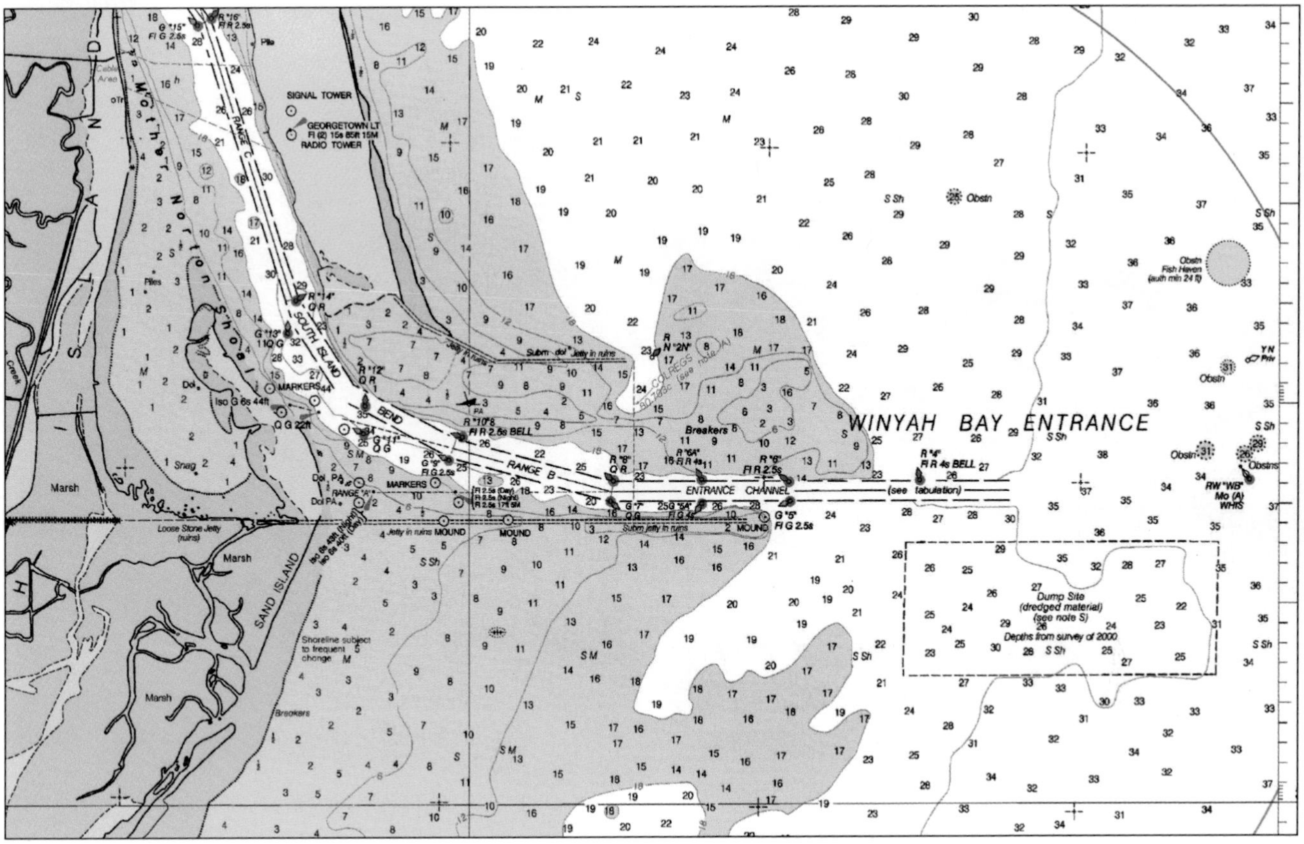

Sea buoy: Lighted red and white Morse (A) whistle buoy "WB" in position 33°11.62N 79°05.18W.

Overview: This inlet is well marked and deep. For underpowered vessels, it presents a challenge with its strong currents. It pays to watch the tide here and enter or leave with the current.

Cautions and hazards: Conditions can be particularly bad at the ends of the jetties when tide opposes wind. Also, much of the south jetty is visible only at low water.

Navigation: Georgetown Light, 85 feet above the water, shines from a white cylindrical tower on the north side of Winyah Bay entrance. Smoke from one or another of the stacks in Georgetown can often be seen from well offshore. The sea buoy is well out; recreational vessels can safely approach waypoint 33°11.57N 79°07.04W which is just east of R '4'. Northbound vessels need to be aware of the shoals to the south and west of the channel and not stray west of this waypoint. Anything under 20 feet indicates you're too far west on your approach. From the waypoint, entry is straightforward on a heading of due west, turning to NW at R '8' and NNW after that. This is an inlet in which a nighttime entry is feasible due to its width, depth and the well marked ranges. The southbound ICW entrance is nearly nine miles in. Georgetown is another 3.5 nm. These distances highlight the need to enter or leave with the current in your favor, or spend a great deal of time needlessly fighting the current.

Average maximum current and direction: 1.9 knots, 320 degrees on the flood; 2 knots, 140 degrees on the ebb.

ICW connection: The channel joins the ICW at Mile 406. Southbound traffic coming from offshore will want to leave the main shipping channel sooner, veering to port at flashing green buoy "17" to enter the ICW via the Western Channel.

Nearest recommended inlets: Murrells Inlet, a good secondary inlet with no connection to the ICW, is 19 nautical miles to the north. The entrance to Cape Fear is 62 nautical miles to the northeast. The entrance to Charleston is 42 nautical miles to the southwest. The latter two are big-ship channels.

Nearby facilities: Marinas and shopping can be found in nearby Georgetown (Mile 403), while an anchorage can be found a few miles to the south on the ICW at Minim Creek. The anchorage in Georgetown proper is crowded, but there is a dinghy dock and downtown Georgetown is well worth the visit. Morsels, on the main street, is especially cruiser friendly, with wifi, fresh vegetables and a good wine selection.

Historical note: The first Europeans to settle the banks of Winyah Bay were actually the Spanish, but after failing as farmers, they built a ship from the towering cypress and oak trees lining the swamps and sailed off to the Spice Islands of the Caribbean, where there was a ready market for their slaves.

Charleston Harbor Entrance, South Carolina

USE CHARTS 11521, 11524

(NOT TO BE USED FOR NAVIGATION.) WATERWAY GUIDE PHOTOGRAPHY.

Sea buoy: Lighted red and white Morse (A) (RACON) whistle buoy "C" in position 32°37.07N 79°35.49W.

Overview: A heavily used ship channel, there is a great deal of commercial traffic here day and night. Smaller vessels are advised to stay to the edge of the channel until reaching the inlet jetties. There is a ship anchorage to the north of the channel farther out, but it is not a place for smaller vessels.

Cautions and hazards: Other than large ships, be aware of the partially submerged jetties north and south of the channel at quick flashing green buoy "17" and quick flashing red buoy "18." After clearing the jetties, do not proceed onto the charted Middle Ground without a harbor chart (11524).

Navigation: This is a Class A inlet for big ships with lots of deep water all about. The sea buoy is 10 miles farther out than necessary for recreational craft. A waypoint at 32°42.86N 79°47.55W between G '15' and R '16' saves considerable time although southbound vessels need to be aware of the shoaling to the north and guide their course appropriately, coming in on a southwesterly heading.

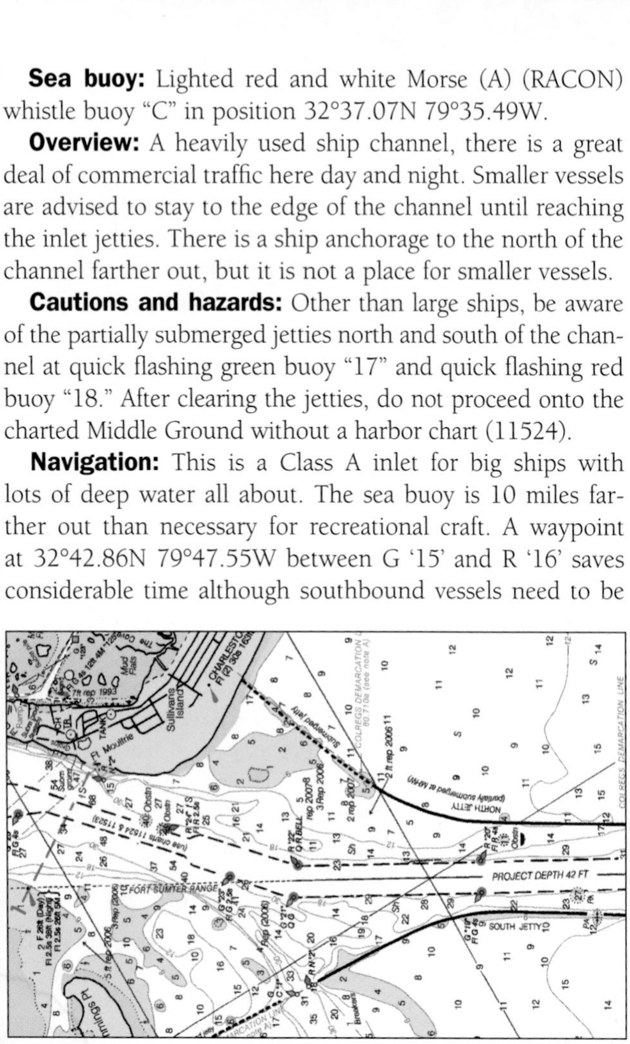

Follow the markers in, and if continuing south on the ICW, bear to the west on the South Channel Range. Those northbound or heading for the Cooper River continue, using the Mount Pleasant Range and following it out of the channel (it's deep here), watching for Fl R '1' about a quarter mile to the east marking the entrance to the northbound ICW.

This inlet can be very confusing for nighttime entries due to the many lights both on the water and land, and the considerable traffic you'll encounter at all hours.

Average maximum current and direction: 1.8 knots, 320 degrees on the flood; 1.8 knots, 121 degrees on the ebb.

ICW connection: The southbound ICW intersects with the entrance channel at Mile 464.1.

Nearest recommended inlets: The Winyah Bay entrance is 46 nautical miles to the northeast. For the southbound cruiser, North Edisto is a fair weather-only inlet 21 nautical miles to the southeast. Port Royal Sound, 57 nautical miles to the southeast, is deep and well marked but has a great disadvantage for slow moving craft: The entrance channel begins nine nautical miles offshore as a cut through shallow banks.

Nearby facilities: There is an abundance of every sort of requirement in Charleston, with many fine marinas and plenty of shoreside facilities, though many require a cab ride.

Historical note: As you enter this harbor, you pass near the site of one of the most famous of shipwrecks, the Confederate submarine H. L. Hunley, which in 1864 became the first sub to sink an enemy vessel; it sunk following its triumph.

Stono River, South Carolina

USE CHART 11521, 11522

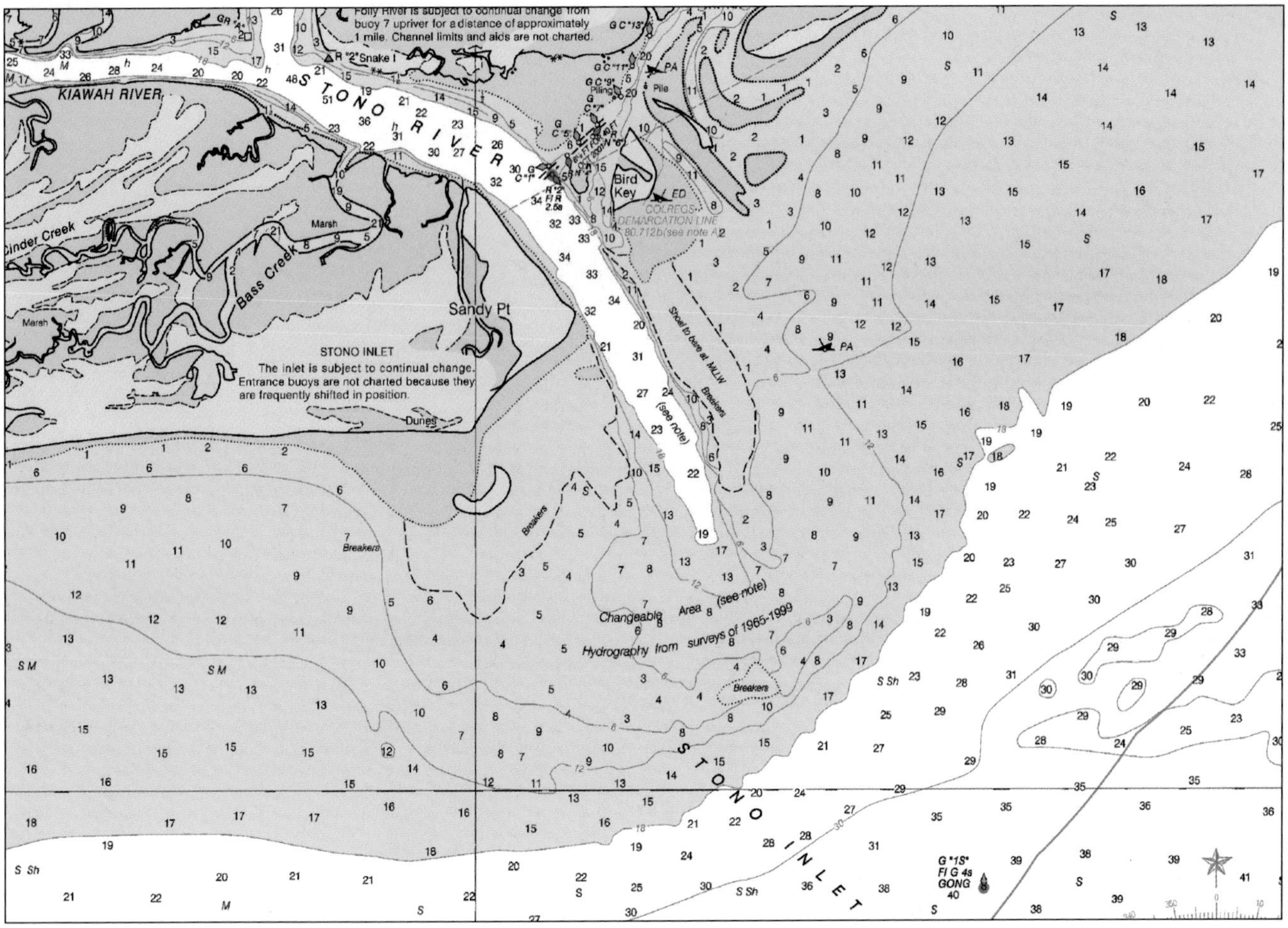

Sea buoy: Lighted flashing green gong buoy "1S" in position32°35.84N 79°56.58W

Overview: This inlet is strictly for local small boat traffic, and then only in settled weather. A shallow bar and breakers surround the entry.

Cautions and hazards: Given the proximity of both Charleston and the North Edisto inlets, this inlet cannot be recommended for cruising vessels. Along with 3- and 4-foot depths, shoals and breakers, there are no aids to navigation here.

Navigation: Not recommended. But if one were foolish enough to try, start at a rising half-tide or better. Run slightly north of west from the sea buoy through a section of 7-foot depths, then north into 20-foot plus depths between breakers into the river. Avoid the 3-foot shoal to port in an area, which is noted on the charts as "changeable." Depths from the river mouth onward to the ICW are generally 20 feet or better.

Average maximum current and direction: 1.9 knots, 315 on the flood; 2.7 knots, 136 degrees on the ebb.

ICW connection: The Stono River connects with the ICW at Elliot Cut, Mile 472.

Nearest recommended inlets: The entrance to the North Edisto River is nine nautical miles to the southwest. Charleston is 11.5 nautical miles to the northeast.

Nearby facilities: See Charleston.

Historical note: Union Naval forces controlled the Stono River during the Civil War but got their comeuppance when a Confederate artillery unit set up on the banks by cover of darkness, bombarded a Union warship and forced her officers to row ashore to surrender.

North Edisto River, South Carolina

USE CHARTS 11518, 11522

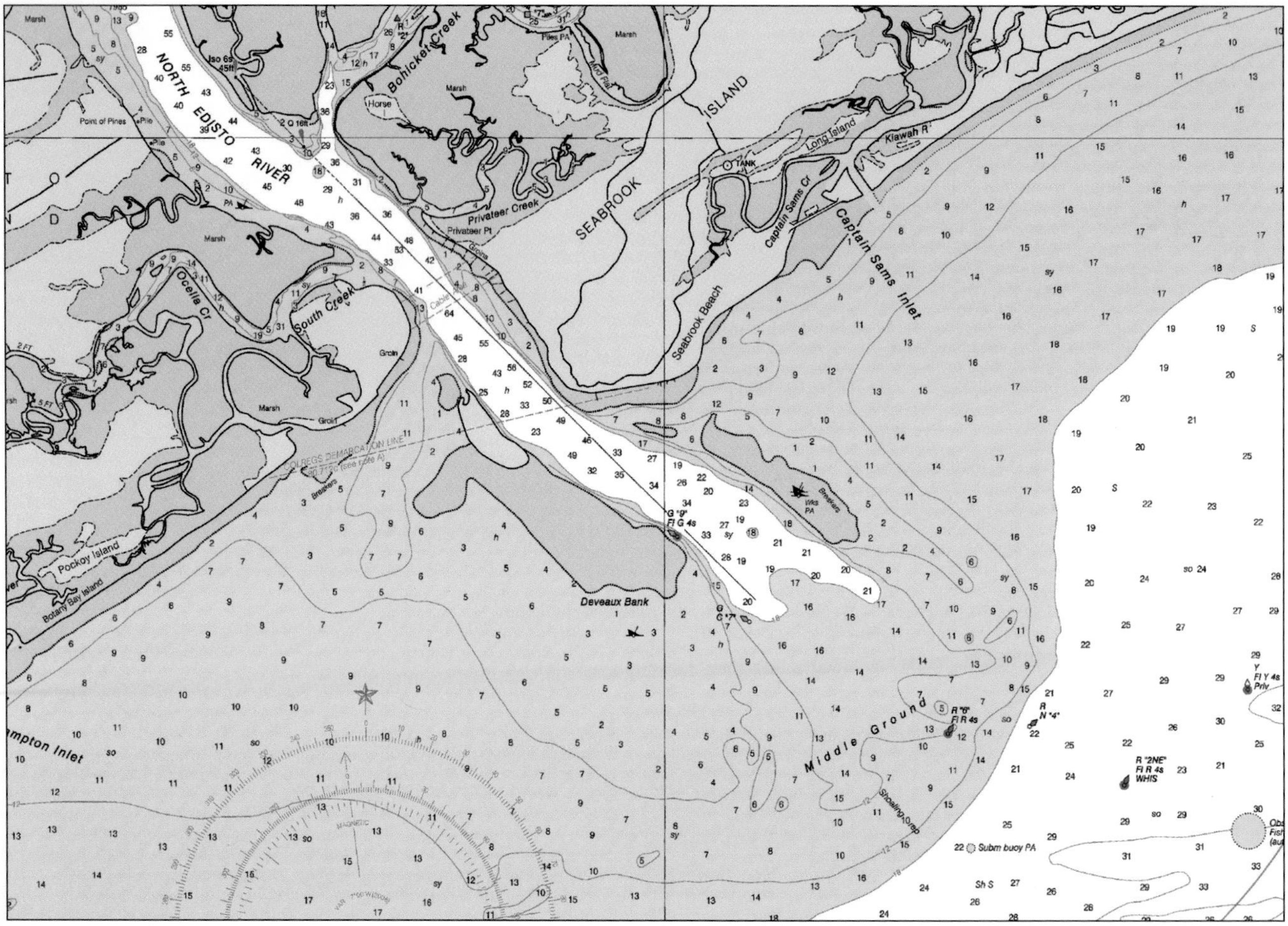

Sea buoy: Flashing red whistle buoy "2NE" in position 32°31.36N 80°06.85W.

Overview: The river entrance is a straight shot in, with shoals to the west and breakers to the northeast.

Cautions and hazards: The chart shows a 5-foot-deep section near flashing red buoy "6," which is no problem provided you keep the marker to starboard on entering.

Navigation: Proceed on a course of 286° M, leaving flashing red buoy "6" to starboard (red nun buoy "4" is close by), turning to 325° M, picking up green can buoy "7" before lining up with the charted range that leads you close alongside flashing green buoy "9."

Average maximum current and direction: 2.9 knots, 332 degrees on the flood; 3.7 knots, 142 degrees on the ebb.

ICW connection: The North Edisto River joins the ICW approximately 7.5 nautical miles from the inlet, at White Point, Mile 496.7.

Nearest recommended inlets: The entrance to Charleston Harbor is 21 nautical miles to the northeast. For southbound vessels, the entrance to Port Royal Sound is 35 nautical miles to the southwest; Tybee Roads, GA and the Savannah River are 46 nautical miles away.

Nearby facilities: Turning north into Bohicket Creek, you will find marinas offering full services, including a restaurant. Several of the creeks here offer anchoring possibilities.

Historical note: The North Edisto River was often used as a back door for Union vessels to attack Charleston, as any vessel proceeding through the Charleston Harbor entrance was a sitting duck, unable to return fire on Fort Moultrie while inbound.

St. Helena Sound, South Carolina

USE CHARTS 11513, 11517, 11518

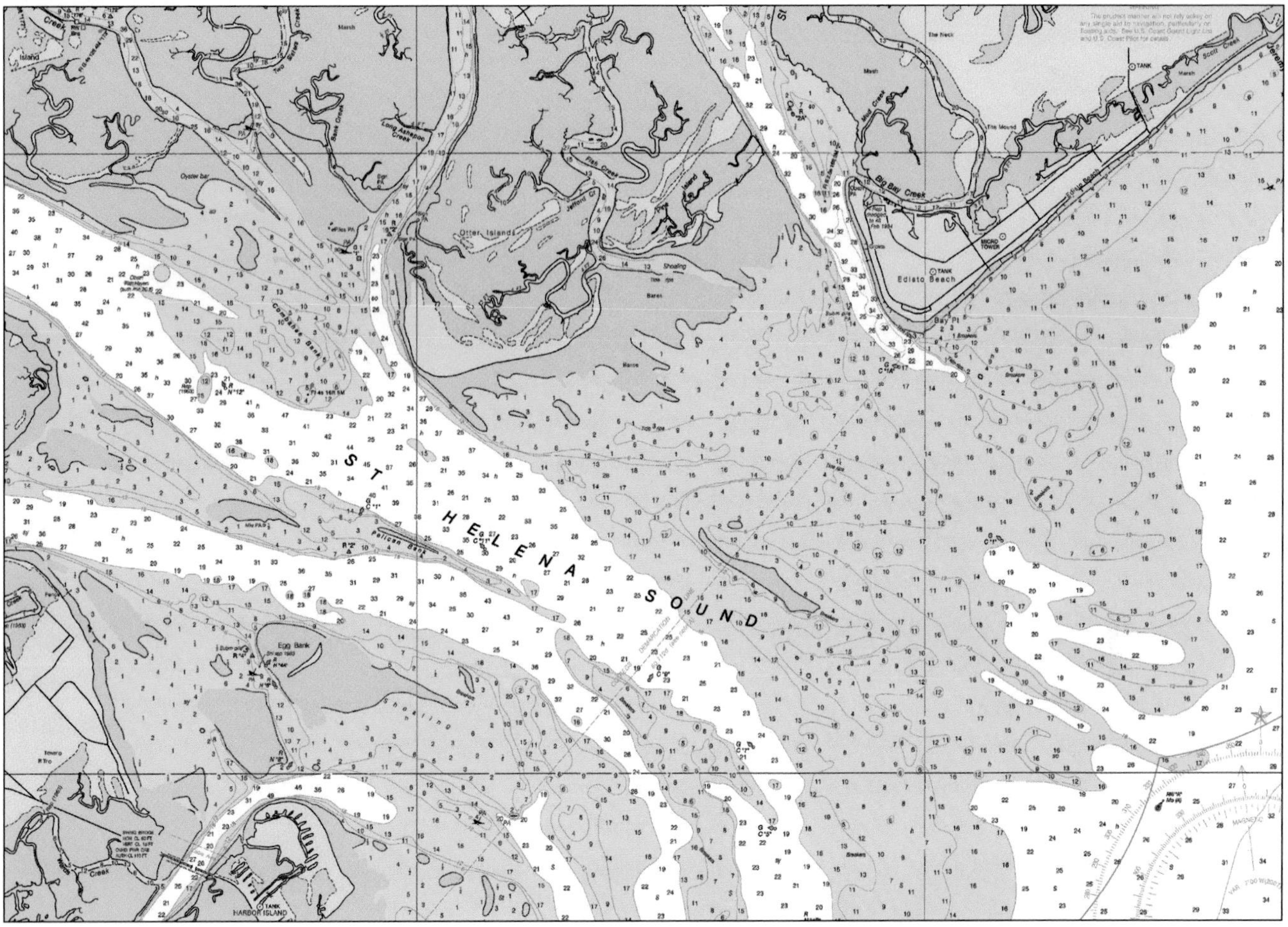

Sea buoy: None as such. For approach, use green can buoy "1" in position 32°21.67N 80°18.36W

Overview: Given the proximity of Port Royal Sound, Charleston and even North Edisto inlets, this is another inlet that should be placed low on your list. It is wide with shoals on either side and would require deft pilotage in anything but clear settled weather. It is, essentially, a northern entrance to the ICW en route to Beaufort.

Cautions and hazards: The channel is not clearly defined, and there are shoals on both sides, with fewer markers than one might like if the weather were deteriorating. The markers are not lit, so this is not an inlet for night entry. There are reports that depths are less than shown on the chart, so a close watch on the depth sounder is advisable.

Navigation: From green can buoy "1," proceed west and then north to green can buoy "7," and then west again towards green can buoy "11," watching for the shoal extending southeast from Pelican Bank. Head for red nun buoy "12," staying north of the shoal and ignoring green can buoy "1" just past Pelican Bank. (This marker is not the same green can buoy "1" used in your approach and leads to the channel to Morgan River.) Continuing northwest, you enter the Coosaw River.

ICW connection: The approach buoy is more than 15 nautical miles from the ICW, which intersects the channel at Mile 518.

Nearest recommended inlet: Northbound, North Edisto Inlet, good in fair weather, is closest at 11.5 nautical miles to the northeast. The entrance to Charleston is 33 nautical miles to the northeast. Southbound sailors will find the entrance to Port Royal Sound 33 nautical miles to the southwest.

Nearby facilities: Dataw Island and Beaufort, SC would be the nearest locations for provisioning, repairs and transient dockage.

Historical note: St. Helena Island is considered the center of African American Gullah culture and is also the site of several forts that have been extensively excavated.

During the Civil War, Fort Walker fell early, leading to the capture of Port Royal. The slaves were freed and measures were undertaken to assist them, including land grants. Black history is such a powerful force in this area that those supporting the Gullah culture have been able to prevent the building of condominiums and gated communities on St. Helena Island.

Port Royal Sound, South Carolina

USE CHART 11513, 11516

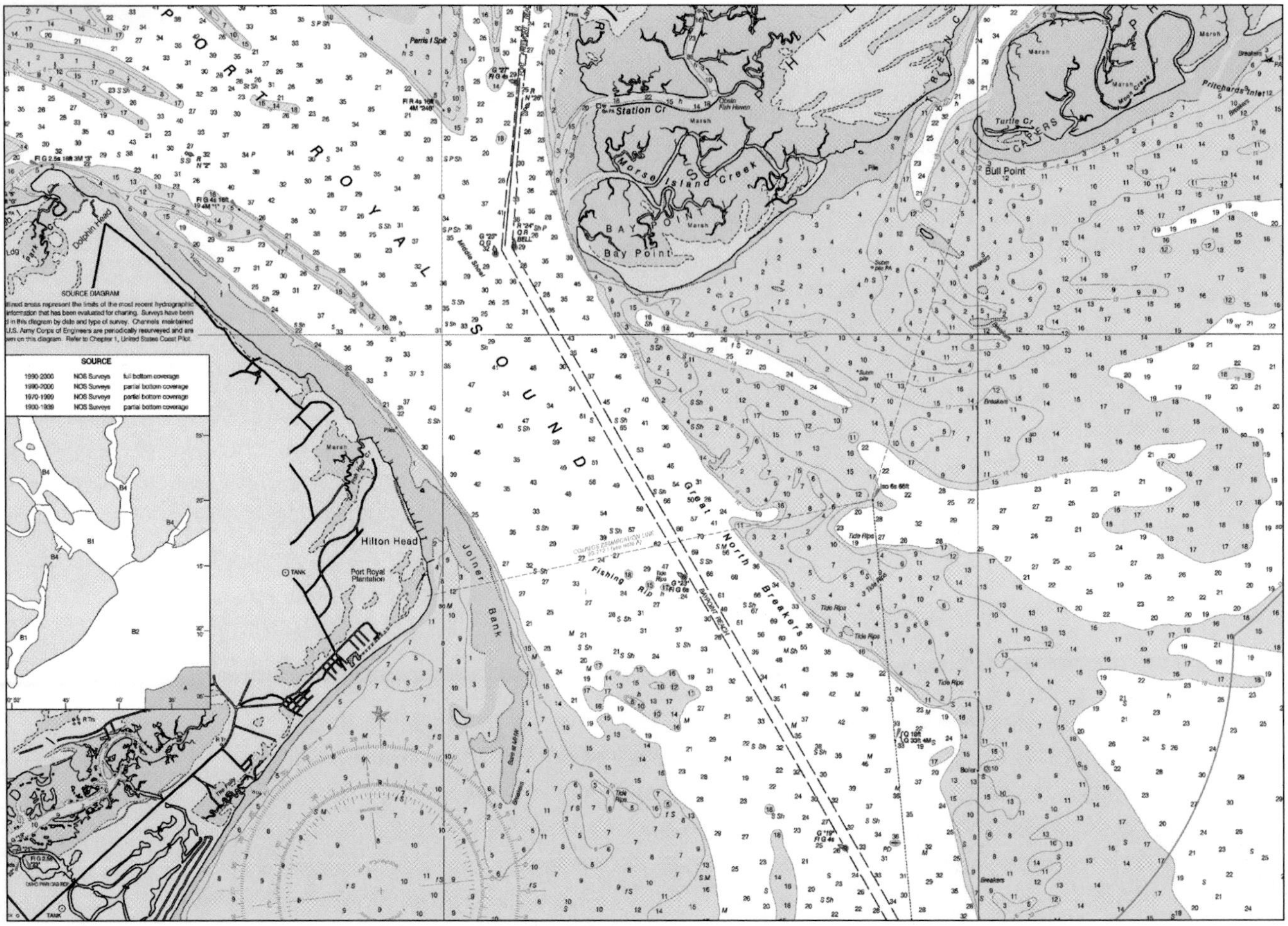

Sea buoy: Lighted red and white Morse (A) whistle buoy "P", in position 32°05.14N 80°34.96W

Overview: Port Royal Sound is a big ship inlet—wide, deep and very long. If you are headed south offshore, this is not always a good option as a point of entry, as you will backtrack some distance to re-enter the ocean. However, it is a great exit to use to make a fast, overnight run south to St. Marys. If your destination is Hilton Head Island, you can turn west at quick flashing green buoy "25" to join the ICW southbound, although that trek is still more than a dozen miles away from the sea buoy.

Cautions and hazards: If there is any sort of wind against tide, or you are bucking the current, things are likely to get a bit rough. Because of its length, this is an inlet where it pays to get the tides behind you.

Navigation: From the sea buoy, head north, and follow the range to flashing red buoy "14," then veer to the west to quick flashing green buoy "25," where you can head west as noted to the southbound ICW and Hilton Head Island, or north to Beaufort, SC. There are ranges northbound to quick flashing green buoy "37" on the Beaufort River. If you are going northbound after dark, not all of the lights are evident, and there are land-based lights that can confuse even the best navigator.

Average maximum current and direction: 1.8 knots, 324 degrees on the flood; 1.8 knots, 146 degrees on the ebb.

ICW connection: The inlet intersects the ICW after quick flashing green buoy "25" approximately at Mile 548.6.

Nearest recommended inlets: To the northeast, about 21 nautical miles away, begins the channel into St. Helena Sound. The North Edisto entrance is 36 nautical miles away and Charleston, SC, 56 nautical miles. Southbound, the Tybee Roads, GA entrance to the Savannah River and Hilton Head, SC is about 10 nautical miles away on a southerly course.

Nearby facilities: Up the Beaufort River, Beaufort and Port Royal both offer transient dockage and facilities. To the south, Hilton Head Island has full marine facilities, although provisioning may require renting a car. Beaufort Municipal Marina has a loaner car.

Historical note: Most mariners are aware that the Parris Island Marine Corps base is here. What most will not know is that Cat Island, at the anchorage at Mile 544, was at one time a nudist colony. (It closed prior to World War II, in case you were wondering!) Hilton Head Island was, at one time, a prominent outpost of the Gullah community.

Calibogue Sound, South Carolina

USE CHART 11512, 11513

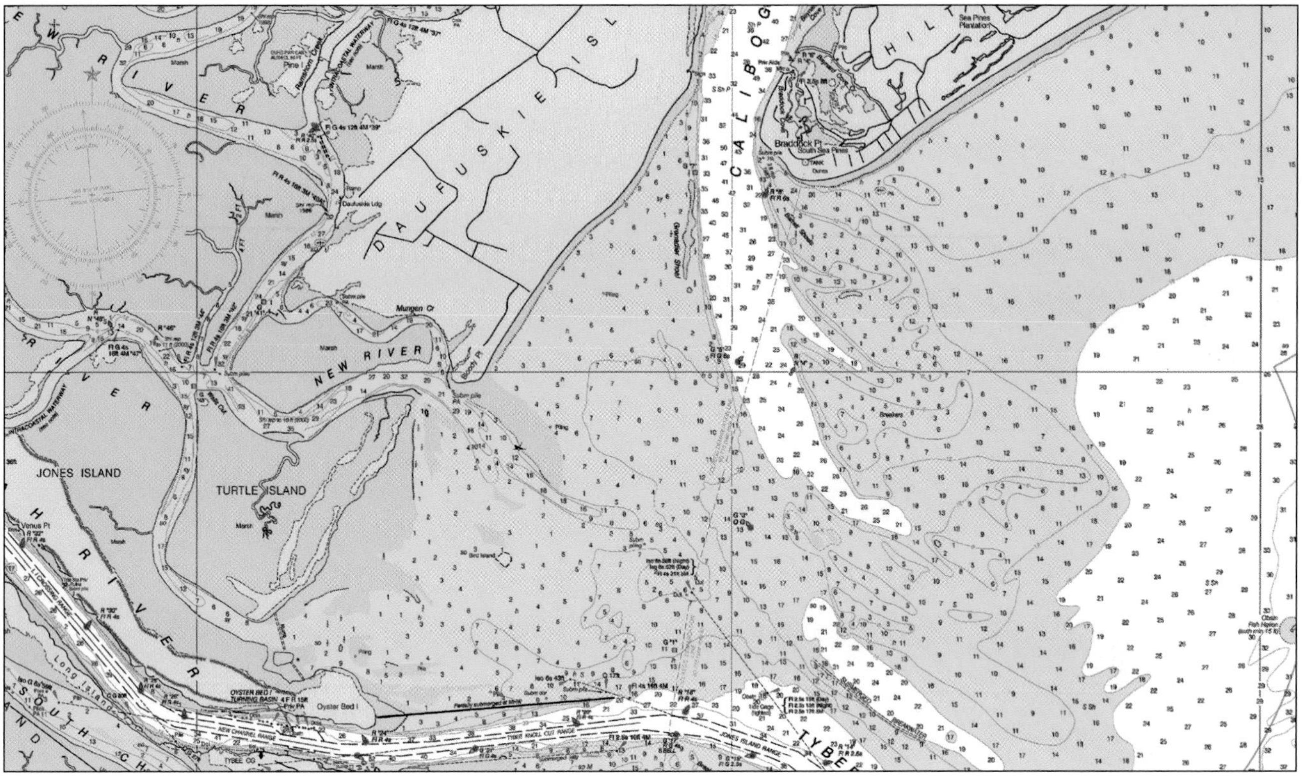

Sea buoy: Use the sea buoy for Tybee Roads, lighted red and white Morse (A) (RACON) buoy "T" in position 31°57.700 N, 80°43.100 W.

Overview: Tybee Roads, a big-ship entrance to Savannah, GA, leads to Calibogue Sound and Hilton Head Island, SC. At night or in poor weather, entering farther north at Port Royal Sound to reach Hilton Head Island is the wiser choice, due to shoal waters and the dearth of lighted markers showing the way from Tybee Roads toward Calibogue Sound.

Cautions and hazards: Coming from the north, mariners need to be aware of Gaskin Banks, an extensive shoal area extending nearly eight nautical miles out from Hilton Head Island. There is also a submerged breakwater north of the Tybee Roads channel that is roughly parallel to flashing red buoys "12" and "14," which must be avoided if one is heading toward Calibogue Sound.

Navigation: For South Hilton Head Island vie Calibogue Sound, use the sailing directions for entering the Savannah River but stay on Bloody Point Range after flashing red buoy "14," passing the lower range light and leaving green daybeacon "1" well to port. Next, keep clear of the 5- to 6-foot deep shoal at the back Bloody Point Range, and then turn north toward quick flashing green buoy "3." Depths will briefly fall to 8 to 10 feet from 14 feet, then rise again as you pass quick flashing green buoy "3." At quick flashing green buoy "3," turn due north, and proceed to flashing green buoy "5," where you can then follow the remaining channel markers into Calibogue Sound.

Average maximum current and direction: 1.6 knots, 06 degrees on the flood; 2 knots, 183 degrees on the ebb.

ICW connection: Rejoin the ICW at the Cooper River, Mile 564.

Nearest recommended inlets: At night or in heavy seas, forgo Calibogue Sound and continue on Tybee Roads to the Savannah River entrance. Port Royal Sound is 10 miles to the northeast. Heading towards Savannah, there are no anchorages unless you re-enter the ICW. Although it is marked as an anchorage in some guides, St. Augustine Creek, off the ICW to the south of Savannah R. is not safe to anchor in due to the gambling cruise boats, which use it day and night. To the north, Wright R. at the north end of Field's Cut, offers the first convenient anchorage. Bull Creek, off Cooper River is a deep and spacious anchorage with good holding close to Daufauskie Island.

Nearby facilities: The nearest marinas are on Hilton Head Island off Calibogue Sound.

Historical note: This entire area was fought over by the Spanish, French and British for years, and the coast was a favorite hunting ground for pirates, including Blackbeard. The area is noted for its Gullah heritage. Today, most of the coast is a major resort region, with Hilton Head Island golf courses being one of the biggest draws. The red-striped replica lighthouse at Harbour Town Yacht Basin is one of the most photographed sights on the Waterway.

Tybee Roads, Savannah River, Georgia

USE CHART 11512, 11513

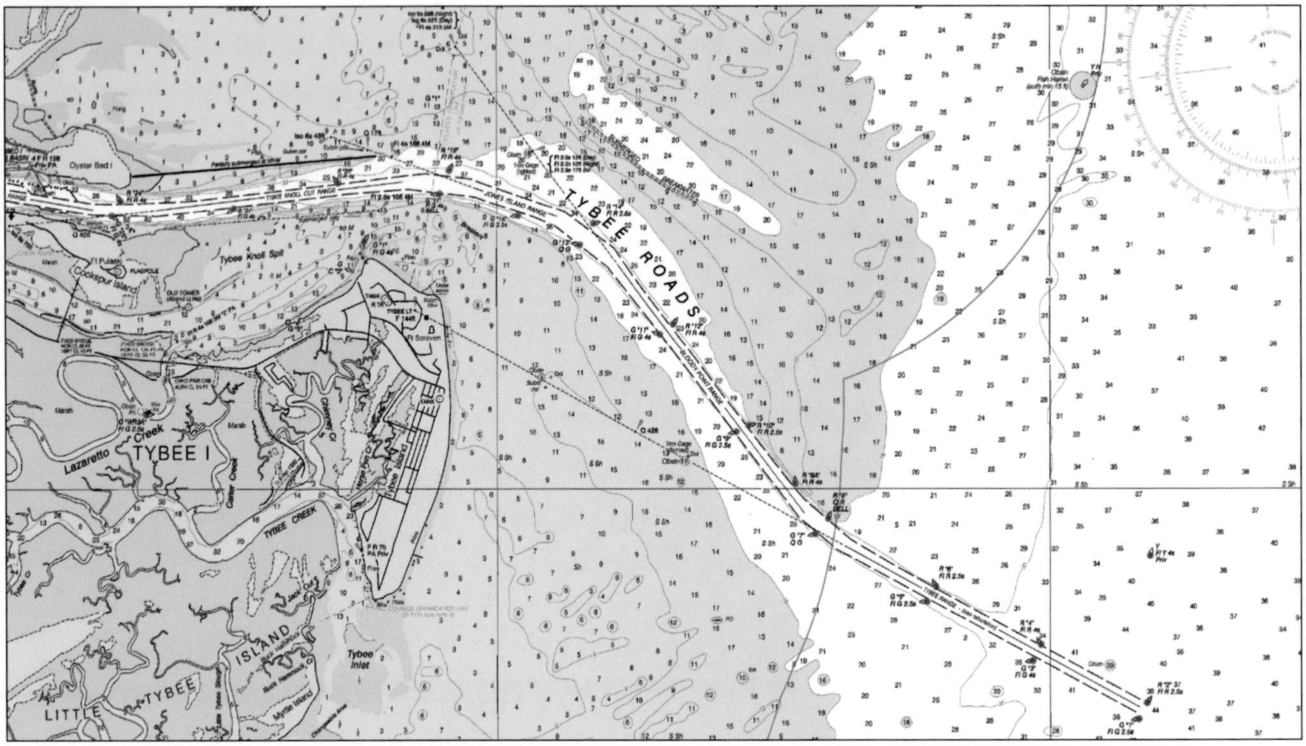

Sea buoy: Lighted red and white Morse (A) (RACON) buoy "T" in position 31°57.700 N, 80°43.100 W.

Overview: Tybee Roads is a big-ship entrance, offering entry to Savannah, GA via the Savannah River.

Cautions and hazards: Coming from the north, mariners need to be aware of Gaskin Banks, an extensive shoal area extending nearly eight nautical miles out from Hilton Head. Also to be avoided is a submerged breakwater north of and roughly parallel to flashing red buoy "12" and flashing red buoy "14."

Navigation: Entering the channel from the sea buoy, follow the Tybee range to quick flashing red bell buoy "8," turning north to follow the Bloody Point Range to flashing red "14." Turning to port here, follow the Jones Island Range to flashing red buoy "18," and then turn slightly southwest and continue in on Tybee Knoll Cut Range to flashing red buoy "24." Here, you will have Oyster Bed Island to your north and Cockspur Island to the south. Pick up New Channel Range and follow the channel markers. Note carefully the partially submerged breakwater that begins just past flashing red buoy "18," which is marked by a flashing white light, noted as "Fl 4s 16ft 4M" on your chart.

Average maximum current and direction: 2 knots, 286 degrees on the flood; 2 knots, 110 degrees on the ebb.

ICW connection: The Savannah River crosses the ICW at Fields Cut, Mile 575.7, which is directly opposite flashing green buoy "35."

Nearest recommended inlets: Northbound cruisers heading for Hilton Head may detour from Tybee Roads to make Calibogue Sound, with an entrance that is usable by day and in settled weather. From Tybee Roads, the sea buoy for Port Royal Sound is 10 nautical miles to the northeast. If southbound, Wassaw Sound, 10 nautical miles to the southwest, is another strictly fair-weather, daylight entrance. Ditto for St. Catherines Sound, 22 nautical miles away.

Nearby facilities: Savannah is 16 miles up the river that bears its name. For southbound cruisers, the closest marine facilities are at Thunderbolt, GA and Isle of Hope, GA (Mile 583); if heading north, marinas may be found at Hilton Head Island, SC, beginning at Mile 555.

Heading towards Savannah, there are no anchorages unless you re-enter the ICW. Although it is marked as an anchorage in some guides, St. Augustine Creek, off the ICW to the south of Savannah River is not safe to anchor in due to the gambling cruise boats, which use it day and night. To the north, Wright River at the north end of Field's Cut offers the first convenient anchorage. Bull Creek, off Cooper River, is a deep and spacious anchorage with good holding close to Daufauskie Island.

Historical note: Like Calibogue Sound, this entire area was fought over by the Spanish, French and British for years, and the coast was a favorite hunting ground for pirates, including Blackbeard. The area is noted for its Gullah heritage. Colonial Savannah, an early "planned city" (by Gen. James Oglethorpe), is regarded as one of the most beautiful in the United States.

Wassaw Sound, Georgia

USE CHARTS 11509, 11512

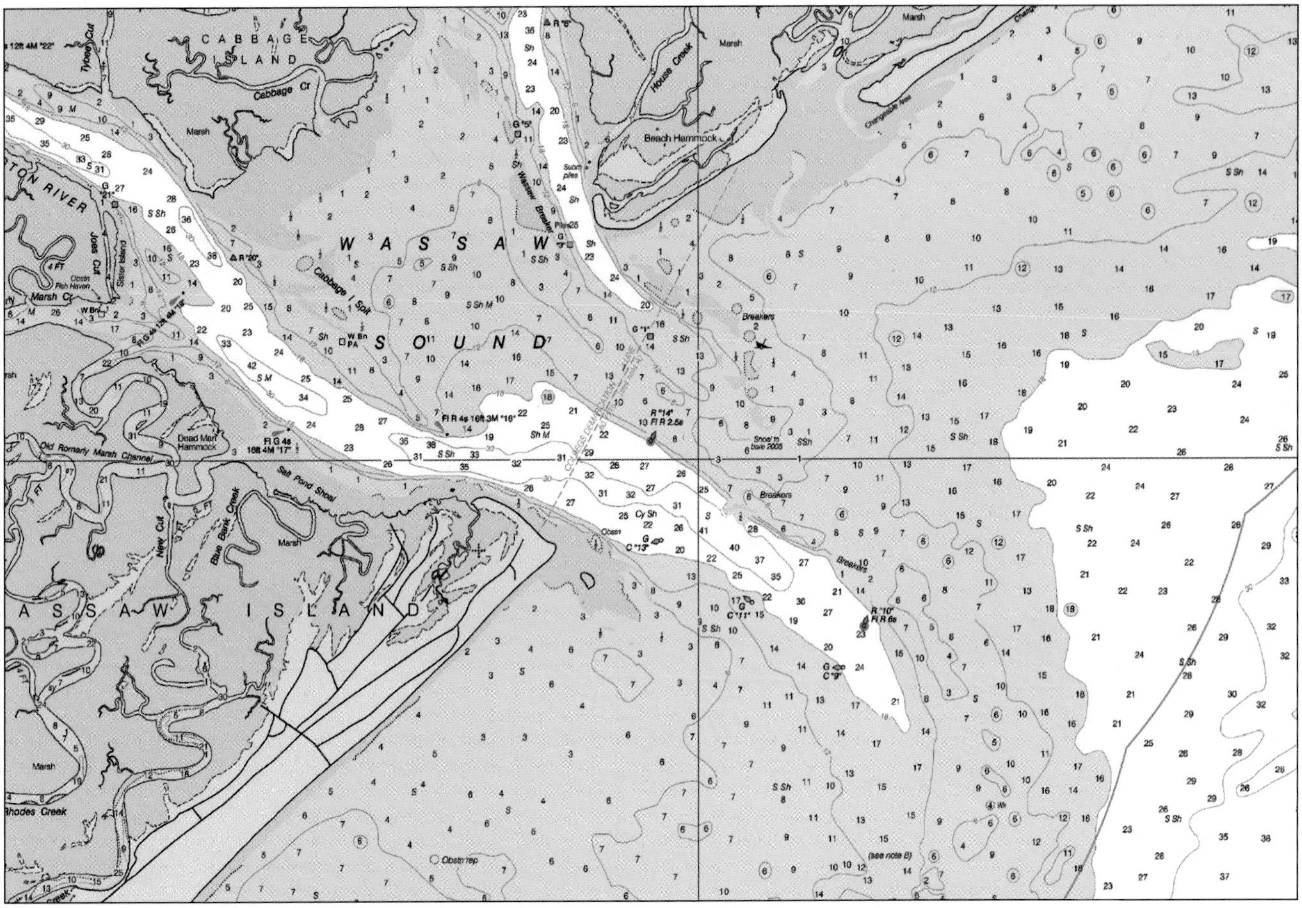

Sea buoy: Flashing red buoy "2W" in position 31°51.56N 80°53W

Overview: Wassaw Sound is a popular local inlet, but not one for dark and stormy arrivals without local knowledge, as it is poorly marked and surrounded by shoals nearly five miles out from the entrance.

Cautions and hazards: The two nautical miles from the sea buoy to the first markers are tricky, with shoals on both sides, breakers and no markers. You will have to rely on your depth sounder and good instincts for this segment. If depths drop below 12 feet, you have probably strayed too far to the southeast and need to recheck your position on your chart. The inlet has no lighted markers until you are inside, and it would be foolhardy to enter at night here.

Navigation: The entrance to Wassaw Sound changes continually, so buoys "4", "6" and "8" are not charted. Before beginning this inlet, mark a boundary line on your chart running due south from flashing red buoy "10." From flashing red buoy "2W," head west-northwest and curve to the north around the shoal to starboard until you reach the above noted line from flashing red buoy "10." Head due north to green can buoy "9" and turn northwest to follow the markers. Depths will now be 20 feet or better. Stay to the center of Wilmington River until you turn to the north after flashing red "22" and then stay to the east side of the river for deep water.

Average maximum current and direction: 1.7 knots, 352 degrees on the flood; 2.2 knots, 156 degrees on the ebb.

ICW connection: The Wilmington River meets the ICW at Mile 585.5, Skidaway Narrows, about three and a half miles north of flashing red buoy "20," which is located at the river's entrance.

Nearest recommended inlets: The deepwater entrance to the Savannah River at Tybee Roads, GA is 10 nautical miles to the northeast. Southbound, fair-weather inlets include St. Catherines at 12.5 nautical miles away and Sapelo Sound at 22 nautical miles.

Nearby facilities: The nearest facilities are in Thunderbolt, GA, about two and a half miles north on the ICW and Isle of Hope, GA, five miles to the south. There are anchorages at Turner Creek and Herb River, as well as at Isle of Hope; however,that anchorage is small and exposed to ICW wakes.

Historical note: Thunderbolt was supposedly named after a lighting bolt struck there, creating a spring at which Indians settled.

Ossabaw Sound, Georgia

USE CHART 11509, 11511

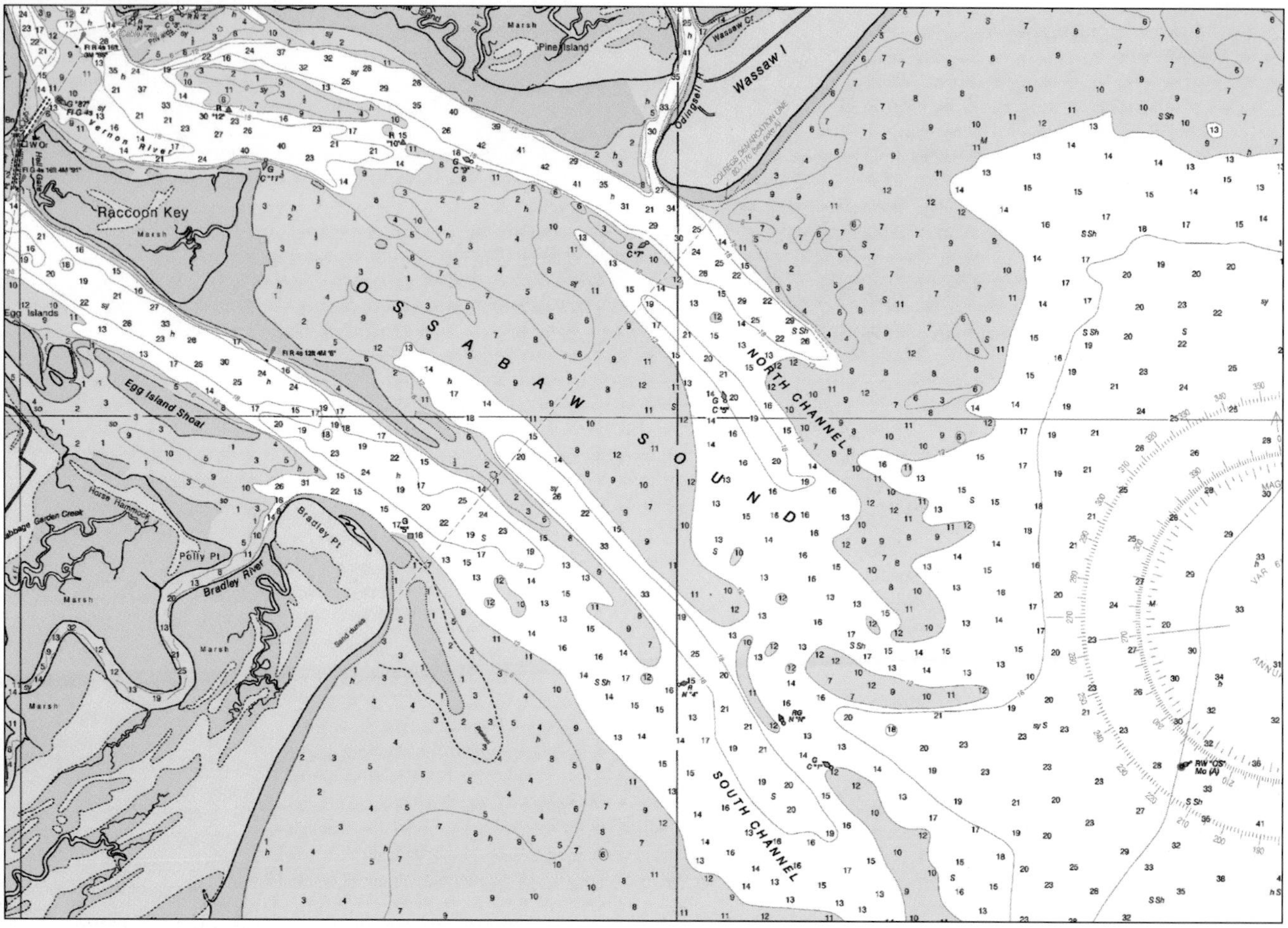

Sea buoy: Lighted red and white Morse (A) buoy "OS" in position 31°47.82N 80°56.20W

Overview: This is another inlet used by small local craft but is not really suitable for use by cruising vessels other than in very calm weather. Tybee Roads, about 15 nautical miles to the north, is a far better choice.

Cautions and hazards: Breakers can extend clear across the entrance to this inlet, making it very hazardous. Both North Channel and South Channel are surrounded by shoal water. Markers are far apart and not lighted.

Navigation: From the sea buoy, head west to green can buoy "1" and then northwest to red and green can buoy "N." To use the North Channel, turn north for two nautical miles to reach green can buoy "5," head north toward Wassaw Island, then veer west at green can buoy "7" and follow the markers in past Steamboat Cut. For the South Channel, proceed from green can buoy "1" to red nun buoy "4," and then continue slightly north of west past green daybeacon "5" at Bradley Point. From there, a heading of approximately 310 degrees magnetic will take you past Egg Island Shoal and Raccoon Key, where you rejoin the ICW at Hell Gate. Controlling depths within either channel will be around 10 feet.

Average maximum current and direction: 1.6 knots, 316 degrees on the flood; 2.3 knots, 123 degrees on the ebb.

ICW connection: It is eight nautical miles in from the sea buoy to the ICW at Hell Gate, Mile 602.4.

Nearest recommended inlets: Five nautical miles away to the northeast is the entrance to Wassaw Sound and at 15 nautical miles away is the entrance to the Savannah River at Tybee Roads, GA. Heading south, St. Catherines Sound, GA is 8 nautical miles away and Sapelo Sound is 17 nautical miles from the Ossabaw sea buoy. Except for Savannah, these inlets are suitable for transit only in fair weather and daylight.

Nearby facilities: There are no nearby facilities. There are anchoring possibilities in several creeks, provided one considers the strength of the current in this area.

Historical note: Archeological evidence indicates Ossabaw Island has been inhabited for 4,000 years. During the last century, it was a hunting retreat and then a privately held scholarly and artistic retreat. When the owners could no longer subsidize the cost, they sold the island to the state of Georgia, thus preserving its natural beauty for the enjoyment of future generations.

St. Catherines Sound, Georgia

USE CHARTS 11507, 11509, 11511

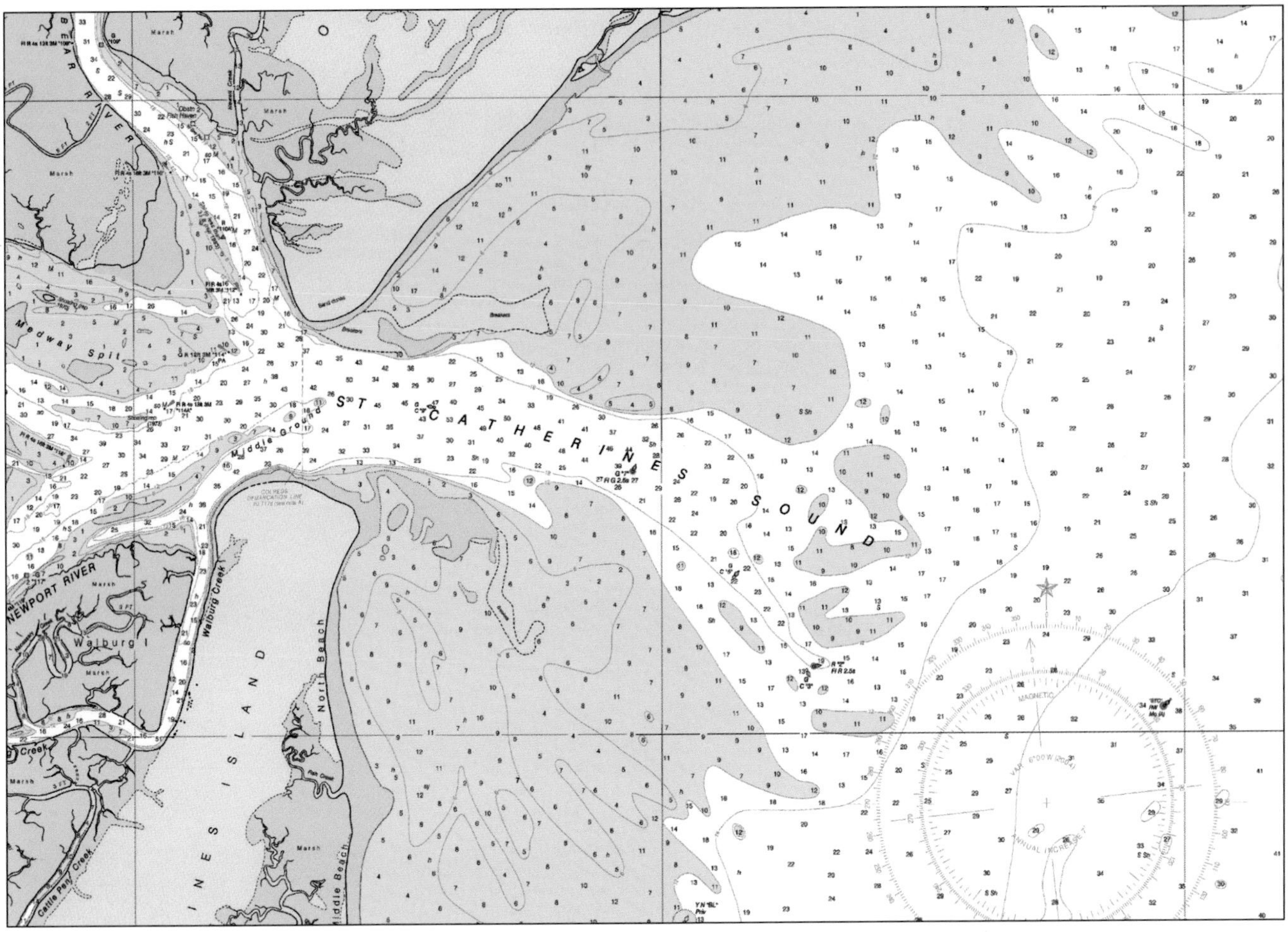

Sea buoy: Lighted red and white Morse (A) buoy "STC" in position 31°40.20N 81°00.19W

Overview: Not recommended for use by recreational craft. St. Catherines Sound is wide and surrounded by shoals and breakers, suitable for daytime use in settled weather only. The sound is generally used by local small fishing boats; there is little other traffic.

Cautions and hazards: The entrance is a shifting bar that extends well offshore. Controlling depths are 10 to 12 feet, except for shoaling from 6 to 6.5 feet near flashing red buoy "2." Due to its size and exposure, the sound becomes rough quickly in moderate weather and very rough in bad weather.

Navigation: From the sea buoy, head west to the red and green channel markers. From there, head west, making a counterclockwise circle into the inlet, about four and a half nautical miles away. Like other secondary inlets in Georgia, channel marks are widely spaced and difficult to spot.

Average maximum current and direction: 1.8 knots, 291 degrees on the flood; 1.7 knots, 126 degrees on the ebb.

ICW connection: The ICW passes through St. Catherines Sound at Mile 617.5.

Nearest recommended inlets: St. Catherines Sound is 21.5 nautical miles from the entrance to the shipping channel at Tybee Roads on a northerly course. Southbound cruisers will find Sapelo Sound's fair weather inlet about nine nautical miles to the south and Doboy Sound, GA, another secondary inlet, 44 nautical miles distant. The next best inlet, however, is St. Simons Sound, GA, 61 nautical miles away.

Nearby facilities: There are no facilities in the immediate area. There is a protected anchorage in Walburg Creek on the south entrance to the sound.

Historical note: General Sherman awarded St. Catherines Island, along with Ossabaw and Sapelo, to freed slaves after the Civil War. This state of affairs lasted for two years, after which the island was returned to its former owner. The new residents relocated to the Georgia mainland. Of historical interest, a Spanish fort dating from 1566 was built on the island. An 1893 hurricane covered the entire island in water. Only one person survived.

Sapelo Sound, Georgia

USE CHART 11509, 11510

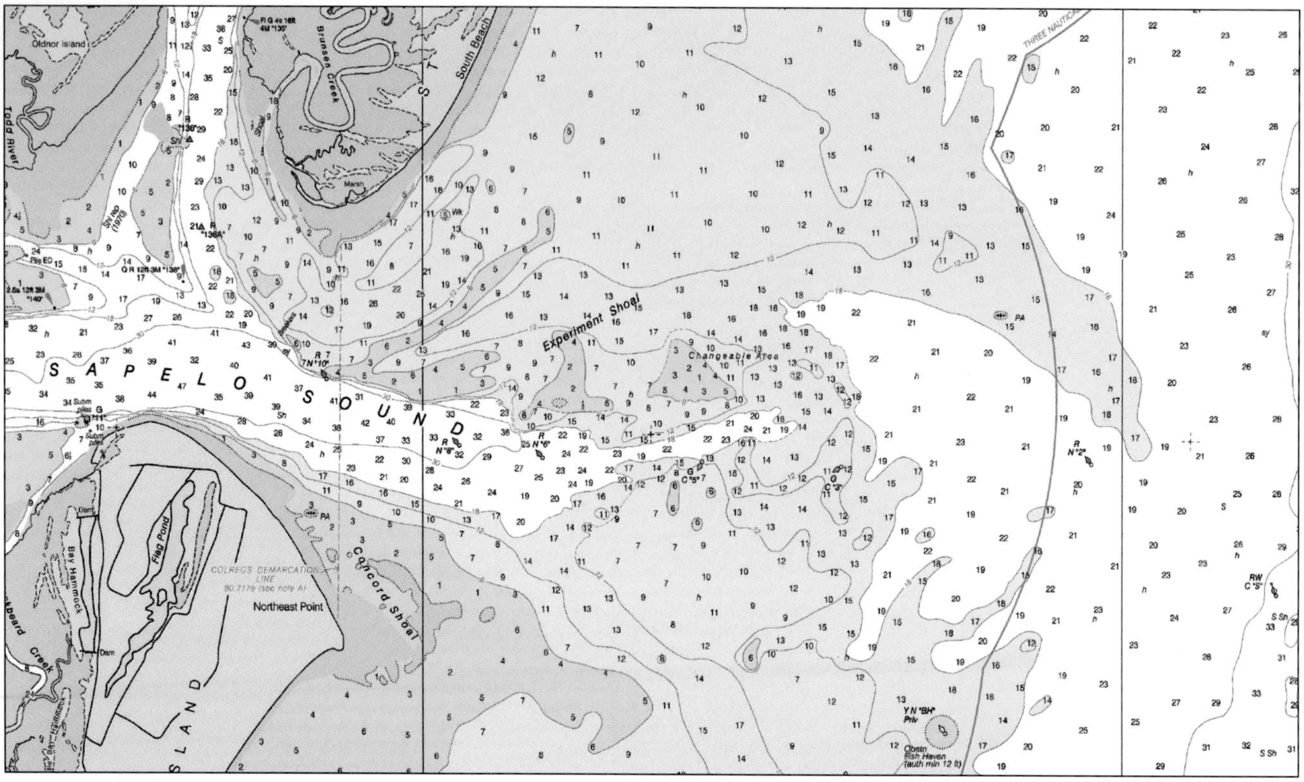

Sea buoy: Red and white can buoy "S" in position 31°31.21N 81°03.89W.

Overview: Sapelo Sound is a favorite of area fishermen and shrimpers, not to mention legendary pirate Edward Teach (Blackbeard). You will pass just north of Blackbeard Island and Blackbeard Creek while transiting this inlet. Southbound cruisers hoping to avoid the Georgia ICW rarely use the inlet, preferring to jump offshore through the big ship channels at Charleston, Port Royal, SC or Savannah, GA.

Cautions and hazards: This is not the best inlet in rougher weather, due to extensive shoals to the north and south of the inlet. Sapelo Sound is quite wide and the aids to navigation are unlighted, making it unfavorable for nighttime passage except by the well experienced. Depths between green can buoy "3" and green can buoy "5" drop to 12 feet in places, and there are breaking shoals to the north of the channel but, otherwise, depths typically run to over 20 feet. Nonetheless, do not succumb to any temptations to cut corners here.

Average maximum current and direction: 1.7 knots, 290 degrees on the flood; 2.2 knots, 118 degrees on the ebb.

Navigation: From the sea buoy, proceed first to red nun buoy "2" and then head slightly south of west to green can buoy "3." Depths will drop from more than 20 feet down to 12 feet along the way. If you see 10-foot depths, you are in trouble, and it is time to reverse course and take stock of the situation. At green can buoy "5," you will see 20-plus-foot depths return, and it is a simple matter of following the red buoys in until you meet up with the ICW past red nun buoy "10."

ICW connection: The junction of Sapelo Sound and the ICW is at Mile 632.

Nearest recommended inlets: Northbound, you should bypass St. Catherines Sound (9.5 nautical miles) and continue to Wassaw Sound (22 nautical miles) if conditions are calm or, best yet, go on to Tybee Roads to the Savannah River (31 nautical miles). Southbound, the ship channel at St. Simons Sound is 29.5 nautical miles away.

Nearby facilities: There are no nearby facilities. There is plenty of room to anchor, if conditions are calm, off High Point in 10-foot depths. A more protected anchorage awaits at Mile Marker 643 on the Crescent River at flashing green "157." There is an anchorage just north of Cabretta Inlet reached via Blackbeard Creek, which reportedly will carry 5 feet at low tide.

Historical note: Sapelo Island has a interesting ownership history. Fleeing revolution at home, a syndicate of French nobles purchased it in 1790, followed by a Danish sea captain, and then a planter who was the only one who ever managed to make a profit from the island's soil. In the 20th century, an executive of the Hudson Motorcar Company took possession, but the Crash of 1929 forced him to sell to R.J. Reynolds of tobacco fame. In 1969, Reynolds's widow donated part of it to the state of Georgia for a wildlife refuge. Now the entire island has protected status under government ownership.

Doboy Sound, Georgia

USE CHART 11509, 11510

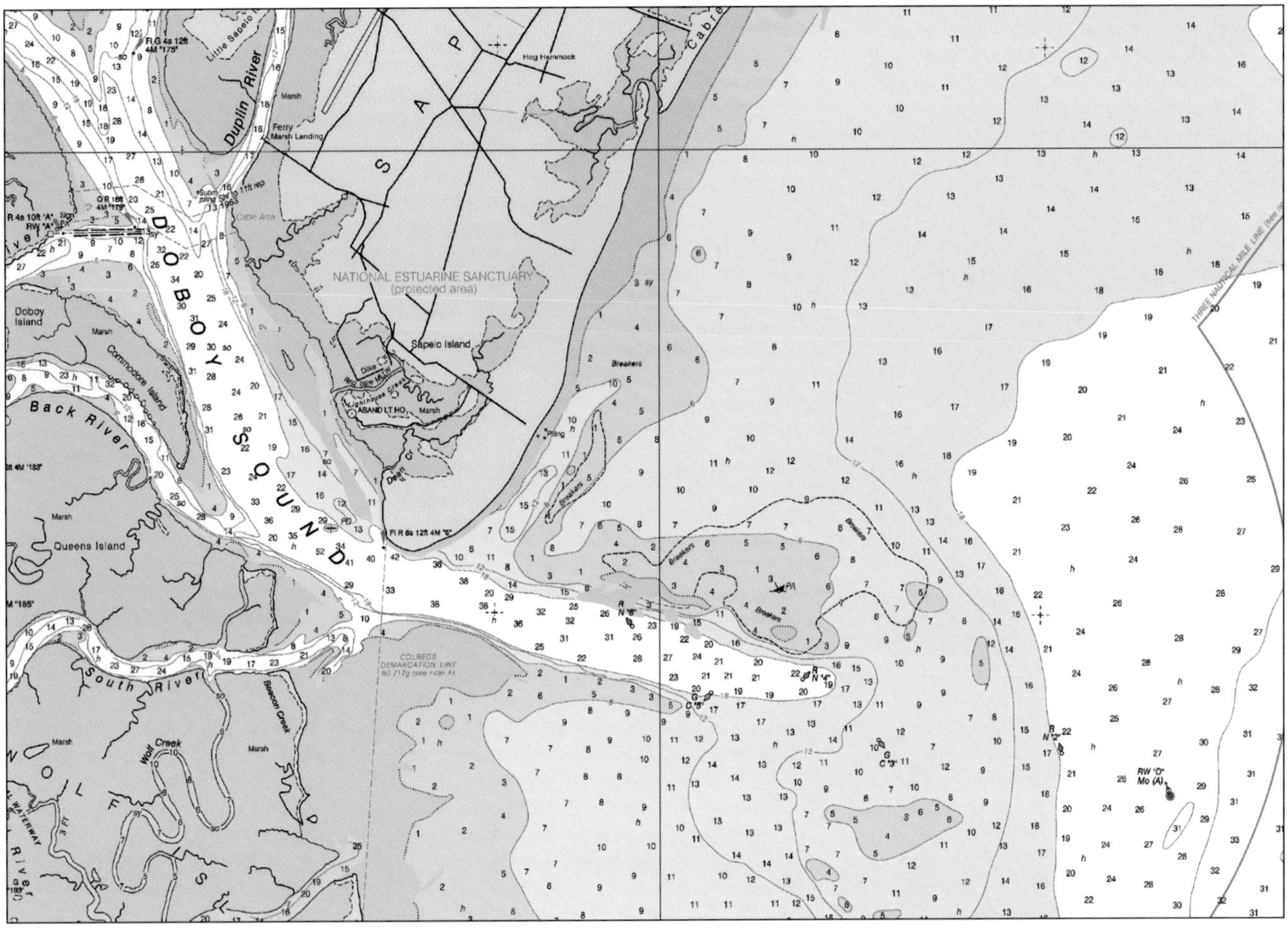

Sea buoy: Lighted red and white Morse (A) buoy "D" in position 31°21.23N 81°11.39W

Overview: Doboy Sound, with 7-foot controlling depths, is not our first choice in bad weather. On the other hand, if you have to get in, it is uncomplicated and the aforementioned breakers may give you some protection from south-setting waves once behind them.

Cautions and hazards: Breakers to the north and a long easterly shoal on the south side are the main hazards here. Aside from the sea buoy and flashing red "8," all of the aids to navigation in this inlet are unlighted, making it a difficult, if not dangerous, nighttime passage.

Navigation: Heading slightly north of west from the sea buoy, continue in past the breakers to the north of red nun buoy "4." The channel shoals to seven feet approaching green nun buoy "3," then deepens again. Continue to flashing red "8" on the northerly point of land in 20- to 40-foot depths.

Average maximum current and direction: 1.6 knots, 289 degrees on the flood; 1.8 knots, 106 degrees on the ebb.

ICW connection: About 2.5 nautical miles from the inlet proper, Doboy Sound meets the ICW just above Commodore and Doboy islands at Mile 649. The ICW runs around the north and west sides of Doboy Island.

Nearest navigable inlets: The big ship channel of St. Simons Sound is 18 nautical miles to the south. Wassaw Sound, a good fair-weather inlet, is 35 nautical miles to the north, while the shipping channel at Tybee Roads (to the Savannah River) is past Wassaw, 44 nautical miles distant.

Nearby facilities: Once inside the inlet, the various rivers and creeks offer a variety of anchoring possibilities, especially in the South and Back rivers.

Historical note: Cruisers using this inlet may well notice mounds of large rocks not native to the area, particularly on Commodore Island. These are ballast stones from tall ships that used these waters in past centuries, tossed overboard to lighten the ships so they could navigate the shallower waters upstream with their cargoes.

Altamaha Sound, Georgia

USE CHART 11507, 11508

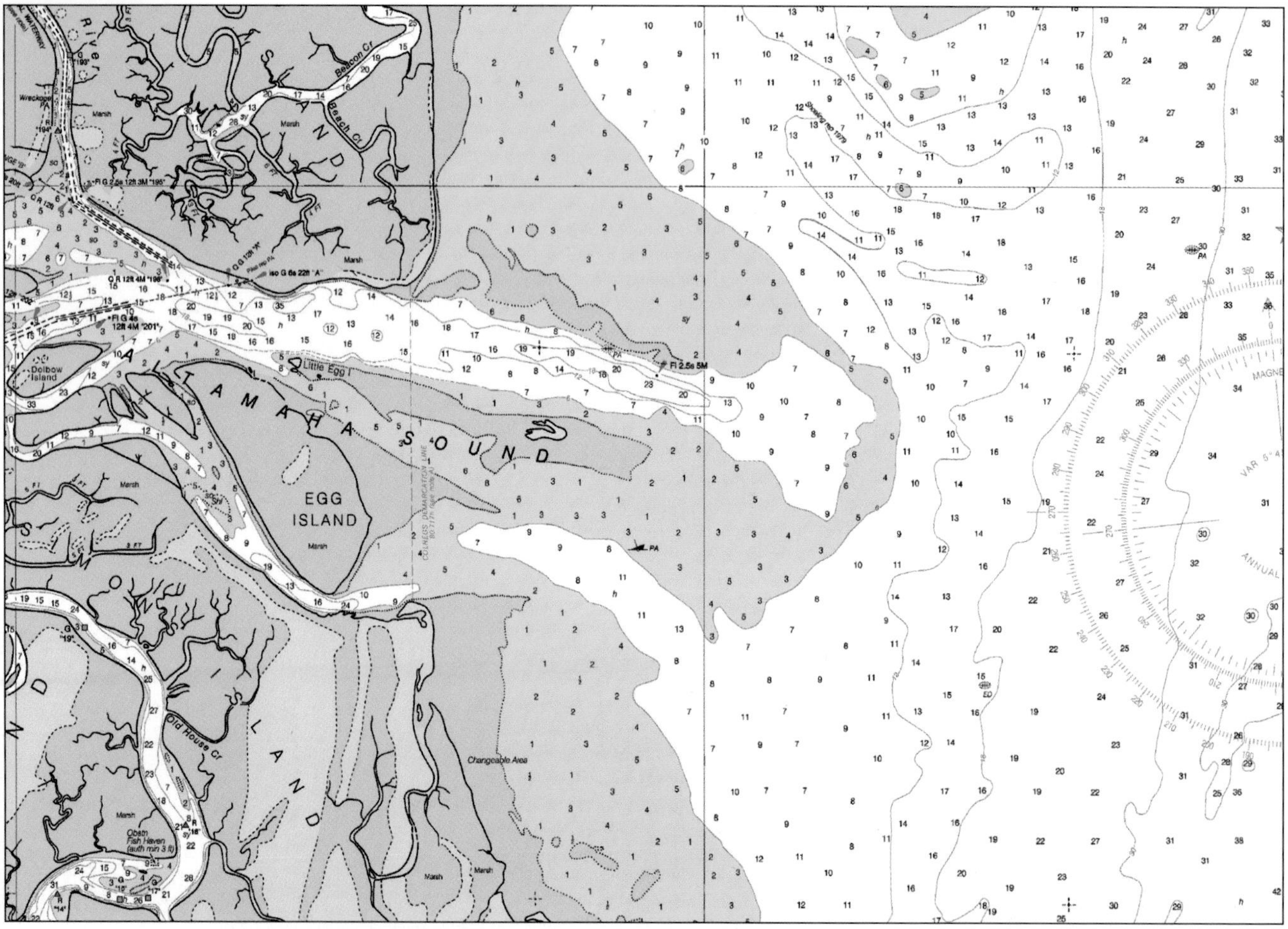

Sea buoy: No sea buoy present.

Overview: Altamaha Sound is entirely unsuitable for use by cruising vessels. In any type of seas, Altamaha would be untenable.

Cautions and hazards: There is no sea buoy and a shallow bar crosses the entrance with charted 4- to 6-foot depths. There is, however, a flashing 5-meter light on the northern side of the entrance marking a shoal. All channel buoys were permanently removed in 2005 and shoal markers put in their stead.

Navigation: Unsuitable for cruising vessels.

ICW connection: The ICW heads out towards the sound at Mile 656.5, then turns and heads up toward Buttermilk Sound. You should too.

Nearest recommended inlets: If you absolutely have to get inside and the weather is not too rough, the fair weather inlet at Doboy Sound is only three and a half nautical miles to the north. Southbound, the entrance to St. Simons Sound, a big ship channel, is an excellent alternative about 15 nautical miles away.

Nearby facilities: None.

Historical note: Altamaha Sound is the northern limit of the area in which the endangered North Atlantic Right Whale bears its young, between December 1 and March 1. Adult right whales are 45 to 55 feet long, while calves are 15 to 20 feet long and usually tag along closely with their mothers. Stay clear of them and report all sightings to the Coast Guard.

St. Simons Sound, Georgia

USE CHARTS 11502, 11506, 11507

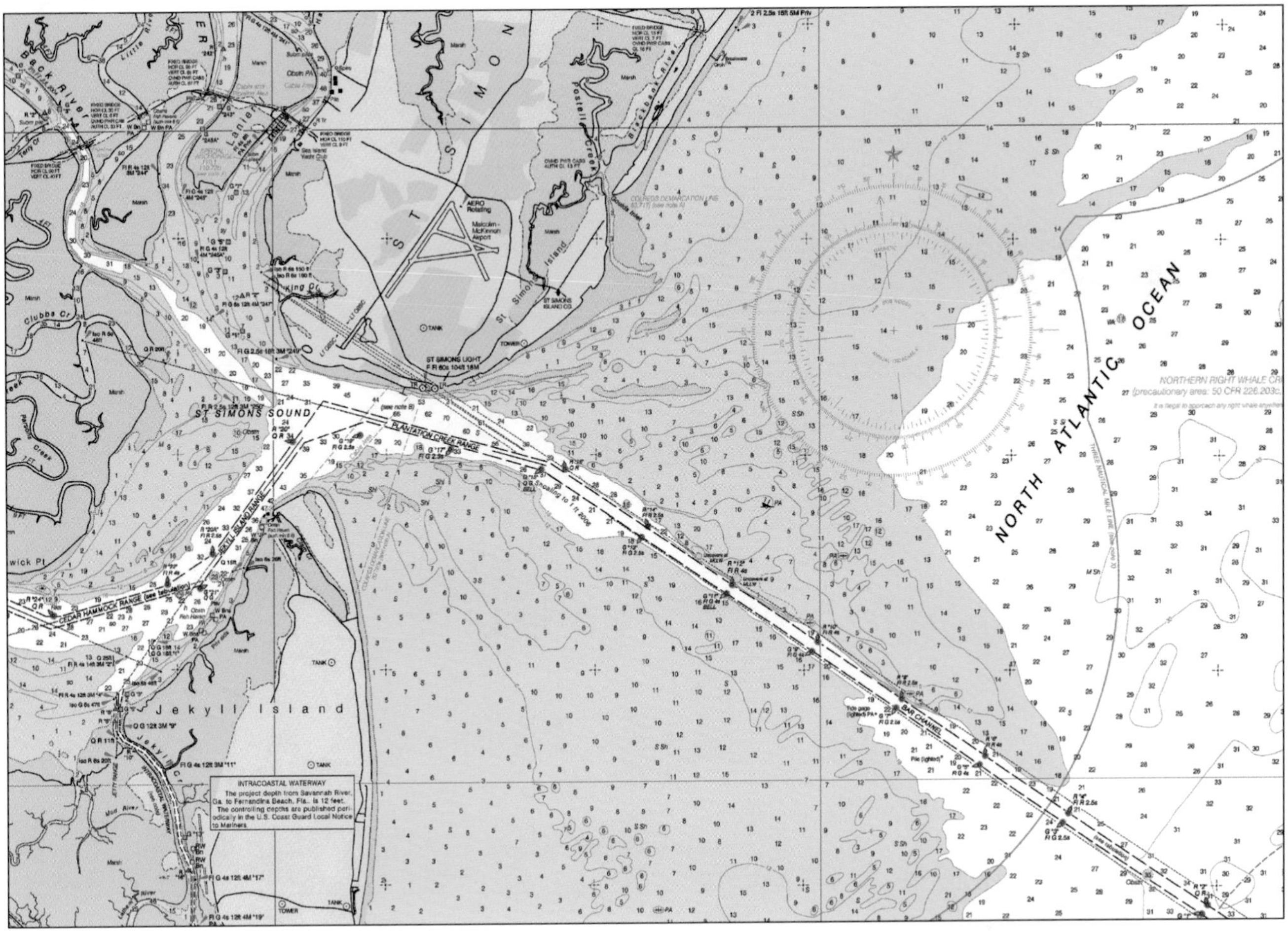

Sea buoy: Lighted red and white Morse (A) (RACON) whistle buoy "STS" located at 31°03.20N 81°15.10W

Overview: St. Simons is the big ship entrance to Brunswick, GA and is an all-weather inlet.

Cautions and hazards: You will need to start from the sea buoy due to shallows that extend quite far from shore. The channel shallows very rapidly outside of the markers, and the ebb current is quite strong at the mouth of the inlet. This is a busy entrance; keep a watch for big ships transiting the inlet.

Navigation: This entrance is very straightforward. From the sea buoy, proceed northwesterly to quick flashing red buoy "16" on the range, then turn to port and pick up Plantation Creek range.

Average maximum current and direction: 0.8 knots, 308 degrees on the flood; 1.7 knots, 119 degrees on the ebb.

ICW connection: The ICW is immediately inside the inlet at Mile 678.

Nearest recommended inlets: The fair weather inlet at Doboy Sound, GA is 18 nautical miles to the north. To the south, St. Andrews Sound should only be attempted with local knowledge, while the big ship channel at the St. Marys Entrance is 21 nautical miles away.

Nearby facilities: There are marinas to the north on the ICW, in Brunswick and south on the ICW at Jekyll Island, as well as full provisioning available there. There is an anchorage to the north at Lanier Island.

Historical note: The St. Simons Lighthouse has an interesting history. Originally built in 1808, it was torn down by Confederate forces in 1862 and replaced in 1872. In 1953, the oil lamps were replaced by a Fresnel lens and the 106 foot structure can be climbed. The view is worth the effort.

St. Andrew Sound, Georgia

USE CHART 11502, 11504

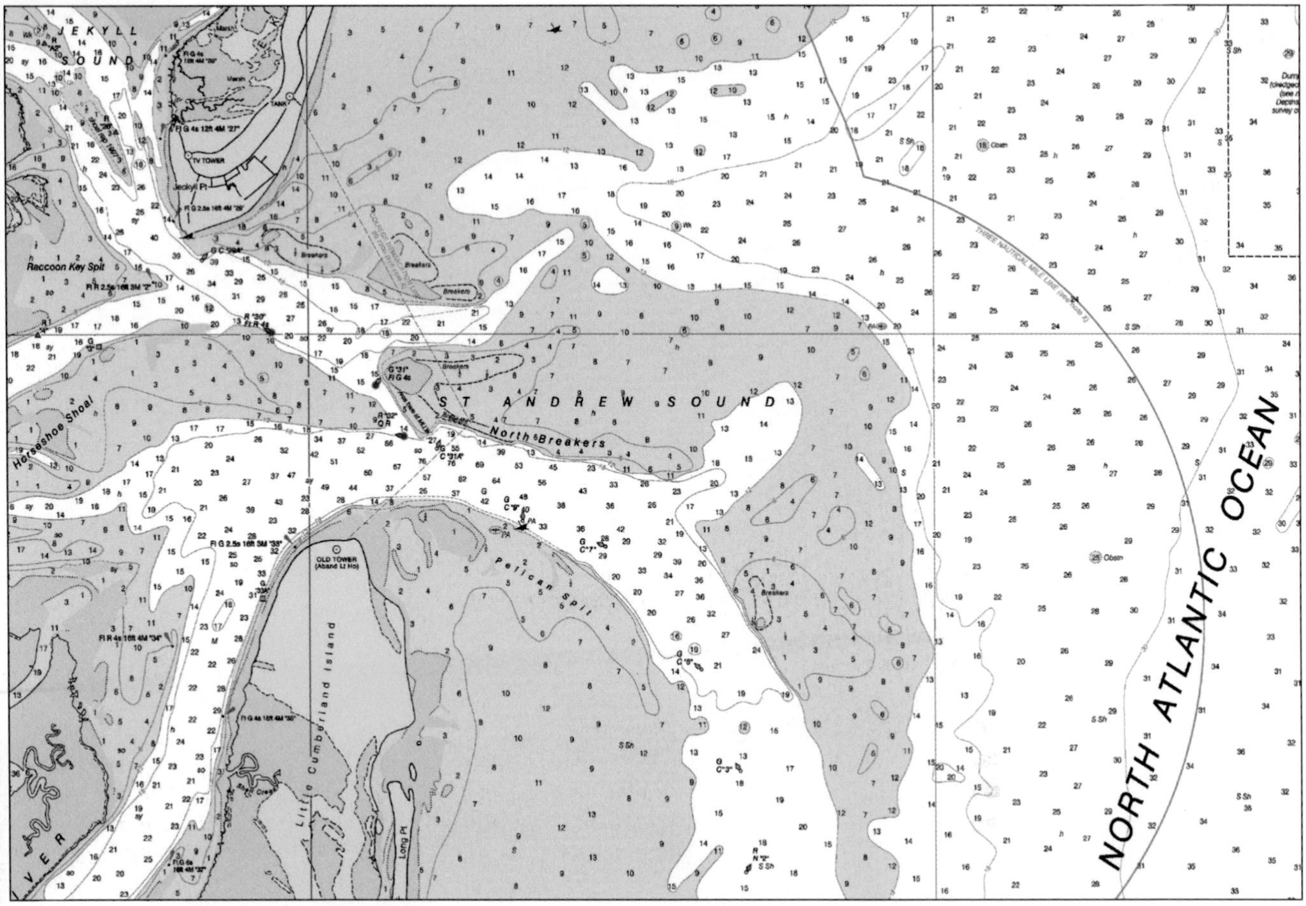

Sea buoy: Unlighted red and white can buoy "STA" in position 30° 55.56N 81° 18.98W

Overview: Use only with great caution. While this is a reasonable inlet in calm weather, it kicks up in any sort of opposing wind or tide and isn't a good choice in deteriorating weather. You are far wiser to use the big ship entrance of St. Simons Sound just a few miles to your north.

Cautions and hazards: A sunken wreck has been reported about 1.9 nautical miles east of the abandoned lighthouse (charted "Old tOWer") at the north tip of Cumberland Island. In the sound are extensive shoals between which channels lead to the principal tributaries: Jekyll Sound to the north, Satilla River to the west and Cumberland River to the south.

Navigation: From the seabuoy, the entrance marker lies 1.4 miles at 277°M. From there, head north following the markers closely as you veer to the west past Pelican Spit. You will see breakers to starboard this entire distance, but the channel itself is 15 feet or better and deepens as you proceed.

At G '31A', you will choose to go north or south on the ICW. North: Keep QR '32' to port—some ICW charts incorrectly show the magenta line inside (west) of this marker. Pass to port of G '31', keeping in mind that the water shallows rapidly to less than 10 feet on your starboard side. You're now past the hard part. Head towards G '29' on the point of land, marking the shoal building out to G '29A' and follow the markers around to Jekyll Sound. South: Lucky you! This is much easier. From G '31A', swing south of west around the point of Little Cumberland Island.

Average maximum current and direction: 2.1 knots, 268 degrees on the flood; 2.2 knots, 103 degrees on the ebb.

ICW connection: The channel junction with the ICW is nearly at the mouth of the sound at quick flashing red buoy "32" at Mile 689.6.

Nearest recommended inlets: St. Simons is eight nautical miles to the north. St. Marys River entrance is 12 nautical miles to the south. Both are deep, well marked and used by big ships.

Nearby facilities: Northbound, marinas can be found about five miles away on Jekyll Island. Numerous anchorages can be found south on the ICW, including Floyd and Shellbine creeks and on the Brickhill River.

Historical note: The lighthouse on Little Cumberland Island operated from 1838 until its deactivation in 1915. The keeper's house was destroyed by fire in 1968.

St. Marys Entrance, Georgia/Florida Border

USE CHART 11502, 11503

(NOT TO BE USED FOR NAVIGATION.) Photo Courtesy of Cloud 9 Photography: Deagle/Kucera.

Sea buoy: Lighted red and white Morse (A) whistle buoy "STM" in position 30° 42.91N 81° 14.65W

Overview: This, the most northerly of the Florida inlets, is a big ship entrance that is easy to transit day or night.

Cautions and hazards: Inside the jetties, there are some shoal sections to the north of the channel. The current in this inlet is very strong. Slower boats are advised to wait for slack water. Wind against current can put a slow boat at a standstill trying to enter.

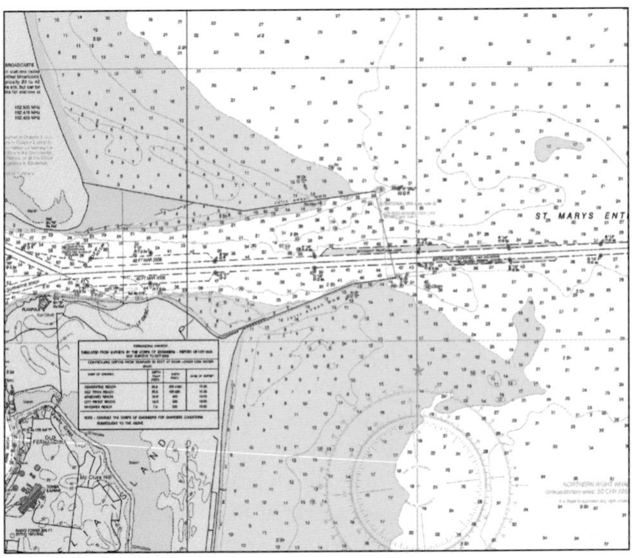

Navigation: Straightforward. For recreational craft, waypoint N 30° 42.690'/W 81° 21.520' will put you in the center of the channel at flashing red buoy "10." From flashing red "10," proceed due west into Cumberland Sound.

ICW connection: The ICW crosses the inlet at Mile 714.

Nearby facilities: Fernandina Beach lies just to the south and offers full facilities. There is an anchorage and mooring balls there as well. There is also an anchorage to the north, just over the Georgia state line, beside Cumberland Island. You can also proceed up river to the town of St. Marys, GA for marinas, anchorages and provisions.

Historical note: Union soldiers, who returned there after having occupied Amelia Island during the war, founded Fernandina Beach, FL; they were drawn to the area's climate and natural beauty. That may explain why the city's downtown resembles a 19th-century New England town.

Fort Clinch, constructed in the mid-1800s, is part of the National Park system. Located south of the entrance on the Florida side, the fort was never fully completed but was restored in the 1930s.

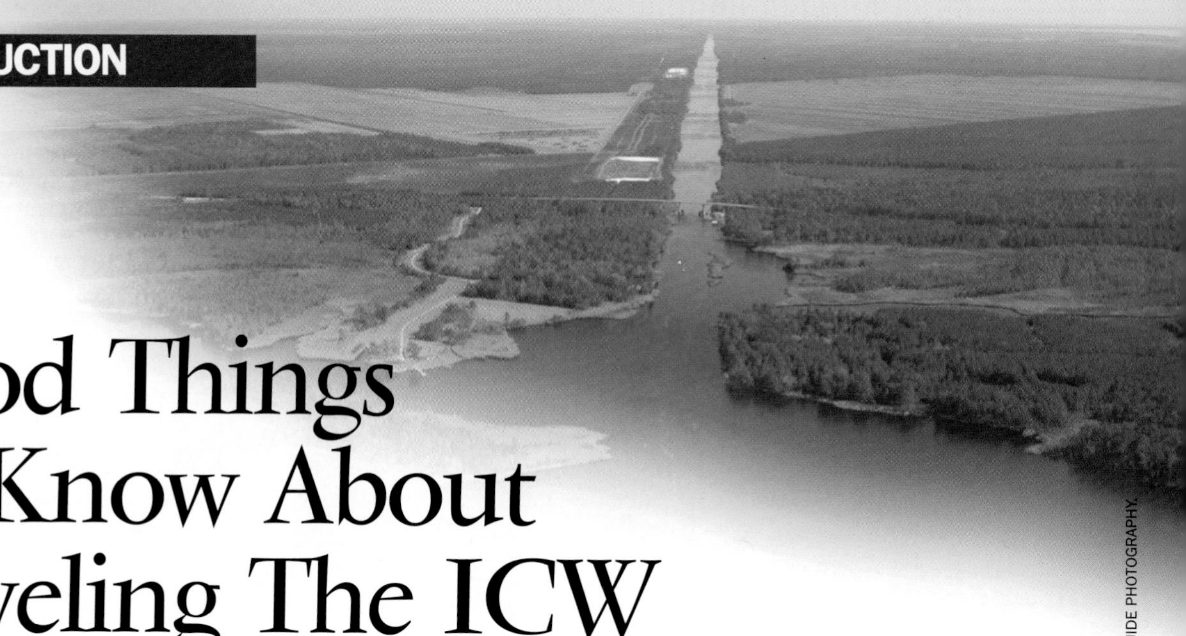

WATERWAY GUIDE PHOTOGRAPHY.

Good Things To Know About Traveling The ICW

Best Times to Make the Trip

Crowds and weather determine the best time to make a trip along the Intracoastal Waterway (ICW). Except for cold spells, which occur mostly in January and February, weather is usually not a serious factor, due to the protection afforded by the waterway. Going south in the fall, you are likely to experience a number of cold fronts. However, these weather fronts have northerly winds and will be at your back, which is often a benefit. Returning home in the spring, days will be longer, the boats spread out more and any cold fronts will likely be weaker, although now on your nose.

Boat traffic can present some inconveniences. Traditionally, a southward migration of cruising boaters ("snowbirds") moves down the ICW from points north during the fall months from September through November, having moved northward from March through June. Now, largely because of insurance restrictions put in place due to heavy hurricane activity during the past decade, many boats are restricted from going below a designated line during the official hurricane season of June 1 to November 30.

For many boats, this line is either the Virginia/North Carolina border or the 35th parallel (roughly Cape Hatteras). This has had the effect of creating a short burst of activity starting the first half of November in the Carolinas, moving down the line as these boats head for points south. During this time, there can be longer waits at bridges and fuel docks, a shortage of berths and anchoring locations and frustration as faster boats and slower boats juggle for position. Another growing trend is the number of southern residents taking a summer trip along the ICW to points north. Already paying for hurricane insurance, these boaters generally proceed north after June 1 and return in August and September.

If you desire a less crowded and hectic trip, head south in the fall well before the Annapolis Boat Shows end and north later in the spring. Hopefully your insurance coverage will permit this adjustment.

NAVIGATION TIPS

One of the favorable characteristics of traveling the ICW is that it is relatively forgiving for many of the types of navigational errors that could be very serious elsewhere. As an example, most of the bottom is either soft mud or sand, and the few rocky areas that do exist are well charted or specifically noted in this edition of WATERWAY GUIDE. Usually, if you go aground, it is merely a matter of backing or kedging off, or perhaps waiting for the tide. But complacency can ruin any good cruise, so keen attention to markers and the "navigation" sections throughout this Guide are essential.

Keep track of where you are on your chart, noting landmarks, buoys or mile markers as you pass them. Not only will this be of general help in normal navigation, it will be important if visibility becomes obscured in rain or fog and may be critical if you suddenly find that you need assistance. Aids to navigation are frequently changed on the ICW, both in characteristic and location. Also, with the increase in population along the ICW, it is not unusual for the shoreline and structures or landmarks to change significantly in a short period of time.

Safety: Rules of the Road

Many types and sizes of vessels use the ICW, so knowledge of and adherence to the rules of the road are important. Vessels you are likely to encounter include tugs with barges, dredges stretching up to one-quarter mile in length, small cruise liners, shrimpers, pleasure boats and megayachts, down to craft as small as canoes and kayaks. Larger vessels (especially commercial vessels) may have very limited maneuverability, requiring a lot of room to stop or change course (if they can), and a close passing with one of them can be dangerous because of prop wash and suction. Monitor your VHF radio (required) and communicate with vessels you wish to pass or who wish to pass you.

Aids to Navigation

Aids to navigation are changed frequently on the ICW in an attempt to keep up with the shifting bottom contours. The ICW is patrolled and checked often, so it is not unusual to see aids to navigation change location in an area. The Coast Guard often moves navigation aids to mark the deepest waters, using floating red nuns and green can buoys.

You will see many private aids to navigation on side creeks and dredged channels. Some of these are quite elaborate, carefully maintained, regulated and reliable. Others are no more than stakes in the mud or small Styrofoam floats put out by whoever lives up the creek. Long-established private aids are sometimes noted on the charts (usually labeled "PA" on the chart itself), but even this does not ensure that the entity responsible for their maintenance is still there and doing their job. These present a dilemma for any navigator. While they can be very helpful, they can also be quite misleading.

Often, as conditions change, these private markers are not changed. Sometimes a new stake will be pushed into the mud (with the old one still remaining), and private floats can and do drag off station. Reliance upon private aids should be taken with great caution.

When you encounter a privately maintained aid to navigation, look first to see if it makes sense with regard to the chart and your observations. If local boats are in the area, see if they are following them. Look also to see if they appear to be fresh. A new stick in the mud or a clean white Styrofoam float is more likely to be in the right place than an obviously old one. Never take them for granted and proceed with care.

Bridges on the ICW

Bridges can be problematic or worse for all but the lowest clearance boats on the ICW. On the positive side, most new bridges being built are constructed to the "official" ICW clearance of 65 feet. Many older low bridges have been replaced with these. A word of caution: A few of the newer 65-foot bridges are actually a foot or two below that height, as noted in our text describing those specific areas. Also, fluctuating water levels from storm events can increase or decrease the actual clearance by as much as several feet over normal tidal fluctuations.

CONTACTING THE BRIDGE TENDER: When you encounter a bridge that must be opened for your passage, the horn signal is one long and one short blast. However, the best way to communicate with them is via VHF radio. This way, you will then know whether they can respond, and they can advise you of any problems or the actual wait time until the next opening. Bridges in most states monitor VHF Channel 13, but South Carolina, Georgia and Florida monitor VHF Channel 09, as noted in our bridge tables.

VERTICAL CLEARANCE: The vertical clearance of each bridge is normally posted on a clearance gauge. It is also noted on the charts, but these do not always reflect recent changes. We have attempted to note these as of our last visit or as charted, but beware that they may now be different. Bridge signs and charts normally note the lowest clearance point, often at the outer edges of the opening. WATERWAY GUIDE normally gives the maximum opening at the center of the bridge, which accounts for the additional arch clearance. It is important, however, to note that obstructions such as bridge-mounted lights or signs may decrease the actual clearance under such attachments.

BRIDGE RESTRICTIONS: Each year, as automobile traffic has increased, more bridges have instituted restricted openings for boats and/or decreased the frequency of openings. These can change, but in our bridge tables in the Skipper's Handbook section (yellow border), we show the latest detailed schedules and restrictions as of publication date. There is also a summary bridge table on the inside back flap of this Guide.

Restrictions of schedules are usually posted on a sign on the bridge, but often the signs are obscured by weathering or have writing that is too small to read until you are too close for safety. Check ahead, or call the bridge tender on VHF radio. See additional bridge information in our Skipper's Handbook section.

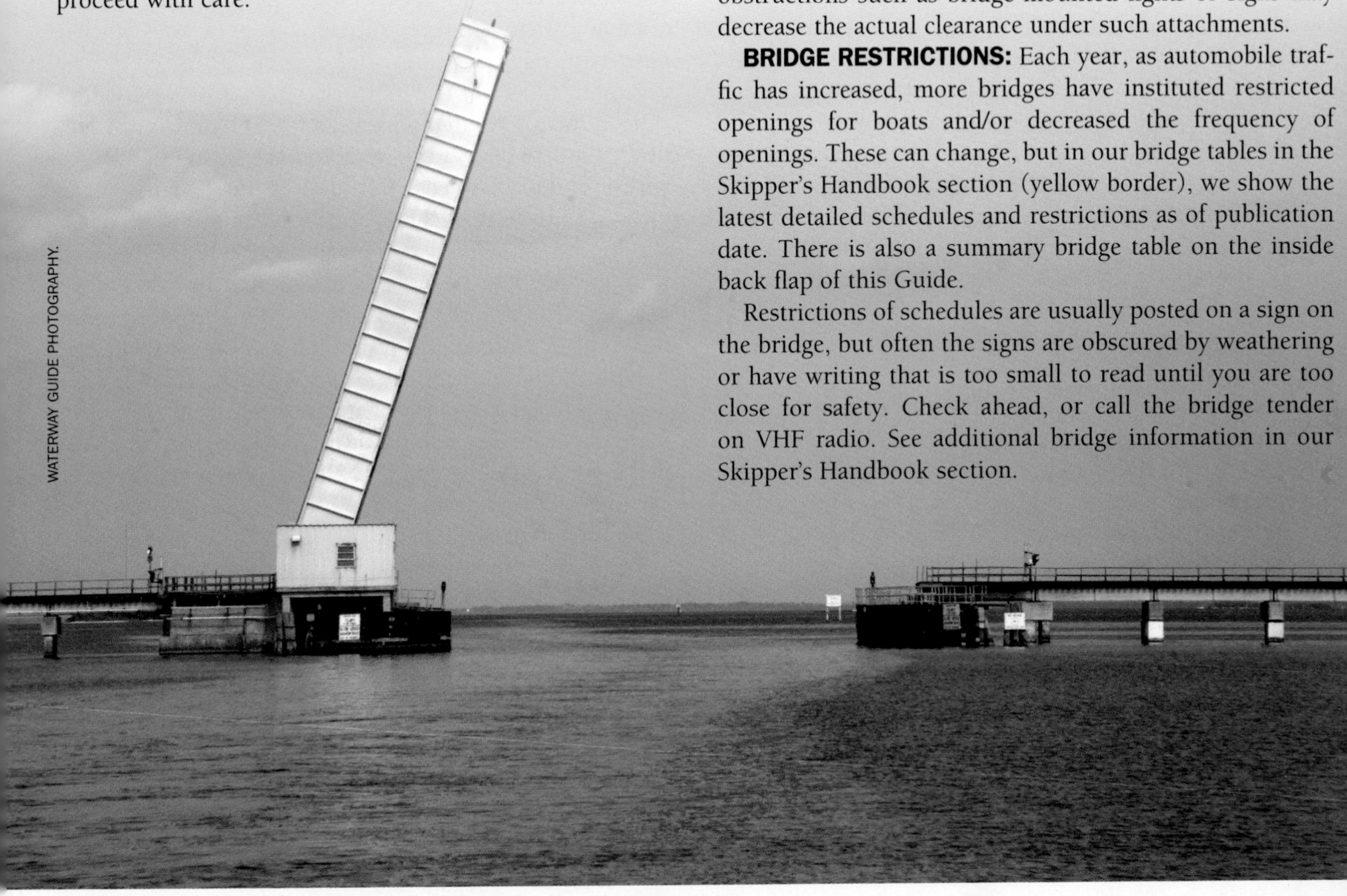

WATERWAY GUIDE PHOTOGRAPHY.

Shoaling

Shoaling is an especially prevalent concern for the ICW traveler as the designated channels are usually narrow, not very deep to begin with and subject to cross currents. This leaves little room for error. It is important to recognize that there are some areas along the ICW where the shifting of shoals is much more likely than others. Inlets and any areas of the ICW that pass close to inlets are prime areas for shoaling.

Also, almost any time you are entering a cut with a channel through shallows that are exposed to a long wind and wave fetch, you should expect shoaling and proceed with the assumption that things have changed since the last chartings. Whenever there is sand or mud to wash around and whenever there are tides or waves to do it, it will happen. We have tried to note most of these problem areas as we noticed them in our travels, but there will be others.

We highlight prevalent areas of shoaling throughout our Guides with a yellow background. Carefully study the text for these areas before you approach them to determine how best to proceed.

CURRENTS AND TIDES

Between the Virginia/North Carolina line and the top of Florida, you will experience a wide range of tide and tidal current conditions, from areas with no tide to areas with 8-foot tides and currents of 3 knots or more. In many of the Carolina sounds, there are no astronomical tides and, therefore, no current from those tides. This is due to their landlocked nature. Wind-driven tides and currents are, however, a regular occurrence. There is no way to predict the height or direction of these, and usually they are insignificant, except during major blows.

Heading south through the sounds, as you approach the coast at Beaufort/Morehead City, astronomical tides and currents become the norm. Here, tides are in the 3-foot range. They gradually increase as you head south along the coast, reaching their maximum range of 7 to 8 feet in the Savannah area and then begin decreasing as you move farther south.

Phases of the moon affect the heights of the tide and, therefore, the strength of the currents. A full or new moon will bring the greatest extremes between highs and lows. Since there is more water moving during these times, there will be more current.

The base stations for high and low tides for the area covered in this edition of Waterway Guide are displayed in the Skipper's Handbook. Tide differences for different locations are given in hours and minutes before or after low and high tide at the base stations. Differences can be considerable, particularly as you move up tributaries and rivers.

The time of high and low time does not correspond with the time of zero current. The current flow will stop and change at different times in relation to the tide peaks, and this will vary with the wind and moon. The book "Tidal Current Tables, Atlantic Coast of North America" (available at most marine stores) will give the norms expected but don't rely on this completely. Predicting when the current will reverse can be important to a slow-moving sailboat or motorboat.

Use tides to get through difficult areas of the ICW. Making shorter runs timed to coincide with high water can made the difference between getting through without incidence or spending hours stuck on the bottom, especially in areas of lower South Carolina and Georgia. Even the deepest-draft boat can pass through easily on high tide.

ANCHORING

Without getting into the eternal debate as to which anchor is best, the prudent mariner will have both CQR- and Danforth-type working anchors. One or the other almost always works, providing you use the proper length and weight of chain. Chain will not be cut by pieces of glass or junk on the bottom, whereas rope will. Also, the weight of the chain will help to set any type of anchor, causing the pull to be more parallel to the bottom rather than up and down, which will tend to pull the anchor out of the bottom, rather than dig it in. A good amount of heavy chain is absolutely critical in areas where the mud is very soft. Some bottoms are so soft that nothing will work, but long chain will sometimes save the day with this type of bottom.

Sand can also be good for holding but not always. Some sand is too hard even for a Danforth-type to easily dig in, although often this type will work in hard sand when a plow type won't. Grass is seldom good. Worse, it can be very misleading. Any anchor may bite hard at first, but in a blow, the roots will often give, a few at a time, until suddenly the last ones break, and you are sailing downwind with a clump of weeds! Fortunately, there is not much grass in most ICW anchorages.

Bottom mixtures are common. Shell and mud is found in many areas. Unless shells are broken up, they often provide a hard surface that most hooks cannot readily penetrate or, if deep, will result in a mixture that will only hold for a light pull. Shells also occasionally catch on the points of the anchor, making it impossible to set. However, many small or broken shells evenly mixed in mud can make good holding. Sand and mud is generally a good mixture, but very heavy concentrates of sand often require a Danforth-type anchor.

There are several ways to find what may be down there when you can't see the bottom. The best way is to dig up some bottom with your anchor and check it. No one wants to do this on purpose, although it is what often happens when you drag on the first try. If you don't want to do this, first look at the charts. They sometimes give cryptic clues such as "stk" (sticky) or "hrd" (hard). (NOAA Chart Number One has abbreviation guides that may indicate a different code than that actually used.) This occasionally helps, but only take it as very general advice.

Also look along the shores for clues. Often, for example, shells on the bank will indicate shell below. If the banks are marsh in mud, with a fair current to keep the bottom free from mush, there may be good mud below. Quiet coves surrounded by beautiful forest often hold slime bottoms caused from years of siltation and decay with little cleansing current. Sandy beaches ashore with a gently sloping bottom indicated on the chart often means sand out where you wish to anchor.

Time spent in properly anchoring could save you from a miserable night, property damage and/or personal injury. Remember that the wind and weather can change. For example, if you are expecting a front or thunder squalls, be sure that your anchor is set from the direction of the anticipated strong wind, unless you are already experiencing strong winds from another direction. Also, anticipate where you will swing when the wind shifts. If it is into a bank, or into another boat or over their anchor rode, reposition yourself or put out a second anchor.

If your anchor does hold after backing, don't stop there, particularly if you expect any weather. Continue backing down with slowly increasing power on the engine until you are sure, while taking a bearing with an object on shore. If your boat jerks a little when the line tightens and the stern swings around straight behind, you are probably in for the night.

Anchor Lights

Because of the heavy amount of commercial and pleasure traffic on the ICW, it is always important that you are operating with the proper lighting configuration, and it is crucial that you show an anchor light. There are many deserted creeks and coves where you would never expect to see anyone when suddenly, around 4 a.m., a workboat with a sleepy waterman at the helm heads out from a little slip up in the woods, comes around a bend and is suddenly upon you. Even in so-called "designated anchorages," if someone can't see you and hits you, there may be substantial civil liability on your part. *Always* show a bright anchor light.

Wrecks and Obstructions

The ICW has been subjected to the march of "civilization" since construction first began in the 1930s, and much longer on the sections that run through rivers and sounds. Since then, boats have been sinking, piers have been built, and pilings have been driven and disappeared with the ages. Remnants of our incursions remain throughout the waters, as the charts constantly remind us.

The problem is that many of these charted "wrecks" and "obstructions reported" are no longer there and have not been for some time. Another problem is if the charted wreck symbol covers the entire cove or channel, when actually the "wreck" is just a few old ribs up in the marsh on the shore or in about 1 foot of water.

In many cases, you will find that wrecks or obstructions are noted in front of active marinas. As a general rule, you can usually assume that the marina has either removed these or marked them if they are still there.

In other cases, you will see the wreck symbol up in an otherwise perfect cove. Often this means that, generations ago, a boat was left there to die on the shore. Check along the marsh to see if this is not the case. There are some areas where there has been a great deal of industrial waterfront use and development over the years, and you should be especially careful to avoid symbols in these areas.

Power Lines, Above and Below

Because of the abundance of civilization around the shores, there are power lines throughout the ICW. Some are stretched overhead, while some are laid or buried along the bottom of the Waterway. In either case, tangling with one can be fatal. Not only can it ensnare your anchor or entangle your mast, it can allow huge voltages of electricity to shoot throughout the boat, causing electrocution and usually fire.

The charts generally denote cable areas. In these areas, there is usually a sign on the shore at each end of an underwater cable so that you know where it is. However, we have noticed places where there were no signs, they were obscured or there were uncharted cables.

The best rule to follow is to never put the anchor down without first checking the chart. (Make sure your chart is up-to-date.) Then check the shore for signage to be sure you are safe. If there are signs, anchor well away from any line between them. If there is a designated underwater cable area and you cannot find signs, anchor outside of that area unless you have a certain local knowledge that nothing is there. Always assume that you might drag in a blow and give yourself enough room to do this without snagging a cable.

Overhead power lines are also a serious danger. We are all accustomed to seeing power and telephone poles and proceeding under them as we drive our automobiles. If you are in a sailboat or any boat with high protrusions such as outriggers, you should never take clearance for granted. First, look up (sometimes a difficult habit to get into) to see if there are wires, and then check the charts for clearance. Wires often sag for various reasons, and even a close passing could allow current to jump to the metal bits of your boat.

WEATHER ALONG THE ICW

Bermuda Highs

A primary consideration for any cruise is weather. The dog days of summer (usually early to mid-July through mid-September) often bring many periods of flat-calm winds, very hot, humid and hazy days and nights, broken by afternoon thunderstorms, sometimes with dangerous winds and lightning. Often during the summer months, dense high-pressure systems will settle off the Eastern Seaboard. These can affect the weather for weeks, causing extreme heat and humidity, stagnant air and haze. These are frequently called "Bermuda Highs."

Thunderstorms

Coastal thunderstorms should be taken very seriously. They come up rapidly, usually from the southwest, west or northwest and often contain damaging hail and deadly cloud-to-ground lightning, with strong winds. The storm and winds seldom last long, but they can be quite serious.

Because of the sudden nature of the wind shifts, and the fact that the wind may go from dead still to over 70 miles per hour very suddenly, most experienced sailors take down their sails and motor into, or run off from, the approaching storm if they are caught out. A knockdown could easily occur in these conditions, even with fully reefed sail.

The weather stations on VHF radio (see the coverage chart in the back of this Guide) usually issue watches and warnings, and the Coast Guard will also issue weather bulletins on VHF Channel 16 when these storms are approaching. However, you should always keep a weather eye. Hot, humid conditions are most likely to produce these storms, particularly if a cold front is approaching.

Usually the sky to the west will begin to gray, sometimes becoming dull blue, green or copper in color. High towering cumulus clouds should always be watched. Often, on the days when the storms are most likely to occur, there is so much haze in the air that you can't see the changes in the sky. In these conditions, it is particularly important to listen for thunder, observe the sky closely, and check the weather stations. If such a storm threatens, seek a safe anchorage or marina, and prepare for strong gusty winds.

Tornadoes and waterspouts also occasionally occur, usually in the spring, particularly associated with severe violent thunderstorms and the systems that produce these storms. Any time that there is a violent thunderstorm watch, and anytime you observe the conditions that create these storms, be also on a lookout for these twisters. If you see one, report it to the Coast Guard, not only to alert others, but also to alert them to your position and situation. If you have not had the time to get in and are still on the water, take evasive action.

We are all familiar with cold fronts; we know that they can bring sudden shifts of very strong wind and preceding thunderstorms. Usually, we relax after they have blown through, knowing that there will probably be at least several days of cool, comfortable, stable weather. Enjoy these postfrontal days, but do not automatically assume that no violent weather can occur and heed any sky and cloud warnings.

Fog and Haze

Fortunately, fog is not very common, although at times it can be a very serious problem, especially in the fall. Most often, it will be associated with warm, moist air over the colder autumn water. The same thinking goes for early spring. Fog is usually predicted over VHF weather radio and visibility can quickly become totally obscured. Pay attention to the weather and listen to the VHF radio for weather updates. (See the NOAA Weather radio station coverage map in the back of this edition.)

Dense haze can not only make it difficult to sight approaching thunderstorms but also obliterates the shoreline and aids to navigation until you are quite close. This sort of haze can sometimes occur on hot muggy days, particularly when there has been a dense high-pressure system dominating the weather. These conditions can, even on a sunny day, cause you to be totally out of sight of land, even in areas where the shore seems very close.

Hurricanes

Hurricanes are of great concern from the Carolinas southward, and for this reason, many insurance companies will not give you storm coverage south of the Chesapeake Bay during the hurricane season, which runs from June 1 to November 30. Storms can sweep in off the nearby ocean in full fury, leaving incredible destruction. Numerous landmarks along the Atlantic coast were either formed or demolished by these storms. Do not become complacent because one never knows what these storms are going to do until they do it.

Hurricane holes are hard to find because of the low coastal plain, proximity to the ocean and tidal surges that

WATERWAY GUIDE PHOTOGRAPHY.

occur. Staying at a dock is usually not an option. At best it is a bad choice, due to the risk of damage by striking pilings from storm surge.

Do not wait for the storm to begin before you make your plans. Start looking and settling on a spot many days before the expected hurricane landfall. Preparing for a hurricane takes a lot of work and time.

If you decide to ride out a storm at anchor, check the type of bottom. Thick mud, preferably mud and gray clay, usually provides the best holding. Mud and sand with a Danforth anchor is another good type of bottom in which to anchor. It is usually better to put down at least two anchors because the winds will shift 180 degrees if the storm passes right over head. Many people will place two anchors against the first expected direction (usually easterly or some quadrant thereof) because that will generally be the strongest wind. Then they place a third to hold after the wind shift with the storm passage.

Observe piers, pilings or other structures on the shore that could cause damage if you drag. Anchor in a place where if you drag in the time of maximum wind, you will drag into a forgiving bank rather than a bunch of broken pilings. No matter how well you have prepared, if your neighbor does a poor job and drags into you or your lines, you may be no better off than he.

Once you are secured to the bottom or shore, remove or tightly tie down everything that is on your deck that could come loose. If you have a leak around a window or port that you haven't gotten around to fixing, cover it with duct tape. If you don't, the driving rain will flood in.

Weather Reports

For 24-hour weather that will include special alerts and sometimes tide information, turn to the weather stations on your VHF radio.

Satellite weather and websites are another source for obtaining current updates. However, remember that conditions can change in a few hours, often making current weather reports inaccurate. Wind conditions are notoriously stronger than generally forecast.

Nothing beats knowledgeable observation with your eyes and instincts and the use of a barometer. We would strongly recommend having a good quality working barometer aboard and learning how to use it. If the barometric pressure starts to drop, you know the weather is going to worsen.

Insects

With warm weather, there will be more problems from mosquitoes, particularly for cruisers seeking the quiet anchorages among the many marsh-lined shores. The best way to handle them is to have screens on your hatches and portholes. Nothing can take the place of these. It also helps to avoid the areas where mosquitoes are most likely to breed, like marshes and low lands. As a rule, the farther you are from marsh or marsh shoreline, and the more breeze you have, the fewer the bites. Close wooded or marshy coves in summer will always bring these pests. They will be the worst just as light is failing, engaging in a feeding frenzy upon whomever they can find.

You should also have a repellent spray aboard, particularly if you don't want to spend a beautiful evening cowering below behind screens. Gnats and "no-see-ums" are also encountered mostly in the evening on quiet warm nights in marshes and wooded areas. Some varieties of these creatures are so small that they can come through most screens, necessitating "no-see-um" netting.

Shells and Other Sharp Objects

Whenever you are swimming or wading, take care where you put your feet until you know what is there. Oysters, clams and barnacles have sharp edges that make dirty cuts if you step on them. Beware also of other sharp objects around areas of civilization. Thoughtless people can throw a bottle overboard that will lie in wait for years until you step on it. Treat any cut immediately with a thorough washing of hydrogen peroxide. Better yet, wear water socks or a similar-type foot covering when wading anywhere but a sandy beach. ■

QUICK FACT:

PASSER VS PASSEE

Passing, or being passed, in a narrow channel is a common, everyday occurrence we all experience on the Waterway. Although simple in theory, it can cause significant conflict, due to a lack of knowledge or lack of courtesy.

The basic rule to remember in a close passing situation is that BOTH boats must slow down.

In a typical situation, a sailboat moving at approximately 6 knots is being overtaken by a powerboat capable of much higher speeds. If the boat being overtaken does not slow down to idle speed, then the faster boat must move past at 9 or 10 knots. The problem is, although the speed differential between the boats is only walking speed, at a speed 9 or 10 knots, the stern of a powerboat is beginning to squat, causing it to pull a large wake, so it cannot prevent rolling the boat being overtaken.

The solution: The faster boat should hail the slower boat via VHF radio to indicate his passing intentions. (Boats are required to monitor and acknowledge VHF.) The slower boat should reduce speed to idle as the faster boat nears. The faster boat can slow at the last minute as its bow draws near the stern of the slower boat. As it does, its wake lifts its stern, allowing the faster boat to slide by at about 6 knots with minimal wake. The slower boat should then turn into the wake of the faster boat, and then resume its course behind the faster boat as it speeds off.

This simple procedure produces minimal wake and minimal lost time for both boats. It also saves a lot of things from being broken during side-to-side rolls.

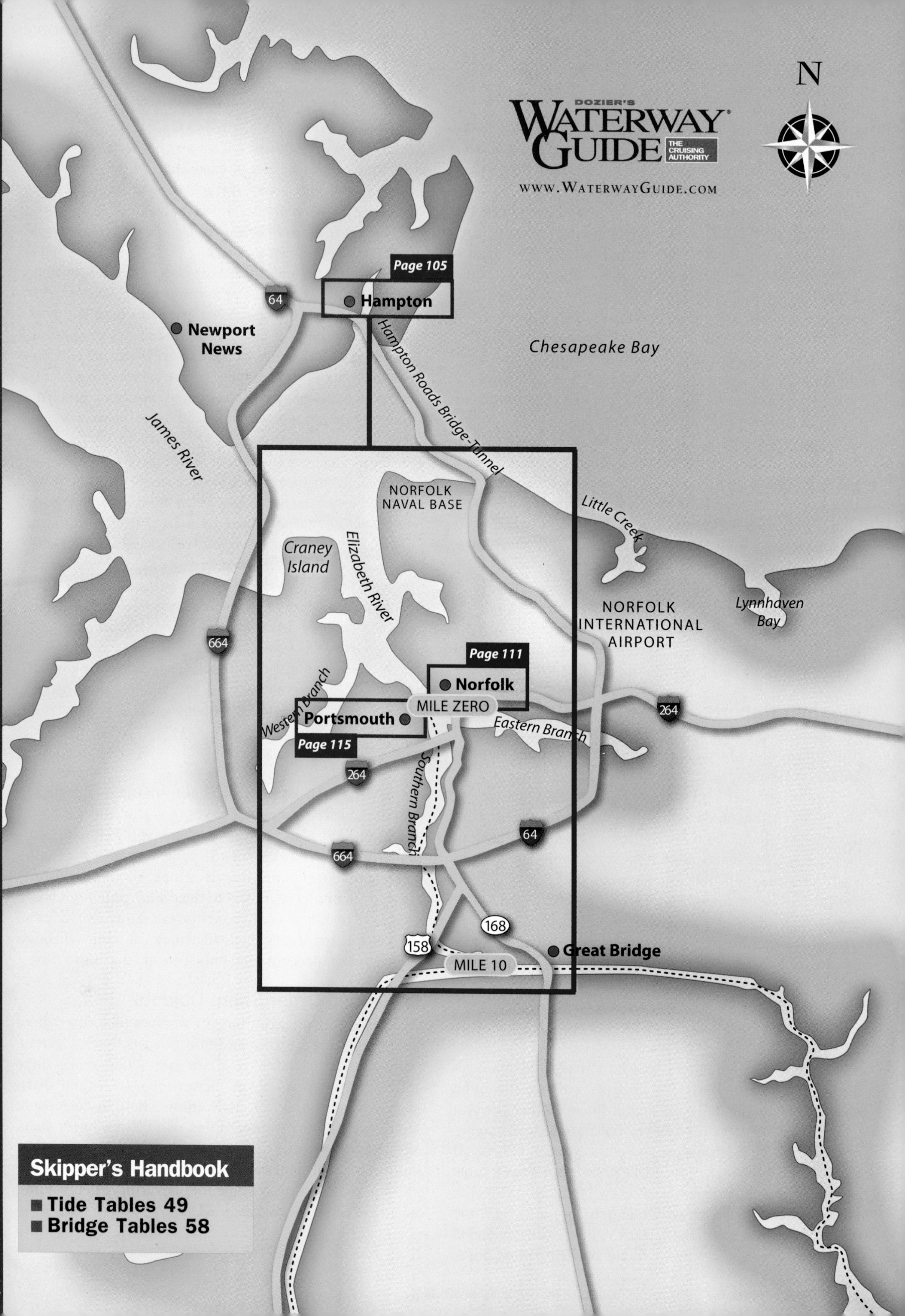

Skipper's Handbook

- Tide Tables 49
- Bridge Tables 58

Hampton Roads, VA

CHARTS 12221, 12222, 12245, 12256

HAMPTON ROADS, VA

Before you can begin your journey down the ICW, you must traverse the 10-mile-stretch through the Hampton Roads area. This huge harbor is home to vessels of all kinds: commercial, military, foreign and recreational. Hampton Roads Harbor begins at the line between Old Point Comfort on the north shore and Willoughby Spit to the south. It is the site of the famous *Monitor* and *Merrimac* naval battle of 1862, and continues today as one of the world's greatest natural harbors. Hampton Roads is also home to the world's largest naval base, a major shipbuilder and several great commercial ports. Mariners must carefully find their way among all these vessels and aids to navigation in this great nautical crossroads. Stay tuned to VHF Channel 16 and, if your radio scans, also to VHF Channel 13, the channel on which commercial traffic will be communicating.

Twin three-mile-long bridge-tunnels join the north and south sides of Hampton Roads (from Hampton to Norfolk) between Old Point Comfort and Willoughby Spit. Channels over the tunnels are well marked, but they also serve as bottlenecks through which all of the big-ship traffic must pass, and currents are strong here. At Old Point Comfort, the conspicuous historical brick landmark, the Chamberlin Hotel is visible from Chesapeake Bay and marks the north side of the entrance to Hampton Roads Harbor. Fort Monroe and Hampton University are on the eastern side of Hampton Harbor. Hampton, just west of Old Point Comfort, is located on both sides of the short, busy Hampton River. Founded in 1610, Hampton is the oldest English-speaking city in America and is now Virginia's main seafood packing center.

Proceeding south through Hampton Roads Harbor, give ships at the Norfolk Naval Base a wide berth. This area is constantly patrolled, and it is advised is to favor the west side of the channel, or even just outside the channel, where there is still adequate water depth. In fact, all military and commercial ships must be given a wide berth at all times, as dictated by the Homeland Security Act. This is not a No-Wake Zone, but caution should be exercised through this congested area.

Hampton Roads, VA

NAVIGATION: Use Chart 12222. On the north side of Hampton Roads Harbor, after you cross the twin tunnels of the Hampton Roads Bridge-Tunnel, pick up flashing red "2" marking the start of the dogleg channel into the Hampton River. Take care not to cut the riprap too closely at the tunnel's entrance islands; some of the rocks extend out farther than one might expect. The channel into the Hampton River makes a turn to port at quick flashing red light "6" and green daybeacon "7," and then to starboard at quick flashing green "11" and red daybeacon "12." Despite the curviness, the channel is deep and easy to follow. Both commercial and recreational boats frequently use the channel.

Dockage: Hampton's marinas are all to port, either up the Hampton River or on Sunset Creek, which leads off to the west from the main Hampton River channel. Bluewater Yachting Center features over 200 slips, all floating, for vessels up to 200 feet. They have three separate fueling stations, along with the Surfrider Restaurant, yacht sales offices, complimentary water shuttle service to downtown, wireless Internet, pump-out facilities and a pool. Bluewater Yacht Yard division is located on Sunset Creek and has space available for transients at its floating docks, a 100-ton lift, pump-out service and full-service repairs. The Hampton Yacht Club holds a few spots for transients who are members of reciprocating yacht clubs.

Below the bridge, the Downtown Hampton Public Piers maintain slips for cruising boats at floating piers just upriver of the visitor's center. The docks have finger piers and enough room for 26 boats docked stern- or bow-to. The tour boat to Fort Wool uses the slip next to the visitor's center. Farther upstream, at the far end of the docks, is the dinghy docking area. Heads and showers are located ashore, and there's a wireless Internet link. Mariners who wish to tie up at the public piers should call ahead to the dockmaster (757-727-1276). Short-term dockage is available for four hours. Stay longer, and you will be charged for a full day, based on the length of your boat. (Note: A hotel on the waterfront features a formal restaurant, a sports lounge, a waterside raw bar, a pool and a fitness center, which are all available to boaters).

Anchorage: You can anchor on the Hampton River above red daybeacon "20," opposite the Downtown Hampton Public Piers, on the Hampton University side out of the channel. A Coast Guard-designated anchorage, marked by three yellow buoys, is located across from the Hampton Public Piers. Boats may anchor anywhere past red daybeacon "20" on the red-marker side of the channel. Depths are 6 to 15 feet—use the depth sounder! Do not block traffic, interfere with the private marina or with the city dock. Boats that can get under the 29-foot fixed vertical clearance of the highway bridge at the end of the channel can find good anchorage upstream, in 8 to 10 feet of water with good holding and plenty of swing room. As always, exercise caution in shoal areas.

See additional information about the town of Hampton in our Chesapeake Bay edition of WATERWAY GUIDE.

Hampton River, VA

HAMPTON RIVER	Phone	Largest Vessel Accommodated	VHF Channel Monitored	Transient Berths / Total Berths	Approach / Dockside Depth (reported)	Floating Docks	Gas / Diesel	Groceries, Ice, Marine Supplies, Snacks	Repairs: Hull, Engine, Propeller	Lift (tonnage), Crane, Rail	1=110V, 2=220V, B=Both, Max Amps	Laundry, Pool, Showers	Pump-Out Station	Nearby: Grocery Store, Motel, Restaurant
		Dockage					Supplies		Services					
1. Bluewater Yachting Center (Internet Access) (Wireless Internet Access)	**757-723-6774**	**225**	**16/72**	**50/208**	**12/8**	**F**	**GD**	**IMS**	**HEP**	**L100**	**B/100**	**LPS**	**P**	**GMR**
2. Bluewater Yacht Yards (Internet Access) (Wireless Internet Access)	**757-723-0793**	**80**	**16/09**	**6/36**	**12/8**	**F**		**M**	**HEP**	**L100**	**B/50**		**P**	**GMR**
3. Sunset Boating Center (Internet Access)	757-722-3325	44	16	10/55	10/8	F	GD	GIMS	HEP		1/30	LS	P	GMR
4. Hampton Yacht Club (Wireless Internet Access)	757-722-0711	100		/200	10/8	F					B/50	S	P	GMR
5. North Sails Hampton Inc.	757-722-4000	70			12/12							S		G
6. Downtown Hampton Public Piers (Internet Access) (Wireless Internet Access)	**757-727-1276**	**110**	**16/68**	**22/22**	**12/11**	**F**		**I**			**B/100**	**LPS**	**P**	**GR**
7. Joys Marina (Wireless Internet Access)	757-723-1022	50		3/70	12/6						B/50	S	P	MR

Corresponding chart(s) not to be used for navigation. Internet Access Wireless Internet Access

Willoughby Bay

A less crowded and less protected layover than Hampton is available at Willoughby Bay on the opposite (south) side of Hampton Roads, behind Willoughby Spit (where the Hampton Roads Bridge-Tunnel ends).

NAVIGATION: Use Chart 12222. Two marked channels take you into Willoughby Bay between Willoughby Spit and Sewells Point. The Navy-maintained south channel by Sewells Point is in a restricted area near the carrier docks, so it is recommended you use the north channel near the bridge tunnel into Willoughby Bay. Be prepared for strong currents at the entrance by Fort Wool. The northern Willoughby Channel depth is 10 feet with a width of 200 feet. When entering the north channel, stay clear of green daybeacon "1" and use flashing red "2" as the entrance point. Give the green markers a wide berth, especially green daybeacon "3."

Dockage: Willoughby Harbor Marina is located on the north side of Willoughby Bay on Willoughby Spit. The large marina offers numerous transient slips at floating docks, a laundry, restrooms and showers. The marina is convenient to the large Norfolk Naval Base nearby. Rebel Marina, just next door, has a few transient slips.

Anchorage: Anchor holding in Willoughby Spit past the marina complex (just past the entry on the north side of the bay) is good in approximately 10 feet of water but watch for submerged, marked pilings and crab markers in the area. In addition to reported debris on the bottom, an unmarked telephone cable crosses this area. This anchorage is also very noisy because of helicopter and Hovercraft training in the area.

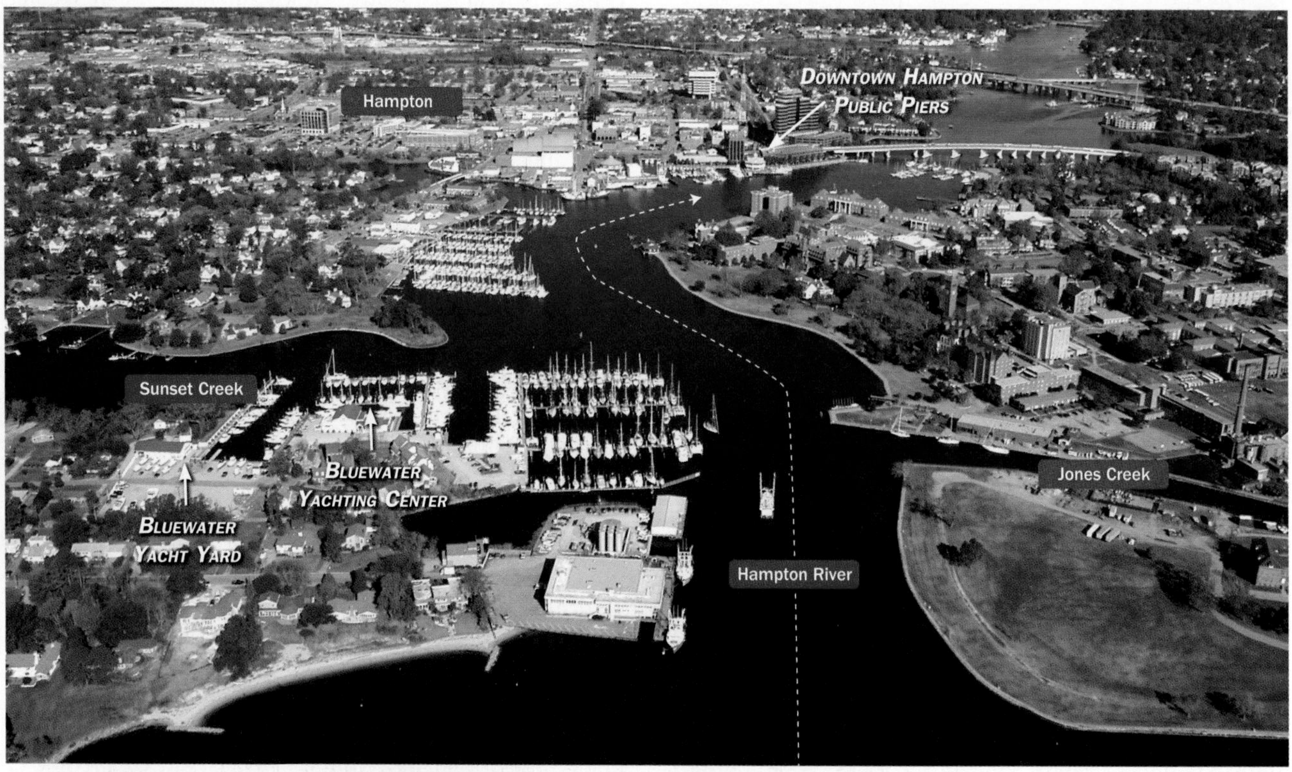

Looking northwest over the Hampton River. (Not to be used for navigation.) Waterway Guide Photography.

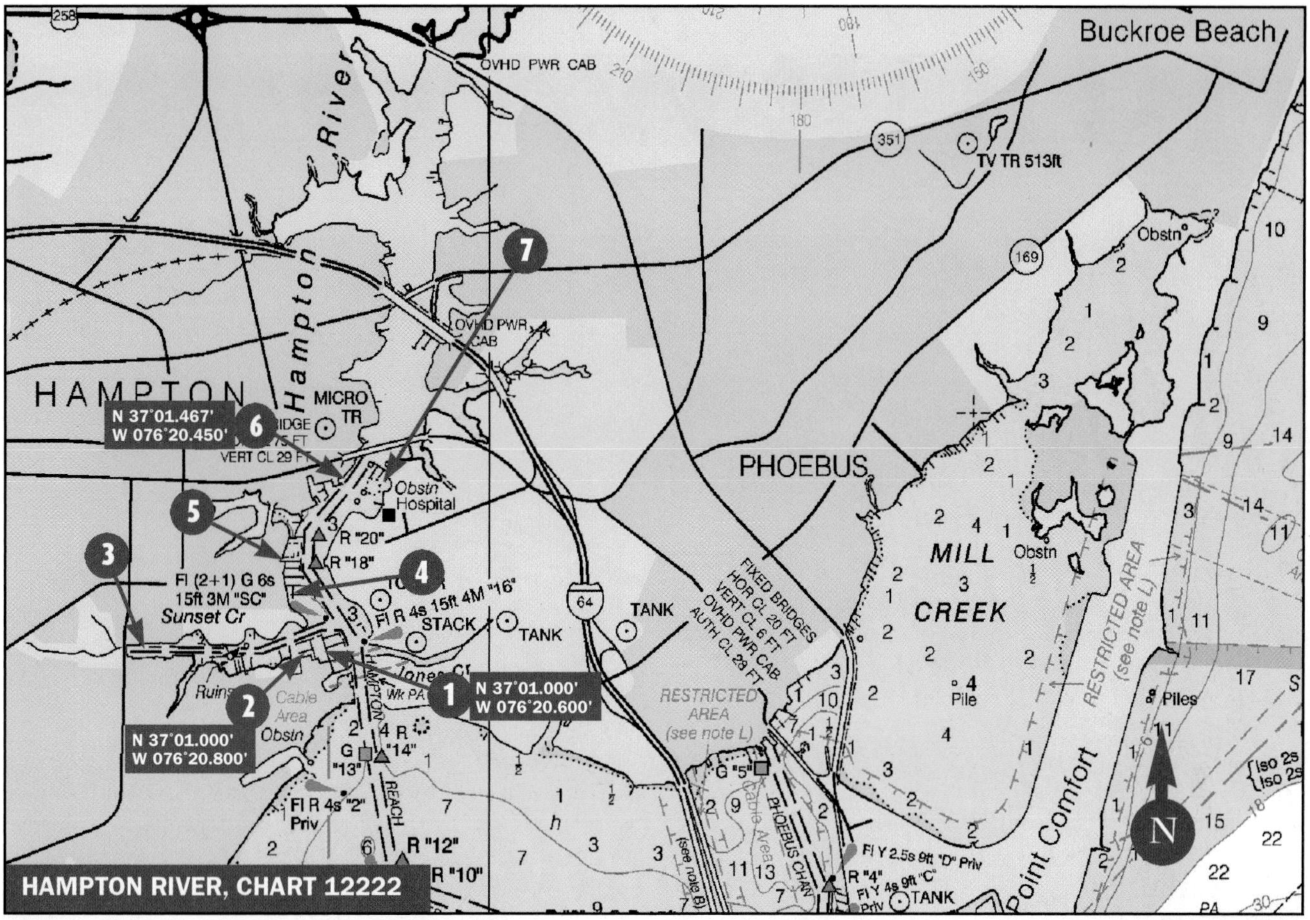

HAMPTON RIVER, CHART 12222

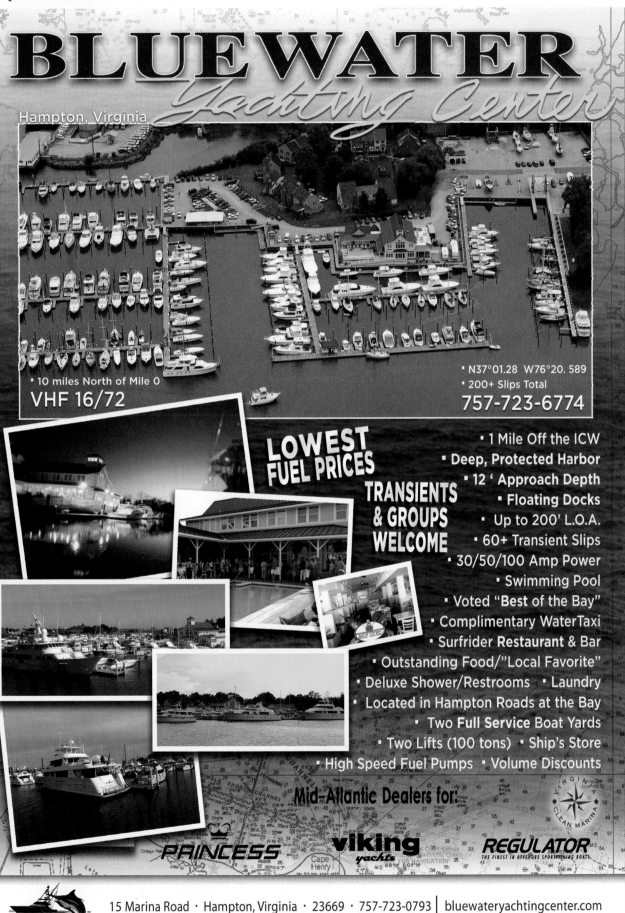

Introduction

Norfolk to Beaufort, NC

For southbound boats, the first 200-mile-long stretch of the Atlantic Intracoastal Waterway (ICW) between Mile Marker 0 at Norfolk and Mile Marker 205 at Morehead City/Beaufort, NC presents a diverse array of navigational challenges. The route passes through a lock (or two depending on the route you choose), canals, land cuts and open-water sounds along the way. Some of the open water offers the challenges associated with long fetches and shallow depths—namely, choppy wave action when the wind kicks up. Still, the run to Morehead City, NC is full of fascinating sights, side trips and ports of call.

Once you have begun the journey south from Norfolk, VA, the trip just gets more interesting as you enter the major Carolina waters of the Albemarle and Pamlico sounds. From the Sounds, side trips to waterside villages, such as Edenton, Washington, and New Bern offer diversion from the ICW proper. Meanwhile, to the east of the ICW, you will find the famous wilds of North Carolina's Outer Banks, with shipwreck-strewn beaches, massive dunes and excellent bird-watching opportunities.

On Croatan Sound, which connects the Albemarle and Pamlico Sounds, boaters can put in to the little port town of Manteo, NC, located on Roanoke Island, where one of the earliest American settlements was established—and from which the same settlement mysteriously vanished.

Along the way, boaters with a bent toward angling can drop a line over and fish for a tremendous variety of species. Some of the more popular in the sounds are bluefish, Spanish mackerel, channel bass, striped bass and spotted trout.

Note: Paper small-craft charts have five-statute-mile increments marked along the "magenta line" of the ICW, and these "Mile Markers" on the charts are commonly used to identify the locations of bridges, businesses, marinas, aids to navigation, anchorage locations, etc. In much, but not all of North Carolina (and sporadically in other ICW states), the Corps of Engineers has placed signs just outside the channel marking each five-mile increment along the route. But the numbers on these signs do not necessarily correspond to the "Mile Markers" on the charts. Some are the same, but some are different by a hundred yards or so, and some by as much as a mile. If you are using the actual signs to determine your location in relation to a timed bridge or marina location, you may find yourself a lot closer or farther away than you thought. Use the paper charts for this information. Also note that the magenta line may have been removed from recent charts in locations that are frequently dredged, where there are shifting shoals or where markers may be moved frequently. In some cases, the magenta line may be drawn on the wrong side of a few markers; if you observe this to be the case, seek local knowledge, but keep in mind that the markers are in place for a reason. ■

Bridges/Distances (Approximate Statute Miles from Mile Zero, Norfolk)

NORFOLK

Location	Mile	Clearance
Norfolk; Mile Zero (ICW flashing red buoy "36")	0	
N&P Beltline Railroad Lift Bridge (Normally open)*	2.6	6'
Norfolk & Western RR Lift Bridge (Norm.open)*	3.6	10'
Gilmerton Bascule Bridge	**5.8**	**11'**
Norfolk & Western Railroad Bridge	5.8	7'
Highway Bridge (Interstate 64)	7.1	65'

VIRGINIA CUT ROUTE

Location	Mile	Clearance
Dominion Boulevard Bridge (aka "Steel Bridge")	**8.8**	**12'**
Great Bridge Lock	**11.3**	
Great Bridge Bascule Bridge (Rte. 168)	**12.0**	**8'**
Highway Bypass Bridge (SR 168 Bypass)		
Albemarle & Chesapeake Railroad Bridge (Normally open)*	13.9	7'
Centerville Tpk. Swing Bridge (SR 170)	**15.2**	**4'**
North Landing Swing Bridge (SR 165)	**20.2**	**6'**
Pungo Ferry Bridge (SR 726)	28.3	65'
North Landing River Marker Q Fl G "87"	39.3	
Coinjock Bridge	49.9	65'
North River Entrance Marker Fl R 4 sec "170"	65.3	
Alligator River Entrance Marker FL G "1AR"	79.0	

DISMAL SWAMP ROUTE

Location	Mile	Clearance
Dismal Swamp Entrance Marker Fl R "30"	7.3	
Deep Creek Lock	**10.5**	
Deep Creek Bridge (U.S. 17)*	**11.1**	**4'**
Visitor Center Foot Bridge	28.0	0'
Highway Bridge	31.5	65'
South Mills Bridge*	**32.6**	**4'**
South Mills Lock	32.7	65'
Pasquotank River Junction	37	
Norfolk Southern Railroad Swing Bridge (Normally open)*	47.7	3'
Highway Bridges (U.S. 158)	**50.7**	**2'**

ICW ROUTES REJOIN

Location	Mile	Clearance
Alligator River Swing Bridge (U.S. 64)	84.2	14'
Alligator/Pungo Canal Entrance Q Fl "54"	105.0	
Fairfield Bridge (SR 94)	113.9	65'
Walter B. Jones Bridge (U.S. 264)	125.9	64'
Durante Point, Belhaven Q Fl R "10"	135.4	
Wades Point Marker Fl (2+1) R 6s "PR"	145.9	
Hobucken Bridge (SR 33/304)	157.2	65'
Neuse River Junction Fl (2+1) R 6s	166.5	
Garbacon Shoal Fl 4 sec "7"	180.6	
Core Creek Bridge (SR 101)	195.8	65'
Beaufort Channel Hwy. Bridge (U.S. 70)	203.8	65'
Beaufort Channel Railroad Bridge	203.8	4'
Beaufort Bridge	**Off ICW**	**13'**

Call 757-201-7500 opt. 3 (Army Engineers Dept. of Waterway Maintenance) for conditions in the Dismal Swamp route. Clearance is vertical, closed, in feet. *Not radio-equipped. Bridges and locks in bold type have restricted openings.

ICW Mile Marker

John Sharp

Norfolk, Elizabeth River

ICW Mile Zero–Mile 7 VHF Virginia Bridges: Channel 13

CHARTS 12206, 12207, 12221, 12222, 12245, 12253

Strategically situated at Mile Zero, the "official" beginning of the Atlantic Intracoastal Waterway (ICW), Norfolk and Portsmouth, VA offer nearly every kind of marine service and equipment and are especially good fitting-out places in preparation for a cruise south or north. Norfolk and Portsmouth are also exciting places to visit, with rejuvenated waterfronts filled with shops, restaurants, hotels, museums and historic sites.

The world's merchant fleet loads and unloads cargo at the Hampton Roads and Elizabeth River piers. Colliers fill their holds here with 100,000 tons of coal at a time. The Norfolk Naval Station, the largest naval installation in the world, is homeport for aircraft carriers, cruisers, destroyers, frigates, nuclear submarines and admiral's barges.

There are four daily bus tours of the naval base, seven days a week, during the spring and fall; nine daily tours in the summer months; and one daily tour in the winter months, excluding Mondays (call 757-444-7955). There is a fee for these tours ($10 for adults and $5 for seniors, 60-plus and children, 3 to 11). The Confederate ironclad *Merrimac*, which famously dueled with the Union's *Monitor* in 1861, was built in the Norfolk Naval Shipyard, which is actually across the river in Portsmouth. Many of today's huge ships are still built at a private shipbuilding and dry-dock company in nearby Newport News; this shipyard also builds giant supercarriers.

Warning: When transiting this area, keep your boat at least 500 yards from Navy ships. Vessels passing within 500 yards must do so at slow speed. No vessel may approach closer than 100 yards of any U.S. Navy vessel. Patrol boats are in abundance around the berthed vessels at the Norfolk Naval Station, Norshipco and the Norfolk Naval Shipyard. This perimeter is strictly enforced. Also, delays can occur as Coast Guard vessels escort ships in and out of the harbor. Commercial ships, especially containerships, are often escorted in and out of the harbor. Rules state that you cannot pass these vessels from behind but are free to go by them from the opposite direction. Be sure to stand by the VHF radio and maintain the largest possible distance between you and large ships. When in doubt, hail the ship on VHF Channel 13. See the "Port Security" section of our Skipper's Handbook in the front of this Guide for details on dealing with security zones and perimeters.

The Norfolk-Portsmouth area is a good centralized spot for sightseeing in the surrounding countryside, for picking up or dropping off guests and for flying in to rejoin a boat. Limousine service to and from Norfolk's airport is easy to arrange.

NAVIGATION: Use Chart 12222. **Use the Hampton Roads Tide Table. For high tide, add 18 minutes; for low tide, add 15 minutes.** Even with all its commercial and military activity, navigating through Norfolk Harbor is relatively easy during daylight hours. If southbound from Hampton Roads, pick up the marked channel past Sewells Point at the western end of Willoughby Bay and continue on into the Elizabeth River. Southbound past Sewells Point, you will see a great array of Naval vessels to port, from aircraft carriers to submarines. The harbor itself begins at Craney Island, where you can switch to Small-Craft Chart 12206. At night, navigation can be a bit more difficult with all the illumination ashore, making aids to navigation more difficult to detect.

As in New York Harbor, you can run outside the marked channel if ship traffic is heavy. Depths alongside the channel are good. The main hazard is flotsam, which can be in the form of wooden planks or piles the size of telephone poles. If you choose to run outside the channel, use the western side until you are past the Norfolk Naval Base and port operations to the east. Patrol boats and security barriers line the Restricted Area (shown as a purple shaded area on your chart) on the eastern side of the channel. From Craney Island southward, remain inside the channel to avoid shallows and military or port facilities.

The current can be strong here and can produce a marked delay in arrival time. Expect less current as you proceed from ICW Mile Zero southward. Heavy commercial traffic, bridge schedules and lock openings can also sometimes cause marked delay in arrival time, so planning ahead is a good idea before proceeding southward. There are frequent construction and diving operations to the north in Hampton Roads. Be alert for these and give a slow pass.

Anchorage: An anchorage up the Lafayette River is directly across from the yacht club and just outside the channel at the red marker. Several boats are here on permanent moorings. Depths are 8 to 9 feet just off the channel, shoaling gradually farther in. Although the club is private and the anchorage exposed to the west, you will find a suburban setting with little traffic. For boats that can clear a 24-foot fixed vertical bridge, there is a lot of additional anchorage farther up the river in 8 to 9 feet of water with ample swing room and protection. The spot is good for a layover if you are not planning to stop in Norfolk or Portsmouth.

Western Branch, Elizabeth River

NAVIGATION: Use Chart 12253. South around the main channel's bend at Lamberts Point, the Western Branch

Looking north over the Elizabeth River. (Not to be used for navigation.) WATERWAY GUIDE PHOTOGRAPHY.

of the Elizabeth River leads off to starboard. Note the magenta restricted area on the chart east of Lovett Point on your approach to Western Branch. A 45-foot fixed vertical clearance bridge just west of Lovett Point makes it impossible for some sailboats to pass farther upstream. Those who can clear the fixed bridge will find depths of 15 to 20 feet all the way to the Churchland Bridge (38-foot fixed vertical clearance) farther on.

Dockage: Virginia Boat and Yacht Service, located on the north side of Western Branch before the 45-foot bridge, has 63 slips with some transient space.

Western Branch Diesel Inc., also conveniently located on the north side before the bridge, offers installation, service and parts for vessels of all sizes.

■ MILE ZERO

NAVIGATION: Use Chart 12253 or 12206. Elizabeth River quick flashing red buoy "36," just east of Hospital Point, marks Mile 0 and the beginning of the 1,243-mile-long ICW. All mileage on the Norfolk-to-Florida segment of the ICW is measured in statute rather than nautical miles. Appropriately named, Hospital Point—located on the western side of the main Elizabeth River channel, south of the Western Branch junction—is home to a huge and recently enlarged Naval hospital, which is the nation's oldest.

Anchorage: Late arrivals and those who prefer to anchor out normally use the harbor's small-boat anchorage, south and west of the channel at flashing red buoy "36," between the large brick Naval hospital and Tidewater Yacht Marina. Unfortunately, it gets shaken up by endless passing traffic, including giant commercial vessels and is relatively exposed to high winds that can tunnel down the river, particularly during summer thunderstorms. The anchorage is popular despite its drawbacks. The bottom is poor here, with irregular holding, but a chain rode helps.

You can take the dinghy (you will need an outboard motor) and, for a small fee, make fast inside the Waterside Marina on the Norfolk waterfront across the river. Dinghy dockage and use of some facilities is available at the Tidewater Yacht Marina adjacent to the Portsmouth side of the river, also for a fee. There is no dinghy dockage available at Tidewater Yacht Marina or Waterside Marina during special events such as Harborfest in early June. Water taxi service is available on weekend evenings and for some special events.

Norfolk—Elizabeth River (East Shore)

Dockage: The city of Norfolk has constructed a wave screen directly in front of the Festival Marketplace at Waterside Marina to provide a protected area for vessels moored there. Transient space is available at modern floating slips with access to restrooms, showers, laundry facilities, an athletic club and complimentary wireless Internet service. The dockmaster will arrange for discount fuel and transportation for reprovisioning for overnight slipholders on request. Call on VHF Channel 16 or phone 757-625-3625 for reservations. The city of Norfolk has recently opened a new smaller marine facility (15 slips) for overflow from Waterside closeby at Nauticus, appropriately named the Nauticus Marina. Call Waterside Marina for information and reservations. A passenger ferry runs every 30 minutes between downtown Norfolk and Portsmouth with a fare of only $1.

GOIN' ASHORE: NORFOLK, VA

For two centuries, Norfolk has been a Navy town, and to this day, it is flanked on north and south by ships in gray livery. Before the Navy came into existence, merchant ships and sailors called Norfolk home, and cargo vessels of all types still call to load, to discharge or to undergo repairs.

A large city and several dormitory communities have grown up around all this maritime activity, flourishing with its booms and languishing with its busts. For several post-WWII decades, America's focus was on its highway systems, and maritime hubs received scant resources with which to maintain their infrastructures, both social and physical. In the 1980s, that tide changed, and Norfolk has ridden it to a new high water mark of civic pride and urban dynamism.

Anyone arriving in Norfolk by boat from either direction, whether from the isolated small towns of the Chesapeake Bay or from the cypress-bound sounds of North Carolina, is in for re-entry shock. It begins with the visual stimulation of the sheer volume of water traffic and intense industrial activity on both banks of the Elizabeth River and culminates with immersion into the din and clamor of a vibrant city. Enjoy it, because when you leave, in either direction, you will go a long way before encountering anything like it again.

History: Norfolk, home of the world's largest Naval base, has roots that begin at the waterfront and are entwined with it throughout history. Long before the arrival of English Colonists in the Chesapeake Bay, the Chesipean Indians had a settlement here, on the right bank of the Elizabeth River. By the time the Jamestown group arrived, Chief Powhatan—with whom the colonists, too, would have their own skirmishes—had wiped them out.

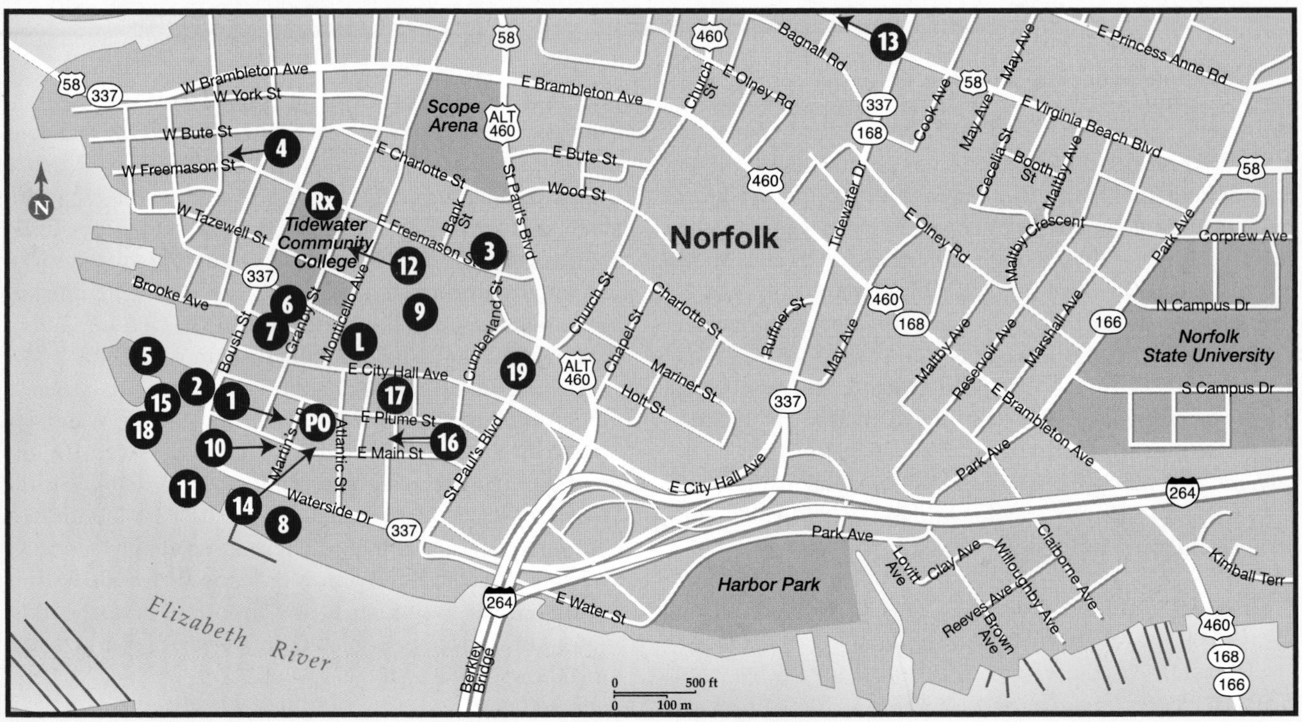

Reference the marina listing tables to see all the marinas in the area.

ARTS
1 Selden Arcade

ATTRACTIONS
2 Nauticus
3 Norfolk History Museum at the Willoughby
4 Hunter House Victorian Museum
5 Hampton Roads Naval Museum

DINING/SHOPPING
6 Espeto na Brasa
7 Rama Garden
8 Waterside Festival Marketplace
9 MacArthur Center
10 Prince Books

ENTERTAINMENT
11 Town Point Park
12 Wells Theater
13 Harrison Opera House

INFORMATION
14, 15 Convention & Visitors Bureaus

MARINE SUPPLIES
16 W.T. Brownley Co.

POINTS OF INTEREST
17 The MacArthur Memorial
18 Armed Forces Memorial
19 St. Paul's Church

L LIBRARY

PO POST OFFICE

Rx PHARMACY

One of the earliest English settlers in the area was Nicholas Wise, who, in 1622, purchased 200 acres of the land on which Norfolk now stands. He was a shipwright, and the surrounding vast forests of cypress, pine and oak laced with deep rivers must have provided bounty of proportions unimaginable in his homeland.

In 1682, in response to a 1680 decree from the Virginia House of Burgesses, Norfolk Towne was established on 50 acres purchased from the trustees of the Wise tract. Strategically located near the entrance to the Chesapeake Bay, and well served with sheltered deep water, Norfolk expanded rapidly to become one of the largest ports in Virginia. At the outbreak of the Revolutionary War, its importance was duly noted by the English, who sent a fleet of ships to bombard it. What they left of the town, Colonial troops razed to prevent the English from occupying it.

Reconstruction of the town began in 1783, and in 1801 the Continental Navy established its first Navy Yard. During the Civil War, Norfolk's strategic location again made it the focus of the attention of both sides, which took turns destroying much of it again—until, shortly after the spectacular but inconclusive battle between the ironclads *Virginia* and *Monitor* in 1862, the city surrendered to the Union Army. The occupation ended when Virginia was re-admitted into the Union in 1870; thereafter, Norfolk grew apace once more. Connected to the north by the Chesapeake Bay, to the west by railroads and to the south by the Albemarle and Chesapeake Canal (which had opened in 1859), it soon became, according to the city's official history, the world's largest seaport.

By itself, Norfolk, with a population approaching 250,000, is the second largest city in Virginia. The urban sprawl it forms with the surrounding towns and cities—Virginia Beach, Chesapeake, Suffolk and Portsmouth—is the largest in the state. It is not surprising that Norfolk supports many of the cultural and recreational outlets associated with bigger cities. It has a symphony orchestra, several museums, professional sports teams and a downtown shopping mall full of high-end retail stores.

At its heart, Norfolk is still a seaport and a Naval base, and the rejuvenation of its city center has been an arduous fight against the grittiness that adheres to port cities everywhere. It has been largely successful in the downtown area of Town Point, where Norfolk's waterfront basks in light reflected off high-rise office buildings and hotels. It is here that visiting boaters will tie up, either at Waterside or at the Nauticus Marina, within walking distance of many of Norfolk's must-sees. An early stop should be the visitors center at the entrance of Nauticus to pick up information on current events and a map.

Attractions: Nauticus is a fusion of science museum, game arcade and theme park, centered around humankind's historic engagement with the ocean and its denizens. Here, you can touch a shark, design a battleship or see how the earth's atmosphere and oceans interact to create and influence climate and weather. In the same building, the Hampton Roads Naval Museum showcases the U.S. Navy's 200-year association with the Hampton Roads region. Berthed alongside is the *USS Wisconsin*, veteran of three wars and the last battleship built for the U.S. Navy. Tours by bus or boat provide a close-up view of active-service ships at Naval Station Norfolk. Call 757-664-1000 for operating hours and information.

A city whose lifeblood is the military must necessarily cope with death, and several memorials remind visitors of the ultimate price our warriors pay. The MacArthur Memorial, where General Douglas MacArthur and his wife are laid to rest, is both a celebration of his life and achievements, and a tribute to the millions of men and women who served in America's wars, from the Spanish-American War to Korea. More evocative at a personal level, the Armed Forces Memorial in Town Point Park tells its story through examples of letters written home by servicemen and women who subsequently died in action. A good time to visit is in late afternoon, when warm light and long shadows highlight the messages, each one borne on cast bronze sheets and displayed as though strewn across the plaza by the wind.

Energetic walkers can follow the marked Cannonball Trail, which loops through the downtown area, taking in many city sights including Town Point, the Freemason Historic District, St. Paul's Church and the MacArthur Memorial. Those who care to make a morning or afternoon of it will find abundant opportunities for refreshment along the way.

A little farther afield, the Norfolk Botanical Gardens (757-441-5830) and the Virginia Zoo (757-441-2374) provide windows on nature contained, for those intimidated by the wildness of the Great Dismal Swamp.

Norfolk is home to a professional ice hockey team, the Admirals, who play at the Norfolk Scope Arena and a baseball team, the Tides, who play at the waterfront Harbor Park.

Getting Around: Norfolk Electric Transit (NET) is a free electric bus service that operates in the downtown area. The weekend route differs from the weekday route, so pick up a map at the visitors center (757-664-6222, www.norfolk.gov/parking).

Hampton Roads Transit connects with destinations beyond downtown and with all the cities in the Hampton Roads area (757-222-6100, www.gohrt.com).

A pedestrian ferry ($1.50 adults and children – seniors and disabled $0.75) connects Waterside to downtown Portsmouth across the Elizabeth River, so whichever side you moor your boat, you will have access to the amenities of both. And because you are in a city, taxicabs and rental cars are available to take you farther afield. Norfolk International Airport is a mere five miles from downtown.

Construction began in 2008 on Norfolk's light-rail transit system, The Tide. The first section opened in spring 2011 and will connect the city center with points west and east, including the waterfront baseball field at Harbor Park.

Shopping: Shopaholics can head for the Waterside Festival Marketplace, where the fare is touristy, or to the MacArthur Center, with its full quota of mid- and upscale mall stores anchored by Dillards and Nordstrom. A variety of emporia line the streets in between, and the Selden Arcade houses art workshops and galleries. If the onboard navigation system or library need updating, or the compass needs adjusting, a visit to W.T. Brownley Co. (established 1932) is a short step away at 226 E. Main St. (757-622-7589).

At Prince Books, 109 E. Main St. (757-622-9223), the discriminating bibliophile can browse a broad and eclectic selection of books and partake of a restorative coffee and a muffin in the on-site Lizard Café.

Culture: Norfolk is home to a symphony orchestra, an opera company, a professional theater and several venues for concerts and other cultural expositions.

The Virginia Stage Company is based in the Wells Theater, 254 Granby St., a restored Beaux Arts landmark that opened in 1913 as a vaudeville theater (757-627-1234, www.vastage.com).

The Attucks Theatre (1010 Church St.), was built in 1919 in what was then the heart of the minority district. After being idle and neglected for decades, it has been refurbished and reopened in 2008 to once again stage performances with an African-American influence (757-662-4763, www.attuckstheatre.org).

In the course of its 42-week season, which runs from September through June, Virginia Symphony plays at several venues in the Hampton Roads area (757-892-6366, www.virginiasymphony.org).

Virginia Opera performs at the Harrison Opera House, located on the corner of Virginia Beach Boulevard and Llewellyn Avenue, about a mile and a half from Waterside (866-763-7282, www.vaopera.org).

Norfolk has museums big and small with focuses broad and narrow. A sampling:

Chrysler Museum of Art: 245 W. Olney Road (757-664-6200, www.chrysler.org).

The Norfolk History Museum at the Willoughby-Baylor House: 601 E. Freemason St. (757-333-6283, www.chrysler.org).

Hermitage Foundation Museum: 7637 N. Shore Road (757-423-2052, www.hermitagefoundation.org).

Hunter House Victorian Museum: 240 W. Freemason St. (757-623-9814, www.hunterhousemuseum.org).

Restaurants: Restaurants in downtown Norfolk serve every gastronomic taste from meatballs to highballs. At Waterside Festival Marketplace, you will find pizza, an Outback Steakhouse and Hooters, and the usual food-court offerings are available at the MacArthur Center.

For a more adventurous dining experience, forage along Granby Street and its neighbors in an area studded with restaurants. Try Brazilian fare at Espeto na Brasa (757-313-4363) or Thai at Rama Garden (757-616-0533). Every continent is represented here, and the restaurants are numerous, but just as Norfolk is to some degree still finding itself, so too are some of these establishments. Take your lead from the visitor's guide, but don't be surprised if you find changes. Norfolk has an active nightlife, so the action at some restaurants doesn't get heavy until late in the evening.

Events: Town Point Park hosts cultural and musical festivals throughout the summer. The annual Harborfest has its origins in Operation Sail, the tall ship tour that was part of the America's Bicentennial celebrations in 1976.

Norfolk Town Point/Tall Ships. Photo courtesy of Norfolk Convention & Visitors Bureau.

ADDITIONAL RESOURCES

- CONVENTION & VISITORS BUREAU: Satellite offices at 232 E. Main St. and One Waterside Dr., 757-441-1852, 800-368-3097 www.norfolkcvb.com
- CITY OF NORFOLK: www.norfolk.gov
- NAUTICUS: One Waterside Dr.; 757-664-1000, 800-664-1080, www.nauticus.org
- HAMPTON ROADS NAVAL MUSEUM: One Waterside Dr., 757-322-2987 www.hrnm.navy.mil
- NAVAL STATION NORFOLK: 757-322-2330 www.navstanorva.navy.mil
- MACARTHUR MEMORIAL: MacArthur Square, Bank Street and City Hall Avenue; 757-441-2965 www.macarthurmemorial.org
- NORFOLK BOTANICAL GARDENS: 6700 Azalea Garden Rd.; 757-441-5830
- VIRGINIA ZOO: 3500 Granby St.; 757-441-2374 www.virginiazoo.org

NEARBY GOLF COURSES
Ocean View Golf Course, 9610 Norfolk Ave.; 757-480-2094, www.oceanviewgc.com (10 miles)

NEARBY MEDICAL FACILITIES
Sentara Norfolk General Hospital, 600 Gresham Dr. Norfolk, VA 23507, 757-388-3000 (3 miles)

Portsmouth—Elizabeth River (West Shore)

Directly on the ICW's first mile, this is a convenient location to regroup for the journey south or to recoup from the rigors of "The Ditch" when heading north. **Use Hampton Roads Tide Table. For high tide, add 9 minutes; for low tide, add 10 minutes.**

The Portsmouth Renaissance Hotel and Conference Center is on the waterfront at the entrance to the Elizabeth River's Southern Branch. The first basin, located just above the hotel, is North Harbor Landing (formerly known as Portside Ferry Landing), which offers ferry service and short-term dockage (no overnights, but dinghies are welcome). Private vessels may make fast for up to two hours, but must stay clear of the ferry.

Free public docking, but no overnight dockage, is also available in High Street Landing, a small basin with an entrance below the hotel. The Olde Towne Portsmouth historic shopping and entertainment district is adjacent to High Street Landing, with numerous shops and restaurants and the restored Art Deco-style Commodore Theatre.

Dockage: Dockage on the Portsmouth side of the Elizabeth River is available on Scotts Creek at Portsmouth Boating Center, also known for its high-speed diesel pumps and reasonable fuel prices.

Directly opposite Town Point, on the Portsmouth (west) side of the Elizabeth River, the full-service Tidewater Yacht Marina has 80 slips available for transients, some fixed and some at floating docks. The marina has six diesel and three gas fueling stations, substantial lift and repair facilities, a well-stocked ship's store with charts,

Looking north over the busy Intracoastal Waterway heading south from Norfolk. (Not to be used for navigation.) WATERWAY GUIDE PHOTOGRAPHY.

clothing and groceries. The Deck Restaurant, situated above the marina store and office, has a commanding view of the harbor and a full selection of seafood dishes to complement the view. Call ahead for reservations on VHF Channel 16. Tidewater Yacht Marina also has a floating swimming pool, a laundry, three bathhouses, a 1,000-square foot conference facility with a kitchen and wireless Internet service. Their new dock offers 12-foot depths. There are six megayacht slips with 100-amp single phase and 100-amp three-phase shore power.

Ocean Marine Yacht Center is easily accessible one half mile south with 122 floating slips, fuel, laundry and a one of the largest yacht service yards in the Mid-Atlantic region. The yard, boastsing an 80-ton Travelift and 1,250-ton Syncrolift, and has become a global refit center for many renowned megayachts, with its 35,000-square-foot indoor paint and repair facility. As an added bonus, the marina is adjacent to Portsmouth's new amphitheater, and marina guests may listen from their boats to concerts performed by famous classical and modern musicians at no extra cost. Wireless Internet is available at Ocean Marine as well as a courtesy car. Portsmouth's waterfront and the adjacent streets offer a wide venue of entertainment features, restaurants, shops and museums (but no grocery), and are all within walking distance of both Tidewater Yacht Marina and Ocean Marine Yacht Center.

Reprovisioning in downtown Portsmouth is possible at a Food Lion grocery about two miles from the marinas. You will still need a taxi (757-235-5099, Portside Taxi) or a marina courtesy car. There is a new store called Mile Marker "0", located at One High Street (at Water Street), that is offering marine supplies as well as transportation for the boating community and other such services. You can go to the supermarket, West Marine and other stores.

Norfolk, Portsmouth, VA

NORFOLK, PORTSMOUTH		Largest Vessel Accommodated	VHF Channel Monitored	Transient Berths / Total Berths	Approach / Dockside Depth (reported)	Floating Docks	Gas / Diesel	Groceries, Ice, Marine Supplies, Snacks	Repairs: Hull, Engine, Propeller	Lift (tonnage), Crane, Rail	1=110V, 2=220V, B=Both, Max Amps	Laundry, Pool, Showers	Pump-Out Station	Nearby: Grocery Store, Motel, Restaurant
		Dockage					Supplies		Services					
1. **Western Branch Diesel**	**757-673-7000**	**200**		**8/52**	**12/12**				**E**	**L35**	**B/50**	**LS**		**R**
2. Virginia Boat & Yacht	757-673-7167	150		5/62	12/8				HEP	L35	B/50	LS		R
3. Scott's Creek Marina 0	757-399-BOAT	65	16/68	8/135	14/12			GIMS			B/50	LPS	P	GR
4. Portsmouth Boating Center 0	757-397-2092	80	16	6/30	8/10		GD	IMS	HEP	L70	B/50	LS	P	GMR
5. **Nauticus Marina 0**	**757-625-3625**	**60**	**16**	**15/15**	**45/20**	**F**		**GIS**			**B/100**	**LS**	**P**	**GMR**
6. **Waterside Marina 0**	**757-625-3625**	**400**	**16/68**	**60/60**	**45/20**	**F**		**GIS**	**EP**		**B/100**	**LS**	**P**	**GMR**
7. **Tidewater Yacht Marina 0**	**757-393-2525**	**170**	**16/68**	**100/300**	**12/10**	**F**	**GD**	**GIMS**	**HEP**	**L60**	**B/100**	**LPS**	**P**	**GMR**
8. **Ocean Marine Yacht Center .6**	**757-399-2920**	**350**	**16/09**	**25/122**	**45/30**	**F**	**GD**	**IMS**	**HEP**	**L125**	**B/100**	**LS**	**P**	**GMR**
9. **Mile Marker 0**	**757-618-8885**			**1/1**	**Full Service Store**			**IMS**						**GR**

Corresponding chart(s) not to be used for navigation. Internet Access Wireless Internet Access

GOIN' ASHORE: **PORTSMOUTH, VA**

Portsmouth has long served as a key point at the beginning or end of a passage through the ICW. For many years before the city began construction on the new face it now presents to the Elizabeth River, it was a place to hit only to take aboard fuel and provisions before running for the less threatening open spaces of the Bay or the ICW. Today, now that the crust of decay has been peeled off to reveal its hoard of historic buildings, it is a destination worth exploring for its own sake.

Two large marinas, Tidewater Yacht Marina and Ocean Marine Yacht Center, provide a large number of transient berths at either end of a bustling waterfront bristling with new, high-rise hotels and fronted by green spaces and a boardwalk. From either one, a short stroll in quest of a morning latte will take you past many of the city's downtown attractions.

Directly across from you, a couple of America's largest warships, berthed in gargantuan floating dry docks, will be undergoing refits. Upstream, shipyards stretch as far as you can see. Downstream, towers of glass and concrete in Norfolk's business district loom above the Waterside Festival Marketplace, Town Point Park and Nauticus. The river itself teems with traffic. Threading its way among it all is the pedestrian ferry on which, when you have seen all you want to of Portsmouth, you can take passage to Norfolk to see what is offered over there.

History: Although complimented in 1607 by Capt. John Smith on its beauty, and blessed with similar natural resources to those of its neighbor across the Elizabeth River, the area that eventually became Portsmouth developed much more slowly than did Norfolk.

In 1620, John Wood, a shipbuilder, obviously impressed by the wealth of timber the region possessed, petitioned King James for a land grant. It appears he was unsuccessful, as little evidence of his enterprise remains in the record. Plantations in the region did flourish, pouring agricultural and timber products into the trade with England, but it was Norfolk that got the nod in 1680 to build one of the 20 official ports through which the Virginia House of Burgesses decreed that all of the Colony's business was to be conducted.

Despite that setback, the settlement steadily grew in size and importance. In 1752, it was established as a town by the Virginia General Assembly. Its founder, Col. William Crawford, named it Portsmouth, after his home town and England's preeminent Naval port, and laid out an area of 65 acres with a grid of streets and squares after the fashion then popular in England.

During the Revolutionary War, squabbles between groups with differing loyalties led to parts of the town being burned, but the defeat of Lord Dunmore at Great Bridge spared the town from the utter destruction the English had wrought on Norfolk.

After the war, the town continued to grow, along with the new nation's expanding international trade and in support of the Navy charged with protecting it. In 1827, the U.S. Navy chose Fort Nelson for the site of the first Naval hospital. In 1833, the Navy expanded the Gosport Navy Yard in Portsmouth but named the facility the Norfolk Naval Shipyard so that it wouldn't be confused with the Portsmouth Naval Shipyard in Kittery, Maine that is named after the town across the Piscataqua River in New Hampshire (proving that the Navy is consistent even in its inconsistencies). At the same time, the Portsmouth and Weldon Railroad came to town, connecting the canal system of the Roanoke River with the port facilities adjacent to Hampton Roads.

Two World Wars brought further growth in the naval and maritime facilities, and the scaling back of activity after each triggered economic setbacks, too. In 1952, the first highway under the Elizabeth River opened, and ferry services, which had driven commercial, cultural and social interaction between Portsmouth and Norfolk for three centuries, shut down, depriving both waterfronts of the foot traffic upon which downtown businesses once flourished. Portsmouth, long dependent on shipbuilding, suffered further when that industry moved to the Far East, and by the 1970s, in common with many American port cities, it was in serious decline.

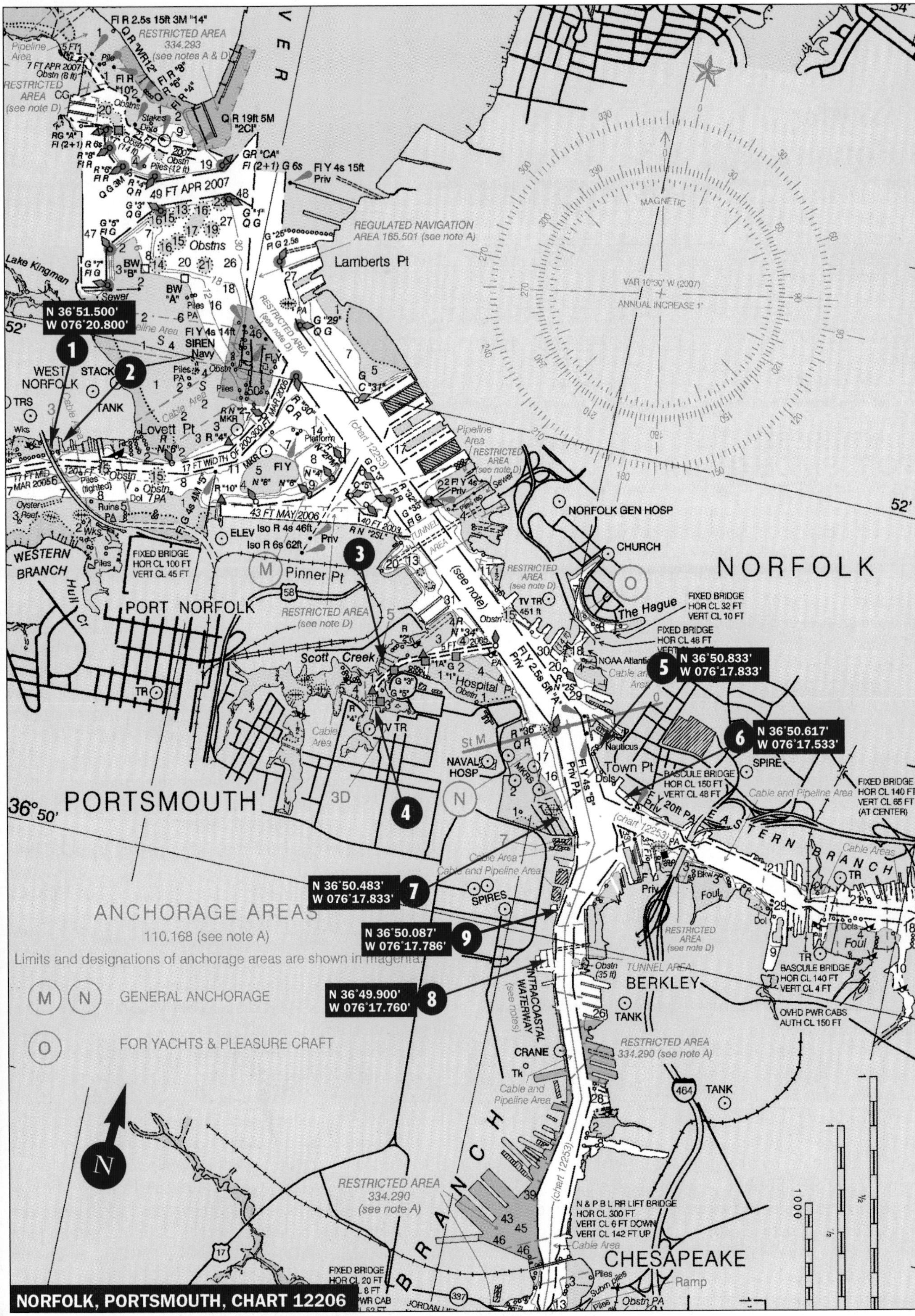

NORFOLK, PORTSMOUTH, CHART 12206

Portsmouth, VA

Dismayed at the town's condition, loyal residents formed civic groups to rescue its historic buildings and its spirit. In the 1980s, Portsmouth began to bounce back. Despite being hampered by its limited tax base, almost half of the town's area is occupied by the U.S. Navy and other tax-exempt organizations. The city, with support from the Olde Towne Business Association and other civic groups, has reinvented itself, beginning with downtown. The waterfront area has been largely rebuilt, High Street is vibrant with commerce once again, and several museums and cultural centers provide distractions enough to fill a visit of several days.

Attractions: A significant number of Portsmouth's attractions, whether culinary, cultural or recreational, are within easy walking distance of both downtown marinas.

In the Olde Towne Historic District, one block from the waterfront, scores of historically and architecturally important structures line leafy streets that still follow the original

QUICK FACT:

MUTE SWANS

Although mute swans improve the aesthetic of any waterfront, the bird is considered an aggressive, invasive species in the Chesapeake Bay and the greater eastern United States. The mute swan is native to Eurasia and was introduced to the United States, where it has become a controversial topic of discussion due to its threat to other wildlife.

Mute swans can be found in coastal and freshwater habitats, including sheltered bays, lakes, ponds and open marshes, as well as parks or on country estates. While several factors have caused U.S. populations to fluctuate, the current mute swan tally is approximately 16,000, a figure which has remained stable for the last 15 years, according to a U.S. Fish and Wildlife report.

Adult mute swans can range from 49 to 67 inches in length, measure up to 4 feet in height and can have a wingspan of 79 to 95 inches. Males, known as cobs, average 27 pounds, and females, or pens, can reach upwards of 19 pounds. At maturity, the swan has an orange-reddish bill and bright white plumage; young birds, known as cygnets, most often have a gray/buff color and a black bill for their first year. The bird has an extreme lifespan of 19 years in the wild and 35 years in captivity.

The swan's expansion in North America has presented serious problems for native species and ecosystems; the mute has been known to aggressively chase off birds equal in size, and it also poses a significant threat to plant life. Because submerged aquatic vegetation is a staple in the mute's diet, it can practically deplete it in feeding areas, disrupting the greater ecosystem.

Although the swan is protected in some states, there are measures in effect to reduce the Mute Swan populations, which unfortunately require lethal methods to control.

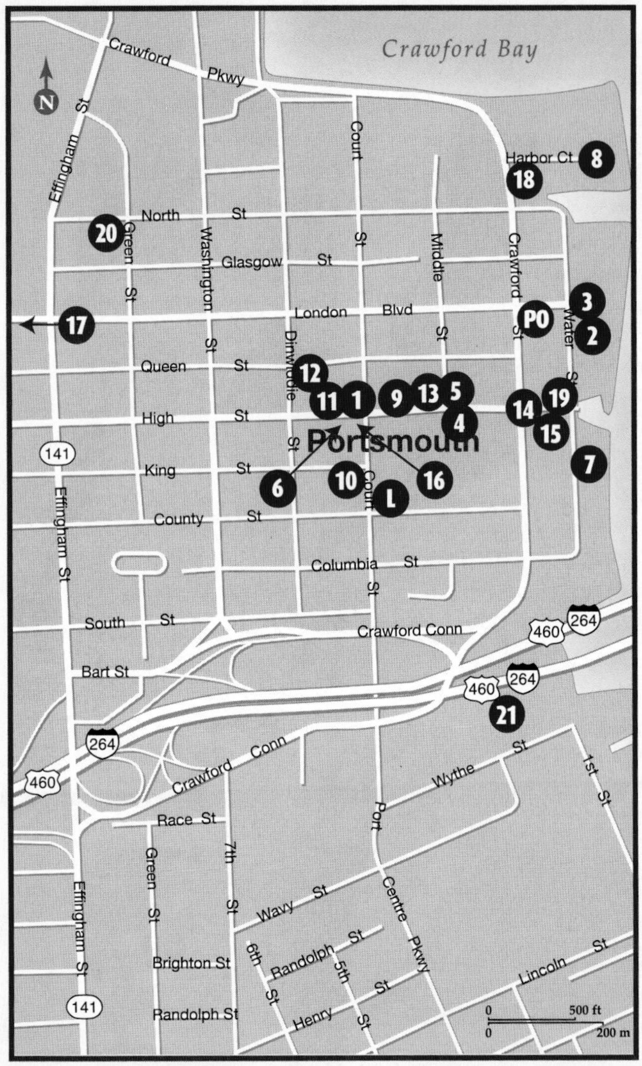

Reference the marina listing tables to see all the marinas in the area.

ARTS/ANTIQUES
1 Courthouse Galleries

ATTRACTIONS
2 Naval Shipyard Museum
3 Lightship Museum
4 The Children's Museum of Virginia
5 The Virginia Sports Hall of Fame
6 Commodore Theatre
7 High Street Elizabeth River Ferry Landing

DINING
9 Roger Brown's Restaurant & Sports Bar
10 Thumpers Olde Towne Bar & Grille
11 Bier Garden
12 Blue Water Seafood Grill
13 The Coffee Shoppe

MARINE SUPPLIES
14 SkipJack Nautical Wares
15 Mile Marker "0" Marine Supplies

GROCERIES/CARRYOUT
16 Organic Food Depot
17 Food Lion

INFORMATION
18 Visitors Center
19 Starboards Kiosk

POINTS OF INTEREST
20 Emanuel AME Church
21 Harbor Center nTelos Pavilion

L LIBRARY

PO POST OFFICE

grid pattern laid out in 1752. Because of the damage inflicted by all sides during both the Revolutionary and Civil wars, few Colonial-era buildings survived, but the private homes, churches and public buildings so far restored reflect every architectural style, from Federal and Queen Anne to Victorian and Art Deco. Stop in at the Visitor Center at 6 Crawford Parkway, pick up the Olde Towne walking tour brochure, and immerse yourself in a fascinating world of art, invention and extemporization, as manifested in two centuries of urban architecture.

Some buildings are as interesting for their social significance as for their age. Emanuel AME Church, at 637 North St., was built in 1857 to replace one on Glasgow Street that burned down in 1856. It is not only the second oldest church building in the town, it was also built by Portsmouth's oldest black congregation, which itself dates to the 1730s.

On the waterfront at the foot of High Street are the Naval Shipyard Museum and the Lightship Museum, the latter housed in a refurbished, but now landlocked, lightship (757-393-8591, www.portsnavalmuseums.com). Two blocks away at 221 High St. is The Children's Museum of Virginia (757-393-5258, www.childrensmuseumva.com). A Key Pass is available that gives access to all three museums and the Courthouse Galleries.

The Virginia Sports Hall of Fame & Museum, at 206 High St., celebrates Virginians who have made important contributions to the world of sports (757-393-8031, www.vshfm.com). Multimedia and interactive exhibits include soccer, baseball, basketball, golf, and auto racing.

Shopping, whether for needs or knickknacks, centers on the first seven blocks of High Street, and its tributaries. You will find art, antiques, organic foods, a pharmacy and sundry specialty stores all within a comfortable walk in attractive and well-maintained surroundings.

Culture: Resurgent and pre-resurgent neighborhoods everywhere are usually initially recolonized by the arts fringe drawn to the creative opportunities presented by antique buildings at low rents. Portsmouth's Olde Towne is no exception and has been a magnet for artists in all media. Their works are on display and on sale in a number of cooperative galleries and work spaces, as well as in businesses that welcome the color and cachet they add to the neighborhood.

More formal exhibits appear in regular sequence in the Courthouse Galleries, housed in the architecturally impressive and historically significant 1846 Courthouse on the corner of High and Court streets (757-393-8543, www.courthousegalleries.com for hours and calendar).

Live concerts by recognized musicians in many genres draw crowds all summer long to the Harbor Center nTelos Pavilion on the waterfront at 901 Crawford St. (757-393-8181, www.pavilionconcerts.com for schedules and advance tickets).

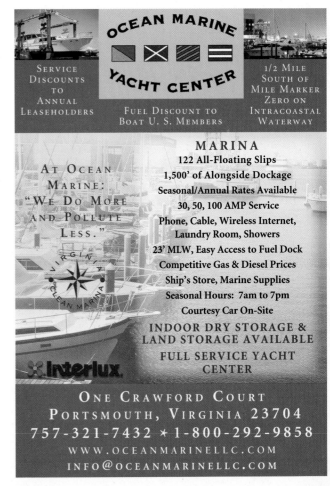

Events: Both the town and its various civic and cultural organizations put on events year-round, most of them centered on Olde Towne and the waterfront. An annual Memorial Day Parade gets summer off to a spirited start, fireworks off the seafront punctuate the sky on Independence Day, and a fleet of schooners arrives in mid-October at the finish of the annual Great Chesapeake Bay Schooner Race. Various art and musical festivals and gatherings fill in the gaps between.

Restaurants: A stroll along High Street will take you past a variety of eateries with offerings from the ordinary to the exotic and from the Mediterranean to the Pacific for breakfast, lunch, cocktails and dinner, as well as baked goods or ice cream for the in-betweens.

Perhaps the most unusual is the Commodore Theatre at 421 High St. A fully-appointed dining room occupies the main auditorium of this restored movie theater built in 1945 in Art Deco style and listed on both the National Register of Historic Places and the Virginia Landmarks Register. Dine while watching first-run movies screened in all their digital and Dolby glory, but be sure to call ahead for schedules and reservations (757-393-6962, www.commodoretheatre.com).

Sports fans and pool players will enjoy the big screens and billiard room at Roger Brown's Restaurant and Sports Bar at 316 High St. (757-399-5377).

Thumpers Olde Towne Bar & Grille, at (600 Court St., 757-399-1001), offers a broad range of fare with a Cajun flavor, from burgers and sandwiches to steaks and seafood, and also features a raw bar.

At the Bier Garden (438 High St., 757-393-6022), you can wash down home-cooked German cuisine with your choice from a menu of 250 beers from around the world.

If you have a craving for seafood, stop by Blue Water Seafood Grill (467 Dinwiddie Street, 757-398-0888).

To get a java fix and a vibe on the Olde Towne social scene in an artsy atmosphere, try The Coffee Shoppe (300 High St., 757-399-0497).

If you need local information and/or a great cup of coffee, try Starboards Coffee Kiosk at the foot of High Street by the ferry landing.

Shopping: W.T. Brownley Co., across the river in Norfolk, sells navigation instruments and charts in various formats and is a compass adjuster (226 E. Main St., Norfolk, 757-622-7589). SkipJack Nautical Wares (One High Street, Portsmouth, 757-399-5012) has a fantastic inventory of nautical gifts and artwork and is very happy to assist boaters. There is a new store right next door called Mile Marker "0" Marine Supplies that has propane, batteries, brass and stainless hardware, and cleaning and maintenance supplies. You can also use this store as a mail-drop. They are also providing transportation to and from the supermarket, West Marine and other stores. This is a really great service and this cruising editor hopes that the boating community supports his efforts by frequenting the store.

For provisioning, there is a Food Lion supermarket and all the usual associated stores, about two miles out (a cab ride) on London Boulevard.

ADDITIONAL RESOURCES

- **PORTSMOUTH VISITOR CENTER:** 6 Crawford Parkway Portsmouth City Hall, 801 Crawford St.; Portsmouth, VA 23704, 757-393-8000, www.portsmouthva.gov
- **ELIZABETH RIVER PASSENGER FERRY** (to Norfolk): 757-222-6100
- **OLDE TOWNE BUSINESS ASSOCIATION** (publishes the Visitors Guide); 757-405-3500 www.oldetowneportsmouth.com

NEARBY GOLF COURSES
Bide-A-Wee Golf Course (about five miles from downtown): 757-393-8600, bideaweegolf.com

NEARBY MEDICAL FACILITIES
Bon Secours Maryview Medical Center:
3636 High St., Portsmouth, VA 23704
757-398-2200 (3 miles)

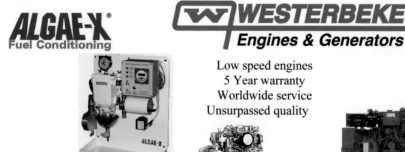

Eastern Branch, Elizabeth River

Do not mistake this for the ICW route, which follows the Southern Branch. Beyond Mile Zero, Town Point on the Norfolk side marks the mouth of the Elizabeth River's Eastern Branch. Commercial traffic is extremely heavy in this area, with tugs passing through and large commercial vessels maneuvering into and out of the docks. It is a good idea to monitor VHF Channel 13 and to call any tug or other vessel whose intentions are unclear. Sometimes, though, listening is enough. Always yield to commercial traffic in this area.

NORFOLK BRIDGES
Mile 2.5-5.8

WATERWAY GUIDE PHOTOGRAPHY

NAVIGATION: Use Chart 12253. Before reaching Town Point, study your chart. The Eastern Branch of the Elizabeth River curves around Norfolk's Waterside development to port, and the Southern Branch (ICW) bears to starboard around Portsmouth. There are no aids to navigation in this area, and none are needed, as the water is deep to the shoreline. Many mariners mistakenly continue along the Eastern Branch thinking it is the ICW, only to turn around two miles later at its end.

Southern Branch, Elizabeth River (ICW)

Norshipco is the yard on the Norfolk side with the huge dry docks that mark the intersection of the Southern Branch. Leave this facility to port heading south to enter the Southern Branch. Large Naval and cruise ships can normally be seen in the dry docks. The Norfolk Naval Shipyard is farther up the Southern Branch of the Elizabeth River (heading south), on the Portsmouth (west) side. As many signs warn, no landings are permitted. Navy and Coast Guard patrol boats guard the Naval vessels docked along both sides of the river.

NAVIGATION: Use Chart 12206. Proceeding southward on the Southern Branch of the Elizabeth River, you will encounter a seven-mile-long congested stretch with a six-mph speed limit (enforced) and six bridges. Be sure to monitor VHF Channel 13, where all commercial vessels communicate and bridge traffic is handled. Most bridges open promptly, except during restricted hours. (See bridge tables in the Skipper's Handbook section in the front of this Guide for opening schedules and restrictions.) Northbound vessels leaving the lock at Great Bridge at the same time are usually required to bunch together for openings of all the bridges in Norfolk, whether the vessels are fast or slow, power or sail.

The Jordan Lift Bridge (state Route 337) at Mile 2.8 was dismantled in 2009 and the center lift span was removed, eliminating one bottleneck in this section of the ICW. The Gilmerton Bridge (11-foot closed vertical clearance) at Mile 5.8 opens on signal, except during restricted hours. The new schedule dictates no openings Monday to Friday from 6:30 a.m. to 9:30 a.m., and 3:30 p.m. to 6:30 p.m., except during an emergency. To avoid a delay of up to three hours while idling in river currents, plan departures and arrivals carefully. The bridge will open hourly on the half hour during non-restricted time periods. The two railroad lift bridges on either side of the Jordan Bridge (the Belt Line Railroad Bridge at Mile 2.6 and the Norfolk and Western Railroad Bridge at Mile 3.6) are usually open, but closures do occur and are announced in advance on VHF Channel 13. Boaters should always monitor VHF Channel 13 while transiting this area.

The Gilmerton Bridge (U.S. 13) at Mile 5.8 (bascule, 11-foot closed vertical clearance) is followed immediately by the Norfolk and Western Railroad Bridge (7-foot closed vertical clearance, normally open). The railroad bridge's openings are announced on VHF Channel 13, and it is operated remotely with light, horn and audio signals when opening and closing. (This is not to be confused with the Norfolk and Western Railroad Bridge, located on the Eastern Branch; when a train passes through, both bridges usually close, one after the other.)

Situated on a bend in the river, these bridges are hard to see until you are nearly upon them. Be sure both are open completely before you start through. The highway bridge will not open unless the railroad bridge is open. You can call the Gilmerton bridge tender on VHF Channel 13, but the railroad bridge is unmanned and does not respond to VHF calls. The railroad spans can get tied up when long trains pass. Of the three railroad bridges in this stretch, the Norfolk and Western is the most frequently closed. Caution: Do not mistake St. Julian Creek, Mile 4.9, for the ICW. (This is easier to do northbound than southbound, just north of the Gilmerton Bridge.) A 45-foot-high overhead power cable crosses this creek. New beacons warning of the power cable were placed at the mouth of St. Julian Creek in late 2007 after two dismastings during the spring and summer.

Cruising Options—Two Routes

Those traveling south from Norfolk on the ICW must now choose between two routes into North Carolina: either Dismal Swamp or Virginia Cut. Each has its advantages, but careful consideration must be given to this decision. Read the chapter immediately following this one, "Virginia Cut, Dismal Swamp," for complete details. ■

WATERWAY GUIDE is always open to your observations from the helm. Email your comments on any navigation information in the guide to: editor@waterwayguide.com.

WATERWAY GUIDE advertising sponsors play a vital role in bringing you the most trusted and well-respected cruising guide in the country. Without our advertising sponsors, we simply couldn't produce the top-notch publication now resting in your hands. Next time you stop in for a peaceful night's rest, let them know where you found them—WATERWAY GUIDE, The Cruising Authority.

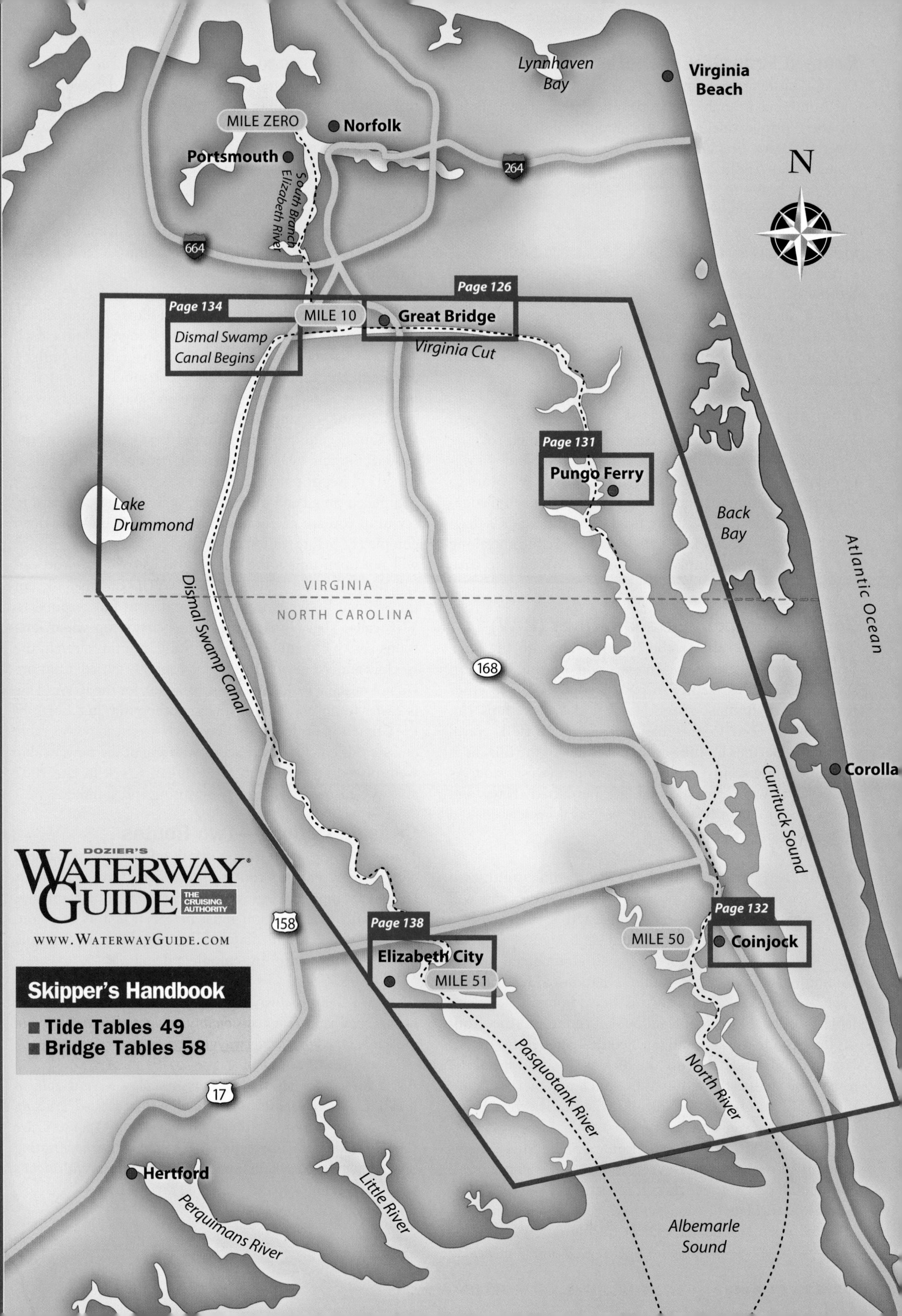
Lynnhaven Bay
Virginia Beach
MILE ZERO
Norfolk
Portsmouth
264
South Branch Elizabeth River
664
N
Page 126
Page 134
MILE 10
Great Bridge
Dismal Swamp Canal Begins
Virginia Cut
Page 131
Pungo Ferry
Lake Drummond
Back Bay
Atlantic Ocean
VIRGINIA
NORTH CAROLINA
Dismal Swamp Canal
168
Corolla
Currituck Sound
DOZIER'S WATERWAY GUIDE
THE CRUISING AUTHORITY
WWW.WATERWAYGUIDE.COM
Page 138
Page 132
158
MILE 50
Coinjock
Elizabeth City
MILE 51
Skipper's Handbook
Tide Tables 49
Bridge Tables 58
17
Pasquotank River
North River
Hertford
Little River
Perquimans River
Albemarle Sound

Virginia Cut, Dismal Swamp

ICW Mile 7–Mile 79

VHF Virginia Bridges: Channel 13
North Carolina Bridges: Channel 13

CHARTS 12204, 12205, 12206

At Mile 7.3, almost immediately south of the high-level (65-foot closed vertical clearance) Interstate 64 Bridge, cruisers must choose one of two very different Intracoastal Waterway (ICW) routes south to Albemarle Sound: the Virginia Cut route (officially the Albemarle and Chesapeake Canal to North Landing River) or the Great Dismal Swamp Canal route to Elizabeth City, NC. A U.S. Army Corps of Engineers sign, positioned on the Waterway, points the way to each route. It states whether the canal at Dismal Swamp is open or closed and gives its controlling depth.

The Virginia Cut has deeper water and only one lock to negotiate, while the Dismal Swamp has a controlling depth of 6 feet and two easy locks. During periods of low water, the Dismal Swamp Canal may be closed to navigation or have limited lock/bridge openings to protect the water levels in the Great Dismal Swamp Wildlife Refuge. It was closed due to drought conditions from the end of October 2007 through late February 2008, but a lack of rain has not been an issue in recent years. Call the Corps of Engineers to confirm the canal's status before proceeding (757-201-7500, Option 3). The Dismal Swamp Canal Welcome Center is also a good source of information for the status of the canal. Call 877-771-8333 for the latest conditions.

The Virginia Cut route winds 13 miles to the headwaters of North Landing River, on to Currituck Sound, into Coinjock Bay and then to the town of Coinjock, NC on the North Carolina Cut. From Coinjock, it follows the North River into Albemarle Sound. The Dismal Swamp route runs 30 miles to the headwaters of North Carolina's Pasquotank River, and then to Elizabeth City and on to the broad expanse of Albemarle Sound. The two routes then rejoin near Mile 79—after crossing Albemarle Sound—at the mouth of the Alligator River.

VIRGINIA CUT ROUTE

Virginia Cut, the primary ICW route, is well-marked and always open for navigation. The Corps of Engineers ICW project depth is 12 feet with a channel width of 90 feet. Direction of this route is at first almost east-west, and then north-south. The fresh-to-brackish waters have no tide, but they may rise or fall with the wind. A strong northerly lowers the water, and southerlies can raise it, both by as much as 2 feet.

NAVIGATION: Use Chart 12206. The Highway Bridge (Interstate 64) at Mile 7.1 has a 65-foot closed vertical clearance. An opening for taller vessels will require 24-hours advance notice. The "Steel Bridge" (Dominion Boulevard Bridge, 12-foot closed vertical clearance) at Mile 8.8 will not open from 7 a.m. to 9 a.m., and from 4 p.m. to 6 p.m., Monday through Friday. The draw opens each hour on the hour from 6 a.m. to 7 a.m., and 9 a.m. to 4 p.m., Monday through Friday, and from 6 a.m. to 6 p.m. on Saturdays, Sundays and federal holidays.

DOCKAGE: At Mile 8.7, Top Rack Marina 9 offers transient dockage for boats in the 45-foot range. There are heads and showers, laundry, power and water as well as a restaurant on the premises. If you dine at the restaurant, that night's dockage fee is waived.

Great Bridge Lock—Mile 11.3, Along Virginia Cut

The Great Bridge Lock, at Mile 11.3, is the only one on this route. The lock raises or lowers boats 2 to 3 feet with little turbulence.

Delays can occur at Great Bridge Lock, especially during periods of heavy traffic. Only one lock opening per hour in each direction is permitted, to synchronize with the hourly openings of the Great Bridge Bascule Bridge (8-foot closed vertical clearance) just east of the lock. Since commercial traffic has first preference in locking through, it is not a good idea to push ahead of a tug, as you will probably have to wait for the vessel once you arrive. Government and commercial vessels have precedence, while fuel barges and vessels transporting hazardous materials are locked through alone.

GREAT BRIDGE LOCK
Mile 11.3

WATERWAY GUIDE PHOTOGRAPHY

The lock is 600 feet long, 72 feet wide and can handle tows up to 530 feet long. Many recreational craft lock through at once when traffic is heavy. The lockmaster monitors VHF Channel 13 (telephone 757-547-3311) and can provide information on the route ahead if needed.

If the lock cannot accommodate all the boats waiting, and you are at the back of the line, prepare for a delay. There is room to maneuver or anchor as you wait on the west end of the lock. If the line is long, late arrivals should not push

Looking southeast over the Great Bridge Lock and the Virginia Cut route of the ICW.
(Not to be used for navigation.) WATERWAY GUIDE PHOTOGRAPHY.

ahead. On the east end of the lock, on the south side of the canal, is a long face dock where you can tie up to wait if you are traveling northbound. Keep the radio on VHF Channel 13, as the lockmaster may wish to contact you.

A speed limit of 3 mph (actively enforced by the Virginia Marine Police) applies until you are past the lock and bridge. It is a good idea to continue at that speed until you are well past the long face dock at the yacht basin on the south bank, east of the bridge. If you think you are about to miss the opening of the lock and bridge, do not speed. The bridge tender can delay the opening for 10 minutes if notified ahead of time on VHF Channel 13. Otherwise, the canal has no speed limit, but the standard rule applies here as elsewhere: You are liable for damage caused by your wake. If yours is a big boat, remember to allow for the "canal effect," a tendency of the stern to swing in toward the bank in narrow waters.

NAVIGATION: Use Chart 12206. As you approach the lock, you will see either a red or a green signal light. Call the lockmaster on VHF Channel 13 to request an opening, but do not approach closer than 300 feet until the light turns green. Should your VHF call go unanswered, the horn signal for opening is two long and two short blasts. Even in cases where boats are already in line ahead of you for an opening, you should call the lockmaster and give him your boat name so that he knows how many boats are ready to lock through. If there are a lot of boats, he will direct who goes where on the lock walls. Enter at idle speed with bow and stern lines and fenders ready to moor as directed by the lockmaster. If there are only a few boats to pass through, you will be directed to make fast on the north or south side of the lock.

The rubber fender system on the south side of the Great Bridge Lock is excellent, which is why the lockmasters are now requesting that all recreational craft tie off here. There are cleats and bollards for making lines fast, but there are no lock attendants to help on this side. Anyone who gets off the boat at Great Bridge Lock is required to wear a personal flotation device.

When there is an overload of recreational vessels, some will be asked to tie off on the lock's north side. In this case, lock attendants will usually assist in getting you properly secured. Be aware that you will definitely need your own fenders—and long dock lines—when tying off to the steel and concrete on the north side. Also, be prepared to adjust your lines during the locking process, especially the stern lines as the stern may want to swing toward the center of the lock as the water level adjusts.

Vessels traveling northbound from Great Bridge Lock will usually be required to group together for the bridge openings north of the lock: the Steel Bridge and Gilmerton Bridge.

Great Bridge—Mile 12, Along Virginia Cut

The Great Bridge Bascule Bridge (8-foot closed vertical clearance, opens daily on the hour between 6:00 a.m. and 7:00 p.m. The face dock west of the bridge (on the south side of the canal) has an adequate number of piles to tie

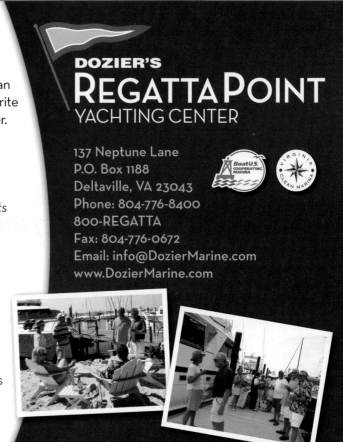

Great Bridge, Virginia Cut, VA

VIRGINIA CUT		Largest Vessel Accommodated	VHF Channel Monitored	Transient Berths / Total Berths	Approach / Dockside Depth (reported)	Floating Docks	Gas / Diesel	Groceries, Ice, Marine Supplies, Snacks	Repairs: Hull, Engine, Propeller	Lift (tonnage), Crane, Rail	1=110V, 2=220V, B=Both, Max Amps	Laundry, Pool, Showers	Pump-Out Station	Nearby: Grocery Store, Motel, Restaurant
		Dockage					Supplies		Services					
1. Top Rack Marina 8.8	757-227-3041	85	13	8+/22	20/6+	F	GD	GIMS	HEP	L14	B/50	S	P	GR
2. Atlantic Yacht Basin, Inc. 12.2 (Internet Access) (Wireless Internet Access)	757-482-2141	ALL	16	100/200	12/10		GD	IMS	HEP	L60,C30,R	B/100	LS	P	GM
3. Virginia Yacht Brokers 12.2	757-482-6630		(Yacht Brokerage at Atlantic Yacht Basin)											
4. Centerville Waterway Marina 15.2	757-547-4498	100	13	6/32	12/5		GD	IMS	EP		B/50	LS	P	GMR

Corresponding chart(s) not to be used for navigation. (Internet Access) (Wireless Internet Access)

DOCKMASTER 757-615-8+7585 16/13

to, and depth alongside is about 10 feet. A sign states that you may stay for 24 hours.

Immediately east of the Great Bridge Bascule Bridge on the north side of the canal, another public dock that used to accommodate five or six boats will be the site of the new Great Bridge Battlefield and Waterways Park and Visitor Center. Both docks are within easy walking distance of stores and restaurants.

Vessels tied to the face docks on either side of the bridge should be prepared for possible commercial traffic and a rise and fall in the water level from the displacement effect of these vessels. It is not a good idea to leave your boat unattended at these docks. There are no facilities, except trash receptacles at the west docks. Vehicular traffic is always heavy on the road here.

Atlantic Yacht Basin offers a free ice advisory service for mariners traveling during the cold-weather months. Call 757-482-2141 for information about ice conditions along the upper freshwater stretches of either the Virginia Cut or Dismal Swamp routes.

NAVIGATION: Use Chart 12206. The Highway Bypass Bridge (state Route 168, 65-foot fixed vertical clearance) crosses the channel at Mile 13.0. The Albemarle and Chesapeake Railroad Bridge (7-foot closed vertical clearance) at Mile 13.9 opens on signal but is rarely closed. The Centerville Turnpike Swing Bridge (4-foot closed vertical clearance) at Mile 15.2 remains closed to vessel traffic Monday through Friday, year-round, except federal holidays, between 6:30 a.m. and 8:30 a.m., and between 4 p.m. and 6 p.m. It will open on the hour and at 20 and 40 minutes after the hour between 8:30 a.m. and 4 p.m., and on signal at all other times. There has been no action on the feasibility study for a replacement bridge for Centerville Turnpike Swing Bridge as of press time in 2011.

The North Landing Swing Bridge (6-foot closed vertical clearance), at Mile 20.2, opens on the hour and half-hour between 6:00 a.m. and 7:00 p.m. The five-mile distance between the Centerville and North Landing bridges is slightly beyond the speed of most sailboats or slower trawlers to make neatly synchronized openings, so you may as well take your time.

In times of low water, use caution in the areas on either side of the North Landing Bridge and the Centerville Turnpike Bridge. Stumps not normally seen may be visible. Stakes usually mark the outer limits of these stumps, which go almost halfway across on the west side but not as far on the east. Occasionally, stumps are unseen, unmarked and uncharted, posing a constant threat to vessels. The first marker north of the North Landing Bridge is flashing green "1," beginning the numbering system from Great Bridge to the Alligator River entrance.

Dockage: Just east of the Great Bridge Bascule Bridge, Atlantic Yacht Basin is a full-service boatyard offering

CENTERVILLE TURNPIKE BRIDGE Mile 15.2

WATERWAY GUIDE PHOTOGRAPHY.

all repair services, transient dockage and a well-stocked marine store. This facility's long dock is along the canal (as always be aware of your wake in this area), and a big protected work and storage basin is behind the wharf. If the courtesy car is not available, both local supermarkets will give you and your groceries a lift to the boatyard but check with the cashier before you start shopping. Atlantic Yacht Basin is the home of Virginia Yacht Brokers, a long established, well-respected firm specializing in the sale of quality motoryachts and trawlers.

On the northwest side of the Centerville Turnpike Bridge is the Centerville Waterway Marina. This marina has 6 slips for transients, can accommodate vessels up to 100 feet and has 5-foot dockside depths. They have diesel and gas, marine supplies, showers and laundry, as well as providing engine and propeller repairs, dry storage, canvas repair and bottoming cleaning and painting.

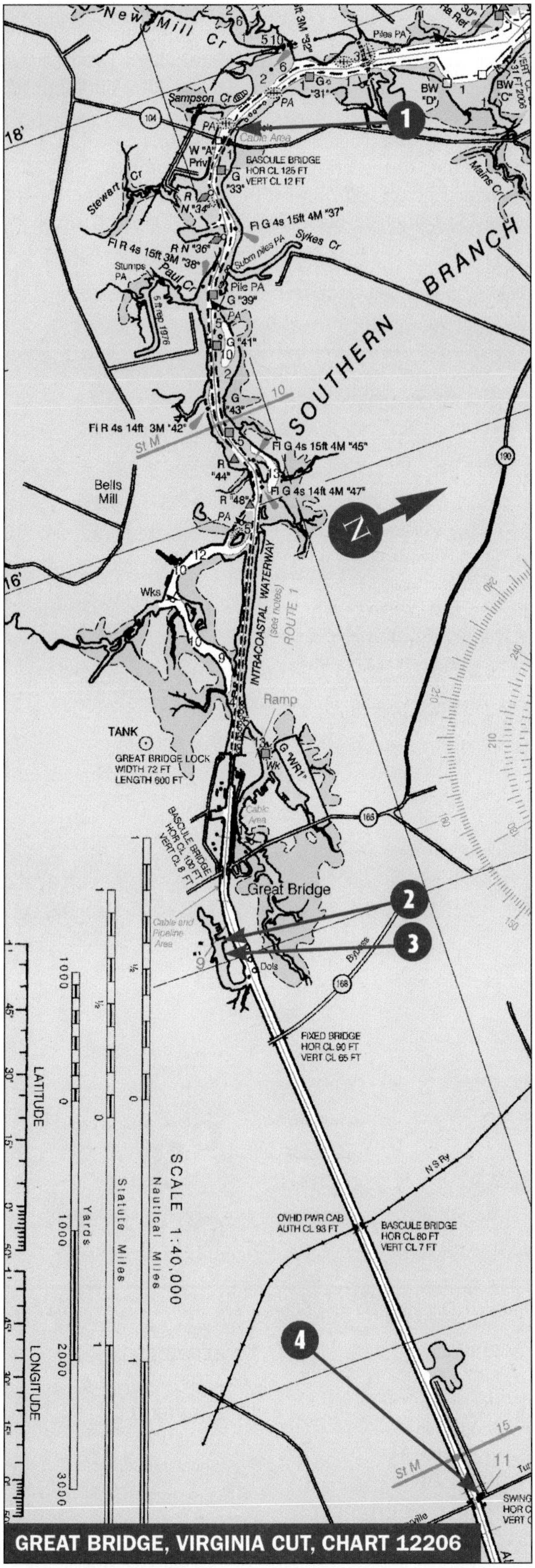

GREAT BRIDGE, VIRGINIA CUT, CHART 12206

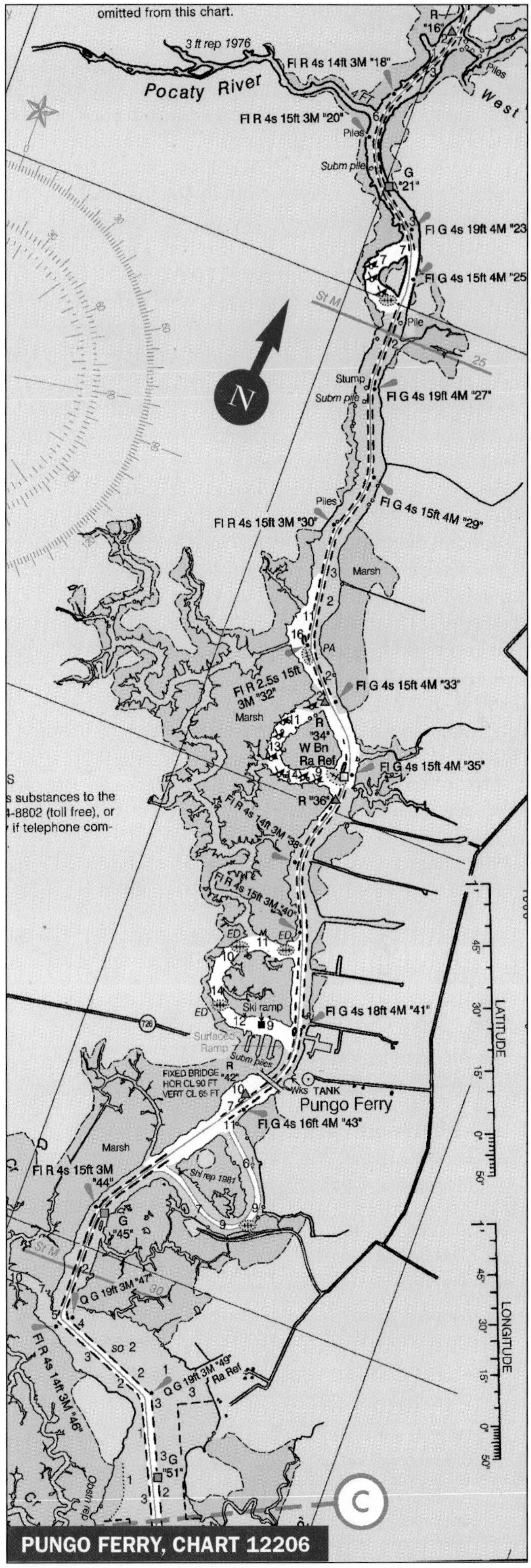

PUNGO FERRY, CHART 12206

GOIN' ASHORE:
GREAT BRIDGE, VA

In Great Bridge, you will find the Chesapeake City Hall and other municipal buildings. Stores, numerous restaurants, shopping centers, banks, a library and a liquor store are all within a short walk of the ICW. Buses run to downtown Norfolk, and a taxi ride to Norfolk International Airport takes around 30 minutes.

History: Great Bridge derives its name from the American Revolutionary War Battle of 1775. While the battles of Lexington and Concord took place several months prior to the event, the Battle of Great Bridge changed the course of history. The complete defeat of the British allowed the local militia to capture Norfolk and give the Americans a naval base from which to harry the British. The battle ended the rule of the British Crown in Virginia. The new Great Bridge Battlefield and Waterways Park and Visitor Center (under construction) lie northeast of the Great Bridge Bascule Bridge.

Special events: The Battle of Great Bridge re-enactment is a two-day event held the first weekend in December at the "bridge." The event centers around the two pivotal battles: the Battle at Kemps Landing and the Battle of Great Bridge. The event also features Revolutionary War encampments, demonstrations, character portrayals, camp life, historical displays and lectures. Skilled artisans demonstrate early American trades and children's crafts and activities. Admission is free.

Attractions: The Great Bridge Lock Park consists of a small peninsula surrounded by the canal on one side and the river on the other.

Shopping: You can get propane refills at the CITGO station (208 Battlefield Blvd.) two blocks south of the ICW. Near that same intersection, you will find the Great Bridge Shopping Center, which includes an Eckerd Drugs, Farm Fresh grocery that offers pick up service, Rite Aid Pharmacy and specialty shops.

Restaurants: There are several restaurants within walking distance of the bridge. Try Moe's Southwest Grill (237 Battlefield Blvd., 757-482-5400), Hometown Heroes Sports Pub (237 Battlefield Blvd., 757-546-2867), or El Toro Loco (146 Battlefield Blvd., 757-482-0623). Kelly's Tavern (136 N. Battlefield Blvd., 757-819-6567) has a varied, casual menu and waterfront dining.

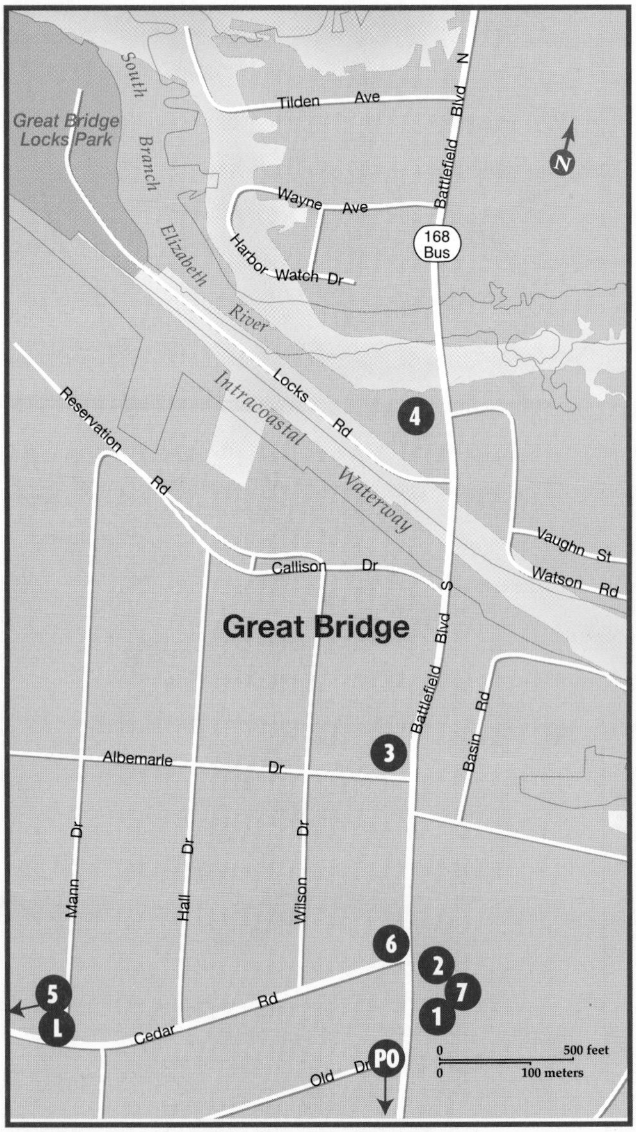

Reference the marina listing tables to see all the marinas in the area.

DINING
1 Moe's Southwest Grill
2 Hometown Heroes Sports Pub
3 El Toro Loco
4 Kelly's Tavern

POINTS OF INTEREST
5 Chesapeake City Hall

SERVICES
6 CITGO

SHOPPING
7 Great Bridge Shopping Center

L LIBRARY

PO POST OFFICE

ADDITIONAL RESOURCES

- CITY OF CHESAPEAKE, 757-382-2489
  www.chesapeake.va.us
- THE BATTLE OF GREAT BRIDGE,
  http://sites.communitylink.org/cpl/battlebridge.html

NEARBY GOLF COURSES
Chesapeake Golf Club, 1201 Club House Drive, Chesapeake, VA 23322, 757-436-2512 (4 miles).

NEARBY MEDICAL FACILITIES
Chesapeake General Hospital, 736 Battlefield Blvd. N., Chesapeake, VA 23320, 757-312-8121 (2 miles)

Charles R Wright DDS, 548 Battlefield Blvd. S., Chesapeake, VA 23322, 757-482-3304 (Dental)

Pedro L Casingal Jr. DDS, 810 Battlefield Blvd. S., Chesapeake, VA 23322, 757-482-7977 (Dental)

Mt Pleasant Veterinary Clinic, 209 Mount Pleasant Road, Chesapeake, VA 23322, 757-482-3534

Amanda Hayden DVM, 417 Centerville Turnpike S., Chesapeake, VA 23322, 757-482-9410 (Veterinary)

Looking southwest over North Carolina Cut and the town of Coinjock. (Not to be used for navigation.) WATERWAY GUIDE PHOTOGRAPHY.

Route to Coinjock, Along Virginia Cut

About eight miles beyond Great Bridge, the heavily wooded and sparsely populated land-cut stretch makes into the headwaters of North Landing River. From here to the Pungo Ferry Bridge, you will notice side sloughs and bypassed bends of the river, which look like secluded anchorages. *Do not be tempted!* All these old river loops are either silted in or may have spoil banks, submerged pilings or wrecks across them. The poles and lines seen along the sides of the channel are catfish lines. Watch for snags and flotsam, and stay to mid-channel. Over the years, wakes have eroded the banks, leaving wide shallows off the channel with stumps just below the surface. What looks like a small limb might actually be attached to a tree trunk suspended just below the surface. Give any suspect debris a wide berth.

Along the Virginia Cut, recreational boat traffic increases significantly during the transient seasons in fall and spring. The cut is narrow in some areas, making it almost impossible for three vessels to pass through at once. Be mindful of other vessels and not just your own schedule. Wakes are especially dangerous in narrow channels. Barges and tugs use the cut and often travel at night.

The North Landing River winds leisurely southward, and a dredged channel cuts through its widening waters. Watch the channel markers in the lower Virginia stretch of the river—shoals tend to encroach from the banks. The route leaves Virginia and enters North Carolina at Mile 34, between flashing green "61" and green daybeacon "63."

NAVIGATION: Use Chart 12206. The area on either side of the Pungo Ferry Bridge at Mile 28.3, from the location of the now-defunct Pungo Ferry Marina immediately north of the spans through the bridge fenders to the south, is a posted No-Wake Zone.

Construction on the North Landing Swing Bridge at Mile 20.2 was completed in early 2010, so should not be an issue by press time. The old swing bridge at Pungo Ferry was removed and replaced with a high-rise bridge (65-foot vertical clearance) a few years ago. There are two tide boards, showing the charted 65-foot vertical clearance, on both sides of the bridge. Some sailboats, however, have reported less than 65-foot clearance here in past years. If you are in doubt, contact the authorities or obtain local knowledge before proceeding. During the summer, the beach north of the bridge is usually full of swimmers, knee-boarders and swarms of personal watercraft, so proceed slowly.

Dockage: The Pungo Ferry Marina, just north of the bridge at Mile 28.3, closed in early 2008 and remained closed in 2011. The restaurant is boarded up and is for sale, and there is a chain across the basin. The face dock is in very poor condition.

Anchorage: There is an oxbow across from the location of the Pungo Ferry Marina, where boats have been observed to anchor, just off the ICW. Depths here are reported to be around 4.5 feet. Ski-boats have been observed using this area in spring and summer. Although the chart indicates 10-foot depths just south of the Pungo Ferry Bridge, boats that have tried to anchor out of the channel here have run into shallower water, with around 5-foot depths reported. In addition, this area is very congested on warm weekends.

Just south of Mile 30, to starboard heading south, Blackwater Creek offers a fair-weather anchorage with good holding. All that remains of the small spit on the north side of the entrance to Blackwater Creek is a tiny marsh island, leaving little protection from wash to boats anchored in the lower creek. Enter the creek between that tiny marsh island and flashing red "46." A 5-foot shoal has been reported at the entrance, but you should find 6- to 9-foot depths up the creek. Local outboard-powered boats rushing up and down the creek on weekends may bother you. Winds from the north quadrant can blow the water out of this spot and leave vessels firmly aground. There is little swinging room for boats longer than 35 to 40 feet.

Currituck Sound, NC—Mile 42

This stretch is generally placid, but Currituck Sound can develop an unpleasant chop. There is little tide, but strong winds can affect water levels and create stiff currents. Government snag-boats check the cuts periodically, but, as always, look out for floating debris.

NAVIGATION: Use Chart 12206. Once in Currituck Sound, observe intermediate daybeacons carefully. A hedge of submerged pilings on the east side protects the narrow dredged channel, and a beam wind from the west can push you right up on them. These may be closer to the marked channel than indicated by the chart. This stretch is subject to shoaling. It is important to stay in the center of

North Carolina Cut, Coinjock, NC

COINJOCK		Largest Vessel Accommodated	VHF Channel Monitored	Transient Berths / Total Berths	Approach / Dockside Depth (reported)	Floating Docks	Gas / Diesel	Groceries, Ice, Marine Supplies, Snacks	Repairs: Hull, Engine, Propeller	Lift (tonnage), Crane, Rail	1=110V, 2=220V, B=Both, Max Amps	Laundry, Pool, Showers	Pump-Out Station	Nearby: Grocery Store, Motel, Restaurant
		Dockage					Supplies		Services					
1. Midway Marina & Motel 49 (Internet Access) (Wireless Internet Access)	252-453-3625	220	16	40/40	14/12		GD	GIMS	EP		B/50	LPS	P	MR
2. Coinjock Marina & Restaurant 50 (Internet Access) (Wireless Internet Access)	**252-453-3271**	**150**	**16/68**	**24/24**	**12/12**		**GD**	**GIMS**	**EP**		**B/100**	**LS**	**P**	**GMR**

Corresponding chart(s) not to be used for navigation. Internet Access; Wireless Internet Access

the channel and to check astern, as well as ahead, to track your progress.

The centerline channel is supposed to carry 12 feet. Prolonged strong northerly winds will lower the depths here by as much as 2 or 3 feet, but tugs and barges drawing more than 9 or 10 feet regularly transit this sound with few problems.

Between flashing green "79" near Mackay Island to red daybeacon "122" at Piney Island, the lowest depth observed was 11 feet. Most of the way it ranged between 12 and 13 feet at low tide. Also in the area, be alert for the passenger-and-auto ferry from Currituck, which crosses the ICW on its route to Knotts Island. Next to flashing green "111," there is a warning daybeacon with a white diamond-shaped daybeacon reading Danger: Shoal. Locals report that this is only one area of persistent shoaling from the east (green daybeacon) side of the ICW in the south end of Currituck Sound. The narrowest and most difficult part of this stretch is between flashing green "111" and flashing red "118." Wind driven current will also try to push you out of the channel through the Sound.

Coinjock to Albemarle Sound—Mile 50 to Mile 65

About a mile south of shallow Coinjock Bay, the quiet hamlet of Coinjock, at Mile Marker 50, announces itself with an array of marine facilities that cater to transients. Centered on a particularly lonely stretch of the ICW, the conveniences here are welcome for those in need of a secure place to rest, plug in, take on reasonably priced fuel and restore basic supplies.

Coinjock, named by the Indians for the berries still growing in the area, includes a hardware store, barbershop and post office. It is a good place to stop, either to wait for good weather on Albemarle Sound or, coming north, to recover from the dusting you can get crossing that unpredictable patch of water.

NAVIGATION: Use Chart 12206. Watch for submerged logs or stumps in the channel in the stretch of Coinjock Bay between Long Point and the entrance to the North Carolina Cut, especially in the narrow cut at Long Point. Vessels regularly report obstructions in the vicinity of flashing red "116" at Long Point. The boat ramp on the east side of the North Carolina Cut can be very busy on weekends. Note: Coinjock is now a state-posted and

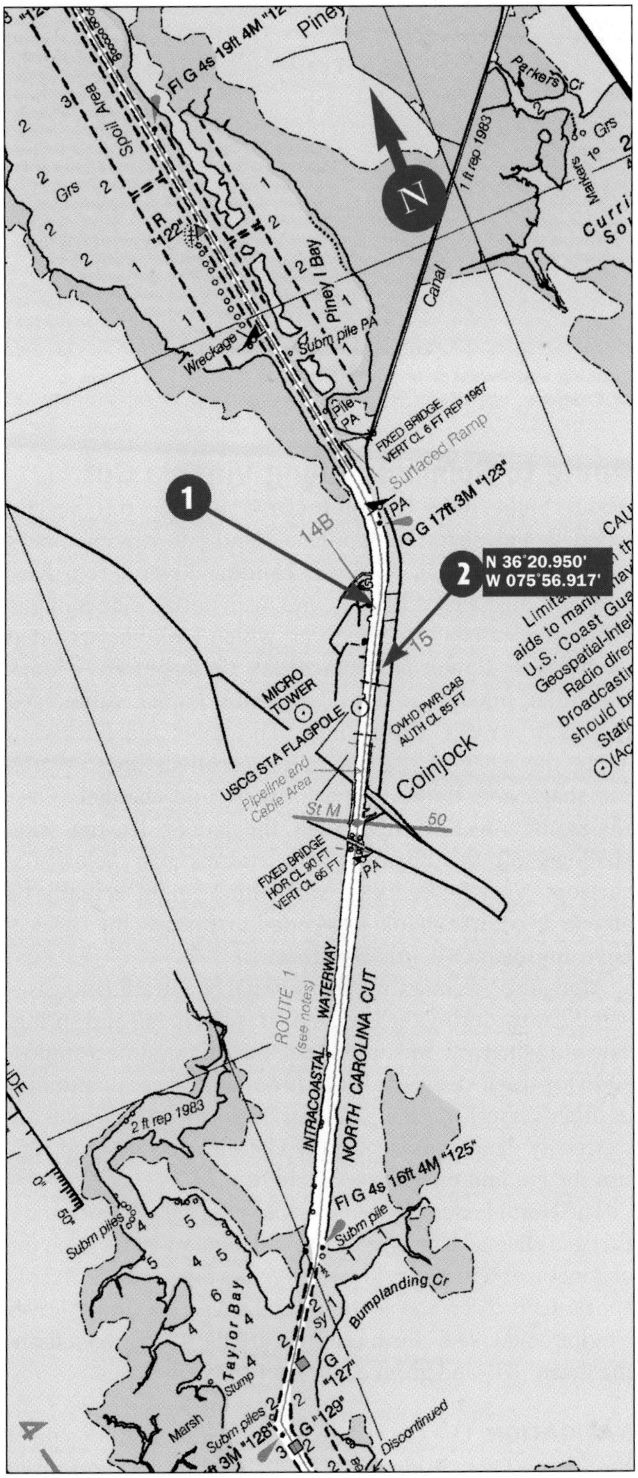

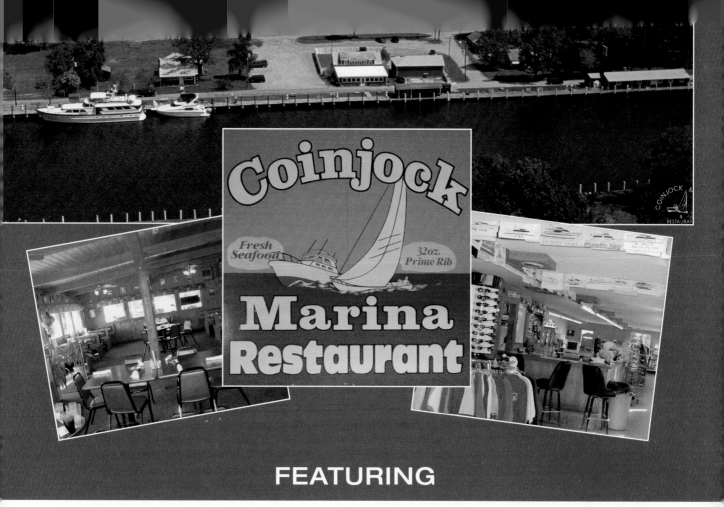

enforced No-Wake Zone. At Mile 49.9 just south of the marinas, you pass beneath the Coinjock Bridge (U.S. 158), a high-level fixed span with a 65-foot vertical clearance.

Check the current before tying up at any of the marinas in Coinjock. Although there is no tidal rise and fall here, the current is wind-driven and can be strong. The wind funnels up and down the cut, and the strongest current will be with northerly or southerly winds. If it is calm, consider the most recent period of strong wind in trying to determine the strength and direction of the current. If northbound, check the current flow against the bridge; if southbound, start checking at the first pilings you come to in the cut or on flashing green "123." And don't forget to check the current before untying from one of the docks after a stay. It may be different than when you docked and can cause just as much trouble when you leave as it did when you arrived.

Heavy fog can be an occasional problem in the morning, especially in the fall, though it usually burns off by 9:00 a.m. The route from Coinjock through the upper North River follows a winding but well-marked channel. Be sure to stay in the center of the narrow dredged stretch between flashing red "128" and red daybeacon "132," as it is very shallow outside the channel. Groundings occur here frequently. Heading south, the river becomes wider and deeper, finally reaching Camden Point and the approach to Albemarle Sound. Fish stakes extend from Buck Island southward to flashing green "155." There are still shoals encroaching upon the channel between green daybeacon "169" and green daybeacon "171" (Mile Marker 65) at Camden Point on the red side of the channel. Numerous groundings have occurred where the chart shows 3-foot depths on the outside edge of the dredged channel. Note that green daybeacon "169" is difficult to see when approaching it from the south.

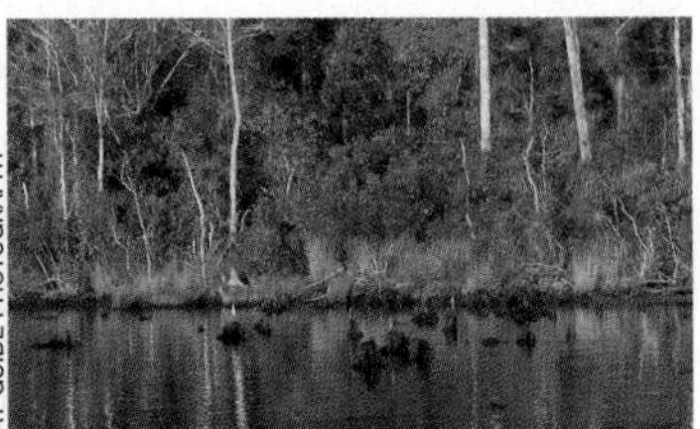

WATERWAY GUIDE PHOTOGRAPHY

STUMPS AT COINJOCK
Mile 49-51

Dockage: Two popular marinas, Coinjock Marina and Midway Marina & Motel, are situated along the North Carolina Cut within a stone's throw across from one another. Because marine facilities and secure berths are scarce along this stretch of the ICW, marinas fill up rapidly during the fall and spring transient seasons. Making an advance call for reservations by phone or on VHF Channel 16 is advised.

Coinjock Marina has a popular restaurant and full-service bar on the premises. Its 32-ounce prime rib and crab-stuffed flounder dinners draw patrons from miles around. The restaurant also serves a modestly priced sandwich and salad menu at lunch. The marina's wide 1,000-foot-long dock provides a friendly reception, fuel at competitive prices and quiet, secure dockage with power, water, a modern bathhouse, wireless Internet service, cable TV and laundry. Basic groceries, beer, wine, ice and a selection of marine-oriented sportswear are available at the marina's convenience store.

On the western side, Midway Marina & Motel is the first encountered on the way south. Midway's 600-foot-long fuel dock faces the ICW. Crabbies Restaurant at Midway Marina is open for lunch and dinner. There is a pool on the property as well. Both of the Coinjock marinas are favored fuel stops.

Anchorage: Several North River anchorages offer good holding and reasonable protection, depending on wind direction. Immediately north of Buck Island, due east of quick flashing green "153" (around Mile 156.5), there is good shelter during a southerly blow with depths of 7 to 8 feet, though boats drawing more than 5 feet should check the chart carefully to avoid shallower areas north of the anchorage area.

Southeast of Buck Island, there is ample anchorage room in 7- to 8-foot depths, with good protection from the east and northeast. Due west of quick flashing red "164" (Mile 61), Broad Creek affords excellent protection in virtually all conditions and carries 7-foot depths. Once beyond the mouth of the creek, however, boats drawing more than 5 feet should proceed slowly with an eye on the depth sounder, since there are reports of an uncharted shallow spot. In westerly winds, it is possible to comfortably anchor off the mouth of Broad Creek if it is crowded, or if you are too deep-drafted or large to go all the way in.

Crossing the Albemarle Sound

Traveling south, Albemarle Sound is the first of the few sometimes-challenging bodies of water on the Norfolk-Miami section of the ICW. The 14-mile-long crossing can be very sloppy because winds from almost any quarter tend to funnel either up or down the long, straight sound. Because of its uniformly shallow depth, even a light wind can quickly create rough, confused seas. Another danger on Albemarle Sound is the collection of trap markers, often right on the route.

Should wind and sea conditions appear unfavorable for an Albemarle crossing, prudent options include a return to Coinjock, as there is no shelter available for the average boat in the lower Pasquotank. Discussion of ICW route is continued in Chapter 5 of this guide.

■ DISMAL SWAMP ROUTE

Mile 7 to Mile 70

Back north, the Dismal Swamp route heads off west of the ICW, just south of the Highway (Interstate 64) Bridge (65-foot closed vertical clearance) at Mile 7.1. The Deep Creek land cut leads to Deep Creek itself and the lock, which introduces you to the Great Dismal Swamp Canal.

Everything—from birds and slithering reptiles to winged insects and mammals, including a few scattered people—inhabits this unique primeval forest. In 1763,

Dismal Swamp Route, VA, NC

DISMAL SWAMP ROUTE		Largest Vessel Accommodated	VHF Channel Monitored	Transient Berths / Total Berths	Approach / Dockside Depth (reported)	Floating Docks	Gas / Diesel	Groceries, Ice, Marine Supplies, Snacks	Repairs: Hull, Engine, Propeller	Lift (tonnage), Crane, Rail	1=110V, 2=220V, B=Both, Max Amps	Laundry, Pool, Showers	Pump-Out Station	Nearby: Grocery Store, Motel, Restaurant
		Dockage					Supplies		Services					
1. Chesapeake Yachts 8.3	757-487-9100	200	16	10/10	16/8	F			HEP	L70,C	1/30			GMR
2. Dismal Swamp Canal Welcome Center 28	**252-771-8333**	**100**	**16/13**		**6/6**			**S**						

Corresponding chart(s) not to be used for navigation. Internet Access; WiFi Wireless Internet Access

George Washington first proposed draining the swamp, harvesting the timber (cypress for shipbuilding and cedar for shingles) and then farming the land. He and other prominent businessmen purchased 40,000 acres of swampland. Washington first supervised the digging for the ditch from the swamp to Lake Drummond, today known as Washington Ditch. Disenchanted with the business venture, Washington sold his interest in the land to "Lighthorse" Harry Lee, father of Robert E. Lee, 30 years later. In 1909, a lumbering company purchased the swamp and continued to harvest virgin timber until they cut the last tree down in the 1950s. In 1973, the Union Camp Company donated its swamp holding to create the Great Dismal Swamp National Wildlife Refuge.

Today, recreational boaters cruise past a number of historical sites on the Dismal Swamp Canal. Astride the Virginia/North Carolina border is the site of the Halfway House Hotel (circa 1820), a popular spot for marriages, duels and those escaping the law. Edgar Allan Poe is said to have written "The Raven" during a stay at this hotel. (There are no actual remains of the hotel visible today.) Boats today follow the same course as Jane Adams' Floating Theatre, which inspired Edna Ferber to write "Showboat."

Boaters should make an effort to take the Dismal Swamp Canal if water levels and their drafts permit. It has remained open because of intense pressure on the part of local politicians. Elizabeth City officials have done their best to welcome transients and drum up support for the canal.

As a rule, skippers using this route are more interested in seeing the magnificent countryside than in making fast time. There is no speed limit here, but you are responsible for your wake. No-Wake signs are posted in the canal proper in a stepped-up effort to reduce the problem of bank erosion. Regardless of restrictions, common sense dictates slow speed through the canal.

NAVIGATION: Use Chart 12206. The sign at the entrance to the Dismal Swamp Canal tells of 6-foot depths, which are maintained as long as there is adequate water in Lake Drummond. Stay to the middle, as the edges are shoal. This route no longer carries commercial traffic except from below South Mills (Mile 32) to Elizabeth City (Mile 50), so the stretch north of South Mills is not as carefully maintained as it once was. The Corps of Engineers, however, cleans the ICW and clips overhanging tree limbs annually. If you encounter the barge, you may have a wait as there is not always ample room to pass. The locks and bridges are in good condition, although boaters in the past few years have reported an increasing amount of debris on the bottom, in some cases causing prop damage.

There are two locks on the Dismal Swamp Canal—one on the north end at Deep Creek and one at South Mills. When the locks are open, the tenders will ask the draft of each vessel and warn those with drafts of more than 6 feet that they may proceed only at their own risk. Tell the tender where you plan to spend the night, so he will know your expected locking needs. The locks at Deep Creek and South Mills open four times daily (unless low water levels cause restricted openings) at 8:30 a.m., 11:00 a.m., 1:30 p.m. and 3:30 p.m. Boats entering the canal are locked first. For instance, at Deep Creek Lock, southbound boats are locked first; at the South Mills Lock, northbound boats are locked first. The lockmasters do double duty as bridge tenders and open the adjacent bridges so you will have to wait for them to drive to the bridge to open it after opening the lock.

For those who choose to decide their route when already underway, the sign at ICW Mile 7.3—just past the 65-foot vertical clearance Highway Bridge (Interstate 64) and at the entrance of the Dismal Swamp Canal—states the lock

QUICK FACT:

TANNIC ACID

Ever wonder why the water is crystal clear one moment and an unpleasant brown the next? The answer is a combination of tannic acid and tides. No, we are not talking dangerous chemicals; the acid is released from decaying vegetation, which happens to be a hallmark of the inland canals of the ICW. Tannins are released from the roots and leaves of decaying trees, such as cypress and juniper. Since incoming tides bring clear ocean water inland through inlets, and outgoing tides pull the brown water from inland canals out, the location and "schedule" of the tannin-tinged water naturally varies with the tides. It can be the color of tea or as dark as strong coffee.

Tannic acid is also responsible for the trademark brown "mustache" that many ICW boats sport on their bow. If you are looking to remove your "boat mustache," try a cleaner called "On-Off," which is available at most marine supply stores.

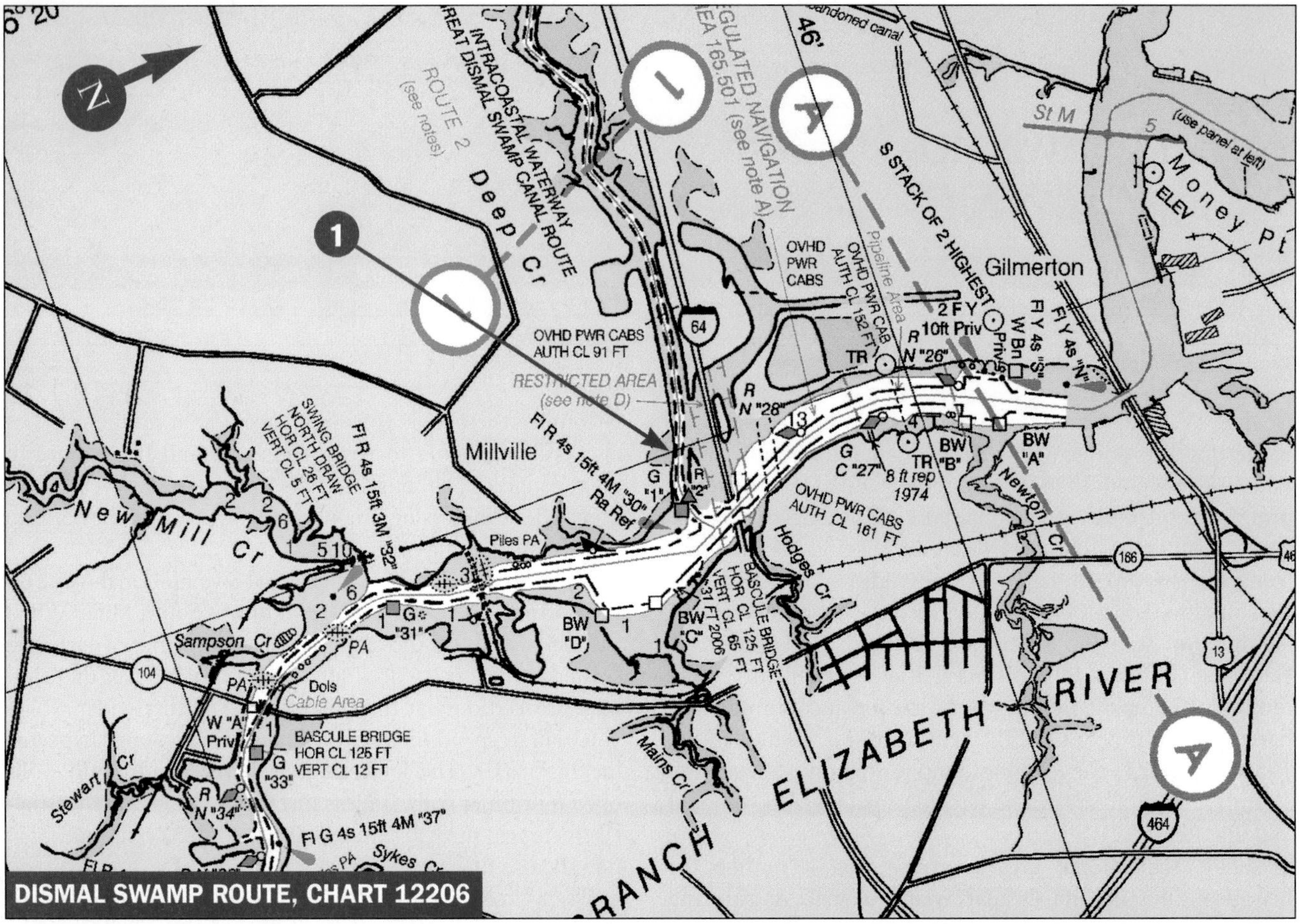

DISMAL SWAMP ROUTE, CHART 12206

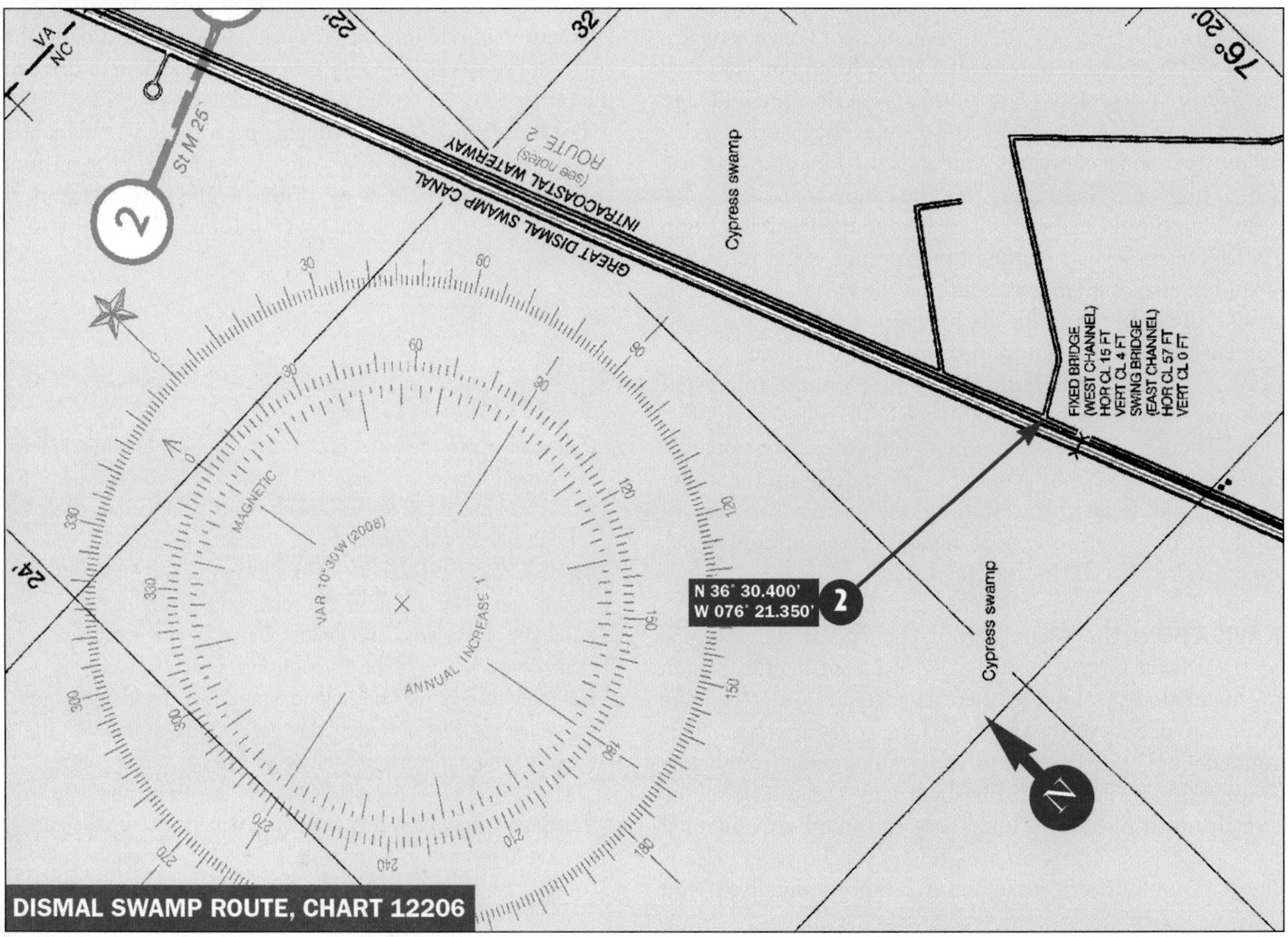

DISMAL SWAMP ROUTE, CHART 12206

Sign at Dismal Swamp entrance.
(Not to be used for navigation.) WATERWAY GUIDE PHOTOGRAPHY.

schedule, the controlling depth and whether the canal is open or closed. Information about the status of the Dismal Swamp Canal is also available from the Corps of Engineers at 757-201-7500 (option 3) or from the Dismal Swamp Canal Welcome Center (877-771-8333).

To run the Dismal Swamp Canal in a single day, a boat traveling 6 knots can enter the Deep Creek Lock at either the 8:30 a.m. or 11 a.m. openings. The distance is approximately 51 miles from Norfolk to Elizabeth City, but the day's travel can be terminated at South Mills Lock. The passage from Deep Creek Lock to South Mills Lock is 22 miles long. Once through South Mills Lock, it is only 18 miles to Elizabeth City.

Dockage: Chesapeake Yachts, located just off the main ICW channel at the northern entrance to the Dismal Swamp route, will accept transient visitors at its face dock, but the facility is not set up for extensive catering to transients.

Deep Creek, to the Dismal Swamp Canal

The three-mile stretch of Deep Creek leads to the Dismal Swamp Canal itself. The creek is pretty, with wooded banks and small beaches used by local inhabitants.

NAVIGATION: Use Chart 12206. While narrow and unmarked, Deep Creek presents no unusual problems. Travel at a reasonable speed and do not be misled by the nice-looking side waters; they are extremely shallow. Keep to the center of the main stream and give points a good berth, as shoaling is chronic.

Just before the Deep Creek Lock, there are dolphins for tie-ups and adequate depth for anchoring. This spot is ideal for overnight or for awaiting the next lock opening. A posted dinghy landing is located nearby.

Deep Creek Lock, South Mills Lock, and Turner Cut—Mile 7 to Mile 70

The lock at Deep Creek (Mile 10.5) raises you 8 feet in elevation, and the lock at Mile 33, just beyond South Mills, lowers you the same amount. At both locks, boats must furnish and tend to their own lines. Be sure to have plenty of line and watch your stern, which may want to swing toward the center during the locking process. The canal is fed primarily by freshwater drainage from Lake Drummond and its feeder system.

Inside the canal, on the west side, in Deep Creek Lock Pond, you will find a long renovated wooden dock with 8-foot depths (except at the far north end) and new gangways and handrails. It is popular with crews wanting to transit the canal the morning after a late-afternoon locking. (It is south of the locks and north of the bascule bridge.) Restaurants and shopping are nearby.

A plaque at Deep Creek tells of a Civil War battle at the quiet and friendly village of South Mills, about three miles from the Dismal Swamp Canal Welcome Center. There, the Confederate soldiers prevented the Yankees from blowing up the locks, and thus were able to keep the canal open. Information about this and other Civil War battles is available at the Dismal Swamp Welcome Center.

NAVIGATION: Use Chart 12206. From Deep Creek, the Dismal Swamp Canal reaches south in two arrow-straight stretches. The feeder ditch from Lake Drummond makes in toward the end of the first of these at Mile 21.5. If your schedule allows, you can travel the three miles up to Lake Drummond in a boat 16 feet or less and with a draft that is less than 3 feet. At the head of the feeder ditch, there is a free rail trolley for carrying boats less than 1,000 pounds over a small peninsula into Lake Drummond. A small dock across from the feeder ditch is available to cruising mariners, compliments of the Corps of Engineers. Rafting is permitted here.

The Corps of Engineers has placed small pipe markers, white with a red top, along every mile of the canal, indicating statute mileage from Norfolk. At about Mile 23, there is a sign marking the beginning of a measured nautical mile.

There is a pontoon pedestrian bridge at the Dismal Swamp Canal Welcome Center to allow visitors to access the Dismal Swamp State Park on the opposite side of the canal. It is reportedly only floated in place when pedestrians need to cross, and navigation takes precedence over pedestrians.

The South Mills lock is at Mile 33. Although you could stay at the fender of the South Mills Bascule Bridge (4-foot closed vertical clearance, Mile 32.6) overnight, we recommend that you stay instead at the welcome station wharf a few miles to the north at Mile 28, or continue south of the bridge. When headed south, make fast to the northwestern fender at the bridge if you have to wait for an opening. The lock tender operates the bridge, and it will not open until all boats have been locked through.

Dockage: A bit more than three miles south of the Virginia/North Carolina border (not marked on the canal), the Dismal Swamp Canal Welcome Center (Mile 28) includes a 150-foot wharf running parallel to the canal. While there are no berths or slips, as many as 25 boats have rafted up at one time here. Tie-up is free, and amenities include water and restrooms that are available 24-hours a day, but there are no electrical hookups. The staff monitors VHF Channel 16 or can be reached by phone at 252-771-8333. You will find a friendly atmosphere here, with charcoal grills and picnic tables, bike trails with rental bikes and a nature trail. Keep an eye out for bears, bobcats, snakes, and other such "locals." The yellow fly can be particularly invasive in June and/or July. These yellowish-green biters will visit in swarms and leave you with whelps! Use screens and cover up before entering the canal during that time of year. If you continue on through the South Mills Bridge, you may be able to find an overnight spot along the west bulkheads between the lock and the bridge, with about 6-foot depths reported alongside. There is a convenience store west of the bridge.

Turner Cut, Pasquotank River to Elizabeth City, Along the Dismal Swamp Canal—Mile 33-52

South Mills is the place to check your time and decide whether to lock through or to stay put for the night. It is 18 miles to Elizabeth City, and the winding, narrow, unmarked headwaters of the Pasquotank River are hazardous to run after dark. The tall cypress and mistletoe-festooned gum trees give the upper Pasquotank a wild and eerie splendor. Here you will see some of the most undisturbed and natural cruising grounds on the entire intracoastal.

NAVIGATION: Use Chart 12206. Give tows all the room you can in the narrow, straight area of Turner Cut and in the twisting upper Pasquotank River. When encountering a tow, slow down or stop, hug the bank and allow the tow as much room as possible. Give points a fair berth, especially where Turner Cut enters the Pasquotank River, and watch out for floating debris.

Farther down, the river straightens out and gradually widens as markers appear. The first, green daybeacon "19," shows up suddenly around a sharp bend near Mile 41. Note that you are now going downstream in a river marked from seaward: keep green to starboard (markers have yellow triangles). Shoaling is a continuing problem between green daybeacons "17" and "15." (Note that green daybeacon "15" is on or near shore, not at the edge of the shoal.)

Farther on at Mile 47.7, a manually operated railroad swing bridge (3-foot closed vertical clearance) is usually left in the open position. If the bridge is closed, this tender is one of the few who will answer to horn signals. The draw is difficult to see until you are almost on top of it. The bascule highway bridges at Mile 50.7 (U.S. 158, 12-foot closed vertical clearance) open on demand except from 7:00 a.m. to 9:00 a.m., and 4:00 p.m. to 6:00 p.m., but will open on the half-hour if vessels are waiting to pass. The No-Wake Zone along the city is strictly enforced with a six-mph speed limit.

Dockage: Elizabeth City (Mile 51) offers 48-hour complimentary dockage at Mariners' Wharf, right in the downtown area. The 14 transient slips, some suitable for boats up to 50 feet, are available on a first-come, first-served basis. The finger piers between slips are quite short, so getting

North-bound boats line up at the Dismal Swamp canal Welcome Center. Photo courtesy of Dismal Swamp Welcome Center.

Elizabeth City, NC

ELIZABETH CITY		Largest Vessel Accommodated	VHF Channel Monitored	Transient Berths / Total Berths	Approach / Dockside Depth (reported)	Floating Docks	Gas / Diesel	Groceries, Ice, Marine Supplies, Snacks	Repairs: Hull, Engine, Propeller	Lift (tonnage), Crane, Rail	1=110V, 2=220V, B=Both, Max Amps	Laundry, Pool, Showers	Pump-Out Station	Nearby: Grocery Store, Motel, Restaurant
		Dockage					Supplies		Services					
1. Lambs Marina 47.2	252-338-1957	55	16	4/46	5/8		GD	GIS			B/50	LS		GR
2. Mariner's Wharf 50.9	**252-335-5330**	**80**		**14/14**	**12/15**			**GIMS**			**1/30**	**LS**		**MR**
3. Elizabeth City Shipyard 51.2	252-335-0171	50		/50	12/20				HEP	L60	B/50			
4. The Pelican Marina Inc. 51.2	252-335-5108	70	16/68	9/58	10/7			IMS			B/50	LS	P	GMR

Corresponding chart(s) not to be used for navigation. Internet Access Wireless Internet Access

on or off your boat can be a problem for the not-so-young-and-nimble. You can dispose of your trash ashore, but no restrooms, water or electrical hookups are available. There is a place to tie dinghies, although there are no attendants.

If you are lucky, it will be "movie night" and you can catch a classic on the huge outdoor screen from the comfort of your boat slip. Classic American films are shown at Mariners Wharf on Tuesdays in June and July. For movie listings, and exact dates and times, check www.marinerswharffilmfestival.com. The adjacent Elizabeth City Shipyard offers some repairs and a 60-ton lift. The Pelican Marina, on the eastern side of the Pasquotank, south of the bascule bridge, offers transient slips. The only fuel available is at Lambs Marina, at Mile 47.2 before you get to Elizabeth City, southbound. Marine supplies can be found at Causeway Marina, within walking distance from Pelican Marina.

Anchorage: A good place to anchor lies not far south from South Mills, off the channel just before it joins Turners Cut (at about Mile 33.5); do not, however, anchor in Turners Cut. There are also three anchorage possibilities on the Pasquotank River. The first, at Mile 44, is behind Goat Island at green daybeacon "13." On weekend evenings, you will likely have to share it with a few water skiers. The second is located in the beautiful deepwater cove at Mile 48. Depths here are deeper than charted. The third is along the eastern shore near Mile 49.5. Anchor to the east of the marina entrance to avoid a wreck in 10 feet of water. This area is often used as an alternative to the Elizabeth City town docks when strong southeastern winds make those docks uncomfortable.

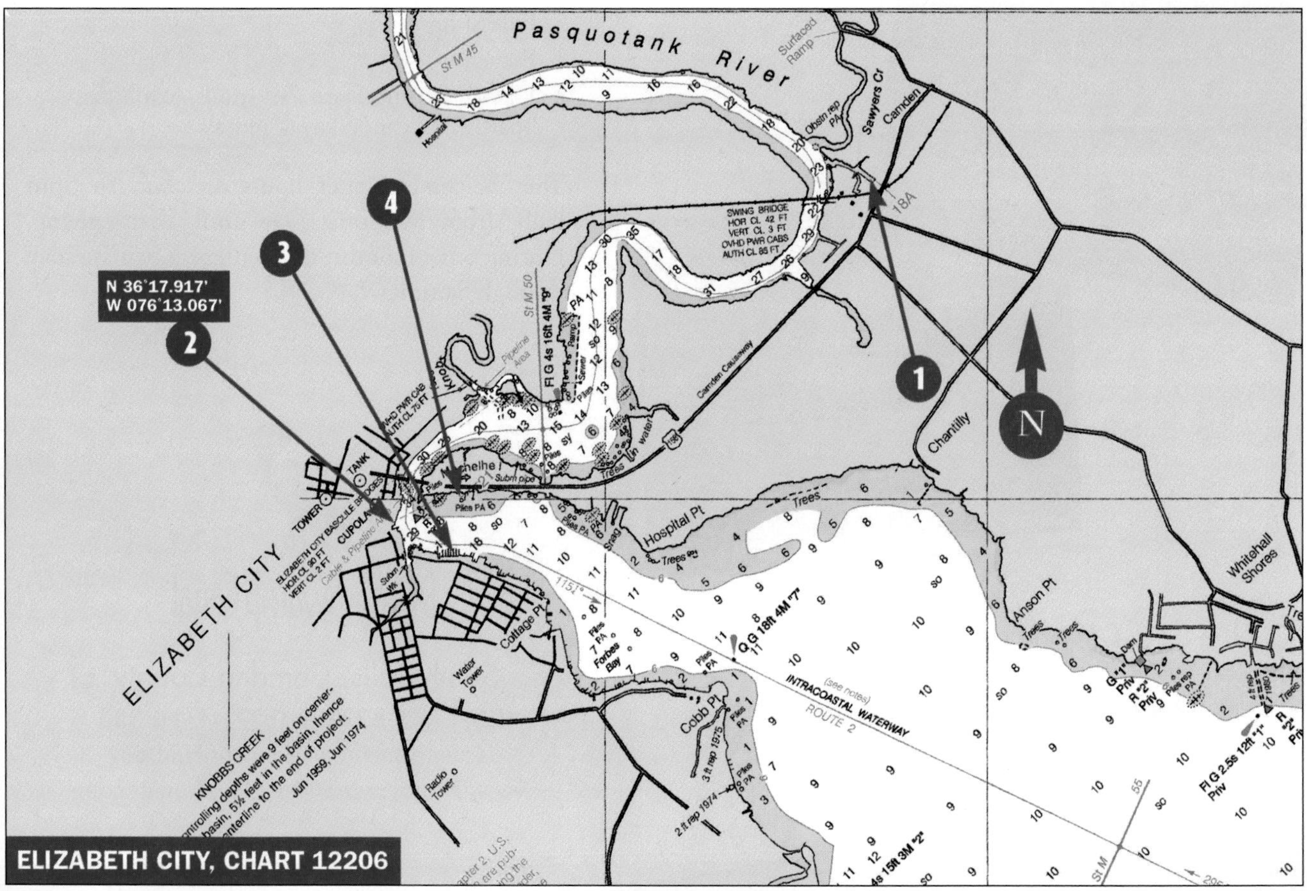

ELIZABETH CITY, CHART 12206

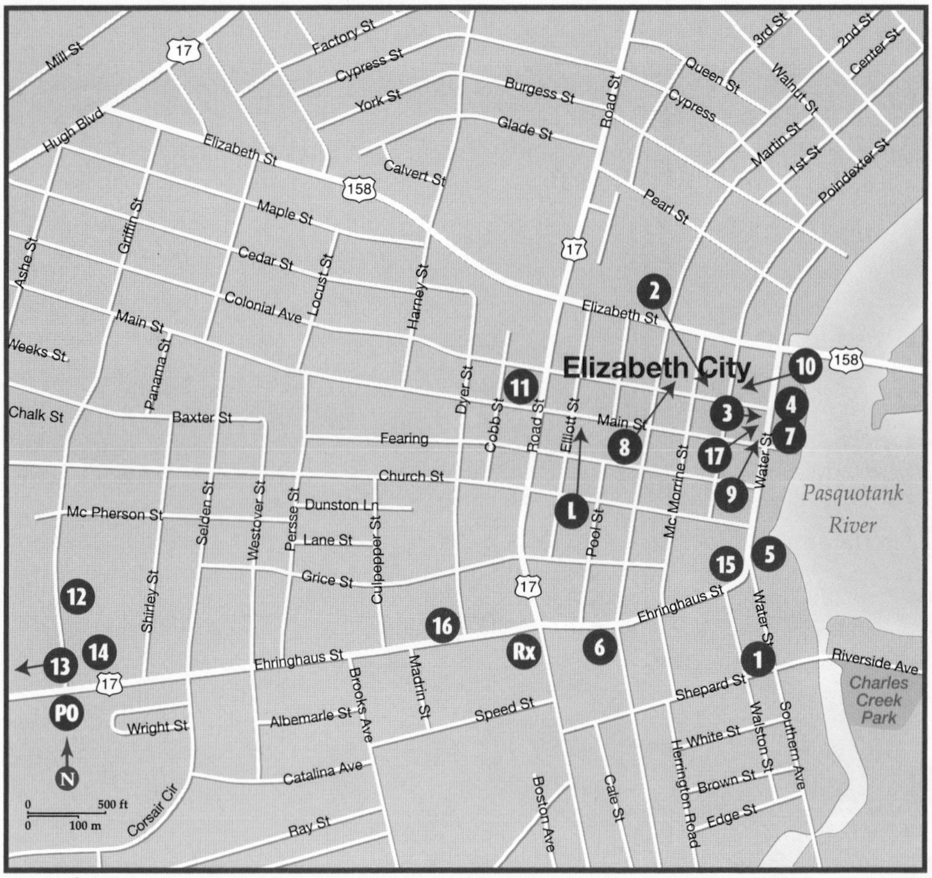

Reference the marina listing tables to see all the marinas in the area.

ATTRACTIONS
1 Museum of the Albemarle
2 Arts of Albemarle
3 Port Discover
4 Moth Boat Park

DINING
5 Grouper's Waterfront Restaurant
6 Quality Seafood Company
7 City Wine Sellar
8 Colonial Restaurant
9 Cypress Creek Grill
10 Thumpers Downtown Bar & Grill
11 Muddy Waters Coffeehouse

GROCERIES/CARRYOUT
12 Soho Organic Market
13 Farm Fresh Market
14 Food Lion

INFORMATION
15 Visitors Center

SERVICES
16 Colonial Cleaners & Laundromat

SHOPPING
17 Page After Page Bookstore

L **LIBRARY**

PO **POST OFFICE**

Rx **PHARMACY**

GOIN' ASHORE:
ELIZABETH CITY, NC

Boaters sailing up the Pasquotank River view Elizabeth City through rose-colored glasses, and with good reason. Along the docks, you will find roses and red wine, new friends and old dogs lounging on the grass beyond a park bench. On the docks at the Mariners' Wharf, the legacy of the Rose Buddies endures. Here, the Harbor of Hospitality still beckons to sailors enjoying life in the slow lane.

In Rose Buddy tradition, the local tourism office often hosts a wine and cheese party for boaters during the week. Depending on your direction, the town docks mark the beginning or end of your trip through the Dismal Swamp Canal. A drought and low water in Lake Drummond can sometimes close the canal for weeks—sometimes months—but it is never a dry run when you visit Elizabeth City. The tourism office and local folks make sure of that.

History: The Dismal Swamp Canal was once the lifeblood of the town. The canal allowed the northeastern region of the state of North Carolina to ship goods to the Port of Norfolk from the rivers and inner bays of the Carolina coast. While Elizabeth City served as an important port from the mid- to late-1700s, it did not become a major economic force until the canal's completion in 1805. During the Civil War, the cut served as a vital link in the Underground Railroad, helping slaves slip through the dense swampland until they could board a vessel sailing north. Today, the Canal provides an

Elizabeth City, NC. Photo courtesty of Justin Falls.

Looking northeast over Elizabeth City and the Pasquotank River. (Not to be used for navigation.) Photo courtesy of Mike Kucera.

alternate route for cruisers sailing to and from the Chesapeake Bay area.

First visited in 1585 by the English, who lived on Roanoke Island, and settled in 1793 by Adam and Elizabeth Tooley, the town was originally known as Redding. In 1794, the town was renamed Elizabeth Town. Lumber companies supplying wood products to the east and north provided a stable economy until the Great Depression.

Culture: The Museum of the Albemarle (501 S. Water St.) is home to a number of galleries. Here, you will find stories of Native Americans, colonists, farmers and fishermen who settled in the Albemarle region. Call 252-335-1453 for museum hours. Arts of the Albemarle, on the corner of Main and Poindexter streets, showcases fine art and traditional crafts from both regional and local artists. Call 252-338-6455 for gallery hours. Live theater happens at the McGuire Theatre (516 E. Main St.). Port Discover, located at 611 E. Main St., is a great place for kids of all ages, housing an interactive science center.

Attractions: A walking tour of the waterfront Historic District begins at the visitors center and includes homes in the Federal, Greek Revival, Neo-Classical Revival and Gothic Revival styles. Maps are available, so grab one, and then relax at one of the two waterside parks as you plan your tour. At the Museum of the Albemarle, you will find over 700 artifacts on display, covering 400 years of local history. The Discovery Room features interactive displays.

Moth Boat Park (501 S. Water St.) pays tribute to the Moth Boat, an 11-foot one-design sailboat that was designed in Elizabeth City. Every September, the Moth Boat Regatta takes over the city's harbor.

Coast Guard Air Station Elizabeth City is home to the largest and most diverse Coast Guard command center in the nation. On the campus of Elizabeth City State University (1704 Weeksville Road), a planetarium presents multimedia productions and laser shows about astronomy and space exploration. Call for reservations at 252-335-3759.

Occasionally, all you have to do is look up to see a few of Elizabeth City's larger attractions. Blimps with names like "Monster.com," "Sanyo" and "Fuji Film" sometimes fly over the city on their way back to the TCOM Blimp Hangar. Tours of the TCOM plant can be pre-arranged. Call 252-330-5555 for more information.

Special events: In May, Elizabeth City hosts the NC Potato Festival. Enjoy the parades, pageants and product samples as local farmers honor North Carolina's number-one cash crop.

In June, the waterfront thunders to the sound of powerboats as participants in the Carolina Cup Regatta race down the Pasquotank River. Call 252-339-3473 for more information.

Professional bull riders come to Elizabeth City in August. The River City Bull Bash brings together professional bull

Moth boats race in front of the Museum of the Albemarle, Elizabeth City. Photo courtesy of Wendy Moody.

riders from across the country as they compete for a purse of more than $32,000.

Shopping: There are three groceries within a few miles of the waterfront: Soho Organic Market is 1.5 miles away (406 S. Griffin St.), and Food Lion is approximately 1.5 miles away; however, Farm Fresh Market (683 S. Hughes Blvd.) will pick you up at Mariners' Wharf and bring you back free of charge. Just call them (252-331-1301), and they will make the arrangements. Page After Page Bookstore (111 S. Water St.) carries a great selection of North Carolina books including "Skipper Bob," nautical titles, art supplies, gifts, toys and stationery. Colonial Cleaners & Laundromat (300 W. Ehringhaus St.) is approximately four blocks from the waterfront.

Restaurants: Elizabeth City provides a number of outstanding dining opportunities. Grouper's Waterfront Restaurant (400 S. Water St., 252-331-2431) is only steps away from Mariners' Wharf and has a deck overlooking the river. City Wine Sellar Bakery, Deli and Wine Bar (102 Water St., 252-335-1163) serves sandwiches and salads. Quality Seafood Company (309 E. Ehringhaus St., 252-335-7648) serves the freshest seafood in town. Colonial Restaurant (418 E. Colonial Ave., 252-335-0212) offers home-style cooking, and the Cypress Creek Grill (113 S. Water St., 252-334-9915) serves gourmet fare in a relaxed atmosphere. Thumpers Downtown Bar & Grill (200 N. Poindexter St., 252-333-1243) offers burgers, nachos and wireless Internet access for their customers. Finally, for the coffee and tea lovers, try Muddy Waters (100 W. Main St., 252-338-BREW).

ADDITIONAL RESOURCES

- ELIZABETH CITY AREA CONVENTION AND VISITORS BUREAU: 252-335-5330, www.discoverelizabethcity.com
- ELIZABETH CITY AREA CHAMBER OF COMMERCE: 252-335-4365, www.elizabethcitychamber.org

NEARBY GOLF COURSES

The Pines Country Club, 1525 N. Road St., Elizabeth City, NC 252-335-7245 (3 miles)

NEARBY MEDICAL FACILITIES

Albemarle Hospital, Highway 17 N., Elizabeth City, NC, 252-335-0531 (2 miles)

First Choice Urgent Care, 615 South Hughes Blvd., Elizabeth City, NC, 252-338-3111

■ LOWER PASQUOTANK RIVER AND ALBEMARLE SOUND

NAVIGATION: Use Charts 12206 and 11553. From Elizabeth City along the Pasquotank River, Camden Point is about 19 miles southeast. When crossing Albemarle Sound, you can save a couple of miles by deserting the chart's magenta-line ICW course to make for flashing green "1PR" east of Wade Point in the mouth of the river, and then directly to flashing green "1AR" at the entrance to the Alligator River. Watch out for crab-trap floats off the point. Crab-trap floats are also scattered throughout the Sound and are difficult to see if the water is rough.

If the wind is up, but you decide to cross Albemarle Sound anyway, it is a good idea to call the tender (on VHF Channel 13 only) of the Alligator River Swing Bridge (Mile 84.2) for a situation report. During unsafe conditions (when the wind speed is 35 mph or greater), the tender need not open, and you should know of this potential obstacle before beginning your crossing.

Two lighted aids to navigation, 6-second white flashing isophase "N" to the north and flashing 4-second white "S" to the south (about 6.5 miles apart), set the course across Albemarle Sound from the mouth of the North River along the Virginia Cut route. (The lighted marker "AS" marking the halfway point across the sound has been permanently removed.) As the course from the Dismal Swamp Canal Route from the Pasquotank River across Albemarle Sound converges with Virginia Cut Route, the second marker, flashing 4-second white "S," will lie close to the course. It is another 3.5 miles to flashing green "1AR" at the mouth of the Alligator River. Note the particulars to the Alligator River Entrance, which are described in detail in Chapter 5.

Anchorage: On the Pasquotank, Newbegun Creek has a shallow, unmarked entrance. In a pinch, you could stop in the bight between Miles Point and Poquoson Point (on the east side at Mile 64), sheltered from northeast to southeast winds. The best advice is to judge the suitability of the weather for making the sound crossing before you leave port.

Crossing the Albemarle Sound

Traveling south, Albemarle Sound is the first of the few sometimes-challenging bodies of water on the Norfolk-Miami section of the ICW. The 14-mile-long crossing can be very sloppy because winds from almost any quarter tend to funnel either up or down the long, straight sound. Because of its uniformly shallow depth, even a light wind can quickly create rough, confused seas. Another danger on Albemarle Sound is the collection of trap markers, often right on the route.

ALBEMARLE SOUND "S" Marker

WATERWAY GUIDE PHOTOGRAPHY

Should wind and sea conditions appear unfavorable for an Albemarle crossing, prudent options include a return to Coinjock, as there is no shelter available for the average boat in the lower Pasquotank. Discussion of ICW route is continued in Chapter 5 of this guide.

To the Carolina Sounds and Outer Banks

Depending on the route, you will find yourself approaching Albemarle Sound either from Elizabeth City or Coinjock. Once in the Sound, cruisers can venture east to the Outer Banks, consulting the next chapter, "Side Trips on the Sounds and Outer Banks." Boaters with a schedule to keep can continue south on the ICW. (See "Albemarle Sound to Morehead City.") Fast boats may wish to take the Croatan Sound route south and rejoin the Waterway at the Neuse River. ■

QUICK FACT:

U.S. Coast Guard Air Station Elizabeth City is located at Mile Marker 55 past Cobb Point on Albemarle Sound, NC, and is roughly midway between the Virginia state line and the Outer Banks. The home of Coast Guard Aviation, the base is located on the Support Center Elizabeth City campus, of which is also home to the Aircraft Repair and Supply Center (AR&SC) and the Aviation Technical Training Center (ATTC).

Commissioned in 1940 with only a handful of officers, enlisted, landplanes, seaplanes and amphibians, the station now employs 500 active duty and 450 civilian employees. It has a roster of four C-130 Hercules aircraft and five HH-60 Jayhawk helicopters. Missions include search and rescue (SAR), Ice Patrol, Maritime Law enforcement, Aids to Navigation and environmental protection.

Air Station personnel carry out missions as far away as the Azores, Greenland and the Caribbean. Recently, Support Center Elizabeth City served as the setting (a double for Coast Guard Air Station Kodiak, AK) in the Kevin Costner film "The Guardian." Support Center staff and personnel were integral in facilitating the filming of the movie. Rescue teams from the station were also featured in several dramatic scenes in "The Perfect Storm," a 2000 film starring George Clooney based on Sebastian Junger's book of the same name.

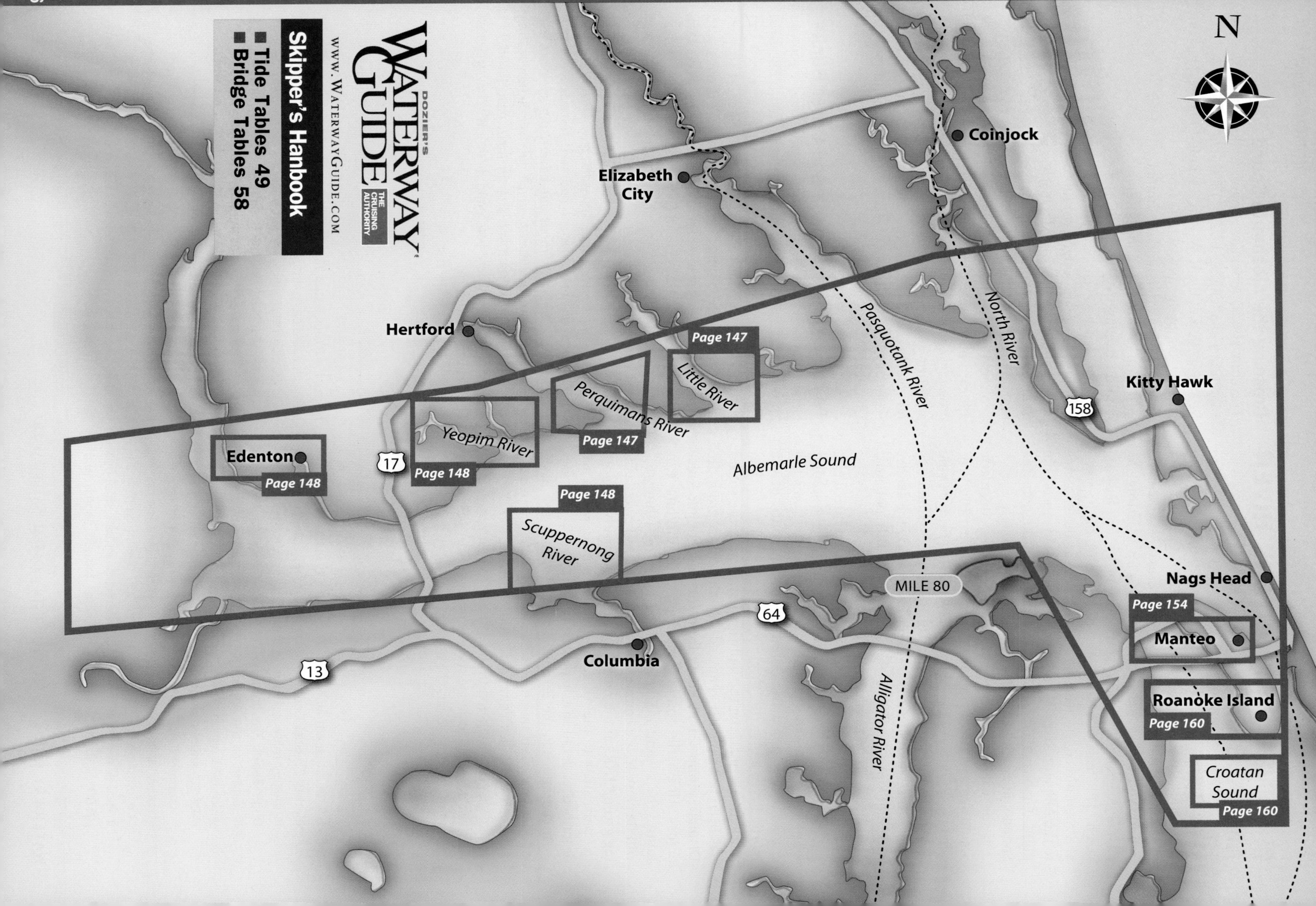
N
Coinjock
Elizabeth City
Hertford
Edenton
Page 148
Yeopim River
Page 148
Perquimans River
Page 147
Little River
Page 147
Pasquotank River
North River
Kitty Hawk
158
17
Albemarle Sound
Page 148
Scuppernong River
MILE 80
Nags Head
Page 154
Manteo
64
Columbia
13
Alligator River
Roanoke Island
Page 160
Croatan Sound
Page 160
DOZIER'S WATERWAY GUIDE THE CRUISING AUTHORITY
WWW.WATERWAYGUIDE.COM
Skipper's Hanbook
Tide Tables 49
Bridge Tables 58

Side Trips on the Albemarle Sound

CHARTS 11544, 11545, 11548, 11550, 11552, 11554, 11555, 12204, 12205

North Carolina's sounds (Inner Banks) and the Outer Banks make a rewarding side trip for those who are willing to depart from the Intracoastal Waterway (ICW) proper. The Albemarle and Pamlico sounds, along with their big rivers, which at times almost become sounds in themselves, are convenient to the ICW and offer isolated side waters and out-of-the-way waterside communities.

In this chapter, Waterway Guide covers the off-ICW sounds. For details of the direct ICW route and its major ports, see Chapter 4, "Albemarle Sound to Morehead City."

The major rivers are moderately deep, largely unobstructed and adequately marked. Some side waters have naturally deep entrances, hold their depths until near the head and are full of unexpected tranquil anchorages and untouched landscapes. Boating facilities are adequate and becoming more oriented toward cruising skippers with families.

East of the sounds lie North Carolina's beguiling Outer Banks. The long chain of low, narrow barrier islands stretches more than 160 miles from just below Virginia Beach, VA, out around Cape Hatteras, and then down to Cape Lookout. The far-reaching Outer Banks enclose four sounds: Albemarle, Pamlico and Currituck sounds to the north and Core Sound to the south.

ALBEMARLE SOUND

Albemarle Sound covers 50 miles, east to west, from Kitty Hawk on the Outer Banks to Edenton at the mouth of the Chowan River. Surprisingly little wind can stir the relatively shallow waters of Albemarle Sound into a short, nasty chop, making conditions uncomfortable—and sometimes dangerous. Many a prudent skipper has holed up on either side of Albemarle Sound for days, waiting for the weather and seas to calm down before making the crossing. Albemarle Sound compensates by offering some picturesque and peaceful cruising waters in the tributaries along its banks. Several of these are deep and easy to enter, with many good anchorages.

HEADING WEST ON ALBEMARLE SOUND

Little River, off Albemarle Sound

About eight miles west of the Pasquotank River Entrance Light flashing green "1PR" (or 14 miles from flashing green "173" at the North River), off the north side of Albemarle Sound, lies the entrance to Little River. Despite the dearth of amenities on this tributary, the abundance of good anchorages makes Little River a natural place where groups of boaters can rendezvous.

NAVIGATION: Use Chart 12205. Little River is easy to enter. The entrance is marked by green daybeacon "1L," and there is a platform to its northwest. Use your chart and depth sounder and, as usual in these waters, watch carefully for fish stakes. Depths in the river run 8 to 10 feet, but be wary of the shoals that extend from Mill and Stevenson points at the entrance. The rest of the river is unmarked.

Anchorage: Depths are suitable for anchoring in the coves upriver. Because of the long fetch, anchorages could be choppy in a strong southeast wind, especially near the mouth of the river. The chart indicates a hard bottom in some places, which may not make for good holding, so make sure your anchor is set well.

Perquimans River, off North Side of Albemarle Sound

Four nautical miles to the west of green daybeacon "1L," at the mouth of Little River, lies the Perquimans River. Boats that can clear the twin fixed bridges (33-foot vertical clearances) at Ferry and Crow points will find Hertford, a true river town well worth visiting. A port of entry as early as 1701, Hertford's records go back to a 1685 deed book. You can visit the restored Newbold-White House, said to be one of North Carolina's oldest. The local chamber of commerce sponsors a walking tour of historical sites.

NAVIGATION: Use Chart 12205. Navigation is fairly straightforward up the well-marked Perquimans River. Start your approach at flashing red "2P," just south of Reed Point, and then head northwest into the river, making sure to honor the markers positioned at most of the points. Eight- to 11-foot depths prevail in the river proper.

Dockage: You will not find boating services at Hertford, but the waterfront does offer boat ramps, a small dock and a picnic area. A restaurant, grocery store and hardware store are an easy stroll away.

Anchorage: The holding ground is good for anchoring, and you can dinghy ashore but be cautious about anchoring east of the twin bridges when strong winds are blowing from the southeast.

Yeopim River

NAVIGATION: Use Chart 12205. The Yeopim River is six miles west of the mouth of the Perquimans River. Enter the river from flashing green "1," and then follow the private aids northward to Albemarle Plantation, or to the unmarked river with charted depths of 5 to 9 feet.

Dockage: Albemarle Plantation is off the entrance channel to the Yeopim River. This beautiful facility is part of a large, upscale residential development in a park-like setting. Transient dockage is available here, as are gas and diesel.

Anchorage: Yeopim River offers good anchorage in protected waters. Water depths are 5 to 7 feet once you have cleared the well-marked entrance channel. Use your chart and mind the depth sounder carefully.

Scuppernong River, off South Side of Albemarle Sound

Across from Perquimans River, broad, open Bull Bay, which forms the entrance to the scenic Scuppernong River, breaks Albemarle Sound's southern shore. About four winding, well-marked miles upriver is the old town of Columbia, once an important shipping point, now popular as a boating center. Sportsmen use Columbia as a year-round base to fish the waters of Albemarle Sound, but some dockage is available for transients.

NAVIGATION: Use Chart 12205. The entrance to the Scuppernong River is marked by flashing green "1SR" and is followed by a series of daybeacons past Mill Point. Be sure to honor the marks precisely as 2- and 3-foot depths border either side of the channel. After passing flashing green "3," the river widens and deepens to 10 feet. Three bridges cross the Scuppernong River—one in Columbia (12-foot closed vertical clearance, removable span), and two other bridges (one fixed bridge at Cross Landing with a 5-foot vertical clearance and the other at Creswell, a removable span with an overhead cable limiting vertical clearance to 25 feet). To continue upriver past Columbia, make prior arrangements for a bridge opening by calling 252-797-4468.

Dockage: Cypress Cove Marina (formerly International Yachting Center) is located on the north shore of the Scuppernong River before the 12-foot vertical clearance movable span bridge in Columbia. In addition to transient dockage, Cypress Cove Marina offers haul-out, complete repair services, gasoline and diesel fuels. The town pier along the downtown waterfront is available for transient dockage (boats up to 35 feet) on a first-come, first-served basis at no charge. No fuel or shore power is present, but water and pump-out service are available. The visitors center, a restaurant, a pharmacy, an art gallery and a grocery store are nearby.

Anchorage: You will find good anchorages in the Scuppernong (refer to the chart for guidance), and Columbia is easily accessible by dinghy from several of them. The cypress swamps of the river's upper reaches warrant exploration by dinghy or the town of Columbia's guided boat tours. Be aware that the projected depths upstream are just 3 feet.

QUICK FACT:

CYPRESS KNEES

As you are cruising through the swampy, wetland portions and an around the ICW, you will no doubt encounter numerous woody projections in the waterway at the base of cypress trees. The protruding "spikes" are cypress knees, part of the root of a mature cypress tree. While their exact purpose is still unknown, some scientists have suggested that the knees, which are one part of the root structure of the cypress, provide oxygen to the roots of trees that grow in the low dissolved oxygen waters characteristic of swamps. However, such trees have continued to sustain themselves even when their knees were removed. Cypress knees also likely serve to anchor and stabilize the flood-tolerant tree in lowland and swampy areas.

Much like a snowflake, no two cypress knees are the same and are consequently popular with artisans for use as carving material. Carved and finished knees can take the shape of people, animals or remain relatively natural.

Edenton, on Albemarle Sound

NAVIGATION: Use Chart 12205. Cruising west on Albemarle Sound toward Edenton, you will pass under the fixed Albemarle Sound/State Highway 32 Bridge (fixed vertical clearance 65 feet). Overhead power lines farther upriver have a 94-foot minimum vertical clearance in the marked channel. Once you have passed the power lines, watch for flashing red "2" leading into Edenton. Submerged fish stakes are off Reedy Point on the west side of Edenton Bay. The entrance channel here is well-marked, with a controlling depth of 7.5 past the turning basin.

Dockage: A breakwater protects the Edenton Harbor Town Docks from the chop that can develop from a southerly breeze. The entrance to this protected area is to the west side of the breakwater. Boaters may dock to visit the charming Edenton Harbor waterfront (two-day complimentary dockage, with a fee for shore power); reservations are accepted. Numerous shops, restaurants and shore accommodations are within easy walking distance. Restrooms, shower facilities and pump-out service are available. Edenton is committed to becoming a destination port for boaters along the ICW. Dockage is also available at Edenton Marina, up Pembroke Creek beyond Edenton Harbor Town Docks. The well-marked channel carries 5.5-foot depths beyond the turning basin.

Located at the mouth of the Chowan River at the base of the U.S. 17 Bridge around Reedy Point, Wharf Landing Marina accommodates vessels up to 60 feet in length and offers a variety of services. Call ahead for availability.

Anchorage: Anchorage is available outside the channels in Edenton Bay, but use caution as the area is exposed in many directions.

GOIN' ASHORE:
EDENTON, NC

Sailing into Edenton harbor is a voyage back in history. Here, stately mansions built of brick and stone were awe-inspiring to a population of settlers accustomed to one-room cabins and outdoor plumbing. Edenton remains a regal town, steeped in tradition, but richly independent, as evidenced by its early revolt against the British Crown.

Today the Courthouse Green remains a gathering place for sailors talking politics and ports. Standing on the broad-columned porch of the Barker House, you can look across Edenton Bay at a row of Revolutionary War cannons supplied by France. The Edenton Battery protects stately homes nestled among cypress trees and serves as a reminder that the town on Queen Anne's Creek began a cultural revolution that changed the future of the Colonies.

From a bluff overlooking the Albemarle River, the open windows of shops and homes catch the full effect of the water's breeze. With over 25 fully restored houses and buildings, visitors begin their walk through history by visiting The Cupola House, built in 1758 for Frances Corbin and restored in 1967 as a museum of the pre-Revolutionary period.

Stroll along the shops and cafés that line the waterfront in the business district. A new 12-slip marina now offers boaters a pleasant berth in the heart of the city.

History: Originally incorporated in 1715 as "The Towne on Queen Anne's Creek," the settlement was renamed Edenton in 1722 in honor of Governor Charles Eden. The custom of drinking tea was a long-standing English tradition, so when the citizens gathered at the court house on August 22, 1774, and publicly denounced the imposition of taxes by condemning the Boston Port Act, they openly declared that the cause of Boston was the cause of us all. A few weeks later, 51 women met and resolved not to drink tea. News of the Edenton Tea Party reached Britain. While political resistance was common, an organized women's movement was not, so news of the Edenton Tea Party rocked Britain's world.

At one time, Edenton was the Colonial Capital of North Carolina, serving as the center of cultural and economic commerce. It became a regular port of call as hundreds of ships sailed up the river to trade European goods.

Culture and cultural references: Chowan Arts Council and Gallery Shop (200 E. Church St., 252-482-8005) features unique and affordable works by local and regional artists. You will find the Edenton Historical Commission (505 S. Broad St., 252-482-7800) in the Barker House, home of the famous Edenton Tea Party. The rivers and creeks around Edenton serve as the backdrop for two novels, "Glory Be!" and "Gone to Glory."

Attractions: Edenton from the water offers a unique perspective. Canoe and kayak rentals are also available through the dockmaster's office at the public docks. A good place to begin your journey is at the Robert Hendrix Park & Cannon's Ferry Heritage River Walk (315 Cannon's Ferry Road). The Edenton National Fish Hatchery (1102 W. Queen St., 252-482-4118) is one of more than 80 federal hatcheries located throughout the country dedicated to the preservation of America's fishing tradition. The hatchery is featured on the Charles Kuralt Trail.

The Edenton Trolley Tour (108 N. Broad St.) runs several times daily, allowing travelers an opportunity to see and hear the richness of the city and its history. The

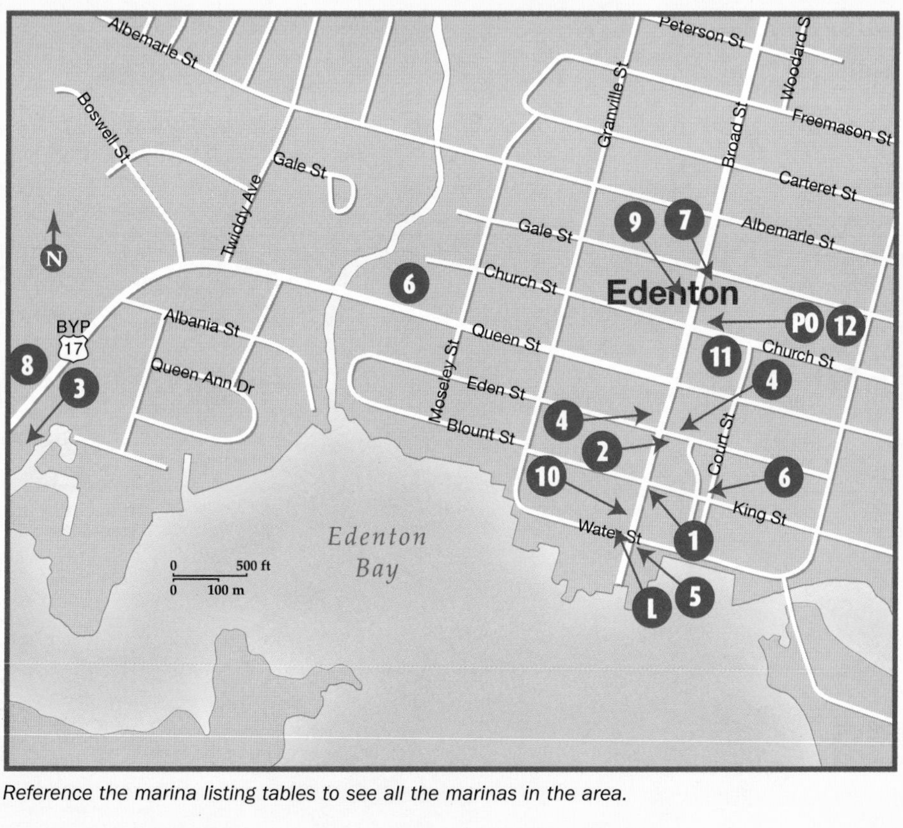

DINING
1 Waterman's Grill
2 Nuttin' Fancy

GROCERIES/CARRYOUT
3 Westover General Store

POINTS OF INTEREST
4 Chowan Arts Council
5 Barker House; Edenton Historical Commission
6 Chowan County Courthouse
7 Ziegler House; Edenton Visitors Center
8 Edenton National Fish Hatchery
9 St. Paul's Episcopal Church
10 Cupola House

SHOPPING
11 Byrum Gift Shop
12 Christian Book Seller

L LIBRARY

PO POST OFFICE

Reference the marina listing tables to see all the marinas in the area.

Albemarle Sound, NC

	Phone	Largest Vessel Accommodated	VHF Channel Monitored	Transient Berths / Total Berths	Approach / Dockside Depth (reported)	Floating Docks	Gas / Diesel	Groceries, Ice, Marine Supplies, Snacks	Repairs: Hull, Engine, Propeller	Lift (tonnage), Crane, Rail	1=110V, 2=220V, B=Both, Max Amps	Laundry, Pool, Showers	Pump-Out Station	Nearby: Grocery Store, Motel, Restaurant
		Dockage					Supplies				Services			
SCUPPERNONG RIVER														
1. Columbia Marina	252-796-8561	45		1/12	9/						1/30	LS	P	GMR
2. Cypress Cove Marina (Internet Access) (Wireless Internet Access)	252-796-0435	55	16/68	15/55	6/8		GD	IMS	HEP	L25	B/50	LS	P	MR
EDENTON														
3. Edenton Marina	252-482-7421	85	16/06	15/110	6/8		GD				B/50	LS	P	
4. Edenton Harbor (Internet Access) (Wireless Internet Access)	252-482-7352	130	16	9/9	6/6	F		I			B/50	S	P	R
5. Wharf Landing Marina (Wireless Internet Access)	252-337-5454	60		100/100	8/8		GD	GIS			B/50	PS	P	
YEOPIM CREEK														
6. Albemarle Plantation Marina	252-426-4037	60	16	15/166	8/6		GD	IMS			B/50	LPS	P	R

Corresponding chart(s) not to be used for navigation. Internet Access, WiFi Wireless Internet Access

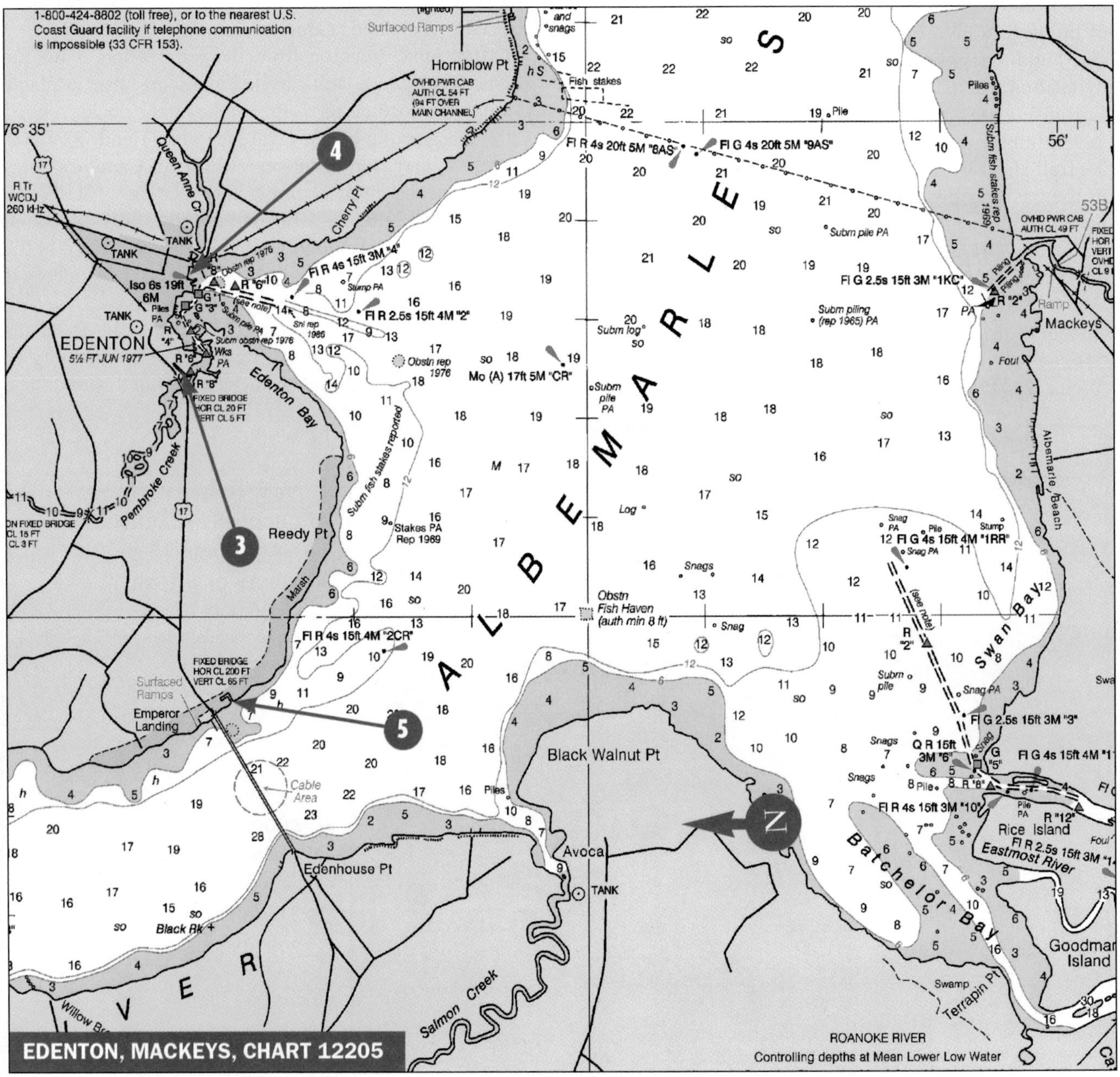

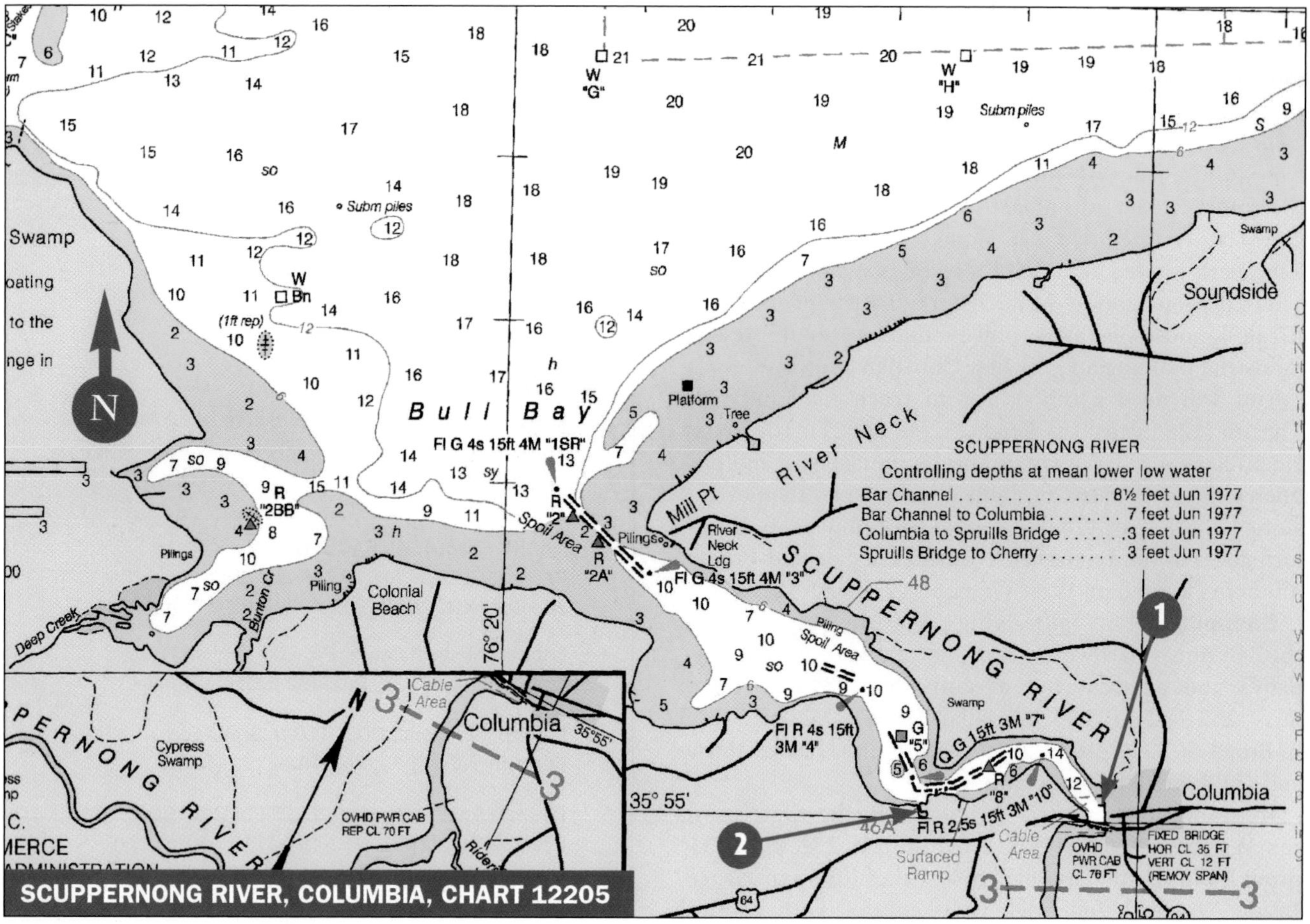

SCUPPERNONG RIVER, COLUMBIA, CHART 12205

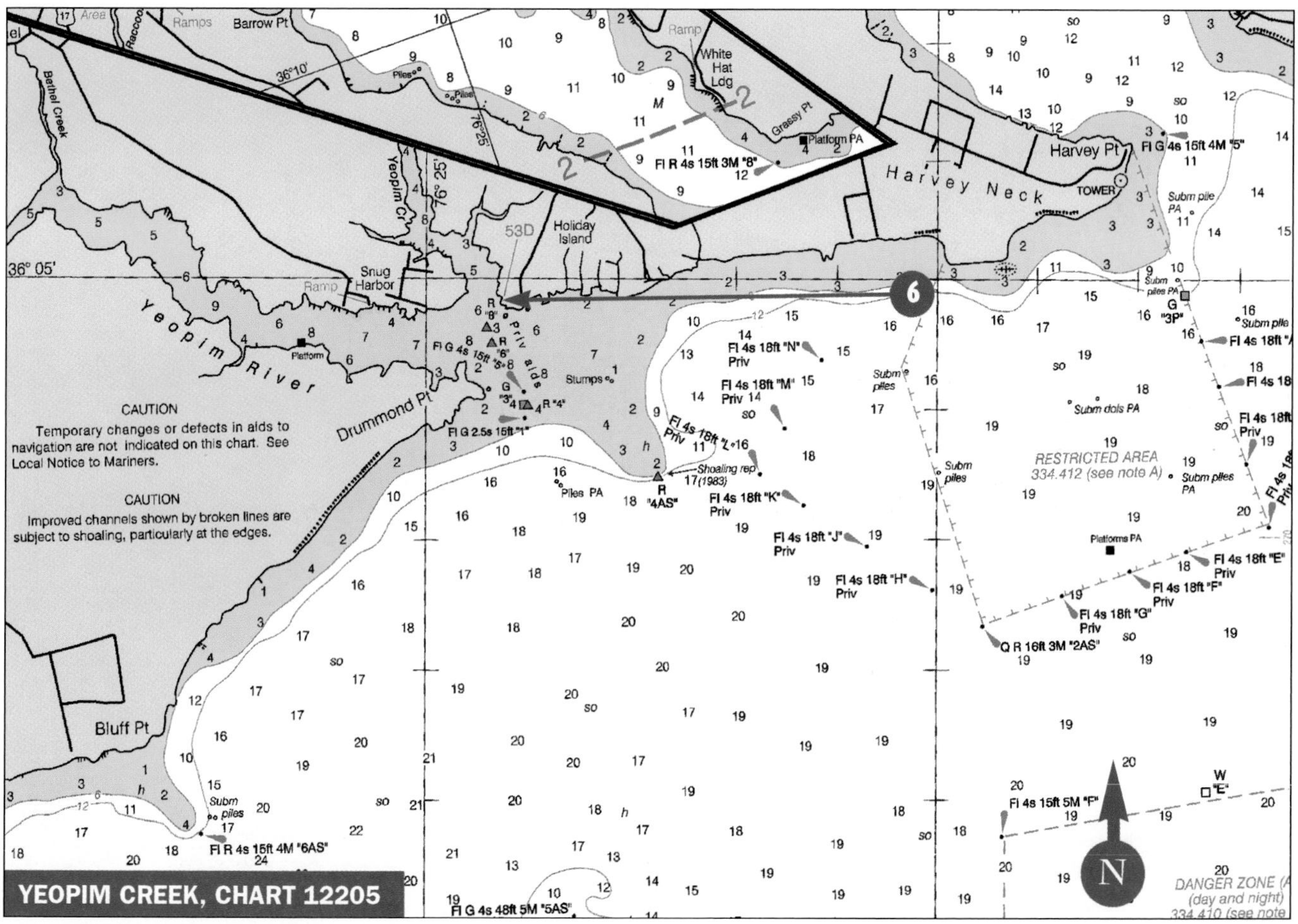

YEOPIM CREEK, CHART 12205

Edenton Visitors Center (108 N. Broad St.) offers a free 14-minute slide show on the history of Edenton.Guided tours begin out front.

St. Paul's Episcopal Church, built in 1736, is the state's second oldest surviving church. The Chowan County Courthouse, built in 1767, is the oldest and the most intact Colonial courthouse in the country. The restored Cupola House, a National Historic Landmark located at 408 S. Broad St., was built in 1758. The Edenton Cotton Mill Historic District consists of 57 mill houses, a brick office building, an impressive industrial building and the first Christian church.

You will need a cab or car to reach the Emmerich Theatre (126 Evans Bass Road, 252-482-4621). The Rocky Hock Playhouse has a family theater atmosphere and premieres musicals based on Biblical characters, themes and stories. More than 125,000 people have now enjoyed performances at the Emmerich Theatre. The Shepard-Pruden Library is located on West Water St. (252-482-4112).

Shopping: For gift-giving and buying, browse the Byrum Hardware Co. (a Radio Shack company) and adjacent Byrum Gift Shop (314 S. Broad St., 252-482-2131). Christian Book Seller (303 S. Broad St., 252-482-7378) carries Bibles, books, music and children's gifts and crafts.

Restaurants: Located a block off the waterfront, the Waterman's Grill (427 S. Broad St., 252-482-7733) provides a rustic setting to a delightful experience. Inside, you will find brick walls covered with nautical photos and artifacts, a spiral staircase and a paneled bar. Nuttin' Fancy (701 N. Broad St., 252-482-1909) serves southern food (meatloaf and fried chicken) and Indian food (curry).

ADDITIONAL RESOURCES

- EDENTON, NC, www.visitedenton.com
- HISTORIC EDENTON, 252-482-2637

NEARBY GOLF COURSES
Chowan Golf and Country Club,
1101 W. Soundshore Drive, Edenton, NC 27932,
252-482-3606, www.chowangolfandcountryclub.com
(8 miles)

NEARBY MEDICAL FACILITIES
Chowan Hospital Inc, 211 Virginia Road,
Edenton, NC 27932, 252-482-8451 (1.5 miles)

Chowan Medical Center PA, 201 Virginia Road,
Edenton, NC 27932, 252-482-2116 (1.5 miles)

Paul S. Richmond, DDS, 410 N. Broad St.,
Edenton, NC 27932, 252-482-2181 (Dental)

Chowan Animal Hospital, 1515 Paradise Road,
Edenton, NC 27932, 252-482-4113 (Veterinary)

Barker House in Edenton. Photo courtesy of Chowan County Tourism Development Authority.

Looking northwest over Edenton, Pembroke Creek and Edenton Bay. (Not to be used for navigation.) WATERWAY GUIDE PHOTOGRAPHY.

Roanoke River, off Albemarle Sound

Across from Edenton, around Black Walnut Point, and then through Batchelor Bay, the Roanoke River leads to the southwest. At Plymouth, six miles upriver, you can tie to Plymouth's commercial dock, behind the police station and next to the town's main street. A short distance from town is the 18,000-acre Pungo Wildlife Refuge.

NAVIGATION: Use Chart 12205. The Roanoke River is much narrower than the Chowan River but is generally deep (about 10-foot depths) and well marked. Shoaling is reported in the area of red daybeacons "8" to "12" along Rice Island, but you can anchor almost anywhere along the cypress shores and marshes. A fixed bridge (50-foot vertical clearance) crosses the river about 2.5 miles upstream.

Chowan River, off Albemarle Sound

Three miles west of Edenton Bay, the wide mouth of Chowan River opens up, with the picturesque river swinging northward for many undeveloped miles. The shores, with their high wooded banks, are especially scenic. These inland freshwater rivers offer many miles of delightful cruising.

NAVIGATION: Use Chart 12205. The high-rise bridge at Emperor Landing and Edenhouse Point has a 65-foot fixed vertical clearance. The river carries 12-foot depths for 80 miles, but is interrupted by a 35-foot fixed vertical clearance bridge 32 miles upriver at Winton. Underwater snags, especially in the bend around Holiday Island, dictate caution. Beyond Winton, near the mouth of the Meherrin River, skippers need to exercise caution in the cable ferry area; do not pass a cable ferry until it has reached the other side of the river and its cables have dropped.

GOIN' ASHORE: WINTON, NC

Winton is the county seat of Hertford County. There is no public dockage but there is a boardwalk that can accommodate dingys. A short walk will bring you to the courthouse, restaurants, banks and convenience stores. The real attraction is the journey—beautiful scenery, abundant wildlife and quiet anchorages. Look for old ballast piles at creek entrances from the days that the Chowan River was a major trading link.

HEADING EAST ON ALBEMARLE SOUND

Roanoke Sound, off the Outer Banks

From the north end of Albemarle Sound, the distant outline of rising dunes to the east heralds the beginning of the Outer Banks.

NAVIGATION: Use Charts 12204 and 12205. From ICW Mile Marker 70, cruise east on Albemarle Sound, setting a course to light "MG," at the head of Croatan and Roanoke sounds. From here, head south from light "MG" to Croatan Sound flashing green approach light "3CS," approximately four miles to the south-southeast. From here, you can go on either side of Roanoke Island—south

QUICK FACT:

DUNES

Cruising the East Coast affords a wonderful opportunity to explore the fragile dune ecosystem. Dunes may appear to be a simple mountain of sand, but their science is anything but mundane. Dunes are hills of sand built by eolian processes or wind's ability to shift the landscape. Along the ICW, it is common for onshore winds to blow sand inland, where it is trapped against vegetation or another form of matter and accumulates over time, forming a dune. Then, the wind begins to erode sand particles from the windward side and deposits them onto the leeward side, creating a slope and a slipface. The "foredune" is the part of the dune directly behind the beach. Here, many dunes "stay put" because of vegetation that anchors them, and these are able to support wildlife such as birds and plants. Some, though, are constantly reshaped due to shifting winds, such as those at Jockey's Ridge State Park in Nags Head, NC. Dunes in the park range in height from 110 to 400 feet, and adventurous visitors can hang glide or fly kites off the peaks.

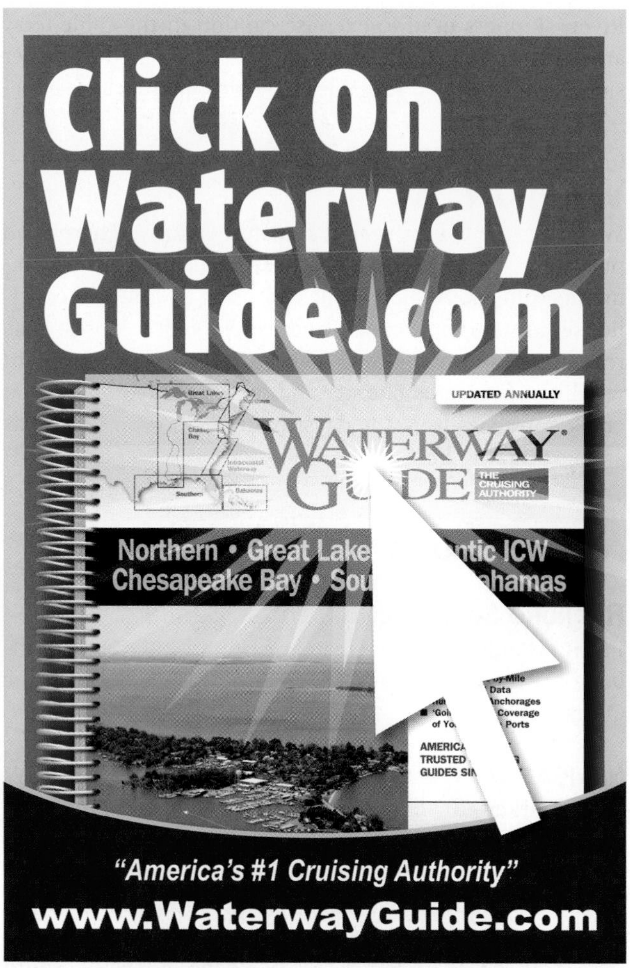

in Croatan Sound if you can clear a 45-foot fixed vertical clearance bridge (local knowledge says that this bridge actually has a vertical clearance of between 42 and 44 feet) or east into Roanoke Sound. Croatan Sound has better depths throughout.

The channel leading through Roanoke Sound (east of Roanoke Island) is well marked. Proceeding southward, keep the red lights and daybeacons on your port side. As of a July 2009 survey, the channel carries minimum charted depths of 7 feet at the entrance by flashing red "36," then shallows to 6 feet as you travel south toward the Washington Baum Bridge. There is a brief period of charted 4-foot depths from the bridge south to flashing red "22," then it increases to 9.5 feet to just past Broad Creek Point. Use caution. It is winding, and aids are not as prevalent south of Shallowbag Bay, which can be confusing, especially farther down at Oregon Inlet. The 65-foot fixed vertical clearance bridge makes passage through this area much simpler than Croatan Sound if the 45-foot vertical clearance bridge there is a limiting factor. Both routes converge in Pamlico Sound south of Roanoke Island.

Manteo, at Roanoke Island

Shallowbag Bay, on Roanoke Sound, is the entrance to Manteo. Manteo's marinas are located off Shallowbag Bay: Shallowbag Bay Club, south of red daybeacon "10," and Manteo Waterfront Marina, north of red daybeacon "10." Marshes Light is a new residential/marina community located along the Manteo waterfront between the other two marinas. The charted depths into Manteo as of the July 2009 survey were 4 feet at mean low water; however, a local dockmaster claims that the average depth into Manteo is 8 to 12 feet and that the depths on the chart cause a lot of confusion. The Elizabeth II replica, which draws 8 feet, transits the channel frequently. They note that shoaling occurs at the entrance to Shallowbag Bay, so slow down and keep an eye on your depth sounder.

DOCKAGE: Manteo Waterfront Marina offers transient slips. The marina is on the historic waterfront of the downtown area, adjacent to 70 shops, inns, a bed and breakfast, restaurants and the mile-long town boardwalk. It is run by the town of Manteo, has 53 slips that can hold vessels up to 140 feet and now also has a pump-out facility.

Marshes Light Marina offers transient dockage at their 60-slip marina on a daily, weekly or monthly basis. They can presently accommodate vessels to 50 feet, with plans in the works to support dockage for larger vessels in the future. From here, you also have access to the boardwalk with its shops and restaurants. A park where concerts are held and a playground are right nearby. If you like your dock space, you can purchase a slip here.

Just on the north side of the Washington Baum Bridge, a mile and a half south of Shallowbag Bay, is Pirate's Cove Marina, part of a large residential development. Shallowbag Bay Marina accommodates vessels up to 75 feet at floating docks with 7-foot depths.

DON'T JUST CROSS THE ALBEMARLE,
TAKE TIME OUT TO DISCOVER
AMERICA'S BEGINNING...
Manteo Waterfront Marina
Sail into Roanoke Island and the Manteo Waterfront Marina. Historic downtown Manteo's waterfront renaissance has turned a quaint little village into a wonderland for visiting yachtsmen. Manteo has recognized that their waterfront is a valuable asset and it's a choice place for a side run. Nestled in this picturesque town and along the boardwalk are over 70 quaint shops and art galleries, an awesome bookstore, America's oldest family owned and operated movie theater and a nationally recognized salon and spa. For those that would like to stay ashore for the evening there are several bed and breakfasts within walking distance and one right on the boardwalk voted "Top Ten Best New Inns in America." The Manteo Waterfront offers excellent protection from the weather and amenities for vessels up to 140 feet.
If you are exiting the Alligator River on a north trek or exiting the North River on a south trek, make a very historic east turn and visit one of the oldest pieces of real estate in the country. Maybe you can help, we lost a colony here over 500 years ago and we haven't found it yet. Call the Dockmaster, Carl Jordan at 252-473-3320 for reservations or any questions you may have and make a point to visit us on your way North or South.
• Transient, weekly, and monthly rates
• 2-30 & 2-50 amp outlets at each slip
• 53 Slips, accommodating boats to 140'
• A small, deep and well-protected harbor
• Modern air-conditioned showers & laundry
• Wi-Fi and cable TV
• Adjacent to great shopping, fine dining, and elegant accomodations in Old Town Manteo
PO Box 1328, Manteo NC 27954-1328
(252) 473-3320 VHF 16 & 9
www.townofmanteo.com

Looking west over Manteo, NC. (Not to be used for navigation.) WATERWAY GUIDE PHOTOGRAPHY.

GOIN' ASHORE:
MANTEO, NC

For centuries, the town of Manteo (pronounced Man-Tea-Oh) has suffered the fate of the overlooked, misplaced and forgotten. Nestled on the northeastern end of Roanoke Island, Manteo truly is a "lost colony" of cruisers. When Ralph Lane and his band of colonists accepted Sir Francis Drake's offer of passage back to England, they set a precedent that would haunt this town for years to come. By some accounts, the colonists left two days too soon. Other historians say it was several weeks later that Sir Walter Raleigh arrived with fresh supplies for the settlers.

Manteo lies due west of and close to the Outer Banks of North Carolina. Along the oceanfront to the east, across Roanoke Sound, lie the beaches and strip malls, traffic jams and tourists cramming a year's worth of relaxation into five days. For cruisers on the ICW, Manteo can be a three-day detour off the magenta line of a GPS display. Here, you will find the legacy of sailors from afar seeking an uncharted island to call their own.

History: The history of Manteo is wrapped in the saga of the first settlers to Roanoke Island and the mystery surrounding the Lost Colony. The name reflects the gratitude felt towards Chief Manteo, an American Indian who acted as a mediator after a couple of unfortunate incidents. The first involved the ambush and killing of George Howe by a group of Roanokes. The second was in retaliation for Howe's murder when Howe's friend, Edward Stafford, and two dozen settlers mistakenly attacked a group of Manteo's people gathering corn. Manteo blamed his own people for not alerting the English that the Roanokes had fled the field. In August 1587, the English showed their appreciation to Manteo by baptizing him. By command of Sir Walter Raleigh, Chief Manteo was named Lord of Roanoke.

Attractions: The North Carolina Aquarium (374 Airport Road, 252-473-3494) draws visitors into the undersea world, allowing a sneak peak at life below the waters around the island. In addition to the attractions on Roanoke Island itself, there are a number of other side trips available, though all will require transportation. The Wright Brothers National Memorial in Kill Devil Hills (252-441-7430) honors the first powered flight. Here, you will find a full-scale reproduction of the original plane, exhibits, a walking tour on the history of the Wright Brothers and other flight-related reproductions. The memorial is $4 for adults, free of charge to those 15 and under, and open year-round. On nearby Jockey's Ridge, you will find a 400-acre state park comprised entirely of sand dunes, providing one of the East Coast's premier hang-gliding locations. Lessons and rentals are available from the main Kitty Hawk Kites, located directly across the street (252-473-2357). The park is open year-round. If you love lighthouses, there are two within an hour's drive of Manteo. Bodie Island Lighthouse sits just north of Oregon Inlet, while farther south, the famous Cape Hatteras Lighthouse stands 208 feet above

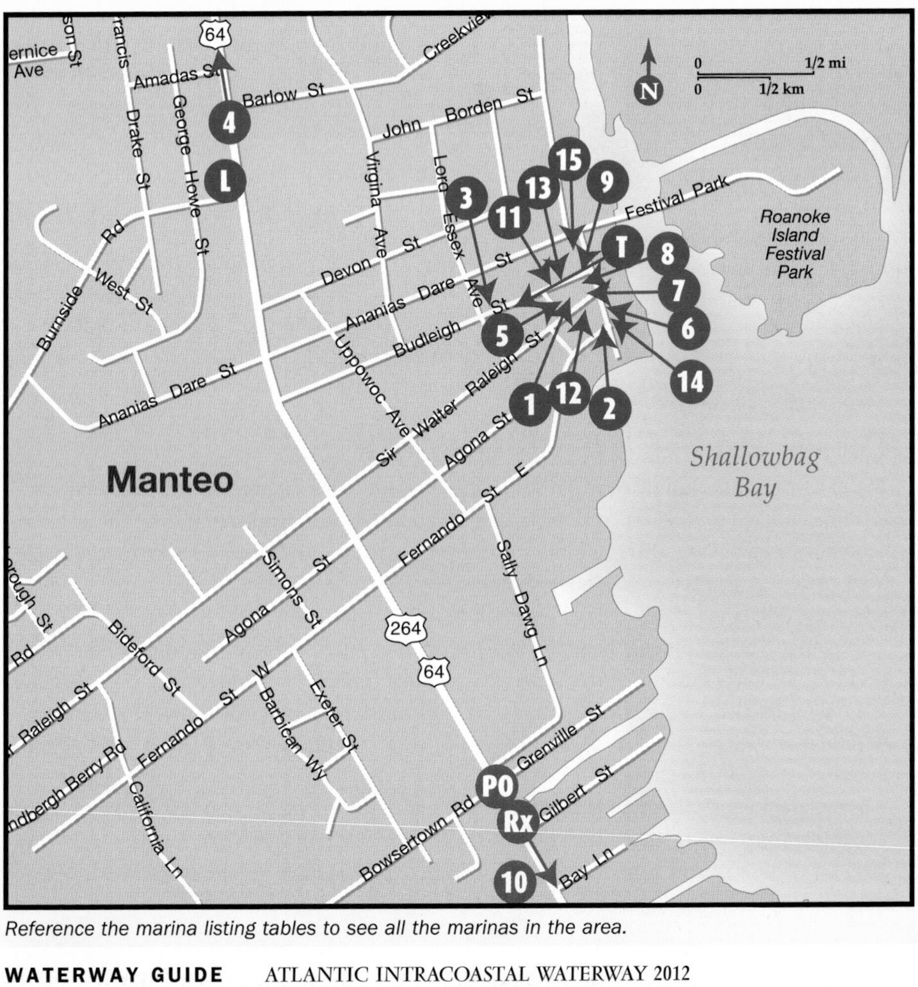

Reference the marina listing tables to see all the marinas in the area.

ART/ANTIQUES
- 1 Outer Banks Quilts & Antiques
- 2 Wanchese Pottery
- 3 Budleigh Street Antique Mall

ATTRACTIONS
- 4 North Carolina Aquarium

DINING
- 5 The Coffeehouse
- 6 The Hungry Pelican
- 7 The Full Moon Cafe
- 8 Poor Richard's Sandwich Shop
- 9 1587

LAUNDRY
- 10 Manteo Speed Wash

SHOPPING
- 11 Endless Possibilities
- 12 Manteo Booksellers
- 13 Georgie's Place
- 13 Something Special
- 14 Charlotte's Ladies' Boutique
- 15 Nancyware Pottery

L LIBRARY

PO POST OFFICE

Rx PHARMACY

T THEATER

Roanoke Island Area, NC

Roanoke Island Area, NC	Phone	Largest Vessel Accommodated	VHF Channel Monitored	Transient Berths / Total Berths	Approach / Dockside Depth (reported)	Floating Docks	Gas / Diesel	Groceries, Ice, Marine Supplies, Snacks	Repairs: Hull, Engine, Propeller	Lift (tonnage), Crane, Rail	1=110V, 2=220V, B=Both, Max Amps	Laundry, Pool, Showers	Pump-Out Station	Nearby: Grocery Store, Motel, Restaurant
		Dockage					Supplies		Services					
MANTEO (ROANOKE ISLAND)														
1. Manteo Waterfront Marina 🖳 WiFi	**252-473-3320**	**150**	**16/09**	**25/53**	**8/6**			**IS**			**B/50**	**LS**	**P**	**GR**
2. Marshes Light Marina 🖳 WiFi	**252-327-9803**	**70**	**16**	**40/158**	**10/9**			**IMS**			**B/50**		**P**	**GMR**
3. Shallowbag Bay Marina	252-473-4946	70	16/69	50/80	6/6	F	GD	GIMS			B/50	LPS	P	GMR
ROANOKE ISLAND														
4. Pirate's Cove Yacht Club & Marina 🖳 WiFi	800-367-4728	180	78	179/179	10/13			GIMS	HEP		B/50	LPS		GMR
WANCHESE (ROANOKE ISLAND)														
5. Bayliss Boatworks & Full Service Yard WiFi	252-473-9797	100	16/09	7/7	11/20	F	GD	IM	HEP	L110	B/100	S	P	GMR
6. Thicket Lump Marina	252-473-4500	40	19	1/30	3/3		GD	IS			B/50			R
OREGON INLET														
7. Oregon Inlet Fishing Center	252-441-6301	65	69	6/55	6/6		GD	GIMS			B/50			G

Corresponding chart(s) not to be used for navigation. 🖳 Internet Access WiFi Wireless Internet Access

sea level, making it the tallest brick lighthouse on the East Coast. Both are open year-round.

Special events: Dare Day, held the first Saturday of June, is an annual celebration of the people and history of Dare County. This event features live music on the waterfront and ends with a street dance. The New World Festival of the Arts, held in August, features over 80 selected artists exhibiting and selling their works on the Manteo Waterfront. Ye Olde Pioneer Theater (113 Budleigh St., 252-473-2216) holds the distinction of being the oldest theater in the U.S. run continuously by one family. This small but cozy venue runs one new movie at a time for $5.00!

Shopping: Downtown Manteo offers a compact shopping experience. Wanchese Pottery (107 Fernando St., 252-473-2099) offers a small gallery of handcrafted items. Manteo Booksellers (105 Sir Walter Raleigh St., 252-473-1221) carries books on Outer Banks lighthouses, shipwrecks along the Outer Banks, America's colonization, natural history and pirate stories. Outer Banks Quilts & Antiques (108 Sir Walter Raleigh St., 252-473-4183) is a good place to pick up a rare artifact. For upscale clothing, check out Charlotte's Ladies' Boutique (207 Queen Elizabeth Ave., 252-473-3078).

Nancyware Pottery (402 Queen Elizabeth Ave., 252-473-9400) has a wide selection of beaded earrings and jewelry. Endless Possibilities (105 Budleigh St., 252-475-1575) offers handcrafted items made from recycled fiber. At the Budleigh Street Antique Mall (400 Budleigh St., 252-473-9339), you can browse through shops of antiques. Something Special (107 Budleigh St., 252-475-1594) is a specialty gift and souvenir shop. Georgie's Place (107 Budleigh St., 252-475-9895) offers a collection of "shabby chic" items for your home. If you need to launder your new outfits, visit Manteo Speed Wash (114 U.S. Highway 64, 252-473-5037).

QUICK FACT:

CAPE HATTERAS LIGHTHOUSE

The black-and-white candy cane stripes of the Cape Hatteras Lighthouse make the beacon an unmistakable marker for cruisers passing Hatteras Island in the Outer Banks. The original lighthouse was built in 1803 to mark the dangerous shoals which extend 10 nautical miles from the cape. The tower was built of dark sandstone, consisted of 18 lamps and 14-inch reflectors, and was visible, in clear weather, from 18 miles away.

Because the lighthouse beacon was so often mistaken for a steamer's light and seemed to lack the necessary intensity, a new tower, constructed out of roughly 1.2 million bricks, was completed in 1870. The tower underwent a series of alterations and upgrades and, between 1999 and 2000, was ultimately moved 2,870 feet inland due to erosion of the shore.

The current lighthouse stands 207.5 feet tall and 210 feet above sea level. Visitors with endurance can make their way up 268 steps to reach the light, which glows with two 1,000-watt lamps and flashes every 7.5 seconds. The light is visible in clear conditions from 20 nautical miles.

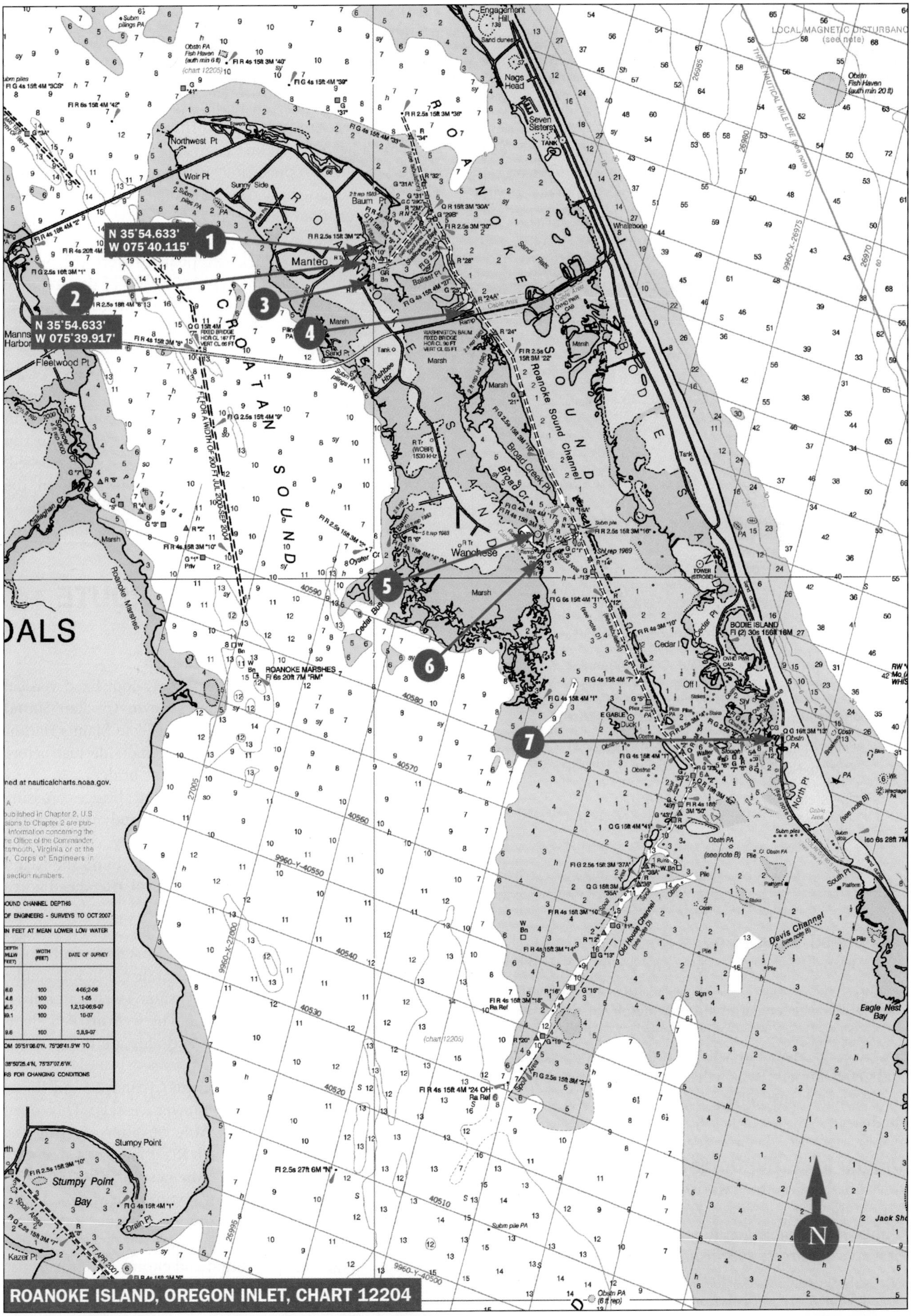

ROANOKE ISLAND, OREGON INLET, CHART 12204

Restaurants: The Full Moon Café (208 Queen Elizabeth Ave., 252-473-6666) is a local favorite. The Washington Post calls it "Delightful and affordable." The Hungry Pelican (207 Queen Elizabeth Ave., 252-473-9441) offers sandwiches on fresh baked bread, homemade soups and fresh salads, milkshakes and smoothies, plus packaged gourmet foods. Poor Richard's Sandwich Shop (302 Queen Elizabeth Ave., 252-473-3333) offers dining in a casual atmosphere. The Coffeehouse (106 Sir Walter Raleigh St., 252-475-1295) has a full espresso bar and serves tea, smoothies, milkshakes and ice cream, plus baked goods.

ADDITIONAL RESOURCES

- ELIZABETHAN GARDENS, 252-473-3234 www.elizabethangardens.org
- FORT RALEIGH HISTORICAL SITE, 252-473-5772 www.nps.gov/fora

NEARBY GOLF COURSES

Nags Head Golf Links, 5615 S. Seachase Drive, Nags Head, NC 27959, 252-441-8073 www.nagsheadgolflinks.com (7 miles)

NEARBY MEDICAL FACILITIES

Outer Banks Hospital, 4800 S. Croatan Highway, Nags Head, NC 27959, 252-449-4500 www.theouterbankshospital.com (8 miles)

Dare Medical Associates Pa, 604 Amanda St., Manteo, NC 27959, 252-473-3478 (1 mile)

Medical House Calls, Manteo, NC, 252-475-2007

Island Medical Center, 715 U.S. Highway 64, Manteo, NC 27959, 252-473-2500 (1.5 miles)

Troy Sluder Dr., 503 Cypress Lane, Manteo, NC 27959, 252-475-9841 (Dental)

County of Dare Medical, 109 Exeter St., Manteo, NC 27959, 252-475-5002 (1 mile)

Wanchese, South End of Roanoke Island

A commercial fishing village at the south end of Roanoke Island, Wanchese is home base for four fishing companies. They receive and ship the catch for the substantial oceangoing fleet that operates from here. It is an interesting place to visit, but while it offers seafood restaurants and retail outlets, you will find no accommodations for recreational boats. Silting has been a serious problem in the harbor.

Oregon Inlet, the Outer Banks

A well-defined channel, with 9- to 10-foot minimum depths, is used by the trawler fleet and leads south from Wanchese 6 miles down to Oregon Inlet. It is also used by one of the East Coast's largest sportfishing fleets. Be aware that aids to navigation change at the Oregon Inlet intersection. *(See page 65 for more information about Oregon Inlet.)*

NAVIGATION: Use Chart 12205. Oregon Inlet was dredged in 2009. Always obtain accurate local information before attempting this inlet, as it can be quite dangerous, even in calm conditions. Check with Coast Guard Station Oregon Inlet at 252-441-6260 for information regarding the marking system at Oregon Inlet. Information about depths can be found at www.saw.usace.army.mil/nav. The most recent surveys available at press time were done in February 2010. East of the bridge, the shoals off Bodie Island are encroaching on the channel and depths of 4 feet were noted near red channel buoy "14." There are 20-foot depths on the green side of the channel, except just before the bridge, where they drop to 9 and 10 feet. Surveys of this inlet are made frequently. The east-west channel inside the inlet is subject to shifting from the inlet to its intersection with the north-south channel.

From Oregon Inlet, Old House Channel carries at least 7-foot depths west into Pamlico Sound. Seek local knowledge or follow one of the local charter or fishing boats in or out of the inlet if you are in doubt. Do not try to run the inlet in foul weather. The channel is well marked, however. Carry the red lights and daybeacons on the starboard side from this point south to Pamlico Sound.

Dockage: Oregon Inlet Fishing Center sits north of the inlet, offering fuel and transient berths.

CROATAN SOUND ROUTE

Western Side of Roanoke Island

Back north, boats that can clear the 45-foot fixed vertical clearance bridge can run 4 miles down Croatan Sound from flashing green Croatan Light "3CS" to Manns Harbor (no transient facilities), on the mainland side just before the new 66-foot fixed vertical clearance bridge.

Vessels that cannot clear the fixed bridge crossing Croatan Sound can reach Manns Harbor and other Croatan Sound points via Roanoke Sound. They can run the dredged channel east of Roanoke Island, round the island via Old House Channel in Pamlico Sound, then head north up Croatan Sound.

NAVIGATION: Use Charts 12204, 12205, 11548, 11553 and 11555. At the north end of Croatan Sound, fixed bridges (45- and 66-foot vertical clearances) link Roanoke Island with the mainland. Check water levels carefully if your mast approaches this height. The well-marked channel carries 7- to 8-foot depths. Red aids are to starboard when heading south.

Many power vessels also use the Croatan Sound Route to circumvent the ICW and slower vessels. This open water route starts at Statute Mile 66 after entering the Albemarle Sound from the North River and ends at Statute Mile 169 in the Neuse River. After clearing both bridges in Croatan Sound heading south, your next waypoint will be Roanoke Marshes, flashing white 20-foot "RM." Your subsequent waypoints from the southern end of Croatan Sound, through Pamlico Sound and ending with the Neuse River, are as follows: Stumpy Point - 27-foot flashing white

Looking southeast over the town of Wanchese and Roanoke Sound. (Not to be used for navigation.) WATERWAY GUIDE PHOTOGRAPHY.

Looking northwest over the Oregon Inlet area. (Not to be used for navigation.) WATERWAY GUIDE PHOTOGRAPHY.

"N," Long Shoal – 15-foot flashing red "LS2," Bluff Shoal – 40-foot isophase "BL," Brant I Shoal – 40-foot flashing white "BI" then finally Neuse River 24-foot flashing white "NR." A licensed boat captain and long-time user of this route says it shaves 18 miles and a lot of aggravation off the trip north or south.

Dockage: At the southern end of Croatan Sound, Stumpy Point Bay has a commercial dock and anchorage for shallow-draft boats. The channel into the bay is well marked. On the eastern side of the Sound, the Sportsman's Boatworks offers a repair yard and is readily accessible from the Croatan Sound side of Wanchese.

GOIN' ASHORE: **ROANOKE ISLAND, NC**

As you head across Albemarle Sound, you will begin to see the island of Roanoke rise from the east. The northwestern shore appears much as it did when the subjects of Queen Elizabeth, under the command of Sir Walter Raleigh, suffered, starved and perished in the first British effort to conquer the New World. The hardships of the first colony under Governor Lane, 1585-86, and the disappearance of the "Lost Colony" in 1587 demonstrated the harsh nature of forging a new civilization so far from home.

History: On April 27, 1584, Captains Philip Amidas and Arthur Barlow sailed two barks across the Atlantic to explore the North American coast for Sir Walter Raleigh. The explorers landed on July 13, 1584, on the North Carolina coast, about 20 miles north of Roanoke Island. Barlow described it as "very sandie and low toward the waters side, but full of scuppernongs (grapes)." Amidas and Barlow presented Raleigh with a glowing report. They had arrived in midsummer and the natives, because it was the season of plenty, welcomed the visitors. Two Indians, Wanchese and Manteo, were taken back to England so that Raleigh could learn more about the character of the coastal Native Americans.

Raleigh sent a party of 108 settlers to Roanoke Island the following spring. A colony was established on the north end of Roanoke Island, and Ralph Lane was made Governor. Lane built a fort called "The New Fort in Virginia," where the present Fort Raleigh National Historic Site is situated. Soon relations between the settlers and Indians grew strained, deteriorating into open warfare.

When Sir Francis Drake arrived on June 9, 1586, and offered Lane and the colonists passage back to England, they accepted. Shortly thereafter, Sir Walter Raleigh arrived at "Hatoraske," found the settlement abandoned and returned to England. A few weeks later, Grenville arrived with three ships. Unwilling to lose possession of this new country, Grenville left 15 men on Roanoke Island with enough provisions to last 2 years. The next July, Sir Walter Raleigh returned with Governor White. When they went ashore to confer with the 15 men, all they found were skeletal remains. The next day Governor White and his party walked to the north end of the island and found the fort destroyed.

Roanoke Island. Photo courtesy Outer Banks Visitors Bureau.

Undaunted, White and his men decided to settle again at Roanoke Island rather than continue on to the Chesapeake Bay. The Native Americans proved to be more hostile than in the past, and George Howe, one of the assistants, was killed soon after the landing. In August, White's daughter, Eleanor, gave birth to a daughter, who was named Virginia because she was the first child of English parentage to be born in the New World. A few weeks later, Governor White sailed home with the fleet to obtain supplies for the colony.

Returning in August 1590, Governor White sent two boats ashore. On the north end of the island, they saw a light and rowed toward it. Anchoring in the darkness, they blew a trumpet but received no answer. In the morning, they landed on the north end of the island and found only the grass and rotten trees burning. One of the chief trees, or posts, had the bark peeled off and carved on it in capital letters was the word CROATOAN, but without the Maltese cross or sign of distress. On entering the palisade, they found iron and other heavy objects thrown about and overgrown with grass, signifying that the place had been abandoned for some time. From the fort and settlement area, White proceeded southward to the Shallowbag Bay but could find no sign of any of the inhabitants. The next day, White and his men tried to sail to Croatoan Island to look for the colonists, but they were turned back by the weather. As late as 1602, Raleigh was still seeking in vain for his lost colony.

Attractions: If you love drama, the nation's oldest running outdoor play, "The Lost Colony," plays throughout the summer. The amazing story of the original settlers plays each evening at the Waterside Theatre, near the site of the colonists' first settlement. Written by North Carolina's Pulitzer Prize-winning playwright, Paul Green, and produced by the Roanoke Island Historical Association, "The Lost Colony" is a first in its own right. It is the first and longest running historical outdoor drama. Combining dance, spectacle and song, the production is the forerunner of the modern American musical. You should choose a seat in the middle to rear sections due to ongoing action on the side stage. Also, be sure to bring bug spray or cover up completely. If the wind is blowing from the "wrong" direction, the mosquitoes can be brutal in the summertime! Locals can help you choose the best weather window. Call 252-473-3414 for ticket information.

The Elizabeth II, anchored across from the Manteo waterfront, is a replica of a 16th-century ship. It is named after one of the seven vessels in Sir Walter Raleigh's fleet.

The North Carolina Maritime Museum teaches visitors about building boats at its Watercraft Center. Visitors can view the building of a shadboat. The George Washington Creek Boathouse shows the traditional workings of a boat shop. (Hours vary, call 252-475-1750 for more information.)- The Roanoke Marshes lighthouse marks the entrance to Dough's Creek. This lighthouse is a replica of the 1877 screwpile lighthouse that was once found at Croatan Sound.

Special events: Tea with the Queen allows visitors to meet the Lost Colony's Queen Elizabeth for tea and dessert in beautiful Elizabethan Gardens. Advance reservations are required. Dare Day is a homespun festival that offers entertainment all day long, including dance troupes, cloggers, bands and barbershop quartets.

ADDITIONAL RESOURCES

- ELIZABETHAN GARDENS, 252-473-3234
  www.elizabethangardens.org
- FORT RALEIGH HISTORICAL SITE, 252-473-5772
  www.nps.gov/fora

NEARBY GOLF COURSES

Nags Head Golf Links, 5615 S. Seachase Drive,
Nags Head, NC 27959, 252-441-8073
www.nagsheadgolflinks.com (8 miles)

NEARBY MEDICAL FACILITIES

Outer Banks Hospital, 4800 S. Croatan Highway,
Nags Head, NC 27959, 252-449-4500
www.theouterbankshospital.com (8 miles)

Dare Medical Associates Pa, 604 Amanda St.,
Manteo, NC 27954, 252-473-3478 (2 miles)

Medical House Calls, Manteo, NC 27954, 252-475-2007

Island Medical Center, 715 US Highway 64,
Manteo, NC 27954, 252-473-2500 (2 miles)

Troy Sluder Dr., 503 Cypress Lane,
Manteo, NC 27954, 252-475-9841 (Dental)

County of Dare Medical, 109 Exeter St.,
Manteo, NC 252-475-5002 (2 miles)

WATERWAY GUIDE is always open to your observations from the helm. E-mail your comments on any navigation information in the guide to: editor@waterwayguide.com.

WATERWAY GUIDE advertising sponsors play a vital role in bringing you the most trusted and well-respected cruising guide in the country. Without our advertising sponsors, we simply couldn't produce the top-notch publication now resting in your hands. Next time you stop in for a peaceful night's rest, let them know where you found them—Waterway Guide, The Cruising Authority.

"The Lost Colony" outdoor drama, Manteo, NC.
Photo courtesy of Jani Parker.

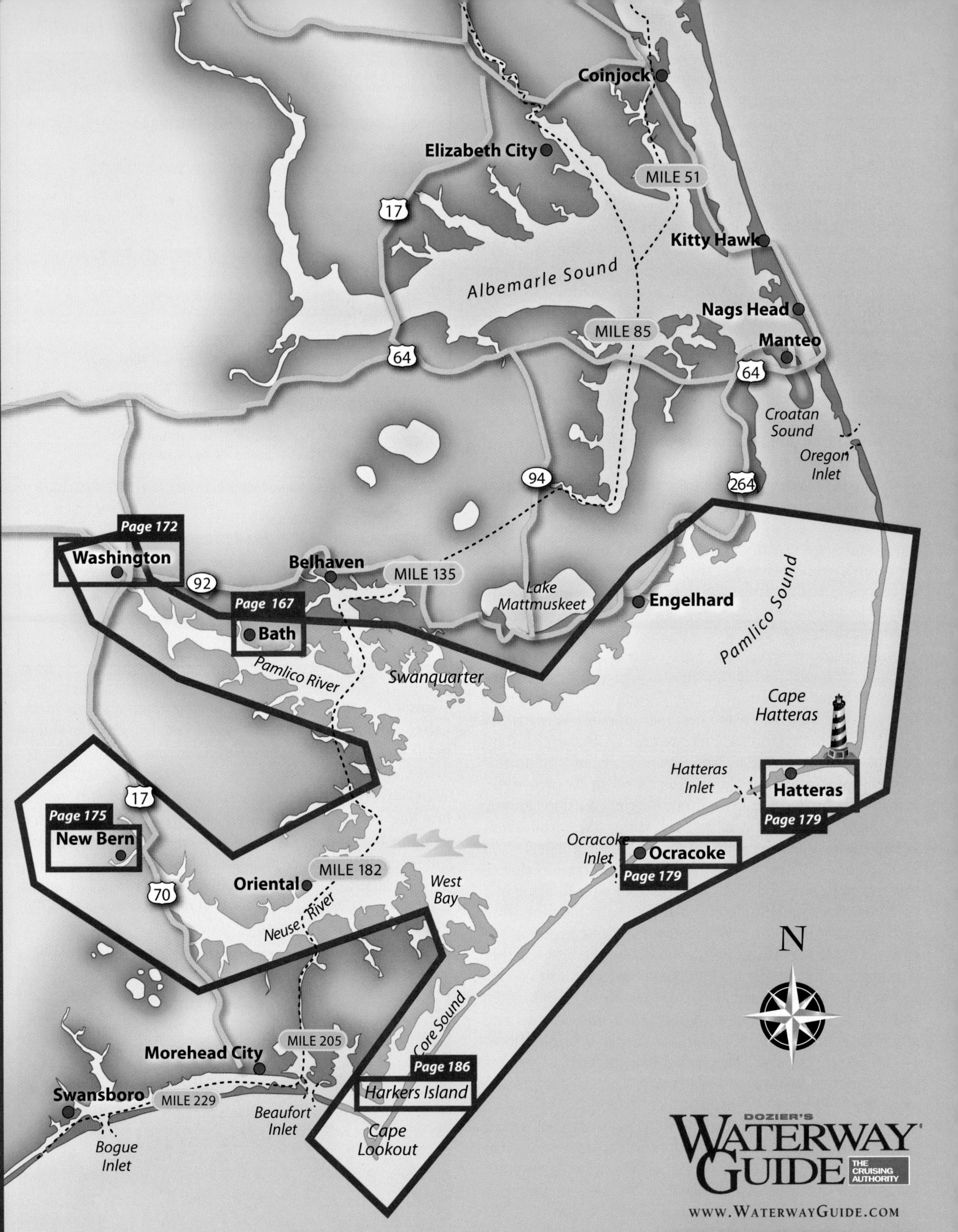

Skipper's Handbook

- Tide Tables 49
- Bridge Tables 58

Side Trips on the Outer Banks, Pamlico Sound

CHARTS 11544, 11545, 11548, 11550, 11552, 11554, 11555, 12204, 12205

North Carolina's Outer Banks, a long strip of barrier islands, are unlike any other islands along the Mid-Atlantic coast. Vulnerable to wind and wave, they extend in a crescent from the Virginia state line, bending farther and farther out to sea until the strip swings back suddenly at Cape Hatteras, leaving an exposed and dangerous cape. They finally meet with the mainland at Cape Lookout, near Morehead City and Beaufort. This route offers those prepared to deal with possibly rough conditions, or those whose vessels can travel at high speeds, with an alternative to the better-protected ICW route off of Albemarle Sound. The reward is some of the most pristine and wild scenery on the East Coast, should you choose to go ashore.

The banks enclose Currituck, Albemarle, Roanoke, Croatan, Pamlico and Core sounds, in that order. Currituck and Core sounds, at the two extremes, are narrow, shoal and suitable only for small or shoal-draft craft with local knowledge. The northern end of the banks has been a popular summer resort for generations, with many cottages, condominiums and commercial services.

Below Nags Head, the Cape Hatteras National Seashore stretches the length of the barrier islands to meet Cape Lookout National Seashore, at Core Sound beyond Ocracoke. The wild beaches, dunes, marshes and woodlands, preserved as National Seashores, are interrupted in only a few places by villages and private property holdings.

The best way to see the Outer Banks is from the inside (not from the Atlantic), and the best time is summer, when the sounds are relatively placid. In the sounds, waters are often shoaling, and channels near inlets shift rapidly. Although channels are marked, they may not be entirely reliable after a storm. Off-channel waters are sprinkled with crabpot floats and fishnet stakes, which warrant a wide berth.

PAMLICO SOUND

Sixty-five miles (via the ICW) south of Albemarle Sound, Pamlico Sound, the second largest ICW estuary after the Chesapeake Bay, deserves the utmost respect. Along with Albemarle Sound and the Neuse River, it can be one of the roughest bodies of water on the entire ICW. The afternoon sea breeze, combined with prevailing southwesterly winds, can often produce winds in excess of 20 knots. The north side of Pamlico Sound, though still primitive, is becoming more popular as boating services develop.

In November, migratory waterfowl transiting the Atlantic Flyway visit the refuge area halfway between Englehard and Swan Quarter. Swan Quarter, the seat of Hyde County, is the trading center for this area and an embarkation point for ferries crossing Pamlico Sound to Ocracoke Island. No marinas are available here.

NAVIGATION: Use Chart 11555. Pamlico Sound markers are generally 5 to 15 miles apart, so we strongly recommend that you run compass courses or GPS routes between them. Currents, often set up by the wind, can cause you to drift 10 to 15 degrees off course. Where these currents begin and end is impossible to predict, but they are indeed there, so you should check your position continually. Pamlico Sound, along with the other sounds, is a good area in which to use the GPS. An alternative route to the ICW, via the Croatan and Pamlico sounds, is covered in Chapter 3.

Dockage: Located on the western shore of Pamlico Sound, Big Trout Marina is up Far Creek with a well-marked channel. Camping, supplies, fuel and restaurants are nearby in the town of Englehard. Swan Quarter Bay, a harbor of refuge that can be buggy on still summer nights, has basic docks that accept transients if space allows. Large trawlers use the entrance, so use caution as you enter. The marked channel leads to Clark's Marina and Seafood, a boat basin at the north end of Swan Quarter Bay, offering fuel, 30-amp shore power and a store. From July to April, the harbor at Wysocking Bay is apt to be busy with commercial fishing boats and availability of dock space may be uncertain.

Pamlico Sound, NC

Pamlico Sound, NC		Largest Vessel Accommodated	VHF Channel Monitored	Transient Berths / Total Berths	Approach / Dockside Depth (reported)	Floating Docks	Gas / Diesel	Groceries, Ice, Marine Supplies, Snacks	Repairs: Hull, Engine, Propeller	Lift (tonnage), Crane, Rail	1=110V, 2=220V, B=Both, Max Amps	Pump-Out Station	Laundry, Pool, Showers	Nearby: Grocery Store, Motel, Restaurant
		Dockage					Supplies		Services					
GERMANTOWN BAY														
1. Van Horn's Bayside Marina	252-926-6621	40	16/01	6/15	4/4		G	IMS	E		1/30	S		M
FAR CREEK														
2. Big Trout Marina	252-925-6651	60	18	/30	5/5		GD				B/50			GMR

Corresponding chart(s) not to be used for navigation. Internet Access Wireless Internet Access

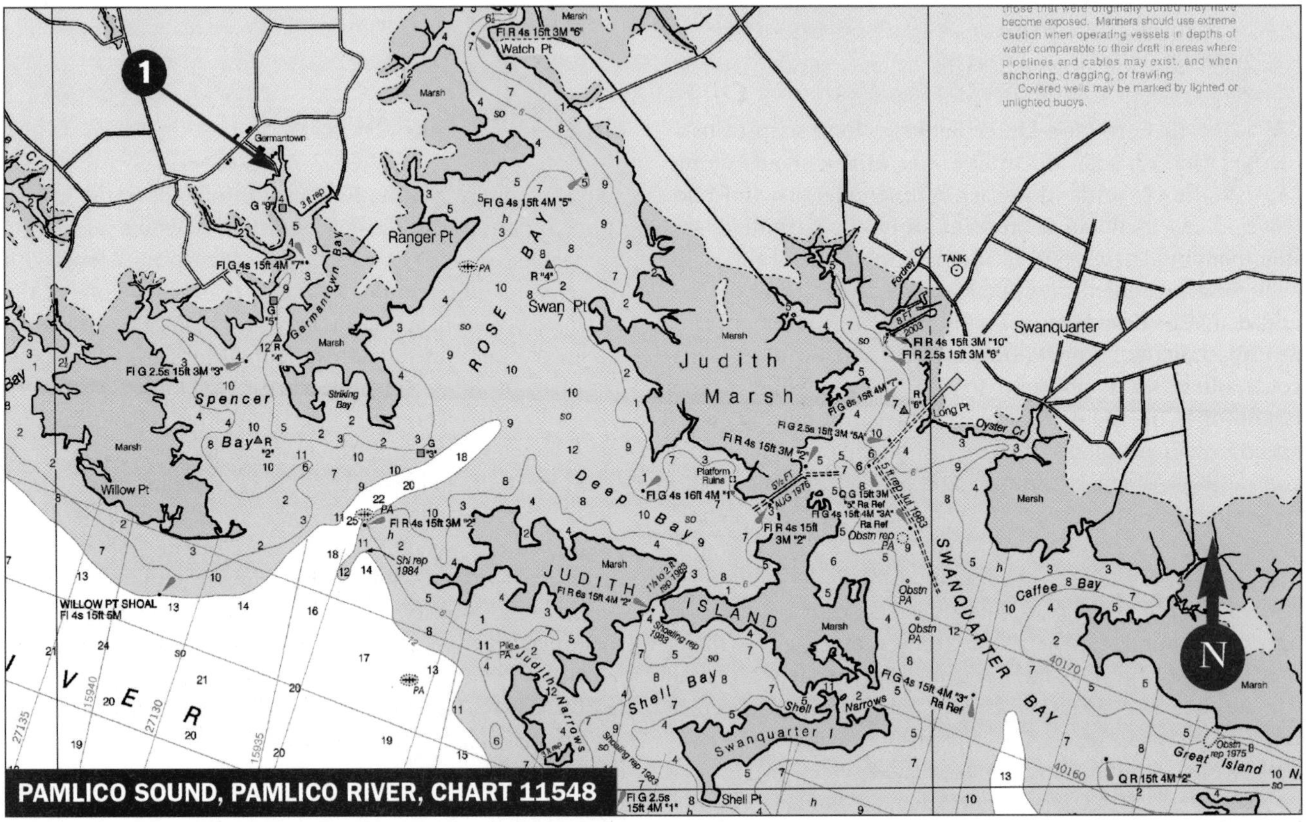

PAMLICO SOUND, PAMLICO RIVER, CHART 11548

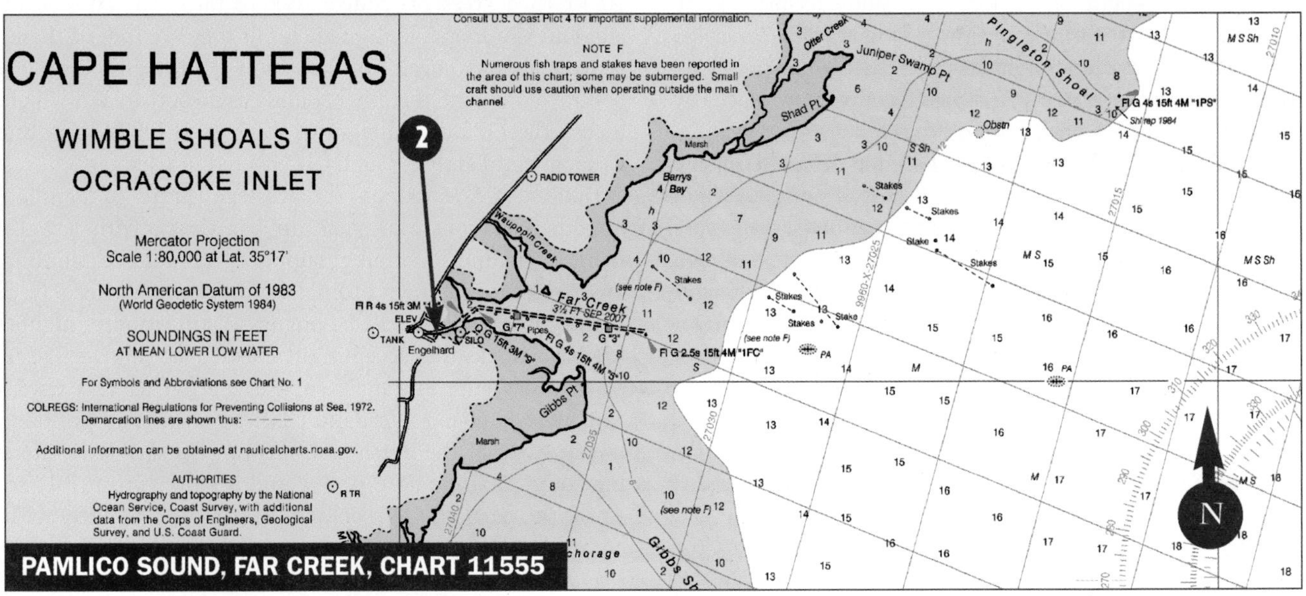

PAMLICO SOUND, FAR CREEK, CHART 11555

■ PAMLICO RIVER

Pamlico River to Washington

Sixty-five miles (via the ICW) south of Albemarle Sound lies the northwestern prong of Pamlico Sound, which reaches up to meet the Pamlico River. The Pamlico River is beautiful, wide and navigable, with wooded banks and only one industrial site: A phosphate mine on the south side of the Pamlico River occupies Durham Creek, a little more than 10 miles from the ICW.

NAVIGATION: Use Charts 11553 and 11554. If you are southbound, the entrance to the Pamlico River from the ICW is around the junction flashing red (2+1) "PR" (Mile 146), marking the shoal off Wades Point at the mouth of the Pungo River. Do not attempt to cut inside the marker unless you are very familiar with the area. Take care not to hit Mile Marker 145. It Is an unmarked, unlighted post on the east side of the Pungo prior to Wades Point. The river winds 27 miles westward to the city of Washington, where the Pamlico River becomes the Tar River.

South Creek

South Creek lies just west of Indian Island on the south shore of the Pamlico River. Deep and well-marked all the way to the town of Aurora, this is an excellent creek for exploration or anchorage, but be aware that there are no facilities for transient boaters. The small marina in Aurora has closed. Boats at anchor can possibly tie to the former town docks, which are now leased by North Carolina Fish and Wildlife.

When approaching Aurora, the channel narrows, and depths shoal to 5 to 7 feet. Follow the daybeacons carefully, and save any shallow-water exploration for your dinghy. Downtown Aurora is about three blocks from the waterfront, but the town's only grocery is considerably farther. The Aurora Fossil Museum (400 Main St.), located near the head of South Creek off the Pamlico River, is well worth a visit. It houses a collection of shark teeth, whalebones and other fossils. Visitors can sift through fossil-bed soil and find their own souvenir shark teeth, free of charge. There is also a history museum in town.

Anchorage: South Creek offers numerous anchorage possibilities off of the well-marked channel, but no protection from the east or west.

North Creek

North Creek lies east of Indian Island on the north shore of the Pamlico River. The entrance to the channel is marked by a red/green day beacon. The channel has about 7 feet of water. It is important to stay in the channel. The channel does a dogleg to the right then left to the red day beacon. Transit dockage is available at Potters Marina. There is fuel and ice available at North Creek Marina, a short walk from Potters, but sailboats cannot make it to the docks due to the shallow depth. Anchoring in North Creek is possible, but be aware of a very soft, muddy bottom that may cause anchors to drag. It recently provided a calm overnight stay for this editor while 50-knot winds roared across the Pamlico from the SW.

Bath Creek, off the Pamlico River

The waterfront here at the little historic town of Bath—which lies a bit farther up the Pamlico, on the north shore across from Durham Creek—cannot accommodate large numbers of transients, but the town is delightful and well worth a visit.

NAVIGATION: Use Chart 11554. Beyond the state ferry crossing, three nautical miles northwest of flashing red "4" off Gum Point, set a northerly course into Bath Creek. Upon entry, avoid the fish stakes, and be wary of any possible submerged pilings after clearing flashing green "1" at the entrance. The harbor is easy to enter if you mind the chart (11554) and watch out for the crab pots around flashing green "1" and red daybeacon "2" (Plum and Archbell points). Inside are good anchorages on the east and west sides, out of the way of any passing traffic.

Dockage: Pass green daybeacon "3" and flashing red "4" to reach dockage at the Bath Harbor Marina, which has transient amenities, or the free state docks (no utilities), both just to the south of the Bath Creek Bridge (13-foot fixed vertical clearance). Both facilities report 5- to 6-foot dockside depths. Gas is available at the Quarterdeck Marina, for shallow-draft boats, up Back Creek. A charming bed and breakfast (to starboard after you enter the creek) offers dockage for a few craft, comfortable lodging and a hearty morning meal. There is a surprisingly good local grocery store, post office, liquor store and bank within walking distance.

Anchorage: Back Creek provides protected anchorage with good holding and depths of 6 to 7 feet up to the fixed bridge (7-foot vertical clearance). A grocery store and restaurant are both a short dinghy ride away.

GOIN' ASHORE: BATH, NC

Located on the Pamlico River, Bath is a town rich in historical roots. Founded in 1696 and listed as the oldest town in North Carolina, perhaps Bath's most notorious citizen was Edward Teach, also known as Blackbeard the Pirate. Standing in front of the historic Bonner House and looking south across the bay, it is easy to see why Blackbeard selected Bath and Plum Point as his base of operation: privacy. That much has not changed.

History: The birth of Bath happened in the 1690s, when European settlers stopped at Bath Creek because of its sheltered location on the Pamlico River and close proximity to the Atlantic Ocean via Ocracoke Inlet. French Protestants were the first to arrive. John Lawson was appointed first surveyor general of the colony, and Christopher Gale became its chief justice. By 1705, Bath was North Carolina's first city and by 1708, there were 12 homes in town.

Pamlico River, NC

		Largest Vessel Accommodated	VHF Channel Monitored	Transient Berths / Total Berths	Approach / Dockside Depth (reported)	Floating Docks	Gas / Diesel	Groceries, Ice, Marine Supplies, Snacks	Repairs: Hull, Engine, Propeller	Lift (tonnage), Crane, Rail	1=110V, 2=220V, B=Both, Max Amps	Laundry, Pool, Showers	Pump-Out Station	Nearby: Grocery Store, Motel, Restaurant
BATH CREEK		Dockage					Supplies				Services			
1. Bath Harbor Marina & Motel 🖳	252-923-5711	60	16	2/43	7/8						1/30	LS	P	GMR
2. Harding's Landing, Bath State Dock	252-923-3971	40		7/7	6/6						1/30			GMR
3. The Quarterdeck Inc.	252-923-2361	75			9/5		G	GIMS						GR
BROAD CREEK														
4. Washington Yacht & Country Club 🖳 WiFi	252-946-6872	55		2/	6/6		GD	I			B/50	LPS	P	R
5. McCotters Marina	252-975-2174	55	16	10/180	6/6			IMS	HEP	L15	B/50	S	P	
6. Captain Sam's Boatyard	252-975-2046							MS	HE	L20				
7. Broad Creek Marina	252-975-2046	36		20/100	4/4						1/30		P	

Corresponding chart(s) not to be used for navigation. 🖳 Internet Access WiFi Wireless Internet Access

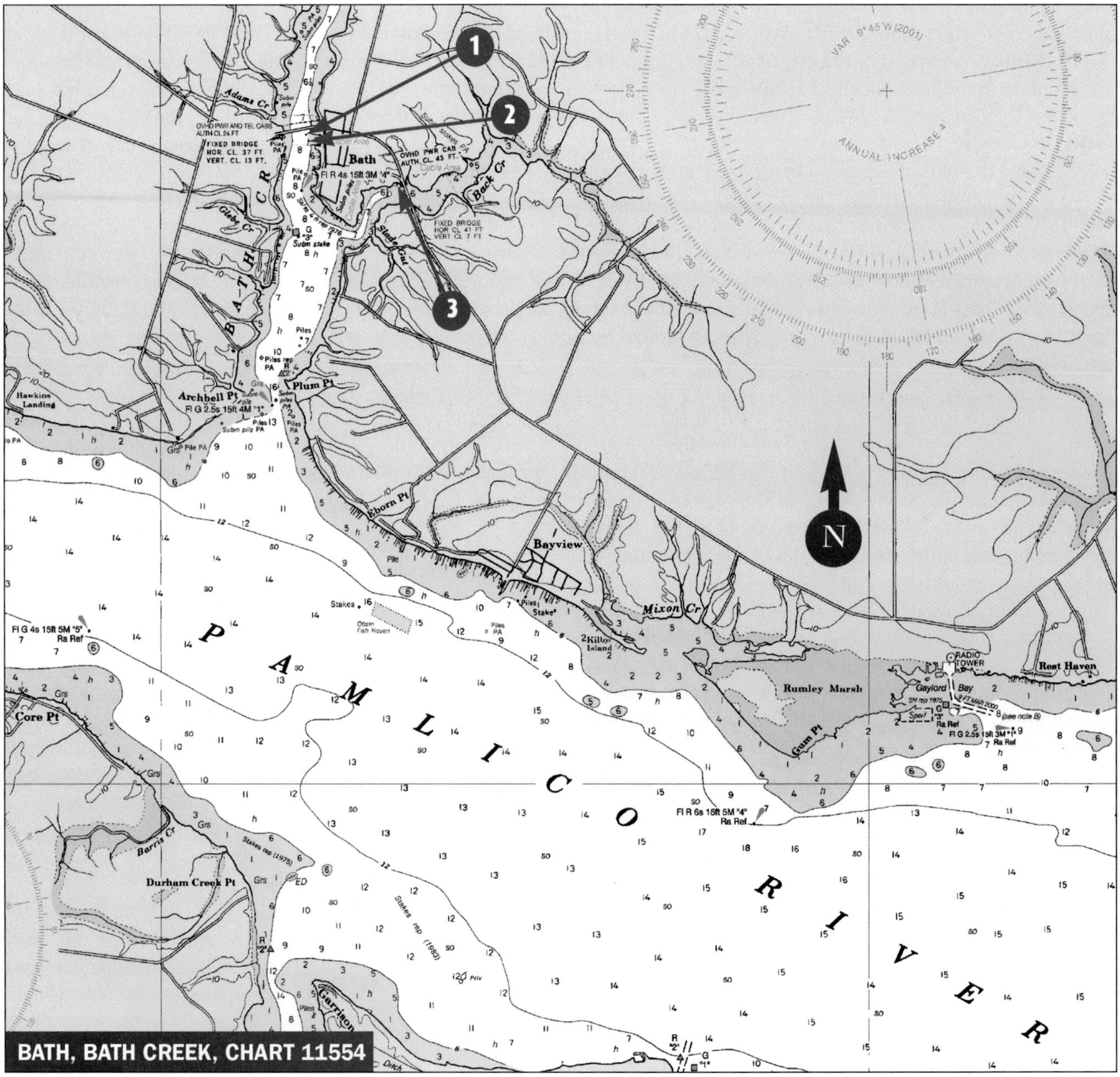

BATH, BATH CREEK, CHART 11554

Residents traded in furs, tobacco, West Indian molasses, salt, wine, sugar, New England rum and English merchandise. Bath became the first port of entry into North Carolina.

In 1707, a gristmill and the colony's first shipyard were built. Books sent to St. Thomas Parish in 1701 became the first public library in the colony. The parish also established a free school for American Indians and African-Americans.

In 1753, 28-year-old Robert Palmer, a lieutenant colonel in the British army, sailed from Scotland with his 32-year-old wife, Margaret, and two small sons, Robert and William, to the port on Bath Creek where he had been appointed as customs collector. He had replaced Lawson as surveyor general. These two posts were important ones, providing Palmer with an annual salary that made him one of the highest paid crown officials in North Carolina. He also surveyed vast tracts of land and smaller plantations for new settlers and recorded their patents with the secretary of the province. Beaufort County's first courthouse was built in Bath in 1723, and later the town was considered the first capital of the Colony.

Soon the town became embroiled in political rivalries, suffered epidemics and endured Indian wars and piracy. Cary's Rebellion of 1711 led to an armed struggle over religion and politics. That same year, a severe drought and an outbreak of yellow fever decimated the colony. When war broke out between the Tuscarora tribe and the settlers, Bath became a refuge for those in the outlying areas.

Attractions: Homes and history are the attractions of Bath. Both the Palmer-Marsh House, built in 1751, and the Bonner House are restored and furnished with period pieces. The Van Der Veer House offers a self-guided exhibit on the history of Bath. When services are not in session, you may also tour the St. Thomas Church.

The Palmer-Marsh House offers a wide central passage that allows for a good breeze from front door to back and into the upstairs. The Palmers had a spacious parlor in the room opening onto Water Street. Because of its outside entrance, Palmer used the northeast corner room as his port collector's office. In this way, ship's officers could come and go without disturbing Margaret, who for several years suffered from poor health. The home also served as the social hub of the town, a need that became more important when Governor Dobbs named Palmer a member of the royal council.

In 1830, Joseph Bonner purchased property on Water Street, known then as Town Point. The home was spacious, as it needed to be for five children. Today, the Bonner House sits among elm, walnut, cedar and dogwood trees and remains one of the best examples of early 19th century Carolina architecture. The house retains many of its original features, including the small blown-glass window panes, wide-board pine floors and delicate hand-carved mantels. Decorative paint treatments of the period, such as wood graining on interior doors and "marbleizing" on baseboards, are evident throughout the home. Several names,

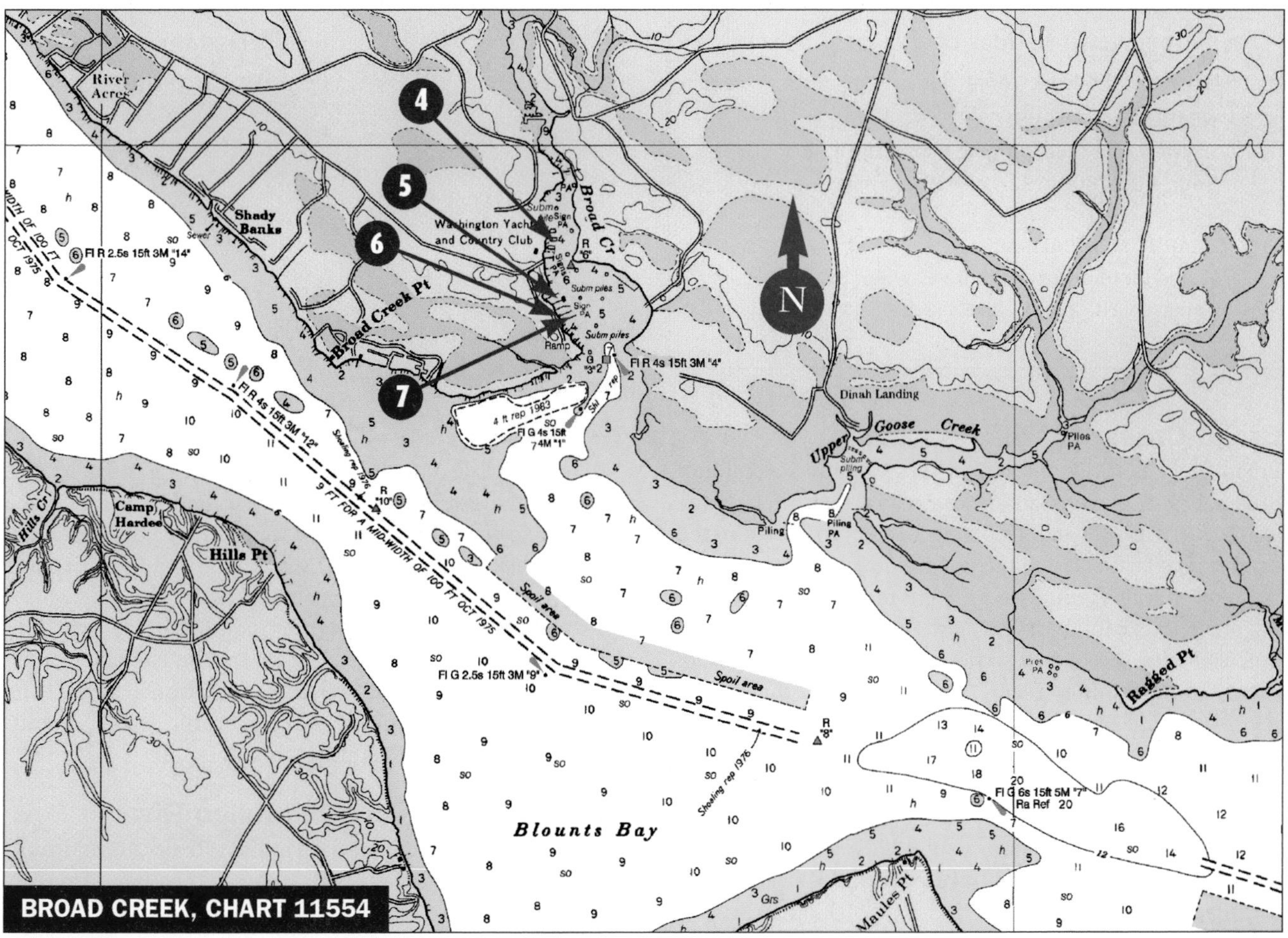

BROAD CREEK, CHART 11554

etched long ago by the Bonner children, remain visible on one of the front window panes.

The Van Der Veer House was constructed around 1790 and features a gambrel roof and double-shouldered Flemish bond chimneys. Named after Jacob Van Der Veer, one of the founders of the Bank of Washington, the house and property changed hands several times during the late 19th century. It was once known as the H. W. Beasley Plantation. In 1970, the dwelling was moved to its present location, and in 1972, the house was restored to its original appearance.

Special events: Each May, Bath sponsors a Croquet Tournament in conjunction with Open House and Bath Fest. This arts festival features free tours of the Palmer-Marsh and Bonner Houses, as well as arts and crafts vendors, music and theatrical performances, food booths, and hands-on arts and craft activities for children and adults. Call Historic Bath at 252-923-3971 for more information.

Restaurants: Blackbeard's Slices & Ices (101 N. Main St., 252-923-9444) serves, pizza, pastas, subs and salads and has live music on many Friday and Saturday nights. It is located at the foot of the bridge, just a short walk from the state docks. About a mile's walk from the state dock is Old Towne Country Kitchen (436 Carteret St., 252-923-1840). They serve breakfast, lunch and dinner. Bath General Store (502 Carteret St., 252-923-4361) is located next door on Highway 92.

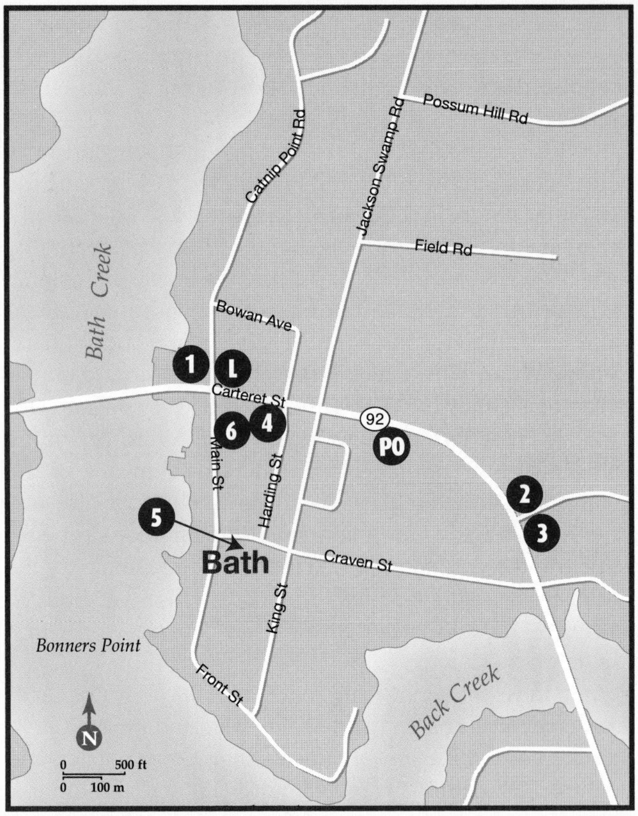

Reference the marina listing tables to see all the marinas in the area.

DINING
1 Blackbeard's Slices & Ices
2 Old Town Country Kitchen

GROCERIES/CARRYOUT
3 Bath General Store

POINTS OF INTEREST
4 Historic Bath Visitors Center
5 St. Thomas Church

LODGING
6 Inn on Bath Creek

L LIBRARY

PO POST OFFICE

ADDITIONAL RESOURCES

- **HISTORIC BATH VISITORS CENTER, 252-923-3971**
  www.nchistoricsites.org/bath/

NEARBY GOLF COURSES
Bayview Golf Club, 49 King Blount Drive, Bath, NC 27808, 252-923-8191 (4 miles)

NEARBY MEDICAL FACILITIES
Pungo District Hospital, 202 E. Water St., Belhaven, NC 27810, 252-943-2111 (18 miles)

Broad Creek, off the Pamlico

Broad Creek is seven miles to the west of Bath. Several hundred sail and powerboats make Broad Creek their homeport, and it is the main boating center for Washington, seven miles farther on to the north-northwest.

Broad Creek's entrance is well marked and easy to negotiate. Steer in a northwesterly direction from flashing green "7" (in the main Pamlico River channel off Maules Point) until flashing green "1" is visible, and then follow the channel to green daybeacon "3" and flashing red "4." Have a current version of Chart 11554 handy, and note the spoil areas south of the entrance. The channel carries 6-foot depths, and there is some anchorage space available.

Dockage: To starboard you will find the Pamlico Plantation private docks. To port are Broad Creek Marina, Captain Sam's Boatyard and McCotters Marina (recognized by the sheds). McCotters and Captain Sam's Boatyard both have haul-out and repair facilities. McCotters monitors VHF Channel 16 and can give advice on the harbor. McCotters is rebuilding a portion of the docks lost in a fire in 2011. Captain Sam's boat yard will allow owners to make repairs under dry dock for a reasonable charge. Washington Yacht and Country Club is beyond red daybeacon "6" (give it good clearance). The club sells gas and diesel fuel, and offers transient dockage and amenities to members of reciprocating clubs, including a restaurant, a swimming pool and golf.

Chocowinity Bay, off Pamlico River

Boaters traveling west on the Pamlico River can find tranquil overnight anchorage in Chocowinity Bay. There is also a marina here.

Washington, NC

WASHINGTON		Largest Vessel Accommodated	VHF Channel Monitored	Transient Berths / Total Berths	Approach / Dockside Depth (reported)	Floating Docks	Gas / Diesel	Groceries, Ice, Marine Supplies, Snacks	Repairs: Hull, Engine, Propeller	Lift (tonnage), Crane, Rail	1=110V, 2=220V, B=Both, Max Amps	Laundry, Pool, Showers	Pump-Out Station	Nearby: Grocery Store, Motel, Restaurant
		Dockage					Supplies		Services					
1. Park Boat Co.	252-946-3248	30			6/4			M	HE	L5				GR
2. Carolina Wind Yachting Center 💻	252-946-4653	48	16	2/22	22/22						B/50	S		GMR
3. Washington Waterfront	252-975-9367	100	16	17/46	10/12			IS			B/50	S	P	GMR
4. Whichard's Marina	252-946-0223	50	16	5/20	7/7		G	GIMS	E		B/50	LS		GMR
5. Cypress Landing Marina	252-975-3955	42	16	7/222	7/6	F		I			B/50	S	P	G

Corresponding chart(s) not to be used for navigation. 💻 Internet Access WiFi Wireless Internet Access

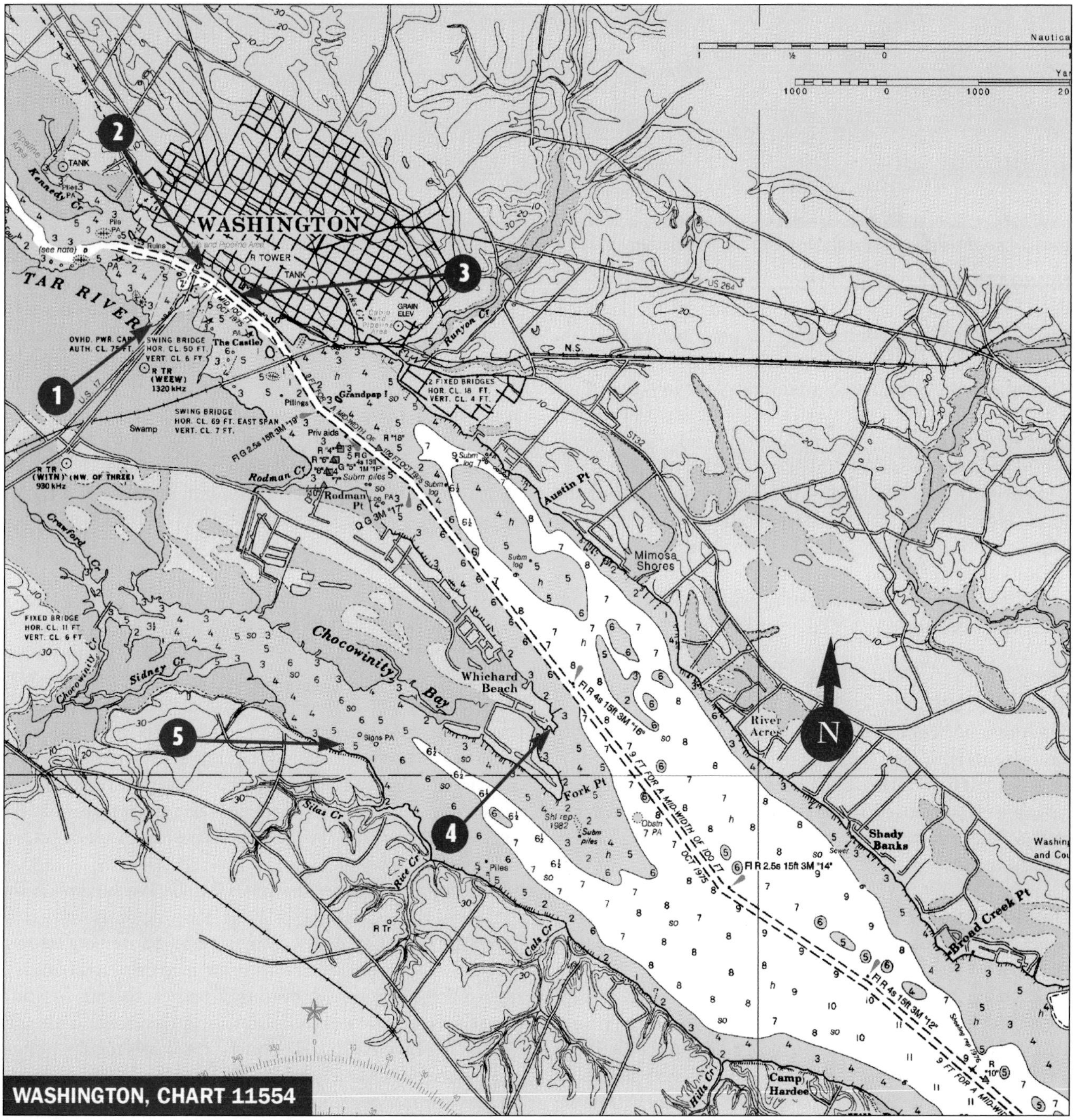

WASHINGTON, CHART 11554

Looking northwest over Washington and the Pamlico River. (Not to be used for navigation.) WATERWAY GUIDE PHOTOGRAPHY.

NAVIGATION: Use Chart 11554. To reach the marina on Chocowinity Bay, stay on the south side of the Pamlico River, south of Fork Point, giving the point plenty of clearance for shoals, submerged pilings and a hard bottom. This is a tricky entrance that requires your full attention! The bay is unmarked but carries 6-foot depths toward the middle almost all the way to Sidney Creek. Go directly to the marina, avoiding the tree stumps to the right. Chocowinity Bay is shallow in places, so call ahead for local advice if you have a deep draft. Cypress Landing Marina monitors VHF Channel 16 during the day.

Dockage: The Cypress Landing Yacht Club and Marina offers pump-out service and transient dockage. Visitors from reciprocating yacht clubs get the first night's dockage free.

Washington, on the Pamlico River

The town of Washington has completely redeveloped its waterfront, with new building faces and an extensive new bulkhead. The riverfront between the two swing bridges (7- and 6-foot closed vertical clearances) is landscaped, and to the east is a city park with picnic tables and a playground.

NAVIGATION: Use Chart 11554. The chart shows plenty of water in the Pamlico River, even outside the channel, until flashing red "14." From there, markers "16," "17," "18" and "19" lead to the railroad swing bridge (7-foot closed vertical clearance, usually left open) and the Washington riverfront. Past the railroad swing bridge is the U.S. Highway 17 Swing Bridge (6-foot closed vertical clearance). When approaching the town, keep The Castle Island to port, and stay within the 9-foot-deep channel.

Dockage: Complimentary city dockage (first-come, first-served, 48-hour tie-up limit) is available at the town waterfront (with five 80-foot-long docks), but no utilities are available. Many of the other slips are now occupied by permanent slipholders, but some transient space with utilities is usually available. More transient slips with utilities are expected to be built soon. For reservations, call 252-975-9367. The facility has showers, restrooms and a pump-out station. There is a dinghy dock for those who anchor out, and the town is considering establishing a mooring field.

GOIN' ASHORE: WASHINGTON, NC

The heart of the Inner Banks beats slowly as the Pamlico River flows along the Washington, NC waterfront. On a given evening, as another Carolina sunset flames out behind the pines and street lamps wink on, visiting cruisers step from their cockpits onto the dock for an evening stroll. Beginning from the brick walkway running the length of the docks, there is much to do and see in Washington, but the best part is what they left behind—bridge schedules, crowded anchorages and a hurried itinerary.

Within the crown of the Inner Banks, Washington is the largest of the jewels. The original Washington is more than a town; it is a city with commerce and conveniences. East Carolina University's state-of-the-art medical school lies less than a half-hour away, providing fast access to some of North Carolina's top medical professionals. And yet for all its amenities, Washington shows best when it shines the light on its cypress oaks and stately homes. Here, you will find a sprawling waterfront with stores, businesses and the historic haunts of pirates, merchants and notable politicians.

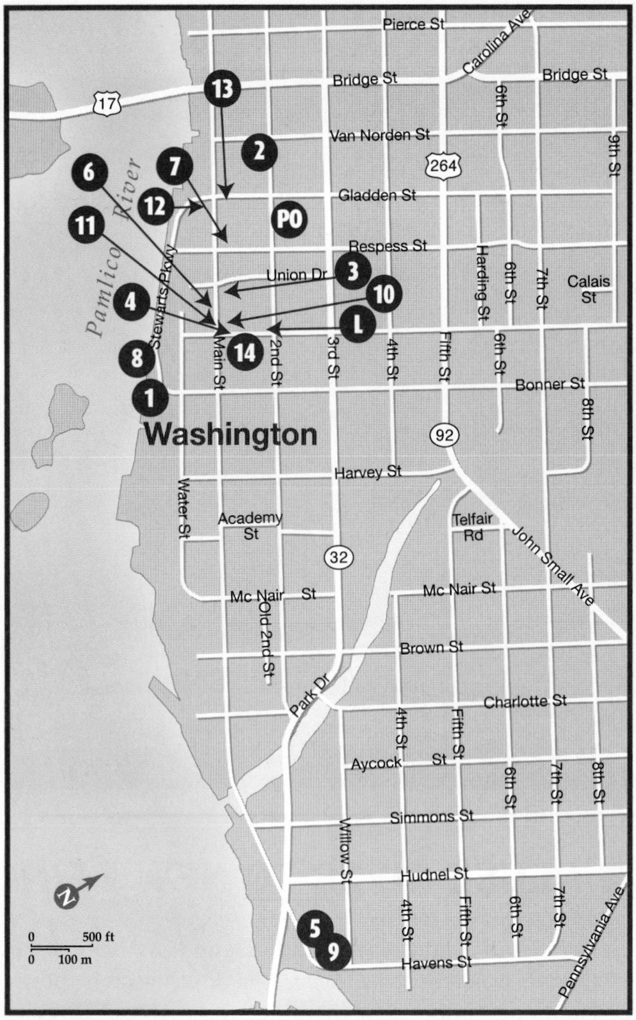

Reference the marina listing tables to see all the marinas in the area.

ATTRACTIONS
1 The Estuarium
2 The Moss House
3 The Turnage Theater

DINING
4 Down on Main Street
5 Backwater Jack's Tiki Bar & Grill
6 The Meeting Place
7 Wine & Words

INFORMATION
8 Visitors Center

RECREATION
9 Inner Banks Outfitters

SHOPPING
10 Russell's Mens Shop
11 Tassels
12 Whimsy
13 Warren's Sport Headquarters
14 Stewart's Jewelry

L LIBRARY

PO POST OFFICE

Washington's new waterfront provides 48-hour free docking, allowing boaters the chance to sample its restaurants, antique shops and art galleries. With the exception of the Piggly Wiggly grocery store, a two-mile trek, most of what you will need is a short walk from the docks.

History: First called Forks of the Tar, the name was changed in 1776 in honor of Gen. George Washington, making the original Washington the first town to be named after our first president. The entire waterfront of Washington is listed in the National Register of Historic Places.

West of the Highway 17 bridge lies one of the scars from the Civil War. The Union ship *SSV Picket* can still be seen in the water. In the spring of 1864, Union forces set fire to Haven's Wharf in an effort to keep naval stores and cotton from falling into the hands of the Confederates. An eyewitness wrote, "The fire rapidly spread north across Main Street, down Van Norden Street, consuming everything to Fifth, the last street in town ... it burned the length of Gladden and Respess streets ... every home on Bridge went down." Chimneys were all that remained. There are two homes that withstood the fires and barrages of the war, cannonballs still lodged in their walls.

Culture: The Turnage Theater (150 W. Main St., 252-975-1711) presents professional performing arts, entertainment and classic movies. Stop by Pia's Restaurant (252-940-0600) next door after the show. The third Saturday of the month, April through October, the "Saturday Market" features a food court with live entertainment and an Artisans' Market.

Attractions: Inner Banks Outfitters (1050 E. Main St., 252-975-3006), located on Runyon Creek at the Haven's Garden public boat ramp, rents kayaks and bikes. The Moss House (129 Van Norden St.) marks the beginning of a self-guided tour of downtown. Maps are available at the Visitors Center at 138 S. Market St. (252-948-9415). The Estuarium (223 E. Water St., 252-948-0000) is an aquarium with unique exhibits about the Pamlico-Tar River System. The Estuarium features over 200 exhibits with unique environmental artworks, living aquariums and the Crab Pot gift shop. Special programs are offered throughout the year. River Roving Educational Tours are seasonal and require reservations. The Beaufort Hyde Martin Library, on Market and Second streets, will guide you through the Civil War battles in and around Washington.

ADDITIONAL RESOURCES

- **WASHINGTON VISITORS CENTER TOURISM INFORMATION, 800-546-0162** **www.visitwashingtonnc.com**
- **NORTH CAROLINA ESTUARIUM, 252-948-0000** **www.pamlico.com/nce**
- **CITY OF WASHINGTON, www.ci.washington.nc.us**
- **www.beaufortedc.com**
- **WASHINGTON HARBOR DISTRICT ALLIANCE** **www.washingtononthewater.com**

NEARBY GOLF COURSES
Cypress Landing, 600 Clubhouse Drive, Chocowinity, NC 27817, 252-946-7788 www.cypresslandinggolf.com (16 miles)

Bayview Golf Club, 49 King Blount Drive, Bath, NC 27808, 252-923-8191 (19 miles)

NEARBY MEDICAL FACILITIES
Beaufort County Regional Health System 628 E. 12th St., Washington, NC 27889, 252-975-4100 (1 mile)

Pitt County Memorial Hospital, 2100 Stantonsburg Road, Greenville, NC 27835 252-847-4100 (29 miles)

Looking north over New Bern. (Not to be used for navigation.) WATERWAY GUIDE PHOTOGRAPHY.

Special events: Race for the River Kayakalon is a fund raising event to support the Pamlico-Tar River Foundation. The race is held at Goose Creek State Park. Pickin' on the Pamlico is a crab feast with crabs harvested fresh from the Pamlico River. Smoke on the Water is an annual chili cook-off with some of the best in the state, plus live music. There is live music on the waterfront sponsored by the Chamber of Commerce on numerous Fridays, Spring through Fall.

Shopping: Washington has a nice collection of shops downtown. Russell's Men's Shop (118 W. Main Street, 252-946-2120) has quality menswear for more than 30 years now. Tassels has unique gifts and accessories (127 W. Main Street, 252-946-0799). Whimsy (221 W. Main St., 252-940-0513) sells women's clothing, original art and gifts. Warren's Sport Headquarters (240 W. Main St., 252-946-0960) is a good choice for hunting and fishing paraphernalia. Stewart's Jewelry (121 N. Market St., 252-946-2611) offers original and distinctive pieces.

Restaurants: Down on Main Street (107 W. Main Street, 252-940-1988) is a family restaurant featuring American cuisine with a downeast flair. Enjoy outdoor seating with views of the Pamlico River. Backwater Jack's Tiki Bar & Grill and Inner Banks Outfitters (1052 E. Main St., 252-975-1090) are located in "The Fun Zone" at the east end of Main Street. Try the amazing half-pound "Buffett Burger" named after the singer. The Meeting Place (225 W. Main St., 252-975-6370) offers a varied menu in a pleasant atmosphere. Wine & Words (220 W. Main St., 252-974-2870) offers wine, beer and wine accessories, specialty foods and books.

NEUSE RIVER TO NEW BERN

Upriver from Adams Creek and off the ICW lies a jewel of the Neuse River, New Bern. The southwestern prong of Pamlico Sound leads 31 miles up the Neuse River to New Bern, where the Trent River makes in. A trip up the Neuse River, the widest river in the United States, can be a great time if the weather cooperates. It can also be challenging, depending on wind direction. The river, one of the least developed in the country, provides one of the best side trips along the Eastern Seaboard.

NAVIGATION: Use Chart 11552. The wind's direction and strength, not the moon, cause the tide fluctuations in the upper Neuse. No tables or regular schedules can be established, but water depths change by a foot or two in each direction. Overall, the depth is adequate for all drafts, but pay attention to your charts.

Dockage: Marinas catering to transients are becoming more numerous here. Between Adams Creek and New Bern, beyond Wilkinson Point and just west of the ferry crossing (look for flashing red "2"), is Wayfarers Cove on the north shore of the Neuse River at Minnesott Beach. Carefully follow the markers, as shoaling can be a problem in this area. Northwest Creek Marina at Fairfield Harbor is about four miles east of New Bern. Beyond the marina to starboard is Spring Creek, the entrance to Fairfield Harbour, a deepwater canal and private resort community. The Cherry Point Marine Corps Air Station has taken over the Hancock Creek/Slocum Creek area on the south side of the river.

New Bern, on the Neuse

Named for the capital of Switzerland and founded by Swiss and German settlers in the 1700s, New Bern is 21 miles from flashing green "1AC," which is near ICW Mile 185 at the mouth of Adams Creek. Gift shops, antiques shops and specialty shops—including woodcarving and stained glass—abound in downtown New Bern.

NAVIGATION: Use Chart 11552. The channel up the Neuse River to New Bern is well-marked and easy to navigate. The lighted clock tower on City Hall is an excellent landmark. The new 65-foot fixed vertical clearance bridge (in channel) across the Neuse River, immediately down from New Bern, is visible for about 10 miles, making an excellent landmark. Be aware that strong northeasterly winds can raise the water level, resulting in reduced bridge clearance.

The Cunningham Bridge, at Mile 0 in the Trent River is a new bascule bridge (14-foot closed vertical clearance) and is closed from 6:30 a.m. to 8:30 a.m. and from 4:00 p.m. to 6:00 p.m. Monday through Friday, except that it will open at 7:30 a.m. and at 5:00 p.m. if vessels are waiting. It is also closed from 2:00 p.m. till 7:00 p.m. on Sundays and federal holidays from May 24 through Sept. 8, but will open at 4:00 p.m. and 6:00 p.m. if vessels are waiting.

A railroad swing bridge (5-foot closed vertical clearance) also crosses the Trent River. This bridge is usually open except for an infrequent train crossing. Two thousand feet upstream are twin fixed highway bridges (45-foot vertical clearances). Note that winds may affect water levels, and there may be less than the charted 45-foot clearances.

Dockage: Transient dockage in New Bern is convenient to town. Located on Union Point on the Neuse River, with no bridge opening to negotiate, is the Skipjack Landing and The Galley Stores, which offer full-service transient dockage, along with gourmet provisioning, restaurant, gas and diesel fuel, boat supplies, restrooms and showers. Try Persimmons, their new waterfront restaurant. Skipjack Landing is located directly on the channel.

The New Bern Grand Marina (formerly the New Bern Sheraton Marina) has a 1,000-foot face dock with 12-foot depths inside a protected breakwater. The marina is located in front of the newly renovated waterfront Hilton. The marina offers full amenities, including shower and laundry facilities, an on-site restaurant and bar. All the Hilton amenities are also available to marina guests, including the fitness center and pool. The SkySail Luxury Condos are adjacent. Slips at the marina are for sale; however, transient dockage, both long and short term, may be available.

New Bern's Union Point has undergone a major renovation, with new public docks (complimentary daytime dockage), but no overnight dockage. Extensive shopping, restaurants and an excellent market are nearby. This development is adjacent to the Comfort Suites Hotel, which no longer offers dockage. Across Front Street from Union Point is the new convention center. On the south side of the river, adjacent to the Ramada Inn, Bridge Pointe Marina offers transient slips.

Ensley's Radio Company, located between the Neuse and Trent rivers, offers sales, service and installation of marine electronics to boaters.

GOIN' ASHORE: NEW BERN, NC

New Bern, NC offers visitors hospitality and Southern charm with the best of modern conveniences. New Bern's greatest assets are its natural resources: abundant water, steady winds and a vibrant waterfront. This is a river town, not a coastal city. The condominiums and beaches are down the road, across the railroad track and several dozen stoplights away. In New Bern, you will find park benches and city sidewalks, restaurants and brick storefronts adorned with polished brass. This is the home of Pepsi-Cola and best-selling author Nicholas Sparks. It is the state's first capital and the final port of call for those seeking small-town living without the big-box feel.

For every sportfish boat speeding down the ditch to the condominium communities on the beach, you will find a couple in a sailboat or trawler yacht making a right-hand turn at Minnesott Beach and following, historically speaking, in the wake of barkentines that once sailed toward the Tryon Palace.

History: Settled in 1710 by Baron von Graffenreid, New Bern began as Chattawka, a small village purchased from the Tuscarora Indians. Chattawka means "where fish were taken out." The name was later changed to New Bern in honor of the descendants of Bern, Switzerland.

A "Carolina Charter" was issued by King Charles II, granting his loyal supporters wide areas of land in the New World. The Carolina Charter spread from Virginia to the Spanish border of Florida. The name "Carolina" came from "Carolus," the Latin word for Charles. William, Earl of Craven, was one of the original Lords Proprietor, and Craven County bears his name. The Royal Governor William Tryon saw the need for a permanent capital in the growing colony and selected New Bern as the site.

By the mid-1700s, New Bern had grown to become a vital port for the new Colonies. Deckhands would offload cargos of rum, sugar and molasses from barkentines arriving from the West Indies, replacing the cargo with pitch, tar and turpentine destined for England.

New Bern is a town of firsts. It was North Carolina's first capital, home of the state's first printing press, first publicly chartered school, home of the first motion picture theater and the first to hang electric Christmas lights above city streets. New Bern residents are quick to point out that Caleb Bradham's soda pop—Pepsi-Cola—has a better kick than the competing brand.

Culture: Tryon Palace (610 Pollock St., 252-639-3500) was originally built between 1767 and 1770, as the first permanent capitol of the Colony of North Carolina and a home for the Royal Governor and his family. Architect John Hawks designed the Palace, in the manner of a number of fashionable houses, in London's Georgian style, with symmetry maintained throughout. It was soon regarded to be the finest public building in the American Colonies. For another dose of historical perspective, you can take a 90-minute trolley ride through Historic New Bern, narrated by knowledgeable local residents. Call New Bern Tours at 800-849-7316.

New Bern, NC

NEW BERN		Largest Vessel Accommodated	VHF Channel Monitored	Transient Berths / Total Berths	Approach / Dockside Depth (reported)	Floating Docks	Gas / Diesel	Groceries, Ice, Marine Supplies, Snacks	Repairs: Hull, Engine, Propeller	Lift (tonnage), Crane, Rail	1=110V, 2=220V, B=Both, Max Amps	Laundry, Pool, Showers	Pump-Out Station	Nearby: Grocery Store, Motel, Restaurant
		Dockage					Supplies		Services					
1. New Bern Grand Marina (Internet Access) (Wireless Internet Access)	252-638-3585	200	16/68	20/225	12/8	F		GI			B/100	LPS	P	GMR
2. Skipjack Landing - The Galley Stores	252-633-4648	100	16	25/		F	GD	GIS			B/50	S		R
3. Bridge Pointe Marina	252-637-7372	100	16	10/125	16/10	F		I			B/50	LPS	P	GMR
4. Duck Creek Marina	252-638-1702			1/58	5/6			M		L35,C		S		
5. Northwest Creek Marina	252-638-4133	75	16/68	12/268	8/12		GD	GIMS			B/50	LPS	P	R

Corresponding chart(s) not to be used for navigation. Internet Access, Wireless Internet Access

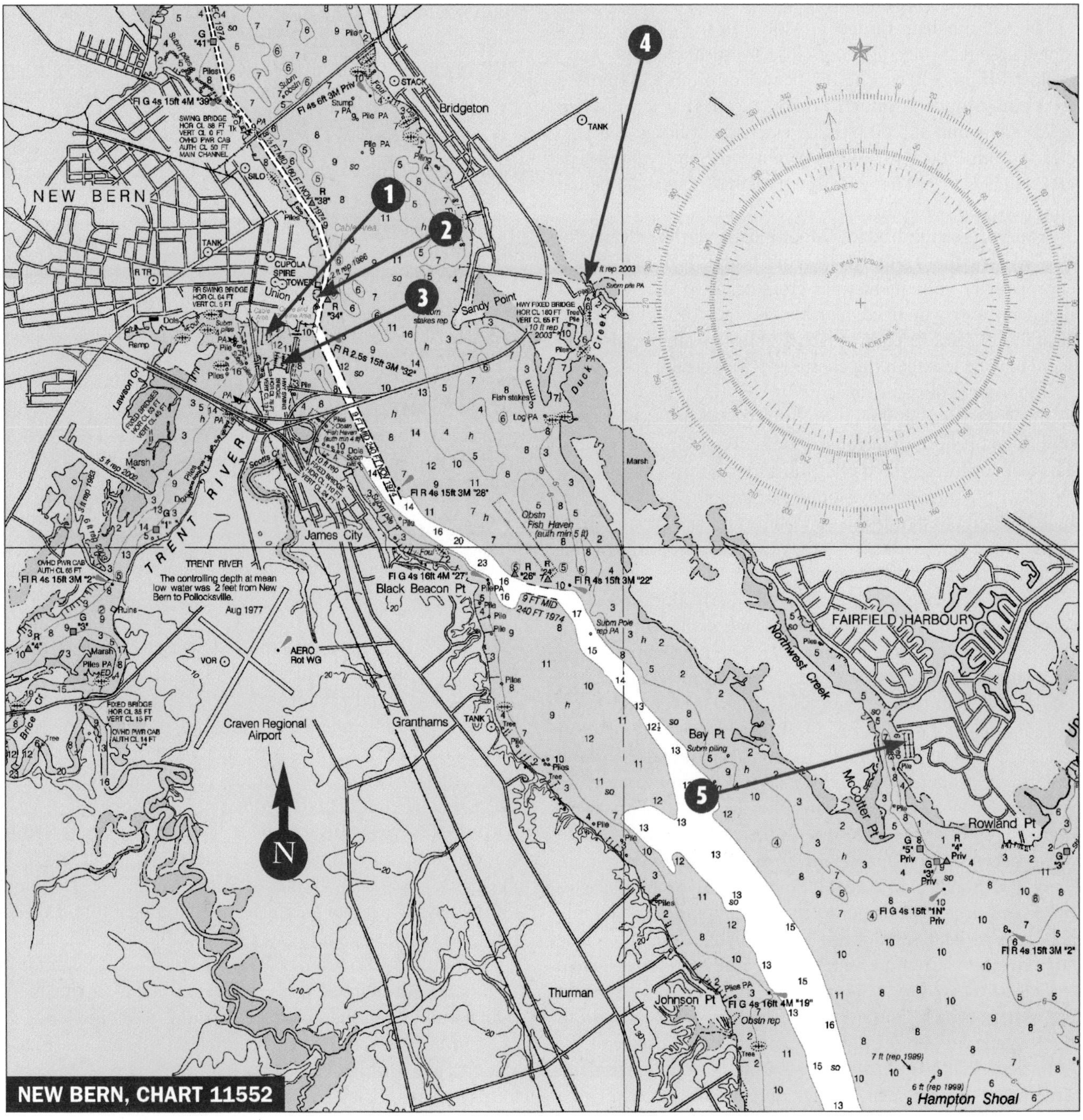

Christ Church Parish (320 Pollock St.) was established in 1715. In 1752, King George II gave the church a silver communion service, a prayer book and a Bible, all of which are still in use today. The Presbyterian Church, built from plans by Sir Christopher Wren, designer of St. Paul's Cathedral in London, served as a hospital during the Civil War. The belfry still shows carved names and initials of Union soldiers.

Attractions: The primary attractions are the Colonial Governor's Mansion, the Tryon Palace Historic Site and Gardens (610 Pollock St.) and the surrounding Historic District homes, many of which are open year-round. The 13-acre estate includes the Palace, George W. Dixon House, John Wright Stanly House, stables, a series of landscaped gardens and the Academy Museum. Demonstrations of the period include cooking, blacksmithing and weaving. The Attmore-Oliver House (512 Pollock St., 252-638-8558) is home to the New Bern Historical Society. Inside, you will also find a doll collection and a Civil War Museum.

The Bank of The Arts (at the Craven Arts Council and Gallery, 317 Middle St., 252-638-2577) features monthly exhibits of painting, sculpture, photography and pottery. At the Fireman's Museum (408 Hancock St., 252-636-4087), you will find early steam pumpers, a brass sliding pole and an extensive collection of early fire-fighting equipment.

The bust of DeGraffenreid is tucked away on Pollock Street beside the gorgeous Christ Church. The Pepsi Store (256 Middle St., 252-636-5898) is in the exact spot where Caleb Bradham invented his "soft" drink. Stop in for a free sample.

The Masonic Theater (516 Hancock St., 252-638-8558) is the oldest theater in America to be used continuously. The first schoolhouse in North Carolina is worth a visit. The Academy Building, on the corner of New and Hancock streets, served as a schoolhouse for boys and girls, and later as a hospital during the Civil War. In 1881, it became part of the New Bern Graded School System. Tours are available from Carolina Carriage and Tours (252-675-5360).

Special events: The MUMfest, held each October, is a combination of fantasy, fun, education and entertainment, attracting more than 80,000 festival-goers to New Bern's historic downtown streets and waterfront.

Shopping: Mitchell Hardware (215 Craven St., 252-638-4261) is an authentic turn-of-the-century hardware store with a little bit of everything, including books and gifts. The Boathouse (220 Middle St., 252-633-5501) carries a nice selection of nautical books and gifts. Four C's Casual Clothing (250 Middle St., 252-636-3285) offers camping gear and travel accessories. At Carolina Creations (317-A Pollock St., 252-633-4369), you will find a wide selection of art, craft and gift gallery items. The Farmer's Market (421 S. Front St.) is a great place to go for fresh vegetables and fruits, seafood, flowers and crafts. At Bear Essentials (309 Middle St., 252-637-6663), you will find organic and natural products including soaps, lotions, cosmetics, balms and more. At Middle Street Landing (225 Middle St., 252-514-0000), you can shop for Vera Bradley handbags and accessories. Art of the Wild, Etc. (218 Middle St., 252-638-1082) carries a wide mix of local and imported art, predominantly

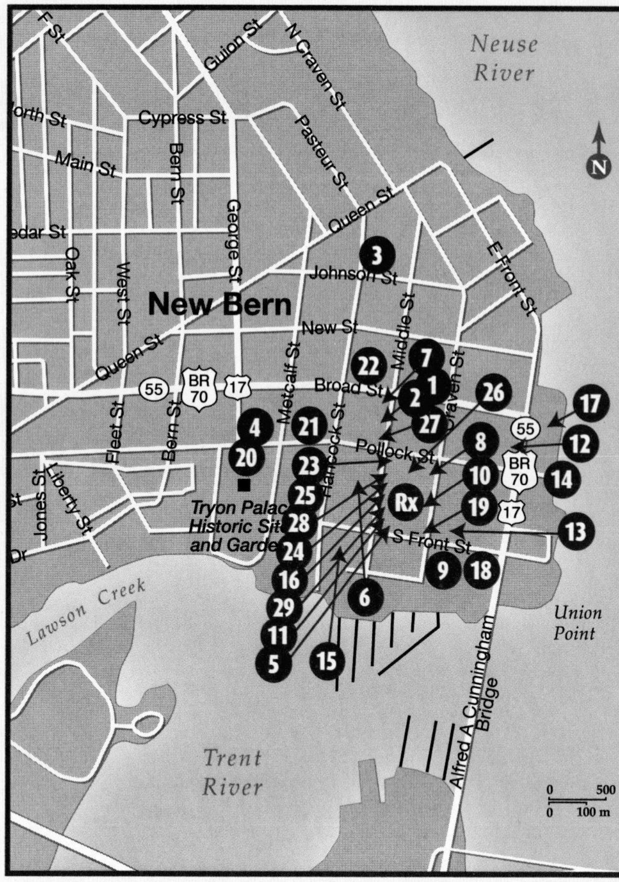

Reference the marina listing tables to see all the marinas in the area.

ART/ANTIQUES
1 Craven Arts Council and Gallery
2 The Bank of The Arts

ATTRACTIONS
3 The Masonic Theater
4 Trolley Tours

DINING
5 Captain Ratty's
6 Baker's Square
7 The Chelsea
8 Saffron & Spoons Kitchen Boutique
9 The Harvey Mansion
10 Morgan's Tavern and Grill
11 MJ's Raw Bar
12 Pollock Street Deli
13 Trent River Coffee Company
14 Persimmons

GROCERIES/CARRYOUT
15 The Farmer's Market
16 Fraser's Wine, Cheese and More
17 Galley Stores

INFORMATION
18 Craven County Convention and Visitors Bureau

MARINE SUPPLIES
19 Mitchell Hardware

POINTS OF INTEREST
20 Tryon Palace Historic Site and Gardens & NC History Center
21 Attmore-Oliver House; New Bern Historical Society
22 Fireman's Museum
23 The Pepsi Store

SHOPPING
24 The Boathouse
25 Four C's Casual Clothing
26 Carolina Creations
27 Bear Essentials
28 Middle Street Landing
29 Art of the Wild, Etc.

PHARMACY

New Bern, NC. (Not to be used for navigation.) WATERWAY GUIDE PHOTOGRAPHY.

of birds and animals, sculpted from wood, marble resin, water buffalo horns, driftwood and tree roots. Fraser's Wine, Cheese and More (210 Middle St., 252-634-2580) offers wine, cheese, chocolate and more, including specialty foods, and imported and domestic beer. Saffron & Spoons Kitchen Boutique (208 Middle St., 252-633-1335) has a large variety of unique products and kitchen accessories. Galley Stores, a gourmet provisioning establishment on the waterfront, offers everything you need to provision the boat (300 E. Front St., 252-633-4648).

Restaurants: Captain Ratty's (202 Middle St., 252-633-2088) features an upstairs piano bar with live entertainment several nights a week. Check out their new rooftop bar with river views. Baker's Square (227 Middle St., 252-637-0304) offers fried chicken with all the trimmings, homemade breads, desserts and their famous Dutch potatoes. The Chelsea (335 Middle St. 252-637-5469) is located in Caleb Bradham's old drug store and offers a 1920s atmosphere. Persimmons, a new restaurant on the waterfront, is located at Skipjack Landing (100 Pollock St., 252-514-0333).

The Harvey Mansion (221 S. Front St., 252-635-3232) offers a wonderful atmosphere and fine dining in this 17th- century mansion. Morgan's Tavern and Grill (235 Craven St., 252-636-2430) serves great steaks, seafood, burgers and drinks. MJ's Raw Bar (216 Middle St., 252-635-6890) is a good choice for fresh seafood. The Pollock Street Deli (208 Pollock St., 252-637-2480) is another local favorite among cruisers. For an early-morning jolt or late-night snack, try Trent River Coffee Company (208 Craven St.), where you will hear live nightly music on weekends.

ADDITIONAL RESOURCES

- **Craven County Convention and Visitors Bureau, 800-437-5767, www.visitnewbern.com**
- **Tryon Palace, 800-767-1560, www.tryonpalace.org**

NEARBY GOLF COURSES

Carolina Pines Golf and Country Club, 465 Carolina Pines Blvd., New Bern, NC 28560 252-444-1000 (13 miles)

Emerald Golf Club, 5000 Clubhouse Drive, New Bern, NC 28561, 252-633-4440 (16 miles)

NEARBY MEDICAL FACILITIES

Craven Regional Medical Center, 2000 Neuse Blvd., New Bern, NC 28560, 252-633-8111 (2 miles)

Hatteras, NC

HATTERAS		Largest Vessel Accommodated	VHF Channel Monitored	Transient Berths / Total Berths	Approach / Dockside Depth (reported)	Floating Docks	Gas / Diesel	Groceries, Ice, Marine Supplies, Snacks	Repairs: Hull, Engine, Propeller	Lift (tonnage), Crane, Rail	1=110V, 2=220V, B=Both, Max Amps	Laundry, Pool, Showers	Pump-Out Station	Nearby: Grocery Store, Motel, Restaurant
		Dockage					Supplies		Services					
1. Scott Boatyard	252-995-4331	55	07	3/9	6/6			M	HEP	L30	1/30			GMR
2. Oden's Dock 🖳	888-544-8115	75	1	19/25	6/10		GD	GIMS			B/50	S		GMR
3. Village Marina, Motel & Campground	252-986-2522	70		3/32	7/6		G	IMS			B/100	LS		GMR
4. Hatteras Harbor Marina 🖳	800-676-4939	60	1	25/44	7/6		D	IMS			B/100	LS		GMR
5. Teach's Lair Marina Inc.	252-986-2460	65		75/90	6/6		GD	GIMS			B/50	S		GMR
6. Hatteras Landing Marina 🖳	800-551-8478	78		20/37	9/9		GD	GIMS			B/50	LS		GMR

Corresponding chart(s) not to be used for navigation. 🖳 Internet Access (WiFi) Wireless Internet Access

Hatteras, the Outer Banks

Hatteras Island is the longest of the barrier islands, stretching from Oregon Inlet south and around the elbow of Cape Hatteras to Hatteras Inlet. Hurricane Isabel created a new inlet in September 2003, which separated Hatteras Village from the remainder of Hatteras Island. The inlet has since been filled, and Hatteras Village has been restored. Hatteras is a major charter-sportfishing harbor. The small village has some interesting shops and restaurants.

Do not fail to visit the Cape Hatteras Lighthouse (10 miles from Hatteras Village), now relocated 2,900 feet inland to protect it from beach erosion. The former lighthouse site is marked with a circle of large granite boulders, which formed part of the stone foundation when the lighthouse occupied the spot. The view from its top toward famous Diamond Shoals, known as "The Graveyard of the Atlantic," is an unforgettable sight. It is 268 steps to the top, but definitely worth the effort. Since the 1500s, more than 600 ships have wrecked along the treacherous coastline surrounding Cape Hatteras. The Graveyard of the Atlantic Museum, a dream for many years, is now open in Hatteras Village, featuring displays on shipwrecks and North Carolina's maritime history.

NAVIGATION: Use Chart 11555. We advise strangers against attempting Hatteras Inlet without local knowledge, as the twisting channel shifts regularly and, at times, may shoal to 4-foot depths or less. The Pamlico Sound side of the island is shoal for a considerable distance out from the shore. Approach Hatteras Village from Pamlico Sound via long, well-marked Rollinson Channel (reported mid-channel depth of 7 feet, but charted at 6.5 feet from a March 2011 survey), leaving red markers to port (this is a continuation of the channel in from the Atlantic Ocean at Hatteras Inlet). Check for local information on the state of the inlets. ***(See page 66 for more information about Hatteras Inlet.)***

Dockage: Several marinas have transient slips and cater to serious sportfishermen. Teach's Lair Marina and Hatteras Landing Marina welcomes transients. Scott Boatyard has full-service repairs. Oden's Dock welcomes transients and has gas and diesel fuel available, as do several others. Village Marina Motel and Campground accepts transient boaters. Be sure to call ahead and check the status of transient dockage before making your way to Hatteras Village.

Ocracoke Island, the Outer Banks

Ocracoke Island is the last link in the Cape Hatteras National Seashore. In sharp contrast to the glamorous resorts springing up all along the Mid-Atlantic coastline, life on tiny Ocracoke Island remains, by choice, much as it was 25, or even 50, years ago. Though motels, cottages, shops and restaurants cater to a large number of tourists, most of the island's longtime residents strive to preserve the small-town atmosphere and staunchly defend its merits. Geography is also a contributing factor: Ocracoke has a road but no bridge. Access is by boat only—motorists must take the ferry from Swan Quarter, Cedar Island or Hatteras Island.

NAVIGATION: Use Chart 11555. **Use the Cape Hatteras Tide Table. For high tide, add 9 minutes; for low tide, add 11 minutes.** Ocracoke Inlet can be an alternative to the long diversion to Beaufort when heading north or south around Cape Hatteras, but check with Coast Guard Sector North Carolina via VHF Channel 16 for current conditions before using the inlet at or near low tide. The inlet is buoyed from the sea, with red markers to starboard. The sea buoy is positioned correctly on the small-scale chart. This arrangement continues through Big Foot Slough Channel into Pamlico Sound. Thus, if you are approaching the island from the sound, you will leave the red channel markers to port. The most current chart for the inlet at publication was Chart 11550 Edition 29 from May 2004. Check the *Local Notice to Mariners* for any changes, or use a Print on Demand chart, which has changes and survey information through August 2009. ***(See page 67 for more information about Ocracoke Inlet.)***

On the inside, Big Foot Slough Channel, routinely used by the large car ferries coming from the mainland, is regularly dredged to carry minimum depths of 10 feet, and is the obvious choice for deep-footed craft and those

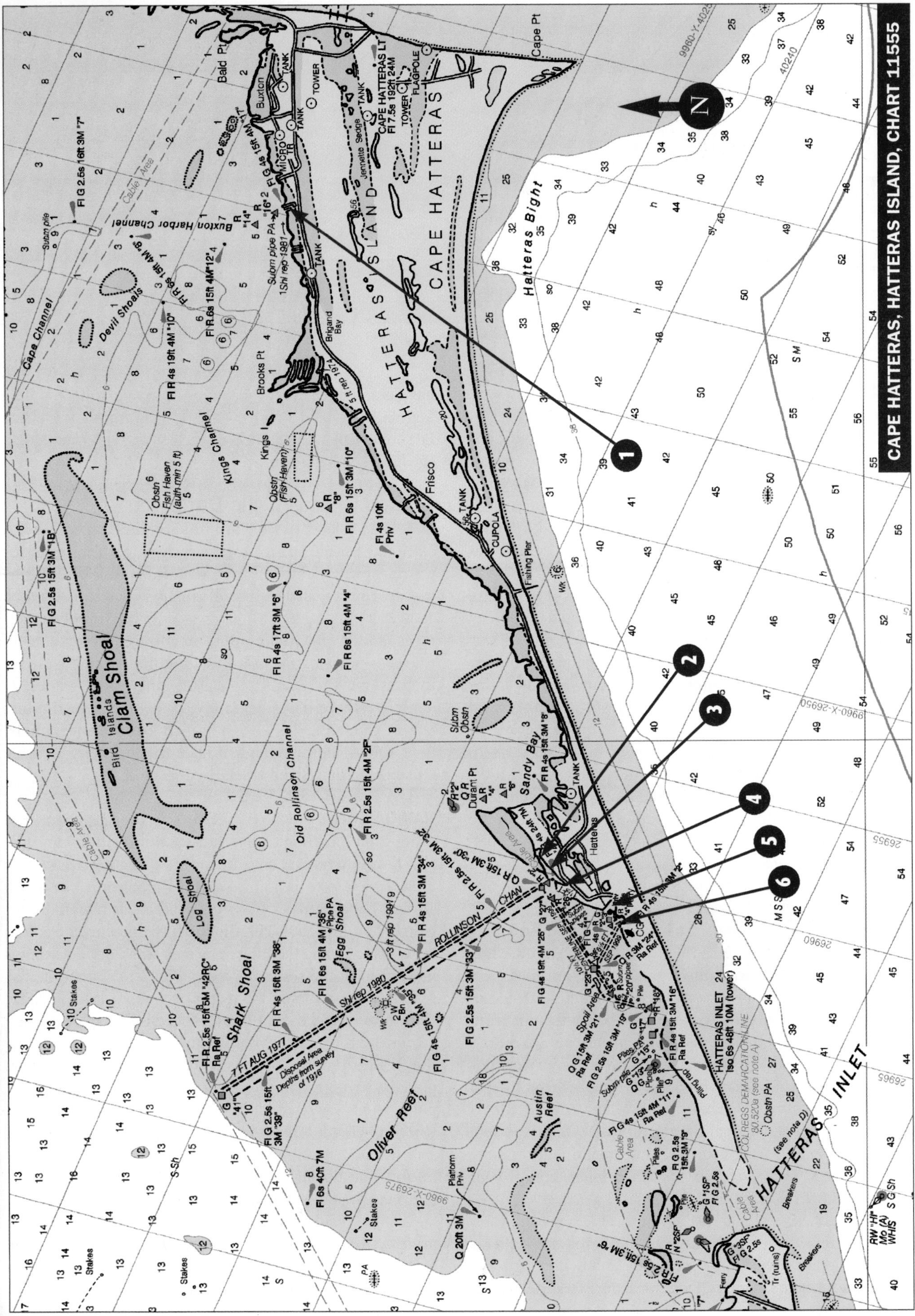
CAPE HATTERAS, HATTERAS ISLAND, CHART 11555
Hatteras Bight
CAPE HATTERAS
HATTERAS ISLAND
HATTERAS INLET
Clam Shoal
Bird Islands
Log Shoal
Shark Shoal
Oliver Reef
Austin Reef
Egg Shoal
Devil Shoals
Kings Channel
Old Rollinson Channel
Buxton Harbor Channel
Cape Channel
Sandy Bay
Durant Pt
Brooks Pt
Kings I
Bald Pt
Cape Pt
Buxton
Frisco
Hatteras
Brigand Bay
Jennette Sedge
CAPE HATTERAS LT Fl 7.5s 192ft 24M
HATTERAS INLET Iso 6s 48ft 10M (tower)
1
2
3
4
5
6

Ocracoke, NC

OCRACOKE		Largest Vessel Accommodated	VHF Channel Monitored	Transient Berths / Total Berths	Approach / Dockside Depth (reported)	Floating Docks	Gas / Diesel	Groceries, Ice, Marine Supplies, Snacks	Repairs: Hull, Engine, Propeller	Lift (tonnage), Crane, Rail	1=110V, 2=220V, B=Both, Max Amps	Laundry, Pool, Showers	Pump-Out Station	Nearby: Grocery Store, Motel, Restaurant
		Dockage					Supplies			Services				
1. Ocracoke Public Dock/Ranger Station	252-928-5111	60		/20	7/6	F					B/50			GMR
2. Anchorage Inn & Marina (WiFi)	**252-928-6661**	**100**	**16**	**25/35**	**10/9**		**GD**	**IMS**			**B/50**	**PS**	**P**	**GMR**
3. Down Creek Marina (Internet)	**252-996-0515**			**3/10**	**12/8**						**B/50**	**S**		**GMR**

Corresponding chart(s) not to be used for navigation. ☐ Internet Access (WiFi) Wireless Internet Access

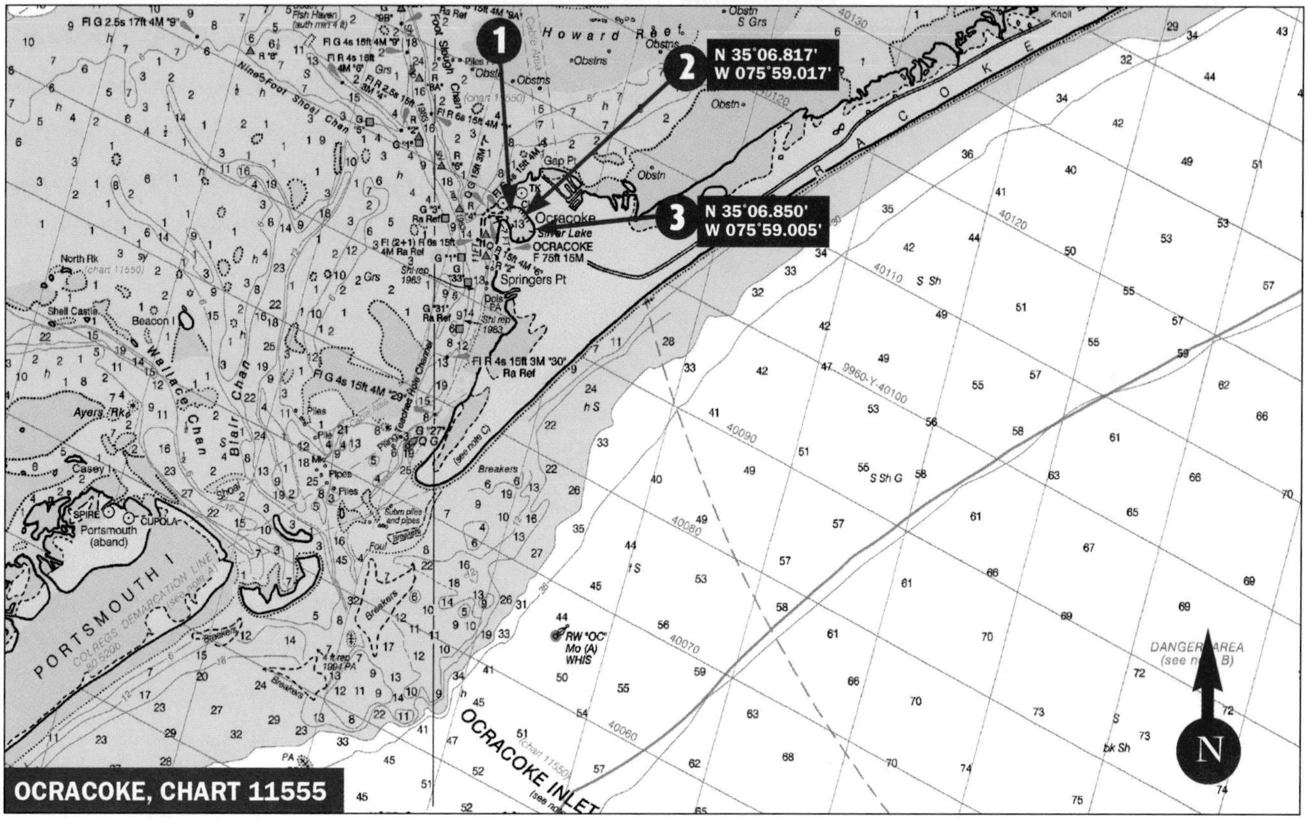

OCRACOKE, CHART 11555

lacking current local knowledge (dredged in March 2009). Big Foot Slough shoals constantly. The channel is marked by temporary buoys. It will change every trip you make. Shoaling causes the channel to become very narrow at points. Care must be taken to watch for ferry traffic. A serious accident occurred this year when a cruiser turned in the path of the ferry. You must stay in the channel. If you pass on the wrong side of the markers, you will ground!

Two steel pipes, protruding far above the water near flashing green "13" at the channel entrance (see Chart 11550), will be visible from the sound well before the channel becomes evident. These pipes are part of a sunken dredge boat that appears (both on the chart and on first sighting) to be a partial obstruction. In fact, the wreck is located off to the east side of the channel. There is also a charted 6-foot spot in that vicinity.

On preparing to enter Ocracoke's harbor, Silver Lake (called Cockle Creek by locals), go around the south side of the junction light with its red-over-green board as you turn to port, thus avoiding the shoal charted here. Do not cut this marker; you will run aground! From this point, the entrance is well marked and straightforward, with reds on the starboard side. Stay in the middle of the channel. Watch for the ferries that will pass slower boats in the channel, leaving bountiful wakes as they churn by. Inside Silver Lake, prop thrust from the ferries can cause a considerable current.

Dockage: The National Park Service offers dockage near its headquarters, just beyond the ferry dock, on the port side of the Silver Lake entrance. Rates are reasonable, with discounts for senior citizens possessing a Park Service "Golden Age Passport." Enter these transient docks between two clusters of huge bollards, and tie-up alongside sturdy piers faced with large, widely spaced bollards. These were originally built for PT boats during World War II. In the summer, the maximum allowable stay here is two weeks. There is room for about a dozen transients on a first-come, first-served basis.

The Anchorage Inn and Marina has slips for transients,

with electricity and water at dockside. There is a bath house with hot showers across the street beside the Inn. This can be a busy place during in-season weekends; it is best to call ahead for reservations. The Anchorage works with slip holders in the area and can often place you in a private slip for a night or weekend. Dockside service is excellent. The new (in 2011) Down Creek Marina has transient space and offers Internet access and showers, with electricity at dockside.

Anchorage: Silver Lake is a perfectly protected harbor, with anchoring depths of 7 to 13 feet or more, except in the shallow cove to the southwest. Holding is good (watch for a weedy bottom, which can give a false sense of security. Make certain you set your anchor). There is ample room for those who want to drop a hook, even on summer weekends. Be sure to anchor away from the ferry channel and dock.

GOIN' ASHORE: OCRACOKE ISLAND, NC

Ocracoke, on the barrier island of the same name, is about as close as you can get to out-island cruising in North Carolina. To reach Ocracoke, you come by boat or you don't come at all. The anchorage is well protected, bordered by beautiful beaches with a marine forest and an ancient lighthouse.

The village offers an assortment of dining opportunities, from pizza to gourmet selections, and has groceries and supplies, too. Exuding a Cape Cod ambience, the island is peppered with pirate legends and a rich nautical heritage. Here, Blackbeard the Pirate met his death off Teach's Hole, the channel that now bears his name.

Foot or bike is the preferred means of touring the village. Ocracoke Island has almost 15 miles of unspoiled beaches and was recently voted the number-one beach in America. The wide swath of shoreline is clean and free of development, which means on many days you will have the beach all to yourself. The dominant physical feature of the village is the Ocracoke Lighthouse, which overlooks Silver Lake and the Pamlico Sound. Ocracokers speak with an old English "brogue," a unique dialect passed down from the early settlers of the Outer Banks. (Note: If you are not from Ocracoke, then you are the one speaking with an accent!)

History: The first light station was built on the island in 1803, but 15 years later was destroyed by lightning and replaced with the current tower. The original fourth-order lens was destroyed during the Civil War, but a new lens installed in 1864 remains today. Since 1953, all of Ocracoke Island, with the exception of Ocracoke Village, has been under federal ownership as a part of the Cape Hatteras National Seashore. During the War of 1812, Ocracoke Inlet served as a base of operations for privateers, funneling supplies to Virginia via the Pamlico and Albemarle sounds.

When a hurricane opened Hatteras Inlet in 1846, boat traffic shifted north, and the Portsmouth villagers had to find other ways to make a living. Leaving seemed to be one solution, so many fled as Union troops advanced and Portsmouth Village's population declined. In 1971, only three remained. One of them died, and the other two left. In 1976, Portsmouth Village was incorporated into the Cape Lookout National Seashore. The village is now on the National Register of Historic Places.

Culture: The Ocracoke Preservation Society's Museum (252-928-7375), located on the National Park Service property, displays photographs, artifacts and exhibits that pertain

Ocracoke Lighthouse. Photo courtesy of Mike Kucera.

Ocracoke Island

The "Pearl of the Outer Banks"

Hand Crafted, American Made, Affordable

FINE ART AND CRAFT

2009 NICHE TOP RETAILER AWARDS WINNER

Fine Jewelry • Art Glass • Pottery
Local Paintings, Prints and Photography
Bath & Body • Cards • Candles
Slip Rentals - Short, Long & Transient Term

down creek gallery & marina

FINE ART & CRAFT

On the Waterfront in the Heart Of the Village
Ocracoke, NC • (252) 928-4400

BACK PORCH
Restaurant & Wine Bar

Over 25 Years of
Ocracoke's Finest Cuisine

Fresh local seafood, steaks, chicken & duck
Premium spirits and cocktails • Extensive wine list

110 Back Road • Ocracoke Island • **252-928-6401**
Open daily at 5 pm for dinner

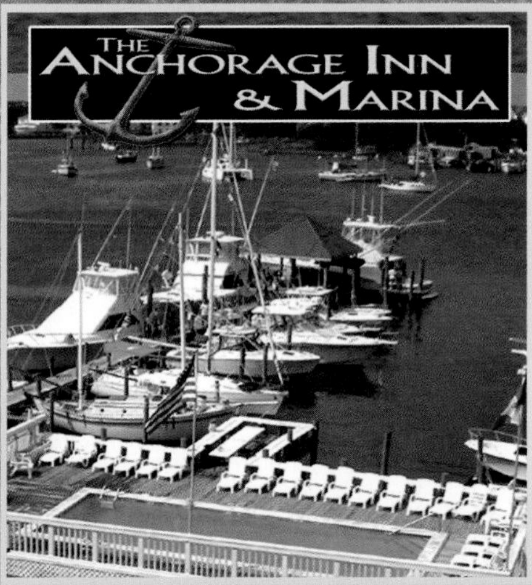

THE ANCHORAGE INN & MARINA

OCRACOKE ISLAND
NORTH CAROLINA

Anchorage Inn
(252) 928-1101

Anchorage Marina
(252) 928-6661

www.theanchorageinn.com
email: info@theanchorageinn.com

Meet Us At...

Zillie's ISLAND PANTRY

For The Good Things In Life!

Over 200 Wines • Cheeses • Gourmet Provisions • Cigars • Gift Baskets
Build Your Own Six Pack – Nearly 300 Beers & Micro Brews • Cold Drinks

WIFI WINE & BEER DECK

538 Back Road • (Near British Cemetery Road) • 252.928.9036
www.ZILLIESPANTRY.com

Looking north over Ocracoke, NC and Silver Lake. (Not to be used for navigation.) WATERWAY GUIDE PHOTOGRAPHY.

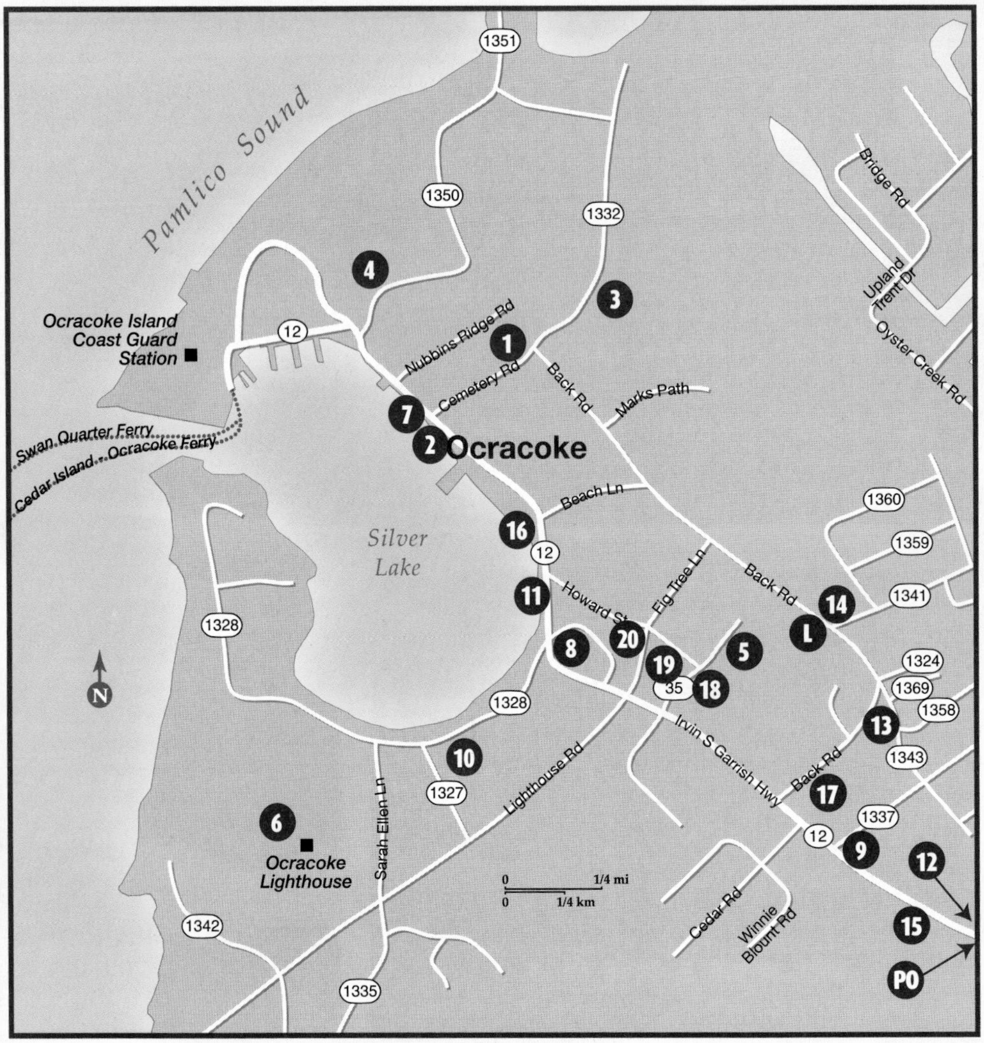

Reference the marina listing tables to see all the marinas in the area.

ART/ANTIQUES
1 Island Artworks
2 Down Creek Gallery

ATTRACTIONS
3 The British Cemetery
4 Ocracoke Preservation Museum
5 Deepwater Theater
6 Ocracoke Lighthouse

BICYCLES
7 Anchorage Marina
8 Slushie Stand
9 Pony Island Motel
10 Ocracoke Harbor Inn

DINING
7 SMacNalley's Bar and Grill (at Anchorage Marina)
11 The Jolly Roger Pub & Marina
12 Howard's Pub
13 Back Porch Restaurant
14 Ocracoke Coffee Company/ Java Books

GROCERIES/CARRYOUT
15 Ocracoke Variety Store

SHOPPING
14 Java Books/Ocracoke Coffee Company
16 The Captain's Cargo
17 The Secret Garden Gallery
18 Books to be Red
18 Deepwater Pottery
19 Natural Selections
20 The Village Craftsman

L LIBRARY

PO POST OFFICE

to island life and culture. A small gift shop exhibits works from local artists. Upstairs is a small research library.

Attractions: You can easily see most of Ocracoke by foot, but bicycles are available for rental from the Anchorage Marina, Slushie Stand, Pony Island Motel, Ocracoke Harbor Inn and Ocracoke Island Realty. The British cemetery and the lighthouse are two popular attractions. If you have the time, visit Portsmouth Island. Boat rentals and day ferries shuttle visitors over during calm weather. Restrooms are available, as are plenty of mosquitoes, so carry insect repellent and drinking water.

Hammock Hills Nature Trail is a .75-mile trail through the island's maritime forest and salt marsh. It is a great stroll for nature lovers and bird watchers. You will find informative signposts along the way. The hike takes about 30 minutes.

In 1959, the National Park Service developed the Ocracoke Pony Pens to protect the herd from traffic. Today around 24 ponies graze on a 180-acre pasture. The Pony Pens are located about seven miles north of the village, just off the main highway. It is free to visit, but donations are welcomed to help pay for the food and veterinary care of the ponies. The ponies are not tame, so do not try to feed or touch them.

Deepwater Theater at 25 School Road (252-928-3411) is home to Molasses Creek, a local band that has built a loyal following, but you will also find other performing artists. Springer's Point covers about 90 acres of maritime forest bordering Pamlico Sound near South Point. On a high point of land overlooking the inlet, Springer's is believed to be the site of the earliest settlements on the island.

According to legend, Blackbeard met here with some fellow pirates shortly before his death and spent several days drinking rum and playing music. The deep hole just off the point is a popular fishing spot and still called "Teach's Hole."

Special events: The annual Howard Street Arts & Crafts Fair and Ocrafolk Festival of Music and Storytelling is held each June. Local musicians perform sea ditties, traditional island ballads and classical music. Island jewelers, potters, woodworkers and artists are joined by other regional craftspeople for the display and sale of fine quality handcrafts. The local Fire and Rescue squad has a Memorial Day weekend BBQ and dance. It is extremely popular with local sailing clubs (Neuse River Sailing Club, River Rat Yacht Club) who make this an annual cruise event. Halloween often draws many boaters and visitors making the last trip of the season.

Shopping: The Captain's Cargo (252-928-9991) is a specialty gift shop located in the old Post Office lobby. The Secret Garden Gallery is located on Back Road (252-928-6793) and offers fine art and crafts. At the corner of School Road and the main highway, you will find Books to be Red and Deepwater Pottery (252-928-3936) together in one building. Check out Island Artworks at 89 British Cemetery Road (252-928-3892). Down Creek Gallery is on the waterfront (252-928-4400). Natural Selections sells environmentally conscious clothing, bags, beads and hats. You will find them on School Road under the oaks (252-928-4367). The Village Craftsmen is located on Howard Street (252-928-5541). Java Books (252-928-7473) is located in the back of Ocracoke Coffee Company on Back Road.

If you are looking for provisions for the next leg of your passage, visit the Ocracoke Variety Store on Highway 12 about a mile from the harbor (252-928-4911).

Restaurants: The Jolly Roger Pub & Marina overlooks Silver Lake and has a large outdoor dining area (252-928-3703). This is a great place to grab a burger and beverage and watch your vessel swing on the hook. Howard's Pub (1175 Irvin H. Garris Highway, 252-928-4441) is a mile from the harbor, but well worth the walk. Of course, a stop in Ocracoke would not be complete without dining at the Back Porch Restaurant (226 Back Road, 252-928-6401) where you will find local seafood, beef and poultry. The Anchorage has an outdoor bar and dining on the docks at SMacNalley's Bar and Grill. It is a great place to see who is in port and very popular with the local boaters. These are just a few of the dining options you will find on the island. Service and specials change, so your best bet is to ask the locals for a recommendation.

ADDITIONAL RESOURCES

- **Ocracoke Island, www.ocracoke-nc.com**
  www.ocracokevillage.com

NEARBY MEDICAL FACILITIES
Ocracoke Health Center, 252-928-1511
305 Back Road, Ocracoke, NC 27960

THE LOWER BANKS

To the south, Core Sound runs behind the narrow ocean barrier of Core Banks. Once part of the ICW route, it was abandoned when the land cuts that link the present ICW were dredged. Cruising boats now usually bypass the sound. On the mainland side, there are numerous bays, several of which have small local marinas. Those unable to make this passage should follow the channel up the Neuse River and use the ICW route to Beaufort/Morehead City. Draft is the limiting factor when transiting Core Sound.

Most skippers heading for the Lower Banks avoid the Core Sound/Pamlico Sound route in favor of the approach from Morehead City or Beaufort. From these cities, access is easy for two popular side trips: Lookout Bight (for fishing) and Harkers Island (for the boatbuilding and island ambience).

Atlantic, opposite Drum Inlet, is a fishing community where you can get repairs and limited supplies.

NAVIGATION: Use Chart 11545. Core Sound is 27 shallow miles long, with widely spaced markers. All the channels call for local knowledge. Shallow-draft boats less than 25 feet long are the only vessels that can reasonably consider cruising here. Drum Inlet is closed to navigation.

Harkers Island and Marshallberg, off the Lower Banks

When North Carolinians talk of the Harkers Island area, they usually include the adjacent mainland villages fronted by The Straits, which separates the island from the mainland.

Cape Lookout, a remote natural territory with limited freshwater access and no garbage service, is reminiscent of the Bahamas. Cape Lookout is best accessed from the ocean from Beaufort Inlet, although it is an easy trip from Taylor Creek along the inside route in a smaller boat. The channels are well marked. Cape Lookout Lighthouse has been a landmark for the coast since 1812.

NAVIGATION: Use Chart 11545. A swing bridge with a 14-foot closed vertical clearance crosses The Straits. An offshoot channel before the bridge, which is marked and has 6-foot depths, leads to Marshallberg after flashing green "42A" (a private aid). Navigation to the marinas is challenging, as some entrance channels only hold 3-foot depths at mean low water. Call for guidance if necessary and plan to enter with a rising tide.

Back Sound, the southern route, leads between Shackleford Banks and Middle Marsh. At its eastern end, a dredged channel leads to Lookout Bight and Cape Lookout. The distinctive black-and-white diamond pattern on the lighthouse helps you locate your position. Black diamonds indicate you are north or south of the light, while white diamonds indicate you are east or west. At the western end of Back Sound, it is easy to get to Beaufort via Taylor Creek in a shallow-drafted boat.

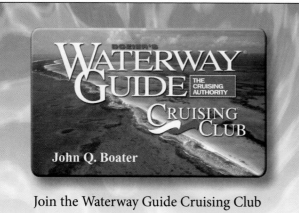

GOIN' ASHORE:

HARKERS ISLAND, NC

Harkers Island marks the southern end of Core Sound. Surrounded by shoals and the shifting sands of Back Sound, this rugged enclave is home to fishermen and boatbuilders, providing a pleasant respite for cruisers without deadlines. Beyond the docks off Calico Jacks, you will find the water alive with mullet (a type of baitfish). To the north, a wind-whipped carpet of khaki sawgrass bows low. If you come to Harkers Island, you come to fish. Its waters lead to Shackleford Banks and Middle Marsh, but the depths run from not much to none at all. Still, the Barden Inlet channel provides quick access to Cape Lookout Bight and the Atlantic Ocean.

In the past few years, large waterfront homes have blossomed as second-home owners or retirees have moved to the island changing, some say, the culture of the island. Outdoor enthusiasts, however, can still get their dose of Down East lore when they visit the Core Sound Waterfowl Museum (1785 Island Road).

History: Harkers Island was originally called Craney Island, once home to the Coree Indians. Part of the Tuscarora tribe, the Coree lived on Core Sound, fishing and hunting along the Core Banks. An effort was made to build a shell bridge across the sound to the Banks. Today this area is known as "Shell Point."

In the early 1700s, Enoch Ward and John Shackleford bought 7,000 acres, creating a permanent settlement. Soon New England whalers arrived on the Banks with their harpoon boats. Ebenezer Harker and the other "Bankers" hunted whales and fished for mullet, transporting their catch to Portsmouth Village where they met with traders. By 1890, Diamond City, a community of fishing families, occupied more than half of Shackleford Banks.

But what the water and tides bring, they take too, and in 1899, a hurricane flooded homes and destroyed livestock. Board-by-board, the residents of Diamond City abandoned the banks and floated their belongings across Back Sound. Today, many of the Diamond City descendents live in communities such as Otway, Marshallberg, Gloucester, Sea Level, Atlantic and Cedar Island.

Culture: With fishing and boatbuilding such a vital link to the island's heritage, the Core Sound Waterfowl Museum (1785 Island Road, 252-728-1500) serves as a repository for treasured artifacts and living history. Here, you will find demonstrations on net making, decoy carving and small boatbuilding. The museum brings the past and future together, serving as a central gathering place for locals and visitors.

Attractions: While arriving in Cape Lookout Bight on your own vessel is the better way to see the bight, you can also go by passenger ferry. Launches are available at Calico Jacks Ferry (1698 Island Road), Harkers Island Fishing Center (1002 Island Road) and Local Yokel Ferry (516 Island Road).

Special events: The Big Decoy Festival is held the first weekend in December. Sponsored by the Core Sound Decoy Carver's Guild, this event draws visitors from

Harkers Island, NC

HARKERS ISLAND		Largest Vessel Accommodated	VHF Channel Monitored	Transient Berths / Total Berths	Approach / Dockside Depth (reported)	Floating Docks	Gas / Diesel	Groceries, Ice, Marine Supplies, Snacks	Repairs: Hull, Engine, Propeller	Lift (tonnage), Crane, Rail	1=110V, 2=220V, B=Both, Max Amps	Laundry, Pool, Showers	Pump-Out Station	Nearby: Grocery Store, Motel, Restaurant
		Dockage					Supplies		Services					
1. Harkers Island Fishing Center	252-728-3907	48	69	/70	4/6		GD	IMS	E			S		G
2. Calico Jack's Inn & Marina	252-728-3575	30	08	40/52	4/4		GD	GIMS						GMR

Corresponding chart(s) not to be used for navigation. ☐ Internet Access (WiFi) Wireless Internet Access

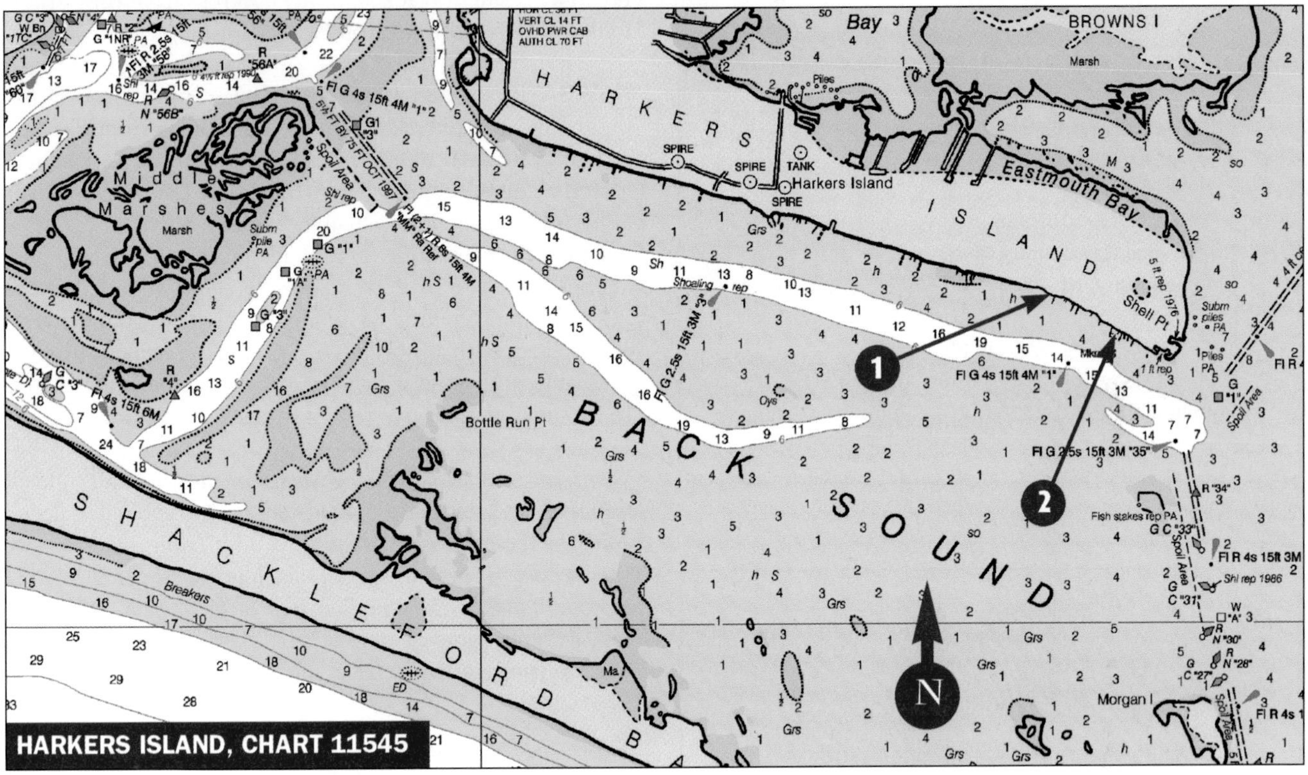

HARKERS ISLAND, CHART 11545

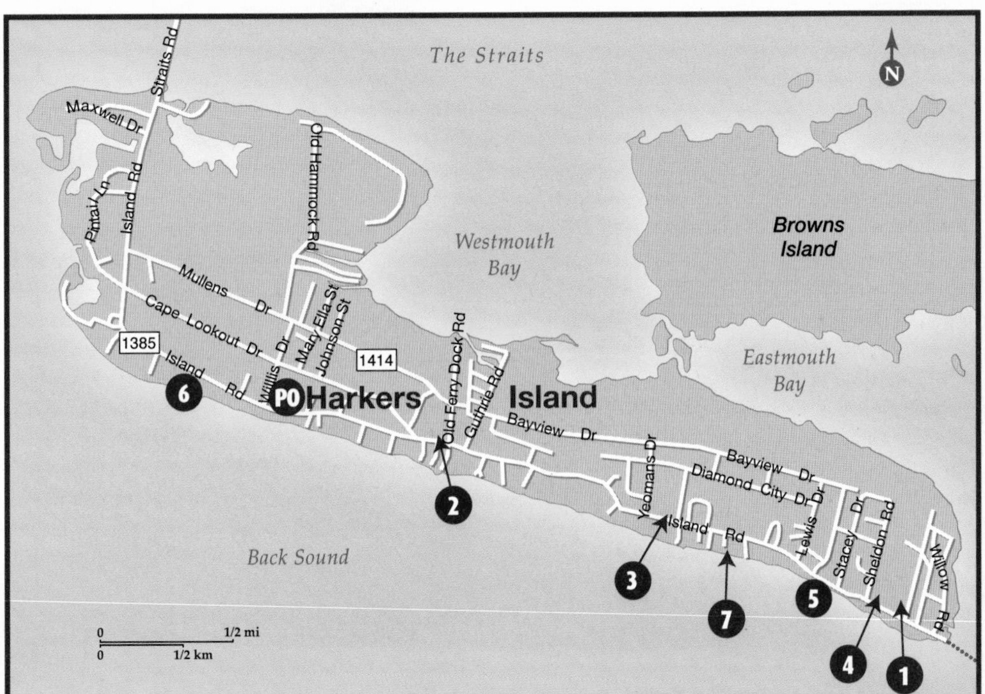

ATTRACTIONS
1 Core Sound Waterfowl Museum

DINING
2 Captains Choice Restaurant

SHOPPING
3 Capt. Henry's Gift Store

TRANSPORTATION
4 Calico Jacks Ferry
5 Harkers Island Fishing Center
6 Local Yokel Ferry
7 Island Ferry Adventures

PO POST OFFICE

Reference the marina listing tables to see all the marinas in the area.

across the country. Call 252-838-8818 for more information. Waterfowl Weekend happens at the same time over at the Core Sound Waterfowl Museum (252-728-1500).

Shopping: Capt. Henry's Gift Store (1341 Island Road, 252-728-7316) sells a wide selection of Down East decoys, nautical items, pottery, baskets, birdhouses and wind chimes. Core Sound Waterfowl Museum Gift Shop carries wildlife art, books, cards, house flags, windsocks, T-shirts, birdhouses, bird feeders and much more.

Restaurants: Captains Choice Restaurant (977 Island Road, 252-728-7122) is a good pick for local seafood.

ADDITIONAL RESOURCES

- **CORE SOUND WATERFOWL MUSEUM, 252-728-1500**
  www.coresound.com

NEARBY GOLF COURSES
Brandywine Bay Country Club,
Morehead City, NC 28557, 252-247-2541 (26 miles)

NEARBY MEDICAL FACILITIES
Carteret General Hospital, 3500 Arendell St.,
Morehead City, NC 28557, 252-808-6000 (22 miles)

Lookout Bight, off the Lower Banks

Miles of unspoiled, dune-backed beaches of the Cape Lookout National Seashore provide the perfect setting to search for shells of the giant whelk or just to gawk and test the rips of this famous cape.

One of the most beautiful anchorages of the Carolinas, Lookout Bight offers a secure place to set the hook in all but the most inclement weather, within the protective arm and elbow of the cape. It is a ringside seat for the antics of laughing gulls, a variety of terns, willets, dunlins, cavorting oystercatchers and the inimitable working patterns flown by resident black skimmers. Across from the harbor, look for the wild horses on Shackleford Banks.

NAVIGATION: Use Chart 11545. The entrance buoy to the bight (flashing red "4") is located 6.2 miles from flashing red "6" on the Beaufort Inlet Channel on an east-southeasterly course coming from the inlet. *(See page 69 for more information about Beaufort Inlet.)*

Anchorage: During summer months, most skippers anchor just east of Power Squadron Spit (depths in the 20-foot range), taking advantage of prevailing southwesterly breezes with a short fetch. Holding is excellent in thick mud at depths ranging from 8 to 26 feet at mean low water. In the next chapter, we return to the ICW-proper. ■

WATERWAY GUIDE advertising sponsors play a vital role in bringing you the most trusted and well-respected cruising guide in the country. Without our advertising sponsors, we simply couldn't produce the top-notch publication now resting in your hands. Next time you stop in for a peaceful night's rest, let them know where you found them—WATERWAY GUIDE, The Cruising Authority.

Cape Lookout, NC. (Not to be used for navigation.) WATERWAY GUIDE PHOTOGRAPHY.

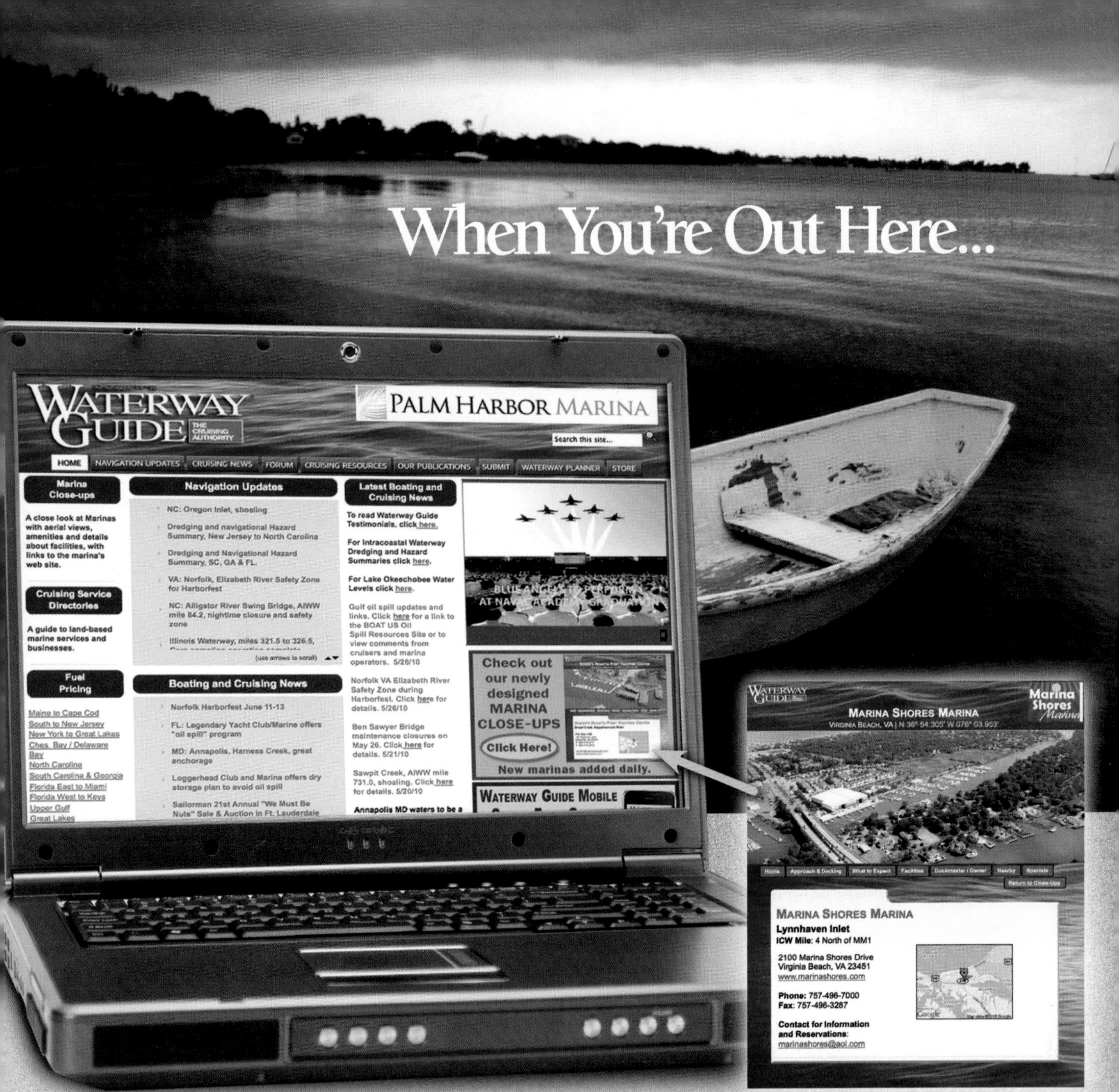
When You're Out Here...
WATERWAY GUIDE
PALM HARBOR MARINA
Navigation Updates
Boating and Cruising News
Check out our newly designed MARINA CLOSE-UPS
Click Here!
New marinas added daily.
WATERWAY GUIDE MOBILE
MARINA SHORES MARINA
Lynnhaven Inlet
ICW Mile: 4 North of MM1
2100 Marina Shores Drive
Virginia Beach, VA 23451
www.marinashores.com
Phone: 757-496-7000
Fax: 757-496-3287
Contact for Information and Reservations:
marinashores@aol.com

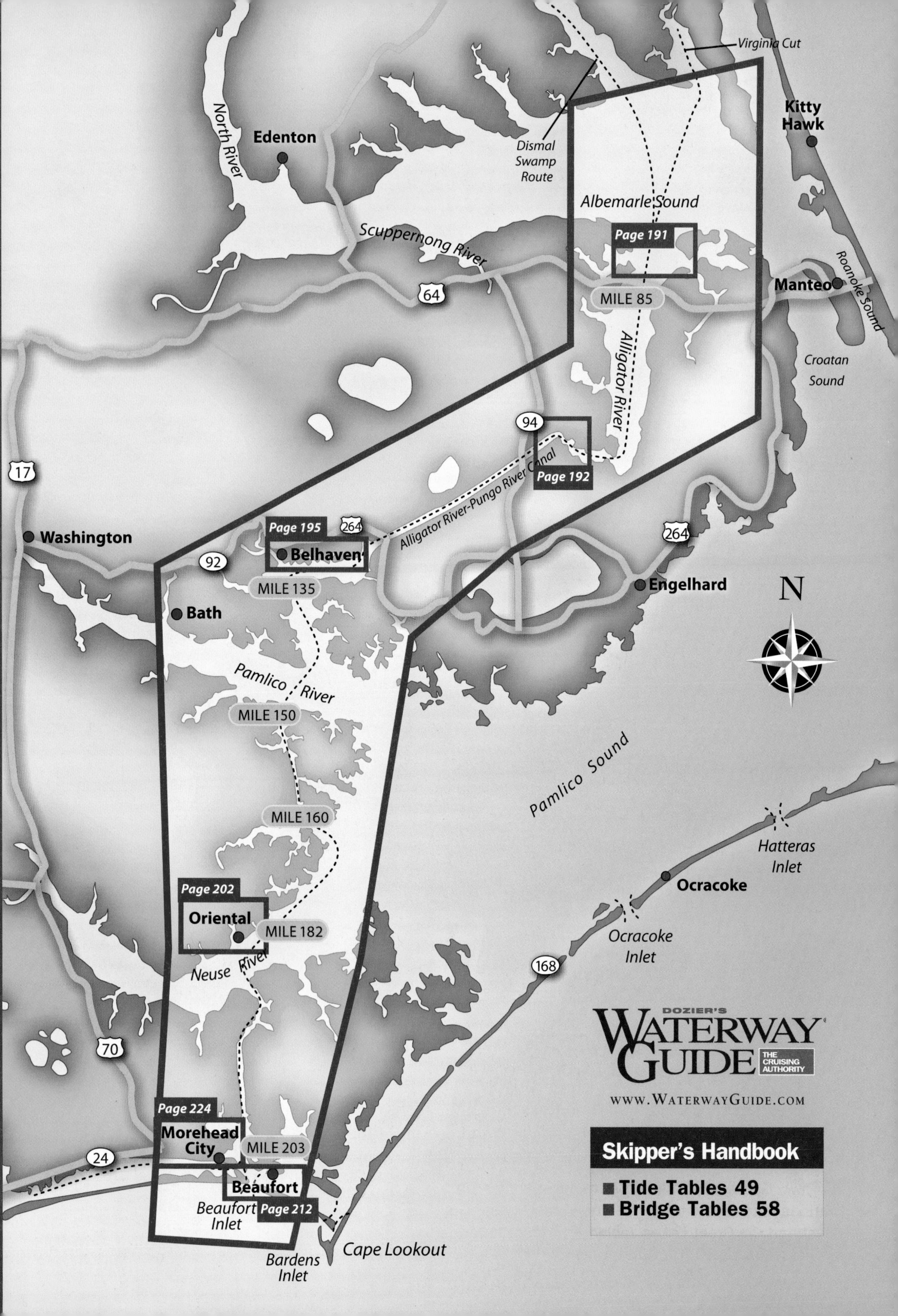
Virginia Cut
Kitty Hawk
Edenton
North River
Dismal Swamp Route
Albemarle Sound
Page 191
Scuppernong River
64
MILE 85
Manteo
Roanoke Sound
Alligator River
Croatan Sound
94
Page 192
Alligator River-Pungo River Canal
17
Washington
Page 195
264
Belhaven
92
264
MILE 135
Engelhard
N
Bath
Pamlico River
MILE 150
Pamlico Sound
MILE 160
Hatteras Inlet
Ocracoke
Page 202
Oriental
MILE 182
Ocracoke Inlet
Neuse River
168
70
DOZIER'S WATERWAY GUIDE
THE CRUISING AUTHORITY
WWW.WATERWAYGUIDE.COM
Page 224
Morehead City
MILE 203
24
Beaufort
Beaufort Inlet
Page 212
Cape Lookout
Bardens Inlet
Skipper's Handbook
Tide Tables 49
Bridge Tables 58

Albemarle Sound to Beaufort, NC

ICW MILE 80–MILE 211

VHF North Carolina Bridges: Channel 13

CHARTS 11541, 11543, 11544, 11545, 11547, 11548, 11553

Two boats that opted for either the 79-mile-long Virginia Cut route (see page 125) or the 82-mile-long Dismal Swamp route (see page 134), respectively, are likely to meet again just north of flashing green "1AR" at the mouth of the Alligator River near Intracoastal Waterway (ICW) Mile Marker 80. Here, on the southern side of Albemarle Sound, the two ICW routes converge. With widths of nearly four miles in certain areas, the Alligator River seems more like a sound than a river. These wide-open stretches continue south-southwest for 20 miles before the Alligator River turns west and narrows for about five miles. ICW mileage is measured from Norfolk using the Virginia Cut. But the Dismal Swamp route is only three miles longer to the mouth of the Alligator River—miles that you might have eliminated by short-cutting across Albemarle Sound from flashing green "1PR" at the mouth of the Pasquotank River.

Crossing the Albemarle Sound

Traveling south, Albemarle Sound is the first of the few sometimes-challenging bodies of water on the Norfolk-Miami section of the ICW. The 14-mile-long crossing can be very sloppy because winds from almost any quarter tend to funnel either up or down the long, straight sound. Because of its uniformly shallow depth, even a light wind can quickly create rough, confused seas. Another danger on Albemarle Sound is the collection of trap markers, often right on the route.

Should wind and sea conditions appear unfavorable for an Albemarle crossing, prudent options include a return to Coinjock or Elizabeth City, as there is no shelter available for the average boat in the lower Pasquotank. Discussion of ICW route is continued in Chapter 5 of this guide.

ALLIGATOR RIVER (MILE 80)

Long Shoal Point, at the mouth of the Alligator River, is popular with the local hunting crowd and can be thick with duck blinds, boats and shotguns during duck season. In late fall, migrating whistling swans settle onto the shallows in large flocks, a sight beautiful to behold.

THE FOLLOWING AREA REQUIRES SPECIAL ATTENTION DUE TO SHOALING OR CHANGES TO THE CHANNEL

ALLIGATOR RIVER

NAVIGATION: Use Chart 11553. Just before Mile 80 is the entrance marker for the Alligator River, flashing green "1AR." Next in line to the south, quick flashing green "3" was moved a few years ago to the west of its former position, which was along a straight line course from flashing green "1AR" to flashing green "5." This new dogleg course to flashing green "3" is difficult to see approaching from either direction. The Mile 80 sign, which used to be between flashing green "1AR" and flashing green "3," was damaged and is submerged. Its wreck was marked with a small green can buoy numbered "1A WR." Flashing green "5" has been realigned so that its board is visible only when approached from the correct direction. This is confusing, especially when using older charts or chartplotters that do not show the new channel. There have been numerous groundings by vessels missing flashing green "3" and heading straight to flashing green "5." Red daybeacon "6" is just north of Long Shoal Point, and quick flashing red "8" marks the shoal southeast of Long Shoal Point.

Long Shoal is aptly named and seems to get longer with each passing year. Flashing green "7" is just east of quick flashing red "8" and marks the eastern boundary of the ICW channel here. Make sure you honor both marks, favoring the green side. The U.S. Coast Guard reported 7-foot depths in the vicinity of flashing green "7." Deeper water was observed here by a Waterway Guide cruising editor in spring 2011. The pole from the charted former white Danger beacon is still on the shoal, but it has no boards. Marker "9" is a green daybeacon, rather than a green can buoy, as indicated on older charts. Favor the east side of the channel between flashing green "7" and green daybeacon "9." Remember, the magenta line on your charts is only a guide. You should always follow the markers especially in this area because the markers are moved frequently. Up-to-date charts are really a necessity for accurate navigation. From here, set your course for the opening span of the Alligator River Swing Bridge at Mile 84.2 (14-foot closed vertical clearance). This remarked channel at the Alligator River entrance is still confusing, even to veteran ICW travelers, so be sure to slow down and take time to sort out the markers.

END SPECIAL CAUTION AREA.

Alligator River, NC

ALLIGATOR RIVER		Largest Vessel Accommodated	VHF Channel Monitored	Transient Berths / Total Berths	Approach / Dockside Depth (reported)	Floating Docks	Gas / Diesel	Groceries, Ice, Marine Supplies, Snacks	Repairs: Hull, Engine, Propeller	Lift (tonnage), Crane, Rail	1=110V, 2=220V, B=Both, Max Amps	Laundry, Pool, Showers	Pump-Out Station	Nearby: Grocery Store, Motel, Restaurant
		Dockage					Supplies				Services			
1. ALLIGATOR RIVER MARINA 1.5 W of 84 ☐	252-796-0333	150	16	30/32	8/8		GD	GIMS	EP		B/100	LS	P	GR

Corresponding chart(s) not to be used for navigation. ☐ Internet Access (WiFi) Wireless Internet Access

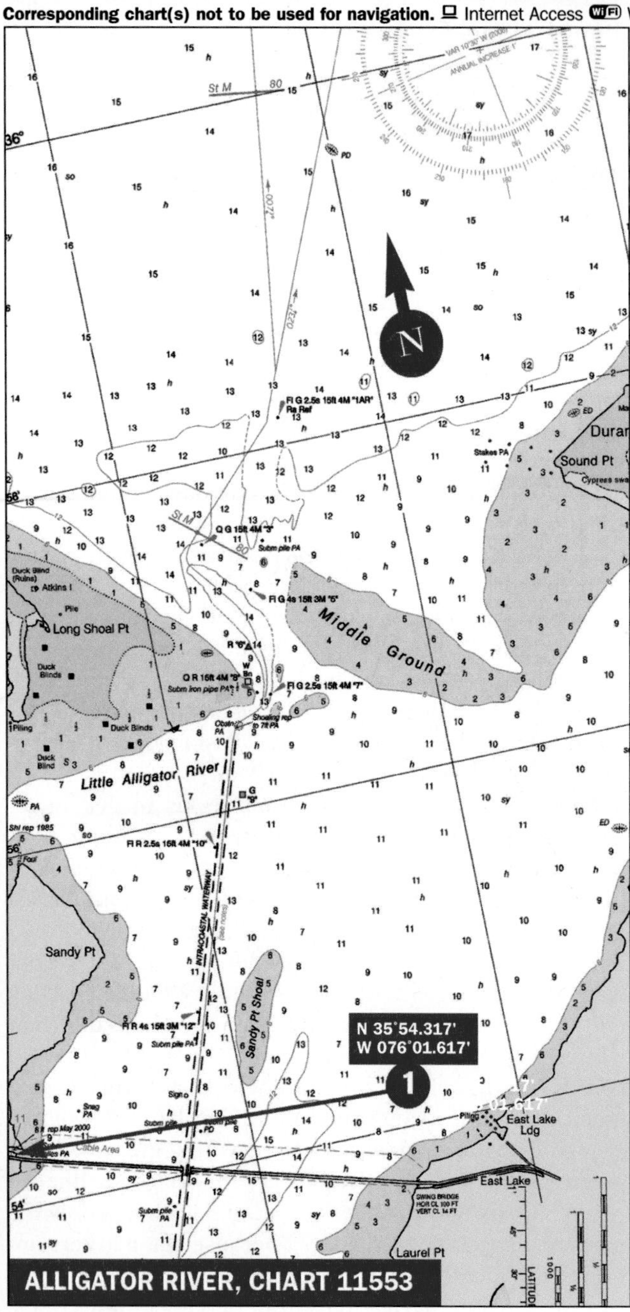

ALLIGATOR RIVER, CHART 11553

While the Alligator River Swing Bridge (Mile 84.2, 14-foot closed vertical clearance) normally opens on signal, it cannot open in winds stronger than 34 knots and, at the discretion of the tender, may remain closed in winds of lesser velocities. In either case, look for a good spot to hole up, should it become necessary. Southbound boats might want to check weather conditions at the bridge before crossing the Albemarle.

Dockage: At the northwestern end of the Alligator River Bridge (Mile 84.2) is Alligator River Marina, with a well-protected harbor and the only fuel available along the 86 miles between Coinjock (Mile 50) and Belhaven (Mile 136). Alligator River Marina accepts transients of all sizes. Call ahead to make sure of the depth in the entrance channel.

Anchorage: If the weather is already getting sloppy, the bridge (as previously noted) may not open. If that is the case, northbound boaters will have to find a spot close to the southwestern end of the bridge to drop the hook and wait it out. Southbound boaters can anchor to the southwest side of Durant Island, the common entrance to East Lake and South Lake. Do not venture into East or South lakes if you draw more than 5 feet; the channel is unmarked and narrow. Although it carries 8 to 10 feet, it shallows to 3 to 5 feet outside of the channel. Little Alligator River offers limited protection, especially in any northerly or easterly wind. It is not a spot to wait out a cold front passage, nor is it a refuge if the Alligator River Bridge cannot open because of strong winds when southbound. In strong winds from any direction, southbound boaters should plan to wait on the other side of Albemarle Sound or go into the Alligator River Marina.

West of quick flashing red "18," and about three miles south of the bridge (near ICW Mile 88), Second Creek leads in south of Second Creek Point. It is shoal; depths of 3 to 4 feet exist south of the point. Shallow-drafted boats can explore anchoring possibilities here, but note that Second Creek can hold even less than charted depths when certain conditions apply, like during long droughts and in strong winds from the west or northwest.

It is recommended that a trip line be used when anchoring in the Alligator River, as there are many snags on the bottom.

Mile 80 to Alligator River—Pungo River Canal

While the Alligator River continues wide and deep almost to its head, snags are frequent outside the channel, and boaters should follow the markers carefully. This keep-to-mid-channel rule holds true for much of the ICW south of Norfolk, VA. *Any departure from the main channel carries the risk of prop damage or worse. Play it safe: Do not short-cut points, do not hug the banks too closely and approach anchorages cautiously.*

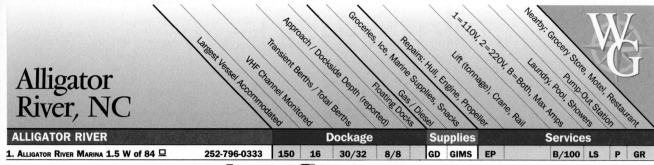

Occasionally, large logs float in the Alligator River channel. These obstructions are often partially submerged and difficult to see, and you may hear other skippers reporting them to the Coast Guard on VHF Channel 16. Over the last three or four, years we have found the worst section to be between red daybeacon "24" and green "37." An extra pair of eyes is always helpful in this area.

Cellular coverage from this area south to Belhaven likely will be lost.

NAVIGATION: Use Chart 11553. South of the swing bridge at Mile 84.2, the east bank of the Alligator River is primitive, with side streams worth exploring only by dinghy. Milltail Creek, east of the bend in the channel at quick flashing red "18" (about Mile 88), is pristine but hard to find. Five miles upstream are the turning basin and the decaying town's wharf of Buffalo City. The creek is narrow, and fallen trees may lie across the creek in areas.

Some of the markers in the Alligator River may have different light characteristics than those indicated on the chart. Colors and numbers are the same, however. Quick flashing lights mark doglegs: There are usually 2.5-second lights before doglegs and 4-second flashers in between.

To the east of Mile 94, The Straits into Babbitt Bay and the Frying Pan may be limited to dinghies—the entrance is 3 to 5 feet (with deeper water beyond), unmarked, littered with snags, and 1- to 3-foot depths are the deepest soundings behind Crane Island Point.

Anchorage: There are two excellent anchorages near the ICW's turn west at Newport News Point (Mile 101). The first, off Deep Point (Mile 102), provides protection from everything but severe easterlies and wakes from passing traffic. When anchoring here, position yourself as far out of the channel as possible to stay away from maneuvering tugs and barges in this vicinity. Drought conditions and prolonged strong winds can lower the water level in all of the Alligator River. The mooring buoy in this anchorage (shown on some charts) may or may not be in place.

The second good anchorage spot is outside the channel off Tuckahoe Point (Mile 104), just before the entrance to the 20-mile-long Alligator River-Pungo River Canal. Turn to the north off the ICW between green daybeacon "49" and red daybeacon "52," and then proceed slowly to Tuckahoe Point. Do not get too close to the point; the area is foul with tree stumps. Holding, swing room and protection are good, and the current is slight. Dense fog develops here during the fall months. At both spots, vessels should anchor well out of the channel and show anchor lights because tugs and barges run through here at night.

Cruising vessels also anchor in the bight south of quick flashing green "37" and "39" (Mile 100-101), especially in strong easterly and southerly winds. Anywhere out of the channel in 7- to 8-foot depths will suffice.

The Route to Belhaven

The Alligator River-Pungo River Canal runs northeast to southwest. Do not be in a hurry; you might see deer near the shore or a black bear swimming across the channel. While enjoying the scenery and wildlife, keep a lookout for stumps and snags outside of the channel. This is another area where deadheads have been spotted in the channel. Keep a watchful eye on the water when transiting this 20-mile canal. It is a good idea to stick to the center of the channel and maintain a radio watch; tugs and recreational boats will frequently point out possible hazards. Channel markers in the vicinity of the Fairfield Bridge (Mile 113.9) and farther west will help you maintain your mid-channel position in those areas.

The Alligator River-Pungo River Canal is scenic and heavily wooded at its upper end. Farther on are areas that have burned in the past, but they now have their second growth. The canal is relatively narrow, and boats dragging huge wakes have a tendency to damage the banks. Each year, more and more trees topple into the water.

The Fairfield Canal (Mile 113.8) leads to Lake Mattamuskeet, part of the Mattamuskeet Wildlife Refuge. The refuge is popular with hunters and naturalists from March through November, when huge flocks of water birds gather in the lake and marshes. Arrangements to visit the refuge can be made in Belhaven.

NAVIGATION: Use Chart 11553. At Mile 113.6, just before the Fairfield Bridge (Highway 94, 65-foot fixed vertical clearance), Fairfield Canal crosses the ICW. While some boats have been observed anchoring here, with lines tied to shore and anchors astern, this is not a recommended anchorage, except possibly in emergency situations.

Looking east over the 21-mile Alligator River-Pungo River Canal. (Not to be used for navigation.) WATERWAY GUIDE PHOTOGRAPHY.

The Fairfield Bridge, Mile 113.9, is just beyond the canal (65-foot fixed vertical clearance). The old Fairfield Swing Bridge was removed, but tree stumps line both sides of the channel, and there can be considerable current present here.

The Alligator River-Pungo River Canal's controlling depth is 12 feet; however, keep a close eye on the depth sounder, stick to the center of the channel and squeeze to the side carefully if you must pass another boat. The U.S. Army Corps of Engineers Wilmington District recently completed dredging on the lower end of the canal. Depths were surveyed at approximately 11 feet or greater in February 2009 along the centerline of the channel, and observed to be those depths as well by Waterway Guide staff in June 2011. Flashing green "59AR," east of the Wilkerson Bridge, is the last ICW marker before the Pungo River marking system takes over. New homes and a few docks are on the canal toward the western end.

At Mile 125.9, you pass under the high-level Wilkerson Bridge, (officially known as the Walter B. Jones Bridge), which has a charted 64-foot fixed vertical clearance, a foot less than the U.S. Army Corps of Engineers' authorized vertical clearance of 65 feet at mean high water. Sailors with masts over 60 feet should know their exact mast height with antennas and exercise extreme caution when passing under the bridge. The slight tidal range here may or may not provide the extra clearance required for safe passage. If the tide boards are missing from this bridge, check locally for information. Debris from Hurricane Isabel in 2003 indicated that the water had risen to the 60-foot vertical clearance line on the tide boards on the Wilkerson Bridge; use caution in this area.

Heading south into the Pungo River, the buoys suddenly reverse, with green aids to starboard—but still with the familiar ICW yellow triangles and squares marking the boards to signify they are ICW markers. This is because you are going downstream here on the Pungo River, which is marked from seaward. Green daybeacon "27PR" is the first Pungo River marker, with red daybeacon "28" just to its south. The river is easy to follow, and you can run the stretch to Belhaven after dark if necessary, although floating logs and submerged obstacles make it inadvisable unless absolutely necessary.

During periods of extreme low water, the tips of several submerged pilings are sometimes visible in the channel between the Wilkerson Bridge and flashing green "23" on the north edge of the channel. Heading southwest on the Pungo River, stay in the channel and give flashing green "21" a wide berth to avoid the chronic shoaling extending from the western bank. The channel is well marked up to Belhaven's entrance channel, which is reached by heading northwest from quick flashing red "10" in the Pungo River.

Dockage: After exiting the Alligator River-Pungo River Canal, Dowry Creek Marina is located on Upper Dowry Creek, just north of the channel at green daybeacon "15" (Mile 131.6). The marked entrance channel has a minimum depth of 7 feet. The marina is well kept, has a pool and offers a courtesy car for the trip into nearby Belhaven. On summer afternoons cruisers may find homegrown vegetables put out for the taking.

Anchorage: When the wind is up, the best protection in the area can be found in the anchorage in the headwaters of the Pungo River, just beyond the lower end of the Alligator River-Pungo River Canal. Enter the creek at flashing green "23" (Mile 127.3) proceeding north (see Chart 11553) to select a spot with desired protection, well off the ICW. Minding the depth sounder, you can pick your way for some distance into the river. The bot-

Belhaven, NC

BELHAVEN		Largest Vessel Accommodated	VHF Channel Monitored	Transient Berths / Total Berths	Approach / Dockside Depth (reported)	Floating Docks	Gas / Diesel	Groceries, Ice, Marine Supplies, Snacks	Repairs: Hull, Engine, Propeller	Lift (tonnage), Crane, Rail	1=110V, 2=220V, B=Both, Max Amps	Laundry, Pool, Showers	Pump-Out Station	Nearby: Grocery Store, Motel, Restaurant
		Dockage					Supplies		Services					
1. Dowry Creek Marina 132 (Internet Access) (Wireless Internet Access)	252-943-2728	120	16/71	53/73	8/8		GD	IMS	HEP		B/100	LPS	P	G
2. River Forest Shipyard 1.1 W of 135.8	252-943-2151	120	16		7/7			M	HEP	L40	B/50	S		GMR
3. River Forest Marina 1.6 W of 136 (Internet Access)	252-943-2151	120	16	38/38	9/9			IS			B/100	LPS	P	
4. Belhaven Waterway Marina 2 W of 136 (Internet Access) (Wireless Internet Access)	252-944-0066	65	16/09	23/23	8/7			M	HEP	R	B/50	LS	P	GMR
5. Pungo Creek Marina 135 (Internet Access) (Wireless Internet Access)	252-964-3777	110	16	10/48	10/10		GD	GIMS	E		B/50	LS		

Corresponding chart(s) not to be used for navigation. Internet Access, Wireless Internet Access

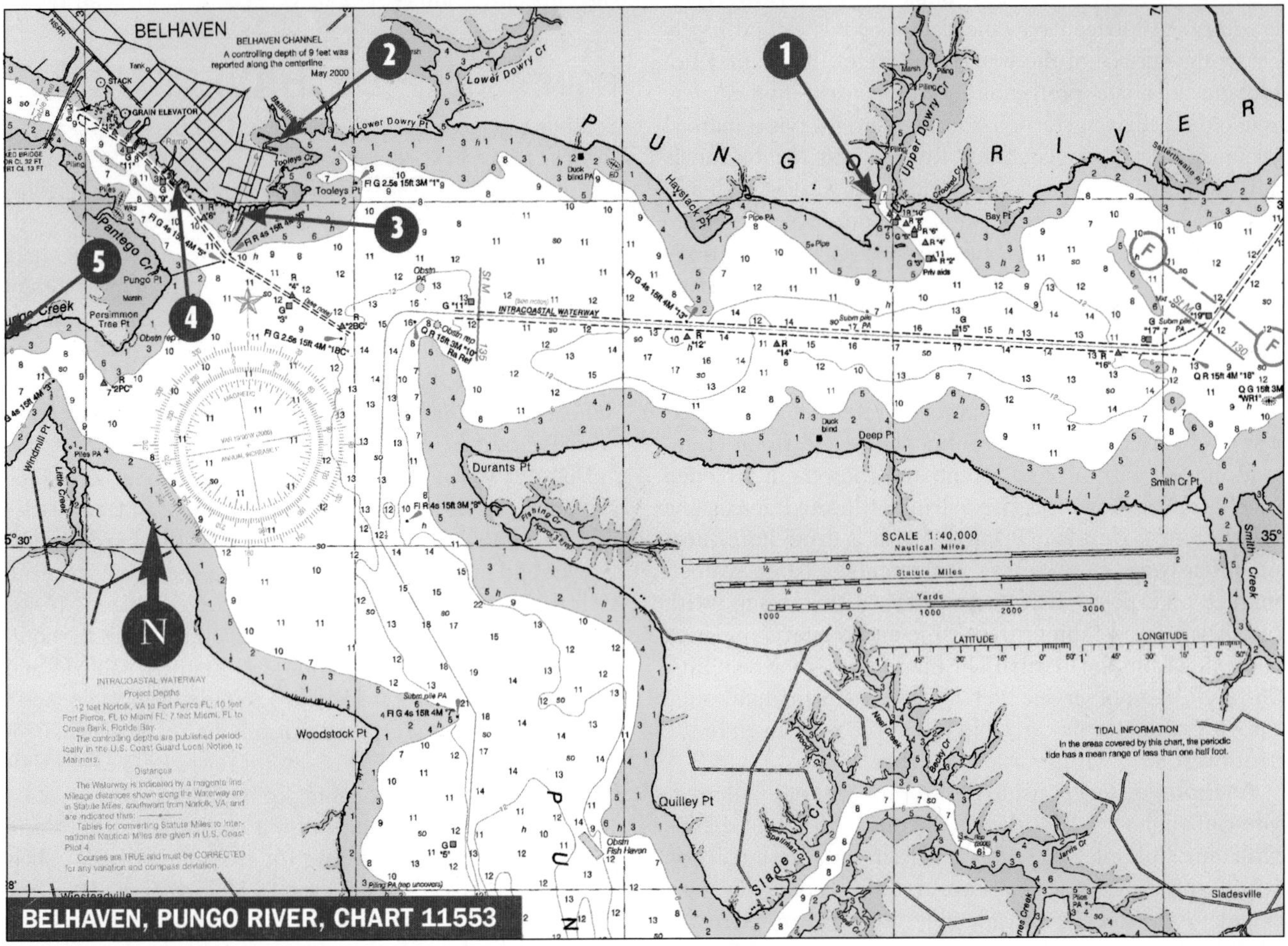

BELHAVEN, PUNGO RIVER, CHART 11553

tom is uneven, soft and given to hump-like shoals, even in what is ostensibly the center channel. It may be difficult at first to get the anchor to set, but it will usually dig in tightly by backing down. At every turn, the scenery in the upper Pungo River is serene and beautiful. This is a large anchorage area, with space for many boats, so spread out upriver if the first cove is crowded.

Another anchorage is available in the center of Upper Dowry Creek (Mile 131.6), north of Dowry Creek Marina. The creek carries 5- to 6-foot depths for about a quarter mile north of the mouth. Secure holding and a short fetch make this location a favorite retreat for local skippers when even the most severe storms approach. Cruisers also frequent this anchorage on a regular basis, arranging for facilities use with Dowry Creek Marina for a modest daily fee.

Several smaller side creeks along the Pungo River are unmarked but are reported to have adequate depths for anchoring shallower drafted boats. Exercise the usual cautions when entering unmarked creeks.

Belhaven—Mile 136

Belhaven is a strategic stop for the ICW traveler—with ample reason. It sits in the middle of one of the most sparsely populated regions on the ICW. Many boats making the yearly north-south trip stop here at least once and some stop in both fall and spring. There is limited dock space, and the marinas can fill up quickly during the travel seasons, so call ahead for reservations by phone or on VHF Channel 16.

NAVIGATION: Use Chart 11553. The approach to the full-service marinas and boatyards of Belhaven is easy and well marked. What appears to be a solid seawall protecting the harbor in Pantego Creek is actually no more than a slatted storm barrier extending only just below the surface. Heavy wakes carry right through it, to the disadvantage of boats berthed or anchored inside. On approach, reduce speed to no-wake level just beyond green daybeacon "3" and red daybeacon "4." The channel carries 9-foot depths along the centerline.

Dockage: The sea wall at the entrance to Belhaven was recently rebuilt at a cost of 6 million dollars. However, it is somewhat ineffective as the slatted boards extend barely below the surface of the water. Because of this, it may not provide adequate protection from the east. Immediately inside the Belhaven storm barrier to the right (via a marked channel), the once glamorous River Forest Manor Inn is partially closed but still offers dockage. Cruisers should radio ahead to ensure the dock master is available. There are diesel and gas pumps at the fuel dock. River Forest Marina's Shipyard Division is located at the end of Battalina Creek just northeast of the Belhaven harbor entrance. They have a service staff and room for do-it-yourself work.

Farther in the creek to starboard is recently renovated Belhaven Waterway Marina, accepting transients for dockage. They are extremely accommodating and run a clean, neat marina with nice bathroom and showers, a screened gazebo and a hot tub. The marina is located across the street from downtown Belhaven with a drug store, hospital, hardware store, several restaurants, a bank, seafood market and post office steps away. For cruisers with bicycles, a Food Lion grocery store and Liquor store are a short ride from the marina. The marina has some boat lifts, 50- and 30-amp service and a heavy tram for haul-outs. Pungo Creek Marina can be found in the next creek to the southwest, also with transient dockage.

Anchorage: Once inside the storm barrier at Belhaven, you can anchor west of the channel in 7- to 9-foot depths with fair holding. The storm barrier has been recently rebuilt, offering somewhat improved protection. This is a popular spot despite considerable wave action when the wind picks up, as it often does in the afternoon. This is not a good anchorage in wind from any southerly quadrant. Holding is marginal, in addition to the uncomfortable wave action. Care should be taken to avoid a shoal in front of the hospital. A town dinghy dock is just past green daybeacon "9" on the northeast side of the channel. A narrow channel into the creek carries 6 feet; be sure to keep to starboard. Commercial fishing boats usually tie up here.

Pungo Creek, just to the south of (and not to be confused with) Pantego Creek, has anchorage with good protection and excellent holding in 7 to 10 feet of water. To find the anchorage, steer between red daybeacon "2PC" and flashing green "3" off the Pungo River, and then run southwest of Windmill Point. Crab trap buoys are scattered throughout the creek; work your way in carefully. This is a great location to sit out strong winds.

Jordan Creek, just to the east of Marker 4, offers very good anchorage throughout the creek and protection from all but strong easterly winds. The entrance is marked but should not be attempted if you draw more than 5 feet. Limited transient dockage is available at the River Rat Yacht Club. There is not a full-time harbour master, but there are usually "Rats" around willing to help. Every second Saturday the Rats have a Pot Luck dinner that has no rivals on the ICW. The Rats gather around 6:30 p.m. with music usually until midnight. There are bathrooms and showers available. Sally's, a small store with groceries, fuel and hardware, is a short bike ride away. Anchorage is available across the Pungo in Slade's Creek with 7 feet of water at all times.

GOIN' ASHORE: **BELHAVEN, NC**

Solitude and serenity are the eternal qualities of Belhaven. The town sits among old forests and wide creeks, good anchorages and dark water. White-tailed deer forage on the shoreline. Overhead, quail, duck and geese fall into formation.

Drop a dock line over a piling, and stroll into town, where you will find most of what you need near the intersection of Main and Pamlico streets. Many of the businesses and shops, including restaurants like the Back Bay Café, are within a short stroll of the intersection. Victorian homes sit along residential streets lined with large oaks, their windows open to catch the river breeze.

History: When Daniel Latham built a hunting and fishing camp in 1868 on what is now the River Forest Manor, Jack's Neck was little more than a small settlement inhabited by a few farmers and fishermen. In time, the town changed its name to Belhaven, and a half-dozen lumber companies began supplying wood products produced from the local mills. With the addition of a rail spur from the Norfolk and Southern Railroad, and the port's location near the Pamlico Sound, the town became a vital transportation artery for the distribution of goods throughout eastern North Carolina. Today, the towns businesses mainly serve the surrounding farming communities.

Many of the grand homes built in the later 1800s and early 1900s remain standing today. The largest of all is River Forest Manor, completed in 1904 (738 E. Main St., 252-943-2151). Its first owner was John Aaron Wilkinson, president of Roper Lumber Company and vice president of the Norfolk and Southern Railroad. Today, the mansion is a country inn, restaurant and marina. You may notice many of the houses in town now sit on raised foundations after flooding from hurricanes in the early 2000s caused extensive damage to the town.

Seafood and farming remain a major source of income for residents in and around Belhaven, but change is showing as developers look to reshape the banks of the Pungo River and Pantego Creek. Day Beacon, a new waterfront townhome community located just inside the breakwater, is one of the first to offer condominium living.

Attractions: The Fourth of July celebration is in old-time style, with fireworks, a parade, concerts, contests, games and a street dance. If you want a break from the bunk, spend a few nights at the Belhaven Water Street Bed and Breakfast (567 E. Water St., 252-943-2825), where you will find private baths, fireplaces, high-speed Internet and a Jacuzzi. Pirates on the Pungo Regatta, held in late May, is a fun event that raises money for the local hospital. Rack Time Pool Hall (333 Pamlico St., 252-944-0212) is an iconic friendly southern bar, with three pool tables, cold beer and is open Monday through Saturday.

Culture: The town offers a number of local historical sites, including the Belhaven Memorial Museum (210 E. Main St., 252-943-3750), located on the second floor of the old Belhaven Town Hall. Here, you will find antiques from Eva Blount Way's collection. Gathered in the early 1900s as a means of raising money for the American Red Cross, the collection includes an eight-legged pig, a wedding party of dressed fleas and more than 30,000 buttons of varying colors and shapes.

Shopping: If you are looking for pipes and fittings or a little red wagon, you will probably find it at Riddick & Windley (235 Pamlico St., 252-943-2205). This Ace Hardware affiliate is located within walking distance of most marinas. To fill a prescription or sample some "good down home cooking," visit O'Neals Drug Store (292 E. Main St., 252-943-2643), a local hang-out. The Food Lion (998 U.S. Highway 264 Bypass, 252-943-3094) requires a trip of nearly two miles. There is also an ABC liquor store on the bypass (968 U.S. Highway 264 Bypass, 252-943-2107).

Restaurants: Gingerbread Bakery & O'Neals Snack Bar (278 E. Main St., 252-944-0099) serves breakfast and lunch. It is a favorite among locals, who enjoy the chicken salad plates or sandwiches, along with daily lunch specials. Breakfast is straight from mother's kitchen. The Fish Hooks Café (231 E. Main St., 252-943-9948) is known for their fresh local seafood entrees, daily lunch buffets, Sunday brunches, and great service. Try the flounder stuffed with local crab. You might also enjoy the beef sandwich at Farm Boy's Restaurant (216 Pamlico St., 252-943-3295), which is crowded with locals at lunchtime. Friday and Saturday night includes service on the deck with beer and wine and often live music. Also while in town, make sure you try Georgie's Sport & Oyster Bar (458 Pamlico St., 252-943-2102) for tasty North Carolina seafood (open Thursday through Saturday). For a relaxed atmosphere, visit Wine & Words and the Back Bay Café (413 Pamlico St., 252-944-2870), where you can sip wine and sample eclectic food in a relaxed atmosphere.

ADDITIONAL RESOURCES

- **BELHAVEN CHAMBER OF COMMERCE, 252-943-3770**
  www.belhavenchamber.com

NEARBY GOLF COURSES
Bayview Golf Club, 49 King Blount Drive,
Bath, NC 27808, 252-923-8191 (16 miles)

NEARBY MEDICAL FACILITIES
Pungo District Hospital, 202 E. Water St.,
Belhaven, NC 27810, 252-943-2111 (less than one mile)

Belhaven Family Practice, PA, 166. E. Water St,
Belhaven, NC 27810, 252-943-6114 (less than one mile)

Pungo Family Medicine, 245 Allen St.,
Belhaven, NC 27810, 252-944-2218 (less than one mile)

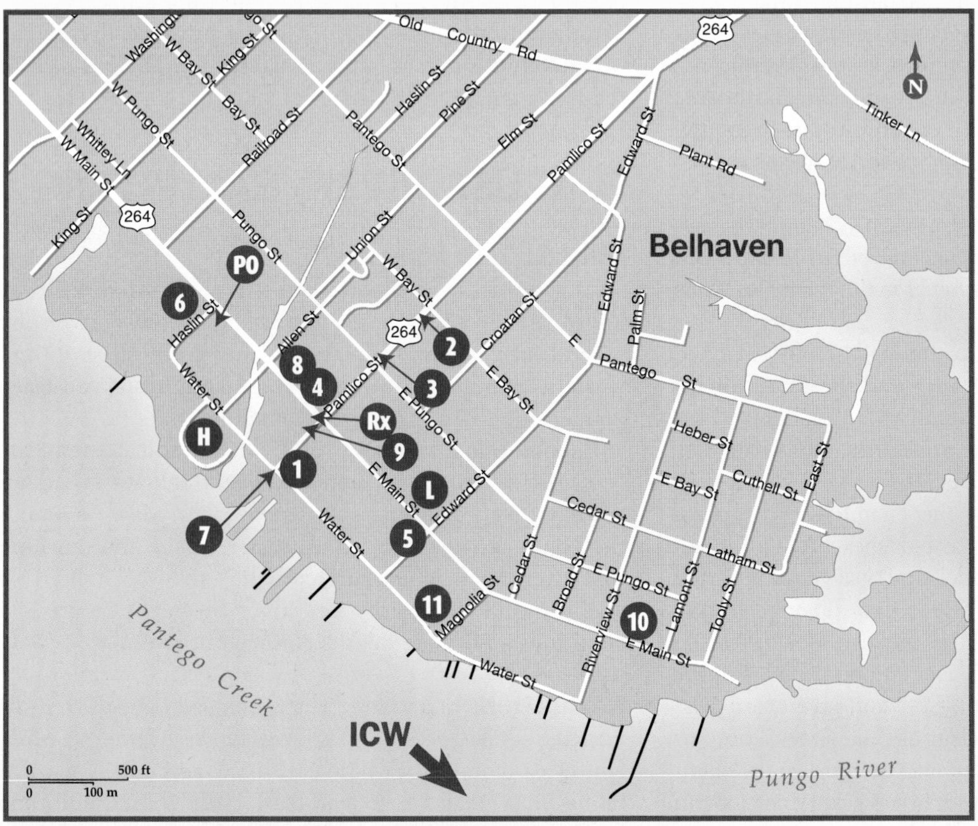

Reference the marina listing tables to see all the marinas in the area.

DINING
1 Farm Boys Restaurant & Front Porch
2 Georgies Sports & Oyster Bar
3 Back Bay Café/Wine & Words
4 Fish Hooks Café
5 Gingerbread Bakery & O'Neals Snack Bar

INFORMATION
6 Community Chamber of Commerce

MARINE SUPPLIES
7 Riddick & Windley (Ace Hardware)

POINTS OF INTEREST
8 Belhaven Memorial Museum

SERVICES
9 Shear Elegance

LODGING
10 Belport Inn
11 Belhaven Water Street Bed & Breakfast

L LIBRARY
PO POST OFFICE
H HOSPITAL

PUNGO RIVER TO HOBUCKEN

Mile 136 to Mile 157

At Belhaven, the Pungo River makes a 90-degree turn to the south for the 10-mile run to the Pamlico River. The Hobucken Coast Guard station on the north side of the Hobucken Bridge (Mile 157.2, 65-foot fixed vertical clearance) can give you information on conditions around the sometimes-dangerous Maw Point (near Mile 165) and Neuse River junction.

Northbound boats will want to check the Corps of Engineers sign, on the eastern shore, concerning the Dismal Swamp route. If rainfall has been insufficient to operate the locks, the sign will indicate that the Dismal Swamp route is closed. If the sign is illegible, call the Coast Guard Station on VHF Channel 16.

NAVIGATION: Use Chart 11553. The ICW follows the broad lower reach of the Pungo River to the junction of the Pamlico River. (Markers are still reversed, green to starboard going south; continue running the yellow squares and triangles.) The markers in the lower Pungo River are spaced far apart and sometimes difficult to locate, but the river is wide and adequately deep.

The Pamlico River crossing is straight going and is usually an easy run. However, conflicting currents meet at the junction of the Pungo and Pamlico rivers. When easterly or westerly winds are strong and gusty, the crossing of the Pamlico River can be rough and wet. Confused seas are common, especially within a mile or so of Wades Point flashing red "PR," which is located around Mile 145.7. The 29-foot-tall flashing red "PR" marker at Wades Point was destroyed in 2006. It was replaced by a flashing red (2+1) 18-foot light, with red over green triangular boards (on three sides, all reading "PR") on a multi-pile structure. It is much shorter and very difficult to locate, especially northbound from Goose Creek.

From the Pamlico River through Goose Creek, aids to navigation return to the ICW configuration of red-to-starboard running south. This is especially important to remember when entering Goose Creek.

At Mile 157.2, the area surrounding the 65-foot fixed vertical clearance Hobucken Bridge and the Coast Guard Station is a No-Wake Zone. At about Mile 159, the land cut (canal) ends at Gale Creek, an arm of the Bay River. Use caution in transiting Gale Creek.

On the red (west) side of the channel at the point between flashing red "22" and green daybeacon "23," shoaling is encroaching on the channel, and boats have reported grounding hard here. Several vessels have reported hitting some type of obstruction in the vicinity of Mile 160.5 where the chart indicates an obstruction on the edge of the channel between red daybeacon "24" and green can "25." It is also a good idea to keep clear of Gale Creek Point, as it is continually building out and encroaching on the channel. Depths outside the markers are a scant half-foot in places. When leaving Gale Creek, do not mistake the Bay River markers that lead to Vandermere for those leading southeast to the Neuse River.

From Gale Creek, the ICW cuts five miles southeastward down Bay River to Maw Point and Maw Point Shoal, which continues to build out into the Neuse River. When strong winds blow down the Bay River, wave action can be almost as bad as on the Neuse.

Dockage: The commercial facilities at R. E. Mayo Co. are on the south side of the Hobucken Bridge (Mile 157.2). Dockage and fuel (gas and diesel) are available at R.E. Mayo, but the dock is usually full of commercial vessels. There can be a considerable wind-driven current at this bridge.

Anchorage: At Mile 140 off the Pungo River is unmarked Slade Creek. This harbor is difficult to enter, due to shoaling on both sides of the entrance. Using a chartplotter is extremely helpful because the channel is twisty when entering the creek and very shallow outside the channel. Slade Creek is nice and wide with good holding. Two possible anchorages are located along Goose Creek across the Pamlico River, but both spots are sometimes so full of crab pots that it may be difficult to find anchorage space.

Turning east at Mile 153.5 (at green daybeacon "13"), you will find six-foot depths in Eastham Creek just northeast of the creek's red daybeacon "4" (a private aid). A bit farther on, at Mile 154, you can turn west into Campbell Creek, which is very exposed with 5-foot-plus depths along the north shore approximately three-quarters of a mile off the ICW. Along Gale Creek (approximately Mile 159), you can anchor in the creek west of flashing red "22" (4- to 6-foot depths).

Anchoring is no longer possible opposite green daybeacon "23." An underwater electric cable runs from the mainland to the Jones Island Club, a private lodge on the island shore just east of green daybeacon "23." A sign in the bay warns, DANGER HIGH VOLTAGE.

NEUSE RIVER/BAY RIVER

Mile 161 to Mile 167

Strong winds over a period of a few days can raise or lower the depth of both the Bay and Neuse rivers by several feet. Winds from the northeast will raise it, and westerly winds will lower it. These conditions can leave you aground in a marina or at anchor.

If conditions at Maw Point Shoal indicate that the Neuse River is rough, you can backtrack westward up the Bay River to several good anchorages. Maw Point and the Neuse River are often an easier run in the morning just after dawn when surface winds may be lighter, so anchoring in the nearby Bay River the night before is a good idea. Adequate depths run well upriver.

NAVIGATION: Use Chart 11553. *Like the Pungo River, the marking system for the Bay River is numbered from seaward.* Southeast along the Bay River, Pine Tree Point is marked by flashing green "3" to starboard (Mile 162.2), and then by flashing green "1," which marks the shoaling off Deep

Goose Creek, Jones Bay, NC

GOOSE CREEK	Largest Vessel Accommodated	VHF Channel Monitored	Transient Berths / Total Berths	Approach / Dockside Depth (reported)	Floating Docks	Gas / Diesel	Groceries, Ice, Marine Supplies, Snacks	Repairs: Hull, Engine, Propeller	Lift (tonnage), Crane, Rail	1=110V, 2=220V, B=Both, Max Amps	Laundry, Pool, Showers	Pump-Out Station	Nearby: Grocery Store, Motel, Restaurant
	Dockage					Supplies		Services					
1. R.E. Mayo Co. Inc. (Commercial Fishing Vessels) 157.3 252-745-5331	90			13/13		GD	IMS			1/30			GM

Corresponding chart(s) not to be used for navigation. Internet Access Wireless Internet Access

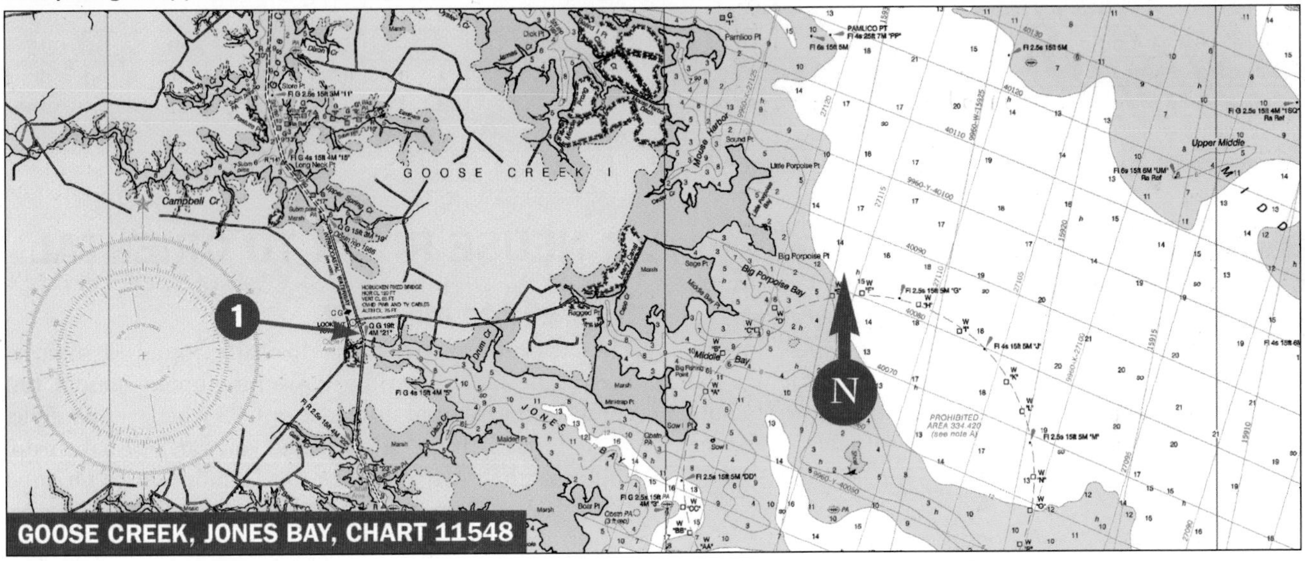

GOOSE CREEK, JONES BAY, CHART 11548

Point. Do not pass too close to flashing green "1," as shoaling has been reported to extend slightly into the channel from the marker.

Maw Point Shoal introduces you to the Neuse River. Follow the magenta line carefully as you make the 90-degree turn around the Neuse River Junction Light (Mile 167). The Neuse River Junction Marker at Maw Point has a flashing red (2+1) light at six-second intervals. Its former distinctly shaped structure has been replaced with a 15-foot multi-pile structure with a red-over-green triangular board.

There are two reasons for special caution here. The three red flashing lights (uncharted) in the prohibited area of Rattan Bay can be confused with the entrance light and, more importantly, there are 30 miles of open water between Maw Point and the Outer Banks. Winds out of the east make it rough and, if you are not careful, you could be set onto the shoal.

If both are on station, flashing green "1" (off Deep Point) and flashing red "2" (off Maw Point Shoal) make a shortcut inside Neuse River junction light, but do not use it if brisk winds make Maw Point Shoal a lee shore. Though depths are at least 8 feet along the shortcut route inside the Neuse River Junction Marker, trap markers are scattered throughout the area and require a close lookout. From Bay River flashing green "1" off Deep Point, run a course that will put you at least a quarter mile off flashing red "2," and then head for flashing red "4," off the tip of the shoal extending from Piney Point (Mile 172.3), on a south-southwesterly course.

Anchorage: One anchorage just off the ICW in the Bay River is to the south in Bonner Bay. To reach Bonner Bay, exit the ICW magenta line at quick flashing green "27" (Mile 161) and head southwest. Feel your way in via the unmarked channel with the depth sounder and go up Long Creek, the left fork. Other anchorages are far up Bay River near Vandermere, about five miles up on the river's north shore.

Vandermere, on Bay River

Vandermere means "village by the sea." At one point, this was the bustling county seat of Pamlico County. The town once boasted a courthouse, the first jail in the county, a hotel and a railroad depot. Today, the jail is in ruins, the depot is a warehouse, and the courthouse and hotel are private homes. The village is a nice place to stretch your legs or wait out bad weather. Near the waterfront is a small overgrown cemetery which some believe "runs blood" when it rains.

Anchorage: Though there are no amenities, you can anchor off Vandermere's village dock, but stay clear of the channel because shrimp boats use it. Steer toward the village docks from flashing green "5," and drop the anchor in 9 to 10 feet of water. Show an anchor light at night and always ask permission to tie up the dinghy if you go ashore.

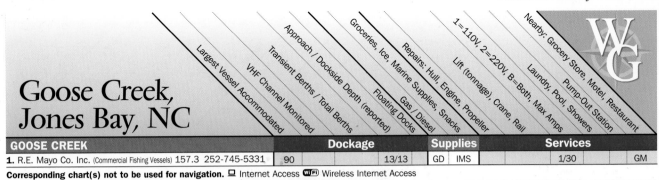

Oriental, Neuse River, NC

NEUSE RIVER		Largest Vessel Accommodated	VHF Channel Monitored	Transient Berths / Total Berths	Approach / Dockside Depth (reported)	Floating Docks	Gas / Diesel	Groceries, Ice, Marine Supplies, Snacks	Repairs: Hull, Engine, Propeller	Lift (tonnage), Crane, Rail	1=110V, 2=220V, B=Both, Max Amps	Laundry, Pool, Showers	Pump-Out Station	Nearby: Grocery Store, Motel, Restaurant
		Dockage					Supplies		Services					
1. Grace Harbor at River Dunes 173 (Internet, WiFi)	**252-249-4908 X2**	**160**	**16/72**	**20/400**	**7.5/8**	**F**	**GD**	**IMS**			**B/200+**	**LPS**	**P**	**MR**
2. Whittaker Pointe Marina 181 (Internet, WiFi)	**252-249-1750**	**100**	**16/11**	**8/53**	**8/6**			**I**			**B/50**	**LPS**		
3. Whittaker Creek Yacht Harbor 181 (Internet, WiFi)	252-249-0666	120	16	15/140	8/7		GD	IMS	E		B/50	LPS	P	GMR
4. Sailcraft Service Inc. 181	252-249-0522	50	16	12/12	8/6				HEP	L25	1/30	LS		GMR
5. Deaton Yacht Service 181 (WiFi)	**252-249-1180**	**50**	**16**	**4/29**	**8/7**			**M**	**HEP**	**L35**	**B/50**	**S**	**P**	**R**
6. Oriental Marina & Inn 181.5 (Internet, WiFi)	**252-249-1818**	**90**	**16**	**27/27**	**8/6.5**		**GD**	**IS**			**B/50**	**LPS**		**GMR**
7. Oriental Harbor 181.5 (WiFi)	252-249-3783	100	16	25/120	8/6			GIMS			B/50	LS		GMR

Corresponding chart(s) not to be used for navigation. (Internet icon) Internet Access (WiFi icon) Wireless Internet Access

Bayboro on Bay River

To reach Bayboro on Bay River, proceed past Vandermere, continuing to follow the markers carefully, especially green daybeacon "11" and red daybeacon "12." Do not mistake red daybeacon "14" for red daybeacon "12," or you will find yourself in 4-foot depths along the southwest shore. Just off red daybeacon "18" is the well-marked channel leading to Hurricane Boat Yard.

NEUSE RIVER TO ORIENTAL

Mile 167 to Mile 182

The Neuse River vies with Albemarle Sound as some of the meanest water on the ICW. First-timers should run compass courses and use radar or GPS whenever possible. With easterly or westerly winds, you can be shaken up, and a southwester can make the 18-mile run to Oriental (Mile 182) very wet going. A fall northwester, however, will leave the river calm with the wind coming from the

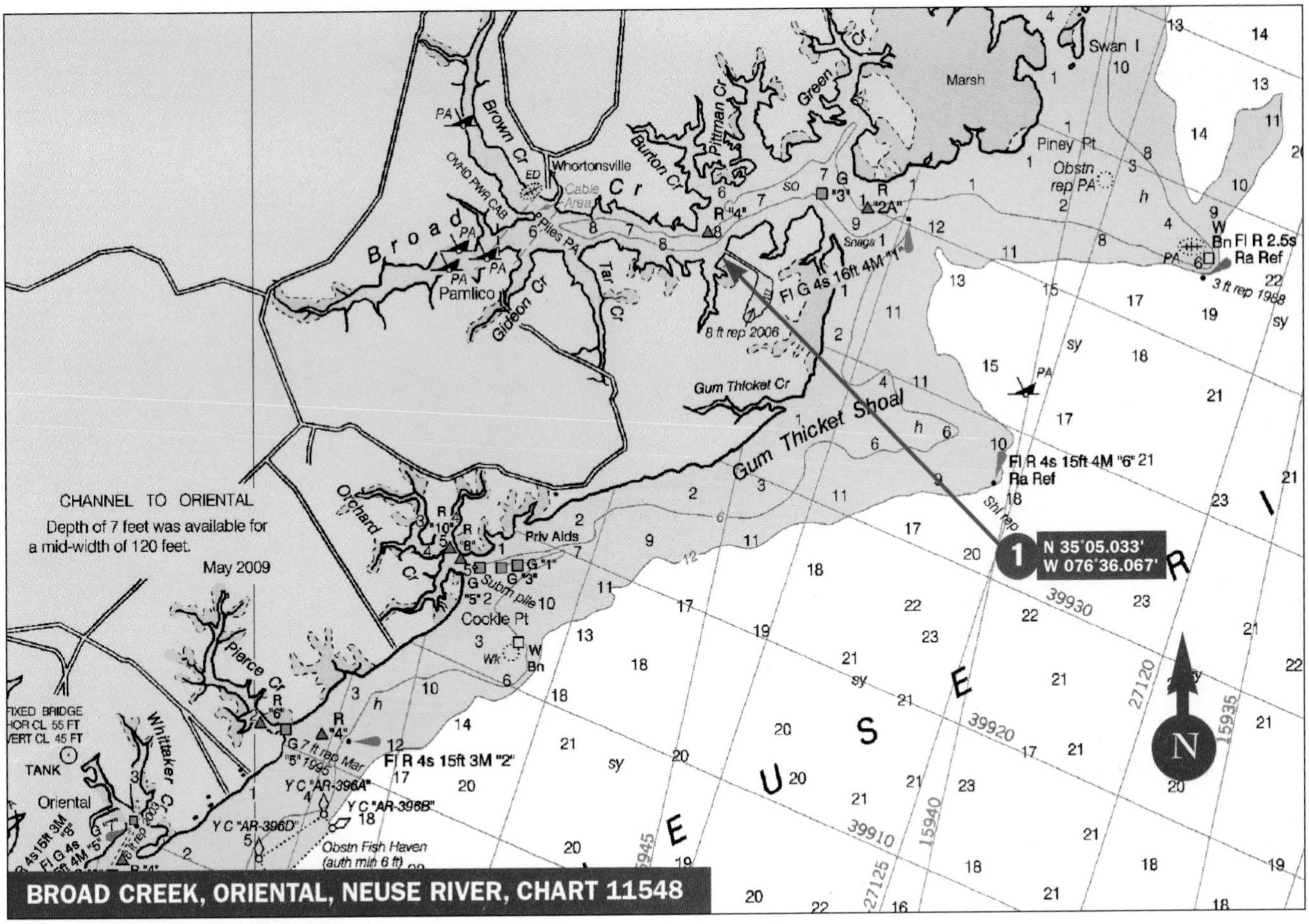

BROAD CREEK, ORIENTAL, NEUSE RIVER, CHART 11548

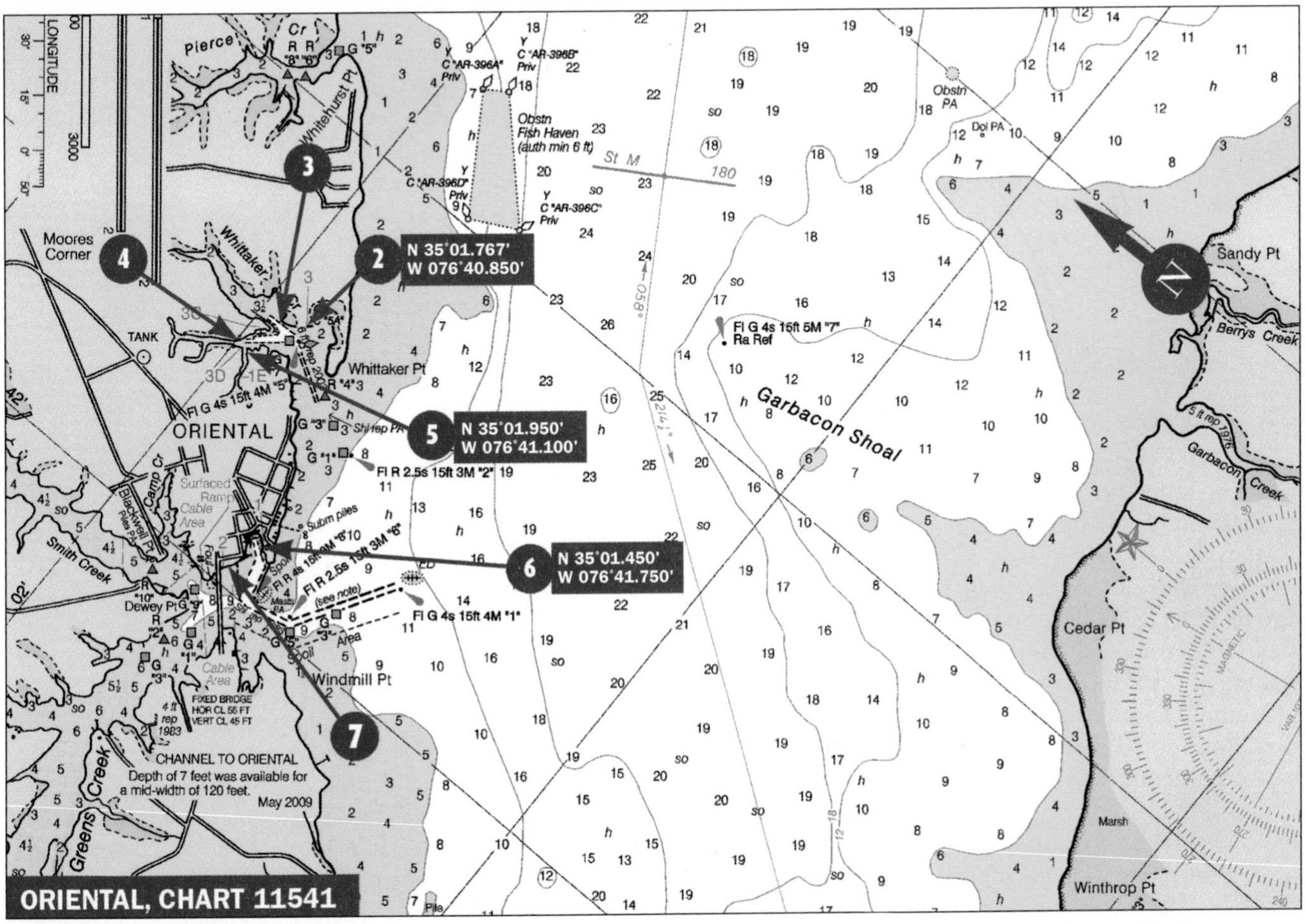

ORIENTAL, CHART 11541

Oriental is widely known as the "sailing capital of North Carolina." (Not to be used for navigation.) Photo courtesy of Mike Kucera.

shore. At those times, the wide, lovely Neuse River can be a pleasant change from the narrow land cuts of the ICW.

NAVIGATION: Use Chart 11541. *Going up the Neuse River, markers revert to the normal red-to-starboard pattern southbound on the ICW.* Watch them carefully and stay off the points in these parts. A danger marker, "BW," guides skippers bound for Broad Creek around the extending shoal south of Piney Point. Shoals at Piney Point and Gum Thicket Shoal continually build out. Do not mistake the more slightly dilapidated white warning daybeacon on a platform for flashing red "4" off Piney Point. Depths inshore of the platform are less than 2 feet in spots. The white danger beacon ("BW") marks the tip of the shoal between flashing red "4" and the platform. All markers off Piney Point should be left well to the north.

Dockage: Just off the ICW on the western side of Broad Creek is Grace Harbor at River Dunes, a new residential and marina facility with luxury accommodations for transients and residents. Among the impressive amenities are a clubhouse, exercise facility, laundry, pool with spa area, restrooms/showers, complimentary wireless Internet, fine dining ashore (Friday through Sunday) and a courtesy car. The facilities here make this a "must stop." River Dunes is reached by heading northwest from the ICW halfway between flashing reds "4" and "6," and then following the marked channel into Broad Creek. The marina is on the port side of the creek at red daybeacon "4." Entry is through a private, well-maintained, bulkheaded channel, with charted 8-foot depths. Unless you have the latest updates on your electronic charts, you will not see the channel marked so do follow the markers.

Anchorage: Northbound boats will appreciate the anchorages in Broad Creek off the Neuse River's western shore at Mile 173. One favorite is Burton Creek, where depths are 5 to 6 feet. From here, an early morning run north around Maw Point Shoal is possible, as is a short run south to Oriental.

If you can get out of the "magenta line mentality" and do not mind being remote from Oriental, the South River, across the Neuse and south of Broad Creek, is worth going four miles off the route. The entrance is well-marked, depths are good, the holding is secure in firm mud with sand or shells, and the high banks provide good wind protection. It is undeveloped, pretty and mercifully clear of crab pots.

Oriental—Mile 182

Oriental has become widely known as the "Sailing Capital of North Carolina," though boating facilities in the area also attract visiting powerboaters. The magnet of sheltered creeks has drawn up-country Carolinians and world-ranging cruisers alike, with immediate access to the country's second largest estuary and sailing, cruising and gunkholing areas. Local marinas welcome transients and offer supply and repair capabilities to handle virtually any

requirement. This is a popular place and space is limited, so reservations are helpful.

NAVIGATION: Use Chart 11541. Marine facilities begin at Mile 181, where a marked entrance leads to Whittaker Creek. There are more markers here than shown on the chart, and they make it easy to stay on the range (not charted), which can be picked up on entry. Be sure to give flashing green "5" a wide berth before turning left into the facility-lined creek. Depths of 8 feet are reported for the channel; nevertheless, southwesterly winds can lower this depth, and some shoaling persists in the area around and south of flashing green "5." In this entire area, it is best to call ahead to the marina of your choice to check for current depths and steering directions at time of entry.

Dockage: Whittaker Creek Yacht Harbor is immediately visible just inside the point. The marina has a resident fleet of more than 100 boats, but also reserves space to accommodate transients. It is also the only facility on Whittaker Creek that offers gas and diesel fuel.

To port heading upstream and slightly farther up the creek, Deaton Yacht Service is a full-capacity boatyard with an excellent reputation. Though primarily intended as a repair and refit facility, Deaton's does rent a few transient slips. Sailcraft Service is located across the canal.

Whittaker Pointe Marina is the newest in the area and is located at the mouth of Whittaker Creek on the east side of the entrance. The marina is now open for transients and offers electricity, showers, courtesy car, wireless Internet and a barbecue area. Credit cards were still not accepted in 2011.

Just past the entrance to Whittaker Creek, a well-marked channel carrying 8.5 feet leads to the basin confluence of Smith Creek and Greens Creek, immediately beyond the fixed bridge (45-foot vertical clearance) spanning the junction. Oriental's harbor (known locally as Raccoon Creek) lies immediately to starboard after passing flashing red "8" at the end of the rock jetty. The dredged channel leads past Oriental Yacht Club—usually packed with boats—and the shrimp boat wharf to Oriental Marina and, at the head of the harbor, "downtown" Oriental's public dock (with up to 48 hours of complimentary dockage where dredging is reported to have increased available depths to 6 feet—no water or shore power).

The recently refurbished Oriental Marina & Inn & Toucan Grill and Fresh Bar is actually a complex of facilities: docks, an inn and lounge, a swimming pool with a tiki bar, a fuel dock for gas and diesel and an on-site restaurant famous for fresh seafood meals. See "Goin' Ashore: Oriental" for additional dining options.

Not to be confused with the Oriental Marina & Inn, Oriental Harbor is a 110-slip marina facility inside the breakwater with transient berths, showers, laundry service and groceries all available on site.

Alternative Dockage: About seven miles up the Neuse River from Oriental (five miles west of the ICW), Wayfarers Cove at Minnesott Beach offers a well-protected alternative to a stopover in Oriental. Also along the way to New Bern, NC, Arlington Place offers some transient slips and services, as does the larger Mathews Point Marina.

Anchorage: Just south of the Oriental Yacht Club, the first structure to port (northwest) as you enter the harbor at Oriental, there is a popular anchorage spot in soft mud with 5- to 8-foot depths. Note that this anchorage is very small and holding is poor. Several boats are usually at anchor, but there is generally room for more. If using two anchors, it is best to set them in a Bahamian moor, with anchors set in opposite directions. (Remember that two poorly set anchors are twice as much trouble as one, and your anchoring should not interfere with the swinging space of the already anchored boats.) The facilities at Oriental Harbor Marina now occupy much of the space between the harbor entrance channel and the bridge, so you can no longer anchor close to the bridge.

Protected anchorage is also available up Greens Creek, if your boat can handle both the 45-foot vertical clearance of the fixed bridge and controlling depths of 5 to 6 feet. Anchorage is possible in Smith Creek, but depths are shallower still, and the length of the creek is open to southerly winds. If your mast is close to the posted 45-foot vertical clearance, enter cautiously. Wind and weather can raise (as well as lower) the water level appreciably. Charted depths in these creeks can be misleading. If winds have been out of the west or southwest for any length of time, a drop in water levels of as much as 3 feet is possible. Sound your way in. Many areas have depths of 6 to 7 feet, but some shoaling exists.

GOIN' ASHORE:
ORIENTAL, NC

Oriental, North Carolina is not at the end of the world, but you can see it from there. Stand on the lawn at Lou Mac Park and look to your left, across the Neuse River, and you will see the earth fall away below the edge of the Pamlico Sound. Somewhere beneath the horizon lies Ocracoke Island, and beyond that, England. So while Oriental isn't really land's end, it does have that feel.

Life moves slowly in the village. Boats and bikes rest against dock pilings and porch railings. The odor—some call it aroma—of shrimp nets drying on trawl doors fills the inner harbor, where sailboats and skiffs thump the town dock. Across the street at The Bean, local politics are discussed over strong coffee.

Talking and walking may not be considered official recreational activities in most towns, but in Oriental, they seem to fit with the feel of a place where biking, sailing, kayaking, fishing and boating are popular pastimes. Long known as the "Sailing Capital of the Carolinas," Oriental is blessed with wide-open waters, steady winds and easy access to creeks and coves.

"Perhaps the best part of Oriental is its location along the Inner Banks," one local yacht broker says. "Northeast of here is Ocracoke, and to the south is Beaufort and Shackleford Banks. You might say Oriental is the hub of boating in eastern North Carolina."

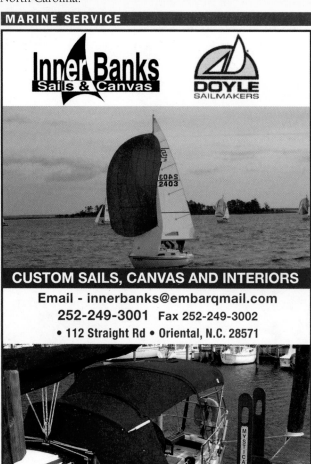

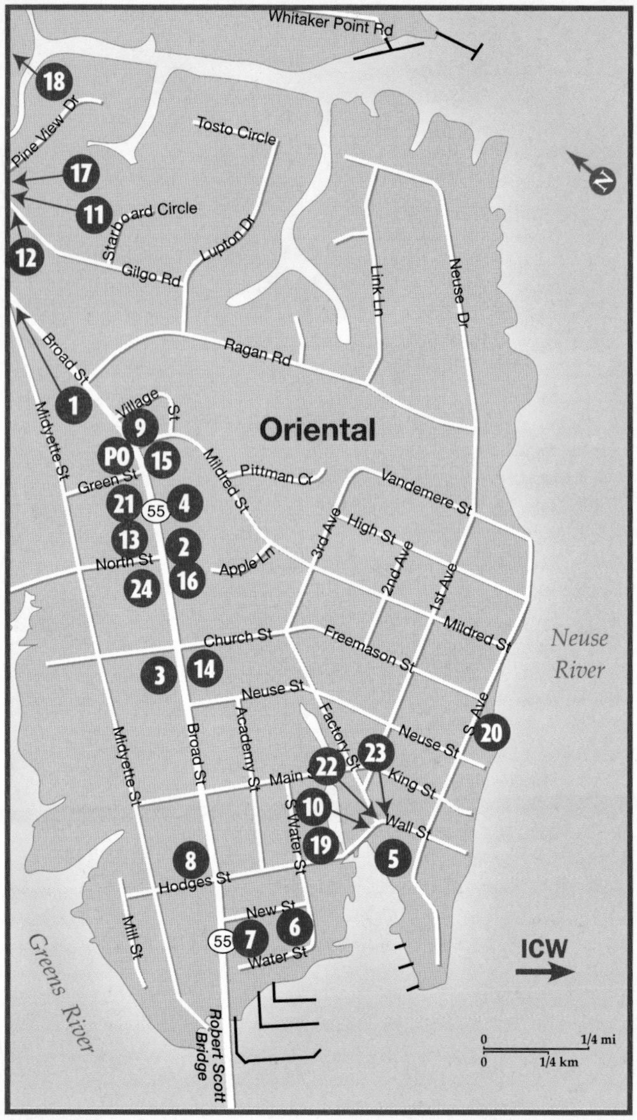

Reference the marina listing tables to see all the marinas in the area.

ART/ANTIQUES
1 The Circle Ten Art Gallery

ATTRACTIONS
2 Oriental's History Museum
3 Old Theater

DINING
4 The Broad Street Grill
5 Toucan Grill & Fresh Bar
6 M&M's Café
7 Oriental Harbor Deli & Bistro
8 Oriental Steamer
9 Brantley's Village Restaurant
10 The Bean
11 The Silos Restaurant

GROCERIES/CARRYOUT
12 Town 'N' Country Grocery
13 The Hungry Dragon Food Store

INFORMATION
14 Town Hall

MARINE SUPPLIES
15 Village Hardware & Marine Supply
16 Marine Consignment of Oriental
17 West Marine
18 Inner Banks Sails & Canvas
19 Inland Waterway Provision Company

POINTS OF INTEREST
20 Lou Mac Park

SHOPPING
21 Croakertown Gifts
22 The Village Gallery
23 Marsha's Cottage
24 Errands Plus Business Center

PO POST OFFICE

History: From the early 1900s, Oriental's economy was supported by lumber, fishing and farming. The train came to town, providing both cargo and passenger service. The last sawmill closed in the early 1960s around the same time recreational sailboats began to call Oriental "home." Today, there are almost 3,000 vessels berthed in the lower Neuse River area, hence Oriental's nickname.

Oriental got its proper name in 1866 when Lou Midyette became postmaster. He wanted to call the town Smith's Creek, but his wife thought the village needed a better name. Rebecca had found the nameplate from the sunken ship *Oriental* on a beach along the Outer Banks. The nameplate itself has been lost to history, its fate unknown.

Culture and cultural references: While casual is the prevailing culture of the community, the village does offer a bit of highbrow fare. The Circle Ten Art Gallery (708 Broad St., 252-249-0298) displays items of local artists working in paint, photograph, pottery, jewelry and textiles. In The Old Theater (608 Broad St., 252-249-0477), the Pelican Players offer real theater with local flavor. Several times a year, this entertainment center plays host to a number of popular musicians including Mike Cross, Livingston Taylor and Al Stewart (of "Year of the Cat" fame). The Dawson's Creek television show took its name from the tributary a few miles up the Neuse River. You will also find a close network of writers and authors living nearby.

Attractions: Oriental's History Museum (252-249-2493) is located on Main Street. Here, you can see model skiffs, oyster scoops, a net pole and a bronze porthole from the *SS Oriental*. A fishing pier in front of Lou Mac Park was added in 2007. If you want to cast a wider net, you can hire one of Oriental's fishing guides. Trailerable boats can be launched for free at the Wildlife Resources Ramp located at the foot of the bridge on Smith Creek. Nearby, there is a special launching area for kayaks and canoes. Within Pamlico County, there are more than 300 miles of mapped tributaries for paddling.

Special events: The Oriental Cup Regatta, held during the summer, is a three-day event that often attracts more than 100 boats. This great event is a fundraiser for a local scholarship fund. The Croaker Festival, held during Fourth of July weekend, is the town's largest event, attracting 10,000 visitors. Here, you will find street bands, a parade, coronation of the Croaker Queen, food, and arts and crafts vendors, all capped by fireworks over the harbor.

Now in its 16th year, the Oriental Rotary Tarpon Tournament hosts up to 75 boats competing for more than $22,000 in prizes. While fishermen come from afar for the competition, the tournament is also for a good cause, raising funds for its scholarship program. Each December, Oriental hosts "The Spirit of Christmas." Boats compete for the best Christmas light decorations, luminaries light the streets, and Santa rings in the season riding on a boat in the Christmas parade. New Year's Eve in Oriental brings out the "heritage of the Orient," with the Running of the Dragon and the dropping of the croaker fish from the top of a sailboat mast docked along the inner harbor.

Shopping: Shops in the area include Village Hardware & Marine Supply (804 Broad St., 252-249-1211), The Village Gallery (300 Hodges St., 252-249-0300), Marsha's Cottage (204 Wall St., 252-249-0334), The Shops at Croakertown (807 Broad St., 252-249-0990), Marine Consignment of Oriental (708 Broad St., 252-249-3222), Town 'N' Country Grocery (approximately a mile from the downtown harbor, 252-249-1317), and Errands Plus Business Center (801 Broad St., 252-249-0006) for fax and shipping services. Contact Inner Banks Sails & Canvas for sail and canvas repairs (112 Straight Rd., 252-249-3001). The popular Inland Waterway Provision Company (305 Hodges St., 252-249-7245) has reopened under new ownership and continues to offer boating supplies and provisions.

Restaurants: Toucan Grill & Fresh Bar (101 Wall St., 252-249-2204) offers visitors a great view of the inner harbor, and M&M's Café (205 S. Water St., 252-249-2000) is a local favorite. The Silo's Restaurant (located in a couple of actual old silos, 252-249-1050) is a local and boater favorite with live acoustic music (Wednesday) as well as weekly breakfast, lunch, and dinner specials and a specialty pizza menu. You might also try Oriental Harbor Deli & Bistro (516 S. Water St., 252-249-0550, the Oriental Steamer (401 Broad St., 252-249-3557), Broad Street Grill (802 Broad St., 252-249-2707), Brantley's Village Restaurant (900 Broad St., 252-249-3509) and, of course, don't forget to grab a cup of coffee at The Bean (304 Hodges St., 252-249-4918), which now offers bike rentals, home of the Porch Pirates profiled in SAIL magazine.

ADDITIONAL RESOURCES

- For free street maps and information about events and attractions visit Town Hall, 507 Church St., 252-249-0555, www.townoforiental.com or www.visitoriental.com
- Pamlico County Chamber of Commerce, 252-745-3008 www.pamlicochamber.com
- Old Theater, www.oldtheater.org
- Town Dock, www.towndock.net/happening.html
- Oriental Rotary Tarpon Tournament, www.orientalrotary.org
- The Bean, www.thebeanorientalnc.com

NEARBY GOLF COURSES

Minnesott Golf & Country Club, 806 Country Club Drive, Minnesott Beach, NC 28510, 252-249-0813 (11 miles)

NEARBY MEDICAL FACILITIES

Oriental Medical Center, 901 Broad St., Oriental, NC 28571, 252-249-2888 (less than one mile)

Craven Regional Medical Center, 2000 Neuse Blvd., New Bern, NC 28561, 252-633-8111 (30 miles)

Pamlico Medical Center, 606 Main St, Bayboro, NC 28515, 252-745-3191 (11 miles)

Oriental Dental, 403 Hodges St., Oriental, NC 28571, 252-249-1551

Oriental Village Veterinary Hospital, 407 Broad St., Oriental, NC 28571, 252-249-2149

Minnesott Beach, Mitchell Creek, NC

		Largest Vessel Accommodated	VHF Channel Monitored	Transient Berths / Total Berths	Approach / Dockside Depth (reported)	Floating Docks	Gas / Diesel	Groceries, Ice, Marine Supplies, Snacks	Repairs: Hull, Engine, Propeller	Lift (tonnage), Crane, Rail	1=110V, 2=220V, B=Both, Max Amps	Laundry, Pool, Showers	Pump-Out Station	Nearby: Grocery Store, Motel, Restaurant
MINNESOTT BEACH		Dockage					Supplies		Services					
1. Wayfarers Cove Marina & Boatyard 185 🖳	252-249-0200	55	16/68	150	6.5/6-7			I	HEP	L60	B/50	LS	P	
MITCHELL CREEK														
2. Matthews Point Marina 6 SW of 185 🖳	252-444-1805	50	16	6/110	6.5/6.5		GD	IM	E		B/50	LS	P	GMR
3. Arlington Place Marina 6 SW of 185	800-967-7639			10			G				1/30	P		R

Corresponding chart(s) not to be used for navigation. 🖳 Internet Access WiFi Wireless Internet Access

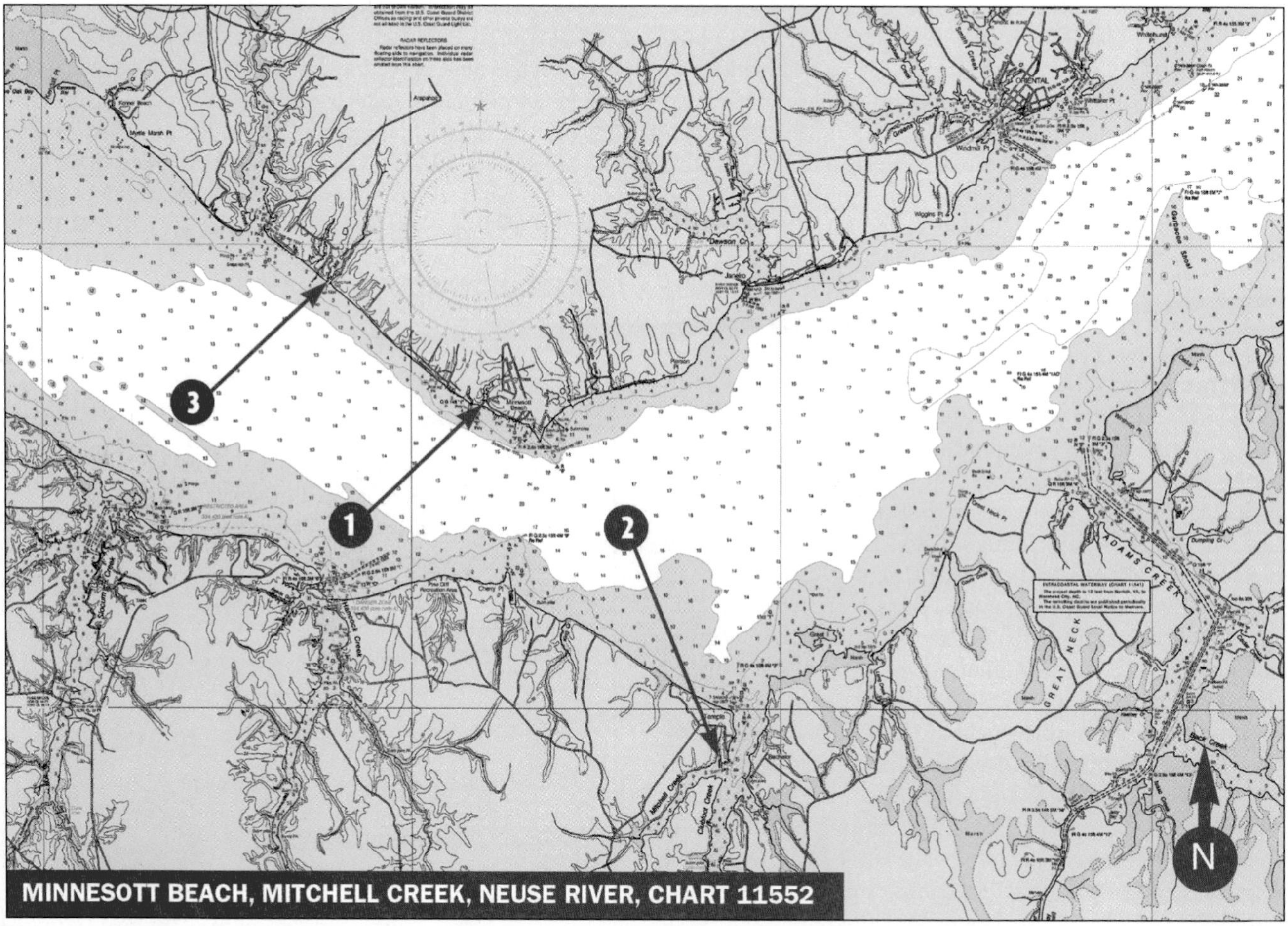

MINNESOTT BEACH, MITCHELL CREEK, NEUSE RIVER, CHART 11552

ADAMS CREEK TO MOREHEAD CITY

Mile 185 to Mile 205

The ICW route leaves the Neuse River at Mile 185 and enters Adams Creek, which underwent dredging in February 2011. Just beyond its entrance, Adams Creek gives you a refresher on the use of ranges. Farther south, Adams Creek is connected to Core Creek via the Adams Creek Canal, a five-mile-long land cut that ends at the headwaters of Core Creek below the Core Creek Bridge. Adams Creek Canal (also recently dredged) is mostly undeveloped but that is changing; keep an eye out for deer, eagles and other wildlife along the way. Both Adams and Core creeks, as well as the canal, may have floating debris, so keep a close eye on the course ahead. The area of Core Creek below the bridge was dredged in late 2007 and was holding its depth in 2011.

NAVIGATION: Use Chart 11541. Do not be tempted to cut inside Garbacon Shoal light "7" in the Neuse River (Mile 180.6) when approaching Adams Creek. The fishermen's markers off Winthrop Point indicate nets just below the surface. Follow the magenta line around flashing green "1AC" (Mile 183.8), which marks the entry to Adams

A view over the Adams Creek Canal, just north of the approach to Beaufort and Morehead City, NC, Looking North.
(Not to be used for navigation.) WATERWAY GUIDE PHOTOGRAPHY.

Creek, and make a dogleg approach. You will then be on a range for a mile and a half.

The aids to navigation along Adams and Core creeks are located 30 to 35 feet outside the channel limits. Although the chart shows 8- to 6-foot depths in Adams Creek opposite marker "9," do not cut this corner, as there are reports of only 6-foot depths. There is a huge new residential development on the Adams Creek Canal, north of the Core Creek Bridge (Mile 195.8, 65-foot fixed vertical clearance), with numerous docks extending toward the ICW channel. Tidal currents from the Beaufort Inlet begin to appear in the vicinity of the Core Creek Bridge. Currents are particularly strong around the bridge, at Bock Marine just below the bridge and at the outside docking area at Jarrett Bay. Strong wind-driven currents can be felt as well in the Adams Creek Canal and into lower Adams Creek in certain conditions. From Core Creek Bridge to the Morehead City/Beaufort area at Mile 205, an ebb current provides strong assistance to southbound craft.

At Mile 199.3, in Core Creek, the Coast Guard has permanently removed the back range marker, and the front part is now lit and numbered (quick flashing red) "24." From there, the ICW route turns to the southeast, following the Newport River as it makes several dogleg turns to approach the 65-foot fixed vertical clearance Morehead City Highway Bridge at Mile 203.8.

Dockage: At Mile 193.3, Sea Gate Marina is located on the west side of the Adams Creek Canal. Just beyond the Core Creek Bridge (Mile 195.8), Bock Marine has lift and repair capabilities and offers good depths for transients to make fast overnight. Eastern Marine Diesel is located here and can perform repairs, maintenance and rebuilds.

Jarrett Bay Boatworks, a Down East Carolina custom builder and full-service boatyard, operates a huge facility in the Jarrett Bay Marine Industrial Park at Mile 198 on Core Creek. With a 175-acre yard, 50- and 220-ton lifts and a 12-foot-deep basin, Jarrett Bay's repair facilities can accommodate sportfishing boats, cruising boats (both power and sail), commercial vessels, megayachts and large multihull craft. Jarrett Bay offers complete paint, marine carpentry, fiberglass, machining, aluminum fabrication, canvas/upholstery, custom marine interiors and propeller, shaft and strut services. A brokerage service is also available here. Transient dockage is available for vessels up to 125 feet, including nine 22-foot-wide slips fronting the ICW. Fuel (gas and diesel) and a well-stocked ship's store are on site. Other businesses in the industrial park include Covington Detroit Diesel, Gregory Poole CAT Marine Power, ZF Marine, Offshore Electronics, Southern Skimmer, Lookout Boats, Moore's Marine Yacht Center and True World Marine. True World Marine offers a 75-ton Travelift, short- and long-term storage, painting, fiberglass and other repairs. They have an 11-acre yard for repair and service.

Anchorage: Just beyond the straight stretch of the first range in Adams Creek and behind quick flashing green "9" is the mouth of Cedar Creek (Mile 187.6), a good anchorage for vessels with drafts of 6 feet or less, with more room than you might think from the chart.

Adams Creek Canal, NC

ADAMS CREEK CANAL		Largest Vessel Accommodated	VHF Channel Monitored	Transient Berths / Total Berths	Approach / Dockside Depth (reported)	Floating Docks	Gas / Diesel	Groceries, Ice, Marine Supplies, Snacks	Repairs: Hull, Engine, Propeller	Lift (tonnage), Crane, Rail	1=110V, 2=220V, B=Both, Max Amps	Laundry, Pool, Showers	Pump-Out Station	Nearby: Grocery Store, Motel, Restaurant
		Dockage					Supplies		Services					
1. Sea Gate Marina 193.3 (Internet Access)	252-728-4126	50	16	/72	6/6			GIMS			B/50	LS	P	
2. Bock Marine Builders Inc. 196	252-728-6855	75	16	7/7	8/8			MS	HEP	L70	B/50	LS		
3. Jarrett Bay Boatworks 198 (Internet Access) (Wireless Internet Access)	**252-728-2690**	**125**	**16**	**9/15**	**12/9**	**F**	**GD**	**IMS**	**HEP**	**L220,C15**	**B/50**	**S**	**P**	**GMR**
4. Gregory Poole Marine Power 198	252-504-2640	350	16	CATERPILLAR ENGINE DISTRIBUTOR							1/30			
5. Moores Marine Yacht Center 198 (Internet Access)	252-504-7060	150	69	2/	12/9		GD	M	HE	L220, C50	B/100	S	P	GMR
6. True World Marine 198.5 (Wireless Internet Access)	252-728-2541	100	16	/4	7/5	F			H	L75	B/50	S		

Corresponding chart(s) not to be used for navigation. Internet Access · Wireless Internet Access

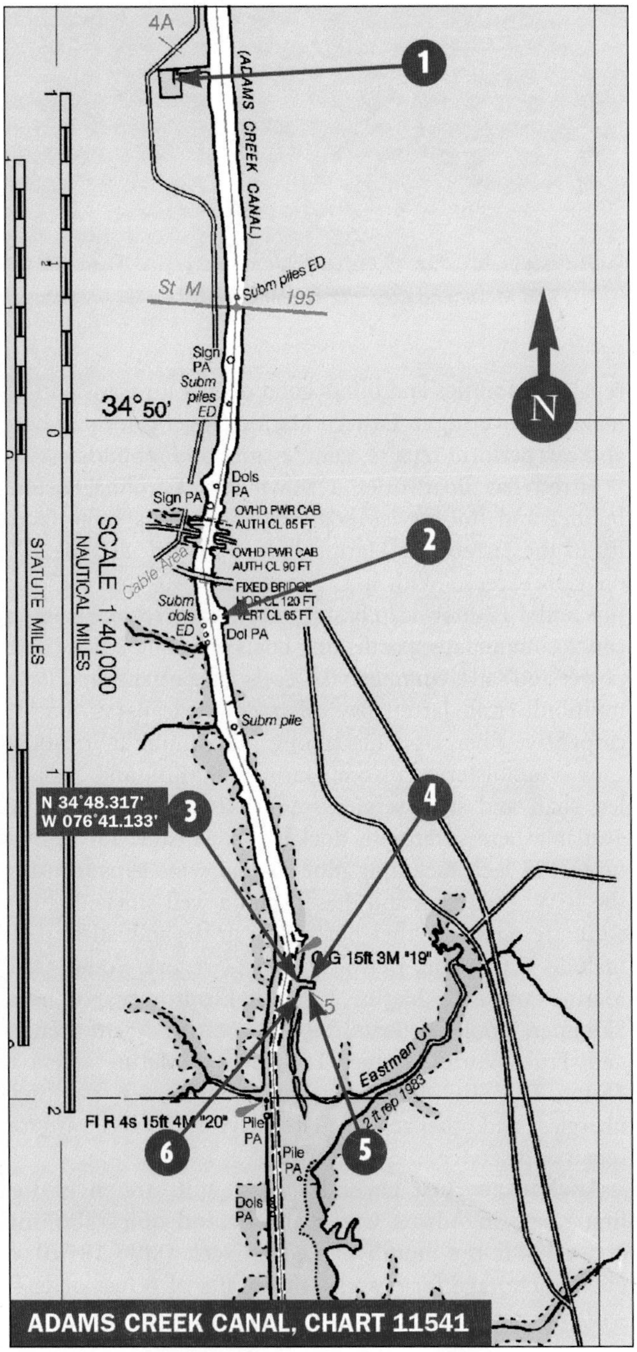

ADAMS CREEK CANAL, CHART 11541

Several years ago, a sailboat sunk in this anchorage. If you anchor here and do not see the mast, assume that the wreckage is likely still on the bottom. The wreck is approximately 150 to 200 yards to the east-northeast of flashing green "9" and generally has floats attached to it. Avoid this anchorage if a southerly wind is blowing water out of Adams Creek—you may find yourself aground in the morning. Vessels drawing less than 5.5 feet can sound their way up past the hook on Cedar Creek for better protection, unless the wind is out of the west. Holding is good, but watch out for possible long seaweed on the bottom. Although the chart shows only 5 feet; 6-foot depths or better are available in the much more protected Jonaquin Creek farther back to port. It provides all-around protection with excellent holding. Back Creek (Mile 189), a mile and a half south of Cedar Creek, can provide excellent protection from southwest and north-east winds for boats drawing 4.5 feet or less.

Morehead City/Beaufort Approaches

THE FOLLOWING AREA REQUIRES SPECIAL ATTENTION DUE TO SHOALING OR CHANGES TO THE CHANNEL

MOREHEAD CITY/BEAUFORT APPROACHES

NAVIGATION: Use Chart 11541. Study the charts, *Local Notice to Mariners* and our color-coded diagram of the Morehead City/Beaufort approaches (on page 213) before trying to make your way into the area. If heading to Town Creek or the Beaufort waterfront from the north, depart the ICW between quick flashing green "29" and flashing green (2+1) junction marker "RS" (Mile 200.8), and then follow the Russell Slough Channel using the detailed instructions under the Beaufort approach and dockage section below.

Those cruisers continuing south to Morehead City will use the right (magenta line) fork of the channel, which has good depths and passes under the Morehead City Highway Bridge (Mile 203.8, 65-foot fixed vertical clearance) and Morehead City Railroad Bascule Bridge (Mile 203.8, 4-foot closed vertical clearance, normally open).

Looking northwest over Beaufort, NC. (Not to be used for navigation.) WATERWAY GUIDE PHOTOGRAPHY.

At quick flashing green "35" on the ICW main channel, there is no longer a dredged side channel leading east into Town Creek. The most recent NOAA charts, dated March 2010, show the shoal now extending across the former dredged channel; however, even some new electronic charts and older paper ones still show this as a viable channel. It is not!

The charted white danger beacon "A" that marked the dangerous shoal east of quick flashing green "35" is reported to have been removed. If you turn here, you will quickly and firmly go aground.

END SPECIAL CAUTION AREA.

There is another entrance to Beaufort from the ocean inlet, known as the Radio Island Route (also called Bulkhead Channel). This route is busier than the northern Russell Slough approach (still referred to locally as the Gallants Channel) because it leads directly off the Beaufort Inlet. To use the Radio Island Route when traveling southbound on the ICW, pass under the 65-foot fixed vertical clearance bridge and railroad span between Beaufort and Morehead City (Mile 203.8), and then head southeast toward the inlet at the charted turning basin at Mile 204. If northbound on the ICW, turn southeast from the turning basin into the Morehead City Channel. Heading toward the inlet, round the southern tip of Radio Island and pick up quick flashing red buoy "2," the entrance marker to Beaufort. The channel bears north from here, between Radio Island on the west and the small unnamed island to the east. Follow the marked channel into Taylor Creek and the Beaufort waterfront. Also, be sure to strictly honor all green aids to navigation on this route—particularly green can "3" at the southern tip of Radio Island, which appears to be off-station on some electronic charts.

ICW, Between Morehead City and Beaufort

The ICW channel that leads to the high-rise railroad span at Mile 203.8 is holding its depths, but has a very strong crosscurrent (1 to 2 knots). The most recent chart, from March 2010, shows red daybeacon "30" (Mile 201) as a small red nun and daybeacon "30A" was located just to its south. The shoal to the west is bare at low tide (rather than 3 feet deep as indicated on the chart) and extends slightly into the ICW channel at the marker. The two green cans, "37" and "39" (Mile 203.3) can be extremely difficult to find—they are very small and lean way over in the current. The horizontal opening at the bridges at Mile 203.8 is very narrow with strong current and is made more difficult by the narrow opening of the railroad bridge (usually open) on the other side.

MOREHEAD CITY/ BEAUFORT, NC

Mile 205

Morehead City and its sister city, Beaufort, are two of the most popular stopovers between Norfolk and Florida. This commercial and sportfishing center operates a large fishing charter fleet year-round. This seaport is also a port of entry, with Customs inspections

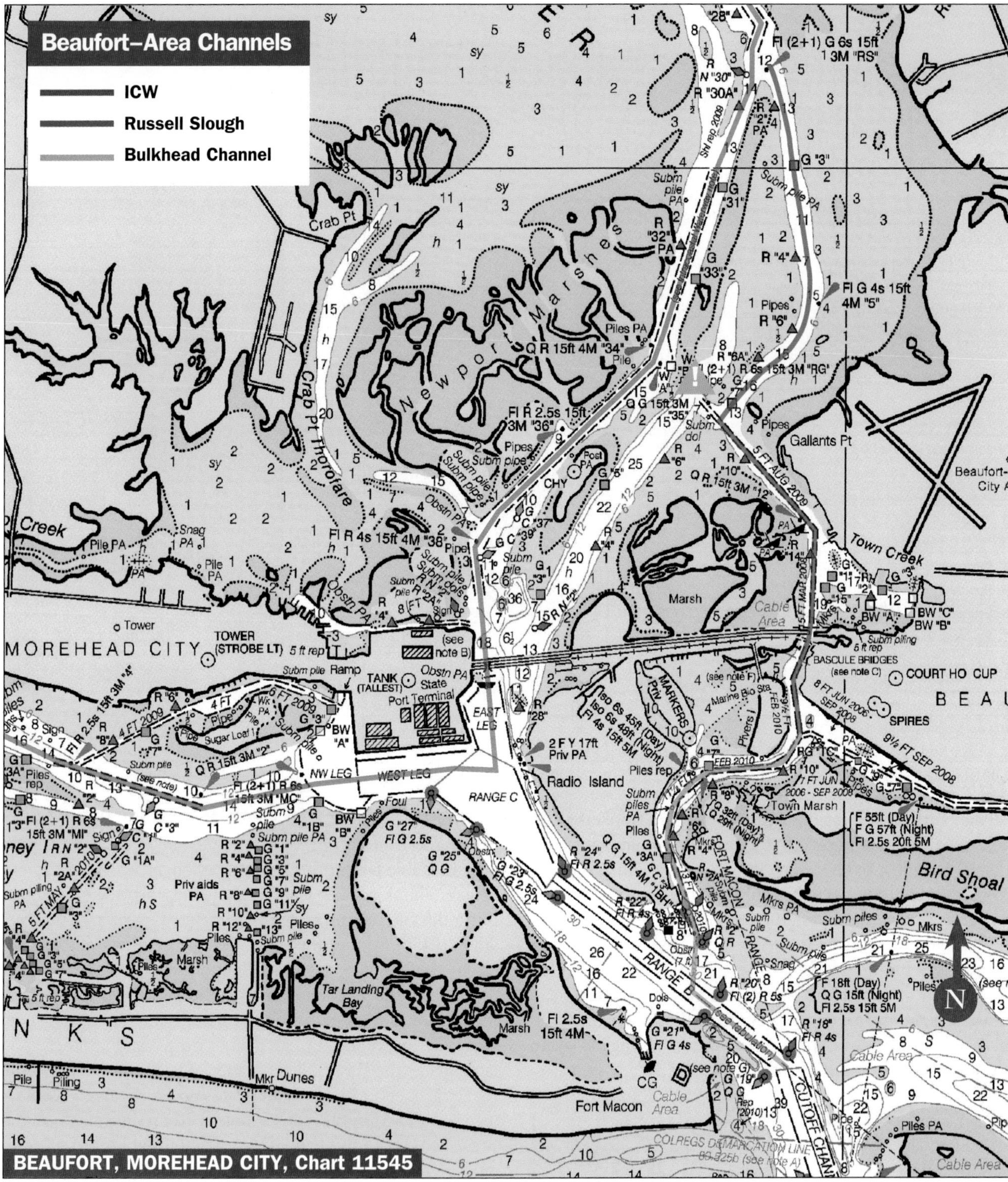

available. Numerous marinas and service facilities can handle the needs of cruisers, both power and sail.

The Morehead City/Beaufort area includes the waters out to Cape Lookout and Core Banks, including Shackleford Banks (now preserved as the Rachel Carson Reserve and part of the Cape Lookout National Seashore Reserve).

Note that tides and currents now begin to be a major consideration as you proceed south on the ICW in close proximity to the coast.

Beaufort—Mile 205

Founded in 1709, the charming city of Beaufort, NC (pronounced "bo-fort"—Beaufort, SC is pronounced "bue-fort"), preserves traces of its nautical history as a backdrop to a thriving modern boating center. Year-round, Beaufort is home to yachts of all descriptions, either moored out or tied up along the town side of the waterfront channel. During the fall, passage-making sailboats dominate the scene with preparations for ocean voyages from this major jumping-off point for trips to the Caribbean.

Beaufort, Morehead City, Bogue Banks, NC

		Largest Vessel Accommodated	VHF Channel Monitored	Transient Berths / Total Berths	Approach / Dockside Depth (reported)	Floating Docks	Gas / Diesel	Groceries, Ice, Marine Supplies, Snacks	Repairs: Hull, Engine, Propeller	Lift (tonnage), Crane, Rail	1=110V, 2=220V, B=Both, Max Amps	Laundry, Pool, Showers	Pump-Out Station	Nearby: Grocery Store, Motel, Restaurant
MOREHEAD CITY		**Dockage**					**Supplies**		**Services**					
1. Russell Yachts .7 W of 205	252-240-2826	100		5/5	12/12			GM	HP	L35	B/50			GMR
2. Captain Bill's Waterfront Restaurant .8 W/204.9	252-726-2166	80		2/7	15/15						1/30			GR
3. Morehead City Docks (Internet Access)	252-726-2457	50	16/71	10/10	8-10/8-10	F					B/50	LS		GR
4. Morehead Gulf Docks .7 W of 204.9	**252-726-5461**	**120**	**16**	**3/9**	**14/14**		**GD**	**GIMS**			**B/50**			**G**
5. Sanitary Fish Market & Restaurant 204.9	252-247-3111	55		4/15	12/12			I						GMR
6. Dockside Yacht Club 203.9 (Internet Access) (WiFi)	252-247-4890	80	16	20/75	16/16	F		GIMS			B/50	LS	P	GMR
7. Morehead City Yacht Basin .7 W/203.5 (Internet Access) (WiFi)	252-726-6862	200	16/71	40/88	12/10	F	GD	IS			B/100	LS	P	R
8. Portside Marina 205 (Internet Access) (WiFi)	**252-726-7678**	**100**	**16/10**	**10/25**	**40/10**	**F**	**GD**	**GIMS**	**HEP**	**L8**	**B/100**	**LS**		**GMR**
BEAUFORT														
9. Radio Island Marina 203.9	252-726-3773	35	16	/35	5/4	F	G	IMS	E		1/30			GMR
10. Island Marina 203.9	252-726-5706	45			4/3			M	HEP	L	1/30			
11. Olde Towne Yacht Club 203	252-726-3066	90	16	20/95	14/10	F	GD	IMS			B/50	LPS		R
12. Beaufort Inn 1.7 E of 202.3	252-728-2600	36		6/12	12/5						1/30			MR
13. Town Creek Marina 1.3 S of 202 (Internet Access) (WiFi)	252-728-6111	180	16/08	25/100	10/12	F	GD	GIMS	HEP	L50	B/50	LS	P	GMR
14. Discovery Diving Co. Inc. 202	252-728-2265	45	10	/42	6/6			IS	EP		B/50	S	P	GMR
15. Spouter Inn Restaurant 1.4 E of 204	252-728-5190	60		/4	8/8						1/30			GMR
16. Scuttlebutt Nautical Books & Bounty 1.4 E/204	**252-728-7765**			**Nautical Books and Charts**										
17. Beaufort Docks 202 (Internet Access) (WiFi)	**252-728-2503**	**300**	**16**	**98/98**	**16/12**	**F**	**GD**	**GIMS**	**HEP**		**B/100**	**LS**	**P**	**GMR**
18. The Boathouse 202	252-838-1524	44					GD	M	HEP			S	P	GMR
BOGUE BANKS														
19. Anchorage Marina 1 S of 205.7	252-726-4423	60	16/68	5/130	6/6	F	GD	GIMS	E		B/50	S		MR
20. Fort Macon Marina 1 S of 205.7	252-726-2055	35	16		6/4	F	G	IMS	HEP					GMR
21. Crow's Nest Yacht Club Inc. .8 S of 206.9	252-726-4048		16		5/6		G				1/30			

Corresponding chart(s) not to be used for navigation. (Internet Access icon) Internet Access (WiFi icon) Wireless Internet Access

The North Carolina Maritime Museum Conservation Lab, located northwest of the marina repair yard on Russell Slough Channel (also known as Gallants Channel from Gallants Point to the Beaufort Bridge), is a receiving and conservation area for the artifacts brought up from the wreck of Blackbeard's *Queen Anne's Revenge*. It is not open to the public, although there are occasional guided tours of the premises. This facility has a new bulkhead on the creek, and there has been considerable expansion ashore. The museum sponsors a junior sailing program and a rowing club, both based here.

GOIN' ASHORE: **BEAUFORT, NC**

Beyond a sliver of beach on Carrot Island, a pony grazes near the inflatable tender of a cruising ketch anchored in Taylors Creek. The skipper of a small sailing dory plays wind shifts as he dodges sterns and stares, tacking his way towards the dinghy dock in front of the post office. The captain of a trawler yacht backs down, tossing a line to the dockmaster as bow thrusters push the hull towards the T dock. From beyond the boardwalk, the sound of a furling headsail announces a new arrival. A hand goes up, an anchor drops, and another crew anticipates the shoreside amenities of Beaufort.

Long hailed as the "Gateway to the Caribbean," Beaufort is often cooled by a brisk sea breeze. Then, in the fall, as the western edge of the Gulf Stream veers to within 40 miles of the inlet, fresh northwest winds carry eager sailors into the Atlantic. It is a four-day sail to the Bahamas, a day more to Bermuda. This close proximity to the Atlantic trade routes was not lost on the early settlers, and today, it is still receiving cargo and sailors from afar.

History: Named after Sir Henry Somerset, Duke of Beaufort, this port city is the third-oldest town in North Carolina. Beaufort has survived pirates and hurricanes, depressions and tourism. Surveyed in 1713 and incorporated in 1722, the British influence of its roots is apparent in the architecture and street names: Ann and Queen, Earl of Craven and Orange for the Prince of Orange. By the mid-1800s, Beaufort had two

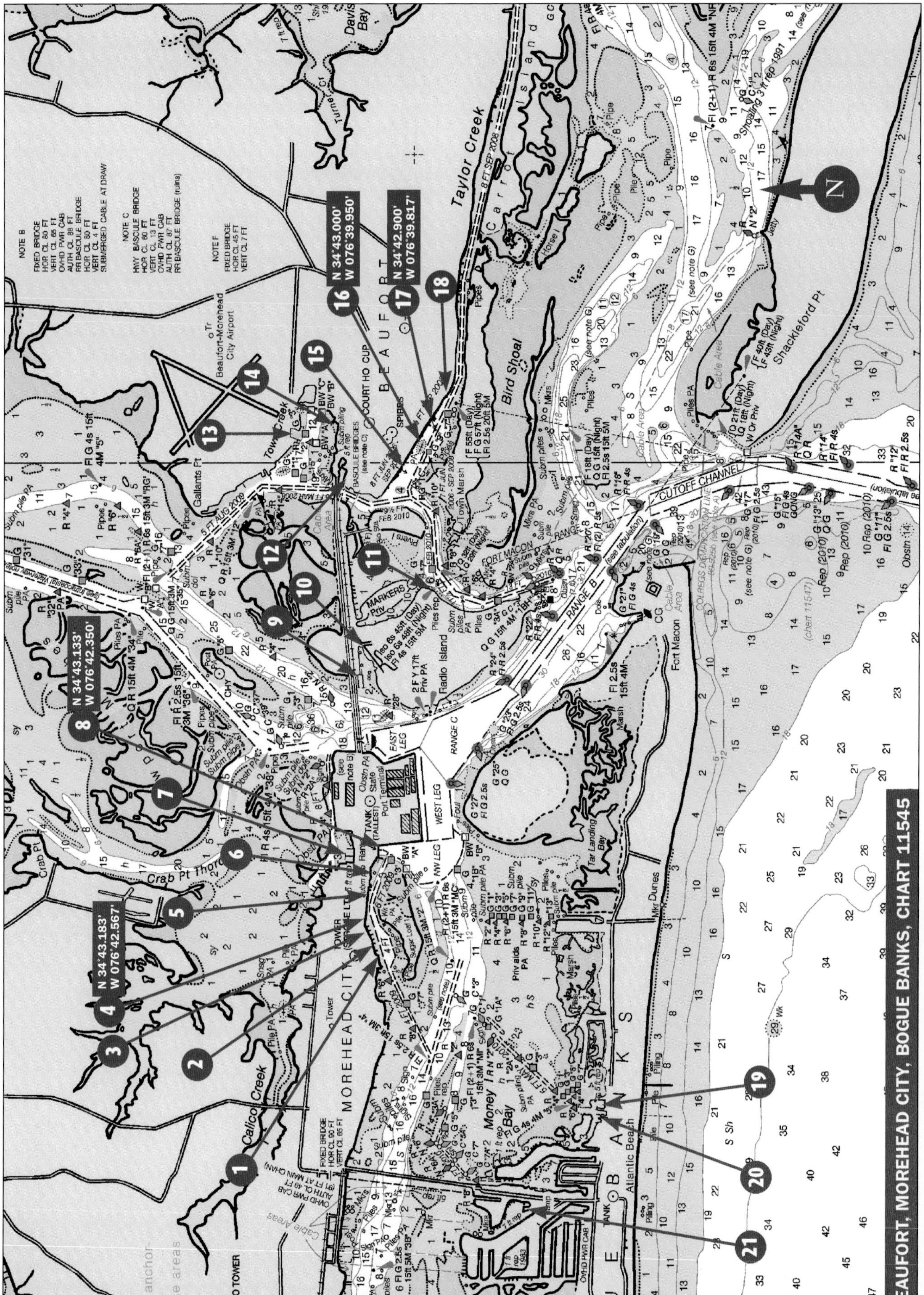
BEAUFORT, MOREHEAD CITY, BOGUE BANKS, CHART 11545
N 34°43.000' W 076°39.950'
N 34°42.900' W 076°39.817'
N 34°43.133' W 076°42.350'
N 34°43.183' W 076°42.567'
NOTE B
FIXED BRIDGE
HOR CL 60 FT
VERT CL 65 FT
OVHD PWR CAB
AUTH CL 88 FT
RR BASCULE BRIDGE
HOR CL 80 FT
VERT CL 4 FT
SUBMERGED CABLE AT DRAW
NOTE C
HWY BASCULE BRIDGE
HOR CL 80 FT
VERT CL 13 FT
OVHD PWR CAB
AUTH CL 87 FT
RR BASCULE BRIDGE (ruins)
NOTE F
FIXED BRIDGE
HOR CL 45 FT
VERT CL 7 FT
Taylor Creek
Bird Shoal
Shackleford Pt
Radio Island
Fort Macon
MOREHEAD CITY
BEAUFORT
Calico Creek
Money Bay
Atlantic Beach
Tar Landing Bay
Gallants Pt
Town Creek
Crab Pt
Davis Bay
Beaufort-Morehead City Airport
CUTOFF CHANNEL
RANGE B
RANGE C
WEST LEG
EAST LEG
NW LEG
State Port Terminal
Carrot Island
Horse I
Turner Cr

hotels, and for a time, was a popular vacation destination for plantation owners.

In 1974, as part of revitalization project, the waterfront began to transform from one of dilapidated fish houses into a yachting center. The renovation involved building a boardwalk and docks. Several homes and buildings scheduled for demolition, including the old brick jail, original courthouse and apothecary shop, were moved from the waterfront to Turner Street.

Culture: In Beaufort, the town is the culture and its seascape the canvas. Here, there is a flourishing arts community of painters, photographers, sculptors and writers. Galleries within walking distance of the docks include Art and Soul (220 Front St., 252-504-2005), Handscapes Gallery (410 Front St., 252-728-6805), Mattie King Davis Art Gallery (130 Turner St., 252-728-5225), and Scott Taylor Photography Gallery (214 Pollack St., 252-728-0900).

Attractions: The North Carolina Maritime Museum and Watercraft Center (315 Front St.) is the highlight of any visit to Beaufort. The museum has an active boatbuilding program and offers environmental education programs, including the Cape Lookout Studies Program. In their maritime store, you will find nautical and coastal books, gifts, prints and souvenirs. At their annex facility on Gallants Channel, next to Town Creek Marina, there is an exhibit on North Carolina shipwrecks. The exhibit consists of two major sections: "Underwater Archeology" and "The Shipwrecks." Photographs and artifacts include what is presumed to be the wreck of *Queen Anne's Revenge*, Blackbeard's flagship. For more information, call 252-728-7317.

On the 400 block of Ann Street, beneath the shade of live oak trees, you will find the Old Burying Ground (252-728-5225). Listed on the National Register of Historic Places, the cemetery was deeded to the town in 1731 by Nathaniel Taylor. The weathered tombstones chronicle the heritage of Beaufort and the surrounding coast. Union soldiers, Confederate soldiers, freed African-Americans and slaves all rest together in the Old Burying Ground.

The Beaufort Historic Site (100 block of Turner St.) consists of 10 buildings, 6 of which have been authentically restored. The Leffers Cottage was the home of Samuel

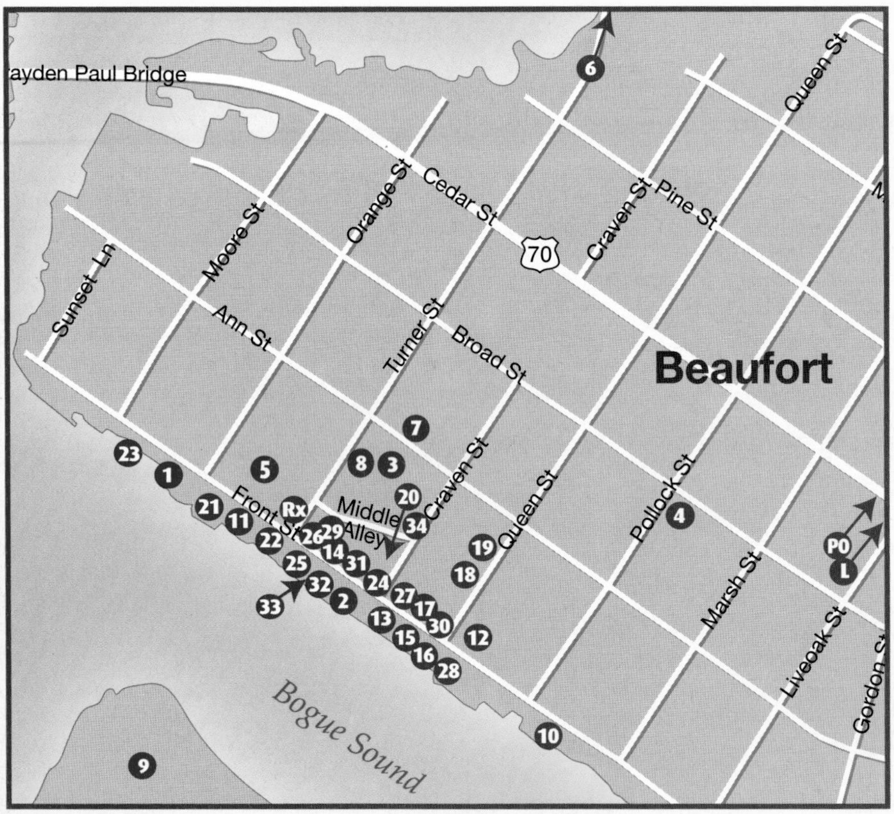

Reference the marina listing tables to see all the marinas in the area.

ART/ANTIQUES

1 Art and Soul
2 Handscapes Gallery
3 Mattie King Davis Art Gallery
4 Scott Taylor Photography

ATTRACTIONS

5 NC Maritime Museum & Watercraft Center
6 Maritime Museum Annex
7 Old Burying Ground
8 Beaufort Historic Society
9 Rachel Carson Reserve
10 Island Ferry Adventures
11 Outer Banks Ferry & Pirate Adventures
12 Ghost Walk (Inlet Inn)

DINING

13 Dockhouse Restaurant
14 Clawson's Restaurant
15 Queen Anne's Revenge
16 Boardwalk Café
17 Ribeyes Steakhouse
18 Beaufort Grocery Co.
19 Blue Moon Bistro
20 Aqua Restaurant
21 Front Street Grill at Stillwater
22 Finz Grill and Eatery
23 The Spouter Inn

SHOPPING

24 Harbor Specialties
25 Beaufort Trading Company
26 Bag Lady of Beaufort
27 Jarrett Bay Boathouse
28 Periwinkles
29 Tierra Fina
30 The General Store
31 Scuttlebutt
32 Top Deck
33 Rocking Chair Bookstore

GROCERIES/CARRYOUT

34 Treasure Chest Provisions

Rx PHARMACY

L LIBRARY

PO POST OFFICE

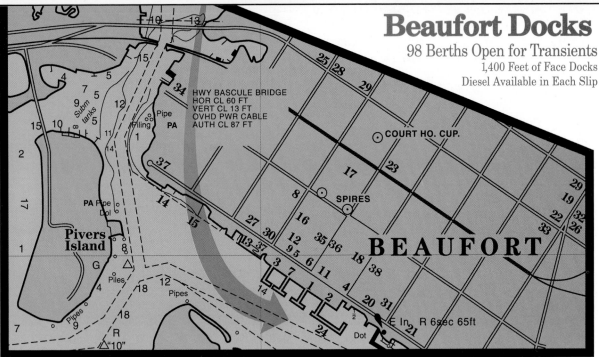

Leffers, a schoolmaster, merchant and clerk of the court. Inside, one can see artifacts relating to the daily chores of cooking, spinning, sewing, candlemaking and weaving. The Carteret County Courthouse is the oldest wood-framed courthouse in North Carolina. The John C. Manson House, with its Bahamian architecture, still stands on its original site. The Josiah Bell House served as the residence of the influential Bell family. The Old Jail has 28-inch-thick walls and boasts legends of ghosts and a single hanging in 1874. Built in 1859, the Apothecary Shop houses a unique collection of medicinal and pharmaceutical artifacts, most of which are original to the shop. For more information, call the Beaufort Historical Association at 252-728-5225.

Beyond the Front Street docks and across Taylors Creek, you will see the Rachel Carson Reserve (252-838-0890), part of the North Carolina National Estuarine Research Reserve. Wild ponies are frequently seen grazing near the anchorage along the shore of Carrot Island. Rent a kayak and paddle over or land in your tender.

There are several ferries that can shuttle you to Shackleford Island and Cape Lookout. Call Island Ferry Adventures (610 Front St., 252-728-7555) or Outer Banks Ferry Service (326 Front St., 252-728-4129) to book your tour of these unspoiled barrier islands. The Beaufort Ghost Walk leaves from the front of the Inlet Inn (601 Front St., 252-728-3600), covers approximately nine blocks and lasts around one hour.

Special events: In April, guests enjoy the Beaufort Food and Wine Weekend, which includes wine tastings, an auction, seminars, dinners, art exhibits and two days of delicious dining. Call 252-728-5225 for more information. In May, catch the Beaufort Music Festival.

Shopping: Immediately across Front Street from the docks, there are two banks, a laundry and a pharmacy. The post office is now located out of town by the Food Lion on Hwy. 70. For many, strolling through the shops and boutiques along Beaufort's waterfront and side streets is a just reward for the offshore passages and long hours on the ICW. Perhaps no store captures the flavor of Beaufort better than Harbor Specialties (127 Middle Lane, 252-838-0059). They sell dock and foredeck apparel including Tilley, Sperry and Henri Lloyd. For women, you will find handbags from Vera Bradley and flip-flops from Douglas Paquette. There is also a specialty shop devoted to model boats and nautical books.

The Beaufort Trading Company (400 Front St., 252-504-3209), located on the second floor of the Somerset Square, is where you can find hats and outdoor wear by Colombia, Teva and Sea Dog. The Bag Lady of Beaufort (413 Front St., 252-728-4200) sells handbags, totes and backpacks. Jarrett Bay Boathouse (507 Front St., 252-728-6363) carries a nice assortment of art, prints and clothing. Periwinkles (510 Front St.) is a stationery and gift shop. For unique home and garden items, visit Tierra Fina (119 Turner St., 252-504-2789). Finally, visit The General Store (515 Front St., 252-728-7707).

There are two excellent bookstores in town, Scuttlebutt Nautical Books (433 Front St., 252-728-7765) and Rocking Chair Bookstore in Somerset Square (400 Front St., 252-728-2671).

ADDITIONAL RESOURCES

- BEAUFORT HISTORIC SITE, 252-728-5225 www.beauforthistoricsite.org
- TOWN OF BEAUFORT, www.beaufortnc.org
- NORTH CAROLINA MARITIME MUSEUM, 252-728-7317 www.ncmaritime.org
- *QUEEN ANNE'S REVENGE* SHIPWRECK PROJECT, www.qaronline.org

NEARBY GOLF COURSES
Brandywine Bay Country Club, 177 Brandywine Blvd., Morehead City, NC 28557, 252-247-2541 (10 miles)
www.brandywinegolf.com/golf/proto/brandywinegolf

NEARBY MEDICAL FACILITIES
Carteret General Hospital, 3500 Arendell St., Morehead City, NC 28557, 252-808-6000 (5 miles)

Medical Park Pharmacy, 1513 Live Oak St, Beaufort, NC 28516, 252-504-2800

Restaurants: You will not need to stroll far to find a great meal in Beaufort. There are more than 10 restaurants within a 5-minute walk of the docks, but you can also dinghy around to Town Creek and enjoy a great meal at Dockhouse Restaurant (500 Front St., 252-728-4506), which offers live music on weekends, making it a popular stop along the boardwalk. Across the street is Clawson's 1905 Restaurant (425 Front St., 252-728-2133), a popular choice due to its ambiance and décor. Queen Anne's Revenge Restaurant (252-504-7272) and Boardwalk Café (252-728-0933) are both located at 510 Front St. Also, be sure to try Ribeyes, which specializes in Omaha steaks (509 Front St., 252-728-6105).

Around the corner on Queen Street is Beaufort Grocery Company (117 Queen St., 252-728-3899) with a reputation for service and quality. Nearby is Blue Moon Bistro (119 Queen St., 252-728-5800), which one local calls "beyond excellent." Another block over you will find the Aqua Restaurant (114 Middle Lane, 252-728-7777). Aqua offers exceptional dining in an urban-chic decor setting.

Try the Front Street Grill at Stillwater (300 Front St., 252-728-4956), serving lunch, dinner and Sunday brunch from a menu featuring regional cuisine with an emphasis on seafood. Finz Grill & Eatery (330 Front St., 252-728-7459) offers waterfront dining in a relaxed setting. The Spouter Inn (218 Front St., 252-728-5190) is a favorite with boaters. Make sure you save room for dessert.

Beaufort NORTH CAROLINA

Looking north over Morehead City, NC. (Not to be used for navigation.) WATERWAY GUIDE PHOTOGRAPHY.

Southbound Approach to Beaufort

NAVIGATION: Use Chart 11545. **Use the Cape Hatteras Tide Table. For high tide, add 7 minutes; for low tide, add 11 minutes.** Southbound vessels heading for Town Creek or the Beaufort waterfront should depart the ICW to port between quick flashing green "29" and flashing green "RS" (Mile 200.8), following the newly marked Russell Slough Channel east of the ICW and west of Russell Creek. Favor the green side of the channel at red daybeacon "4," and then, after making the turn to starboard at flashing green "5," plot a course to green daybeacon "7." Red daybeacon "6A," beyond red daybeacon "6," assists you in reaching green daybeacon "7." Where "8" used to be, there is now a lighted junction marker, flashing red "RG," with red at the top and green at the bottom of its board. Once past green daybeacon "7," turn immediately to port toward red daybeacon "10," and continue on to quick flashing red "12."

Vessels headed to the Beaufort waterfront should bear south and follow the Russell Slough Channel (also known locally as "Gallants Channel" where it passes Gallants Point and leads towards the Beaufort Bridge) markers through the Beaufort Bridge (13-foot closed vertical clearance, opening every 30 minutes from 6 a.m. to 10 p.m., no openings Monday through Friday between 6:30 a.m. and 8 a.m., and again between 4:30 p.m. and 6 p.m., otherwise on signal) and on to the Beaufort waterfront and Taylor Creek. Boaters needing assistance in entering Beaufort should contact Coast Guard Sector North Carolina or TowBoatU.S. in Beaufort.

Dockage: Town Creek Marina is located on Town Creek to port (turn at green daybeacon "1"), where you can find transient dockage, take on fuel at the marina's floating dock, pick up a complimentary map of town and catch the latest report on the Weather Channel. Restrooms and showers here are large, clean and air-conditioned. This is a major repair facility with a 50-ton lift. The popular Sand Bar Restaurant is upstairs. The marina provides a courtesy car for trips to the nearby supermarket or the Beaufort waterfront. It is also easy enough to take a ride to the waterfront via powered dinghy; you can tie up at the dinghy dock east of the Beaufort Docks.

Anchorage: Sometimes boats anchor to the northwest of Town Creek Marina. Due to the remains of sunken boats in the anchorage, as well as a few private moorings, anchorage space is minimal. The holding in this anchorage is poor. Anchoring space here is further limited by the docks and shoreside activities at the North Carolina Maritime Museum Conservation Lab.

To enter the local harbor of refuge on Town Creek, follow the marked channel to the Town Creek Marina. Then go past the marina into the triangular anchorage, with the apexes of the triangle marked by three black-and-white checkered daybeacons ("A," "B" and "C"). Although several vessels usually moor here, there is generally enough room remaining for a few more boats to anchor. The holding here is reported to be poor. Land

Looking over Beaufort Inlet and Morehead City Channel, NC. (Not to be used for navigation.) WATERWAY GUIDE PHOTOGRAPHY.

your dinghy on the small sandy beach to the southwest. If your tender is reasonably well powered, you can make the trip to the Beaufort waterfront via Russell Slough Channel and land at the dinghy dock at the southeast end of the town docks.

Southbound for the ICW from Town Creek

NAVIGATION: Use Charts 11545 and 11547. From Town Creek, head back out to Russell Slough Channel past Gallants Point, and make a 90-degree turn to the southwest around flashing red junction marker "RG," then into the deepwater cut that runs southeast of Chimney Island down to the Morehead City Highway Bridge and adjacent railroad span (Mile 203.8). This channel—the Chimney Island Channel—is wide and deep. The shallowest part (6.5 feet) is just north of the bridge. Be aware of markers in the Chimney Island Channel and those of Beaufort Inlet and Morehead City Channel, on the opposite side of the bridge; green is on starboard if southbound.

Beaufort: Taylor Creek Waterfront

The Beaufort waterfront along Taylor Creek is most easily accessed from the Radio Island Route (also known as the Bulkhead Channel) if coming in from the inlet or if northbound on the ICW.

NAVIGATION: Use Chart 11545. To reach Beaufort on the Taylor Creek waterfront, vessels northbound on the ICW should turn southeast from the ICW channel into the Turning Basin and enter the Morehead City Channel toward the inlet. After passing the southern tip of Radio Island, turn to port (northward) towards quick flashing red buoy "2" at the entrance to the Radio Island route into Beaufort. The Morehead City Channel was dredged in late 2010 into early 2011. Bulkhead Channel was dredged in early 2008. The previous dogleg from the main shipping channel was eliminated, and the channel into Beaufort makes a straight line from flashing red buoy "20" north to quick flashing red buoy "2" near the southern tip of Radio Island. The approach carries 16-foot depths and accommodates the resident fishing trawlers, up to 180 feet, that dock beyond the Beaufort Docks. Favor the green markers.

Remember that the numerous range markers for the entrance from the Beaufort Inlet are different from the red or green ICW lateral system or the lateral markers for the inlet. Many boats have mistaken these range markers (especially at night) for other navigation aids in this area, realizing their errors only once they have run aground.

Dockage: Beaufort Docks, on Taylor Creek, is convenient to all the waterfront attractions, businesses and services. Located on deep, protected water, Beaufort Docks has 98 slips maintained solely for transients. Six of the slips have single-phase 100-amp power for large vessels and four have three-phase 100-amp power. On approach, hail Beaufort Docks for directions on VHF Channel 16. The marina personnel will direct you to an appropriate slip. All slips exposed to the current run parallel to the shore to make docking easier. Check with the dockmaster on the state of the current as you make your approach and also be sure to ask for assistance when docking or getting underway. Unique features of the Beaufort Docks include diesel fuel available at each slip and complimentary wireless Internet service for guests. Courtesy cars are available for trips around town. The Dock House Restaurant and Lookout Lounge are conveniently located on premises. The bathhouse at the western end of the docks is available for a modest charge to boaters at anchor.

Anchorage: The large anchorage in Taylor Creek is convenient to town and also more crowded than the anchorages in Town Creek. The swift tidal current and the close quarters dictate that you use caution when anchoring. Anchor only on the southern side of the channel and consider using a Bahamian moor (two anchors in opposite directions, usually up and down the direction of the current), especially if other boats nearby are also using a Bahamian moor or are on moorings. This will help to limit your swinging distance and to better plant yourself in the swift currents. Be mindful of the precipitous shoaling along the southern side of the anchorage.

Huge menhaden ships use the channel at all hours to get to their docks upstream, and the Coast Guard frowns on anchored boats that encroach upon the channel. The town dock, across the street from the post office, has a convenient floating dinghy dock—look for the gazebo at the shore end. There is a second dinghy dock two blocks away, at the foot of Orange Street. There are a few private moorings within the anchorage and at least one new donation-based mooring off the post office/dinghy dock. Look for a sign for donation information.

BEAUFORT INLET

This inlet is deep, safe, easy, all-weather passage has made Morehead City/Beaufort an important port of entry. Note that older charts will not reflect the sea buoy's location farther offshore than in previous years, nor the channel's increased length and renumbering. The most recent chart at press time is dated March 2010.

If coming in from abroad, call the Customs and Border Protection Office at 252-726-5845 to request an inspector to clear you. When going out to a foreign port, order a U.S. Customs decal (apply online or download Form CF-339 at www.cbp.gov and click on Forms) before you go to save yourself time and paperwork upon returning to the United States. This will only benefit those who are returning to the United States within the calendar year of departure, as decals are purchased for a specific year. As part of the Department of Homeland Security's new clearing-in requirements, all persons aboard will have to also report to the immigrations office at the North Carolina State Port in Morehead City located in the North Carolina Maritime Building.

From inside the inlet, you can follow the fleet of sportfishermen to the Lookout Bight fishing spots for a sample of the ocean, even if you are not planning to run any distance outside. Charter captains can give you timely tips for running the inlet. If you do not have time to visit Cape Lookout in your own boat, water taxi service and speedboat trips are available from Beaufort.

From the Beaufort Inlet area, you can take the dinghy and do some real exploring. The long dinghy trip east through Taylor Creek out into Back Sound past Harkers Island and down to Cape Lookout provides a glimpse of North Carolina that transients do not often witness. This trip is for anyone with a large, sturdy, fast and reliable dinghy or shoal-draft cruiser and time on their schedule to play. On the return trip, follow Shackleford Banks on the inside from Middle Marsh to the inlet. There is some beautiful, clear water with many deserted sandy islands, quaint shoreline and plentiful wildlife—birds, fish and turtles. Be sure to leave time to explore Cape Lookout.

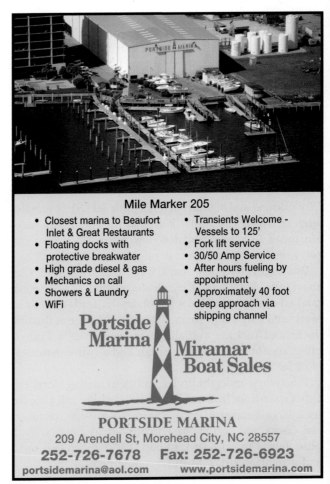

NAVIGATION: Use Chart 11541. To reach the inlet from the Beaufort waterfront in Taylor Creek, head west out of the creek, following the marked channel that swings to port past Radio Island and then joins the Morehead City and inlet channels. The inlet channel leads south past Shackleford Banks, then south-southwestward out to sea. Lights on the Shackleford Range markers at night are bright green, and skippers should identify them when making a night entry through the inlet. The range markers are much brighter than channel markers and have different characteristics. *(See page 69 for more information about Beaufort Inlet.)*

Morehead City—Mile 205

Like its sister city, Beaufort, Morehead City is a strategic spot on the southeast coast, and it has become a favorite for offshore skippers heading north to avoid the offshore rigors of Cape Hatteras. It is also popular with ICW boaters who are heading south and looking for a jaunt along the open Atlantic. Thus, a large marine community serving both commercial and recreational boats flourishes here. All repairs, from electronics and propellers to diesel engines, are available at Morehead City.

NAVIGATION: Use Charts 11545 and 11541. **Use the Cape Hatteras Tide Table. For high tide, add 26 minutes; for low tide, add 27 minutes.** From the north, the city is easily approached "from behind," by turning to starboard into the canal at red nun "2," about a quarter mile north of the fixed 65-foot vertical clearance Morehead City Highway Bridge and adjacent railroad bridge (both at Mile 203.8, railroad bridge normally open). Do not confuse this buoy with the red nun buoy on Chimney Island Channel farther north and east of the bridges. This approach leads to Morehead City Yacht Basin, the only facility for recreational vessels on the back side of the Morehead City waterfront.

As an alternative, the Morehead City waterfront-proper is approached from the ICW by taking a turn to starboard (west) around the Port Terminal Turning Basin (Mile 204.2), and then a sharp turn to the north at the west end of the Port Terminal before reaching junction light "MC" (Mile 205) to the west. Stay well off the bulkhead and be alert for ship and tug traffic around the terminal. Local authorities enforce a No-Wake Zone here 24 hours a day. Since currents run swiftly at 1 to 2 knots through the harbor cut, skippers of underpowered or slow-turning craft should pick a slack tide for docking duties.

Slow boats take note: Ebb tide begins at the Morehead City railroad and highway bridges (Mile 203.8) 11 minutes after the times given for Charleston Harbor. If you leave Morehead City southbound at low water slack, you can carry the flood tide south to around Mile 220.

Dockage: The first "back way" into Morehead City above the Morehead City Bridge, which has a well-marked canal dredged to 9.5-foot depths, leads directly to Morehead City Yacht Basin. Transient dockage at floating docks and fuel are available here, as well as a lounge/office area overlooking the harbor and a convenience car ($10 for 2 hours).

Proceeding under the bridge, and then entering Morehead City's waterfront from the Turning Basin, you will encounter a large number of establishments—marinas, commercial docks and seafood restaurants—that shoulder each other busily to starboard; to port, the uninhabited island and marshland strike a natural counterpoint.

Traveling west from the Turning Basin, Portside Marina is the first facility to starboard and offers transient slips on floating docks behind a protective breakwater, along with fuel and easy access to Beaufort Inlet. Dockside Yacht Club is second to starboard. Sanitary Fish Market is next, with face-dock moorage available to its restaurant patrons (without service or dockside amenities). Sanitary Fish Market also has a large retail seafood market. Morehead Gulf Docks next door (pumping gas and diesel) can accommodate large, deep-draft vessels at its face dock and has additional space at its new floating inner slips. Full water and shore power hookups are available and high-pressure pumps facilitate rapid gas and diesel delivery. Chef 105 is across the street. Captain Bill's Seafood Restaurant, just to the south, permits patron tie-ups for boats up to about 30 feet. Russell Yachts is next in line with repair capabilities.

Anchorage: Unfortunately, anchorage across from the waterfront is not advisable. Swinging room is limited, and high-speed reversing tidal currents rip through the area, although folks have been seen anchoring in the lee of Sugar Loaf Island.

GOIN' ASHORE:
MOREHEAD CITY, NC

Beyond the tip of Sugar Loaf Island, a skiff drifts with the current as an eddy forms near a channel marker. Ghosting behind a shoal at the edge of the ICW, a Sunfish tacks against a sticky summer breeze. A motorboat nudges a dock piling as the skipper tosses a boat fender over the side, a pair of ambitious boys leaping onto the dock as the boat comes to a stop. Past the cluster of deep sea charter fishing boats docked stern in, bow out, a crowd stands in line, waiting for a table at the Sanitary Fish Market and Restaurant.

While other towns boast of their "cute and quaint" coastal charm, Morehead City serves as a major port of entry, but it is not the freighters that draw boaters to town. It is the fish: king mackerel, yellowfin tuna, blue marlin, sailfish and amber jack. The head boats pull out in pre-dawn darkness and race out to the Gulf Stream to give their crew a chance at the big ones. The Big Rock is the granddaddy of the fishing tournaments, but there are others: The Calcutta Wahoo Challenge, Ducks Unlimited Billfish Tournament, Barta Boys and Girls Club and the Strike It Rich King Mackerel Tournament.

Along the waterfront, patrons file into the shops and stores, buying fresh seafood, books, beach toys and art. The town spills westward towards the high-rise bridge and strip malls, but for the boater, most of what you will need is within a 5- to 10-block walk from the marinas. Grocery stores, a post office, history museum and bookstore are all within walking distance. There is a dive shop nearby that can deliver you to some great wreck diving.

History: The area was originally called Shepherd's Point and marked the confluence of Newport River, Bogue Sound and Beaufort Inlet. However, Governor John Motley Morehead envisioned a great commercial hub, so he designed a town built around city blocks with a system of alleys between

Morehead City West, NC

MOREHEAD CITY WEST		Largest Vessel Accommodated	VHF Channel Monitored	Transient Berths / Total Berths	Approach / Dockside Depth (reported)	Floating Docks	Gas / Diesel	Groceries, Ice, Marine Supplies, Snacks	Repairs: Hull, Engine, Propeller	Lift (tonnage), Crane, Rail	1=110V, 2=220V, B=Both, Max Amps	Laundry, Pool, Showers	Pump-Out Station	Nearby: Grocery Store, Motel, Restaurant
		Dockage					Supplies		Services					
1. 70 West Marina 209.2	252-726-5171	55	16	/70	5/5		GD	GIMS	HEP	L20	B/50			GMR
2. Harbor Master Inc. 209.2	252-726-2541	50	16	2/30	8/5			M	HEP	L35,C	1/30	S		GMR
3. Taylor Boat Works 209.2	252-726-6374	60		3/8	8/6			M	HEP	R50	B/50	S		GMR
4. Coral Bay Marina 209.2	252-247-6900	50	16	/26	6/6		GD	IMS	HE		B/50	S		GMR
5. Spooners Creek Marina 210 (Internet Access) (Wireless Internet Access)	252-726-2060	100		10/85	7/8	F	GD	I			B/50	PS	P	GMR

Corresponding chart(s) not to be used for navigation. Internet Access; WiFi Wireless Internet Access

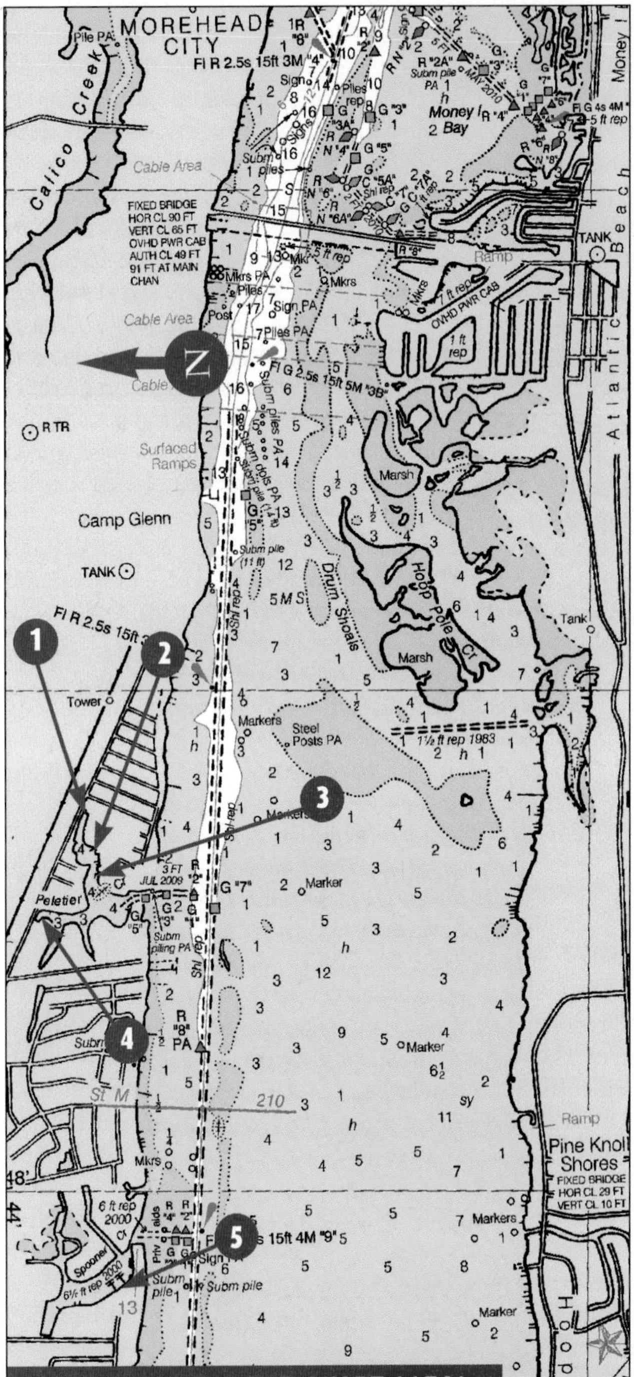

MOREHEAD CITY WEST, CHART 11541

each block in the form of an H. In this way, all houses and businesses could be serviced from the alleys. Each block contained 16 lots, and much of that "Philadelphia plan" remains today. Lots were sold to the public. Around the same time, rail service reached Shepherd's Point, and soon the town had grown to more than 300 citizens.

The Civil War interrupted Morehead's grand vision, and his project faltered, but after the war, the railroad allowed local fishermen to provide fresh seafood to markets in the Piedmont and the state capital. The hurricane of 1899 drove the residents in Diamond City off Shackleford Banks, and many found their way to Morehead City. These fisherman became the nucleus of a fishing industry that continues to thrive, shipping to restaurants throughout the country.

Culture: The Crystal Coast Jamboree (1311 Arendell St., 252-726-1501) features comedy, gospel, bluegrass, dance and musical tributes in the tradition of Nashville, Branson and Myrtle Beach.

Throughout the year, The History Place (1008 Arendell St., 252-247-7533) hosts classical music concerts in conjunction with The American Music Festival. Carolina Artists Studio Gallery (801 Arendell St., 252-726-7550) is a non-profit cooperative offering a diverse selection of original two-and-three dimensional art and a limited number of prints.

The Carteret County Curb Market, located at the corner of 13th and Evans streets, runs the oldest continuously operating curb market in North Carolina. Stalls open each Saturday through Labor Day at 7:30. Come and pick from fresh vegetables, local seafood, cut flowers and baked goods.

Special events: In October, the Morehead City waterfront hosts the North Carolina Seafood Festival, where you can sample fresh seafood while listening to live entertainment. Morehead City is also home to the Bald-Headed Men of America, whose motto boast that they are the; "World's only organization that grows because of a lack of growth." The BHMA hold their annual convention the second weekend of September.

Attractions: A good place to begin your tour of Morehead City is at the Crystal Coast Visitors Center (3409 Arendell St., 252-726-8148) Here, you will find brochures and directions to local attractions. The History Place Museum (1008 Arendell St., 252-247-7533) houses a collection of Carteret County artifacts and an excellent research library, which contains one of the best collections of Civil War materials in eastern North Carolina. A gift shop offers books on a wide variety of subjects, and unique gifts for children and adults.

The Olympus Dive Center (713 Shepard St., 252-726-9432) offers deep sea diving. Depending on conditions, you may be able to dive on an 18th century schooner, cargo ship, British fishing trawler, World War I gunboat or German submarine.

In calm conditions, you can dinghy to Fort Macon State Park (2300 E. Fort Macon Rd., Atlantic Beach, 252-726-3775), although it may be more convenient to rent a car. The pentagon-shaped fortress, built between 1826 and 1834, is the centerpiece of a 398-acre state park that offers swimming, fishing, nature programs and trails, and guided tours of the Fort. If you rent a car, make sure you visit the North Carolina Aquarium in Pine Knoll Shores (1 Roosevelt Blvd., Pine Knoll Shores, 252-247-4003). The Precious Waters exhibit features a 2,000-gallon salt marsh aquarium and a riverbank display with live alligators.

Shopping: For boat and hardware supplies, stop in at Ace Marine Rigging & Supply (600 Arendell St., 252-726-6620), or try Big Rock Propellers (111 Turner's Dairy Road, 252-222-3618) and Crystal Coast Cordage (1103 Evans St., 252-726-8452).

Dee Gee's Gifts & Books (508 Evans St., 252-726-3314) carries a great selection of nautical books, fiction, non-fiction and works by local authors. The City News Stand (514 Arendell St., 252-726-6820) is a good choice for magazines and periodicals.

If you are shopping for the rare and collectable, visit one of the many antiques shops along the waterfront. Here are just a few of the antiques stores that are near the waterfront: Evans Street Company Antiques (706 Evans St., 252-240-2077), Light Tender's Cottage (510 Arendell St., 252-247-3382), Jib Street Museum (713 Evans St., 252-222-4838), Old Towne Theater Antiques (1308 Arendell St., 252-247-7478), and Seaport Antique Market (509 Arendell St., 252-726-6606).

For art, pottery and sculpture, visit Carteret Contemporary Arts (1106 Arendell St., 252-726-4071). Waterfront Junction (412 Evans St.) and the Windward Gallery (508-C Evans St., 252-726-6283) are also located near the waterfront.

Restaurants: For dining, try Captain Bill's Restaurant (710 Evans St., 252-726-2166) or Bistro by the Sea (4031 Arendell St., 252-247-2777). Of course, no visit to Morehead City is complete without a meal at the Sanitary Restaurant (501 Evans St., 252-247-3111). With such an abundance of fine dining options, however, you might want to stroll the downtown waterfront before making your final choice. Floyd's 1921 Restaurant (400 Bridges St., 252-727-1921), Piccata's (506 Arendell St., 252-240-3380), Beach Bumz Pub & Pizzaria (515 Arendell St., 252-726-7800), Shepard's Point (913 Arendell St., 252-727-0815), Ruddy Duck Tavern (509 Evans St., 252-726-7500) and Jack's Waterfront Bar (513 Evans St., 252-247-2043) all come highly recommended. Coffee, tea and sweets are available at Seaside Cheesecake Dessert Shoppe (1002 Arendell St., 252-726-2339). Just a short walk from the waterfront is Raps Grill and Bar (709 Arendell St., 252-240-1213).

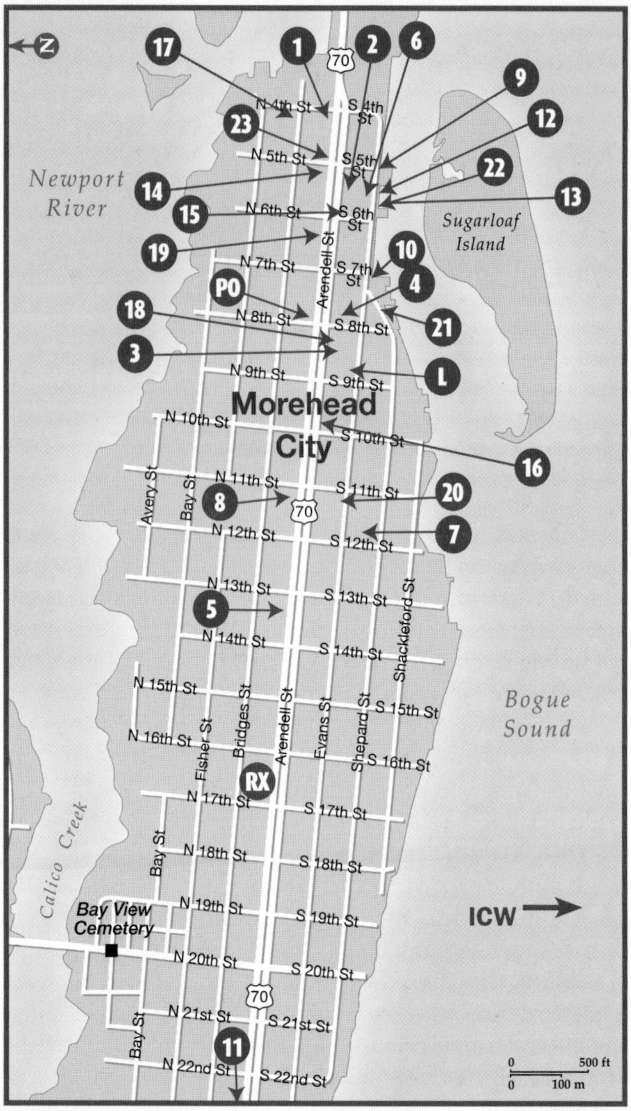

Reference the marina listing tables to see all the marinas in the area.

ART/ANTIQUES
1 Light Tender's Cottage
2 Seaport Antique Market
3 Carolina Artists Studio Gallery
4 Jib Street Museum
5 Old Towne Theater Antiques
6 Windward Gallery

ATTRACTIONS
7 The Crystal Coast Jamboree
8 The History Place

DINING
9 Sanitary Restaurant
10 Captain Bill's Restaurant
11 Bistro by the Sea
12 Ruddy Duck Tavern
13 Jack's Waterfront Bar
14 Piccatta's
15 Beach Bumz Pub Pizzaria
16 Shephard's Point
17 Floyd's 1921 Restaurant

INFO
18 Chamber of Commerce

MARINE SUPPLIES
19 Ace Marine Rigging & Supply
20 Crystal Coast Cordage

RECREATION
21 The Olympus Dive Center

SHOPPING
22 Dee Gee's Gifts & Books
23 The City News Stand

L LIBRARY
PO POST OFFICE
Rx PHARMACY

ADDITIONAL RESOURCES

- MOREHEAD CITY INFORMATION, www.morehead.com
- NORTH CAROLINA PORTS, www.ncports.com
- NORTH CAROLINA SEAFOOD FESTIVAL, www.ncseafoodfestival.org

NEARBY GOLF COURSES

Brandywine Bay Country Club, 177 Brandywine Blvd., Morehead City, NC 28557, 252-247-2541 (7 miles) www.brandywinegolf.com/golf/proto/brandywinegolf

NEARBY MEDICAL FACILITIES

Carteret General Hospital, 3500 Arendell St., Morehead City, NC 28557, 252-808-6000 (3 miles)

Coastal Eye Clinic, 3504 Bridges St., Morehead City, NC 28557, 252-726-1064 (3 miles)

Beachcare Urgent Care Center, 5059 U.S. 70, Morehead City, NC 28557, 252-808-3696 (3 miles)

Walgreens Pharmacy, 2202 Arendell St., Morehead City, NC 28557, 252-222-3643

Morehead City Drug Co., 1704 Arendell St., Morehead City, NC 28557, 252-726-2106

Robertson, David P. DDS, 3002 Bridges St., Morehead City, NC 28557, 252-726-1461

Rejoining the ICW

If your vessel draws 4 feet or more, and you want to continue southbound down the ICW, it is safest to go back around the island to the Morehead City Harbor's east entrance, follow the buoys carefully, and then rejoin the ICW channel. The western exit, which is adequately marked, shows 4-foot depths on the most current chart (dated March 2010), and shoaling has been reported.

Atlantic Beach—Mile 206 (Oceanside)

The north end of Bogue Banks (the long barrier strip running south from Beaufort Inlet, protecting Morehead City and nearby communities from Atlantic swells) is a resort area. Money Island and Atlantic Beach are set on grassy sand dunes that are among the highest and most scenic on the East Coast. Atlantic Beach, like Long Island, NY, runs east to west and faces south. Restaurants, motels, condominiums and an amusement park are here. Some of the approach channels were reportedly shoaling, so check locally for depths. The Atlantic Beach Causeway Marina can provide information and assistance on VHF Channel 16, as can local towboat operators.

At the east end of Atlantic Beach is Fort Macon, which was built between 1826 and 1834. The pentagon-shaped fortress is part of a 400-acre state park. In 1862, the fort came under attack for 30 days. Union troops eventually captured the fort, which gave them control of North Carolina's coastline. Now, the fort is an interesting place to experience guided tours, audio-visual displays and other various historical exhibits. Swimming, fishing, nature trails and picnic tables are also available at the state park. If time permits, another interesting stop is the North Carolina Aquarium at Pine Knoll Shores.

NAVIGATION: Use Chart 11541. At Mile 206, the markers to the side-channels in Atlantic Beach become very confusing. Be sure to sort them out before proceeding along the ICW or up one of the side channels.

To reach the westernmost of Morehead City's services, follow the marked ICW channel through the Atlantic Beach Bridge (Mile 206.7, 65-foot fixed vertical clearance). The bridge's tide boards and cruisers consistently report 2 to 3 feet less than the charted 65-foot fixed vertical clearance here and also at the Morehead City Bridge at Mile 203.8. Do not mistake the RESUME SPEED sign just above the bridge for green daybeacon "3A." The sign is in shallow water, and boats have gone aground here by making that mistake.

The marked side channel through Money Bay carries 6-foot depths and leads to the Anchorage Marina (fuel, supplies and transient dockage) and Fort Macon Marina (boat repairs). The channel along the fixed bridge is subject to shoaling. Call the Atlantic Beach Causeway Marina for the latest information on channel depths. The marina offers dockage, fuel and supplies. Note that there is a large docking facility for research vessels just west of the Atlantic Beach Bridge.

Peletier Creek—Mile 209

On the western outskirts of Morehead City and considered part of its general area, Peletier Creek is a couple of miles west of the city proper. The Peletier Creek marinas and anchorage are popular with locals and transients.

NAVIGATION: Use Chart 11541. The entrance is well marked and has a controlling depth of 6 feet at mean low water from a July 2009 survey and 8 feet at mid-tide. Stay in the middle between the creek's green daybeacons "3" and "5." Do not go near green daybeacon "3" or the private docks. Inside the creek, 5-foot depths (or better) continue to the complex of yards and marine installations up the right-hand prong. Inside, at the junction of the two prongs, is room for four or five boats to anchor. Dredging of Bogue Sound, between the Atlantic Beach Bridge (Mile 206.7) and the Cedar Point Bridge (Mile 226) was last completed in March 2008.

Dockage: Peletier Creek has good repair yards, boatbuilders, and a restaurant and bar for pickup and delivery. There is also a shopping center with a grocery store, liquor store and deli. The marine railways are capable of hauling both sailboats and powerboats. Mechanics, too, are available here. Several marinas have transient slips, including Taylor Boat Works and Harbor Master. Entrance depths are reportedly holding steady at 6 feet, with 5-foot or better depths up the creek into the marinas. Each offers a variety of services.

Spooner Creek—Mile 210.7

A mile farther down the ICW, the large basin at Spooner Creek (or Spooners Creek as it is referred to by locals) is surrounded by nice homes and docks. It has a marked entrance channel off the ICW at flashing green "9." A condominium development, which had been under construction at the mouth of Spooner Creek for a few years, is now complete and is known as The Shores. Spooners Creek Marina has been totally rebuilt. The entrance depth in the marked channel leading into Spooner Creek is reported to be 7 feet deep at mean low water. Also, note that the former range markers are no longer in place. High tide is approximately two and a half hours later here than at Beaufort.

Dockage: Spooners Creek Marina has all-new facilities. Transient dockage on floating piers, fuel (both gas and diesel) and pump-out facilities are available, though the slips are also offered for private sale. There is no store, but a 24-hour Walmart is within walking distance, as are restaurants.

Anchorage: Boats sometimes anchor in the middle of the widest part of the creek, but the area may offer poor holding. Numerous new docks on Spooner Creek have reduced anchorage space. The small dock at the head of the creek is no longer available for landing.

To Wrightsville Beach

Coverage of the ICW continues in the next chapter, "Bogue Sound to Southport." An offshore jaunt from Beaufort Inlet to Masonboro Inlet at Wrightsville Beach is approximately 73 miles, while the inside route is about 70 miles. ■

WATERWAY GUIDE advertising sponsors play a vital role in bringing you the most trusted and well-respected cruising guide in the country. Without our advertising sponsors, we simply couldn't produce the top-notch publication now resting in your hands. Next time you stop in for a peaceful night's rest, let them know where you found them—WATERWAY GUIDE, The Cruising Authority.

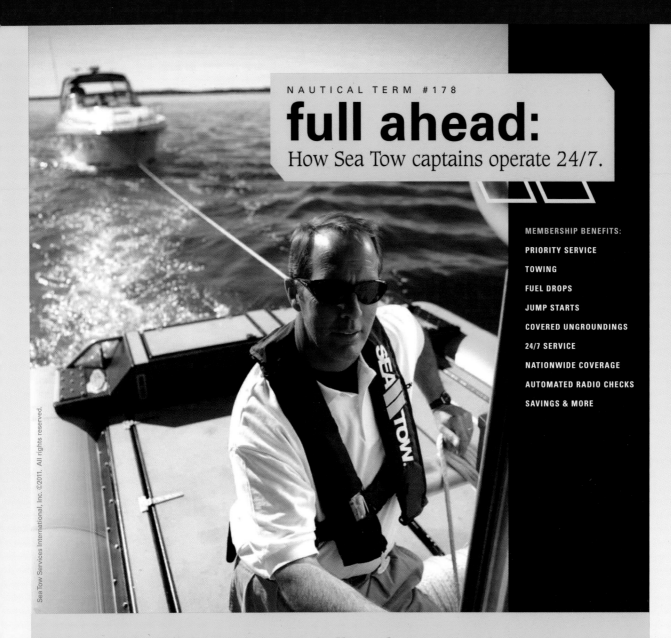

Morehead City to Charleston

■ MOREHEAD CITY TO CAPE FEAR ■ CAPE FEAR TO CHARLESTON ■ CHARLESTON AND ENVIRONS

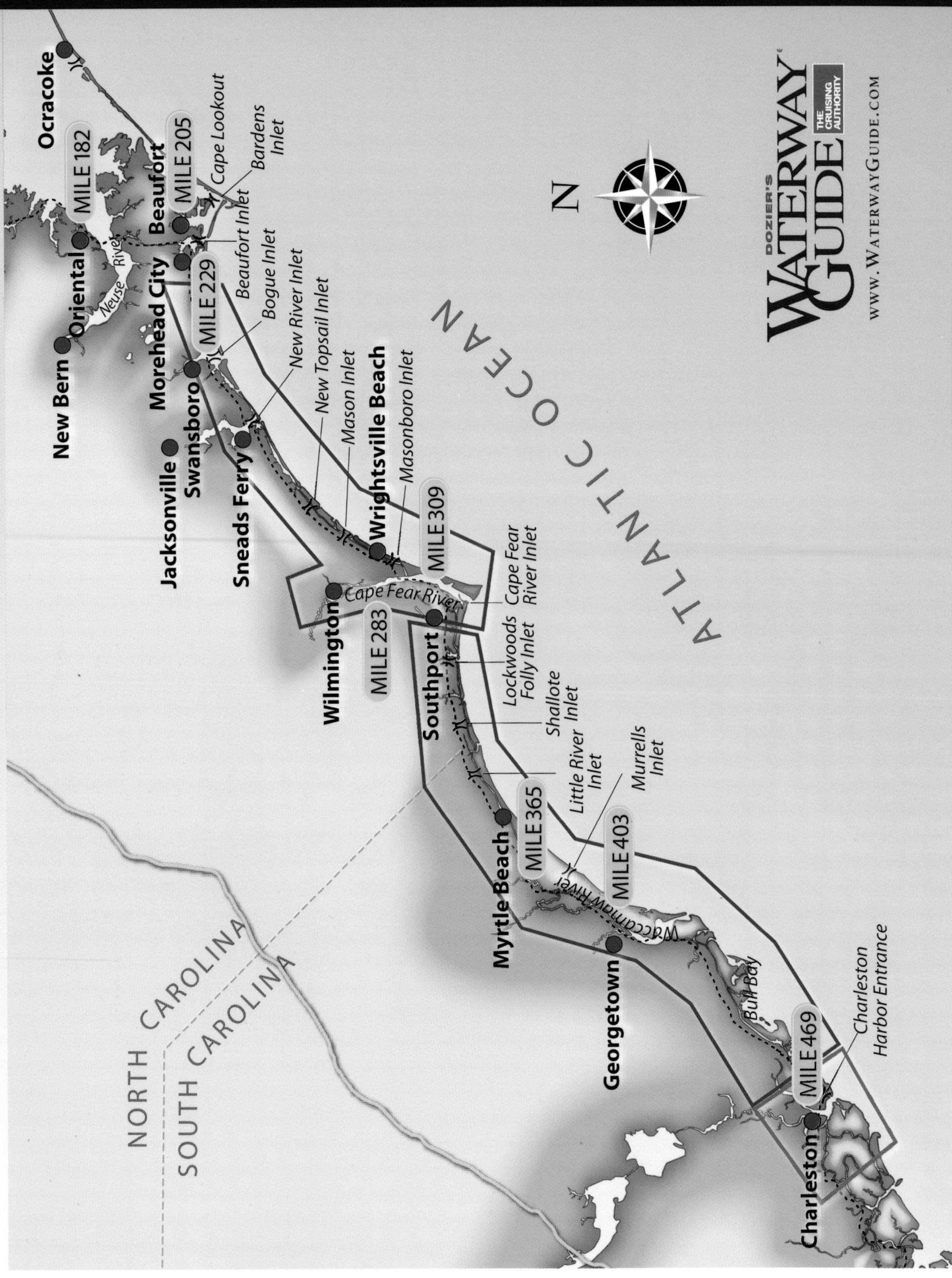

Charleston Area Convention and Visitors Bureau

Introduction

Morehead City to Charleston

Roughly 265 miles along the Intracoastal Waterway (ICW) from Bogue Sound in North Carolina to Charleston, SC, this passage will slowly reveal different kinds of waterways and scenery. The wide, deep waters of the North Carolina sounds are behind you, and the route now follows a succession of dredged channels through small sounds, shallow sloughs and salt marshes, all connected by a series of land cuts. Halfway along the passage, North Carolina gives way to South Carolina.

Cruising Characteristics

This section of the ICW has more than its fair share of bridges, particularly in the stretch between Swansboro and Georgetown (South Carolina). Seventeen of these are fixed high-level bridges. Boats with masts taller than 65 feet must run outside from Beaufort Inlet, NC to Georgetown or Charleston, SC, both of which have safe big-ship entrances.

With the reduction of dredging funds, shoaling continues to be an issue in some sections of this stretch of the ICW. While we cover these areas in detail in this section, certain areas require your utmost attention, including Bear to Browns Inlet crossings, Carolina Beach Inlet Crossing, New River Crossing, Lockwoods Folly Inlet Crossing and Shallotte Inlet Crossing. The Bear to Browns Inlet area (around Mile 238) was dredged in March 2010, dredging took place in April 2010 in Carolina Beach Inlet Crossing and in December 2010, the New River Crossing was dredged. The Bogue Inlet Crossing area was dredged in January 2010, moving 65,000 cubic yards of sand to Emerald Isle Beach. The entire Bogue Sound from the Atlantic Beach Bridge (Mile 206.7) to the Cedar Point Highway Bridge (Mile 226) north of Swansboro was dredged in early 2008 and parts were redredged in 2010. Check the *Local Notice to Mariners* (www.navcen.uscg.gov/lnm/d5) for possible changes in the markers. Also check the U.S. Army Corps of Engineers (USACE) for current surveys at www.saw.usace.army.mil/nav for North Carolina and www.sac.usace.army.mil/?action=navigation.surveymaps for South Carolina.

When shoaling becomes a problem, the USACE does its best to survey these areas and frequently gives specific GPS waypoints that you can use to avoid the shoals. Be aware that conditions may change between the survey date and the time you pass through. The State of North Carolina and some localities are providing funds for dredging, along with some money appropriated in the fiscal year 2011. The Federal Budget for the USACE to dredge parts of the ICW is around $4.75 million for North Carolina and slightly less than $1 million for South Carolina. *(See page 61 for more detailed information about Inlets.)*

Keeping an eye on tidal currents is important in this area; beginning at Morehead City, you suddenly encounter

Bridges / Distances

(Approximate Statute Miles from Mile Zero, Norfolk, VA)

LOCATION	MILE	CLEARANCE
Morehead City Bridge (SR 1182)	206.7	65'
Peletier Creek Green Daybeacon "7"	209.5	
Spooner Creek Flashing Green "9"	210.4	
Cedar Point Highway Bridge	226.0	65'
Swansboro Flashing Red "46C"	229.4	
Onslow Beach Swing Bridge	**240.7**	**12'**
Highway Bridge	252.3	65'
Surf City Swing Bridge	**260.7**	**12'**
Figure Eight Island Swing Bridge	**278.1**	**20'**
Wrightsville Beach Bridge	**283.1**	**20'**
Carolina Beach Entrance Light "161"	295.2	
Snows Cut Highway Bridge (U.S. 421)	295.7	65'
Southport Flashing Red "1"	308.7	
Highway Bridge (SR 133)	311.8	65'
Highway Bridge (SR 110)	316.8	65'
Highway Bridge (SR 130)	323.6	65'
Ocean Isle Bridge (SR 904)	333.7	65'
Sunset Beach Pontoon Bridge (SR 1172)	**337.9**	**0'**
Highway Bridge	347.2	65'
Little River Swing Bridge (SR 20)	**347.3**	**7'**
Myrtle Beach Connector Bridge	349.1	65'
Barefoot Landing Swing Bridge	**353.3**	**31'**
Conway Bypass Bridge (U.S. 17)	355.5	65'
Grande Dunes High-rise Bridge	357.5	65'
Grissom Parkway Bridge	360.5	65'
SCL Railroad Bridge	365.4	16'
Highway Bridge (U.S. 501)	365.4	65'
Fantasy Harbor Bridge	366.4	65'
Socastee Swing Bridge (SR 544)	**371.0**	**11'**
Highway Bridge	371.3	65'
Bucksport Flashing Red "38"	377.5	
Wachesaw Landing Flashing Green "57"	383.7	
Highway Bridge (U.S. 17)	402.1	65'
Georgetown Entrance	402.8	
Estherville Minim Creek Canal Ferry	411.5	
McClellanville Flashing Green "35"	430.0	
Andersonville Flashing Red "68"	444.2	
Isle of Palms Connector Bridge	458.9	65'
Ben Sawyer Memorial Swing Bridge	**462.2**	**31'**
James Island Expressway Bridge	469.9	67'
Wappoo Creek Bridge	**470.8**	**33'**

*Clearance is vertical, closed, in feet. *Not radio equipped. Bridges and locks in bold type have restricted openings. SR=State Route*

tide and tidal current conditions quite different from those on the run down from Norfolk. The 3-foot tidal fluctuation becomes progressively greater and peaks at 9 feet in Georgia. It is important to have accurate tide and current information available when traveling this portion of the ICW. This information is available at http://tidesonline.nos.noaa.gov, or you may already have tide and tidal current tables on your chartplotter or in your computer navigation program. If these options are not available, then obtain a tide and current table book for this area. They are usually sold at the same stores that sell charts.

Tidal currents, growing stronger as you head south, are strongest around inlets, bridges and converging waterways, which have a side-sweeping effect. Try to visualize beforehand which way the current might push (or pull) your boat and consider how an ebb or flood tide might affect the situation. (In some places, it is difficult to tell which direction the ebb and flood will travel.) Learn to check your course astern from the relative position of the markers and steer to compensate. Places where the side-setting effect of the current can be serious are detailed in the text.

When approaching a bridge with the current, have your boat under control and do not move in too close while waiting for the bridge to open. There is no regulation on these waters as to which boat has the right-of-way passing through bridges, but it is generally accepted that a boat going against the current should yield to one going with the current. It is foolish and dangerous to contest the channel with another boat under any circumstance.

Keep track of the tidal currents, whether flooding or ebbing, and at what stage. Be careful to follow the marked channel, particularly on a falling tide, as going aground then can be serious. Your boat might wind up high and dry, allowing for the possibility of a swamping when the tide begins to rise.

Note: Small-craft paper charts have each five statute-mile increment marked along the "magenta line" of the ICW, and these "Mile Markers" on the charts are commonly used to identify the locations of bridges, businesses, marinas, aids to navigation, anchorage locations, etc. In much, but not all, of North Carolina and a very few other areas of the ICW, the Corps of Engineers has placed signs just outside the channel marking each five-mile increment along the route. Note that the numbers on these signs do not necessarily correspond to the "Mile Markers" on the charts. Some are the same, some are different by a hundred yards or so, and some by as much as a mile. If you are using the actual signs to determine your location in relation to a timed bridge or marina location, you may find yourself a lot closer or farther away than you thought. Use the paper charts for this information, but make sure you have the most current edition of the chart.

While the mile marker figures do not change, aids to navigation are frequently moved or relocated to reflect the current deep part of navigable channels. If a marker or two on your chart appears to be on the wrong side of the magenta line, don't be alarmed. In most cases, the marker has been moved as conditions have changed and is in the correct position on the chart, but the magenta line has not been changed. Rather than constantly changing the magenta line, it has been removed on some charts in areas where there is frequent shoaling and markers are changed often. ■

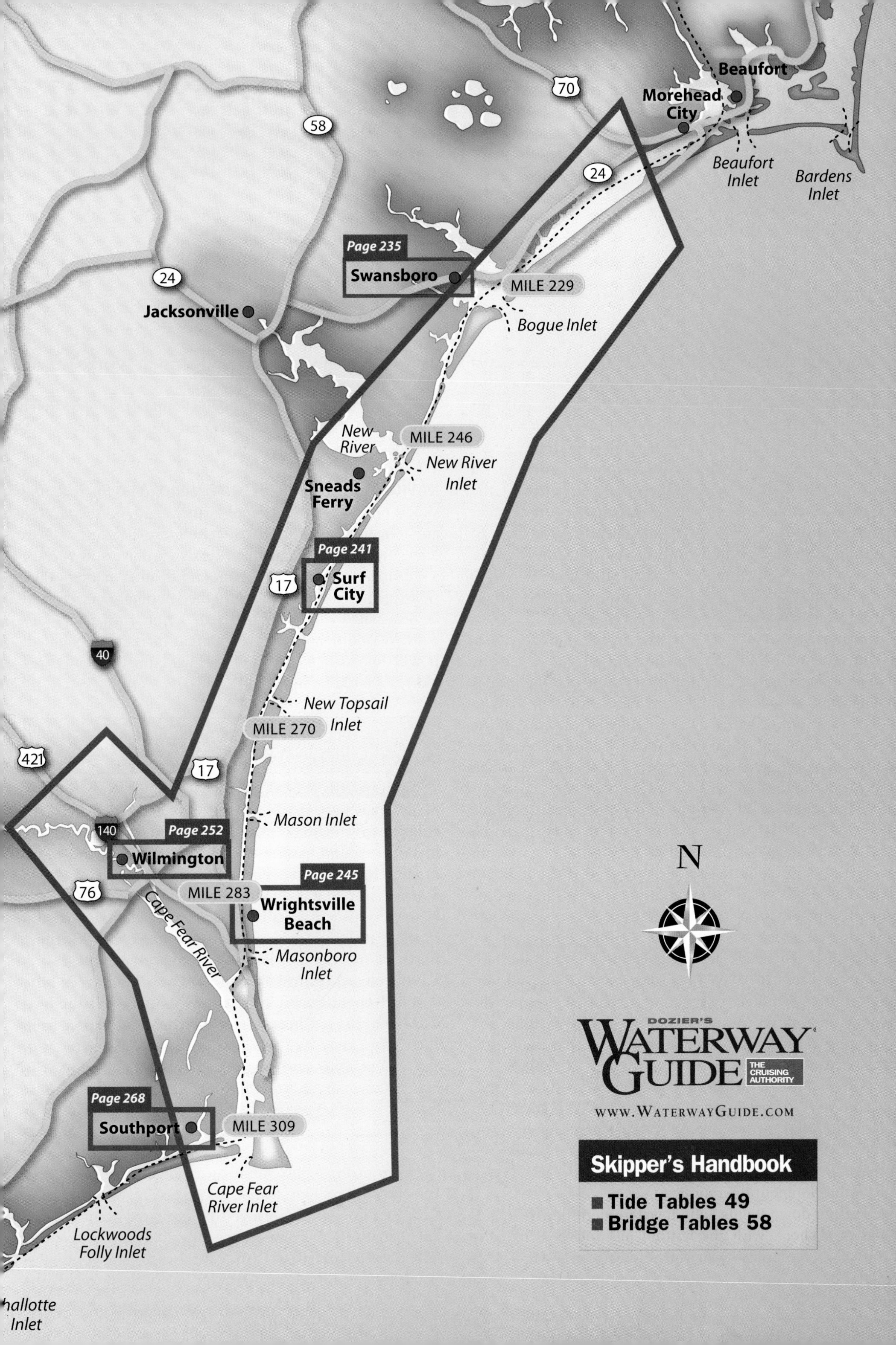

Skipper's Handbook

- Tide Tables 49
- Bridge Tables 58

Morehead City to Cape Fear

ICW Mile 211–Mile 315

VHF North Carolina Bridges: Channel 13

CHARTS 11534, 11536, 11537, 11539, 11541, 11542, 11543, 11544, 11545

Below Morehead City (Mile 205), the Intracoastal Waterway (ICW) follows Bogue Sound almost 25 miles to Swansboro (Mile 229), the port for Bogue Inlet. The ICW channel to Swansboro is marked with daybeacons and lights; green and red are staggered, with few exceptions. The only possible hazard is that a beam wind will set you on the often-hard edge of the dredged channel. Watch behind you and be sure to steer toward the windward side of the channel so if you go aground, the wind will help push you off. Currents and tides are also something to contend with here. Be aware of tides and the timing of their occurrences; you can use them to your advantage with proper planning.

Bogue Sound was last dredged by the United States Army Corps of Engineers in spring 2010. It is a narrow channel so it is a good idea to set your depth sounder alarm at 8 feet; if it sounds and the depth continues to decrease, slow down. This method helps you stay in the channel and spot shoal areas. With its sometimes scattered shoaling and shallow water outside the channel, Bogue Sound is a good place to use this technique.

The Bogue Sound route is by no means monotonous. Covered with tall pines and windswept oaks, the high mainland side is dotted with beautiful homes, many with private docks along the sound. Dolphins often frequent the sound's lower portion, and goats sometimes appear on the spoil islands. You can also expect to see people digging for clams.

Opposite the mainland, Bogue Banks stands in stark contrast. From the ICW, this long barrier island no longer appears as a dense growth of scrub pine and myrtle. More and more, vacation homes, condominiums and resorts, all vulnerable to frequent hurricanes, are covering the sand dunes.

The explorer Verrazzano sighted this island in 1524, recording what historians believe is the first written description of America. Early American Indians lived on the island, and archaeology teams have excavated the remains of several of their villages, uncovered during land development operations.

Farther down Bogue Sound, waters alongside the channel turn shoal, with the bottom just inches below the surface. Commercial watermen sometimes wade rather than work from their boats, and often the workboats are deliberately grounded on tiny islets.

The aids to navigation in Bogue Sound on to New River and then to the Cape Fear River are located 30 to 35 feet outside the channel limits.

NAVIGATION: Use Charts 11541 and 11534. Encroaching shoals on Bogue Sound—and farther south on the ICW—are frequently marked with temporary floating aids to navigation until dredging can correct problems. If you see a stationary beacon and a temporary floating marker of the same identification (sometimes the temporary marker will be designated with an "A" or a "B"), honor the temporary marker. Additionally, if the original marker was lighted, it will be extinguished and the light on the temporary marker should be honored.

THE FOLLOWING AREA REQUIRES SPECIAL ATTENTION DUE TO SHOALING OR CHANGES TO THE CHANNEL

BROWNS INLET CROSSING

Many areas between Morehead City and Swansboro are subject to shoaling, despite frequent dredging. Parts of Bogue Sound can be especially shallow at the edges of the channel. Keep current with the *Local Notice to Mariners* regarding shoaling in this stretch, or check the Waterway Guide website. The worst shoaling is usually in the vicinity of Browns Inlet Crossing (Mile 238) just north of the Onslow Beach Swing Bridge (Mile 240.7, 12-foot closed vertical clearance). The area between Mile 235 at Bear Inlet and 238 at Browns Inlet was dredged in March 2010. Check for up-to-date information from the Coast Guard and the most recent USACE surveys of the area at www.saw.usace.army.mil/nav/aiww.htm. The current reverses at around Mile 238.

END SPECIAL CAUTION AREA.

Currents in Bogue Sound occasionally run swiftly at velocities up to 1 to 2 knots. Be especially careful at the Cedar Point Highway Bridge (65-foot fixed vertical clearance) at Mile 226. From here to Mile 290, current reversals at the various inlets work to cancel each other out. Slow boats leaving Morehead City during the last part of the flood tide usually catch the first of the ebb tide at about Mile 220. Then, a fair tide carries to the point where Bogue Inlet meets at Swansboro, a few miles below the Cedar Point high-level bridge (Mile 226). Be careful here to avoid mistaking inlet channel markers for ICW aids to navigation; the inlet markers do not have the yellow squares and triangles characteristic of the ICW. Favor the mainland side. Since it is subject to shifting bars and shoaling, Bogue Inlet should not be used except by smaller boats with local knowledge. Note: In early 2011, shoaling was noted by a Waterway Guide cruising editor just north of red daybeacon "40A" Mile 224.5. ***(See page 61 for more detailed information about Inlets.)***

Swansboro—Mile 229

Popular with inland anglers, Swansboro also has a sizable charter fishing fleet of considerable commercial importance because of its inlet. Swansboro is a friendly town with good dining, convenient provisioning and numerous small antiques shops, all making it increasingly popular as a tourist destination.

NAVIGATION: Use Chart 11541. In approaching Swansboro, be wary of crosscurrents and their side-setting effect, particularly on the ebb. Here, and at other places like it, the flow out of the river accelerates the current. Stay to mid-channel, favoring the mainland side between green can "45A" and red daybeacon "46A" and keep an eye on the depth sounder. Local boaters consider the area from red daybeacon "44" to quick-flashing red "48" (Mile 227 to Mile 229) a No-Wake Zone, and these otherwise friendly folks do not take kindly to boaters who ignore it.

Directly off the ICW at the mouth of the White Oak River is the Swansboro town harbor. Red nun buoy "2" and red daybeacon "4" (no yellow triangle) guide the boater into the harbor. Although clearly charted, these marks seem to confuse strangers. Periodically, a boat will try to go between them, but with little success. An immediate grounding awaits those who attempt to go between these markers.

Dockage: Cruising boaters can tie up comfortably or have most hull and engine repairs handled at Dudley's Marina, which has a large-boat marine railway at Mile 227. They also offer fuel, approach depths of 7 to 8 feet and hot showers. Dockage is also available at Casper's Marina, located adjacent to Swansboro's Historic District.

Anchorage: Boats frequently anchor in the 11- to 12-foot depths along the north shore, between Casper's Marina and the state Route 24 Highway Bridge (fixed vertical clearance 12 feet). Holding is good despite the swift current here, although we recommend backing down hard on your anchor.

GOIN' ASHORE: SWANSBORO, NC

A yellow kayak is tethered to shore, its bow parting the hedge of marsh grass while the stern swings near the brow of a beach. Past the beach and beyond the point, a sailboat lies at anchor near the bridge spanning the White Oak River. There may be better anchorages on the ICW, but if you are looking for a place to paddle and get lost in the backwaters of the Carolina Coast, it is a good bet you will love Swansboro.

Known as "The Friendly City by the Sea," Swansboro sits at the intersection of the White Oak River and Brown's Inlet. Here, you will find a picturesque Colonial port built on fishing and boatbuilding. Like so many of North Carolina's small coastal towns, Swansboro is experiencing a rebirth within its historic and waterfront area, and it is here that you will discover the soul of Swansboro.

From beyond Bear Island and Huggins Island, a salt-laden sea breeze scuffs the waters of the anchorage. From the top-story window of a gift store you can see the wide expanse of Hammocks Beach State Park, an 890-acre island with forest and salt marsh. This park is nationally recognized as a coastal wildlife nature preserve and a nesting area for the loggerhead sea turtle. Access to Bear Island is by private boat or ferry service operated by the park service.

History: The first permanent settlement was established in 1740, on the former site of an Algonquin Indian Village on the White Oak River. The port was called Swansborough and incorporated in 1783 in honor of the former speaker of the North Carolina Commons. The town thrived as a port, with shipbuilding as its major industry. Swansboro's most famous shipbuilder was Captain Otway Burns, builder of the *Prometheus*, the first steamboat built in North Carolina.

The town flourished until the end of the Civil War. As the shipping and lumber industries declined, Swansboro's residents returned to their roots—the sea. Commercial fishing became its economic base. During World War II, the Marine Corps opened bases at Cherry Point and Camp Lejeune, bringing new growth to the community.

Attractions: Hammocks Beach State Park is accessible only by ferry or private boat. This beach is secluded, providing the perfect day trip for boaters looking to escape the crowds. For a less strenuous trek, stroll around the Bicentennial Park, and feed the ducks. Make sure you visit Yanamama's '50s Memorabilia Shoppe (117 Front St.), where you can find Marilyn Monroe, Elvis Presley and James Dean memorabilia. A lovely way to see the Swansboro area is by bike, and the 25-mile-long bicycle trail takes you through historic downtown Swansboro, into the Croatan National Forest, and past historic landmarks and country stores. You can rent bikes on the eastern side of the bridge at Bikes-R-In (1020 Cedar Point Blvd., 888-393-7161).

Special events: Military Appreciation Day now includes the Sea Story Telling Festival and occurs in May. Call 910-326-1174 for more information. The town celebrates the Fourth of July in a big way, with band concerts, games, local foods and fireworks over the water. In October, the Mullet (a local fish) Festival attracts locals and tourists for a town parade, arts and crafts and a variety of food vendors.

ICW/Bogue Inlet Area, NC

ICW/BOGUE INLET AREA		Largest Vessel Accommodated	VHF Channel Monitored	Transient Berths / Total Berths	Approach / Dockside Depth (reported)	Floating Docks	Gas / Diesel	Groceries, Ice, Marine Supplies, Snacks	Repairs: Hull, Engine, Propeller	Lift (tonnage), Crane, Rail	1=110V, 2=220V, B=Both, Max Amps	Laundry, Pool, Showers	Pump-Out Station	Nearby: Grocery Store, Motel, Restaurant
		Dockage					Supplies		Services					
1. Island Harbor Marina 224.8	252-354-3106	40	16	/65	3.5/3.5		GD	IMS			1/30			GR
2. Dudley's Marina 228.7 (Internet Access)	**252-393-2204**	**125**	**16**	**14/26**	**7/7**	**F**	**GD**	**IMS**	**HEP**	**R**	**B/50**	**S**		**GMR**
3. Casper's Marina 229.3 (Internet Access) (Wireless Internet Access)	910-326-4462	180	16/09	10/20	10/9		GD	IMS		L	B/50	S	P	GMR

Corresponding chart(s) not to be used for navigation. Internet Access Wireless Internet Access

Shopping: The nearest supermarket, a Piggly Wiggly, is within walking distance of the downtown waterfront area (715 W. Corbett Ave.). Waters Ace Hardware (778 W. Corbett Ave.) is on Highway 24 and a longer walk. Suzanne's Fudge Factory (114 Main St.) is a sweet stop after a long day on the water. Silver Thimble (137 N. Front St.) is a small, but nice gift shop. There is a good selection of art and antiques at Front Porch Pottery (105 W. Church St.). A North Carolina ABC Store (1073 W. Corbett Ave.) is a short walk from the waterfront.

Restaurants: Captain Charlie's Seafood Paradise (106 Front St., 910-326-4303) specializes in fresh seafood and steaks and offers a full-service bar. For a light lunch or a good cup of coffee, try Church Street Coffee and Deli (105 Church St., 910-326-7572). The Chamber of Commerce also recommends Yana's Ye Olde Restaurant (119 Front St., 910-326-5501), a 1950s restaurant serving breakfast and lunch daily, featuring fruit fritters and burgers. The Ice House Restaurant, offering seafood, steaks and chicken, (103 Moore St., 910-325-0501) and Riverside Steak and Seafood (506 W. Corbett Ave., 910-326-8847) are both within walking distance of the waterfront.

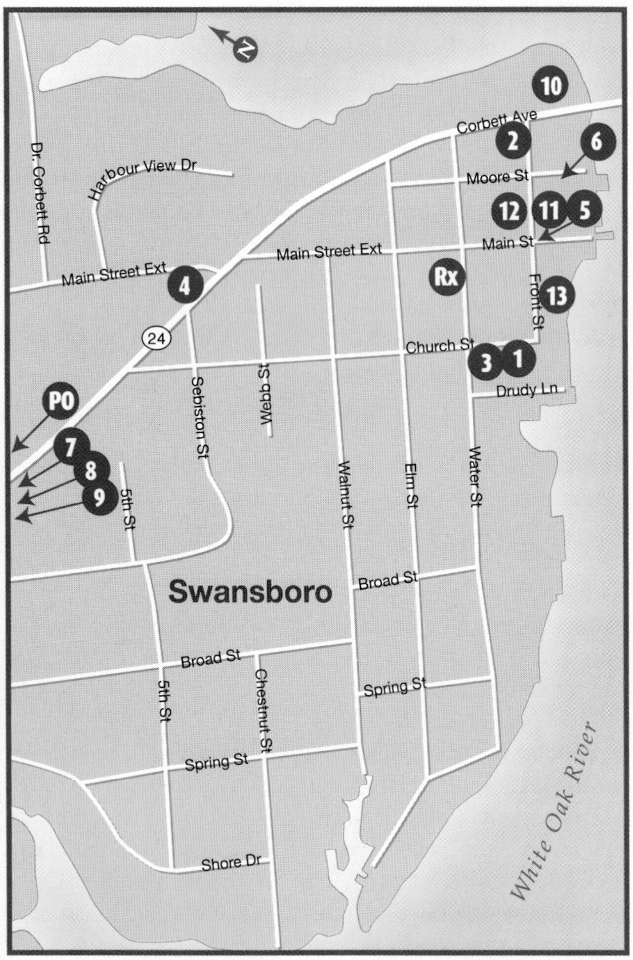

Reference the marina listing tables to see all the marinas in the area.

ADDITIONAL RESOURCES

- SWANSBORO CHAMBER OF COMMERCE, 910-326-1174
  www.swansborochamber.org

NEARBY GOLF COURSES
Silver Creek Golf Club, 601 Pelletier Loop Road, Swansboro, NC 28584, 800-393-6605 (6 miles)

NEARBY MEDICAL FACILITIES
Western Carteret Medical Center, 718 Cedar Point Blvd., Swansboro, NC 28584, 252-393-6543 (3 miles)

Crystal Coast Family Practice, 540 Cedar Point Blvd., Swansboro, NC 28584, 252-393-6374 (3 miles)

ART/ANTIQUES
1 Front Porch Pottery

DINING
2 Captain Charlie's Seafood Paradise
3 Church Street Coffee and Deli
4 Riverside Steak & Seafood
5 Yana's Ye Olde Restaurant
6 Ice House Waterfront Restaurant

GROCERIES/CARRYOUT
7 Piggly Wiggly
8 North Carolina ABC Store

MARINE SUPPLIES
9 Waters Ace Hardware

POINTS OF INTEREST
10 Bicentennial Park

SHOPPING
11 Yanamama's '50s Memorabilia Shoppe
12 Suzanne's Fudge Factory
13 Silver Thimble

PO POST OFFICE

Rx PHARMACY

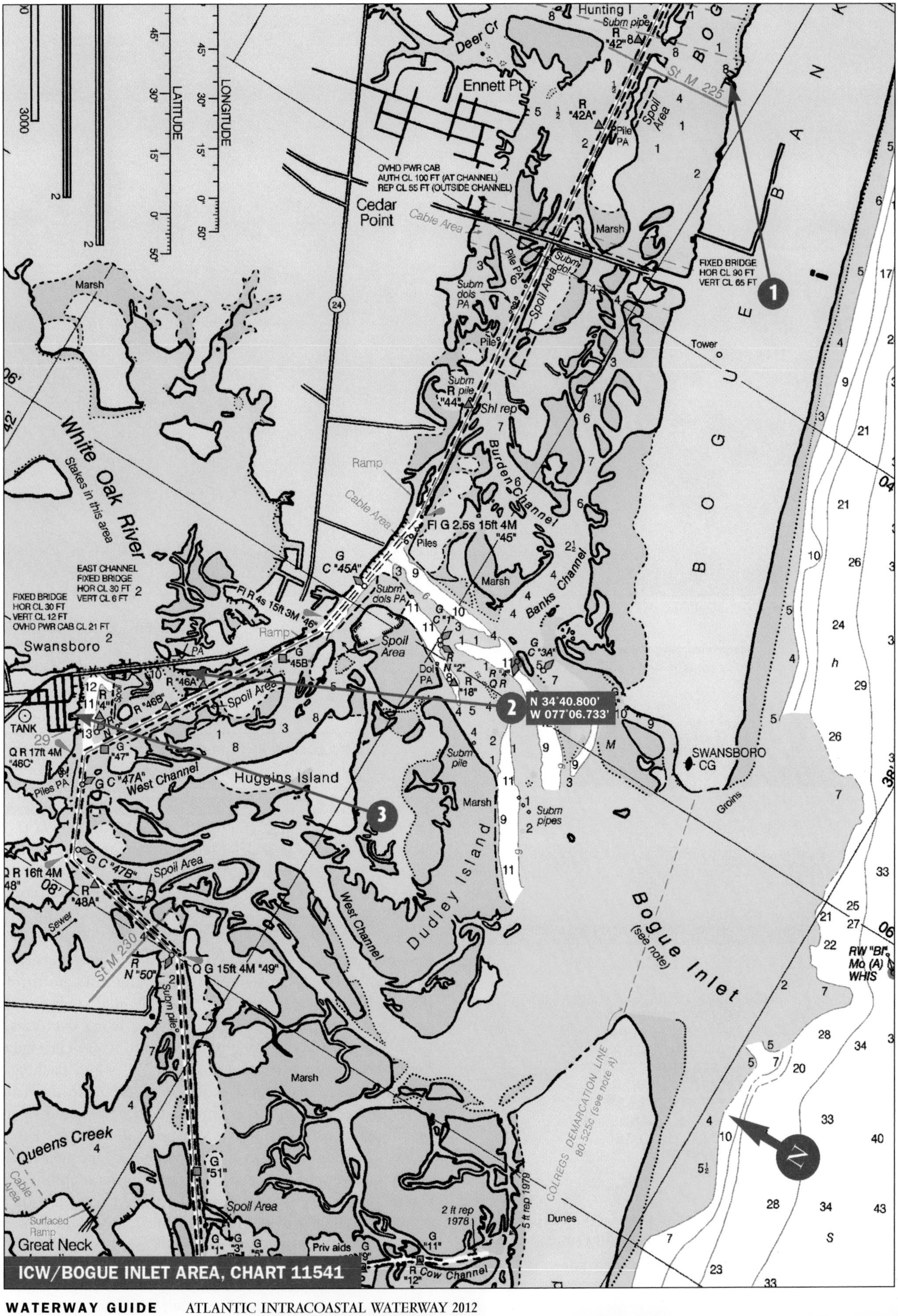

ICW/BOGUE INLET AREA, CHART 11541

Looking northeast over Swansboro. (Not to be used for navigation.) WATERWAY GUIDE PHOTOGRAPHY.

SWANSBORO TO NEW RIVER

THE FOLLOWING AREA REQUIRES SPECIAL ATTENTION DUE TO SHOALING OR CHANGES TO THE CHANNEL

RESTRICTED AREA

Camp Lejeune extends about 18 miles upstream on the New River, almost to Jacksonville, and encompasses parts adjacent to the ICW from Mile 235 to the New River at Mile 245. The ICW through Camp Lejeune occasionally closes for artillery, small-weapons firing and beach-landing exercises. The area along the ICW that closes for bombing exercises starts just south of red daybeacon "58" (Mile 235.2) and ends around Mile 240, north of the Onslow Beach Bridge. Prominent lighted signs stand at both ends of the range area. During firing exercises, these signs display flashing lights and red flags. The signs direct boaters to tune to AM Radio 530 when flashing. Manned stake-boats stand watch at each end to prevent ICW traffic from running into danger. The stake-boat personnel can usually advise you as to the length of the delay. As a rule, it is only one to two hours, but delays of up to four hours have been reported. During amphibious troop-landing exercises, this stretch may close for a day or more. When this happens, marinas above and below the reservation post notices. Coast Guard Sector North Carolina gives notice of firing exercises at 5:30 a.m. and

8:30 p.m. on the "Broadcast Notice to Mariners" (the time given in the broadcast is Universal Time Code, not local). The Coast Guard first comes up on VHF Channel 16, and then switches to Channel 22A. Other information given includes the weather, changes in bridge status, shoaling and hazards to navigation.

There continues to be considerable shoaling in the 70-mile stretch between Swansboro and Carolina Beach. Many areas along this stretch are 8- to 10-feet deep at mean low water. The persistently shallow area at Bogue Inlet Crossing north of Swansboro was dredged during January 2010, and the New River Crossing (Mile 245.9 between red nuns "72A" and "72B") was dredged in December 2010. Even though dredging solves the shoaling problems for a while, cruisers should still exercise caution in transiting these areas, and seek local knowledge. Note that the dredging referred to here is in the ICW where the inlets cross or meet the waterway, not in the inlets to the ocean.

END SPECIAL CAUTION AREA.

NAVIGATION: Use Chart 11541. Departing from Swansboro (Mile 229), the ICW zigzags its way southwest with two bends, one at quick flashing red "48" and another at quick flashing green "49." Around Mile 232, a narrow marked channel leads southeast to Hammocks Beach State Park. This side trip is for small boats only. Severe shoaling in this small side channel was partially alleviated by spot dredging in May 2007 and was completely dredged by the year's end. The dunes at Hammocks Beach State Park are impressive, and you can visit them via the park service's pontoon ferryboats if you make prior arrangements. The park's phone number is 910-326-4881.

In the short channel off the ICW at Mile 234, there are docks associated with a yacht building facility that has changed hands three times in recent years. The facility, most recently operated by Hatteras, was closed in March 2008. There is not much space for boats to anchor here because of the docks. Watch for shoaling on the northwest side of flashing green "55" where there are less than 8-foot depths at mean low water.

THE FOLLOWING AREA REQUIRES SPECIAL ATTENTION DUE TO SHOALING OR CHANGES TO THE CHANNEL

MILE 235 TO NEW RIVER

From Mile 235 to New River at Mile 246, the ICW cuts through the U.S. Marine Corps' Camp Lejeune military reservation, where signs along the way prohibit landing. A persistent shoaling area is at Mile 238, where temporary markers may be placed. It was dredged in January 2010 and depths were around 12 feet. In June 2011, however, depths had shoaled to 6 feet mean low water just south of marker 60. Favor the mainland side of the ICW at this point. Check with the Coast Guard, or look at the Waterway Guide website to find out about new channel markers. Expect this area to continue to shoal, due to the strong currents flowing in and out of the small inlets to the ocean (Bear and Browns inlets).

END SPECIAL CAUTION AREA.

At the southern end of the Camp Lejeune range at Onslow Beach, Mile 240.7, is the Onslow Beach Swing Bridge, owned and operated by the Marine Corps. Use the northwest draw, which has a 12-foot closed vertical clearance. This bridge opens on the hour and half-hour from 7:00 a.m. to 7:00 p.m. In 2008, this bridge underwent extensive repairs. This bridge is very slow to open (openings usually take about 8 to 10 minutes). The bridge tender will only open for vessels actually at the bridge at the appointed times and only if you contact them on VHF Channel 13 to request an opening. Heading south after the bridge, you have passed the danger area. However, there is still heavy military activity along the sides of the ICW, where the Marines practice amphibious landings. Watch for shallow water near the edge of the channel in the long straight stretch below the Onslow Beach Swing Bridge.

Anchorage: About two miles north of the three-way junction where the ICW, New River and New River Inlet channel meet, a large dredged basin in Mile Hammock Bay (Mile 244) offers a very good and popular anchorage. Dredging a few years ago left Mile Hammock Bay with 12-foot depths. Check ahead for local knowledge about the state of the entrance channel, although it had adequate depths in October 2010 for deep-draft vessels to enter the channel and to anchor. Do not go too far east of the eastern wharf—depths there are only 1 or 2 feet. Use your best anchoring techniques, as holding is poor in some spots. Stay clear of the docks—a U.S. Army Corps of Engineers dredge often ties up here. This is Marine Corps property, and civilians are prohibited from going ashore. Frequent military activity and exercises in this basin can sometimes make this a less-than-tranquil anchorage. You may be buzzed by a helicopter or inflatables full of well-armed soldiers.

New River Inlet—Mile 246

THE FOLLOWING AREA REQUIRES SPECIAL ATTENTION DUE TO SHOALING OR CHANGES TO THE CHANNEL

NEW RIVER INLET

While there has been some dredging of the New River Inlet (from the ICW to the ocean), this inlet still frequently shoals, and markers are sometimes off station. Those unfamiliar with the inlet should avoid using it to access the ocean. There has been considerable shoaling of the ICW channel at the New River Crossing (between red nuns "72A" and "72B") for years. Even though this area is regularly dredged, less than 5.5-foot depths were observed off red nun "74" in late 2011 at mean low water; however, a dredge was on station working to correct this chronic problem. Be aware that some charts inaccurately show the magenta line on the wrong side of red nun "72A." Check the Fifth District Coast Guard's *Local Notice to Mariners* (www.navcen.uscg.gov/lnm/d5) for updates on dredging and the Wilmington District Army Corps of Engineers site for the latest survey information: www.saw.usace.army.mil. Some areas of the New River above its intersection with the ICW are shoal. Seek local knowledge before heading up this river.

END SPECIAL CAUTION AREA.

New River, NC

NEW RIVER		Largest Vessel Accommodated	VHF Channel Monitored	Transient Berths / Total Berths	Approach / Dockside Depth (reported)	Floating Docks	Gas / Diesel	Groceries, Ice, Marine Supplies, Snacks	Repairs: Hull, Engine, Propeller	Lift (tonnage), Crane, Rail	1=110V, 2=220V, B=Both, Max Amps	Laundry, Pool, Showers	Pump-Out Station	Nearby: Grocery Store, Motel, Restaurant
		Dockage					Supplies		Services					
1. Swan Point Marina and Boatyard 247 (WiFi)	910-327-1081	100	16/12	10/25	8/6		GD	IMS	HEP	L40	B/50	LS		R
2. New River Marina 247	910-327-2106	90	16/09	2/13	6/9		GD	GIMS	E		1/30	S		R

Corresponding chart(s) not to be used for navigation. ☐ Internet Access (WiFi) Wireless Internet Access

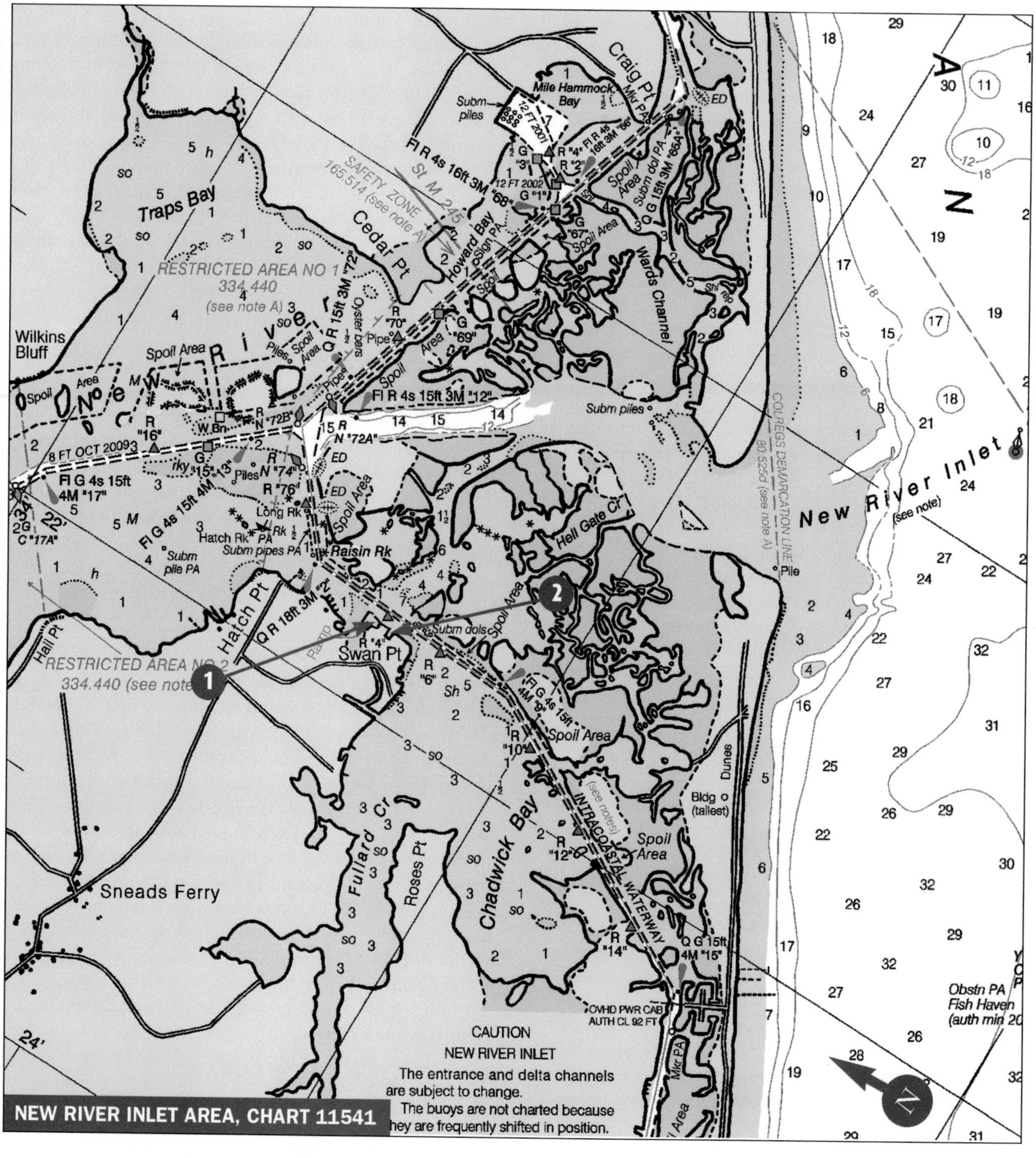

NEW RIVER INLET AREA, CHART 11541

NAVIGATION: Use Chart 11541. At the junction of the New River Inlet and the ICW at Mile 246, be prepared for strong side currents and favor the ocean side. Be aware of depths in the area (see notice above). Take time beforehand to sort out markers, as the upriver channel buoys can be confusing. Note that at the junction of the ICW and inlet channels, red buoys mark inshore shoals—they are moved as required to show deepwater limits. At this point, New River, with a well-marked channel, heads off sharply to starboard. *(See page 71 for more information about New River Inlet.)*

New River/Swan Point

From here, it is possible to journey up the New River to the city of Jacksonville, NC. (Be sure to obtain local knowledge before venturing upriver.) Chart 11541 covers the first mile or so, and 11542 will take you the rest of the 19-mile-long route. Upstream, the route takes you through the Marine Corps training base, Camp Lejeune.

Dockage: At Jacksonville, you will find transient dockage at Tideline Marine and dining at the Fisherman's Wharf Restaurant. South on the ICW at Swan Point (Mile 247), there is transient dockage at Swan Point Marina. Here, you will find a mix of local recreational boats, small-scale commercial fishermen and cruisers, immediately off the ICW just north of red daybeacon "4." Fuel is available, as is a 40-ton lift. Sneads Ferry is just a few miles away, where you can replenish the food lockers at Food Lion and find a post office, bank, liquor store and drugstore. The Riverview Restaurant in town and the Green Turtle restaurant offer transportation from the marinas. Immediately south of red daybeacon "4," the New River Marina's fuel dock faces the ICW. Deep-draft vessels should call ahead for docking information. They consistently have excellent fuel prices and may allow overnight dockage once the fuel pumps have closed for the evening.

NEW RIVER TO WRIGHTSVILLE BEACH

Mile 246 to Mile 283

In this stretch to Wrightsville and beyond, a wide expanse of channel and slough-threaded marsh separates the ICW from barrier beaches. Most of these small waterways dead-end inside the barrier beach dunes. (Watch for side-setting currents and shoaling where these meet the ICW.) Others provide access to small inlets, and some are even deep enough for anchoring if you feel adventurous.

The bottom is very sandy here, and currents can run swiftly. Because of increased hurricane activity over the past decade, last year's good anchorage may be too shallow this year, or a formerly shoaled entrance channel may have been scoured deep. The ICW channel tends to shoal near small inlets. Deep-draft boats should proceed cautiously in such areas.

On the way, you will pass several loading basins used by pulpwood barges, but many are abandoned and shoaled, so we do not recommend anchoring. Small communities of watermen's cottages have landings but are not set up to handle transients.

The countryside begins to change in this section. Inlets appear with more frequency, and the high wooded shores gradually become lined with houses, as well as vacation cottages. Since this is popular fishing and boating territory, most homes have their own boats at small off-the-ICW docks, snuggled up side creeks or in dredged private channels.

NAVIGATION: Use Chart 11541. Below New River, the ICW doglegs around such that the Swan Point and New River marina (Mile 247) facilities become visible. The route then runs southwest along a mostly straight dredged path for about 10 miles. At Mile 252.3 is a highway bridge with a 65-foot fixed vertical clearance. Before the highway bridge, along Alligator Bay, shoaling has been noted between flashing green "23" and green daybeacon "25." Favor the green side of the channel. Farther southwest at Mile 257.6, shoaling is continually a problem between green daybeacons "51" and "53," with depths of 7 to 8 feet reported at mean low water.

Surf City Swing Bridge, Mile 260.7

NAVIGATION: Use Chart 11541. Watch out for strong currents at the Surf City Swing Bridge ("Sears Landing Bridge," 12-foot closed vertical clearance). Both this bridge and the Wrightsville Beach Bridge (20-foot closed vertical clearance), 22 miles farther south, open only on the hour between 7:00 a.m. and 7:00 p.m. The Figure Eight Island Swing Bridge (20-foot closed vertical clearance) between them, five miles before Wrightsville, opens every hour on the half-hour, 24 hours a day. These bridges will not delay their openings if boats are already waiting, so you must know your speed and calculate your transit here carefully; slow boats may not be able to synchronize their passages with the openings. However, the bridges will open for commercial vessels and do allow recreational vessels to transit with them. During periods of strong winds, these bridges may be closed. Swing bridges are especially vulnerable to damage from high winds. The Figure Eight Island Swing Bridge will not open when the sustained wind is stronger than 30 miles per hour. The current can be strong and may cause trouble for low-powered boats in a strong tailwind. Scan VHF Channels 13 and 16 to determine if there are any problems in the area.

SURF CITY BRIDGE
Mile 260.7

WATERWAY GUIDE PHOTOGRAPHY

Dockage: The Beach House Marina is strategically located just north of the Surf City Bridge, where many boaters arrive late for the bridge opening and have no place to anchor overnight. Their docks have 7-foot depths, gas and diesel fuel, up to 40-foot finger piers and the staff monitors VHF Channel 16. This convenient stop is just inside the first small channel on the ocean side, north of the Surf City Bridge.

ICW—Mile 263.5

NAVIGATION: Use Chart 11541. **Use the Cape Hatteras Tide Table. For New Topsail Inlet high tide, add 20 minutes; for low tide, add 1 hour.** At junction flashing green "BC," about Mile 263.5, a channel makes off to the southeast and meanders along the backside of the barrier island, past Topsail Beach to New Topsail Inlet. Used extensively by locals, this scenic side trip is suitable only for shallow-draft boats. Use caution if you decide to anchor just inside flashing green "BC" at Topsail Beach; the channel is very narrow. Uncharted buoys mark New Topsail Inlet. The inlet frequently shoals, and markers may be off station. This is a local-knowledge inlet for smaller boats, and dredging of this inlet only occurs when funds are available. *(See page 72 for more information about New Topsail Inlet.)*

Dockage: For skippers in need of yard work before they reach Wilmington, Anchors Away Boat Yard at Mile 264 is an option. A channel at Mile 267 on the mainland side leads into Harbour Village Marina. The marina itself is private and closed to transients; however, monthly slip rentals can be arranged through the individual slip holders. The fuel dock operates as a separate concession and offers fuel and transient dockage along its 150-foot-long face dock. It is necessary to make an appointment for dockage by calling ahead. The entrance channel was dredged in late 2008 when the new floating docks were installed.

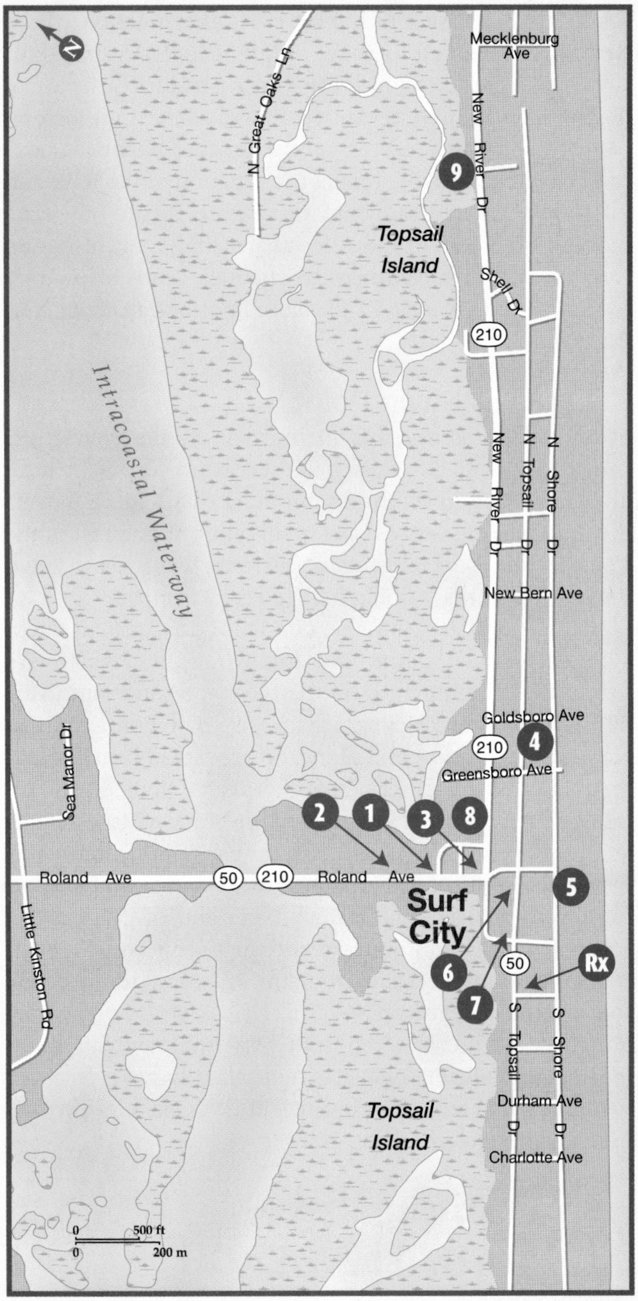

Reference the marina listing tables to see all the marinas in the area.

DINING

1 Cheri's
2 Crab Pot
3 Mainsail Restaurant
4 New York Corner
5 Buddy's Crab House & Oyster Bar

SHOPPING

6 Surf City Shopping Center
7 Topsail Art Gallery
8 Topsail Island Trading Company
9 Herring's Outdoor Sports

Rx PHARMACY

GOIN' ASHORE:
TOPSAIL ISLAND, NC

There was a time, not too long ago, when you could camp beneath the concert launch pad of a space rocket. A tent was still necessary for privacy, but the launch pad kept out the rain better than the canvas. Cars and pick-ups carved narrow tracks in soft sand, and some nights you would spend as much time pulling vehicles off the beach as you would reeling in bluefish. Fishing off the Jolly Roger pier was the reward for a hard week's work, and fish in the cooler provided dinner for days to come. But the tides of change are sweeping over the dunes of Topsail Island. While Surf City and the surrounding island remain a blue-collar beach area, most of the single-wide trailers have been trucked away and replaced with two-story cottages on spider-leg stilts.

There remains a middle-class culture to Topsail, but it is harder to find these days. You still see the putt-putt course and surf shops, small motels and breakfast cafés. Men and women still walk into the diner wearing waders before heading out in the pre-dawn light to fish. The area has grown a lot, but you can still find a shop foreman and a bank executive conversing side by side as they cast into a school of mullet.

History: Much has been made about the name Topsail Island. Folklore became fact and now many historians attribute the name to pirate ships anchored in the lee of the dunes. When a vessel laden with gold or goats strayed too close to shore, the pirates would hoist the topsail to give them steerage as they raced for the inlet to begin the chase.

Topsail Island almost became Cape Canaveral. Or, at least, the base for space exploration. Today, you can still still find several observation towers strategically placed on the island.

These silos, and the concrete slab that serves as the Jolly Roger Motel's patio, are all that remain of the island's contribution to space exploration. In 1946, Topsail was a barrier island that the military called "the sand spit." Following World War II, the U.S. government seized the island and used it to develop a long-range defense missile for the Navy.

The goal of the project was to develop a supersonic missile that would swiftly reach a target up to 20 miles away. A six-inch diameter rocket, fashioned from the tailpipe of a Navy Thunderbolt airplane and fueled by a mixture of propylene oxide and oxygen, provided the thrust. During the next 2 years, the military launched more than 200 experimental rockets. The test launchings resulted in the ramjet rocket, which was the foundation of the U.S. guided missile program.

Due to the success of the rockets, Topsail Island became too small. The project was divided and transferred to other test sites, one of which would become Cape Canaveral. Now, the towers built to track the flight of the missiles are all that remain of the project.

Shopping: Shopping on-island is a compact experience. At the intersection of Roland Avenue and NC 1547, you will find the Surf City Shopping Center (106 S. Topsail Drive, 910-328-0835). Nearby is Topsail Art Gallery (121 S. Topsail Drive, 910-328-2138), carrying a good selection of original art and reproductions, pottery, sculptures and fine glass. Topsail Island Trading Company (201 N. New River Drive, 910-328-1905) carries a good selection of resort wear, gifts and fudge. Herring's Outdoor Sports (701 N. New River Drive, 910-329-3291) is a long hike from the bridge, so you are advised to grab a ride.

Restaurants: Cheri's (602 Roland Ave., 910-328-2580) features a cozy, wood-paneled dining room overlooking Topsail Sound. At the Crab Pot (508 Roland Ave., 910-328-5001), your dinner arrives in a Styrofoam box with a roll of paper towels to sop up the sauce and fixings. Mainsail Restaurant (404 Roland Ave., 910-328-0010) serves seafood, steaks and pasta. New York Corner (206 N. Topsail Drive, 910-328-2808) serves deli-style food. Buddy's Crab House & Oyster Bar (101 Roland Ave., 910-328-1515) has a great neighborhood feel and serves steamed seafood.

ADDITIONAL RESOURCES

- **TOPSAIL ISLAND CHAMBER OF COMMERCE, 910-329-4446,**

NEARBY GOLF COURSES
North Shore Country Club, 101 N. Shore Drive, Sneads Ferry, NC 28460, 800-828-5035, (4 miles)

NEARBY MEDICAL FACILITIES
Beach Care PA, 204 N. New River Drive #D, Surf City, NC 28445, 910-328-4729 (5 miles)

Hampstead Medical Center, 14980 U.S. Highway 17 N., Hampstead, NC 28443, 910-270-2722 (10 miles)

⚠ THE FOLLOWING AREA REQUIRES SPECIAL ATTENTION DUE TO SHOALING OR CHANGES TO THE CHANNEL

BLACK MUD CHANNEL

NAVIGATION: Use Chart 11541. **Use the Cape Hatteras Tide Table. For Masonboro Inlet high tide, add 23 minutes; for low tide, add 22 minutes.** Continuing from New Topsail Inlet at Mile 270 to Wrightsville Beach at Mile 283, the ICW channel is straight, well-marked and easy-to-run. The markers in narrow Old Topsail Creek leading from the ICW at Mile 270 to New Topsail Inlet have been removed due to shoaling. Shoaling in the ICW off Black Mud Channel, Mile 270.5, occurs frequently. In the vicinity of the shoal prone area off Old Topsail Creek near ICW red flashing "98" and green can buoy "99," depths were at least 10.5 feet from a December 2009 survey. Remember that conditions can change where inlets cross the ICW, and you may find something entirely different when you pass through. This area was last dredged in March 2011

END SPECIAL CAUTION AREA.

At Figure Eight Island, Mile 278.1, the Figure Eight Island Swing Bridge (charted 20-foot closed vertical clearance) was noted to have tide boards that read 21.5 feet at high tide in early 2011. Note: The bridge opens every hour on the half-hour, 24 hours a day. The schedule change for the bridge began in the spring of 2010. (It used to open on the hour and half-hour.) It will not open in winds of 30 mph or greater and can remain closed at the discretion of the tender in bad weather. The area behind Figure Eight Island was also dredged in March 2011.

Going through Middle Sound after mid-afternoon, watch for commercial mullet fishermen with their nets stretched across the channel. (It is hard to identify on today's charts, but it extends from around Mile 278 to Mile 283.) Ordinarily, fishermen tend to the nets and promptly lower them so that approaching boats can pass over them. To be on the safe side, boaters should travel at a reasonable speed and allow ample time for the nets to reach the bottom. The Coast Guard at Wrightsville Beach has stated that the nets are to be at least 6 feet below the surface of the water and tended.

In the five miles between Figure Eight Island Swing Bridge, Mile 278.1 (boat passage on the west opening only), and the Wrightsville Beach Bridge, Mile 283, the route is straightforward, although aids to navigation are fewer and farther apart. When the marshes flood at high tide, it is hard to make out the channel. At such times, run compass courses between markers. Shoaling has been reported along the ICW near Mason Inlet, Mile 280.5. Green can buoy "121" marks a shoal that extends partially into the Waterway at the point where Mason Inlet intersects the ICW channelward of green daybeacon "123." Depths in late 2010 were around 7 feet at low tide, but dredging was completed in January 2011. *(See page 73 for more information about Mason Inlet.)*

Surf City, Topsail Beach, NC

TOPSAIL BEACH		Largest Vessel Accommodated	VHF Channel Monitored	Transient Berths / Total Berths	Approach / Dockside Depth (reported)	Floating Docks	Gas / Diesel	Groceries, Ice, Marine Supplies, Snacks	Repairs: Hull, Engine, Propeller	Lift (tonnage), Crane, Rail	1=110V, 2=220V, B=Both, Max Amps	Laundry, Pool, Showers	Pump-Out Station	Nearby: Grocery Store, Motel, Restaurant
		Dockage					Supplies		Services					
1. Beach House Marina 261	910-328-2628	60	16	4/24	7.5/7	F	GD	GIMS			B/50	LS	P	GMR
2. Anchors Away Boatyard 264 ☐	910-270-4741	70	16		8/8	F			HEP	L68	B/50			
3. Harbour Village Marina Fuel Dock 267 ☐ WiFi	910-270-4017	100			8/8	F		IS			B/50	S	P	

Corresponding chart(s) not to be used for navigation. ☐ Internet Access WiFi Wireless Internet Access

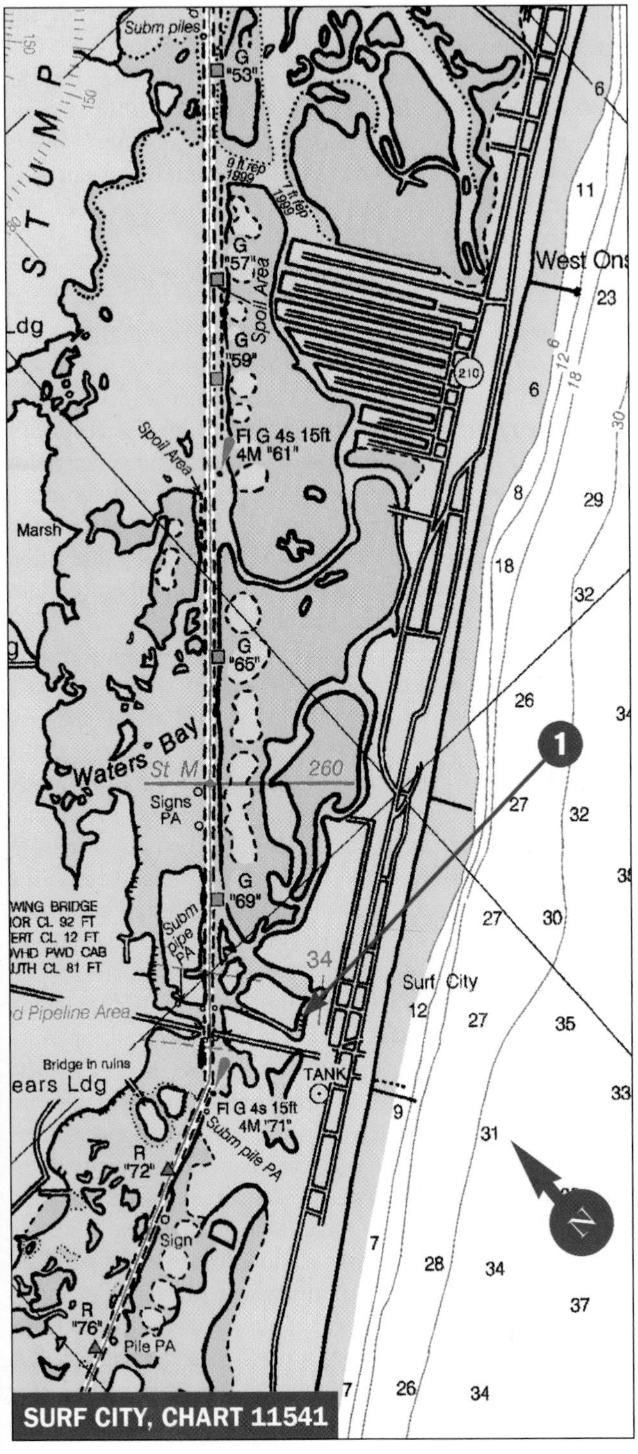

SURF CITY, CHART 11541

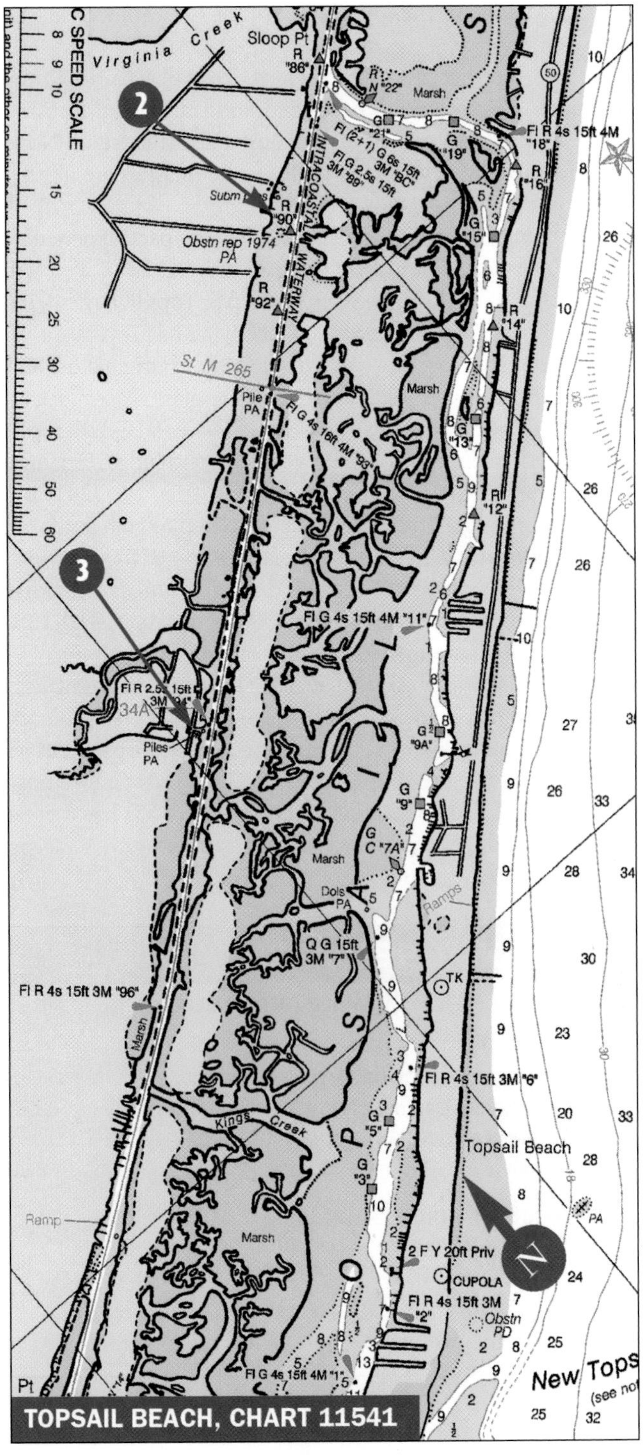

TOPSAIL BEACH, CHART 11541

Looking south over the Wrightsville Beach area. (Not to be used for navigation.) WATERWAY GUIDE PHOTOGRAPHY.

Wrightsville Beach, Mile 283

Wrightsville Beach is a burgeoning water-oriented community. Boating is what makes the place tick, and the activities throughout its waterways are perhaps greater here than in any other North Carolina region. Wrightsville Beach has attracted boating types from all over the world, and for the ICW traveler, it is well worth a visit.

Note that the Wrightsville Beach Bridge at Mile 283.1, 20-foot closed vertical clearance, opens on the hour between 7:00 a.m. and 7:00 p.m., year-round. The current picks up as one closes with the Wrightsville Beach Bridge, and then reverses just north of the bridge, making it difficult for slower vessels to correctly time arrivals at the bridge. Sailboats and slower trawlers have a difficult time making the five miles between these two bridges in a half-hour. Slower boats southbound will now have to go through Figure Eight on the half-hour, and then take a leisurely hour and a half ride to Wrightsville. Currents are particularly strong directly at the bridge and at the marinas adjacent to the ICW below the bridge. Exercise care in holding for this bridge on either side. You may receive instructions to bunch with other boats during the unrestricted hours. Traffic from a busy launching ramp just north of the bridge adds to the congestion. Boats waiting on the south side of the bridge will also see congestion from marina traffic and Motts Channel.

Motts Channel, at Wrightsville Beach

Motts Channel, a short distance south of the Wrightsville Beach Bridge, runs east from the ICW at green daybeacon "25" (not an ICW number) to Banks Channel, with a large (and sometimes, uncomfortably busy) anchorage area. Banks Channel extends southwest to Atlantic Ocean access at Masonboro Inlet.

THE FOLLOWING AREA REQUIRES SPECIAL ATTENTION DUE TO SHOALING OR CHANGES TO THE CHANNEL

MOTTS CHANNEL

NAVIGATION: Use Chart 11541. There has been a persistent area of shoaling in Motts Channel where it joins the ICW in the vicinity of green daybeacon "25" and red daybeacon "24." This area was last dredged in 2008. In October 2010, depths in this area were charted at 4 feet at a very low tide. Even with frequent dredging, this is an area to watch because it fills in quickly. Between green daybeacons "21" and "19," favor the "red side" of the channel, giving those two markers a wide berth. Local knowledge says to hug the green side of the channel until past Seapath, then stay close to the red side from that point on. Call or radio Seapath Yacht Club for help if needed.

END SPECIAL CAUTION AREA.

Dockage: When you pass the Wrightsville Beach Bridge, Wrightsville Beach Marina immediately becomes visible to port. The Bluewater American Grill (910-256-8500) is adjacent to Wrightsville Beach Marina. Cruisers can call the marina on VHF Channel 16 (or 910-256-6666) to

Wrightsville Beach, NC

WRIGHTSVILLE BEACH		Largest Vessel Accommodated	VHF Channel Monitored	Transient Berths / Total Berths	Approach / Dockside Depth (reported)	Floating Docks	Gas / Diesel	Groceries, Ice, Marine Supplies, Snacks	Repairs: Hull, Engine, Propeller	Lift (tonnage), Crane, Rail	1=110V, 2=220V, B=Both, Max Amps	Laundry, Pool, Showers	Pump-Out Station	Nearby: Grocery Store, Motel, Restaurant
		Dockage					Supplies		Services					
1. Dockside Marina/Restaurant 284 (WiFi)	910-256-3579	170	16	15/25	10/10	F	GD	IS			B/50			GMR
2. Bearing Marine Group	910-401-3079			1					HEP					
3. Bridge Tender Marina 283.3	910-256-6550	200	16	15/65	18/18	F	GD	IMS			B/50			GMR
4. Bluewater-American Grill 283.3	910-256-8500			/10		F					1/30			GMR
5. Wrightsville Beach Marina 283.3 (Internet) (WiFi)	910-256-6666	150	16	/20	18/18	F	GD	IMS	HEP		B/100	LPS	P	GMR
6. Seapath Yacht Club & Transient Dock 284 (Internet) (WiFi)	910-256-3747	150	16	10/200	8/10	F	GD	GIS			B/50	LS	P	GR
7. Atlantic Marine 284	910-256-9911	26	16/09		8/5	F	G	IMS	HEP			S		GMR
8. Marine Max of NC 284	910-256-8100		16					M	HEP	L50				MR

Corresponding chart(s) not to be used for navigation. (Internet) Internet Access (WiFi) Wireless Internet Access

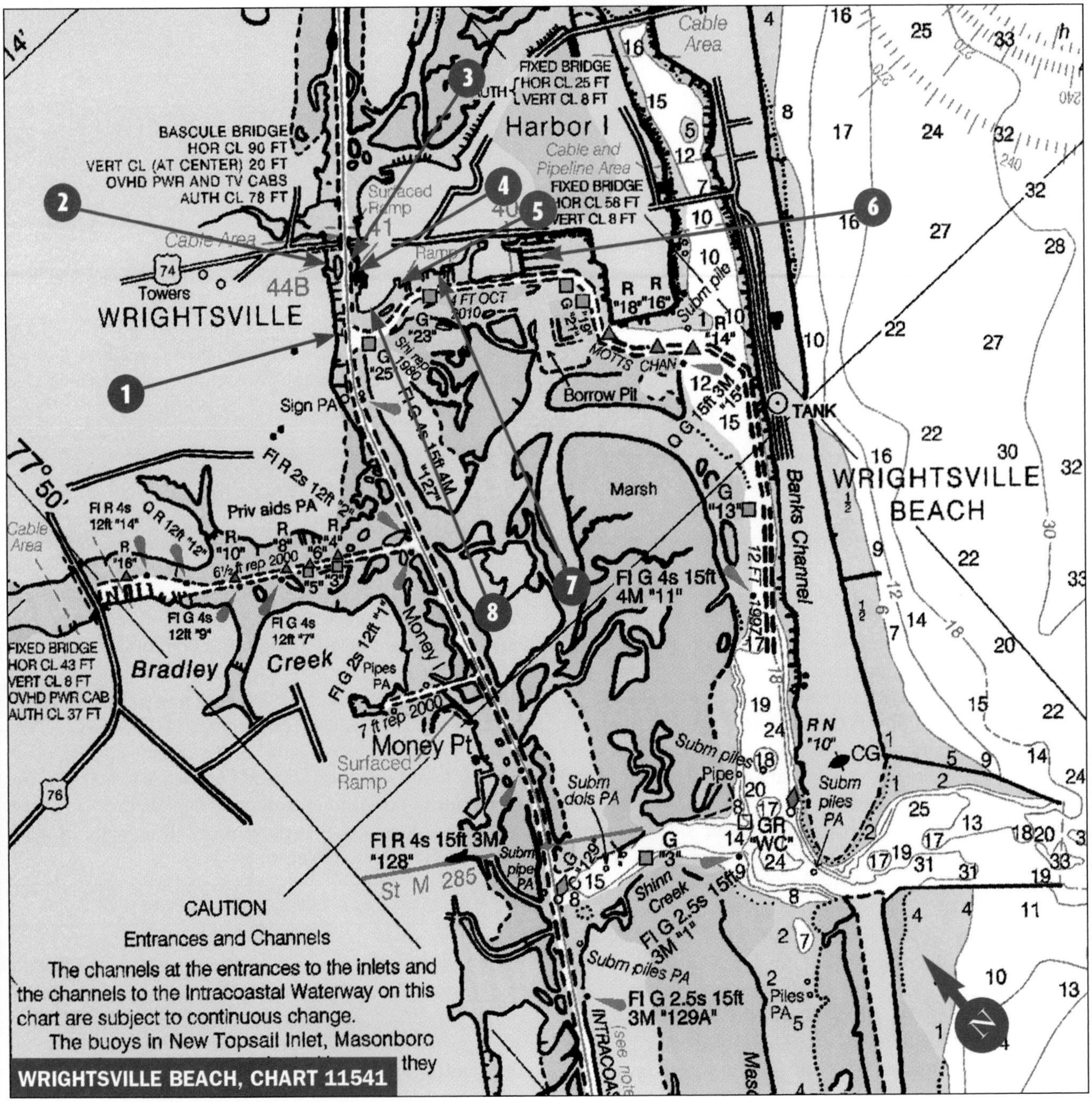

see if there is an available slip or large enough spot along the front wall. Across the ICW on the mainland side, just south of the Wrightsville Beach Bridge, the Bridge Tender Marina (910-256-6550) has face dock space available for transients. Farther south, Dockside Restaurant and Marina (910-256-3579) has face dock space with 10-foot depths and features casual river view dining and a convenient fuel dock. When docking at face docks at any of these marinas, exercise caution and dock against the current. Seapath Yacht Club, on the northern side of Motts Channel, offers 600 feet of floating face docks for transients. This full-service marina has fuel, a ship's store with a lounge, a laundry, a pump-out station, a courtesy car and is convenient to nearby restaurants and beach attractions.

Shinn Creek, Masonboro Inlet and Banks Channel, at Wrightsville Beach

Deep-draft boats can also enter the anchorage area via Shinn Creek (10- to 15-foot water depths) farther south at Mile 285.1, and then follow Banks Channel northeast. The Coast Guard maintains dockage on Banks Channel, just north of Masonboro Inlet, and responds quickly to emergency calls. The channel from the inlet to Shinn Creek is marked and readily passable. On summer weekends, however, this area resembles Fort Lauderdale, FL and is packed with boats of all types.

Note that when you use these channels, you are off the ICW and away from its marking system. Refer to your chart for buoy information before leaving the ICW. The area is wide with good water depths.

Masonboro Inlet is safe under ordinary wind and weather conditions. Depths are maintained at 12 feet in the 400-foot-wide channel running midway between the jetties. The uncharted buoys in Masonboro Inlet are frequently relocated. This inlet and parts of Banks Channel were dredged in early 2010, and the sand was used to replenish Wrightsville Beach. *(See page 74 for more information about Masonboro Inlet.)*

NAVIGATION: Use Chart 11541. When turning off the ICW into Shinn Creek, watch for current set, and treat ICW green can "129" (Mile 285.1) as a green for the ICW as well as for Shinn Creek, which is marked with red on the right coming from the sea. Cut halfway between green can "129" and the sandy north shore of Shinn Creek, for low-tide depths of 8 feet. Check the most recent USACE survey for Shinn Creek Crossing (www.saw.usace.army). Just north of Shinn Creek, about 12-foot mean low water depths were surveyed in May 2009 in the ICW channel. To enter Banks Channel and approach the anchorage, proceed toward the inlet until you reach junction marker "WC," then turn northeast, leaving the Coast Guard Station to starboard.

Back on the ICW, just south of Mile 285, strong cross-currents can make it difficult to maintain a mid-channel course. Favor the ocean side of the main channel on the flood tide and the mainland side on the ebb. Tidal range is from 3 to 4 feet.

Anchorage: A favorite (but busy) anchorage is in the bight just southwest of the Motts Channel junction with Banks Channel (southwest of red daybeacon "14"), inside the protective arm of Wrightsville Beach. There are 12- to 15-foot depths with a hard sand bottom, which may require a Danforth-type anchor for a good set. This spot is so popular that private owners maintain several moorings here.

An equally good anchorage (better protected from the wakes of passing boats) lies northeast of Motts Channel and south of the fixed bridge between Harbor Island and Wrightsville Beach. This anchorage has a varied type of bottom in 10-foot depths. The shallower parts have a very hard bottom with poor holding, while the deeper areas have a softer bottom and usually will hold with some extra work in backing down. In both anchorages, boats will swing, sometimes rather wildly, with the current rather than the wind, unless the wind is quite strong. Those dropping the hook here should plan accordingly. The municipal dinghy dock is located just south of the bridge on the beach side at the Wrightsville Beach Fishing Center.

Photo courtesy of Jani Parker.

QUICK FACT:

DRAGONFLY

Dragonflies are common on the ICW and often will "hitch a ride" from one destination to another aboard passing boats. Despite their name, they are not related to flies and belong to an entirely different order of insects. Dragonflies are actually of the Odonata order of insects, of which there are over 5,000 species. They are usually located near bodies of water—mostly lakes, ponds, streams, and wetlands—which is where they lay their eggs. They are predatory from birth and eat mosquitoes, flies, bees, and ants, as well as the occasional butterfly! Like butterflies, dragonflies spend the majority of their short lives (about 3 years) in the larva stage; by the time they grow wings, they are nearing the end of their lives. Dragonflies, such as the one shown above, often travel in swarms, usually related to weather changes, such as the passage of a cold front. They are some of the fastest insects on earth; they can fly over 30 mph but usually "cruise" at around 10 mph.

Masonboro Inlet, Wrightsville Beach, NC. (Not to be used for navigation.) WATERWAY GUIDE PHOTOGRAPHY.

GOIN' ASHORE:
WRIGHTSVILLE BEACH, NC

For cruisers, Wrightsville (west side of the ICW) and Wrightsville Beach (east side of the ICW) offer a convenient stopover for replenishing, dining or sightseeing. Marinas line both sides of the ICW beginning immediately south of the Wrightsville Beach Bascule Bridge and just off the ICW on Motts Channel, but a word of caution: This is a popular stopover so make a reservation in advance.

Just a short ½-mile walk to the west of the ICW and within easy reach of all the marinas you will find Lumina Commons Shopping Center, an open shopping center with a large 24-hour Harris Teeter grocery, West Marine, bank, restaurants, fast food and numerous specialty shops. Craft American Hardware (7002 Wrightsville Ave., 910-256-4782) is located just south of the Harris Teeter and is known for locating hard-to-find specialty items. Between the ICW and Plaza East look for Harbor Island Ship Models (7232 Wrightsville Avenue, 910-256-1110), a store featuring upper-end nautical artifacts.

The Post Office is one block east of the Wrightsville Beach Bridge. Adjacent to it is Redix, a store with sharply contrasting offerings. On entering you will find yourself among rows of ordinary beach and tourist items, but go to the right, and you'll enter a separate area well stocked with upper-end clothing brands, all at discount prices.

The tourist area of Wrightsville Beach along the oceanside is old school, a family-style beach that has matured in a manner that makes it the envy of other seaside communities. Here, you will find parking meters and public rinse stations, fishing piers and municipal parks, soccer fields and surfing and a whole lot of sunning. Wrightsville doesn't lure visitors with perforated coupons from a welcome center vacation packet. Guests flock here because they have discovered that it is a great place to retreat, relax and rinse away the stress of mainland living.

On the west side of the ICW just beyond the bascule bridge spanning the ICW lie the perks of the American dream. Gated communities and golf courses, townhomes above upscale shops and five-star restaurants. But on the beach, the breeze blows up Banks Channel, turning an average day into a memorable moment as skiffs and day sailors work the tidal currents. On Wrightsville Beach, the "coast of living" is always within reach if you have a boat or float to get you onto the water.

History: One of the earliest buildings on the island was a camping lodge used by sailors near the current location of the Carolina Yacht Club (CYC), the first structure on the island. The CYC remains the second oldest yacht club residing in its original location (401 S. Lumina Ave., 910-256-3396). During the initial dredging of the ICW, sand and clay were deposited in the area called The Hammocks. Today, this area sits between the mainland and the beach and is known as Harbor Island.

In 1887, the railroad was extended across the marsh, but it stopped at the eastern tip of Harbor Island, leaving visitors to unload their towels and blankets and hike across a foot bridge to the beach. In 1889, the railroad was extended, fueling development along the island. Transported by trolley-powered "beach cars," visitors made Wrightsville a popular

Masonboro, NC

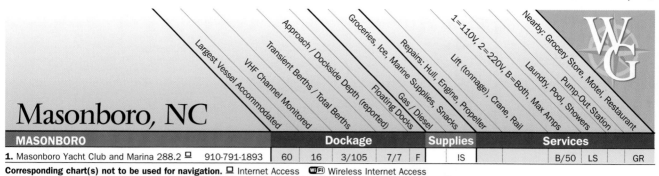

MASONBORO	Largest Vessel Accommodated	VHF Channel Monitored	Transient Berths / Total Berths	Approach / Dockside Depth (reported)	Floating Docks	Gas / Diesel	Groceries, Ice, Marine Supplies, Snacks	Repairs: Hull, Engine, Propeller	Lift (tonnage), Crane, Rail	1=110V, 2=220V, B=Both, Max Amps	Laundry, Pool, Showers	Pump-Out Station	Nearby: Grocery Store, Motel, Restaurant
	Dockage						**Supplies**			**Services**			
1. Masonboro Yacht Club and Marina 288.2 (Internet Access) 910-791-1893	60	16	3/105	7/7	F		IS			B/50	LS		GR

Corresponding chart(s) not to be used for navigation. Internet Access   Wireless Internet Access

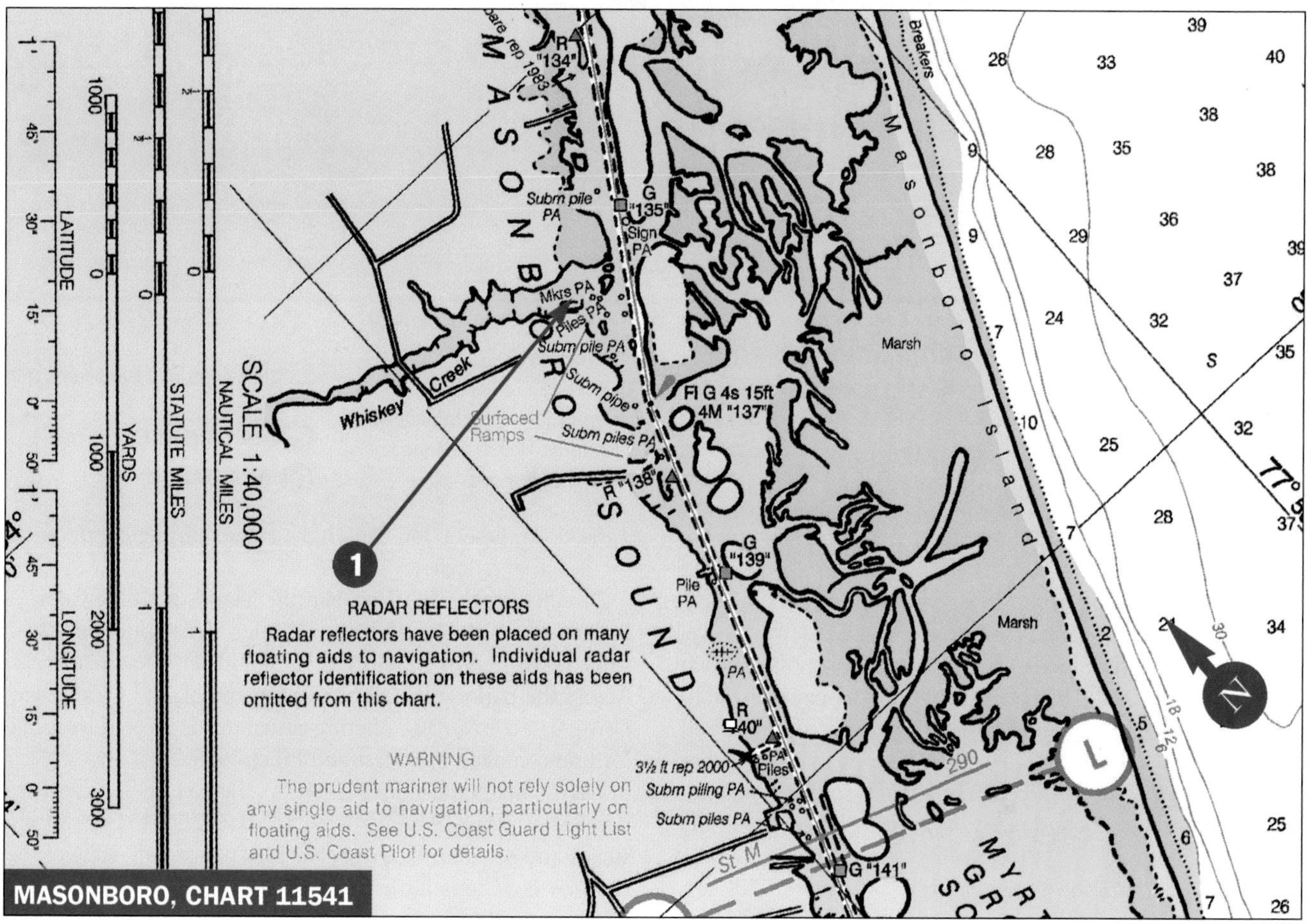

MASONBORO, CHART 11541

summer destination. Places like Station One, a condominium complex, still retain the name of the "beach car" stops. After the 1920s, a new highway connected the island to the mainland, and within a few years the "beach cars" ceased to run. In 1905, the Lumina Pavilion was opened. The 12,500-square-foot complex hosted many of the day's big bands. The pavilion included an outdoor movie screen aimed towards the ocean so viewers could sit in the sand.

Culture: The Wrightsville Beach Museum of History (303 W. Salisbury St., 910-256-2569) is located in the Myers Cottage.

Attractions: Wrightsville's top attraction is the beach itself. Framed by the two inlets and shadowed by both old and new cottages, the sand and surf remain the best parts of the town. Masonboro Island, just south of Masonboro Inlet, is a protected wildlife preserve and makes a pleasant dinghy trip. Wrightsville Beach Park is a great place to walk pets, shoot hoops or toss a Frisbee. There is a walking path to Lee's Nature Park. You can take kite surfing lessons at Blowing in the Wind (222 Causeway Drive, 910-509-9989).

Special events: Each May, Wrightsville Beach hosts the Surf-Sun-Sand Volleyball and Bocce Ball Tournament. This four- or six-person coed volleyball tournament has divisions for skill levels from novice to intermediate. Call 910-256-7925 for more information. In June, join locals for Jazz in the Park on the lawn. Call 910-256-9880 for details.

Drop by Crystal Pier for the annual East Coast Wahine Championships held each August. Competition includes surfing in the categories of shortboard, longboard, pro longboard, advanced shortboard, bodyboard and novice divisions.

In October, there is the Bark in the Park Skyhoundz Hyperflight Canine Disc Championships. Mutts and purebreds compete to catch flying discs. The event takes place at Wrightsville Beach Park from 11:00 a.m. until about 1:00 p.m. Call 910-256-7925 for more information.

ATTRACTIONS
1 Wrightsville Beach Museum of History

DINING
2 Tower 7 Baja Mexican Grill
3 22 North
4 South Beach Grill
5 Banks Channel Pub & Grill
6 Jerry Allen's Sports Bar
7 Oceanic
8 Bluewater
9 Causeway Café
10 The Bridge Tender Restaurant
11 Dockside Restaurant

GROCERIES/CARRYOUT
12 Robert's Market
13 Lumina Commons Shopping Center
14 Lighthouse Beer & Wine

LAUNDRY
15 Coastal Dry Cleaners and Coin Laundry

MARINE SUPPLIES
13 West Marine, Lumina Commons Shopping Center

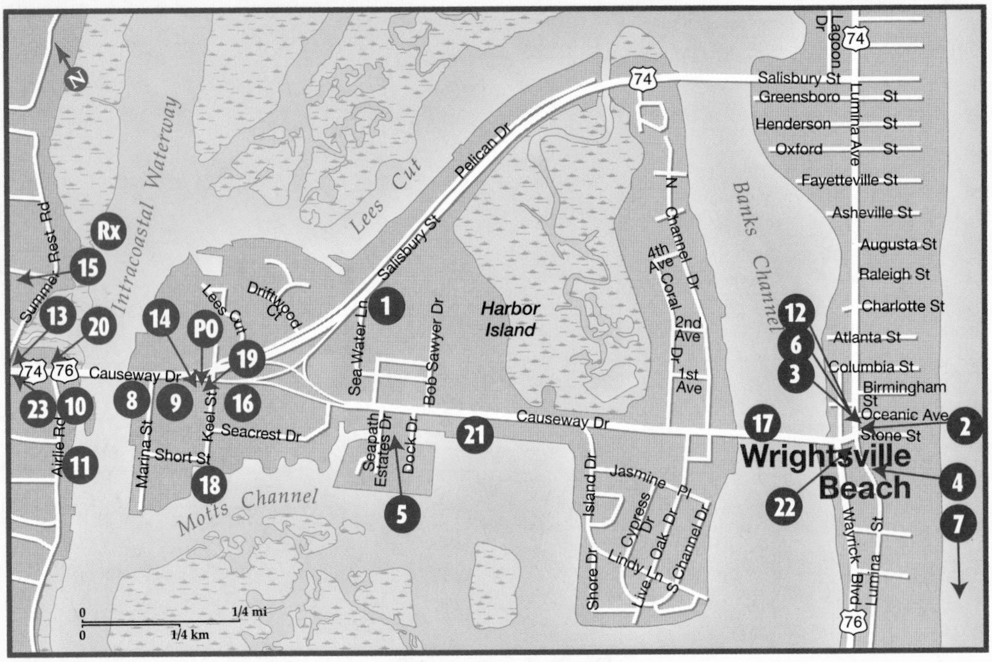

Reference the marina listing tables to see all the marinas in the area.

RECREATION
16 Blowing in the Wind
17 Wrightsville Beach Supply Co.

SEAFOOD
18 Motts Channel Seafood

SHOPPING
19 Redix
20 Harbor Island Ship Models
21 Hatteras House Antiques
22 Hallelu Boutique
23 Craft American Hardware

PO POST OFFICE

Rx PHARMACY

Shopping: Near the dinghy dock on Banks Channel is Robert's Market (32 N. Lumina Ave., 910-256-2641). They carry a good selection of produce, dry goods, meats and seafood and offer an in-store ATM. Redix (120 Causeway Drive, 910-256-2201) is a good bet for basic fishing supplies, beach ware and beverages. They also carry over-the-counter medicines. The post office is next door. Motts Channel Seafood (120 Short St., 910-256-3474) will be happy to put together a seafood sampler of shrimp, fish steaks and scallops. You can rent bikes and beach equipment at Wrightsville Beach Supply Co. (1 N. Lumina Ave., 910-256-8821).

Hallelu Boutique (84 Waynick Blvd., 910-509-0570) carries a great selection of gently used clothes. Hatteras House Antiques (426 Causeway Drive, 910-256-3667) is a high-end antique shop specializing in Victorian art glass and European porcelains. Lighthouse Beer & Wine (220 Causeway Drive, 910-256-8622) carries a wide variety of wine. They have over 400 different types of beers along with cigars, cheese, gourmet snacks and gift baskets.

Restaurants: Over on the beach a short taxi ride away you will find several good dining options. For southwestern fare, try Tower 7 Baja Mexican Grill (4 N. Lumina Ave., 910-256-8585). 22 North (22 N. Lumina Ave., 910-509-0177) serves fresh seafood, steaks, burgers and chicken. Overlooking Banks Channel, South Beach Grill (100 S. Lumina Ave., 910-256-4646) is a local favorite, serving a good mix of sandwiches. Banks Channel Pub & Grille (530 Causeway Drive, 910-256-2269), open until 2:00 a.m., is a favorite with the late night crowd. You can get burgers and beverages at Jerry Allen's Sports Bar (38 N. Lumina Ave., 910-256-8286). And don't miss Oceanic Restaurant (703 S. Lumina Ave., 910-256-5551), where you can enjoy indoor dining overlooking the beach and ocean.

Directly on the ICW on Harbor Island, try Bluewater (4 Marina St., 910-256-8500) for dinner. This sprawling two-story restaurant overlooks the ICW and serves a great meal. Across the parking lot is The Causeway Cafe (114 Causeway Drive, 910-256-3730), offering casual meals favored by locals for home cooked breakfast and lunch.

On the mainland side of the ICW, there is The Bridge Tender Restaurant (1414 Airlie Road, 910-256-4519) serving steaks and seafood with a spectacular panoramic view of the ICW. A few steps farther, you will find the Dockside Restaurant (1308 Airlie Road, 910-256-2752). The menu boasts fresh seafood, both broiled or fried, snow crab legs, shrimp Creole and Baja tuna.

A tugboat on the ICW. WATERWAY GUIDE PHOTOGRAPHY.

ADDITIONAL RESOURCES

- WRIGHTSVILLE BEACH CHAMBER OF COMMERCE: www.wrightsville.com
- TOWN OF WRIGHTSVILLE BEACH: 910-256-7900 www.townofwrightsvillebeach.com

NEARBY GOLF COURSES

Inland Greens Golf Course, 5945 Inland Greens Drive, Wilmington, NC 28405, 910-452-9900 www.inlandgreens.com (5 miles)

Wilmington Municipal Golf Course, 311 S. Wallace Ave., Wilmington, NC 28409, 910-791-0558 (15 miles)

NEARBY MEDICAL FACILITIES

New Hanover Regional Medical Center, 2131 S. 17th St., Wilmington, NC 28401, 910-343-7000 (9 miles)

New Hanover Medical Group, PA, 1960 S. 16th St., Wilmington, NC 28401, 910-343-9991 (10 miles)

Phyllis B Cook DDS, 7028 Wrightsville Ave., Wilmington, NC 28403, 910-256-8486 (Dentistry)

Salling and Tate, 2002 Eastwood Rd #105, Wilmington, NC 28403, 910-256-9040 (Dentistry)

Wrightsville Beach to Cape Fear River—Mile 283 to Mile 297

Below Wrightsville Beach, the route follows a dredged channel through a succession of marshy sloughs for about 12 miles to Snows Cut, at Mile 295, the connecting link with the Cape Fear River. Stay in the channel, because parts of this area tend to shoal, and the current runs swiftly. Note that Carolina Beach is one of the state's busiest summer resorts, but its grocery stores and restaurants stay open during the off-season as well.

THE FOLLOWING AREA REQUIRES SPECIAL ATTENTION DUE TO SHOALING OR CHANGES TO THE CHANNEL

MASONBORO AND MYRTLE GROVE SOUND

NAVIGATION: Use Charts 11541 and 11534. Through Masonboro Sound and Myrtle Grove Sound, the route runs straight and narrow. Shoaling frequently occurs here, especially at the many junctions where side creeks cross the ICW, and temporary buoys are placed to mark the shallow areas. Our cruising editor reported 10-foot depths in this area in spring 2011. The Carolina Beach Inlet Crossing of the ICW at Mile 293.5 was dredged in February 2011. (Boaters had been running aground near green can "155.") The Corps of Engineers regularly surveys the Carolina Beach Inlet Crossing, and survey results are posted at www.saw.usace.army.mil/nav. Conditions can change quickly, and this is an area very prone to shoaling, so caution and seeking local knowledge are advised in transiting between red nun "154" and red daybeacon "156." The shallow ocean inlet at Carolina Beach is marked, but shifting shoals make this a local knowledge, small-boat inlet, although it is often dredged by the USACE and was dredged again in early 2011. At Mile 295, immediately before the ICW turns to enter Snows Cut, a deep, well-marked channel leads to Carolina Beach.

END SPECIAL CAUTION AREA.

The fixed Snows Cut Highway Bridge (65-foot vertical clearance, Mile 295.7) and the overhead power cables (68-foot vertical clearance) at Snows Cut should provide enough room for most. Exercise care here, as the current runs strong at the bridge, and eddies can make boat handling difficult.

The high ancient sand dune at the west end of Snows Cut is eroding substantially into the otherwise well-dredged channel. While passing this dune (on the north side of the cut), deep-footed boats should favor the south side and honor the new movable markers: red nun "162," green can "161A" and red nun "162A." The Snows Cut area was also dredged in spring 2010. The ranges (Range "A" and Range "B") at the exit from Snows Cut were discontinued in 2008. Look for new markers here and be sure to compensate for side-setting currents from the Cape Fear River as you exit the cut.

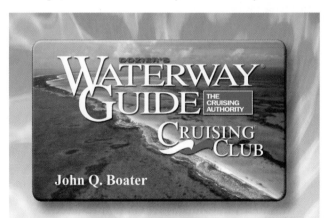

Dockage: Five miles south of Wrightsville Beach at Whiskey Creek, the Masonboro Yacht Club and Marina is visible to starboard. The marina has floating docks with 100 slips, water and electricity. Its two-story clubhouse

Looking west over Snows Cut and the ICW. (Not to be used for navigation.) WATERWAY GUIDE PHOTOGRAPHY.

for boaters has a fantastic view, along with showers and laundry facilities.

At the entrance to Snows Cut, you will find transient facilities to port, at Joyner Marina, Mile 295, at the north end of Snows Cut. Be aware that its fuel and transient dock is just off the ICW beyond flashing green "161" and should be passed without a wake.

Across the channel to the west—immediately south of the entrance to Snows Cut at red daybeacon "2" in Carolina Beach Bight—is Waterfront Villas and Yacht Club, a private facility. Carolina Beach Municipal Marina, at the southern end of the bight, has a fuel dock and may have short-term mooring available. The Federal Point Marina, across from green daybeacon "7," on the starboard side, caters mainly to locals. It has a few transient spots and no fuel. The City of Carolina Beach has received some grant monies to invest and build a mooring field in the bight. The field of 10 moorings, which were not yet in place prior to the printing of this guide, will be a welcome addition to an otherwise marginal anchorage. It will accommodate boats between 26 and 55 feet. New dinghy docks are also part of the plan.

The small marina at Carolina Beach State Park in a basin at the southeast end of Snows Cut has been completely rebuilt and opened on November 1, 2010 with shower facilities, restrooms and fuel (gas and diesel). The largest boat allowed is 40-foot overall length. The basin has been dredged and now has 7 feet at low tide.

Anchorage: The entire bight at Carolina Beach (south of Snows Cut and behind the beach) has more than adequate water off the marked channel, except where specifically noted on the chart. Anchorage is good along the channel, but space is limited, and boat traffic, particularly on summer weekends, is intense. The most popular spot is outside the channel between the last islet and green daybeacon "7," although the soft bottom here makes for difficult holding; be sure to back down on the anchor hard. Note that a mooring field is in the planning stages for this area. Beware of sharp shoaling and submerged pilings in the harbor near red daybeacon "4." Holding is fair here but be prepared for an eddy effect under certain wind and tide conditions. The shoreside area is mostly developed. Do not anchor by the camp on the Pleasure Island side, as there are submerged piles. From here, it is easy to get an early morning start through Snows Cut and down the Cape Fear River.

Cape Fear River to Wilmington

While you could use a rental car to drive from Wrightsville Beach to Wilmington, the trip upriver on the deep, well-marked shipping channel provides a routine passage with interesting features. Renting a car from Wrightsville Beach might still be your best bet if you want to see the surrounding area, but the tour will take several days. If you choose the ICW route, you will find dockage within walking distance of shopping and restaurants. You can see a battleship, museums, beautiful gardens and a battlefield. Historic Orton Plantation comes abreast to port as you pass out of Snows Cut and head north on the main river channel. Nine miles upriver, also on the west bank, stands Clarendon Plantation.

NAVIGATION: Use Chart 11537. **Use Wilmington Tide Tables.** The easiest way to make this upriver run is to go with the flood tide but be prepared for a rough chop if the wind is against the current. Conditions will improve in the upper reaches where the river narrows, but currents will be strong during the ebb tide. From Snows Cut, set a course northwest along the well-marked, but narrow channel (8-foot depths). Just past red daybeacon "4," the channel becomes wider and deeper as you head northward to Wilmington.

Dockage: Upriver at flashing green buoy "59" (approximately seven nautical miles north of ICW Mile 297), a well-marked channel leads off to starboard to Wilmington Marine Center. Wilmington Marine Center maintains 6-foot depths (at extremely low tide) in its entrance channel and basin. Even with a tidal range of about 4 feet, deep-draft vessels find good water depths. This marina has full transient facilities, new floating docks, pump-out service and fuel. Call ahead for reservations. A 75-ton lift and 400-ton railway facilitate repairs and maintenance of very large vessels.

The Wilmington City Docks (just across from flashing green "63" or approximately 12 nautical miles from ICW Mile 297) offer over 1,000 feet of transient dockage (most of which is at floating docks) with public restrooms; no showers or laundry. For reservations, call the city dockmaster at 910-520-6875. Limited long-term dockage is available between October 1 and March 31. (Make arrangements through the dockmaster.) The City Docks are located downtown in the center of the Historic District, with museums, shops, restaurants and nightlife all within walking distance.

Bennett Bros. Yachts at Cape Fear Marina is located a short distance upriver, beyond the Interstate 117 Bascule Bridge (26-foot closed vertical clearance). This full-service boatyard, located a few miles from downtown, also provides transient dockage for vessels up to 176 feet, pump-out facilities at every slip, free ice, wireless Internet, showers and a laundry.

QUICK FACT:

OSPREYS

A common species to spot along the ICW is the osprey, a large bird of prey found on all continents except Antarctica. Worldwide, there are an estimated 460,000 ospreys. Ospreys live near bodies of water such as rivers, marshes, lakes, mangroves and seashores. The raptor weighs three to four pounds, grows to 2 feet in length and has a 5- to 6-foot wingspan. The bird is whitish on the head and underparts, and has a glossy brown coloration on the upperparts, wings and eyepatch. The osprey's feet are white with four toes (with black talons), one of which is reversible. Its short tail can be both white and dark brown, and its narrow wings have four finger-like feathers.

The osprey's diet is almost exclusively fish. Ospreys typically spot their prey from 32 to 130 feet above water, hover, then plunge, feet first, into the water. The bird adjusts the angle of its dive into the water depending on the type of prey in pursuit; steep and slow dives are used for slower-moving fish deeper in the water, while faster fish require fast, long dives. Once the osprey has acquired its meal, talons and barbed pads on the soles of its feet help the bird hold its prey tight, and it will turn the fish face-forward to minimize wind resistance. Ospreys usually mate for life. Females lay two to four eggs in March, which usually hatch sequentially, one to five days apart. A common sight on top of many ICW daybeacons is the osprey nest. Ospreys build their nests on manmade structures and those made specifically for nests. Be careful not to pass too closely by a nest or you may get an angry peck on the head! Ospreys migrate to South America and reappear in the mid-Atlantic around St. Patrick's Day.

Snows Cut, Carolina Beach, NC

CAROLINA BEACH		Largest Vessel Accommodated	VHF Channel Monitored	Transient Berths / Total Berths	Approach / Dockside Depth (reported)	Floating Docks	Gas / Diesel	Groceries, Ice, Marine Supplies, Snacks	Repairs: Hull, Engine, Propeller	Lift (tonnage), Crane, Rail	1=110V, 2=220V, B=Both, Max Amps	Laundry, Pool, Showers	Pump-Out Station	Nearby: Grocery Store, Motel, Restaurant
		Dockage					Supplies		Services					
1. Joyner Marina 295 (Internet Access) (Wireless Internet Access)	910-458-5053	100	16/11	15/69	6/6	F	GD	IMS	HEP		B/50	LPS	P	GMR
2. Carolina Beach State Park 297.1	910-458-7770	45	16	8/42	4/4	F	GD	IMS			1/30	LS	P	GR

Corresponding chart(s) not to be used for navigation. (Internet Access icon) Internet Access (WiFi icon) Wireless Internet Access

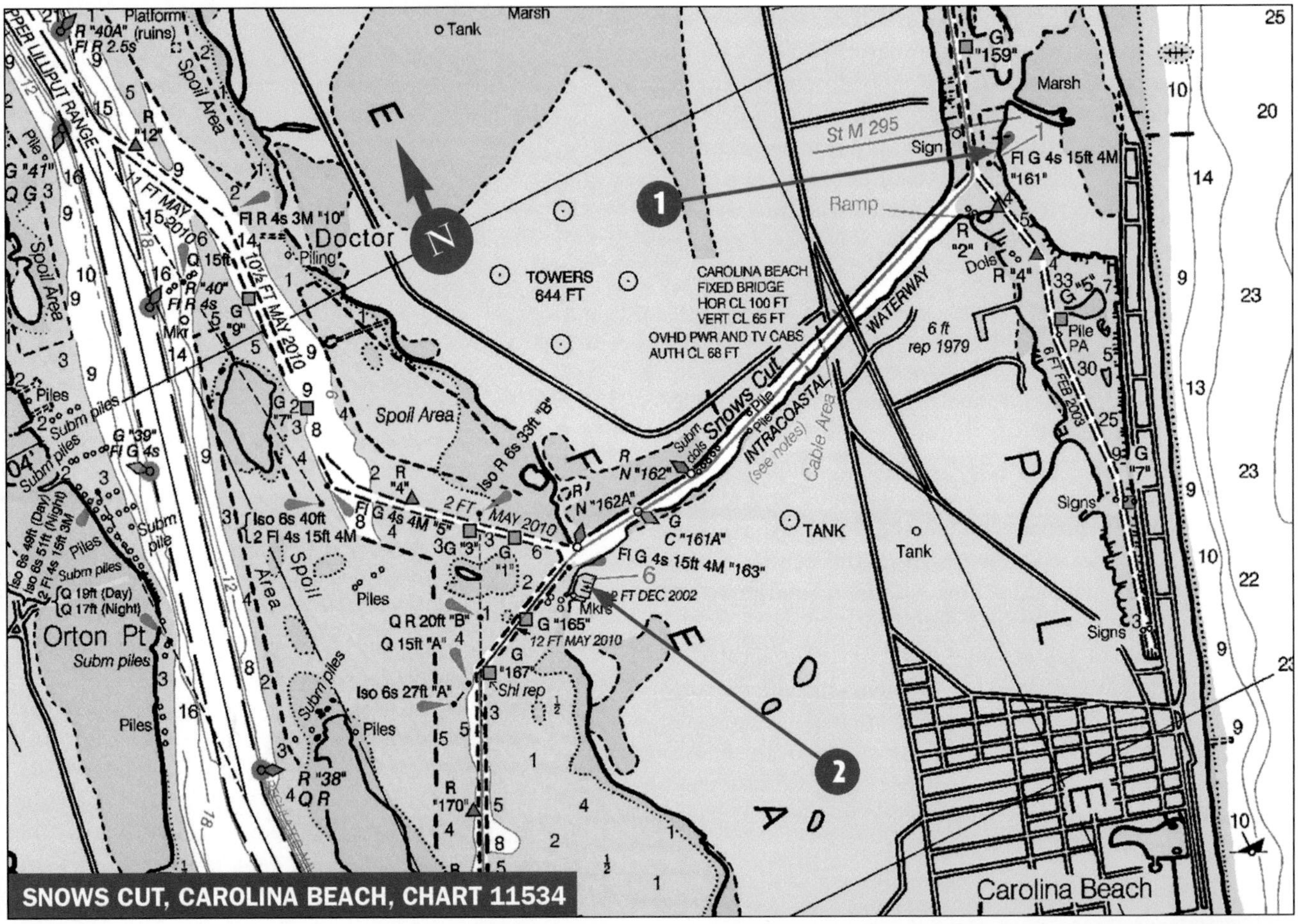

Looking south over Carolina Beach. (Not to be used for navigation.) WATERWAY GUIDE PHOTOGRAPHY.

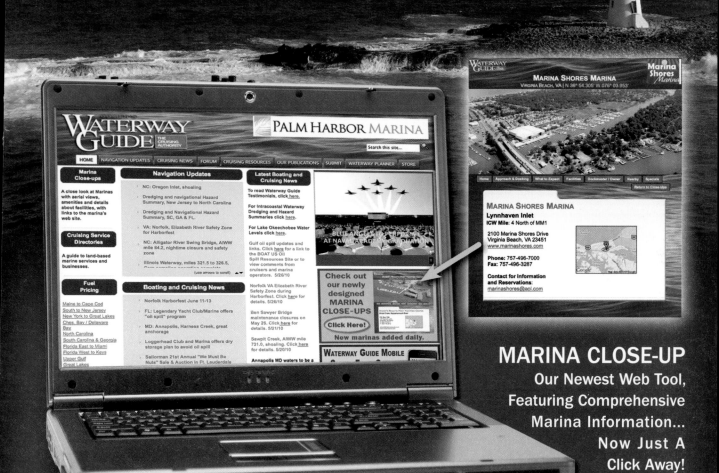

GOIN' ASHORE:
WILMINGTON, NC

The heart of downtown Wilmington is its riverfront. Once a bustling wharf of warehouses, boatsheds, docks and stables, today, a cluster of shops and restaurants span several city blocks along the Cape Fear River. Stroll along cobblestone streets, and listen to the river breeze blowing through branches gray-bearded with Spanish moss. You can also hear the clip-clopping of hooves as carriage tours pass antebellum homes wrapped in picket fences, jasmine and magnolias.

For more than a century, the Chandler's Wharf (225 S. Water St.) was the center of commerce with warehouses brimming with naval supplies, tools, cotton and turpentine. A fire destroyed much of the wharf, but the flavor of the 1870s has been restored, giving Wilmington the feel of the Old South without the heat and humidity of Charleston, SC.

History: For more than a century, railroading was Wilmington's chief industry. In 1840, the Wilmington & Weldon Railroad drove the last spike, making it the longest continuous rail line in the world. Near the turn of the century, several railroads merged to become the Atlantic Coast Line Railroad. During this time, the railroad was referred to as the "aorta" of Wilmington, contributing to the commercial and industrial growth of the region. In 1960, the Atlantic Coast Line moved its headquarters from Wilmington to Jacksonville, FL.

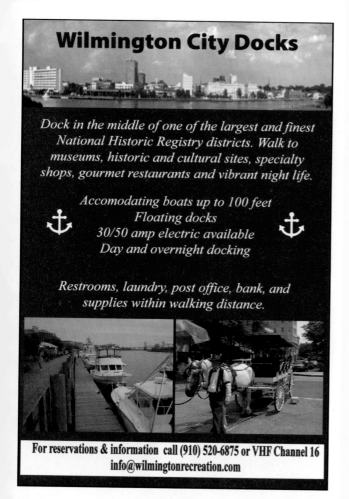

Culture: Wilmington is home to several film companies, and the waterfront has been featured in television shows such as "Dawson's Creek." A tour of the Screen Gems Studios (1223 23rd St. N) is available. Call 910-343-3500 for more information. At Cinematique of Wilmington (254 N. Front St., 910-632-2285), you can catch foreign and classic films several nights a week. Thalian Hall (310 Chestnut St.,910-632-2241) is the home of the country's oldest community theater and currently hosts national touring companies as well as numerous local theater companies. One of the best ways to see the waterfront area is by buggy. Call Horsedrawn Carriage & Trolley Tours (910-251-8889) to reserve your ride. Tours leave from the corner of Market Street between Water and Front streets.

Attractions: One of Wilmington's best known attractions lies across the river. Visitors to the *USS North Carolina* battleship (1 Battleship Rd., 910-251-5797) can tour the main deck, interior rooms and gun turrets. There is a Roll of Honor in the wardroom listing the names of North Carolinians who died in the line of duty during World War II. The site also features a gift shop, visitors center and picnic area.

The Bellamy Mansion (503 Market St., 910-251-3700) is a great example of antebellum architecture. After the fall of Fort Fisher in 1865, Federal troops used the home as their headquarters. Inside, you will find historical exhibits, arts and exhibitions. Carriage and walking tours begin out front. Burgwin-Wright House (224 Market St., 910-762-0570) is distinguished by its wrap-around, two-story porches and tiered gardens. The massive ballast-stone foundation is the remains of an abandoned town jail.

The Cape Fear Museum (814 Market St., 910-798-4370) is the oldest history museum in North Carolina. Inside, there is a 20-foot-tall giant ground sloth skeleton, a miniature recreation of the second battle of Fort Fisher and a room dedicated to native son and basketball great Michael Jordan. The Discovery Gallery includes a giant, crawl-through beaver lodge, dinosaur fossils and an entertaining Venus flytrap model. Wilmington Railroad Museum (505 Nutt St., 910-763-2634) has an extensive library of railroading history. It is conveniently located on the waterfront and open year-round.

Cape Fear Serpentarium (20 Orange St., 910-762-1669) houses over 100 species of snakes, most of them deadly. It claims to be the largest collection of venomous reptiles in the world. The serpentarium boasts the world's only breeding colony of the nearly extinct black-headed bushmaster. At the Wilmington Children's Museum (116 Orange St., 910-254-3534) kids can climb aboard a pirate ship, experiment in the science lab or make souvenirs in the art room.

Special events: The Azalea Festival comes to town every April, drawing big stars and big crowds. The street fair, parade and garden tours attract many; make sure to book your reservations early. Call 910-794-4650 for more information.

The Riverfest is held the first weekend of October and includes the Great Waiter's Wine Race, boat rides, military exhibits and a handmade self-powered Riverfest Raft Regatta. A Kids Zone set up in the Cotton Exchange parking lot offers face painting, interactive games, arts and crafts activities,

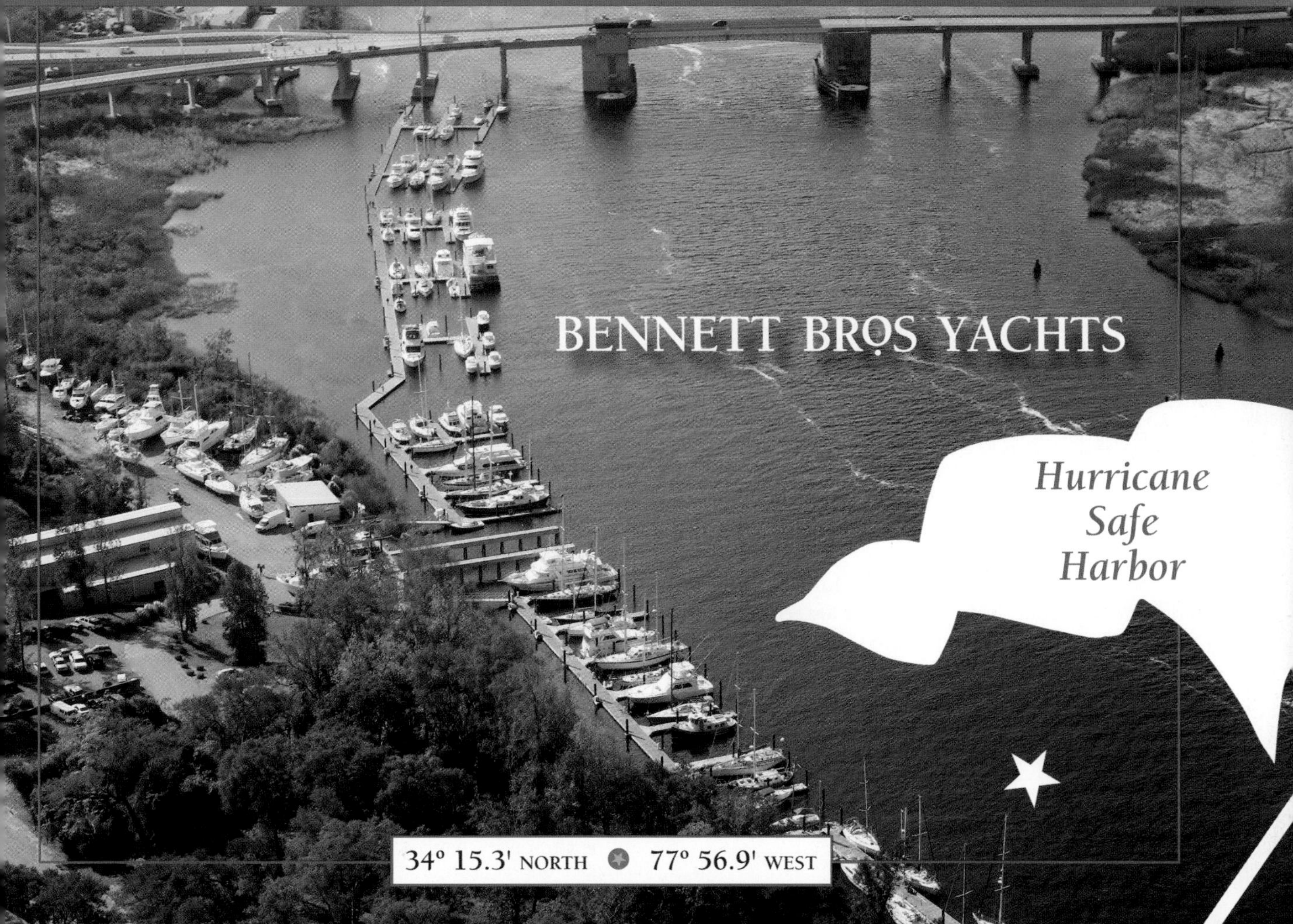

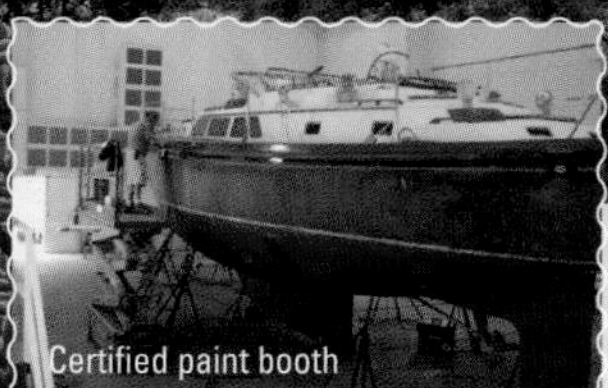
Certified paint booth

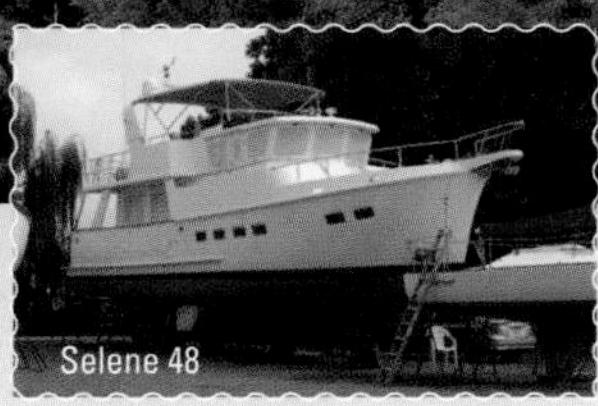
Selene 48

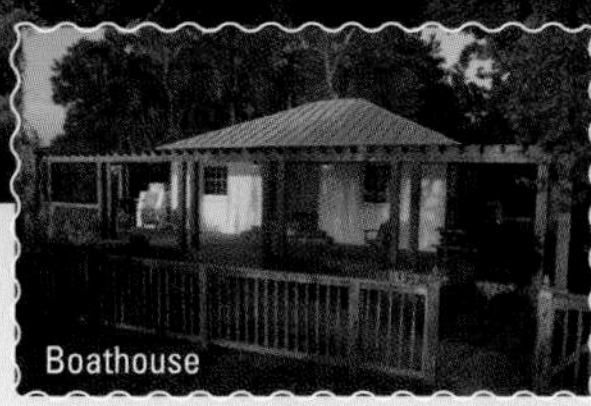
Boathouse

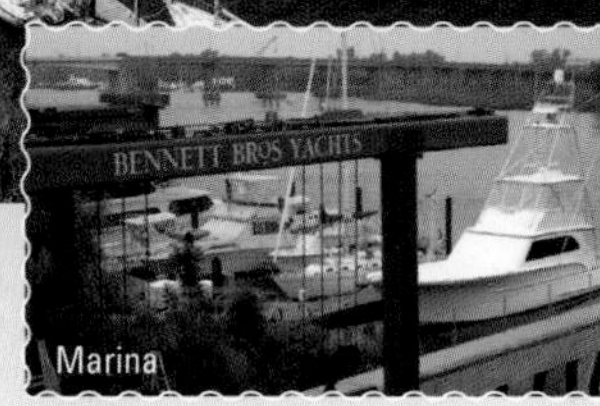

Marina

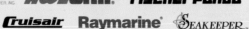

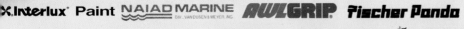

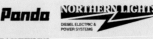

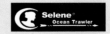

Wilmington, Cape Fear River, NC

WILMINGTON	Largest Vessel Accommodated	VHF Channel Monitored	Transient Berths / Total Berths	Approach / Dockside Depth (reported)	Floating Docks	Gas / Diesel	Groceries, Ice, Marine Supplies, Snacks	Repairs: Hull, Engine, Propeller	Lift (tonnage), Crane, Rail	1=110V, 2=220V, B=Both, Max Amps	Laundry, Pool, Showers	Pump-Out Station	Nearby: Grocery Store, Motel, Restaurant
	Dockage					Supplies		Services					
1. Bennett Brothers Yachts Inc. 14.4 N of 297 910-772-9277	175	13	25/75	28/18	F		GIMS	HEP	L70	B/200+	LS	P	GMR
2. Cape Fear Marina 14.4 N of 297 910-772-9277	175	13	25/75	15/8	F		GIMS	HEP	L70	B/200+	LS	P	GMR
3. Wilmington City Docks 13.6 N of 297 910-520-6875	100	16/68	30/30	38/16	F					B/50			GMR
CAPE FEAR RIVER													
4. Wilmington Marine Center 7 N of 297 910-395-5055	120	16/09	6/106	6/6	F	GD	IM	HEP	L75,R400	B/50	S	P	R
5. Champney Yacht Sales & Service 7 N of 297 910-395-5008	110	16			F			HEP	L75,R	B/50	S	P	
6. Gregory Poole Marine Services 7 N of 297 910-791-8002	CATERPILLAR ENGINE DISTRIBUTOR												

Corresponding chart(s) not to be used for navigation. Internet Access Wireless Internet Access

entertainment, rides, displays, a petting zoo and more. Call 910-452-6862, or check www.wilmingtonriverfest.com for more information.

Join sailors and other scary folks for the Halloween History-Mystery Tour. This popular Halloween tour begins at the Bellamy Mansion Museum (503 Market St.) and continues through historic downtown Wilmington. Experience the Port City's haunted and mysterious past as you visit historic homes and other venues, including a haunted cemetery. Costumed storytellers appear at various sites along the tour, offering insights into Wilmington's rich and spooky past. Wear comfortable shoes and bring a flashlight. Call 910-251-3700 for more information.

At the end of Market Street on the waterfront, you will find free live concerts on Friday nights during the summer months and a farmers markets on Saturday mornings from April through December.

Shopping: At the turn of the century, cotton was still king, and one of the largest and busiest cotton export companies in the world was located in Wilmington. Today, eight restored buildings, connected by brick walkways and open-air courtyards, house 30 unique specialty shops and restaurants, each a charming reflection of the style and feel of Wilmington's 19th-century working port days. If you are looking for a gift, book, art or home décor item, spend time strolling through the Cotton Exchange (321 N. Front St., 910-254-9281).

Looking upriver over Wilmington, NC.
(Not to be used for navigation.) WATERWAY GUIDE PHOTOGRAPHY.

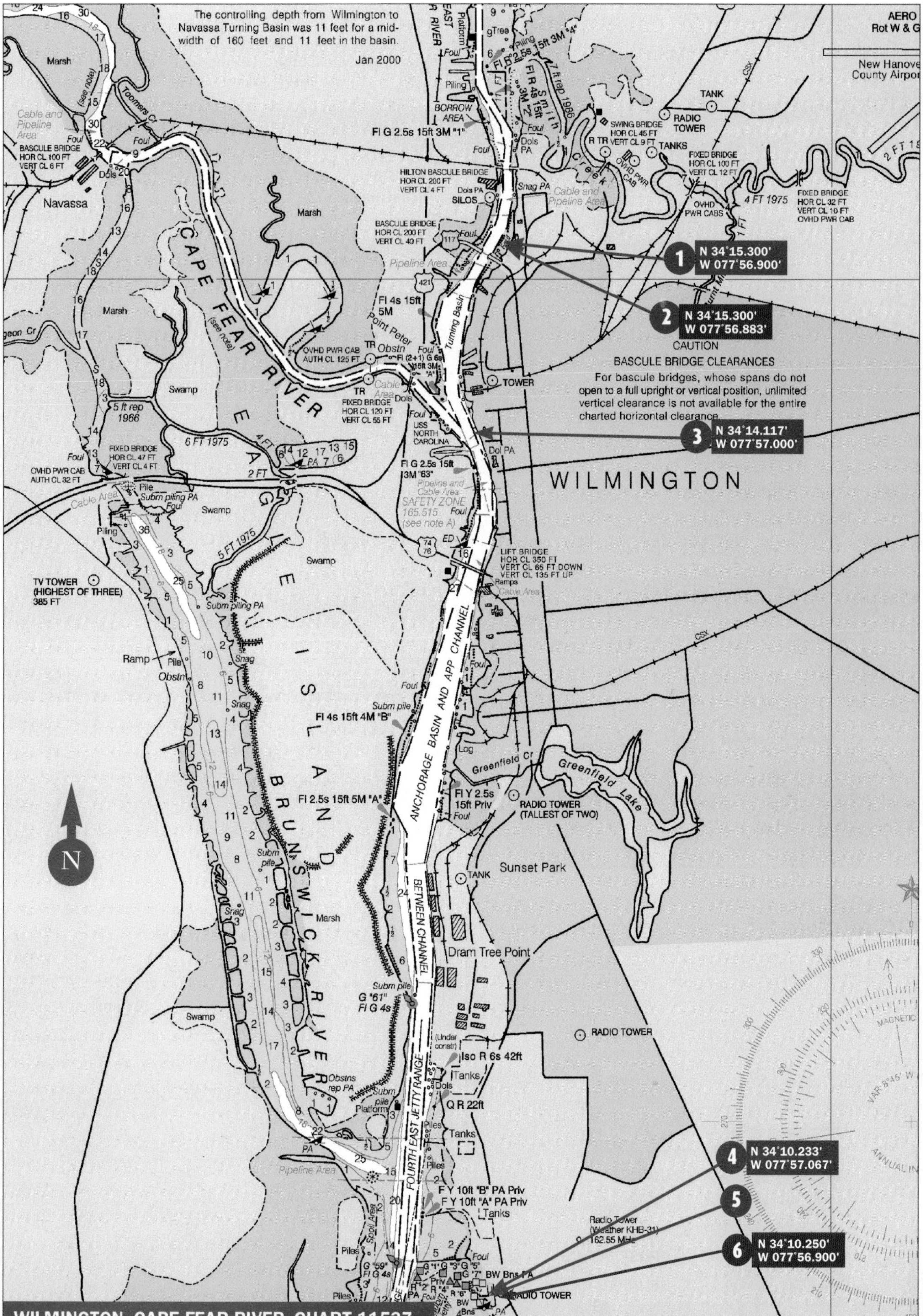

WILMINGTON, CAPE FEAR RIVER, CHART 11537

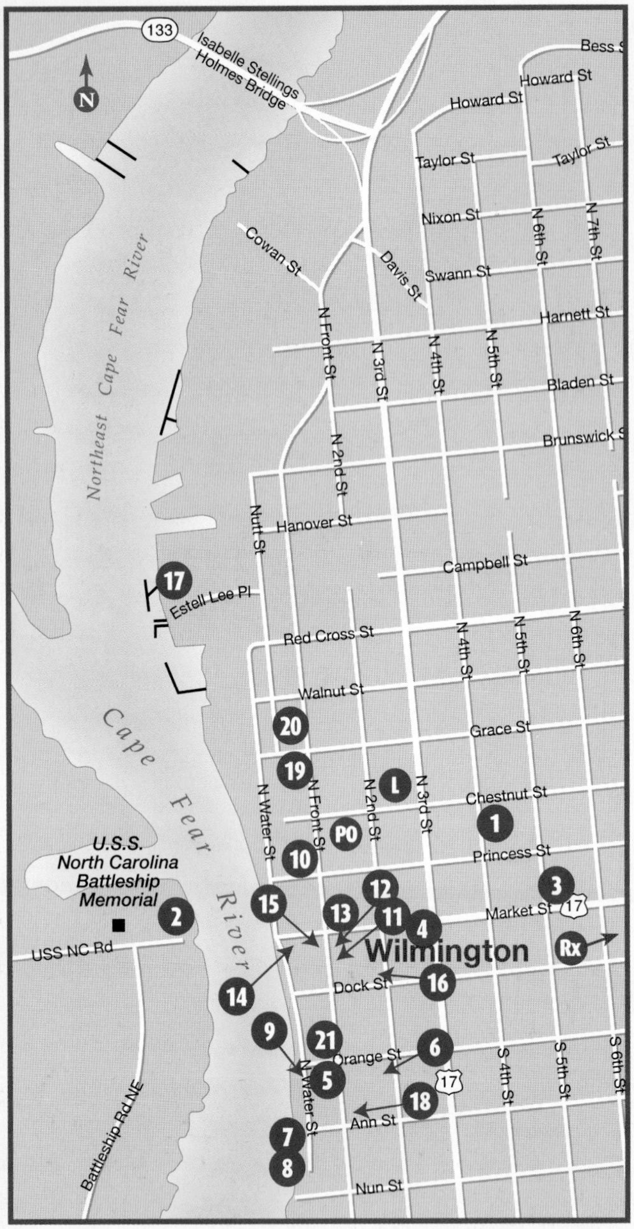

Reference the marina listing tables to see all the marinas in the area.

ATTRACTIONS
1 Thalian Hall
2 *USS North Carolina*
3 Bellamy Mansion Museum
4 Burgwin-Wright House
5 Cape Fear Serpentarium
6 Wilmington Children's Museum

DINING
7 Elijah's Restaurant
8 The Pilot House
9 George on the Riverwalk
10 Fat Tony's Italian Pub
11 Caffè Phoenix
12 Deluxe Café
13 Circa 1922
14 Union Café
15 Caprice Bistro

GROCERIES/CARRYOUT
16 Village Supermarket

INFORMATION
17 Visitor Information

POINTS OF INTEREST
18 Chandler's Wharf

SERVICES
19 Soapbox Laundro Lounge

SHOPPING
20 Cotton Exchange
21 Old Wilmington City Market

LIBRARY

POST OFFICE

PHARMACY

You will find the Village Supermarket (26 S. 2nd St., 910-762-6229) a few blocks from the waterfront, close to Market Street. Soapbox Laundro Lounge (255 N. Front St., 910-251-8500) is a laundry and bar with live music. Clean your clothes and check out the local artwork on display. Also, don't miss the Old Wilmington City Market (120 Front St.) that was established in 1880. It is a collection of eclectic and unique merchandise offered by numerous independent vendors.

Restaurants: In the Chandler's Wharf Complex, Elijah's Restaurant (2 Ann St., 910-343-1448) is one of Wilmington's finest eating establishments, and some contend the crab dip is the best on the coast. The Pilot House (2 Ann St., 910-343-0200) comes highly recommended by locals and offers a great view of the river. George on the Riverwalk (128 S. Water St., 910-763-2052) is favored for the atmosphere; Fat Tony's Italian Pub (131 N. Front St., 910-343-8881) offers good food and excellent service. Try their mussels marinara.

Caffè Phoenix (35 N. Front St., 910-343-1395) draws praise from the hard-to-please. At the Deluxe Café (114 Market St., 910-251-0333) there is a Sunday brunch that is hard to beat. The Circa 1922 (8 N. Front St., 910-762-1922), a tapas restaurant, has great ambience and good prices. Union Café (2 Market St., 910-763-7227) is famous for its wine selection and food. Also check out Caprice Bistro (10 Market St., 910-815-0810) for good steaks and service. This is a wonderful town for strolling and exploring. There are shops and restaurants too numerous to list.

ADDITIONAL RESOURCES

- CAPE FEAR COAST CONVENTION AND VISITORS CENTER, 877-406-2356, www.capefearcoast.com
- BATTLESHIP *USS NORTH CAROLINA*, 910-251-5797 www.battleshipnc.com

NEARBY GOLF COURSES
Inland Greens Golf Course, 5945 Inland Greens Drive, Wilmington, NC 28405, 910-452-9900
www.inlandgreens.com (7 miles)

NEARBY MEDICAL FACILITIES
New Hanover Regional Medical Center, 2131 S. 17th St., Wilmington, NC 28401, 910-343-7000 (3 miles)

Looking over Southport, NC. (Not to be used for navigation.) WATERWAY GUIDE PHOTOGRAPHY.

Carolina Beach to Southport, Mile 295 to Mile 309

Back on the ICW, the route to Southport leads through Snows Cut and down the Cape Fear River. A good procedure along this 12-mile-long downstream run to Southport is to run compass courses for each leg to assist in identifying the navigational aids that mark the course. The color of the marks change from side to side and also the numbering changes as you go down the Cape Fear River. Studying the charts before departure is, as always, a very wise decision.

NAVIGATION: Use Chart 11534. *(Note that the buoys are reversed from the normal ICW system when you reach the Cape Fear River at Mile 299: The yellow squares and triangles are what count for the ICW skipper—keep the yellow triangles on your starboard side, even if the aid is painted green, and leave the yellow squares to port.)* South of Snows Cut, additional buoys have been added in the Cape Fear River, increasing the ease of maintaining a visual ICW channel course from the helm. These additions have occasioned the renumbering of existing buoys in the area, and the new marker numbers are now correct on current charts. The numerous ranges used by the large ships in the Cape Fear River have been changed recently and may not correspond with those on your chart.

Currents: As you head south, you will experience strong tidal currents on the Cape Fear River from Snows Cut to Southport (Mile 297 to Mile 309). Slow-boat skippers take note: **Currents can run in excess of 2 knots during flood tide. Low-water slack, before flood tides, occurs in the river off Southport 1 hour and 16 minutes after the time listed in the tide tables for Charleston Harbor.** Adjust your departure time to arrive in Southport at or before the slack before flood tide begins. If you are going to press on past the harbor, arrive right at slack water to take advantage of the flood tide as you proceed on to Mile 320. With a strong wind against the current out on the river, a nasty sea can develop. In such conditions, you will have a calmer, albeit longer, trip if you buck the current instead of the waves.

There is also a strong current at Snows Cut, Mile 295.5. However, with low-water slack here being 5 hours and 54 minutes later than at Charleston, you will have some difficulty keeping with the current both in this area and on the Cape Fear River during the same trip. The Snows Cut current ebbs and floods from Carolina Beach Inlet, and the Cape Fear River's tides ebb and flood from the Cape Fear Inlet. That is why the current in Snows Cut will likely be from the opposite direction than in the Cape Fear River.

To sum up, Southport is another spot where you can't go wrong if you arrive at low-water slack, going either north or south. If you ride the maximum ebb down the Cape Fear River, you will be facing into a wicked current as you turn into the ICW at Southport. If you have a favorable current in Snows Cut, it will be against you in the Cape Fear River. When the tide and wind are opposing, batten down for a wet, uncomfortable ride to Southport.

Between Mile 299 and 302 on the west side of the Cape Fear River, you will pass the Army's Military Ocean Terminal at Sunny Point with its three large piers. This is

Southport, Bald Head Island, Oak Island, NC

		Largest Vessel Accommodated	VHF Channel Monitored	Transient Berths / Total Berths	Approach / Dockside Depth (reported)	Floating Docks	Gas / Diesel	Groceries, Ice, Marine Supplies, Snacks	Repairs: Hull, Engine, Propeller	Lift (tonnage), Crane, Rail	1=110V, 2=220V, B=Both, Max Amps	Laundry, Pool, Showers	Pump-Out Station	Nearby: Grocery Store, Motel, Restaurant
		Dockage					Supplies		Services					
SOUTHPORT														
1. Deep Point Marina 307 WiFi	**910-269-2380**	**100**	**16**	**20/82**	**10/10**	**F**	**GD**	**IS**			**B/100**	**LPS**	**P**	**R**
2. Southport Marina 309.3 Internet WiFi	**910-457-9900**	**180**	**16/09**	**20/200**	**8/6**	**F**	**GD**	**IMS**	**HEP**	**L65**	**B/100**	**LS**	**P**	**GMR**
3. Indigo Plantation & Marina 310	910-457-7380	50	16	1/49	10/6	F					B/50			R
4. South Harbour Village Marina 311.4 Internet WiFi	**910-454-7486**	**200**	**16**	**35/152**	**12+/12+**	**F**	**GD**	**GIMS**			**B/100**	**LS**	**P**	**GMR**
5. American Fish Company 312	910-457-5488	FISH WHOLESALER & DISTRIBUTOR								L50				
BALD HEAD ISLAND														
6. Bald Head Island Marina 2.8 S of 309 Internet	**910-457-7380**	**115**	**16**	**25/150**	**8/7**	**F**	**GD**	**GIS**			**B/100**	**LPS**	**P**	**GMR**
OAK ISLAND														
7. St. James Plantation Marina 315 Internet WiFi	**910-253-0463**	**120**	**16**	**50/155**	**7/7**	**F**	**GD**	**GIMS**	**HEP**	**L**	**B/50**	**LS**	**P**	**GMR**

Corresponding chart(s) not to be used for navigation. Internet Access WiFi Wireless Internet Access

a restricted area protected by a security barrier marked by 45 dolphins connected to each other with cables with three openings for ships to pass. Each dolphin pile shows a white light and white and orange sign worded DANGER RESTRICTED AREA. This is the largest ammunitions port in the United States and is patrolled by smaller vessels. Steer clear of this area. Also of note in navigating the Cape Fear River is the Fishers Island Ferry, which makes regular runs across the river between Federal Point and the Ferry Terminal just north of Price Creek. You may also encounter large ships going to and from the port of Wilmington.

Dockage: At mile 307, Deep Point Marina has transient slips, along with gas and diesel. This new 82-slip marina has a snack bar that also serves beverages. The marina is convenient to the ocean, ICW and Southport's historic district. The ferry departing Deep Point Marina to Bald Head Island takes approximately 20 minutes.

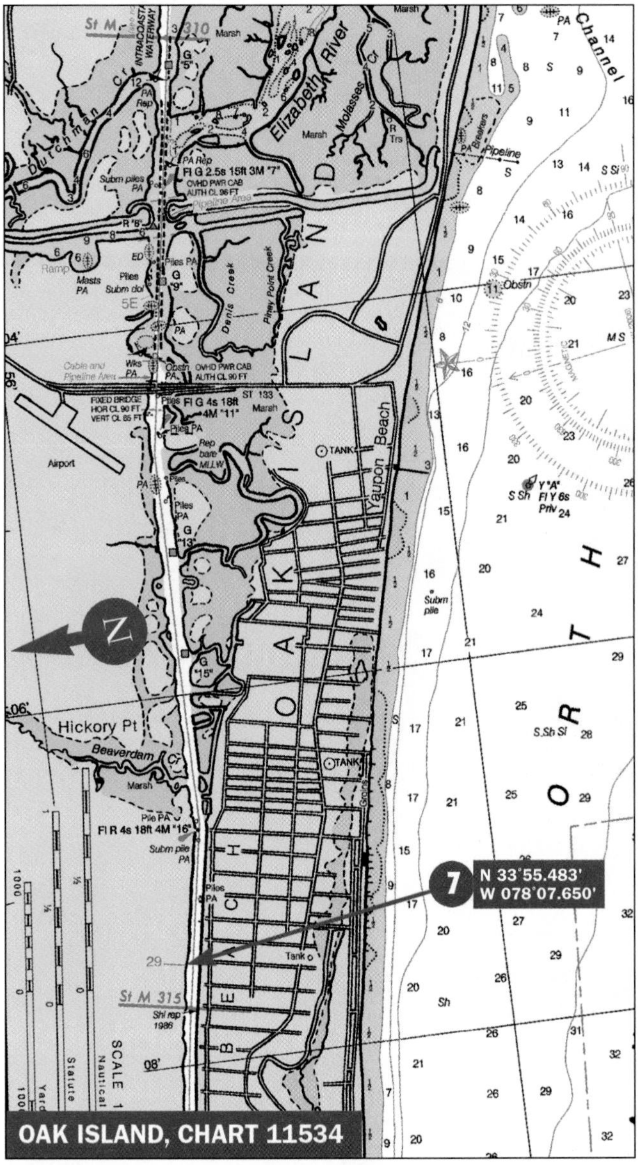

OAK ISLAND, CHART 11534

Bald Head Island, at the Mouth of the Cape Fear River

Bald Head Island, on the northeastern shore at the mouth of the Cape Fear River, offers a destination marina and shore development well worth the two-mile diversion off the ICW. Its remoteness (accessible only by water), its 14 miles of wide, unspoiled beaches and magnificent dunes, and its oak, pine and palm forests—juxtaposed against meandering creeks through inland seas of waving marsh grass, monitored by flocks of white ibis—conspire to make the pristine beauty of this natural barrier island stand out. There is a place for man here, too, in a low-density, revisionist version of Cape Cod or Martha's Vineyard.

Bald Head Island is an excellent jumping-off or landing point to or from a voyage south. For cruisers heading "outside" on a Florida run, the passage from Cape Fear Entrance is preferable to the route via Beaufort Inlet because of the long stretch of shoals north of Cape Fear. Frying Pan Shoals extends into the Atlantic Ocean for many miles.

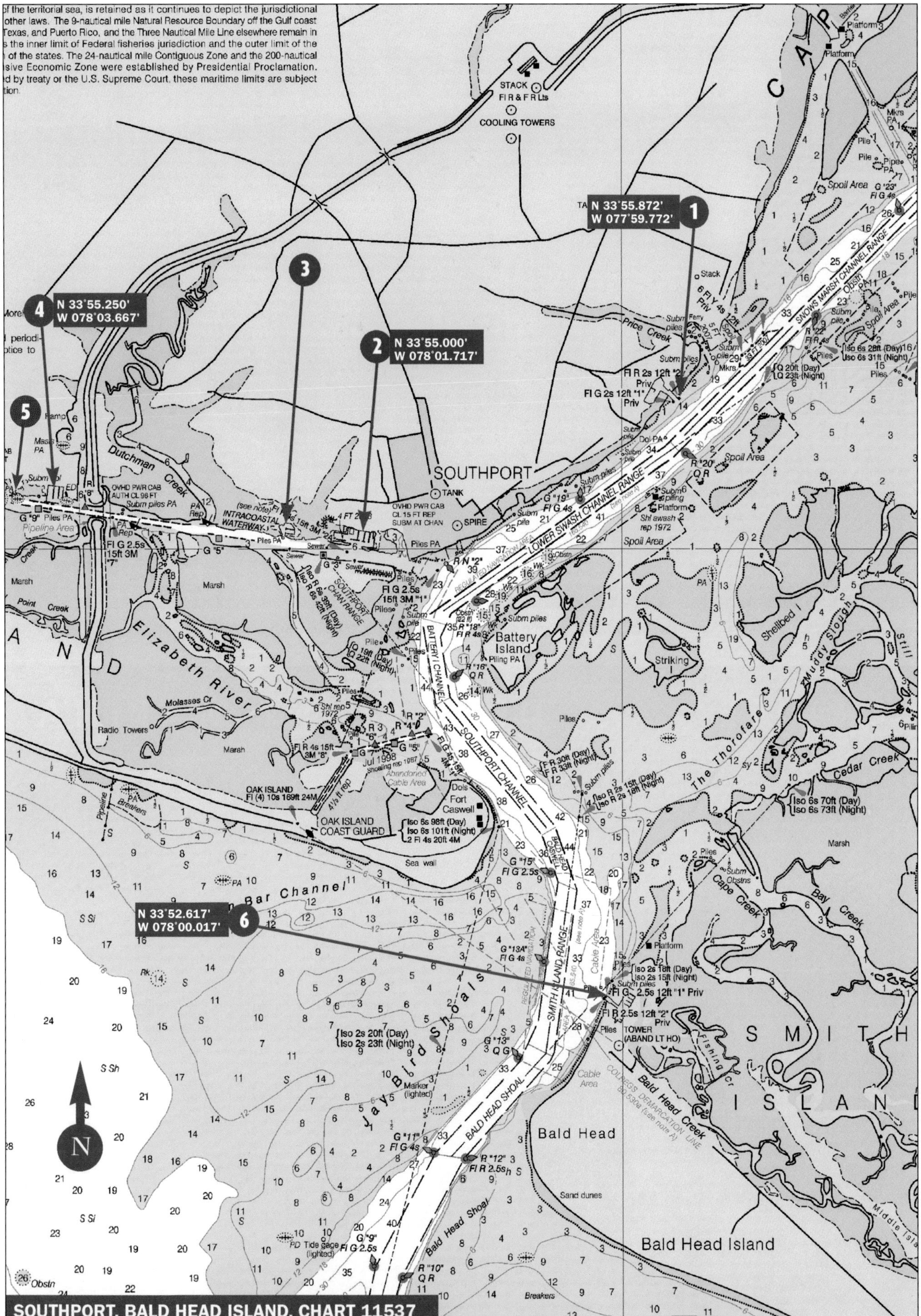

SOUTHPORT, BALD HEAD ISLAND, CHART 11537

Looking north over the Cape Fear River Entrance. (Not to be used for navigation.) WATERWAY GUIDE PHOTOGRAPHY.

Visit Southport Marina Today!

ICW Marker 2A at the mouth of the Cape Fear River

www.southport-marina.com

Southport Marina is a full service facility offering:

Gregory Poole full service center onsite
Great restaurants within walking distance
Medical facilities within two miles
Cumaru docks with dock boxes, wireless internet, cable TV, water, and 30/50/100 amp power
Dockhouse overlooking transient dockage with high speed gas/diesel pumps and pump out system
Valvtect fuel
Freshly dredged basin (as of Fall 2011)
Bath, shower, and laundry facilities
Our very own Live Oak Park, available for relaxing and private functions
An inviting Tiki Bar for summer fun

Now Open–
Phase 1 of the Dry Storage Boat Facility!
Racks Available for Rent

Hurricane rated for winds up to 140 mph, this facility features space for 128 boats, security cameras, a sprinkler system, and mini-storage availability.

2A
SOUTHPORT
MARINA

In-water slips also available for rent!

North Carolina Clean Marina

Southport Marina is proud to have received the Clean Marina Designation... Come see why!

VALVTECT
MARINE FUEL

Southport Marina | 606 W. West Street | Southport, NC 28461 | (910) 457-9900
email: info@southport-marina.com | www.southport-marina.com

WATERWAY GUIDE PHOTOGRAPHY.

The grocery store on Bald Head Island has an excellent selection of fine food and wine as well as staples, a café and deli. Renamed the Maritime Market, it has been moved from the marina to a location 1.5 miles inland. An informal restaurant, Ebb and Flo's, now remains open year-round. The River Pilot Café, with an attractive selection of light luncheon and dinner specials, is just steps away from the slips. Marina guests may purchase temporary memberships at the Bald Head Island Club for superb golf, tennis, pool and croquet facilities and more elegant dining, and at the new Shoals Club, with a pool, a beach and fine dining.

Except for a few service vehicles, there are no cars on the island, so transportation is by foot, bicycle and electric cart (similar to Smith and Tangier islands on the Chesapeake Bay). You can rent bikes and carts near the marina office at "Island Passage." All Bald Head beaches are public, with access via paths from the road. You need wheeled transportation to reach most of them.

If you want a break from boat bunks or are meeting overflow guests at this resort location, Theodosia's Bed & Breakfast is a charming inn. Or try The Elements, four new efficiency-style rental units located at the harbor side.

NAVIGATION: Use Chart 11534. Bald Head Island is easily reached either from the ICW, which turns to the west at Southport, or from the ocean. Bald Head Island's deep-dredged and well-marked channel lies southeast of flashing green "13A" on the Smith Island Range of the Cape Fear River (east of Jay Bird Shoals). The ebb and flood currents range from 2 to 3 knots and run perpendicular to the island's entrance channel. The entrance channel is narrow and care must be exercised to maintain control of your vessel in the current. Do not try to enter if another boat is exiting the channel fairway.

Dockage: Transient dockage is usually available at Bald Head Island Marina's floating docks, but call ahead for availability, docking instructions and assistance (monitoring VHF Channel 16). The dock house has air-conditioned restrooms, showers and laundry, a small convenience store, a high-speed fueling station and a business office for use by transient boaters.

Southport/Cape Fear River Entrance

About two miles north of the Cape Fear River Entrance (to the Atlantic), the ICW leaves the river, takes a hard turn to the west, enters a dredged land cut and arrives in the peaceful little village of Southport. Cape Fear Inlet is the first port south of Morehead City suitable for all sizes of oceangoing vessels via a major deepwater channel. The Cape Fear River Entrance is a deep, well-marked, all-weather inlet. Many charts still show the old entrance channel to the west of the new channel that replaced it. Follow the markers. This area was dredged in spring 2010. *(See page 76 for more information about Cape Fear River Entrance.)*

Southport's numerous restaurants and much of its business district are within easy walking distance of the

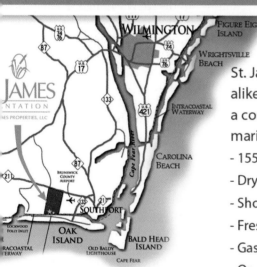

Southport, NC. Photo courtesy of Bald Head Island Limited.

waterfront, but the nearest supermarket is several miles away. Fortunately, Southport does have taxi service on call. A short taxi ride can take you to the Walmart Superstore and Lowe's, located just outside of Southport.

NAVIGATION: Use Chart 11534. Because of Jay Bird Shoals, buoys on Cape Fear's main shipping channel should be observed, and the Western Bar Channel should be avoided. Shoaling continues along Southport's waterfront and the nameless island just southwest of the village. When entering the ICW channel from the Cape Fear River, there is no shortcut. Pass between flashing green "1" and red nun "2." The two new rectangular condo buildings on the point at Southport make a prominent landmark.

Dockage: Dockage is sometimes available at a few of the private slips in the town basin (check the posted signs). The City Pier on the west side of the basin can accommodate one vessel at its end. Stays here are limited to 24 hours, with dockage provided at no charge, although there are no water or electric hookups. The new floating docks at the entrance to the basin are private and associated with the new condos on the point.

A short distance farther into the southbound ICW land cut, a channel opens to the right at flashing red "2A" into Southport Marina. Transient space is available along both sides of a 388-foot-long floating face dock, 90-foot T-head piers and in some of the marina slips. Fuel can be pumped at both high and low speeds along most of the face dock, and the marina's dock house features a ship's store. Haul-out and repair services are also available, along with showers and laundry facilities. A public boardwalk surrounds the marina along the bulkhead as part of Southport's Riverwalk.

Immediately south on the ICW, Indigo Plantation has additional deepwater slips for transients at floating docks with water and electricity. Unfortunately, the road to town from here is circuitous, making a taxi ride necessary for shopping or dining out. The Bald Head Island ferry terminus has recently relocated from here to a new terminal just above Southport on the Cape Fear River. The ferry offers a high-speed run to the island's gorgeous beaches.

South Harbour Village Marina, Mile 311, has a long face dock directly on the ICW for transients, with four diesel-fuel stations, two gas-fuel stations and dockside depths of 12 feet. They can accommodate vessels up to 200 feet. The restaurant, market and deli (open for breakfast and lunch, except Sundays) and a bed and breakfast are next to the marina. Don't miss Joseph's Italian Bistro, open daily (except Sundays) for dinner. It features genuine homemade sauces and pasta with an exceptional wine list, and is very popular with the locals. Limited shopping is within a mile's walk from the marina; transportation is needed for extensive provisioning. Enterprise rental cars are nearby at the local airport.

The American Fish Company, a seafood wholesale company formerly located in Southport, occupies the docks on the west side of the ICW north of the Oak Island Bridge at Mile 311.8.

At Mile 315, the large St. James Plantation Marina has floating docks and fuel. They also have repair facilities. This is part of a large residential development, including three golf courses and other amenities.

The approach is easy and directly on the ICW. Their friendly staff is ready to assist you.

Anchorage: At Southport, there is room for up to three small craft to anchor in the Old Southport Basin at the beginning of the land cut. This basin was dredged in January 2010. Dinghies from anchored boats can land at the Southport City Pier. The anchorage in the North Carolina Wildlife Park basin north of the ICW at red daybeacon "8" has spotty holding, several permanently moored boats, as well as heavy weekend small boat traffic using the nearby ramp. However, there is space for a few boats to anchor. Because of shoaling over the years, Dutchman Creek is narrow and not recommended as an anchorage.

GOIN' ASHORE:
SOUTHPORT, NC

In Southport, you will find that fish, fowl and foul-weather sailors all enjoy the passing of tides along the Cape Fear River.

History: Southport was originally named Smithville, after Benjamin Smith who served under Gen. George Washington in the Revolutionary War. What began as a small fishing and military town has blossomed into a community for retirees and commuters working in Wilmington.

The first Spanish explorers arrived in 1521 and settled up the Cape Fear River in what became known as Brunswick Town. Between 1745 and 1754, Fort Johnson was built as a quarantine service for incoming seamen and to protect settlements farther up the river. Located at the mouth of the Cape Fear, Fort Johnson attracted a small community of river pilots and fishermen, and the area began to thrive. At the close of the war, local businessmen sought to create a major port by combining the city's river transportation with the new railroad system. The town's name was changed from Smithville to Southport, but the project failed to attract commercial shipping.

Still, Southport benefited from the swirling eddies of the Gulf Stream. The warmer waters allowed the village to enjoy seasonal temperatures nearly as high as those found along Florida's northern counties. These mild temperatures and the deep waters of the Cape Fear River attracted vacationers and soon the town blossomed.

Culture and cultural references: If you enjoy arts and crafts, visit the Franklin Square Gallery (130 E. West St., 910-457-5450), where you will find classes and workshops taught by local and national instructors. Classes are open to the public. Be sure to check out the Captain Thompson Home for a look at the life of a blockade runner captain. The Adkins-Ruark House is the former home of Robert Ruark, author of "The Old Man and the Boy."

Southport has served as the backdrop for a number of movies. The Inn At River Oaks on Howe Street was John

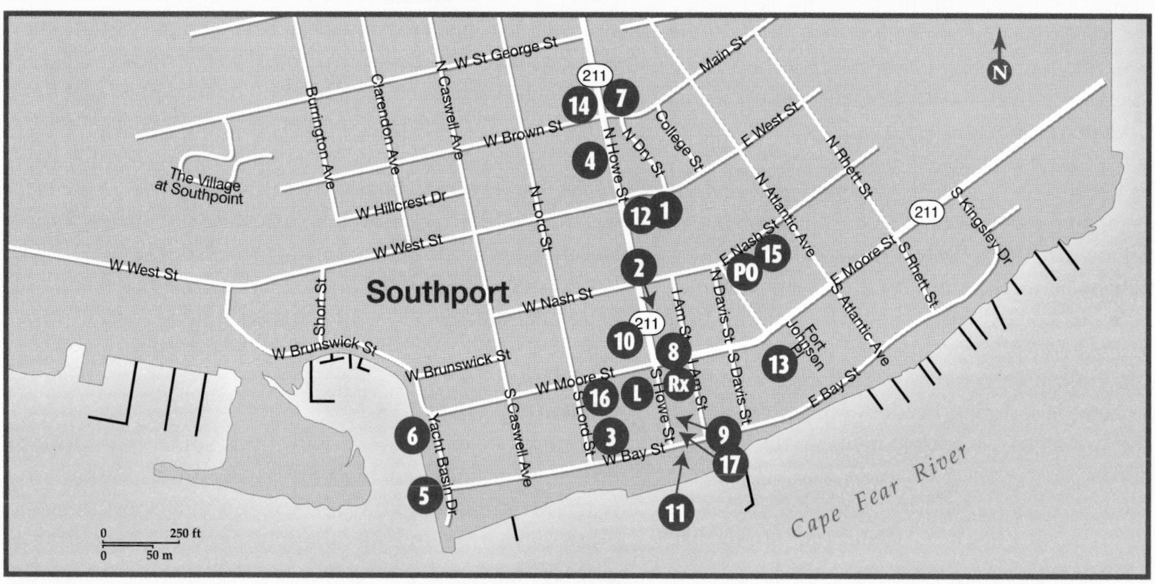

Reference the marina listing tables to see all the marinas in the area.

ART/CRAFTS

1 Franklin Square Gallery

ATTRACTIONS

2 Southport Maritime Museum
3 Kiziah Park

DINING

4 Mr. P's Bistro
5 The Yacht Basin Provision Company
6 Fishy Fishy Café
7 Dry Street Pub & Pizza
8 Thai Peppers
9 Trolly Stop
10 Port City Java
11 Cape Fear Restaurant & Lounge

ENTERTAINMENT

12 Franklin Square Park
13 Garrison Lawn

GROCERIES/CARRYOUT

14 The Wine Rack
15 Live Oak Nutrition

INFORMATION

16 Visitor Information

SHOPPING

17 Waterfront Gifts and Antiques

L LIBRARY

PO POST OFFICE

Rx PHARMACY

Travolta's motel in the movie "Domestic Disturbance." In 1987, the movie "Crimes of the Heart," starring Sissy Spacek, Jessica Lange and Diane Keaton, was shot at 211 Caswell Ave. The home is still known as "The Crimes of the Heart House." In the early '90s, "Spies" was filmed in homes along Bay Street. More recent movies filmed in Southport include "I Know What You Did Last Summer" and "Summer Catch," as well as the television series "Dawson's Creek."

Attractions: Southport is a walk-about town. Maps are available at the Visitor Information Center on West Moore Street. From there, you can begin your stroll down Howe Street, where you will find the Southport Maritime Museum (116 N. Howe St., 910-457-0003). A self-guided tour takes you through the history of the Lower Cape Fear region. There is also a nice collection of nautical memorabilia.

Every Tuesday evening, from June through September, the Brunswick Arts Council holds their Concerts On The Coast series in Franklin Square Park (Howe and E. West streets). If you enjoy outdoor entertainment, drop by Garrison Lawn for Southport Film Nights. Guests are invited to bring lawn chairs, blankets, picnics, family and friends. The post office (206 E. Nash St., 910-457-4633) is a couple of blocks from the waterfront. The highlight of any stop in Southport is a trip to Bald Head Island. With miles of uncluttered beaches, Bald Head makes a great day trip. Transportation is by foot, bike or golf cart. Cars are not allowed. A 10,000-acre wildlife preserve provides several viewing towers overlooking the salt marsh and marine forest. As you stroll along the path, watch for deer and gator crossings.

Special events: In May, the Cape Fear Yacht Club hosts the North Carolina Leukemia Cup Regatta. This is a sailing regatta, powerboat race, auction and raffle. Call 919-677-3993 for additional information. Also in May, Southport hosts their annual Heritage Days festival. In October, check out the Fall Craft Bonanza, where you can find wood crafts, wreaths, hand-painted pottery, needlework, toys and baby items.

For over 200 years, Southport has celebrated America's independence, making this one of the state's largest Fourth of July celebrations. Each year, between 40,000 and 50,000 people set up chairs along the main roads and enjoy an old-fashioned Independence Day celebration. You will find over 100 handmade arts and crafts on display, beach music on the waterfront, a naturalization ceremony, veterans recognition ritual, flag retirement observance, freedom run and walk and, of course, a huge fireworks display that lights up the sky over the Cape Fear River.

The Stede Bonnet Regatta, held in October, requires all participants to arrive in buccaneer costumes and act like pirates during the race.

Shopping: If you are looking for boating and outdoor clothing, visit Ocean Outfitters (424 N. Howe St., 910-457-0433). They carry Columbia, Woolrich, Crocs, Teva, Royal Robbins, Sperry, Guy Harvey and many other nautical brands. You might also try Stewart Hardware (8848 River Road SE, 910-457-5544) a couple miles from the waterfront. The Wine Rack (102 W. Brown St., 910-457-5147) offers a good selection of wines. There is an ABC store (714 N. Howe St., 910-457-6924) near Napa Atlantic Auto & Marine Supply (721 N. Howe St., 910-457-5022) and the Shop Girl boutique is at 701 N. Howe St. (910-457-9575).

ADDITIONAL RESOURCES

- **SOUTHPORT-OAK ISLAND CHAMBER OF COMMERCE,** 800-457-6964, www.southport-oakisland.com

NEARBY GOLF COURSES

Clubs at St. James Plantation,
3779 Members Club Blvd. SE,
Southport, NC 28461, 910-253-3010 (6 miles)
www.theclubsatstjames.com

Lakes Country Club, 591 South Shore Drive,
Southport, NC 28461, 910-845-2625 (9 miles)

South Harbour Golf Links, 4188 Vanessa Drive,
Southport, NC 28461, 910-454-0905 (5 miles)

Bald Head Island Club, 910-457-7300
www.bhiclub.net (10 miles)

NEARBY MEDICAL FACILITIES

Dosher Memorial Hospital, 924 N. Howe St.,
Southport, NC 28461, 910-457-3800 (1 mile)

Southport Dental Care, 621A N. Fodale Ave.,
Southport, NC 28641, 910-457-5026

C. Richard Conrad Family Dentistry, 302 E. Moore St.,
Southport, NC 28641, 910-457-6152

Restaurants: Mr. P's Bistro (309 N. Howe St., 910-457-0801) is a local favorite, serving seafood and beef in a cozy atmosphere. Don't leave town before you try the yummy items at the Baked with Love Café (302 N. Howe St., 910-454-0044). The Yacht Basin Provision Company (130 Yacht Basin Drive, 910-457-0654) is another local favorite. Featured in a few movies, it offers outdoor seating overlooking the ICW. For seafood, you might also try Fishy Fishy Café (106 Yacht Basin St., 910-457-1881). For subs and sandwiches, try Dry Street Pub & Pizza (101 E. Brown St., 910-457-5994). Thai Peppers (115 E. Moore St., 910-457-0095) is said to have great Thai food. The Cape Fear Restaurant (101 W. Bay St., 910-457-9222) is on the water with a seafood menu.

Cruising Options

Looking ahead, boaters will find some true "ditch" cruising, punctuated by side-setting inlets. When you reach Myrtle Beach at Mile 346, you may want to spend a few days enjoying the shopping centers, restaurants, golf courses and public beaches. Then it's on to the beautiful Waccamaw River as you get even closer to the Low Country. ■

Skipper's Handbook

- Tide Tables 49
- Bridge Tables 58

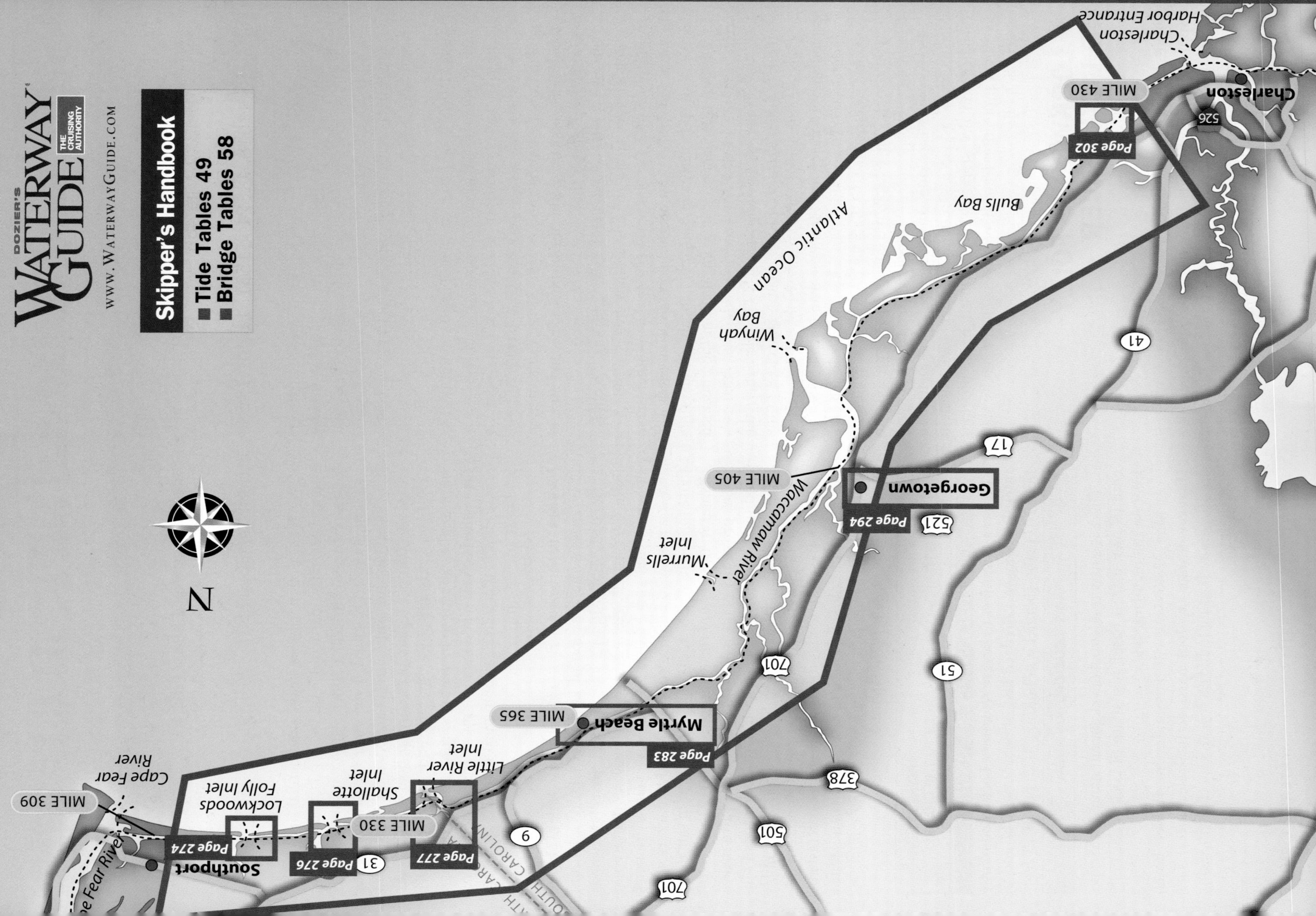

Cape Fear to Charleston

ICW Mile 310–Mile 436

VHF North Carolina Bridges: Channel 13
South Carolina Bridges: Channel 09

CHARTS 11518, 11521, 11531, 11532, 11534, 11535, 11536, 11537

After the swift currents of the Cape Fear River, beyond the Southport area, Intracoastal Waterway (ICW) cruisers will enter an area of the ICW that lives up to its nickname, "The Ditch." A series of beach developments is evident on the ocean side from Oak Island through Long Beach.

NAVIGATION: Use Chart 11534. The state Route 133 Bridge (65-foot fixed vertical clearance) at Mile 311.8 is the first bridge encountered after Snows Cut. There is another high-level bridge between Oak Island and the mainland under construction at Mile 316.8. Construction should be beyond the point of causing delays and should be completed by press time.

This area is relatively straightforward cruising, except for a couple of shoal areas. The first shallow area is at Mile 315 on the south side (as charted—"Shl rep"). Another shoal spot is at Mile 317.4, west of Southport at flashing red "18" on the north side. Here, an unmarked shoal extends some 50 feet into the channel; it may be silt from the unnamed creek near the marker. At dead low tide, the shoal is a foot above water. At flashing green "29" (Mile 318.9) the channel makes a sharp turn to starboard. Stay close to the marker—an uncharted shoal, partly visible at low water, extends toward the channel from the mainland side.

From Mile 310 to Mile 396 below Myrtle Beach, the National Ocean Service (NOS) tables do not provide information on currents. In general, the flood seems to run south in this area, but expect current reversals as you pass each inlet.

Dockage: Near Mile 315, the St. James Plantation Marina, with easy access to the ICW, offers fuel, transient dockage and dry storage. This enclosed basin provides excellent protection from ICW wakes. Their friendly staff is very helpful.

LOCKWOODS FOLLY TO LITTLE RIVER

Mile 321 to Mile 330

Approaching Lockwoods Folly Inlet, the shoreline shifts to low marshland extending back to scrub trees. Along the banks at Holden Beach, just below the inlet, an increasing number of houses have appeared on the ocean side of the ICW. This section carries heavy commercial and recreational boat traffic, particularly on weekends, and there are long stretches of No-Wake Zones. Although this stretch is increasingly resort oriented, if you make the passage in late June when North Carolina rivers are open for fishing, you will find "bumper-to-bumper" shrimp boat traffic. Boats vary from outboard-powered skiffs and center consoles with families aboard to miniature shrimp boats. Although the traffic is chaotic and some skippers are uncooperative, one reward is that a fresh shrimp meal is readily available at almost any tie-up.

NAVIGATION: Use Chart 11534. Just past Mile 321, the ICW crosses the junction of Lockwoods Folly Inlet and Lockwoods Folly River. The channel past Lockwoods Folly Inlet usually has extra floating markers that are not shown on the chart. Look for the ICW yellow triangles and squares so you do not confuse the inlet markers with those for the ICW. See additional information in our inlets chapter in the front of this Guide.

The proximity of the ICW to the ocean in this area makes conditions extremely changeable at both Lockwoods Folly Inlet Crossing and Shallotte Inlet Crossing a few miles farther south. Strong ebb and flow currents alone continually move the sand, while storms off the ocean can reshape the bottom in hours. Be aware of crosscurrents and adjust your heading as required. *(See pages 77 for more information about Lockwoods Folly Inlet.)*

THE FOLLOWING AREA REQUIRES SPECIAL ATTENTION DUE TO SHOALING OR CHANGES TO THE CHANNEL

LOCKWOODS FOLLY INLET CROSSING

This area is subject to severe shoaling. Lockwoods Folly Inlet Crossing was dredged last in February 2011 and in June 2011, the channel was holding its depth of 12 feet.

END SPECIAL CAUTION AREA.

There is a new residential development named SeaScape, with its own marina basin, just south of Lockwoods Folly Inlet on the mainland side.

At Mile 323.6, you will pass under the Holden Beach Highway Bridge (65-foot fixed vertical clearance). This area has more boating traffic each year, especially in spring and summer.

Lockwoods Folly Inlet, NC

MILE 320		Largest Vessel Accommodated	VHF Channel Monitored	Transient Berths / Total Berths	Approach / Dockside Depth (reported)	Floating Docks	Gas / Diesel	Groceries, Ice, Marine Supplies, Snacks	Repairs: Hull, Engine, Propeller	Lift (tonnage), Crane, Rail	1=110V, 2=220V, B=Both, Max Amps	Laundry, Pool, Showers	Pump-Out Station	Nearby: Grocery Store, Motel, Restaurant
		Dockage					Supplies		Services					
1. Blue Water Point Motel and Marina	910-278-1230	60	16	10/40	5/5	F	GD	IMS			B/50	PS		MR

Corresponding chart(s) not to be used for navigation. Internet Access Wireless Internet Access

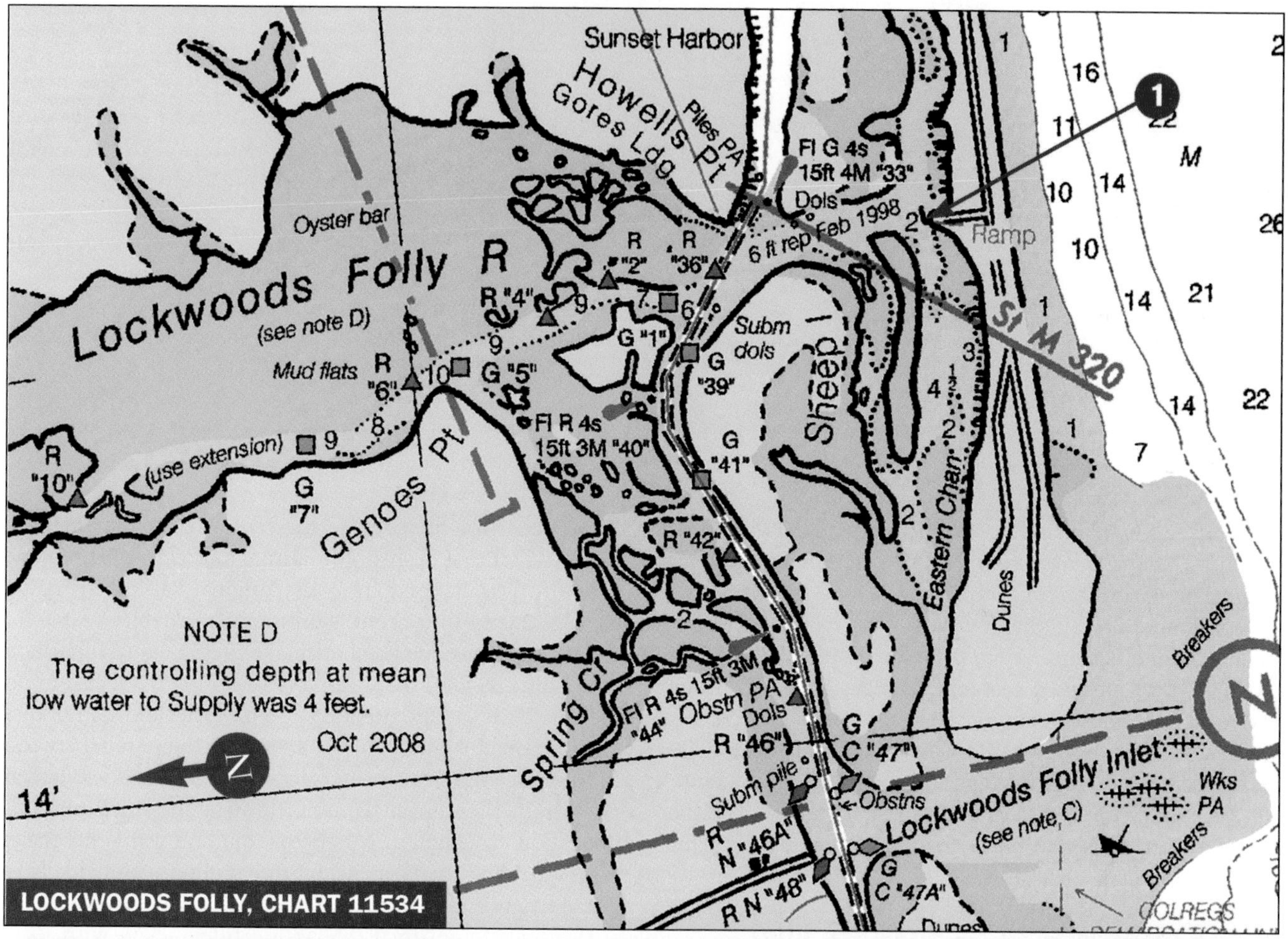

Lockwoods Folly Inlet, NC. (Not to be used for navigation.) WATERWAY GUIDE PHOTOGRAPHY.

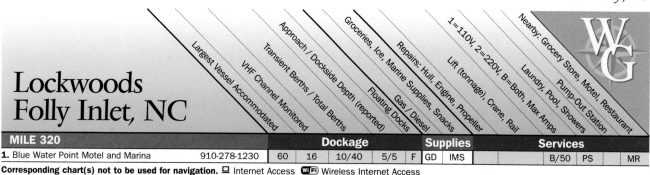

Shallotte Inlet, NC. (Not to be used for navigation.) WATERWAY GUIDE PHOTOGRAPHY.

Dockage: Just one mile north of Lockwoods Folly Inlet, at Mile 320 and ICW flashing green "33," is Blue Water Point Motel and Marina, reporting 5-foot depths (both approach and dockside) at low tide.

The Holden Beach Marina, just above Mile 323, accommodates boats up to 35 feet and sells gas and diesel fuel. You can walk to a grocery store, and several restaurants are nearby. The restaurant Provisions has good seafood, a casual atmosphere, dockage and live music on weekends. Hewett Marine, about a quarter mile north of Holden Beach Marina, has haul-out capabilities for larger yachts and floating docks just off the ICW.

Mile 325 to Mile 342—Shallotte Inlet

At both Holden Beach and Ocean Isle Beach, long colonies of oceanfront houses (many on stilts) stand on dredged canals slicing through the fill, Florida-style, from the ICW to the ocean. Houses on the mainland side are more substantial, spaced farther apart and appear among the trees facing toward the ocean beach. At Mile 330, Shallotte Inlet leads into Saucepan Creek. Just beyond, there are some very large new houses at Shallotte Inlet on the mainland side with long docks extending out to the ICW channel. From Holden Beach to Shallotte Inlet, be sure to stay in the middle of the channel because of rapid shoaling outside the channel.

NAVIGATION: Use Chart 11534. The Shallotte River makes off northward at Mile 329.6 and carries 3- to 5-foot depths at mean low water to the country town of Shallotte, NC. Call Coastal Machine and Welding on VHF Channel 16 for advice if you are considering venturing up the Shallotte River, which has a spring tidal range of 6 feet. The name Shallotte was derived from the original settlement name Charlotte, and the accent is on the first syllable.

The markings on the chart make the Shallotte Inlet look especially bad for crossing as you follow the ICW. Just mind the markers, paying attention to any local knowledge that you may obtain. On the ICW at Shallotte Inlet itself, between the floating markers, boaters can expect a sudden lateral push from the current coming through the inlet during a flood tide. You will experience a "pull" toward the ocean during an ebb tide. This pushing and pulling is more likely to put you aground than any shoaling along the ICW channel.

Do not attempt to use Shallotte Inlet—even with local knowledge. It sometimes has markers, but none were on station in late 2010. *(See page 78 for more information about Shallotte Inlet.)*

THE FOLLOWING AREA REQUIRES SPECIAL ATTENTION DUE TO SHOALING OR CHANGES TO THE CHANNEL

SHALLOTTE RIVER AND INLET

The Shallotte River and inlet crossing of the ICW is subject to severe shoaling. Although recently dredged (February 2011 to approximately 12-foot depths), a bar had built across most of the ICW channel close to the inlet side at the Southern end. Minimum depth observed was 8 feet at mean low water. Best water is on mainland side of channel. Check for the most recent survey before you pass through, as the controlling depth route is usually indicated with waypoints. Deepest water is generally on the red (west) side. Shoaling conditions can develop

Holden Beach, NC

HOLDEN BEACH		Largest Vessel Accommodated	VHF Channel Monitored	Transient Berths / Total Berths	Approach / Dockside Depth (reported)	Floating Docks	Gas / Diesel	Groceries, Ice, Marine Supplies, Snacks	Repairs: Hull, Engine, Propeller	Lift (tonnage), Crane, Rail	1=110V, 2=220V, B=Both, Max Amps	Laundry, Pool, Showers	Pump-Out Station	Nearby: Grocery Store, Motel, Restaurant
		Dockage					Supplies		Services					
1. Hewett Marina 322.5	910-842-9104					F					1/30			
2. Holden Beach Marina 325	910-842-5447	45	16	2/14	6/6	F	GD	IS	E		1/30	S		GR

Corresponding chart(s) not to be used for navigation. Internet Access Wireless Internet Access

quickly, so also check for local knowledge when transiting Shallotte Inlet Crossing. Local towing services are often excellent sources of information regarding current conditions.

END SPECIAL CAUTION AREA.

The next eight miles are straightforward. The Ocean Isle Bridge, at Mile 333.7, is a fixed 65-foot span. There is a small fuel dock inside the first canal on the ocean side, just north of this bridge. The entrance channel is from the south side of the bridge and leads under it.

After over 20 years of resistance from locals, development pressure won the battle, and replacement of the 500-foot floating pontoon bridge, built in 1961, has been completed. A new 65-foot bridge now stands at Mile 337.9. The completion of this bridge has eliminated the delays that used to occur.

Between the Sunset Beach Bridge (Mile 337.9) and Little River (Mile 343), stay in mid-channel to avoid the frequent shoals, which often crop up where creeks cross to the ocean. Flashing greens "117" and "119" are out of the water, about 20 feet up on the bank at very low tide, so give both a wide berth, being mindful also that there is a shoal at flashing green "117"on the opposite side of the channel.

Dockage: Ocean Isle Marina and Yacht Club is located at Mile 335.5 at the site of the former Pelican Point Marina. The long fuel face dock has been removed, and a launching slipway has been constructed. There is a large dry storage building on-site.

NOW ENTERING SOUTH CAROLINA
SOUTH CAROLINA BRIDGES MONITOR VHF CHANNEL 09

Little River Inlet—Mile 342

Just inside the South Carolina State Line, the ICW crosses Little River, which offers relatively easy and well-marked access to the ocean through the maintained channel between jetties. This inlet is used regularly by casino boats and head boats docked at Little River, SC. *(See page 79 for more information about Little River Inlet.)*

Little River—Mile 343

About one mile above the junction of the ICW and the channel from the Little River Inlet, the route crosses the border from North Carolina into South Carolina (Mile 340.9). A sign marks the spot, but it is often faded and difficult to read.

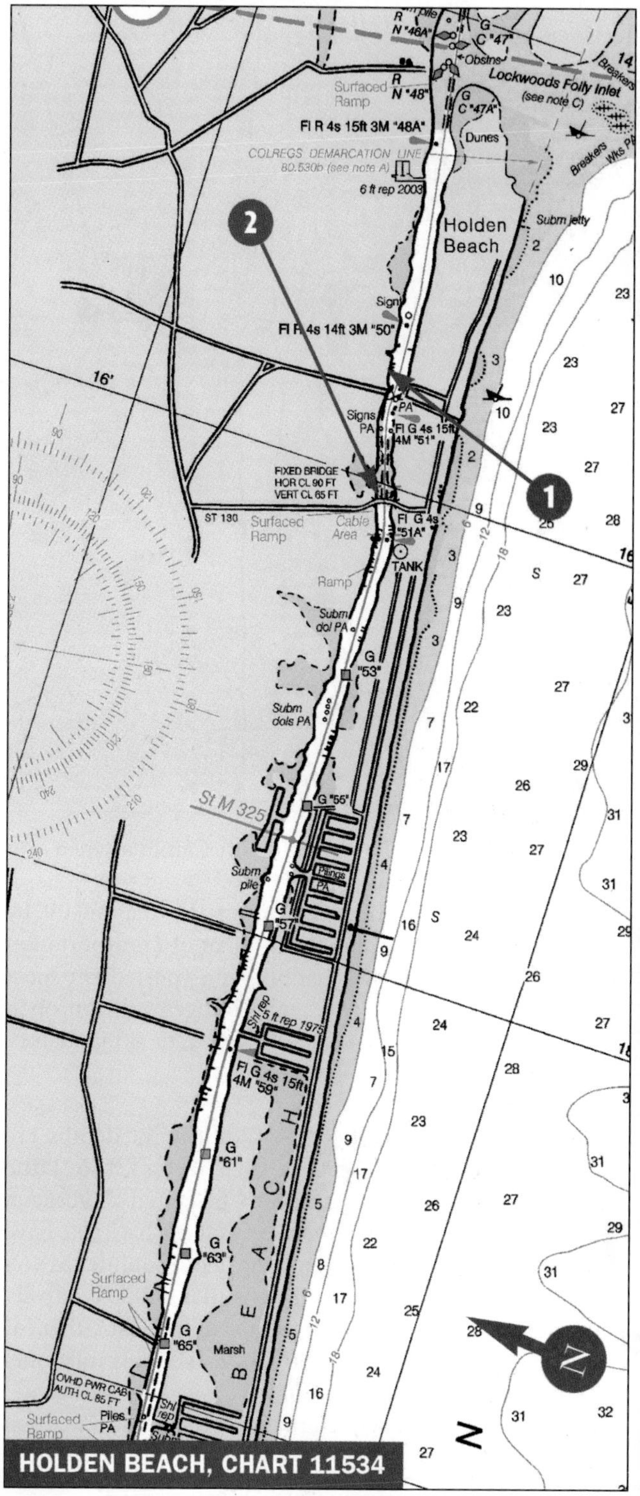

HOLDEN BEACH, CHART 11534

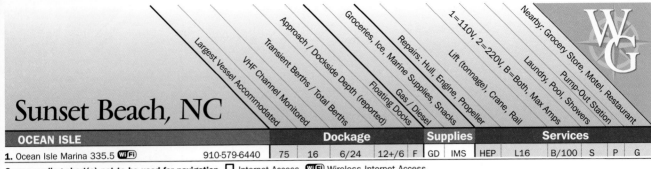

Sunset Beach, NC

OCEAN ISLE	Phone	Largest Vessel Accommodated	VHF Channel Monitored	Transient Berths / Total Berths	Approach / Dockside Depth (reported)	Floating Docks	Gas / Diesel	Groceries, Ice, Marine Supplies, Snacks	Repairs: Hull, Engine, Propeller	Lift (tonnage), Crane, Rail	1=110V, 2=220V, B=Both, Max Amps	Laundry, Pool, Showers	Pump-Out Station	Nearby: Grocery Store, Motel, Restaurant
1. Ocean Isle Marina 335.5 (WiFi)	910-579-6440	75	16	6/24	12+/6	F	GD	IMS	HEP	L16	B/100	S	P	G

Dockage: columns Largest Vessel through Floating Docks; Supplies: Gas / Diesel, Groceries; Services: Repairs through Nearby.

Corresponding chart(s) not to be used for navigation. Internet Access (WiFi) Wireless Internet Access

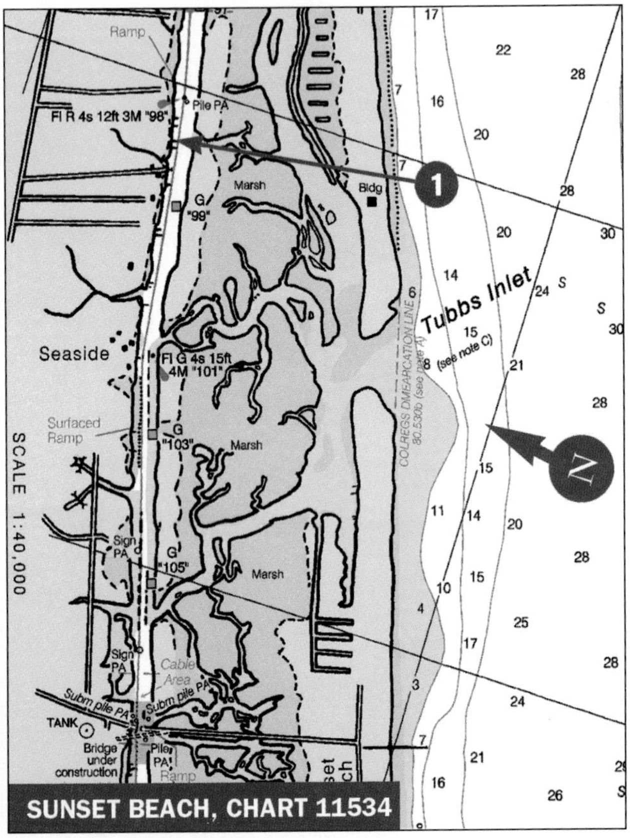

SUNSET BEACH, CHART 11534

You can assume that you are in South Carolina when you make the turn below flashing red "116."

All South Carolina bridges monitor VHF Channel 09. Be aware of the South Carolina Department of Transportation (SC DOT) Hurricane Evacuation Rule (posted on most opening bridges): Draw and swing bridges will not open when wind reaches a sustained 25 knots, or if mandatory evacuation is ordered.

NAVIGATION: Use Chart 11534. While ICW depths are stable, the entrance to Calabash Creek across from Little River Inlet has a bar building out from red daybeacon "2." Depths across the entrance to Calabash Creek have shoaled to 5 feet in places; watch the depth sounder as you proceed. Little River Inlet itself has jetties and is relatively stable. In daily use by local boats, it is of interest either for going offshore or for rejoining the ICW. Use this inlet only in settled weather, as it is shallow.

Dockage: The Marsh Harbour Marina on Calabash Creek has closed.

Anchorage: You can anchor in Calabash Creek on the mainland side of the junction between the ICW and the inlet. At extreme low tides, the entrance bar carries around 5 feet at low tide. You will be subject to wakes from the ICW if you anchor toward the mouth of the creek. This is a pleasant spot otherwise, with a golf course on the wooded northern shore. Give Calabash Creek's red daybeacon "2" (not the ICW red daybeacon "2," which features the distinctive ICW yellow triangle) a wide berth to avoid the shoal mentioned above. Then, turn toward the row of charted dolphins, and drop the hook near the north side of the center of the river. The opposite shore, just upstream of the dolphins, has increased shoaling. Do not anchor near the entrance, as other vessels may arrive after you. Use two anchors in bad weather or if the anchorage is too crowded for normal swinging room. As always, show an anchor light. Shrimp boats and sightseeing vessels, whose wakes may disturb you, use the channel at night. You can visit the town of Calabash by dinghy from this anchorage.

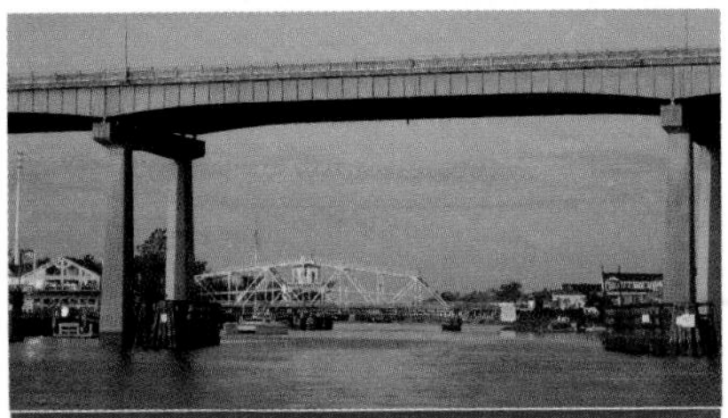
LITTLE RIVER BRIDGES Mile 347.2/3
WATERWAY GUIDE PHOTOGRAPHY

The chart shows a deceivingly inviting spot on the north side of the ICW channel at about Mile 342.5, near red daybeacon "6." Do not attempt to enter. It has shoaled badly, and most of it is bare at low tide.

Village of Little River—Mile 345

The village of Little River is a good stopping point for boats coming from the north or south. About a one-day run from Wrightsville Beach to the north, and just before the long stretch of the ditch behind Myrtle Beach, it is the northern gateway to popular vacation resorts, which line the ocean beach for more than 20 miles as you head south. The mild climate has attracted permanent residents as well as vacationers. Shoreline change consistent with the degree of development around the booming Myrtle Beach area—new homes, condominiums, 130 golf courses, docks and dredged basins—has created increased boat traffic and a need for slower speeds through the ICW. With increasing development, the natural state of the ICW here may soon disappear.

Sunset Beach new high-level fixed bridge.
(Not to be used for navigation.) WATERWAY GUIDE PHOTOGRAPHY.

NAVIGATION: Use Chart 11534. **Use Myrtle Beach tide tables.** South Carolina bridges monitor VHF Channel 09. New construction is evident near flashing green "11" and green daybeacon "13." A few miles farther on—your heading is nearly due west here—Nixon Crossroads has two bridges: the highway bridge at Mile 347.2 (fixed vertical clearance 65 feet) and Little River Swing Bridge at Mile 347.3 (closed vertical clearance 7 feet, opens on request). The Little River Swing Bridge is old and frequently in need of repair. It is sometimes left in the "open to navigation" position for long periods, but don't count on it being open when you pass through. These two bridges denote the dividing line between fresh and saltwater. Southwest of the bridges, where the water becomes fresh, you need a freshwater fishing license to do any angling.

Keep an eye out for a Danger Submerged Rock sign just northeast of the fixed bridge, about a third of the way out into the channel from the east (or ocean) side. Below the swing bridge, be careful of shoals along the sides (and submerged obstructions, likely pilings, on the ocean side) for the next quarter mile or so.

Dockage: The town of Little River attracts anglers who come to patronize its charter fishing boats. At the face dock close to the commercial sportfishing boats, BW's Marina offers fuel and some services, but no transient dockage. You may have to wait while the two casino boats maneuver at the dock here in the narrow waterway. Nearby, Captain Juel's Hurricane Restaurant, one of three restaurants at Little River's docks, serves seafood year-round.

Two long face docks downriver from BW's Marina are in a dangerous state of disrepair and have No Docking signs posted. Crickett Cove Marina is at Mile 345, directly on the ICW.

Coquina Harbor, a large deepwater basin on the west side of the ICW at Mile 346 near green daybeacon "13," is home to several marinas serving transients. Deep-draft vessels need to call ahead for entrance information. A black and white lighthouse replica marks the harbor entrance. Upon entering the harbor, Lightkeeper's Marina, home of Harbourside Marine Services, is to port. Myrtle Beach Yacht Club and Coquina Yacht Club are located to the rear and starboard area of the harbor, both with amenities and services. Fuel is available at Lightkeeper's Marina and the Myrtle Beach Yacht Club.

Dredging was completed at the Myrtle Beach Yacht Club in April 2008. Restaurants are within walking distance. They also provide complimentary wireless Internet and have a dock store with snacks. Silver Coast Marina and Boating Center (formerly North Myrtle Beach Marina) is on the mainland side, just past Coquina Harbor. There is dry stack storage here and a lift but no wet slips. The Anchor Marina, with a Travelift and complete repair capabilities, is located just before the Nixon Crossroads bridges on the south side of the ICW. Anchor Marina's basin was dredged in 2008.

ROCK PILE
Mile 350 to Mile 365
WATERWAY GUIDE PHOTOGRAPHY

PINE ISLAND CUT TO WACCAMAW RIVER

Mile 347 to Mile 355—Rock Pile

Below Little River, at Mile 347, the ICW route enters a 26-mile-long high-banked land cut known as Pine Island Cut. For some unexplained reason, its name is not on the charts, and the cut is labeled only "Intracoastal Waterway." The new North Myrtle Beach Connector Bridge, a 65-foot

Looking east over Harbourgate Resort, Little River Swing Bridge and the ICW. (Not to be used for navigation.) WATERWAY GUIDE PHOTOGRAPHY.

fixed bridge at Mile 349.5 is shown on the latest chart edition dated August 2009.

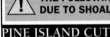

THE FOLLOWING AREA REQUIRES SPECIAL ATTENTION DUE TO SHOALING OR CHANGES TO THE CHANNEL

PINE ISLAND CUT

Some travelers call this stretch the most worrisome segment of the whole ICW trip. Check on VHF Channels 13 or 16 to see if any tug or barge traffic is passing through the area. Boaters should exercise caution since boats do go aground on the rock ledges along both sides of the channel.

NAVIGATION: Use Chart 11534. Pine Island Cut's edges are prone to shoaling. The bottom is hard shale or rock. Rock ledges abut the deep part of the channel between Mile 347 and Mile 365.5. The worst stretch, known as The Rock Pile, begins at ICW Mile 349 and ends at the VORTAC aviation tower installation on the ocean side, around Mile 352. A number of charted daybeacons mark the most worrisome of the rock ledges from Mile 350 to Mile 365, many of which are visible only at low tide. Not all of them are marked, so keep a sharp watch. New development and clearing along this once-heavily wooded area give the illusion that the channel is wider than it really is. Be extremely careful to remain in the center, especially at high tide. Green daybeacon "19" is in the correct place, even though it appears to be too close to the middle of the cut due to clearing of the surrounding shoreline.

END SPECIAL CAUTION AREA.

Keep to mid-channel and watch for shoaling at bends and places where drainage ditches make in. When passing or being passed by another boat, do not crowd too close to the edge of the channel. Keep an eye out for flotsam and snags. Numerous trees have toppled into the cut, and many woodpiles on the banks appear ready to follow. There is heavy development—condominiums, docks, basins, single-family homes and golf courses—along much of this stretch.

Barefoot Landing Swing Bridge crosses the ICW (31-foot closed vertical clearance), at Mile 353.3. The bridge tender monitors VHF Channel 09, and the bridge opens on signal. Two dolphins are on the edges of the channel, on the east side of the bridge between the bridge and the docks. The Barefoot Landing Resorts development has now expanded to both sides of the ICW above and below the swing bridge. There are waterfront residential communities, condominiums, golf courses, clubs and hotels.

BAREFOOT LANDING BRIDGE
Mile 353.3
WATERWAY GUIDE PHOTOGRAPHY

Dockage: Harbourgate Resort & Marina is located directly on the ICW at Mile 347.7, just before the Little River Swing Bridge when headed south. The resort-style facility features transient slips at floating docks, gas and diesel fuel, a ship's store, a restaurant, laundry facilities and restrooms/showers. The marina can accommodate vessels up to 150 feet in length. Overnight lodging is also on-site.

The marina at Dock Holidays, Mile 348.2, is located just inside Pine Island Cut, with access to the nearby private airport. This marina offers transient dockage and fuel. Numerous restaurants, markets, West Marine and Walmart are all within a short walking distance. This is a good provisioning stop.

At approximately Mile 354, upon reaching the No-Wake Zone, you can visit the Barefoot Landing shopping and entertainment complex on the ocean side. Transient dockage is available at the adjacent Barefoot Landing Marina, which provides on-site access to 14 restaurants and more than 100 shops, plus live entertainment. The docks have been renovated and provide electric, water and cable connections.

The Barefoot Marina is open across the ICW from the shopping area. They offer transient dockage, gas and diesel fuel, 142 slips at concrete floating docks, shore power, wireless Internet access, golf, laundry, a spa and an exercise room.

Mile 355 to Mile 375

There has been almost continuous new shoreside development between Barefoot Landing, Mile 354, and about Mile 362, on both sides of the ICW for over a decade. Golf is popular here, with over 120 courses nearby. New single-family homes, docks and huge condominium developments surrounding golf courses line much of the ICW, and new construction begins almost daily.

NAVIGATION: Use Chart 11534. Just beyond Barefoot Landing, you will pass under the Conway Bypass Bridge, Mile 355.5 (65-foot fixed vertical clearance). Several new markers have been placed in shoaling areas north of the Conway Bypass Bridge. Shoaling is particularly bad near the drainage ditches between the Conway Bypass Bridge and the Combination Bridges at Mile 365.4.

At Mile 356, cables for an overhead tramway giving access to a golf course across the ICW may look too low for comfort, but the clearance is at least 67 feet, as clearly charted.

At Mile 357.5 is the Grande Dunes Bridge (65-foot fixed vertical clearance), which is private and of a unique style, leading to the private residential community of Grande Dunes, spanning both sides of the ICW. It is shown on the current chart, although previous chart revisions may show this bridge as "Under Construction." The Marina at Grande Dunes is located in a dredged basin just south of the bridge on the ocean side of the ICW (see dockage). Be careful not to confuse the small floating markers at the two entrances to the Marina at Grande Dunes with ICW markers.

GRANDE DUNES BRIDGE
Mile 357.5
WATERWAY GUIDE PHOTOGRAPHY

Another fixed 65-foot high-rise bridge, the Grissom Parkway Bridge, is at Mile 360.5. There is shoaling at the drainage pipe at Mile 361.5 on the north side of the ICW. Favor the dock on the south side of the channel when passing. Watch for an obstruction on the north side of the shoal.

At Mile 362.5, between green daybeacons "23" and "25," there is a very conspicuous shoal at another drainage ditch on the north side of the ICW. Additional markers are near Mile 363 to mark shoaling.

The fixed 65-foot U.S. 501 Bridge crosses the ICW at Mile 365.4, along with a railroad bridge that is usually open. ICW veterans, especially commercial skippers, call these two bridges the "Combination Bridges." Six-tenths of a mile farther (Mile 366), numerous cypress stumps and a lone tree significantly encroach into the north side of the ICW from the extensive stone riprap meant to prevent soil erosion around a new condominium development (one of many along this stretch).

A new 65-foot bridge, Fantasy Harbour Bridge (Mile 366.4), is the connector to reach the Freestyle Music Park which replaced Hard Rock Park, a theme park that opened in May 2008, then closed in September of the same year due to financial woes.

At Mile 371.0, the Socastee (pronounced sock-a-stee) Swing Bridge (which opens on the hour and every 15 minutes thereafter) has an official closed vertical clearance of 11 feet, although its tide board shows less. Like the Little River Swing Bridge (Mile 347.3), the Socastee Swing Bridge is old and frequently in need of repair. Call the bridge tender on VHF Channel 09 or by phone to find out its current status. The No-Wake Zone on both sides of the swing bridge is locally enforced.

The highway bridge, Mile 371.3, frequently shows less than the charted 65 feet of clearance on its tide board (often less than 64 feet). Sailboats with tall masts should check conditions carefully here. You may no longer anchor in the county basin, as there is now a small residential marina, Harbor Oaks, and ramp located here. The dock at Socastee Landing has been taken over by a busy personal-watercraft rental operation; exercise extreme caution.

Dockage: The Marina at Grande Dunes is at Mile 357. The 144-slip luxury marina, with 1,150 feet of face dockage, reserves 18 transient slips with 8- to 10-foot depths at dockside. The Inn at Grande Dunes, a resort and conference center located at the marina, is available along with a Ruth's Chris Steak House. Across the ICW, Grand Dunes has golf courses and tennis, along with its residential development.

At around Mile 368, another No-Wake Zone protects the two entrances to Hague Marina, the oldest marina and boatyard in the area. Note the presence of a new private marina, Harbor Oaks Marina, just south of the Socastee Highway Bridge, in the old turning basin at Mile 371.

Osprey Marina, located at red daybeacon "26" (Mile 373), has fuel, floating transient slips, pump-out service and a dockmaster's building with restrooms, showers, laundry and a ship's store, all in a protected basin on the east side of the ICW. Dockside depth is 9 feet at mean low water. The entrance is well-marked and has 10-foot depths. There is a small, short-order grill at Osprey Marina that is open until 5:00 p.m. on weekdays and 7:00 p.m. on weekends. This marina has become an ICW favorite.

Myrtle Beach, SC. Photo courtesy of the Myrtle Beach Area Chamber of Commerce.

Myrtle Beach, SC. Photo courtesy of Myrtle Beach Area Chamber of Commerce.

GOIN' ASHORE: **MYRTLE BEACH, SC**

Myrtle Beach can be a welcome diversion after many lazy days of cruising the ICW. Here is where you go for action: golfing on championship courses or themed putt-putt courses, entertainment at nightclubs and music halls, amusement parks, shopping or dining in more than 1,500 restaurants. All this, plus the 60 miles of beaches that make up the Grand Strand, has made Myrtle Beach, as Diane Sawyer on "Good Morning America" decreed, "the number-one family vacation destination in America." Boaters can partake in the fun from any of the marinas in Little River, North Myrtle Beach and Myrtle Beach itself, although the Marina at Grande Dunes is the only full-service marina actually within the Myrtle Beach city limits.

History: Myrtle Beach, originally called New Town, did not become a city until 1957. The northern portion of South Carolina was mostly swamp and timberlands until after the Civil War, when Conway businessman F.G. Burroughs came up with the idea of a resort area on the beach to be reached by riverboats and a railway. His and his partner's sons actually completed the railroad, beginning the surge of development by building the Seaside Inn in 1901. North Myrtle Beach was still four sleepy little villages along a scrub-filled beach into the 1950s when the local Nixon family began digging channels and canals, also promoting development.

S.B. Chapin, from Chicago, joined the group and the Burroughs & Chapin Company began accumulating real estate to develop, including the landmark Myrtle Beach Pavilion, which closed in 2006. The company remains an important influence in the area today and donated 320 acres of oceanfront land to the state for the Myrtle Beach State Park as well as the public access areas to the beach in the city. In fact, the Grande Dunes Resort is one of their projects.

Attractions: If you have any interest in golf, this is the place to go. With well over 100 golf courses to choose from, your best bet is to consult the harbormaster for suggestions or go to www.golfholiday.com. You can even book tee times online at some of the courses these days.

The birthplace of the Shag, the state's official dance, Myrtle Beach is big on musical entertainment, offering everything from Broadway, to country, to blues and Jimmy Buffett.

Barefoot Landing, in North Myrtle Beach, has dockage along the ICW edge of a large complex featuring two theaters, plus a variety of restaurants and specialty shops. The Alabama Theatre features shows with country, rock, gospel, Broadway and Motown as well as a guest artists concert series. It also features the "South's Grandest Holiday Production," playing from early November through New Year's Eve. The House of Blues has top bands performing until late—also with a good restaurant. Another favorite place to dine here is Greg Norman's Australian Grille, overlooking the ICW.

Broadway at the Beach has more than the average person can keep up with in a short visit, including the Pavilion Nostalgia Park, with a collection of the rides and games that were part of the old Myrtle Beach Pavilion Amusement Park. The Palace Theatre features live Broadway-style performances as well as celebrity concerts. Jimmy Buffett's Margaritaville showcases his music and a casual island style for dining. Plus, there are 10 nightclubs, several hotels, specialty shops and at least 20 restaurants. Family entertainment is also close, from Ripley's Aquarium with its touch tank and sea life exhibits and a Ripley's Believe It or Not! exhibit to an IMAX Discovery Theatre. Even more entertainment can be enjoyed at Legends in Concert, with live performers impersonating some of the world's greatest entertainers, and Medieval Times, which offers a medieval banquet and a tournament show, complete with sword fights and jousting.

For sports action, fishing and kayak tours are favorite

activities in the area, but there is also a NASCAR Speedpark and the Myrtle Beach Pelicans, an Atlanta Braves class A minor league team, playing at Coastal Federal Field. A more unusual excursion is a visit to La Belle Amie Vineyard (Highway 90 west of North Myrtle Beach), part of a former tobacco plantation, for a vineyard tour and tasting. The vineyard also hosts music and arts festivals throughout the year.

Special Events: Bike Week takes place over five days in May ending on Mother's Day, when some 300,000 bikers descend upon the beach, along with numerous vendors. Myrtle Beach is also home to the Hootie and the Blowfish Monday after the Masters Pro-Am tournament.

Shopping: Supermarkets, marine supplies and beverages are within walking distance of most marinas. Many of the marinas now have Internet service; the Chapin Memorial Library (400 14th Ave. N.) has Internet stations for public use as well as periodicals, a reference room and business collection. Ground transportation is plentiful with taxis and rental cars. The Myrtle Beach International Airport, at the city's south edge near the ICW, is served by several airlines and has a new shopping mall. Several visitors centers provide maps, brochures and schedules of events as well as discount tickets for restaurants and attractions.

Restaurants: Be sure to sample the local style of seafood offered by the nearby town of Calabash. At Harbourgate Marina, Filet's (2121 Sea Mountain Highway, 843-280-5200) is well-known for its sushi bar and casual atmosphere. Its tiki bar overlooks the famous Little River Swing Bridge. Another favorite spot is Flamingo's Seafood Grill (7050 N. Kings Highway, 843-449-5388), a locally owned and operated restaurant with great seafood and beef dishes; others claim that Martini's (98 Highway 17 S., 843-249-1134) has the best prime rib. Don't overlook Greg Norman's Australian Grille (4930 Highway 17, 843-361-0000) that is conveniently located along the waterfront at Barefoot Landing.

ADDITIONAL RESOURCES

- MYRTLE BEACH AREA CONVENTION AND VISITORS BUREAU: 800-356-3016, www.visitmyrtlebeach.com
- CITY OF MYRTLE BEACH: www.cityofmyrtlebeach.com
- BROADWAY AT THE BEACH: www.broadwayatthebeach.com
- BAREFOOT LANDING: www.bflanding.com
- GRANDE DUNES RESORT: www.grandedunes.com

NEARBY GOLF COURSES
Ask your dockmaster for a recommendation or visit www.golfholiday.com for more details.

NEARBY MEDICAL FACILITIES
Grand Strand Regional Medical Center,
809 82nd Parkway, Myrtle Beach, SC 29572
843-692-1000

WACCAMAW RIVER

Mile 375 to Mile 403

The Waccamaw River, deep to its wooded banks, is possibly the most scenic part of the ICW route. Moss-draped cypresses line its side streams, and turtles sometimes sun themselves along the shore. Wildflowers of all descriptions grow in cypress stumps, and the water looks like tea. Your boat's bow will get a brown mustache, but it is easy to remove with proper cleaners. (For those who enjoy this section of the Waccamaw River, the upper reaches of the St. Johns River, from Palatka to Lake Monroe, FL are equal in scenic beauty. See Waterway Guide's Southern edition for full coverage of the St. Johns.)

A beautiful and interesting side trip off the ICW, the upper Waccamaw River, while not completely charted, is well marked. Stay to the outside of the bends and be prepared to face a speeding bass boat or two as you round the curves. Set your depth sounder alarm to 5 feet (it will beep merrily in spots) and hold down your speed. Conway, SC has two marinas, both catering to local boats, usually in the 30-feet-or-less category. The first has a shoal entrance and is only for small boats, but you can also anchor off and dinghy ashore. The second, slightly farther up the river, has a deeper entrance and can accommodate larger boats. An upriver bridge, with no clearance gauge, appears to have about 35 feet of vertical clearance.

NAVIGATION: Use Chart 11534. At Enterprise Landing, Mile 375, the ICW enters the upriver waters of Waccamaw River. Note that at Mile 375.2, charted green daybeacon "1" appears on the red-marker side of the channel. Its location can be confusing until you realize that it is not an ICW marker, but actually the first in a series of aids that mark the upper Waccamaw River leading off to the north. Although the ICW route continues downriver on the Waccamaw, the upriver 15-mile-long stretch to Conway carries 4.5-foot depths.

Watch for flotsam along the entire length of the Waccamaw. It can vary from harmless bundles of reeds to a whole tree or a water-soaked log (or deadhead) with only the top exposed. In October 2010, our cruising editor observed numerous logs in the channel. Tugs with tows frequently announce their presence in the narrow and winding upper Waccamaw River with a Sécurité call on VHF Channel 16, or occasionally on Channel 13.

There is a large, busy public boat ramp on the southeast side of the ICW at Enterprise Landing, between green daybeacon "27" and flashing green "27A" (around Mile 375), so watch for small-boat traffic. There is also a series of new private docks here extending toward the ICW channel, with a few new homes nestled in the

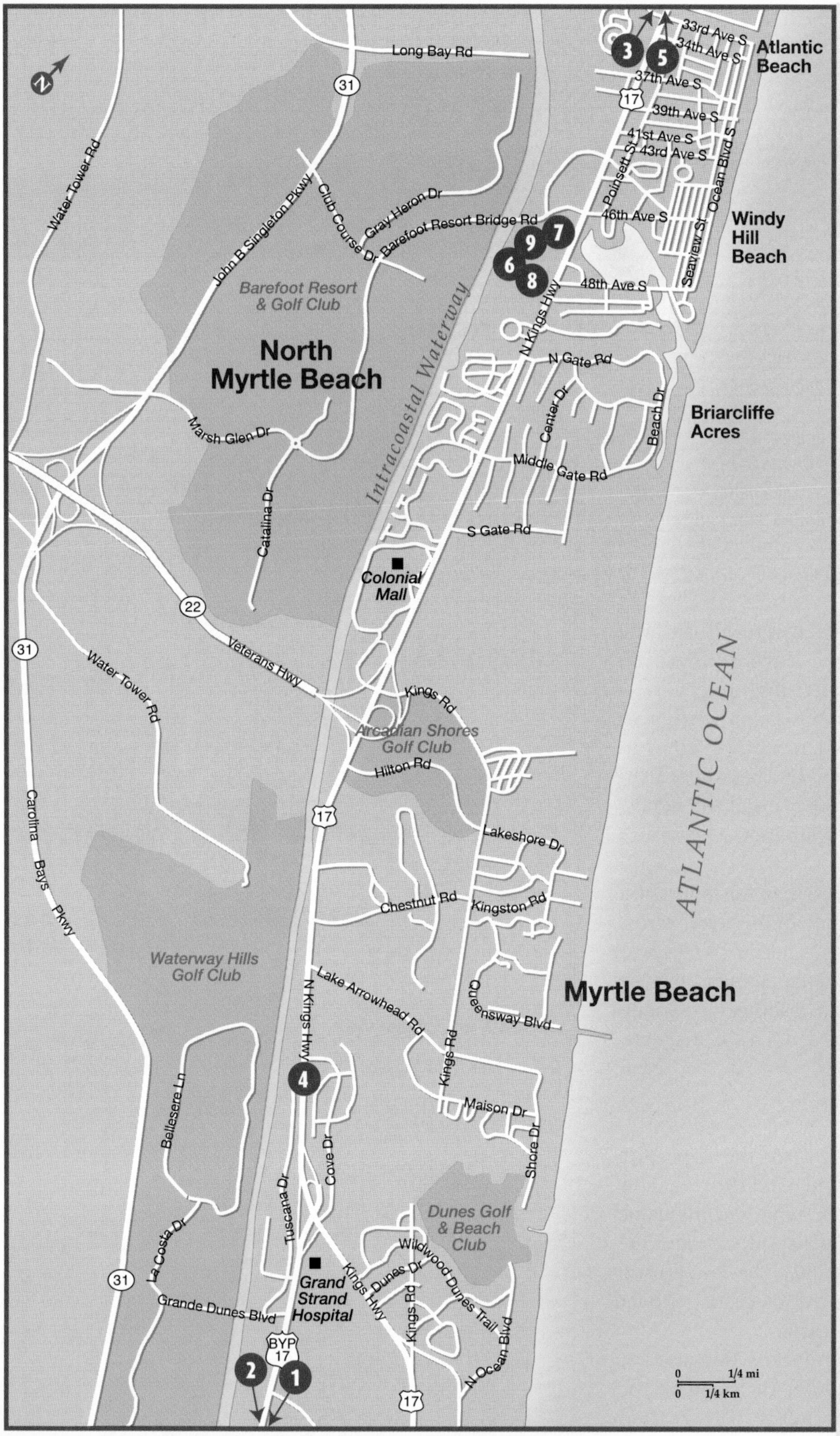

Reference the marina listing tables to see all the marinas in the area.

ATTRACTIONS
1 Broadway at the Beach
2 NASCAR Speedpark

DINING
3 Filet's
4 Flamingo's Seafood Grill
5 Martini's
6 Barefoot Landing
7 House of Blues
8 Greg Norman's Australian Grille
9 Alabama Theater

ENTERTAINMENT
6 Barefoot Landing
7 House of Blues

QUICK FACT:

CORMORANTS

It is not uncommon to see black birds perched on markers along the ICW, wings spread as if waiting for a big hug. This peculiarly-staged bird is the cormorant, a sea bird found on freshwater and saltwater shores throughout the world. Six cormorant species can be found throughout the United States: the double-crested cormorant, great cormorant, neotropic cormorant, Brandt's cormorant, pelagic cormorant and red-faced cormorant. The double-crested is the most widespread cormorant in North America and is the only one of its kind that can be found inland as well as on the coast. The bird is recognizable by its black plumage, webbed feet, long tail, yellow throat patch and its bill, which is usually hooked at the tip. During breeding season, the double head crest (white tufts) can be seen in western birds.

Cormorant varieties range in size from 18 to 40 inches and weigh between 12 ounces and 11 pounds. They have a wingspan of approximately 4 feet. Their coloration can vary from dark brown to black.

Interestingly, the cormorant does not have well-developed oil glands, so its feathers are not well waterproofed. As a result, it spends significant time drying its feathers by holding its wings out in the sun.

The bird is clumsy on land, and colonies tend to establish themselves in areas that are difficult for predators to reach, such as cliffs, dead trees and offshore islets. Here, the bird makes its nest of sticks, seaweed and oftentimes pieces of dead bird. Its diet consists mostly of fish but can include amphibians and crustaceans. To feed, the double-crested cormorant dives for fish and marine invertebrates from the water's surface. After catching a fish, the cormorant surfaces, flips the fish in the air and swallows it head-first.

Myrtle Beach, Little River, SC

MYRTLE BEACH, LITTLE RIVER		Largest Vessel Accommodated	VHF Channel Monitored	Transient Berths / Total Berths	Approach / Dockside Depth (reported)	Floating Docks	Gas / Diesel	Groceries, Ice, Marine Supplies, Snacks	Repairs: Hull, Engine, Propeller	Lift (tonnage), Crane, Rail	1=110V, 2=220V, B=Both, Max Amps	Laundry, Pool, Showers	Pump-Out Station	Nearby: Grocery Store, Motel, Restaurant
		Dockage					Supplies		Services					
1. BW's Marina 344.5	843-249-1941		16		/8	F	GD	GIMS	E		1/30			GMR
2. Crickett Cove Marina 345	843-249-7169	130	16	10/90	10/7	F	GD	GIMS	EP	L8	B/100	LS	P	GMR
3. Coquina Yacht Club 346	843-249-9333	100	16	12/113	8/12	F	GD	I	EP		B/50	LS	P	
4. Lightkeeper's Marina 346 (Internet) (WiFi)	843-249-8660	125	16	10/125	7/12	F		IS			B/50	LPS		MR
5. Myrtle Beach Yacht Club 346 (Internet) (WiFi)	843-249-5376	120	16/14	50/153	7/12	F	GD	GIMS			B/100	LPS	P	MR
6. Anchor Marina 347	843-249-7899	45	16	10/95	7/6	F	GD	IMS	HEP	L35	1/30	S	P	GMR
7. Harbourgate Resort & Marina 347.7 (Internet) (WiFi)	**843-249-8888**	**150**	**16/12**	**8/98**	**8/6**	**F**	**GD**	**IMS**	**HEP**		**B/50**	**LPS**	**P**	**GMR**
8. Dock Holidays Marina 348.2	843-280-6354	150	16	10/96	7/7	F	GD	IMS			B/50	S	P	GMR
9. Barefoot Landing Marina 354	843-663-0838	200	16		10/5	F		MS			B/100			GMR
10. Barefoot Marina 354 (Internet) (WiFi)	**843-390-2011**	**300**	**16**	**32/160**	**12/12**	**F**	**GD**	**IMS**			**B/50**	**LPS**	**P**	**GMR**
11. Marina at Grande Dunes 357 (Internet) (WiFi)	843-315-7777	130	16/12	18/136	12/10	F	GD	IMS			B/100	LPS	P	GMR

Corresponding chart(s) not to be used for navigation. (Internet) Internet Access (WiFi) Wireless Internet Access

trees. Slower boats will carry a fair current all the way to Georgetown, SC (Mile 403) when leaving Enterprise Landing about an hour and a half after high tide.

Anchorage: The Waccamaw River is laden with great anchorages. This is one of the most rewarding areas to anchor south of the Chesapeake Bay, but bass-boat fishermen may sometimes come full-bore around the bends, so bear that in mind when picking your spot. Always use your anchor light.

Our editor likes to anchor at Mile 375.5, in the loop south of Enterprise Landing on the north side of the river, across from flashing green "29." The holding is fair in 13 feet near of the southern part of the oxbow. We recommend the use of an anchor trip line in case you snare a submerged stump or log and make sure your anchor is set. This is a serene, quiet anchorage after dark.

Bucksport—Mile 377

Enterprise Landing (Mile 375) was once the departure point for huge shipments of yellow pine and cypress. This was the domain of Capt. Henry Buck, who lent his name to the shipbuilding community of Bucksport, ME and the timbering community of Bucksport, SC. The latter community lies on a sharp bend where the Waccamaw River begins to widen, making navigation easier.

Dockage: The Bucksport Plantation Marina & Restaurant, located on the west side at the bend in the river, changed ownership and was under construction at press time. The new owners have many renovations planned.

Anchorage: One of the prettiest, most secluded anchorages anywhere is at Prince Creek, east of the ICW across from flashing red "44" and Mile 380.4. The few houses here are well hidden, and only an occasional fisherman uses the creek. You can go part way or all the way in, depending on your whim. The north and south entrances both have approximately 15-foot depths, but neither end

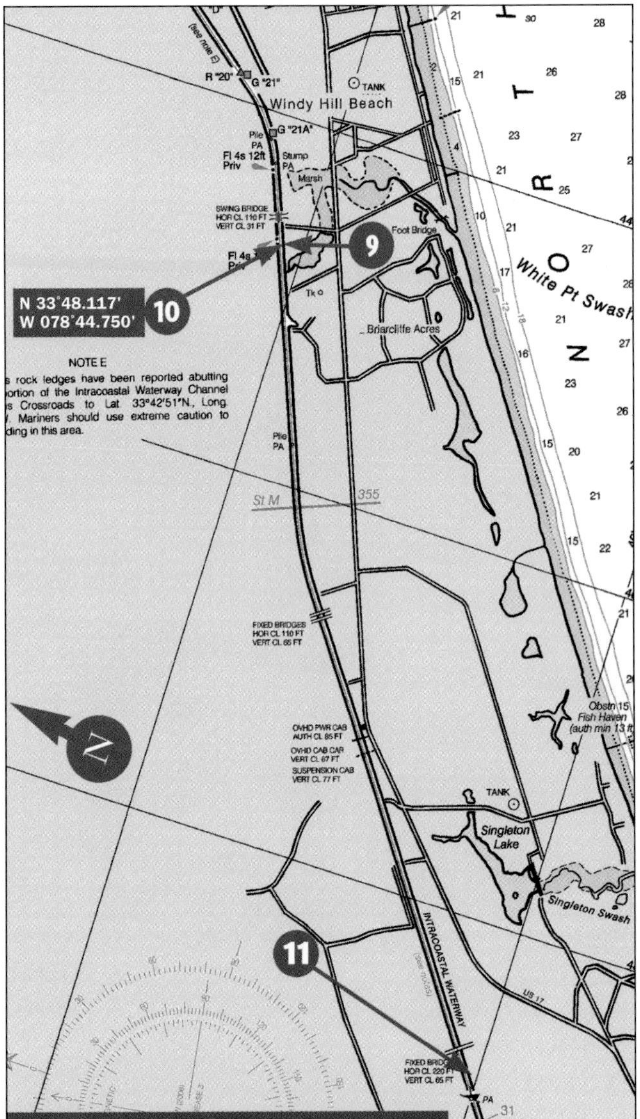

MYRTLE BEACH, CHART 11534

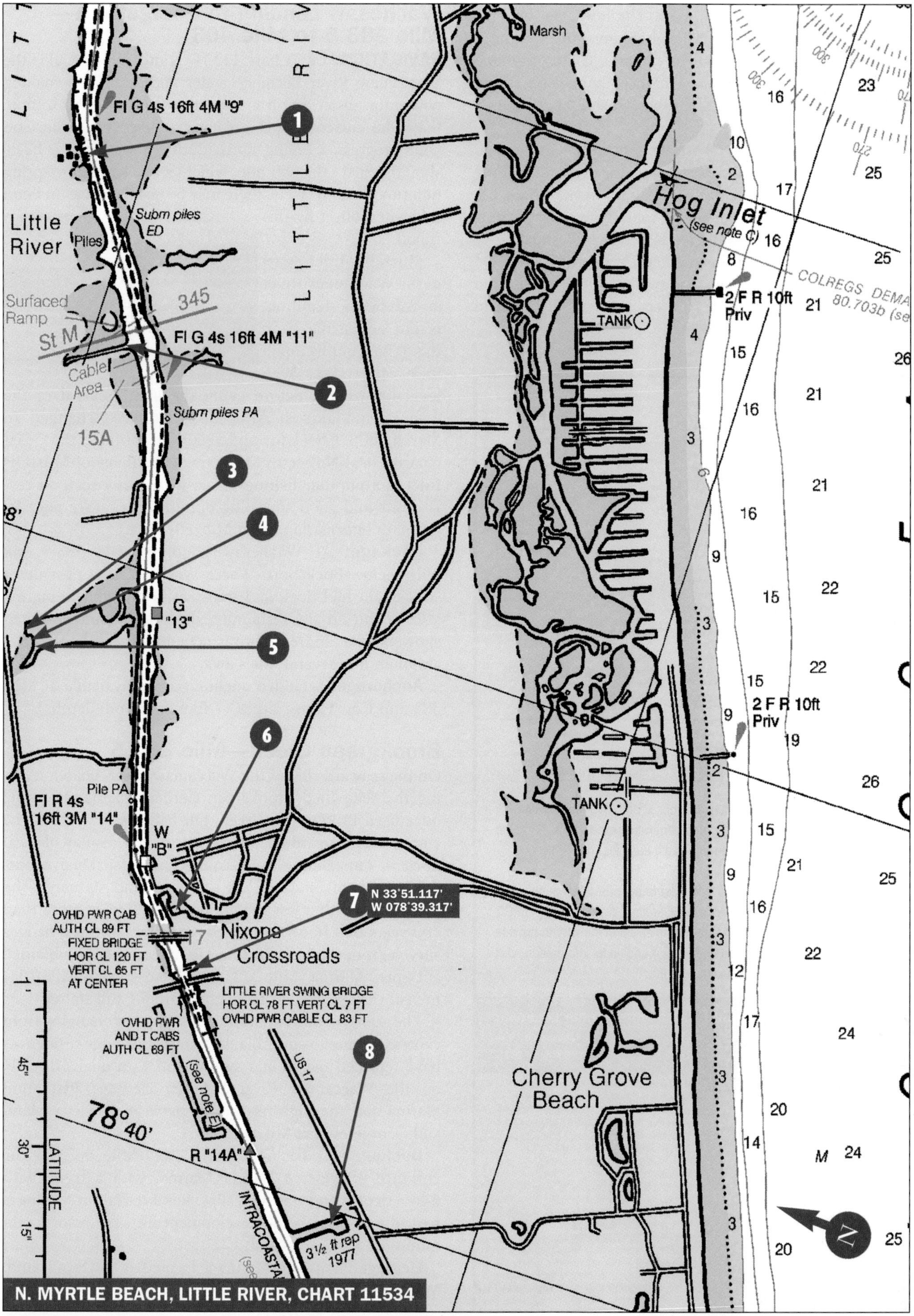

N. MYRTLE BEACH, LITTLE RIVER, CHART 11534

offers protection from ICW wash. The lower end is wide enough to warrant only one anchor, but you may need two at the upper end or narrower parts. Giving points a good berth, you can run the length of Longwood Island and rejoin the ICW south of Mulberry Landing at flashing green "53" (Mile 381.7).

Just south (Mile 381.2) of the northern entrance to Prince Creek, you may turn west off the ICW at flashing red "48" marking the entrance to Bull Creek, which has better holding and more swinging room than other anchorages on the Waccamaw River. Be careful of shoaling at flashing red "48." Give this marker a very wide berth! Go up past the first bend to avoid the wake of ICW traffic, and anchor where depths suit. Hunters frequent this area in season, so prepare to awaken early.

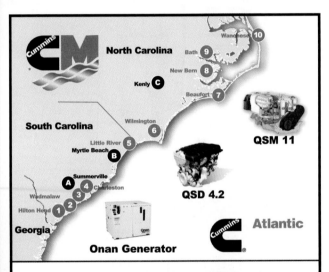

Wachesaw Landing to Georgetown—Mile 383.5 to Mile 403

NAVIGATION: Use Chart 11534. South of Mile 385, the Waccamaw River becomes wider and straighter, making navigation easier, but it is important for slow boats to note that tidal currents here can have an impressive effect on your progress. Coming north during a wet spring, boats should respect the ebb tide, which is accelerated by spring rain runoff. Conversely, there may be no advantage on flood tide when offset by this runoff.

WACCAMAW RIVER
Mile 375 to Mile 403
WATERWAY GUIDE PHOTOGRAPHY

Murrells Inlet, east of the Waccamaw River at Wachesaw Landing, is not accessible from the ICW, but is open to ocean traffic. Seek local knowledge before using the inlet. Several of the navigational aids at Murrells Inlet were changed in March 2008. Check for updated information in the Coast Guard Local Notice to Mariners. The village of Murrells Inlet is a popular fishing resort with many seafood restaurants and good shopping opportunities. *(See page 80 for more information about Murrells Inlet.)*

Dockage: At Wachesaw Landing, Mile 383.5, six miles below Bucksport, Wacca Wache Marina provides a convenient fuel dock and transient berthing. The marina also has an on-site restaurant, dock store and renovated showers. The address here is actually Murrells Inlet, SC, although it is several miles away.

Anchorage: Secluded anchorages are available at Mile 383.5 in Cow House Creek (7-foot minimum depths).

Brookgreen Creek—Mile 387.5

On the seaward side of the Waccamaw River, boaters visiting the renowned Brookgreen Gardens plantation home once used Brookgreen Creek, but barriers now block the entrances. The gardens offer a spectacular display of local flowers, outstanding landscaping and an extensive outdoor museum of American sculpture and statuary. The plantation, with a few remaining structures, is more than 100 years old. Rows of gnarled oaks and boxwood hedges survive from original plantings. Rental cars can be obtained at Osprey Marina (Mile 373) or in Georgetown (Mile 403) to visit the spectacular landscape gardens and statuary.

The scenery south of Brookgreen Creek is changing from cypress swamp to suburbia. In some areas, huge residences have replaced marsh and swampland with docks directly on the Waccamaw River between Heritage Plantation Marina and the high-rise bridge between Pawleys Island and Georgetown at Mile 401.1.

Dockage: At flashing green "71" (Mile 388) is the entrance to Reserve Harbor Marina, with a basin with 6-foot depths and transient slips. Reserve Harbor Marina is part of a major upscale development near the resort community of Pawleys Island.

Heritage Plantation Marina is located at Pawleys Island, Mile 394, directly on the ICW. The marina is part of a

Waccamaw River, SC

WACCAMAW RIVER		Largest Vessel Accommodated	VHF Channel Monitored	Transient Berths / Total Berths	Approach / Dockside Depth (reported)	Floating Docks	Gas / Diesel	Groceries, Ice, Marine Supplies, Snacks	Repairs: Hull, Engine, Propeller	Lift (tonnage), Crane, Rail	1=110V, 2=220V, B=Both, Max Amps	Laundry, Pool, Showers	Pump-Out Station	Nearby: Grocery Store, Motel, Restaurant
		Dockage					Supplies		Services					
1. Hague Marina 368.2 (Internet Access) (WiFi)	843-293-2141	100	16/09	15/35	6/6			IMS	HEP	L	B/50			GMR
2. Osprey Marina 373 (Internet Access) (WiFi)	**843-215-5353**	**100**	**16**	**10/100**	**10/9**	**F**	**GD**	**GIMS**			**B/100**	**LS**	**P**	
3. Bucksport Plantation Marina & Rest. 377.5	843-397-5566	230	16	50/50	15/8	F	GD	GIMS			B/100	S	P	GR
4. Wacca Wache Marina 383 (Internet Access) (WiFi)	843-651-2994	150	16/10	10/180	25/6	F	GD	IMS		L15	B/100	S	P	R

Corresponding chart(s) not to be used for navigation. (Internet Access icon) Internet Access (WiFi icon) Wireless Internet Access

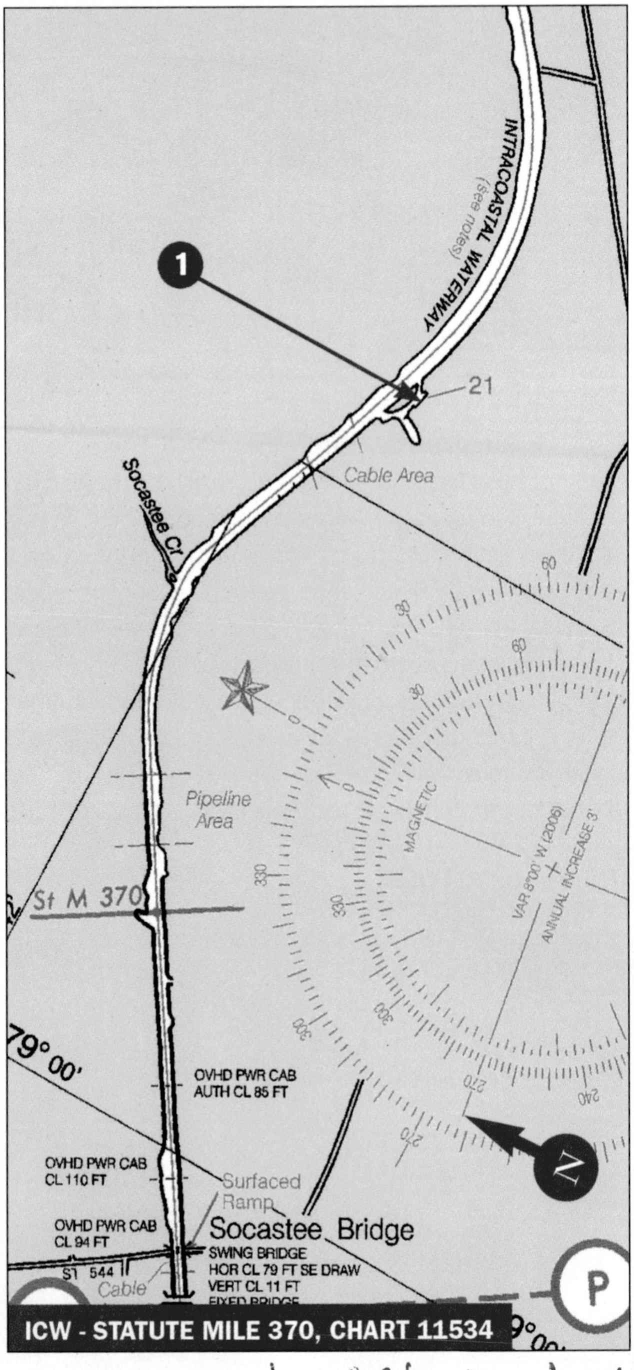

ICW - STATUTE MILE 370, CHART 11534

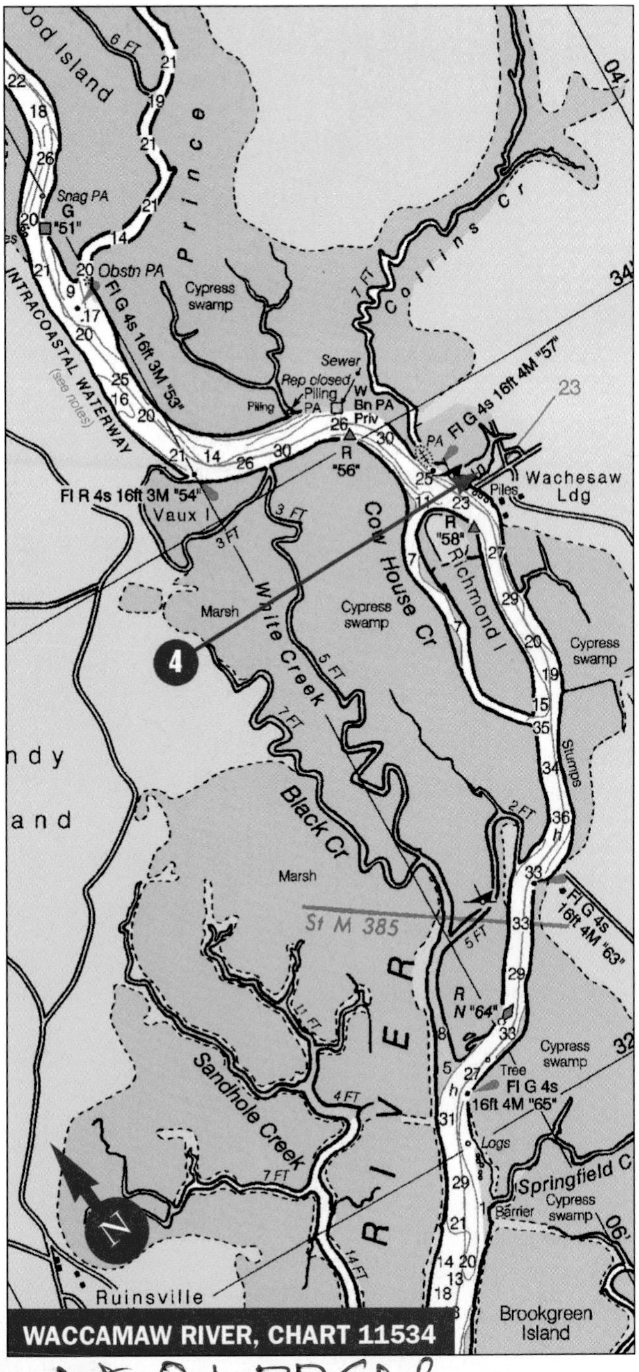

WACCAMAW RIVER, CHART 11534

804-814 6836 - DIVER AT OSPREY

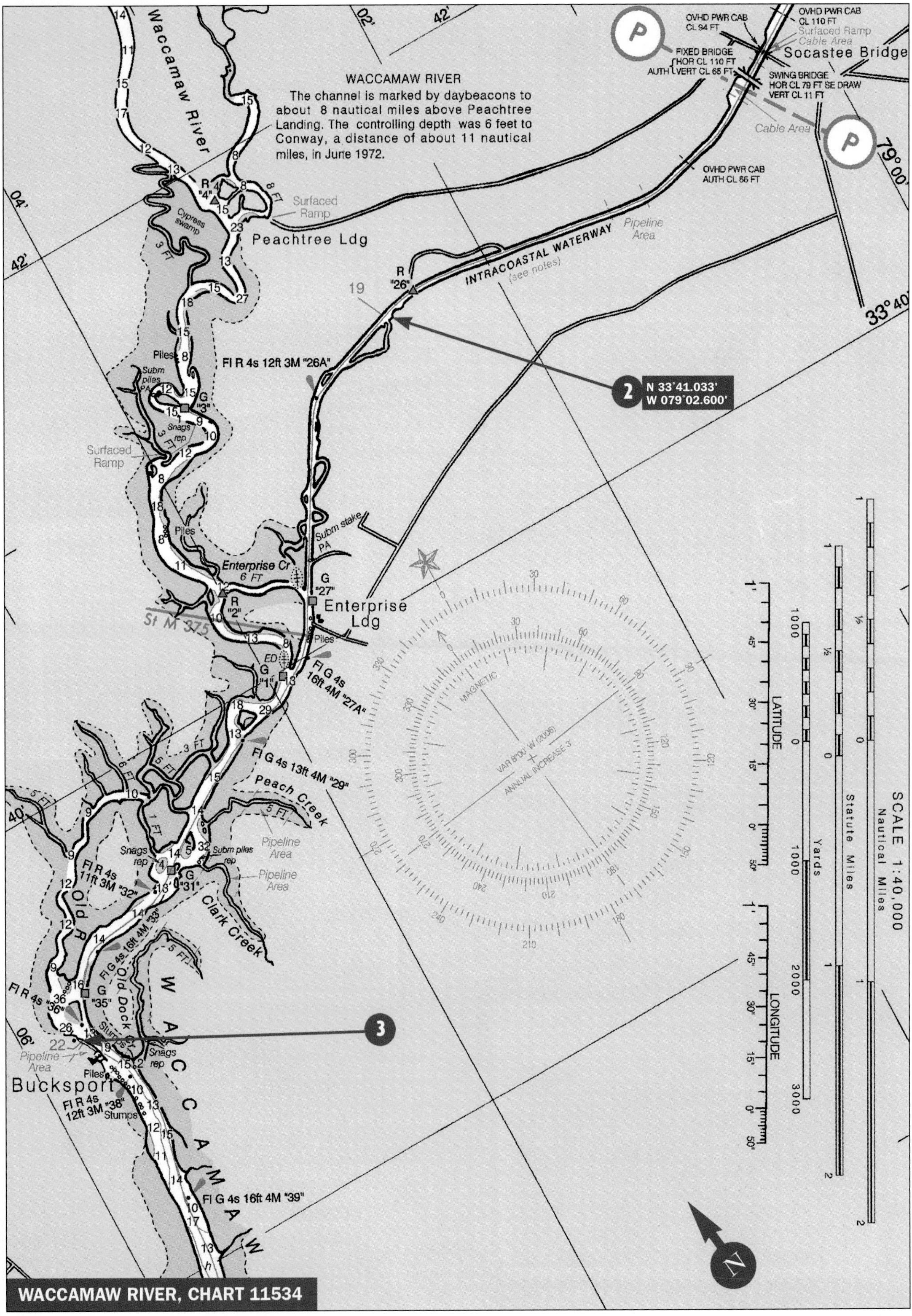

WACCAMAW RIVER, CHART 11534

larger community development that also has a fitness center, pool and spa.

Thoroughfare Creek to Butler Island—Mile 389 to Mile 396

NAVIGATION: Use Chart 11534. Two long private community docks extending into the channel affect navigation in the Butler Island area, where the river narrows and the ICW channel turns around the east side of the island. The ends of both docks are marked with flashing white lights. Charts up to the 1980s showed abandoned rice paddies in the marshes along the west side of the river along this area, indicative of an earlier time when rice was a major export crop for the area plantations.

Anchorage: A good spot to drop the hook is at Mile 389 in Thoroughfare Creek, which carries 14-foot minimum depths, or at Mile 395 in Jericho Creek, which has 8-foot charted minimum depths at the entrance but deepens as you proceed. Be aware, however, that Thoroughfare Creek is heavily used by locals on the weekends and it may not be the same tranquil spot it is during the week.

Butler Island, near Mile 396, is a very scenic and natural area with nesting eagle families. Behind Butler Island, there is good holding in 20 to 28 feet but use an anchor trip-line near the island. The anchorage behind Butler Island is well protected from east through south winds. If you anchor on the channel side north of Butler Island, you will be jostled by wakes from passing boats.

On the north end of Butler Island, there is an underwater high voltage cable crossing. It is indicated on the chart as a cable area, and there are signs ashore, but they are difficult to read. Avoid this area in choosing your anchorage. Remember that tidal currents affect anchorages in the lower Waccamaw River.

Mile 401 to Mile 403

This stretch of the Waccamaw River, which includes Georgetown, has become increasingly touristy and popular. There has been a proliferation of tour boats of many types, even amphibious craft, along the river and around the inlet at Winyah Bay. There are island tours, plantation tours and wilderness tours. Even vessels that create minimum wake should give these tour boats a slow pass.

NAVIGATION: Use Chart 11534. A high-level bridge on the Waccamaw River, the U.S. 17 Highway Bridge (65-foot fixed vertical clearance) at Mile 401.1, is a short distance above Georgetown. After passing under the bridge, take the time to sort out the markers leading to the Georgetown harbor entrance channel. Here, below the big shoal extending south from Waccamaw Point, four bodies of water converge: Waccamaw River, Winyah Bay, Great Pee Dee River and Georgetown's Sampit River. The buoys can be confusing. There is green daybeacon "95" opposite flashing red "96" south of the bridge. Near the junction of the four bodies of water is flashing red "W." Read your chart carefully and do not cut behind flashing red "W." Leave it to starboard heading south and to port if heading north, as it sits in 5 feet of water.

Dockage: The Great Pee Dee River channel is marked with red and green daybeacons leading upriver toward Georgetown Landing, the marina just before the U.S. 17 fixed bridge (20-foot vertical clearance). The Coast Guard station at Georgetown is next to the marina, on the Great Pee Dee River.

Waccamaw River. WATERWAY GUIDE PHOTOGRAPHY.

■ GEORGETOWN TO MCCLELLANVILLE

Mile 403 to Mile 430

NAVIGATION: Use Chart 11534. For boats making the ocean run along the coast, Winyah Bay is the first shipping inlet south of the Cape Fear River and Southport, NC. If you bypass Georgetown to go down Winyah Bay, note that the aids to navigation from there are colored and numbered as from seaward. This change occurs at the junction of Georgetown's harbor channel and the ICW. The ICW markers resume where Winyah Bay divides into two channels: one leading to the inlet, while the other, Western Channel, continues as part of the ICW. Careful navigation is necessary to ensure that you take the desired route. Low-powered boats headed north should leave Georgetown an hour after slack tide, before flood at Charleston, to carry a fair current up the Waccamaw River.

If the Winyah Bay ocean inlet is your goal, follow the main shipping channel beginning at Frazier Point. If you should end up in the wrong channel, note the shoal between the two channels and be cautious. There are swift currents and whirlpools on the ebb tide. The tremendous volume of water that passes through the jetties at this entrance should not be underestimated. Use caution when transiting the inlet at Winyah Bay, especially on the ebb with opposing winds. The rock jetty here has claimed a number of vessels over the years. The Western Channel to the inlet, though unmarked beyond the ICW turn into the Estherville Minim Creek Canal, is true to its charted depths.

Recent years have seen extensive dredging of the inlet and levee construction along the ICW in this area. Flashing red "96" at the ICW was relocated but not far from its former position. (It is always a difficult one to locate.)

Green daybeacon "97" is on the opposite side of the channel, marking the end of an area of broken-off pilings, visible at low to mid-water, extending from the marshy island.

Georgetown—Mile 403

NAVIGATION: Use Chart 11534. **Use the Charleston Tide Table. For high tide, add 1 hour and 25 minutes; for low tide, add 2 hours and 9 minutes.** The channel into Georgetown Harbor is wide and deep; it was surveyed in 2009 with at least 9-foot depths. Once off the ICW and heading in toward town, the channel for yachts and small commercial craft bears off to starboard just before flashing red "S." The Sampit River turns abruptly to port, and the factory basin is straight ahead. You can explore either of the last two but, assuming that you want to visit Georgetown, take the channel to starboard. Exercise some care and do not cut too close to the starboard shore, as it is infested with broken and submerged pilings. Once abeam of the first docking area, the harbor is relatively clear of obstacles.

Above Georgetown, on the Sampit River, is a twin-span 65-foot fixed bridge. The upper reaches of this small, but attractive river are readily open to exploration. Unmarked and uncharted, the river poses a do-it-yourself challenge.

Dockage: Approaching from the ICW, Hazzard Marine is the first facility along the waterfront in Georgetown. This is the only haul-out facility between the Myrtle Beach area, 40 miles to the north, and Charleston, 65 miles to the south. The Boat Shed marina, with floating docks and fuel, is located just beyond Hazzard Marine.

Next is Harborwalk Marina, adjacent to Georgetown's business district. Floating docks with updated electric hookups have been added recently at Harborwalk as well as a new bathhouse. All of the marinas are just a short walk from the restaurants, museums and shopping.

Anchorage: Because of its convenient location, the Georgetown waterfront has always been a popular spot to drop the hook, and it can get crowded. Much of the harbor is now taken up by boats on permanent moorings and anchoring space may only be available downstream of the moorings. Check with the marinas for availability of moorings. Anchoring in the area is not highly recommended by our cruising editor because of poor holding in very deep, soft mud.

GOIN' ASHORE: GEORGETOWN, SC

Georgetown's small-town, quiet façade, coupled with surrounding natural beauty, belies the historic and economic significance of the area. Its downtown is a National Historic District, where visitors can stroll the streets and adjacent neighborhood, admiring the city homes of former plantation owners. The town and its residents welcome transients with a wealth of services, interesting land tours, good restaurants and interesting shopping.

History: An important port, South Carolina's third oldest city was founded in 1729 and became an official port of entry in 1732. The confluence of the Waccamaw, Black and Pee Dee rivers, at the head of Winyah Bay, was the hub of the main avenues carrying plantation produce to market and supplies to the plantations. Rice and indigo plantations were established along the waterways, their products later replaced by lumber and turpentine. By the 1840s, this area produced about half of the rice consumed in the entire United States, including the special Carolina Gold rice, which is back in production today. With the abolition of slavery, rice and indigo were no longer viable enterprises and lumber, followed by paper products and steel, became the major economic influence. Today, residential development is a booming business.

The beauty of the town is largely due to W.D. Morgan, a New Yorker whose family moved to Georgetown before the Civil War. Among his many accomplishments as mayor was the planting of the live oaks along the city streets a century ago. He continually advanced ideas to improve Georgetown, including keeping the harbor dredged, digging a deep water channel from the inlet and building rock jetties at the entrance to Winyah Bay to keep a sandbar from blocking the inlet. The jetty construction was completed in 1904.

Attractions: A visit to Georgetown certainly calls for at least a day's layover, longer if you want to explore some of the outlying plantations. While a car is helpful for this, there are boat tours

Downtown Georgetown, SC. Photo courtesy of Mike Kucera.

to some of the plantation areas, the marsh islands and beaches. First Lady Michelle Obama has family roots in the area.

Georgetown is actually located just off the ICW on a loop of the Sampit River. Any of the marinas can arrange a car rental. The Trolley Tour leaves from the Visitors Center (1001 Front St.) to tour the revitalized downtown. The center also offers brochures and a comprehensive map pinpointing the commercial and public activities in the business district. The marinas can supply the packets of information when you register for dockage. A small powerboat also frequently delivers these packets to boats in the anchorage.

The city built a harborwalk along the Sampit River side of the buildings that line Front Street. The stores and restaurants that abut it have privately owned slips along this section. It is a lovely walk along the river, lined with flower boxes maintained by the residents and plant-filled balconies overlooking the water.

Aside from strolling along the tree-lined streets enjoying the pre-Revolutionary and antebellum homes, a visit to the Kaminski House Museum next to the visitors center should be part of your itinerary. Built in 1769 by a local merchant, it is now used as a teaching tool for the area's history. Another must-stop is the Rice Museum (originally the Old Market built in 1842) at the opposite end of Front Street, which includes a 45-minute guided tour about the local rice culture, featuring the 1842 Clock Tower and the Kaminski Hardware Building. The third floor of the Rice Museum houses the skeleton of America's oldest known vessel, the Brown's ferry vessel, an 18th-century all-purpose freighter. The Georgetown County Museum, located in the heart of the historic district, features 300 years of local history and culture. See relics of local plantation culture while learning about the rice culture, thriving lumber industry, and the making of paper from Southern yellow pine. The Georgetown Maritime Museum is located on the ground floor of the Georgetown County's historic Chamber of Commerce Building on Front Street. The historic Prince George Winyah Episcopal Church, built around 1750 with brick from the ballast on British ships, is worth a visit as well.

The closest golf course, Wedgefield Plantation Golf Club, is just north of Georgetown along the banks of the Black River. To play multiple courses, check out the newly created Waccamaw Golf Trail packages that include the 12 most awarded courses in Georgetown County.

Special Events: The third weekend in October is a great time to be in Georgetown for the Georgetown Wooden Boat Show, put on by the Georgetown Harbor Historical Association. Proceeds go toward establishing a permanent home for the Maritime Museum and adding to its exhibits. The Winyah Bay Heritage Festival is held the third week of January, featuring art exhibits, hunting and fishing crafts, decoy painting and carvings, storytelling and the state's championship duck calling contest.

Shopping: For groceries, the Piggly Wiggly (on High-

Georgetown, Waccamaw River, Winyah Bay, SC

WACCAMAW RIVER, WINYAH BAY		Largest Vessel Accommodated	VHF Channel Monitored	Transient Berths / Total Berths	Approach / Dockside Depth (reported)	Floating Docks	Gas / Diesel	Groceries, Ice, Marine Supplies, Snacks	Repairs: Hull, Engine, Propeller	Lift (tonnage), Crane, Rail	1=110V, 2=220V, B=Both, Max Amps	Laundry, Pool, Showers	Pump-Out Station	Nearby: Grocery Store, Motel, Restaurant
		Dockage					Supplies		Services					
1. Reserve Harbor Yacht Club 388.2 WiFi	843-314-5133	60	16	2/50	6/6	F	GD	IMS			B/50	S	P	GR
2. Heritage Plantation Marina 394	843-237-3650	100	16	10/40	30/30	F		IS			B/100	LS	P	
3. Hazzard Marine .9 N of 403 ☐	843-527-3625	200	16	5/35	10/9	F	GD	IMS	HEP	L50	B/100	LS	P	GMR
4. The Boat Shed 1 N of 403 ☐	843-546-4415	100	16	10/10	10/9	F	GD	IMS	E		B/50	S	P	GMR
5. Harborwalk Marina 1.1 N of 403 ☐ WiFi	**843-546-4250**	**200**	**16/68**	**30/40**	**12/7-10**	**F**	**GD**	**IM**			**B/100**	**LS**	**P**	**GMR**
6. Georgetown Landing Marina 402 ☐ WiFi	**843-546-1776**	**200**	**16/10**	**25/171**	**19/17**	**F**	**GD**	**IMS**			**B/100**	**LS**	**P**	**MR**
7. Belle Isle Marina 405.9 WiFi	843-546-8491	55	16/9	10/81	5/7	F	GD	IMS			**B/50**	**LS**	**P**	

Corresponding chart(s) not to be used for navigation. ☐ Internet Access WiFi Wireless Internet Access

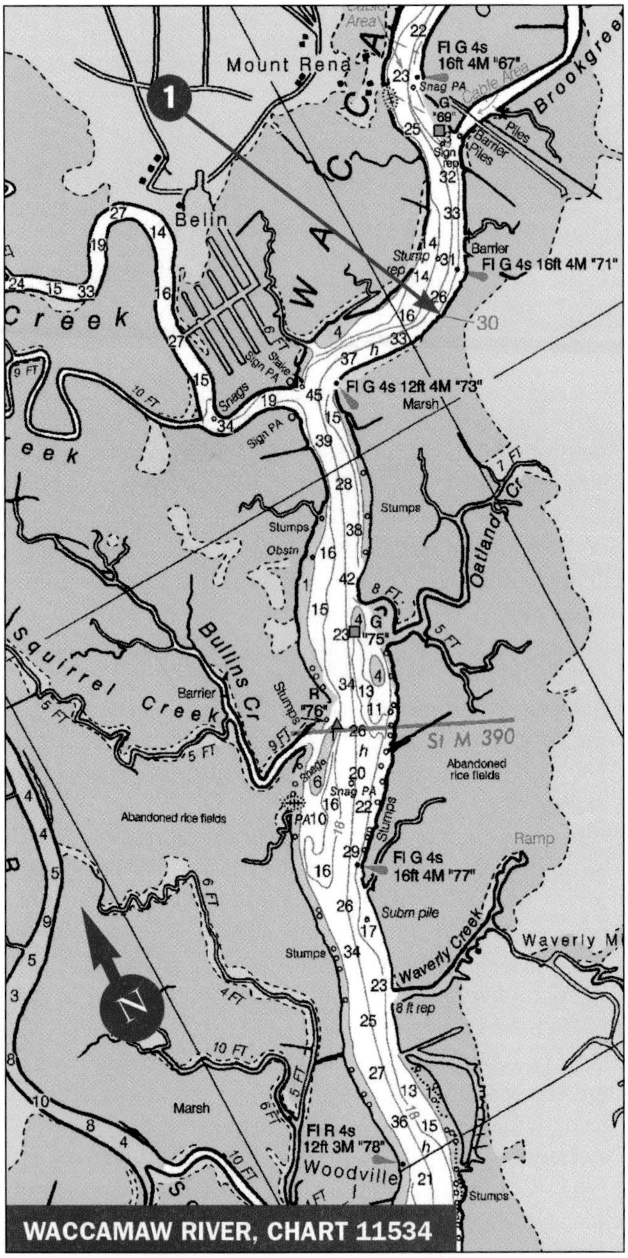

WACCAMAW RIVER, CHART 11534

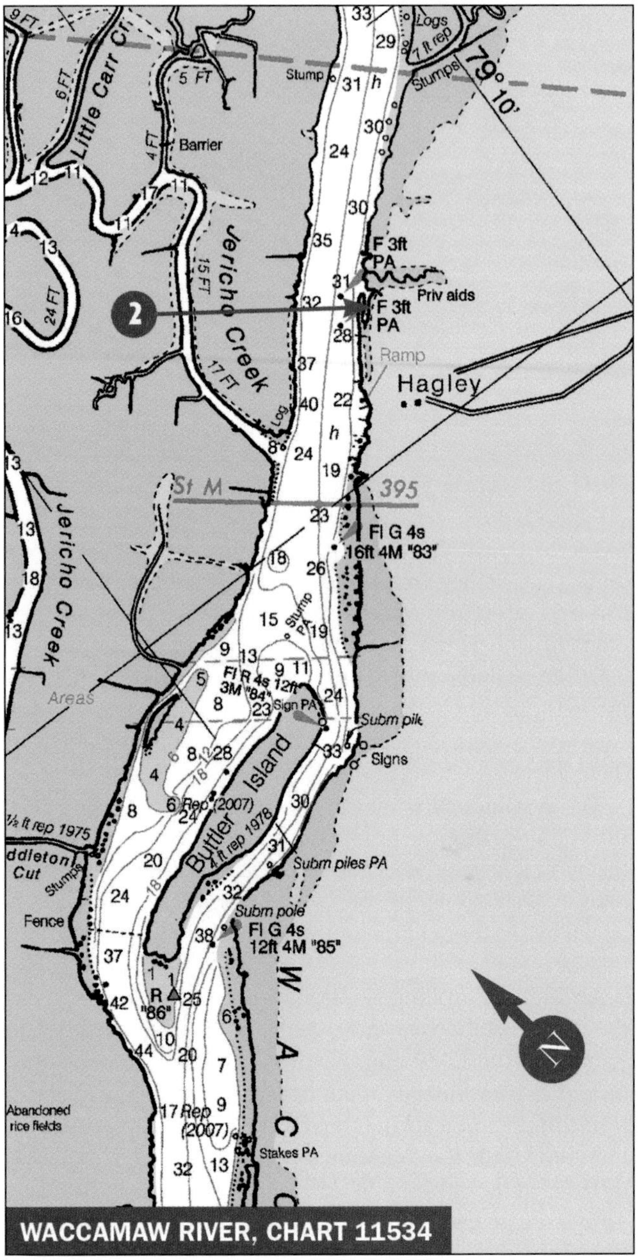

WACCAMAW RIVER, CHART 11534

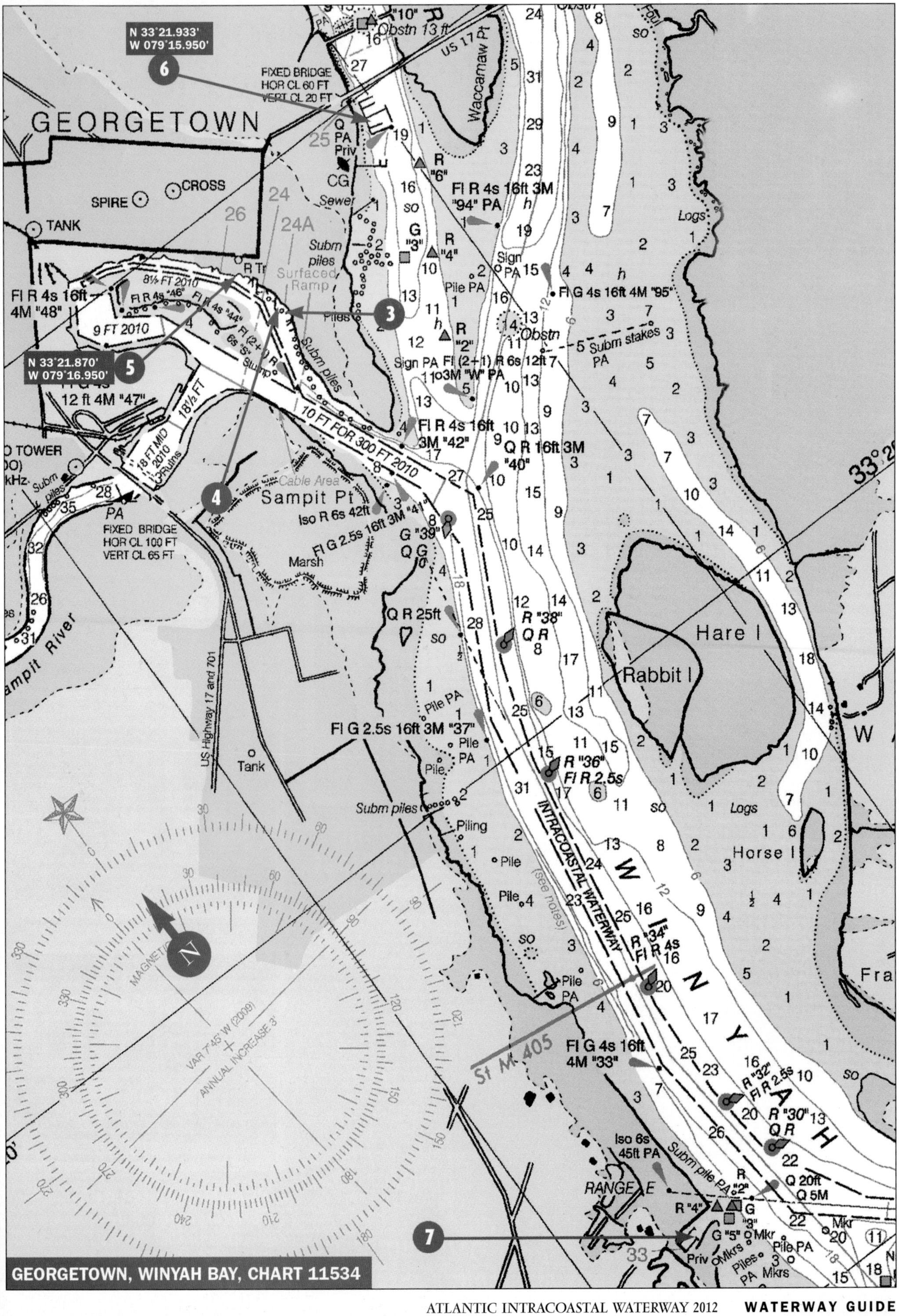

GEORGETOWN, WINYAH BAY, CHART 11534

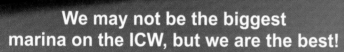

Looking southeast over Georgetown, SC. (Not to be used for navigation.) WATERWAY GUIDE PHOTOGRAPHY.

market Street) used to send a car for transients, but now only sends someone if they aren't busy. A Food Lion is farther south of town. The Kudzu Bakery, several blocks away (120 King St.), but worth the walk, has gourmet items, including delicious fresh baked breads and sandwiches, a good wine selection, Carolina Plantation rice, local relishes, chutneys and preserves. Very convenient to the waterfront is Morsels Market (619 Front Street). They carry essentials, such as milk and eggs, and also have gourmet meats, dry goods and pastries. Georgetown has its own shrimp dock and fishing fleet, so freshly caught seafood is available at Independent Seafood (1 Cannon St.) and Stormy Seas Seafood (130 S. Meeting St.). After touring the Rice Museum, buy their brown rice for an original flavor and aroma.

Stroll along Front Street to shop antiques and gift shops, small department stores and a great bookstore, Harborwalk Books (723 Front St.), with a large selection of books about Georgetown and South Carolina. The Humidor has an Internet café, or you can check email at the public library. To satisfy your "sweet tooth," stop in at Sweeties (707 Front St.) for one of their famous pralines or homemade ice cream plus many other tempting treats.

Restaurants: For a break from galley preparation, check out Thomas Café (703 Front St.), which, for locals, is a place "where everyone knows your name." It has a steady lunch and breakfast business. Breakfasts are old-fashioned, hearty and inexpensive. The fried green tomatoes are highly recommended, as are the fluffy biscuits and grits.

The River Room (801 Front St.), on the water, is in the J.B. Steele Building, built in 1888. It originally housed a dry goods store on one side, with a food store on the other, and hats were made upstairs. The River Room had outgrown its space down the street and moved to this location 100 years after the building first opened. The original walls and hardwood floors were uncovered and restored, giving the restaurant a comfortable, cozy feel. The enclosed dining porch is bright and cheery, even in winter. Order anything seafood and the homemade soups. A special treat is a slice of the Mud Pie that has to be at least six inches tall.

The Rice Paddy (732 Front St.), for fine dining, is across Front Street in an old bank building on the site of a Revolu-tionary War headquarters. The wine cellar is in the old vault. Open for lunch and dinner, tables on the sidewalk are available in nice weather. Favorite choices are Bahamian grouper or snapper piccata, although it is hard not to choose rack of lamb or osso buco. There are a number of other restaurants along the waterfront to choose from during your stay. Some of them are: Goat Island Grill (719 Front St.); The Big Tuna, formerly known as The Old Fish House (807 Front St.); Portofino's at Fogel Wharf (815 Front St.); and Aunny's Country Kitchen (906 Front St.).

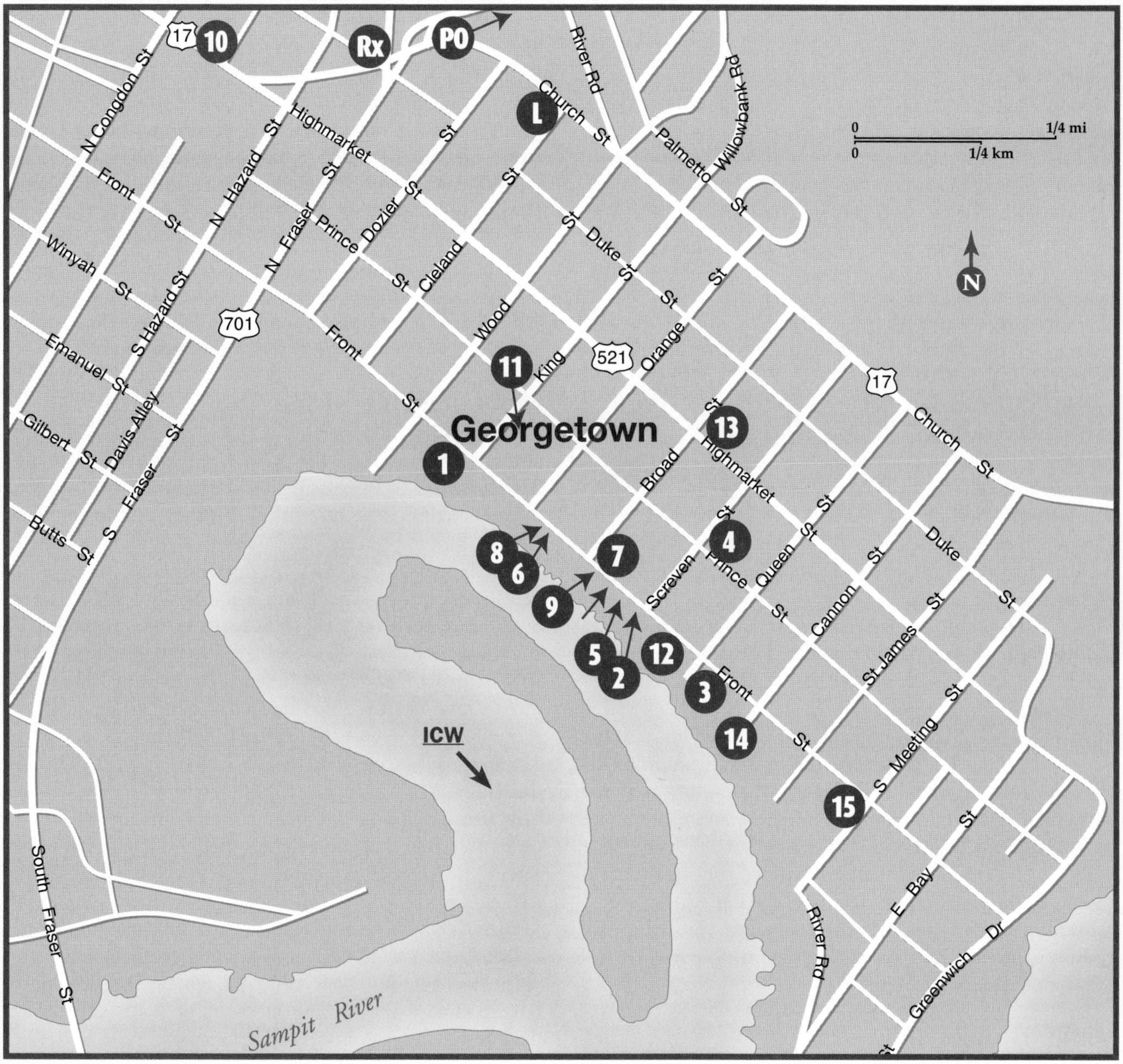

Reference the marina listing tables to see all the marinas in the area.

ATTRACTIONS
1 Kaminski House Museum
2 Rice Museum
3 Georgetown Maritime Museum
4 Georgetown County Museum

DINING
5 Thomas Café
6 The River Room
7 The Rice Paddy
8 Big Tuna
9 Buzz's Roost

GROCERIES/CARRYOUT
10 Piggly Wiggly
11 Kudzu Bakery
12 Morsels Market

INFORMATION
3 Visitors Center/Georgetown Maritime Museum

POINTS OF INTEREST
13 Prince George Winyah Episcopal Church

SEAFOOD
14 Independent Seafood
15 Stormy Seas Seafood

L LIBRARY

PO POST OFFICE

Rx PHARMACY

ADDITIONAL RESOURCES

- GEORGETOWN COUNTY VISITORS BUREAU: 866-368-8687, www.visitgeorgetowncountysc.com
- GEORGETOWN COUNTY CHAMBER OF COMMERCE: 800-777-7705, www.georgetownchamber.com or www.seaportgeorgetown.com
- GEORGETOWN WOODEN BOAT SHOW: www.WoodenBoatShow.com

NEARBY GOLF COURSES
Wedgefield Plantation Golf Club, 129 Clubhouse Lane, Highway 701 N., 843-448-2124, www.wedgefield.com

NEARBY MEDICAL FACILITIES
Georgetown Memorial Hospital, 606 Black River Road, Georgetown, SC 29440, 843-527-7000

ICW—Mile 406 to Mile 415

South of Georgetown (Mile 405.9), the Winyah Bay Channel is subject to maintenance dredging for shipping depths to serve the factories in Georgetown. If you plan to exit the ICW to go offshore at this point, check locally for current conditions affecting passage through the inlet. *(See page 81 for more information about Winyah Bay Channel.)*

Three miles below Georgetown, the ICW route leaves the Winyah Bay ship channel, bears off to the south and continues down the well-marked Western Channel to just past Mile 410. The ICW marking system resumes at the western channel. The ICW makes a sharp departure southward from the Western Channel at flashing red "2" into the Estherville Minim Creek Canal. Currents in the Western Channel are strong, up to 3 knots on the ebb. Don't be tempted to anchor here.

ESTHERVILLE MINIM CREEK
Mile 411.5

WATERWAY GUIDE PHOTOGRAPHY

From this point, the ICW leaves the Waccamaw River and follows mostly straight dredged cuts through vast marshlands for the next 50 miles to Charleston Harbor.

At Mile 411.5, the free-running South Island cable ferry crosses the ICW channel. Signals indicate when it is making a crossing, and a 5-mph speed limit is strictly enforced for a quarter mile on either side of the crossing, not only for the benefit of the ferry, but also for the small-boat activity on the adjacent boat ramp. Allow time for the ferry cable to drop before passing through. Currents run up to 2.5 to 3 knots in the canal in the vicinity of the ferry dock.

Dockage: The marked entry channel to Belle Isle Marina is just to the west of the ICW at Mile 406. It has floating docks and amenities.

Minim Creek—Mile 415

⚠ THE FOLLOWING AREA REQUIRES SPECIAL ATTENTION DUE TO SHOALING OR CHANGES TO THE CHANNEL

MINIM CREEK

NAVIGATION: Use Chart 11534. Heading south on the ICW, the channel turns to starboard just past Mile 415 and immediately crosses Minim Creek, where it enters a long cut with shoal edges and two ranges. One range is just before the North Santee River and the other is on the river. Shoals and strong currents are prevalent, so take extra care. There is also a lot of debris in the water. In April 2011, there were several areas of 7.5-foot depths (mean low water) observed in the ICW between green daybeacon "5" and flashing red "12" between Minim Creek and the North Santee River. The charted mudbank and shoal just north of flashing red "12" has been observed to be bare at low tide and very close to the channel. It is very important to follow charted Range "A" to avoid this shallow area.

END SPECIAL CAUTION AREA.

Anchorage: Although it has a good deal of tidal current, Minim Creek is the best anchorage for many miles to come. Either side has good holding, but the west side offers the most protection with 8- to 13-foot depths. A few miles south, the west branches of the North and South Santee rivers may also present options for overnight anchoring in calm conditions. The anchorage on the west side of the South Santee River at Mile 420 has 10- to 12-foot depths, a sand and mud bottom and good holding. Crab pots usually line both sides of the river. From the South Santee River, it is 10 miles to the next good stopping place at McClellanville. Several channels lead off the ICW just past Mile 425, but depths are suspect for anchoring.

McClellanville—Mile 430

NAVIGATION: Use Chart 11518. There are shallow stretches of water on the ICW from Mile 429.5 to just past Mile 435.6. Details of this shoaling are in the "ICW to Andersonville" section below. Leading off the mainland side at flashing green "35," Jeremy Creek takes you to McClellanville, SC, a small fishing community dating from the 1700s. Jeremy Creek has some shallow depths at its entrance. Check for local knowledge before entering. The shallowest part is at the south side of the entrance. There is no room to anchor in Jeremy Creek—the channel is too narrow. Be aware that the ICW channel here has been renumbered. Green can "31" marks the shoal just north of green daybeacon "33." Green daybeacon "35A" lies on the ICW just southwest of the Jeremy Creek entrance. This marker and its two green counterparts are so close to each other that they need to be sorted out if entering either Jeremy Creek or Five Fathom Creek, which makes off the east side of the ICW. Many new private docks extend out to the channel both above and below McClellanville.

Dockage: Leland Marine Service in McClellanville provides dockage and fuel. With limited dock space, many boats emulate the shrimpers by rafting up, particularly during the annual shrimp festival each spring. The former shrimp boathouse and dock along the northern entrance to Jeremy Creek has given way to huge waterfront homes with private docks. There is also a boat ramp just beyond the first few houses. Fresh seafood is available at the retail store at the shrimp boat dock west of Leland Marine.

Five Fathom Creek, at McClellanville

Leaving the ICW via Five Fathom Creek, shrimp boats and U.S. Army Corps of Engineers boats use a surprisingly well-marked channel across from Jeremy Creek, day and night. Five Fathom Creek is deep with strong currents (like all creeks in this area), but boats do anchor here outside the main channel. There are uncharted side creeks, possibly of questionable depths for the tidal range. Even if you only want to explore the Cape Romain area, it is an easy run out to the ocean. For a dinghy side-trip behind the barrier islands, or for overnight anchorage, Five Fathom Creek and environs are virtually pristine. The USACE reports that dredging took place in Town Creek (between Jeremy Creek and Five Fathom Creek) in 2008.

McClellanville, SC

MCCLELLANVILLE		Largest Vessel Accommodated	VHF Channel Monitored	Transient Berths / Total Berths	Approach / Dockside Depth (reported)	Floating Docks	Gas / Diesel	Groceries, Ice, Marine Supplies, Snacks	Repairs: Hull, Engine, Propeller	Lift (tonnage), Crane, Rail	1=110V, 2=220V, B=Both, Max Amps	Laundry, Pool, Showers	Pump-Out Station	Nearby: Grocery Store, Motel, Restaurant
		Dockage						Supplies		Services				
1. Leland Oil Co. .5 N of 430	843-887-3641	75	16/68	4/8	10/6	F	GD	I			B/50	LS		GR

Corresponding chart(s) not to be used for navigation. Internet Access Wireless Internet Access

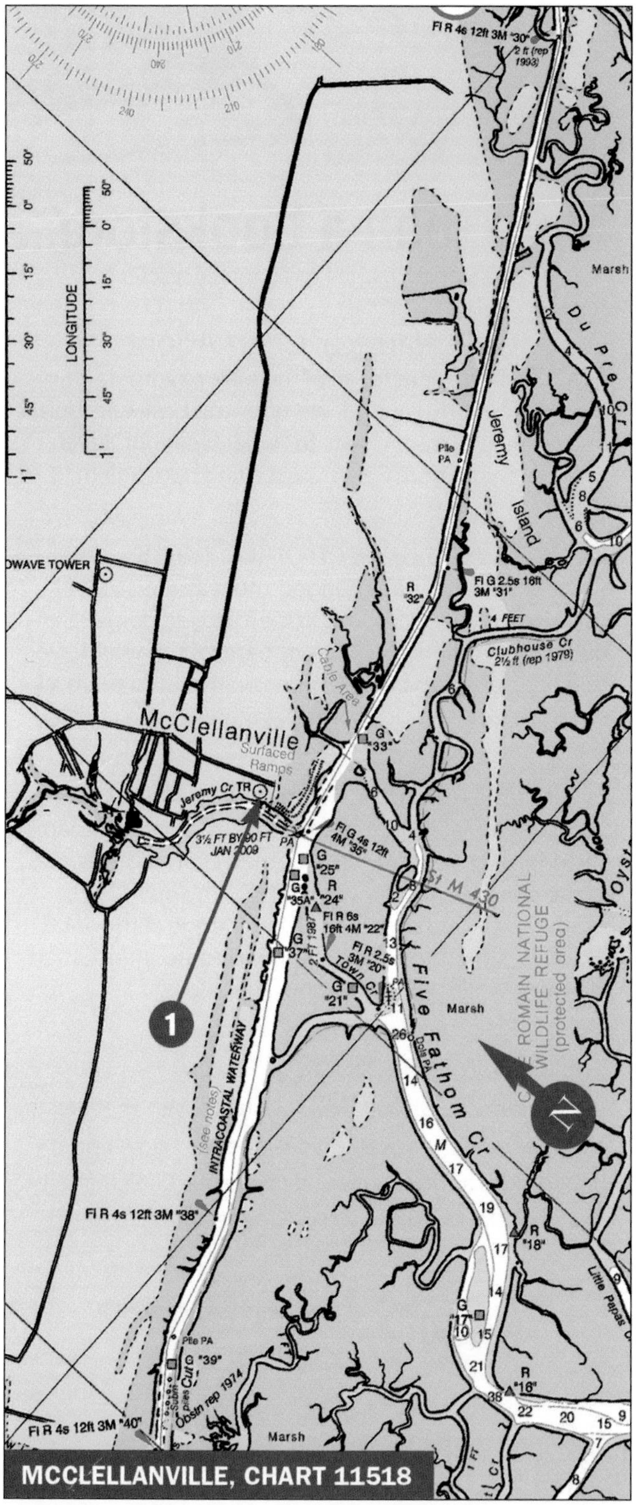

MCCLELLANVILLE, CHART 11518

Looking northwest over McClellanville, SC.
(Not to be used for navigation.) WATERWAY GUIDE PHOTOGRAPHY.

ICW to Andersonville

THE FOLLOWING AREA REQUIRES SPECIAL ATTENTION DUE TO SHOALING OR CHANGES TO THE CHANNEL

SOUTH OF MCCLELLANVILLE

There are shallow areas in the ICW south of McClellanville, and even with frequent dredging, the channel is quick to fill in. Two shallow areas were observed in the ICW channel in early 2011: There were 7-foot depths observed at Mile 431, and additionally, 5- to 6-foot depths were between reds "46" and "48" (Mile 435.7, north of Awendaw Creek). The shallowest part was off green daybeacon "47." These are mean low water depths; there is a 5- to 6-foot tide range.

END SPECIAL CAUTION AREA.

From Mile 436, the ICW follows a land cut for about 10 miles. On the mainland side is Francis Marion National Forest Recreation Area, which offers picnic areas, campsites and a boat ramp, but no facilities for transient boaters.

About Mile 444, the area of Andersonville, SC appears with a development on the mainland side. For the next mile or more, a wake is undesirable, so use caution. This stretch of the ICW is subject to shoaling at the edges, so it is prudent to stay to mid-channel. Use caution in the area of the ferry docks at Mile 445.5. There is a lot of activity around them.

Anchorage: You can anchor east of the ICW at Mile 435.6 in Awendaw Creek, opposite flashing red "48." Go around the bend heading east and anchor in the 13-foot spot shown on the chart. The bottom is irregular here. There is space for several boats. The ICW at the entrance has shoaled, as mentioned above.

South to Charleston

Charleston is another 35 miles or so south along a straight dredged cut with vast marshlands to the east. Watch for persistent shoaling, especially where natural creeks cross the ICW. Plan to stop and enjoy this historic and beautiful city, with its burgeoning yachting facilities. ■

Waterway Guide advertising sponsors play a vital role in bringing you the most trusted and well-respected cruising guide in the country. Without our advertising sponsors, we simply couldn't produce the top-notch publication now resting in your hands. Next time you stop in for a peaceful night's rest, let them know where you found them—Waterway Guide, The Cruising Authority.

Waterway Guide is always open to your observations from the helm. Email your comments on any navigation information in the Guide to: editor@waterwayguide.com.

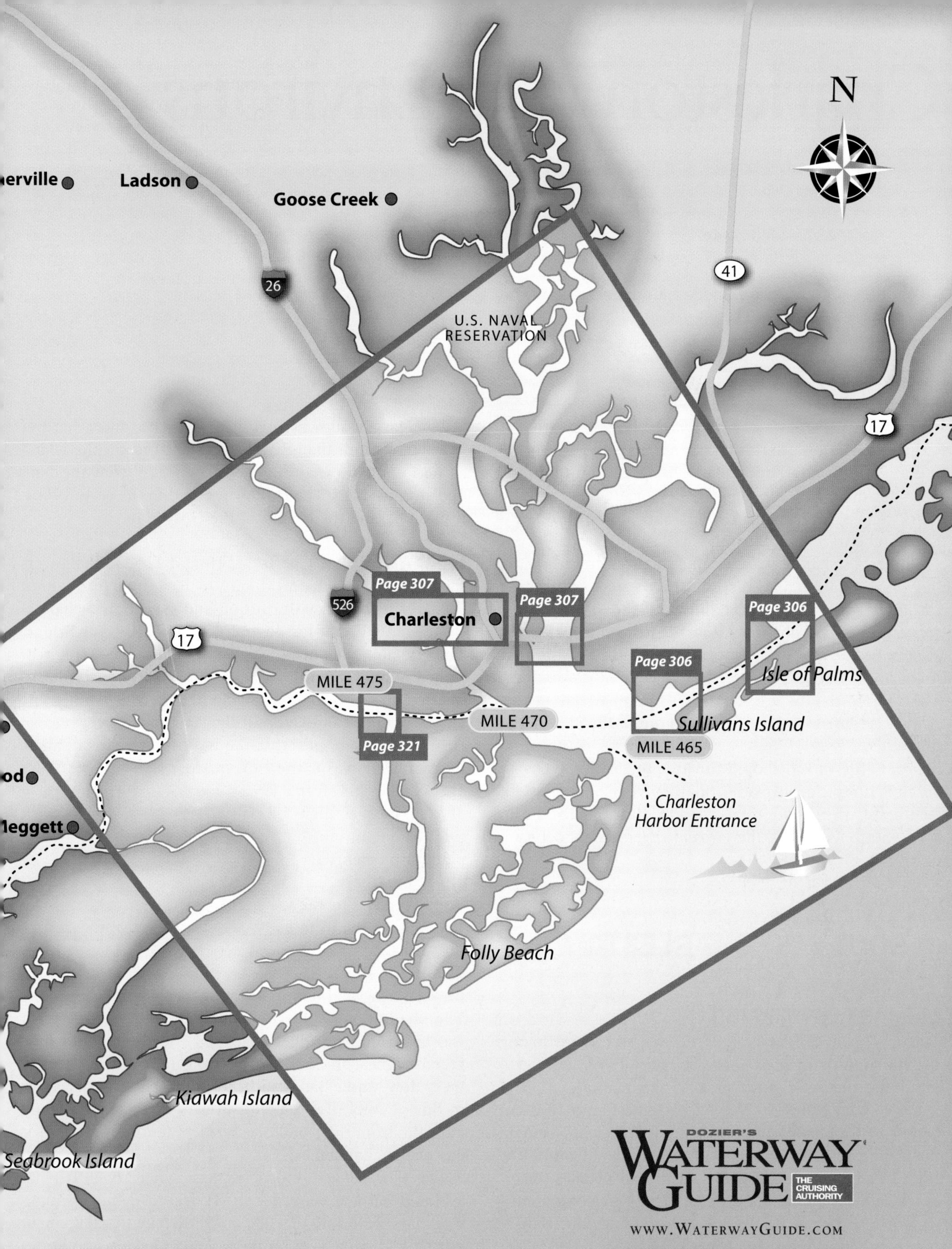

Skipper's Handbook

- Tide Tables 49
- Bridge Tables 58

Charleston and Environs

ICW Mile 437—Mile 474

VHF South Carolina Bridges: Channel 09

CHARTS 11518, 11521, 11522, 11523, 11524, 11527

The Intracoastal Waterway (ICW) north of Charleston offers wide scenic marsh views to the east and alternating marsh and forest on the west. Here, the dredged ICW channel cuts through low marshy islets, across several small rivers and finally through a long land cut before reaching Charleston Harbor.

Numerous marsh streams and small rivers cross the ICW channel from all directions in this area. All of these can affect the tidal current flow and the side currents crossing the ICW channel. Slow boats need to pay more attention than fast ones, but both need to be aware that shoal areas can and do creep out near these crossings. The charted depths are somewhat optimistic along this stretch, so be more precise in keeping to the channel at low tide.

From Mile 415 to about Mile 450, the National Ocean Service does not provide tidal current information. Generally, the flood tidal current runs north. From Mile 450 to Mile 460, the current reversals cancel each other out.

SOUTH TO CHARLESTON

Mile 437 to Mile 469

The ICW channel between Mile 437 and Mile 456 is among the straightest stretches along the entire ICW. Be sure to mind the markers. After passing the marinas at Wild Dunes (about Mile 456.7), you pass through a land cut between Isle of Palms on the ocean side and Goat Island on the mainland side. The two islands are quite different. The Isle of Palms is well developed with golf courses, resort hotels and restaurants. (Hurricane Hugo totally flattened the Isle of Palms in 1989. Almost everything you see here now was built from scratch since then.)

Goat Island was formerly inhabited by only a few hearty souls who commuted to their jobs by boat. Now, although the island remains relatively isolated, more and more weekend getaway cottages have appeared. From 1931 to the early '60s, Goat Island's only inhabitants were Henry "Goat Man" Holloway, his wife, Blanche, and a herd of goats. For more than 30 years, they lived on the island as hermits and, according to legend, ate what the land and sea provided. The Holloways died in the early 1960s, leaving behind the legend of the Goat Man.

NAVIGATION: Use Charts 11518 and 11523. Shallower-than-charted depths are likely to be found throughout this area. Proceed with caution and stay to mid-channel from Mile 447 until Mile 462 at the Ben Sawyer Bridge. There is an "Idle Speed, No-Wake" zone that starts near Mile 456 and green daybeacon "115" and ends at flashing red buoy "116" (Mile 456.5). At Mile 458.9, the Isle of Palms Connector Bridge (65-foot fixed vertical clearance) stretches across the ICW to the Isle of Palms. Based on stains on the tide boards, this bridge shows only 63 to 64 feet of clearance at high tide. Dredging took place in February 2011, but there had been shoaling in the 3.3-mile stretch from the Isle of Palms Connector Bridge to the Ben Sawyer Memorial Swing Bridge at Mile 462.2. The shallowest water observed by our cruising editor was between the bridges at around 7 feet at low tide near green daybeacon "117A." Shoaling to around 7 feet at mean low water had also been observed in other spots in this vicinity. Depths tend to vary in this stretch, and currents from the small ocean inlets tend to pull vessels out of the channel.

BEN SAWYER BRIDGE
Mile 462.2

WATERWAY GUIDE PHOTOGRAPHY

The Ben Sawyer Bridge (replaced in early 2010) has a closed vertical clearance of 31 feet with no openings weekdays, 7:00 a.m. to 9:00 a.m., 4:00 p.m. to 6:00 p.m. or during high winds—25 mph or higher against the bridge span. The swing bridge opens on the hour from 9:00 a.m. to 7:00 p.m. on weekends and holidays. Be sure to use the west side of the span.

Dockage: Along this stretch at Mile 456, near flashing red "116," is the 35-slip Isle of Palms Marina, owned by the city of Isle of Palms. This is the public part of the former Wild Dunes Yacht Harbor. (The interior section offers permanent condominium slips only and is still called Wild Dunes Yacht Harbor.) The fuel dock, the Morgan Creek Grill, a convenience store and transient docks are all part of the Isle of Palms Marina. The marina rents out space for the Dewees Island ferry, a parasail boat, jet skis, eco-tours and fishing charters. Resort amenities (pool, tennis, golf course, etc.) are reserved only for permanent slip holders at the private Wild Dunes Yacht Harbor.

Just through the Ben Sawyer Memorial Swing Bridge on the mainland side at Mile 462.5 is Toler's Cove Marina. It is best to call on VHF Channel 16 for slip availability, as most slips are now privately owned as part of a condominium development.

Anchorage: You will find several lovely spots to drop the hook along the way to Charleston Harbor. Price Creek, at Mile 448, is a local favorite for weekend and holiday outings. Feel your way in near flashing red "86," below the islet blocking the entrance (submerged at high tide), then proceed a short distance to a suitable spot. Proceeding seaward, this winding creek widens into Price Inlet.

Because of its proximity to Capers Island State Park, Whiteside Creek at Mile 451.1 is a favorite overnight anchorage for skippers who are ready for an ocean swim or a hike along the beach. Anchor west of the ICW and take the dinghy across the ICW three-quarters of a mile to the park dock at the western tip of Capers Island. The trail from the dock leads to the ocean beach after passing an impounded lake, which is home to numerous alligators. Whiteside Creek can get extremely congested during the spring and fall. It is too deep for anchoring at the bend, and shoals unpredictably upriver of the bend. Depths are generally shallower before the bend than shown on charts.

The mainland side of Dewees Creek (near Mile 455) also provides suitable anchorage. Dewees Creek is wide and deep, but the current flows swiftly, and the island residents are served by a commuter boat from the mainland, so bear these things in mind when dropping the hook. Dewees Island is privately owned, so cruising boaters should not venture above the high-water line while walking the beach. Hamlin Creek, at Mile 458 (crossed by the Isle of Palms Connector Bridge), offers protected anchorage off the south side of the ICW near green daybeacon "117." However, the area tends to shoal and is very narrow.

At Mile 461, Inlet Creek branches off on the mainland side of the ICW. In the past few years, there have been reports of boats hitting obstructions (steel I-beams) in this creek and of anchors snagging the same. It is no longer a recommended anchorage.

Looking southwest over the ICW and Isle of Palms.
(Not to be used for navigation.) WATERWAY GUIDE PHOTOGRAPHY.

CHARLESTON HARBOR

NAVIGATION: Use Charts 11521, 11523 and 11524. **Use the Charleston Tide Table.** During daylight, the entrance markers and the forest of harbor buoys leading to Charleston Harbor are easy to sort out. If yours is a first-time passage, however, it is best to run rough compass courses without shortcutting any of the buoys. Starting at flashing red "130," set a course for flashing red buoy "2" (Mile 465) to the South Channel Range. Follow your chart's ICW magenta line to the Ashley River and allow for the stiff current (about 3 knots at flood). If the current is flowing contrary to a wind of any strength, prepare yourself for a rough crossing.

When entering Charleston Harbor from the ICW—anytime after low-water slack tide to about two hours before high-water slack for Charleston Harbor—the current will give slower boats a healthy boost up to the various marinas on the Ashley River. When leaving Charleston to head north, slow boats should leave a couple of hours before low-water slack tide for an easier run.

Markers in Charleston Harbor's entrance channel and the channel leading into the Cooper River were renumbered

Isle of Palms, SC

ISLE OF PALMS		Largest Vessel Accommodated	VHF Channel Monitored	Transient Berths / Total Berths	Approach / Dockside Depth (reported)	Floating Docks	Gas / Diesel	Groceries, Ice, Marine Supplies, Snacks	Repairs: Hull, Engine, Propeller	Lift (tonnage), Crane, Rail	1=110V, 2=220V, B=Both, Max Amps	Laundry, Pool, Showers	Pump-Out Station	Nearby: Grocery Store, Motel, Restaurant
		Dockage					Supplies				Services			
1. Isle of Palms Marina 458 (Internet Access, Wireless Internet Access)	**843-886-0209**	**220**	**16/71**	**10/50**	**12/9**	**F**	**GD**	**GIMS**	**EP**		**B/50**	**LS**	**P**	**GMR**
2. Toler's Cove Marina 462.3	843-881-0325	70	16	/140	8/8	F	GD	IS			B/50	LS	P	GR

Corresponding chart(s) not to be used for navigation. Internet Access Wireless Internet Access

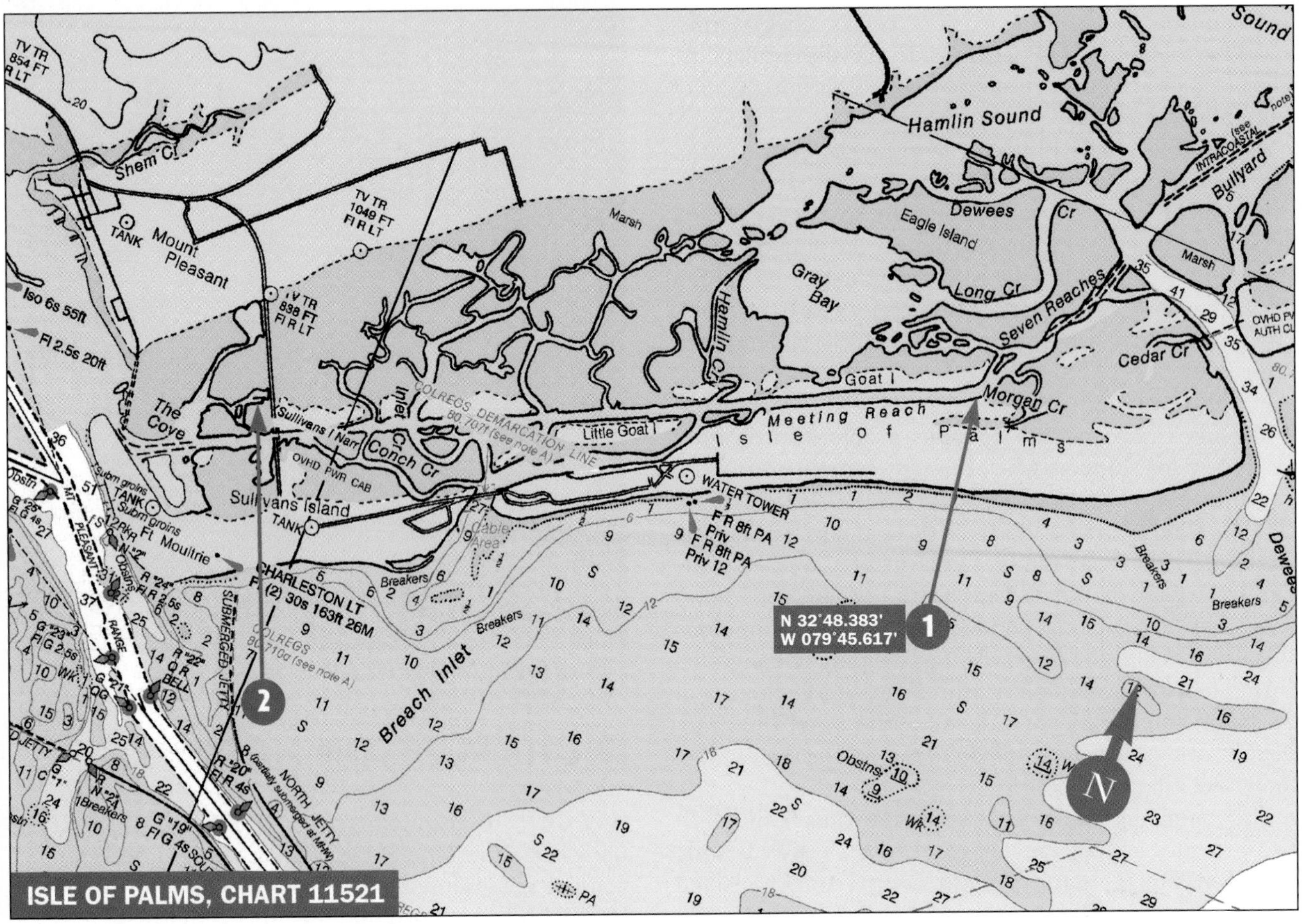

ISLE OF PALMS, CHART 11521

a few years ago, following extensive harbor dredging. The newer numbers may not appear on older charts. Refer to the most recent charts, dated January 2010 (for chart 11523) and October 2010 (for chart 11524), for these changes. *(See page 82 for more information about Charleston Harbor Entrance.)*

If Charleston Harbor is busy (which it normally is), you may want to leave the ICW's magenta line and take a shortcut to Charleston. Skirt the southern edge of the charted Middle Ground to pick up the ICW again at flashing red buoy "BP" south of Potts Shoal, using flashing yellow "L" as a mid-way point. This route crosses an anchorage for large ships, so exercise caution.

You can also turn northward from Sullivans Island and follow the well-marked channel to reach the facilities of Mount Pleasant or those on Town Creek off the Cooper River. Alternatively, boaters can head for the Charleston Harbor Marina at Patriots Point or the Charleston Maritime Center. Be alert for commercial and naval traffic when crossing the harbor and give these big vessels plenty of room.

Mount Pleasant, North of Charleston

NAVIGATION: Use Chart 11524. South along the ICW, just before Charleston Harbor, a well-marked channel arcs northward inside Crab Bank, leading to Mount Pleasant and Shem Creek. Depths in the Mount Pleasant Channel are at least 8 feet.

Dockage: Dockage is somewhat hard to come by, and while there are several spots to make fast, rafting to a commercial shrimper might be necessary. Mount Pleasant is a short car ride away from Charleston Harbor Marina.

Shem Creek Marina is a dry storage facility with no transient services. The original village of Mount Pleasant is a picture-perfect community of tree-lined streets with large, handsome and lovingly maintained homes. Here, following recent growth, you will find an assortment of popular waterfront restaurants and nightspots spread out over several miles.

Cooper River, at Charleston

On the east side of Charleston's peninsula, the Cooper River enters from the north to meet the harbor at Shutes Folly Island, where historic Castle Pinckney stands. A yacht club is nearby on the Charleston mainland. Above Drum Island, the Wando River feeds into the Cooper from the northeast.

On the east side of the Cooper River at Hog Island is Patriots Point, where the aircraft carrier *USS Yorktown*, the submarine *USS Clamagore*, and the U.S. Coast Guard Cutter *Ingham* and the destroyer *USS Laffey* are permanently berthed and open for tours. The *Yorktown* is the most heavily visited tourist attraction in South Carolina, with about 700,000 visitors each year. Charleston Harbor Resort and Marina at Patriots Point is a convenient place to dock to visit this attraction, with easy access to the adjoining the *Yorktown* and Patriots Point Maritime Museum.

The South Carolina Aquarium at Liberty Square (on the west side of the river in the city of Charleston), extending 200 feet over the Cooper River, highlights aquatic life from all five regions of South Carolina in a state-of-the-art facility. The aquarium displays more than 10,000 living organisms. For information, call 843-720-1990 or visit the website at www.scaquarium.org.

Meanwhile, Luden's, a chandlery, has moved a block from its old location to Alexander Street, around the corner from the public library.

The Ravenel suspension bridge over the Cooper River at Drum Island opened in 2007 and the old twin bridges were removed.

Dockage: The Charleston Harbor Resort and Marina at Patriots Point has 450 slips, with 30 available for transient vessels up to 200 feet. Turn in at quick flashing red buoy "34." You can get fuel at some of the slips and at the fuel dock near the entrance. The resort offers shopping, restaurants, an outdoor pool and spa, tennis and golf. They also provide shuttle transportation to a well-stocked gourmet Harris Teeter grocery store nearby in Mount Pleasant, and downtown Charleston is a short ride away. The view out to the inlet and ocean is incredible from the hurricane-tested dock and breakwater system. In this swift-current area, you will appreciate help from dockside personnel.

The Charleston Maritime Center offers some dockage adjacent to Liberty Square, within walking distance of downtown attractions as well as the Harris Teeter market. Also, a trolley stops in front of the marina. Numerous events and festivals are held here and on the adjacent grounds throughout the year. Water taxi service between the marinas and attractions is available. Check www.charlestonwatertaxi.com for details or call 843-330-2989.

Charleston City Boatyard is located up the Wando River in the river's shoreside namesake of Wando, SC. The full-service boatyard specializes in electrical, engine, fiberglass, woodwork and propeller repairs. A 75-ton Travelift and 300-ton railway are available for haul-outs. They also have deepwater floating docks and hot showers.

Ashley River, at Charleston—Mile 468

This river forms the left fork of the two rivers that flow along the peninsula of downtown Charleston. Note that the ICW leaves the Ashley River and enters Wappoo Creek across from, and just past, the Coast Guard Station in Charleston. The shoreline along the city side of the Ashley River, marked by the row of colonial mansions, is known as The Battery. The name dates back to Charleston's earliest days, when gun emplacements protected the city here.

Above the bascule bridges (18- and 14-foot closed vertical clearances, respectively), on the west side of the Ashley River at Old Town Creek, is Charles Towne Landing, site of the first permanent English settlement in South Carolina. This historic site recreates the colonists' daily lives and includes a full-scale replica of the trading vessel *Adventure*.

Additionally, several beautiful plantation homes and gardens—Middleton Place, Drayton Hall, Magnolia Plantation and the Audubon Swamp Gardens—are upriver on the Ashley. Both Charles Towne Landing and the plantations are best visited by car.

Two large grocery stores are a short taxi ride away from Charleston's Ashley River waterfront, and the shuttle bus to downtown Charleston stops nearby. The upscale Harris Teeter grocery store is located at 290 E. Bay St. (843-722-6821), and the marina courtesy vans make regular stops here.

NAVIGATION: Use Chart 11524. **Use the Charleston Tide Table.** When heading into the Ashley River, use the two ranges, the South Channel and the Ashley River Approach (both clearly charted), to assist you. If you wish to cruise up the Ashley River past the marinas and cannot clear the twin bascule bridges, with their respective 18- and 14-foot controlling vertical clearances, you will need to call ahead to have the bridges opened. (Note that a 24-hour notice is sometimes required for bridge openings here because this is a major traffic artery into downtown Charleston; check locally to see if it is required when you are coming through.) Also note that the high-rise fixed bridge crossing the Ashley River at the municipal marina has a 56-foot fixed vertical clearance. Beyond the turning basin, the Ashley River's minimal depths prohibit all but small shallow-draft boats from proceeding.

Dockage: The Coast Guard base is to starboard about a mile up the river beyond The Battery, followed by the Charleston City Marina, then The Harborage at Ashley Marina. A convenient walkway under the fixed bridge connects the two marinas.

The Charleston City Marina, at Mile 469.5, welcomes transients. It offers 3,000 feet of floating docks, with high-speed fueling stations, deep-draft slips with no height limitations and an impressive floating bathhouse with laundry. A marina courtesy van makes hourly trips to the downtown area and once a day makes a trip to West Marine. The Charleston City Marina is also home to the Marine Variety Store and Waterfront Restaurant.

The Harborage at Ashley Marina, with full services, offers a free shuttle into town. A 56-foot fixed vertical clearance bridge adjacent to The Harborage at Ashley Marina restricts large sailboats from entering, though the marina's outside docks can accommodate very large vessels (up to 150 feet). The docks have recently been renovated. Adjacent to The Harborage at Ashley Marina is a Courtyard by Marriott hotel.

Note that the current can be extremely swift, from 1 to 2 knots, with tides ranging 4 to 6 feet in this area. Check the currents and winds carefully before entering any of the marinas, and call for assistance if needed. Space during the traveling seasons can be at a premium, so reservations are recommended.

Looking east over the Wando River. (Not to be used for navigation.) Photo courtesy of Mike Kucera.

The Bristol Marina, adjacent to the Citadel, is full of yearly slip holders. There is a 14-foot height restriction for this marina. The city of Charleston plans to connect Bristol Marina to The Harborage at Ashley Marina and the Charleston City Marina with a "Riverwalk," which will eventually go all the way around Charleston's waterfront.

Anchorage: One popular anchorage is across from the Charleston City Marina. Boats swing differently in the current here, so pay careful attention to how the boats around you are swinging (some on a single anchor, some on two—some on rode, some on chain) when you set the hook. The Charleston City Marina no longer has moorings for rent.

Holding is good (in 15 to 20 feet) despite the current. However, this anchorage fills quickly, and a number of private permanent moorings have been established. Anchored vessels may find dinghy dockage at the Charleston City Marina for a fee, at the nearby ramp or possibly at the Charleston Yacht Club. The dinghy dockage fee at the Charleston City Marina covers dockage only, not van service or use of marina facilities.

In addition, cruisers frequently anchor just north of the entrance to Ripley Light Marina and in the small area adjacent to the Coast Guard Station, between it and the Charleston City Marina.

The most protected overnight anchorage in the Charleston area, however, is about a mile farther south, just beyond the Wappoo Creek Bascule Bridge (33-foot closed vertical clearance, very restricted schedule), behind the little island at Mile 471. This anchorage is narrow, not very large (with space for only a few small to mid-size boats) and subject to strong current but is a quiet, secluded spot for those who get there early. Use two anchors for the current and for limited space. It is in a residential area and there are docks on the south side. Although it is a long dinghy ride to downtown, southbound boats staying here overnight do not need to be concerned with the early morning Wappoo Creek Bascule Bridge restrictions.

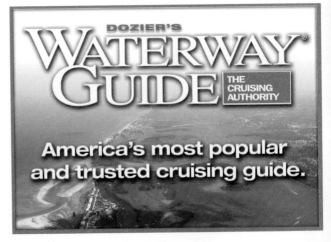

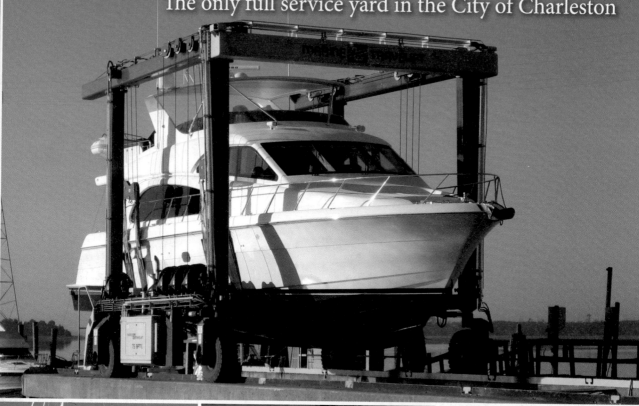

Charleston, SC

CHARLESTON		Largest Vessel Accommodated	VHF Channel Monitored	Transient Berths / Total Berths	Approach / Dockside Depth (reported)	Floating Docks	Gas / Diesel	Groceries, Ice, Marine Supplies, Snacks	Repairs: Hull, Engine, Propeller	Lift (tonnage), Crane, Rail	1=110V, 2=220V, B=Both, Max Amps	Laundry, Pool, Showers	Pump-Out Station	Nearby: Grocery Store, Motel, Restaurant
		Dockage					Supplies		Services					
1. RiversEdge Marina (Internet Access) (Wireless Internet Access)	843-554-8901	45	16	20/60	5/5	F	G	IMS		L	B/50	S	P	GMR
2. Charleston City Boatyard	**843-884-3000**	**125**	**16**		**15/10**	**F**		**M**	**HEP**	**L60,C,R**	**B/50**	**S**		**R**
3. Pierside Boatworks	843-554-7775	90			10/10	F			HEP	L70,C	B/100			
4. Dolphin Cove Marina	843-744-2562	45	16	10/100	32/32	F	G	IS	HEP	L25	1/30	LS	P	GMR
5. Cooper River Marina (Internet Access) (Wireless Internet Access)	843-554-0790	125	16/11	35/200	25/15	F		GIMS	HEP	L,C,R	B/50	LS	P	G
6. Ripley Light Marina 469.5	843-766-2100	65	16		5/6		GD				1/30		P	
7. Harborage at Ashley Marina 469.5 (Internet Access) (Wireless Internet Access)	**843-722-1996**	**150**	**16**	**50/254**	**15/22**	**F**	**GD**	**GIMS**	**EP**		**B/200+**	**LS**	**P**	**GMR**
8. Charleston Yacht Club 469.5	843-722-4968	PRIVATE CLUB			/8						1/30			
9. Charleston City Marina 469.5 (Internet Access) (Wireless Internet Access)	**843-723-5098**	**300**	**16/68**	**125/415**	**25/25**	**F**		**GIMS**	**HEP**		**B/100**	**LS**	**P**	**GMR**
10. Charleston Maritime Center 0.5 N of 467 (Internet Access)	843-853-3625	120	16	24/30	30/20	F	GD	I			B/100	LS	P	GMR
11. Carolina Yacht Club 1 N of 467	843-722-0209	100			12/7	F				L5	B/100			GMR
12. Charleston Harbor Resort & Marina 2 NW of 465 (Internet Access) (Wireless Internet Access)	**843-284-7062**	**200**	**16**	**30/428**	**10/10**	**F**	**GD**	**IMS**			**B/100**	**LPS**	**P**	**G**

Corresponding chart(s) not to be used for navigation. (Internet Access icon) Internet Access (WiFi icon) Wireless Internet Access

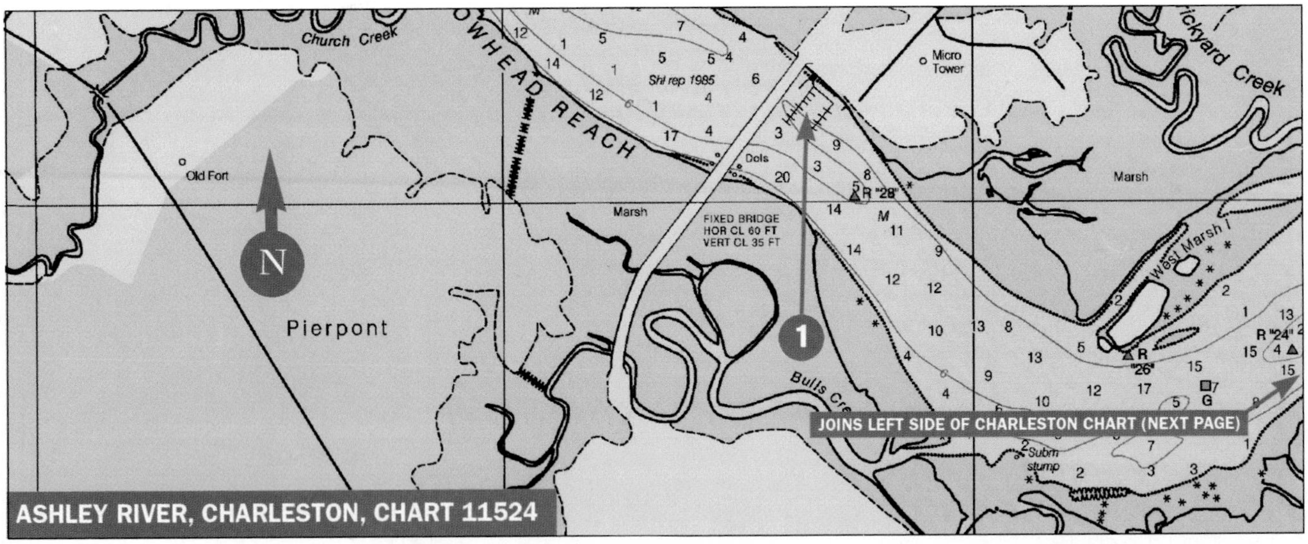

ASHLEY RIVER, CHARLESTON, CHART 11524

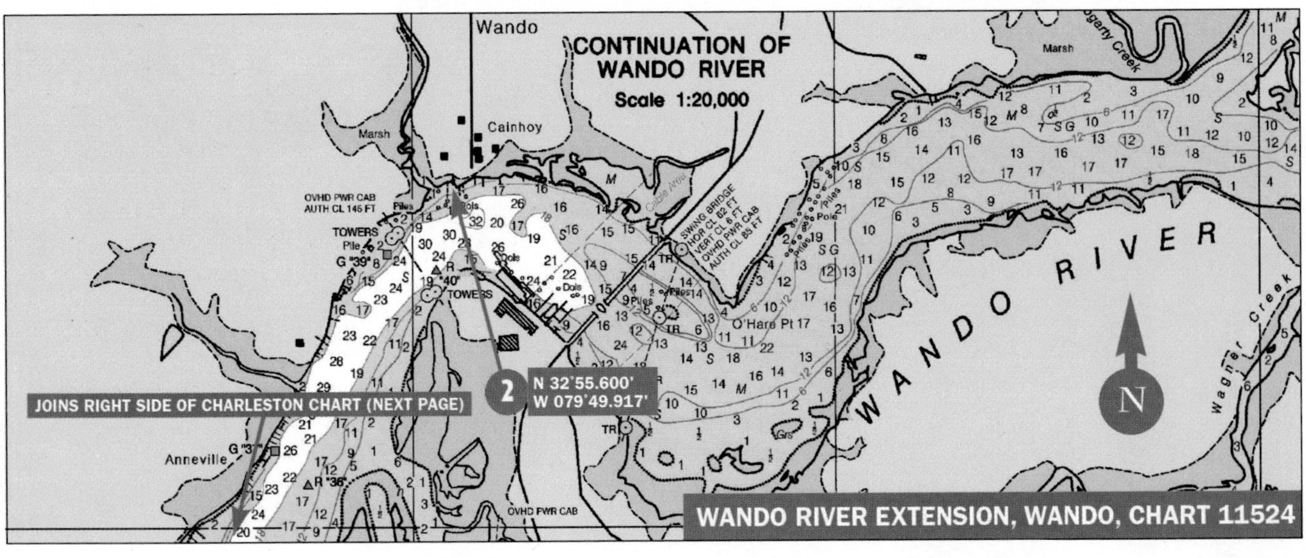

WANDO RIVER EXTENSION, WANDO, CHART 11524

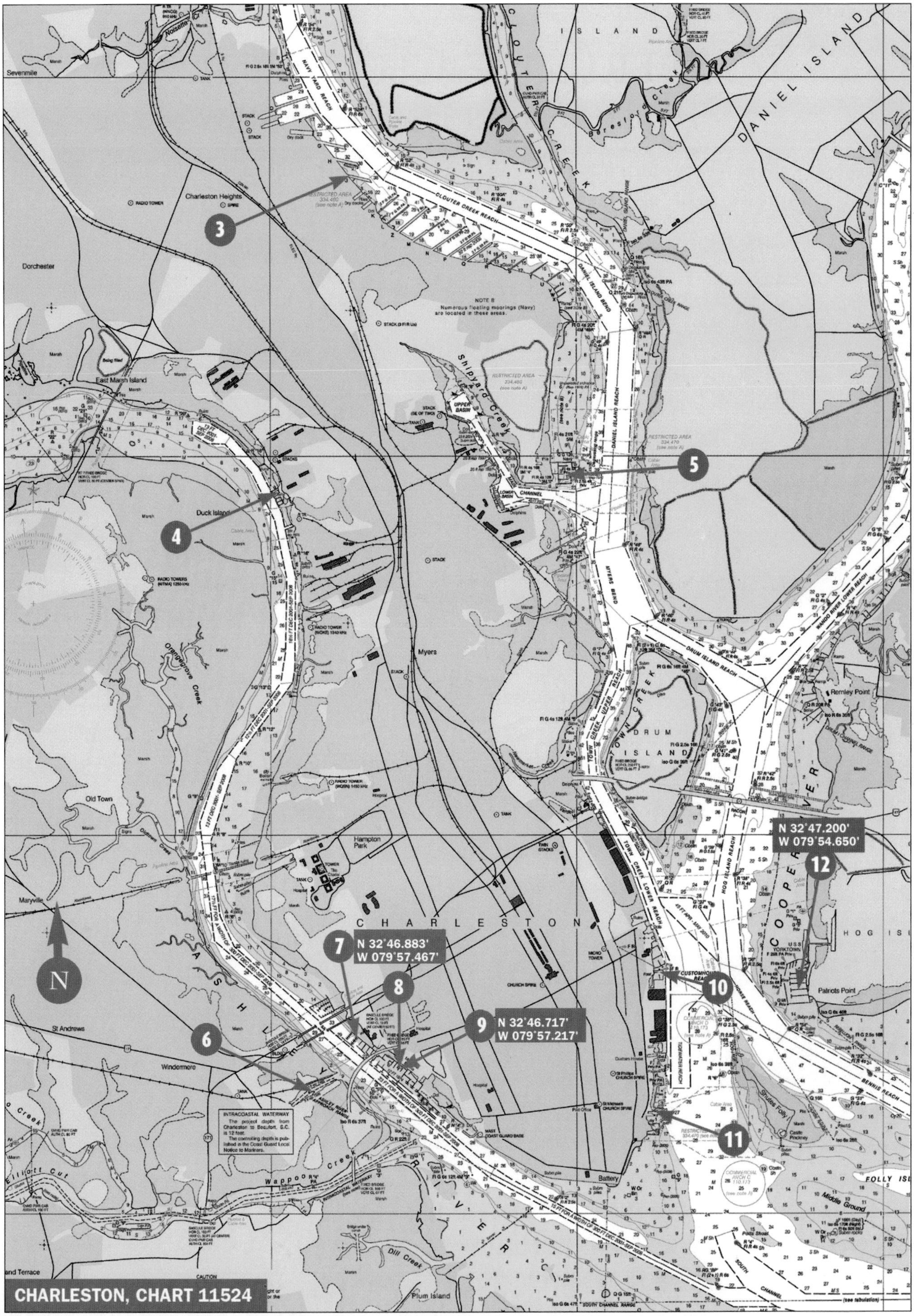
CHARLESTON, CHART 11524
N 32°46.883'
W 079°57.467'
N 32°46.717'
W 079°57.217'
N 32°47.200'
W 079°54.650'
3
4
5
6
7
8
9
10
11
12
N
CHARLESTON
DANIEL ISLAND
DRUM ISLAND
COOPER RIVER
ASHLEY RIVER
CLOUTER CREEK
Charleston Heights
Dorchester
Sevenmile
East Marsh Island
Duck Island
Myers
Old Town
Hampton Park
Maryville
St Andrews
Windermere
Wappoo Creek
Elliott Cut
Dill Creek
Plum Island
Remley Point
Patriots Point
Battery
Shipyard Creek
NOTE B
Numerous floating moorings (Navy) are located in these areas.
INTRACOASTAL WATERWAY
The project depth from Charleston to Beaufort, S.C. is 12 feet.
The controlling depth is published in the Coast Guard Local Notice to Mariners.

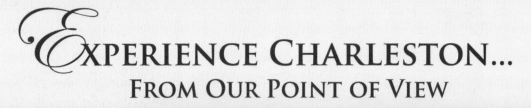

Looking south over Charleston Harbor and the Ashley River. (Not to be used for navigation.) Photo Courtesy of Mike Kucera.

GOIN' ASHORE: **CHARLESTON, SC**

Charleston is a perennial favorite destination in magazines such as *Southern Living, Condé Nast Traveler* and *Travel + Leisure*. Given the attention, residents may be forgiven if they describe Charleston as the place "where the Ashley and Cooper rivers meet to form the Atlantic Ocean."

For cruisers, the fourth largest shipping port on the East Coast offers superb protection in bad weather. Its numerous marinas and boatyards make it an excellent stopover point to attend to you and your boat's needs. Have the boat serviced, replenish the larder and take a break from the galley with gourmet restaurants onshore. Tours of plantations, battlefield sites and monuments, concerts, art walks, museums, garden tours and a myriad of festivals provide welcome diversions.

History: Charleston's culture and love for the good life has its roots in the man for whom it is named, England's King Charles II. A Charleston historian has written that the king was, "one of the most hedonistic of English monarchs," and that the colonists came, "to recreate the luxurious, cosmopolitan, pleasure-filled world of Restoration England ... inhabited by a landed gentry."

The British founded Charleston in 1670 on what is now Charles Towne Landing, on the western bank of the Ashley River. The colonists aboard the English ship *Carolina* originally planned to settle at Port Royal, but the chief of the Kiawah Indians convinced them to move farther north. Within 10 years, they had relocated to what locals refer to as "the Peninsula," or the site of current downtown Charleston. Not two years later, there were nearly 100 houses built, perhaps foretelling the ongoing real estate boom.

The culture is a mélange of influences. The English ideas soon blended with those of the French Huguenots fleeing religious persecution. Many came by way of Barbados and added a Caribbean flair to the city's lifestyle. The Spanish were here, and slaves certainly had a huge impact on the population from food to the arts and language. Gullah, a patois of all the languages, is still spoken on the sea islands today.

Culture and cultural references: Dock Street Theatre is an experience, if only to see its stunning interior. Reopened in 1937, the theater is the first building in the United States designed specifically for theatrical performances. The Theatre reopened in March of 2010 after undergoing a 3-year, 19 million dollar renovation. It has been improved in every way, from sound and seats to climate control. The Charleston Symphony Orchestra and the Charleston Ballet perform frequently at the Gaillard Auditorium, and the Charleston Coliseum and Performing Arts Theater book top performers and Broadway acts. When scenes from "The Patriot," starring Mel Gibson, were filmed in Charleston, the streets were covered with dirt for authenticity.

Attractions: Start your visit downtown with a trip to the Charleston Visitors Center at Meeting and John streets. A short film will acquaint you with the history and layout of the city, and brochures are available for the many adventures available in the Charleston area. The Charleston Museum is across the street. The changing exhibits include a replica of the CSA submarine *Hunley*, as well as tours of the *Hunley* restoration project, which is currently housed at a former Navy base in North Charleston. Walking and carriage tours of the historic area can be booked, just beware of what the guides tell you. Many have extraordinary imaginations when it comes to history. Do take one of the ghost tours. Even if it does not make your hair stand on end, you will have a new insight into the city's past.

A boat tour along The Battery on the Cooper River gives visitors a unique view of the antebellum mansions built by merchants for easy access to arriving ships. Return to walk the area on the cobblestone streets built from the rocks used as ship's ballast. Up the river, cruise underneath a magnificent engineering marvel, the impressive Ravenel Bridge, North America's longest cable-stayed bridge, which connects Mt. Pleasant and downtown. Across the Cooper, Patriots Point and the *USS Yorktown* house a wealth of naval history. Head out to Fort Sumter, which Citadel (the Military College of South Carolina) cadets shelled to begin the Civil War, at least in local lore. (The U.S. Park Service rangers who maintain the site have a slightly different interpretation).

Don't miss the architecture of the unique Charleston single houses. Built one room wide, they are entered through a door onto a piazza, giving the occupants privacy in town. The most "desirable" area is South of Broad, on the tip of the Peninsula.

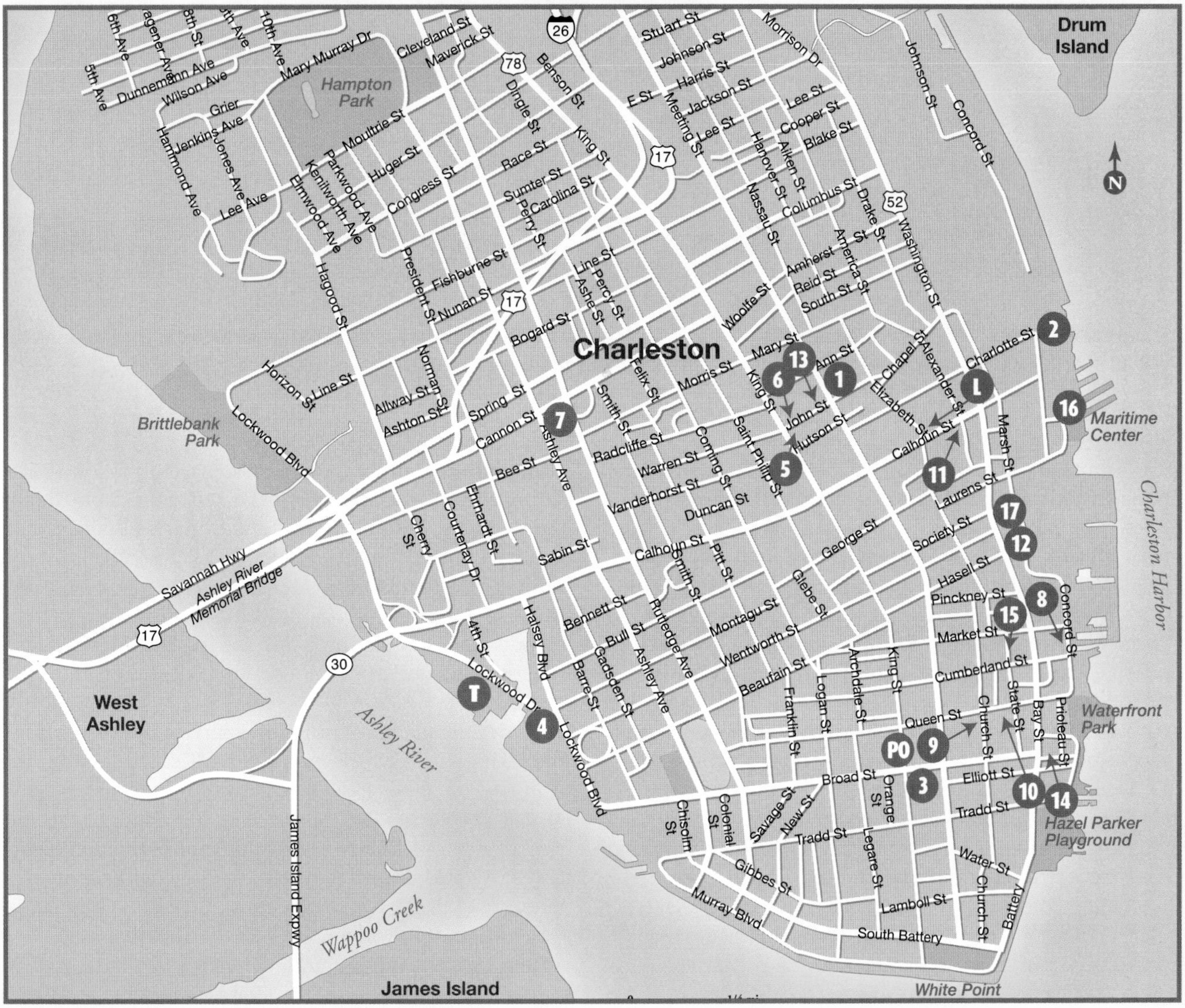

Reference the marina listing tables to see all the marinas in the area.

ATTRACTIONS
1 Charleston Museum
2 South Carolina Aquarium

DINING
3 Gaulart et Maliclet
4 The Variety Store
5 30 Rue de Jean
6 La Fourchette
7 Hominy Grill
8 Fleet Landing

ENTERTAINMENT
9 Dock Street Theatre

GROCERIES/CARRYOUT
10 Farmer's Market
11 Kennedy's Market
12 Harris Teeter Groceries

INFORMATION
13 Charleston Visitors Center

POINTS OF INTEREST
14 Old Exchange Building
15 The Old Market

SHOPPING/DINING
16 The New Liberty Square
17 East Bay True Value Hardware

L LIBRARY

PO POST OFFICE

T TROLLEY STOP

Looking west from Charleston Harbor up the Cooper River towards Patriots Point.
(Not to be used for navigation.) Photo Courtesy of Charleston Harbor Resort & Marina.

Its residents are fondly known as "SOBs." Frequent tours by the Historic Charleston Foundation and the Preservation Society offer a peek inside the old homes and their glorious gardens. Historic Charleston Foundation's annual Festival of Homes and Gardens runs from mid-March to mid-April. Tickets are limited and normally sell out by the end of January.

Be sure to visit the Old Exchange Building that used to house a prison; the Old Market that really was a market for food items, not slaves (the Slave Market is a few blocks away) and may now be the best spot to see the sweet grass basket weavers at work; and the new Liberty Square with the South Carolina Aquarium, shops and restaurants. A tour boat runs from here to Fort Sumter; another, run by Spirit Line Cruises, leaves from Patriots Point. A water taxi travels between the docks here and the Charleston Harbor Resort and Marina, next to Patriots Point.

The Charleston River Dogs, a Class A minor league baseball team affiliated with the New York Yankees, play at Joe Riley Park on the banks of the Ashley River.

Special Events: The Charleston River Food and Wine Festival, in early March, showcases the talents of local and nationally-known chefs with lectures, classes and tastings. The Spoleto Festival, held in May, is world renowned for its symphonies, operas, plays, music festivals and the many gala events that accompany it. What was the Charleston Maritime Heritage Festival, now called Charleston HarborFest, is in mid-June, coinciding with the start of the Charleston to Bermuda Race in odd-numbered years.

Shopping: Provisioning is easy. The City Marina, The Harborage at Ashley in Charleston and Charleston Harbor Marina in Mt. Pleasant have shuttles that will take you to the Harris Teeter grocery store on East Bay Street, or you can pop into the Farmers' Market at Marion Square, every Saturday from mid-March until Christmas. Kennedy's Market on Calhoun Street probably has the best French bread in the area, as well as delicious desserts and prepared heat-and-eat casseroles.

Besides the marina shuttles, bus service is also available. The CARTA trolleys leave on a regular schedule from the Visitors Center and circle most of the downtown area, arriving near the Variety Store. To visit Mt. Pleasant and the outlying plantations (Boone Hall, Middleton Plantation, Drayton Hall), you will need to rent a car. Golf courses abound in the area, but the closest to downtown is Patriots Point Links, a fairly flat course with great views of the harbor.

Restaurants: Restaurants in every price range and to suit every taste abound in Charleston. Locals find it difficult to name a favorite. For a quick, good breakfast, lunch or dinner, try Gaulart et Maliclet, locally known as "Fast & French" (98 Broad St., 843-577-9797). You may have to wait for a seat, but tables are communal. Homemade soups and desserts and the daily lunch special accompanied by a glass of wine, are great choices.

Another long-standing choice is The Variety Store (17 Lockwood Drive., 843-723-6325) at The City Marina. The Altine family has been feeding visiting sailors and local business folk for years, with good, down-home cooking and

The Battery. Photo courtesy of Perry Baker/SCPRT.

a view of the harbor and marina. Pick the homemade chips to go with sandwiches and burgers.

For good French food, it is hard to beat 39 Rue de Jean (39 John St, 843-722-8881), a true French bistro near the Visitors Center. The daily specials instantly transport you to a Parisian café. (There is sidewalk dining.) Mussels are served seven different ways, and the steak and fish are *très delicieux!* Another good choice is La Fourchette, around the corner on King Street. The owners are from Bretagne, and the menu choices are authentic.

For some good low country cooking, try Hominy Grill (207 Rutledge Ave., 843-937-0930), a cruisers favorite that can't be beat. Sit in the garden if the weather is good. Innovative versions of old recipes please, whether it is chicken livers or shrimp and grits. Fleet Landing (186 Concord St.), a unique spot with terrace dining over the Cooper River, has great grouper dishes and a fantastic view of the Ravenel Bridge.

ADDITIONAL RESOURCES

- **THE CHARLESTON INTERNATIONAL AIRPORT:** 5500 International Blvd., Charleston, SC 29418 843-767-1100, **www.chs-airport.com**
- **CHARLESTON CONVENTION AND VISITORS BUREAU:** 800-774-0006, **www.charlestoncvb.com**
- **HISTORIC CHARLESTON FOUNDATION:** 843-723-1623 **www.historiccharleston.org**
- **SOUTH CAROLINA AQUARIUM:** 843-720-1990 **www.scaquarium.org**
- **SOUTH CAROLINA MARITIME FOUNDATION:** 843-722-1030, **www.scmaritime.org**

NEARBY GOLF COURSES
Patriots Point Links, One Patriots Point Road, Mt. Pleasant, SC 29464, 843-881-0042
www.patriotspointlinks.com

NEARBY MEDICAL FACILITIES
Roper Hospital, 316 Calhoun St., Charleston, SC 29401, 843-724-2000

MUSC Medical Center, 171 Ashley Ave., Charleston, SC 29403, 843-792-2300

WAPPOO CREEK TO STONO RIVER

Mile 469.5 to Mile 473.5

From Mile 472 at Elliott Cut to Mile 535 at Beaufort, SC—a beautiful stopping place and the next community of any size—the South Carolina low country scenery is lush and beautiful with water birds and marsh grass creating picture-postcard sights everywhere you look.

NAVIGATION: Use Charts 11518. Continuing down the ICW on the Ashley River from Charleston, you enter Wappoo Creek (which then leads into narrow Elliott Cut) opposite the Charleston City Marina. The passage through Wappoo Creek and Elliott Cut used to be shallow between

Looking east over Wappoo Creek and Elliott Cut. (Not to be used for navigation.) WATERWAY GUIDE PHOTOGRAPHY.

green daybeacon "9" and the charted overhead power cables at the northern entrance to Elliott Cut. However, a USACE survey, completed in February 2009, only shows shoaling to a depth of 7.7 feet at mean lower low water on the red side of the channel, adjacent to green daybeacon "9." The rest of the stretch has 12- to 20-foot depths.

Immediately inside Wappoo Creek's northern entrance, at Mile 469.9, is the James Island Expressway Bridge (official fixed vertical clearance of 67 feet, but there are no tide boards), followed by the Wappoo Creek Bascule Bridge (33-foot closed vertical clearance) at Mile 470.8. This bridge has restricted opening schedules as follows:

■ From April 1 to November 30, Monday through Friday (except federal holidays), from 9:00 a.m. to 4:00 p.m., and on weekends and federal holidays from 9:00 a.m. to 7:00 p.m., the bridge opens on the hour and half-hour.

■ From June 1 to September 30 and from December 1 to March 30, Monday through Friday (except federal holidays), there are no openings from 6:30 a.m. to 9:00 a.m, and from 4:00 p.m. to 6:30 p.m.

■ From April 1 to May 31 and October 1 to November 30, Monday through Friday (except federal holidays), there are no openings from 6:00 a.m. to 9:00 a.m., and 4:00 p.m. to 6:30 p.m.

Just before the bascule bridge on Wappoo Creek, if you are southbound on the ICW (your heading will be west at this point), a boat ramp is on the north (starboard) side. This entire section, through Elliott Cut, is a patrolled No-Wake Zone. Go as slowly as you can, even though it may be difficult when the strong current is dead against you. When the current is with you, you must be able to maintain steerage. Slow boats might do better by waiting until the current moderates. The flood tide runs west in the cut toward the Stono River; ebb tides run east toward Charleston Harbor.

WATERWAY GUIDE PHOTOGRAPHY

For slower, southbound boats, the best time to leave Charleston for Beaufort is toward the end of a flood tide. You can save between two and three hours on this 65-mile-long stretch. Moreover, a passage through Elliott Cut's narrow channel against a 2- to 4-knot current can guarantee an all-too-memorable experience. Ebb tide begins at the Wappoo Creek entrance 45 minutes before it begins at Charleston Harbor. Leaving at other times, slower auxiliary-powered craft may prefer to make the trip to Beaufort in two days and take advantage of the many excellent anchorages en route.

Elliott Cut to Stono River

NAVIGATION: Use Chart 11518. From Elliott Cut, the ICW enters the Stono River just beyond Mile 472.

Stono River, SC

STONO RIVER		Largest Vessel Accommodated	VHF Channel Monitored	Transient Berths / Total Berths	Approach / Dockside Depth (reported)	Floating Docks	Gas / Diesel	Groceries, Ice, Marine Supplies, Snacks	Repairs: Hull, Engine, Propeller	Lift (tonnage), Crane, Rail	1=110V, 2=220V, B=Both, Max Amps	Laundry, Pool, Showers	Pump-Out Station	Nearby: Grocery Store, Motel, Restaurant
		Dockage						**Supplies**			**Services**			
1. ST. JOHNS YACHT HARBOR 1S OF 472.5 (WiFi)	843-557-1027	150	16/71	45/224	25/8	F	GD	GIMS			B/50	LPS	P	GR
2. ROSS MARINE 476	843-559-0379	150	16/79	20/40	12/12	F	D	IM	HEP	L75	B/50			

Corresponding chart(s) not to be used for navigation. Internet Access (WiFi) Wireless Internet Access

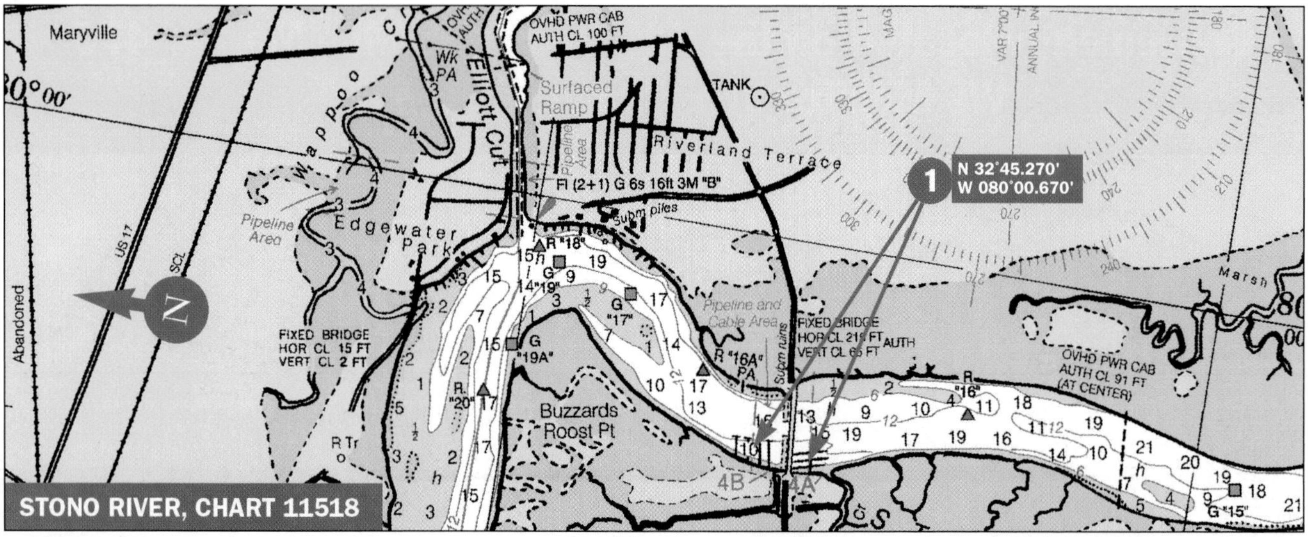

STONO RIVER, CHART 11518

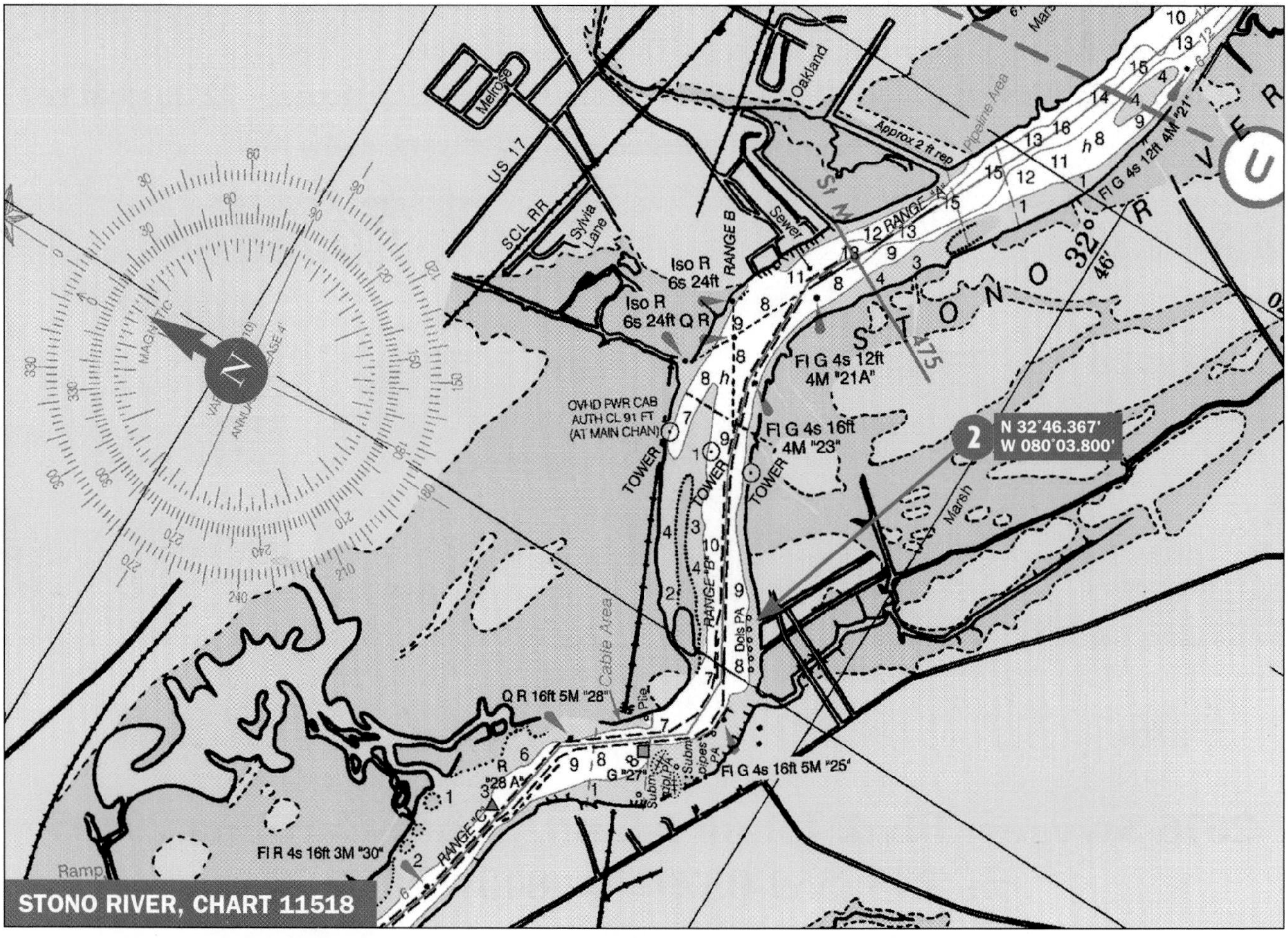

STONO RIVER, CHART 11518

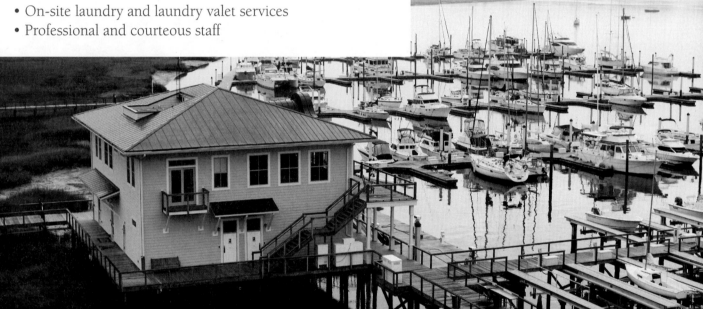

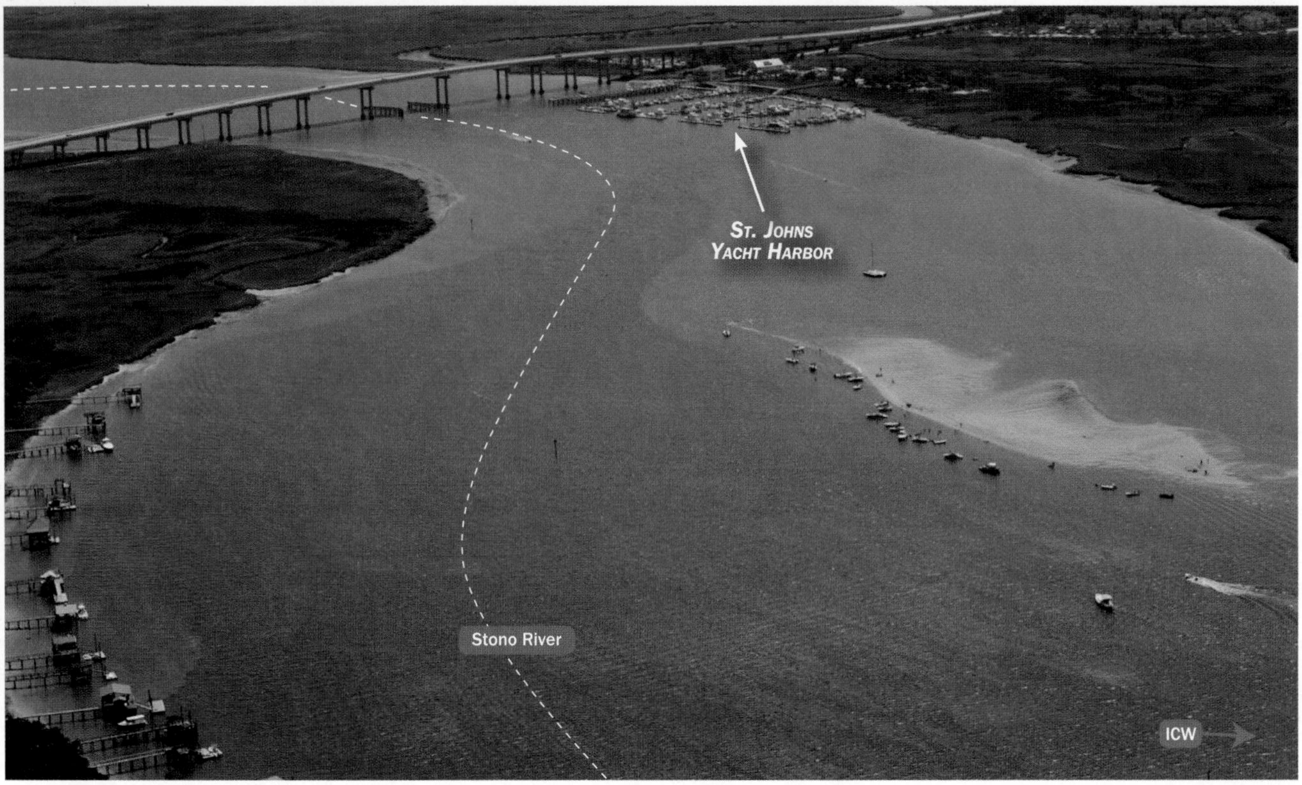

Looking south over the Stono River. (Not to be used for navigation.) Photo courtesy of Mike Kucera.

Shoaling has been reported at the confluence of Elliott Cut and the Stono River near red daybeacon "18." Note that red daybeacon "18" and green daybeacon "19" are not ICW markers but mark the Stono River channel leading in from its inlet to intersect the ICW at this point. The ICW channel up the Stono River begins with green daybeacon "19A."

In late 2010, several markers in the Stono were changed. There is now a new red "28A" and marker red "34" is missing. Red day-beacon "40" has been replaced with a red nun. All of these changes are present on the most current chart at publication in summer 2011, which is dated January 2010. *(See page 83 for more information about Stono River.)*

Dockage: As you turn slightly to starboard coming out of Elliott Cut to continue along the ICW, Ross Marine, a full-service yacht repair yard located about 3 miles ahead near flashing green "25" to port (Mile 476), is equipped to handle major repairs on any size boat with their 75-ton lift. Alternately, a short side trip to port from Elliott Cut, down the Stono River, brings you to the newly developed St. John's Yacht Harbor. They sell non-ethanol gas and diesel and have an on-site ship's and sundries store, in-slip pump-out services, and a pool. They also offer a shuttle service. Farther downstream, the Stono River leads to the Folly and Kiawah rivers, frequented by local recreational boaters. Folly and Kiawah islands are home to several ocean resorts with beaches, shopping, restaurants and several golf courses.

Anchorage: If you wish to anchor on this side of the cut to await favorable tides or bridge openings at the Wappoo Creek Bridge, try a spot several hundred yards southwest of flashing green (2+1) "B," marking the entrance to Elliott Cut from the Stono River, being mindful of the shoaling beyond green daybeacon "19" off Buzzards Roost Point. There is no longer much room to anchor northwest of the exit from Elliott Cut—docks fill the space.

The best anchorage in this immediate area is across the Stono from red daybeacon "16A" in the 10-foot charted area near St. Johns Yacht Harbor. The long shoal area keeps ICW wakes from bothering you, and it is pleasant and quiet at night.

To Low Country

Ahead on your southbound journey down the ICW lies the lush and lovely Low Country. The following chapters offer trips off the ICW via the North Edisto River or South Edisto River to Seabrook and Edisto islands, respectively. Different in character and amenities, each has something to offer. Back on the ICW, Beaufort, SC and Hilton Head, SC await. ■

Charleston to Florida

■ CHARLESTON TO THUNDERBOLT □ THUNDERBOLT TO FLORIDA ■ FLORIDA BORDER TO JACKSONVILLE

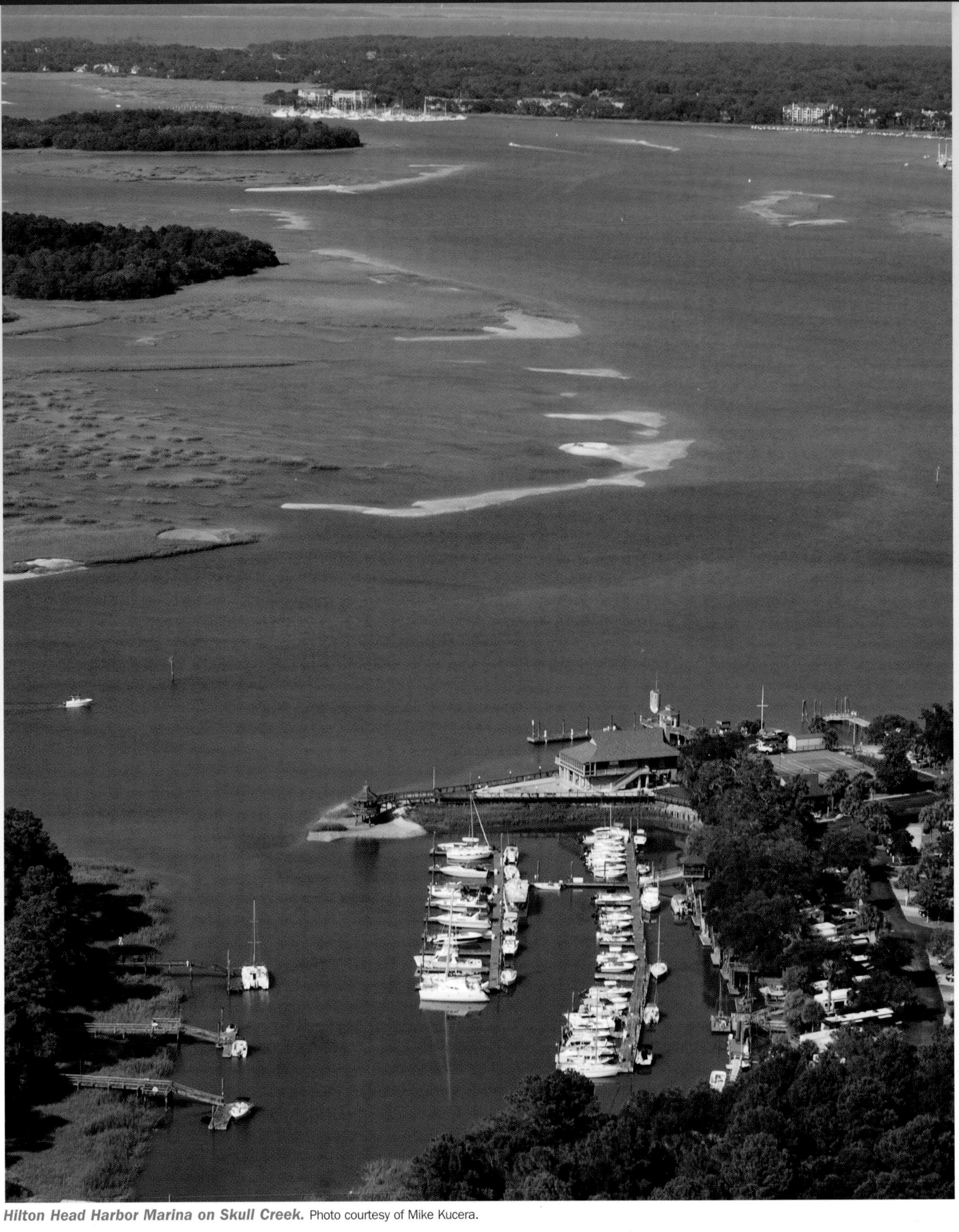

Hilton Head Harbor Marina on Skull Creek. Photo courtesy of Mike Kucera.

Charleston to Florida

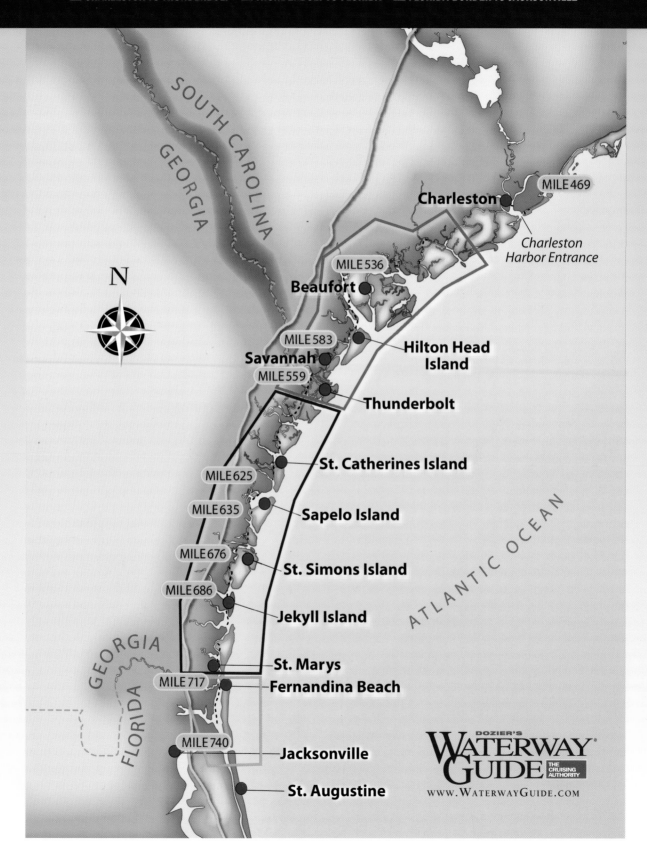

CHARLESTON TO THUNDERBOLT | THUNDERBOLT TO FLORIDA | FLORIDA BORDER TO JACKSONVILLE

Introduction

Charleston to Florida

Courtesy of Susan Land

Along the 244 miles of the Intracoastal Waterway (ICW) from Charleston, SC (Mile 469) to Florida's state line (just south of St. Marys, GA at Mile 714), the route departs from the canals and dredged cuts common in North Carolina. Instead, expect to wend your way across wide river mouths, through sounds and past coastal inlets.

The low, marshy grassland appears almost pristine in this area: You can cruise for 10 miles without seeing any signs of human habitation. The landscape's predominant feature is marshland, backed by woods or hummocks of trees. In some places, the marsh gives way to wooded banks, some with stately moss-covered oaks. You will also pass some big sand dunes and even catch occasional glimpses of the Atlantic Ocean.

At low tide, the vast salt marshes and exposed fringes of mud teem with bird life. You might see porpoises playing alongside your boat or cruising along with your bow wake. You also might catch glimpses of the majestic great blue herons that patrol the water's edge, hunting for fish.

Cruising Conditions

This portion of the ICW is made up of natural waterways, which are usually deep to the banks. This results in straightforward piloting. It is a good idea to keep in mind that the broader waters can make it easier to lose your way. Keep track of the markers and run approximate compass courses at a minimum. Shoals still exist here; make sure you follow this guide closely and heed the warnings of shallow water along the way.

QUICK FACT:

BOTTLENOSE DOLPHINS

Of all the wildlife you will encounter along the expanses of the ICW, the Atlantic bottlenose dolphin is one of the most common and exciting species to spot.

Bottlenose dolphins, toothed whales that belong to the order *Cetacea*, live and travel in fluid social groups called pods near the coast and inshore waters from northern Cape Hatteras, south to Florida and westward through the Gulf of Mexico. They can also be spotted off the New Jersey coast near the continental shelf.

Much like a shark, the bottlenose's streamlined body and tall dorsal fin can be seen jetting through the water. The dolphin's defining characteristics are its rounded head and, of course, its short, stubby beak (rostrum), which resembles a bottle. The bottlenose is light to slate gray on the upper part of its body and light gray to pink on its belly. Its tail fins are curved with a median notch, and its pectoral fins are medium length and pointed. The dolphin has 86 to 100 sharp, cone-shaped teeth in its upper and lower jaws. Adult bottlenose dolphins reach between 6 to 12 feet in length and can weigh 400 to 800 pounds.

Atlantic bottlenose dolphins hunt fish and squid, mostly at the water's surface but have been known to dig into the sand to find crustaceans. They sometimes hunt in pods,

A happy bottlenose dolphin posing with its head above water.
©IstockPhoto/cbpix.

assisting each other by encircling schools of fish and forcing them into a dense pack for easy feeding. Bottlenoses swim at speeds of 3 to 11 mph and can often be seen riding the bow or stern wake of boats. They have been known to jump as high as 16 feet out of the water and land on their backs or sides, a behavior called breaching.

While cruising, you may see the dolphins beach themselves, with a flurry of silver. This practice allows them to catch fish by driving them onto the shore. Whether on shore or in the water, do not approach bottlenoses; federal law prohibits feeding or attempting to feed marine mammals.

WATERWAY GUIDE PHOTOGRAPHY

Money was again allocated for South Carolina with almost 20 million designated for the dredging of Charleston Harbor and the Cooper River in FY2012. Georgia will receive $20 million in the FY2012 with several projects to be completed in the Savannah and Brunswick areas. The Economic Recovery stimulus package funded additional ICW dredging projects in an attempt to keep the ICW usable. South Carolina received an additional $4 million while Georgia received $5.9 million. Check our website, www.waterwayguide.com, regularly for the latest status and dredging updates.

When you encounter a working dredge, contact them via VHF (Channels 9 or 13) and wait for clearance before passing. In the meantime, shallow areas remain, and strong tidal currents throughout the region can change depths almost overnight, creating shoals in previously dredged spots.

With careful navigation and waiting for the tide in just a few areas, even deeper-draft boats can pass through this entire area of South Carolina's and Georgia's beautiful coastal waters with no problems. USACE Savannah District quarterly surveys of the shoal-prone areas can be found at www.sas.usace.army.mil/navrprts.htm.

Weather plays an important role as you cruise these waters. The ICW route is designed for maximum protection from the elements, but crossing large sounds can still call for caution. Larger sounds and the mouths of many rivers are exposed to weather, with tidal ranges of up to 9 feet throughout much of Georgia. When a stiff wind runs contrary to the strong currents, or a sudden thunderstorm kicks up, the going can get uncomfortably rough. You should consider tidal conditions (i.e., rising, falling or slack) and currents when running, docking or selecting an anchorage. For safety's sake, you should run navigational ranges whenever they are present.

Marinas and Anchorages

Marinas, docks and marine repair facilities are few and far between along this stretch, particularly when compared to the high concentrations of marinas on the Chesapeake Bay and in Florida waters. As a plus, marina owners along the ICW between Charleston and Florida are generally top-drawer and knowledgeable.

Remember that there is a 6- to 9-foot tidal range along this stretch. When approaching any marina, exercise caution, especially if your boat draws more than 4 feet, and dock into the current if at all possible. This portion of the ICW—not surprisingly—is prone to shoaling, with channels and basins often silting in to varying degrees. Dredging is a costly business, and environmental concerns have made dredging permits increasingly difficult to obtain for marina owners. Thus, a marina with 6-foot depths in January might have shoaled appreciably by June. Before you tie up, tell the attendant what your draft is so they can assign you an appropriate berth. WATERWAY GUIDE'S marina listings are updated every year with approach and dockside depths for each marina; use these as a guide and, if in doubt, call ahead.

Your other choice, of course, is to anchor out. Anchorages are plentiful along the ICW for those who like to take a break from the marina lifestyle. Be mindful of the silted conditions you will often encounter when dropping the hook along this stretch. ■

Bridges / Distances

(Approximate Statute Miles from Mile Zero, Norfolk)

LOCATION	MILES	CLEARANCE
Ben Sawyer Memorial Swing Bridge	**462.2**	**31'**
Wappoo Creek Entrance, Range	469.4	
James Island Expressway Bridge	469.9	67'
Wappoo Creek Bridge	**470.8**	**33'**
John F. Limehouse Highway Bridge	479.3	65'
McKinley Washington Jr. Bridge (SR 174)	501.3	65'
Coosaw River Marker "184" Fl R 4sec	520.2	
Ladies Island Swing Bridge (U.S. 21)	**536.0**	**30'**
Highway Bridge (SR 802)	539.7	65'
Twin Highway Bridges (U.S. 278)	557.6	65'
~~Causton Bluff Bridge~~	**579.9**	**21'**
State of Georgia Memorial Bridge (U.S. 80)	582.8	65'
Isle of Hope Anchorage Buoys	589.5	
Skidaway Bridge	**592.9**	**22'**
Kilkenny Creek "106" Fl R	613.4	
Front River "151" Fl G 4sec	639.0	
Highway Bridge	674.5	65'
Jekyll Island Bridge (SR 50)	684.2	65'

*Clearance is vertical, closed, in feet. *Not radio equipped. Bridges in bold type have restricted openings.*

SAN VARNEDOE

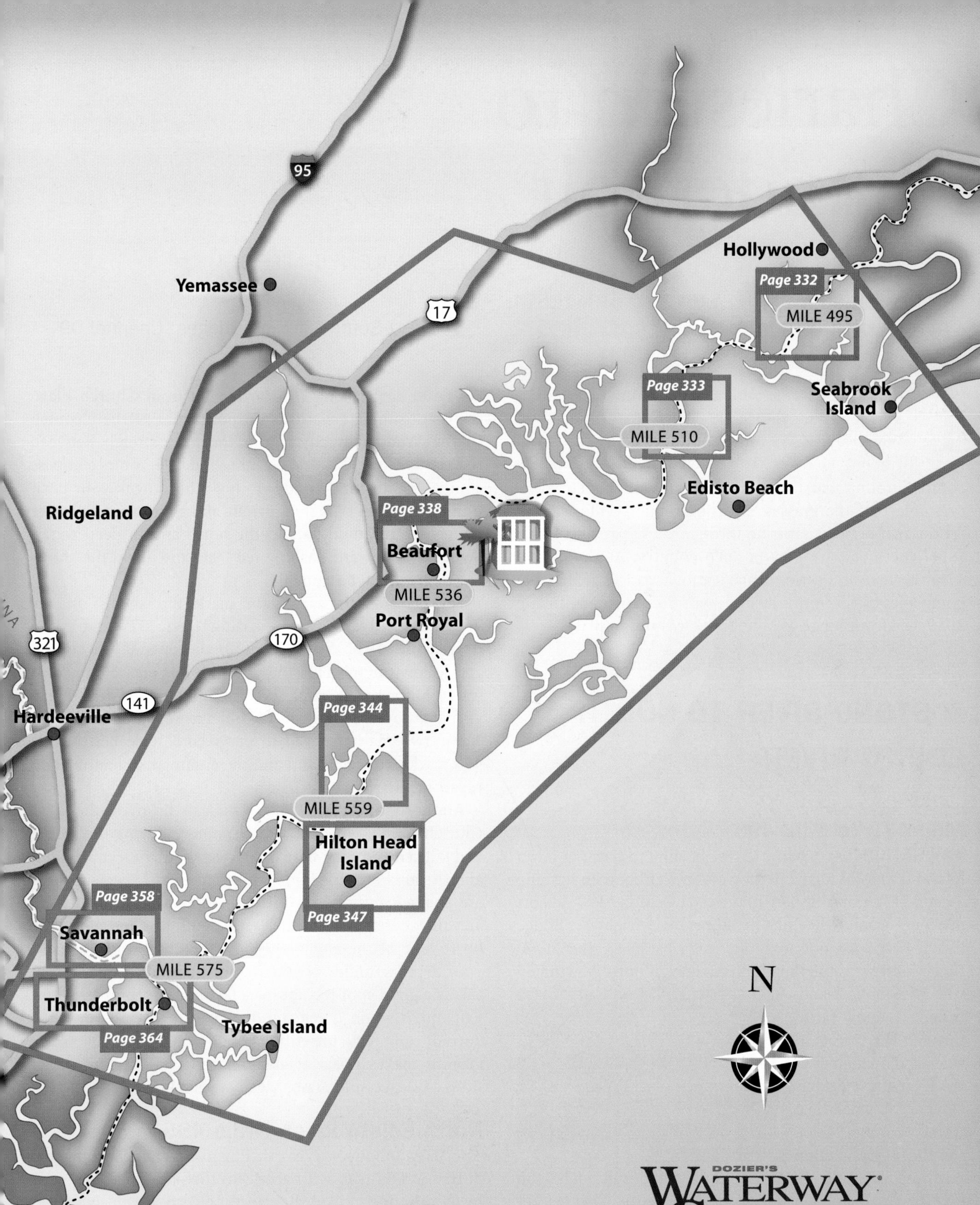

Skipper's Handbook

- Tide Tables 49
- Bridge Tables 58

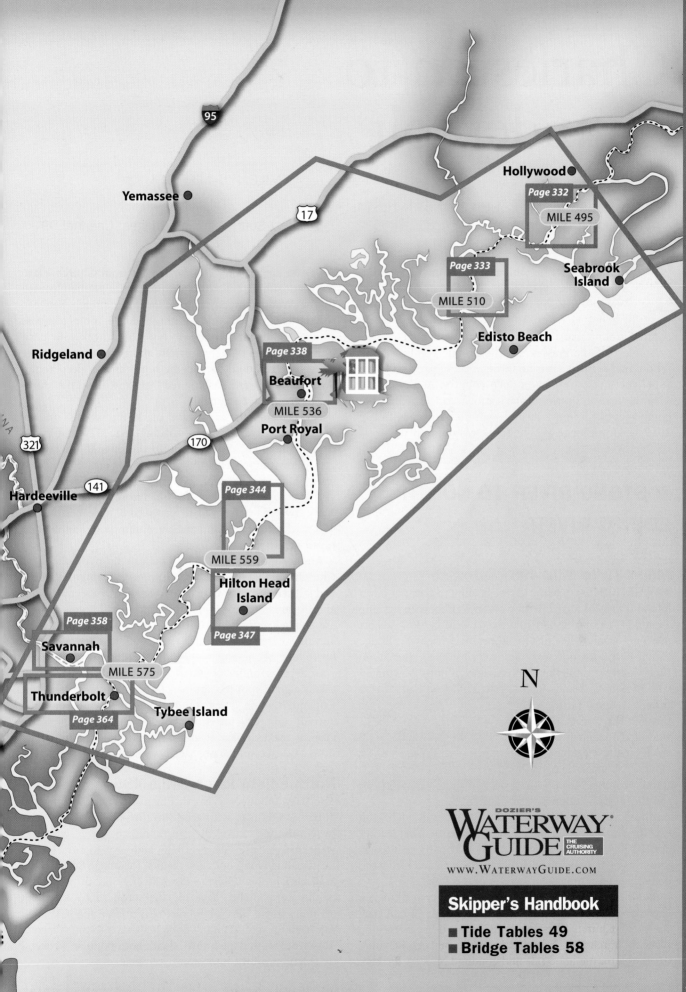

Charleston to Thunderbolt

ICW MILE 475–MILE 615

CHARTS 11505, 11507, 11512, 11513, 11514, 11516, 11517, 11518, 11519, 11521, 11522

(VHF) South Carolina Bridges: Channel 09

From Elliott Cut, which leads from Charleston, SC, south to the Stono River, the Intracoastal Waterway (ICW) route continues along the Stono River for about 12 miles. This stretch of lush and lovely South Carolina marsh is teeming with wildlife. The delicate colors of the grasses and the unique scents wafting off the marsh make cruising through these parts a unique experience. You are now in open country. At about Mile 475, the first of a series of navigational ranges makes the going a lot easier in this area of swift tidal currents. In late 2010, the front range at Mile 475.3 was not in place.

STONO RIVER TO NORTH EDISTO RIVER

Mile 475 to Mile 495

NAVIGATION: Use Chart 11518. Shoaling to 6 feet at mean low water has occurred in the Stono River between flashing green "31" (near Mile 478) and red daybeacon "36." A short distance beyond the John F. Limehouse Highway Bridge (Mile 479.3, 65-foot fixed vertical clearance), the Stono River narrows, and the ICW channel follows a winding path past Johns Island. When heading north through the starboard side of the channel at the Limehouse Bridge, beware of small-boat traffic coming from the busy boat ramp north of the bridge. Just beyond Mile 480, red daybeacon "40" marks a shoal off the creek to the north. This marker appears to be in the wrong place, but it is not. Give it space, as a shoal extends slightly farther into the channel from the creek. The current usually reverses at this point.

LIMEHOUSE BRIDGE
Mile 479.3

WATERWAY GUIDE PHOTOGRAPHY

At Mile 485, the ICW leaves the Stono River and enters a short land cut leading to the headwaters of the Wadmalaw River. At Church Flats (Mile 485), the tides meet—the name "Church Flats" derived from the practice of going to church on the flood tide and coming home on the ebb.

Near red daybeacon "78," farther on from Church Flats, there are submerged rocks on both sides of the channel. In the Wadmalaw River, run the long stretch between red daybeacon "92" and flashing red "94" on a compass course. If transiting at mid- to high tide, check your position with respect to the current along the way, in order to stay off the mud flats to the north and in deep water. Swing wide toward flashing red "94" and avoid the shortcut to green daybeacon "95."

Several aids to navigation mark the shoals on the Wadmalaw River between flashing red "82" and green daybeacon "101." Swing wide to the outside on curves, and follow the magenta line through this area for the best water. Markers "98" and "100" indicate a shoal area that is visible at low tide but can be difficult to spot at high tide. These two markers need to be given a wide berth. Mile 490 marks Yonges Island and the commercial hauling and repair facility there.

Anchorage: At Mile 487, you can drop the hook in Church Creek, which is always popular during the spring and fall. The holding here is good in about 15 feet of water, and the anchorage is fairly well protected. However, there are shallow oyster bars on both sides of Church Creek, and they extend out farther at the entrance and along the north side of the anchorage than the chart indicates; use your depth sounder. If you are northbound to Charleston, this is a good spot to wait for a favorable current in Elliott Cut and Wappoo Creek, although contrary winds and tidal current can create unsettling conditions for keelboats. The current makes boats at anchor swing in different directions, so leave sufficient space between boats.

North Edisto River—Mile 495

The ICW follows the North Edisto River to flashing red "110." A side trip, with access to the ocean, can be made by continuing down the North Edisto River, which is well charted (use Chart 11522) and easy to run, except for shoaling along both riverbanks. (*See page 84 for more information about North Edisto River.*) Stay in the center of the river, slightly favoring the southern bank. About six miles down the North Edisto River from the ICW, you can head up swift-running Bohicket Creek to the village of Rockville, SC and Seabrook Island, both popular weekend destinations with Charleston-based boaters.

Dockage: Up the North Edisto River's Bohicket Creek, Bohicket Marina and Yacht Club lies just north of the village of Rockville. Maximum ebb and flood currents call for both advance planning and dockside help to assure a smooth docking and departure. In addition to restrooms and showers, there are coin-operated laundry machines, bike rentals and a marine supply/fishing equipment store on premises, and resort amenities are nearby.

MILE 495 TO MILE 536

Beyond the North Edisto River at flashing red "110," the ICW channel enters the Dawho River at White Point (Mile 496.7). Remember that at low tide, floating aids in areas of extreme tidal range such as this will pull in the direction of the current, away from their anchored position. In all anchorages, be sure to use your anchor light at night.

NAVIGATION: Use Chart 11518. Use great caution if you attempt to enter Toogoodoo Creek, at Mile 495 off the North Edisto River. There are large areas of mudbanks on both sides at its entrance. Grounding on a mudbank in this area of the waterway can make for a sticky removal process.

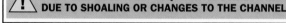

THE FOLLOWING AREA REQUIRES SPECIAL ATTENTION DUE TO SHOALING OR CHANGES TO THE CHANNEL

DAWHO RIVER

For the first couple of miles on the Dawho River, pay close attention to markers and be wary of shoaling in the curves just past White Point. Depths just to the west of White Point were observed to be 6.5 feet at mean low water in late 2010 and the latest chart shows "shoaling to 6 ft rep." Depths are reported to be even shallower when straying from the magenta line. The January 2010 chart shows green cans "111" and "113" marking the S-curve that ends at green daybeacon "117." There are several areas here with depths from 5.7 to 6.3 feet at mean low water in the right half of the channel from the Dawho River to Fenwick Cut, according to the most recent survey. It is best to go through here on a rising tide. Dredging in the spring of 2010 has relieved the shoaling issues for now. But still use caution...This can be a nasty area.

END SPECIAL CAUTION AREA.

At Mile 501, you will notice a pair of sloughs making into the Dawho River from the north. These little slivers of water actually connect behind marshland to form an oxbow. Do not be tempted to try to anchor in either slough, as shoals become bare at low tide.

Just before the McKinley Washington Jr. Bridge (65-foot fixed vertical clearance, Mile 501.3), the ICW enters a land cut. (The tide boards at this bridge show 63- and 64-feet vertical clearance.) A portion of the old remaining swing bridge is used as a fishing pier. Beyond the bridge, the ICW passes through narrow North Creek and Watts Cut before emptying into the broad and swiftly flowing South Edisto River.

Anchorage: Tom Point Creek, at Mile 495.5, offers a more easily accessed anchorage than Toogoodoo Creek, mentioned above. Enter cautiously to avoid the 3-foot-deep shoal to starboard, and you will find at least eight-foot depths inside.

MCKINLEY WASHINGTON JR. BRIDGE, Mile 501.3
WATERWAY GUIDE PHOTOGRAPHY

Just south of the McKinley Washington Jr. Bridge, it is possible to anchor in the approach to Fishing Creek. Be aware that the charted depth at its entrance is 4 feet and that there are charted submerged piles outside the ICW channel here. Favor the red daybeacon "132" side when entering Fishing Creek. You will find 9- to 19-foot depths. Despite some highway noise, this is one of the best anchorages along this section of the ICW.

South Edisto River—Mile 510

The main destination along the South Edisto River is Edisto Island, overlooking the Atlantic Ocean. Edisto Island is home of the community of Edisto Beach and offers nearby deep-sea fishing areas. The town also boasts beautiful, well-preserved Colonial homes, a popular residential resort with golf course, an oceanfront state park and good stores and boutiques. You will find a slower pace that harks back to the 1950s; there are no high-rise motels or bungee-jumping concessions here.

NAVIGATION: Use Charts 11517 and 11518. The South Edisto River is easy to follow. Remember, however, that you are in a strong tidal zone, so do not cut too close to the markers or the bends in the channels.

Two ranges, at Mile 506 (Range "A") and Mile 510 (Range "C"), respectively, mark the ICW course along the South Edisto River between Watts Cut and Fenwick Cut. These ranges keep boaters off the river's wide shoals and projecting points.

Green daybeacon "161A" (Mile 510.7), in the South Edisto River, is not shown on older charts (the current edition of Chart 11518 from January 2010 shows this mark). Green daybeacon "161B," shown on some older charts, no longer exists.

At Fenwick Cut, Mile 511, the ICW heads southwest along the Ashepoo River, while the South Edisto River meanders in a southeasterly direction toward the Atlantic Ocean. Shoals continually build at both entrances to Fenwick Cut and along its entire length. Honoring red daybeacon "162A" and giving the reds a wide berth will keep you in deeper water.

Dockage: Behind Edisto Island on Big Bay Creek—4.5 miles south from the ICW, near the mouth of the South Edisto River—lies another transient-oriented facility, Edisto Marina, with gas and diesel fuel, groceries and

Seabrook I., Wadmalaw I., Edisto I., SC

WADMALAW ISLAND	Phone	Largest Vessel Accommodated	VHF Channel Monitored	Transient Berths / Total Berths	Approach / Dockside Depth (reported)	Floating Docks	Gas / Diesel	Groceries, Ice, Marine Supplies, Snacks	Repairs: Hull, Engine, Propeller	Lift (tonnage), Crane, Rail	1=110V, 2=220V, B=Both, Max Amps	Laundry, Pool, Showers	Pump-Out Station	Nearby: Grocery Store, Motel, Restaurant
		Dockage					Supplies		Services					
1. Bohicket Marina & Market 7.2 S of 497 (Internet Access) (Wireless Internet Access)	**843-768-1280**	**140**	**16/68**	**50/200**	**14/12**	**F**	**GD**	**GIMS**			**B/100**	**LS**	**P**	**GMR**
2. Rockville Marine	843-559-1124	100	16	/17	10/16	F		M	HEP	L60,C15	B/50			
3. Edisto Marina 4.5 S of 511	843-869-3504	42	16/68	5/72	17/12	F	GD	GIMS			B/50	S		R

Corresponding chart(s) not to be used for navigation. ☐ Internet Access (WiFi) Wireless Internet Access

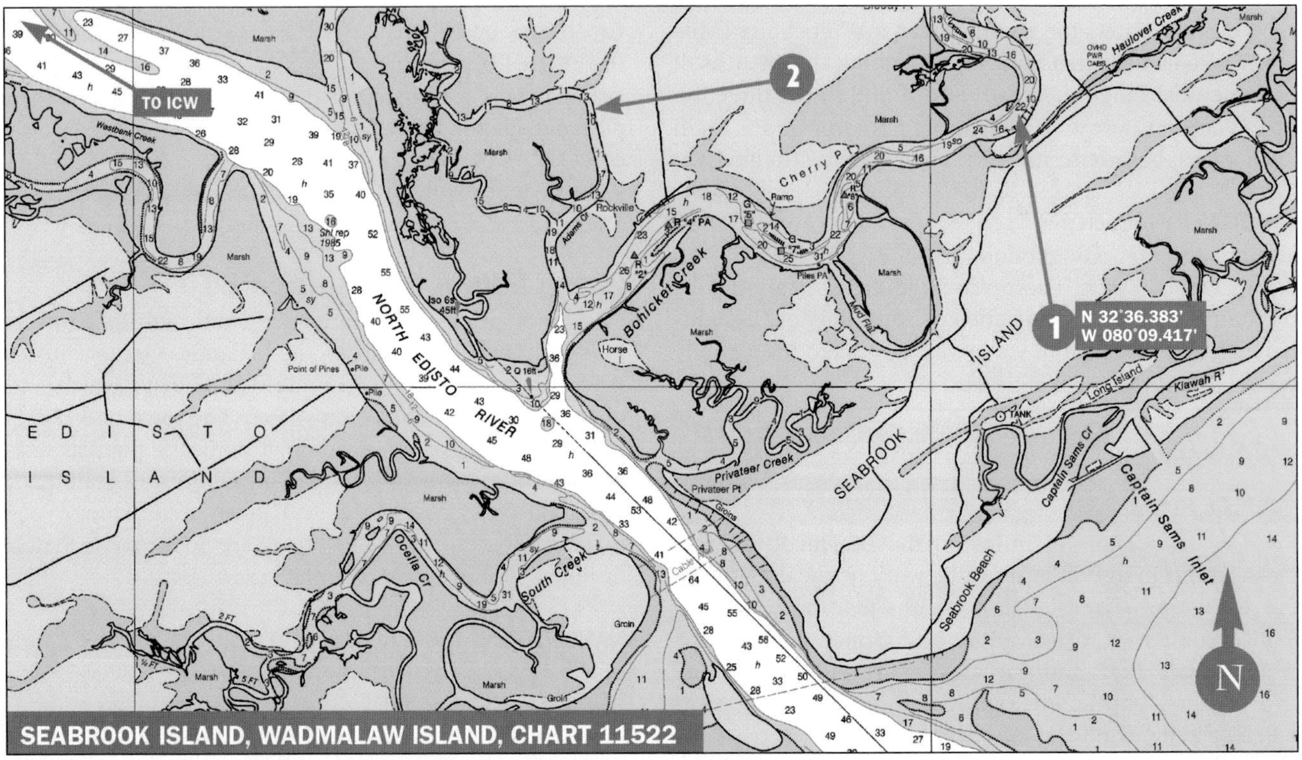

SEABROOK ISLAND, WADMALAW ISLAND, CHART 11522

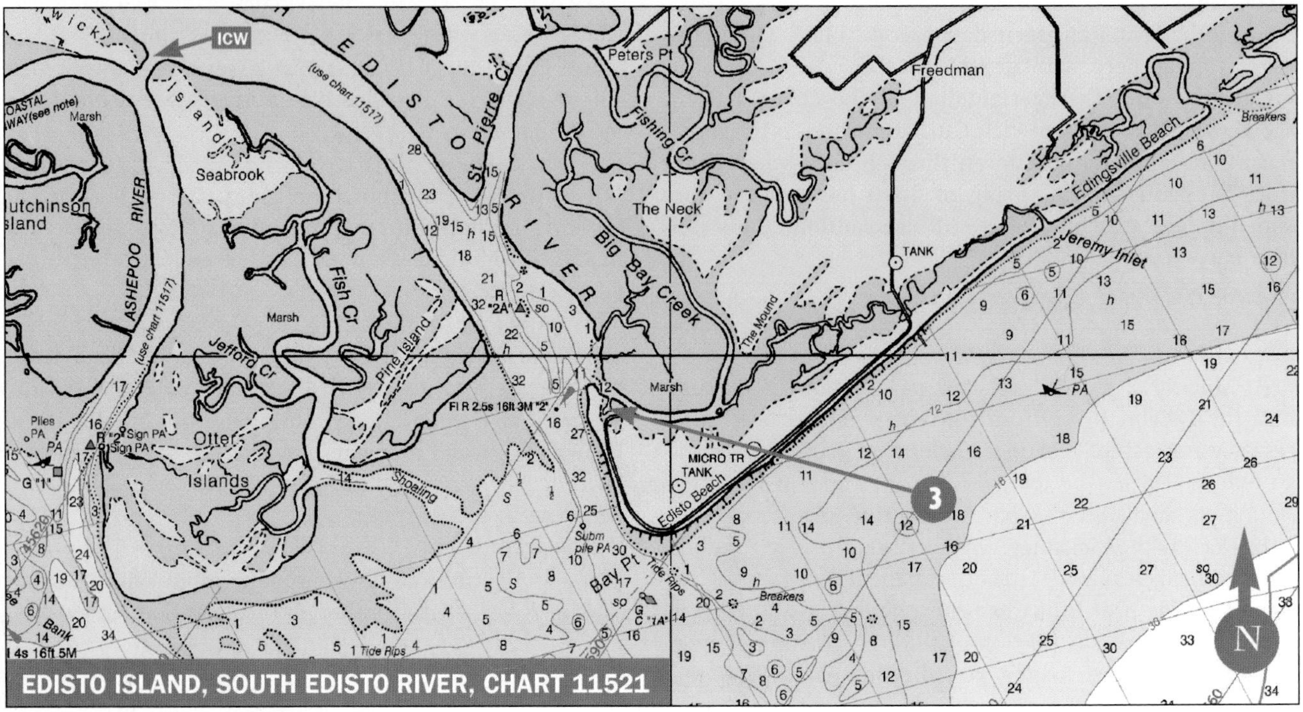

EDISTO ISLAND, SOUTH EDISTO RIVER, CHART 11521

showers. The nearby beachfront community on Edisto Island offers a few shops, restaurants and provisions.

Anchorage: The South Edisto River provides good fair-weather anchorage. When southbound out of Watts Cut, bear off to starboard into the South Edisto River. Anchor in the middle about a mile from Watts Cut where the chart shows 10 and 11 feet with a soft bottom. This is a wide open, relatively quiet spot with good holding, although we advise against anchoring here in any strong wind. There is considerable current (1 to 2 knots) here, just as with all the rivers in this area of the ICW, and conditions can become very uncomfortable with opposing wind and current.

Just past the lower end of Alligator Creek, Mile 509, and opposite green daybeacon "157," is an anchorage for settled weather, with good protection from the northwest. Sound toward the shore to avoid trap markers, and anchor in 8 to 11 feet, well off the channel. The current may reach 1.5 knots, so vessels may lay to the current, rather than the wind. Holding is good here.

Ashepoo River—Ashepoo Coosaw Cutoff

The ICW route continues to the southwest, leading from the South Edisto River through Fenwick Cut and into a short section of the Ashepoo River.

NAVIGATION: Use Chart 11518. Do not get too close to the Ashepoo River's north shore between flashing green "165" and quick flashing red "166," due to increased shoaling along the north bank. Follow the curve of the channel as shown by the magenta line on the chart. If heading up the Ashepoo River toward B&B Seafood, be aware that there is less water just beyond quick flashing red "166" than indicated on the chart. Once you have transited this section of the Ashepoo River, the ICW enters the first part of the Ashepoo Coosaw Cutoff.

THE FOLLOWING AREA REQUIRES SPECIAL ATTENTION DUE TO SHOALING OR CHANGES TO THE CHANNEL

ASHEPOO COOSAW CUTOFF

The Ashepoo Coosaw Cutoff soon jags in a northwesterly direction—entering Rock Creek at Mile 515—before it continues as a narrow land cut toward the wide Coosaw River. When transiting the Ashepoo Coosaw Cutoff, be especially cautious rounding the bend into Rock Creek, marked by flashing green "173" and red daybeacon "172." Do not attempt to shortcut the distance between red daybeacon "172" and red daybeacon "176." There is less than the 9-foot charted depths on the range between red daybeacon "176" and flashing green "177." Do not follow the magenta line, rather favor the southwest shore opposite "176." Crab pot floats are normally placed in the shallow water on the northeast side of the channel.

As in the past few years, flashing green "177" was more than a foot out of the water at low tide, with a shoal extending far into the ICW channel, especially just beyond that marker. There is deep water on the red side of the channel passing flashing green "177," so give it a wide berth.

Additional daybeacons (green daybeacon "181" and red daybeacon "180") were added in the lower Ashepoo Coosaw Cutoff and may not appear on older charts, but do appear in the latest one. There was shoaling noted in the area of green daybeacon "181" in fall 2010.

Carefully follow the slight "S" curve of the charted ICW magenta line where the Ashepoo Coosaw Cutoff meets the Coosaw River to avoid shoaling at the lower end of the cutoff. Recent dredging has removed this as one of the trickiest and shallowest parts of the entire ICW, but it is still subject to persistent shoaling. In early 2011, green daybeacon "185" was in its charted position outside the cut, although it is sometimes moved up into the cut or replaced with a moveable can buoy to mark the deeper water in the exit from this cut. It is important to follow the magenta line on the chart passing between flashing red "184" and green daybeacon "185," as well as around flashing red "186." The shallowest depth observed here was 7 feet at mean low wa-ter, both north of and across the entire channel south of flashing red "184."

END SPECIAL CAUTION AREA.

Anchorage: Anchorages along the Ashepoo River are open but pleasant, with good holding. The headwaters of Rock Creek, north of the ICW at Mile 516, provide a narrow but well-protected deepwater anchorage with minimum 7-foot depths to the second bend. Use the depth sounder to avoid the shoals on the inside of the turns in the creek. Deep-drafted boats swinging on the current have frequently grounded in this anchorage.

Coosaw River

While the Coosaw River is wide and unobstructed, it is best to keep to the channel and run at least rough compass courses to help you spot the markers, which are spaced fairly far apart.

NAVIGATION: Use Chart 11518. The Bull River (Mile 521.5) and the Combahee River at Mile 518.5—an area once fished for sturgeon—make off of the Coosaw River. Around Mile 521.5, Parrot Creek leads south off of the Coosaw River, with a well-marked entrance. The large shoal shown on older charts does not exist and was deleted from the most current chart editions. In fact, depths exceed 10 feet for the entire approach to Parrot Creek from the ICW. Follow green daybeacon "1" and red daybeacon "2" into Parrot Creek.

Dockage: Dataw Island, a quiet, water-oriented residential development situated three miles up Parrot Creek, has a picturesque full-service marina that welcomes transients. They have friendly staff, gas and diesel fuel, a Travelift, an on-site restaurant, elegant showers and restrooms, laundry facilities and courtesy bikes to give a self-guided tour of the beautiful, shaded homes on the island.

Mosquito Creek, Ashepoo River, SC

MOSQUITO CREEK (ASHEPOO RIVER)		Largest Vessel Accommodated	VHF Channel Monitored	Transient Berths / Total Berths	Approach / Dockside Depth (reported)	Floating Docks	Gas / Diesel	Groceries, Ice, Marine Supplies, Snacks	Repairs: Hull, Engine, Propeller	Lift (tonnage), Crane, Rail	1=110V, 2=220V, B=Both, Max Amps	Laundry, Pool, Showers	Pump-Out Station	Nearby: Grocery Store, Motel, Restaurant
		Dockage					Supplies		Services					
1. B & B Seafood House 1.8 N of 513.5	843-844-2322	50	68	2/2	10/10	F	GD	GIMS						R

Corresponding chart(s) not to be used for navigation. Internet Access Wireless Internet Access

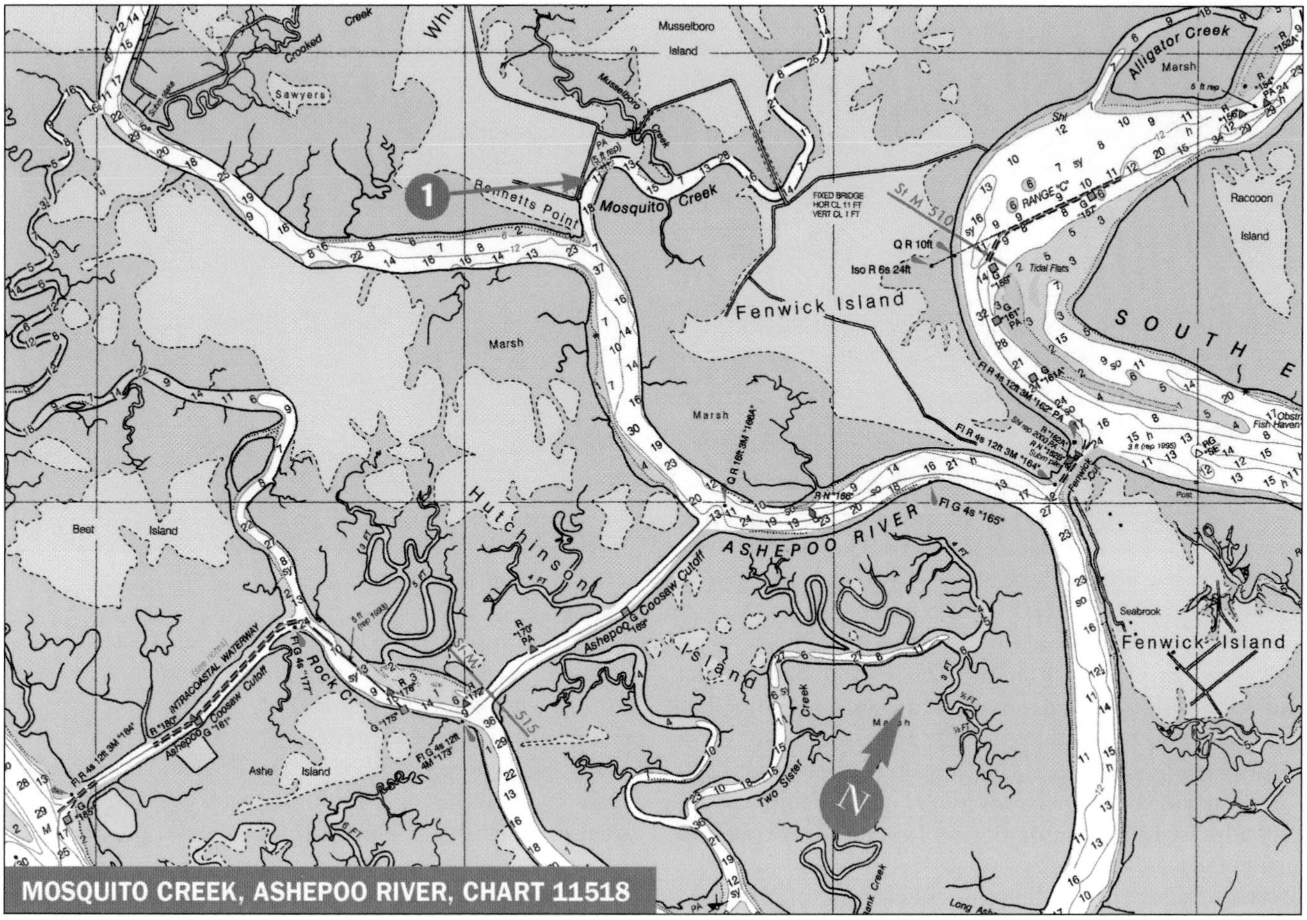

MOSQUITO CREEK, ASHEPOO RIVER, CHART 11518

Anchorage: Many spots in this area are suitable for anchoring. At Mile 521.5, you can anchor inside Bull River, just off the ICW. The mouth of Bull River has less water than shown on the chart, and the bottom here is mostly hard shells. While holding is good, it can be difficult to get the anchor to set. Shrimp boats frequently use this anchorage. For more protected anchorage, go up the Bull River to Wimbee Creek. Watch for the shoal below Summerhouse Point and leave the island to starboard. Holding is good here in 8 to 16 feet, although the bottom also is hard with shells in some areas.

Brickyard Creek to Beaufort

The ICW leaves the Coosaw River at Mile 529, where you will find a well-marked entrance range heading into Brickyard Creek. As you travel south on Brickyard Creek, military aircraft might buzz you. At around Mile 532, a large dock to starboard is the only evidence of the U.S. Marine Corps Air Station. The two Marine Corps installations in the Beaufort, SC area—the other is the famous Parris Island Recruit Depot—are major contributors to the local economy. The noise from the military aircraft in this area can make anchoring here unpleasant.

NAVIGATION: Use Chart 11518. Where the ICW begins its four-mile run along Brickyard Creek—the headwaters of the Beaufort River—stay to mid-channel. There are flats along both sides of the channel, particularly where the Coosaw River enters Brickyard Creek. Following the magenta line on your chart will keep you off the shoal and in deep water between the range marker and green daybeacon "209." The worst shoaling in this area is on the red side of the channel between red daybeacons "210" and "214."

A view over the Morgan River off the Coosaw. (Not to be used for navigation.) Photo courtesy of Mike Kucera.

Slow boats should note that the current between Brickyard Creek and Beaufort changes at about flashing red "224" (Mile 532). If you catch the end of the flood or the slack, you can usually ride the current to Beaufort.

Dockage: At Mile 533, just north of green daybeacon "233," a marked channel leads into Marsh Harbor Boatyard on Ladys Island. Marsh Harbor is a first-rate yard that does meticulous work.

Anchorage: The two loops on the east side of Brickyard Creek between Mile 529 and 530.5 appear to be possible anchorages. Their deep water channels are very narrow and residential docks extend far out from the shore, limiting space in both, so we recommend exercising caution if anchoring in either loop.

BEAUFORT/PORT ROYAL

Mile 536 to Mile 553

The city of Beaufort appears to starboard at about the point where Brickyard Creek becomes the Beaufort River. Beaufort's attractions include an entire downtown on the National Register of Historic Places, a multi-purpose park along the waterfront, an amphitheater, a water garden, markets and a bandstand, all within sight of bed and breakfasts, attractive shops and meticulously restored houses set against the backdrop of a rustic marsh scene across the river. Beaufort (pronounced Bew'-fort; not Boe'-fort, as when referring to Beaufort, NC) has spread gently southward along the western bank of the river toward Port Royal, SC, where Jean Ribault, the Frenchman who made early explorations of the southeastern coast of America, tried to establish a colony in 1562.

NAVIGATION: Use Chart 11518. **Use the Savannah River Entrance Tide Table. For high tide, add 1 hour and 9 minutes; for low tide, add 51 minutes.** Heading south along the ICW, Brickyard Creek reaches Beaufort and the Ladies Island Swing Bridge (Mile 536, closed vertical clearance 30 feet). To port (south), just above the Ladies Island Swing Bridge, is Factory Creek, with ample water depth and Lady's Island Marina.

While there is ample maneuvering room both above and below the Ladies Island Swing Bridge, the strong side-current is tricky—adequate power and careful boat handling are required. The Ladies Island Swing Bridge (indeed, it's "Ladies" when referring to the bridge, not "Ladys," as with the proper spelling of Ladys Island) is closed from 7:00 a.m. to 9:00 a.m., at 11:00 a.m. and at 1:00 p.m., and 4:00 p.m. to 6:00 p.m., and opens on the hour between 9:00 a.m. and 4:00 p.m., Monday through Friday, except weekends and federal holidays. (Note that during construction on the McTeer Bridge, south of here,

"SETTING THE NEW STANDARD FOR MARINAS."

Wet slips, dry stack, full service boatyard with long term storage

- Restaurant and market on-site
- Deep water concrete floating docks with breakwater consisting of 83 wet slips
- Full-service boatyard with 50-ton travel lift and 20,000 lb. fork lift
- Cable on transient docks and free Wi-Fi
- Non-ethanol gasoline and diesel fuels
- New showers, restrooms and laundry
- BBQ grills, bicycles and playground
- 600 plus ft. of face dock • Dry stack available
- Four miles from the Beaufort County airport

DATAW ISLAND MARINA

Providing a state-of-the-art facility and complete marine services, Dataw Island Marina caters to seasoned mariners as well as families casting off on their first adventures afloat.

We are located on the Morgan River just three miles from the I.C.W. and only minutes from the St. Helena Sound and Atlantic Ocean. A nine mile car ride and you will find yourself in Beaufort where you can relish in history, cuisine, and shopping.

A hub of activities, Dataw Marina is perfect for all kinds of activities and seafaring explorations: pristine inlets, marshes, creeks, gunk holing and for the more adventurous, deep sea fishing expeditions of the Atlantic!

843.838.8410 – www.datawmarina.com – 100 Marina Drive, Dataw Island, SC 29920

the bridge will only open on the hour. The construction is expected to continue through the end of 2011.)

The Ladies Island Bridge is slow, cumbersome to open and is frequently under repair. There may be lengthy delays, so check ahead to see if there are any problems. A strictly enforced No-Wake Zone extends nearly four miles all the way from the Ladies Island Swing Bridge to the fixed highway bridge (J.E. McTeer Bridge, 65-foot fixed vertical clearance) over the Beaufort River at Port Royal. (Signs on both bridges warn that violators, if caught, will pay a fine of $1,025 or spend 30 days in a nicely appointed South Carolina jail cell.)

LADIES ISLAND SWING BR. Mile 536

WATERWAY GUIDE PHOTOGRAPHY

South of Beaufort on the Beaufort River, there is shoaling between Spanish Point and the Port Royal Landing Marina, on the west side of the channel.

Dockage: Immediately across the Ladies Island Bridge from Beaufort, on protected Factory Creek, is Lady's Island Marina, with transient space at floating docks and a location that is convenient to shopping, an ABC package store and nearby restaurants. The marina also has showers and laundry facilities. This is a good place to restock groceries. It is protected from ICW wakes.

Downtown Marina of Beaufort lies just south of the Ladies Island Bridge and the Waterfront Park seawall and is within a block or two of most of the town's amenities, shops, restaurants and historic sites. Currents are very strong here, with 7- to 9-foot tides, so use considerable caution in docking. Call ahead to the marina for dockage availability and assistance from the marina's capable staff. Floating docks on the T-head accommodate transient cruisers. Even so, set ample fenders on approach. There is a pump-out service boat available to boats in the marina and anchorage for a reasonable fee. The courtesy "day dock" (the 140-foot-long floating dock south of the marina) is owned by the city and is available except between 1:00 a.m. and 6:00 a.m. Depths at the courtesy dock are 8 feet at the west end and 5 feet at the east end. Smaller boats may tie up along the Seawall at the Waterfront Park, administered by the Downtown Marina. However, these docks are useful only for short tie-ups during periods of high or slack tide because of the strong currents, tidal range and oyster shells on the seawall.

Three miles south of downtown, immediately north of the highway bridge (Mile 539.7, J.E. McTeer Bridge, 65-foot fixed vertical clearance) to starboard, Port Royal Landing Marina offers complete amenities in a serene and secure setting. The easy access T-dock offers gas and diesel fuel, the ship's store is fully stocked, and the marina's courtesy car puts you downtown in just a few minutes. This is a very friendly and well-run marina that goes out of its way to accommodate transients' needs. There is no dinghy dock at this marina. It is right on the ICW and vessels do not always honor it as a No-Wake Zone as they should.

Within less than a mile's drive or walk from Port Royal Landing Marina are a Piggly Wiggly Supermarket, ABC Package Store, drugstore and ATM plus a West Marine store. Be sure to phone or hail the marina on VHF Channel 16 before you approach to check for dockage availability and directions to a berth on its floating docks.

Anchorage: A protected anchorage is available in Factory Creek, which opens just north of and parallel to the Ladies Island Swing Bridge (Mile 536). This anchorage is somewhat narrow for larger vessels. Enter as if heading to the Lady's Island Marina, favoring the red side of the channel as there is only 6 feet at mean low water near green daybeacon "1." Then anchor in a minimum of 9 feet of water past the marina. Anchored boats pay a fee to dock dinghies at the marina. Or you can anchor closer to the public boat ramp before the marina and dinghy ashore there. The current is less intense here than on the ICW, and you will not be rolled by nighttime traffic.

It is possible to anchor west of the Downtown Marina of Beaufort if you keep well clear of ICW traffic and anticipate the effects of strong southerlies, substantial tidal-current swings and lots of boat traffic. A number of private moorings are within this anchorage. You can dock your dinghy behind Beaufort's courtesy dock, next to the Downtown Marina. The depths here are generally 15 to 20 feet.

A city ordinance was put into effect in March 2006 and remained in place at press time for transient vessels anchored in Beaufort City limits: "Vessels anchoring longer than 72 hours must be registered with the Harbormaster (at the Downtown Marina of Beaufort) the occupants of which must show to his satisfaction, evidence of current registration, liability insurance of not less than $100,000 per occurrence, and sewage facilities compliant with State and Federal legislation." Staff at the Downtown Marina of Beaufort also state that vessels must be anchored at least 200 feet away from their facility. Some locals were not even aware of this ordinance and doubt it is being enforced, especially in Factory Creek.

Another anchorage is located in the eastern fork of the Beaufort River, just south of the city. Enter from the south near flashing red "242" (Mile 538.6) off Spanish Point. Proceed east, and then turn north between the marsh island to the west and the marshes to the east. Set your hook in 10 to 20 feet of water over a sandy bottom. Do not try to reenter the Beaufort River proper, to the north, because of the shoals there.

GOIN' ASHORE: **BEAUFORT, SC**

Queen of the Carolina sea islands, Beaufort exudes Southern hospitality and charm, and a strong sense of place. Besides its many historic and architectural treasures, Beaufort has a modern-day military presence, hosting the Beaufort Naval Hospital and the Marine Corps Air Station, home to seven F/A-18 Hornet squadrons. If you spend any time in Beaufort, you will hear and see the jets overhead.

History: Since 1514, this lovely location has been settled by the Spanish, then the French, followed by the English. It has endured Indian uprisings as well as occupations by British, then Union forces. Indigo, rice and later, Sea Island cotton were major moneymakers, allowing wealthy plantation owners to build spacious homes in town along the river with its cooling breezes.

Cultural references: The imposing homes along the high banks of the river have drawn the attention of filmmakers who have used the setting for filming "The Big Chill," "The Prince of Tides" and "Forrest Gump." Noted Southern writers such as Pat Conroy and Cassandra King live nearby on the sea islands.

Attractions: Many of those homes have been restored and still exist today. Unlike Charleston's single homes, the ones in Beaufort are more of a West Indies-style in a T-shaped floor plan, with a raised first floor, high ceilings and double porches. Petit Point (503 Washington St.) is a smaller house but with extensive gardens overlooking the Beaufort River. The John Mark Verdier House (801 Bay St.), now a museum, was built around 1790 and was headquarters for the Union forces in the area during the Civil War. It also hosted the aged Marquis de Lafayette upon his return to the country after the Revolutionary War. The George Elliott House (1001 Bay St.) was built around 1840 and still has its original slate mantels, crown molding, chandeliers and authentic furnishings, which survived its use as a Union hospital during the Civil War. It is privately owned but can occasionally be toured during one of Beaufort's House Tours.

The Beaufort Visitors Center is located in a historic house at 1106 Carteret St., within walking distance north of the waterfront park. It has information on Beaufort's many museums and can arrange horse and carriage tours of the town, plus supply maps for walking tours. There is also a booking office just around the corner from Downtown Marina, and carriages leave from the marina parking lot.

Museums in the area include the Beaufort Arsenal Museum at 713 Craven St., the Parris Island Museum in the War Memorial Building on Parris Island and the York W. Bailey Museum in Beaufort's Penn Center Historic District. St. Helena's Episcopal Church, erected in 1724, is surrounded by a wall built of bricks arriving from England as ships' ballast. The church has an ancient graveyard where tombstones served as operating tables for wounded soldiers during the Civil War. Historic forts in the area include Fort Beauregard at Bay Point, Fort Charles at Parris Island and old Spanish forts like Fort San Felipe and Fort San Marcos, both at Parris Island.

Special Events: Beaufort is a destination for many events, particularly the Annual Spring Tour of Homes in March and the Fall Festival of Houses & Gardens in late October. A Taste of Beaufort takes place in early May, and

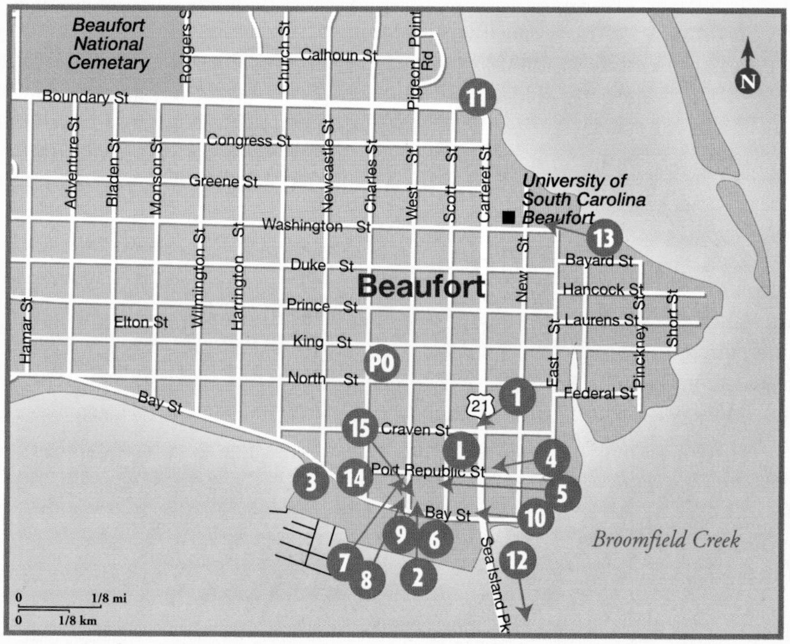

Reference the marina listing tables to see all the marinas in the area.

ATTRACTIONS
1 Beaufort Arsenal Museum
2 The John Mark Verdier House Museum
3 Carolina Buggy Tours

DINING
4 Beaufort Inn
5 Blackstone's Deli & Café
6 The Saltus River Grill
7 Emily's Restaurant and Tapas Bar
8 Breakwater
9 Plum's

GROCERIES/ CARRYOUT
10 Low Country Winery

INFORMATION
11 The Beaufort Visitors Center

MARINE SUPPLIES
12 Grayco True Value Hardware

POINTS OF INTEREST
13 Petit Point
14 The George Elliott House

SHOPPING
15 Old Bay Market Place

L LIBRARY

PO POST OFFICE

Looking south over Beaufort, SC. (Not to be used for navigation.) WATERWAY GUIDE PHOTOGRAPHY.

the Gullah Festival at the end of May celebrates the sea island culture. The two most popular festivals—and you may need to book dockage up to a year ahead of time—are the annual Water Festival in July and the Beaufort Shrimp Festival in early October. All the festivals are held in Waterfront Park and along Bay Street.

Shopping: For provisioning, grocery stores from downtown require the use of a car, but both Downtown Marina and Port Royal Landing Marina offer the use of courtesy cars. From Lady's Island Marina, numerous stores are within walking distance, as is the Grayco True Value Hardware, Bill's Liquors, a Publix as well as a Food Lion supermarket. On the Beaufort side of the river, restaurants and unique shops abound on Bay and adjacent streets, including banks, a pharmacy and the library. The nearest major airports are in Charleston and Savannah, an hour and a half and 45-minute drives, respectively.

Restaurants: While not having as extensive a choice, Beaufort is beginning to rival Charleston in its quality restaurants. Visitors can select from five-star fine dining at the Beaufort Inn (809 Port Republic St., 843-379-4667), to a local favorite, Blackstone's Deli & Café (205 Scott St., 843-524-4330), that serves breakfast and lunch. Its Low Country shrimp and grits is the real deal, made with stone-ground grits.

The Saltus River Grill (802 Bay St., 843-379-3474) offers dinners of fresh-caught seafood as well as a sushi bar. Emily's Restaurant & Tapas Bar (906 Port Republic St., 843-522-1866) features tapas dishes in addition to seafood, lamb and duck. Breakwater (203 Carteret St., 843-379-0052) also has a tapas menu, but includes intriguing items such as lemon ginger pan-roasted flounder. A less expensive choice is Plum's (904 Bay St., 843-525-1946), which makes its own ice cream and serves salads and sandwiches. The Old Bay Market Place (917 Bay St.) houses numerous individual shops and the Southern Sweets Ice Cream Parlor. (Ask them about their pumpkin pie sundae. It's to die for!)

ADDITIONAL RESOURCES

- BEAUFORT, SC, 843-524-3163, www.beaufort.com, www.downtownbeaufort.com
- BEAUFORT CHAMBER OF COMMERCE, 800-638-3525 www.beaufortsc.org

NEARBY GOLF COURSES
Sanctuary Golf Club, 8 Waveland Ave., Beaufort, SC 29902, 843-524-0300
www.sanctuarygolfcatisland.com

NEARBY MEDICAL FACILITIES
Beaufort Memorial Hospital, 955 Ribaut Road, Beaufort, SC 29902, 843-522-5200

DOWNTOWN MARINA *of Beaufort in the Historic District*

If you're looking for a pleasant layover in the heart of one of South Carolina's oldest and most beautiful cities, the Downtown Marina of Beaufort is a must. Moor your boat within 300 yards of restaurants, B&B's and a variety of shops located in Beaufort's lovely and historic business district. Directly adjacent to the marina is the newly renovated Henry C. Chambers Waterfront Park. Enjoy the scenic vista of Beaufort River while relaxing in the park swings or taking a stroll.

For the history enthusiasts, Beaufort's downtown area is located in the National Register of Historic Places. The streets are lined with grand oaks, historic homes and churches just minutes from your boat.

The marina itself offers a well stocked Ship's Store as well as newly renovated showers and a laundromat that are always clean. Engine repairs, hull and shaft work and many other marine services may be arranged by the marina staff.

Stop at our marina and experience our Lowcountry hospitality. The convenient location makes us a perfect historic downtown boating destination.

DOWNTOWN-MARINA
Beaufort S.C.

Located on the ICW at Marker #239

- 1,140 feet of transient dockage
- ValvTect Marine Fuels
- Floating docks with gated entry
- 30 & 50 amp service
- Courtesy car • ATM • Pumpout
- NOAA charts
- Showers • Laundry • Ice
- Sperry Top-Siders
- Costa Del Mar sunglasses
- Visa, Mastercard, Discover & AMEX
- Complimentary Wireless Internet

For more information contact us at: 1006 Bay Street, Beaufort, SC 29902
Ph: (843) 524-4422 • Fax: (843) 524-8437

Dataw I, Port Royal, Beaufort, SC

BEAUFORT AREA		Largest Vessel Accommodated	VHF Channel Monitored	Transient Berths / Total Berths	Approach / Dockside Depth (reported)	Floating Docks	Gas / Diesel	Groceries, Ice, Marine Supplies, Snacks	Repairs: Hull, Engine, Propeller	Lift (tonnage), Crane, Rail	1=110V, 2=220V, B=Both, Max Amps	Laundry, Pool, Showers	Pump-Out Station	Nearby: Grocery Store, Motel, Restaurant
		Dockage					Supplies		Services					
1. Dataw Island Marina 3 S of 521 💻 WiFi	**843-838-8410**	**200**	**16/68**	**20/82**	**25/15**	**F**		**IMS**	**HEP**	**L50**	**B/50**	**LS**	**P**	**R**
2. Marsh Harbor Boat Works 534.4	843-521-1500	65	16	4/16	6/6	F			HP	L50	B/50	S		MR
3. Lady's Island Marina .8 S of 536 💻 WiFi	843-522-0430	100	16/69	20/80	10/12	F		GIS			B/50	LS	P	GR
4. Downtown Marina of Beaufort 536.2 WiFi	**843-524-4422**	**200**	**16/68**	**25/100**	**20/15**	**F**	**GD**	**IMS**	**HEP**		**B/50**	**LS**	**P**	**GMR**
5. Port Royal Landing Marina 539 💻 WiFi	**800-326-7678**	**120**	**16/12**	**15/140**	**20/15**	**F**	**GD**	**GIMS**	**HEP**		**B/50**	**LS**	**P**	**GMR**

Corresponding chart(s) not to be used for navigation. 💻 Internet Access WiFi Wireless Internet Access

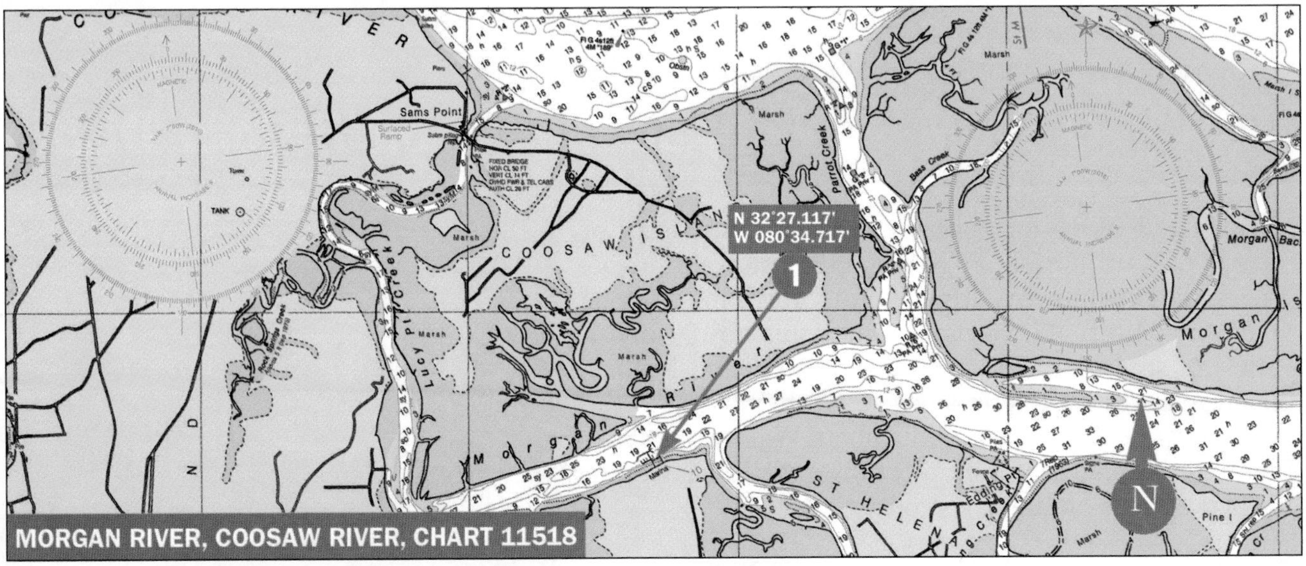

MORGAN RIVER, COOSAW RIVER, CHART 11518

Battery Creek—Mile 542

Battery Creek joins the Beaufort River from the west. On Battery Creek's north shore is Port Royal, the deepwater commercial shipping center for the Beaufort area. Lovely old houses still stand in Port Royal, and the town is beginning to revitalize its oldest section. If headed up Battery Creek, keep red daybeacon "42" to starboard, and follow the channel to Port Royal. Farther upstream are two bridges: a swing bridge (12-foot closed vertical clearance) and a fixed highway bridge (45-foot vertical clearance). The creek, which carries 12-foot depths or more for 4 miles upstream from the bridges, is charted (refer to Chart 11516), but no markers are present.

When northbound on the ICW, be sure to make the turn to the north on the Beaufort River between red nun "40" and quick flashing green "41," beyond which you will pick up the ICW markers again, rather than continuing straight westerly into Battery Creek. Both have high-rise bridges visible ahead, and this mistake has been known to dismast sailboats.

Beaufort River to Port Royal Sound

Beaufort River runs broad and deep, and its well-marked main channel is easy to follow past Parris Island, the Marine Corps Recruit Depot. There is plenty of commercial fishing traffic in the channel and much to see ashore, as the river arcs along between Parris Island and St. Helena Island.

NAVIGATION: Use Charts 11507 and 11516. *At the junction of Battery Creek and the Beaufort River, the familiar ICW marker system reverses: Keep red to port for the next 6.5 miles.* The ICW system returns near Parris Island Spit as you make the turn to cross Port Royal Sound towards Hilton Head Island. *(See page 86 for more information about Port Royal Sound.)*

Port Royal Sound

Jean Ribault once described Port Royal Sound, a little farther down the Beaufort River, as "one of the greatest and fairest havens ... where without danger all the ships in the world might be harbored." In the past, Port Royal Sound, reputedly the deepest natural harbor south of the Chesapeake Bay, played host to phosphate-cargo vessels from many countries.

NAVIGATION: Use Chart 11507. *Markers return to the normal ICW system of leaving reds to starboard going south after you pass flashing green buoy "27" in the Beaufort River.* Stay clear of Parris Island Spit and the shoaling in that area.

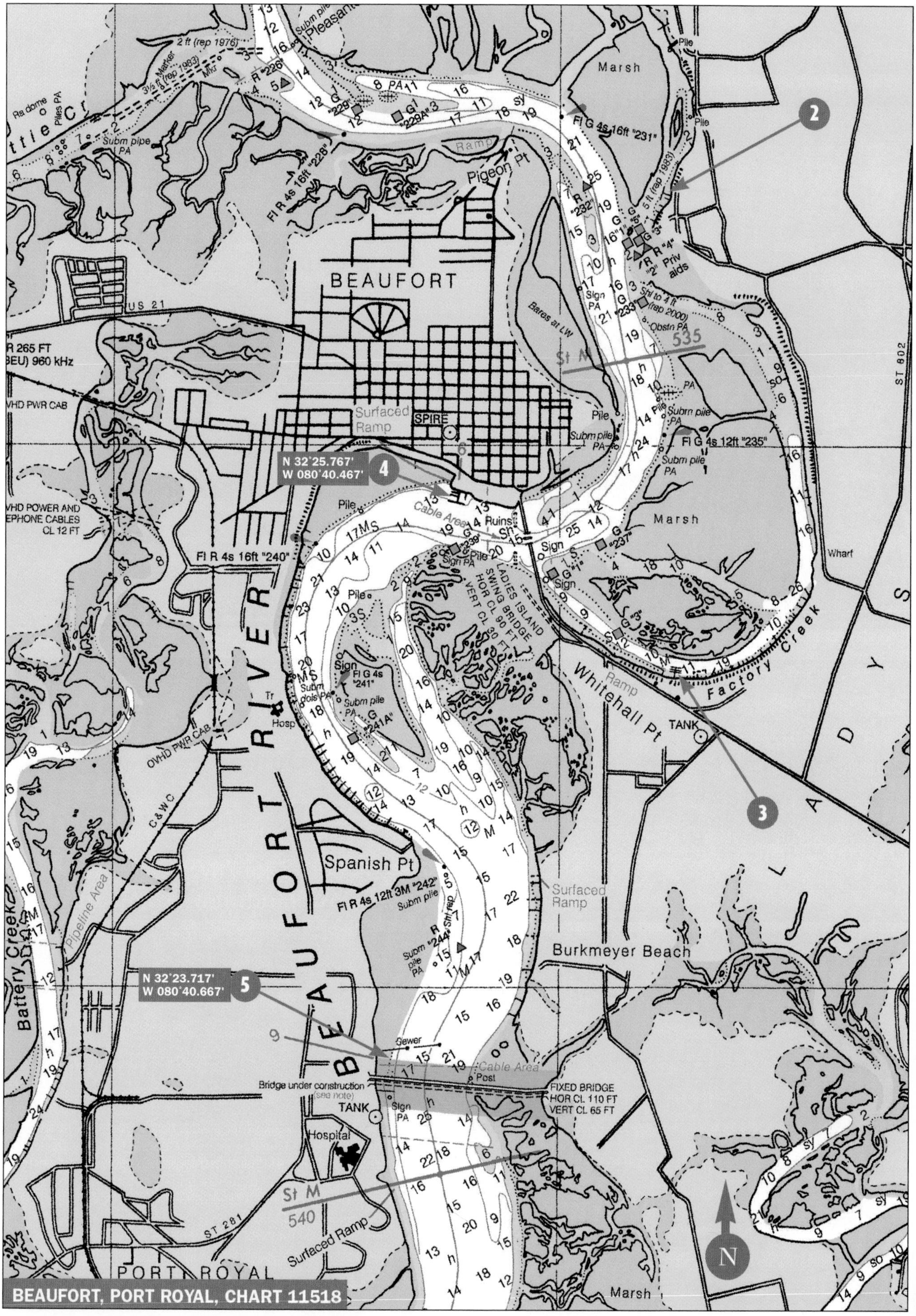

BEAUFORT
BEAUFORT RIVER
N 32°25.767'
W 080°40.467'
N 32°23.717'
W 080°40.667'
Pigeon Pt
Spanish Pt
Whitehall Pt
Burkmeyer Beach
Factory Creek
Battery Creek
PORT ROYAL
LADIES ISLAND SWING BRIDGE HOR CL 90 FT VERT CL 30 FT
FIXED BRIDGE HOR CL 110 FT VERT CL 65 FT
Bridge under construction (see note)
Fl R 4s 16ft "240"
Fl G 4s 16ft "231"
Fl G 4s 12ft "235"
Fl R 4s 16ft "228"
Fl R 4s 12ft 3M "242"
Fl G 4s "241"
Surfaced Ramp
Hospital
Marsh
St M 535
St M 540
BEAUFORT, PORT ROYAL, CHART 11518

Looking north toward Beaufort, SC. (Not to be used for navigation.) WATERWAY GUIDE PHOTOGRAPHY.

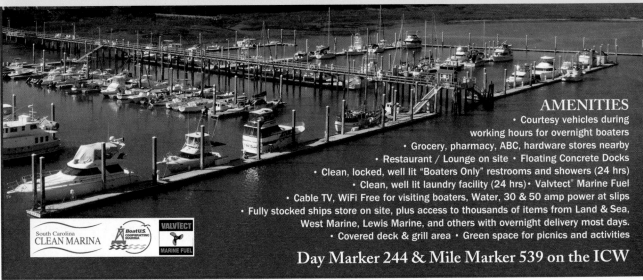

Leaving the Beaufort River channel, lay a course from ICW flashing red "246" off Parris Island Spit to red nun "2," and then to flashing green "3" just past Dolphin Head as you make the five-mile-long crossing of Port Royal Sound. It can be bumpy if wind and tide oppose. At Mile 553, you enter Skull Creek between Hilton Head Island and Pinckney Island (a wildlife refuge).

Port Royal Inlet

The Atlantic Ocean entrance to Port Royal Sound is deep and well marked for commercial ship traffic and accessible to recreational craft under most conditions. This inlet is great for an exit when heading south or an entry going north.

NAVIGATION: Use Chart 11507. When a cold front passes through the area, expect breaking ocean swells throughout the channel until rounding Bay Point. Under these conditions, the going will be tedious but still negotiable for well-found vessels. More difficult is the combination of a stiff onshore breeze against an ebb tide (driven here by local tides of 9 feet)—a situation best avoided. *(See page 86 for more information about Port Royal Sound.)*

HILTON HEAD ISLAND

Mile 553 to Mile 564

A bustling but beautiful year-round resort, Hilton Head Island, named after 17th-century explorer William Hilton, is probably the best-known of South Carolina's sea islands. As one of the largest barrier islands on the Atlantic Coast, it is amply endowed by nature and history, and offers something nearly year-round for everyone, including a choice of excellent marina resorts. The ICW amenities offered on Hilton Head range from the ultra-luxurious to the more basic. As you progress through Skull Creek, you will notice many commercial and private docks along the way.

NAVIGATION: Use Chart 11507. **Use the Savannah River Entrance Tide Table. For Skull Creek high tide, add 22 minutes; for low tide, add 26 minutes.** Some spots are No-Wake Zones around Hilton Head Island; proceed at slow speed in these areas, especially in Broad Creek. The May River, which makes off the ICW at Mile 560, offers an interesting side trip to the small town of Bluffton. Bluffton, easy to reach from Calibogue Sound, about eight miles away, appears on Chart 11516. Flood tide at Mile 560, at the head of Calibogue Sound, begins an hour and 23 minutes before the flood tide at the Savannah River entrance and ebbs 54 minutes before. The numerous ferry boats plying the waters of Calibogue Sound between Hilton Head and Daufuskie Island can leave large wakes. They usually slow down to No-Wake speed when passing recreational boats. The Twin Highway Bridges (Wilton J. Graves Bridge, 65-foot fixed vertical clearance) provide the only automobile access to and from Hilton Head Island. Just south of Last End Point (known locally as Lands End Point) under the bridges, a range leads to the best water for entering deep, wide Calibogue Sound (pronounced Cal-eh-BOE-gie).

Dockage: Markers lead past oyster beds until Mile 555, where the first of Hilton Head Island's seven major marinas—Skull Creek Marina—shows up to port. At Skull Creek Marina, slack tide is 2 hours after slack tide at the south end of Skull Creek. Watch for the shoal just in front of the marina. The No-Wake Zone around Skull Creek Marina is strictly enforced. Note that the No-Wake signs are small and hard to spot. Be courteous, and do not let your wake roll into the docks.

Hilton Head Harbor, at Mile 557, has an easily accessed fuel dock right on the ICW. Note the direction and velocity of the current carefully as you approach the marina. Independently owned Hilton Head Harbor offers dockage in an enclosed basin, health spa amenities and an on-site restaurant. Car rentals and shuttle service are available upon request. When approaching from the north, favor flashing green "19" and give red daybeacon "20," just below the entrance channel, a fair berth. A bar extends well up from the daybeacon.

In Calibogue Sound on the port side (to the east) before Jarvis Creek, a pier marks the entrance to the lock leading into Windmill Harbour Marina, which lies in one of two secure, tide-free, lock-controlled harbors along the ICW. (The other is at private Wexford Plantation, also on Hilton Head.) Their harbormaster monitors the lock and stands by on VHF Channels 14 and 16. Windmill Harbour is home to the South Carolina Yacht Club and is surrounded by a gated residential community.

Anchorage: To reach the northernmost anchorage in the Hilton Head area, bear east off the ICW at Seabrook Landing, Mile 553.5. Anchor along the east or south shore of the island that is three-tenths of a mile to the southeast of Seabrook Landing—the island shown on the NOS chart with 10- to 25-foot depths on the east side. Past the pier at Windmill Harbour, and across to the west, the May River offers good anchorage almost anywhere past the bar at the mouth of its tributary stream, Bass Creek. The southernmost anchorage is at Mile 563 in Bryan Creek, across the ICW from Harbour Town Yacht Basin. When entering, take care to clear the 2-foot bar extending from the north. Once inside, favor the west shore.

Hilton Head, SC

HILTON HEAD		Largest Vessel Accommodated	VHF Channel Monitored	Transient Berths / Total Berths	Approach / Dockside Depth (reported)	Floating Docks	Gas / Diesel	Groceries, Ice, Marine Supplies, Snacks	Repairs: Hull, Engine, Propeller	Lift (tonnage), Crane, Rail	1=110V, 2=220V, B=Both, Max Amps	Laundry, Pool, Showers	Pump-Out Station	Nearby: Grocery Store, Motel, Restaurant
		Dockage					Supplies		Services					
1. Skull Creek Marina 555 WiFi	843-681-8436	200	16/09	10/165	12/10	F	GD	I	HEP	L30	B/100	LS	P	GR
2. Hilton Head Boathouse 555.6	843-681-2628	35	69		6/6	F	G	IMS	E	L20		S		GMR
3. Hilton Head Harbor Marina 557 WiFi	**843-681-3256**	**100**	**16/12**	**15/100**	**30/20**	**F**	**GD**	**GIMS**			**B/50**	**LPS**		**GMR**
4. Windmill Harbour Marina 558.3 □ WiFi	843-681-9235	72	16/14	25/258	8/8	F	GD	GIMS	EP		B/50	LPS	P	GMR
5. Harbour Town Yacht Basin 565 □ WiFi	**843-671-2704**	**150**	**16/68**	**25/85**		**F**	**GD**	**GIMS**			**B/100**	**LPS**	**P**	**GMR**
6. Palmetto Bay Yacht Center 3.5 E of 563.8	843-686-5989	70		2/	20/20	F			HEP	L75,C	B/50			GMR
7. Palmetto Bay Marina 3.5 E of 563.8	843-785-3910	70	16	15/140	20/20	F	GD	GIMS	HEP	L75	B/50	LS	P	GMR
8. Wexford Plantation-Private Harbour	843-686-8813	70	14/14		7/7						B/50			G
9. Broad Creek Marina 4.5 E of 563.8 □ WiFi	**843-681-3625**	**80**	**16**	**/52**	**23/23**	**F**	**GD**	**GIMS**	**HEP**	**L20**	**B/50**	**LS**	**P**	**R**
10. Shelter Cove Marina 5.8 E of 563.8 □ WiFi	**843-842-7001**	**140**	**16/71**	**20/175**	**9/9**	**F**	**GD**	**GIMS**			**B/100**	**LS**	**P**	**GMR**

Corresponding chart(s) not to be used for navigation. □ Internet Access WiFi Wireless Internet Access

GOIN' ASHORE: **HILTON HEAD, SC**

Most people know Hilton Head Island for its a red and white striped lighthouse and fine golf courses, but it is also a great family getaway with long beaches, and walking and bicycling trails through its well-preserved natural areas. Dozens of restaurants cater to every taste. The island has more than its share of celebrities in residence, so you never know when you will be sharing the dining room with a well-known author, musician or athlete.

History: English Navy Capt. William Hilton laid claim to the island for his homeland in 1663. His "discovery" belied the fact that the Spanish had been here as early as 1526. Even after its discovery, Hilton Head remained rural, with only 25 families living on the island in 1766. Between the Revolutionary War and the Civil War, plantations prospered, growing indigo, Sea Island cotton and sugar, but most owners kept town homes in Charleston, Savannah and Beaufort.

Following its stint as the headquarters of the South Atlantic Blockading Squadron for the Union forces, the island sank back into time, inhabited only by former slaves who were farmers, fishermen and basket weavers. By the late 1800s, Northerners returned, this time acquiring land for hunting. As late as 1931, the only access was by water. Twenty-five years later, electricity, telephone and bridge service to Hilton Head enabled the beginning of extensive real estate development. This began with the construction of Sea Pines Plantation by Charles Fraser on the lower third of the island, which he purchased from his father's timber company. The growth has continued, mostly with the addition of vacation homes and golf courses.

Fortunately, Hilton Head incorporated as a town in 1983, passing strict zoning laws limiting signage and building materials so that the image of the island is preserved. Even the Walmart is tastefully hidden behind lush foliage and a discreet sign, as are the fast-food chains that have begun to proliferate. The 12-mile stretch of ocean beach is still beautiful, with houses set well back behind the dunes.

Cultural references: In 2005, Sea Pines Resort was showcased in a major motion picture, starring Gregg Russell and Lea Thompson, titled "Come Away Home." Best-selling author Patricia Cornwell lives here, as do rocker John Mellencamp, hockey player Mark Messier and tennis pro Stan Smith.

Activities: Wildlife sanctuaries ensure that forest and marshland with abundant wildlife are untouched. Access is carefully controlled, but winding nature paths and catwalks for walking and biking allow you to explore. You can also take museum-sponsored beach walks, and the local Audubon Society organizes and leads regular bird walks.

Lawton Stables at the Sea Pines Resort offers trail rides and pony rides and has a small animal farm. Call 843-671-2586 for hours and directions. The Coastal Discovery Museum (100 William Hilton Parkway) offers a wide range of activities including guided tours (walking and by boat or kayak) of the local area, led by museum curators and trained volunteers who teach about the ecology and history of the region. The Sea Island Classroom teaches children and adults about the biodiversity of nature with presentations and displays. A butterfly garden and the Museum Store round out the offerings. The visitors center is located in the same building. The Sandbox, an interactive children's museum, has hands-on exhibits, including sailing away on Capt. Hilton's ship and a loggerhead sand castle.

Special Events: The Verizon Heritage PGA Tournament is played every April after the Masters.

Shopping: Shopping centers, more than 250 restaurants, and golf courses have proliferated on the island. Perhaps the most well-known area is Harbour Town Yacht Basin, with its signature red and white striped lighthouse (and yes, you can climb to the top for $1). The marina has a shopping center with specialty shops (book shops, clothing, gift and nautical shops) and restaurants, including a grocery and deli. A larger supermarket is nearby, as well as golf, tennis, a pool and, of course, the ocean. It offers a superb view of

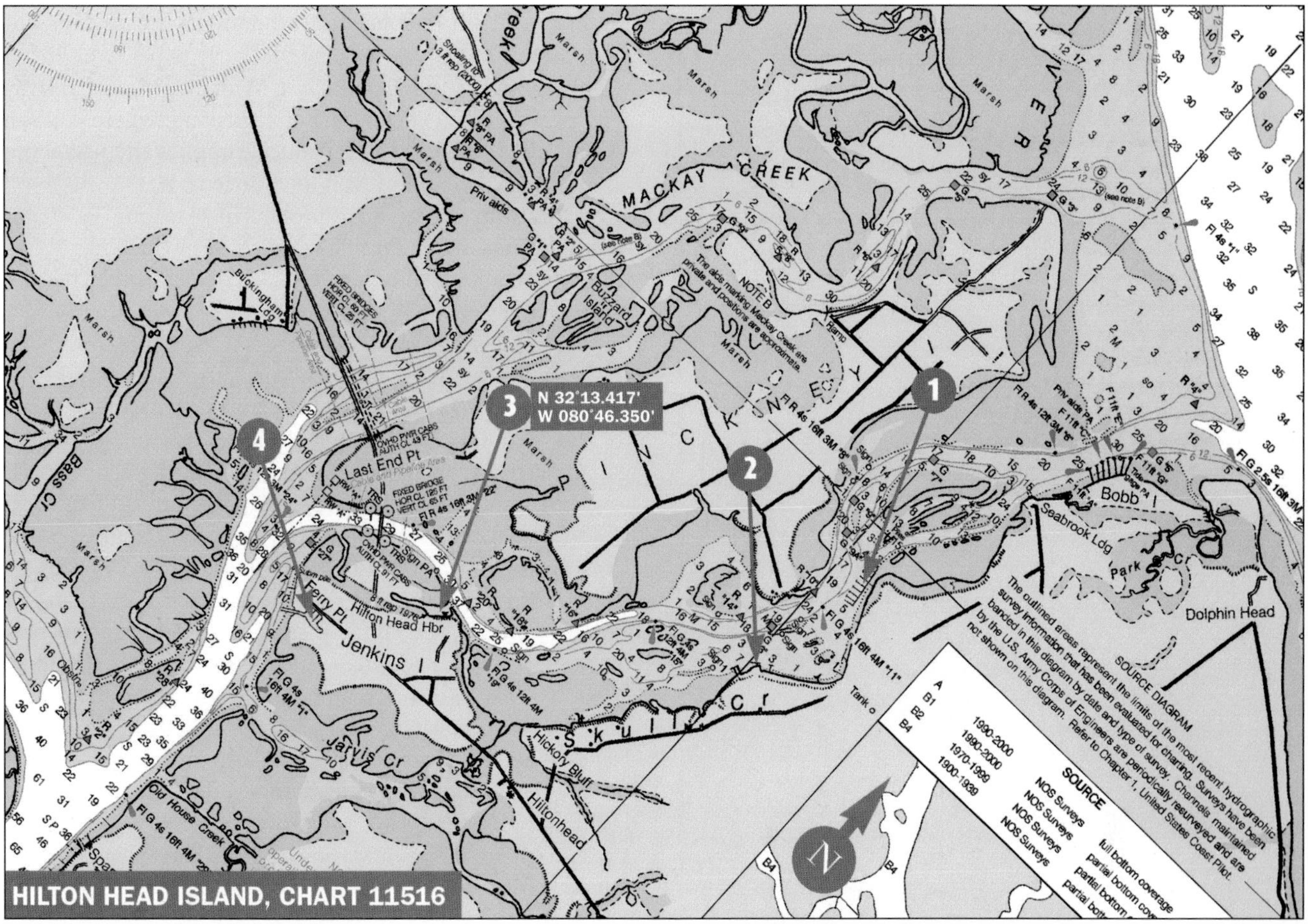

HILTON HEAD ISLAND, CHART 11516

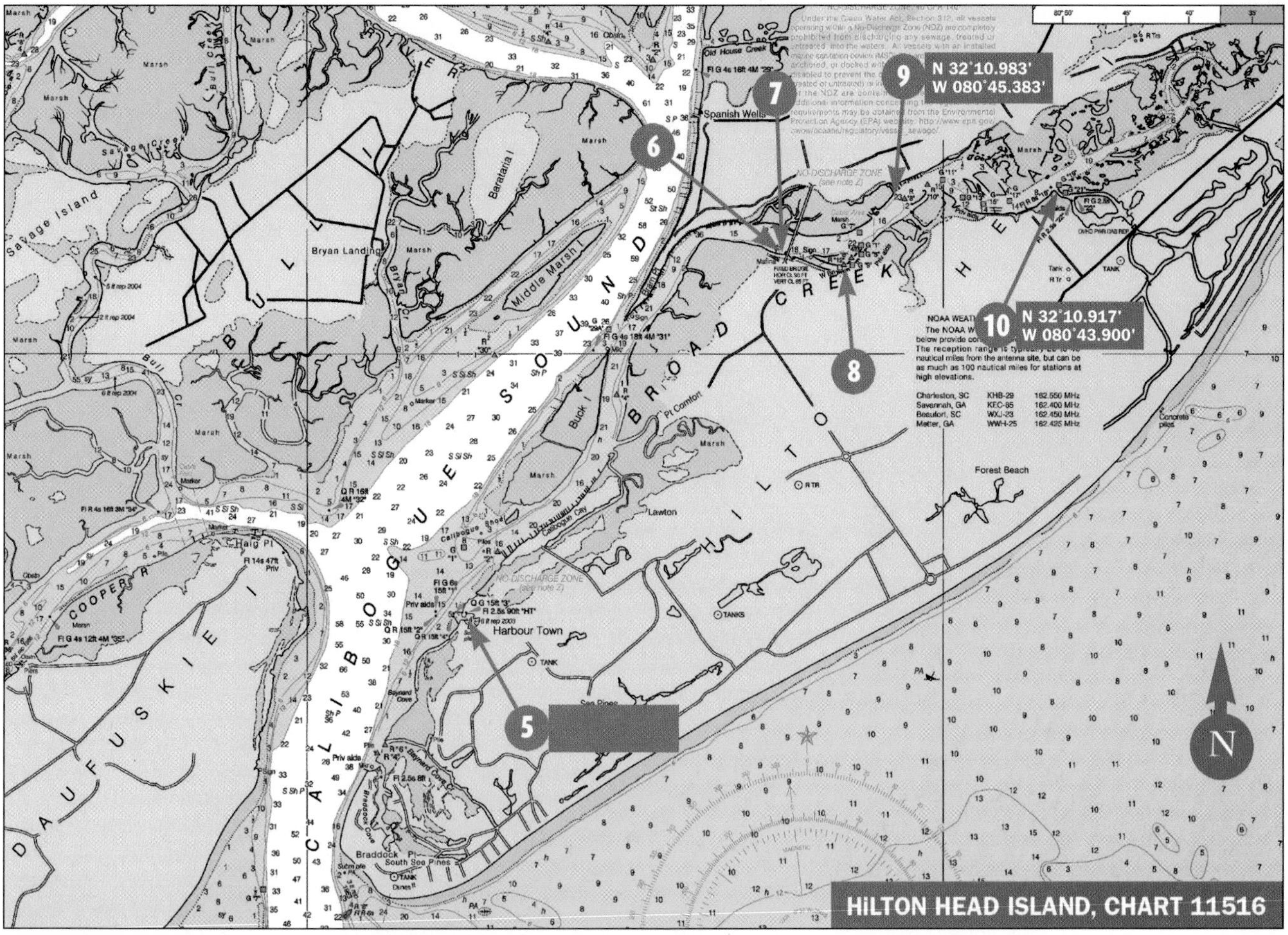

HILTON HEAD ISLAND, CHART 11516

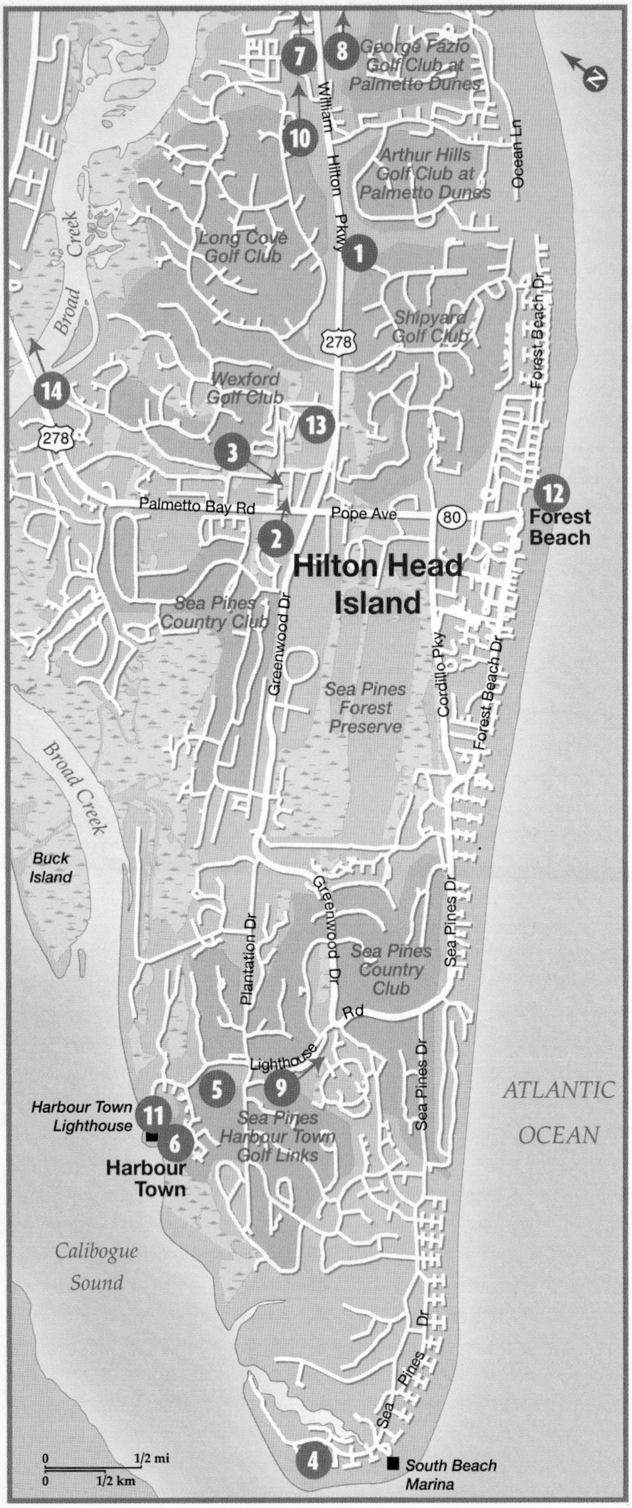

Reference the marina listing tables to see all the marinas in the area.

DINING

1 211 Park Wine Bar & Bistro
2 Red Fish
3 Signe's Heaven Bound Bakery & Cafe
4 Salty Dog Café
5 Truffles Café
6 Crazy Crab
7 Santa Fe Cafe
8 Sunset Grille

RECREATION

9 Lawton Stables
10 Coastal Discovery Museum

SHOPPING/DINING

11 Harbour Town Yacht Basin
12 Coligny Plaza
13 The Village Shoppes at Wexford

the famous 18th hole at the Harbour Town Golf Links. It is an interesting course to play but fairly expensive. Bigger shopping areas are located along William Hilton Parkway (Highway 278), the main drag on the island, where you can find all the "big-box" stores, nautical supplies and just about anything you even think you might need.

Restaurants: The favorite spot in Harbour Town for dining is The Crazy Crab (843-363-2722), which has everything from fabulous burgers to good fried shrimp. The staff at the Harbour Town Marina has eaten lunch there every day for the last 25 years. Also recommended, just outside the Sea Pines gates, is 211 Park Wine Bar & Bistro (211 Park Place, 843-686-5212), which has an extensive wine bar. The top choice might be the tuna appetizer, a tenderloin with garlic mashed potatoes and Southern collard greens, finishing with tiramisu. Santa Fe Café (mid-island 807 William Hilton Parkway, 843-785-3838) is great for southwestern food. An unexpected find is the Sunset Grille (43 Jenkins Island Road, 843-689-6744) in the Outdoor Resort, an RV/camper facility. The smoked seafood appetizer is recommended. Red Fish (8 Archer Rd., 843-686-3388) utilizes fresh fish, natural or free-range meats and vegetables from their own or other local gardens to create innovative meals. Nearby, Signe's Heaven Bound Bakery and Cafe has been serving meals and sweets for visitors and residents of Hilton Head for almost 40 years (93 Arrow Road, 843-785-9118). Located in South Beach Marina Village, The Salty Dog Café offers waterfront dining for lunch and dinner (232 S. Sea Pines Dr., 843-363-2198). Truffles Café offers creative twists on old favorites (Sea Pines Center, 843-671-6136).

ADDITIONAL RESOURCES

- HILTON HEAD ISLAND-BLUFFTON CHAMBER OF COMMERCE: 800-523-3373, www.hiltonheadisland.org
- HILTON HEAD VISITORS GUIDE: www.hiltonhead.com
- COASTAL DISCOVERY MUSEUM: 843-689-6767 www.coastaldiscovery.org

NEARBY GOLF COURSES
Sea Pines Resort, 32 Greenwood Drive, Hilton Head Island, SC 29926, 843-842-8484
www.seapines.com/golf

NEARBY MEDICAL FACILITIES
Hilton Head Medical Center, 25 Hospital Center Blvd., Hilton Head Island, SC 29926, 843-681-6122

ATTRACTIONS

14 Broad Creek Marina Land & Water Adventures

Looking north over Broad Creek. (Not to be used for navigation.) Photo courtesy of Mike Kucera.

Calibogue Sound Area

NAVIGATION: Use Chart 11507. Just opposite the spot where the ICW leaves Calibogue Sound for the Cooper River (Mile 565) is Broad Creek. Green daybeacon "29A," to the north of Buck Island, is not shown on older charts but is on the most recent one dated December 2010. Do not attempt to use Broad Creek's secondary entrance here without local knowledge: The break between Bram Point and Buck Island is too tricky for strangers. Instead, run down to green daybeacon "1" at the proper entrance to Broad Creek. Give the marker a rather wide berth at low tide and enter between it and red daybeacon "2" on the opposite side. The shoal extends northeast of green daybeacon "1," so use caution. Once you are inside, Broad Creek runs deep to its banks all the way to the marinas well upstream. Use Charts 11507 and 11516, with detailed coverage of the creek's markers, to reach these facilities. Remember, this is a No-Wake Zone that is strictly enforced. Additionally, Broad Creek is a designated No-Discharge Zone. No onboard sewage, even that which has been treated, may be pumped overboard here. Y-valves and seacocks for overboard discharge must be wire-tied shut; simply closing them will not do. Fines will be levied if you are boarded and inspected, which can happen in this area.

Many boats use the ocean entrance to Calibogue Sound in fair weather and seas. It is a shortcut to reach the ICW from the ocean and is much shorter than the Savannah River approach. The markers, however, are widely spaced and sometimes difficult to locate. It is approached from the Jones Island Range area of Tybee Roads. Note that if using this route to the Tybee Roads channel, the shoal to the east of quick flashing green buoy "3" has built to the west to within about 200 feet of that buoy. ***(See page 87 for more information about Calibogue Sound.)***

Dockage: The first marina you will encounter as you head up Broad Creek is Palmetto Bay Marina, home of the private Yacht Club of Hilton Head. The Cross-Island Expressway Bridge (65-foot fixed vertical clearance) crosses Broad Creek just east of Palmetto Bay Marina. Vessels with mast heights greater than 65 feet are no longer able to go up Broad Creek beyond the bridge except by playing the tides. Palmetto Bay Marina is the last accessible marina for these vessels.

Broad Creek Marina, on the port side, recently underwent a multi-million dollar renovation. They welcome transients and offer pump-out service, fuel, laundry and showers. They also have an on-site restaurant. At press time, plans were in the works for Broad Creek Marina Land & Water Adventures to include a rope course, climbing wall and zip-line tour.

Beyond the bridge, Shelter Cove Marina is the largest marina on the Island. This luxury marina is part of the 2,000-acre Palmetto Dunes Oceanfront Resort, stretching from Broad Creek to the ocean. Unique shops, art galleries and restaurants line the protected marina basin. The resort offers three world-class golf courses, tennis and an 11-mile inland salt water lagoon system for kayaking. Its central location offers ready access to all of Hilton Head Island's attractions. Here, you will find courteous and professional service. This is a popular spot for cruisers who leave their boats for extended periods. Handsome houses, many with their own docks, line the creek; oyster beds line the banks; crab pot markers dot the marsh flats; and fishing drops are at the entrance to tidal streams along the way. On the starboard side of Broad Creek, above Palmetto Bay Marina, is the other Hilton Head facility with its own dock. This marina is for private use of the residents of Wexford Plantation, members of its club or invited guests. The facilities are not open to the public.

Perhaps one of the best-known features along this stretch of the ICW is the red and white striped 90-foot-tall lighthouse, east of Mile 564 and south of the entrance to Broad Creek. This marks Harbour Town Yacht Basin, entrance to the original residential development on Hilton Head Island, Sea Pines Plantation. Enter between two jetties—the one to port is an observation pier—into Harbour Town's circular basin, with its floating concrete docks. A 270-foot-long floating face dock across from the fuel dock at the marina's entrance offers additional linear footage. This is a full-service marina with many amenities. Condominiums, shops, restaurants and the Inn at Harbour Town rim the circular basin. The Verizon Heritage PGA Golf Tournament is played here each April on the Harbour Town Links, the best of four golf courses within the resort. Make reservations at the marina well in advance for this event.

Anchorage: At the head of Broad Creek, you can anchor in the channel near green daybeacon "19." Holding is good here, with 10-foot depths in the middle of the creek. Access to Hilton Head is easy. It is possible to anchor outside the channel in Broad Creek, just off Buck Island and above the first bend, before Palmetto Bay Marina, as well as off the marina itself. You may want to set two anchors because the area outside the channel is narrow and the current reverses strongly. The holding in Broad Creek is excellent in thick mud.

CALIBOGUE SOUND TO SAVANNAH RIVER

Mile 565 to Mile 576

Heading south on the ICW, Daufuskie Island awaits at the confluence of Calibogue Sound and the Cooper River. (The ICW continues to run past Daufuskie Island as the channel goes south along the Cooper River, Ramshorn Creek and the New River.) Daufuskie Island has undergone big changes in recent years. The old lighthouse on Haig Point, a landmark for spotting the lighted buoy at the entrance to the Cooper River, serves as the centerpiece of a major land-based development.

Looking northeast over Skull Creek and the ICW.
(Not to be used for navigation.) Photo courtesy of Mike Kucera.

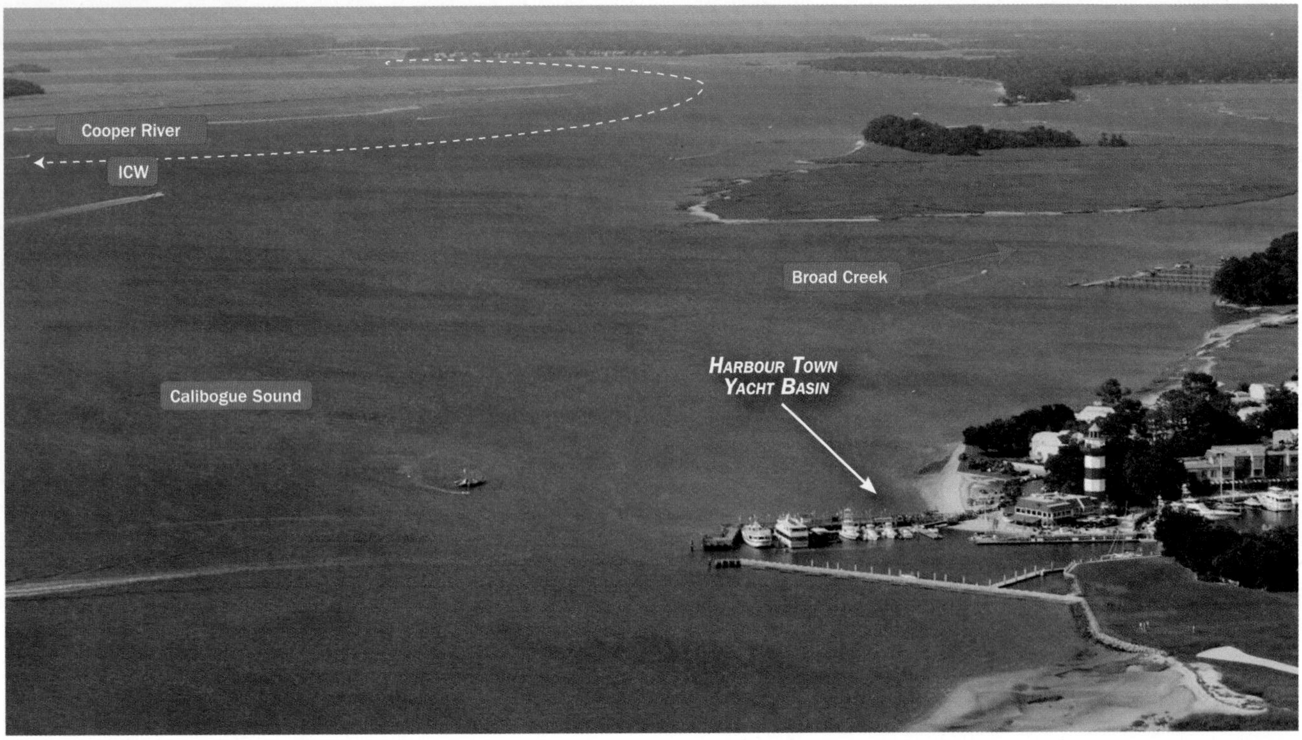

Looking north over Calibogue and Port Royal Sound. (Not to be used for navigation.) Photo courtesy of Mike Kucera.

The name Daufuskie originated from the early settlers identifying their island as "Da Fus Key" ("the first key"). Author Pat Conroy chronicled his experience as a schoolteacher on the island in his book "The River is Wide." With no bridge linking the island to the mainland, the small native population (direct descendants of slaves brought from Africa) lived an isolated life, having little contact with the outside world. The movie based on the book ("Conrack") was filmed on St. Simons Island.

Until 2009, there had been no funding for the previous five years for maintenance dredging of the ICW south of Port Royal Sound, SC to Cumberland Sound, GA above the submarine base at Kings Bay, and there continues to be very little money for dredging. Consequently, some areas of lower South Carolina and most of Georgia become shallower with each passing year. Fields Cut in South Carolina is the first of these areas you will encounter. The tidal range here is around 8 or 9 feet, so most boats will have no trouble at mid- to high tide. It is important to stay in the channel, follow the magenta line and give markers a wide berth.

Dockage: Inspired by Hilton Head Island's development, Daufuskie Island continues to undergo extensive development of its own, with resorts and residential areas springing up each year. There is no vehicular access to Daufuskie Island. Along the Cooper River side of the island, Freeport Marina has some transient dockage. The former Melrose Landing Marina was still not operational at press time in 2011.

⚠ THE FOLLOWING AREA REQUIRES SPECIAL ATTENTION DUE TO SHOALING OR CHANGES TO THE CHANNEL

RAMSHORN CREEK AND SOUTH

NAVIGATION:

Use Chart 11507. When passing Daufuskie Landing on the ICW, follow the dredged channel of narrow Ramshorn Creek into the New River, favoring the east (port) side of the channel at flashing green "39" (Mile 570). Extensive shoaling has been reported in the vicinity of Ramshorn Creek flashing red daybeacon "40A." Reports of shoaling in this area are confirmed by the most recent U.S. Army Corps of Engineers (USACE) survey in 2010, which reports 6 feet to be the centerline depth in the channel at mean low water. Run slowly to flatten your wake and pass this area at half-tide or on a rising tide. This area is congested and strictly policed. Over the years, the wakes of passing vessels have damaged locally berthed craft at the floating dock and boat ramp at Daufuskie Landing. There are several new floating docks north of the landing, apparently for residential development. Along this stretch, the tidal current reverses every two or three miles.

Going south through Walls Cut and entering the Wright River (Mile 572.5), follow the magenta line carefully past flashing red "42" and green daybeacon "43." The mid-channel depth was 9 feet in the 2010 survey.

The chronic shoaling in Fields Cut has been alleviated, for now. The USACE survey in 2010 reported 14 feet to be the depth at mean low water along the centerline of Fields Cut. Fields Cut was dredged in January 2010. Be warned, however, that if you continue south on the ICW, after crossing the Savannah River, Elba Cut had

Savannah River, GA

SAVANNAH, 8 W OF ICW 576		Largest Vessel Accommodated	VHF Channel Monitored	Transient Berths / Total Berths	Approach / Dockside Depth (reported)	Floating Docks	Gas / Diesel	Groceries, Ice, Marine Supplies, Snacks	Repairs: Hull, Engine, Propeller	Lift (tonnage), Crane, Rail	1=110V, 2=220V, B=Both, Max Amps	Laundry, Pool, Showers	Pump-Out Station	Nearby: Grocery Store, Motel, Restaurant
		Dockage					Supplies		Services					
1. Westin Savannah Harbor Golf Resort & Spa ☐ WiFi	912-201-2000	400		25	27/16	F		IS	Championship Golf		B/200+	LPS		GMR
2. River Street Market Place Dock ☐ WiFi	**912-398-6038**	**190**			**24/14**	**F**		**IS**			**B/100**			**GMR**
3. River Street LLC ☐	**912-232-4252**	**200**			**27/14**	**F**					**B/100**			**GMR**
4. Hyatt Regency Savannah ☐ WiFi	912-721-4654	300			35/27	F					B/100	PS		GMR

Corresponding chart(s) not to be used for navigation. ☐ Internet Access WiFi Wireless Internet Access

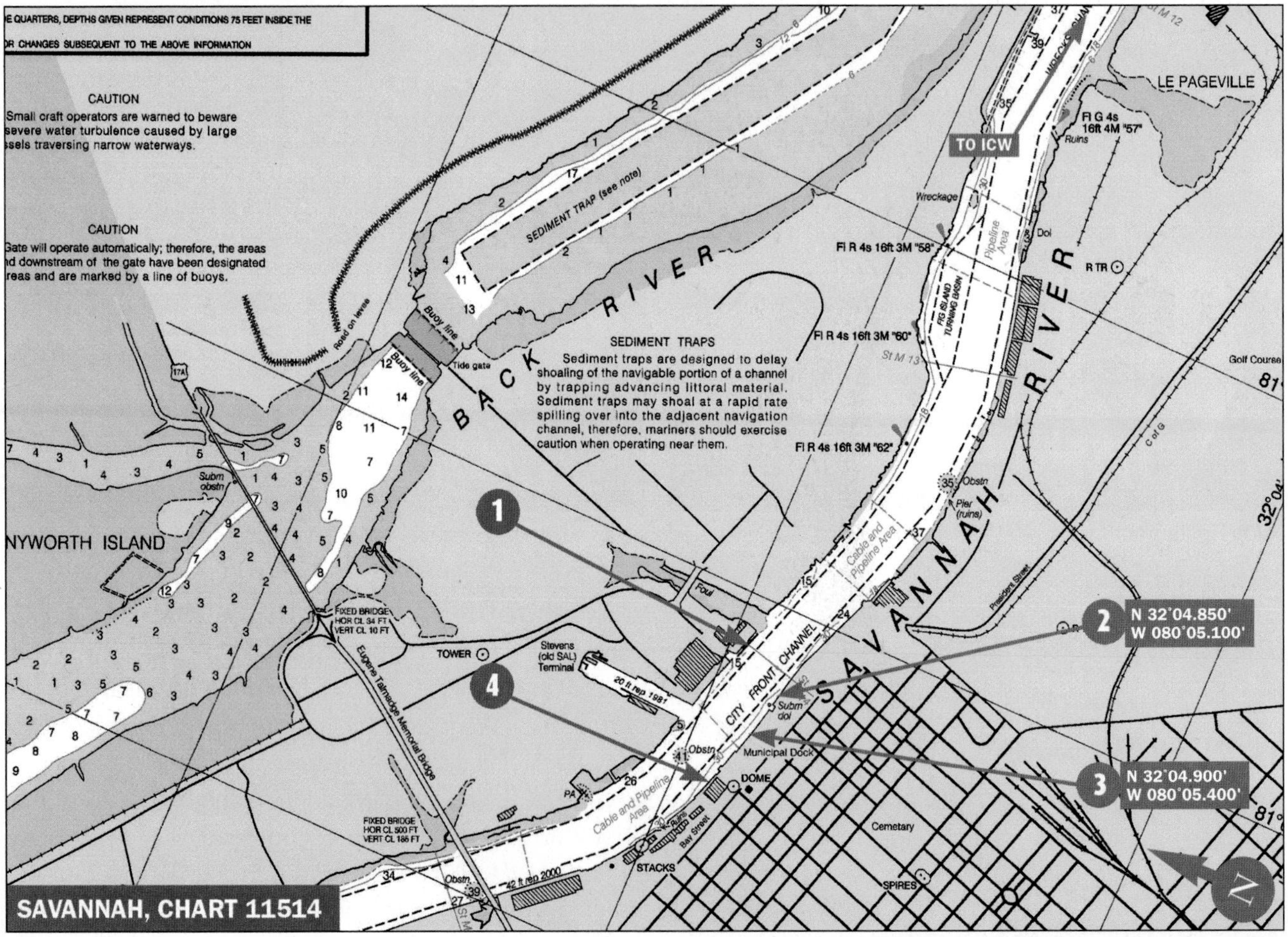

5 feet mid-channel at mean low water. According to the February 2010 survey, 10-foot depths were found in the green side of the channel.

Plan on playing the tides when passing through these channels to avoid grounding. Check our website, www.waterwayguide.com, for the latest updates.

END SPECIAL CAUTION AREA.

Anchorage: Bull Creek, which enters the ICW from the Cooper River just past Mile 565, is a favorite anchorage and rafting site for local boats and ICW travelers alike. Just inside the entrance is good holding in lots of water, but currents are strong, and there is no place to go ashore. This is another anchorage favored by shrimp boats and slow-moving boats traveling between Beaufort and Savannah, GA. The best spot to anchor on Bull Creek is past the little creek to the west because the shrimp boats use the lower part of Bull Creek.

In calm weather, cruisers often anchor just south of the ICW in the Wright River at Mile 572.2. There is also a good anchorage in the New River, just below Ramshorn Creek (Mile 570). Enter from the south side of the river, watch your depth gauge and avoid the shallow water to the northwest. Anchoring in the 10- to 11-foot area offers excellent holding.

Looking southeast over Savannah, GA. (Not to be used for navigation.) WATERWAY GUIDE PHOTOGRAPHY.

South to Georgia

Continuing south on the ICW, you will cross into Georgia as the route winds across swift rivers and choppy sounds. From here until the sheltered waters of Florida, pay close attention to currents and depths, as well as markers and ranges.

Study your charts before beginning this passage—the next 140 miles down the ICW are visually interesting and physically demanding. You will use your GPS, compass, depth sounder and binoculars as you wind along serpentine rivers and cross open sounds that can be choppy when the wind kicks up. The route winds past Georgia's barrier islands and then becomes an entirely different kind of ICW in Florida.

Leaving South Carolina, you pass through several shallow land cuts before reaching the Savannah River at the end of Fields Cut. Here, you have a choice of continuing on the ICW through the Elba Island Cut, turning east to head out the Savannah River to Tybee Roads and out to sea, or heading west up the river to the beautiful city of Savannah, GA.

The tidal range here is about 8 or 9 feet, so most boats will have no trouble at mid- to high tide. In this area, it is important to stay in the channel, follow the charted magenta ICW line (except where noted in the text), make use of the numerous navigational ranges, and give markers, especially at turns in natural rivers, a wide berth. There is some funding allocated to Georgia for dredging in the FY 2012 budget. Waterway Guide posts updated information on surveys by the Savannah District U.S. Army Corps of Engineers (USACE) on our website (www.waterwayguide.com), or you can access them directly at www.sas.usace.army.mil/navrprts.htm. Conditions change, so check for the latest in-formation before you go. Plan ahead in timing your arrival at the known trouble spots. If it is low tide when you arrive, drop the hook for a while to wait for higher water—it doesn't take long for the tide to come up a foot or two. "Mid-tide and rising" is always preferable in these areas. Remember that strong winds and the lunar cycle affect tidal range.

SAVANNAH

Savannah is about eight miles up the Savannah River from where the river crosses the ICW at Mile 576. Dockage is available on the city waterfront, but strong currents, a 9-foot tide and heavy commercial traffic sometimes make docking along the city bulkhead difficult. The city is a short trip from Thunderbolt (Mile 583) or Isle of Hope (Mile 590), both with extensive boating facilities, described below. (Actually, many recreational boaters who wish to visit Savannah opt to bus or taxi in from either Thunderbolt or Isle of Hope.)

Currents are swift on the Savannah River, but floating docks at the various marinas run parallel to shore and eliminate the problem of the river's 9-foot tidal range. Those with low-powered boats should check the tide tables and plan arrivals and departures accordingly.

Dockage: The River Street Marina has 200 feet of docks on the city side of the river. River Street Market Place Dock also offers floating dockage with direct access to downtown. These marinas are located in the heart of Savannah's historic area. From here, you can step off of your boat and enjoy the many fine restaurants and shops just across the street. These docks can accommodate vessels up to 250 feet and provide ample electrical service and wireless Internet access.

The riverfront Hyatt Regency Hotel in Savannah has docks for transient boats and is also located in historic downtown. Included with your dockage are the amenities of the Hyatt: pool and shower facilities, fitness center, wireless Internet and even dockside room service. They can accommodate deep draft vessels and those up to 300 feet in length. Here again, you are just steps away from all that historic downtown Savannah has to offer.

Another overnight option is the Westin Savannah Harbor Resort, on Hutchinson Island, directly across from River Street. Water ferry service is available to reach the other side of the harbor.

GOIN' ASHORE: SAVANNAH, GA

Savannah sits serenely on a bluff 40 feet above the banks of the Savannah River, where General James Oglethorpe and 120 passengers landed in 1733 to found Britain's last American colony. That colonial heritage is well preserved, and synchronizes nicely (if a bit counterintuitively) with Savannah's youthful vibe. Southern hospitality manifests itself in a desire to entertain, welcoming visitors to dine and drink, enjoy carriage or riverboat tours and explore spooky cemeteries.

History: Oglethorpe laid out the city in a series of 24 squares, 21 of which remain as lovely parks surrounded by a mix of architectural styles, including Federal, Georgian, Victorian and Italianate. At the time of the original charter, religious freedom was guaranteed, but lawyers, rum and slavery were forbidden. In the 1950s, a group of women founded the Historic Savannah Foundation, which has worked to restore many of the old buildings. At two square miles, the Historic District is the largest urban National Landmark, with more than 1,000 architecturally or historically significant structures restored and in use.

Cotton was the major source of income in the area, especially after the cotton gin was invented on a plantation outside the city. The Savannah Cotton Exchange, which still exists, is said to have set the world's cotton prices, and Savannah rivaled Charleston as a commercial port. Today, tourism plays a major role in the economy, although the port is still a vital part.

Culture and cultural references: In February, the Savannah Black Heritage Festival takes place, as well as the Book Festival, and October is active with the Savannah Jazz Festival and the Savannah Film Festival, but there is some sort of festival every month.

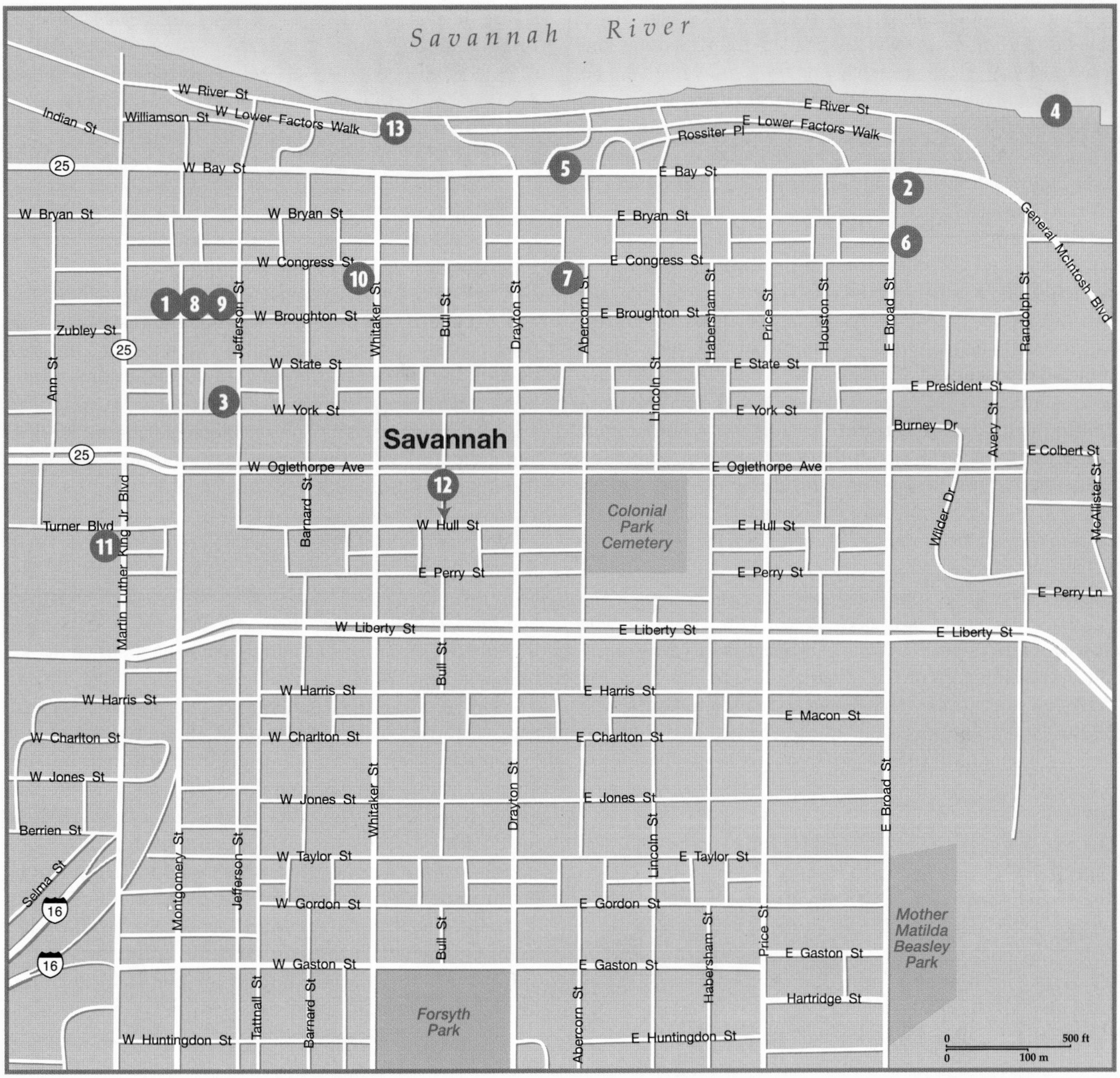

Reference the marina listing tables to see all the marinas in the area.

ART/DINING/SHOPPING

1 City Market Art Center

ATTRACTIONS

2 Herb House

3 Telfair Academy of Arts and Sciences

4 The Waving Girl

5 The Savannah Cotton Exchange

6 1754 Pirate's House

7 Olde Pink House Restaurant

DINING

5 The Savannah Cotton Exchange

6 1754 Pirate's House

7 Olde Pink House Restaurant

8 Vinnie Van Go-Go's

9 Tapas by Anna

10 Paula Deen's Lady & Sons

INFORMATION

11 Visitors Center/ Railroad Museum

POINTS OF INTEREST

12 Forrest Gump Bench

SHOPPING/DINING

13 Factor's Walk

ADDITIONAL RESOURCES

- SAVANNAH CONVENTION AND VISITORS BUREAU: 877-SAVANNAH, www.savannahvisit.com
- VISIT SAVANNAH: www.savannah.com
- OLD SAVANNAH TOURS: 800-517-9007 www.oldsavannahtours.com
- CHATHAM AREA TRANSIT: 912-233-5767 catchacat.org/content

NEARBY GOLF COURSES

Club at Savannah Harbor, #2 Resort Drive, Savannah, GA 31421, 912-201-2400 www.theclubatsavannahharbor.net

NEARBY MEDICAL FACILITIES

Candler Hospital, 5353 Reynolds St., Savannah, GA 31405, 912-819-6000

Savannah is the birthplace of such diverse characters as Juliette Gordon Low, who founded the Girl Scouts, and Johnny Mercer, singer and songwriter best known for "Moon River" among other great hits. The Mercer House, which was featured in the movie "Midnight in the Garden of Good and Evil," was built by Mercer's great-grandfather in the 1860s. Other movies filmed here include "Forrest Gump" and "The Legend of Bagger Vance."

Attractions: Walking and driving tours, carriage tours, taped tours and guided bus tours—highlighting the historic homes built around Savannah's squares—are all available. A good way to explore the city is Oglethorpe Trolley Tours, which offers a 90-minute outing with narration and also allows you to hop on and off until 5:30 p.m. If you wander on your own, be sure to visit the 1754 Pirate's House mentioned in "Treasure Island," now a restaurant (20 E. Broad St.); the site of Georgia's first bank, now the Olde Pink House Restaurant, built in 1789 (23 Abercorn St.); and the oldest building in Georgia, the Herb House, built in 1734. One of the south's first public museums, The Telfair Academy of Arts and Sciences, was built as a mansion in 1812 (121 Barnard St.).

Two young ladies have become icons for Savannah. The Waving Girl, a statue of Florence Martus, waves a handkerchief at passing ships on the Savannah River in hopes that her departed sailor-lover would be on one of them. During the 1996 Olympics, a bronze Olympic torch joined her in honor of Savannah hosting the sailing competitions. The other is The Bird Girl statue, made famous on the cover of John Berendt's novel "Midnight in the Garden of Good and Evil." After its publication, the 1938 bronze sculpture was removed from the Bonaventure Cemetery and is now on display at the Telfair Museum.

Special Events: Savannah's more well-known party is the St. Patrick's Day Celebration, said to be the second largest in the country. Throngs of revelers gather on historic River Street to sample fresh seafood, drink green beer and watch the parade.

Shopping: Don't miss Factor's Walk, blocks of four- and five-story brick warehouses along River Street, built hard against the bluff but rising to connect with Bay Street by iron and wooden bridges. The lower levels are now filled with shops, restaurants, boutiques, inns and art galleries, while street musicians, acrobats and mimes play along the river walkway. On a foggy evening, you can just picture drunken sailors spilling out of tavern doors and being shanghaied!

The City Market (Jefferson and West St. Julian) has gone through several renditions, the first in 1755, when it was a hub of commercial and social activity, with fishermen and farmers selling fresh fish and produce, farriers shoeing horses and barbers trimming hair. The first two market buildings burned down, and two were torn down, the last in 1954. Today, it is a revitalized area with a series of courtyards featuring art, entertainment, shopping and dining. Private art galleries abound, or one can visit the City Market Art Center. Various entertainers hold forth in the courtyards, while the surrounding shops offer everything from handmade cigars to gourmet gifts and souvenirs. Provisioning and marine supplies are farther from the waterfront and require a taxi or rental car. Bus service, called Catch A Cat, is provided by the Chatham Area Transit and includes a line to the Savannah/Hilton Head International Airport.

Restaurants: Dining options include "the best pizza in Savannah" from Vinnie Van Go-Go's (317 W. Bryan St., 912-233-6394), tapas with an Italian twist from Tapas by Anna (314 W. Saint Julian St., 912-236-2066), which offers fresh-made gelato, bistro food and more. For fine dining, Elizabeth on 37th (105 E. 37th St., 912-236-5547) gets rave reviews for its coastal cuisine served in an elegant 1900 mansion. The restaurant is known for fresh local ingredients, so try the black-eyed pea cake with greens and a curry sauce, smothered chicken or salmon in a mustard glaze. Save room for the Savannah cream cake or a pecan-and-almond tart. Another stalwart on the dining scene is Paula Deen's Lady & Sons (102 W. Congress St., 912-233-2600) for scrumptious Southern-style fried chicken, lump crab cakes, shrimp and grits, or go whole hog with the Southern buffet.

Savannah via the Atlantic Ocean and Tybee Roads

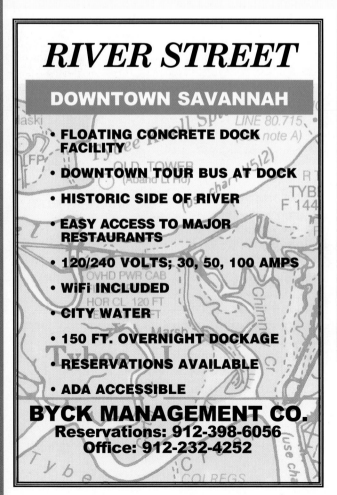

Coming down the Atlantic Coast on the outside run, you have access to the ICW and the Savannah River via the inlet at Tybee Roads. (Slower boats bound for the Savannah River on this route should try to enter

Amenities, Convenience, Luxury:

Delegal Creek Marina

Located just off the Intracoastal Waterway, Delegal Creek Marina offers a serene haven for your watercraft and yourself. It also provides complete fuel services, shower and laundry facilities and free Wi-Fi. To solidify the convenience, the marina offers a courtesy golf cart and a temporary membership card which will grant you access to four unique clubhouses along with other amenities such as six championship golf courses and a 48,000 square foot fitness and wellness center.

Just outside the community's gates lies The Village, a golf cart accessible shopping center, which features a supermarket, a restaurant, banks, a gas station, dental office, liquor store, hair salon and more.

For slip reservations or information call the dockmaster at (912) 598-0023. Hailing: VHF Ch. 16
Working Channel: VHF Ch. 68. Find us on waterwayguide.com under marina close up.

The Landings Company
One Landings Way North, Savannah, GA 31411 | (800) 841-7011/(912) 598-0500 | info@TheLandings.com | www.TheLandings.com

Tybee Island, GA

TYBEE ISLAND		Largest Vessel Accommodated	VHF Channel Monitored	Transient Berths / Total Berths	Approach / Dockside Depth (reported)	Floating Docks	Gas / Diesel	Groceries, Ice, Marine Supplies, Snacks	Repairs: Hull, Engine, Propeller	Lift (tonnage), Crane, Rail	1=110V, 2=220V, B=Both, Max Amps	Laundry, Pool, Showers	Pump-Out Station	Nearby: Grocery Store, Motel, Restaurant
		Dockage					Supplies		Services					
1. Lazaretto Creek Marina (Internet Access)	912-786-5848	60	16	1/12	8/14	F	GD	GIMS	EP			S		GMR
2. Tybee Island Marina (Wireless Internet Access)	912-786-5554		16/16	8/54	18/16	F	GD	GIMS	EP	L7	B/100	LS	P	GMR

Corresponding chart(s) not to be used for navigation. Internet Access, Wireless Internet Access

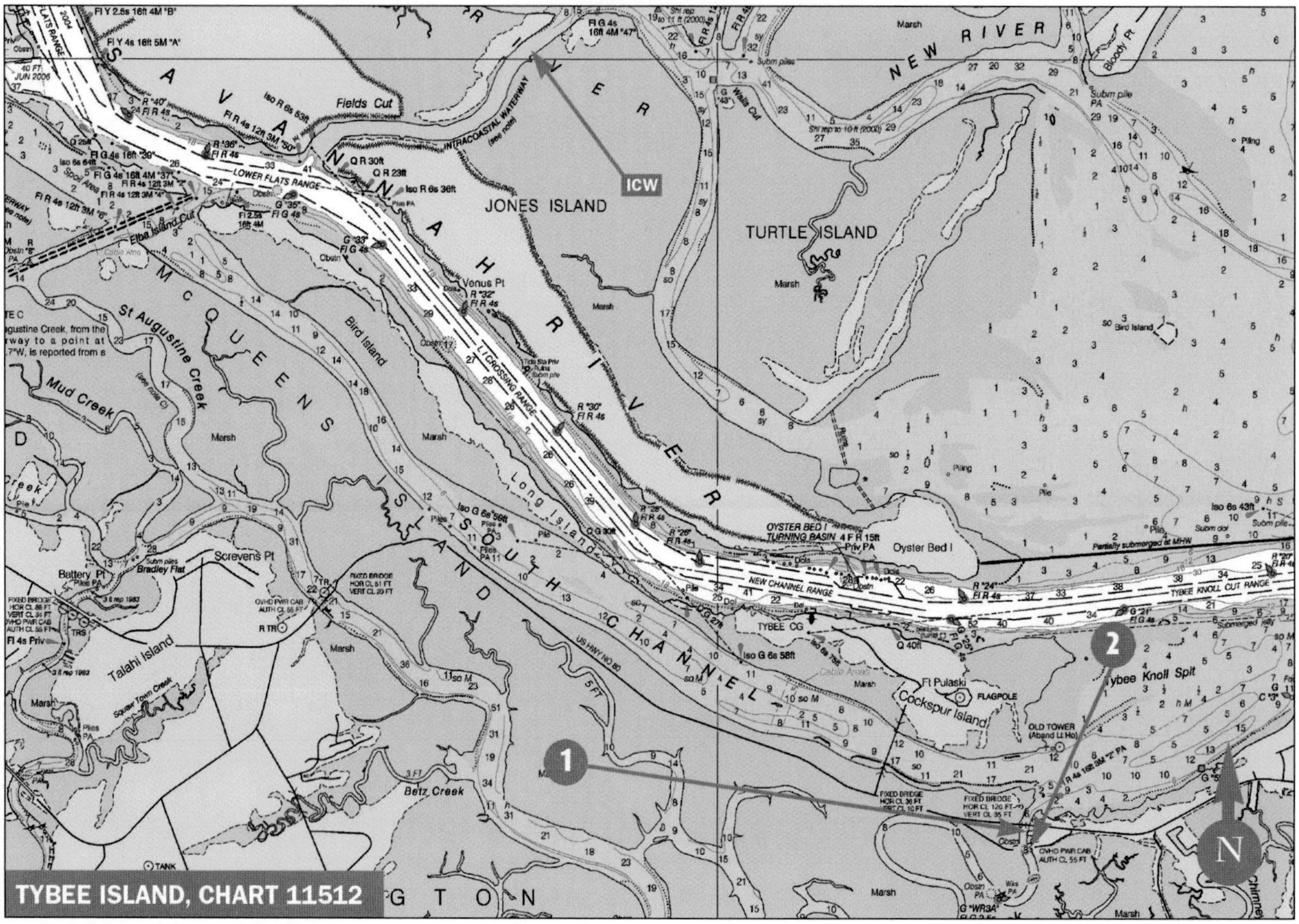

TYBEE ISLAND, CHART 11512

Tybee Roads with a favorable current, if possible, as the effects of the current start many miles offshore in the Atlantic.) *(See page 88 for more information about Tybee Roads.)* Sixteen miles up the Savannah River from the Tybee Roads inlet is the city of Savannah. Following the Savannah River another 170 miles will bring you to Augusta, home of the Professional Golf Association's annual Masters Championship.

Dockage: Tybee Island Marina, at the entrance to the Savannah River near Tybee Island, Savannah's primary beach area, makes a good fuel stop for powerboaters going south on the outside run down the Atlantic. Their fuel dock is open 24 hours a day. The marina is on the south side of the Savannah River's mouth and has 8-foot charted depths, but the 35-foot fixed vertical clearance bridge over the marina's access channel restricts usage by sailboats. You can also enjoy their dockside tiki bar. An additional marina, Lazaretto Creek Marina, is also located here.

Wassaw Sound to Wilmington River, an Alternative Route to Savannah

Wassaw Sound, the next Atlantic inlet south of the one at Tybee Roads, provides quick access to the Savannah area from the Atlantic Ocean. A fair amount of local traffic regularly uses this inlet, but we do not recommend it except with up-to-date local knowledge, excellent visibility, calm seas and at mid-tide. This is the Atlantic inlet used by vessels bound for Thunderbolt Marina and unable to clear the 65-foot State of Georgia Memorial Bridge over the Wilmington River at Mile 582.8. Local boats anchor off a beautiful sandy beach at a spit on the northeast corner of Wassaw Island for day outings.

NAVIGATION: Use Charts 11507 and 11512. Wassaw Sound leads from the Atlantic Ocean into the Wilmington River, which, in turn, leads north to Thunderbolt, GA (Mile 583) and Savannah. This is a shorter route in from the ocean than Tybee Roads when northbound. From the Wassau Sound sea buoy, flashing red "2W," red buoys "4," "6" and "8" are not charted because they are frequently moved. Depths in this area are shallower than upriver (charted at 6- to 14-foot at mean low water in February 2010). The channel is deep and easy to follow after making the turn at green can "9" and flashing red buoy "10." Wassaw Sound and the Wilmington River carry about 25-foot depths between flashing red buoy "10" in the Atlantic Ocean to flashing green "29" at Skidaway River (Mile 585.5). Local smaller boats have been observed cutting corners in running this inlet, so don't count on locating the channel markers by following them in. *(See page 89 for more information about Wassaw Sound.)*

Dockage: There is a marina at Priests Landing on the Wilmington River. You can also go to Bull River Marina, on the Bull River, which is accessible from Wassaw Sound, with no bridges or other height restrictions but with a shallow bar (6- to 7-foot spots charted) across its entrance channel. Reports from locals indicated that the charted channel into Bull River from Wassau Sound has severely shoaled at its entrance and should not be attempted except with up-to-date local knowledge. This shoaling is not shown on the most recent chart, which still indicates a 6-foot bar from red buoy "14" to green buoy "1."

Anchorage: If your provisions are low, head up Turner Creek, and anchor before or after the fixed Spence Grayson Bridge (35-foot vertical clearance) and dinghy into Hogan's Marina. Remember to get permission to leave the dinghy while you shop. Beware of the charted 4-foot area soon after the first bend.

Savannah River to Thunderbolt —Mile 576 to Mile 583

As you cross the Savannah River, going from Fields Cut to Elba Island Cut, traveling south along the ICW, you leave South Carolina and enter Georgia. The Bonaventure Cemetery, made famous in the book "Midnight in the Garden of Good and Evil," is visible from the ICW along the Wilmington River between flashing red "30" and flashing green "31" on the west side of the route.

Heading north on the ICW, one can pick up the beginning of the ebb just south of Thunderbolt (Mile 585) and carry a fair (ebb) current all the way through Fields Cut and Walls Cut (Mile 572). A flood current gives the same advantage to southbound vessels.

THE FOLLOWING AREA REQUIRES SPECIAL ATTENTION DUE TO SHOALING OR CHANGES TO THE CHANNEL

SAVANNAH RIVER

NAVIGATION: Use Chart 11507. The ICW passage is not straight across the Savannah River, but diagonal. When you cross the Savannah River, allow for the strong river current. Slow boats may have to correct course several times.

Watch for big ships that will have announced their presence on VHF Channels 13 and 16. They approach fast from both directions, and port pilots have had many close encounters with pleasure boats in the river where the ships have no room to maneuver in the narrow, swiftly running channel.

A rock jetty at Elba Island Cut's confluence with the Savannah River—on the southeast side of the river—is submerged at high tide but marked with a white danger beacon. Because of the shoal on the west side in Elba Cut, flashing red "2" and flashing red "4" have been moved eastward and appear to be in the middle of the channel. The channel passes close to the eastern quarter for 10-foot depths mean low water. This area has not seen dredging in some time. Favor the green side.

END SPECIAL CAUTION AREA.

From Elba Island Cut, the ICW heads briefly westward along St. Augustine Creek. It then enters the winding upper reaches of the Wilmington River, which is not nearly as intricate as it appears on the chart, and then approaches the town of Thunderbolt (Mile 583). Multiple sets of ranges guide you through this area. The back board of Range "A" was almost completely obscured by trees in late 2010.

Depths are well maintained here, but since the tidal range is between 8 and 9 feet, be sure to stay in the channel. From flashing green "19" (Mile 578.7) to flashing red "36" (Mile 583.5), stay in the center of the channel, following the chart's magenta line to avoid shoals along the banks.

The Sam Varnedoe Bascule Bridge (Causton Bluff Bridge, closed vertical clearance 21 feet), Mile 579.9, is the first opening bridge in Georgia (and one of only two on Georgia's portion of the ICW—the other being the Skidaway Bridge at Mile 592.9) for southbound vessels. Georgia bridges monitor VHF Channel 09, as they do in South Carolina and Florida. The bridge tender will often request that boats bunch together for openings. Note that the approaches are No-Wake Zones on both sides. The Causton Bluff Bridge is restricted year-round, Monday through Friday, except federal holidays: Between 6:30 a.m. and 9 a.m., and 4:30 p.m. and 6:30 p.m., the draw will only open for waiting traffic at 7:00 a.m., 8:00 a.m. and 5:30 p.m. At all other times it will open on request. If you have any questions about passage or clearance, call the bridge tender on VHF Channel 09.

The tidal current reverses between the Sam Varnedoe Bascule (Causton Bluff) Bridge and the high-rise span at Thunderbolt.

■ THUNDERBOLT

Mile 583

Thunderbolt, close to Savannah and located on the ICW, is an important seafood-packing center with good marinas and restaurants. The town hall, a laundry, an electronics firm and a marine supply store are located on the riverfront. The shore is lined with shrimp boats, often rafted two abreast. Bus service is available, with stops about three-tenths of a mile from Thunderbolt's marinas. (A taxi is better for the trip to Savannah).

NAVIGATION: Use Chart 11507. **Use the Savannah River Entrance Tide Table. For high tide, add 32 minutes; for low tide, add 12 minutes.** Here at Thunderbolt, and farther down the ICW at Isle of Hope (Mile 590), the current and direction of flow must be considered when docking. Marina personnel are generally knowledgeable and, in assigning berths, try to put the less maneuverable, single-screw boats in slips that are easy to enter and leave in this area of high tides and swift currents. If no attendant is around, it is best to put in at the fuel dock to size up the situation and then locate someone who can give directions or lend a hand. The marinas at Thunderbolt all conveniently have floating docks.

Dockage: Hinckley Yachts, to starboard just northwest of the Thunderbolt Bridge (fixed vertical clearance 65 feet), is one of the company's service facilities. Directly across the ICW, at Mile 582, is Savannah Bend Marina.

At Mile 582, Morningstar Marinas at Bahia Bleu, on the south side of the Thunderbolt Bridge, offers fuel, floating docks, full mechanical repairs and large boat dockage that is convenient to the ICW and to Thunderbolt's restaurants and shops.

Thunderbolt Marine is at Mile 583 with transient dockage close to town and full-service repairs. Their lifts are capable of hauling the smallest to the largest of yachts. They also have a ship's store, 24-hour security, laundry, restroom and pump-out facilities.

The Savannah Yacht and Country Club is about two miles past Thunderbolt to port. The yacht club has limited space and its reciprocation policy varies, so contact the club before you arrive.

Anchorage: A mile or so below Thunderbolt, the Wilmington River widens, and the channel begins to straighten out. The popular Herb River anchorage is located at Mile 584.5. Most skippers anchor along the east bank before the first turn. Above the first bend, the Herb River's bottom is a bit irregular and very deep at the bend, but holding is better than in the lower stretch of the river, where there is an oyster bank. Be prepared for considerable local traffic and tidal current. Depths are good, at 7 to 17 feet, but set the anchor well.

GOIN' ASHORE:

THUNDERBOLT, GA

Looking at the marinas, boatyard facilities and condominium development along Thunderbolt's waterfront today, it is hard to believe the town used to be Savannah's weekend playground. With the advent of the streetcar and electricity, people flocked to the casino, horse racing track and dance pavilion, finishing with dinner at the world-famous Bannon Lodge.

History: First settled by American Indians, legend has it that lightning struck Wilmington Bluff, creating a freshwater spring. The American Indians named the area Thunderbolt. English settlers also came to the area, enjoying the access to the Wilmington River that created a shipping point for the local plantations. By 1856, Thunderbolt had incorporated into the town of Warsaw. Not long after that, the Thunderbolt Battery was constructed to ward off Union attacks from Wassaw Sound. Although Union gunboats anchored near Thunderbolt, the Battery never fell.

Thunderbolt's era as a river resort lasted from the late 19th century into the early 20th century. By 1898, it was an exciting place to visit with a horse racing track, Tivoli Park, the casino and Varn & Byrd Music Park, all with bandstands and live music. The casino was actually built by the Savannah Electric Company, owner of the streetcar company, to increase ridership and to promote the use of electricity. In the early 1900s, Savannah started a series of car races to compete with Long Island's Vanderbilt Cup Race. The road races were

Mile 582 to Mile 590, GA

THUNDERBOLT (WILMINGTON RIVER)		Largest Vessel Accommodated	VHF Channel Monitored	Transient Berths / Total Berths	Approach / Dockside Depth (reported)	Floating Docks	Gas / Diesel	Groceries, Ice, Marine Supplies, Snacks	Repairs: Hull, Engine, Propeller	Lift (tonnage), Crane, Rail	1=110V, 2=220V, B=Both, Max Amps	Laundry, Pool, Showers	Pump-Out Station	Nearby: Grocery Store, Motel, Restaurant
		Dockage					Supplies		Services					
1. Hinckley Yacht Services 582.4	**912-629-2400**	**65**	**16/68**	**8/30**	**12/12**	**F**		**IM**	**HEP**	**L50**	**B/50**	**S**		**GR**
2. Savannah Bend Marina 582.3	912-897-3625	100	16/68	10/32	12/10	F	GD	IMS			B/50	LS		GR
3. Morningstar Marinas at Bahia Bleu 582.6 (Internet Access) (Wireless Internet Access)	**912-354-2283**	**200**	**16/68**	**20/45**	**26/20**	**F**	**GD**	**IMS**	**EP**		**B/50**	**LS**		**GMR**
4. Thunderbolt Marine 583 (Internet Access) (Wireless Internet Access)	**912-356-3875**	**200**	**16/11**	**15/45**	**20/20**	**F**	**GD**	**GIMS**	**HEP**	**L160**	**B/100**	**LS**	**P**	**GR**
TURNER CREEK														
5. Sail Harbor Marina and Boatyard SE of 585.4 (Wireless Internet Access)	912-897-2896	50	16/71	5/85	7/10	F		IMS	HEP	L35	B/50	LS	P	GR
6. Hogan's Marina	912-897-3474						GD	IMS	HE	L10	B/50	S	P	GR
BULL RIVER														
7. Bull River Marina 4 NE of 586 (Internet Access) (Wireless Internet Access)	**912-897-7300**	**110**	**16/07**	**6/80**	**25/18**	**F**	**GD**	**IMS**	**E**		**B/50**	**S**	**P**	**GR**
WILMINGTON AND SKIDAWAY RIVERS														
8. Isle of Hope Marina Inc. 590 (Internet Access) (Wireless Internet Access)	**912-354-8187**	**220**	**16/68**	**15/125**	**12/15**	**F**	**GD**	**GIMS**	**HEP**		**B/100**	**LPS**	**P**	**GR**
9. Landings Harbor Marina	912-598-1901	50	16	/30	20/7	F	GD	IMS	HE	L4	B/50		P	GR

Corresponding chart(s) not to be used for navigation. Internet Access, Wireless Internet Access

long enough to require camps for pit crews, and the Fiat team ensconced themselves at Thunderbolt, which was also one of the guard stations.

The advent of the automobile and improved roads was a double-edged sword, as people began to travel farther for entertainment and Thunderbolt's attractions began to decline. However, the demand for seafood was increasing, and packing-houses were built along the river to accommodate the shrimp fishing fleet. In fact, it was in Thunderbolt where frozen, breaded, pan-ready shrimp was developed by the Trade Winds Company. At the peak of the shrimping industry, there were around 150 boats fishing from Thunderbolt.

Yachting has long been part of life in Thunderbolt. The Savannah Yacht Club was originally located in Thunderbolt, then relocated to north of the business district. It is now on the other side of the river and farther south. The townspeople still work along the river, refurbishing luxury yachts and servicing boats cruising the ICW. Several marinas within walking distance provide transient services with restaurants, provisioning and nautical supplies. Commercial fishing boats still thrive in Thunderbolt, and fresh seafood is available at Thunderbolt Fisherman's Seafood (3110 River Drive, 912-354-0417).

Attractions: The Thunderbolt Museum Society (2702 Mechanics Ave., 912-351-0836) was established in the old town hall to recapture the town's history with exhibits and a staff of informative volunteers. Honey Park and Thompson Park are located near the marinas for leisurely strolls along the river.

Shopping: Chu's Convenience Mart (3019 E. Victory Drive, 912-352-8538) has basic necessities, and there is a Kroger (1900 E. Victory Drive, 912-236-9321) less than a mile away for groceries, produce, fresh meats and seafood. Marine supplies and services are readily available.

Dining: A favorite dining spot is Tubby's Tank House (2909 River Drive, 912-354-9040), serving lunch and dinner and featuring fresh seafood with a full-service bar and live entertainment in a casual atmosphere.

ADDITIONAL RESOURCES

- SAVANNAH CONVENTION AND VISITORS BUREAU: 877-SAVANNAH, www.savannahvisit.com
- COASTAL GEORGIA: www.coastalgeorgiaexperience.com
- NEARBY GOLF COURSES
  Club at Savannah Harbor, #2 Resort Drive, Savannah, GA 31421, 912-201-2400
  www.theclubatsavannahharbor.net
- NEARBY MEDICAL FACILITIES
  Memorial University Medical Center,
  4700 Waters Ave., Savannah, GA 31404
  912-350-8000

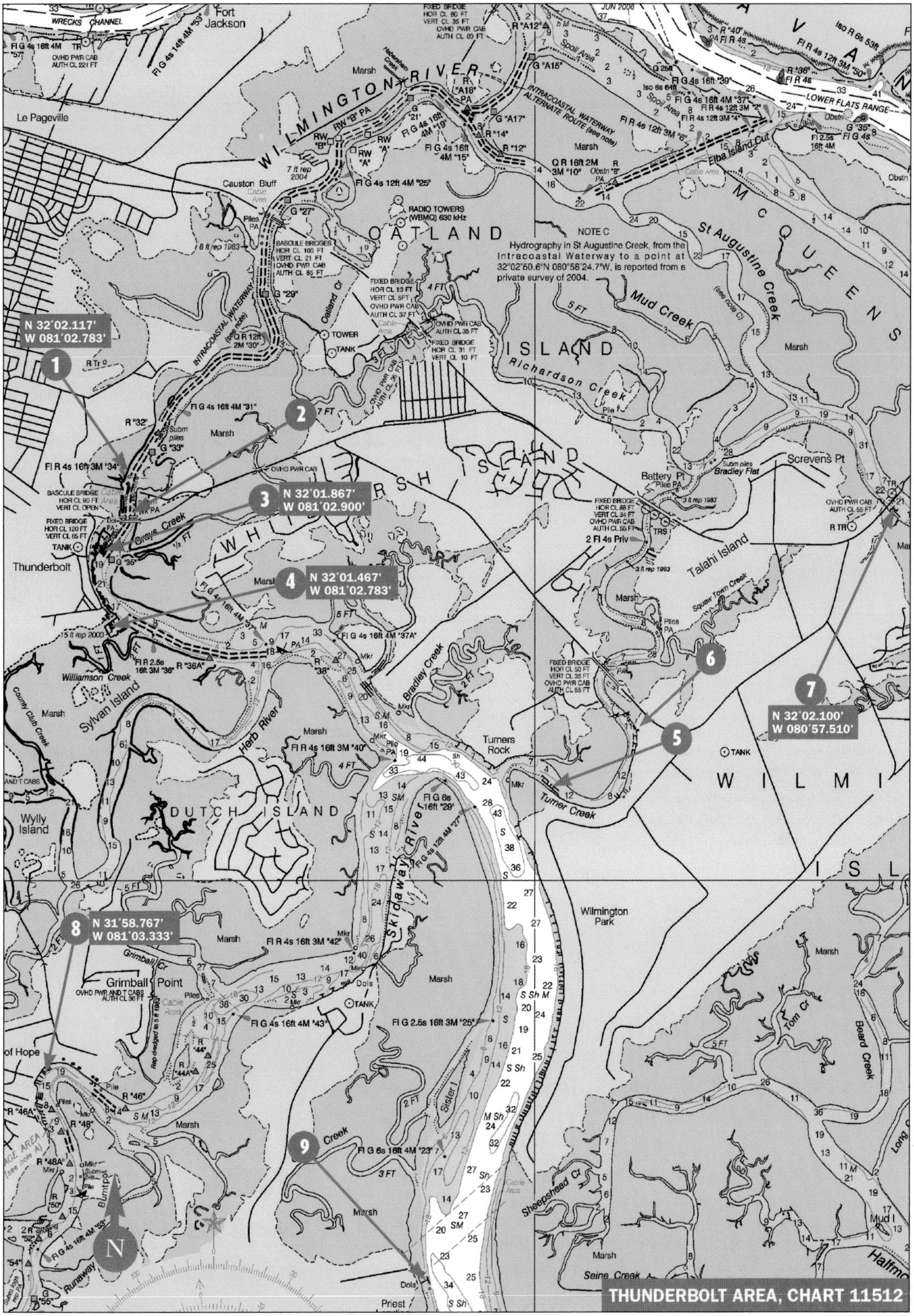
THUNDERBOLT AREA, CHART 11512
1 N 32˚02.117' W 081˚02.783'
3 N 32˚01.867' W 081˚02.900'
4 N 32˚01.467' W 081˚02.783'
7 N 32˚02.100' W 080˚57.510'
8 N 31˚58.767' W 081˚03.333'
NOTE C
Hydrography in St Augustine Creek, from the Intracoastal Waterway to a point at 32°02'50.6"N 080°58'24.7"W, is reported from a private survey of 2004.
WILMINGTON RIVER
OATLAND
ISLAND
WHITEMARSH ISLAND
DUTCH ISLAND
McQUEENS
WILMI
ISL
Fort Jackson
Le Pageville
Causton Bluff
Thunderbolt
Wylly Island
Grimball Point
Wilmington Park
Turners Rock
Talahi Island
Battery Pt
Screvens Pt
Sylvan Island
Williamson Creek
Herb River
Bradley Creek
Skidaway River
Richardson Creek
Mud Creek
St Augustine Creek
Squaw Town Creek
Turner Creek
Sheepshead Cr
Seine Creek
Beard Creek
Elba Island Cut
Bradley Flat
Oatland Cr
Grimball Cr
Mud I
Priest
RADIO TOWERS (WBMQ) 630 kHz
INTRACOASTAL WATERWAY ALTERNATE ROUTE (see note)
LOWER FLATS RANGE
WRECKS CHANNEL
BASCULE BRIDGE HOR CL 90 FT VERT CL OPEN
FIXED BRIDGE HOR CL 120 FT VERT CL 65 FT
Marsh

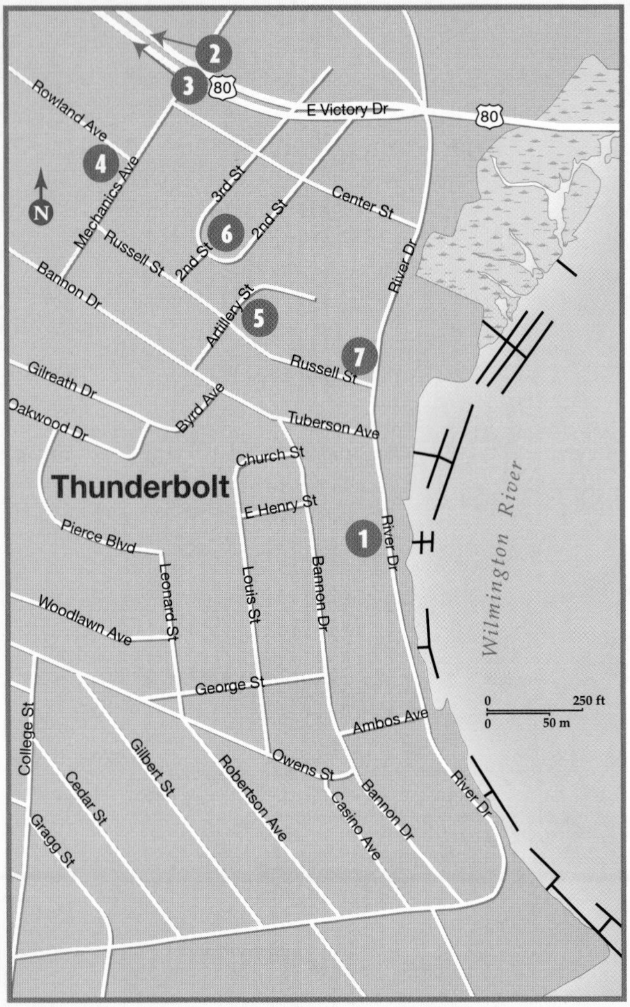

Reference the marina listing tables to see all the marinas in the area.

DINING
1 Tubby's Tank House

GROCERIES/CARRYOUT
2 Chu's Convenience Mart
3 Kroger

INFORMATION/ POINTS OF INTEREST
4 Thunderbolt Museum Society

POINTS OF INTEREST
5 Bonaventure Cemetery

RECREATION
6 Thompson Park

SEAFOOD
7 Thunderbolt Fisherman's Seafood

ISLE OF HOPE TO OSSABAW ISLAND

Mile 584 to Mile 615—Isle of Hope

Isle of Hope, GA (Mile 590), a charming village of winding roads and old houses scattered among the tall pines and oaks located on the shore of the Skidaway River, is seven miles by water down the twisting ICW from Thunderbolt, but only half that by road. The town, its name of unknown origin, stands on a bend high above the river and is listed on the National Register of Historic Places. Signs politely request that you slow down as you pass and keep your wake to a minimum; better yet, stop to walk the streets and view the restored houses.

About a mile from the Isle of Hope Marina is the Wormsloe Historic Site (7601 Skidaway Road) with a museum, ruins of a fortified house and a nature walk. Wild deer and pigs leave their tracks and sometimes appear on the grounds. The Wormsloe Mansion itself is not open to the public. It is a private residence still occupied by the descendants of Noble Jones, one of the earliest Georgia settlers and the original owner of the property. You can visit Wormsloe Historic Site on foot, bike or by tour bus from Savannah.

NAVIGATION: Use Chart 11507. When heading south from Thunderbolt, take flashing green "37" a little wide, and then favor flashing green "37A," avoiding the shoal near red daybeacon "38." The charted wreck of a shrimp boat just outside the ICW channel beyond the Herb River entrance was long ago removed.

Dockage: Located in one of the most beautiful settings on the entire ICW, the convenient Isle of Hope Marina provides complimentary courtesy cars, wireless Internet and large slips at concrete floating docks. Tie up here to enjoy a walk among the antebellum homes. This is the logical jumping-off point for the long run south, and the first landing near Savannah when you are headed north, with bus service to the city. Note that it is the last fuel stop on the ICW for 90 miles.

Anchorage: There is an anchorage area just below the Isle of Hope Marina on the same side of the channel, but it is full of locally anchored and moored boats, with little space for transients. It is reported to have only 4-foot depths, except directly adjacent to the ICW channel, a dangerous spot with barge traffic swinging around the curve.

Skidaway Narrows

Skidaway Narrows, immediately below Isle of Hope, is a twisting, challenging stretch of the ICW, weaving erratically back and forth around curves and bends. Take your time, cut your speed as necessary, watch your course, and enjoy this winding creek with its fringes of salt marsh extending back to distant woods. Skidaway Narrows is the preferred swimming hole of the local river otter population.

NAVIGATION: Use Chart 11507. The most recent edition of this chart is Edition 34 from December 2010. The channel narrows from red daybeacon "46A" (Mile 590) to the Skidaway Bridge. Favor the eastern bank until red daybeacon "50." The Skidaway Bridge at Mile 592.9 (22-foot closed vertical clearance) is restricted year-round. Monday through Friday, except federal holidays, from 7:00 a.m. to 9:00 a.m., the bridge opens on the hour. From 4:30 p.m. to 6:30 p.m., the bridge opens on the half-hour. The bridge opens on signal at all other times. Remember that all Georgia ICW bridges use VHF Channel 09. A boat ramp just below the bridge creates considerable small-boat traffic, so keep alert. There is also a buoyed-off swimming area. Note the SLOW-SPEED signs here.

Slow boats should note that high slack water at Mile 592 (Skidaway Narrows) occurs 49 minutes before it does at the Savannah River Entrance. This is good to keep in mind, as arriving at Skidaway Narrows at slack water provides the most favorable currents from Mile 585 to Mile 603. Tidal currents reverse in the vicinity of the Skidaway Bridge.

The pretty Vernon View (Mile 596), another Savannah suburb overlooking the Burnside River portion of the ICW, begins at Skidaway Narrows' southern end, about six miles below Isle of Hope. Private docks line the shore (and are well charted), but there is no public marina. Remember, you are responsible for your wake here.

On the Burnside River, favor the north side of the channel between red daybeacon "76" and flashing green "79," which marks the turn into the Vernon River. A shoal is building out along the southeast side of the Burnside River, so don't cut flashing green "79" too closely, even

Looking north over Isle of Hope, GA. (Not to be used for navigation.)
WATERWAY GUIDE PHOTOGRAPHY.

though the magenta line takes you there. Shoaling exists between flashing green "79" and flashing green "81."

Anchorage: Moon River, made famous by songwriter Johnny Mercer and singer Andy Williams, is just short of Mile 595. Boaters have reported shoaling to around 4-foot depths at the entrance, but with deeper water inside, although depths are still charted at 9 feet with shoaling indicated. 9mber that in periods of strong and prolonged westerly wind, and during the new and full moon phases, tides can be much lower than normal charted depths. Enter this anchorage at your own risk. Stay clear of flashing red "74" and the shoaling before heading northwest up the river.

If you give the long shoal off Possum Point a wide berth, you can turn northward up the Vernon River, well off the ICW, to drop the hook south of the village of Montgomery. Currents can be strong here, and you should allow for an 8-foot tidal range. You will probably share this anchorage with a shrimp boat or two during the season. They usually anchor on one long stretchy nylon rode and keep their arms down, so give them plenty of space to swing. This is a pleasant anchorage in 8 to 14 feet. Anchor before the charted 1-foot bar, which extends out to the middle of the river.

Mile 601 to Mile 615— Hell Gate and Florida Passage

Vernon River runs wide and deep until you reach Hell Gate, a land cut leading from the Vernon River to the Ogeechee River. If strong northeast winds kick up, you might see swells breaking up the long fetch of the Vernon and Ogeechee rivers. The Georgia coast's second largest river, the Ogeechee, has a particularly strong ebb current.

From the Ogeechee River, the ICW channel leads south through the Florida Passage, which flows into the Bear River, running the length of Ossabaw Island. One of Georgia's eight major sea islands, Ossabaw Island is pierced by a number of narrow, but deep creeks fanning out from the Bear River. *(See page 90 for more information about Ossabaw Sound.)*

⚠ THE FOLLOWING AREA REQUIRES SPECIAL ATTENTION DUE TO SHOALING OR CHANGES TO THE CHANNEL

HELL GATE

NAVIGATION: Use Chart 11507. Although dredging at Hell Gate (Mile 601.4 to Mile 602.4) was performed in 2009, the mid-channel depth report from our cruising editor was 6 feet in fall of 2010 at marker "89" a half hour after low tide. This is one of the most notorious sections of the ICW for shoaling, and it may not improve any time soon. The area is always subject to rapid shoaling even after dredging so check our website, www.waterwayguide.com, for the latest updates. The chart for Hell Gate shows no magenta line for the southern half of this passage.

There are extremely strong side-sweeping currents at Hell Gate, especially on the ebb when entering from the north (Vernon River), so keep track of your progress by looking both ahead and astern. Before going through Hell

Ossabaw Sound Area, GA

OSSABAW SOUND AREA	Phone	Largest Vessel Accommodated	VHF Channel Monitored	Transient Berths / Total Berths	Approach / Dockside Depth (reported)	Floating Docks	Gas / Diesel	Groceries, Ice, Marine Supplies, Snacks	Repairs: Hull, Engine, Propeller	Lift (tonnage), Crane, Rail	1=110V, 2=220V, B=Both, Max Amps	Laundry, Pool, Showers	Pump-Out Station	Nearby: Grocery Store, Motel, Restaurant
		Dockage					Supplies		Services					
1. Delegal Creek Marina 1 E of 601 🖳 WiFi	912-598-0023	100	16/68	10/66	5/15	F	GD	IM	HEP		B/50	LS	P	GR
2. Fort McAllister Marina & Inn 6 W of 605.5 🖳	912-727-2632	60	16/68	9/30	7/20	F	GD	GIMS	E	LC	B/50	LS	P	R

Corresponding chart(s) not to be used for navigation. 🖳 Internet Access WiFi Wireless Internet Access

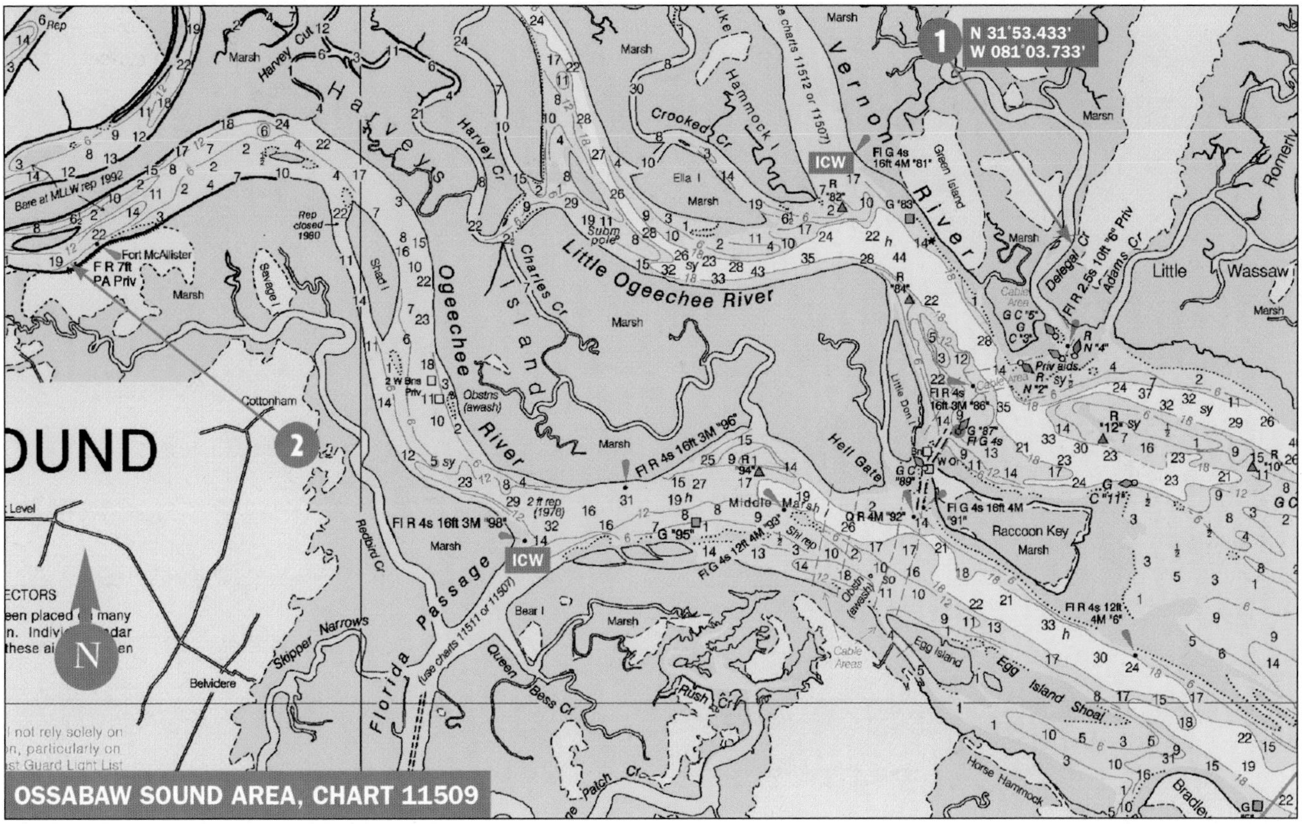

OSSABAW SOUND AREA, CHART 11509

Gate, it is a good idea to check the most recent quarterly USACE Savannah survey, find out if the Coast Guard has recently moved the markers and also seek local knowledge. Mid-tide and rising is the safest time to go through these questionable areas of the ICW.

There is a charted route around Hell Gate: southbound, out the Vernon River to the North Channel of Ossabaw Sound, and then back in through the South Channel of Ossabaw Sound. This is not a recommended alternative route to bypass Hell Gate due to the length, the open ocean water, strong reversing currents, uncharted shallows and the far spacing of markers. It is better to wait for higher tides at Hell Gate. With an 8-foot tidal range, patience will pay off.

Leaving Hell Gate, run beyond flashing green "91," and round quick flashing red "92" to make the turn for the three-mile run up the Ogeechee River. Pay particular attention to the markers at the passage through Middle Marsh. Carefully follow the magenta ICW line on the chart, changing course as indicated to pass safely between Middle Marsh to the south (obscure at high tide) and the shoal north of red daybeacon "94" off Charles Creek's entrance. Near Mile 606, at flashing red "98," is the entrance to Florida Passage, which leads south to the Bear River. The shallowest part is usually at the exit into the Bear River, heading towards red daybeacon "102" (formerly red nun "102"), and flashing green "101" was missing in late 2010. Range "B" near red daybeacon "104C" at Mile 612 has been replaced with quick flashing green "105."

END SPECIAL CAUTION AREA.

Dockage: At Mile 601, just above Hell Gate across the Vernon River, Delegal Creek makes off to the north. The marked channel leads to Delegal Creek Marina, a compact marina in a beautiful setting. The marina is part of The Landings on Skidaway Island, a luxury community with six golf courses. Call the dockmaster's office at 912-598-

Kilkenny Creek, GA

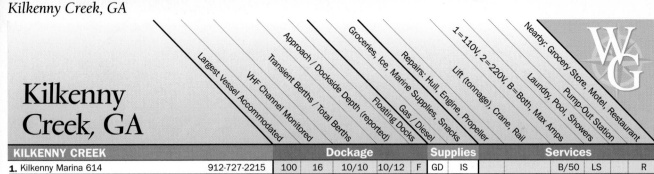

KILKENNY CREEK		Largest Vessel Accommodated	VHF Channel Monitored	Transient Berths / Total Berths	Approach / Dockside Depth (reported)	Floating Docks	Gas / Diesel	Groceries, Ice, Marine Supplies, Snacks	Repairs: Hull, Engine, Propeller	Lift (tonnage), Crane, Rail	1=110V, 2=220V, B=Both, Max Amps	Laundry, Pool, Showers	Pump-Out Station	Nearby: Grocery Store, Motel, Restaurant
		Dockage					Supplies		Services					
1. Kilkenny Marina 614	912-727-2215	100	16	10/10	10/12	F	GD	IS			B/50	LS		R

Corresponding chart(s) not to be used for navigation. Internet Access Wireless Internet Access

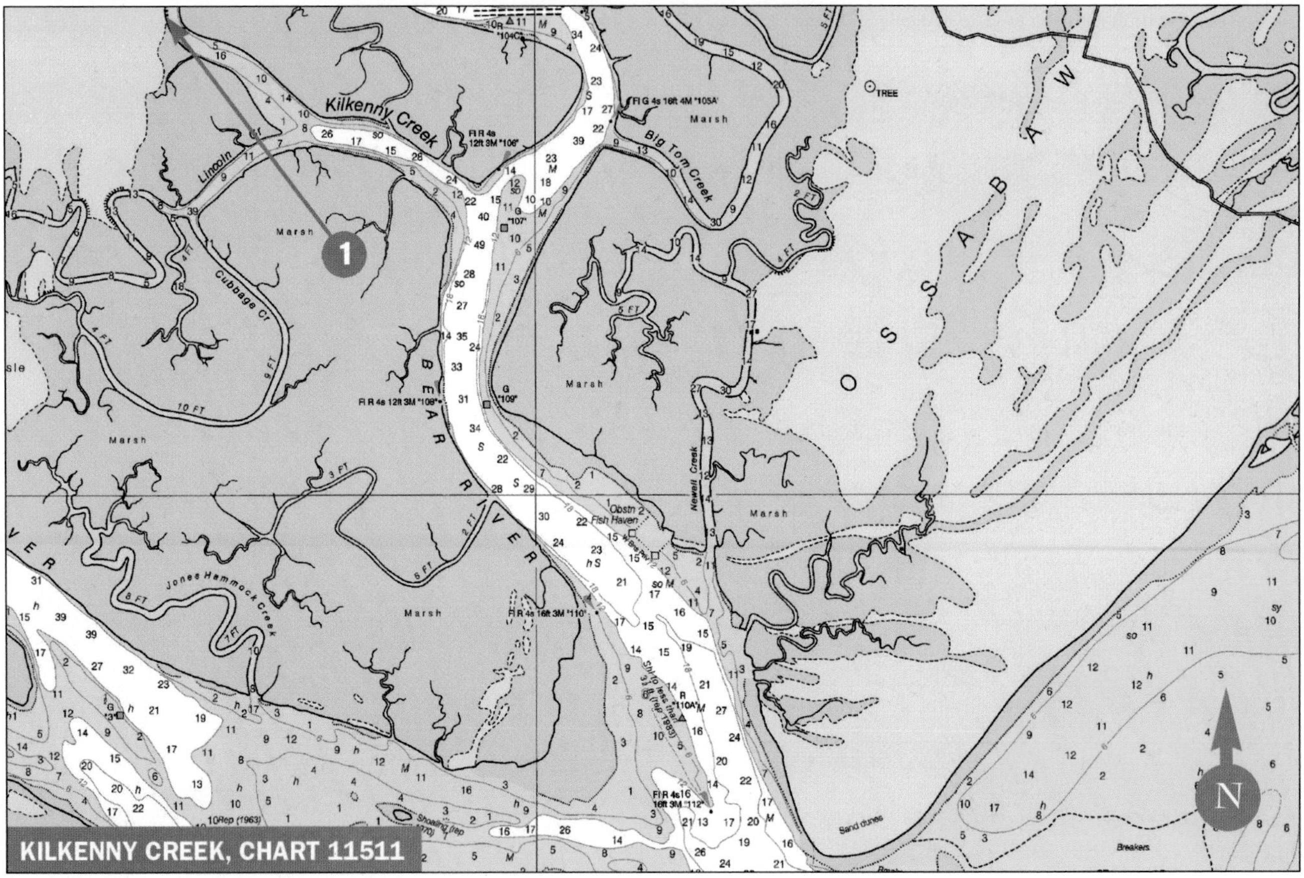

KILKENNY CREEK, CHART 11511

0023, or on VHF Channels 16 or 68, to check depths and to get directions for entering the marked channel. Five miles up the Ogeechee River from flashing red "98" (Florida Passage) is the Fort McAllister Marina & Inn. Study the charts (11507, 11509 and 11511) and the markers before heading upriver.

At Mile 614 on the Bear River, at ICW green daybeacon "107," you can turn westward into Kilkenny Creek, with a Texaco sign at its entrance. About a mile and a half up from flashing red "106" is rural Kilkenny Marina, which welcomes transients. The marina reports that its entrance channel carries 10 feet if you stay 30 feet north of the center of the creek.

Anchorage: There is a fine selection of anchorages with 10-foot-plus depths and good holding in Redbird Creek off the Florida Passage at Mile 607. At Mile 608.5, stay on the range until you are well past red daybeacon "102," then turn eastward up the Bear River to Cane Patch Creek or Buckhead Creek, pick a spot with suitable depths, and set the anchor well. Depths vary from 10 to 30 feet here, and the current is strong. At Mile 612, you can turn north and anchor in 9- to 14-foot depths with good holding. Big Tom Creek, at Mile 612.5, is another popular overnight anchorage. Anchor either near its entrance or around the first bend in 9-foot depths. Kilkenny Creek, Mile 614, provides a well-known, but peaceful spot to drop the hook, with 15-foot depths and a mud bottom. This anchorage borders the marsh, making insect screens and repellent essential. There is considerable nighttime traffic from shrimp boats in Kilkenny Creek during the harvesting season, so be sure your anchor light is working properly. Anchor past the marina in a sheltered cove for protection from strong westerly winds. ■

Waterway Guide is always open to your observations from the helm. Email your comments on any navigation information in the Guide to: editor@waterwayguide.com.

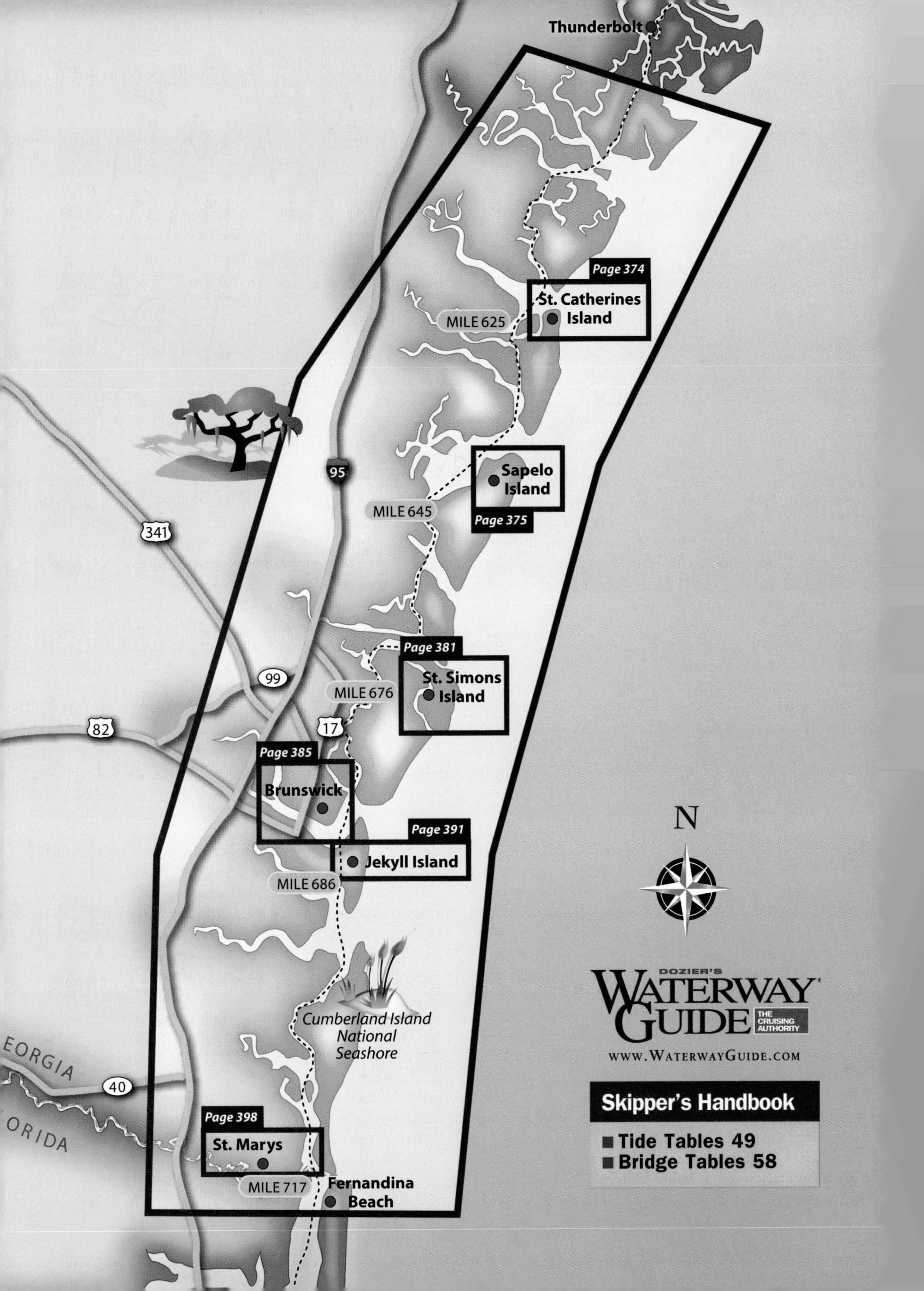

Skipper's Handbook

- Tide Tables 49
- Bridge Tables 58

Savannah River to Florida

ONLY run at High TIDE!

ICW MILE 616–MILE 717 VHF Georgia Bridges: Channel 09

CHARTS 11489, 11502, 11504, 11506, 11507, 11508, 11509, 11510, 11511, 11512, 11513, 11514

GEORGIA'S SOUNDS

The Intracoastal Waterway (ICW) follows the Bear River as it empties into St. Catherines Sound (Mile 618). This is the first in a series of sounds—connected by rivers—that you will pass through as you transit the Georgia portion of the ICW. Other sounds along this stretch include Sapelo Sound, Doboy Sound, Altamaha Sound, Buttermilk Sound, St. Simons Sound and Jekyll Sound. Some of these sounds are large and exposed enough to get a little rough, but they also provide a nice change of pace from the rivers and land cuts to the north.

When the sounds are open for shrimping, keep an eye on all shrimp boats in your vicinity. They move fast when heading to and from their shrimping grounds. When they are working, however, their movements will be erratic, and they will be occupied with their trailing nets, so you will be the one to take evasive action. They often travel with their long "arms" down, so even if you are under sail, do not expect shrimp boats to alter course or raise their booms. There have been reports of dismastings in narrow passages. Keep your horn handy; five blasts is the danger signal.

NAVIGATION: Use Chart 11507. Watch your course between Mile 616 through Mile 617 (and flashing red "110" and flashing red "112") and take care that wind and current do not set your vessel too far to the west. The shoal reported on the charts does indeed exist near red daybeacon "110A," which is not shown on older charts. (The most recent edition of this chart is from December 2010.) Give flashing red "112," flashing red "114" and flashing red "114A" a wide berth, and keep to the charted ICW magenta line. Green flashing "C," which formerly marked the end of the shoal at Middle Ground in St. Catherines Sound off Walburg Creek, was removed.

For slow-moving north or southbound boats, the best time to arrive at St. Catherines Sound is at low slack water, when the sea is calmest and the currents are most favorable. **Expect low slack water at Mile 618 to be 39 minutes earlier than at the Savannah River Entrance. Refer to tide tables in our Skipper's Handbook section.** Tidal range is 7 to 8 feet. Heading south, once you transit the two miles of the ICW route across St. Catherines Sound, you will enter the North Newport River, at Mile 620.

St. Catherines Sound and Inlet

St. Catherines Inlet is a "fair weather" entrance and exit from the ocean. The inlet should be used only on mid-tide and rising tide, with calm seas. Shoaling is reported from 6 to 6.5 feet at mean low water in the center of the channel near flashing red buoy "2." Local towboat operators do not recommend this inlet. Most electronic charts will show the sea buoys and the position of the other channel markers in some of these minor inlets, while paper charts may just give the position of the sea buoys. However, keep in mind the buoys are moved or changed as needed. ***(See page 91 for more information about St. Catherines Sound and Inlet.)***

For St. Catherines and the other minor inlets in Georgia (Sapelo, Doboy and St. Andrews), channel markers are so widely placed that it is difficult to visually pick them out, although the offshore sea buoys are in their charted position and easy to locate with GPS. Radar helps to locate uncharted channel markers, but it is best to also be able to see their position on an electronic chart. St. Catherines Inlet, like most unimproved inlets (i.e. not dredged or jettied but left in its natural state) is shallowest at its entrance bar, just inside the sea buoy, with deeper water closer inshore. Just like the ICW, these inlet entrances can shift and shoal at any time.

Walburg Creek is a convenient anchorage when using St. Catherines Sound as an entry or exit from the ICW to the Atlantic Ocean. The long shoal at Middle Ground in St. Catherines Sound, north of Walburg Creek, extends farther south toward St. Catherines Island than charted. St. Catherines Sound would be a dangerous passage in poor weather, at low tide or with ebb tide against strong onshore winds.

Remember that shoals and bars shift, especially in areas of strong current flowing into the ocean or following major storms, so approach all unimproved inlets with caution. Shoaling to 4 feet has been reported recently at the entrance to Georgia's St. Andrew Sound (inlet from the ocean, not the ICW). Shoaling was so severe in Altamaha Sound that all aids to navigation in that sound's ocean entrance (not the ICW) were removed by the Coast Guard in 2004.

Dockage: About seven miles northwest of Saint Catherines Sound (from ICW Mile 618) on the Medway River, Sunbury Crab Company Restaurant & Marina offers transient facilities including laundry, pool, showers and fuel. The restaurant features fresh steamed blue crabs caught daily, wild Georgia shrimp and local oysters in a relaxed, laid-back atmosphere.

Walburg Creek, off the ICW—Mile 623

Walburg Creek flows past the western shore of St. Catherines Island to join with the ICW route at Mile 623. The St. Catherines Island Foundation owns the island and limits visitation. Halfway down the route is the St. Catherines Island Foundation Survival Center for endangered species, operated in conjunction with the New York Zoological Society. The climate of St. Catherines Island is suitable for breeding colonies of rare and endangered animals like gazelles, parrots and Madagascar turtles.

NAVIGATION: Use Chart 11507. A protected, but seldom-used alternate to the ICW route along the exposed North Newport River, Walburg Creek's channel is charted as a dotted magenta line. Follow this course to avoid shoals. Green flashing "C," marking the end of the Middle Ground shoal off Walburg Creek, has been removed, although the shoal it marked extends farther south toward St. Catherines Island than charted. Although the northern entrance to Walburg Creek (from St. Catherines Sound) is straightforward, the southern passage back into the North Newport River is tricky, with depths of 4 to 5 feet, as shown on the chart.

Anchorage: Walburg Creek's waters provide for splendid anchorages. You can drop the hook across from houses near the northern entrance to Walburg Creek. Shrimp boats often use this anchorage too, so be sure that your anchor light is working properly. Avoid anchoring in the bend of the creek off the southern tip of Walburg Island, where the water is deep and currents run swiftly. A dinghy ride to the north end of St. Catherines Island reveals a desolate, but beautiful sandy barrier island beach.

North Newport River—Mile 620 to Mile 624

Beyond Mile 620, the ICW enters the mouth of the North Newport River and follows along that river to about Mile 623, where the North Newport River bears off to the west. The ICW channel continues south along Johnson Creek. At the entrance to the North Newport River, on its west side, there is an unmarked shoal, so be sure to favor the green side as you follow the ICW channel. There is another area of shoaling on the red side of the North Newport River marked by red daybeacons "122," "124" and "124A" off the southern end of Walburg Creek. Continue to favor the green side here. Don't cut the corner before flashing green "125." Round it as the charted magenta line indicates and continue into Johnson Creek.

North Newport River, off the ICW

From flashing green "125" (Mile 623.7), you can cruise seven miles up the North Newport River to the small Half Moon Marina, which offers space for transients. Seven markers on shore, not in the water, indicate the best route; call the marina for directions as some of the markers may be down. The Half Moon Marina has no groceries or restaurants, but it is the last marina near the ICW southbound for the next 40 miles.

Johnson Creek—Mile 624 to Mile 629

NAVIGATION: Use Chart 11507. The ICW route continues down Johnson Creek's serpentine, deep and unobstructed natural channel. Water depths between flashing green "125" and red daybeacon "126" range from 10 to 12 feet, 3 to 5 feet less than charted. Green daybeacons "131" and "131A," at the lower bend of Johnson Creek, mark an extensive shoal making out from the east.

Anchorage: Cattle Pen Creek, off Johnson Creek, south of Mile 625, provides a fine overnight anchorage for smaller boats, but may be too narrow for larger boats that need more swinging room. While the charted depths inside Cattle Pen Creek are good, expect mean low water entrance depths to be only 7 feet, rather than the 14 feet shown on the chart.

Southbound out of Johnson Creek, the Wahoo River makes off the South Newport River portion of the ICW at Mile 630. The Wahoo River is a fine overnight anchorage if you are willing to backtrack about two miles. The tidal range throughout this area is 7 to 9 feet.

■ SAPELO SOUND—Mile 632

Heading south along the ICW, you exit Johnson Creek for a short run along the South Newport River to its mouth. Then comes Sapelo Sound, with similar cruising characteristics to St. Catherines Sound to the north. Skippers of slow boats: **Note that low slack water on Sapelo Sound** (at Mile 632) **occurs 30 minutes before it occurs at the Savannah River Entrance.**

The ICW route heads up Sapelo Sound to the Sapelo River, running past Sapelo Island. Once owned by tobacco magnate R.J. Reynolds, this island now houses the University of Georgia's Marine Institute, one of the East Coast's outstanding research centers.

On Sapelo Sound, as well as other large sounds, give both lighted aids and daybeacons a wider berth than usual, especially around low tide. Keep track of your markers, running a compass course between distant ones. Many boats have erroneously run for an outlying sea buoy instead of a marker leading into a nearby tributary.

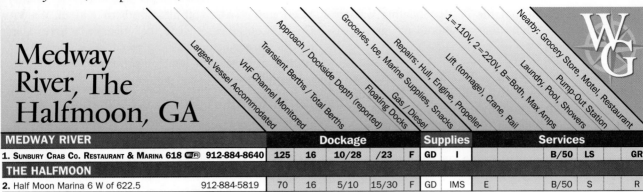

Medway River, The Halfmoon, GA

MEDWAY RIVER	Largest Vessel Accommodated	VHF Channel Monitored	Transient Berths / Total Berths	Approach / Dockside Depth (reported)	Floating Docks	Gas / Diesel	Groceries, Ice, Marine Supplies, Snacks	Repairs: Hull, Engine, Propeller	Lift (tonnage), Crane, Rail	1=110V, 2=220V, B=Both, Max Amps	Laundry, Pool, Showers	Pump-Out Station	Nearby: Grocery Store, Motel, Restaurant
	Dockage					Supplies				Services			
1. Sunbury Crab Co. Restaurant & Marina 618 (WiFi) 912-884-8640	**125**	**16**	**10/28**	**/23**	**F**	**GD**	**I**			**B/50**	**LS**		**GR**
THE HALFMOON													
2. Half Moon Marina 6 W of 622.5 912-884-5819	70	16	5/10	15/30	F	GD	IMS	E		B/50	S		R

Corresponding chart(s) not to be used for navigation. Internet Access (WiFi) Wireless Internet Access

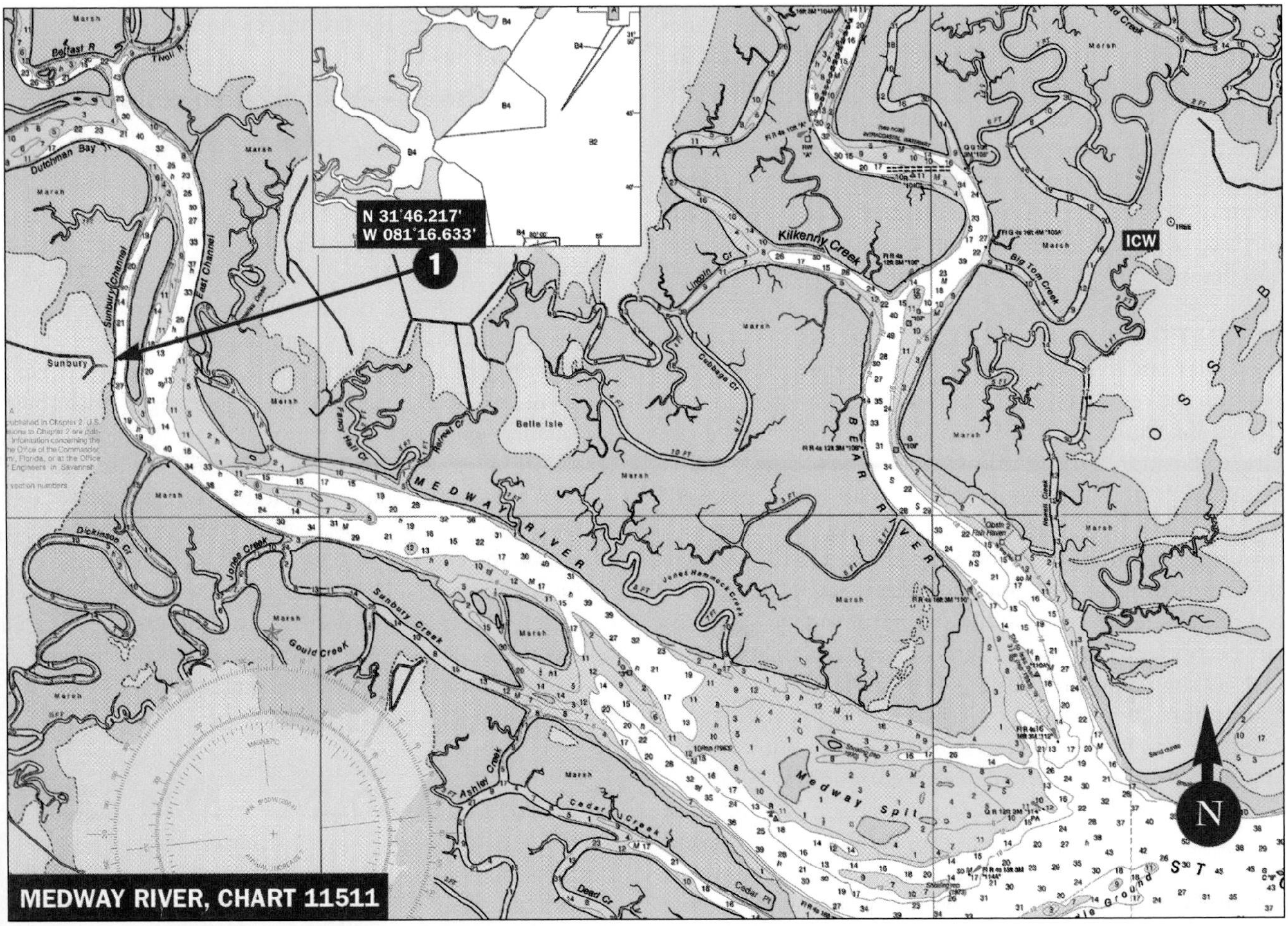

MEDWAY RIVER, CHART 11511

NAVIGATION: Use Chart 11507. As you cruise along Sapelo Sound, red daybeacon "136," red daybeacon "136A" and flashing red "138" need an especially wide berth—shoaling seems to extend farther out every year. Marker "137" on the "breakers" area, between red daybeacon "136" and flashing red "138," is no longer present and is not shown on recent charts. It had marked a 5-foot-deep bank to the east. There is less than 12 feet of water between red daybeacon "136" and flashing red "138" at mid-tide. Red daybeacon "136A," south of red daybeacon "136," marks the shoal. The most recent charts show the magenta line on the wrong side of red daybeacon "136A," but remember that the markers are placed for a reason, and you should honor them.

Mind the markers at the western end of Sapelo Sound, where the ICW route enters the Sapelo River. At low tide,

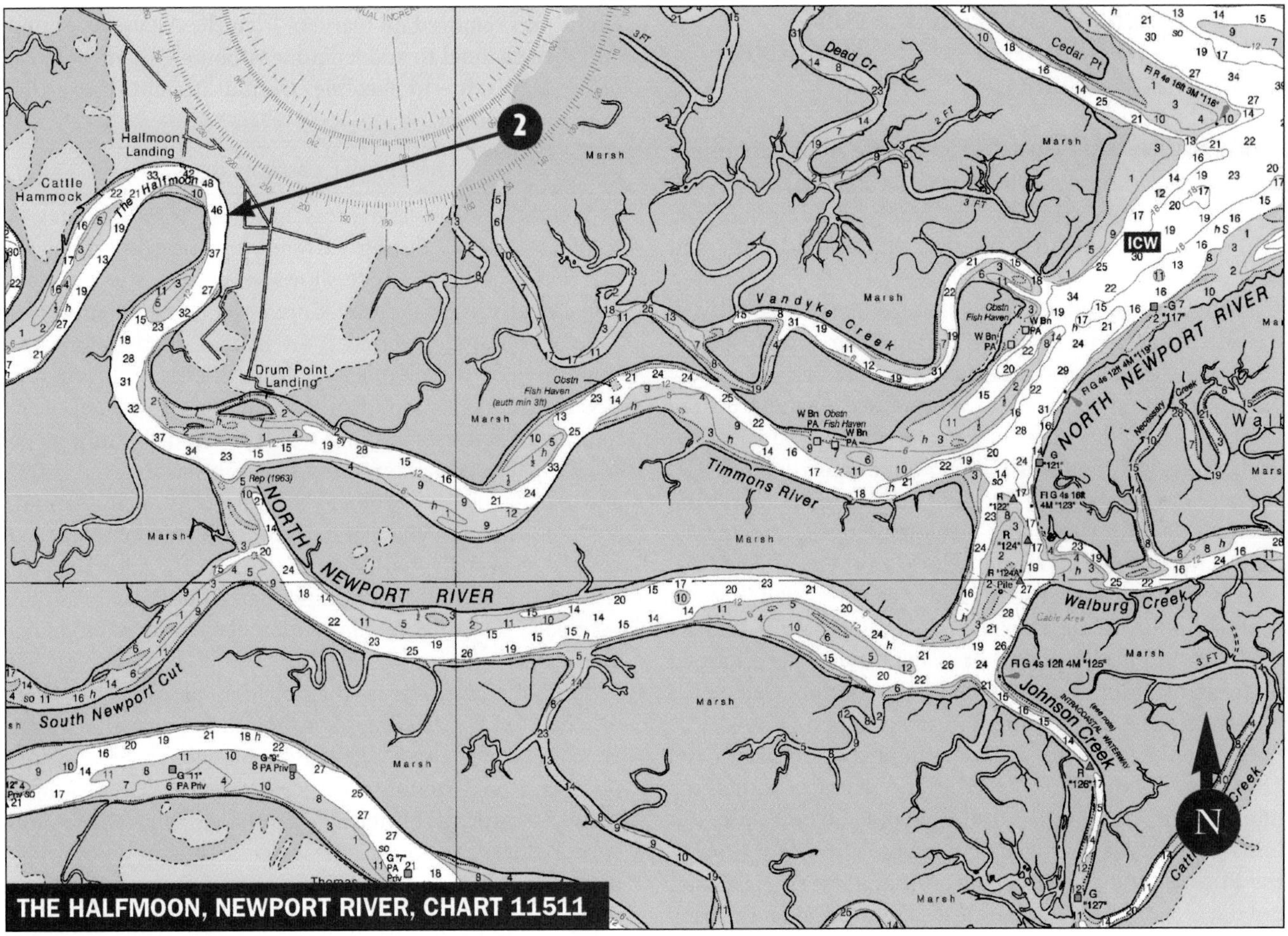

THE HALFMOON, NEWPORT RIVER, CHART 11511

approach the whole stretch with caution. Water depths of 10 to 12 feet (less than charted) exist between red daybeacons "150" and "150A." *(See page 92 for more information about Sapelo Sound and Inlet.)*

Front River to Doboy Sound—Mile 640 to Mile 649

Heading south, the ICW route leaves the Sapelo River and enters the Front River. The Front River is narrow but deep in mid-channel. Many of the hummocks of land west of the channel show piles of ballast stone, all that remains of a once-prosperous riverside community.

SHOALING Mile 643.7

WATERWAY GUIDE PHOTOGRAPHY

NAVIGATION: Use Chart 11507. The ICW route continues south along the Front River, before heading into Creighton Narrows (Mile 642). Back north on the Front River, observe red daybeacon "150A," which marks shoals and a submerged wreck to the west. Along this stretch through Creighton Narrows, you are aided by a succession of daybeacons and lights; observe them all carefully. At Mile 640, red daybeacon "154" marks shoaling along the west bank. When leaving Creighton Narrows and entering the Crescent River, run straight past red daybeacon "156" until passing flashing green "157" to avoid shallow depths to the west. You will be lined up on a navigational range and then turn to round a shoal where the remains of a wrecked shrimp boat lie. The shoal, which is bare at low tide, is marked by red daybeacons "158," "158A" and "160." Give these red daybeacons a wide berth to avoid both the wreckage and the mud shoal that extends into the channel. If you go aground here, try powering off toward the eastern bank for deeper water. These aids lead you into unobstructed Old Teakettle Creek, which widens as it reaches Doboy Sound at Mile 649.

If your boat is slow, **note that low slack water in Doboy Sound at Mile 649 occurs 32 minutes before it does at the Savannah River Entrance.** Arriving at Doboy Sound at low slack water will speed up your run from Mile 644 to Mile 654. (Trying to hit low slack water at either Sapelo Sound or Buttermilk Sound is not quite as critical, as both of these sounds provide more open waters and easier currents to navigate.)

Anchorage: Some boats anchor to the west of where Creighton Narrows empties into the Crescent River, but a large shrimping fleet goes through the anchorage area at all hours. The most popular anchorage between Sapelo Sound and Doboy Sound is New Teakettle Creek at Mile 646.5. The charted depths are good, and the best protection lies around the first bend to starboard. Be careful to avoid the charted 2-foot lump in New Teakettle Creek just past Mary Creek. An attractive, but seldom-used anchorage is up the Duplin River at Mile 649. Go past the very busy ferry dock at Marsh Landing a mile or so to the high ground of Little Sapelo Island. Note the overhead power cable upstream on the Duplin River with a 38-foot vertical clearance.

Doboy Sound to Buttermilk Sound—Mile 650 to Mile 660 (Little Mud River & Altamaha Sound)

NAVIGATION: Use Chart 11507. The ICW continues down Doboy Sound to flashing red "178" at the mouth of the North River. Follow the range carefully here and in the dredged areas past the Darien, Rockdedundy and South rivers.

The Coast Guard has placed channel markers all the way to Darien, seven miles up the Darien River, which shrimp boats use heavily. Shoaling to 5-foot depths (mean low water) has been reported in the marked channel up the Darien River, and further shoaling on the west side between daybeacons "27" and "29" was reported in early 2011.

Plan your passage for mid-tide and rising going off the ICW up the river. Cruising boats making the trip up the Darien River can find transient dockage at Darien Landing, with water and electricity and nearby restaurants. A second option is the Downtown Development Authority docks (free but no power or water), which are located in front of Skipper's Fish Camp Restaurant. Call (912) 437-6686 ext. 6 for docking information/permission.

Back in the ICW, the shallow water between flashing red "184" and flashing green "185" in the channel south of the mouth of the Darien River can be avoided by carefully following the ICW's charted magenta line. The 5-foot shoal in the Rockdedundy River between flashing green "185" and red daybeacon "188" can be cleared by staying on the back range until you reach flashing red "190."

THE FOLLOWING AREA REQUIRES SPECIAL ATTENTION DUE TO SHOALING OR CHANGES TO THE CHANNEL

LITTLE MUD RIVER

The ICW follows a dredged channel down Little Mud River to the Altamaha Sound and on into Buttermilk Sound. Although the Little Mud River is one of the shallowest areas on the entire ICW, this area was not on the list of locations to be dredged with the stimulus money. The reported reason is that environmental restrictions have prevented approval of a designated spoil disposal site.

A U.S. Army Corps of Engineers (USACE) survey, dated April 2010, reported less than 5-foot mean low water depth along the centerline of the North and Little Mud River channels, with 3-foot depths in both the east quarter and west quarters (between flashing red "190" and "198"). The most shoal-prone area remains between red daybeacon "194" and flashing green "195." In early 2011, it was noted by our cruising editors that there was 6.9 feet just prior to red daybeacon "194" at about three hours before low water. Boaters consistently report shallower depths than does the USACE. It is best to plan this transit for a rising two-thirds tide. Crosscurrents can quickly push slow vessels out of the channel when exiting narrow stretches like the Little Mud River to enter open water like Altamaha Sound. Follow Range "B" carefully. Note that Range "A," noted on older charts, no longer exists. The Coast Guard has removed all markers from the Altamaha Sound entrance channel to and from the Atlantic Ocean (not part of the ICW) due to shoaling. Do not attempt to use this inlet to the ocean.

END SPECIAL CAUTION AREA.

Watch for bare-land areas near the ICW channel in Altamaha Sound during extreme low tides, particularly in areas where the chart shows less than 3 feet at low tide. An April 2010 Army Corps of Engineers survey of Altamaha Sound reported 8- to 12-foot depths along the centerline of the channel, at least 8-foot depths in the east quarter and 7-foot depths in the west quarter at mean low water between flashing red "198" and flashing green "213." There is shallow water between flashing red "202" and red daybeacon "208" as you leave Altamaha Sound, so do not hug the channel markers (four red markers) too closely, especially red daybeacon "208." Cruisers report shallow water and groundings near red daybeacon "208." *(See page 94 for more information about Altamaha Sound and Inlet.)*

The narrow dredged channel that passes green daybeacon "211," heading southbound toward a range ahead, is especially shallow along the edges. Strong currents and encroaching shoals warrant the use of ranges to well south of Buttermilk Sound. Strong winds and spring tides can lower the water a foot or two below mean low water depths. If you know that the tide will be too low when you reach one of the well-known shallow areas, like the Little Mud River, anchor for a while and let the tide rise before you enter.

Low slack water at Mile 655 occurs 38 minutes before it occurs at the Savannah River Entrance. At Mile 660, only 5 miles away, low slack water occurs two hours and 6 minutes before it does at Savannah.

Buttermilk Sound to Hampton River—Mile 660 to Mile 664

NAVIGATION: Use Chart 11507. Buttermilk Sound was dredged in November 2009. Check our website, www.waterwayguide.com, for the latest updates. This area is historically prone to shoaling.

Heading south from Buttermilk Sound, several sets of ranges guide you over the flats to the headwaters of the southward-flowing Mackay River. Watch for new or revised buoys here, and be especially wary of the charted shoals near the mouth of the South Altamaha River between red daybeacon "216A" and flashing red "218," at Mile 662: They are encroaching on the channel.

An April 2010 USACE survey, the most recent at press time, indicated a controlling depth of 10.5 feet (mean low water) along the centerline of the channel in Buttermilk Sound between red daybeacon "216A" and flashing green "223." The shallowest depths in the west and east quarters was 10.5 feet. Follow the charted ranges and the magenta line to stay in the deepest water. For now, shoaling is not a problem here.

Sapelo River, Altamaha River, GA

SAPELO RIVER, ALTAMAHA RIVER		Largest Vessel Accommodated	VHF Channel Monitored	Transient Berths / Total Berths	Approach / Dockside Depth (reported)	Floating Docks	Gas / Diesel	Groceries, Ice, Marine Supplies, Snacks	Repairs: Hull, Engine, Propeller	Lift (tonnage), Crane, Rail	1=110V, 2=220V, B=Both, Max Amps	Laundry, Pool, Showers	Pump-Out Station	Nearby: Grocery Store, Motel, Restaurant
		Dockage					Supplies		Services					
1. Pine Harbor Marina	912-832-5999	23	16	/2	15/15	F	G							
2. Two Way Fish Camp	912-265-0410	175	16	10/110	10/15	F	GD	GIMS	HEP	L35	B/50	LS		G

Corresponding chart(s) not to be used for navigation. Internet Access Wireless Internet Access

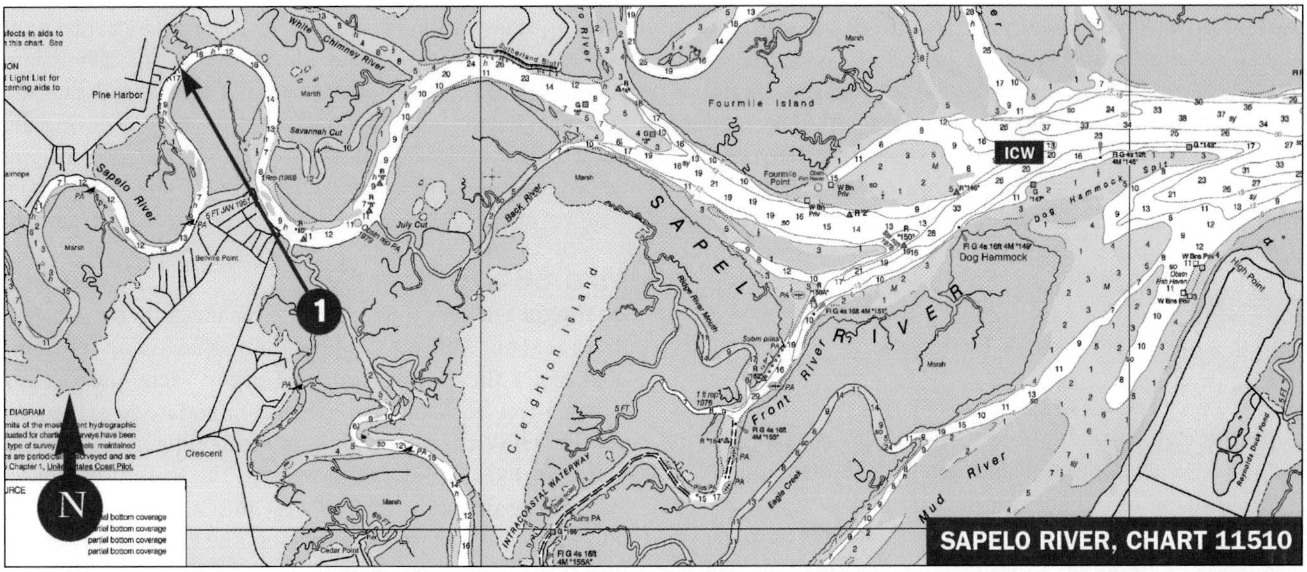

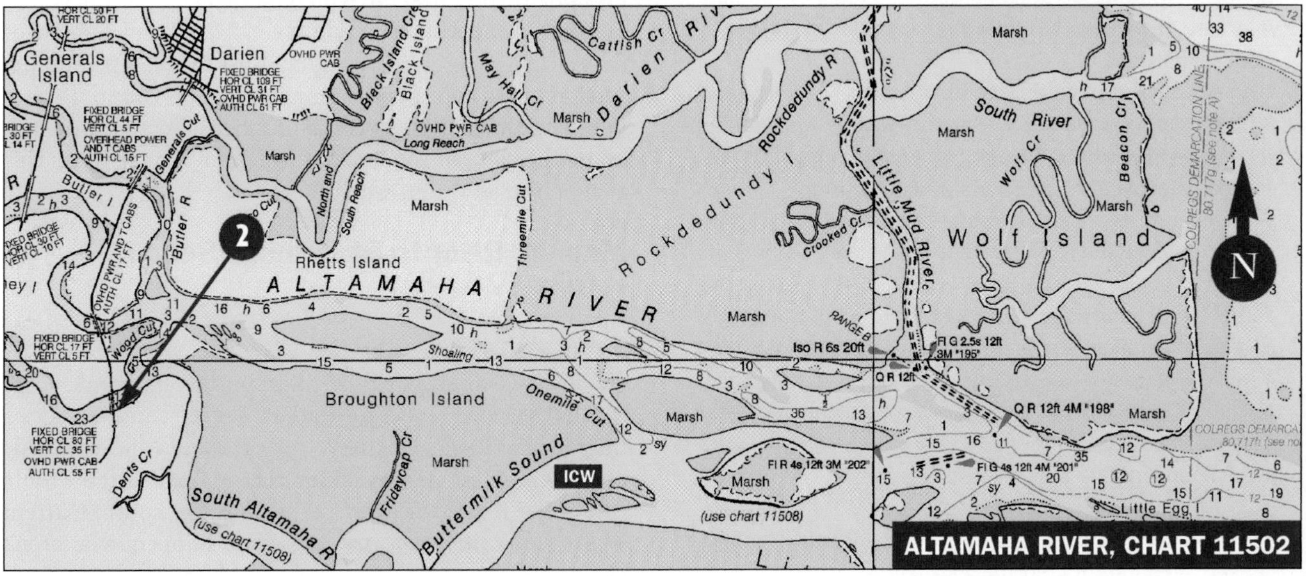

Anchorage: You can anchor up the South Altamaha River, off the ICW. Two Way Marina is up this river. The river is deep and well-marked with a 7-foot bar at the entrance near red daybeacon "218."

Hampton River, off the ICW

NAVIGATION: Use Chart 11507. At Mile 664, between red daybeacon "222" and flashing green "223," the Hampton River leads abruptly back to port. Shoaling extends into the channel from both riverbanks up to green daybeacon "27." Proceed slowly and watch the depth sounder. Daybeacons farther downstream mark some of the shoals, so pass wide of the markers. At green daybeacon "21," the charted obstruction is less than 4 feet underwater.

Dockage: About three miles up its marked channel, you will find the Hampton River Marina, set amidst the naturally beautiful marsh. The marina welcomes transients and offers some engine repair on site as well as other amenities. Across the Hampton River from the Hampton River Club is private Little St. Simons Island, a 10,000-acre barrier island accessible only by boat, with a resort limited to 24 overnight guests. Nature watching is the main activity on this pristine island, and the elegant, but rustic lodge-style accommodations include guided interpretive programs, canoeing through tidal creeks, fishing, horseback riding, bicycling and three meals a day. Dockage is available for guests arriving by private boat or for passengers aboard the resort's daily ferry service from Hampton River Marina.

Frederica River, off the ICW

At Mile 666 and flashing green "229," the Frederica River heads off the ICW to the east. This makes for a fun side trip as you wend your way north or south along the ICW. Slightly more scenic than the ICW in this area, the Frederica River flows past Fort Frederica National Monument on St. Simons Island, rejoins the ICW farther down the Mackay River at approximately Mile 674 and then continues under the fixed bridge east of the ICW. Morningstar Marina at Golden Isles is on the western shore south of the fixed bridge.

QUICK FACT:

FORT FREDERICA

Off the ICW on the Frederica River south of Mile 670, Fort Frederica National Monument, on St. Simons Island, GA, is home to the archeological remains of a fort and town built by James Oglethorpe in 1736. The fort was established to protect the southern boundary of his new colony (today's Georgia) from raids by Spanish forces in Florida and Cuba.

Known as the "Debatable Land," the land lying between British South Carolina and Spanish Florida was highly volatile and considered the epicenter of the ongoing conflict between Spain and Britain. Colonists from England, Scotland and the Germanic states assisted Oglethorpe in the establishment of the fort, which was named for Frederick Louis, the Prince of Wales (1702-1754). The name was feminized to distinguish it from Fort Frederick in South Carolina. The fort proved effective in 1742, when the garrison and Oglethorpe's forces successfully repelled the Spanish during the War of Jenkins' Ear. The fray, which included the battle at "Bloody Marsh," found the Spanish unable to retake St. Simons. They retreated from Georgia after a short time.

Fort Frederica was no longer needed once the Spanish ceased their threats, so the garrison at Frederica was disbanded in 1749. The town declined and was eventually abandoned by the early 1760s. Nearly two centuries later, the fort was authorized as a National Monument and, starting in 1947, archaeologists unearthed sections of the fort and town with support of the National Park Service and the Fort Frederica Association. The Fort Frederica National Monument was listed on the National Register of Historic Places in 1966. Today, visitors can explore the fort and its history through tours, films and events.

NAVIGATION: Use Chart 11507. Take care if you are entering the Frederica River with the current. A bar protrudes from below flashing green "229," and the current seems to split here. Keep well to the north side at the entrance and don't hesitate. Flashing green "229" is now lighted (flashing every 2.5 seconds). Do not confuse it with flashing green "231" (flashing every four seconds) at the entrance to Wallys Leg.

Though winding and unmarked, this slightly longer side route runs deep to the shore, except at the mouth of the lower end at Manhead Sound, where the water depth is 5 feet midway between the two banks.

Many cruisers like to anchor in the Frederica River off the Fort Frederica National Monument. Visits ashore are possible at some states of the tide, but be mindful that the tide can sometimes rise and fall 2 feet in an hour during the middle of the cycle. Dinghies can be left high and dry, making reentry to the water difficult, if not impossible. The fort is well worth a visit, but it may be easier by car from a marina.

Mile 664 to Mile 675

Dockage: On Troup Creek, which makes into the Mackay River at about Mile 670, you might be able to find transient dockage at the private Hidden Harbor Yacht Club. They have 15-feet dockside and can accommodate vessels up to 100 feet. Call ahead to check for availability.

Anchorage: At Mile 666, west off the main ICW route, Wallys Leg opens up to the west into a good anchorage, but only in fair weather. Wind from the east can be annoying; out of the west, it will blow your socks off! Enter mid-stream opposite flashing green "231," and then favor the north shore; go in slowly and use the depth sounder. Anchor in 10-foot depths or more off the clump of trees to the north. Holding is good, but the current is strong, so know the state of the tide and set your anchor well. This anchorage can get crowded in season.

Mackay River to St. Simons Sound —Mile 675

NAVIGATION: Use Charts 11507 and 11506. Flashing green "237" marks shallow water on the east bank. Keep red daybeacon "238" to starboard and continue along the Mackay River. The ICW now tracks to the west side of Lanier Island, versus taking the original easterly route (the lower Frederica River), when heading south. Current charts show this correctly, but some skippers who aren't paying attention may still attempt to take the wrong route around the eastern side of Lanier Island, only to be stopped by the welded-shut 9-foot clearance bridge. While boats sometimes anchor off the eastern side of Lanier Island, southeast of flashing green "241," we do not recommend it, particularly with winds out of the northeast.

A fixed highway bridge (65-foot vertical clearance) spans the Mackay River portion of the ICW at Mile 674.5. The current under this bridge is very strong. This five-mile stretch from Mile 673 to Mile 678 is straightforward; the only problem area is the shoal south of Lanier Island. Leave flashing greens "245," "247" and "249" well to port when passing. Flashing green "249" has been moved so that it appears to be far to the east of the ICW channel. Quick flashing red buoy "20" in the St. Simons entrance channel should be left to starboard southbound on the ICW heading towards Jekyll Creek. Heading north, you can arrive at Mile 678 at low slack water, and ride the flood current up the Mackay River. St. Simons Sound can be rough when the wind and current are opposed *(See page 95 for more information about St. Simon's Sound and Inlet.)*.

■ ST. SIMONS ISLAND

Mile 676

At the southern tip of St. Simons Island, an old village serves as a permanent resort colony. On the island's ocean side, exclusive Sea Island is home to the fashionable five-star Cloister Hotel and beautifully landscaped residences. When entering and exiting the marked channel to Morningstar Marinas at Golden Isles, follow the chart carefully, and do not confuse these channel markers with the ICW markers nearby. The markers have recently been reconfigured and may differ from what is shown on your chart. **Use the Savannah River Entrance Tide Table. For St. Simon's Sound Bar high tide, subtract one minute; for low tide, subtract two minutes.** Refer to the tide tables in our Skipper's Handbook section.

WATERWAY GUIDE PHOTOGRAPHY

Dockage: The Morningstar Marina at Golden Isles is two miles north of Mile 676, on the east side of Lanier Island. This facility is south of the welded-shut bridge (9-foot vertical clearance) across the Frederica River connecting Lanier Island with St. Simons Island, so it must be approached from the south. Enjoying much-deserved popularity, Golden Isles offers knowledgeable personnel, ample amenities and immediate access to historic St. Simons Island, just over the bridge. The marina staff report that former difficulties with the current setting boats into the docks, especially on the ebb, has been alleviated with the present configuration of the docks. There is still strong current running parallel to the docks, so be sure you have fenders rigged before you come alongside.

Anchorage: Just downstream from Morningstar Marinas at Golden Isles, at the head of St. Simons Sound, the Coast Guard has established a special anchorage area. Yachts measuring 65 feet or less are not required to show anchor lights in the area, but it is a good idea to do so anyway. The bottom is hard in some places, and it is difficult to get the anchor set. Pick a spot clear of the few moorings and be mindful of the current. Wakes can be a problem at the outer end of the anchorage, near green daybeacon "7." Morningstar Marina provides dinghy dockage for a modest fee.

The Saint Simons Island Lighthouse framed by palm trees.
©IstockPhoto/lightasafeather.

St. Simons Island Area, GA

ST. SIMONS ISLAND AREA		Largest Vessel Accommodated	VHF Channel Monitored	Transient Berths / Total Berths	Approach / Dockside Depth (reported)	Floating Docks	Gas / Diesel	Groceries, Ice, Marine Supplies, Snacks	Repairs: Hull, Engine, Propeller	Lift (tonnage), Crane, Rail	1=110V, 2=220V, B=Both, Max Amps	Laundry, Pool, Showers	Pump-Out Station	Nearby: Grocery Store, Motel, Restaurant
		Dockage					Supplies		Services					
1. **Hampton River Marina 3.5 E of 664** Internet Access, Wireless Internet Access	912-638-1210	55	16/68	12/25	12/12	F	GD	IMS	E	L5	B/50	S		
2. **Hidden Harbor Yacht Club** Internet Access, Wireless Internet Access	918-261-1049	100	16	10/	15/15	F		G	Transient and long-term slips available					
3. Morningstar Marinas at Golden Isles 2 S of 677 Wireless Internet Access	912-634-1128	200	16/68	50/137	10/18	F		GIMS	EP	L10	B/50	LPS	P	R

Corresponding chart(s) not to be used for navigation. Internet Access, Wireless Internet Access

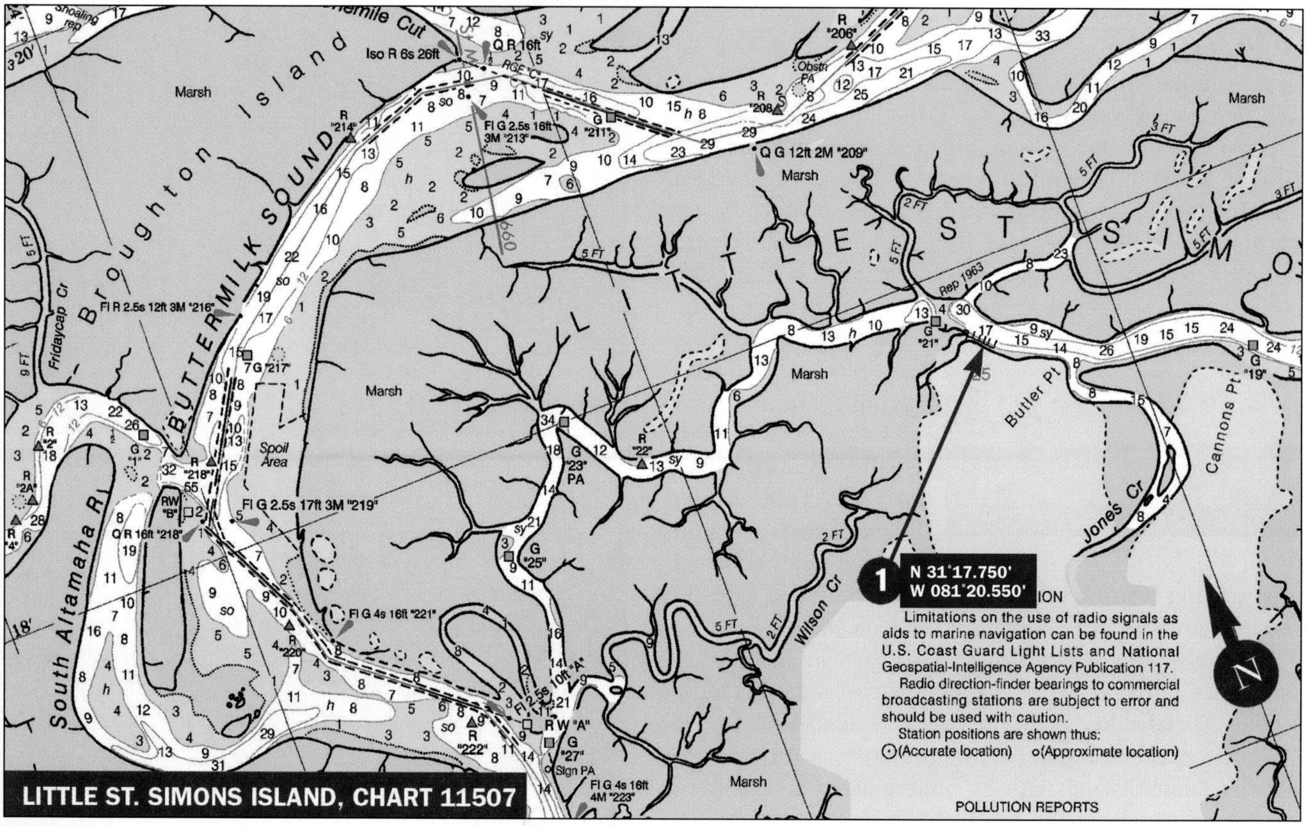

LITTLE ST. SIMONS ISLAND, CHART 11507

GOIN' ASHORE:
ST. SIMONS ISLAND, GA

One of Georgia's Golden Isles and largest of its sea islands, St. Simons Island is a draw for history buffs, golf and tennis players, nature lovers and, of course, boaters.

History: Gen. James Oglethorpe brought colonists and soldiers to St. Simon's in 1736, building Fort Frederica as Georgia's first military outpost on the banks of the Frederica River. Today, it is a national monument where visitors can still see the tabby powder magazine, cannons and the foundations of many of the original town buildings.

In 1742, the English repulsed a Spanish attempt to add Georgia to its territories in the Battle of Bloody Marsh, supposedly named because the marsh turned red with Spanish blood. Locals say it is why Georgians speak English rather than Spanish. Another contribution to warfare came from Gascoigne Bluff, where live oaks were harvested for our new country's battleships, including the *USS Constitution,* known as "Old Ironsides."

In the 1740s, the reverends John and Charles Wesley, Anglican priests, accompanied Gen. Oglethorpe to St. Simons Island where John Wesley, the father of Methodism, preached a sermon at a site south of the fort—the eventual site of Christ Church. The original church, the third oldest Episcopal church in the country, was built in 1820. It was destroyed by Union troops during the Civil War but was rebuilt in 1886 by Anson Phelps Dodge as a memorial to his wife.

During the 19th century, many antebellum plantations were established on the island to grow cotton and indigo. Hampton Plantation, on the northern coast, served as the hiding place for Vice President Aaron Burr after he shot Alexander Hamilton to death in an 1804 duel. The ruins of many of the plantations can still be seen, particularly Retreat Plantation, which is now part of the Sea Island Golf Club. The slave burial ground and ruins of the slave hospital

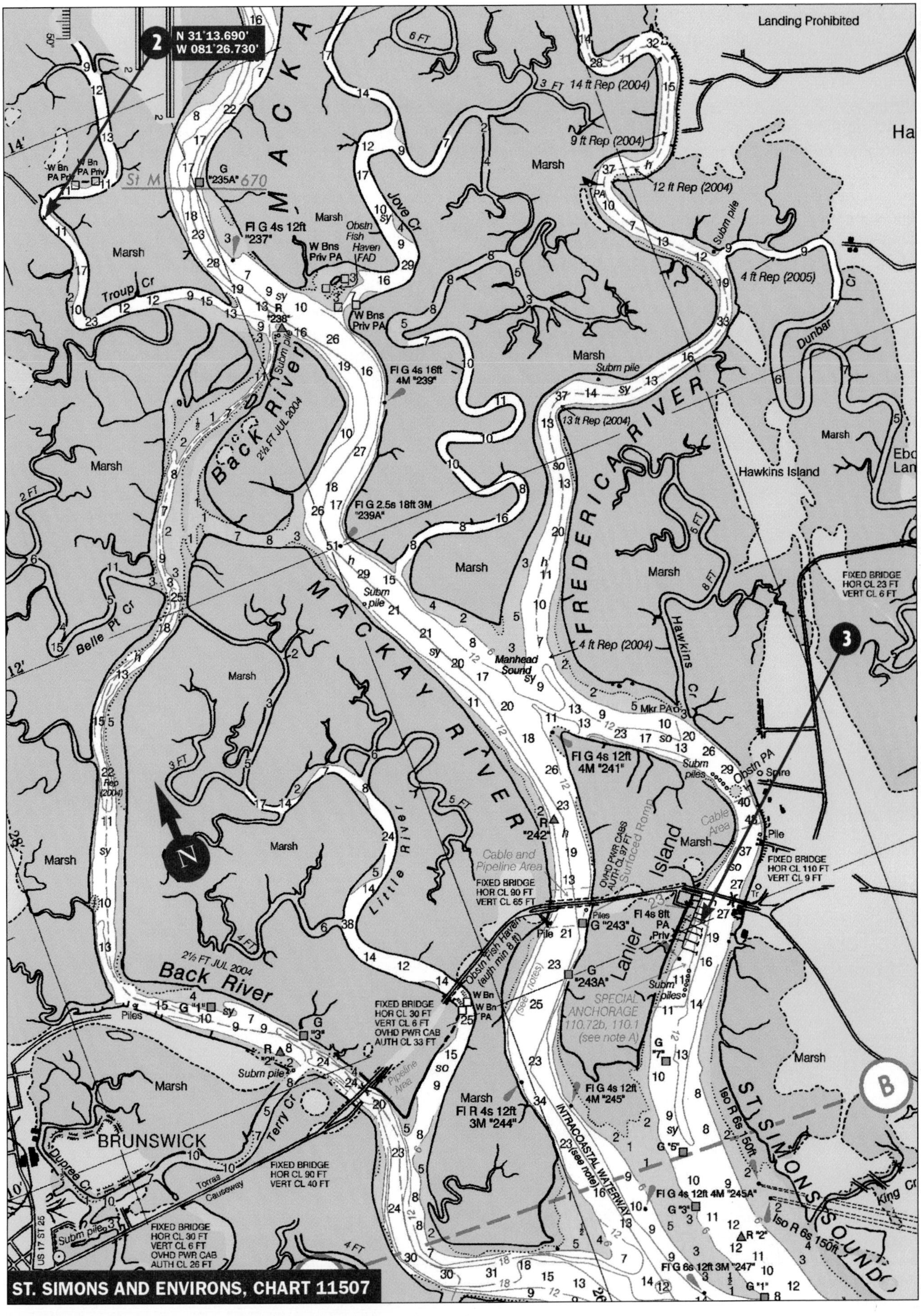

ST. SIMONS AND ENVIRONS, CHART 11507

and plantation house still exist. The golf courses, however, are only open to members of the club or guests staying at the Lodge or the Cloisters. Visitors can drive along the Avenue of Oaks, the entrance to the club, to view some of the ruins.

Attractions: Now a popular tourist destination, St. Simons was named one of the best places to retire by *Money Magazine*. The southern tip of the island is a hub of activity centered around the Village and Pier (along Mallery St.). Here, you will find a concentration of tourist-oriented shops and restaurants. Just east of the pier is Neptune Park, a beachfront picnic area, playground and the site of numerous festivals. On the far side of the park is the St. Simons Island Visitors Center, housed in the St. Simons Island Casino, and the landmark lighthouse, the original keeper's dwelling and the A.W. Jones Heritage Center.

Do make the strenuous climb up the narrow, winding staircase of the 1872 lighthouse for a great view of the island and St. Simons Sound. The keeper's cottage has a museum with the history of the lighthouse. The original, built in 1807, was destroyed by Confederate troops in 1862 to prevent the Union forces from using it. The Heritage Center has exhibits about island history.

Farther along at East Beach, the old Coast Guard Station houses the Maritime Center and the Honey Creek Coastal Encounters Nature Center. Meet Ollie, a 1940s "coastie," who describes the Coast Guard and local natural history. For other environmental education experiences, there are beach and marsh explorations, maritime forest ecology walks, kayaking and paddleboat rentals.

Shopping: For provisioning, banks, drugstores and a number of shopping centers populate Frederica and Demere roads. Also, there is a Harris Teeter market (600 Sea Island Rd., 912-638-8100). The Morningstar Marinas at Golden Isles does have a courtesy car with a limit of one-hour use. A fun way to explore is to rent a two-, four- or six-seat electrical car, available by the hour or day from Beachcomber Buggies. Be mindful of the fact that when renting one of these vehicles, you need transportation to get to their facility. The Brunswick Golden Isles Airport is serviced by Delta Airlines and is less than 30 minutes away.

Restaurants: Eateries are widely available, from ice cream and sandwich spots to full-service restaurants. The Coastal Kitchen, at Morningstar Marinas at Golden Isles (102 Marina Drive, 912-638-7790) offers lunch, dinner and Sunday brunch. It is worth visiting just for the view from the deck, overlooking the marina and out to St. Simons Sound. Another casual spot is Mullet Bay Seafood Restaurant (512 Ocean Blvd., 912-634-9977), with a wide porch, where you can dine on fresh local seafood as well as a good pasta selection. There are a lot of fine restaurants scattered throughout the village.

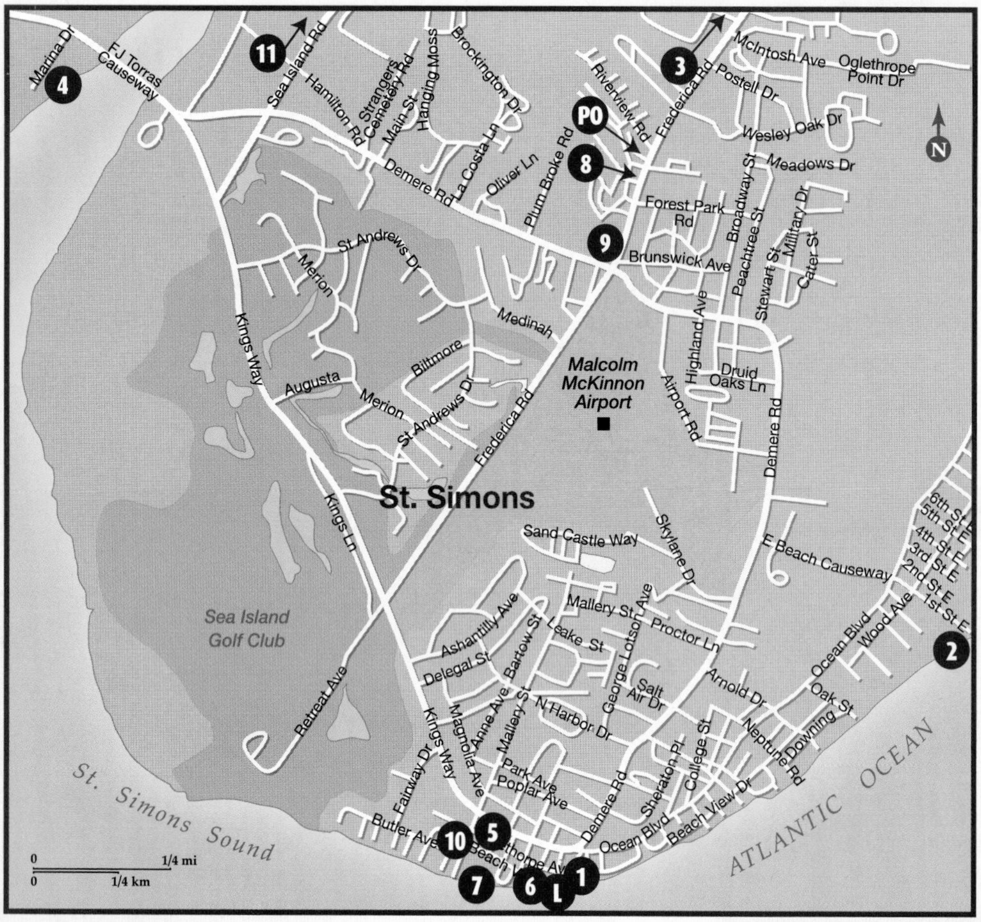

ATTRACTIONS
1 Lighthouse & Museum
2 Maritime Center
3 Fort Frederica

DINING
4 The Coastal Kitchen
5 Mullet Bay

INFORMATION/ POINTS OF INTEREST
6 St. Simons Island Visitors Center

RECREATION
7 Neptune Park

SHOPPING
8 Retreat Village
9 Redfern Village
10 Village and Pier
11 Harris Teeter Market

L LIBRARY

PO POST OFFICE

Reference the marina listing tables to see all the marinas in the area.

ADDITIONAL RESOURCES

- ST. SIMONS ISLAND, GA: www.saintsimons.com
- GEORGIA COAST: www.visitcoastalgeorgia.com
- BEACHCOMBER BUGGIES: 541 Ocean Blvd., St. Simons Island, 912-638-2966 www.beachcomberbuggies.com

NEARBY GOLF COURSES
Sea Palms Golf & Tennis Resort,
5445 Frederica Road, St. Simons Island, GA 31522
912-638-3351, www.seapalms.com

NEARBY MEDICAL FACILITIES
Southeast Georgia Health System
St. Simons Immediate Care Center
500 Wellness Way, St. Simons Island, GA 31522
912-466-5900

BRUNSWICK

Heading south from St. Simons Island, the ICW crosses St. Simons Sound and runs three miles up the wide Brunswick River to the mouth of Jekyll Creek (Mile 681), which flows between Jekyll Island and marshland. From there, the ICW proper continues south down Jekyll Creek, which eventually hooks up with Jekyll Sound, farther south.

NAVIGATION: Use Charts 11489 or 11506. **Use the Savannah River Entrance Tide Table. For Brunswick, East River high tide, add 59 minutes; for low tide, add 51 minutes.** You can follow the main shipping channel, which branches off the ICW at flashing red "22" on the Brunswick River. In heading up the Brunswick River in the vicinity of red flashing "20A" and "22," note that the charted sand bars to the north are now a huge spoil island appearing to be at least 10 feet above the high tide line. It was created with dredge material from a deepening of the entrance to St. Simons Sound, and a rock bulkhead surrounds the island. The warning beacons around this island are not lit or currently charted. The island is highly visible in daylight, but if you are traveling at night or in other conditions of poor visibility, be sure to stay in the marked channel. This route leads in a westerly direction before turning north at flashing green "1" and heading to downtown Brunswick. Crossing the shipping channel is the Sidney Lanier Bridge, which carries Route 17. It is a suspension bridge with more than 230 feet of vertical clearance. The old lift bridge has been removed.

Dockage: Unfortunately, anchoring off the Brunswick city docks is strictly prohibited, but Brunswick does have a nice marina, Brunswick Landing Marina, north of the Sidney Lanier Bridge. At flashing green buoy "1," head north, following the Brunswick Harbor range markers to the marina just beyond the shrimp boat docks. This full-service marina is in the center of Brunswick's Historic District, protected from all directions, and its surrounding waters have little current, making maneuvering easy. With dockside depths of at least 12 feet, it can accommodate vessels up to 230 feet. The marina's boatyard and lift are north of the transient facilities. Amenities include an air-conditioned captain's lounge and laundry facilities (free for boats docked at the marina). There are currently plans to enlarge the marina so that docks will extend northward all the way to the boatyard. The boatyard has expanded its dry storage area.

Ocean Petroleum, with very reasonable fuel prices, is located just before Brunswick Landing in the historic district. They offer gas and diesel with quantity discounts. You may be able to secure overnight dockage here in a pinch.

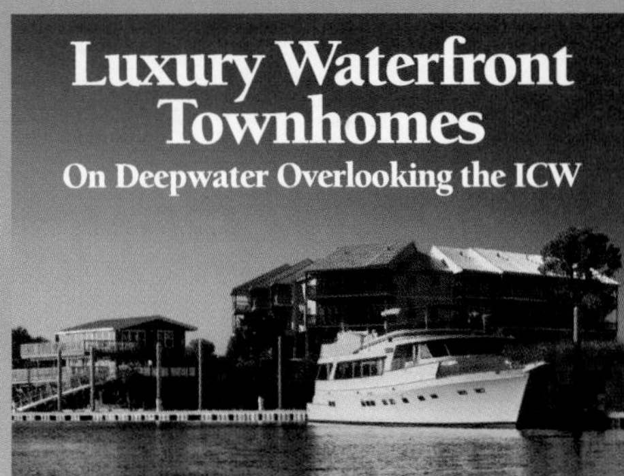

GOIN' ASHORE:

BRUNSWICK, GA

Known as the "Gateway to the Golden Isles," the "Land of Five Flags" and the birthplace of the original Brunswick stew, Brunswick now boasts a revitalized commercial and residential historic district. It is delightful to walk around this section of town under the old live oaks festooned with Spanish moss, admiring the stately old homes and specialty shops or to stroll along the waterfront park with a farmers' market, shrimp boats and the marina.

History: The British gave the town its name from Braunsweig, Germany, the ancestral home of King George III; however, five nations have claimed this area of Georgia as their own. First, explorer Hernando de Soto raised the Spanish flag in 1540, followed by Frenchman Jean Ribault in 1562, who sought to establish a haven for French Huguenots. In 1565, the Spanish expelled the French and ruled again until Gen. James Oglethorpe established Fort Frederica on St. Simons Island in 1736. The British flag flew until the Revolutionary War. The American flag was lowered during the Civil War, replaced by the stars and bars of the Confederate flag until 1865, when the United States flag was raised once again.

Brunswick has been a port city since the 1700s and continues its commercial heritage. Besides the cargo and shrimp traffic, the J.A. Jones Company built Liberty Ships during World War II. The shipyard set an unbroken record in December 1944 by constructing seven ships in one month with only six under-construction berths available.

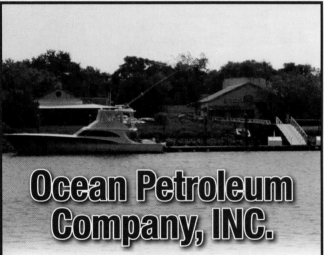

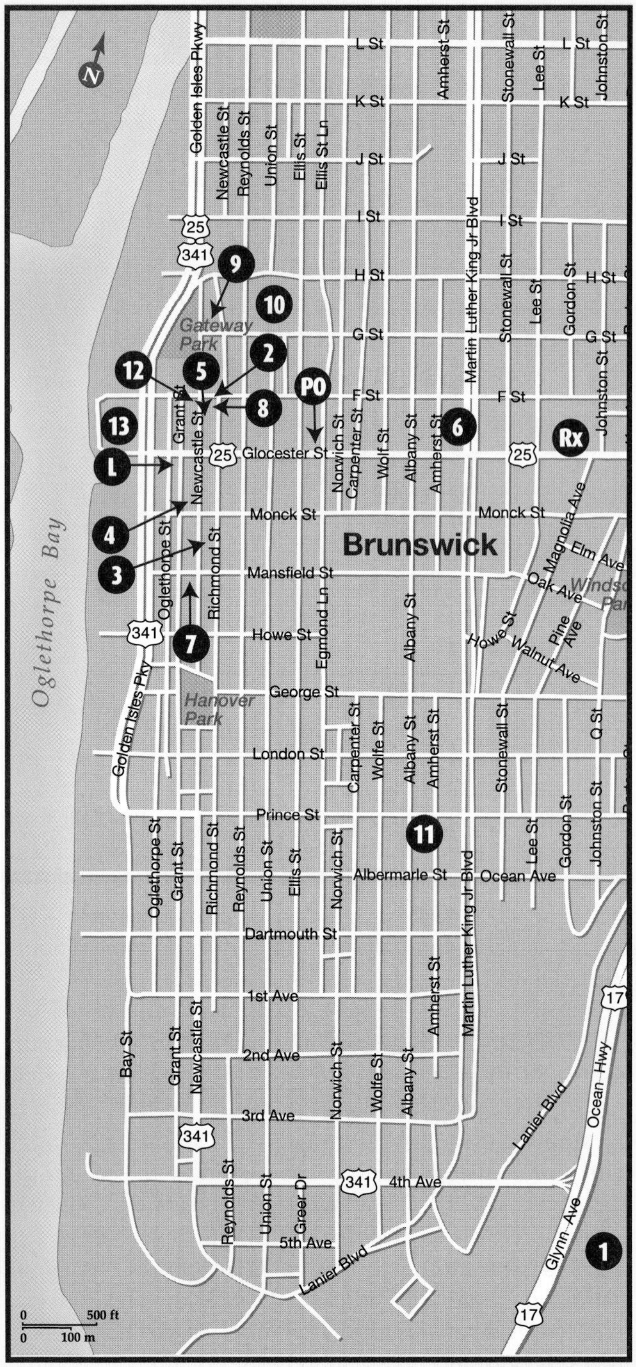

Reference the marina listing tables to see all the marinas in the area.

ATTRACTIONS
1 Marshes of Glynn

DINING
2 Brewburgers & the Riva Club Lounge
3 Jim's Corner Cafe
4 Fox's Pizza Den

GROCERIES/CARRYOUT
5 True Vine Wine and Gourmet
6 Brunswick Farmers' Market

INFORMATION
7 Brunswick Historic City Hall

POINTS OF INTEREST
8 The Ritz Theatre
9 The Mahoney-McGarvey House
10 Glynn County Courthouse
11 The Lover's Oak
12 Hatties Books

RECREATION
13 Mary Ross Waterfront Park

LIBRARY

POST OFFICE

PHARMACY

Brunswick, GA

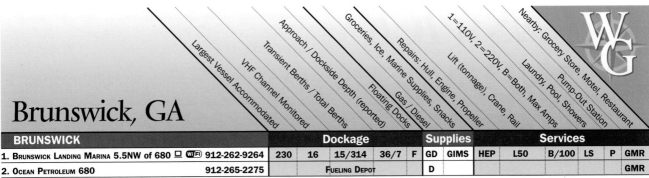

BRUNSWICK	Largest Vessel Accommodated	VHF Channel Monitored	Transient Berths / Total Berths	Approach / Dockside Depth (reported)	Floating Docks	Gas / Diesel	Groceries, Ice, Marine Supplies, Snacks	Repairs: Hull, Engine, Propeller	Lift (tonnage), Crane, Rail	1=110V, 2=220V, B=Both, Max Amps	Laundry, Pool, Showers	Pump-Out Station	Nearby: Grocery Store, Motel, Restaurant
	Dockage					Supplies		Services					
1. Brunswick Landing Marina 5.5NW of 680 □ WiFi 912-262-9264	230	16	15/314	36/7	F	GD	GIMS	HEP	L50	B/100	LS	P	GMR
2. Ocean Petroleum 680 912-265-2275	Fueling Depot					D							GMR

Corresponding chart(s) not to be used for navigation. □ Internet Access WiFi Wireless Internet Access

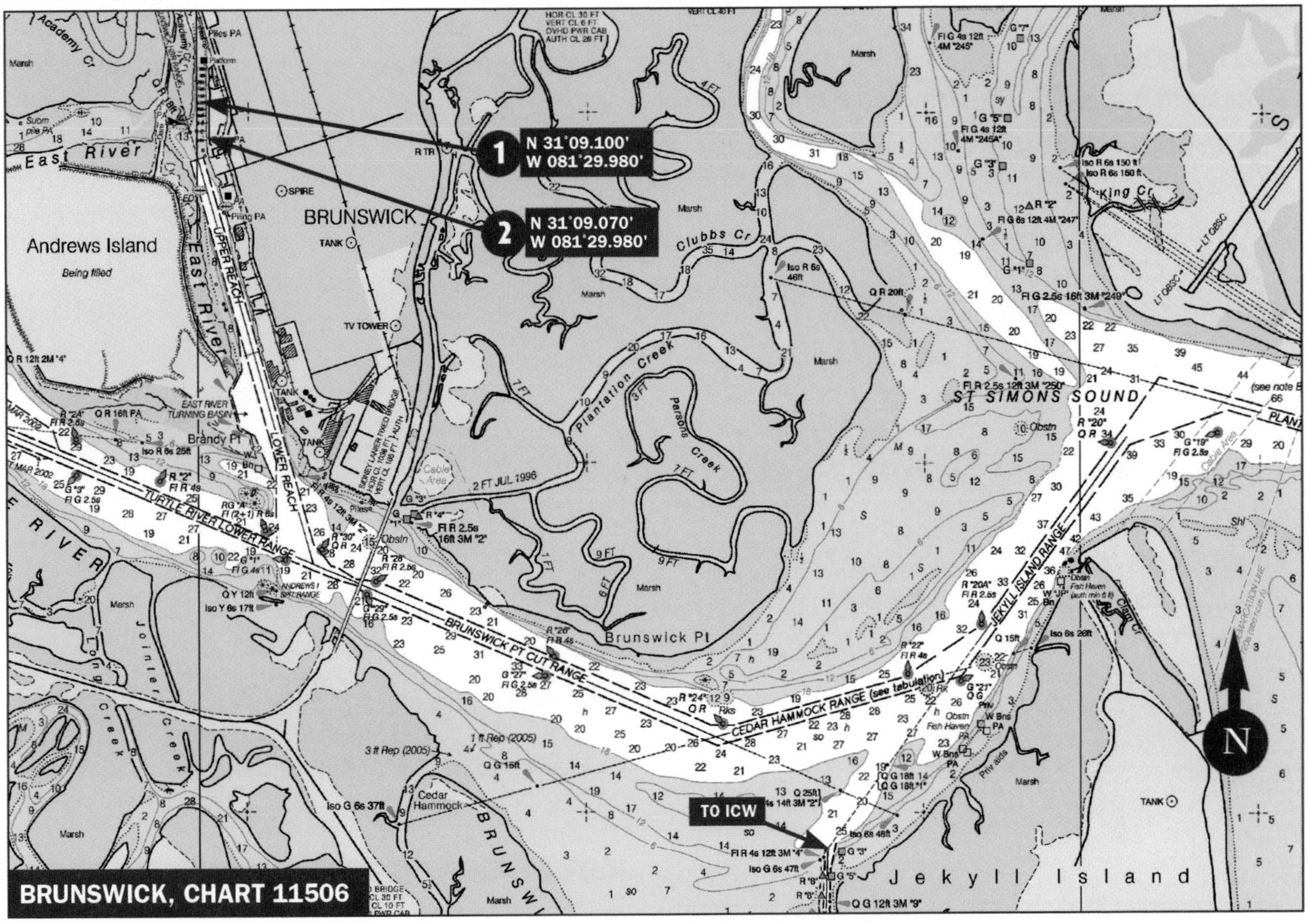

Looking east over Brunswick, GA, with the ICW and Atlantic Ocean in the distance. (Not to be used for navigation.) WATERWAY GUIDE PHOTOGRAPHY.

BRUNSWICK LANDING MARINA, INC

The areas only full service marina:

- 50 ton travellift
- Full shaft, propeller, strut, and rudder repairs.
- Diesel and gas engine mechanics.
- Fiberglass repairs.
- Painting and gelcoat work.
- Bottom cleaning and painting.
- Full detailing services available.
- Electronics repairs and sales.
- Holding tank pump-out facilities.
- Towing service.
- Charter fishing and sightseeing services.
- Rental cars available.
- Restaurants and lounges.
- A large assortment of clothing stores, drug stores, jewelry stores, marine hardwares, groceries, and other speciality stores.

Dockage:

- Well marked channel with 32′ maintained depth to lead dock, 12′ throughout marina.
- Diesel and gasoline sales available.
- 314 Slips and Transient dockage up to 225′ with up to 100 amp service
- Phone and cable T.V. hook-ups available upon requests.
- Restroom, shower, and laundry facilities.
- Free Wireless Internet

Olde Town Brunswick Historic District, Established 1771

The marina is located in the center of downtown Brunswick. The main street, Newcastle Street, passes in front of the marina. Newcastle Street has original store fronts on all its retail stores, restaurants and offices. This business district is reminiscent of a turn-of-the-century, thriving southern town.

Within walking distance of:

- banks, lawyers, doctors, hair salons, restaurants and lounges.
- A large assortment of retail stores to serve all your needs, including antiques, books, jewelry, clothing, pharmaceuticals, health foods, marine hardware, groceries and other specialties.

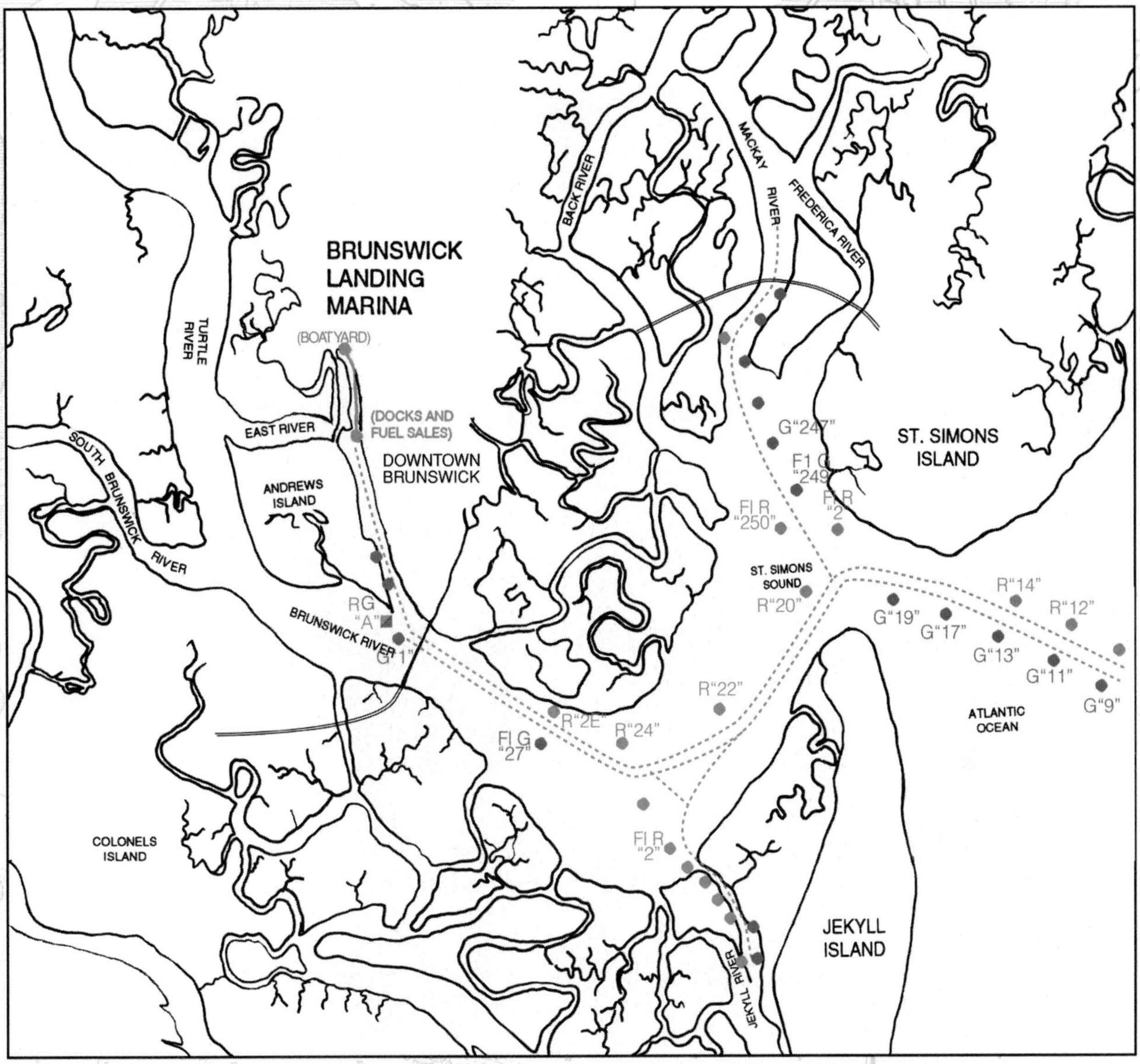

Not for Navigational purposes.

We monitor Channel 16

We honor Discover MasterCard and VISA

DISCOVER

MasterCard

VISA

Brunswick Landing Marina is a state-of-the-art facility. This modern marina will please you with its covered piers, concrete floating docks, and landscaped riverfront. Located in the heart of Historic Downtown Brunswick, you will enjoy this 1771 seaport town.

Brunswick Landing Marina, Inc.
2429 Newcastle Street
Brunswick, GA 31520

Phone: 912-262-9264
Fax: 912-262-9327
E-mail: blmarina@bellsouth.net

Culture: The Ritz Theatre (1530 Newcastle St.) in the Old Town opened in 1898 as the Grand Opera House, a three-story ornate Victorian building that also housed the offices of the Brunswick & Birmingham Railroad as well as retail establishments. It turned into a vaudeville stage, and in the 1930s became a movie theater. In the process, the brickwork was covered, and a marquee and the present sign were added, turning it into the art deco Ritz Theatre. The city purchased it in 1980 and altered it again but left the sign. It is slowly being restored to the original brickwork and glass look, and live performances once again are seen on its stage.

Attractions: The magnet that draws visitors to Brunswick is Old Town, a National Historic District, originally laid out by Oglethorpe in a series of squares, much like a mini Savannah. The area is delineated by H Street, Newcastle Street, First Avenue and Martin Luther King, Jr., with most of the streets retaining their original names honoring English royalty and military officers. The district is known for its turn-of-the-century architecture and eclectic mix of styles encompassing Victorian, Gothic Revival, Italianate, Queen Anne, Tudor and Craftsman, among others.

The Mahoney-McGarvey House on Reynolds Street is considered one of the finest examples of Carpenter Gothic architecture in the South. The old Glynn County Courthouse, built in 1907, is across the street, surrounded by live oaks and exotic trees like tung and Chinese pistachio. The Lover's Oak at the intersection of Albany and Prince Streets, a live oak purported to be 900 years old, has served as a romantic rendezvous spot for courting couples for centuries. Walking and driving tours are available. Check with the Information Station in Old City Hall on the corner of Mansfield and Newcastle Streets for downtown and area events, activities and services.

Along the river, stroll Mary Ross Waterfront Park with access to Brunswick Landing Marina, the shrimp boats, and the Brunswick Farmers' Market, held every Tuesday, Thursday and Saturday from 8:00 a.m. to dark. Other Brunswick-area attractions include the Marshes of Glynn, idealized by poet Sidney Lanier, and the Hofwyl-Broadfield Plantation on the banks of the Altamaha River. Built on the site of a cypress swamp in 1807, this well-preserved rice plantation had 350 slaves cultivating its 7,000 acres.

Special Events: The Brunswick Stewbilee is held annually on the second Saturday in October. Amateur and professional chefs, some with "secret" recipes, face off to compete for the coveted title of "Brunswick Stewmaster."

Shopping: Newcastle Street in the Old Town has a bookstore (Hatties, 1531 Newcastle St., 912-554-8677), a drugstore, clothing, antique and gift shops, and even a gourmet store. True Vine Wine & Gourmet (1523 Newcastle St., 912-280-0380) is open Tuesday through Saturday 10:00 a.m.-6:00 p.m. and offers beer, cheese, wine and chocolate. The first Friday of every month they combine with other local stores and have wine and beer tastings. For larger supermarkets and the mall, you will need a car to head west, closer to the interstate.

Restaurants: The Old Town district has a number of dining options. Brewburgers & the Riva Club Lounge (1618 Newcastle St., 912-262-5443) is open seven days a week for lunch and dinner. They specialize in burgers but also offer pasta, steak and seafood dishes. Jim's Corner Café (1312 Newcastle St., 912-267-5630) is great for home-style breakfasts, lunches and and everything in between. For pizza, try Fox's Pizza Den (1435 Newcastle St., 912-265-4490).

ADDITIONAL RESOURCES

- **BRUNSWICK, GA: www.glynncounty.com**

NEARBY GOLF COURSES
Sea Palms Golf & Tennis Resort,
5445 Frederica Road, St. Simons Island, GA 31522
912-638-3351 www.seapalms.com

NEARBY MEDICAL FACILITIES
Glynn Immediate Care Center, 3400 Parkwood Drive,
Brunswick, GA 31520, 912-466-5800

THE FOLLOWING AREA REQUIRES SPECIAL ATTENTION DUE TO SHOALING OR CHANGES TO THE CHANNEL

JEKYLL CREEK TO JEKYLL SOUND—MILE 678 TO MILE 686

NAVIGATION: Use Chart 11489. Jekyll Creek, an area of persistent shoaling, is not scheduled for dredging as of press time. The tidal range is 7 to 9 feet. This area should only be traversed near high tide on a rising tide.

The charted Jekyll Island Range is used to approach Jekyll Creek. It has new characteristics as of a few years ago, so if your charts are old, observe and follow the aids carefully. The dayboard for green daybeacon "1," located on the front structure of this set of range markers, is difficult to see northbound and confusing to line up when southbound. A range (labeled "Jetty Range" on the chart) leads past a single stone jetty on the red side between the red daybeacons at the entrance to the creek, which is submerged at high tide. Be aware that this jetty extends from the shore all the way out to flashing red "4." Because the current sets strongly to the side, be sure to follow the range until past this jetty.

Green daybeacons "1" and "5," flashing greens "9" and "11" and red daybeacon "20A" were added in recent years and are not shown on older charts. The channel follows a centerline course until a set of ranges and lights guides you across mud flats to Jekyll Island's main waterfront area along Jekyll Creek. Jekyll Creek is particularly shoal-prone, so keep to mid-channel. A survey in spring 2010 indicated that the least depth in Jekyll Creek under normal conditions is around 2.5 feet at mean low water. The shallowest (and narrowest) part is in the middle of the creek between the range markers and the bridge. Local knowledge cautions that you stay on the range here, and even though the depths are very shallow, this is as good as it gets.

This area is being studied by the U.S. Army Corps of Engineers to determine some method to improve the flow of water through the creek to keep silt from settling out. Use caution and proceed with the depth sounder in plain view. Flashing green "25" is a short marker (about 10 feet) and very difficult to see at high tide. The area outside the channel to the southwest of Jekyll Harbor Marina is shallow and not a recommended anchorage. This is one of the worst areas of shoaling on the entire ICW in spring 2011. The good news is that the tidal range is 8 to 9 feet.

END SPECIAL CAUTION AREA.

Dockage: Two marinas are on either side of the high-rise Jekyll Island Bridge (65-foot fixed vertical clearance) at approximately Mile 684.4. These are the last marinas before St. Marys, nearly on the Florida border, so be sure to fuel up and provision if necessary. Fuel will not be available again until Fernandina Beach at about Mile 716.

The northernmost facility, Jekyll Wharf Marina, is adjacent to Jekyll Island's restored historic district. Excursion boats operate from this marina, as well as from Morningstar Marinas at Golden Isles. The restaurant on the wharf has been remodeled. Docking is now limited due to shoaling.

Jekyll Harbor Marina, on the south side of the bridge, has 10-foot depths, transient dockage alongside a long floating dock parallel to the channel, fuel, a pool and hot tub, propane grills, SeaJay's Grill and a ship's store.

If you need to provision or wish to explore Jekyll Island, Jekyll Harbor Marina will provide courtesy transportation. The shopping center on the island includes a small IGA grocery, a drugstore, a liquor store, several gift shops and a handful of restaurants. Be sure to visit the Georgia Sea Turtle Center while you are here. There are currently development plans which could change the face of Jekyll Island, transforming it from the pristine environmental treasure it is now into an upscale tourist area.

GOIN' ASHORE:
JEKYLL ISLAND, GA

Jekyll Island, the smallest of Georgia's sea islands, is a place of contrasts. Once a playground for families such as the Rockefellers, Morgans and Vanderbilts, it is now a state park with a national historic district and a commitment to preserving its natural elements. Under state law, 65 percent of the island must remain undeveloped.

History: William Horton, a member of Gen. Oglethorpe's military group at Fort Frederica on St. Simons Island, was the first settler on Jekyll Island in 1738, establishing a 500-acre plantation on which he raised enough beef and corn to supply Frederica. By the 1790s, the island was owned by the DuBignon family, who fled to this country to escape the French Revolution.

In 1885, the French family sold the island to a group of wealthy northerners for a hunting resort for $125,000. The 60-room clubhouse on Jekyll Creek was officially opened in January 1888. Golf courses, tennis courts and a marina to handle their yachts (the only way to arrive at the island) soon followed, as well as individual mansion-sized "cottages."

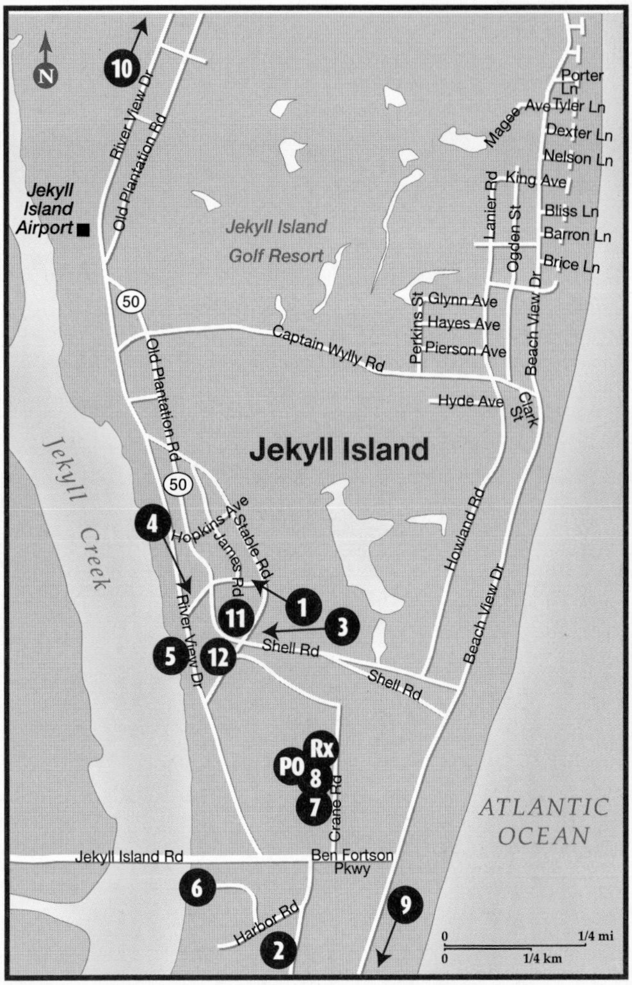

Reference the marina listing tables to see all the marinas in the area.

ATTRACTIONS
1 The Georgia Sea Turtle Center
2 Tidelands Nature Center
3 Jekyll Island Museum

DINING
4 The Grand Dining Room
5 Latitude 31
6 SeaJay's Waterfront Café & Pub

GROCERIES/CARRYOUT
7 IGA Supermarket
8 Flash Food Convenience Store

INFORMATION
3 Jekyll Island Museum

RECREATION
9 St. Andrews Picnic Area
10 Fishing Pier

SHOPPING/DINING
11 Pier Road Shops
12 Jekyll Books

PO POST OFFICE

Rx PHARMACY

During the "Club Era," a group of influential men met secretly in 1908 to form what would become a modern monetary system for the United States that led to the formation of the Federal Reserve System. In 1915, Jekyll Island took part in the first transcontinental telephone call when Theodore Vail, president of AT&T, spoke on the line to

Jekyll Island, GA

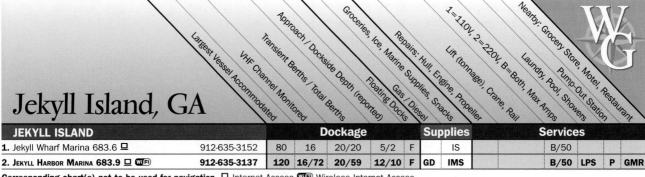

JEKYLL ISLAND		Largest Vessel Accommodated	VHF Channel Monitored	Transient Berths / Total Berths	Approach / Dockside Depth (reported)	Floating Docks	Gas / Diesel	Groceries, Ice, Marine Supplies, Snacks	Repairs: Hull, Engine, Propeller	Lift (tonnage), Crane, Rail	1=110V, 2=220V, B=Both, Max Amps	Laundry, Pool, Showers	Pump-Out Station	Nearby: Grocery Store, Motel, Restaurant
		Dockage					Supplies		Services					
1. Jekyll Wharf Marina 683.6 (Internet Access)	912-635-3152	80	16	20/20	5/2	F		IS			B/50			
2. Jekyll Harbor Marina 683.9 (Internet Access) (Wireless Internet Access)	**912-635-3137**	**120**	**16/72**	**20/59**	**12/10**	**F**	**GD**	**IMS**			**B/50**	**LPS**	**P**	**GMR**

Corresponding chart(s) not to be used for navigation. Internet Access, Wireless Internet Access

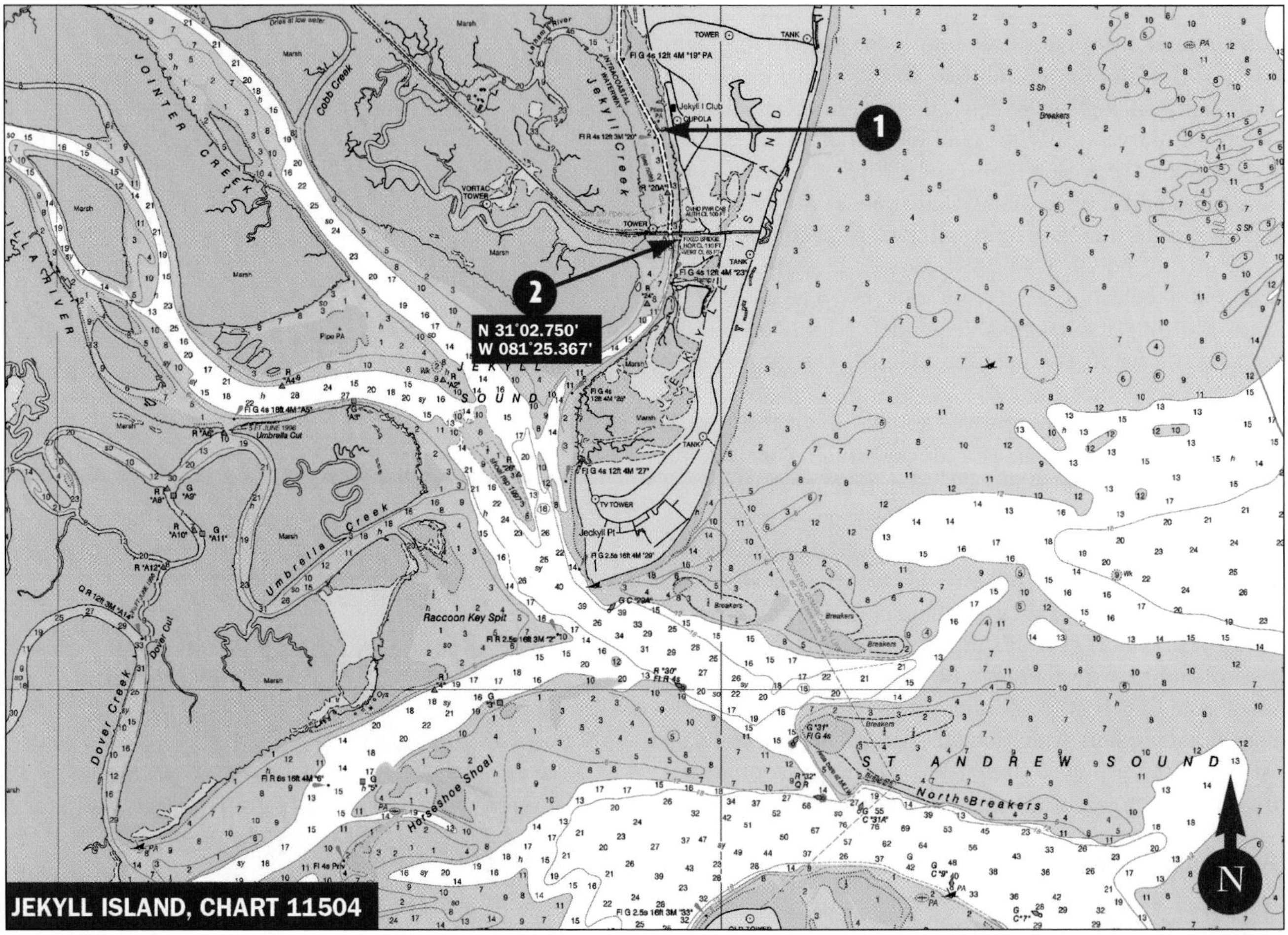

JEKYLL ISLAND, CHART 11504

Alexander Graham Bell, Thomas Watson and President Woodrow Wilson.

The club declined following the Great Depression and was closed permanently after World War II. The State of Georgia purchased the island in 1947, but restoration work on the historic buildings did not begin until 1985.

Cultural References: Jekyll Island is the site for some of the scenes in the movies "Glory," "The Legend of Bagger Vance" and "The View from Pompey's Head."

Attractions: The national historic district, known better as "The Millionaires' Village," has 29 of the 34 historic structures that have been restored, including the Club House, now the luxurious Jekyll Island Club Hotel where guests still play croquet on the lawn. The Jekyll Island Museum, in the old club stables on Stable Road, is the place to start. From here, you can also embark on self-guided walking or narrated tram tours. The Georgia Sea Turtle Center (214 Stable Road) cares for sick and injured sea turtles but also has interactive exhibits on sea turtle biology and life history. The 4-H Tidelands Nature Center (100 S. Riverview Drive) has nature exhibits, touch-tanks and also conducts guided kayak marsh tours and nature walks. With only 35 percent of the island developed, there are shell-dotted ocean beaches to explore, surf fishing at the St. Andrews Picnic Area on the island's south end or fishing on the north end Fishing Pier, miles of bike trails, four golf courses, miniature golf and a water park to keep everyone as busy or relaxed as they would like to be.

Special Events: Some type of festival or sporting event takes place every month, including the New Year's Bluegrass

Festival in late December/early January, the Beach Music Festival in August, the Wild Georgia Shrimp Festival in September and Holiday in History during the month of December. In addition, the Jekyll Island Museum has special themed historical tours, and the Jekyll Island Club Hotel hosts a series of lectures on historical, environmental and economic issues.

Shopping: The IGA Supermarket and the Flash Food Convenience Store are both located in the Beachside Shopping Center (South Beachview Drive and Ben Fortson Parkway), as are a hardware store, gift shop and pharmacy. The Pier Road Shops in the Historic District has gift, art and clothing shops, including the Commissary, a treasure trove of Georgia food products—jams, jellies, sauces and Georgia Peach and Vidalia onion items—and regional cookbooks. Don't miss Jekyll Books, located at the old Infirmary (Shell and Stable Road), for local and regional books, bestsellers and gifts. Getting around can be by car, but, in keeping with the preservation efforts, try a pedal-powered surrey with the fringe on top from Wheel Fun Rentals (912-635-9801) or an open-air electric car from Red Bug Motors (912-635-9330).

Restaurants: For a special treat, try the Victorian Sunday Brunch in the Grand Dining Room at the Jekyll Island Club Hotel (371 Riverview Dr., 912-635-2400). It is also open for breakfast, lunch and dinner, although gentlemen are requested to wear jackets at dinner. Also at the hotel, Café Solterra offers fresh-baked muffins and pastries as well as deli sandwiches, homemade soups, pizza and frozen yogurt. Latitude 31 (912-635-3800) at the Jekyll Wharf is known for its seafood, including the "Rah" Bar, and the sunset views over the marsh and ICW. SeaJay's Waterfront Café & Pub (1 Harbor Road, 912-635-3200), at the Jekyll Harbor Marina, has a "Low Country Boil" buffet dinner nightly, fresh local seafood, Brunswick stew and crab chowder.

ADDITIONAL RESOURCES

- JEKYLL ISLAND, GA: 877-453-5955
  www.jekyllisland.com
- GEORGIA SEA TURTLE CENTER: 912-635-4444
  www.georgiaseaturtlecenter.org

NEARBY GOLF COURSES
Jekyll Island Golf Courses, 322 Captain Wylly Road, Jekyll Island, GA 31527, 912-635-2368

NEARBY MEDICAL FACILITIES
Glynn Immediate Care Center, 3400 Parkwood Drive, Brunswick, GA 31520, 912-466-5800

Jekyll Creek to Cumberland River—Mile 686 to Mile 689

The ICW route at the mouth of St. Andrew Sound, just north of Cumberland Island, marks the closest spot to the ocean on the ICW south of Norfolk, VA. Look to the northwest, and you will be looking back at the ocean side of Jekyll Island. A stiff onshore wind running against the current can make the short passage across St. Andrew Sound very wet and uncomfortable. As always, the seas will be calmest when the wind and current are in the same direction.

Low slack water at Mile 690 occurs 58 minutes earlier than at Savannah River. Timed correctly, you will have a fair current from about Mile 685 to a little past Mile 700. Otherwise, the current will be going with you in one direction and against you when you make the turn at red flashing buoy "32," with seas behaving accordingly.

The Coast Guard has reported that St. Andrew Sound's inlet from the ocean has shoaled to 4 feet at its southern entrance. Knowledgeable locals advise against using this inlet to approach Jekyll Sound. *(See page 96 for more information about St. Andrew Sound and Inlet.)*

NAVIGATION: Use Chart 11489. To continue south after transiting Jekyll Creek, give a wide berth to Jekyll Island's Jekyll Point, with its light and green can. The point continues to build out. You can see the remains of a sunken shrimp boat at low tide close inshore of flashing green "29." Set your course for flashing red buoy "32," the more easterly of two red lighted buoys far out in the sound. The markers in the sound can be hard to spot from a distance. Green can "29A" marks the end of a shoal in the seaward part of St. Andrew Sound; this point continues to build out. In St. Andrew Sound, flashing green buoy "31" marks the breakers to the northwest of flashing red buoy "32." Green can "31A" was added beyond red flashing buoy "32," and it may not appear on older charts. This area of shallow water and breakers, marked by the two green floating aids ("31" and "31A"), is slowly building southward, and the strip of deep water marked by flashing red buoy "32" has narrowed. Inside the two red flashing buoys "30" and "32," the bottom not only shoals but also shelters the sunken remains of old wrecks. A shoal has built out approximately 150 feet east of red buoy "32." Once you round flashing red buoy "32," you can safely head into the wide entrance of the Cumberland River and southward down the ICW.

Note that the magenta line on your chart may be drawn on the wrong side of flashing red buoy "32." Remember that aids to navigation may be moved frequently as the bottom shifts and sand bars move, but the magenta line usually just stays as a mark on the chart or, in some cases, is removed. Seek local knowledge from your marina or a local tow boat operator if you have questions or check www.waterwayguide.com for the latest updates. When in doubt, honor the buoys.

Cumberland River—Mile 690 to Mile 700

NAVIGATION: Use Chart 11489. Heading south into the Cumberland River, you will pass two markers at the northern tip of Little Cumberland Island: flashing green "33" on the northern tip and green daybeacon "33A" just beyond. Signs on Little Cumberland Island warn against any landings, as this is a wildlife sanctuary, although there is a large house on the St. Andrew Sound shore of Little Cumberland Island. A green offshore buoy, broken from its mooring in a storm, can still be seen washed ashore on the beach below the abandoned lighthouse on the northern tip of Little Cumberland Island.

Anchorage: On the Cumberland River, in the bight just east of flashing green "37," you will find a fair-weather anchorage, protected only from east and southeast winds. Avoid the shoal marked by flashing green "37," and drop the hook in about 10 feet. This anchorage is away from the Cumberland River traffic but gets uncomfortable with wind from any direction except east. Keep an eye out for wild horses on the shore here.

ALTERNATE ROUTE: Umbrella Creek, off the ICW—Umbrella Cut & Dover Cut

NAVIGATION: Use Chart 11489. If you want to avoid St. Andrew Sound and the Cumberland River, a 15-mile-long alternate, foul-weather route avoids the direct crossing. This route, via Umbrella, Dover and Floyd creeks, is charted and reasonably easy to run. It will add approximately five miles to the ICW route and has very shallow spots.

To pick up the alternate route coming from Jekyll Creek, a set of markers leads you across Jekyll Sound and into the Little Satilla River, where you can enter Umbrella Creek via the land cut at flashing green "A5." Shallow-draft vessels may attempt this route, but only on a rising tide. A Corps of Engineers survey from April 2010 showed a controlling depth in Umbrella Cut at the beginning of the route between flashing green "A5" and red daybeacon "A6" of 6.5 feet at mean low water. Umbrella Creek between red daybeacon "A6" and flashing red "A14" showed depths of less than a foot at mean low water in some places. The tidal range here is 8 feet or better; run this route on a rising tide, near high tide.

Enter Umbrella Cut dead on its centerline instead of trying to line up with the two markers. During strong northeast winds, high water makes it more difficult to navigate by obscuring much of the marsh grass along the shores of Umbrella Creek.

Be especially cautious in two areas, the first of which is Dover Cut, connecting Umbrella Creek with Dover Creek. The cut is narrow and winding, and some spots are reported in the USACE survey to have 5-foot controlling depths at mean low water. Continuing along this alternate route, a straight land cut connects Dover Creek to the Satilla River, easily followed for a mile and three quarters to the entrance of Floyd Creek, the next section of the alternate route.

The second shoal area to watch for is at the junction of Floyd Creek and Floyd Basin, from green daybeacon "A21" to just past green daybeacon "A31." Floyd Creek, between green daybeacons "A21" and "A31," was reported to have a controlling depth of 6 feet at mean low water in the latest Corps of Engineers survey, with the lowest depth recorded at 2 feet. From here on, it is smooth sailing out to red daybeacon "40," in the center of the Cumberland River, back on the ICW at Mile 696. Nighttime commercial shrimp boat traffic makes Floyd Creek a less desirable anchorage. Daybeacons were renumbered and additional daybeacons installed in recent years. Use current charts when taking this alternate route and for safe passage, use only near or at high tide.

■ ICW SOUTH TO FLORIDA

THE FOLLOWING AREA REQUIRES SPECIAL ATTENTION DUE TO SHOALING OR CHANGES TO THE CHANNEL

CUMBERLAND RIVER TO KINGS BAY—MILE 695 TO MILE 707

NAVIGATION:

Use Chart 11489. The ICW route becomes progressively more complicated as it approaches the Cumberland Dividings channel and Cumberland Sound. This whole route is subject to shoaling. It is a good idea to favor the green-marker side of the channel, and proceed with extreme caution from red daybeacon "58A" to just south of flashing red daybeacon "64." The shoaling from the west bank extends toward the channel farther than indicated on the charts. Favor the green side from green daybeacon "59A" until flashing green "63A" for reported 12-foot depths at mean low water all the way through. Stay away from the reds. Most chartplotters will show you on an "island" at flashing red "60." This island does not exist. This area snared many unsuspecting boaters in recent years. The Corps of Engineers has been made aware of the issue.

At Mile 703, the deep, but unmarked Brickhill River joins the ICW route above Cumberland Sound at flashing red "60A." The Cumberland Sound Range starts at Mile 705.

END SPECIAL CAUTION AREA.

Anchorage: Two particularly well-protected anchorages along this stretch are in Shellbine Creek at Mile 698. Depths found in the north fork of Shellbine Creek are somewhat less than shown on the chart. Delaroche Creek at Mile 702 has anchorage up to the first bend to the north and has good holding in 12 to 18 feet of water. Stay well off the ICW to avoid traffic from barges and speeding powerboats.

On the Brickhill River, 1.5 miles northeast of the ICW, you can anchor in 11 to 15 feet of water, just north of the Plum Orchard Plantation dock on Cumberland Island. Plum Orchard, one of the Carnegie family estates, was built in 1898. After you dinghy ashore, you will be rewarded with a walk among huge live oaks draped with Spanish moss and a view of the well-preserved mansion. If you are fortunate, you may encounter a family of wild horses grazing on the lawn or alligators swimming in the anchorage. The area where the Brickhill River meets Cumberland Dividings is subject to shoaling. Enter the Brickhill River slowly, and watch the depth sounder.

South of the Brickhill River, you can anchor in the Crooked River west of the ICW, with charted depths of 8 to 13 feet at Mile 703.8.

Cumberland Sound—Mile 708

The complications of Cumberland Sound are compounded by the activity at the Navy's Kings Bay Submarine Base, home to six Trident-class submarines. Frequent changing of navigational aids and dredging operations between Mile 708 and Mile 711 make navigation challenging. Be sure to use the latest (38th dated January 2009) edition of Chart 11489, as many marks were renumbered. Kings Bay, and the area west of the ICW channel here, are strictly off limits to cruising skippers. No-Wake Zones have been established in this vicinity and are strictly enforced. Expect to see patrol boats throughout this area.

Submarines returning from the Atlantic Ocean to the base at Kings Bay will have surfaced well before they reach the inlet portion of the St. Marys Entrance Channel (the Atlantic inlet just south of Cumberland Sound). The submarines create huge wakes, especially when steaming fast in the exposed entrance channel, but they slow down upon entering the jetties and heading up into Kings Bay. The aforementioned patrol boats will likely escort you through the area if a submarine is present.

NAVIGATION: Use Chart 11489. Shoaling continues in the vicinity of ICW green daybeacon "75," while green daybeacon "79" is frequently relocated as shoaling dictates. This stretch is well marked and sufficiently deep—still, watch the depth sounder. Make sure that you keep green daybeacon "75" to port and avoid cruising in the eastern side of Cumberland Sound. Shoaling exists near the range markers northwest of Drum Point Island.

Take time here to sort out the mosaic of lights, markers and ranges now serving the huge government installation on Kings Bay at Mile 708. *Note that navigational aids read from the ocean up Cumberland Sound. Once past ICW red daybeacon "78" and green daybeacon "79" heading south, keep green markers to starboard and red ones to port as you proceed, south to the intersection with the ICW at quick flashing green buoy "1" at Fernandina Beach, FL.*

Cumberland Island

Cumberland Island, behind which the ICW route winds for more than 20 miles, was once the center of controversy over development plans. It achieved its protected status as a National Seashore decades ago, ensuring that

QUICK FACT:
CUMBERLAND ISLAND

Georgia's largest and southernmost barrier island, Cumberland Island, at Mile 710, stretches 17.5 miles and contains more than 36,000 acres of habitat.

Cumberland Island was first inhabited by the Timucua Indians nearly 4,000 years ago. The island was part of the Mocama missionary province of Spanish Florida during the 16th century. The majority of the Timucuans converted to Christianity and either perished from European disease or left once the Spanish departed the island.

In 1783, Nathaniel Greene, who earned fame as one of George Washington's most successful officers during the Revolutionary War, purchased nearly 11,000 acres on Cumberland Island. In 1803, Greene's widow, Catherine, built a large home on the land which she called Dungeness. The mansion burned to the ground mid-century. In 1881, Thomas Carnegie, brother of steel magnate Andrew Carnegie, and his wife, Lucy, built another mansion named Dungeness on the foundation of the Greene estate. Carnegie didn't live to see the completion of the mansion, which stood until 1945, when it also burned. Mrs. Carnegie commissioned several other mansions for her family, including Plum Orchard, a Georgian Revival-style mansion, which was donated to the National Park Foundation by Carnegie family members in 1971.

Today, Cumberland Island is composed of Great and Little Cumberland Islands. There is no bridge to the island, and visitors come ashore via the Cumberland Ferry, usually from the town of St. Marys, GA. Visitors can enjoy hiking trails, tours of the Dungeness Historic District, camping and the island's extensive wildlife. Boating is also permitted. Day-use dockage is available at the north end of the Dungeness and Sea Camp docks. Space is limited, and slips are available on a first-come, first-served basis. A $4 per person entrance fee is requested for those over 16. Overnight docking is prohibited.

most of the island will remain in its primitive state. No road or causeway from the mainland will ever be constructed. Public land acquisition continues today, and the federal government owns approximately 85 percent of the island. Private property includes Greyfield Inn and several cottages passed down through several generations of Cumberland Island families.

All island visitors must bring their own food and supplies and transport all their garbage back to the mainland. Nothing is available beyond campsites, water and restroom facilities. You will need insect repellent in spring, summer and fall. Most visitors arrive via ferry service from St. Marys, a 45-minute trip. Make reservations by calling 912-882-4335.

Dockage: Limited daytime dockage is available at the Sea Camp dock on a floating pier maintained by the National Park Service with 10- to 11-foot minimum depths for boats 20 feet or less. The ferry from St. Marys occupies the major portion of the dock, and National Park Service boats take most of the inside section. That leaves room for about two 20-foot boats or a number of dinghies on the outside docking area aft of the ferry. After hours, there is more space. There is a small fee to visit the National Park. There are no power or water hookups available, but this is an excellent base from which to explore the island. It is an easy half-mile hike east to the beach, and a little more than a mile south to the ruins of Dungeness, a good spot for viewing some of the island's wild horses. Private boats may not dock at the National Park Service's Dungeness Dock. Greyfield Inn may have limited dockage available for dinner or overnight guests. For information on Greyfield Inn, call 904-261-6408.

Anchorage: North of the St. Marys Entrance Channel, off Cumberland Sound, is an anchorage that will give you access to Cumberland Island. Head east near Mile 711 in the vicinity of flashing red "34," and then proceed north along the shore of Cumberland Island, following the eastern branch of Cumberland Sound, about one and a quarter miles to Sea Camp Dock and Visitor Center. Anchor near the docks, avoiding the shoal that makes out to the south of the marsh island off Greyfield. You can dinghy into the docks and go ashore. Holding is good but mind the 7- to 9-foot tides and consider the effects of reversing current in the narrow channel. There is a long southwest exposure here, and the anchorage can become uncomfortable in wind-against-tide situations. This anchorage is often very crowded during warm weekends and during spring and fall transient seasons. It is a good place to wait for weather to make passage from the St. Marys Entrance Channel.

Georgia/Florida Line

The next stretch to the mouth of the St. Marys River, which marks the boundary between Georgia and Florida, presents no problems. The St. Marys Entrance Channel, into which Cumberland Sound and St. Marys River discharge into the Atlantic, is a safe, big-ship inlet. Its close proximity to the ICW and short entry channel makes it a popular inlet for boats running offshore. *(See page 97 for more information about St. Marys River and Inlet.)*

NAVIGATION: Use Chart 11489. The St. Marys Entrance Channel through the outer bars has lights and ranges, but the stone jetties of the entrance are awash at half-tide. In recent years, the St. Marys Entrance Channel buoys were changed and the buoy that formerly was "10" is now "2." Every buoy in the St. Marys Entrance and in Cumberland Sound up to the head of Kings Bay was renumbered accordingly. ICW daybeacon numbers were not changed. Continuing south on the ICW, arrive at Mile 714 at low slack water (**33 minutes earlier than Miami**) to carry a fair current from Mile 704 to about Mile 720. St. Marys Entrance Channel was dredged in late summer 2008. This

St. Marys, GA

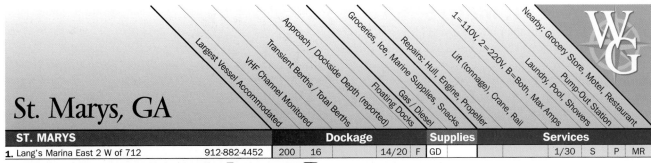

ST. MARYS		Largest Vessel Accommodated	VHF Channel Monitored	Transient Berths / Total Berths	Approach / Dockside Depth (reported)	Floating Docks	Gas / Diesel	Groceries, Ice, Marine Supplies, Snacks	Repairs: Hull, Engine, Propeller	Lift (tonnage), Crane, Rail	1=110V, 2=220V, B=Both, Max Amps	Laundry, Pool, Showers	Pump-Out Station	Nearby: Grocery Store, Motel, Restaurant
		Dockage					Supplies		Services					
1. Lang's Marina East 2 W of 712	912-882-4452	200	16		14/20	F	GD				1/30	S	P	MR

Corresponding chart(s) not to be used for navigation. Internet Access Wireless Internet Access

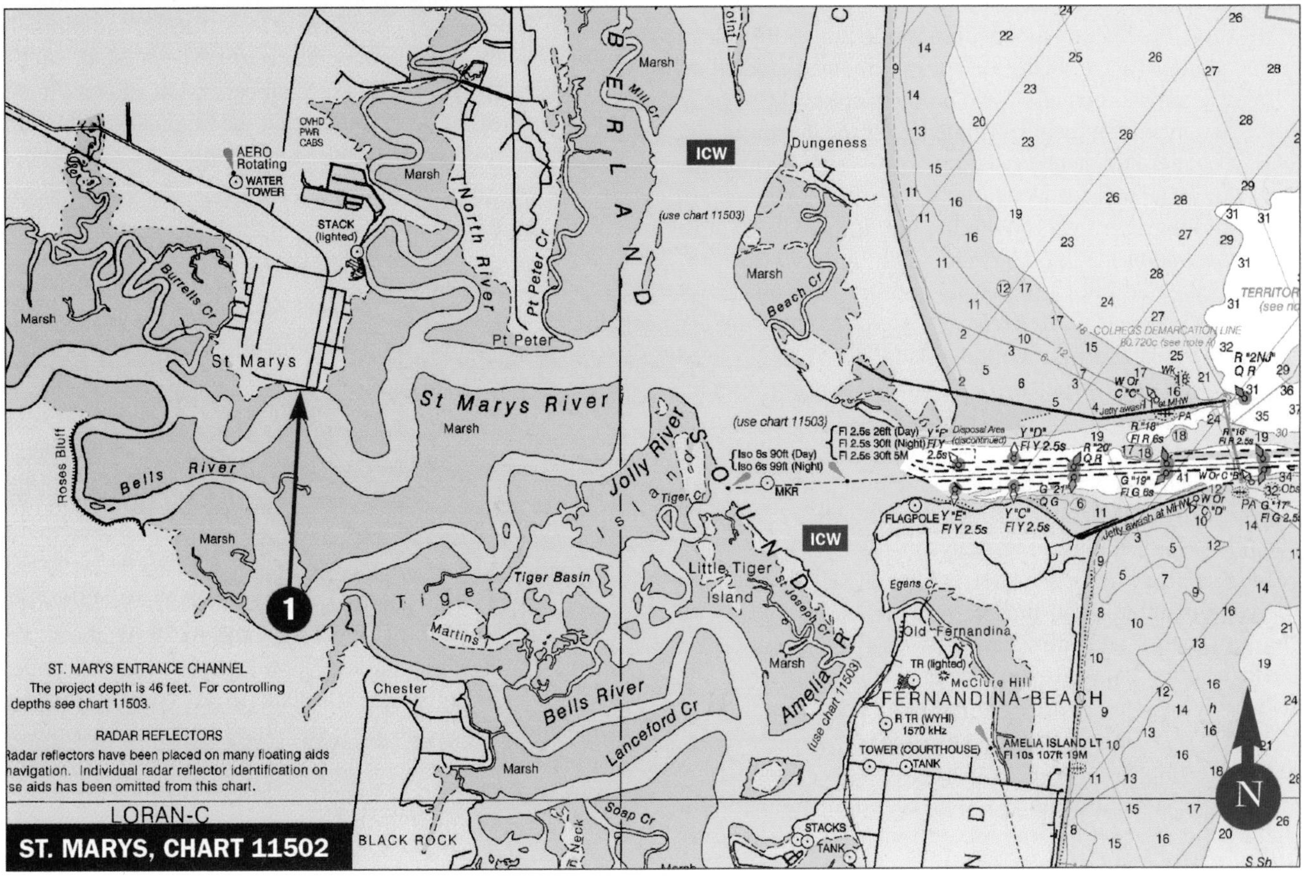

channel is a favorite departure and arrival point for boats making offshore jaunts along the coast.

St. Marys River, off the ICW

NAVIGATION: Use Chart 11489. St. Marys River, charted and marked, enters Cumberland Sound from the west. Favor the center of the river, and take flashing green "3" wide to starboard. Follow the markers to avoid shoaling of the west bank from red daybeacon "6" to flashing red "10."

Dockage: Lang's Marina docks—at the Georgia town of St. Marys, roughly two miles up the St. Marys River—are distinctive at the end of the town waterfront, where the river veers away from the town to port. There is a small office at the head of the dock. The marina office doubles as a seafood market, with restroom and shower facilities in the same building. NOTE: This marina does not take reservations; it is first-come, first-served only. This is the only transient dockage in St. Marys, with the exception of a free town dock that will accommodate three or four 35-foot vessels for a 24-hour period.

Anchorage: There is a substantial anchorage area in front of the long deepwater bulkhead (tie-ups with electricity and water available). Tidal currents run swiftly here, so consider them when both dropping anchor or docking. There is a "Cruisers Net" at 8:00 a.m. every morning on VHF Channel 68. During the net, you can get information about town activities and announcements along with help, if needed, and also make arrangements for transportation.

GOIN' ASHORE: **ST. MARYS, GA**

St. Marys has more to it than meets the eye. It is one of the oldest cities in the United States. It sits aside the St. Marys River, looking the part of a fishing village with a dash of charm—lovely Victorian homes, inns, restaurants and shops. But the "Gateway to Cumberland Island" is quickly growing like every other town along the ICW, in large part because St. Marys enjoys the added economic benefit of having Kings Bay submarine base nearby. Wars and their aftermaths, in fact, have been a historical constant, shaping life in St. Marys since its beginnings.

History: St. Marys sits on Buttermilk Bluff, the site of an old Indian village. Plans for a town emerged as early as 1767, when it was owned by two brothers of Royal Governor James Wright. Upon their banishment after the Revolutionary War, a planter and state legislator, Jacob Weed, became the owner. He sold acreage along the river to a group of men in 1788, and together they laid out the new town. The Georgia legislature established St. Marys in 1792, but it wasn't actually incorporated until 1802. From 1869 to 1923, St. Marys served as Camden County's seat.

Although shelled by Union gunboats, the town survived the Civil War and by the 1870s, was prospering as a seaport. Besides the British, early settlers included Acadian French. First deported from Canada by the victorious British, the Acadians fled to Hispaniola in the Caribbean, then a French colony. When Hispaniola's slaves rebelled, many Acadians fled once again, landing at St. Marys in 1791.

Industrialization began shortly after the Civil War with the establishment of a lumber mill, followed by several canning plants and more sawmills. In the 20th century, fertilizer and chemical plants were established, while the riverfront was lined with cotton and tobacco warehouses. In 1941, the Gilman Paper Company was built, becoming the Durango-Georgia Company in 2000. The company closed in 2002 and, while it was an economic hardship for the area, it was a welcome relief to visitors who no longer had to suffer the papermill odor. Also, the Kings Bay Naval Submarine Base opened in 1979. St. Marys has continued to prosper from a growing retirement and tourist population.

Cultural References: Roy Crane, creator of comics such as "Buzz Sawyer," also wrote the 1935 "Wash Tubbs & Easy" comic strip based on local St. Marys residents who used to ride the Toonerville Trolley from St. Marys to Kingsland, GA in the late 1920s. You can still take a historic ride through St. Marys on a tram. Also, Marjorie Kinnan Rawlings, author of "The Yearling," used to stay at the Riverview Hotel.

Attractions: The Welcome Center (406 Osborne St.) can provide maps and brochures of the historic downtown and other attractions. The Orange Hall Museum (311 Osborne St.), so-named for a large sour-orange grove behind the house, was first started between 1826 and 1829, and through various owners, became an architectural showcase of Greek Revival style. Strolling the wide, cabbage palm and oak-lined streets is a pleasant way to check out the Colonial, antebellum and Victorian homes, several which are now inns. The First Presbyterian Church (110 W. Conyers St.), built in 1808, is believed to be the second oldest church in Georgia. The Cumberland Island National Seashore Museum (129 Osborne St.) was opened in 2001 to house a collection of artifacts in a climate-controlled atmosphere. A small portion of the items are on exhibit, including a Native American Indian canoe, pottery and arrowheads, as well as old black-and-white photos of people who lived on the island in the late 1800s and early 1900s. The ferry to take visitors to Cumberland Island makes several trips a day from the waterfront. Nature lovers might see wild horses in the marshes in addition to mink, armadillos, alligators and deer. You can also explore the ruins of Dungeness, the old Carnegie Estate.

At the St. Marys Submarine Museum (102 W. St. Marys St.), learn everything you ever wanted to know about the underwater machines and check out the working periscope. Also, walk through the 1788 Oakgrove Cemetery (corner of Bartlett and Weed streets), where you can find much history of the area. It is believed that graves of veterans representing every war fought in and by America are there. The Riverview Hotel (105 Osborne St.), built in 1916 and

ATTRACTIONS
1 The Orange Hall Museum
2 Cumberland Island National Seashore Museum
3 St. Marys Submarine Museum
4 Cumberland Island Visitors Center

DINING
5 Lang's Marina Restaurant
6 Pauly's Cafe
7 Seagle's Restaurant

GROCERIES/CARRYOUT
8 Market on the Square

INFORMATION
9 The Welcome Center

POINTS OF INTEREST
10 Riverview Hotel
11 The First Presbyterian Church
12 Oakgrove Cemetery

SHOPPING/DINING
13 Once Upon A Bookseller
14 The Cottage Shop

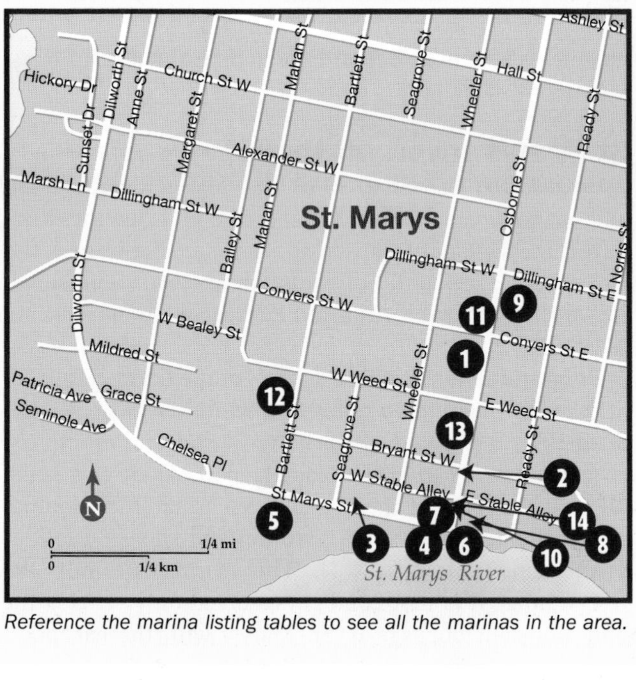

Reference the marina listing tables to see all the marinas in the area.

renovated in the 1970s, is open for business, some say with a resident ghost.

Special Events: Join the Mardi Gras Festival the Saturday before Ash Wednesday in February, the Rock Shrimp Festival on the first Saturday in October or the Candlelight Tour of Homes on the second Saturday in December.

In November 2000, several boaters gathered in Seagle's Pub at the Riverview Hotel with no plans for their Thanksgiving dinner. So the Pub fried a turkey, the boaters all brought a side dish to share and a "tradition" was started. That first year there were about 10 or 12 people, but in 2010 they had about 300 so be prepared to wait in line. This has become an annual event and most of the volunteers are the local people. If you are in the area, don't miss it!

Shopping: Shops in St. Marys are small and delightful. For provisioning, you will need to head west. But do check out the local stores on Osborne and St. Marys streets, especially Once Upon a Bookseller (207 Osborne St.), with a collection of NOAA charts, and The Cottage Shop (112D Osborne St.) for unique gifts. Visit 1926 Osborne St. or call 912-576-8170 to rent a golf cart. Be sure to visit The Market on the Square (100 Osborne St.) for delicious fudge and also the only washer/dryer within walking distance.

Restaurants: Lang's Marina Restaurant (307 W. St. Marys St., 912-882-4432) is on the water and has fresh-from-the-water fried shrimp. Pauly's Cafe, a small eatery near the waterfront, gets rave reviews (102 Osborne St., 912-882-3944). In the Riverview Hotel (105 Osborne St., 912-882-3242), Captain Seagle's Restaurant has fresh seafood and steaks and a weekly lunch buffet. Locals have made a neighborhood tradition of Seagle's Saloon & Patio Bar, with music and sports.

Silver Star Steakhouse (219 Osborne St., 912-882-1845) has great steaks. The Mad Hatter Restaurant (122 Osborne St., 912-576-3645) specializes in quiches, crepes and homemade soups. Cedar Oak & Java Joe'z (304 Osborne St., 912-882-9555) serve breakfast, lunch and good coffee. If you have transportation, Borrell Creek Landing (1101 Highway 40 East, 912-673-6300) is open for lunch and dinner overlooking a creek and marshes. The fish, pasta and veal dishes are all good.

ADDITIONAL RESOURCES

- ST. MARYS TOURISM COUNCIL: 866-868-2199
  www.stmaryswelcome.com

NEARBY GOLF COURSES

Trident Lakes Golf Club, Kings Bay Naval Submarine Base, St. Marys, GA 31558, 912-573-8475

Laurel Island Links, 233 Marsh Harbour Parkway, Kingsland, GA 31548, 888-480-7277
www.laurelislandlinks.com

NEARBY MEDICAL FACILITIES

Southeast Georgia Health System
Camden Campus Center, 2000 Dan Proctor Drive, St. Marys, GA 31558, 912-576-6200

When Mrs. Carnegie died, she willed that her horses on Cumberland Island, GA, be allowed to roam wild on the island. The horses continue to roam wild, fending for themselves to this day. ©IstockPhoto/goldnugget.

Heading South Into Florida

Fernandina Beach, FL, at Mile 716, is the next town to the south on the ICW once you leave the St. Marys River area.

Ahead lies more than 1,000 miles of Florida coastline and 1,000 more if you continue to Texas, all covered in WATERWAY GUIDE's Southern edition. The Bahamas are covered in our Bahamas edition. ■

WATERWAY GUIDE advertising sponsors play a vital role in bringing you the most trusted and well-respected cruising guide in the country. Without our advertising sponsors, we simply couldn't produce the top-notch publication now resting in your hands. Next time you stop in for a peaceful night's rest, let them know where you found them—WATERWAY GUIDE, The Cruising Authority.

WATERWAY GUIDE is always open to your observations from the helm. Email your comments on any navigation information in the guide to: editor@waterwayguide.com.

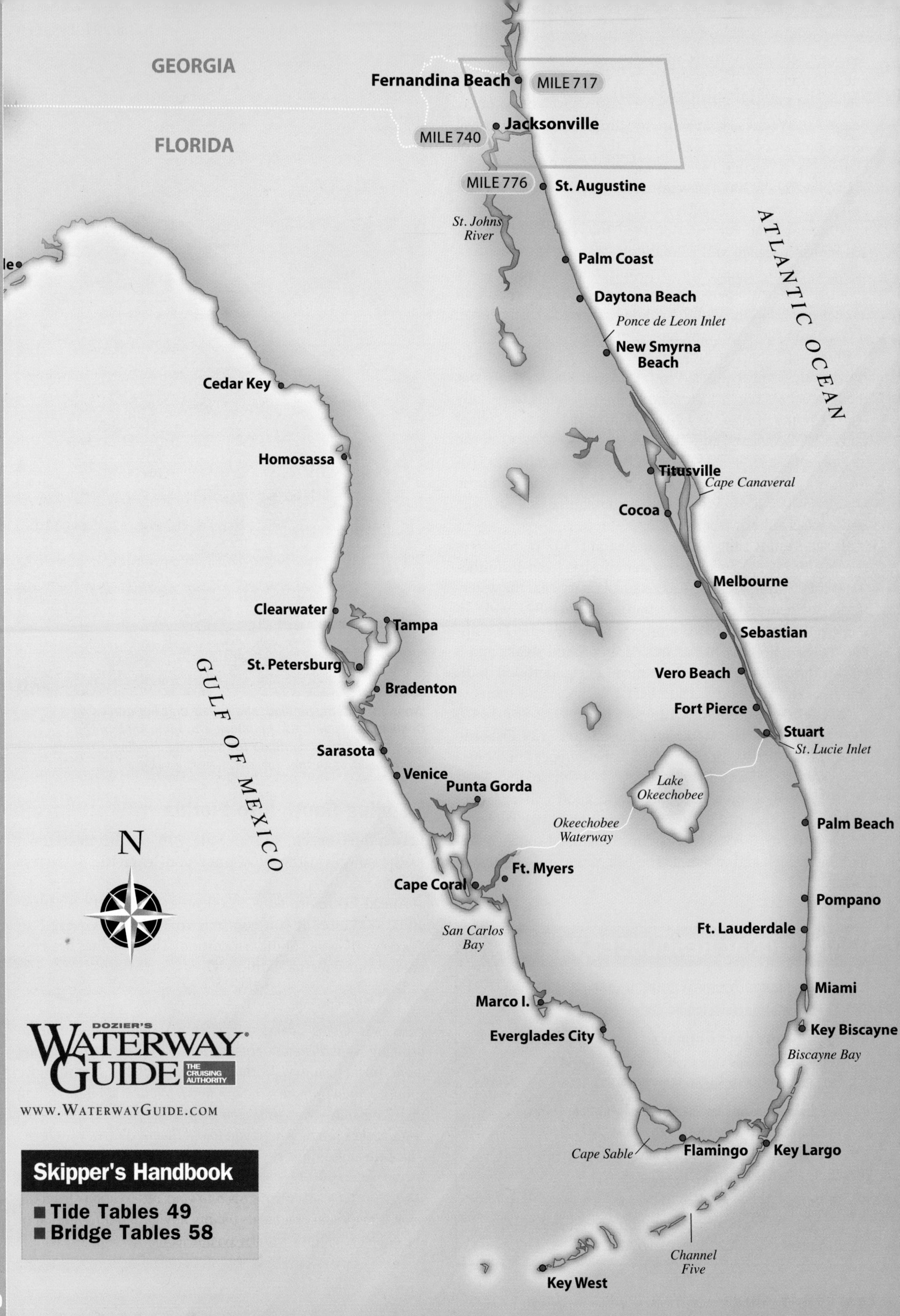

DOZIER'S WATERWAY GUIDE THE CRUISING AUTHORITY

WWW.WATERWAYGUIDE.COM

Skipper's Handbook

- Tide Tables 49
- Bridge Tables 58

Florida Border to Jacksonville

CHARTS 11488, 11489, 11490, 11491, 11502, 11503

As you cross the St. Marys River and enter the state of Florida, you will notice a change in the characteristics of the Intracoastal Waterway (ICW). Georgia's long, open sounds and wide rivers gradually transform into a series of creeks and rivers connected by narrow land cuts, and you see much more development. The ICW crosses several navigable inlets that no doubt attracted the early explorers. The first settlers built strategic, profitable ports along these protected inside waters. Today's cruisers use improved and connected passages that link many of these original settlements.

NAVIGATION: Use Chart 11489. The St. Marys Entrance is deep, wide, jettied and well marked, but exercise caution when going through, as the jetties become submerged at mid-tide. It is a relatively easy entry and exit point, conveniently located just off the ICW. The short offshore jump from here to the St. Johns River at Mayport (near Jacksonville) or to the inlet at St. Augustine bypasses the sometimes shallow, shifting channels at Nassau Sound, and a northerly leg to St. Simons will cut out the meandering shallows found in Cumberland Sound and Jekyll Creek. Both the St. Johns and the St. Simons inlets do involve long entry channels and strong currents to return to the ICW; be careful and try to plan exits and entries with a slack current or fair tide.

The active Kings Bay Naval Submarine Base, located in Cumberland Sound north of the junction of the St. Marys River, continues to be the reason for frequent dredging and renumbering of buoys, beginning where the ICW joins the head of Cumberland Sound and continuing to the ocean inlet. The channel is consequently quite deep and was again dredged in summer 2008. The St. Marys Entrance Channel buoys, offshore of the entrance, were eliminated several years ago. The buoy that formerly was "10" is now flashing red buoy "2," and every buoy in Cumberland Sound up to the head of Kings Bay was renumbered accordingly. ICW daybeacon numbering remains unchanged. Older charts may not show this change.

When passing from Cumberland Dividings into Cumberland Sound, there is a tricky spot in the ICW channel just south of green daybeacon "75" (Mile 707.8 just east of Kings Bay). Heading south, alter course westward to favor red daybeacon "76," leaving it close to starboard, and then continue south in the channel, avoiding the charted four- to five-foot-deep shoal to port. Also be sure to leave green daybeacon "79" well to port heading south. You will probably see a Navy patrol boat as you pass Kings Bay entering Cumberland Sound. *Here, the green markers will be left to starboard southbound out of Cumberland Sound to the Florida line until you pick up quick flashing green buoy "1" in the Amelia River near Mile 715.*

The ICW fronts the Kings Bay Naval Submarine Base near Mile 708, and Navy security patrols carefully monitor traffic from both directions, especially when submarines are passing through Cumberland Sound and St. Marys Entrance. They will ask you to move outside of the channel if a submarine is in the vicinity. Patrol boats respond on VHF Channel 16. The submarines travel at high speeds in open water, creating very large wakes. For more information on security zones around U.S. Naval vessels, see the "Port Security Procedures" section found in the Skipper's Handbook in the front of this Guide.

On the Amelia River at Mile 718 past the Fernandina Beach waterfront, swing wide between red daybeacons "14" and "16" and favor the north side between red daybeacons "16" and "18" due to six-foot depths on the magenta line between the two. Red daybeacon "18" appears to be too far to the west but head toward it to give the shoal at the bend marked by flashing green "1" a wide berth, both above and below. After passing flashing green "1," swing to the east side of the channel as indicated by the magenta line on the chart. The shoal making out here from the west side is about six feet or less at low water, as noted by our cruising editor in Spring 2011.

Fernandina Beach–Mile 716

Florida's northernmost city, Fernandina Beach, is on Amelia Island east of the ICW. Discovered in 1562 by the French explorer Jean Ribault, who named it Isle de Mai, the Spanish settled the island in 1567. They renamed it Santa Maria, established a mission and built Fort San Fernando. In 1702, the British captured the island and gave it the name that finally stuck: Amelia, in honor of King George II's daughter. Amelia Island has enjoyed a colorful history. In its earlier years, pirates and smugglers used it as their stronghold, and during Prohibition, rumrunners continued the tradition. Eight different flags have flown over Amelia Island, among them the standard of the conquistadors and the French Huguenots, the British Union Jack and the Stars and Bars of the Confederacy. The island is the only place in the United States to have been claimed by so many governments.

Dockage: At Mile 715.3 is the entrance to Egans Creek (east of the Waterway), which leads to Tiger Point Marina and Boat Works, the first marina you will encounter as you

Looking towards Fernandina Beach. (Not to be used for navigation.) WATERWAY GUIDE PHOTOGRAPHY.

enter Florida from the north and Amelia Island's only natural deepwater marina. Tiger Point is a full-service repair yard with approach depths of 7 to 8 feet. It is protected from ICW wakes. Tiger Point also offers unique, long-term storage in hurricane cradles. Diesel fuel (no gas) can be found at Florida Petroleum Corp., but no transient dockage is available there. It is usually best to dock alongside Florida Petroleum's fixed dock during higher tides. Many commercial vessels fuel up here, so there may be a wait.

The Fernandina Harbor Marina is located at Mile 716.7. Dredging of the interior part of this marina was completed in 2007, so transient dockage is available on both sides of the floating face dock as well as at several slips on the interior of the marina. It is still a good idea to call ahead for reservations, as this is a popular stop. Fernandina Harbor Marina also has gas and diesel fuel, pump-out service, a laundry facility, an on-site restaurant and restrooms/showers.

About a block from Fernandina Harbor Marina is a small store that carries limited staples, but serious grocery shopping at Winn-Dixie or Publix is about two miles away and requires a cab. The historic downtown district, next to the waterfront, has several restaurants, taverns and gift shops. The Tourist Information Center can provide a helpful map.

Moorings: Fernandina Harbor Marina has installed 20 moorings in the anchorage area across the channel from their marina. Seven are reserved for transient boaters who call ahead, while most are available on a first-come, first-served basis. The mooring fee includes dinghy dockage,

Looking east at the St. Marys Entrance and Cumberland Sound. Fernandina Beach is to the right.
(Not to be used for navigation.) WATERWAY GUIDE PHOTOGRAPHY.

use of the marina showers, trash disposal and free pump-out service at the dock.

Anchorage: The mooring area is marked with yellow buoys, but anchoring is still permitted outside the marked area. Anchored boats may use the dinghy dock and showers for a modest fee. If you choose to anchor, take care that your swinging circle does not extend into the channel or the mooring area. Also, make sure that you have adequate scope on your anchor for the varying depths. Caution is advised, as sunken boats have been present in this area in the past, and their debris may still be on the bottom. Several sunken boats have been observed outside of the channel between red daybeacons "14" and "16."

Boats have been observed anchoring up the Amelia River in Bells River and also in Lanceford Creek. These anchorages should be approached with caution, as the chart contours show varied depths with snags and mud banks. The tidal range is greater than seven feet, and tidal currents run up to 2 knots here. Although it is a relatively short dinghy ride to the marina dinghy dock, the anchorage and mooring areas are open to winds, wakes and considerable tidal current. Always display anchor lights, as commercial and other traffic can be heavy at all hours.

At Mile 719.5, entering the Amelia River and the ICW from the east, Jackson Creek provides seven-foot depths at mean low water, although its entrance is recently reported to have shoaled to four feet. Like all anchorages in the area, it has swift tidal currents. It is relatively narrow, and the north side should be favored to avoid the charted shoal. The Amelia River breaks off to the west of the ICW at Mile 719.8 with six- to seven-foot depths at mean low water. Although it is preferred over Jackson Creek to the north, it is also quite narrow. Enter slowly with an eye on the depth sounder. Use of two anchors in a Bahamian moor might be wise due to the narrowness and swift currents in either of these anchorages.

GOIN' ASHORE: FERNANDINA BEACH, FL

The downtown historic district, a 50-block section surrounding Centre Street, is an attractive and popular gingerbread seaport dating from the 1850s, when Florida's first cross-state railroad ran from Fernandina to Cedar Key. (The railroad tracks still run past the waterfront with occasional traffic.) The area is listed on the National Historic Register and is worth a visit. The old train depot is a satellite office for the Chamber of Commerce and serves as the Tourist Information Center. Several restaurants, specialty shops, a pharmacy and banks are within walking distance of the waterfront, including the Palace Saloon (117 Centre St., 904-491-3332), Florida's oldest tavern. The Beech Street Grill (801 Beech St., 904-277-3662) serves creative dinner specials, complemented by their extensive wine list. There is piano music nightly, and Sunday brunch is served from 11:00 a.m. to 2 p.m. Dine inside or out at España Restaurant and Tapas (22 S. 4th St., 904-261-7700) specializing in dishes from Spain and Portugal. Brett's Waterway Cafe is

Fernandina Beach Area, FL

FERNANDINA BEACH AREA		Largest Vessel Accommodated	VHF Channel Monitored	Transient Berths / Total Berths	Approach / Dockside Depth (reported)	Floating Docks	Gas / Diesel	Groceries, Ice, Marine Supplies, Snacks	Repairs: Hull, Engine, Propeller	Lift (tonnage), Crane, Rail	1=110V, 2=220V, B=Both, Max Amps	Laundry, Pool, Showers	Pump-Out Station	Nearby: Grocery Store, Motel, Restaurant
		Dockage					Supplies		Service					
1. Tiger Point Marina 715.3 (Internet Access) (Wireless Internet Access)	904-277-2720	55	16/11	4/50	7/8	F		M	HEP	L35	B/50	S		GMR
2. Florida Petroleum Corp. 716.5	904-261-3200 x117	285	16	3/13	50/30		D				B/50			GMR
3. Fernandina Harbor Marina 716.7 (Internet Access) (Wireless Internet Access)	904-491-2090	205	16/68	60/101	18/8	F		GIMS	E		B/100	LS	P	MR
4. Oyster Bay Harbour - Private	800-261-4759	PRIVATE SLIPS												
5. Amelia Island Yacht Basin 721 (Internet Access) (Wireless Internet Access)	904-277-4615	110	16/72	30/135	5.5/7	F	GD	GIMS	HEP	L36	B/50	LS	P	GMR

Corresponding chart(s) not to be used for navigation. Internet Access Wireless Internet Access

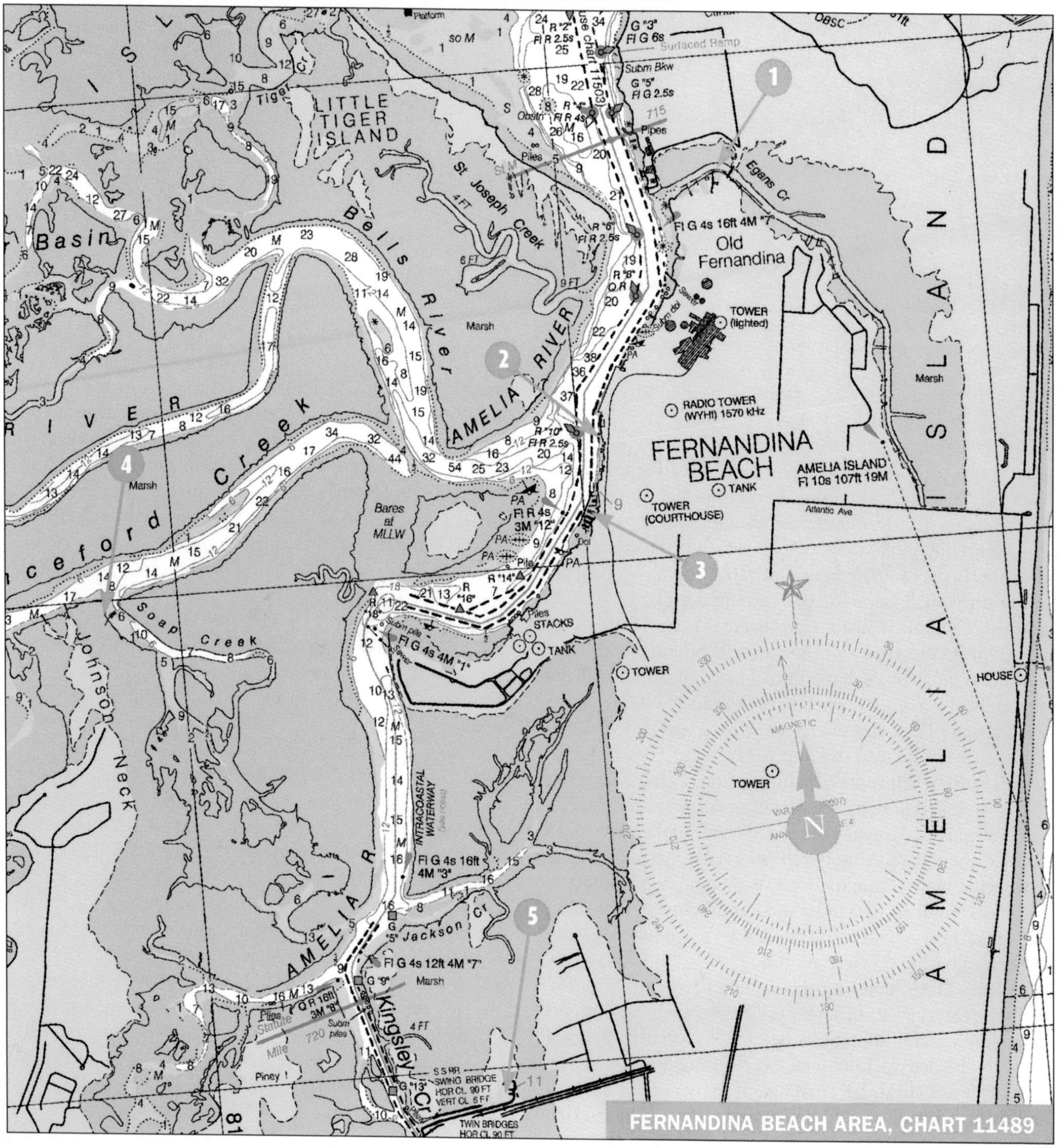

FERNANDINA BEACH AREA, CHART 11489

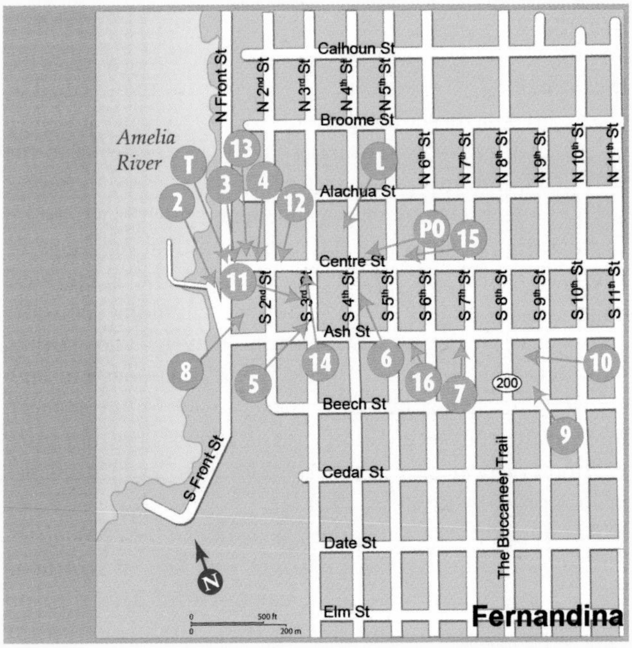

Reference the marina listing tables to see all the marinas in the area.

ATTRACTIONS
1 Fort Clinch State Park

DINING
2 Brett's Waterway Cafe
3 Marina Seafood
4 Palace Saloon
5 29 South
6 Espana Restaurant and Tapas
7 Beech Street Grill

LODGING
8 Hampton Inn & Suites
9 Addison on Amelia
10 Williams House

SHOPPING
11 French Market Antiques
12 Books Plus
13 Fantastic Fudge
14 The General Store and Corner Deli

MARINE SUPPLIES
15 Amelia Island Paint and Hardware

GROCERIES
16 Winn-Dixie & Publix

LIBRARY

POST OFFICE

located at Fernandina Harbor Marina. You can't find a better view in town (1 S. Front St., 904-261-2660). 29 South is getting great reviews. Find them two blocks from the waterfront (29 S. 3rd St., 904-277-7919). An old favorite in town is Marina Seafood Restaurant, located just across the street and the railroad tracks from the marina (101 Centre St., 904-261-5310).

For lodging, the Hampton Inn and Suites is located right on the waterfront in the middle of all of the great downtown shopping and eateries (19 S. 2nd St., 904-491-4911). There are also a number of bed and breakfasts in the downtown district. The Addison on Amelia (614 Ash St., 904-277-1604) provides an elegant setting to soothe the weary traveler. The Williams House (103 S. 9th St., 904-277-2328) is mere blocks from the downtown district in one direction and the Atlantic beaches in the other.

For shopping, try French Market Antiques (203 Centre St., 904-491-0707), Fantastic Fudge (218 Centre St., 904-277-4801), Books Plus (107 Centre St., 904-261-0303) and The General Store and Corner Deli (520 Centre St., 904-310-6080). If you are in need of a post office, you will find one located at the corner of Centre St. and S. 4th St. Amelia Island Paints (516 Ash St., 904-261-6604) not only has hardware but also some boating supplies. There are plans to expand the marine section of the store in the future. There are a surprising number of shops and restaurants in this small town, too numerous to mention, so take time to explore the side streets.

With local attractions such as Fort Clinch State Park, Cumberland Island National Seashore, Amelia Island State Park and the island itself, Fernandina makes a pleasant stopover. Luxury resorts such as the Ritz Carlton and Amelia Island Plantation at the south end of the island draw tourists and conferees from afar, and housing development in the area is attracting a wave of new residents. There is an area of strip malls and large stores of the popular home improvement, drug and department variety usually found in booming residential areas, just off-island, near Yulee. When exploring beyond the downtown Fernandina Beach area, however, you will need to arrange for transportation.

South of the historic area, you can see a white discharge from the chimneys of two paper mills in Fernandina Beach. Although the huge paper mills are still busy, better emissions controls have improved the quality of the air and water. A sizable commercial fishing fleet, consisting mainly of shrimp boats, lies docked above and below the marina. A commercial dock to the north accommodates freighters and containerships.

ADDITIONAL RESOURCES

- CITY OF FERNANDINA BEACH, 904-277-7305, www.fbfl.us
- FERNANDINA BEACH ONLINE, www.fernandinabeach.com

NEARBY GOLF COURSES
Fernandina Beach Municipal Golf Course,
2800 Bill Melton Road, Fernandina Beach, FL 32034,
904-277-7370

NEARBY MEDICAL FACILITIES
Baptist Medical Center Nassau
1250 S. 18th St., Fernandina Beach, FL 32034,
904-321-3500

Mile 720 to Mile 735

NAVIGATION: Use Chart 11489. Just southwest of the Jackson Creek entrance to the Amelia River (near Mile 720), the ICW turns south and leaves the Amelia River for Kingsley Creek. The Kingsley Creek Railroad Swing Bridge (five-foot closed vertical clearance, normally open except for train traffic) and twin fixed high-level highway bridges carrying U.S. A1A (65-foot vertical clearances) span the ICW at Mile 720.7. The high-level bridges here are unofficially considered to be among the "lowest" of the

65-foot bridges on the ICW; expect no more than 64 feet at high tide. If in doubt, check the clearance boards and go through at half tide. With the wide tidal range (seven feet), currents can be unexpectedly strong here.

Although the railroad bridge is usually open, trains hauling logs to the area's two paper mills can delay your journey. The bridge gives no warning when it is going to close, and it does not have a VHF radio. If you are in this area and you hear train whistles, be aware that the bridge could close as you approach it. After passing beneath the bridges, you could see either a wide expanse of water or mud flats on either side of the channel, depending on the state of the tide.

Dockage: Amelia Island Yacht Basin, in a cove just north of the bridges to the east past green daybeacon "13," is a full-service marina with haul-out capabilities that welcomes transients. The narrow channel leading to the marina may look questionable, but locals report good depths, particularly after a dredging project a few years ago increased mean low water depths to 5.5 feet. Contact marina personnel on VHF Channel 16 for current channel depths. Amelia Island Yacht Basin is a good choice in strong winds when other marinas may be too exposed, but the 30 transient slips fill quickly in bad weather, so call ahead. They also have an on-site restaurant.

Amelia City to Fort George River—Mile 725 to Mile 735

NAVIGATION: Use Chart 11489. South from the bridges to flashing red "14," shoaling reduces depths along the west side of the channel to five- to eight-foot depths. In the ICW channel at green daybeacon "21" and flashing red "24," just north of the entrance to Alligator Creek, the narrow channel makes a sharp sweep to the east. Unwary skippers will find two-foot depths outside of the channel at flashing red "24," green daybeacon "25" and red daybeacon "26." From red daybeacon "26" to flashing red "28," follow the magenta line on the chart and avoid the shoaling and submerged pilings to starboard.

Just past flashing red "28" (about Mile 724), you will pass Amelia City, a small waterside hamlet tucked into a bend on the east side of the river. You will see bulkheads, some private docks and a few houses. Inside the marsh, past the bulkhead area, are more houses.

The shallowest part of the South Amelia River is between red daybeacon "34" and red daybeacon "36." Although charted at 9 feet in May 20011, there is around 6 feet of water during extremely low tides. Favor the green side between red daybeacon "34" and flashing green "37." Head toward red daybeacon "36" to follow the magenta line, rounding red daybeacon "38" and green daybeacon "39." The charted seven- to eight-foot depths are the best you will get through here. Follow the magenta line on your chart carefully around red daybeacon "42," then favor green daybeacon "43" rather than flashing red "44."

The last dredging was during spring and summer 2006 between South Amelia River (in Nassau Sound) quick flashing red "46" and south to Sisters Creek flashing red "74." Beyond quick flashing red "46" there had been a temporary red nun "46A" in place for many years (shown on some older charts as red daybeacon "46A"). Following this dredging, red nun buoy "46A" was removed. The charted red daybeacon at the entrance to the cut just north of Mile 730 has been renumbered "46A," according to the May 2011 edition of the chart.

Since this is such a changeable area, remember to be on the alert for shoaling and the possibility that there may be additional aids in place when you make passage here. New charts do not have a magenta line drawn along the route across Nassau Sound. The current may be very strong, so watch your set and drift; slow boats may have to crab across. The swing bridge across Nassau Sound's ocean inlet, at the southern end of Amelia Island, is still in place (15-foot vertical clearance), but closed to traffic and has been replaced with a fixed bridge.

Anchorage: As the chart clearly shows, the ICW channel hugs the Amelia Island shore just south of Amelia City. There is an anchorage just north of Mile 726 off the entrance to Alligator Creek. Enter by turning to the northeast between red daybeacon "36" and flashing green "37." However, be careful; its entrance is shallow, carrying only six-foot depths at low water, and then increasing to eight-foot depths off Alligator Creek. Tugboats have been observed taking a shortcut through this anchorage area at high tide.

LOWER AMELIA ISLAND

The lower portion of Amelia Island is home to a large and lovely resort community, Amelia Island Plantation. The resort still hosts several major annual tennis tournaments. No dockage is available on the premises, however. The closest place to stay is Amelia Island Yacht Basin near Mile 721, described earlier. The island is also the site of an oceanfront Ritz-Carlton Hotel.

Sawpit Creek and Gunnison Cut—Mile 730 to Mile 735

NAVIGATION: Use Chart 11489. Between Miles 730 and 735 (at Mile 735 the ICW meets the Fort George River), shorelines close in somewhat as the channel runs through narrow land cuts and two natural creeks. Sawpit Creek is shoaling in the vicinity of flashing green "49." It is a good idea to favor the deep natural channel along the west (red) side of the ICW when rounding the bend marked by flashing green "49." Sawpit Creek and Gunnison Cut lead to Sisters Creek and the St. Johns River crossing. The May 2011 survey shows three-foot depths on the green side of the channel at mean low water, so staying to starboard is recommended.

Fort George Island—Mile 735 to Mile 740

NAVIGATION: Use Chart 11489. East of the ICW channel, Fort George Island makes an attractive side trip, with its Indian mounds, wildlife sanctuary and lush jungle growth.

There is an area of shoaling between green daybeacon "73" and flashing red "74" reported at seven feet. We recommend against cruising on the Fort George River because of shoaling in the marked channel, a fixed bridge with a 15-foot vertical clearance and a shoaled inlet. The once-popular anchorage here is reported to be shoaled to the point that it can no longer be recommended. If possible, explore this unspoiled natural area by land.

TO ST. JOHNS RIVER

South of the ICW junction with the Fort George River, the ICW route runs a straightforward path through Sisters Creek to the St. Johns River. As you travel along some sections of Sisters Creek, you may see the superstructures of large ships headed up or down the St. Johns River. The suspension bridge at Dames Point, at the western end of Blount Island, can be used as a landmark when you are headed south. Favor the east bank just south of flashing red "82," because shoaling has created water depths of six to eight feet along the west bank. Opening of the Sisters Creek Bridge (Mile 739.2, 24-foot closed vertical clearance) is unrestricted, but you may have to wait; the tender usually waits for several boats before opening the span. Watch for crosscurrents at the bridge. A high-level fixed replacement bridge is planned by 2013. A sign on the bridge warns of heavy traffic at the intersection of Sisters Creek and the St. Johns River.

The city of Jacksonville operates boat ramps and small-boat facilities on both sides of the bridge, which causes congestion, particularly on weekends. The old slips that were part of Sisters Creek Marina on the creek to the north of the ramps are in disrepair, and there is no other dockage for transients in this area.

Sisters Creek/St. Johns River Intersection

NAVIGATION: Use Chart 11489. The pilots and captains of large vessels in this area always announce their approach and intentions at the Sisters Creek and St. Johns River intersection via Sécurité warning. Listen on VHF Channel 16. Smaller vessels in the area should answer them back if in close proximity and stay clear of these large vessels.

ICW INTERSECTION/ST. JOHNS R. Mile 740

WATERWAY GUIDE PHOTOGRAPHY

SISTERS CREEK BRIDGE Mile 739.1

WATERWAY GUIDE PHOTOGRAPHY

At this point, the St. Johns River is narrow, compared to some of its broad expanses south of Jacksonville. Crossing can present problems to lightly powered vessels, given the strong currents (2 to 3 knots on the ebb), obstructed visibility and continuous commercial traffic. Observe markers closely until you are safely into the ICW land cut beyond the St. Johns River. Do not attempt to pass between what appears to be islets downriver from the land cut entrance; there are rocks between them. Keep in mind that large oceangoing vessels have the right of way, so watch out for them while transiting the St. Johns River. Also, remember that the shipyard on the east side of the Sisters Creek entrance to the St. Johns River creates a blind spot for small boats heading into the river.

The land cut from this point southward through the Jacksonville Beach area is well marked but, at low tide, the dredged channel is narrow. Follow the markers carefully to stay on the channel's centerline and be prepared to squeeze over for tugs with barges. On weekends and holidays, small boats often anchor in the land cut just beyond the river crossing. The current in the land cut below the St. Johns River flows toward the river on the ebb and can be very strong. Eddies may be present between red nun buoy "2" and flashing green "1," requiring close attention to the helm. There is a No-Wake Zone after crossing the St. Johns River that extends almost to the first bridge. It is often patrolled and enforced by a small Coast Guard boat. When entering the channel, favor the green daybeacons until you reach red daybeacon "8."

Continuing South

You are now at the St. Johns River. A turn to the west will lead you up the St. Johns River toward Jacksonville, FL and many other fine destinations, while continuing south will take you down the ICW and farther into Florida. Waterway Guide coverage of Florida and the Gulf Coast continues in our Southern edition. To order your copy, visit www.WaterwayGuide.com or a marine store in your area.

Waterway Guide is always open to your observations from the helm. Email your comments on any navigation information in the Guide to: editor@waterwayguide.com.

Waterway Guide advertising sponsors play a vital role in bringing you the most trusted and well-respected cruising guide in the country. Without our advertising sponsors, we simply couldn't produce the top-notch publication now resting in your hands. Next time you stop in for a peaceful night's rest, let them know where you found them—Waterway Guide, The Cruising Authority.

Extended Cruising

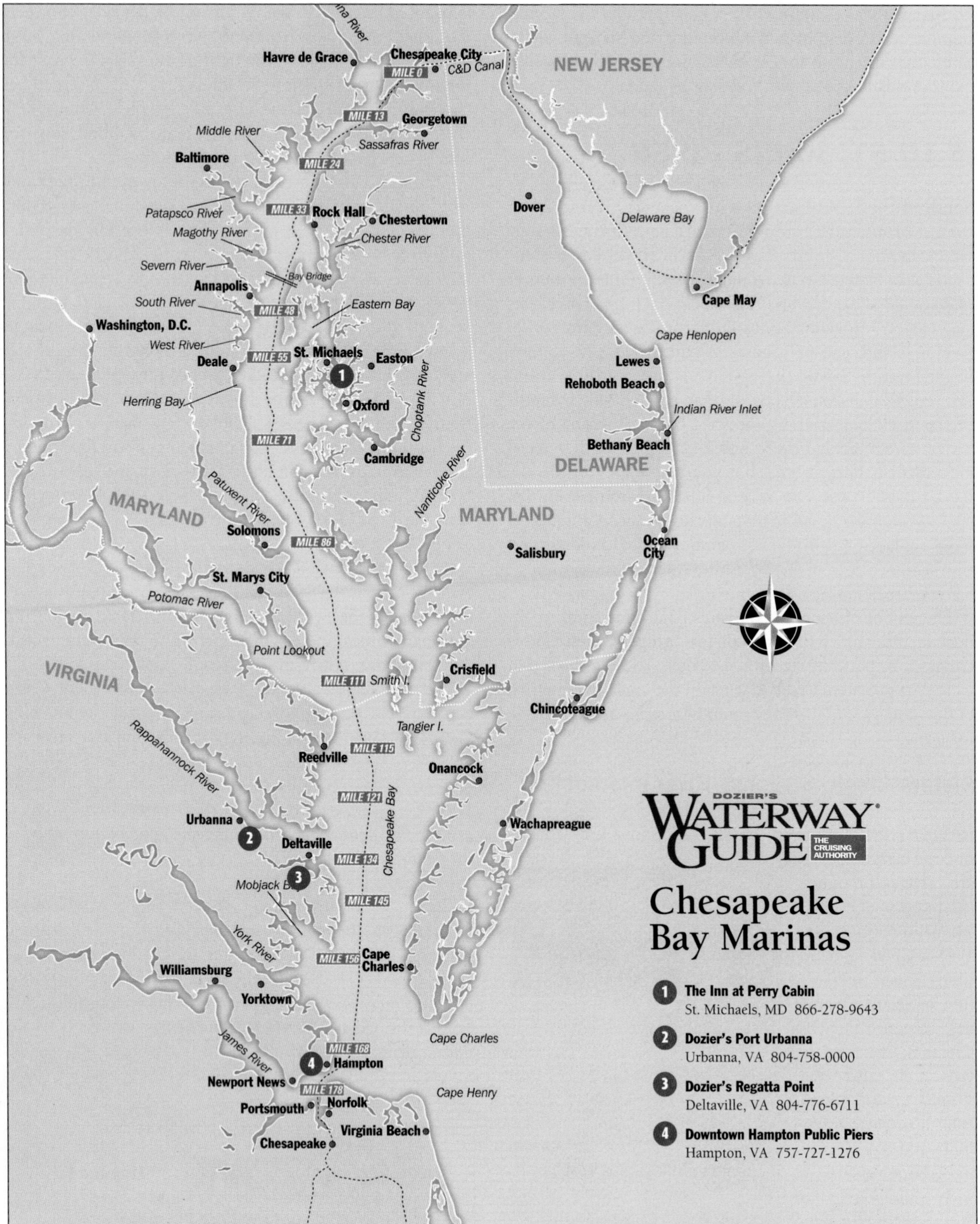

For detailed navigational information, charts and extensive marina coverage see WATERWAY GUIDE, 2011 Chesapeake Bay Edition. Purchase online: www.waterwayguide.com or call 800-233-3359.

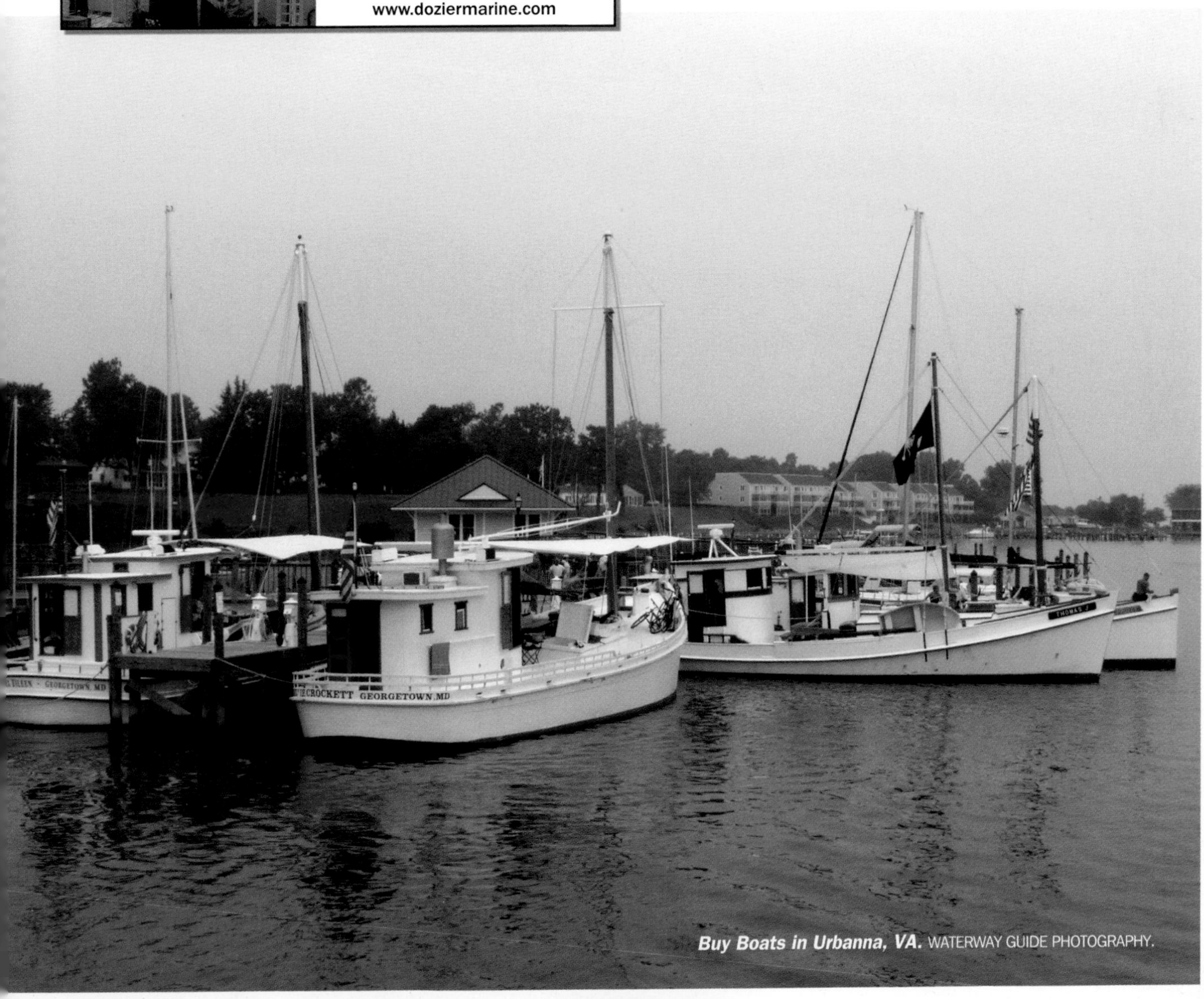

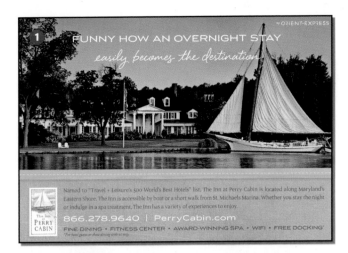

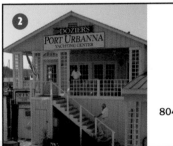

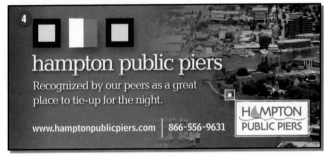

Buy Boats in Urbanna, VA. WATERWAY GUIDE PHOTOGRAPHY.

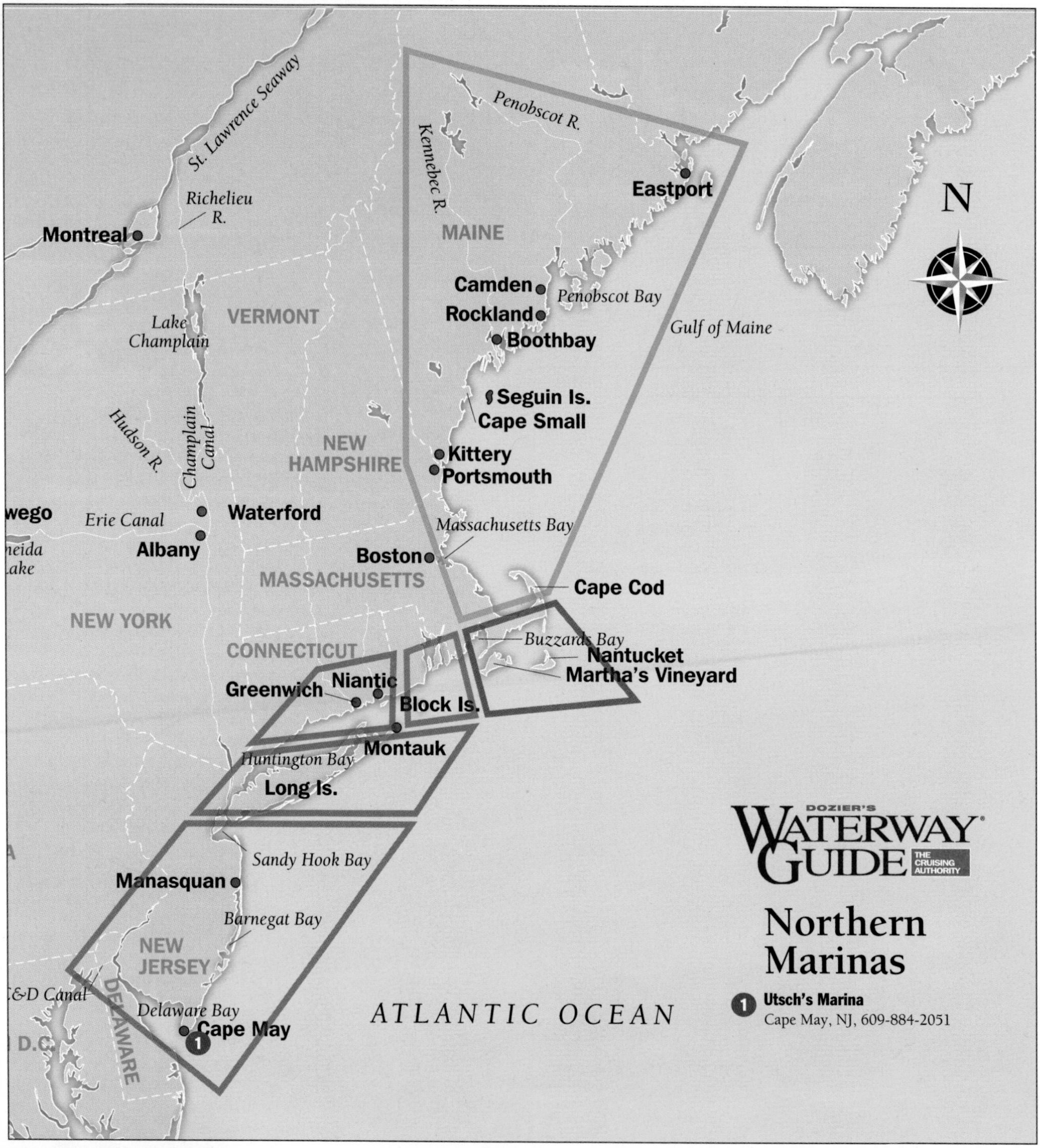

For detailed navigational information, charts and extensive marina coverage see WATERWAY GUIDE, 2011 Northern Edition. Purchase online: www.waterwayguide.com or call 800-233-3359.

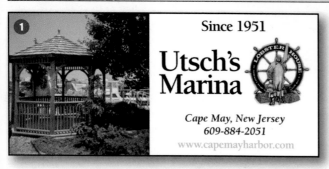

Southern Marinas

1. **Huckins Yachts**
   Jacksonville, FL, 904-389-1125
2. **Camachee Island Yacht Harbor**
   St Augustine, FL, 904-829-5676
3. **Williams Island Marina**
   Aventura, FL, 305-937-7813

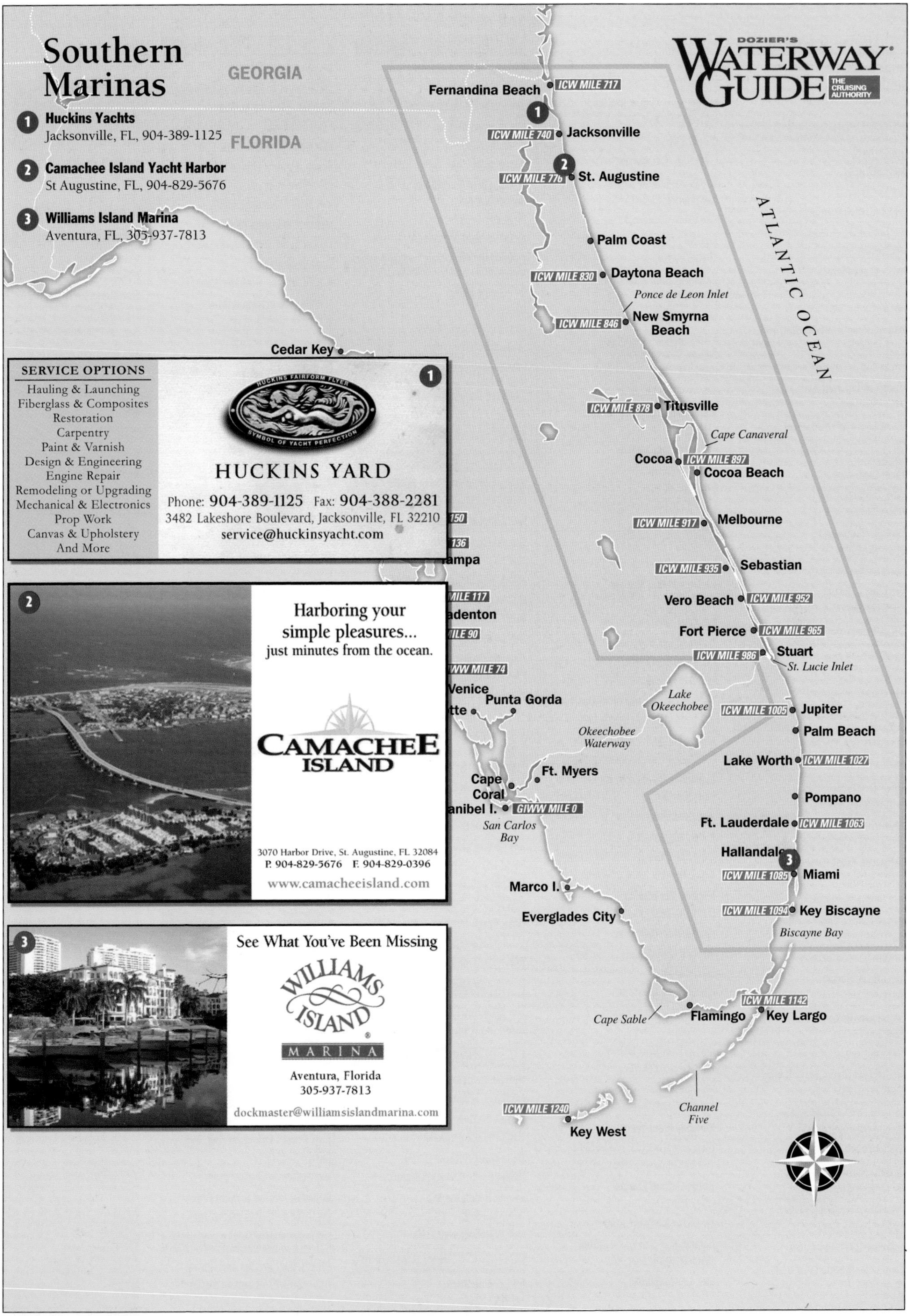

Waterway Guide Cruising Club Participating Partners

ALABAMA

Turner Marine Supply Inc.
(251) 476-1444
www.turnermarine.com

BAHAMAS

Abaco Inn
(800) 468-8799
www.abacoinn.com

Brendals Dive Center
(242) 365-4411
www.brendal.com

Port Lucaya Marina
(242) 373-9090
www.portlucaya.com

Sunrise Resort and Marina
(800) 932-4959
www.sunriseresortandmarina.com

Marina at Emerald Bay
(242) 336-6100
www.marinaatemeraldbay.com

CONNECTICUT

North Cove Yacht Club
(860) 388-9132
www.northcoveyc.com

Landfall Navigation
(203) 487-0775
www.landfallnavigation.com

West Cove Marina
(203) 933-3000

D.C. WASHINGTON

Capital Yacht Club
(202) 488-8110
www.capitalyachtclub.com

FLORIDA

Turnberry Isle Marina Yacht Club (305) 933-6934
www.turnberryislemarina.com

Twin Dolphin Marina
(941) 747-8300
www.twindolphinmarina.com

Adventure Yacht Harbor Inc.
(386) 756-2180
www.adventureyachtharbor.com

Delray Harbor Club Marina
(561) 276-0376
www.delrayharborclub.com

Cape Haze Marina
(941) 698-1110

Everglades National Park Boat Tours
(239) 695-2553

City of Fort Myers Yacht Basin
(239) 321-7080
www.cityftmyers.com/attractions

Florida Marina's Clubs
(239) 489-2969

Loblolly Marina
(772) 546-3136
www.loblollymarinainfo.com

City of Jacksonville
(904) 630-0839 www.coj.net

Palm Cove Marina
(904) 223-4757
www.palmcovemarina.com

The Jacksonville Landing
(904) 353-1188
www.jacksonvillelanding.com

Loggerhead Club & Marina
(561) 747-8980

Dolphin Marina
(305) 872-2685 www.dolphinmarina.net

Sombrero Marina Condo Association (305) 743-0000
www.sombreromarina.com

Austral International Marina
(305) 325-0177

Palm Bay Club & Marina
(305) 751-3700
www.palmbayclubmarina.com

Sandy Beach Catamaran Sailing Charters
(954) 218-0042
www.catamaransailcharter.com

Marina at Naples Bay Resort
(239) 530-5134
www.naplesbayresort.com

Night Swan Intracoastal Bed/Breakfast
(386) 423-4940 www.nightswan.com

Gulf Harbor Marina
(941) 488-7734
www.gulfharbormarina.com

Regatta Pointe Marina
(941) 729-6021
www.regattapointemarina.com

All American Covered Boat Storage (941) 697-9900
www.aaboatstorage.com

Fishermen's Village Yacht Basin
(800) 639-0020 www.fishville.com

Always For Sail
(904) 625-7936 www.alwaysforsail.com

Camachee Cove Yacht Harbor
(904) 829-5676
www.camacheeisland.com

Rivers Edge Marina
(904) 827-0520
www.29riveredgemarina.com

Mariner Cay Marina
(772) 287-2900
www.marinercaymarina.org

Pirate's Cove Resort & Marina
(772) 223-9216
www.piratescoveresort.com

Sailfish Marina of Stuart
(772) 283-1122
www.sailfishmarinastuart.com

Anclote Isles Marina
(727) 939-0100
www.ancloteisles-marina.com

Kennedy Point Yacht Club & Marina (321) 383-0280
www.kennedypointyachtclub.com

Nettles Island Marina
(772) 229-2811
www.nettlesislandmarina.com

Palafox Pier and Yacht Harbor
(850) 432-9620
www.marinamgmt.com

GEORGIA

Hinckley Yacht Services
(912) 629-2400
www.hinckleyyachtservices.com

Isle of Hope Marina
(912) 354-8187
www.iohmarina.com

Morningstar Marinas at Golden Isles
(912) 634-1128
www.morningstarmarinas.com

LOUISIANA

Retif Oil & Fuel
(985) 872-3111

Mariners Village Marina
(800) 360-3625

MASSACHUSETTS

Vineyard Haven Marina
(508) 693-0720
www.vineyardhavenmarina.com

MARYLAND

Annapolis Harbor Boat Yard
(410) 268-0092
www.annapolisharbor.net

Sunset Harbor Marina
(410) 687-7290
www.sunsetharbor.com

Galloway Creek Marina
(410) 335-3575
www.dredgeanddock.com

Campbell's Bachelor Pt. Yacht Co.
(410) 226-5592
www.campbellsboatyards.com

Campbell's Boatyard @ Jack's Point
(410) 226-5105
www.campbellsboatyards.com

Campbell's Town Creek Boatyard
(410) 226-0213
www.campbellsboatyard.com

Point Lookout Marina
(301) 872-5000
www.pointlookoutmarina.com

Back Creek Inn Bed & Breakfast
(410) 326-2022
www.backcreekinnbnb.com

MAINE

The Landings Restaurant & Marina (207) 596-6573

MICHIGAN

Detroit Yacht Club
(313) 824-1200 www.dyc.com

Terry's Marina
(586) 709-9559 www.terrysmarina.com

Belle Maer Harbor
(586) 465-4534 www.bellemaer.com

Toledo Beach Marina
(734) 243-3800
www.toledobeachmarina.com

MISSISSIPPI

Isle Casino Biloxi
(916) 834-4112
www.biloxi.isleofcapricasinos.com

NORTH CAROLINA

Joyner Marina
(910) 458-5053 www.joynermarina.com

Whittaker Pointe Marina
(252) 249-1750
www.whittakerpointe.com

South Harbour Village Marina
(910) 454-7486
www.southharbourvillage.com

Bennett Brothers Yachts Inc.
(910) 772-9277 www.bbyachts.com

Cape Fear Marina
(910) 772-9277 www.bbyachts.com

Wilmington Marine Center
(910) 395-5055
www.wilmingtonmarine.com

NEW JERSEY

Miss Chris Marina
(609) 884-3351
www.misschrismarina.com

Hinckley Yacht Services
(732) 477-6700 www.hinckleyyachts.com

NEW YORK

Ess-Kay Yards Inc.
(315) 676-2711 www.ess-kayyards.com

Minneford Marina
(718) 885-2000
www.minnefordmarina.com

Sunset Harbour Marina
(631) 289-3800 www.ILoveMyMarina.com

Glen Cove Marina
(516) 759-3129
www.glencovemarina.com

Hyde Park Marina
(845) 473-8283
www.hydeparkmarina.com

Patsy's Bay Marina
(845) 786-5270
www.patsysbaymarina.com

RHODE ISLAND

Newport Yachting Center
(800) 653-3625
www.newportyachtingcenter.com

SOUTH CAROLINA

Lady's Island Marina
(843) 522-0430

UK-Halsey Charleston Sailmakers
(843) 722-0823
www.ukhalseycharleston.com

Osprey Marina
(843) 215-5353 www.ospreymarina.com

Pierside Boatworks
(843) 554-7775
www.piersideboatworks.com

Port Royal Landing Marina, Inc.
(800) 326-7678
www.portroyallandingmarina.com

Bohicket Marina & Yacht Club
(843) 768-1280 www.bohicket.com

VIRGINIA

River's Rest Marina and Resort
(804) 829-2753 www.riversrest.com

Top Rack Marina
(757) 227-3041
www.toprackmarina.com

Chesapeake Boat Works
(804) 776-8833
www.chesapeakemarinerailway.com

Dozier's Regatta Point Yachting Center
(804) 776-6711
www.doziermarine.com

Schroeder Yacht Systems Ltd.
(804) 776-7500
www.schroederyachtsystems.com

Downtown Hampton Public Piers
(757) 727-1276
www.downtownhampton.com

The Tides Inn & Marina
(804) 438-5000
www.tidesinn.com

White Point Marina
(804) 472-2977
www.whitepointmarina.com

Bay Point Marina
(757) 362-3600
www.littlecreekmarina.com

Cobb's Marina Inc.
(757) 588-5401
www.cobbsmarina.com

Little Creek Marina
(757) 362-3600
www.littlecreekmarina.com

Vinings Landing Marine Center
(757) 587-8000
www.Viningslanding.com

Willoughby Harbor Marina
(757) 583-4150

Ocean Marine Yacht Center
(757) 399-2920
www.oceanmarinellc.com

Scott's Creek Marina
(757) 399-BOAT

Smithfield Station
(757) 357-7700
www.smithfieldstation.com

Regent Point Marina and Boatyard
(804) 758-4457
www.regent-point.com

Dozier's Port Urbanna Marine Center
(804) 758-0000
www.doziermarine.com

Urbanna Town Marina at Upton's Point
(804) 758-5440

As of August, 2011

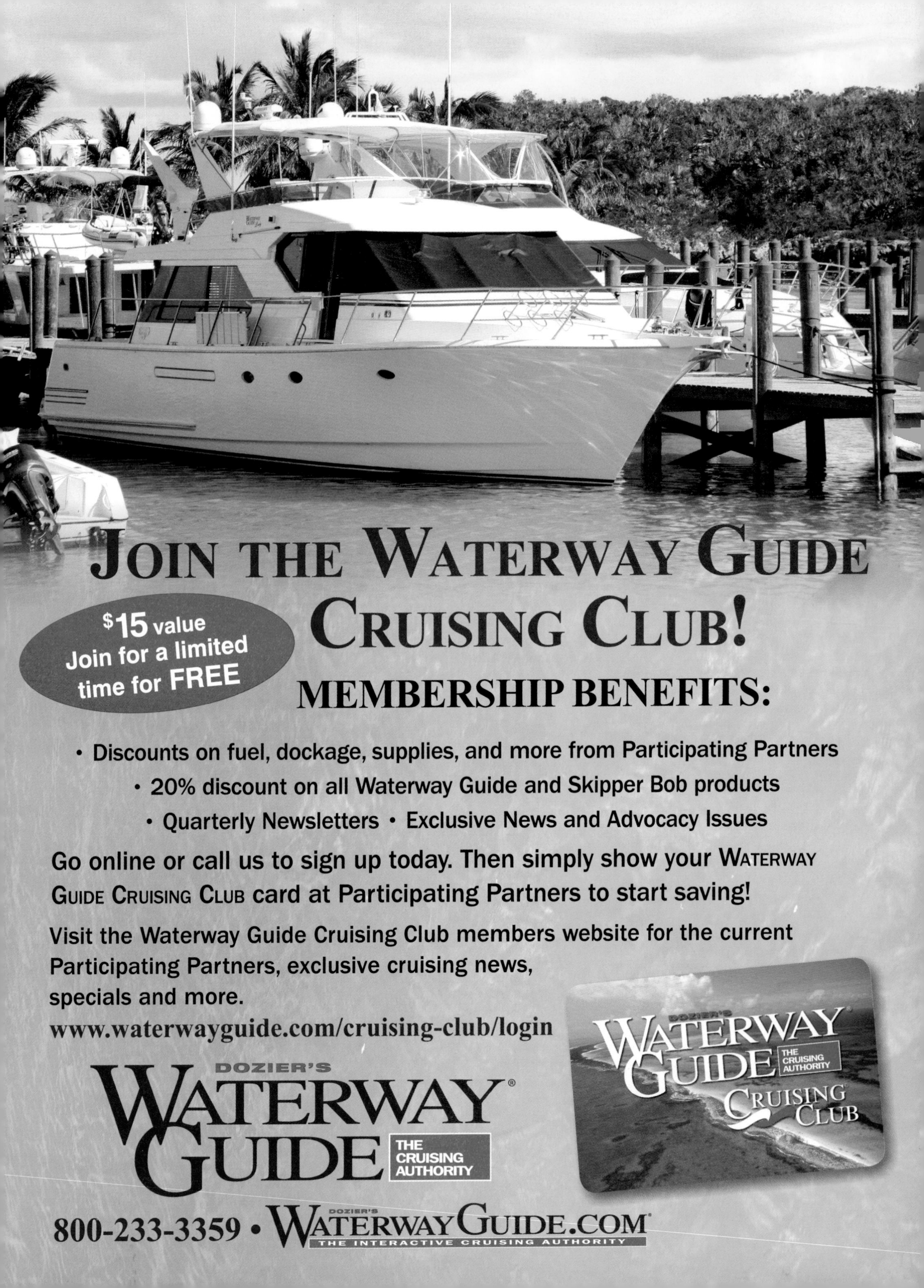
JOIN THE WATERWAY GUIDE CRUISING CLUB!
$15 value Join for a limited time for FREE
MEMBERSHIP BENEFITS:
• Discounts on fuel, dockage, supplies, and more from Participating Partners
• 20% discount on all Waterway Guide and Skipper Bob products
• Quarterly Newsletters • Exclusive News and Advocacy Issues
Go online or call us to sign up today. Then simply show your WATERWAY GUIDE CRUISING CLUB card at Participating Partners to start saving!
Visit the Waterway Guide Cruising Club members website for the current Participating Partners, exclusive cruising news, specials and more.
www.waterwayguide.com/cruising-club/login
DOZIER'S WATERWAY GUIDE® THE CRUISING AUTHORITY
DOZIER'S WATERWAY GUIDE® THE CRUISING AUTHORITY CRUISING CLUB
800-233-3359 • DOZIER'S WATERWAYGUIDE.COM® THE INTERACTIVE CRUISING AUTHORITY

Marina Index

Sponsors are listed in **BOLD**.

Subject Index

Most relevant pages are listed in **BOLD.**

D

E

F

G

SUBJECT INDEX

U

V

W

Y

GOIN' ASHORES

INLETS

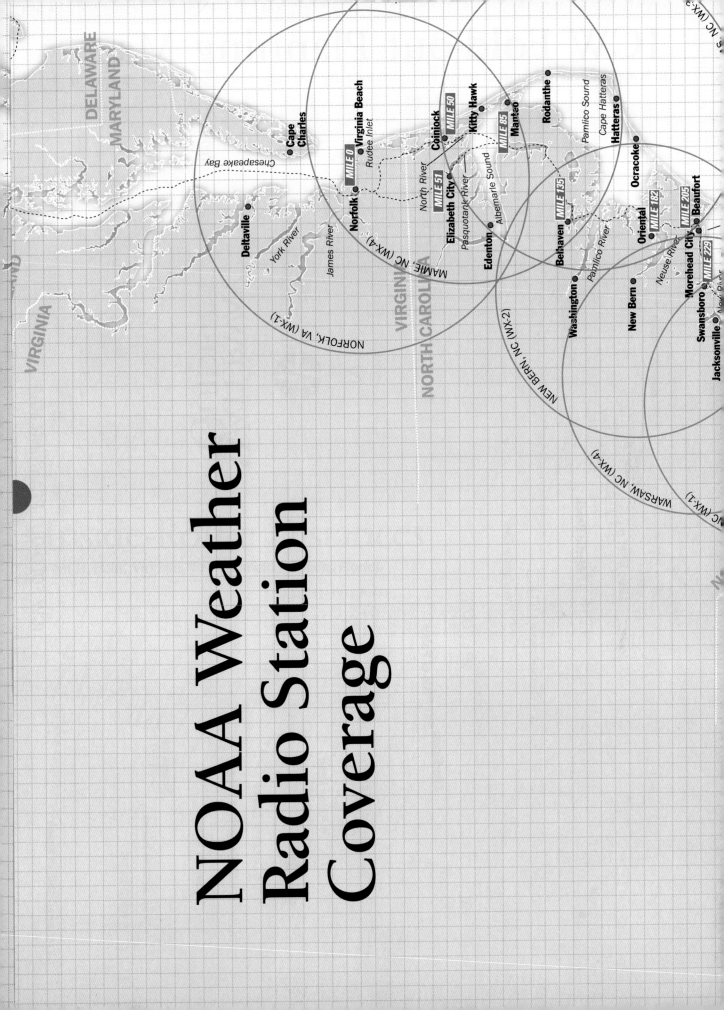

NOAA Weather Radio Station Coverage

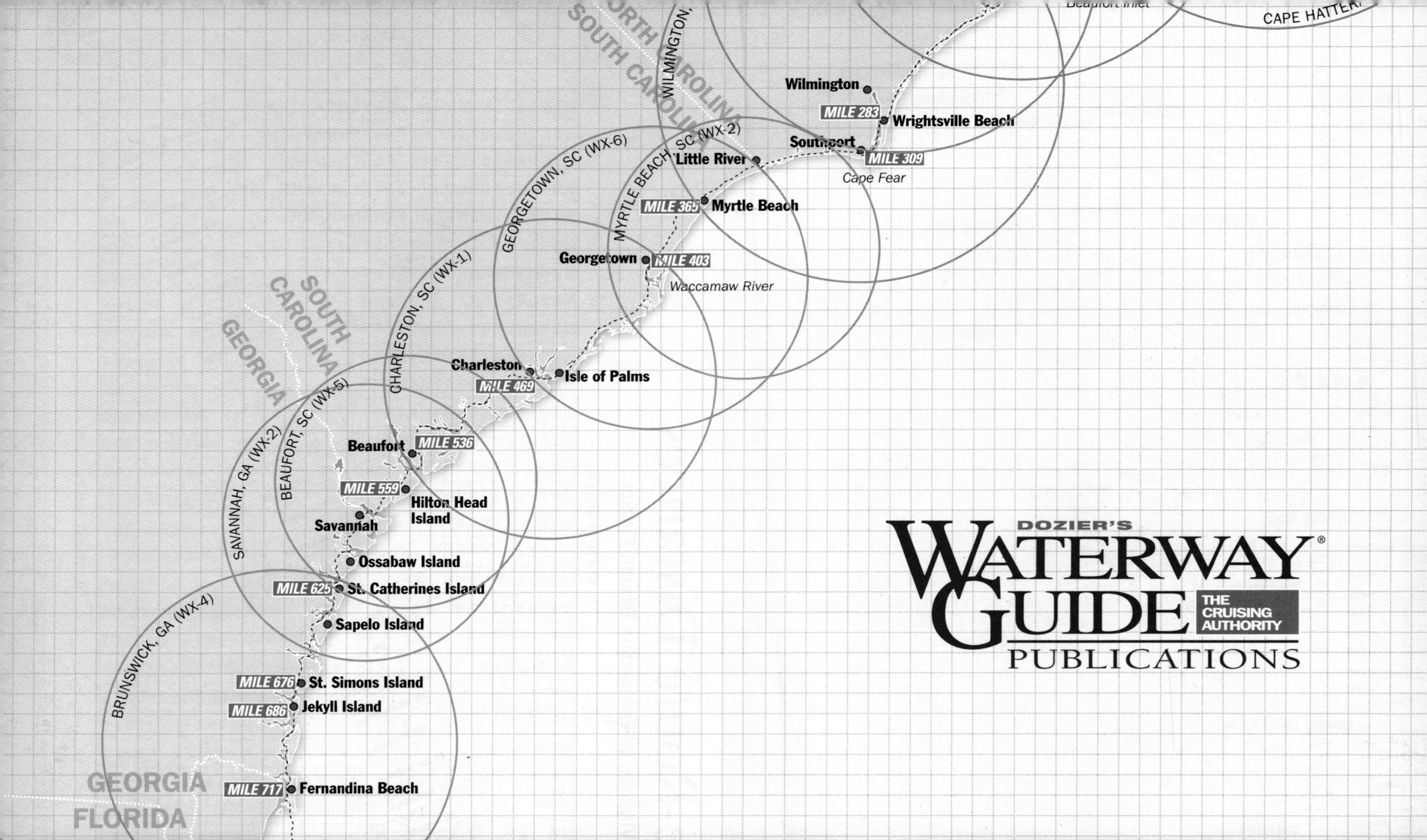

Rings show approximate coverage area for each listed station.

Tune to the following frequencies, as listed:

WX1: 162.550 MHz
WX2: 162.400 MHz
WX3: 162.475 MHz
WX4: 162.425 MHz
WX5: 162.450 MHz
WX6: 162.500 MHz
WX7: 162.525 MHz